Success Stories Start Here

Leaders for the Long Run

Staying Power The ability to survive and thrive in any business climate. It's a special quality that only a select few corporations enjoy. On the cover of this 7th edition of *Financial Accounting,* we pay tribute to a number of firms that have prospered not for a few years, but for many decades. These firms embody the rare ability to build upon a strong product or service and evolve with changing social and market conditions. For instance, AT&T, once strictly a telephone company, also brought us the transistor, the laser, and innumerable other technology innovations. Procter and Gamble, which posted $35.8 billion in sales in 1997, was once just a small soap manufacturer.

Financial Accounting has rare staying power, as well. This marks its 7th edition, going to print 69 years since the first edition of the text from which it is derived, *Accounting,* was published in 1929. A lot has happened in American business and in the field of accounting since *Accounting* and *Financial Accounting* were introduced. Innumerable accounting texts have come and gone since then. But this family of texts has kept pace with students, instructors, and the business world. As a result of these efforts, over 10 million students have been introduced to accounting via this family of texts.

Make that 10 million and counting.

Putting People First

It is a common practice for authors to conclude a text's preface with an acknowledgements section thanking colleagues who contributed ideas to or reviewed their work. It is an important tribute to the people who bring a text to life.

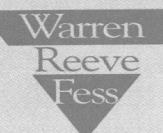

In the case of this text, however, a simple acknowledgements section alone is not enough. We must go against tradition and begin this preface by saluting the people who have secured the position of this family of texts as the most widely used textbooks for accounting. Quite simply, *Financial Accounting* and *Accounting* represent collaboration at its highest level. Users of the previous editions provided valuable classroom feedback. Numerous focus groups and questionnaire respondents shared their personal insights. And dozens of reviewers kept us on track as we made many difficult choices during the revision process. Reviewers offered many specific comments for improving the texts; we took these comments very seriously and the texts are stronger because of them.

And while current *Financial Accounting* and *Accounting* users and reviewers made tremendous contributions, they represent only part of the reason that this family of texts dominates the market. Hundreds of scholars, as users and reviewers, have helped to shape these texts through their many editions. Just as Hershey, pictured on our cover and featured throughout the texts, has grown and changed throughout this century through the efforts of many special individuals, so too have *Financial Accounting* and *Accounting* evolved through their long history. This evolution has been marshaled by a long list of authors, editors, and reviewers, all making unique and invaluable contributions.

A Tradition of Success

When the first edition of *Accounting* was published in 1929, author James McKinsey could have only hoped for the kind of success and influence this family of texts has enjoyed. Its dominance in the introductory accounting market has continued to grow for seven decades. As the current authors, we appreciate the responsibility to protect the spirit of McKinsey's vision, while continuing to shape the texts to the evolving needs of students and instructors. We sincerely thank our many colleagues who have helped to make it happen.

"The teaching of accounting is no longer designed to train professional accountants only. With the growing complexity of business and the constantly increasing difficulty of the problems of management, it has become essential that everyone who aspires to a position of responsibility should have a knowledge of the fundamental principles of accounting."

—James O. McKinsey,
author, first edition, 1929

11. Format for Bank Reconciliation:

Cash balance according to bank statement			$xxx
Add: Additions by depositor not on bank statement		$xx	
Bank errors		xx	xx
			$xxx
Deduct: Deductions by depositor not on bank statement		$xx	
Bank errors		xx	xx
Adjusted balance...			$xxx
Cash balance according to depositor's records			$xxx
Add: Additions by bank not recorded by depositor..		$xx	
Depositor errors.......................................		xx	xx
			$xxx
Deduct: Deductions by bank not recorded by depositor		$xx	
Depositor errors.......................................		xx	xx
Adjusted balance...			$xxx

12. Inventory Costing Methods:
1. First-in, First-out (fifo)
2. Last-in, First-out (lifo)
3. Average Cost

13. Interest Computations:
Interest = Face Amount (or Principal) × Rate × Time

14. Methods of Determining Annual Depreciation:

STRAIGHT-LINE: $\dfrac{\text{Cost} - \text{Estimated Residual Value}}{\text{Estimated Life}}$

DECLINING-BALANCE: Rate* × Book Value at Beginning of Period

*Rate is commonly twice the straight-line rate (1 ÷ Estimated Life).

15. Cash Provided by Operations on Statement of Cash Flows (indirect method):

Net income, per income statement			$xx
Add: Depreciation of fixed assets		$xx	
Amortization of bond payable discount and intangible assets..................................		xx	
Decreases in current assets (receivables, inventories, prepaid expenses).................		xx	
Increases in current liabilities (accounts and notes payable, accrued liabilities)		xx	
Losses on disposal of assets and retirement of debt		xx	xx
Deduct: Amortization of bond payable premium......		$xx	
Increases in current assets (receivables, inventories, prepaid expenses).................		xx	
Decreases in current liabilities (accounts and notes payable, accrued liabilities)		xx	
Gains on disposal of assets and retirement of debt		xx	xx
Net cash flow from operating activities....................			$xx

16. Contribution Margin Ratio $= \dfrac{\text{Sales} - \text{Variable Costs}}{\text{Sales}}$

17. Break-Even Sales (Units) $= \dfrac{\text{Fixed Costs}}{\text{Unit Contribution Margin}}$

18. Sales (Units) $= \dfrac{\text{Fixed Costs} + \text{Target Profit}}{\text{Unit Contribution Margin}}$

19. Margin of Safety $= \dfrac{\text{Sales} - \text{Sales at Break-Even Point}}{\text{Sales}}$

20. Operating Leverage $= \dfrac{\text{Contribution Margin}}{\text{Operating Income}}$

21. Variances

$\dfrac{\text{Direct Materials}}{\text{Price Variance}} = \left(\begin{array}{c}\text{Actual Price per Unit} - \\ \text{Standard Price}\end{array}\right) \times \begin{array}{c}\text{Actual Quantity} \\ \text{Used}\end{array}$

$\dfrac{\text{Direct Materials}}{\text{Quantity Variance}} = \left(\begin{array}{c}\text{Actual Quantity Used} - \\ \text{Standard Quantity}\end{array}\right) \times \begin{array}{c}\text{Standard Price} \\ \text{per Unit}\end{array}$

$\dfrac{\text{Direct Labor}}{\text{Rate Variance}} = \left(\begin{array}{c}\text{Actual Rate per Hour} - \\ \text{Standard Rate}\end{array}\right) \times \begin{array}{c}\text{Actual Hours} \\ \text{Worked}\end{array}$

$\dfrac{\text{Direct Labor}}{\text{Time Variance}} = \left(\begin{array}{c}\text{Actual Hours Worked} - \\ \text{Standard Hours}\end{array}\right) \times \begin{array}{c}\text{Standard Rate} \\ \text{per Hour}\end{array}$

$\begin{array}{c}\text{Variable Factory} \\ \text{Overhead Controllable} \\ \text{Variance}\end{array} = \begin{array}{c}\text{Actual} \\ \text{Variable Factory} \\ \text{Overhead}\end{array} - \begin{array}{c}\text{Budgeted Variable} \\ \text{Factory Overhead for} \\ \text{Actual Amount Produced}\end{array}$

$\begin{array}{c}\text{Fixed Factory} \\ \text{Overhead Volume} \\ \text{Variance}\end{array} = \left(\begin{array}{c}\text{100\% of Normal} \\ \text{Capacity} - \text{Std. Capacity} \\ \text{for Amount Produced}\end{array}\right) \times \begin{array}{c}\text{Std. Fixed Factory} \\ \text{Overhead} \\ \text{Rate}\end{array}$

22. Rate of Return on Investment (ROI) $= \dfrac{\text{Income from Operations}}{\text{Invested Assets}}$

Alternative ROI Computation:

$\text{ROI} = \dfrac{\text{Income from Operations}}{\text{Sales}} \times \dfrac{\text{Sales}}{\text{Invested Assets}}$

23. Capital Investment Analysis Methods:
1. Methods That Ignore Present Values:
   A. Average Rate of Return Method
   B. Cash Payback Method
2. Methods That Use Present Values:
   A. Net Present Value Method
   B. Internal Rate of Return Method

24. Average Rate of Return $= \dfrac{\text{Estimated Average Annual Income}}{\text{Average Investment}}$

25. Present Value Index $= \dfrac{\text{Total Present Value of Net Cash Flow}}{\text{Amount to Be Invested}}$

26. Present Value Factor for an Annuity of $1 $= \dfrac{\text{Amount to Be Invested}}{\text{Equal Annual Net Cash Flows}}$

Guided by the Experts: Content Changes

Extensive feedback from current users, independent reviews by educators, and market research ensures that the texts balance the fundamentals of accounting with thorough coverage of today's important topics. As a result, *Financial Accounting, 7e,* and *Accounting, 19e,* focus squarely on the business of business–how accounting contributes to effective management while emphasizing the most important accounting procedures.

We recognize an important reality–80% of accounting courses are filled with non-accounting majors. Our texts speak to anyone who takes an introductory accounting course. Consider these changes in content and organization:

■ Ch. 1
Introduction to Accounting and Business. This chapter begins with a new section that defines business and describes common types of businesses, forms of organization, and the diverse interests of a business's stakeholders.

■ Ch. 3 The Matching Concept and the Adjusting Process.** A new table summarizes each type of adjustment, adjusting entry, and the financial statement effect of omitting an adjusting entry. The discussion of adjustments ends with the adjusted trial balance, rather than a partial work sheet.

■ Ch. 4 Completing the Accounting Cycle.** The work sheet is now introduced and completed in this chapter. Lines on the work sheet illustrations are numbered to assist you in your classroom presentation.

■ Ch. 5 Accounting Systems and Internal Controls.** An illustration of the revenue and collection cycle in a computerized accounting system, using QuickBooks® has been added.

PROVIDING INFORMATION TO USERS

STAKEHOLDERS

Internal: Owners, managers, employees

External: Customers, creditors, government

1 Identify stakeholders

2 Assess stakeholders' information needs

3 Design the accounting information system to meet stakeholders' needs

4 Record economic data about business activities and events

5 Prepare accounting reports for stakeholders

ACCOUNTING INFORMATION SYSTEM

■ **Ch. 6 Accounting for Merchandising Businesses.** The discussion of perpetual inventory systems gives students a clear understanding of inventory accounting by drawing connections to buying groceries or fast food meals. Purchases are recorded at gross rather than net amounts. A new appendix describes a merchandiser's special journals in a manual system and electronic forms in a computerized system using QuickBooks.

■ **Ch. 8 Receivables.** The discussion of discounting notes receivable was moved to a chapter appendix. The discussion of temporary investments was moved to a later chapter and combined with the discussion of long-term investments.

■ **Ch. 9 Inventories.** A new section introduces the concept of inventory cost flows without reference to the perpetual or periodic systems. The journal entries in a perpetual system are presented alongside the inventory subsidiary ledger to illustrate the FIFO and LIFO flow of costs.

Purchased goods

Sold goods

■ **Ch. 10 Fixed Assets and Intangible Assets.** Gains and losses on exchanges of fixed assets are discussed only from a GAAP viewpoint.

■ **Ch. 13 Corporations: Income and Taxes, Stockholders' Equity, and Investments in Stocks.** A new section on reporting stockholders' equity was added. The discussion of appropriated retained earnings and prior-period adjustments was significantly reduced. A new section covering short-term investments in stocks was added at the end of the chapter. The discussion of international transactions was moved to an appendix.

Purchased goods

Sold goods

■ **Ch. 16 Financial Statement Analysis.** This is a new chapter, adapted from the appendix material included in the previous edition.

■ NEW! **Appendixes on Foreign Currency Transactions** and **Partnerships** are at the end of the text.

Leading by Listening: Special Features

The distinguished team of users and reviewers guided us to numerous format and feature changes for the new editions. Starting with a dynamic and colorful new design, the resulting texts are perfect for a broad spectrum of students and classes. Among the feature changes that will help students make the connection between accounting and business are the following:

Setting the Stage. This feature (formerly You and Accounting) at the beginning of each chapter relates students' personal experiences to the chapter's topic. The immediate relevance of these passages provides excellent motivation to read on.

NEW! Business on Stage. This brief presentation of a business concept introduces students to the business context in which accounting functions.

Intermission. This feature (formerly Using Accounting To Understand Business) uses excerpts from current media coverage to demonstrate how managers and others use accounting information. Pieces from *The Wall Street Journal, Forbes, Business Week,* and other periodicals help students see the real world application of chapter subjects.

NEW! Encore. At the end of each chapter, the texts present a brief, interesting narrative about the success or failure of a real business.

Other features that will help students understand accounting as well as the way business works are:

NEW! Questions & Answers. At appropriate points in the margin of the texts, questions with answers are provided to help students check their understanding of the material they have just read.

NEW! Points of Interest. These margin notes offer insight into subjects of special interest to students, such as careers and current events.

NEW! Summaries. Brief summary statements within each chapter bring special attention to important points.

NEW! Business Transactions. In Chapters 1 and 2, students are introduced to business transactions through non-business events that help them better understand the nature of transactions.

Accounting is an information system that provides reports to stakeholders about the economic activities and condition of a business.

NEW! Real World Notes. J.C. Penney Co. and General Electric are just a couple of the familiar examples that provide a close-up look at how accounting operates in the marketplace. These examples are highlighted in the margin of the text:

AT&T
Campbell Soup Company
Coca-Cola Enterprises Inc.
Delta Air Lines
Ford Motor Co.

Gillette
Hewlett Packard
Mercedes-Benz
UPS

NEW! Financial Analysis and Interpretation. At the end of each chapter, a section describing an important element of financial analysis helps students understand the information in financial statements and how that information is used.

Student Success Starts Here: End-of-Chapter Excellence

This edition takes students well beyond procedures into truly pertinent applications. Consider the following tools that will help students succeed in the business world:

Receive Payments

Customer Payment		DATE	BALANCE
		03/28/00	5,200.00

Customer:Job Handler Co.

Amount 2,200.00
Pmt. Method
Check No.

Memo

○ Group with other undeposited funds
● Deposit To First National Bank

Existing Credits	0.00	Total to Apply	2,200.00
☐ Apply Existing Credits?		Unapplied Amount	0.00

Invoices paid (with this payment) and those still outstanding

✓	Date	Type	Number	Orig. Amt.	Disc. Date	Amt. Due	Payment
✓	03/02/00	Invoice	615	2,200.00		2,200.00	2,200.00
	03/27/00	Invoice	618	3,000.00		3,000.00	0.00
					Totals	5,200.00	2,200.00

■ **NEW! QuickBooks Problems** at the end of Chs. 5, 6, 8, and 11 can be solved using the invoice/billing features in QuickBooks.

■ **Critical-Thinking and Decision-Making Activities.** Students need to develop analytical abilities, not just memorize rules. These activities focus on understanding and solving issues. Some are presented in dialogue format–a conversation in which students can "observe" and "participate" when they respond to the issue being discussed.

■ **NEW! Group Learning Activities** let students learn accounting and business concepts while building teamwork skills at the same time.

■ NEW! **Internet Activities** launch students into accounting-related areas of the Worldwide Web's ever-expanding universe.

■ **"What Do You Think?"** These exercises and activities take students beyond the scope of the texts to apply newly learned material.

■ **"What's Wrong With This?"** These innovative exercises challenge students to analyze and discover what is wrong with a financial statement, a report, or a management decision.

■ **Communications Items.** These activities help students develop communication skills that will be essential on the job, regardless of the fields they pursue.

Accounting, perhaps more than any other discipline, is a field that must be practiced to be understood and retained. The quantity and quality of the following end-of-chapter resources have always been distinguishing characteristics of *Financial Accounting* and *Accounting*:

■ **Continuing Problem** in Chs. 1-4. Here's a great opportunity for students to practice what they've learned. As they study each step of the accounting cycle, they can follow a single company–Music Today–from its transactions to the effect of those transactions on its financial statements.

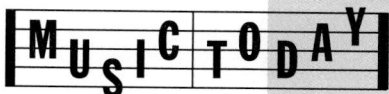

■ **Illustrative Problem and Solution.** A solved problem models one or more of a chapter's assignment problems, helping students make the most of the chapter and end-of-chapter materials.

■ NEW! **Self-Examination Questions** now include a matching activity to help students review and retain terms and definitions.

■ **Exercises.** An average of 20 exercises at the end of each chapter–more than any other text on the market–can be assigned or used as examples in the classroom. Each exercise focuses on only one specific chapter objective.

■ **Problems.** Each chapter includes two full sets of problems for use as classroom illustrations, for assignments, for alternate assignments, or for independent studying. This edition features shortened problems to provide better focus on key chapter topics.

■ **Comprehensive Problems.** At the end of Chs. 4, 6, 11, and 14, cumulative learning applications integrate and summarize the concepts of several chapters to test students' comprehension. Two of these problems can be solved using the debit/credit features of QuickBooks.

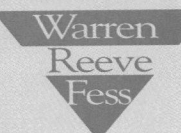

A Collaborative Success: Comprehensive Resource Package

We've designed our entire supplement package around the comments instructors have provided about their courses and teaching needs. These comments have made this supplement package the best in the business.

Available to Students—Because every class, instructor, and student has different needs, *Financial Accounting 7e,* and *Accounting, 19e,* offer a broad range of supplements. Both print material and easy-to-use, affordable technologies help students succeed in the course and in the business world. Some of these supplements are:

PROBLEM 5–2B Jayco Co.
Revenue and Cash receipts journals;
accounts receivable and general ledgers
Objective 4

Name:

Note: The working papers that follow Problem 5–2A may be used with this problem.

Transactions related to revenue and cash receipts completed by Jayco Co. during the period June 15–30 of the current year are as follows.

June   15. Issued Invoice No. 717 to Yamura Co., $6,780.
16. Received cash from AGI Co. for the balance owed on its account.
17. Issued Invoice No. 718 to Hardy Co., $5,340.
18. Issued Invoice No. 719 to Ross and Son, $6,500.
Post all journals to the accounts receivable ledger.
21. Received cash from Hardy Co. for the balance owed on June 15.
24. Issued Invoice No. 720 to Hardy Co., $2,960.
Post all journals to the accounts receivable ledger.
25. Received cash from Yamura Co. for the balance due on invoice of June 15.
27. Received cash from Hardy Co. for invoice of June 17.
29. Issued Invoice No. 721 to AGI Co., $1,600.
30. Recorded cash sales for the second half of the month, $11,340.
30. Received $4,000 of supplies for services rendered to Breck Company.
Post all journals to the accounts receivable ledger.

Letha JeanPierre
Sales Manager

- **Working Papers.** The traditional Working Papers are available both with and without problem-specific forms.

- **Working Papers Plus,** prepared by John Wanlass of DeAnza College. This alternative to traditional working papers integrates the chapter learning objectives and glossary with forms for solving all textbook exercises and selected textbook problems.

- **Study Guide,** prepared by James Heintz of the University of Connecticut and Carl Warren. The Study Guide includes quiz and test tips and multiple choice, fill-in-the-blank, and true-false questions with solutions. The Study Guide is packaged with a disk that allows students to score their own practice tests.

- **PowerNotes,** prepared by John Wanlass. In a classroom where the PowerPoint™ transparencies are utilized, this workbook provides students with printed versions of the transparencies, along with critical-thinking activities and self-study review questions related to those slides.

- **General Ledger Software,** prepared by Dale Klooster and Warren Allen. This best-selling educational general ledger package (formerly Solutions Software) is enhanced with planning tools, a Journal Wizard, more tool tips, a new color-coded system, and additional prob-

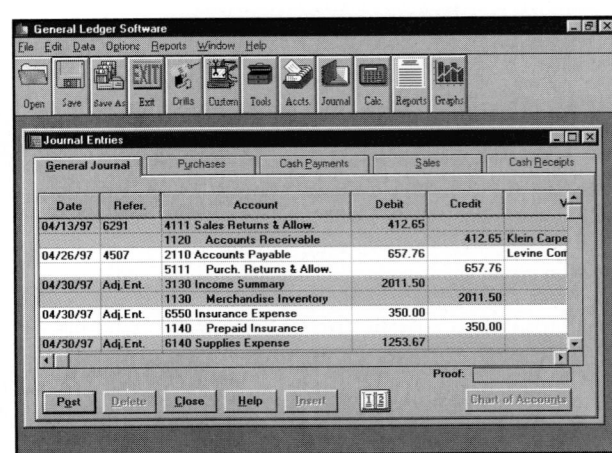

lems for the managerial chapters. Solving end-of-chapter problems, comprehensive problems, as well as practice sets is as easy as clicking icons with a mouse.

■ **Homework Assistant and Tutor (HAT),** prepared by Ray Meservy of Brigham Young University. This user-friendly software for Windows visually teaches students the relationships between journals, ledgers, and financial statements as they solve selected end-of-chapter problems. A built-in tutor function includes numerous hints and help screens.

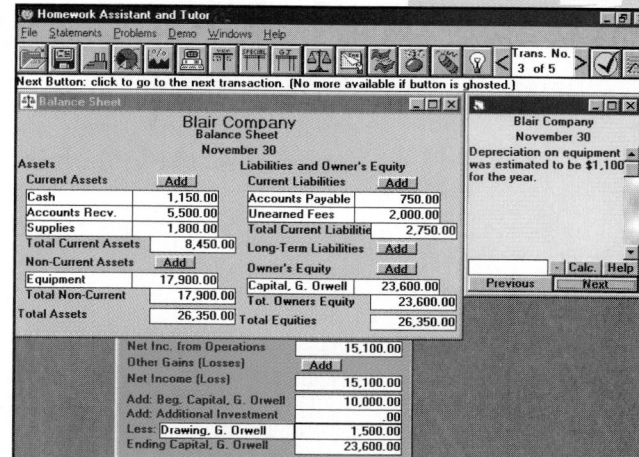

■ **Spreadsheet Applications Software.** Students can solve dozens of problems by using any of the standard spreadsheet packages, such as Lotus 1-2-3® and Excel.® Alternative "what-if" scenarios are also presented and explored.

Available to Instructors–South-Western Publishing continues to lead the field in supplements for instructors, from traditional printed materials to the latest integrated classroom technology. Among these support tools are:

■ ***Virtual Community***–A variety of instructor resources are now available through South-Western's Web site. Organized by chapter and topic, this hyper-linked syllabus includes text-specific and other accounting-related resources. Many of these online resources are also available on CD-ROM. We invite you to be part of this community by sampling what we've provided and by sharing your own material, ideas, and comments with your colleagues and students. Visit our discussion forum and exchange information on current developments in the profession, and share ideas on the course and curriculum.

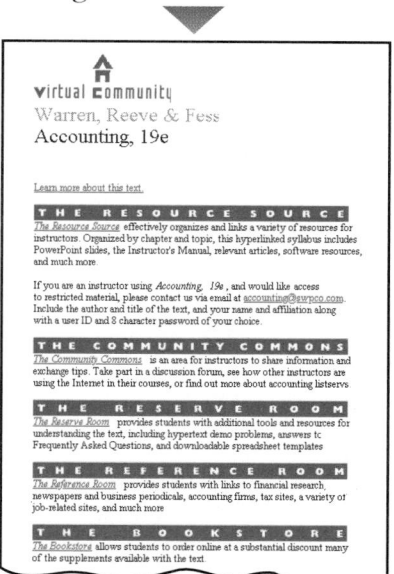

warren.swcollege.com

■ **PowerPoint™ Transparencies,** prepared by John Wanlass. PowerPoint Transparencies enhance lectures and simplify class preparation. You can also add your own custom slides, using this popular presentation package.

■ **Traditional Ancillaries.** The Instructor's Manual, Test Bank, and other traditional elements are available in separate bound volumes as well as on the instructor's CD-ROM. A wide range of writing exercises, group learning activities, demonstration problems, and accounting scenarios are included in the Instructor's Manual and the on-line Accounting Virtual Community.

A Triumph of Teamwork: Acknowledgements

As we have described throughout this preface, our texts are a tribute to the power of collaboration and collegial support. We thank the many people who have made the new editions a reality.

The following people kept diaries of their experience with the texts:

Sam Allred
Forsyth Technical Community College

Thelma Bushong
Delta College

Patricia Conn
Atlantic Community College

Terry Elliott
Morehead State University

Richard Howden
Delta College

George Johnson
Norfolk State University

Ed Krohn
Miami-Dade Community College - South

Linda Kropp
Modesto Junior College

Michael Landers
Middlesex County College

Jim Lentz
Moraine Valley Community College

Larry Lofton
Hinds Community College

William Rencher
Seminole Community College

Ronald Richard
Westark Community College

John Teter
St. Petersburg Junior College

Henry Wilk, Jr.
Fisher College

The following people participated in focus groups:

William Allen
Camden County College

John Atella
Harrisburg Area Community College

Clarence Brown, Jr.
Harold Washington College

Yvonne Brown
University of Cincinnati

Donna Chadwick
Sinclair Community College

Robert Dan
San Antonio College

David Darst
Central Ohio Technical College

Sid Davidson
Foothill College

Carl Essig
Montgomery County Community College

Preston Ford
Malcolm X College

James Genseal
Joliet Junior College

Mary Govan
Sinclair Community College

Betty Habershon
Prince George's Community College

Ken Harper
DeAnza College

Paul Harris
Camden County College

George Heyman
Oakton Community College

Gloria Jackson
San Antonio College

Letha Jeanpierre
DeAnza College

Tom Joyce
Pasadena City College

Sanford Kahn
University of Cincinnati

Arthur Katz
Canada College
Sierra College

Hana Kovanic
Bergen Community College

Cathy Landers
San Antonio College

Jim Lentz
Moraine Valley Community College

Jane Loprest
Bucks County Community College

Florence McGovern
Bergen Community College

Hector Martinez
San Antonio College

Ken Miller
San Antonio College

Deborah Most
Dutchess Community College

Gene Pinchuk
Pasadena City College

Jim Puthoff
Sinclair Community College

Ed Riechman
Central State University

Jill Russell
Camden County College

Nancy Sheridan
Bucks County Community College

Barry Smith
DeAnza College

Doug Staley
Pasadena City College

Martin Stub
DeVry Institute of Technology

Larry Tartaglino
Cabrillo College

Russell Vermillion
Prince George's Community College

John Wanlass
DeAnza College

Tom Welsch
Harold Washington College

Phyllis Yasuda
DeAnza College

The following people reviewed manuscript for the texts:

Sheryl J. Alley
Ball State University

Carl Ballard
Central Piedmont Community College

Frank R. Beigbeder
Santa Ana College

Clifford Bellers
Washtenaw Community College

John R. Blahnik
Lorain County Community College

Donna Chadwick
Sinclair Community College

Ken Coffey
Johnson County Community College

Ana Cruz
Miami-Dade Community College - Wolfson

Alan Davis
Community College of Philadelphia

Lyle Dehning
Metropolitan State College of Denver

Pamela Donahue
Northern Essex Community College

Estelle Faier
Metro Community College

Leonard Goldman
Kingsborough Community College

Debra Goorbin
Westchester Community College

Cynthia Greeson
Ivy Tech State College

Robert Gregrich
Brevard Community College

James L. Haydon
East Los Angeles Community College

Robert Held
Harper College

Tim Helton
Joliet Junior College

Brenda Hester
Volunteer State Community College

Margaret Hicks
Howard University

Bob Hildenbrand
Albuquerque T-VT Community College

Anita Hope
Tarrant County Junior College - Northeast

George Katz
St. Philip's College

Rebecca Kerr
Midlands Technical College

Jack Klett
Indian River Community College

Ed Krohn
Miami-Dade Community College - South

George Lazar
Owens Technical College

Jim Lentz
Moraine Valley Community College

Florence McGovern
Bergen Community College

Sal Marchionna
Triton College

S. A. Marino
Westchester Community College

Salah Negm
Prince George's Community College

Harris O'Brien
North Harris County College

Frank A. Paliotta
Berkeley College

Paige Paulsen
Salt Lake Community College

Loretta Burch Rojo
Central Piedmont Community College

Larry Roman
Cuyahoga Community College

Jill Russell
Camden County College

John J. Sabbagh
Northern Essex Community College

Richard Sarkisian
Camden County College

Lois Slutsky
Boward Community College - South

Steve Teeter
Utah Valley State College

Philip L. Trees
Broward Community College

Shafi Ullah
Broward Community College - South

Joan Weaver
Volunteer State Community College

Charles Wellens
Fitchburg State College

Thomas Welsch
Harold Washington College

Kathleen Wessman
Montgomery College

Preston Wilks
Big Bend Community College

Brief Contents

Ch. 1   Introduction to Accounting and Business   1

Ch. 2   Analyzing Transactions   43

Ch. 3   The Matching Concept and the Adjusting Process   97

Ch. 4   Completing the Accounting Cycle   135

Ch. 5   Accounting Systems and Internal Controls   177

Ch. 6   Accounting for Merchandising Businesses   224

Ch. 7   Cash   277

Ch. 8   Receivables   310

Ch. 9   Inventories   343

Ch. 10   Fixed Assets and Intangible Assets   381

Ch. 11   Current Liabilities   420

Ch. 12   Corporations: Organization, Capital Stock Transactions, and Dividends   464

Ch. 13   Corporations: Income and Taxes, Stockholders' Equity, and Investments in Stocks   497

Ch. 14   Bonds Payable and Investments in Bonds   536

Ch. 15   Statement of Cash Flows   576

Ch. 16   Financial Statement Analysis   625

Appendixes:

A   Interest Tables   A-2

B   Codes of Professional Ethics   B-1

C   Alternative Methods of Recording Deferrals   C-1

D   Periodic Inventory Systems for Merchandising Businesses   D-1

E   Foreign Currency Transactions   E-1

F   Partnerships   F-1

G   Hershey Foods Corporation Annual Report   G-1

Glossary   GL-1

Subject Index   SI-1

Company Index   CI-1

Index of Web Site Addresses   WI-1

7TH EDITION

Financial Accounting

Carl S. Warren, Ph.D., C.P.A., C.I.A.
Professor of Accounting
University of Georgia, Athens

James M. Reeve, Ph.D., C.P.A.
Professor of Accounting
University of Tennessee, Knoxville

Philip E. Fess, Ph.D., C.P.A.
Professor Emeritus of Accountancy
University of Illinois, Champaign-Urbana

Accounting Team Director: Richard Lindgren
Senior Acquisitions Editor: David L. Shaut
Senior Marketing Manager: Sharon Oblinger
Senior Developmental Editor: Ken Martin
Production Editor: Mark Sears
Production House: Litten Editing and Production with GGS Information Services
Cover and Internal Design: Lou Ann Thesing
Cover Illustration: © 1997 Rob Schuster, product photography by Joe Higgins
Internal Illustrations: Rob Schuster and GGS Information Services
Photo Editor: Cary Benbow
Photo Researchers: Feldman & Associates, Inc.
Media and Technology Editor: Diane M. Van Bakel
Media Production Editor: Lora Craver
Copy Writer, Preface: Steve Mott, Words & Occasional Wisdom
Cover Illustration Acknowledgments:
      Ford Expedition used with permission of Ford Motor Company.
      L.L. Bean catalog cover courtesy of L.L. Bean and Francis Golden.
      Motorola logo and cellular phones courtesy of the Cellular Subscriber Sector of Motorola, Inc.
      Tide detergent box © The Procter & Gamble Company. Reprinted with permission.
      Wrigley's gum packages reprinted courtesy of the Wm. Wrigley Jr. Company.
      Mattel logo © 1997 Mattel, Inc. All rights reserved. Used with permission.
      McDonald's Golden Arches used with permission from McDonald's Corporation.
      Levi's Jeans courtesy of Levi Strauss & Company.

International Thomson Publishing
South-Western is an ITP Company. The ITP trademark is used under license.

Library of Congress Cataloging-in-Publication Data

The complete version of the text is catalogued as follows:
Warren, Carl S.
     Accounting / Carl S. Warren, James M. Reeve, Philip E. Fess. —
19th ed.
   p. cm.
Includes index.
ISBN 0-538-86972-0 (alk. paper)
  1. Accounting. I. Reeve, James M., II. Fess, Philip E. III. Title.
HF5635.F386 1998   98-18438
657—dc21   CIP

ISBN: 0-538-87413-9

2 3 4 5 6 7 VH 4 3 2 1 0 9 8

Printed in the United States of America

CARL S. WARREN

Dr. Carl S. Warren is the Arthur Andersen & Co. Alumni Professor of Accounting at the J.M. Tull School of Accounting at the University of Georgia, Athens. Professor Warren received his Ph.D. from Michigan State University in 1973. Dr. Warren's experience in listening to users of his texts sharpens his keen focus on helping students learn. When he is not teaching classes or writing textbooks, Dr. Warren enjoys golf, racquetball, and fishing.

JAMES M. REEVE

Dr. James M. Reeve is Professor of Accounting at the University of Tennessee, Knoxville. He received his Ph.D. from Oklahoma State University in 1980. Dr. Reeve is founder of the Cost Management Institute and a member of the Institute for Productivity Through Quality faculty at the University of Tennessee. In addition to his teaching experience, Dr. Reeve brings to this text a wealth of experience consulting on managerial accounting issues with numerous companies, including Procter & Gamble, AMOCO, Rockwell International, Harris Corporation, and Freddie Mac. Dr. Reeve's interests outside the classroom and the business world include golf, skiing, reading, and travel.

PHILIP E. FESS

Dr. Philip E. Fess is the Arthur Andersen & Co. Alumni Professor of Accountancy Emeritus at the University of Illinois, Champaign-Urbana. He received his Ph.D. from the University of Illinois. Dr. Fess has been involved in writing textbooks for over twenty-five years, and his knowledge of how to make texts userfriendly is reflected on the pages of this edition. Dr. Fess plays golf and tennis, and he has represented the United States in international tennis competition.

Contents

1 Introduction to Accounting and Business 1

Nature of a Business 2
Types of Businesses 2
Types of Business Organizations 3
Business Stakeholders 4

The Role of Accounting in Business 5

Business Ethics 6

Profession of Accounting 7
Private Accounting 8
Public Accounting 8
Specialized Accounting Fields 9

Generally Accepted Accounting Principles 9
Business Entity Concept 10
The Cost Concept 10

Assets, Liabilities, and Owner's Equity 11

Business Transactions and the Accounting Equation 11

Financial Statements 16
Income Statement 16
Statement of Owner's Equity 16
Balance Sheet 18
Statement of Cash Flows 18

Financial Analysis and Interpretation 19

2 Analyzing Transactions 43

Usefulness of an Account 44

Characteristics of an Account 46

Analyzing and Summarizing Transactions in Accounts 47
Transactions and Balance Sheet Accounts 47
Income Statement Accounts 49
Withdrawals by the Owner 50
Normal Balances of Accounts 51

Illustration of Analyzing and Summarizing Transactions 51

Trial Balance 64

Discovery and Correction of Errors 65
Discovery of Errors 65
Correction of Errors 66

Financial Analysis and Interpretation 67

3 The Matching Concept and the Adjusting Process 97

The Matching Concept 98

Nature of the Adjusting Process 99

Recording Adjusting Entries 101
Deferred Expenses (Prepaid Expenses) 102
Deferred Revenue (Unearned Revenue) 103
Accrued Expenses (Accrued Liabilities) 104
Accrued Revenues (Accrued Assets) 106
Fixed Assets 107

Summary of Adjustment Process 108

Financial Analysis and Interpretation 112

4 Completing the Accounting Cycle 135

Work Sheet 136
Unadjusted Trial Balance Columns 136
Adjustments Columns 136
Adjusted Trial Balance Columns 136A
Income Statement and Balance Sheet Columns 136A

Financial Statements 136D
Income Statement 136D
Statement of Owner's Equity 137
Balance Sheet 137

Adjusting and Closing Entries 139
Journalizing and Posting Closing Entries 140
Post-Closing Trial Balance 146

Fiscal Year 146

Accounting Cycle 147

Financial Analysis and Interpretation 148

Appendix: Reversing Entries 150

Comprehensive Problem 1 172

Practice Set: Larry's Lawn Care
This set is a service business operated as a proprietorship. It is a manual set that includes a narrative of transactions and instructions for an optional solution with no debits and credits.

5   Accounting Systems and Internal Controls   177

Basic Accounting Systems   178

Internal Control   179
Objectives of Internal Control   179
Elements of Internal Control   180

Manual Accounting Systems   184
Subsidiary Ledgers   185
Special Journals   185
Manual Accounting System: The Revenue and Collection Cycle   187
Manual Accounting System: The Purchase and Payment Cycle   191

Adapting Manual Accounting Systems   195
Additional Subsidiary Ledgers   195
Modified Special Journals   196

Computerized Accounting Systems   196
Computer Hardware Basics   196
Computer Software Basics   197
Computerized System: An Illustration of the Revenue and Collection Cycle   197

QuickBooks Problem 1: The Revenue and Collection Cycle   219

QuickBooks Problem 2: The Purchase and Payment Cycle   220

6   Accounting for Merchandising Businesses   224

Nature of Merchandising Businesses   225

Accounting for Purchases   226
Purchases Discounts   227
Purchases Returns and Allowances   229

Accounting for Sales   230
Cash Sales   230
Sales on Account   231
Sales Discounts   232
Sales Returns and Allowances   232
Sales Taxes   233
Trade Discounts   234

Transportation Costs   234

Illustration of Accounting for Merchandise Transactions   236

Chart of Accounts for a Merchandising Business   237

Income Statement for a Merchandising Business   238
Multiple-Step Form   239
Single-Step Form   241

The Accounting Cycle for a Merchandising Business   241
Merchandise Inventory Shrinkage   242
Work Sheet   242
Statement of Owner's Equity   242
Balance Sheet   243
Closing Entries   244

Financial Analysis and Interpretation   244

Appendix 1: Accounting Systems for Merchandisers   245
Manual Accounting System   245
Computerized Accounting Systems   247

Appendix 2: Work Sheet and Adjusting and Closing Entries for a Merchandising Business   249

QuickBooks Problem (Appendix 1): Buying and Selling Inventory   270

Comprehensive Problem 2   271

Practice Set: Pacific Poolworks
This set is a merchandising business operated as a proprietorship. It includes business documents and an optional narrative of transactions. It can be solved manually or with the General Ledger Software.

Practice Set: Hazzard Travel
This set involves maintaining an accounting system for the first two months of operations of a small business. The operating, financing, and investing decisions made in completing the set result in different financial outcomes. The set can be solved manually or with the General Ledger Software.

7   Cash   277

Nature of Cash and the Importance of Controls Over Cash   278

Control of Cash Receipts   278
Controlling Cash Received from Cash Sales   279
Controlling Cash Received in the Mail   280

Internal Control of Cash Payments   280
Basic Features of the Voucher System   281
Electronic Funds Transfer   282

Bank Accounts: Their Nature and Use as a Control Over Cash   282
Business Bank Accounts   283
Bank Statement   284
Bank Accounts as a Control Over Cash   285

Bank Reconciliation   286

Petty Cash   289

Presentation of Cash on the Balance Sheet   291

Financial Analysis and Interpretation   291

8   Receivables   310

Classification of Receivables   311
Accounts Receivable   311
Notes Receivable   311
Other Receivables   312

Internal Control of Receivables   312

Uncollectible Receivables   313

Allowance Method of Accounting for Uncollectibles   314
Write-Offs to the Allowance Account   315
Estimating Uncollectibles   316

Direct Write-Off Method of Accounting for Uncollectibles   318

Characteristics of Notes Receivable   319
Due Date   320
Interest   320
Maturity Value   321

Accounting for Notes Receivable   321

Receivables on the Balance Sheet   322

Financial Analysis and Interpretation   323

Appendix: Discounting Notes Receivable   325

QuickBooks Problem: Aging of Accounts Receivable   339

9   Inventories   343

Internal Control of Inventories   344

Effect of Inventory Errors on Financial Statements   346

Inventory Cost Flow Assumptions   347

Inventory Costing Methods Under a Perpetual Inventory System   350
First-In, First-Out Method   350
Last-In, First-Out Method   351
Average Cost Method   352
Computerized Perpetual Inventory Systems   352

Inventory Costing Methods Under a Periodic Inventory System   353
First-In, First-Out Method   354
Last-In, First-Out Method   355
Average Cost Method   355

Comparing Inventory Costing Methods   356
Use of the First-In, First-Out Method   356
Use of the Last-In, First-Out Method   357
Use of the Average Cost Method   357

Valuation of Inventory at Other Than Cost   357
Valuation at Lower of Cost or Market   358
Valuation at Net Realizable Value   358

Presentation of Merchandise Inventory on the Balance Sheet   359

Estimating Inventory Cost   359
Retail Method of Inventory Costing   359
Gross Profit Method of Estimating Inventories   360

Financial Analysis and Interpretation   361

10   Fixed Assets and Intangible Assets   381

Nature of Fixed Assets   382
Costs of Acquiring Fixed Assets   382
Nature of Depreciation   384

Accounting for Depreciation   385
Straight-Line Method   386
Units-of-Production Method   386
Declining-Balance Method   387
Comparing Depreciation Methods   388
Depreciation for Federal Income Tax   388
Revising Depreciation Estimates   389
Composite-Rate Method   390

Capital and Revenue Expenditures   390
Types of Capital Expenditures   390
Summary of Capital and Revenue Expenditures   391

Disposal of Fixed Assets   392
Discarding Fixed Assets   392
Selling Fixed Assets   393
Exchanging Similar Fixed Assets   393

Leasing Fixed Assets   396

Internal Control of Fixed Assets   396

Natural Resources   397

Intangible Assets   398
Patents   398
Copyrights and Trademarks   398
Goodwill   399

Financial Reporting for Fixed Assets and Intangible Assets   399

Financial Analysis and Interpretation   400

Appendix: Sum-of-the-Years-Digits Depreciation   401

11   Current Liabilities   420

The Nature of Current Liabilities   421

Short-Term Notes Payable   421

Contingent Liabilities   423

Payroll and Payroll Taxes   425
Liability for Employee Earnings   425
Deductions from Employee Earnings   426
Computing Employee Net Pay   429
Liability for Employer's Payroll Taxes   429

Accounting Systems for Payroll and Payroll Taxes   430
Payroll Register   431
Employee's Earnings Record   433
Payroll Checks   435
Payroll System Diagram   436
Internal Controls for Payroll Systems   437

Employees' Fringe Benefits   438
Vacation Pay   438
Pensions   439
Postretirement Benefits Other than Pensions   440

Financial Analysis and Interpretation   440

QuickBooks Problem: Payroll   457

Comprehensive Problem 3   458

Practice Set: Water Works
This set is a merchandising business operated as a proprietorship. It includes business documents and an optional narrative of transactions, including payroll transactions. It can be solved manually or with the General Ledger Software.

12   Corporations: Organization, Capital Stock Transactions, and Dividends   464

Nature of a Corporation   465
Characteristics of a Corporation   465
Forming a Corporation   466

Stockholders' Equity   467

Sources of Paid-In Capital   468
Stock   468
Other Sources of Paid-In Capital   471

Issuing Stock   471
Premium on Stock   473
No-Par Stock   473

Treasury Stock Transactions   474

Stock Splits   475

Accounting for Dividends   476
Cash Dividends   476
Stock Dividends   478

Financial Analysis and Interpretation   479

13   Corporations: Income and Taxes, Stockholders' Equity, and Investments in Stocks   497

Corporate Income Taxes   498
Payment of Income Taxes   498
Allocation of Income Taxes   499

Unusual Items that Affect the Income Statement   501
Discontinued Operations   502
Extraordinary Items   502
Changes in Accounting Principles   503

Earnings per Common Share   503

Reporting Stockholders' Equity   505
Reporting Paid-In Capital   505
Reporting Retained Earnings   506
Statement of Stockholders' Equity   507

Comprehensive Income   507

Accounting for Investments in Stocks   508
Short-Term Investments in Stocks   508
Long-Term Investments in Stocks   510
Sale of Investments in Stocks   512

Business Combinations   513
Mergers and Consolidations   513
Parent and Subsidiary Corporations   513
Consolidated Financial Statements   514

Financial Analysis and Interpretation   515

Practice Set: First Designs Inc.
This set is a departmentalized merchandising business operated as a corporation. It includes a narrative of transactions, and can be solved manually or with the General Ledger Software.

Practice Set: SEMO Sporting Goods Supply Inc.
This set is a wholesaling business operated as a corporation. It requires manual correcting entries and financial statements.

14   Bonds Payable and Investments in Bonds   536

Financing Corporations   537

Characteristics of Bonds Payable   539

The Present-Value Concept and Bonds Payable   539
Present Value of the Face Amount of Bonds   541
Present Value of the Periodic Bond Interest Payments   542

Accounting for Bonds Payable   543
Bonds Issued at Face Amount   543
Bonds Issued at a Discount   545
Amortizing a Bond Discount   545
Bonds Issued at a Premium   546
Amortizing a Bond Premium   546
Zero-Coupon Bonds   547

Bond Sinking Funds   547

Bond Redemption   548

Investments in Bonds   549
Accounting for Bond Investments—Purchase, Interest, and Amortization   549
Accounting for Bond Investments—Sale   551

Corporation Balance Sheet   552
Balance Sheet Presentation of Bonds Payable   552
Balance Sheet Presentation of Bond Investments   554

Financial Analysis and Interpretation   554

Appendix: Effective Interest Rate Method of Amortization   555
Amortization of Discount by the Interest Method   556
Amortization of Premium by the Interest Method   557

Comprehensive Problem 4   571

Practice Set: Electronic Play Inc.
This set is a merchandising business operated as a corporation. It includes a narrative of transactions, which are to be recorded in a general journal. It can be solved manually or with the General Ledger Software.

15   Statement of Cash Flows   576

Purpose of the Statement of Cash Flows   577

Reporting Cash Flows   577
Cash Flows from Operating Activities   578
Cash Flows from Investing Activities   579
Cash Flows from Financing Activities   580
Noncash Investing and Financing Activities   580
No Cash Flow per Share   581

Statement of Cash Flows—The Indirect Method   581
Retained Earnings   582
Common Stock   586
Bonds Payable   586
Building   587
Land   587
Preparing the Statement of Cash Flows   588

Statement of Cash Flows—The Direct Method   589
Cash Received from Customers   590
Cash Payments for Merchandise   590
Cash Payments for Operating Expenses   591
Gain on Sale of Land   591
Interest Expense   591
Cash Payments for Income Taxes   592
Reporting Cash Flows from Operating Activities—Direct Method   592

Financial Analysis and Interpretation   593

Appendix: Work Sheet for Statement of Cash Flows   595
Work Sheet—Indirect Method   595
Work Sheet—Direct Method   597

16   Financial Statement Analysis   625

Basic Analytical Procedures   626
Horizontal Analysis   626
Vertical Analysis   629
Common-Size Statements   630
Other Analytical Measures   630

Solvency Analysis   631
Current Position Analysis   632
Accounts Receivable Analysis   633
Inventory Analysis   634
Ratio of Fixed Assets to Long-Term Liabilities   635
Ratio of Liabilities to Stockholders' Equity   636
Number of Times Interest Charges Earned   636

Profitability Analysis   637
Ratio of Net Sales to Assets   637
Rate Earned on Total Assets   638
Rate Earned on Stockholders' Equity   638

Rate Earned on Common Stockholders'
Equity 639
Earnings per Share on Common Stock 640
Price-Earnings Ratio 640
Dividends per Share and Dividend Yield 641

Summary of Analytical Measures 642

Corporate Annual Reports 643
Financial Highlights 643
President's Letter to the Stockholders 644
Management Report 644
Independent Auditors' Report 644
Historical Summary 644
Other Information 644

Hershey's Food Corporation Problem: Financial Statement Analysis 663

QuickBooks Problem: Vertical Analysis 664

Appendix A: Interest Tables A-2

Appendix B: Codes of Professional Ethics B-1

Appendix C: Alternative Methods of Recording Deferrals C-1

Appendix D: Periodic Inventory Systems for Merchandising Businesses D-1

Appendix E: Foreign Currency Transactions E-1

Appendix F: Partnerships F-1

Appendix G: Hershey Foods Corporation Annual Report G-1

Glossary GL-1

Subject Index SI-1

Company Index CI-1

Index of Web Site Addresses WI-1

Photo Credits

I

Introduction to Accounting and Business

Do you use accounting? Yes, we all use accounting information in one form or another. For example, when you think about buying a car, you use accounting information to determine whether you can afford it. Similarly, when you decided to attend college, you considered the costs (the tuition, textbooks, and so on). Most likely, you also considered the benefits (the ability to obtain a higher-paying job or a more desirable job).

Is accounting important to you? Yes, accounting is important in your personal life as well as in your career, even though you may not become an accountant. For example, you may be the manager of a chain of pizza restaurants who is deciding on whether to buy new delivery cars. Accounting information about the restaurants will be a major factor in your decision to acquire the cars and the bank's decision to finance the purchase.

Our primary objective in this text is to illustrate basic accounting concepts that will help you to make good personal and business decisions. We begin by discussing what a business is, how it operates, and the role that accounting plays.

After studying this chapter, you should be able to:

1 Describe the nature of a business.

2 Describe the role of accounting in business.

3 Describe the importance of business ethics and the basic principles of proper ethical conduct.

4 Describe the profession of accounting.

5 Summarize the development of accounting principles and relate them to practice.

6 State the accounting equation and define each element of the equation.

7 Explain how business transactions can be stated in terms of the resulting changes in the three basic elements of the accounting equation.

8 Describe the financial statements of a proprietorship and explain how they interrelate.

9 Use the ratio of liabilities to owner's equity to analyze the ability of a business to withstand poor business conditions.

Nature of a Business

OBJECTIVE 1

Describe the nature of a business.

Name an example of a business. Your example might be a large company such as **General Motors**, **McDonald's**, or **AT&T**. It might be a local company, such as a gas station or a grocery store, or perhaps it might be your employer. It might be a restaurant, a law firm, or a medical office. These examples are all businesses, but what do they have in common that identifies them as businesses?

In general, a **business** is an organization in which basic resources (inputs), such as materials and labor, are assembled and processed to provide goods or services (outputs) to customers.[1] Businesses come in all sizes, from a local coffee house to a General Motors, which sells several billion dollars worth of cars and trucks each year. The customers of a business are individuals or other businesses who purchase goods or services in exchange for money or other items of value. In contrast, a church is not a business because those who receive its services are not obligated to pay for them.

The objective of most businesses is to maximize profits. **Profit** is the difference between the amounts received from customers for goods or services provided and the amounts paid for the inputs used to provide the goods or services. Some businesses operate with an objective other than to maximize profits. The objective of such nonprofit businesses is to provide some benefit to society, such as medical research or conservation of natural resources. In other cases, governmental units such as cities operate water works or sewage treatment plants on a nonprofit basis. Our focus in this text will be on businesses operated to earn a profit. However, many of the concepts and principles also apply to nonprofit businesses.

Types of Businesses

There are three different types of businesses that are operated for profit: manufacturing, merchandising, and service businesses. Each type of business has unique characteristics.

Manufacturing businesses change basic inputs into products that are sold to individual customers. Examples of manufacturing businesses and some of their products are shown below.

---

[1] A complete glossary of terms appears at the end of the text.

BUSINESS ON STAGE

Businesses convert basic inputs into goods and services for customers. These inputs are known as *factors of production*. The factors of production common to all businesses are natural resources, labor, capital, and entrepreneurs. Natural resources are the basic raw materials, including farmland, forests, and mineral deposits. Labor is the employees who contribute their intellectual and physical efforts to a business. Capital represents the financial resources (money) invested in the business to purchase such items as machinery and buildings. Entrepreneurs are the people who combine natural resources, labor, and capital together to produce goods and services.

Let's examine a small pizza restaurant as an example of a business. The pizza ingredients of tomato sauce, dough, sausage, pepperoni, and cheese represent the natural resources that are derived from farming the land. The employees (labor) are the waitresses, the delivery person, the cash register clerk, and the baker. The money required to purchase the land, building, and equipment is the capital. The owner/manager who began the business and operates it on a daily basis is the entrepreneur. ∎

The Factors of Production

Manufacturing Business	Product
General Motors	Automobiles, trucks, vans
General Mills	Breakfast cereals
Boeing	Jet aircraft
Nike	Athletic shoes
Coca-Cola	Beverages
Sony	Stereos, televisions, radios

Merchandising businesses also sell products to customers. However, they do not make the products, but purchase them from other businesses (such as manufacturers). In this sense, merchandisers bring products and customers together. Examples of merchandising businesses and some of the products they sell are shown below.

Merchandising Business	Product
Wal-Mart	General merchandise
Barnes and Noble	Books
Toys "R" Us	Toys
Circuit City	Consumer electronics
Lands' End	Apparel

Service businesses provide services rather than products to customers. Examples of service businesses and the types of services they offer are shown below.

Service Business	Service
Disney	Entertainment
Delta Air Lines	Transportation
Marriott Hotels	Hospitality and lodging
Merrill Lynch	Financial
Sprint	Telecommunications

 Roughly eight out of every ten workers in the United States are employed in providing services. In the past twenty years, 90 percent of the new jobs created in the United States have been in service businesses.
Source: Walter Kiechel III, "How We Will Work in the Year 2000," *Fortune,* May 17, 1993, p. 46.

Types of Business Organizations

A business is normally organized as one of three different forms: proprietorship, partnership, or corporation. In the following paragraphs, we briefly describe each form and discuss its advantages and disadvantages.

A **proprietorship** is owned by one individual. More than 70% of the businesses in the United States are organized as proprietorships. The popularity of this form is due to the ease and the low cost of organizing. The primary disadvantage of proprietorships is that the financial resources available to the business are limited to the individual owner's resources. Small local businesses such as hardware stores, repair shops, laundries, restaurants, and maid services are often organized as proprietorships.

As a business grows and more financial and managerial resources are needed, it may become a partnership. A **partnership** is owned by two or more individuals. Like proprietorships, small local businesses such as automotive repair shops, music stores, beauty shops, and men's and women's clothing stores may be organized as partnerships. Currently, about 10% of the businesses in the United States are organized as partnerships.

A **corporation** is organized under state or federal statutes as a separate legal entity. The ownership of a corporation is divided into shares of stock. A corpora-

Successful Entrepreneurs

What are the characteristics of entrepreneurs who start and manage a new business successfully?

It goes without saying that an entrepreneur must have a thorough technical knowledge of the business. For example, a successful computer consultant must have a thorough knowledge of computers. Entrepreneurs must also have basic management skills, such as the ability to organize and interact with others. Finally, entrepreneurs are often described using the following terms:

Vision	Need for
Perseverance	achievement
Independent	Self-starter
Self-confident	Sense of com-
Risk taker	mitment
High energy level	Willingness to
Motivated	make personal
Personal drive	sacrifices
Spirit of adventure	Communication skills

Examples of some well-known entrepreneurs and their companies are listed below.

Entrepreneur	Company
Henry Ford	Ford Motor Company
George Eastman	Kodak
King C. Gillette	Gillette Company
Steven Jobs	Apple Computer
Bill Gates	Microsoft
Frederick Smith	Federal Express
Sam Walton	Wal-Mart

Examples of entrepreneurs also include the owners of many small businesses in your community, from local restaurants to video rental stores. ■

tion issues the stock to individuals or other businesses, who then become owners or stockholders of the corporation.

A primary advantage of the corporate form is the ability to obtain large amounts of resources by issuing stock. For this reason, most companies that require large investments in equipment and facilities are organized as corporations. For example, **Toys "R" Us** has raised over $800 million by issuing shares of common stock to finance its operations. Other examples of corporations include **General Motors**, **Ford**, **International Business Machines (IBM)**, **Coca-Cola**, and **General Electric**.

About 20% of the businesses in the United States are organized as corporations. However, since most large companies are organized as corporations, over 90% of the total dollars of business receipts are received by corporations. Thus, corporations have a major influence on the economy.

The three types of businesses we discussed earlier—manufacturing, merchandising, and service—may be either proprietorships, partnerships, or corporations. However, because of the large amount of resources required to operate a manufacturing business, most manufacturing businesses are corporations. Likewise, most large retailers such as **Wal-Mart**, **Sears**, and **JC Penney** are corporations.

> **Manufacturing, merchandising, and service businesses are commonly organized as either proprietorships, partnerships, or corporations.**

Business Stakeholders

A **business stakeholder** is a person or entity that has an interest in the economic performance of the business. These stakeholders normally include the owners, managers, employees, customers, creditors, and the government.

The **owners** who have invested resources in the business clearly have an interest in how well the business performs. Most owners want to get the most economic value for their investments. To the extent that the business is profitable, owners will expect to share in the business profits. Since owners may eventually decide to sell their business, they also have an interest in the total economic worth of the business. This economic worth may reflect results of past profits as well as prospects for future profits.

The **managers** are those individuals who the owners have authorized to operate the business. Managers are primarily evaluated on the economic performance of the business. The managers of businesses that perform poorly are often fired by the owners. Thus, managers have an incentive to maximize the economic value of the business. Owners may offer managers salary contracts that are tied directly to how well the business performs. For example, a manager might receive a percent of the profits or a percent of the increase in profits. Such contracts are often referred to as profit-sharing plans.

The **employees** provide services to the business in exchange for their pay. The employees have an interest in the economic performance of the business because their jobs depend upon it. During business downturns, it is not unusual for a business to lay off workers for extended periods of time. In the extreme, a business may fail and the employees lose their jobs permanently. Employee labor unions often use the good economic performance of a business to argue for wage increases. In contrast, businesses often use poor economic performance to argue for employee concessions such as wage decreases.

The **customers** may also have an interest in the continued success of a business. For example, if **Apple Computer** were to fail, customers might not be able to get hardware and software for their computers. Likewise, customers who purchase advance tickets on **Southwest Airlines** have an interest in whether Southwest will continue in business. Frequent flyers on **Eastern Airlines** lost their accumulated frequent-flyer points when Eastern went out of business.

Like the owners, the **creditors** invest resources in the business by extending credit. Therefore, the creditors of a business have an interest in how well the business performs. In order for the creditors to recover their investment, the business must generate enough cash to pay them. In addition, the business is the creditors' customer, and thus creditors have an interest in the continued success of the business.

Various **governments** have an interest in the economic performance of businesses. City, county, state, and federal governments collect taxes from businesses within their jurisdictions. The better a business does, the more taxes the government can collect. In addition, workers are taxed on their wages. In contrast, workers who are laid off and are unemployed can file claims for unemployment compensation, which results in a financial burden for the government. City and state governments often provide incentives for businesses to locate in their jurisdictions.

The state of Alabama offered **Mercedes** millions of dollars in incentives to locate a Mercedes plant in Alabama.

The Role of Accounting in Business

OBJECTIVE 2

Describe the role of accounting in business.

What is the role of accounting in business? The simplest answer to this question is that accounting provides information for managers to use in operating the business. In addition, accounting provides information to other stakeholders to use in assessing the economic performance and condition of the business.

In a general sense, **accounting** can be defined as an information system that provides reports to stakeholders about the economic activities and condition of a business. As we indicated earlier in this chapter, we will focus our discussions on accounting and its role in business. However, many of the concepts in this text also apply to individuals, governments, and other types of organizations. For example, individuals must account for activities such as hours worked, checks written, and bills due. Stakeholders for individuals include creditors, dependents, and the government. A main interest of the government is making sure that individuals pay the proper taxes.

> **Accounting is an information system that provides reports to stakeholders about the economic activities and condition of a business.**

You may think of accounting as the "language of business." This is because accounting is the means by which business information is communicated to the stakeholders. For example, accounting reports summarizing the profitability of a new product help **Coca-Cola's** management decide whether to continue offering the new product for sale. Likewise, financial analysts use accounting reports in deciding whether to recommend the purchase of Coca-Cola's stock. Banks use accounting reports in deciding the amount of credit to extend to Coca-Cola. Suppliers use accounting reports in deciding whether to offer credit for Coca-Cola's purchases of supplies and raw materials. State and federal governments use accounting reports as a basis for assessing taxes on Coca-Cola.

The process by which accounting provides information to business stakeholders is illustrated in Exhibit 1. First, a business must identify its stakeholders. Then, it must assess their various information needs and design its accounting system to meet those needs. Finally, the accounting system records the economic data about business activities and events, which it reports to the stakeholders according to their information needs.

EXHIBIT 1
Accounting Information and the Stakeholders of a Business

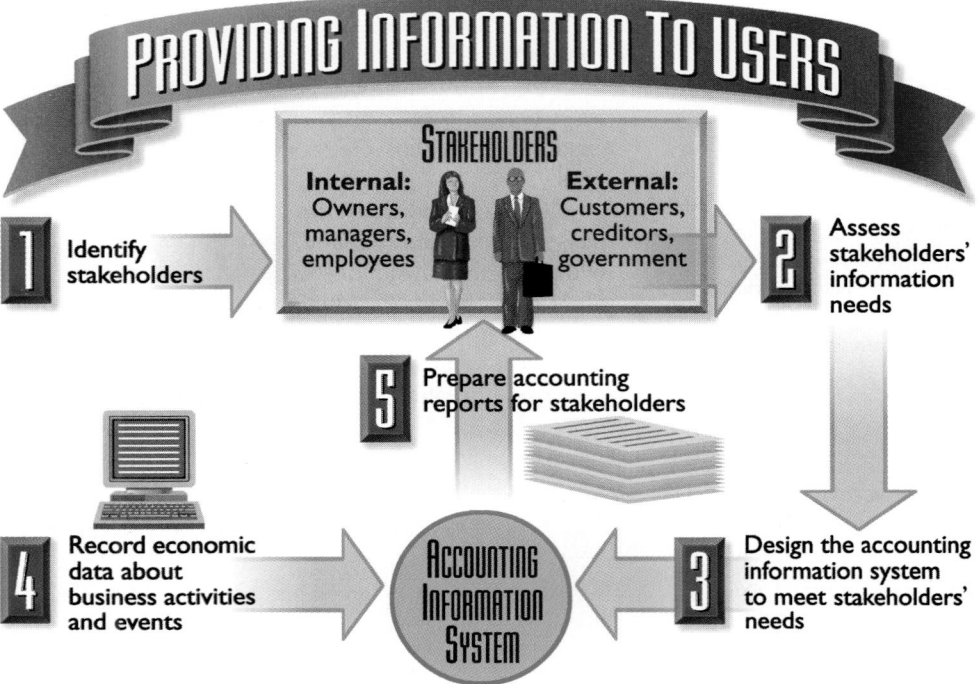

Stakeholders use accounting reports as a primary source of information on which they base their decisions. Stakeholders also use other information in making decisions about a business. For example, in deciding whether to extend credit to an appliance store, a banker might use economic forecasts to assess the future demand for the store's products. During periods of economic downturn, the demand for consumer appliances normally declines. The banker might inquire about the ability and reputation of the managers of the business. For small corporations, bankers may require major stockholders to personally guarantee the loans of the business. Finally, bankers might consult industry publications that rank similar businesses as to their quality of products, customer satisfaction, and future prospects for growth.

Business Ethics

OBJECTIVE 3

Describe the importance of business ethics and the basic principles of proper ethical conduct.

Individuals may differ as to what is "right" or "wrong" in a given situation. For example, you may believe it is wrong to copy another student's homework and hand it in as your own. Other students may feel that it is acceptable to copy homework if the instructor has no stated rule against it. Unfortunately, business managers are often in situations where they may feel pressure to violate personal ethics. For example, managers of **Sears** automotive service departments were accused of recommending unnecessary repairs and overcharging customers for actual repairs in order to meet company goals and earn bonuses.

Ethics are the moral principles that guide the conduct of individuals. Regardless of differences among individuals, proper ethical conduct implies a behavior that considers the impact of one's actions on society and others. In other words, proper ethical conduct implies that you not only consider what's in your best interests, but also what's in the best interests of others.

Ethical conduct is good business. For example, an automobile manufacturer that fails to correct a safety defect to save costs may later lose sales from the loss of consumer confidence. Likewise, a business that pollutes the environment may find itself the focus of lawsuits and customer boycotts.

Businessmen and businesswomen should work within an ethical framework.[2] Although an ethical framework is based on individual experiences and training, there are a number of sound principles that form the foundation for ethical behavior:

REAL WORLD A survey of top managers by the accounting firm of **Deloitte & Touche** reports that "an enterprise actually strengthens its competitive position by maintaining high ethical standards." *Ethics in Business,* Deloitte & Touche, January 1988.

1. *Avoid small ethical lapses.* Small ethical lapses may appear harmless in and of themselves. Unfortunately, such lapses can compromise your work. Small ethical lapses can build up and lead to larger consequences at a later point in time.
2. *Focus on your long-term reputation.* One characteristic of an ethical dilemma is that it places you under severe short-term pressure. The ethical dilemma is created by the stated or unstated threat that failure to "go along" may result in undesirable consequences. You should respond to ethical dilemmas by removing focus from the short-term pressures and instead focusing on long-term reputation. Your reputation is very valuable. You will lose your effectiveness if your reputation becomes tarnished.
3. *Expect to suffer adverse personal consequences for holding to an ethical position.* In some unethical organizations, managers have endured career setbacks for not budging from their ethical positions. Some managers have resigned their positions because they were unable to support management in what was perceived as unethical behavior. Thus, in the short term, ethical behavior can sometimes adversely affect your career.

REAL WORLD Stanley James Cardiges, the top U.S. sales representative for **American Honda** from 1988 to 1992, admitted to receiving $2 million to $5 million in illegal kickbacks from dealers. After being sentenced to five years in prison, he admitted to "falling into a pattern [of unethical behavior] early in my career . . . and went along with the crowd."

Source: "Ex-Honda Executive Handed 5-Year Sentence," The Associated Press, *Knoxville News Sentinel,* August 26, 1995.

Profession of Accounting

Accountants engage in either (1) private accounting or (2) public accounting. Accountants employed by a business firm or a not-for-profit organization are said to be engaged in **private accounting**. Accountants and their staff who provide services on a fee basis are said to be employed in **public accounting**.

Because all functions within a business use accounting information, experience in private or public accounting provides a solid foundation for a career. Many positions in industry and in government agencies are held by individuals with ac-

---

[2] An ethics discussion case is provided at the end of each chapter to focus attention on meaningful ethical situations that accountants often face in practice.

counting backgrounds. For example, in its 1990 Special Bonus Issue on "The Corporate Elite," *Business Week* reported the career paths for the chief executives of the 1,000 largest public corporations. These career paths are shown in Exhibit 2.

EXHIBIT 2
Career Paths of Corporate
Executives

Private Accounting

The scope of activities and duties of private accountants varies widely. Private accountants are frequently called management accountants. If they are employed by a manufacturing concern, they may be called *industrial* or *cost accountants*. The chief accountant in a business may be called the **controller**. Various state and federal agencies and other not-for-profit agencies also employ accountants.

The Institute of Certified Management Accountants, an affiliate of the Institute of Management Accountants (IMA), sponsors the **Certified Management Accountant (CMA)** program. The CMA certificate is evidence of competence in management accounting. To become a CMA requires a college degree, two years of experience, and successful completion of a two-day examination. Continuing professional education is required for renewal of the CMA certificate. In addition, members of the IMA must adhere to standards of ethical conduct.

The Institute of Internal Auditors sponsors a similar program for internal auditors. Internal auditors are accountants who review the accounting and operating procedures prescribed by their firms. Accountants who specialize in internal auditing may be granted the **Certified Internal Auditor (CIA)** certificate.

Public Accounting

In public accounting, an accountant may practice as an individual or as a member of a public accounting firm. Public accountants who have met a state's education, experience, and examination requirements may become **Certified Public Accountants (CPAs)**.

Information on a state's requirements for the CPA certification is available from that state's board of accountancy.

The requirements for obtaining a CPA certificate differ among the various states. All states require a college education in accounting, and most states require 150 semester hours of college credit. In addition, a candidate must pass a two-day examination prepared by the American Institute of Certified Public Accountants (AICPA).

Most states do not permit individuals to practice as CPAs until they have had from one to three years' experience in public accounting. Some states, however, accept similar employment in private accounting as equivalent experience. All states also require continuing professional education and adherence to standards of ethical conduct.[3]

Specialized Accounting Fields

You may think that all accounting is the same. However, you will find several specialized fields of accounting in practice. The two most common are financial accounting and managerial accounting. Other fields include cost accounting, environmental accounting, tax accounting, accounting systems, international accounting, not-for-profit accounting, and social accounting.

Financial accounting is primarily concerned with the recording and reporting of economic data and activities for a business. Although such reports provide useful information for managers, they are the primary reports for owners, creditors, governmental agencies, and the public. For example, if you wanted to own a portion of **PepsiCo**, **American Airlines**, or **McDonald's**, how would you know in which company to invest? One way is to review financial reports and compare the financial performance and condition of each company. The purpose of financial accounting is to provide such reports.

Managerial accounting, or **management accounting**, uses both financial accounting and estimated data to aid management in running day-to-day operations and in planning future operations. Management accountants gather and report information that is relevant and timely to the decision-making needs of management. For example, management might need information on alternative ways to finance the construction of a new building. Alternatively, management might need information on whether to expand its operations into a new product line. Thus, reports to management can differ widely in form and content.

Generally Accepted Accounting Principles

OBJECTIVE 5

Summarize the development of accounting principles and relate them to practice.

If the management of a company could record and report financial data as it saw fit, comparisons among companies would be difficult, if not impossible. Thus, financial accountants follow **generally accepted accounting principles (GAAP)** in preparing reports. These reports allow investors and other stakeholders to compare one company to another.

To illustrate the importance of generally accepted accounting principles, assume that each sports conference in college football used different rules for counting touchdowns. For example, assume that the Pacific Athletic Conference (PAC 10) counted a touchdown as six points and the Atlantic Coast Conference (ACC) counted a touchdown as two points. It would be difficult to evaluate the teams under such different scoring systems. A standard set of rules and a standard scoring system help fans compare teams across conferences. Likewise, a standard set of generally accepted accounting principles allows for the comparison of financial performance and condition across companies.

Accounting principles and concepts develop from research, accepted accounting practices, and pronouncements of authoritative bodies. Currently, the **Financial**

---

[3] The text of the *Code of Professional Conduct* (American Institute of Certified Public Accountants, New York, 1992) is reproduced in Appendix B.

INTERMISSION

Why Do We Need Accounting Principles?

In an editorial in *The Wall Street Journal,* Dennis R. Beresford, former Chairman of the Financial Accounting Standards Board, discussed the role of generally accepted accounting principles. He asserted that the primary role of accounting principles should be to truthfully portray the economic consequences of events on the financial statements of a business enterprise. In doing so, Mr. Beresford asserted, ". . . the truth will set investors free." Mr. Beresford goes on to state that ". . . Truth in accounting means telling it like it is, without bias or intent to encourage any particular mode of behavior by the user of the information." ■

Source: "In Accounting, Truth Above All," Letters to the Editor, *The Wall Street Journal,* March 21, 1994.

Accounting Standards Board (FASB) is the authoritative body that has the primary responsibility for developing accounting principles. The FASB publishes *Statements of Financial Accounting Standards* and *Interpretations* to these Standards.

Because generally accepted accounting principles impact how companies report and what they report, all stakeholders are interested in the setting of these principles. For example, the FASB proposed a standard on how to account for options granted employees and managers to purchase shares of ownership in the company. The proposal was opposed by managers because it would impact negatively the financial results of many companies. Managers and others, including the United States Senate, urged the FASB to revise or drop the proposal.[4] In response to these comments, the FASB significantly revised the proposed standard.

In this chapter and throughout this text, we emphasize accounting principles and concepts. It is through this emphasis on the "why" of accounting as well as the "how" that you will gain an understanding of the full significance of accounting. In the following paragraphs, we discuss the business entity concept and the cost principle.

 The FASB is also developing a broad conceptual framework for financial accounting. Six *Statements of Financial Accounting Concepts* have been published to date.

Business Entity Concept

The individual business unit is the business entity for which economic data are needed. This entity could be an automobile dealer, a department store, or a grocery store. The business entity must be identified, so that the accountant can determine which economic data should be analyzed, recorded, and summarized in reports.

The **business entity concept** is important because it limits the economic data in the accounting system to data related directly to the activities of the business. In other words, the business is viewed as an entity separate from its owners, creditors, or other stakeholders. For example, the accountant for a business with one owner (a proprietorship) would record only activities of the business and not the personal activities, property, or debts of the owner.

Under the business entity concept, the activities of a business are recorded separately from the activities of the stakeholders.

The Cost Concept

If a building is bought for $150,000, that amount should be entered into the buyer's accounting records. The seller may have been asking $170,000 for the building up to the time of the sale. The buyer may have initially offered $130,000 for the building. The building may have been assessed at $125,000 for property tax purposes. The buyer may have received an offer of $175,000 for the building the day after it was acquired. These latter amounts have no effect on the accounting records because they did not result in an exchange of the building from the seller to the buyer. The **cost concept** is the basis for entering the *exchange price, or cost, of $150,000* into the accounting records for the building.

[4] Glenn Alan Cheney, "Senate Rips FASB on Stock Options," *Accounting Today,* May 23, 1994.

Continuing the illustration, the $175,000 offer received by the buyer the day after the building was acquired indicates that it was a bargain purchase at $150,000. To use $175,000 in the accounting records, however, would record an illusory or unrealized profit. If, after buying the building, the buyer accepts the offer and sells the building for $175,000, a profit of $25,000 is then realized and recorded. The new owner would record $175,000 as the cost of the building.

Using the cost concept involves two other important accounting concepts—objectivity and the unit of measure. The objectivity concept requires that the accounting records and reports be based upon objective evidence. In exchanges between a buyer and a seller, both try to get the best price. Only the final amount agreed upon is objective enough for accounting purposes. If the amounts for which properties were recorded were constantly revised upward and downward based on offers, appraisals, and opinions, accounting reports would soon become unstable and unreliable.

The unit of measure concept requires that economic data be recorded in dollars. Money is a common unit of measurement that allows for the reporting of uniform financial data and reports.

Assets, Liabilities, and Owner's Equity

OBJECTIVE 6

State the accounting equation and define each element of the equation.

The resources owned by a business are called assets. Examples of assets include cash, land, buildings, and equipment. The rights or claims to the properties are normally divided into two principal types: (1) the rights of creditors and (2) the rights of owners. The rights of creditors represent debts of the business and are called liabilities. The rights of the owners are called owner's equity. The relationship between the two may be stated in the form of an equation, as follows:

$$\text{Assets} = \text{Liabilities} + \text{Owner's Equity}$$

This equation is known as the accounting equation. It is usual to place liabilities before owner's equity in the accounting equation because creditors have first rights to the assets. The claim of the owners is sometimes given greater emphasis by transposing liabilities to the other side of the equation, which yields:

Assets − Liabilities = Owner's Equity

To illustrate, if the assets owned by a business amount to $100,000 and the liabilities amount to $30,000, the owner's equity is equal to $70,000, as shown below.

Assets	−	Liabilities	=	Owner's Equity
$100,000	−	$30,000	=	$70,000

Q&A *If a company's assets increase by $20,000 and its liabilities decrease by $5,000, how much did the owner's equity increase or decrease?*

Change in assets	=	Change in liabilities	+	Change in owner's equity
+20,000	=	−5,000	+	X
+25,000	=			X

Business Transactions and the Accounting Equation

OBJECTIVE 7

Explain how business transactions can be stated in terms of the resulting changes in the three basic elements of the accounting equation.

Paying a monthly telephone bill of $68 affects a business's financial condition because it now has less cash on hand. Such an economic event or condition that directly changes an entity's financial condition or directly affects its results of operations is a business transaction. For example, purchasing land for $50,000 is a business transaction. In contrast, a change in a business's credit rating does not directly affect cash or any other element of its financial condition.

All business transactions can be stated in terms of changes in the three elements of the accounting equation.

All business transactions can be stated in terms of changes in the three elements of the accounting equation. You will see how business transactions affect the accounting equation by studying some typical transactions. For example, assume that on November 1, 1999, Pat King begins a business that will be known as Computer King. Using Pat's knowledge of microcomputers, the business will offer computer consulting services for a fee. Each transaction or group of similar transactions during the first month of operations is described in the following paragraphs. The effect of each transaction on the accounting equation is then shown.

Transaction a. Pat King deposits $15,000 in a bank account in the name of Computer King. The effect of this transaction is to increase the asset (cash), on the left side of the equation, by $15,000. To balance the equation, the owner's equity, on the right side of the equation, is increased by the same amount. The equity of the owner is referred to by using the owner's name and "Capital," such as "Pat King, Capital." The effect of this transaction on Computer King's accounting equation is shown below.

Assets	=	**Owner's Equity**
Cash	=	Pat King, Capital
a. 15,000		15,000 Investment
		by Pat King

Note that since Pat King is the sole owner, Computer King is a proprietorship. In addition, note that the accounting equation shown above relates only to the business, Computer King. Under the business entity concept, Pat King's personal assets, such as a home or personal bank account, and personal liabilities are excluded from the equation.

Transaction b. If you purchased this textbook by paying cash, you entered into a transaction in which you exchanged one asset for another. That is, you exchanged cash for the textbook. Businesses often enter into similar transactions. Computer King, for example, exchanged $10,000 cash for land. The land is located near a shopping mall that contains three microcomputer stores. Pat King plans to rent office space and equipment for several months. If the business is a success, the company will build on the land.

The purchase of the land changes the makeup of the assets but does not change the total assets. The items in the equation prior to this transaction and the effect of the transaction are shown next. The new amounts or *balances* of the items are also shown.

If Computer King had purchased a minivan for $18,000, paying $4,000 cash and signing a loan agreement (note payable) for $14,000, how would the transaction be recorded using the accounting equation?

Cash	+	Truck	=	Notes Payable
−4,000	+	18,000		+14,000

	Assets			=	**Owner's Equity**
	Cash	+	Land		Pat King, Capital
Bal.	15,000			=	15,000
b.	−10,000		+10,000		
Bal.	5,000		10,000		15,000

Transaction c. At one time or another, you have probably used a credit card to buy clothing or other merchandise. In this type of transaction, you received clothing for a promise to pay your credit card bill in the future. That is, you received an asset and incurred a liability to pay a future bill. During the month, Computer King entered into a similar transaction, buying supplies for $1,350 and agreeing to pay the supplier in the near future. This type of transaction is called a purchase *on ac-*

count. The liability created is called an **account payable**. Items such as supplies that will be used in the business in the future are called **prepaid expenses**, which are assets. The effect of this transaction is to increase assets and liabilities by $1,350, as follows:

 Other examples of common prepaid expenses include insurance and rent. Businesses usually report these assets together as a single item, prepaid expenses.

| | Assets | | | = | Liabilities | + | Owner's Equity |
	Cash	+ Supplies	+ Land	=	Accounts Payable	+	Pat King, Capital
Bal.	5,000		10,000				15,000
c.		+1,350			+1,350		
Bal.	5,000	1,350	10,000		1,350		15,000

Transaction d. You may have earned money by mowing lawns. If so, you received money for rendering services to a customer. Likewise, a business earns money by selling goods or services to its customers. This amount is called **revenue**.

During its first month of operations, Computer King provided services to customers, earning fees of $7,500 and receiving the amount in cash. The receipt of cash increases Computer King's assets and also increases Pat King's equity in the business. Thus, this transaction increased cash and the owner's equity by $7,500, as shown here.

| | Assets | | | = | Liabilities | + | Owner's Equity |
	Cash	+ Supplies	+ Land	=	Accounts Payable	+	Pat King, Capital
Bal.	5,000	1,350	10,000		1,350		15,000
d.	+ 7,500						+ 7,500 Fees earned
Bal.	12,500	1,350	10,000		1,350		22,500

Special terms may be used to describe certain kinds of revenue, such as **sales** for the sale of merchandise. Revenue from providing services is called **fees earned**. For example, a physician would record fees earned for services to patients. Other examples include **rent revenue** (money received for rent) and **interest revenue** (money received for interest).

Instead of requiring the payment of cash at the time services are provided or goods are sold, a business may accept payment at a later date. Such revenues are called *fees on account* or *sales on account*. In such cases, the firm has an **account receivable**, which is a claim against the customer. An account receivable is an asset, and the revenue is earned as if cash had been received. When customers pay their accounts, there is an exchange of one asset for another. Cash increases and accounts receivable decreases.

Transaction e. If you mowed lawns to earn money, you probably used your own lawn mower and bought your own gas. Computer King also spent cash or used up other assets in earning revenue. The amounts used in this process of earning revenue are called **expenses**. Expenses include supplies used, wages of employees, and other assets and services used in operating the business.

For Computer King, the expenses paid during the month were as follows: wages, $2,125; rent, $800; utilities, $450; and miscellaneous, $275. Miscellaneous expenses include small amounts paid for such items as postage due, coffee, and newspaper and magazine purchases. The effect of this group of transactions is the opposite of the effect of revenues. These transactions reduce cash and owner's equity, as shown at the top of the next page.

	Assets			=	Liabilities	+	Owner's Equity
					Accounts		Pat King,
	Cash	+ Supplies	+ Land		Payable	+	Capital
Bal.	12,500	1,350	10,000	=	1,350		22,500
e.	−3,650						−2,125 Wages expense
							− 800 Rent expense
							− 450 Utilities expense
							− 275 Misc. expense
	8,850	1,350	10,000		1,350		18,850

Usually businesses record each revenue and expense transaction separately as it occurs. However, to simplify this illustration, we have summarized Computer King's revenues and expenses for the month in transactions (d) and (e).

Transaction f. When you pay your monthly credit card bill, you decrease the cash in your checking account and also decrease the amount you owe to the credit card company. Likewise, when Computer King pays $950 to creditors during the month, it reduces both assets and liabilities, as shown below.

	Assets			=	Liabilities	+	Owner's Equity
					Accounts		Pat King,
	Cash	+ Supplies	+ Land		Payable	+	Capital
Bal.	8,850	1,350	10,000	=	1,350		18,850
f.	−950	___	___		−950		___
Bal.	7,900	1,350	10,000		400		18,850

You should note that paying an amount on account is different from paying an amount for an expense. The payment of an expense reduces owner's equity, as illustrated in transaction (e). Paying an amount on account reduces the amount owed on a liability.

Transaction g. At the end of the month, the cost of the supplies on hand (not yet used) is $550. The remainder of the supplies ($1,350 − $550) was used in the operations of the business and is treated as an expense. This decrease of $800 in supplies and owner's equity is shown as follows:

If supplies of $2,500 were purchased during the month and supplies of $350 are on hand at the end of the month, how much is supplies expense for the month?

$2,150 ($2,500 supplies purchased − $350 on hand)

	Assets			=	Liabilities	+	Owner's Equity
					Accounts		Pat King,
	Cash	+ Supplies	+ Land		Payable	+	Capital
Bal.	7,900	1,350	10,000	=	400		18,850
g.	___	−800	___				− 800 Supplies expense
Bal.	7,900	550	10,000		400		18,050

Transaction h. At the end of the month, Pat King withdraws $2,000 in cash from the business for personal use. This transaction is the exact opposite of an investment in the business by the owner. Cash and owner's equity are decreased. The cash payment is not a business expense but a withdrawal of a part of the owner's equity. The effect of the $2,000 withdrawal is shown as follows:

	Assets			=	Liabilities	+	Owner's Equity
					Accounts		Pat King,
	Cash	+ Supplies	+ Land		Payable	+	Capital
Bal.	7,900	550	10,000	=	400		18,050
h.	−2,000	___	___		___		−2,000 Withdrawal
Bal.	5,900	550	10,000		400		16,050

You should be careful not to confuse withdrawals by the owner with expenses. Withdrawals *do not* represent assets or services used in the process of earning revenues. The owner's equity decrease from the withdrawals is listed in the equation under Capital. This is because withdrawals are considered a distribution of capital to the owner.

Summary. The transactions of Computer King are summarized as follows. They are identified by letter, and the balance of each item is shown after each transaction.

	Assets			=	Liabilities +		Owner's Equity	
	Cash	+ Supplies	+ Land	=	Accounts Payable	+	Pat King, Capital	
a.	+15,000						+15,000	Investment by Pat King
b.	−10,000		+10,000					
Bal.	5,000		10,000				15,000	
c.		+1,350			+1,350			
Bal.	5,000	1,350	10,000		1,350		15,000	
d.	+ 7,500						+ 7,500	Fees earned
Bal.	12,500	1,350	10,000		1,350		22,500	
e.	− 3,650						− 2,125	Wages expense
							− 800	Rent expense
							− 450	Utilities expense
							− 275	Misc. expense
Bal.	8,850	1,350	10,000		1,350		18,850	
f.	− 950				− 950			
Bal.	7,900	1,350	10,000		400		18,850	
g.		− 800					− 800	Supplies expense
Bal.	7,900	550	10,000		400		18,050	
h.	− 2,000						− 2,000	Withdrawal
Bal.	5,900	550	10,000		400		16,050	

In reviewing the preceding summary, you should note the following, which apply to all types of businesses:

1. The effect of every transaction is *an increase or a decrease in one or more of the accounting equation elements*.
2. The two sides of the accounting equation are *always equal*.
3. The owner's equity is *increased by amounts invested by the owner* and is *decreased by withdrawals by the owner*. In addition, the owner's equity is *increased by revenues* and is *decreased by expenses*. The effects of these four types of transactions on owner's equity are illustrated in Exhibit 3.

EXHIBIT 3
Effects of Transactions on Owner's Equity

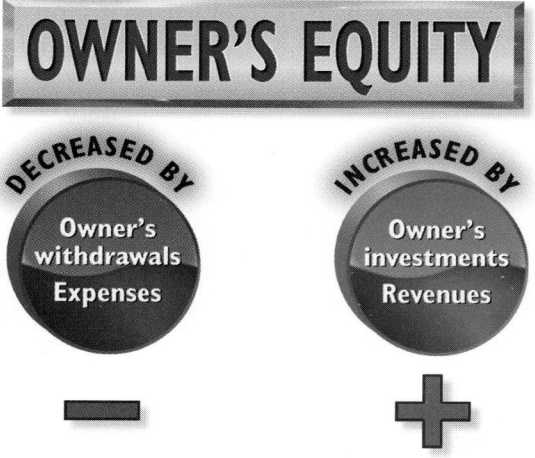

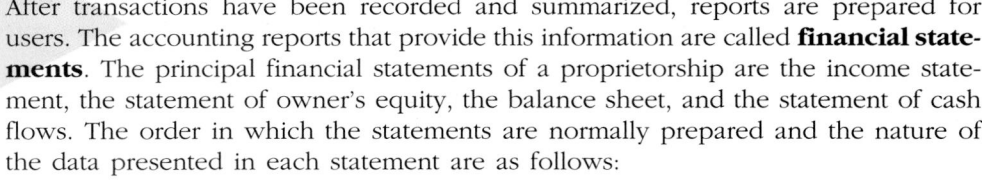

Financial Statements

OBJECTIVE 8

Describe the financial statements of a proprietorship
and explain how they interrelate.

After transactions have been recorded and summarized, reports are prepared for users. The accounting reports that provide this information are called **financial statements**. The principal financial statements of a proprietorship are the income statement, the statement of owner's equity, the balance sheet, and the statement of cash flows. The order in which the statements are normally prepared and the nature of the data presented in each statement are as follows:

- **Income statement**—A summary of the revenue and expenses *for a specific period of time,* such as a month or a year.
- **Statement of owner's equity**—A summary of the changes in the owner's equity that have occurred *during a specific period of time,* such as a month or a year.
- **Balance sheet**—A list of the assets, liabilities, and owner's equity *as of a specific date,* usually at the close of the last day of a month or a year.
- **Statement of cash flows**—A summary of the cash receipts and cash payments *for a specific period of time,* such as a month or a year.

The basic features of the four statements and their interrelationships are illustrated in Exhibit 4. The data for the statements were taken from the summary of transactions of Computer King.

All financial statements should be identified by the name of the business, the title of the statement, and the *date* or *period of time.* The data presented in the income statement, the statement of owner's equity, and the statement of cash flows are for a period of time. The data presented in the balance sheet are for a specific date.

You should note the use of indents, captions, dollar signs, and rulings in the financial statements. They aid the reader by emphasizing the sections of the statements.

Income Statement

When you buy something at a store, you may *match* the cash register total with the amount you paid the cashier and with the amount of change, if any, you received.

The income statement reports the revenues and expenses for a period of time, based on the **matching concept**. This concept is applied by *matching* the expenses with the revenue generated during a period by those expenses. The income statement also reports the excess of the revenue over the expenses incurred. This excess of the revenue over the expenses is called **net income** or **net profit**. If the expenses exceed the revenue, the excess is a **net loss**.

Net income—the excess of revenue over expenses—increases owner's equity.

The effects of revenue earned and expenses incurred during the month for Computer King were shown in the equation as increases and decreases in owner's equity (capital). Net income for a period has the effect of increasing owner's equity (capital) for the period, whereas a net loss has the effect of decreasing owner's equity (capital) for the period.

The revenue, expenses, and the net income of $3,050 for Computer King are reported in the income statement in Exhibit 4. The order in which the expenses are listed in the income statement varies among businesses. One method is to list them in order of size, beginning with the larger items. Miscellaneous expense is usually shown as the last item, regardless of the amount.

Statement of Owner's Equity

The statement of owner's equity reports the changes in the owner's equity for a period of time. It is prepared *after* the income statement because the net income or net loss for the period must be reported in this statement. Similarly, it is prepared *before* the balance sheet, since the amount of owner's equity at the end of the pe-

EXHIBIT 4
Financial Statements

Computer King
Income Statement
For the Month Ended November 30, 1999

Fees earned			$7 5 0 0 00
Operating expenses:			
Wages expense	$2 1 2 5 00		
Rent expense	8 0 0 00		
Supplies expense	8 0 0 00		
Utilities expense	4 5 0 00		
Miscellaneous expense	2 7 5 00		
Total operating expenses		4 4 5 0 00	
Net income		$3 0 5 0 00	

Computer King
Statement of Owner's Equity
For the Month Ended November 30, 1999

Pat King, capital, November 1, 1999		$	0
Investment on November 1, 1999	$15 0 0 0 00		
Net income for November	3 0 5 0 00		
	$18 0 5 0 00		
Less withdrawals	2 0 0 0 00		
Increase in owner's equity		16 0 5 0 00	
Pat King, capital, November 30, 1999		$16 0 5 0 00	

Computer King
Balance Sheet
November 30, 1999

Assets		Liabilities	
Cash	$ 5 9 0 0 00	Accounts payable	$ 4 0 0 00
Supplies	5 5 0 00	**Owner's Equity**	
Land	10 0 0 0 00	Pat King, capital	16 0 5 0 00
		Total liabilities and	
Total assets	$16 4 5 0 00	owner's equity	$16 4 5 0 00

Computer King
Statement of Cash Flows
For the Month Ended November 30, 1999

Cash flows from operating activities:		
Cash received from customers	$ 7 5 0 0 00	
Deduct cash payments for expenses and		
payments to creditors	4 6 0 0 00	
Net cash flow from operating activities		$ 2 9 0 0 00
Cash flows from investing activities:		
Cash payments for acquisition of land		(10 0 0 0 00)
Cash flows from financing activities:		
Cash received as owner's investment	$15 0 0 0 00	
Deduct cash withdrawal by owner	2 0 0 0 00	
Net cash flow from financing activities		13 0 0 0 00
Net cash flow and November 30, 1999 cash balance		$ 5 9 0 0 00

Financial statements are used to evaluate the current financial condition of a business and to predict its future operating results and cash flows. For example, bank loan officers use a business's financial statements in deciding whether to grant a loan to the business. Once the loan is granted, the borrower may be required to maintain a certain level of assets in excess of liabilities. The business's financial statements are used to monitor this level.

riod must be reported on the balance sheet. Because of this, the statement of owner's equity is often viewed as the connecting link between the income statement and balance sheet.

Three types of transactions affected owner's equity for Computer King during November: (1) the original investment of $15,000, (2) the revenue and expenses that resulted in net income of $3,050 for the month, and (3) a withdrawal of $2,000 by the owner. This information is summarized in the statement of owner's equity in Exhibit 4.

Balance Sheet

The balance sheet in Exhibit 4 reports the amounts of Computer King's assets, liabilities, and owner's equity at the end of November. These amounts are taken from the last line of the summary of transactions presented earlier. The form of balance sheet shown in Exhibit 4 is called the **account form** because it resembles the basic format of the accounting equation, with assets on the left side and the liabilities and owner's equity sections on the right side. An alternative form of balance sheet, called the **report form**, presents the liabilities and owner's equity sections below the assets section. We illustrate this form of balance sheet in a later chapter.

The assets section of the balance sheet normally presents assets in the order that they will be converted into cash or used in operations. Cash is presented first, followed by receivables, supplies, prepaid insurance, and other assets. Then, the assets of a more permanent nature are shown, such as land, buildings, and equipment.

In the liabilities section of the balance sheet in Exhibit 4, accounts payable is the only liability. When there are two or more categories of liabilities, each should be listed and the total amount of liabilities presented as shown below.

Liabilities		
Accounts payable	$12,900	
Wages payable	2,570	
Total liabilities		$15,470

Statement of Cash Flows

The statement of cash flows in Exhibit 4 consists of three sections: (1) operating activities, (2) investing activities, and (3) financing activities. Each of these sections is briefly described below.

Cash Flows from Operating Activities. This section reports a summary of cash receipts and cash payments from operations. The net cash flow from operating activities ($2,900 in Exhibit 4) will normally differ from the amount of net income for the period ($3,050 in Exhibit 4). This difference occurs because revenues and expenses may not be recorded at the same time that cash is received from customers and cash is paid to creditors.

Cash Flows from Investing Activities. This section reports the cash transactions for the acquisition and sale of relatively permanent assets.

Cash Flows from Financing Activities. This section reports the cash transactions related to cash investments by the owner, borrowings, and cash withdrawals by the owner.

Preparing the statement of cash flows requires an understanding of concepts that we have not discussed in this chapter. Therefore, we will illustrate the preparation of the statement of cash flows in a later chapter.

FINANCIAL ANALYSIS AND INTERPRETATION

OBJECTIVE 9

Use the ratio of liabilities to owner's equity to analyze the ability of a business to withstand poor business conditions.

As we discussed earlier in this chapter, financial statements are useful to bankers, creditors, owners, and other stakeholders in analyzing and interpreting the financial performance and condition of a business. Throughout this text, we will discuss various tools that are often used in practice to analyze and interpret the financial performance and condition of a business. The first such tool we will introduce is especially useful in analyzing the ability of a business to pay its creditors.

The relationship between liabilities and owner's equity, expressed as a ratio, is calculated as follows:

$$\text{Ratio of liabilities to owner's equity} = \frac{\text{Total liabilities}}{\text{Total owner's equity (or Total stockholders' equity)}}$$

To illustrate, Computer King's ratio of liabilities to owner's equity at the end of 1999 is 0.025, as calculated below.

$$\text{Ratio of liabilities to owner's equity} = \frac{\$400}{\$16,050} = 0.025$$

For corporations, it is normal to refer to total owner's equity as total stockholders' equity. Thus, when computing this ratio for a corporation, you should substitute total stockholders' equity for total owner's equity.

The rights of creditors to a business's assets take precedence over the rights of the owners or stockholders. Thus, the lower the ratio of liabilities to owner's equity, the more able the business is to withstand poor business conditions and still fully meet its obligations to creditors.

To illustrate, a ratio of 1 indicates that the liabilities and owner's equity are equal. In other words, if the business suffers a loss equal to the total liabilities, the amount of total assets available to creditors will not drop below their claims on the assets. If this were to happen, the creditors could collect their claims and the owner would be left with nothing. In contrast, if the ratio were 3, a loss greater than one-third of the liabilities would drop the total assets below the creditors' claims.

ENCORE

Barbie and Ken

Many of today's large businesses began with an idea and a commitment of individuals to pursue that idea as far as possible.

In 1945, Elliott and Ruth Handler started a small toy company in their garage. The husband-and-wife team worked well together, with Elliott, an artist, focusing on the design of the toys and Ruth managing the business affairs and finding sales outlets for the toys. After struggling more than ten years to make the

company a success, it was worth just over $500,000. In 1955, the Handlers decided to take a bold step to expand sales by advertising on a popular children's television program, The Mickey Mouse Club. The cost of the advertising campaign, if unsuccessful, would have potentially bankrupted the company. However, the campaign was successful and sales increased dramatically.

In 1959, the Handlers took another gamble by introducing a full-figured, teenage doll. The market experts predicted that such a doll

Barbie and Ken dolls

would not appeal to three- to eleven-year-old girls. The experts were wrong. The Barbie Doll, named after the Handlers' daughter Barbara, was a huge success. The Barbie Doll, which

sold 350,000 its first year, has now sold over 500 billion. Later, the Handlers introduced a male doll, Ken, as a friend of Barbie. The Ken Doll was named after the Handlers' son.

Mattel Inc. has grown dramatically since its beginning in 1945. In 1996, Mattel reported revenues of over $3.7 billion and total assets of over $2.8 billion. ▪

KEY POINTS

1 Describe the nature of a business.

A business is an organization in which basic resources (inputs), such as materials and labor, are assembled and processed to provide goods or services (outputs) to customers. The objective of most businesses is to maximize profits.

There are three different types of businesses that are operated for profit: manufacturing, merchandising, and service businesses. A business is normally organized in one of three different forms: proprietorship, partnership, or corporation. A business stakeholder is a person or entity (such as an owner, manager, employee, customer, creditor, or the government) that has an interest in the economic performance of the business.

2 Describe the role of accounting in business.

Accounting is an information system that provides reports to stakeholders about the economic activities and condition of a business. Accounting is the "language of business."

3 Describe the importance of business ethics and the basic principles of proper ethical conduct.

Ethics are moral principles that guide the conduct of individuals. Proper ethical conduct implies a behavior that considers the impact of one's actions on society

and others. Sound ethical principles include (1) avoiding small ethical lapses, (2) focusing on your long-term reputation, and (3) being willing to suffer adverse personal consequences for holding to an ethical position.

4 Describe the profession of accounting.

Accountants are engaged in either private accounting or public accounting. The two most common specialized fields of accounting are financial accounting and managerial accounting. Other fields include cost accounting, environmental accounting, tax accounting, accounting systems, international accounting, not-for-profit accounting, and social accounting.

5 Summarize the development of accounting principles and relate them to practice.

Financial accountants follow generally accepted accounting principles (GAAP) in preparing reports so that stakeholders can compare one company to another. Accounting principles and concepts develop from research, accepted accounting practices, and pronouncements of authoritative bodies. Currently, the Financial Accounting Standards Board (FASB) is the authoritative body that has the primary responsibility for developing accounting principles.

The business entity concept views the business as an entity separate from its owners, creditors, or other stakeholders. The business entity limits the economic data in the accounting system to that related directly to the activities of the business. The cost concept requires that properties and services bought by a business be recorded in terms of actual cost. The objectivity concept requires that the accounting records and reports be based upon objective evidence. The unit of measure concept requires that economic data be recorded in dollars.

6 State the accounting equation and define each element of the equation.

The resources owned by a business and the rights or claims to these resources may be stated in the form of an equation, as follows:

$$\text{Assets} = \text{Liabilities} + \text{Owner's Equity}$$

7 Explain how business transactions can be stated in terms of the resulting changes in the three basic elements of the accounting equation.

All business transactions can be stated in terms of the change in one or more of the three elements of the accounting equation. That is, the effect of every transaction can be stated in terms of increases or decreases in one or more of these elements, while maintaining the equality between the two sides of the equation.

8 **Describe the financial statements of a proprietorship and explain how they interrelate.**

The principal financial statements of a proprietorship are the in-come statement, the statement of owner's equity, the balance sheet, and the statement of cash flows. The income statement reports a period's net income or net loss, which also appears on the statement of owner's equity. The ending owner's capital reported on the statement of owner's equity is also reported on the balance sheet. The ending cash balance is reported on the balance sheet and the statement of cash flows.

9 **Use the ratio of liabilities to owner's equity to analyze the ability of a business to withstand poor business conditions.**

The ratio of liabilities to owner's equity is useful in analyzing the ability of a business to pay its creditors. The lower the ratio, the more able the business is to withstand poor business conditions and still fully meet its obligations to creditors.

ILLUSTRATIVE PROBLEM

On July 1 of the current year, the assets and liabilities of Cecil Jameson, Attorney-at-Law, are as follows: cash, $1,000; accounts receivable, $3,200; supplies, $850; land, $10,000; accounts payable, $1,530. Cecil Jameson, Attorney-at-Law, is a proprietorship owned and operated by Cecil Jameson. Currently, office space and office equipment are being rented, pending the construction of an office complex on land purchased last year. Business transactions during July are summarized as follows:

a. Received cash from clients for services, $3,928.
b. Paid creditors on account, $1,055.
c. Received cash from Cecil Jameson as an additional investment, $3,700.
d. Paid office rent for the month, $1,200.
e. Charged clients for legal services on account, $2,025.
f. Purchased office supplies on account, $245.
g. Received cash from clients on account, $3,000.
h. Received invoice for paralegal services from Legal Aid Inc. for July (to be paid on August 10), $1,635.
i. Paid the following: wages expense, $850; answering service expense, $250; utilities expense, $325; and miscellaneous expense, $75.
j. Determined that the cost of office supplies on hand was $980; therefore, the cost of supplies used during the month was $115.
k. Jameson withdrew $1,000 in cash from the business for personal use.

Instructions

1. Determine the amount of owner's equity (Cecil Jameson's capital) as of July 1 of the current year.
2. State the assets, liabilities, and owner's equity as of July 1 in equation form similar to that shown in this chapter. In tabular form below the equation, indicate the increases and decreases resulting from each transaction and the new balances after each transaction. Explain the nature of each increase and decrease in owner's equity by an appropriate notation at the right of the amount.
3. Prepare an income statement for July, a statement of owner's equity for July, and a balance sheet as of July 31.

Solution

1. Assets − Liabilities = Owner's Equity (Cecil Jameson, capital)
$15,050 − $1,530 = Owner's Equity (Cecil Jameson, capital)
$13,520 = Owner's Equity (Cecil Jameson, capital)

2.

			Assets			=	Liabilities	+	Owner's Equity	
			Accounts				Accounts		Cecil Jameson,	
	Cash	+	Receivable	+ Supplies +	Land	=	Payable	+	Capital	
Bal.	1,000		3,200	850	10,000		1,530		13,520	
a.	+3,928								+ 3,928	Fees earned
Bal.	4,928		3,200	850	10,000		1,530		17,448	
b.	−1,055						−1,055			
Bal.	3,873		3,200	850	10,000		475		17,448	
c.	+3,700								+ 3,700	Investment
Bal.	7,573		3,200	850	10,000		475		21,148	
d.	−1,200								− 1,200	Rent expense
Bal.	6,373		3,200	850	10,000		475		19,948	
e.			+2,025						+ 2,025	Fees earned
Bal.	6,373		5,225	850	10,000		475		21,973	
f.				+ 245			+ 245			
Bal.	6,373		5,225	1,095	10,000		720		21,973	
g.	+3,000		−3,000							
Bal.	9,373		2,225	1,095	10,000		720		21,973	
h.							+1,635		− 1,635	Paralegal exp.
Bal.	9,373		2,225	1,095	10,000		2,355		20,338	
i.	−1,500								− 850	Wages exp.
									− 250	Answ. svc. exp.
									− 325	Utilities exp.
									− 75	Misc. exp.
Bal.	7,873		2,225	1,095	10,000		2,355		18,838	
j.				− 115					− 115	Supplies exp.
Bal.	7,873		2,225	980	10,000		2,355		18,723	
k.	−1,000								− 1,000	Withdrawal
	6,873		2,225	980	10,000		2,355		17,723	

3.

Cecil Jameson, Attorney-at-Law Income Statement For the Month Ended July 31, 20—			
Fees earned			$5 9 5 3 00
Operating expenses:			
Paralegal expense	$1 6 3 5 00		
Rent expense	1 2 0 0 00		
Wages expense	8 5 0 00		
Utilities expense	3 2 5 00		
Answering service expense	2 5 0 00		
Supplies expense	1 1 5 00		
Miscellaneous expense	7 5 00		
Total operating expenses			4 4 5 0 00
Net income			$1 5 0 3 00

Cecil Jameson, Attorney-at-Law
Statement of Owner's Equity
For the Month Ended July 31, 20—

Cecil Jameson, capital, July 1, 20—			$13 5 2 0 00
Additional investment by owner	$3 7 0 0 00		
Net income for the month	1 5 0 3 00		
	$5 2 0 3 00		
Less withdrawals	1 0 0 0 00		
Increase in owner's equity		4 2 0 3 00	
Cecil Jameson, capital, July 31, 20—		$17 7 2 3 00	

Cecil Jameson, Attorney-at-Law
Balance Sheet
July 31, 20—

Assets		Liabilities	
Cash	$ 6 8 7 3 00	Accounts payable	$ 2 3 5 5 00
Accounts receivable	2 2 2 5 00	**Owner's Equity**	
Supplies	9 8 0 00	Cecil Jameson, capital	17 7 2 3 00
Land	10 0 0 0 00	Total liabilities and	
Total assets	$20 0 7 8 00	owner's equity	$20 0 7 8 00

SELF-EXAMINATION QUESTIONS
Answers at End of Chapter

Matching

Match each of the following statements with its proper term. Some terms may not be used.

A.	**Account form**
B.	**Account payable**
C.	**Account receivable**
D.	**Accounting**
E.	**Accounting equation**
F.	**Assets**
G.	**Balance sheet**
H.	**Business**
I.	**Business entity concept**
J.	**Business stakeholder**
K.	**Business transaction**
L.	**Corporation**
M.	**Cost concept**
N.	**Ethics**
O.	**Expenses**

____ 1. An organization in which basic resources (inputs), such as materials and labor, are assembled and processed to provide goods or services (outputs) to customers.

____ 2. A type of business that changes basic inputs into products that are sold to individual customers.

____ 3. A type of business that purchases products from other businesses and sells them to customers.

____ 4. A business owned by one individual.

____ 5. A business owned by two or more individuals.

____ 6. A business organized under state or federal statutes as a separate legal entity.

____ 7. A person or entity that has an interest in the economic performance of a business.

____ 8. Individuals who the owners have authorized to operate the business.

____ 9. An information system that provides reports to stakeholders about the economic activities and condition of a business.

____ 10. Moral principles that guide the conduct of individuals.

____ 11. A specialized field of accounting primarily concerned with the recording and reporting of economic data and activities to stakeholders outside the business.

(*continues*)

P.	**Financial accounting**
Q.	**Financial Accounting Standards Board (FASB)**
R.	**Generally accepted accounting principles (GAAP)**
S.	**Income statement**
T.	**Liabilities**
U.	**Managerial accounting**
V.	**Managers**
W.	**Manufacturing**
X.	**Matching concept**
Y.	**Merchandising**
Z.	**Net income**
AA.	**Net loss**
BB.	**Objectivity concept**
CC.	**Owner's equity**
DD.	**Partnership**
EE.	**Prepaid expenses**
FF.	**Proprietorship**
GG.	**Report form**
HH.	**Revenue**
II.	**Service**
JJ.	**Statement of cash flows**
KK.	**Statement of owner's equity**
LL.	**Unit of measure concept**

____ 12. A specialized field of accounting that uses estimated data to aid management in running day-to-day operations and in planning future operations.

____ 13. The authoritative body that has the primary responsibility for developing accounting principles.

____ 14. A concept of accounting that limits the economic data in the accounting system to data related directly to the activities of the business.

____ 15. A concept of accounting that requires that economic data be recorded in dollars.

____ 16. The resources owned by a business.

____ 17. The rights of creditors represent debts of the business.

____ 18. The rights of the owners.

____ 19. Assets = Liabilities + Owner's Equity

____ 20. An economic event or condition that directly changes an entity's financial condition or directly affects its results of operations.

____ 21. The liability created by a purchase on account.

____ 22. Items such as supplies that will be used in the business in the future.

____ 23. A claim against the customer.

____ 24. The amounts used in the process of earning revenue.

____ 25. The amount a business earns by selling goods or services to its customers.

____ 26. A summary of the revenue and expenses *for a specific period of time,* such as a month or a year.

____ 27. A summary of the changes in the owner's equity that have occurred *during a specific period of time,* such as a month or a year.

____ 28. A list of the assets, liabilities, and owner's equity *as of a specific date,* usually at the close of the last day of a month or a year.

____ 29. A summary of the cash receipts and cash payments *for a specific period of time,* such as a month or a year.

____ 30. A concept of accounting in which expenses are matched with the revenue generated during a period by those expenses.

____ 31. The form of balance sheet that resembles the basic format of the accounting equation, with assets on the left side and the liabilities and owner's equity sections on the right side.

Multiple Choice

1. A profit-making business that is a separate legal entity and in which ownership is divided into shares of stock is known as a:
   A. proprietorship   C. partnership
   B. service business   D. corporation

2. The resources owned by a business are called:
   A. assets
   B. liabilities
   C. the accounting equation
   D. owner's equity

3. A list of assets, liabilities, and owner's equity of a business entity as of a specific date is:
   A. a balance sheet
   B. an income statement
   C. a statement of owner's equity
   D. a statement of cash flows

4. If total assets increased $20,000 during a period of time and total liabilities increased $12,000 during the same period, the amount and direction (increase or decrease) of the period's change in owner's equity is:
   A. $32,000 increase   C. $8,000 increase
   B. $32,000 decrease   D. $8,000 decrease

5. If revenue was $45,000, expenses were $37,500, and the owner's withdrawals were $10,000, the amount of net income or net loss would be:
   A. $45,000 net income   C. $37,500 net loss
   B. $7,500 net income   D. $2,500 net loss

CLASS DISCUSSION QUESTIONS

1. What is the objective of most businesses?
2. Who are normally included as the stakeholders of a business?
3. What is the role of accounting in business?
4. What are three sound principles that form the foundation for ethical behavior?
5. Distinguish between private accounting and public accounting.
6. Identify what the abbreviation FASB stands for and describe how the FASB sets generally accepted accounting principles.
7. Jamie Niles is the owner of Niles Delivery Service. Recently, Jamie paid interest of $1,500 on a personal loan of $50,000 that she used to begin the business. Should Niles Delivery Service record the interest payment? Explain.
8. On February 15, Adams Repair Service extended an offer of $75,000 for land that had been priced for sale at $100,000. On February 25, Adams Repair Service accepted the seller's counteroffer of $80,000. Describe how Adams Repair Service should record the land.
9. a. Land with an assessed value of $100,000 for property tax purposes is acquired by a business for $125,000. Ten years later, the plot of land has an assessed value of $210,000 and the business receives an offer of $240,000 for it. Should the monetary amount assigned to the land in the business records now be increased?
   b. Assuming that the land acquired in (a) was sold for $240,000, how would the various elements of the accounting equation be affected?
10. What are the two principal rights to the properties of a business?
11. Name the three elements of the accounting equation.
12. Describe the difference between an account receivable and an account payable.
13. A business had revenues of $90,000 and operating expenses of $120,000. Did the business (a) incur a net loss or (b) realize a net income?
14. A business had revenues of $300,000 and operating expenses of $270,000. Did the business (a) incur a net loss or (b) realize a net income?
15. Name the two types of transactions that increase the owner's equity of a proprietorship.
16. Briefly describe the nature of the information provided by each of the following financial statements:
    1. income statement
    2. statement of owner's equity
    3. balance sheet
    4. statement of cash flows
17. Indicate whether each of the financial statements in Question 16 (a) covers a period of time or (b) is for a specific date.
18. What particular item of financial or operating data appears on (a) both the income statement and the statement of owner's equity and (b) both the balance sheet and the statement of owner's equity?
19. Name the three types of activities reported in the statement of cash flows.

Success Stories Start Here

Congratulations! You are using the most successful, most widely used accounting text of all time. More than 10 million students have started their own personal success stories with this very text.

Everyone Wins

Accounting, by Warren, Reeve, and Fess, is designed to introduce accounting concepts in a practical and interesting way. Whether you're headed for a career as an entrepreneur, a manager of a business, or an accounting professional, here are some tips to get your success story started:

1. Read the chapter prior to your instructor's lecture.

2. Work the assigned problems.

3. Complete the Continuing Problem in Chapters 1-4 to learn one of the foundations of accounting - the accounting cycle.

4. Review the illustrative problems in each chapter as preparation for completing problems.

5. Attend class - there's no substitute for listening and note-taking to absorb accounting concepts.

6. Use the tools described on this page to make the most of your study time.

Resources for Your Success On-Line at **warren.swcollege.com**

This high impact site includes current articles on accounting and downloadable resources, organized by chapter for easy navigation. Visit the text's Web site now to check out the supplements listed below.

▼ **Study Guide.** The Study Guide provides ample opportunity for practice and study. It includes quiz and test tips and multiple choice, fill-in-the-blank, and true-false questions with solutions. The Study Guide is also packaged with a disk that allows you to score your own practice tests. (Chs. 1-16: ISBN 0-538-87421-X, Chs. 12-24: ISBN 0-538-87422-8)

▼ **Working Papers.** Working Papers guide you through solutions to selected end-of-chapter assignments. Included forms help you organize your calculations and see how it all fits together. (Chs. 1-16: ISBN 0-538-87415-5, Chs. 12-24: ISBN 0-538-87416-3)

▼ **Working Papers Plus.** This special edition of Working Papers integrates chapter learning objectives and glossary terms with forms for solving all textbook exercises and selected textbook problems. (Chs. 1-16: ISBN 0-538-87417-1, Chs. 12-24: ISBN 0-538-87418-X)

▼ **Blank Working Papers**. This set of blank forms allows you to work exercises and problems for Chapters 1-24. (ISBN 0-538-87414-7)

▼ **PowerNotes.** If your instructor utilizes PowerPoint™ transparencies, this workbook will significantly aid note-taking and comprehension. PowerNotes provide printed versions of the transparencies and room to take detailed notes, plus critical-thinking activities and self-study review questions related to the transparencies. (Chs. 1-16: ISBN 0-538-87419-8, Chs. 12-24: ISBN 0-538-87420-1)

▼ **General Ledger Software.** This educational general ledger package allows for point-and-click solutions to end-of-chapter problems, comprehensive problems, as well as practice sets. (ISBN 0-538-87423-6)

▼ **Homework Assistant and Tutor (HAT).** This user-friendly software for Windows visually demonstrates the relationships between journals, ledgers, and financial statements as you solve selected end-of-chapter problems. A built-in tutor function includes numerous hints and help screens. (ISBN 0-538-87431-7)

▼ **Spreadsheet Applications Software.** Use these spreadsheet templates to solve dozens of problems via popular spreadsheet packages, such as Lotus 1-2-3® and Excel.® Alternative "what-if" scenarios are also presented and explored. (Chs. 1-16: ISBN 0-538-87437-6, Chs. 12-24: ISBN 0-538-87438-4)

Order Now!

To order any of these supplements, visit "The Bookstore" at **warren.swcollege.com** or call the ITP Academic Resource Center at **1-800-423-0563**

EXERCISES

Exercise 1–1
Professional ethics

Objective 3

A fertilizer manufacturing company wants to relocate to Collier County. A 13-year-old report from a fired researcher at the company says the company's product is releasing toxic by-products. The company has suppressed that report. A second report commissioned by the company shows there is no problem with the fertilizer.

➤ Should the company's chief executive officer reveal the context of the unfavorable report in discussions with Collier County representatives? Discuss.

Source: "Business Leaders Ponder Ethical Questions," *Naples Daily News,* May 12, 1991, p. 1E.

Exercise 1–2
Accounting equation

Objective 6

✓ a. $62,000

Determine the missing amount for each of the following:

	Assets	=	Liabilities	+	Owner's Equity
a.	X	=	$20,500	+	$41,500
b.	$32,750	=	X	+	10,000
c.	57,000	=	18,000	+	X

Exercise 1–3
Accounting equation

Objectives 6, 8

✓ b. $303,000

David Plymouth is the owner and operator of Dyn-A-Go, a motivational consulting business. At the end of its accounting period, December 31, 1999, Dyn-A-Go has assets of $325,000 and liabilities of $85,000. Using the accounting equation and considering each case independently, determine the following amounts:

a. David Plymouth, capital, as of December 31, 1999.
b. David Plymouth, capital, as of December 31, 2000, assuming that during 2000, assets increased by $84,000 and liabilities increased by $21,000.
c. David Plymouth, capital, as of December 31, 2000, assuming that during 2000, assets decreased by $5,000 and liabilities increased by $17,000.
d. David Plymouth, capital, as of December 31, 2000, assuming that during 2000, assets increased by $75,000 and liabilities decreased by $35,000.
e. Net income (or net loss) during 2000, assuming that as of December 31, 2000, assets were $425,000, liabilities were $105,000, and there were no additional investments or withdrawals.

Exercise 1–4
Asset, liability, owner's equity items

Objective 7

Indicate whether each of the following is identified with (1) an asset, (2) a liability, or (3) owner's equity:

a. fees earned
b. supplies
c. wages expense
d. land
e. accounts payable
f. cash

Exercise 1–5
Effect of transactions on accounting equation

Objective 7

Describe how the following business transactions affect the three elements of the accounting equation.

a. Invested cash in business.
b. Received cash for services performed.
c. Purchased supplies for cash.
d. Paid for utilities used in the business.
e. Purchased supplies on account.

Exercise 1–6
Effect of transactions on accounting equation

Objective 7

✓ (a)(1) increase $70,000

a. A vacant lot acquired for $90,000, on which there is a balance owed of $30,000, is sold for $160,000 in cash. What is the effect of the sale on the total amount of the seller's (1) assets, (2) liabilities, and (3) owner's equity?
b. After receiving the $160,000 cash in (a), the seller pays the $30,000 owed. What is the effect of the payment on the total amount of the seller's (1) assets, (2) liabilities, and (3) owner's equity?

Exercise 1–7

Effect of transactions on owner's equity

Objective 7

Indicate whether each of the following types of transactions will (a) increase owner's equity or (b) decrease owner's equity:

1. owner's investments
2. revenues
3. expenses
4. owner's withdrawals

Exercise 1–8

Transactions

Objective 7

The following selected transactions were completed by On Time Delivery Service during May:

1. Received cash from cash customers, $6,250.
2. Paid creditors on account, $250.
3. Received cash from owner as additional investment, $25,000.
4. Paid advertising expense, $625.
5. Billed customers for delivery services on account, $2,900.
6. Purchased supplies for cash, $750.
7. Paid rent for July, $2,500.
8. Received cash from customers on account, $900.
9. Determined that the cost of supplies on hand was $180; therefore, $570 of supplies had been used during the month.
10. Paid cash to owner for personal use, $1,000.

Indicate the effect of each transaction on the accounting equation by listing the numbers identifying the transactions, (1) through (10), in a vertical column, and inserting at the right of each number the appropriate letter from the following list:

a. Increase in an asset, decrease in another asset.
b. Increase in an asset, increase in a liability.
c. Increase in an asset, increase in owner's equity.
d. Decrease in an asset, decrease in a liability.
e. Decrease in an asset, decrease in owner's equity.

Exercise 1–9

Nature of transactions

Objective 7

✓ d. $3,950

Joe Norwood operates his own catering service. Summary financial data for August are presented in equation form as follows. Each line designated by a number indicates the effect of a transaction on the equation. Each increase and decrease in owner's equity, except transaction (5), affects net income.

	Cash	+	Supplies	+	Land	=	Liabilities	+	Owner's Equity
Bal.	5,500		750		29,000		3,750		31,500
1.	+16,000								+16,000
2.	− 2,000				+ 2,000				
3.	−11,250								−11,250
4.			+600				+ 600		
5.	− 1,950								− 1,950
6.	− 2,300						−2,300		
7.			−800						− 800
Bal.	4,000		550		31,000		2,050		33,500

a. Describe each transaction.
b. What is the amount of net decrease in cash during the month?
c. What is the amount of net increase in owner's equity during the month?
d. What is the amount of the net income for the month?
e. How much of the net income for the month was retained in the business?

Exercise 1–10

Net income and owner's withdrawals

Objective 8

The income statement of a proprietorship for the month of February indicates a net income of $28,000. During the same period, the owner withdrew $35,000 in cash from the business for personal use.

Would it be correct to say that the business incurred a net loss of $7,000 during the month? Discuss.

Exercise 1–11

Net income and owner's equity for four businesses

Objective 8

✓ Company G: Net loss, $60,000

Four different proprietorships, E, F, G, and H, show the same balance sheet data at the beginning and end of a year. These data, exclusive of the amount of owner's equity, are summarized as follows:

	Total Assets	Total Liabilities
Beginning of the year	$325,000	$120,000
End of the year	570,000	325,000

On the basis of the above data and the following additional information for the year, determine the net income (or loss) of each company for the year. (Suggestion: First determine the amount of increase or decrease in owner's equity during the year.)

Company E: The owner had made no additional investments in the business and had made no withdrawals from the business.

Company F: The owner had made no additional investments in the business but had withdrawn $25,000.

Company G: The owner had made an additional investment of $100,000 but had made no withdrawals.

Company H: The owner had made an additional investment of $100,000 and had withdrawn $25,000.

Exercise 1–12

Balance sheet items

Objective 8

From the following list of selected items taken from the records of Reliable Appliance Service as of a specific date, identify those that would appear on the balance sheet:

1. Utilities Expense
2. Fees Earned
3. Supplies
4. Wages Expense
5. Accounts Payable
6. Cash
7. Supplies Expense
8. Land
9. Julie McCarthy, Capital
10. Wages Payable

Exercise 1–13

Income statement items

Objective 8

Based on the data presented in Exercise 1–12, identify those items that would appear on the income statement.

Exercise 1–14

Statement of owner's equity

Objective 8

✓ Meg Tewksbury, capital September 30, 2000: $350,250

Financial information related to Eldora Company, a proprietorship, for the month ended September 30, 2000, is as follows:

Net income for September	$ 91,250
Meg Tewksbury's withdrawals during September	12,000
Meg Tewksbury, capital, September 1, 2000	271,000

Prepare a statement of owner's equity for the month ended September 30, 2000.

Exercise 1–15

Income statement

Objective 8

✓ Net income: $19,700

Temporary Help Services was organized on November 1. A summary of the revenue and expense transactions for November are as follows:

Fees earned	$75,400
Wages expense	37,700
Miscellaneous expense	2,250
Rent expense	12,500
Supplies expense	3,250

Prepare an income statement for the month ended November 30.

Exercise 1–16
Missing amounts from balance sheet and income statement data

Objective 8

✓ (a) $211,000
✓ (d) $335,000

One item is omitted in each of the following summaries of balance sheet and income statement data for four different proprietorships, I, II, III, and IV.

	I	II	III	IV
Beginning of the year:				
Assets	$500,000	$ 95,000	$90,000	(d)
Liabilities	360,000	45,000	76,000	$150,000
End of the year:				
Assets	855,000	125,000	94,000	310,000
Liabilities	465,000	35,000	87,000	170,000
During the year:				
Additional investment in the business	(a)	22,000	5,000	50,000
Withdrawals from the business	46,750	8,000	(c)	75,000
Revenue	197,750	(b)	88,100	140,000
Expenses	112,000	52,000	89,600	160,000

Determine the amounts of the missing items, identifying them by letter. (Suggestion: First determine the amount of increase or decrease in owner's equity during the year.)

Exercise 1–17
Balance sheets, net income

Objective 8

✓ b. $10,170

Financial information related to the proprietorship of Lynch Interiors for May and June of the current year is as follows:

	May 31, 20—	June 30, 20—
Accounts payable	$ 5,720	$ 6,900
Accounts receivable	9,300	10,400
Kate Lynch, capital	?	?
Cash	15,000	25,500
Supplies	1,000	750

a. Prepare balance sheets for Lynch Interiors as of May 31 and as of June 30 of the current year.
b. Determine the amount of net income for June, assuming that the owner made no additional investments or withdrawals during the month.
c. Determine the amount of net income for June, assuming that the owner made no additional investments but withdrew $5,000 during the month.

Exercise 1–18
Financial statements

Objective 8

Each of the following items is shown in the financial statements of **Exxon Corporation**. Identify the financial statement (balance sheet or income statement) in which each item would appear.

a. Operating expenses
b. Crude oil inventory
c. Income taxes payable
d. Sales
e. Investments
f. Marketable securities
g. Exploration expenses
h. Notes and loans payable

i. Cash equivalents
j. Long-term debt
k. Selling expenses
l. Notes receivable
m. Equipment
n. Accounts payable
o. Prepaid taxes

Exercise 1–19
Statement of cash flows

Objective 8

Indicate whether each of the following activities would be reported on the statement of cash flows as (a) an operating activity, (b) an investing activity, or (c) a financing activity:

1. Cash received as owner's investment
2. Cash paid for land
3. Cash received from fees earned
4. Cash paid for expenses

Exercise 1–20
Financial statements

Objective 8

What's Wrong

WITH THIS?

✓ Correct Amount of Total Assets is $13,875

Vineyard Realty, organized July 1, 2000, is owned and operated by Barbara Straud. How many errors can you find in the following financial statements for Vineyard Realty, prepared after its second month of operations?

Vineyard Realty
Income Statement
August 31, 2000

Sales commissions		$26,100.00
Operating expenses:		
Office salaries expense	$18,150.00	
Rent expense	2,800.00	
Automobile expense	1,750.00	
Miscellaneous expense	550.00	
Supplies expense	225.00	
Total operating expenses		23,475.00
Net income		$12,625.00

Barbara Straud
Statement of Owner's Equity
August 31, 1999

Barbara Straud, capital, August 1, 2000	$ 8,450.00
Less withdrawals during August	1,000.00
	$ 7,450.00
Additional investment during August	2,500.00
	$ 9,950.00
Net income for the month	12,625.00
Barbara Straud, capital, August 31, 2000	$22,575.00

Balance Sheet
For the Month Ended August 31, 2000

Assets		Liabilities	
Cash	$ 3,350.00	Accounts receivable	$ 9,200.00
Accounts payable	1,300.00	Supplies	1,325.00
		Owner's Equity	
		Barbara Straud, capital	22,575.00
Total assets	$ 4,650.00	Total liabilities and owner's equity	$33,100.00

Exercise 1–21
Ratio of liabilities to stockholders' equity

Objective 9

REAL WORLD

The financial statements for **Hershey Foods Corporation** are presented in Appendix G at the end of the text.

a. Determine the ratio of liabilities to stockholders' equity for Hershey Foods Corporation at the end of 1996 and 1995.
b. What conclusions regarding the margin of protection to the creditors can you draw from your analysis?

PROBLEMS SERIES A

Problem 1–1A
Transactions

Objective 7

✓ Cash Bal. at End of July:
$23,895

Chris Oxnard established an insurance agency on July 1 of the current year and completed the following transactions during July:

a.   Opened a business bank account with a deposit of $25,000.
b.   Purchased supplies on account, $850.
c.   Paid creditors on account, $625.
d.   Received cash from fees earned, $4,250.
e.   Paid rent on office and equipment for the month, $1,000.
f.   Paid automobile expenses for month, $780, and miscellaneous expenses, $250.
g.   Paid office salaries, $1,200.
h.   Determined that the cost of supplies on hand was $275; therefore, the cost of supplies used was $575.
i.   Billed insurance companies for sales commissions earned, $3,350.
j.   Withdrew cash for personal use, $1,500.

Instructions

1.   Indicate the effect of each transaction and the balances after each transaction, using the following tabular headings:

Assets	=	**Liabilities**	+	**Owner's Equity**
Cash + Accounts Receivable + Supplies	=	Accounts Payable	+	Chris Oxnard, Capital

Explain the nature of each increase and decrease in owner's equity by an appropriate notation at the right of the amount.
2.   ✏ Briefly explain why the owner's investment and revenues increased owner's equity, while withdrawals and expenses decreased owner's equity.

Problem 1–2A
Financial statements

Objective 8

✓ Net income: $26,300

Following are the amounts of the assets and liabilities of Las Posas Travel Service at June 30, 2000, the end of the current year, and its revenue and expenses for the year ended on that date. The capital of Gabriela Sanchez, owner, was $18,000 at July 1, 1999, the beginning of the current year, and the owner withdrew $15,000 during the current year.

Accounts payable	$ 6,100
Cash	33,725
Fees earned	108,775
Miscellaneous expense	1,825
Rent expense	18,900
Supplies	1,675
Supplies expense	3,550
Taxes expense	2,800
Utilities expense	10,500
Wages expense	44,900

Instructions

1.   Prepare an income statement for the current year ended June 30, 2000.
2.   Prepare a statement of owner's equity for the current year ended June 30, 2000.
3.   Prepare a balance sheet as of June 30, 2000.

Problem 1–3A
Financial statements

Objective 8

✓ Net income: $4,770

Joe Oakley established Joe's Desktop Computer Services on August 1 of the current year. The effect of each transaction and the balances after each transaction for August are as follows:

			Assets			=	Liabilities	+	Owner's Equity	
			Accounts				Accounts		Joe Oakley,	
	Cash	+	Receivable	+	Supplies	=	Payable	+	Capital	
a.	+10,000								+10,000	Investment
b.					+550		+550			
Bal.	10,000				550		550		10,000	
c.	+ 6,500								+ 6,500	Fees earned
Bal.	16,500				550		550		16,500	
d.	− 1,500								− 1,500	Rent expense
Bal.	15,000				550		550		15,000	
e.	− 250						−250			
Bal.	14,750				550		300		15,000	
f.			+3,750						+ 3,750	Fees earned
Bal.	14,750		3,750		550		300		18,750	
g.	− 1,155								− 780	Auto expense
									− 375	Misc. expense
Bal.	13,595		3,750		550		300		17,595	
h.	− 2,500								− 2,500	Salaries expense
Bal.	11,095		3,750		550		300		15,095	
i.					−325				− 325	Supplies expense
Bal.	11,095		3,750		225		300		14,770	
j.	− 1,000								− 1,000	Withdrawal
Bal.	10,095		3,750		225		300		13,770	

Instructions

1. Prepare an income statement for the month ended August 31.
2. Prepare a statement of owner's equity for the month ended August 31.
3. Prepare a balance sheet as of August 31.

Problem 1–4A

Transactions; financial statements

Objectives 7, 8

✓ Net income: $5,775

On May 1 of the current year, Tom O'Hare established Rabbit Realty. O'Hare completed the following transactions during the month of May:

a. Opened a business bank account with a deposit of $7,000.
b. Paid rent on office and equipment for the month, $4,600.
c. Paid automobile expenses (including rental charge) for month, $900, and miscellaneous expenses, $550.
d. Purchased supplies (pens, file folders, and copy paper) on account, $1,325.
e. Earned sales commissions, receiving cash, $16,500.
f. Paid creditor on account, $800.
g. Paid office salaries, $3,950.
h. Withdrew cash for personal use, $2,000.
i. Determined that the cost of supplies on hand was $600; therefore, the cost of supplies used was $725.

Instructions

1. Indicate the effect of each transaction and the balances after each transaction, using the following tabular headings:

Assets	=	Liabilities	+	Owner's Equity
Cash + Supplies	=	Accounts Payable	+	Tom O'Hare, Capital

Explain the nature of each increase and decrease in owner's equity by an appropriate notation at the right of the amount.

2. Prepare an income statement for May, a statement of owner's equity for May, and a balance sheet as of May 31.

Problem 1–5A
Transactions; financial statements

Objectives 7, 8

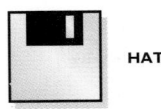

HAT

✓ Net income: $7,625

Camarillo Dry Cleaners is owned and operated by Kelly Camarillo. Currently, a building and equipment are being rented, pending expansion to new facilities. The actual work of dry cleaning is done by another company at wholesale rates. The assets and the liabilities of the business on November 1 of the current year are as follows: Cash, $5,400; Accounts Receivable, $18,750; Supplies, $1,560; Land, $35,000; Accounts Payable, $5,880. Business transactions during November are summarized as follows:

a. Paid rent for the month, $2,450.
b. Charged customers for dry cleaning sales on account, $7,150.
c. Paid creditors on account, $1,680.
d. Purchased supplies on account, $840.
e. Received cash from cash customers for dry cleaning sales, $14,600.
f. Received cash from customers on account, $14,750.
g. Received monthly invoice for dry cleaning expense for November (to be paid on December 10), $7,400.
h. Paid the following: wages expense, $1,800; truck expense, $725; utilities expense, $510; miscellaneous expense, $190.
i. Determined that the cost of supplies on hand was $1,350; therefore, the cost of supplies used during the month was $1,050.

Instructions

1. Determine the amount of Kelly Camarillo's capital as of November 1 of the current year.
2. State the assets, liabilities, and owner's equity as of November 1 in equation form similar to that shown in this chapter. In tabular form below the equation, indicate increases and decreases resulting from each transaction and the new balances after each transaction. Explain the nature of each increase and decrease in owner's equity by an appropriate notation at the right of the amount.
3. Prepare an income statement for November, a statement of owner's equity for November, and a balance sheet as of November 30.

Problem 1–6A
Financial statements

Objective 8

HAT

✓ Net income: $122,375

Dreamaker Designs is an architectural firm. Following are the amounts of the assets and liabilities of Dreamaker Designs at March 31, 2000, the end of the current year, and its revenue and expenses for the year ended on that date. The capital of Cindy Lopez, owner, was $99,990 on April 1, 1999, the beginning of the current year. During the current year, the owner withdrew $35,000.

Accounts payable	$ 28,000
Accounts receivable	39,750
Advertising expense	20,000
Cash	24,515
Fees earned	527,500
Land	150,000
Miscellaneous expense	6,125
Rent expense	98,000
Supplies	4,250
Supplies expense	9,750
Taxes expense	23,500
Utilities expense	35,750
Wages expense	212,000
Wages payable	3,150

Instructions

1. Prepare an income statement for the current year ended March 31, 2000.
2. Prepare a statement of owner's equity for the current year ended March 31, 2000.
3. Prepare a balance sheet as of March 31, 2000.

PROBLEMS SERIES B

Problem 1–1B
Transactions

Objective 7

✓ Cash Bal. at End of Feb.
$27,670

On February 1 of the current year, Diane Winn established a business to manage rental property. She completed the following transactions during February:

a. Opened a business bank account with a deposit of $30,000.
b. Purchased supplies (pens, file folders, and copy paper) on account, $1,250.
c. Received cash from fees earned, $5,500.
d. Paid rent on office and equipment for the month, $3,000.
e. Paid creditors on account, $575.
f. Billed customers for fees earned, $3,250.
g. Paid automobile expenses (including rental charges) for month, $980, and miscellaneous expenses, $775.
h. Paid office salaries, $1,500.
i. Determined that the cost of supplies on hand was $315; therefore, the cost of supplies used was $935.
j. Withdrew cash for personal use, $1,000.

Instructions

1. Indicate the effect of each transaction and the balances after each transaction, using the following tabular headings:

Assets	=	Liabilities	+	Owner's Equity
Cash + Accounts Receivable + Supplies	=	Accounts Payable	+	Diane Winn, Capital

Explain the nature of each increase and decrease in owner's equity by an appropriate notation at the right of the amount.

2. ✎➤ Briefly explain why the owner's investment and revenues increased owner's equity, while withdrawals and expenses decreased owner's equity.

Problem 1–2B
Financial statements

Objective 8

✓ Net income: $46,655

Following are the amounts of the assets and liabilities of Seven Seas Travel Agency at December 31, 2000, the end of the current year, and its revenue and expenses for the year ended on that date. The capital of Trent Baker, owner, was $24,500 on January 1, 2000, the beginning of the current year. During the current year, Trent withdrew $30,000.

Accounts payable	$ 3,200
Cash	42,490
Fees earned	127,530
Miscellaneous expense	1,750
Rent expense	27,000
Supplies	1,865
Supplies expense	2,125
Utilities expense	4,500
Wages expense	45,500

Instructions

1. Prepare an income statement for the current year ended December 31, 2000.
2. Prepare a statement of owner's equity for the current year ended December 31, 2000.
3. Prepare a balance sheet as of December 31, 2000.

Problem 1–3B
Financial statements

Objective 8

✓ Net income: $4,950

Tanya Maguire established Five Star Services on March 1 of the current year. Five Star Services offers financial planning advice to its clients. The effect of each transaction and the balances after each transaction for March are as follows:

	Assets				=	Liabilities	+	Owner's Equity	
			Accounts				Accounts		Tanya Maguire,	
	Cash	+	Receivable	+	Supplies	=	Payable	+	Capital	
a.	+18,000								+18,000	Investment
b.	____				+1,725		+1,725		____	
Bal.	18,000				1,725		1,725		18,000	
c.	− 1,225				____		−1,225		____	
Bal.	16,775				1,725		500		18,000	
d.	+ 7,750								+ 7,750	Fees earned
Bal.	24,525				1,725		500		25,750	
e.	− 2,500								− 2,500	Rent expense
Bal.	22,025				1,725		500		23,250	
f.	− 1,600								− 1,250	Auto expense
									− 350	Misc. expense
Bal.	20,425				1,725		500		21,650	
g.	− 1,900				____		____		− 1,900	Salaries expense
Bal.	18,525				1,725		500		19,750	
h.					−1,150				− 1,150	Supplies expense
Bal.	18,525				575		500		18,600	
i.			+4,350		____		____		+ 4,350	Fees earned
Bal.	18,525		4,350		575		500		22,950	
j.	− 3,000		____		____		____		− 3,000	Withdrawal
Bal.	15,525		4,350		575		500		19,950	

Instructions

1. Prepare an income statement for the month ended March 31.
2. Prepare a statement of owner's equity for the month ended March 31.
3. Prepare a balance sheet as of March 31.

Problem 1–4B

Transactions; financial statements

Objectives 7, 8

✓ Net income: $9,250

On September 1 of the current year, Corean Pace established Rapid Realty. Pace completed the following transactions during the month of September:

a. Opened a business bank account with a deposit of $8,500.
b. Purchased supplies (pens, file folders, fax paper, etc.) on account, $1,250.
c. Paid creditor on account, $750.
d. Earned sales commissions, receiving cash, $18,200.
e. Paid rent on office and equipment for the month, $2,000.
f. Withdrew cash for personal use, $3,000.
g. Paid automobile expenses (including rental charge) for month, $1,900, and miscellaneous expenses, $350.
h. Paid office salaries, $4,150.
i. Determined that the cost of supplies on hand was $700; therefore, the cost of supplies used was $550.

Instructions

1. Indicate the effect of each transaction and the balances after each transaction, using the following tabular headings:

Assets	=	Liabilities	+	Owner's Equity
Cash + Supplies	=	Accounts Payable	+	Corean Pace, Capital

Explain the nature of each increase and decrease in owner's equity by an appropriate notation at the right of the amount.

2. Prepare an income statement for September, a statement of owner's equity for September, and a balance sheet as of September 30.

Problem 1–5B
Transactions; financial statements

Objectives 7, 8

✓ Net income: $6,050

Magic Dry Cleaners is owned and operated by Gail Fox. Currently, a building and equipment are being rented, pending expansion to new facilities. The actual work of dry cleaning is done by another company at wholesale rates. The assets and the liabilities of the business on July 1 of the current year are as follows: Cash, $7,250; Accounts Receivable, $22,100; Supplies, $2,200; Land, $50,000; Accounts Payable, $6,800. Business transactions during July are summarized as follows:

a. Received cash from cash customers for dry cleaning sales, $17,750.
b. Paid rent for the month, $2,000.
c. Purchased supplies on account, $1,650.
d. Paid creditors on account, $6,800.
e. Charged customers for dry cleaning sales on account, $6,920.
f. Received monthly invoice for dry cleaning expense for July (to be paid on August 10), $9,700.
g. Paid the following: wages expense, $2,400; truck expense, $1,580; utilities expense, $960; miscellaneous expense, $630.
h. Received cash from customers on account, $12,100.
i. Determined that the cost of supplies on hand was $2,500; therefore, the cost of supplies used during the month was $1,350.

Instructions

1. Determine the amount of Gail Fox's capital as of July 1 of the current year.
2. State the assets, liabilities, and owner's equity as of July 1 in equation form similar to that shown in this chapter. In tabular form below the equation, indicate increases and decreases resulting from each transaction and the new balances after each transaction. Explain the nature of each increase and decrease in owner's equity by an appropriate notation at the right of the amount.
3. Prepare an income statement for July, a statement of owner's equity for July, and a balance sheet as of July 31.

Problem 1–6B
Financial statements

Objective 8

✓ Net income: $136,400

Design Services is an architectural firm. Following are the amounts of the assets and liabilities of Design Services at December 31, the end of the current year, and its revenue and expenses for the year ended on that date. The capital of Marc Conrad, owner, was $84,950 at January 1, the beginning of the current year, and the owner withdrew $50,000 during the current year.

Accounts payable	$ 13,100
Accounts receivable	52,000
Advertising expense	7,500
Cash	37,200
Fees earned	329,250
Land	90,000
Miscellaneous expense	1,250
Rent expense	42,000
Supplies	6,750
Supplies expense	13,800
Taxes expense	10,500
Utilities expense	18,100
Wages expense	99,700
Wages payable	1,500

Instructions

1. Prepare an income statement for the current year ended December 31.
2. Prepare a statement of owner's equity for the current year ended December 31.
3. Prepare a balance sheet as of December 31 of the current year.

CONTINUING PROBLEM

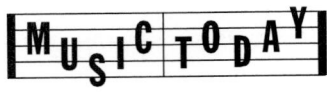

HAT

✓ 2. Net income: $305

Chris Stipe enjoys listening to all types of music and owns countless CDs and tapes. Over the years, Chris has gained a local reputation for knowledge of music from classical to rap and the ability to put together sets of recordings that appeal to all ages.

During the last several months, Chris served as a guest disc jockey on a local radio station. In addition, Chris has entertained at several friends' parties as the host deejay.

On November 1, 1999, Chris established a proprietorship known as Music Today. Using his extensive collection of CDs and tapes, Chris will serve as a disc jockey on a fee basis for weddings, college parties, and other events. During November, Chris entered into the following transactions:

Nov. 1. Deposited $1,500 in a checking account in the name of Music Today.
    2. Received $500 from a local radio station to serve as the guest disc jockey for November.
    2. Agreed to share office space with a local real estate agency, Picasso Realty. Music Today will pay ¼ of the rent. In addition, Music Today agreed to pay $110 a month toward the salary of the receptionist and to pay ¼ of the utilities. Paid $250 for the rent of the office.
    3. Purchased supplies (blank cassette tapes, poster board, extension cords, etc.) from Ideal Office Supply Co. for $250. Agreed to pay $100 within 10 days and the remainder by December 3, 1999.
    5. Paid $75 to a local radio station to advertise the services of Music Today twice daily for two weeks.
    8. Paid $325 to a local electronics store for rent on two CD players, two cassette players, and eight speakers.
  12. Paid $100 (music expense) to The Music Store for the use of its current demo CDs and tapes to make cassette tapes of various music sets.
  13. Paid Ideal Office Supply Co. $100 on account.
  16. Received $50 from a dentist for providing two music sets for the dentist to play for her patients.
  22. Served as disc jockey for a wedding party. The father of the bride agreed to pay $400 the 1st of December.
  25. Received $250 from a friend for serving as the disc jockey for a cancer charity ball hosted by the local hospital.
  29. Paid $120 (music expense) to Crescendo Music for the use of its library of demo CDs and tapes.
  30. Received $350 for serving as disc jockey for a local club's monthly dance.
  30. Paid Picasso Realty $110 for Music Today's share of the receptionist's salary for November.
  30. Paid Picasso Realty $100 for Music Today's share of the utilities for November.
  30. Determined that the cost of supplies on hand is $160. Therefore, the cost of supplies used during the month was $90.
  30. Paid for miscellaneous expenses, $75.
  30. Withdrew $50 of cash from Music Today for personal use.

Instructions

1. Indicate the effect of each transaction and the balances after each transaction, using the following tabular headings:

Assets	=	Liabilities	+	Owner's Equity
Cash + Accounts Receivable + Supplies	=	Accounts Payable	+	Chris Stipe, Capital

Explain the nature of each increase and decrease in owner's equity by an appropriate notation at the right of the amount.

2. Prepare an income statement for Music Today for the month ended November 30, 1999.
3. Prepare a statement of owner's equity for Music Today for the month ended November 30, 1999.
4. Prepare a balance sheet for Music Today as of November 30, 1999.

SPECIAL ACTIVITIES

Activity 1–1
Gay Enterprises

Ethics and professional conduct in business

Nicole Gay, president of Gay Enterprises, applied for a $100,000 loan from Western National Bank. The bank requested financial statements from Gay Enterprises as a basis for granting the loan. Nicole has told her accountant to provide the bank with a balance sheet. Nicole has decided to omit the other financial statements because there was a net loss during the past year.

In groups of three or four, discuss the following questions:

1. Is Nicole behaving in a professional manner by omitting some of the financial statements?
2. a. What types of information about their businesses would owners be willing to provide bankers? What types of information would owners not be willing to provide?
   b. What types of information about a business would bankers want before extending a loan?
   c. What common interests are shared by bankers and the business owners?

Activity 1–2
Second Opinion

Net income

On January 3, 1999, Dr. Brittany Clark established Second Opinion, a medical practice organized as a proprietorship. The following conversation occurred the following August between Dr. Clark and a former medical school classmate, Dr. Herman Ryder, at an American Medical Association convention in Mexico City.

Dr. Ryder: Brittany, good to see you again. Why didn't you call when you were in Reno? We could have had dinner together.

Dr. Clark: Actually, I never made it to Reno this year. My husband and kids went up to our Lake Tahoe condo twice, but I got stuck in New York. I opened a new consulting practice this January and I haven't had any time for myself since.

Dr. Ryder: I heard about it . . . Second . . . something . . . right?

Dr. Clark: Yes, Second Opinion. My husband chose the name.

Dr. Ryder: I've thought about doing something like that. Are you making any money? I mean, is it worth your time?

Dr. Clark: You wouldn't believe it. I started by opening a bank account of $25,000, and my July bank statement has a balance of $225,000. Not bad for seven months—all pure profit.

Dr. Ryder: Maybe I'll try it in Reno. Let's have breakfast together tomorrow and you can fill me in on the details.

➤ Comment on Dr. Clark's statement that the difference between the opening bank balance ($25,000) and the July statement balance ($225,000) is pure profit.

Activity 1–3
Match Point

Transactions and financial statements

HAT

Reva Inman, a junior in college, has been seeking ways to earn extra spending money. As an active sports enthusiast, Reva plays tennis regularly at the Racquet Club, where her family has a membership. The president of the club recently approached Reva with the proposal that she manage the club's tennis courts on weekends. Reva's primary duty would be to supervise the operation of the club's four indoor and six outdoor courts, including court reservations.

In return for her services, the club would pay Reva $75 per weekend, plus Reva could keep whatever she earned from lessons and the fees from the use of the ball machine. The club and Reva agreed to a one-month trial, after which both would consider an arrangement for the remaining two years of Reva's college career. On this basis, Reva organized Match Point. During September, Reva managed the tennis courts and entered into the following transactions:

a. Opened a business account by depositing $500.
b. Paid $180 for tennis supplies (practice tennis balls, etc.).
c. Paid $75 for the rental of videotape equipment to be used in offering lessons during September.

d.   Arranged for the rental of two ball machines during September for $100. Paid $60 in advance, with the remaining $40 due October 1.

e.   Received $875 for lessons given during September.

f.   Received $120 in fees from the use of the ball machines during September.

g.   Paid $300 for salaries of part-time employees who answered the telephone and took reservations while Reva was giving lessons.

h.   Paid $90 for miscellaneous expenses.

i.   Received $300 from the club for managing the tennis courts during September.

j.   Determined that the cost of supplies on hand at the end of the month totaled $75; therefore, the cost of supplies used was $105.

k.   Withdrew $500 for personal use on September 30.

As a friend and accounting student, you have been asked by Reva to aid her in assessing the venture.

1.   Indicate the effect of each transaction and the balances after each transaction, using the following tabular headings:

Assets	=	Liabilities	+	Owner's Equity
Cash + Supplies	=	Accounts Payable	+	Reva Inman, Capital

Explain the nature of each increase and decrease in owner's equity by an appropriate notation at the right of the amount.

2.   Prepare an income statement for September.

3.   Prepare a statement of owner's equity for September.

4.   Prepare a balance sheet as of September 30.

5.   a.   Assume that Reva Inman could earn $7 per hour working 20 hours each of the four weekends as a waitress. Evaluate which of the two alternatives, working as a waitress or operating Match Point, would provide Reva with the most income per month.

      b.   Discuss any other factors that you believe Reva should consider before discussing a long-term arrangement with the Racquet Club.

Activity 1–4
Into the Real World
Certification requirements for accountants

By satisfying certain specific requirements, accountants may become certified as public accountants (CPAs), management accountants (CMAs), or internal auditors (CIAs). Find the certification requirements for *one* of these accounting groups by accessing the appropriate Internet site listed below.

Site	Description
www.ais-cpa.com	This site lists the address and/or Internet link for each state's board of accountancy. Find your state's requirements.
www.rutgers.edu/Accounting/raw/ima/icma.htm	This site lists the requirements for becoming a CMA.
www.rutgers.edu/Accounting/raw/iia	This site lists the requirements for becoming a CIA.

ANSWERS TO SELF-EXAMINATION QUESTIONS

Matching

1. H	5. DD	9. D	13. Q	17. T	21. B	25. HH	29. JJ
2. W	6. L	10. N	14. I	18. CC	22. EE	26. S	30. X
3. Y	7. J	11. P	15. LL	19. E	23. C	27. KK	31. A
4. FF	8. V	12. U	16. F	20. K	24. O	28. G	

Multiple Choice

1. **D** A corporation, organized in accordance with state or federal statutes, is a separate legal entity in which ownership is divided into shares of stock (answer D). A proprietorship (answer A) is an unincorporated business owned by one individual. A service business (answer B) provides services to its customers. It can be organized as a proprietorship, partnership, or corporation. A partnership (answer C) is an unincorporated business owned by two or more individuals.

2. **A** The resources owned by a business are called assets (answer A). The debts of the business are called liabilities (answer B), and the equity of the owners is called owner's equity (answer D). The relationship between assets, liabilities, and owner's equity is expressed as the accounting equation (answer C).

3. **A** The balance sheet is a listing of the assets, liabilities, and owner's equity of a business at a specific date (answer A). The income statement (answer B) is a summary of the revenue and expenses of a business for a specific period of time. The statement of owner's equity (answer C) summarizes the changes in owner's equity for a proprietorship or partnership during a specific period of time. The statement of cash flows (answer D) summarizes the cash receipts and cash payments for a specific period of time.

4. **C** The accounting equation is:

Assets = Liabilities + Owner's Equity

Therefore, if assets increased by $20,000 and liabilities increased by $12,000, owner's equity must have increased by $8,000 (answer C), as indicated in the following computation:

Assets	=	Liabilities	+	Owner's Equity
$20,000	=	$12,000	+	Owner's Equity
$20,000 − $12,000	=			Owner's Equity
$8,000	=			Owner's Equity

5. **B** Net income is the excess of revenue over expenses, or $7,500 (answer B). If expenses exceed revenue, the difference is a net loss. Withdrawals by the owner are the opposite of the owner's investing in the business and do not affect the amount of net income or net loss.

2

Analyzing Transactions

Setting the STAGE

Assume that you have been hired by a pizza restaurant to deliver pizzas, using your own car. You will be paid $5.00 per hour plus $0.20 per mile plus tips. What is the best way for you to determine how many miles you have driven each day in delivering pizzas?

One method would be to record the odometer mileage before work and then at quitting time. The difference would be the miles driven. For example, if the odometer read 56,743 at the start of work and 56,889 at the end of work, you would have driven 146 miles. However, this method is subject to error if you copy down the wrong reading or make a math error.

In the same way, managers of a business need information about the status of the business at different points in time. Such information is useful for analyzing the effects of transactions on the business and for making decisions. For example, the manager of your neighborhood dry cleaners needs to know how much cash is available, how much has been spent, and what services have been provided customers.

In Chapter 1, we analyzed and recorded this kind of information by using the accounting equation, Assets = Liabilities + Owner's Equity. Since such a format is not practical for most businesses, in Chapter 2 we will study more practical methods of recording transactions. We will conclude this chapter by discussing how accounting errors may occur and how they may be detected by the accounting process.

After studying this chapter, you should be able to:

1 Explain why accounts are used to record and summarize the effects of transactions on financial statements.

2 Explain the characteristics of an account.

3 List the rules of debit and credit and the normal balances of accounts.

4 Analyze and summarize the financial statement effects of transactions.

5 Prepare a trial balance and explain how it can be used to discover errors.

6 Discover errors in recording transactions and correct them.

7 Use horizontal analysis to compare financial statements from different periods.

Usefulness of an Account

OBJECTIVE 1

Explain why accounts are used to record and summarize the effects of transactions on financial statements.

Before making a major cash purchase, such as buying a CD player, you need to know the balance of your bank account. Likewise, managers need timely, useful information in order to make good decisions about their businesses.

How are accounting systems designed to provide this information? We illustrated a very simple design in Chapter 1, where transactions were recorded and summarized in the accounting equation format. However, this format is difficult to use when thousands of transactions must be recorded daily. Thus, accounting systems are designed to show the increases and decreases in each financial statement item in a separate record. This record is called an **account**. For example, since cash appears on the balance sheet, a separate record is kept of the increases and decreases in cash. Likewise, a separate record is kept of the increases and decreases for supplies, land, accounts payable, and the other balance sheet items. Similar records would be kept for income statement items, such as fees earned, wages expense, and rent expense.

> **The increases and decreases in each financial statement item are shown in an account.**

A group of accounts for a business entity is called a **ledger**. A list of the accounts in the ledger is called a **chart of accounts**. The accounts are normally listed in the order in which they appear in the financial statements. The balance sheet accounts are usually listed first, in the order of assets, liabilities, and owner's equity. The income statement accounts are then listed in the order of revenues and expenses. Each of these major account classifications is briefly described below.

Assets are resources that are owned by the business entity. These resources are physical items or rights that have value. Examples of assets include cash, accounts receivable, supplies, prepaid expenses (such as insurance), buildings, equipment, land, and patent rights.

Liabilities are debts owed to outsiders (creditors). Liabilities are often identified on the balance sheet by titles that include the word *payable*. Examples of liabilities include accounts payable, notes payable, and wages payable. Cash received

INTERMISSION

What does a chart of accounts reveal about a business's operations? Look at the following revenue and expense accounts taken from the chart of accounts for a newspaper:

The Telltale Chart of Accounts

- Revenue accounts:
  - Circulation—carriers
  - Circulation—vending machines
  - Circulation—mail subscriptions
  - Advertising—commercial
  - Advertising—classified

- Expense accounts:
  - Newsprint
  - News ink
  - Wire services
  - Correspondent fees
  - Photography
  - Telephone
  - Postage
  - Delivery
  - Wages

These accounts tell us that the newspaper receives its primary revenues from circulation and advertising. In addition, the accounts reflect some of the decision-making needs of management. For example, matching the revenues from commercial and classified advertising with the related expenses helps management determine whether these services are profitable. This might lead management to consider expanding the paper's advertising space to take advantage of this profitability. ■

before services are delivered creates a liability to perform the services. These future service commitments are often called *unearned revenues.* Examples of unearned revenues are magazine subscriptions received by a publisher and tuition received by a college at the beginning of a term.

Owner's equity is the owner's right to the assets of the business. For a proprietorship, the owner's equity on the balance sheet is represented by the balance of the owner's *capital* account. A **drawing** account represents the amount of withdrawals made by the owner.

Revenues are increases in owner's equity as a result of selling services or products to customers. Examples of revenues include fees earned, fares earned, commissions revenue, and rent revenue.

Assets used up or services consumed in the process of generating revenues are **expenses.** Examples of typical expenses include wages expense, rent expense, utilities expense, supplies expense, and miscellaneous expense.

A chart of accounts is designed to meet the information needs of a company's managers and other users of its financial statements. Within the chart of accounts, the accounts are numbered for use as references. A flexible numbering system is normally used, so that new accounts can be added without affecting other account numbers.

Exhibit 1 is Computer King's chart of accounts that we will be using in this chapter. Additional accounts will be introduced in later chapters. In Exhibit 1, each account number has two digits. The first digit indicates the major classification of the ledger in which the account is located. Accounts beginning with 1 represent assets; 2, liabilities; 3, owner's equity; 4, revenue; and 5, expenses. The second digit indicates the location of the account within its class.

 **Procter & Gamble's** account numbers have over 30 digits to reflect P&G's many different operations and regions.

EXHIBIT I
Chart of Accounts for Computer King

Balance Sheet Accounts		Income Statement Accounts	
	1. Assets		4. Revenue
11	Cash	41	Fees Earned
12	Accounts Receivable		5. Expenses
14	Supplies	51	Wages Expense
15	Prepaid Insurance	52	Rent Expense
17	Land	54	Utilities Expense
18	Office Equipment	55	Supplies Expense
	2. Liabilities	59	Miscellaneous Expense
21	Accounts Payable		
23	Unearned Rent		
	3. Owner's Equity		
31	Pat King, Capital		
32	Pat King, Drawing		

Characteristics of an Account

The simplest form of an account has three parts. First, each account has a title, which is the name of the item recorded in the account. Second, each account has a space for recording increases in the amount of the item. Third, each account has a space for recording decreases in the amount of the item. The account form presented below is called a **T account** because it is similar to the letter T. The left side of the account is called the *debit* side, and the right side is called the *credit* side.[1]

Point of INTEREST

Many times when accountants analyze complex transactions, they use T accounts to simplify the thought process. In the same way, you will find T accounts a useful device in this and later accounting courses.

Title

Left side	Right side
debit	*credit*

Amounts entered on the left side of an account, regardless of the account title, are called **debits** to the account. When debits are entered in an account, the account is said to be *debited* (or charged). Amounts entered on the right side of an account are called **credits**, and the account is said to be *credited*. Debits and credits are sometimes abbreviated as *Dr.* and *Cr.*

In the cash account shown below, transactions involving receipts of cash are listed on the debit side of the account. The transactions involving cash payments are listed on the credit side. If at any time the total of the cash receipts

Amounts entered on the left side of an account are debits, and amounts entered on the right side of an account are credits.

is needed, the entries on the debit side of the account may be added and the total ($10,950) inserted below the last debit.[2] The total of the cash payments, $6,850 in the example, may be inserted on the credit side in a similar manner. Subtracting the smaller sum from the larger, $10,950 − $6,850, identifies the amount of cash on hand, $4,100. This amount is called the **balance of the account**. It may be inserted in the account, next to the total of the debit column. In this way, the balance is identified as a **debit balance**. If a balance sheet were to be prepared at this time, cash of $4,100 would be reported.

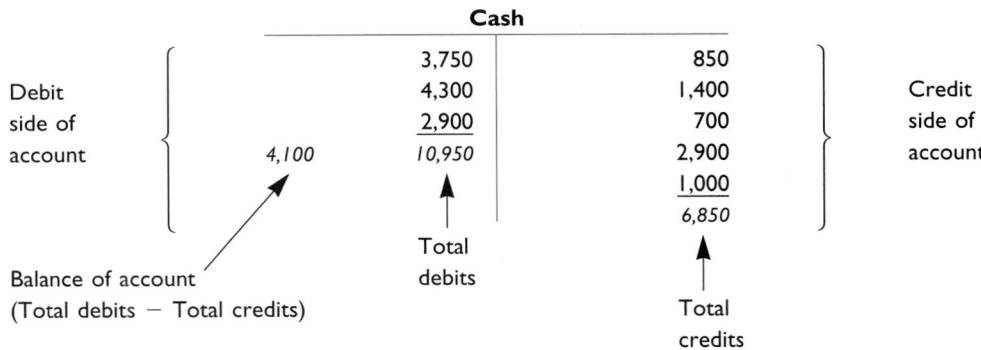

---

[1] The terms *debit* and *credit* are derived from the Latin *debere* and *credere*.
[2] This amount, called a *memorandum balance,* should be written in small figures or identified in some other way to avoid mistaking the amount for an additional debit.

Analyzing and Summarizing Transactions in Accounts

OBJECTIVE 3

List the rules of debit and credit and the normal balances of accounts.

OBJECTIVE 3

List the rules of debit and credit and the normal balances of accounts.

Every business transaction affects at least two accounts. To illustrate how transactions are analyzed and summarized in accounts, we will use the Computer King transactions from Chapter 1, with dates added. First, we illustrate how transactions (a), (b), (c), and (f) are analyzed and summarized in balance sheet accounts (assets, liabilities, and owner's equity). Next, we illustrate how transactions (d), (e), and (g) are analyzed and summarized in income statement accounts (revenues and expenses). Finally, we illustrate how the withdrawal of cash by Pat King, transaction (h), is analyzed and summarized in the accounts.

Every transaction affects at least two accounts.

Transactions and Balance Sheet Accounts

Pat King's first transaction, (a), was to deposit $15,000 in a bank account in the name of Computer King. The effect of this November 1 transaction on the balance sheet is to increase cash and increase the owner's equity, as shown below.

Computer King Balance Sheet November 1, 1999											
Assets						**Owner's Equity**					
Cash	$15	0	0	0	00	Pat King, capital		$15	0	0	0	00

Point of INTEREST

A journal can be thought of as being similar to an individual's diary.

This transaction is initially entered in a record called a **journal**. The title of the account to be debited is listed first, followed by the amount to be debited. The title of the account to be credited is listed below and to the right of the debit, followed by the amount to be credited. This process of recording a transaction in the journal is called **journalizing**. This form of recording a transaction is called a **journal entry**. The journal entry for transaction (a) is shown below.

		JOURNAL			PAGE 1	
Date		**Description**	**Post. Ref.**	**Debit**	**Credit**	
1999 Nov.	1	Cash		15 0 0 0 00		
		Pat King, Capital			15 0 0 0 00	
		Invested cash in Computer King.				

Entry A

The increase in the asset (Cash), which is reported on the left side of the balance sheet, is debited to the cash account. The increase in owner's equity, which is reported on the right side of the balance sheet, is credited to the Pat King, capital account. When other assets are acquired, the increases will also be recorded as debits to asset accounts. Likewise, other increases in owner's equity will be recorded as credits to owner's equity accounts.

The effects of this transaction are shown in the accounts by transferring the amount and the date of the journal entry to the left (debit) side of Cash and to the right (credit) side of Pat King, Capital, as follows:

Cash			Pat King, Capital	
Nov. 1	15,000		Nov. 1	15,000

On November 5 (transaction b), Computer King bought land for $10,000, paying cash. This transaction increases one asset account and decreases another. It is entered in the journal as a $10,000 increase (debit) to Land and a $10,000 decrease (credit) to Cash, as shown below.

Entry B

4						4
5		5	Land	10 0 0 0 00		5
6			Cash		10 0 0 0 00	6
7			Purchased land for building site.			7

The effect of this entry is shown in the accounts of Computer King as follows:

Cash		Land		Pat King, Capital	
Nov. 1 15,000	Nov. 5 10,000	Nov. 5 10,000			Nov. 1 15,000

On November 10 (transaction c), Computer King purchased supplies on account for $1,350. This transaction increases an asset account and increases a liability account. It is entered in the journal as a $1,350 increase (debit) to Supplies and a $1,350 increase (credit) to Accounts Payable, as shown below. To simplify the illustration, the effect of entry (c) and the remaining journal entries for Computer King will be shown in the accounts later.

Entry C

8						8
9		10	Supplies	1 3 5 0 00		9
10			Accounts Payable		1 3 5 0 00	10
11			Purchased supplies on account.			11

On November 30 (transaction f), Computer King paid creditors on account, $950. This transaction decreases a liability account and decreases an asset account. It is entered in the journal as a $950 decrease (debit) to Accounts Payable and a $950 decrease (credit) to Cash, as shown below.

Entry F

23						23
24		30	Accounts Payable	9 5 0 00		24
25			Cash		9 5 0 00	25
26			Paid creditors on account.			26

The left side of all accounts is the debit side, and the right side is the credit side.

In the preceding examples, you should observe that the left side of asset accounts is used for recording increases and the right side is used for recording decreases. Also, the right side of liability and owner's equity accounts is used to record increases, and the left side of such accounts is used to record decreases. The left side of all accounts, whether asset, liability, or owner's equity, is the debit side, and the right side is the credit side. Thus, a debit may be either an increase or a decrease, depending on the account affected. A credit likewise may be either an increase or a decrease, depending on the account. The general rules of debit and credit for balance sheet accounts therefore may be stated as follows:

	Debit		Credit	
Asset accounts	Increase	(+)	Decrease	(−)
Liability accounts	Decrease	(−)	Increase	(+)
Owner's equity (capital) accounts	Decrease	(−)	Increase	(+)

The rules of debit and credit may also be stated in relationship to the accounting equation, as shown below.

Balance Sheet Accounts

ASSETS Asset Accounts		LIABILITIES Liability Accounts	
Debit for increases (+)	Credit for decreases (−)	Debit for decreases (−)	Credit for increases (+)

OWNER'S EQUITY Owner's Equity Accounts	
Debit for decreases (−)	Credit for increases (+)

Income Statement Accounts

The analysis of business transactions affecting the income statement focuses on how each transaction affects owner's equity. Transactions that increase revenue will increase owner's equity. Just as increases in owner's equity are recorded as credits, so are increases in revenue accounts. Transactions that increase expense will decrease owner's equity. Just as decreases in owner's equity are recorded as debits, increases in expense accounts are recorded as debits.

We will use Computer King's transactions (d), (e), and (g) to illustrate the analysis of transactions and the rules of debit and credit for revenue and expense accounts. On November 18 (transaction d), Computer King received fees of $7,500 from customers for services. This transaction increases an asset account and increases a revenue account. It is entered in the journal as a $7,500 increase (debit) to Cash and a $7,500 increase (credit) to Fees Earned, as shown below.

Entry D

12						12
13	18	Cash		7 5 0 0 00		13
14		Fees Earned			7 5 0 0 00	14
15		Received fees from customers.				15

Throughout the month, Computer King incurred the following expenses: wages, $2,125; rent, $800; utilities, $450; and miscellaneous, $275. To simplify the illustration, the entry to journalize the payment of these expenses is recorded on November 30 (transaction e), as shown below. This transaction increases various expense accounts and decreases an asset account.

Entry E

17	30	Wages Expense	2 1 2 5 00		17
18		Rent Expense	8 0 0 00		18
19		Utilities Expense	4 5 0 00		19
20		Miscellaneous Expense	2 7 5 00		20
21		Cash		3 6 5 0 00	21
22		Paid expenses.			22

Point of INTEREST

In 1494, Luca Pacioli, a Franciscan monk, invented the double-entry accounting system that is still used today.

Regardless of the number of accounts, the sum of the debits is always equal to the sum of the credits in a journal entry. This equality of debit and credit for each transaction is built into the accounting equation: Assets = Liabilities + Owner's Equity. It is also because of this double equality that the system is known as **double-entry accounting**.

On November 30, Computer King recorded the amount of supplies used in the operations during the month (transaction g). This transaction increases an expense account and decreases an asset account. The journal entry for transaction (g) is shown below.

> **The sum of the debits must always equal the sum of the credits.**

Entry G

28	30	Supplies Expense	8 0 0 00		28
29		Supplies		8 0 0 00	29
30		Supplies used during November.			30

The general rules of debit and credit for analyzing transactions affecting income statement accounts are stated below.

	Debit		Credit	
Revenue accounts	Decrease	(−)	Increase	(+)
Expense accounts	Increase	(+)	Decrease	(−)

The rules of debit and credit for income statement accounts may also be summarized in relationship to the owner's equity in the accounting equation, as shown below.

Income Statement Accounts

Expense Accounts		Revenue Accounts	
Debit for increases (+)	Credit for decreases (−)	Debit for decreases (−)	Credit for increases (+)

Withdrawals by the Owner

The owner of a proprietorship may withdraw cash from the business for personal use. This practice is common if the owner devotes full time to the business. In this case, the business may be the owner's main source of income. Such withdrawals have the effect of decreasing owner's equity. Just as decreases in owner's equity are recorded as debits, increases in withdrawals are recorded as debits. Withdrawals are debited to an account with the owner's name followed by *Drawing* or *Personal*.

In transaction (h), Pat King withdrew $2,000 in cash from Computer King for personal use. The effect of this transaction is to increase the drawing account and decrease the cash account. The journal entry for transaction (h) is shown below.

Entry H

	1999					
1	Nov.	30	Pat King, Drawing	2 0 0 0 00		1
2			Cash		2 0 0 0 00	2
3			Pat King withdrew cash for			3
4			personal use.			4

Normal Balances of Accounts

The sum of the increases recorded in an account is usually equal to or greater than the sum of the decreases recorded in the account. For this reason, the normal balances of all accounts are positive rather than negative. For example, the total debits (increases) in an asset account will ordinarily be greater than the total credits (decreases). Thus, asset accounts normally have debit balances.

The rules of debit and credit and the normal balances of the various types of accounts are summarized as follows:

	Increase (Normal Balance)	Decrease
Balance sheet accounts:		
Asset	Debit	Credit
Liability	Credit	Debit
Owner's Equity:		
Capital	Credit	Debit
Drawing	Debit	Credit
Income statement accounts:		
Revenue	Credit	Debit
Expense	Debit	Credit

Q&A *A debit balance in which of the following accounts—Cash, Drawing, Wages Expense, Supplies, Fees Earned— would indicate that an error has occurred?*

Fees Earned

When an account that normally has a debit balance actually has a credit balance, or vice versa, an error may have occurred or an unusual situation may exist. For example, a credit balance in the office equipment account could result only from an error. On the other hand, a debit balance in an accounts payable account could result from an overpayment.

Illustration of Analyzing and Summarizing Transactions

OBJECTIVE 4

Analyze and summarize the financial statement effects of transactions.

How does a transaction occur in a business? First, a manager or other employee authorizes the transaction. The transaction then occurs. The businesses involved in the transaction usually prepare documents that describe the details of the transaction. These documents then become the basis for analyzing and recording the transaction. For example, Pat King might authorize the purchase of supplies for Com-

Point of INTEREST

Business documents that you are likely to see often include checks, sales slips, deposit tickets, utility bills, and credit card receipts.

puter King by telling an employee to buy computer paper at the local office supply store. The employee purchases the supplies for cash and receives a sales slip from the office supply store listing the details of the supplies bought. The employee then gives the sales slip to Pat King, who verifies and records the transaction.

As we discussed in the preceding section, a transaction is first recorded in a journal. Periodically, the journal entries are transferred to the accounts in the ledger. This process of transferring the debits and credits from the journal entries to the accounts is called **posting**. The flow of a transaction from its authorization to its posting in the accounts is shown in Exhibit 2.

Point of INTEREST

In computerized accounting systems, some transactions may be automatically authorized and recorded when certain events occur. For example, the salaries of managers may be paid automatically at the end of each pay period.

EXHIBIT 2
Flow of Business Transactions

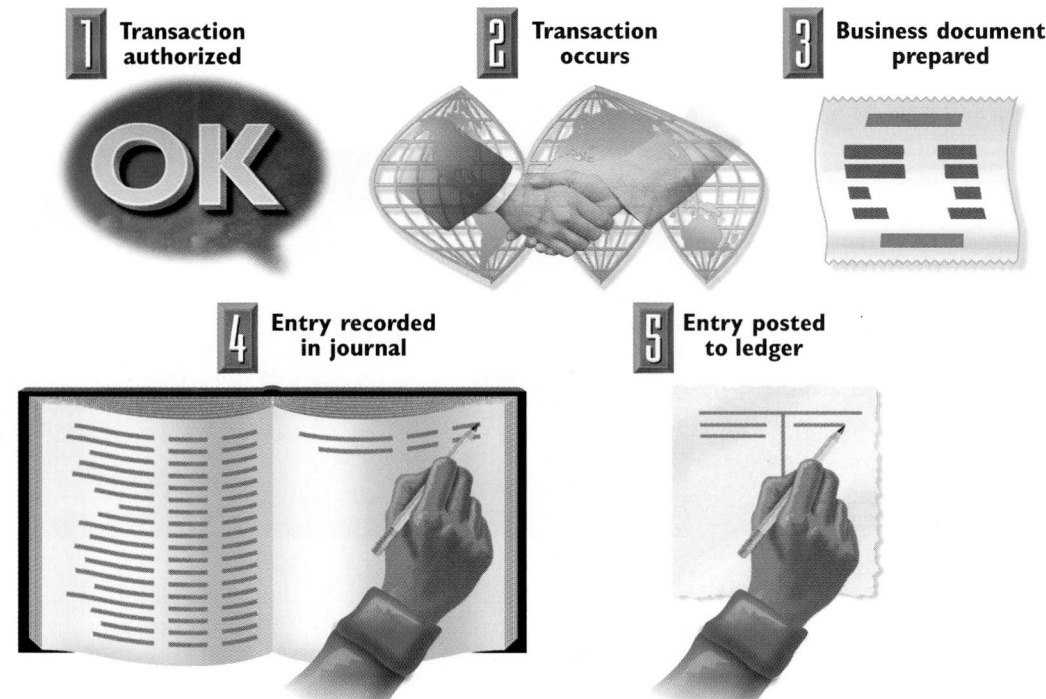

1. Transaction authorized
2. Transaction occurs
3. Business document prepared
4. Entry recorded in journal
5. Entry posted to ledger

The double-entry accounting system is a very powerful tool in analyzing the effects of transactions. Using this system to analyze transactions is summarized as follows:

1. Determine whether an asset, a liability, owner's equity, revenue, or expense account is affected by the transaction.
2. For each account affected by the transaction, determine whether the account increases or decreases.
3. Determine whether each increase or decrease should be recorded as a debit or a credit.

In practice, businesses use a variety of formats for recording journal entries. A business may use one all-purpose journal, sometimes called a **two-column journal**, or it may use several journals. In the latter case, each journal is used to record different types of transactions, such as cash receipts or cash payments. The journals may be part of either a manual accounting system or a computerized accounting system.[3]

To illustrate recording a transaction in an all-purpose journal and posting in a manual accounting system, we will use the December transactions of Computer King. The first transaction in December occurred on December 1.

Dec. 1. Computer King paid a premium of $2,400 for a comprehensive insurance policy covering liability, theft, and fire. The policy covers a two-year period.

Analysis: When you purchased insurance for your automobile, you may have been required to pay the insurance premium in advance. In this case, your transaction was similar to Computer King's. Advance payments of expenses such as insurance are prepaid expenses, which are assets. For Computer King, the asset acquired for the cash payment is insurance protection for 24 months. The asset Prepaid Insurance increases and is debited for $2,400. The asset Cash decreases and is credited for $2,400.

The recording and posting of this transaction is shown in Exhibit 3.

EXHIBIT 3
Diagram of the Recording and Posting of a Debit and a Credit

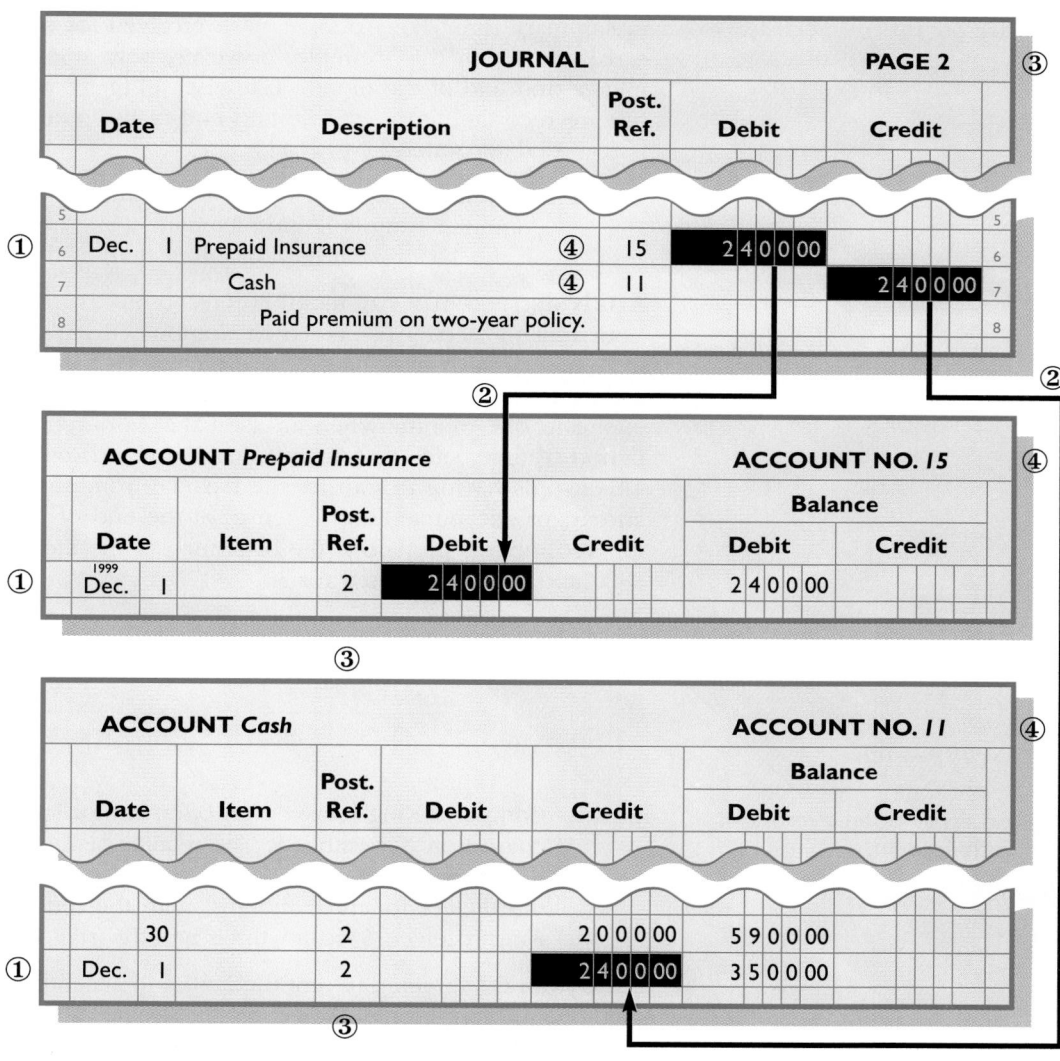

[3] The use of special journals and computerized accounting systems is discussed in later chapters, after the basics of accounting systems have been presented.

In the journal, you should note where the date of the transaction is recorded. Also note that the entry is explained as the payment of an insurance premium. Such explanations should be brief. For unusual and complex transactions, such as a long-term rental arrangement, the journal entry explanation may include a reference to the rental agreement or other business document.

You will note that the T account form is not used in this illustration. Although the T account clearly separates debit entries and credit entries, it is inefficient for summarizing a large quantity of transactions. In practice, the T account is usually replaced with the standard form shown in Exhibit 3.

The debits and credits for each journal entry are posted to the accounts in the order that they occur in the journal. In posting to the standard account, (1) the date is entered, and (2) the amount of the entry is entered. For future reference, (3) the journal page number is inserted in the Posting Reference column of the account, and (4) the account number is inserted in the Posting Reference column of the journal.

The remaining December transactions for Computer King are analyzed in the following paragraphs. These transactions are posted to the ledger in Exhibit 4, shown later. To simplify and reduce repetition, some of the December transactions are stated in summary form. For example, cash received for services is normally recorded on a daily basis. In this example, however, only summary totals are recorded at the middle and end of the month. Likewise, all fees earned on account during December are recorded at the middle and end of the month. In practice, each fee earned is recorded separately.

Dec. 1. Computer King paid rent for December, $800. The company from which Computer King is renting its store space now requires the payment of rent on the 1st of each month, rather than at the end of the month.

Analysis: You may pay monthly rent on an apartment on the first of each month. Your rent transaction is similar to Computer King's. The advance payment of rent is an asset, much like the advance payment of the insurance premium in the preceding transaction. However, unlike the insurance premium, this prepaid rent will expire in one month. When an asset that is purchased will be used up in a short period of time, such as a month, it is normal to debit an expense account initially. This avoids having to transfer the balance from an asset account (Prepaid Rent) to an expense account (Rent Expense) at the end of the month. Thus, when the rent for December is prepaid at the beginning of the month, Rent Expense is debited for $800 and Cash is credited for $800.

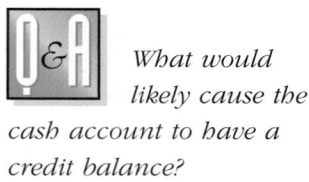

What would likely cause the cash account to have a credit balance?

An error or an overdrawn cash account.

10	1	Rent Expense	52	8 0 0 00		10
11		Cash	11		8 0 0 00	11
12		Paid rent for December.				12

Dec. 1. Computer King received an offer from a local retailer to rent the land purchased on November 5. The retailer plans to use the land as a parking lot for its employees and customers. Computer King agreed to rent the land to the retailer for three months, with the rent payable in advance. Computer King received $360 for three months' rent beginning December 1.

Analysis: By agreeing to rent the land and accepting the $360, Computer King has incurred an obligation (liability) to the retailer. This obligation is to make the land available for use for three months and not to interfere with its use. The liability created by receiving the cash in advance of providing the service is called **unearned revenue**. Thus, the $360 received is an increase in an asset and is debited to Cash. The liability account Unearned Rent increases and is credited for $360. As time passes, the unearned rent liability will decrease and will become revenue.

Magazines that receive subscriptions in advance must record the receipts as unearned revenues. Likewise, airlines that receive ticket payments in advance must record the receipts as unearned revenues until the passengers use the tickets.

14	1	Cash	11	3 6 0 00			14
15		Unearned Rent	23		3 6 0 00		15
16		Received advance payment for					16
17		three months' rent on land.					17

Dec. 4. Computer King purchased office equipment on account from Executive Supply Co. for $1,800.

Analysis: The asset account Office Equipment increases and is therefore debited for $1,800. The liability account Accounts Payable increases and is credited for $1,800.

19	4	Office Equipment	18	1 8 0 0 00			19
20		Accounts Payable	21		1 8 0 0 00		20
21		Purchased office equipment					21
22		on account.					22

Dec. 6. Computer King paid $180 for a newspaper advertisement.

Analysis: An expense increases and is debited for $180. The asset Cash decreases and is credited for $180. Expense items that are expected to be minor in amount are normally included as part of the miscellaneous expense. Thus, Miscellaneous Expense is debited for $180.

24	6	Miscellaneous Expense	59	1 8 0 00			24
25		Cash	11		1 8 0 00		25
26		Paid for newspaper ad.					26

Dec. 11. Computer King paid creditors $400.

Analysis: This payment decreases the liability account Accounts Payable, which is debited for $400. Cash also decreases and is credited for $400.

28	11	Accounts Payable	21	4 0 0 00			28
29		Cash	11		4 0 0 00		29
30		Paid creditors on account.					30

Dec. 13. Computer King paid a receptionist and a part-time assistant $950 for two weeks' wages.

Analysis: This transaction is similar to the December 6 transaction, where an expense account is increased and Cash is decreased. Thus, Wages Expense is debited for $950 and Cash is credited for $950.

		JOURNAL			**PAGE 3**
	Date	**Description**	**Post. Ref.**	**Debit**	**Credit**
1	1999 Dec. 13	Wages Expense	51	9 5 0 00		1
2		Cash	11		9 5 0 00	2
3		Paid two weeks' wages.				3

Dec. 16. Computer King received $3,100 from fees earned for the first half of December.

Analysis: Cash increases and is debited for $3,100. The revenue account Fees Earned increases and is credited for $3,100.

5	16	Cash	11	3 1 0 0 00		5
6		Fees Earned	41		3 1 0 0 00	6
7		Received fees from customers.				7

Dec. 16. Fees earned on account totaled $1,750 for the first half of December.

Analysis: Assume that you have agreed to take care of a neighbor's dog for a week for $100. At the end of the week, you agree to wait until the first of the next month to receive the $100. Like Computer King, you have provided services on account and thus have a right to receive the payment from your neighbor. When a business agrees that payment for services provided or goods sold can be accepted at a later date, the firm has an **account receivable**, which is a claim against the customer. The account receivable is an asset, and the revenue is earned even though no cash has been received. Thus, Accounts Receivable increases and is debited for $1,750. The revenue account Fees Earned increases and is credited for $1,750.

9	16	Accounts Receivable	12	1 7 5 0 00		9
10		Fees Earned	41		1 7 5 0 00	10
11		Fees earned on account.				11

Dec. 20. Computer King paid $900 to Executive Supply Co. on the $1,800 debt owed from the December 4 transaction.

Analysis: This is similar to the transaction of December 11.

13	20	Accounts Payable	21	9 0 0 00		13
14		Cash	11		9 0 0 00	14
15		Paid part of amount owed to				15
16		Executive Supply Co.				16

Dec. 21. Computer King received $650 from customers in payment of their accounts.

Analysis: When customers pay amounts owed for services they have previously received, one asset increases and another asset decreases. Thus, Cash is debited for $650, and Accounts Receivable is credited for $650.

18	21	Cash	11	6 5 0 00		18
19		Accounts Receivable	12		6 5 0 00	19
20		Received cash from customers				20
21		on account.				21

Dec. 23. Computer King paid $1,450 for supplies.

Analysis: The asset account Supplies increases and is debited for $1,450. The asset account Cash decreases and is credited for $1,450.

23		23	Supplies	14		1	4	5	0	00							23
24			Cash	11								1	4	5	0	00	24
25			Purchased supplies.														25

Dec. 27. Computer King paid the receptionist and the part-time assistant $1,200 for two weeks' wages.

Analysis: This is similar to the transaction of December 13.

27		27	Wages Expense	51		1	2	0	0	00							27
28			Cash	11								1	2	0	0	00	28
29			Paid two weeks' wages.														29

Dec. 31. Computer King paid its $310 telephone bill for the month.

Analysis: Each month you pay a telephone bill. Businesses, such as Computer King, also must pay monthly utility bills. Such transactions are similar to the transaction of December 6. The expense account Utilities Expense is debited for $310, and Cash is credited for $310.

31		31	Utilities Expense	54		3	1	0	00							31
32			Cash	11							3	1	0	00	32
33			Paid telephone bill.													33

Dec. 31. Computer King paid its $225 electric bill for the month.

Analysis: This is similar to the preceding transaction.

				JOURNAL			**PAGE 4**							
	Date		**Description**	**Post. Ref.**		**Debit**			**Credit**				
1	1999 Dec.	31	Utilities Expense	54		2 2 5 00							1
2			Cash	11					2 2 5 00				2
3			Paid electric bill.										3

Dec. 31. Computer King received $2,870 from fees earned for the second half of December.

Analysis: This is similar to the transaction of December 16.

5		31	Cash	11		2 8 7 0 00								5
6			Fees Earned	41					2 8 7 0 00					6
7			Received fees from customers.											7

Dec. 31. Fees earned on account totaled $1,120 for the second half of December.

Analysis: This is similar to the transaction of December 16.

	31	Accounts Receivable	12	1 1 2 0 00		
10		Fees Earned	41		1 1 2 0 00	10
11		Fees earned on account.				11

Dec. 31. Pat King withdrew $2,000 for personal use.

Analysis: This transaction resulted in an increase in the amount of withdrawals and is recorded by a $2,000 debit to Pat King, Drawing. The decrease in business cash is recorded by a $2,000 credit to Cash.

	31	Pat King, Drawing	32	2 0 0 0 00		13
14		Cash	11		2 0 0 0 00	14
15		Pat King withdrew cash for				15
16		personal use.				16

The journal for Computer King since it was organized on November 1 is shown in Exhibit 4. Exhibit 4 also shows the ledger after the transactions for both November and December have been posted.

EXHIBIT 4
Journal and Ledger—
Computer King

		JOURNAL			PAGE 1	
	Date	Description	Post. Ref.	Debit	Credit	
1	1999 Nov. 1	Cash	11	15 0 0 0 00		1
2		Pat King, Capital	31		15 0 0 0 00	2
3		Invested cash in Computer King.				3
4						4
5	5	Land	17	10 0 0 0 00		5
6		Cash	11		10 0 0 0 00	6
7		Purchased land for building site.				7
8						8
9	10	Supplies	14	1 3 5 0 00		9
10		Accounts Payable	21		1 3 5 0 00	10
11		Purchased supplies on account.				11
12						12
13	18	Cash	11	7 5 0 0 00		13
14		Fees Earned	41		7 5 0 0 00	14
15		Received fees from customers.				15
16						16
17	30	Wages Expense	51	2 1 2 5 00		17
18		Rent Expense	52	8 0 0 00		18
19		Utilities Expense	54	4 5 0 00		19
20		Miscellaneous Expense	59	2 7 5 00		20
21		Cash	11		3 6 5 0 00	21
22		Paid expenses.				22
23						23
24	30	Accounts Payable	21	9 5 0 00		24
25		Cash	11		9 5 0 00	25
26		Paid creditors on account.				26
27						27
28	30	Supplies Expense	55	8 0 0 00		28
29		Supplies	14		8 0 0 00	29
30		Supplies used during November.				30

EXHIBIT 4 (*continued*)

	Date		Description	Post. Ref.	Debit	Credit	
1	1999 Nov.	30	Pat King, Drawing	32	2 0 0 0 00		1
2			Cash	11		2 0 0 0 00	2
3			Pat King withdrew cash for				3
4			personal use.				4
5							5
6	Dec.	1	Prepaid Insurance	15	2 4 0 0 00		6
7			Cash	11		2 4 0 0 00	7
8			Paid premium on two-year policy.				8
9							9
10		1	Rent Expense	52	8 0 0 00		10
11			Cash	11		8 0 0 00	11
12			Paid rent for December.				12
13							13
14		1	Cash	11	3 6 0 00		14
15			Unearned Rent	23		3 6 0 00	15
16			Received advance payment for				16
17			three months' rent on land.				17
18							18
19		4	Office Equipment	18	1 8 0 0 00		19
20			Accounts Payable	21		1 8 0 0 00	20
21			Purchased office equipment				21
22			on account.				22
23							23
24		6	Miscellaneous Expense	59	1 8 0 00		24
25			Cash	11		1 8 0 00	25
26			Paid for newspaper ad.				26
27							27
28		11	Accounts Payable	21	4 0 0 00		28
29			Cash	11		4 0 0 00	29
30			Paid creditors on account.				30

JOURNAL **PAGE 2**

	Date		Description	Post. Ref.	Debit	Credit	
1	1999 Dec.	13	Wages Expense	51	9 5 0 00		1
2			Cash	11		9 5 0 00	2
3			Paid two weeks' wages.				3
4							4
5		16	Cash	11	3 1 0 0 00		5
6			Fees Earned	41		3 1 0 0 00	6
7			Received fees from customers.				7
8							8
9		16	Accounts Receivable	12	1 7 5 0 00		9
10			Fees Earned	41		1 7 5 0 00	10
11			Fees earned on account.				11

JOURNAL **PAGE 3**

EXHIBIT 4 (continued)

		JOURNAL				PAGE 3	
	Date	Description	Post. Ref.	Debit		Credit	
13	20	Accounts Payable	21	9 0 0 00			13
14		Cash	11			9 0 0 00	14
15		Paid part of amount owed to					15
16		Executive Supply Co.					16
17							17
18	21	Cash	11	6 5 0 00			18
19		Accounts Receivable	12			6 5 0 00	19
20		Received cash from customers					20
21		on account.					21
22							22
23	23	Supplies	14	1 4 5 0 00			23
24		Cash	11			1 4 5 0 00	24
25		Purchased supplies.					25
26							26
27	27	Wages Expense	51	1 2 0 0 00			27
28		Cash	11			1 2 0 0 00	28
29		Paid two weeks' wages.					29
30							30
31	31	Utilities Expense	54	3 1 0 00			31
32		Cash	11			3 1 0 00	32
33		Paid telephone bill.					33

		JOURNAL				PAGE 4	
	Date	Description	Post. Ref.	Debit		Credit	
1	1999 Dec. 31	Utilities Expense	54	2 2 5 00			1
2		Cash	11			2 2 5 00	2
3		Paid electric bill.					3
4							4
5	31	Cash	11	2 8 7 0 00			5
6		Fees Earned	41			2 8 7 0 00	6
7		Received fees from customers.					7
8							8
9	31	Accounts Receivable	12	1 1 2 0 00			9
10		Fees Earned	41			1 1 2 0 00	10
11		Fees earned on account.					11
12							12
13	31	Pat King, Drawing	32	2 0 0 0 00			13
14		Cash	11			2 0 0 0 00	14
15		Pat King withdrew cash for					15
16		personal use.					16
17							17
18							18
19							19

EXHIBIT 4 (*continued*)

LEDGER

ACCOUNT *Cash*   **ACCOUNT NO. 11**

Date		Item	Post. Ref.	Debit	Credit	Balance Debit	Balance Credit
1999 Nov.	1		1	15 000 00		15 000 00	
	5		1		10 000 00	5 000 00	
	18		1	7 500 00		12 500 00	
	30		1		3 650 00	8 850 00	
	30		1		950 00	7 900 00	
	30		2		2 000 00	5 900 00	
Dec.	1		2		2 400 00	3 500 00	
	1		2		800 00	2 700 00	
	1		2	360 00		3 060 00	
	6		2		180 00	2 880 00	
	11		2		400 00	2 480 00	
	13		3		950 00	1 530 00	
	16		3	3 100 00		4 630 00	
	20		3		900 00	3 730 00	
	21		3	650 00		4 380 00	
	23		3		1 450 00	2 930 00	
	27		3		1 200 00	1 730 00	
	31		3		310 00	1 420 00	
	31		4		225 00	1 195 00	
	31		4	2 870 00		4 065 00	
	31		4		2 000 00	2 065 00	

ACCOUNT *Accounts Receivable*   **ACCOUNT NO. 12**

Date		Item	Post. Ref.	Debit	Credit	Balance Debit	Balance Credit
1999 Dec.	16		3	1 750 00		1 750 00	
	21		3		650 00	1 100 00	
	31		4	1 120 00		2 220 00	

ACCOUNT *Supplies*   **ACCOUNT NO. 14**

Date		Item	Post. Ref.	Debit	Credit	Balance Debit	Balance Credit
1999 Nov.	10		1	1 350 00		1 350 00	
	30		1		800 00	550 00	
Dec.	23		3	1 450 00		2 000 00	

EXHIBIT 4 (*continued*)

ACCOUNT *Prepaid Insurance*					ACCOUNT NO. 15	
					Balance	
Date	Item	Post. Ref.	Debit	Credit	Debit	Credit
1999 Dec. 1		2	2 4 0 0 00		2 4 0 0 00	

ACCOUNT *Land*					ACCOUNT NO. 17	
					Balance	
Date	Item	Post. Ref.	Debit	Credit	Debit	Credit
1999 Nov. 5		1	10 0 0 0 00		10 0 0 0 00	

ACCOUNT *Office Equipment*					ACCOUNT NO. 18	
					Balance	
Date	Item	Post. Ref.	Debit	Credit	Debit	Credit
1999 Dec. 4		2	1 8 0 0 00		1 8 0 0 00	

ACCOUNT *Accounts Payable*					ACCOUNT NO. 21	
					Balance	
Date	Item	Post. Ref.	Debit	Credit	Debit	Credit
1999 Nov. 10		1		1 3 5 0 00		1 3 5 0 00
30		1	9 5 0 00			4 0 0 00
Dec. 4		2		1 8 0 0 00		2 2 0 0 00
11		2	4 0 0 00			1 8 0 0 00
20		3	9 0 0 00			9 0 0 00

ACCOUNT *Unearned Rent*					ACCOUNT NO. 23	
					Balance	
Date	Item	Post. Ref.	Debit	Credit	Debit	Credit
1999 Dec. 1		2		3 6 0 00		3 6 0 00

ACCOUNT *Pat King, Capital*					ACCOUNT NO. 31	
					Balance	
Date	Item	Post. Ref.	Debit	Credit	Debit	Credit
1999 Nov. 1		1		15 0 0 0 00		15 0 0 0 00

EXHIBIT 4 (*continued*)

ACCOUNT Pat King, Drawing — ACCOUNT NO. 32

Date		Item	Post. Ref.	Debit	Credit	Balance Debit	Balance Credit
1999 Nov.	30		2	2 0 0 0 00		2 0 0 0 00	
Dec.	31		4	2 0 0 0 00		4 0 0 0 00	

ACCOUNT Fees Earned — ACCOUNT NO. 41

Date		Item	Post. Ref.	Debit	Credit	Balance Debit	Balance Credit
1999 Nov.	18		1		7 5 0 0 00		7 5 0 0 00
Dec.	16		3		3 1 0 0 00		10 6 0 0 00
	16		3		1 7 5 0 00		12 3 5 0 00
	31		4		2 8 7 0 00		15 2 2 0 00
	31		4		1 1 2 0 00		16 3 4 0 00

ACCOUNT Wages Expense — ACCOUNT NO. 51

Date		Item	Post. Ref.	Debit	Credit	Balance Debit	Balance Credit
1999 Nov.	30		1	2 1 2 5 00		2 1 2 5 00	
Dec.	13		3	9 5 0 00		3 0 7 5 00	
	27		3	1 2 0 0 00		4 2 7 5 00	

ACCOUNT Rent Expense — ACCOUNT NO. 52

Date		Item	Post. Ref.	Debit	Credit	Balance Debit	Balance Credit
1999 Nov.	30		1	8 0 0 00		8 0 0 00	
Dec.	1		2	8 0 0 00		1 6 0 0 00	

ACCOUNT Utilities Expense — ACCOUNT NO. 54

Date		Item	Post. Ref.	Debit	Credit	Balance Debit	Balance Credit
1999 Nov.	30		1	4 5 0 00		4 5 0 00	
Dec.	31		3	3 1 0 00		7 6 0 00	
	31		4	2 2 5 00		9 8 5 00	

EXHIBIT 4 (concluded)

ACCOUNT Supplies Expense					ACCOUNT NO. 55	
		Post.			**Balance**	
Date	Item	Ref.	Debit	Credit	Debit	Credit
1999 Nov. 30		1	8 0 0 00		8 0 0 00	

ACCOUNT Miscellaneous Expense					ACCOUNT NO. 59	
		Post.			**Balance**	
Date	Item	Ref.	Debit	Credit	Debit	Credit
1999 Nov. 30		1	2 7 5 00		2 7 5 00	
Dec. 6		2	1 8 0 00		4 5 5 00	

Trial Balance

OBJECTIVE 5

Prepare a trial balance and explain how it can be used to discover errors.

How can you be sure that you have not made an error in posting the debits and credits to the ledger? One way is to determine the equality of the debits and credits in the ledger. This equality should be proved at the end of each accounting period, if not more often. Such a proof, called a **trial balance**, may be in the form of a computer printout or in the form shown in Exhibit 5.

Point of INTEREST

The proof of the equality of the debit and credit balances is called a trial balance because a "trial" is a process of proving or testing.

EXHIBIT 5
Trial Balance

Computer King Trial Balance December 31, 1999					
Cash	2 0 6 5 00		
Accounts Receivable	2 2 2 0 00		
Supplies	2 0 0 0 00		
Prepaid Insurance	2 4 0 0 00		
Land	10 0 0 0 00		
Office Equipment	1 8 0 0 00		
Accounts Payable		9 0 0 00
Unearned Rent		3 6 0 00
Pat King, Capital		15 0 0 0 00
Pat King, Drawing	4 0 0 0 00		
Fees Earned		16 3 4 0 00
Wages Expense	4 2 7 5 00		
Rent Expense	1 6 0 0 00		
Utilities Expense	9 8 5 00		
Supplies Expense	8 0 0 00		
Miscellaneous Expense	4 5 5 00		
	32 6 0 0 00	32 6 0 0 00

If you incorrectly record $1,000 received on account as a debit to Cash and a credit to Accounts Payable, will the trial balance totals be equal?

Yes.

The first step in preparing the trial balance is to determine the balance of each account in the ledger. When the standard account form is used, the balance of each account appears in the balance column on the same line as the last posting to the account.

The trial balance does not provide complete proof of the accuracy of the ledger. It indicates only that the debits and the credits are equal. This proof is of value, however, because errors often affect the equality of debits and credits. If the two totals of a trial balance are not equal, an error has occurred. In the remainder of this chapter, we will discuss procedures for discovering and correcting errors.

Discovery and Correction of Errors

OBJECTIVE 6

Discover errors in recording transactions and correct them.

Errors will sometimes occur in journalizing and posting transactions. In the following paragraphs, we describe and illustrate how errors may be discovered and corrected. In some cases, however, an error might not be significant enough to affect the decisions of management or others. In such cases, the **materiality concept** implies that the error may be treated in the easiest possible way. For example, an error of a few dollars in recording an asset as an expense for a business with millions of dollars in assets would be considered immaterial, and a correction would not be necessary. In the remaining paragraphs, we assume that errors discovered are material and should be corrected.

Many large corporations such as **Microsoft** and **Quaker Oats** round their financial statements to millions of dollars.

Discovery of Errors

As mentioned previously, the trial balance is one of the primary ways for discovering errors in the ledger. However, it indicates only that the debits and credits are equal. If the two totals of the trial balance are not equal, it is probably due to one or more of the errors described in Exhibit 6.

EXHIBIT 6
Errors Causing Unequal Trial Balance

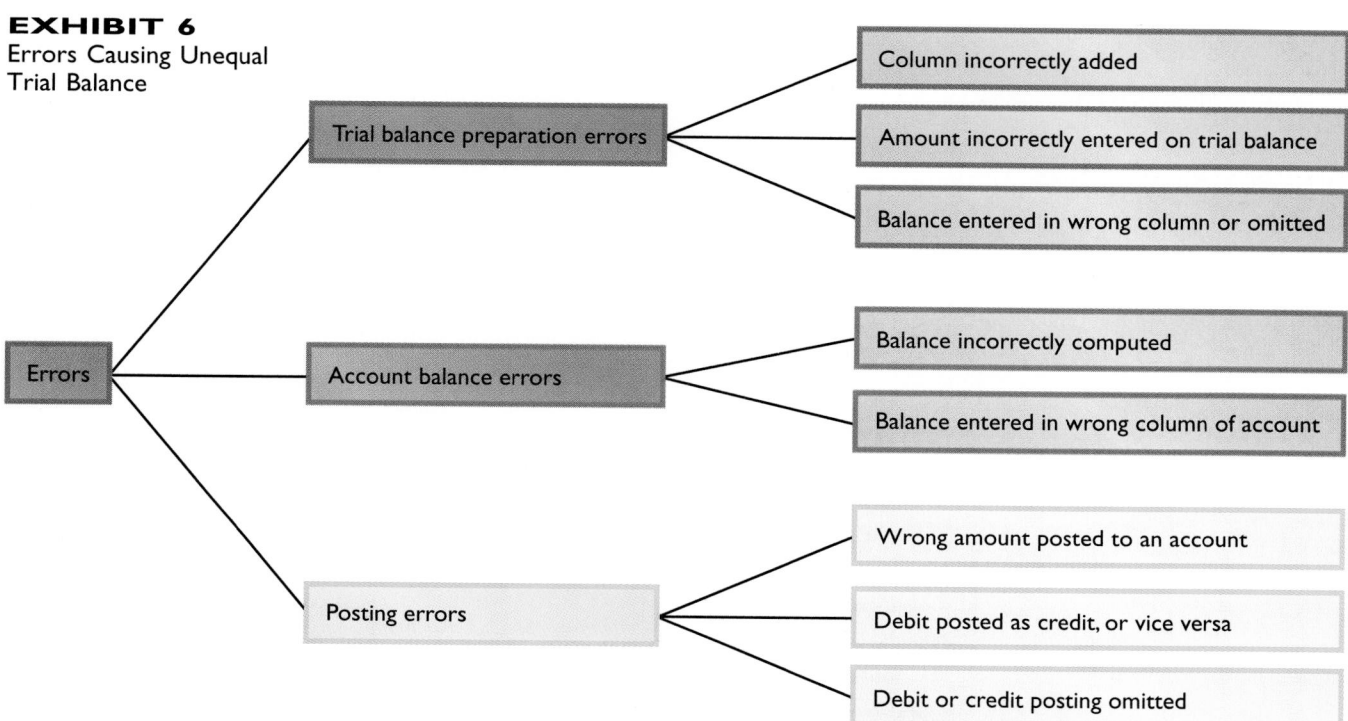

Among the types of errors that will not cause an inequality in the trial balance totals are the following:

1. Failure to record a transaction or to post a transaction.
2. Recording the same erroneous amount for both the debit and the credit parts of a transaction.
3. Recording the same transaction more than once.
4. Posting a part of a transaction correctly as a debit or credit but to the wrong account.

It is obvious that care should be used in recording transactions in the journal and in posting to the accounts. The need for accuracy in determining account balances and reporting them on the trial balance is also obvious.

Errors in the accounts may be discovered in various ways: (1) through audit procedures, (2) by chance, or (3) by looking at the trial balance. If the two trial balance totals are not equal, the amount of the difference between the totals should be determined before searching for the error.

The amount of the difference between the two totals of a trial balance sometimes gives a clue as to the nature of the error or where it occurred. For example, a difference of 10, 100, or 1,000 between two totals is often the result of an error in addition. A difference between totals can also be due to omitting a debit or a credit posting. If the difference can be evenly divided by 2, the error may be due to the posting of a debit as a credit, or vice versa. For example, if the debit total is $20,640 and the credit total is $20,236, the difference of $404 may indicate that a credit posting of $404 was omitted or that a credit of $202 was incorrectly posted as a debit.

Two other common types of errors are known as transpositions and slides. A **transposition** occurs when the order of the digits is changed mistakenly, such as writing $542 as $452 or $524. In a **slide**, the entire number is mistakenly moved one or more spaces to the right or the left, such as writing $542.00 as $54.20 or $5,420.00. If an error of either type has occurred and there are no other errors, the difference between the two trial balance totals can be evenly divided by 9.

If an error is not revealed by the trial balance, the steps in the accounting process must be retraced, beginning with the last step and working back to the entries in the journal. Usually, errors causing the trial balance totals to be unequal will be discovered before all of the steps are retraced.

What type of error occurs when $14,500 is recorded as $15,400?

- -

A transposition.

Correction of Errors

The procedures used to correct an error in journalizing or posting vary according to the nature of the error and when the error is discovered. These procedures are summarized in Exhibit 7.

Correcting the first two types of errors shown in Exhibit 7 involves simply drawing a line through the error and inserting the correct title or amount. The person making corrections should normally initial the correction in case questions later arise.

EXHIBIT 7
Procedures for Correcting Errors

	Error	Correction Procedure
1.	Journal entry is incorrect but not posted.	Draw a line through the error and insert correct title or amount.
2.	Journal entry is correct but posted incorrectly.	Draw a line through the error and post correctly.
3.	Journal entry is incorrect and posted.	Journalize and post a correcting entry.

Correcting the third type of error in Exhibit 7 is more complex. To illustrate, assume that on May 5 a $12,500 purchase of office equipment on account was incorrectly journalized and posted as a debit to Supplies and a credit to Accounts Payable for $12,500. This posting of the incorrect entry is shown in the following T accounts.

	Supplies			Accounts Payable	
Incorrect:	12,500				12,500

Before making a correcting entry, it is best to determine the debit(s) and credit(s) that should have been recorded. These are shown in the following T accounts.

	Office Equipment			Accounts Payable	
Correct:	12,500				12,500

Comparing the two sets of T accounts shows that the incorrect debit of $12,500 to Supplies may be corrected by debiting Office Equipment for $12,500 and crediting Supplies for $12,500. The following correcting entry is then journalized and posted:

Entry to Correct Error:

18	May	31	Office Equipment	18	12 5 0 0 00		18
19			Supplies	14		12 5 0 0 00	19
20			To correct erroneous debit				20
21			to Supplies on May 5. See invoice				21
22			from Bell Office Equipment Co.				22

FINANCIAL ANALYSIS AND INTERPRETATION

OBJECTIVE 7

Use horizontal analysis to compare financial statements from different periods.

A single item appearing in a financial statement is often useful in interpreting the financial results of a business. However, comparing this item in a current statement with the same item in prior statements often makes the financial information more useful. **Horizontal analysis** is the term used to describe such comparisons.

In horizontal analysis, the amount of each item on the current financial statements is compared with the same item on one or more earlier statements. The increase or decrease in the *amount* of the item is computed, together with the *percent* of increase or decrease. When two statements are being compared, the earlier statement is used as the base for computing the amount and the percent of change.

To illustrate, the horizontal analysis of two income statements for J. Holmes, Attorney-at-Law, is shown in Exhibit 8.

EXHIBIT 8
Horizontal Analysis of Income Statement

J. Holmes, Attorney-at-Law Income Statement For the Years Ended December 31, 2000 and 2001			Increase (Decrease)	
	2001	2000	Amount	Percent
Fees earned	$187,500	$150,000	$37,500	25.0%
Operating expenses:				
Wages expense	$ 60,000	$ 45,000	$15,000	33.3%
Rent expense	15,000	12,000	3,000	25.0%
Utilities expense	12,500	9,000	3,500	38.9%
Supplies expense	2,700	3,000	(300)	(10.0)%
Miscellaneous expense	2,300	1,800	500	27.8%
Total operating expenses	$ 92,500	$ 70,800	$21,700	30.6%
Net income	$ 95,000	$ 79,200	$15,800	19.9%

Exhibit 8 indicates both favorable and unfavorable trends affecting the income statement of J. Holmes, Attorney-at-Law. The increase in fees earned is a favorable trend, as is the decrease in supplies expense. Unfavorable trends include the increase in wages expense, utilities expense, and miscellaneous expense. These expenses increased faster than the increase in revenues, with total operating expenses increasing by 30.6%. Overall, net income increased by $15,800, or 19.9%, a favorable trend.

The significance of the various increases and decreases in the revenue and expense items in Exhibit 8 should be investigated to see if operations could be further improved. For example, the increase in utilities expense was the result of renting additional office space for use by a part-time law student in performing paralegal services. This explains the increase in rent expense of 25% and the increase in wages expense of 33.3%. Likewise, the increase in revenues reflects the fees generated by the new paralegal. Thus, it appears that hiring the paralegal was a good decision.

The preceding example illustrates how horizontal analysis can be useful in interpreting and analyzing financial statements. Horizontal analyses similar to that shown in Exhibit 8 can also be performed for the balance sheet, the statement of owner's equity, and the statement of cash flows.

ENCORE

The Hijacking Receivable

A company's chart of accounts should reflect the basic nature of its operations. Occasionally, however, transactions occur that give rise to unusual accounts. The following is a story of one such account.

During the early 1970s, before strict airport security was implemented across the United States, several airlines experienced hijacking incidents. One such incident occurred on November 10, 1972, when a Southern Airways DC-9 en route from Memphis to Miami was hijacked during a stopover in Birmingham, Alabama. The three hijackers boarded the plane in Birmingham armed with handguns and hand grenades. At gunpoint, the hijackers took the plane, the plane's crew of four, and 27 passengers to nine American cities, Toronto, and eventually to Havana, Cuba.

During the long flight, the hijackers threatened to crash the plane into the Oak Ridge, Tennessee nuclear facilities, demanded to talk with President Nixon, and demanded a ransom of $10 million. Southern Airways, however, was only able to come up with $2 million. Eventually, the pilot talked the hijackers into settling for the $2 million when the plane landed in Chattanooga for refueling.

Upon landing in Havana, the Cuban authorities arrested the hijackers and, after a brief delay, sent the plane, passengers, and crew back to the United States. The hijackers and $2 million stayed in Cuba.

How did Southern Airways account for and report the hijacking payment in its subsequent financial statements? As you might have analyzed, the initial entry credited Cash for $2 million. The debit was to an account entitled "Hijacking Payment."

This account was reported as a type of receivable under "other assets" on Southern's balance sheet. The company maintained that it would be able to collect the cash from the Cuban government and that, therefore, a receivable existed. In fact, in August 1975, Southern Airways was repaid $2 million by the Cuban government, which was, at that time, attempting to improve relations with the United States. ■

KEY POINTS

1 Explain why accounts are used to record and summarize the effects of transactions on financial statements.

The record used for recording individual transactions is an account. A group of accounts is called a ledger. The system of accounts that make up a ledger is called a chart of accounts. The accounts are numbered and listed in the order in which they appear in the balance sheet and the income statement.

2 Explain the characteristics of an account.

The simplest form of an account, a T account, has three parts: (1) a title, which is the name of the item recorded in the account; (2) a left side, called the debit side; (3) a right side, called the credit side. Amounts entered on the left side of an account, regardless of the account title, are called debits to the account. Amounts entered on the right side of an account are called credits. Periodically, the debits in an account are added, the credits in the account are added, and the balance of the account is determined.

3 List the rules of debit and credit and the normal balances of accounts.

General rules of debit and credit have been established for recording increases or decreases in asset, liability, owner's equity, revenue, expense, and drawing accounts. Each transaction is recorded so that the sum of the debits is always equal to the sum of the credits. Transactions are initially entered in a record called a journal.

The sum of the increases recorded in an account is usually equal to or greater than the sum of the decreases recorded in the account. For this reason, the normal balance of an account is indicated by the side of the account (debit or credit) that receives the increases.

The rules of debit and credit and normal account balances are summarized in the following table:

	Increase (Normal Balance)	Decrease
Balance sheet accounts:		
Asset	Debit	Credit
Liability	Credit	Debit
Owner's Equity:		
Capital	Credit	Debit
Drawing	Debit	Credit
Income statement accounts:		
Revenue	Credit	Debit
Expense	Debit	Credit

4 Analyze and summarize the financial statement effects of transactions.

Transactions are analyzed by determining whether: (1) an asset, liability, owner's equity, revenue, or expense account is affected, (2) each account affected increases or decreases, and (3) each increase or decrease is recorded as a debit or a credit. A journal is used for recording the transaction initially. The journal entries are periodically posted to the accounts.

5 Prepare a trial balance and explain how it can be used to discover errors.

A trial balance is prepared by listing the accounts from the ledger and their balances. If the two totals of the trial balance are not equal, an error has occurred.

6 Discover errors in recording transactions and correct them.

Errors may be discovered (1) by audit procedures, (2) by chance, or (3) by looking at the trial balance. The procedures for correcting errors are summarized in Exhibit 7.

7 Use horizontal analysis to compare financial statements from different periods.

In horizontal analysis, the amount of each item on the current financial statements is compared with the same item on one or more earlier statements. The increase or decrease in the *amount* of the item is computed, together with the *percent* of increase or decrease.

ILLUSTRATIVE PROBLEM

J. F. Outz, M.D., has been practicing as a cardiologist for three years. During April, Outz completed the following transactions in her practice of cardiology.

April 1. Paid office rent for April, $800.
   3. Purchased equipment on account, $2,100.
   5. Received cash on account from patients, $3,150.
   8. Purchased X-ray film and other supplies on account, $245.

April 9. One of the items of equipment purchased on April 3 was defective. It was returned with the permission of the supplier, who agreed to reduce the account for the amount charged for the item, $325.

12. Paid cash to creditors on account, $1,250.

17. Paid cash for renewal of a six-month property insurance policy, $370.

20. Discovered that the balance of the cash account and of the accounts payable account as of April 1 were overstated by $200. A payment of that amount to a creditor in March had not been recorded. Journalize the $200 payment as of April 20.

24. Paid cash for laboratory analysis, $545.

27. Paid cash from business bank account for personal and family expenses, $1,250.

30. Recorded the cash received in payment of services (on a cash basis) to patients during April, $1,720.

30. Paid salaries of receptionist and nurses, $1,725.

30. Paid various utility expenses, $360.

30. Recorded fees charged to patients on account for services performed in April, $5,145.

30. Paid miscellaneous expenses, $132.

Outz's account titles, numbers, and balances as of April 1 (all normal balances) are listed as follows: Cash, 11, $4,123; Accounts Receivable, 12, $6,725; Supplies, 13, $290; Prepaid Insurance, 14, $465; Equipment, 18, $19,745; Accounts Payable, 22, $765; J. F. Outz, Capital, 31, $30,583; J. F. Outz, Drawing, 32; Professional Fees, 41; Salary Expense, 51; Rent Expense, 53; Laboratory Expense, 55; Utilities Expense, 56; Miscellaneous Expense, 59.

Instructions

1. Open a ledger of standard four-column accounts for Dr. Outz as of April 1 of the current year. Enter the balances in the appropriate balance columns and place a check mark (✓) in the posting reference column. (It is advisable to verify the equality of the debit and credit balances in the ledger before proceeding with the next instruction.)

2. Journalize each transaction in a two-column journal.

3. Post the journal to the ledger, extending the month-end balances to the appropriate balance columns after each posting.

4. Prepare a trial balance as of April 30.

Solution

2. and **3.**

	Date		Description	Post. Ref.	Debit	Credit	
	JOURNAL					**PAGE 27**	
1	20— April	1	Rent Expense	53	8 0 0 00		1
2			Cash	11		8 0 0 00	2
3			Paid office rent for April.				3
4							4
5		3	Equipment	18	2 1 0 0 00		5
6			Accounts Payable	22		2 1 0 0 00	6
7			Purchased equipment on account.				7
8							8
9		5	Cash	11	3 1 5 0 00		9
10			Accounts Receivable	12		3 1 5 0 00	10
11			Received cash on account.				11
12							12
13		8	Supplies	13	2 4 5 00		13
14			Accounts Payable	22		2 4 5 00	14
15			Purchased supplies.				15

JOURNAL **PAGE 27**

	Date	Description	Post. Ref.	Debit	Credit	
17	9	Accounts Payable	22	3 2 5 00		17
18		Equipment	18		3 2 5 00	18
19		Returned defective equipment.				19
20						20
21	12	Accounts Payable	22	1 2 5 0 00		21
22		Cash	11		1 2 5 0 00	22
23		Paid creditors on account.				23
24						24
25	17	Prepaid Insurance	14	3 7 0 00		25
26		Cash	11		3 7 0 00	26
27		Renewed 6-month property policy.				27
28						28
29	20	Accounts Payable	22	2 0 0 00		29
30		Cash	11		2 0 0 00	30
31		Recorded March payment				31
32		to creditor.				32

JOURNAL **PAGE 28**

	Date		Description	Post. Ref.	Debit	Credit	
1	20—April	24	Laboratory Expense	55	5 4 5 00		1
2			Cash	11		5 4 5 00	2
3			Paid for laboratory analysis.				3
4							4
5		27	J. F. Outz, Drawing	32	1 2 5 0 00		5
6			Cash	11		1 2 5 0 00	6
7			J. F. Outz withdrew cash for				7
8			personal use.				8
9							9
10		30	Cash	11	1 7 2 0 00		10
11			Professional Fees	41		1 7 2 0 00	11
12			Received fees from patients.				12
13							13
14		30	Salary Expense	51	1 7 2 5 00		14
15			Cash	11		1 7 2 5 00	15
16			Paid salaries.				16
17							17
18		30	Utilities Expense	56	3 6 0 00		18
19			Cash	11		3 6 0 00	19
20			Paid utilities.				20
21							21
22		30	Accounts Receivable	12	5 1 4 5 00		22
23			Professional Fees	41		5 1 4 5 00	23
24			Fees earned on account.				24
25							25
26		30	Miscellaneous Expense	59	1 3 2 00		26
27			Cash	11		1 3 2 00	27
28			Paid expenses.				28

1. and **3.**

ACCOUNT *Cash*   **ACCOUNT NO. 11**

Date		Item	Post. Ref.	Debit	Credit	Balance Debit	Balance Credit
20— April	1	Balance	✓			4 1 2 3 00	
	1		27		8 0 0 00	3 3 2 3 00	
	5		27	3 1 5 0 00		6 4 7 3 00	
	12		27		1 2 5 0 00	5 2 2 3 00	
	17		27		3 7 0 00	4 8 5 3 00	
	20		27		2 0 0 00	4 6 5 3 00	
	24		28		5 4 5 00	4 1 0 8 00	
	27		28		1 2 5 0 00	2 8 5 8 00	
	30		28	1 7 2 0 00		4 5 7 8 00	
	30		28		1 7 2 5 00	2 8 5 3 00	
	30		28		3 6 0 00	2 4 9 3 00	
	30		28		1 3 2 00	2 3 6 1 00	

ACCOUNT *Accounts Receivable*   **ACCOUNT NO. 12**

Date		Item	Post. Ref.	Debit	Credit	Balance Debit	Balance Credit
20— April	1	Balance	✓			6 7 2 5 00	
	5		27		3 1 5 0 00	3 5 7 5 00	
	30		28	5 1 4 5 00		8 7 2 0 00	

ACCOUNT *Supplies*   **ACCOUNT NO. 13**

Date		Item	Post. Ref.	Debit	Credit	Balance Debit	Balance Credit
20— April	1	Balance	✓			2 9 0 00	
	8		27	2 4 5 00		5 3 5 00	

ACCOUNT *Prepaid Insurance*   **ACCOUNT NO. 14**

Date		Item	Post. Ref.	Debit	Credit	Balance Debit	Balance Credit
20— April	1	Balance	✓			4 6 5 00	
	17		27	3 7 0 00		8 3 5 00	

ACCOUNT *Equipment*   **ACCOUNT NO. 18**

Date		Item	Post. Ref.	Debit	Credit	Balance Debit	Balance Credit
20— April	1	Balance	✓			19 7 4 5 00	
	3		27	2 1 0 0 00		21 8 4 5 00	
	9		27		3 2 5 00	21 5 2 0 00	

ACCOUNT *Accounts Payable*   **ACCOUNT NO. 22**

Date		Item	Post. Ref.	Debit	Credit	Balance Debit	Balance Credit
20— April	1	Balance	✓				7 6 5 00
	3		27		2 1 0 0 00		2 8 6 5 00
	8		27		2 4 5 00		3 1 1 0 00
	9		27	3 2 5 00			2 7 8 5 00
	12		27	1 2 5 0 00			1 5 3 5 00
	20		27	2 0 0 00			1 3 3 5 00

ACCOUNT *J. F. Outz, Capital*   **ACCOUNT NO. 31**

Date		Item	Post. Ref.	Debit	Credit	Balance Debit	Balance Credit
20— April	1	Balance	✓				30 5 8 3 00

ACCOUNT *J. F. Outz, Drawing*   **ACCOUNT NO. 32**

Date		Item	Post. Ref.	Debit	Credit	Balance Debit	Balance Credit
20— April	27		28	1 2 5 0 00		1 2 5 0 00	

ACCOUNT *Professional Fees*   **ACCOUNT NO. 41**

Date		Item	Post. Ref.	Debit	Credit	Balance Debit	Balance Credit
20— April	30		28		1 7 2 0 00		1 7 2 0 00
	30		28		5 1 4 5 00		6 8 6 5 00

ACCOUNT *Salary Expense*   **ACCOUNT NO. 51**

Date		Item	Post. Ref.	Debit	Credit	Balance Debit	Balance Credit
20— April	30		28	1 7 2 5 00		1 7 2 5 00	

ACCOUNT *Rent Expense*   **ACCOUNT NO. 53**

Date		Item	Post. Ref.	Debit	Credit	Balance Debit	Balance Credit
20— April	1		27	8 0 0 00		8 0 0 00	

ACCOUNT *Laboratory Expense*   **ACCOUNT NO. 55**

Date	Item	Post. Ref.	Debit	Credit	Balance Debit	Balance Credit
20— April 24		28	5 4 5 00		5 4 5 00	

ACCOUNT *Utilities Expense*   **ACCOUNT NO. 56**

Date	Item	Post. Ref.	Debit	Credit	Balance Debit	Balance Credit
20— April 30		28	3 6 0 00		3 6 0 00	

ACCOUNT *Miscellaneous Expense*   **ACCOUNT NO. 59**

Date	Item	Post. Ref.	Debit	Credit	Balance Debit	Balance Credit
20— April 30		28	1 3 2 00		1 3 2 00	

4.

J. F. Outz, M.D.
Trial Balance
April 30, 20—

	Debit	Credit
Cash	2 3 6 1 00	
Accounts Receivable	8 7 2 0 00	
Supplies	5 3 5 00	
Prepaid Insurance	8 3 5 00	
Equipment	21 5 2 0 00	
Accounts Payable		1 3 3 5 00
J. F. Outz, Capital		30 5 8 3 00
J. F. Outz, Drawing	1 2 5 0 00	
Professional Fees		6 8 6 5 00
Salary Expense	1 7 2 5 00	
Rent Expense	8 0 0 00	
Laboratory Expense	5 4 5 00	
Utilities Expense	3 6 0 00	
Miscellaneous Expense	1 3 2 00	
	38 7 8 3 00	38 7 8 3 00

Matching

Match each of the following statements with its proper term. Some terms may not be used.

A. account

B. assets

C. balance of the account

D. chart of accounts

E. credits

F. debits

G. double-entry accounting

H. drawing

I. expenses

J. horizontal analysis

K. journal

L. journal entry

M. journalizing

N. ledger

O. liabilities

P. materiality concept

Q. objectivity concept

R. owner's equity

S. posting

T. revenues

U. slide

V. T account

W. transposition

X. trial balance

Y. two-column journal

Z. unearned revenue

AA. vertical analysis

___ 1. An accounting form that is used to record the increases and decreases in each financial statement item.

___ 2. A group of accounts for a business.

___ 3. A list of the accounts in the ledger.

___ 4. Resources that are owned by the business.

___ 5. Debts owed to outsiders (creditors).

___ 6. The owner's right to the assets of the business.

___ 7. Increases in owner's equity as a result of selling services or products to customers.

___ 8. Assets used up or services consumed in the process of generating revenues.

___ 9. The simplest form of an account.

___ 10. Amounts entered on the left side of an account.

___ 11. Amounts entered on the right side of an account.

___ 12. The amount of the difference between the debits and the credits that have been entered into an account.

___ 13. The initial record in which the effects of a transaction are recorded.

___ 14. The process of recording a transaction in the journal.

___ 15. The form of recording a transaction in a journal.

___ 16. A system of accounting for recording transactions, based on recording increases and decreases in accounts so that debits equal credits.

___ 17. The account used to record amounts withdrawn by an owner of a proprietorship.

___ 18. The process of transferring the debits and credits from the journal entries to the accounts.

___ 19. An all-purpose journal.

___ 20. The liability created by receiving revenue in advance.

___ 21. A summary listing of the titles and balances of accounts in the ledger.

___ 22. A concept of accounting that implies that an error may be treated in the easiest possible way.

___ 23. An error in which the order of the digits is changed, such as writing $542 as $452 or $524.

___ 24. An error in which the entire number is moved one or more spaces to the right or the left, such as writing $542.00 as $54.20 or $5,420.00.

___ 25. Financial analysis that compares an item in a current statement with the same item in prior statements.

Multiple Choice

1. A debit may signify:
   A. an increase in an asset account
   B. a decrease in an asset account
   C. an increase in a liability account
   D. an increase in the owner's capital account

2. The type of account with a normal credit balance is:
   A. an asset   C. a revenue
   B. drawing   D. an expense

3. A debit balance in which of the following accounts would indicate a likely error?
   A. Accounts Receivable
   B. Cash
   C. Fees Earned
   D. Miscellaneous Expense

4. The receipt of cash from customers in payment of their accounts would be recorded by a:
   A. debit to Cash; credit to Accounts Receivable
   B. debit to Accounts Receivable; credit to Cash
   C. debit to Cash; credit to Accounts Payable
   D. debit to Accounts Payable; credit to Cash

5. The form listing the titles and balances of the accounts in the ledger on a given date is the:
   A. income statement
   B. balance sheet
   C. statement of owner's equity
   D. trial balance

CLASS DISCUSSION QUESTIONS

1. What is the difference between an account and a ledger?
2. Describe in general terms the sequence of accounts in the ledger.
3. Do the terms *debit* and *credit* signify increase or decrease, or may they signify either? Explain.
4. Explain why the rules of debit and credit are the same for liability accounts and owner's equity accounts.
5. What is the effect (increase or decrease) of debits to expense accounts (a) in terms of owner's equity and (b) in terms of expense?
6. What is the effect (increase or decrease) of credits to revenue accounts (a) in terms of owner's equity and (b) in terms of revenue?
7. Activewear Company adheres to a policy of depositing all cash receipts in a bank account and making all payments by check. The cash account as of October 31 has a credit balance of $1,200, and there is no undeposited cash on hand. (a) Assuming that there were no errors in journalizing or posting, what caused this unusual balance? (b) Is the $1,200 credit balance in the cash account an asset, a liability, owner's equity, a revenue, or an expense?
8. Rearrange the following in proper sequence: (a) entry is posted to ledger, (b) business transaction occurs, (c) entry is recorded in journal, (d) business document is prepared, (e) business transaction is authorized.
9. Describe the three procedures required to post the credit portion of the following journal entry (Fees Earned is account no. 41):

	JOURNAL			PAGE 32
Date	Description	Post. Ref.	Debit	Credit
20— June 11	Accounts Receivable	12	875 00	
	Fees Earned			875 00

10. In the journal, what indicates that an entry has been posted to the accounts?
11. Lofton Company performed services in June for a specific customer, and the fee was $11,500. Payment was received the following July. (a) Was the revenue earned in June or July? (b) What accounts should be debited and credited in (1) June and (2) July?
12. What proof is provided by a trial balance?
13. If the two totals of a trial balance are equal, does it mean that there are no errors in the accounting records? Explain.
14. Assume that a trial balance is prepared with an account balance of $18,500 listed as $15,800 and an account balance of $8,000 listed as $800. Identify the transposition and the slide.
15. When a purchase of supplies of $580 for cash was recorded, both the debit and the credit were journalized and posted as $850. (a) Would this error cause the trial balance to be out of balance? (b) Would the answer be the same if the $580 entry had been journalized correctly, but the credit to Cash had been posted as $850?

16. How is a correction made when an error in an account title or amount in the journal is discovered before the entry is posted?
17. In journalizing and posting the entry to record the purchase of supplies on account, the accounts receivable account was credited in error. What is the preferred procedure to correct the error?
18. Banks rely heavily upon customers' deposits as a source of funds. Demand deposits normally pay interest to the customer, who is entitled to withdraw at any time without prior notice to the bank. Checking and NOW (negotiable order of withdrawal) accounts are the most common form of demand deposits for banks. Assume that The Package Company has a checking account at National Savings Bank. What type of account (asset, liability, owner's equity, revenue, expense, drawing) does the account balance of $21,500 represent from the viewpoint of (a) The Package Company and (b) National Savings Bank?

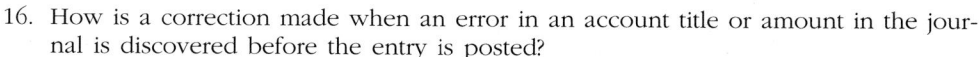

Resources for Your Success On-Line at **warren.swcollege.com**
Remember! If you need additional help, visit South-Western's Web site. See page 26 for a description of the online and printed materials that are available.

EXERCISES

Exercise 2–1
Chart of accounts
Objective 1

Adcock Interiors is owned and operated by Harold Adcock, an interior decorator. In the ledger of Adcock Interiors, the first digit of the account number indicates its major account classification (1—assets, 2—liabilities, 3—owner's equity, 4—revenues, 5—expenses). The second digit of the account number indicates the specific account within each of the preceding major account classifications.

Match each account number with its most likely account in the list below. The account numbers are 11, 12, 13, 21, 31, 32, 41, 51, 52, and 53.

Accounts:

Accounts Payable	Harold Adcock, Drawing
Accounts Receivable	Land
Cash	Miscellaneous Expense
Fees Earned	Supplies Expense
Harold Adcock, Capital	Wages Expense

Exercise 2–2
Chart of accounts
Objective 1

The Charm School is a newly organized business that teaches young people how to behave in a socially acceptable way. The list of accounts to be opened in the general ledger is as follows:

Accounts Payable	Heather Mock, Capital	Supplies
Accounts Receivable	Heather Mock, Drawing	Supplies Expense
Cash	Miscellaneous Expense	Unearned Rent
Equipment	Prepaid Insurance	Wages Expense
Fees Earned	Rent Expense	

List the accounts in the order in which they should appear in the ledger of The Charm School and assign account numbers. Each account number is to have two digits: the first digit is to indicate the major classification (*1* for assets, etc.), and the second digit is to identify the specific account within each major classification (1*1* for Cash, etc.).

Exercise 2–3
Identifying transactions
Objectives 2, 3

Sunrise Co. is a travel agency. The nine transactions recorded by Sunrise during June, its first month of operations, are indicated in the following T accounts:

Cash			Equipment		Cheng Sun, Drawing	
(1) 50,000	(2) 2,500		(3) 30,000		(8) 2,500	
(7) 9,500	(3) 10,000					
	(4) 6,050					
	(6) 6,000					
	(8) 2,500					

Accounts Receivable		Accounts Payable		Service Revenue	
(5) 12,500	(7) 9,500	(6) 6,000	(3) 20,000		(5) 12,500

Supplies		Cheng Sun, Capital		Operating Expenses	
(2) 2,500	(9) 1,450		(1) 50,000	(4) 6,050	
				(9) 1,450	

Indicate for each debit and each credit: (a) whether an asset, liability, owner's equity, drawing, revenue, or expense account was affected and (b) whether the account was increased (+) or decreased (−). Present your answers in the following form [transaction (1) is given as an example]:

	Account Debited		Account Credited	
Transaction	Type	Effect	Type	Effect
(1)	asset	+	owner's equity	+

Exercise 2–4
Journal entries
Objectives 3, 4

Based upon the T accounts in Exercise 2–3, prepare the nine journal entries from which the postings were made. Journal entry explanations may be omitted.

Exercise 2–5
Trial balance
Objective 5

✓ Total Debit Column: $76,500

Based upon the data presented in Exercise 2–3, prepare a trial balance, listing the accounts in their proper order.

Exercise 2–6
Normal entries for accounts
Objective 3

During the month, Dexter Labs Co. has a substantial number of transactions affecting each of the following accounts. State for each account whether it is likely to have (a) debit entries only, (b) credit entries only, or (c) both debit and credit entries.

1. Accounts Payable
2. Accounts Receivable
3. Cash
4. Fees Earned

5. Justin Sykes, Drawing
6. Miscellaneous Expense
7. Supplies Expense

Exercise 2–7
Normal balances of accounts
Objective 3

Identify each of the following accounts of Elrod Services Co. as asset, liability, owner's equity, revenue, or expense, and state in each case whether the normal balance is a debit or a credit.

a. Accounts Payable
b. Accounts Receivable
c. Cash
d. Chester Elrod, Capital
e. Chester Elrod, Drawing

f. Equipment
g. Fees Earned
h. Rent Expense
i. Salary Expense
j. Supplies

Exercise 2–8
Rules of debit and credit

Objective 3

The following table summarizes the rules of debit and credit. For each of the items (a) through (l), indicate whether the proper answer is a debit or a credit.

	Increase	Decrease	Normal Balance
Balance sheet accounts:			
Asset	(a)	Credit	Debit
Liability	(b)	(c)	(d)
Owner's Equity:			
Capital	(e)	(f)	Credit
Drawing	(g)	(h)	Debit
Income statement accounts:			
Revenue	Credit	(i)	(j)
Expense	(k)	Credit	(l)

Exercise 2–9
Capital account balance

Objective 2

✓ Negative $7,000

As of January 1, Wanda Deaton, Capital had a credit balance of $8,000. During the year, withdrawals totaled $10,000 and the business incurred a net loss of $5,000.

a. Calculate the balance of Wanda Deaton, Capital as of the end of the year.
b. ➤ Assuming that there have been no recording errors, will the balance sheet prepared at December 31 balance? Explain.

Exercise 2–10
Cash account balance

Objective 2

✓ b. $100,000

During the month, a business received $712,800 in cash and paid out $630,000 in cash.

a. ➤ Do the data indicate that the business earned $82,800 during the month? Explain.
b. If the balance of the cash account was $17,200 at the beginning of the month, what was the cash balance at the end of the month?

Exercise 2–11
Account balances

Objective 2

✓ c. $13,800

a. On April 1, the cash account balance was $11,250. During April, cash receipts totaled $31,800 and the April 30 balance was $12,500. Determine the cash payments made during April.
b. On June 1, the accounts receivable account balance was $23,900. During June, $21,000 was collected from customers on account. If the June 30 balance was $27,500, determine the fees billed to customers on account during June.
c. During August, $40,500 was paid to creditors on account and purchases on account were $77,700. If the August 31 balance of Accounts Payable was $51,000, determine the account balance on August 1.

Exercise 2–12
Transactions

Objectives 3, 4

The Wildlife Co. has the following accounts in its ledger: Cash; Accounts Receivable; Supplies; Office Equipment; Accounts Payable; Erin Fox, Capital; Erin Fox, Drawing; Fees Earned; Rent Expense; Advertising Expense; Utilities Expense; Miscellaneous Expense.

Journalize the following selected transactions in a two-column journal. Journal entry explanations may be omitted.

July 1. Paid rent for the month, $3,000.
   2. Paid advertising expense, $500.
   4. Paid cash for supplies, $770.
   6. Purchased office equipment on account, $8,500.
   8. Received cash from customers on account, $3,600.
   12. Paid creditor on account, $2,150.
   20. Withdrew cash for personal use, $1,500.
   25. Paid cash for repairs to office equipment, $120.
   30. Paid telephone bill for the month, $195.
   31. Fees earned and billed to customers for the month, $11,150.
   31. Paid electricity bill for the month, $430.

Exercise 2–13
Journalizing and posting
Objectives 3, 4

On April 8, 2000, Parshall Co. purchased $2,720 of supplies on account. In Parshall Co.'s chart of accounts, the supplies account is No. 15 and the accounts payable account is No. 21.

a. Journalize the April 8, 2000 transaction on page 12 of Parshall Co.'s two-column journal. Include an explanation of the entry.

b. Prepare a four-column account for Supplies. Enter a debit balance of $1,200 as of April 1, 2000. Place a check mark (✓) in the posting reference column.

c. Prepare a four-column account for Accounts Payable. Enter a credit balance of $11,734 as of April 1, 2000. Place a check mark (✓) in the posting reference column.

d. Post the April 8, 2000 transaction to the accounts.

Exercise 2–14
Transactions and T accounts
Objectives 2, 3, 4

The following selected transactions were completed during February of the current year:

1. Billed customers for fees earned, $5,210.
2. Purchased supplies on account, $520.
3. Received cash from customers on account, $3,200.
4. Paid creditors on account, $400.

a. Journalize the foregoing transactions in a two-column journal, using the appropriate number to identify the transactions. Journal entry explanations may be omitted.

b. Post the entries prepared in (a) to the following T accounts: Cash, Supplies, Accounts Receivable, Accounts Payable, Fees Earned. To the left of each amount posted in the accounts, place the appropriate number to identify the transactions.

Exercise 2–15
Trial balance
Objective 5

✓ Total Debit Column: $485,000

The accounts in the ledger of Asbury Park Co. as of August 31 of the current year are listed in alphabetical order as follows. All accounts have normal balances. The balance of the cash account has been intentionally omitted.

Accounts Payable	$ 18,710
Accounts Receivable	20,500
Cash	?
Dillon Garcia, Capital	110,290
Dillon Garcia, Drawing	20,000
Fees Earned	315,000
Insurance Expense	5,000
Land	125,000
Miscellaneous Expense	9,900
Notes Payable	35,000
Prepaid Insurance	3,150
Rent Expense	58,000
Supplies	4,100
Supplies Expense	5,900
Unearned Rent	6,000
Utilities Expense	41,500
Wages Expense	175,000

Prepare a trial balance, listing the accounts in their proper order and inserting the missing figure for cash.

Exercise 2–16
Effect of errors on trial balance
Objective 5

Indicate which of the following errors, each considered individually, would cause the trial balance totals to be unequal:

a. Payment of a cash withdrawal of $2,000 was journalized and posted as a debit of $200 to Salary Expense and a credit of $200 to Cash.

b. A payment of $5,000 for equipment purchased was posted as a debit of $5,000 to Equipment and a credit of $50,000 to Cash.

c. A fee of $3,100 earned and due from a client was not debited to Accounts Receivable or credited to a revenue account, because the cash had not been received.

d. A receipt of $500 from an account receivable was journalized and posted as a debit of $500 to Cash and a credit of $500 to Fees Earned.

e. A payment of $850 to a creditor was posted as a debit of $850 to Accounts Payable and a debit of $850 to Cash.

Exercise 2–17
Errors in trial balance

Objective 5

✓ Total of Credit Column: $143,280

The following preliminary trial balance of The Montana Co., a sports ticket agency, does not balance:

The Montana Co.
Trial Balance
December 31, 20—

Cash	83,000	
Accounts Receivable	23,600	
Prepaid Insurance		3,300
Equipment	4,500	
Accounts Payable		9,450
Unearned Rent		1,480
Ted Turner, Capital	68,550	
Ted Turner, Drawing	10,000	
Service Revenue		64,940
Wages Expense		33,400
Advertising Expense	5,200	
Miscellaneous Expense		1,380
	194,850	113,950

When the ledger and other records are reviewed, you discover the following: (1) the debits and credits in the cash account total $83,000 and $65,300, respectively; (2) a billing of $3,700 to a customer on account was not posted to the accounts receivable account; (3) a payment of $1,500 made to a creditor on account was not posted to the accounts payable account; (4) the balance of the unearned rent account is $1,840; (5) the correct balance of the equipment account is $45,000; and (6) each account has a normal balance.

Prepare a corrected trial balance.

Exercise 2–18
Effect of errors on trial balance

Objective 5

The following errors occurred in posting from a two-column journal:

1. A credit of $500 to Accounts Payable was posted as a debit.
2. An entry debiting Accounts Receivable and crediting Fees Earned for $4,500 was not posted.
3. A credit of $250 to Cash was posted as $520.
4. A debit of $750 to Cash was posted to Wages Expense.
5. A debit of $1,200 to Supplies was posted twice.
6. A debit of $1,575 to Wages Expense was posted as $1,755.
7. A credit of $1,830 to Accounts Receivable was not posted.

Considering each case individually (i.e., assuming that no other errors had occurred), indicate: (a) by "yes" or "no" whether the trial balance would be out of balance; (b) if answer to (a) is "yes," the amount by which the trial balance totals would differ; and (c) whether the debit or credit column of the trial balance would have the larger total. Answers should be presented in the following form [error (1) is given as an example]:

Error	(a) Out of Balance	(b) Difference	(c) Larger Total
1.	yes	$1,000	debit

Exercise 2–19
Errors in trial balance

Objective 5

What's Wrong WITH THIS?

✓ Total of Credit Column:
$105,100

How many errors can you find in the following trial balance? All accounts have normal balances.

The Peasley Co.
Trial Balance
For the Month Ending March 31, 20—

Cash	3,010	
Accounts Receivable	16,400	
Prepaid Insurance		2,400
Equipment	41,200	
Accounts Payable	1,850	
Salaries Payable		750
Nikki Swoopes, Capital		34,600
Nikki Swoopes, Drawing		5,000
Service Revenue		67,900
Salary Expense		28,400
Advertising Expense	7,200	
Miscellaneous Expense	1,490	
	139,050	139,050

Exercise 2–20
Entries to correct errors

Objective 6

Errors in journalizing and posting transactions are described as follows:

a.   A withdrawal of $15,000 by T. Woods, owner of the business, was recorded as a debit to Salary Expense and a credit to Cash.

b.   Rent of $1,800 paid for the current month was recorded as a debit to Accounts Payable and a credit to cash.

Journalize the entries to correct the errors. Omit explanations.

Exercise 2–21
Entries to correct errors

Objective 6

Errors in journalizing and posting transactions are described as follows:

a.   A $1,050 purchase of supplies on account was recorded as a debit to Cash and a credit to Accounts Payable.

b.   Cash of $1,350 received on account was recorded as a debit to Accounts Payable and a credit to Cash.

Journalize the entries to correct the errors. Omit explanations.

Exercise 2–22
Horizontal analysis of income statement

Objective 7

The financial statements for **Hershey Foods Corporation** are presented in Appendix G at the end of the text.

a.   For Hershey Foods Corporation, comparing 1996 with 1995, determine the amount of change and the percent of change for
  1.   net sales (revenues) and
  2.   selling, marketing, and administrative expenses.

b.   ━━━► What conclusions can you draw from your analysis of the net sales and the selling, marketing, and administrative expenses?

PROBLEMS SERIES A

Problem 2–1A
Entries into T accounts and trial balance

Objectives 2, 3, 4, 5

HAT

✓ 3. Total of Debit Column: $50,100

Robin Reich, an architect, opened an office on April 1 of the current year. During the month, he completed the following transactions connected with his professional practice:

a. Transferred cash from a personal bank account to an account to be used for the business, $30,000.
b. Purchased used automobile for $18,300, paying $6,000 cash and giving a non-interest-bearing note for the remainder.
c. Paid April rent for office and workroom, $2,200.
d. Paid cash for supplies, $300.
e. Purchased office and drafting room equipment on account, $4,200.
f. Paid cash for insurance policies on automobile and equipment, $810.
g. Received cash from a client for plans delivered, $2,725.
h. Paid cash to creditors on account, $2,100.
i. Paid cash for miscellaneous expenses, $120.
j. Received invoice for blueprint service, due in following month, $275.
k. Recorded fee earned on plans delivered, payment to be received in May, $3,500.
l. Paid salary of assistant, $1,500.
m. Paid cash for miscellaneous expenses, $60.
n. Paid installment due on note payable, $800.
o. Paid gas, oil, and repairs on automobile for April, $170.

Instructions

1. Record the foregoing transactions directly in the following T accounts, without journalizing: Cash; Accounts Receivable; Supplies; Prepaid Insurance; Automobiles; Equipment; Notes Payable; Accounts Payable; Robin Reich, Capital; Professional Fees; Rent Expense; Salary Expense; Automobile Expense; Blueprint Expense; Miscellaneous Expense. To the left of each amount entered in the accounts, place the appropriate letter to identify the transaction.
2. Determine the balances of the T accounts having two or more debits or credits. A memorandum balance should be inserted in accounts having both debits and credits, in the manner illustrated in the chapter. For accounts with entries on one side only (such as Professional Fees), there is no need to insert the memorandum balance in the item column. For accounts containing only a single debit and a single credit (such as Notes Payable), the memorandum balance should be inserted in the appropriate item column. Accounts containing a single entry only (such as Prepaid Insurance) do not need a memorandum balance.
3. Prepare a trial balance for Robin Reich, Architect, as of April 30 of the current year.

Problem 2–2A
Journal entries and trial balance

Objectives 2, 3, 4, 5

HAT
GENERAL LEDGER

✓ 4. a. $32,600
✓   b. $12,700

On October 1 of the current year, Clay Bryant established Northside Realty, which completed the following transactions during the month:

a. Clay Bryant transferred cash from a personal bank account to an account to be used for the business, $25,000.
b. Purchased supplies on account, $2,900.
c. Earned sales commissions, receiving cash, $32,600.
d. Paid rent on office and equipment for the month, $4,500.
e. Paid creditor on account, $1,000.
f. Withdrew cash for personal use, $2,000.
g. Paid automobile expenses (including rental charge) for month, $1,900, and miscellaneous expenses, $1,050.
h. Paid office salaries, $4,000.
i. Determined that the cost of supplies used was $1,250.

Instructions

1. Journalize entries for transactions (a) through (i), using the following account titles: Cash; Supplies; Accounts Payable; Clay Bryant, Capital; Clay Bryant, Drawing; Sales Commissions; Rent Expense; Office Salaries Expense; Automobile Expense; Supplies Expense; Miscellaneous Expense. Journal entry explanations may be omitted.

2. Prepare T accounts, using the account titles in (1). Post the journal entries to these accounts, placing the appropriate letter to the left of each amount to identify the transactions. Determine the account balances, after all posting is complete, for all accounts having two or more debits or credits. A memorandum balance should be inserted in accounts having both debits and credits, in the manner illustrated in the chapter. For accounts with entries on one side only, there is no need to insert a memorandum balance in the item column. For accounts containing only a single debit and a single credit, the memorandum balance should be inserted in the appropriate item column.

3. Prepare a trial balance as of October 31, 20—.

4. Determine the following:
   a. Amount of total revenue recorded in the ledger.
   b. Amount of total expenses recorded in the ledger.
   c. Amount of net income for October.

Problem 2–3A
Journal entries and trial balance

Objectives 2, 3, 4, 5

HAT
GENERAL LEDGER

✓ 3. Total of Credit Column: $36,425

On July 10 of the current year, Jong Woo established an interior decorating business, Asian Designs. During the remainder of the month, Jong Woo completed the following transactions related to the business:

July 10. Jong transferred cash from a personal bank account to an account to be used for the business, $20,000.

10. Paid rent for period of July 10 to end of month, $1,500.

11. Purchased a truck for $15,000, paying $5,000 cash and giving a note payable for the remainder.

12. Purchased equipment on account, $2,500.

14. Purchased supplies for cash, $1,050.

14. Paid premiums on property and casualty insurance, $750.

15. Received cash for job completed, $3,100.

21. Paid creditor for equipment purchased on July 12, $2,500.

24. Recorded jobs completed on account and sent invoices to customers, $3,100.

26. Received an invoice for truck expenses, to be paid in August, $225.

27. Paid utilities expense, $1,205.

27. Paid miscellaneous expenses, $173.

28. Received cash from customers on account, $1,420.

31. Paid wages of employees, $2,100.

31. Withdrew cash for personal use, $1,500.

Instructions

1. Journalize each transaction in a two-column journal, referring to the following chart of accounts in selecting the accounts to be debited and credited. (Do not insert the account numbers in the journal at this time.) Journal entry explanations may be omitted.

11	Cash	31	Jong Woo, Capital
12	Accounts Receivable	32	Jong Woo, Drawing
13	Supplies	41	Fees Earned
14	Prepaid Insurance	51	Wages Expense
16	Equipment	53	Rent Expense
18	Truck	54	Utilities Expense
21	Notes Payable	55	Truck Expense
22	Accounts Payable	59	Miscellaneous Expense

2. Post the journal to a ledger of four-column accounts, inserting appropriate posting references as each item is posted. Extend the balances to the appropriate balance columns after each transaction is posted.
3. Prepare a trial balance for Asian Designs as of July 31.

Problem 2–4A
Journal entries and trial balance

Objectives 2, 3, 4, 5

HAT

✓ 4. Total of Debit Column: $314,500

Cherokee Realty acts as an agent in buying, selling, renting, and managing real estate. The account balances at the end of April of the current year are as follows:

11	Cash	29,500	
12	Accounts Receivable	38,600	
13	Prepaid Insurance	750	
14	Office Supplies	625	
16	Land	0	
21	Accounts Payable		13,250
22	Notes Payable		0
31	Eva Wheless, Capital		63,025
32	Eva Wheless, Drawing	10,000	
41	Fees Earned		158,725
51	Salary and Commission Expense	123,075	
52	Rent Expense	19,000	
53	Advertising Expense	8,900	
54	Automobile Expense	3,950	
59	Miscellaneous Expense	600	
		235,000	235,000

The following business transactions were completed by Cherokee Realty during May of the current year:

May 1. Purchased office supplies on account, $1,100.
2. Paid rent on office for month, $2,500.
3. Received cash from clients on account, $34,200.
9. Paid insurance premiums, $1,925.
10. Returned a portion of the office supplies purchased on May 1, receiving full credit for their cost, $150.
15. Paid advertising expense, $2,150.
20. Paid creditors on account, $7,650.
29. Paid miscellaneous expenses, $215.
30. Paid automobile expense (including rental charges for an automobile), $850.
31. Discovered an error in computing a commission; received cash from the salesperson for the overpayment, $500.
31. Paid salaries and commissions for the month, $30,850.
31. Recorded revenue earned and billed to clients during the month, $46,200.
31. Purchased land for a future building site for $50,000, paying $10,000 in cash and giving a note payable for the remainder.
31. Withdrew cash for personal use, $2,500.

Instructions

1. Record the May 1 balance of each account in the appropriate balance column of a four-column account, write *Balance* in the item section, and place a check mark (✓) in the posting reference column.
2. Journalize the transactions for May in a two-column journal. Journal entry explanations may be omitted.
3. Post to the ledger, extending the account balance to the appropriate balance column after each posting.
4. Prepare a trial balance of the ledger as of May 31.

Problem 2–5A
Errors in trial balance

Objectives 5, 6

What's Wrong

WITH THIS?

✓ 7. Total of Debit Column:
$33,338.10

If the working papers correlating with this textbook are not used, omit Problem 2–5A. The following records of Couch TV Repair are presented in the working papers:

- Journal containing entries for the period March 1–31.
- Ledger to which the March entries have been posted.
- Preliminary trial balance as of March 31, which does not balance.

Locate the errors, supply the information requested, and prepare a corrected trial balance according to the following instructions. The balances recorded in the accounts as of March 1 and the entries in the journal are correctly stated. If it is necessary to correct any posted amounts in the ledger, a line should be drawn through the erroneous figure and the correct amount inserted above. Corrections or notations may be inserted on the preliminary trial balance in any manner desired. It is not necessary to complete all of the instructions if equal trial balance totals can be obtained earlier. However, the requirements of instructions (6) and (7) should be completed in any event.

Instructions

1. Verify the totals of the preliminary trial balance, inserting the correct amounts in the schedule provided in the working papers.
2. Compute the difference between the trial balance totals.
3. Compare the listings in the trial balance with the balances appearing in the ledger, and list the errors in the space provided in the working papers.
4. Verify the accuracy of the balance of each account in the ledger, and list the errors in the space provided in the working papers.
5. Trace the postings in the ledger back to the journal, using small check marks to identify items traced. Correct any amounts in the ledger that may be necessitated by errors in posting, and list the errors in the space provided in the working papers.
6. Journalize as of March 31 the payment of $113.40 for gas and electricity. The bill had been paid on March 31 but was inadvertently omitted from the journal. Post to the ledger. (Revise any amounts necessitated by posting this entry.)
7. Prepare a new trial balance.

Problem 2–6A
Corrected trial balance

Objectives 5, 6

SPREADSHEET

✓ 1. Total of Debit Column:
$103,090

Newman Photography has the following trial balance as of December 31 of the current year:

Cash	4,025	
Accounts Receivable	9,350	
Supplies	1,277	
Prepaid Insurance	330	
Equipment	12,500	
Notes Payable		12,500
Accounts Payable		3,025
Jake Newman, Capital		13,240
Jake Newman, Drawing	6,000	
Fees Earned		80,750
Wages Expense	48,150	
Rent Expense	750	
Advertising Expense	5,250	
Gas, Electricity, and Water Expense	3,150	
	90,782	109,515

The debit and credit totals are not equal as a result of the following errors:

a. The balance of cash was overstated by $1,500.
b. A cash receipt of $1,200 was posted as a credit to Cash of $2,100.
c. A debit of $750 to Accounts Receivable was not posted.
d. A return of $252 of defective supplies was erroneously posted as a $225 credit to Supplies.
e. An insurance policy acquired at a cost of $310 was posted as a credit to Prepaid Insurance.

f.   The balance of Notes Payable was overstated by $5,000.

g.   A credit of $75 in Accounts Payable was overlooked when the balance of the account was determined.

h.   A debit of $1,500 for a withdrawal by the owner was posted as a credit to Jake Newman, Capital.

i.   The balance of $7,500 in Rent Expense was entered as $750 in the trial balance.

j.   Miscellaneous Expense, with a balance of $915, was omitted from the trial balance.

Instructions

1.   Prepare a corrected trial balance as of December 31 of the current year.

2.   ◼◼◼▶ Does the fact that the trial balance in (1) is balanced mean that there are no errors in the accounts? Explain.

PROBLEMS SERIES B

Problem 2–1B

Entries into T accounts and trial balance

Objectives 2, 3, 4, 5

✓ 3. Total of Debit Column: $39,410

Veronica Mays, an architect, opened an office on January 1 of the current year. During the month, she completed the following transactions connected with her professional practice:

a.   Transferred cash from a personal bank account to an account to be used for the business, $20,000.

b.   Paid January rent for office and workroom, $2,500.

c.   Purchased used automobile for $11,500, paying $2,500 cash and giving a non-interest-bearing note for the remainder.

d.   Purchased office and drafting room equipment on account, $6,200.

e.   Paid cash for supplies, $900.

f.   Paid cash for insurance policies, $1,050.

g.   Received cash from client for plans delivered, $3,100.

h.   Paid cash for miscellaneous expenses, $75.

i.   Paid cash to creditors on account, $2,950.

j.   Paid installment due on note payable, $400.

k.   Received invoice for blueprint service, due in February, $310.

l.   Recorded fee earned on plans delivered, payment to be received in February, $4,150.

m.   Paid salary of assistant, $1,150.

n.   Paid gas, oil, and repairs on automobile for January, $175.

Instructions

1.   Record the foregoing transactions directly in the following T accounts, without journalizing: Cash; Accounts Receivable; Supplies; Prepaid Insurance; Automobiles; Equipment; Notes Payable; Accounts Payable; Veronica Mays, Capital; Professional Fees; Rent Expense; Salary Expense; Automobile Expense; Blueprint Expense; Miscellaneous Expense. To the left of the amount entered in the accounts, place the appropriate letter to identify the transaction.

2.   Determine the balances of the T accounts having two or more debits or credits. A memorandum balance should be inserted in accounts having both debits and credits, in the manner illustrated in the chapter. For accounts with entries on one side only (such as Professional Fees), there is no need to insert the memorandum balance in the item column. For accounts containing only a single debit and a single credit (such as Notes Payable), the memorandum balance should be inserted in the appropriate item column. Accounts containing a single entry only (such as Prepaid Insurance) do not need a memorandum balance.

3.   Prepare a trial balance for Veronica Mays, Architect, as of January 31 of the current year.

Problem 2–2B
Journal entries and trial balance

Objectives 2, 3, 4, 5

GENERAL LEDGER

✓ 4. a. $20,750
✓   b. $11,200

On July 1 of the current year, Lamar Todd established Sky Realty, which completed the following transactions during the month:

a.   Lamar Todd transferred cash from a personal bank account to an account to be used for the business, $15,000.
b.   Paid rent on office and equipment for the month, $2,500.
c.   Purchased supplies on account, $1,500.
d.   Paid creditor on account, $900.
e.   Earned sales commissions, receiving cash, $20,750.
f.   Paid automobile expenses (including rental charge) for month, $2,400, and miscellaneous expenses, $1,250.
g.   Paid office salaries, $4,000.
h.   Determined that the cost of supplies used was $1,050.
i.   Withdrew cash for personal use, $1,500.

Instructions

1.   Journalize entries for transactions (a) through (i), using the following account titles: Cash; Supplies; Accounts Payable; Lamar Todd, Capital; Lamar Todd, Drawing; Sales Commissions; Office Salaries Expense; Rent Expense; Automobile Expense; Supplies Expense; Miscellaneous Expense. Explanations may be omitted.
2.   Prepare T accounts, using the account titles in (1). Post the journal entries to these accounts, placing the appropriate letter to the left of each amount to identify the transactions. Determine the account balances, after all posting is complete, for all accounts having two or more debits or credits. A memorandum balance should also be inserted in accounts having both debits and credits, in the manner illustrated in the chapter. For accounts with entries on one side only, there is no need to insert a memorandum balance in the item column. For accounts containing only a single debit and a single credit, the memorandum balance should be inserted in the appropriate item column.
3.   Prepare a trial balance as of July 31, 20—.
4.   Determine the following:
     a.   Amount of total revenue recorded in the ledger.
     b.   Amount of total expenses recorded in the ledger.
     c.   Amount of net income for July.

Problem 2–3B
Journal entries and trial balance

Objectives 2, 3, 4, 5

GENERAL LEDGER

✓ 3. Total of Credit Column: $46,040

On June 5 of the current year, Dave Chapman established an interior decorating business, Modern Designs. During the remainder of the month, Dave completed the following transactions related to the business:

June 5. Dave transferred cash from a personal bank account to an account to be used for the business, $25,000.
5.   Paid rent for period of June 5 to end of month, $1,700.
7.   Purchased office equipment on account, $10,500.
8.   Purchased a used truck for $18,000, paying $10,000 cash and giving a note payable for the remainder.
10. Purchased supplies for cash, $1,315.
12. Received cash for job completed, $3,300.
20. Paid premiums on property and casualty insurance, $800.
22. Recorded jobs completed on account and sent invoices to customers, $1,950.
24. Received an invoice for truck expenses, to be paid in July, $290.
29. Paid utilities expense, $490.
29. Paid miscellaneous expenses, $195.
30. Received cash from customers on account, $1,200.
30. Paid wages of employees, $1,900.
30. Paid creditor a portion of the amount owed for equipment purchased on June 7, $3,000.
30. Withdrew cash for personal use, $2,500.

Instructions

1.   Journalize each transaction in a two-column journal, referring to the following chart of accounts in selecting the accounts to be debited and credited. (Do not insert the account numbers in the journal at this time.) Explanations may be omitted.

11	Cash	31	Dave Chapman, Capital
12	Accounts Receivable	32	Dave Chapman, Drawing
13	Supplies	41	Fees Earned
14	Prepaid Insurance	51	Wages Expense
16	Equipment	53	Rent Expense
18	Truck	54	Utilities Expense
21	Notes Payable	55	Truck Expense
22	Accounts Payable	59	Miscellaneous Expense

2. Post the journal to a ledger of four-column accounts, inserting appropriate posting references as each item is posted. Extend the balances to the appropriate balance columns after each transaction is posted.
3. Prepare a trial balance for Modern Designs as of June 30.

Problem 2–4B

Journal entries and trial balance

Objectives 2, 3, 4, 5

✓ 4. Total of Debit Column: $260,200

Sycamore Realty acts as an agent in buying, selling, renting, and managing real estate. The account balances at the end of March of the current year are as follows:

11	Cash	28,150	
12	Accounts Receivable	38,750	
13	Prepaid Insurance	1,100	
14	Office Supplies	1,050	
16	Land	0	
21	Accounts Payable		11,510
22	Notes Payable		0
31	Shirley Collins, Capital		29,840
32	Shirley Collins, Drawing	1,000	
41	Fees Earned		126,500
51	Salary and Commission Expense	84,100	
52	Rent Expense	5,500	
53	Advertising Expense	3,900	
54	Automobile Expense	2,750	
59	Miscellaneous Expense	1,550	
		167,850	167,850

The following business transactions were completed by Sycamore Realty during April of the current year:

April 1. Paid rent on office for month, $2,500.
    3. Purchased office supplies on account, $1,375.
    5. Paid insurance premiums, $1,650.
    7. Received cash from clients on account, $30,200.
    15. Purchased land for a future building site for $75,000, paying $15,000 in cash and giving a note payable for the remainder.
    18. Paid creditors on account, $7,150.
    20. Returned a portion of the office supplies purchased on April 3, receiving full credit for their cost, $275.
    24. Paid advertising expense, $1,550.
    27. Discovered an error in computing a commission; received cash from the salesperson for the overpayment, $350.
    28. Paid automobile expense (including rental charges for an automobile), $715.
    29. Paid miscellaneous expenses, $215.
    30. Recorded revenue earned and billed to clients during the month, $38,400.
    30. Paid salaries and commissions for the month, $21,500.
    30. Withdrew cash for personal use, $1,500.

Instructions

1. Record the April 1 balance of each account in the appropriate balance column of a four-column account, write *Balance* in the item section, and place a check mark (✓) in the posting reference column.

2. Journalize the transactions for April in a two-column journal. Journal entry explanations may be omitted.
3. Post to the ledger, extending the account balance to the appropriate balance column after each posting.
4. Prepare a trial balance of the ledger as of April 30.

Problem 2–5B
Errors in trial balance

Objectives 5, 6

What's Wrong

WITH THIS?

✓ 7. Total of Debit Column:
$33,338.10

If the working papers correlating with this textbook are not used, omit Problem 2–5B.
The following records of Couch TV Repair are presented in the working papers:

- Journal containing entries for the period March 1–31.
- Ledger to which the March entries have been posted.
- Preliminary trial balance as of March 31, which does not balance.

Locate the errors, supply the information requested, and prepare a corrected trial balance according to the following instructions. The balances recorded in the accounts as of March 1 and the entries in the journal are correctly stated. If it is necessary to correct any posted amounts in the ledger, a line should be drawn through the erroneous figure and the correct amount inserted above. Corrections or notations may be inserted on the preliminary trial balance in any manner desired. It is not necessary to complete all of the instructions if equal trial balance totals can be obtained earlier. However, the requirements of instructions (6) and (7) should be completed in any event.

Instructions

1. Verify the totals of the preliminary trial balance, inserting the correct amounts in the schedule provided in the working papers.
2. Compute the difference between the trial balance totals.
3. Compare the listings in the trial balance with the balances appearing in the ledger, and list the errors in the space provided in the working papers.
4. Verify the accuracy of the balance of each account in the ledger, and list the errors in the space provided in the working papers.
5. Trace the postings in the ledger back to the journal, using small check marks to identify items traced. Correct any amounts in the ledger that may be necessitated by errors in posting, and list the errors in the space provided in the working papers.
6. Journalize as of March 31 the payment of $200 for advertising expense. The bill had been paid on March 31 but was inadvertently omitted from the journal. Post to the ledger. (Revise any amounts necessitated by posting this entry.)
7. Prepare a new trial balance.

Problem 2–6B
Corrected trial balance

Objectives 5, 6

SPREADSHEET

✓ 1. Total of Debit Column:
$78,190

Doolittle Carpet has the following trial balance as of March 31 of the current year:

Cash	2,070	
Accounts Receivable	6,150	
Supplies	1,010	
Prepaid Insurance	250	
Equipment	15,500	
Notes Payable		15,000
Accounts Payable		4,810
Ellisa Doolittle, Capital		16,300
Ellisa Doolittle, Drawing	6,000	
Fees Earned		49,980
Wages Expense	28,500	
Rent Expense	6,400	
Advertising Expense	320	
Miscellaneous Expense	945	
	67,145	86,090

The debit and credit totals are not equal as a result of the following errors:

a. The balance of cash was understated by $750.
b. A cash receipt of $2,100 was posted as a debit to Cash of $1,200.
c. A debit of $2,000 for a withdrawal by the owner was posted as a credit to Ellisa Doolittle, Capital.

d. The balance of $3,200 in Advertising Expense was entered as $320 in the trial balance.

e. A debit of $975 to Accounts Receivable was not posted.

f. A return of $125 of defective supplies was erroneously posted as a $215 credit to Supplies.

g. The balance of Notes Payable was overstated by $5,000.

h. An insurance policy acquired at a cost of $150 was posted as a credit to Prepaid Insurance.

i. Gas, Electricity, and Water Expense, with a balance of $3,150, was omitted from the trial balance.

j. A debit of $900 in Accounts Payable was overlooked when determining the balance of the account.

Instructions

1. Prepare a corrected trial balance as of March 31 of the current year.
2. 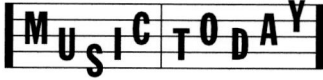 Does the fact that the trial balance in (1) is balanced mean that there are no errors in the accounts? Explain.

CONTINUING PROBLEM

HAT

✔ 4. Total of Debit Column:
$13,155

The transactions completed by Music Today during November 1999 were described at the end of Chapter 1. The following transactions were completed during December, the second month of the business's operations:

Dec. 1. Chris Stipe made an additional investment in Music Today by depositing $2,500 in Music Today's checking account.

1. Instead of continuing to share office space with a local real estate agency, Chris decided to rent office space near a local music store. Paid rent for December, $720.

1. Paid a premium of $1,680 for a comprehensive insurance policy covering liability, theft, and fire. The policy covers a two-year period.

2. Received $400 on account.

3. On behalf of Music Today, Chris signed a contract with a local radio station, KPRG, to provide guest spots for the next three months. The contract requires Music Today to provide a guest disc jockey for 40 hours per month for a monthly fee of $500. Any additional hours beyond 40 will be billed to KPRG at $15 per hour. In accordance with the contract, Chris received $1,500 from KPRG as an advance payment for the first three months.

3. Paid $150 on account.

4. Paid an attorney $75 for reviewing (on December 2) the contract with KPRG. (Record as Miscellaneous Expense.)

5. Purchased office equipment on account from One-Stop Office Mart, $2,500.

8. Paid for a newspaper advertisement, $100.

11. Received $300 for serving as a disc jockey for a college fraternity party.

13. Paid $250 to a local audio electronics store for rental of various equipment (speakers, CD players, etc.).

14. Paid wages of $400 to receptionist and part-time assistant.

16. Received $550 for serving as a disc jockey for a wedding reception.

18. Purchased supplies on account, $375.

21. Paid $120 to The Music Store for use of its current demo CDs and tapes in making cassettes of various music sets.

22. Paid $50 to a local radio station to advertise the services of Music Today twice daily for the remainder of December.

23. Served as disc jockey for an annual holiday party for $780. Received $200, with the remainder due January 6, 2000.

27. Paid electric bill, $280.

28. Paid wages of $400 to receptionist and part-time assistant.

Dec. 29. Paid miscellaneous expenses, $85.

30. Served as a disc jockey for a pre-New Year's Eve charity ball for $600. Received $300, with the remainder due on January 10, 2000.

31. Received $1,000 for serving as a disc jockey for a New Year's Eve party.

31. Withdrew $500 cash from Music Today for personal use.

Music Today's chart of accounts and the balance of accounts as of December 1, 1999 (all normal balances), are as follows:

11	Cash	$1,345
12	Accounts Receivable	400
14	Supplies	160
15	Prepaid Insurance	—
17	Office Equipment	—
21	Accounts Payable	150
23	Unearned Revenue	—
31	Chris Stipe, Capital	1,500
32	Chris Stipe, Drawing	50
41	Fees Earned	1,550
50	Wages Expense	110
51	Office Rent Expense	250
52	Equipment Rent Expense	325
53	Utilities Expense	100
54	Music Expense	220
55	Advertising Expense	75
56	Supplies Expense	90
59	Miscellaneous Expense	75

Instructions

1. Enter the December 1, 1999 account balances in the appropriate balance column of a four-column account. Write *Balance* in the Item column, and place a check mark (✓) in the Posting Reference column. (It is advisable to verify the equality of the debit and credit balances in the ledger before proceeding with the next instruction.)

2. Analyze and journalize each transaction in a two-column journal. Omit journal entry explanations.

3. Post the journal to the ledger, extending the account balance to the appropriate balance column after each posting.

4. Prepare a trial balance as of December 31, 1999.

SPECIAL ACTIVITIES

**Activity 2–1
City Services Co.**
Ethics and professional conduct in business

At the end of the current month, Oliva Ohl prepared a trial balance for City Services Co. The credit side of the trial balance exceeds the debit side by a significant amount. Oliva has decided to add the difference to the balance of the miscellaneous expense account in order to complete the preparation of the current month's financial statements by a 5 o'clock deadline. Oliva will look for the difference next week when there is more time.

▬▬► Discuss whether Oliva Ohl is behaving in a professional manner.

**Activity 2–2
State College**
Account for revenue

State College requires students to pay tuition each term before classes begin. Students who have not paid their tuition are not allowed to enroll or to attend classes.

What journal entry do you think would be used by State College to record the receipt of the students' tuition payments? Describe the nature of each account in the entry.

Activity 2–3
Aero Data Company
Record transactions

The following discussion took place between Anita Cain, the office manager of Aero Data Company, and a new accountant, Bob Nunez.

Bob: I've been thinking about our method of recording entries. It seems that it's inefficient.

Anita: In what way?

Bob: Well—correct me if I'm wrong—it seems like we have unnecessary steps in the process. We could very easily develop a trial balance by posting our transactions directly into the ledger and bypassing the journal altogether. In this way we could combine the recording and posting process into one step and save ourselves a lot of time. What do you think?

Anita: We need to have a talk.

→ What should Anita say to Bob?

Activity 2–4
Crestview Construction Co.
Debits and credits

The following is an excerpt from a conversation between Judy Parker, the president and chief operating officer of Crestview Construction Co., and her neighbor, Jack Vancel.

Jack: Judy, I'm taking a course in night school, "Intro to Accounting." I was wondering—could you answer a couple of questions for me?

Judy: Well, I will if I can.

Jack: Okay, our instructor says that it's critical that we understand the basic concepts of accounting, or we'll never get beyond the first test. My problem is with those rules of debit and credit . . . you know, assets increase with debits, decrease with credits, etc.

Judy: Yes, pretty basic stuff. You just have to memorize the rules. It shouldn't be too difficult.

Jack: Sure, I can memorize the rules, but my problem is I want to be sure I understand the basic concepts behind the rules.

For example, why can't assets be increased with credits and decreased with debits like revenue? As long as everyone did it that way, why not? It would seem easier if we had the same rules for all increases and decreases in accounts.

Also, why is the left side of an account called the debit side? Why couldn't it be called something simple . . . like the "LE" for Left Entry? The right side could be called just "RE" for Right Entry.

Finally, why are there just two sides to an entry? Why can't there be three or four sides to an entry?

In a group of four or five, select one person to play the role of "Judy" and one person to play the role of "Jack."

1. After listening to the conversation between Judy and Jack, help Judy answer Jack's questions.
2. What information (other than just debit and credit journal entries) could the accounting system gather that might be useful to Judy in managing Crestview Construction Co.?

Activity 2–5
Eagle Caddy Service
Transactions and income statement

HAT

During June through August, Dale Wells is planning to manage and operate Eagle Caddy Service at Cordele Golf and Country Club. Dale will rent a small maintenance building from the country club for $200 per month and will offer caddy services, including cart rentals, to golfers. Dale has had no formal training in record keeping. During June, he kept notes of all receipts and expenses in a shoe box.

An examination of Dale's shoe box records for June revealed the following:

June 1. Withdrew $2,000 from personal bank account to be used to operate the caddy service.
    1. Paid rent to Cordele Golf and Country Club, $200.
    2. Paid for golf supplies (practice balls, etc.), $200.
    3. Arranged for the rental of forty regular (pulling) golf carts and ten gasoline-driven carts for $1,000 per month. Paid $750 in advance, with the remaining $250 due June 20.
    7. Purchased supplies, including gasoline, for the golf carts on account, $325. Cordele Golf and Country Club has agreed to allow Dale to store the gasoline in one of its fuel tanks at no cost.

June 15. Received cash for services from June 1–15, $1,020.
    17. Paid cash to creditors on account, $180.
    20. Paid remaining rental on golf carts, $250.
    22. Purchased supplies, including gasoline, on account, $280.
    25. Accepted IOUs from customers on account, $410.
    28. Paid miscellaneous expenses, $125.
    30. Received cash for services from June 16–30, $1,475.
    30. Paid telephone and electricity (utilities) expenses, $85.
    30. Paid wages of part-time employees, $260.
    30. Received cash in payment of IOUs on account, $150.
    30. Supplies on hand at the end of June, $180.

Dale has asked you several questions concerning his financial affairs to date, and he has asked you to assist with his record keeping and reporting of financial data.

a. To assist Dale with his record keeping, prepare a chart of accounts that would be appropriate for Eagle Caddy Service.
b. Prepare an income statement for June in order to help Dale assess the profitability of Eagle Caddy Service. For this purpose, the use of T accounts may be helpful in analyzing the effects of each June transaction.
c. Based on Dale's records of receipts and payments, calculate the amount of cash on hand on June 30. For this purpose, a T account for cash may be useful.
d.   ➤ A count of the cash on hand on June 30 totaled $2,135. Briefly discuss the possible causes of the difference between the amount of cash computed in (c) and the actual amount of cash on hand.

Activity 2–6
Into the Real World
Opportunities for
accountants

The increasing complexity of the current business and regulatory environment has created an increased demand for accountants who can analyze business transactions and interpret their effects on the financial statements. In addition, a basic ability to analyze the effects of transactions is necessary to be successful in all fields of business as well as in other disciplines, such as law. To better understand the importance of accounting in today's environment, search the Internet or your local newspaper for job opportunities. One possible Internet site is **www.jobweb.com**. Then do *one* of the following:

1. Print a listing of at least two ads for accounting jobs. Alternatively, bring to class at least two newspaper ads for accounting jobs.
2. Print a listing of at least two ads for nonaccounting jobs for which some knowledge of accounting is preferred or necessary. Alternatively, bring to class at least two newspaper ads for such jobs.

ANSWERS TO SELF-EXAMINATION QUESTIONS

Matching

1. A	5. O	8. I	11. E	14. M	17. H	20. Z	23. W
2. N	6. R	9. V	12. C	15. L	18. S	21. X	24. U
3. D	7. T	10. F	13. K	16. G	19. Y	22. P	25. J
4. B							

Multiple Choice

1. **A** A debit may signify an increase in an asset account (answer A) or a decrease in a liability or owner's capital account. A credit may signify a decrease in an asset account (answer B) or an increase in a liability or owner's capital account (answers C and D).

2. **C** Liability, capital, and revenue (answer C) accounts have normal credit balances. Asset (answer A), drawing (answer B), and expense (answer D) accounts have normal debit balances.

3. **C** Accounts Receivable (answer A), Cash (answer B),

and Miscellaneous Expense (answer D) would all normally have debit balances. Fees Earned should normally have a credit balance. Hence, a debit balance in Fees Earned (answer C) would indicate a likely error in the recording process.

4. **A** The receipt of cash from customers on account increases the asset Cash and decreases the asset Accounts Receivable, as indicated by answer A. Answer B has the debit and credit reversed, and answers C and D involve transactions with creditors (accounts payable) and not customers (accounts receivable).

5. **D** The trial balance (answer D) is a listing of the balances and the titles of the accounts in the ledger on a given date, so that the equality of the debits and credits in the ledger can be verified. The income statement (answer A) is a summary of revenue and expenses for a period of time. The balance sheet (answer B) is a presentation of the assets, liabilities, and owner's equity on a given date. The statement of owner's equity (answer C) is a summary of the changes in owner's equity for a period of time.

3

The Matching Concept and the Adjusting Process

Setting *the* **STAGE**

Assume that you rented an apartment last month and signed a nine-month lease. When you signed the lease agreement, you were required to pay the final month's rent of $500. This amount is not returnable to you.

You are now applying for a student loan at a local bank. The loan application requires a listing of all your assets. Should you list the $500 deposit as an asset?

The answer to this question is "yes." The deposit is an asset to you until you receive the use of the apartment in the ninth month.

A business faces similar accounting problems at the end of a period. A business must determine what assets, liabilities, and owner's equity should be reported on its balance sheet. It must also determine what revenues and expenses should be reported on its income statement.

As we illustrated in previous chapters, transactions are normally recorded as they occur. Periodically, financial statements are prepared, summarizing the effects of the transactions on the financial position and the operations of the business.

At any one point in time, however, the accounting records may not reflect all transactions. For example, most businesses do not record the daily use of supplies. Likewise, revenue may have been earned from providing services to customers yet the customers have not been billed by the time the accounting period ends. Thus, at the end of the period, the revenue and the receivable accounts must be updated.

In this chapter, we describe and illustrate this updating process. We will focus on accounts that normally require updating and the journal entries that update them.

objectives

1 Explain how the matching concept relates to the accrual basis of accounting.

2 Explain why adjustments are necessary and list the characteristics of adjusting entries.

3 Journalize entries for accounts requiring adjustment.

4 Summarize the adjustment process and prepare an adjusted trial balance.

5 Use vertical analysis to compare financial statement items with each other and with industry averages.

The Matching Concept

OBJECTIVE 1

Explain how the matching concept relates to the accrual basis of accounting.

American Airlines uses the accrual basis of accounting. Revenues are recognized when passengers take flights, not when the passenger makes the reservation or pays for the ticket.

When accountants prepare financial statements, they are assuming that the economic life of the business can be divided into time periods. Using this **accounting period concept**, accountants must determine in which period the revenues and expenses of the business should be reported. To determine the appropriate period, accountants will use either (1) the cash basis of accounting or (2) the accrual basis of accounting.

Under the **cash basis**, revenues and expenses are reported in the income statement in the period in which cash is received or paid. For example, fees are recorded when cash is received from clients, and wages are recorded when cash is paid to employees. The net income (or net loss) is the difference between the cash receipts (revenues) and the cash payments (expenses).

Under the **accrual basis**, revenues are reported in the income statement in the period in which they are earned. For example, revenue is reported when the services are provided to customers. Cash may or may not be received from customers during this period. The concept that supports this reporting of revenues is called the **revenue recognition concept**.

Under the accrual basis, expenses are reported in the same period as the revenues to which they relate. For example, employee wages are reported as an expense in the period in which the employees provided services to customers and not necessarily when the wages are paid.

A bank loan officer requires an individual, who normally keeps records on a cash basis, to list assets (automobiles, homes, investments, etc.) on an application for a loan or a line of credit. In addition, the application often asks for an estimate of the individual's liabilities, such as credit card amounts outstanding and balances of automobile loans. In a sense, the loan application converts the individual's cash-basis accounting system to an estimated accrual basis. The loan officer uses this information in assessing the individual's ability to repay the loan.

The accounting concept that supports reporting revenues and the related expenses in the same period is called the **matching concept** or **matching principle**. Under this concept, an income statement will report the resulting income or loss for the period.

Generally accepted accounting principles require the use of the accrual basis. However, small service businesses may use the cash basis because they have few receivables and payables. For example, attorneys, physicians, and real estate agents often use

The matching concept supports reporting revenues and related expenses in the same period.

The business environment is a dynamic one in which there is constant change, with challenges and opportunities. The current technology revolution affects all businesses.

Technology and Business

Computer and telecommunication technologies affect the production, storage, and use of information by business. Many businesses have developed Web sites for use in marketing products and services and for communicating with stakeholders. New software applications range from accounting software that provides updated accounting information to business simulation software capable of gauging the impact of alternative business decisions on operations.

The technological revolution challenges businesses to adapt quickly to software and hardware improvements. Such improvements offer opportunities for businesses to develop new products, reach more customers, develop new channels of product distribution, lower operating costs, improve product quality, obtain immediate customer feedback, and react quickly to market changes. Businesses unable to adapt quickly to the technological revolution may find themselves at a competitive disadvantage.

Technology also provides you with new and exciting opportunities. To the extent that you develop your computer and technological skills and talents, you will improve your chances of finding a job and advancing rapidly in your career. ■

the cash basis. For them, the cash basis will yield financial statements similar to those prepared under the accrual basis.

For most large businesses, the cash basis will not provide accurate financial statements for user needs. For this reason, we will emphasize the accrual basis in the remainder of this text. The accrual basis and its related matching concept require an analysis and updating of some accounts when financial statements are prepared. In the following paragraphs, we will describe and illustrate this process, called the **adjusting process**.

Nature of the Adjusting Process

OBJECTIVE 2

Explain why adjustments are necessary and list the characteristics of adjusting entries.

At the end of an accounting period, many of the balances of accounts in the ledger can be reported, without change, in the financial statements. For example, the balance of the cash account is normally the amount reported on the balance sheet.

Some accounts in the ledger, however, require updating. For example, the balances listed for prepaid expenses are normally overstated because the use of these assets is not recorded on a day-to-day basis. The balance of the supplies account usually represents the cost of supplies at the beginning of the period plus the cost of supplies acquired during the period. To record the daily use of supplies would require many entries with small amounts. In addition, the total amount of supplies is small relative to other assets, and managers usually do not require day-to-day information about supplies.

The journal entries that bring the accounts up to date at the end of the accounting period are called **adjusting entries**. All adjusting entries affect at least one income statement account and one balance sheet account. Thus, an adjusting entry will *always* involve a revenue or an expense account *and* an asset or a liability account.

Is there an easy way to know when an adjusting entry is needed? Yes, four basic items require adjusting entries. The first two items are **deferrals**. Deferrals are created by recording a transaction in a way that *delays* or *defers* the recognition of an expense or a revenue, as described below.

> **All adjusting entries affect at least one income statement account and one balance sheet account.**

- **Deferred expenses** or **prepaid expenses** are items that have been initially recorded as assets but are expected to become expenses over time or through the normal operations of the business. Supplies and prepaid insurance are two examples of prepaid expenses that may require adjustment at the end of an accounting period. Other examples include prepaid advertising and prepaid interest.

- **Deferred revenues** or **unearned revenues** are items that have been initially recorded as liabilities but are expected to become revenues over time or through the normal operations of the business. An example of deferred revenue is unearned rent. Other examples include tuition received in advance by a school, an annual retainer fee received by an attorney, premiums received in advance by an insurance company, and magazine subscriptions received in advance by a publisher.

The second two items that require adjusting entries are accruals. **Accruals** are created by an unrecorded expense that has been incurred or an unrecorded revenue that has been earned, as described below.

- **Accrued expenses** or **accrued liabilities** are expenses that have been incurred *but have not been recorded* in the accounts. An example of an accrued expense is accrued wages owed to employees at the end of a period. Other examples include accrued interest on notes payable and accrued taxes.
- **Accrued revenues** or **accrued assets** are revenues that have been earned *but have not been recorded* in the accounts. An example of an accrued revenue is fees for services that an attorney has provided but hasn't billed to the client at the end of the period. Other examples include unbilled commissions by a travel agent, accrued interest on notes receivable, and accrued rent on property rented to others.

How do you tell the difference between deferrals and accruals? Determine when cash is received or paid, as shown in Exhibit 1. If cash is received (for revenue) or if cash is paid (for expense) in the *current* period, but the revenue or expense relates to a future period, the revenue or expense is a deferred item. If cash will not be received or if cash will not be paid until a *future* period, but the revenue or expense relates to the current period, the revenue or expense is an accrued item.

EXHIBIT 1
Deferrals and Accruals

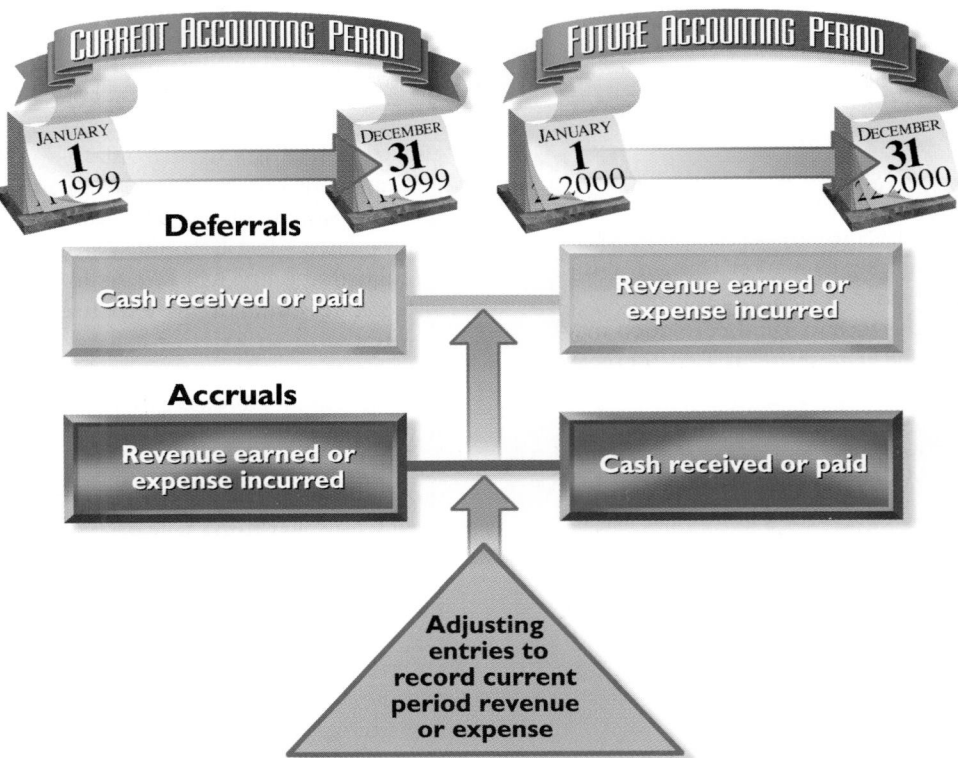

Recording Adjusting Entries

OBJECTIVE 3

Journalize entries for accounts requiring adjustment.

The examples of adjusting entries in the following paragraphs are based on the ledger of Computer King as reported in the December 31, 1999 trial balance in Exhibit 2. To simplify the examples, T accounts are used. The adjusting entries are shown in color in the accounts to separate them from other transactions.

EXHIBIT 2
Unadjusted Trial Balance for Computer King

Computer King Trial Balance December 31, 1999		
Cash	2 0 6 5 00	
Accounts Receivable	2 2 2 0 00	
Supplies	2 0 0 0 00	
Prepaid Insurance	2 4 0 0 00	
Land	10 0 0 0 00	
Office Equipment	1 8 0 0 00	
Accounts Payable		9 0 0 00
Unearned Rent		3 6 0 00
Pat King, Capital		15 0 0 0 00
Pat King, Drawing	4 0 0 0 00	
Fees Earned		16 3 4 0 00
Wages Expense	4 2 7 5 00	
Rent Expense	1 6 0 0 00	
Utilities Expense	9 8 5 00	
Supplies Expense	8 0 0 00	
Miscellaneous Expense	4 5 5 00	
	32 6 0 0 00	32 6 0 0 00

An expanded chart of accounts for Computer King is shown in Exhibit 3. The additional accounts that will be used in this chapter are shown in color.

EXHIBIT 3
Expanded Chart of Accounts for Computer King

Balance Sheet Accounts	Income Statement Accounts
1. Assets	**4. Revenue**
11 Cash	41 Fees Earned
12 Accounts Receivable	42 Rent Revenue
14 Supplies	**5. Expenses**
15 Prepaid Insurance	51 Wages Expense
17 Land	52 Rent Expense
18 Office Equipment	53 Depreciation Expense
19 Accumulated Depreciation	54 Utilities Expense
2. Liabilities	55 Supplies Expense
21 Accounts Payable	56 Insurance Expense
22 Wages Payable	59 Miscellaneous Expense
23 Unearned Rent	
3. Owner's Equity	
31 Pat King, Capital	
32 Pat King, Drawing	

Deferred Expenses (Prepaid Expenses)

The concept of adjusting the accounting records was introduced in Chapters 1 and 2 in the illustration for Computer King. In that illustration, supplies were purchased on November 10 (transaction c). The supplies used during November were recorded on November 30 (transaction g).

The balance in Computer King's **supplies** account on December 31 is $2,000. Some of these supplies (computer diskettes, paper, envelopes, etc.) were used during December, and some are still on hand (not used). If either amount is known, the other can be determined. It is normally easier to determine the cost of the supplies on hand at the end of the month than it is to keep a daily record of those used. Assuming that on December 31 the amount of supplies on hand is $760, the amount to be transferred from the asset account to the expense account is $1,240, computed as follows:

Supplies available during December (balance of account)	$2,000
Supplies on hand, December 31	760
Supplies used (amount of adjustment)	$1,240

As we discussed in Chapter 2, increases in expense accounts are recorded as debits and decreases in asset accounts are recorded as credits. Hence, at the end of December, the supplies expense account should be debited for $1,240 and the supplies account should be credited for $1,240 to record the supplies used during December. The adjusting journal entry and T accounts for Supplies and Supplies Expense are as follows:

2	1999 Dec.	31	Supplies Expense	55	1 2 4 0 00		2
3			Supplies	14		1 2 4 0 00	3

Supplies				**Supplies Expense**		
Bal.	2,000	Dec. 31	1,240	Bal.	800	
760				Dec. 31	1,240	
					2,040	

After the adjustment has been recorded and posted, the supplies account has a debit balance of $760. This balance represents an asset that will become an expense in a future period.

The debit balance of $2,400 in Computer King's **prepaid insurance** account represents a December 1 prepayment of insurance for 24 months. At the end of December, the insurance expense account should be increased (debited) and the prepaid insurance account should be decreased (credited) by $100, the insurance for one month. The adjusting journal entry and the T accounts for Prepaid Insurance and Insurance Expense are as follows:

American Greetings Corporation, which designs and distributes greeting cards, reported prepaid expenses for rent and insurance on its balance sheet.

The balance of a prepaid (deferred) expense is an asset that will become an expense in a future period.

5		31	Insurance Expense	56	1 0 0 00		5
6			Prepaid Insurance	15		1 0 0 00	6

Prepaid Insurance				Insurance Expense	
Bal.	2,400	Dec. 31	100	Dec. 31	100
2,300					

After the adjustment has been recorded and posted, the prepaid insurance account has a debit balance of $2,300. This balance represents an asset that will become an expense in future periods. The insurance expense account has a debit balance of $100, which is an expense of the current period.

What is the effect of omitting adjusting entries? If the preceding adjustments for supplies ($1,240) and insurance ($100) are not recorded, the financial statements prepared as of December 31 will be misstated. On the income statement, Supplies Expense and Insurance Expense will be understated by a total of $1,340 and net income will be overstated by $1,340. On the balance sheet, Supplies and Prepaid Insurance will be overstated by a total of $1,340. Since net income increases owner's equity, Pat King, Capital will also be overstated by $1,340 on the balance sheet. The effects of omitting these adjusting entries on the income statement and balance sheet are shown below.

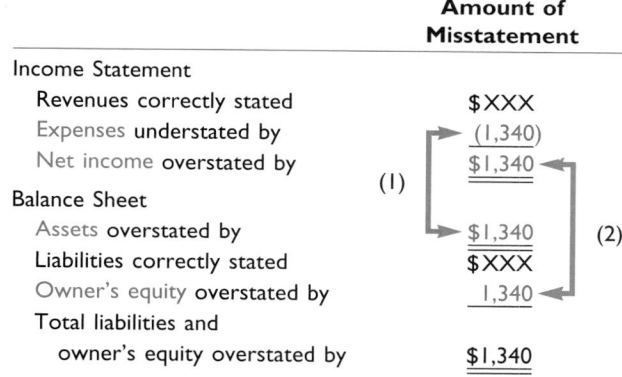

	Amount of Misstatement
Income Statement	
Revenues correctly stated	$XXX
Expenses understated by	(1,340)
Net income overstated by	$1,340
(1)	
Balance Sheet	
Assets overstated by	$1,340 (2)
Liabilities correctly stated	$XXX
Owner's equity overstated by	1,340
Total liabilities and	
owner's equity overstated by	$1,340

Q&A

Supplies of $1,250 were on hand at the beginning of the period, supplies of $3,800 were purchased during the period, and supplies of $1,000 were on hand at the end of the period. What is the supplies expense for the period?

- -

$4,050 ($1,250 + $3,800 − $1,000)

Arrow (1) indicates the effect of the understated expenses on assets. Arrow (2) indicates the effect of the overstated net income on owner's equity.

Prepayments of expenses are sometimes made at the beginning of the period in which they will be *entirely consumed*. On December 1, for example, Computer King paid rent of $800 for the month. On December 1, the rent payment represents the asset prepaid rent. The prepaid rent expires daily, and at the end of December, the entire amount has become an expense (rent expense). In cases such as this, the initial payment is recorded as an expense rather than as an asset. Thus, if the payment is recorded as a debit to Rent Expense, no adjusting entry is needed at the end of the period.[1]

Deferred Revenue (Unearned Revenue)

According to Computer King's trial balance on December 31, the balance in the **unearned rent** account is $360. This balance represents the receipt of three months' rent on December 1 for December, January, and February. At the end of December, the unearned rent account should be decreased (debited) by $120 and the rent revenue account should be increased (credited) by $120. The $120 represents the

---

[1] This alternative treatment of recording the cost of supplies, rent, and other prepayments of expenses is discussed in Appendix C.

rental revenue for one month ($360/3). The adjusting journal entry and T accounts are shown below.

8	31	Unearned Rent	23	1 2 0 00		8
9		Rent Revenue	42		1 2 0 00	9

Unearned Rent		Rent Revenue
Dec. 31 120 │ Bal. 360		Dec. 31 120
│ 240		

After the adjustment has been recorded and posted, the unearned rent account, which is a liability, has a credit balance of $240. This amount represents a deferral that will become revenue in a future period. The rent revenue account has a balance of $120, which is revenue of the current period.[2]

If the preceding adjustment of unearned rent and rent revenue is not recorded, the financial statements prepared on December 31 will be misstated. On the income statement, Rent Revenue and the net income will be understated by $120. On the balance sheet, Unearned Rent will be overstated by $120, and Pat King, Capital will be understated by $120. The effects of omitting this adjusting entry are shown below.

If Computer King's adjustment for unearned rent had been made incorrectly for $180 instead of $120, what would have been the effect on the financial statements?

Revenues would have been overstated by $60; net income would have been overstated by $60; liabilities would have been understated by $60; and owner's equity would have been overstated by $60.

Sears, Roebuck and Co. sells extended warranty contracts with terms between 12 and 36 months. The receipts from sales of these contracts are reported as unearned revenue (deferred revenue) on Sears's balance sheet. Revenue is recorded as the contracts expire.

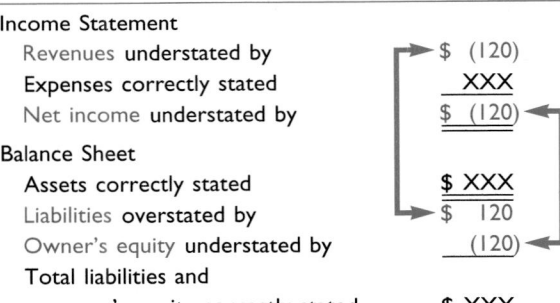

	Amount of Misstatement
Income Statement	
Revenues understated by	$ (120)
Expenses correctly stated	XXX
Net income understated by	$ (120)
Balance Sheet	
Assets correctly stated	$ XXX
Liabilities overstated by	$ 120
Owner's equity understated by	(120)
Total liabilities and	
owner's equity correctly stated	$ XXX

Accrued Expenses (Accrued Liabilities)

Some types of services, such as insurance, are normally paid for *before* they are used. These prepayments are deferrals. Other types of services are paid for *after* the service has been performed. For example, wages expense accumulates or *accrues* hour by hour and day by day, but payment may be made only weekly, biweekly, or monthly. The amount of such an accrued but unpaid item at the end of the accounting period is both an expense and a liability. In the case of wages expense, if the last day of a pay period is not the last day of the accounting period, the accrued wages expense and the related liability must be recorded in the accounts by an adjusting entry. This adjusting entry is necessary so that expenses are properly matched to the period in which they were incurred.

Callaway Golf Company, a manufacturer of such innovative golf clubs as the "Big Bertha" driver, reports accrued warranty expense on its balance sheet.

----

[2] An alternative treatment of recording revenues received in advance of their being earned is discussed in Appendix C.

At the end of December, accrued wages for Computer King were $250. This amount is an additional expense of December and is debited to the **wages expense** account. It is also a liability as of December 31 and is credited to Wages Payable. The adjusting journal entry and T accounts are shown below.

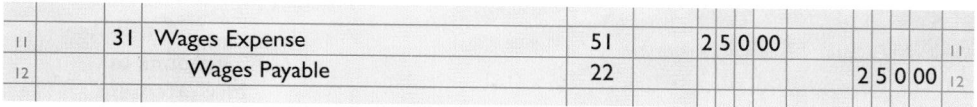

| | 31 | Wages Expense | 51 | 2 5 0 00 | | |
| 12 | | Wages Payable | 22 | | 2 5 0 00 | 12 |

Wages Expense		Wages Payable	
Bal. 4,275			Dec. 31 250
Dec. 31 250			
4,525			

After the adjustment has been recorded and posted, the debit balance of the wages expense account is $4,525, which is the wages expense for the two months, November and December. The credit balance of $250 in Wages Payable is the amount of the liability for wages owed as of December 31.

The accrual of the wages expense for Computer King is summarized in Exhibit 4. You should note that Computer King paid wages of $950 on December 13 and $1,200 on December 27. These payments covered the biweekly pay periods that ended on those days. The wages of $250 incurred for Monday and Tuesday, December 30 and 31, are accrued at December 31. The wages paid on January 10 totaled $1,275, which included the $250 accrued wages of December 31.

EXHIBIT 4
Accrued Wages

1. Wages are paid on the second and fourth Fridays for the two-week periods ending on those Fridays. The payments were $950 on December 13 and $1,200 on December 27.

2. The wages accrued for Monday and Tuesday, December 30 and 31, are $250.

3. Wages paid on Friday, January 10, total $1,275.

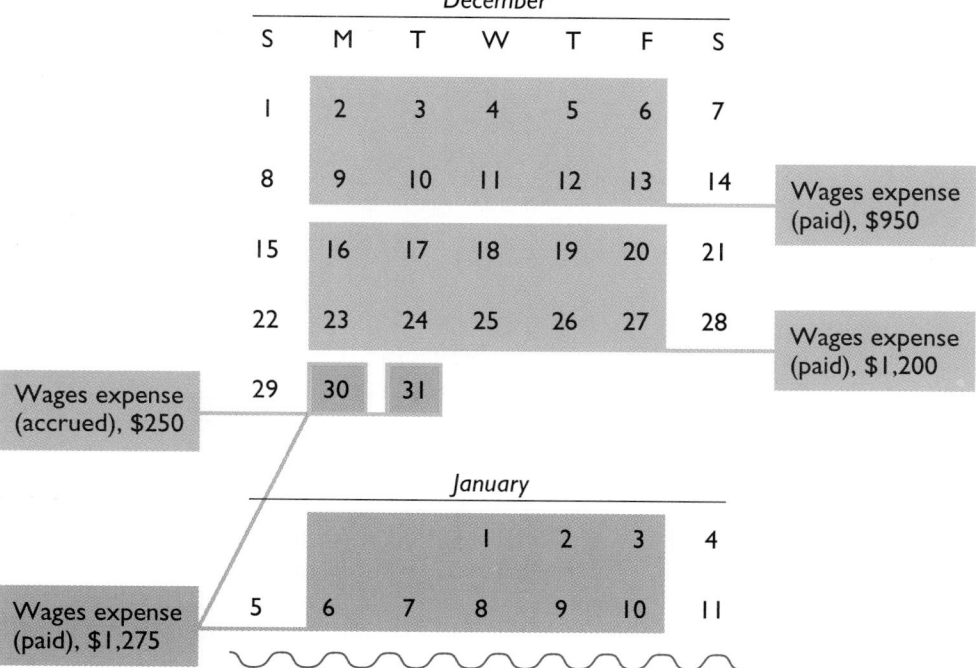

What would be the effect on the financial statements if the adjustment for wages ($250) is not recorded? On the income statement, Wages Expense will be understated by $250, and the net income will be overstated by $250. On the balance sheet, Wages Payable will be understated by $250, and Pat King, Capital will be overstated by $250. These effects of omitting the adjusting entry are shown below.

Assume that weekly wages of $1,500 are paid on Fridays. If wages are incurred evenly throughout the week, what is the accrued wages payable if the accounting period ends on a Tuesday?

$600 ($1,500/5 × 2 days)

	Amount of Misstatement
Income Statement	
Revenues correctly stated	$XXX
Expenses understated by	(250)
Net income overstated by	$ 250
Balance Sheet	
Assets correctly stated	$XXX
Liabilities understated by	$ (250)
Owner's equity overstated by	250
Total liabilities and owner's equity correctly stated	$XXX

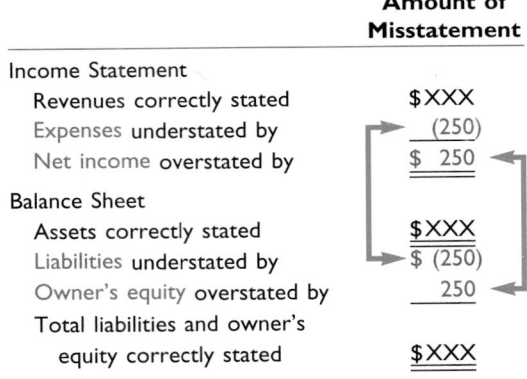

Accrued Revenues (Accrued Assets)

During an accounting period, some revenues are recorded only when cash is received. Thus, at the end of an accounting period, there may be items of revenue that have been earned *but have not been recorded*. In such cases, the amount of the revenue should be recorded by debiting an asset account and crediting a revenue account.

To illustrate, assume that Computer King signed an agreement with Dankner Co. on December 15. The agreement provides that Computer King will be on call to answer computer questions and render assistance to Dankner Co.'s employees. The services provided will be billed to Dankner Co. on the fifteenth of each month at a rate of $20 per hour. As of December 31, Computer King had provided 25 hours of assistance to Dankner Co. Although the revenue of $500 (25 hours × $20) will be billed and collected in January, Computer King earned the revenue in December. The adjusting journal entry and T accounts to record the claim against the customer (an account receivable) and the **fees earned** in December are shown below.

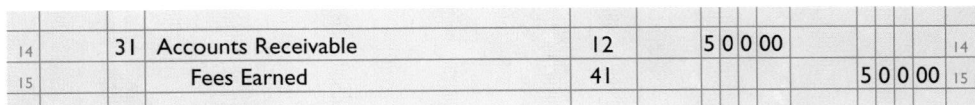

	31	Accounts Receivable	12	5 0 0 00		14
		Fees Earned	41		5 0 0 00	15

Accounts Receivable				Fees Earned	
Bal.	2,220			Bal.	16,340
Dec. 31	500			Dec. 31	500
	2,720				16,840

If the adjustment for the accrued asset ($500) is not recorded, Fees Earned and the net income will be understated by $500 on the income statement. On the balance sheet, Accounts Receivable and Pat King, Capital will be understated by $500. These effects of omitting the adjusting entry are shown below.

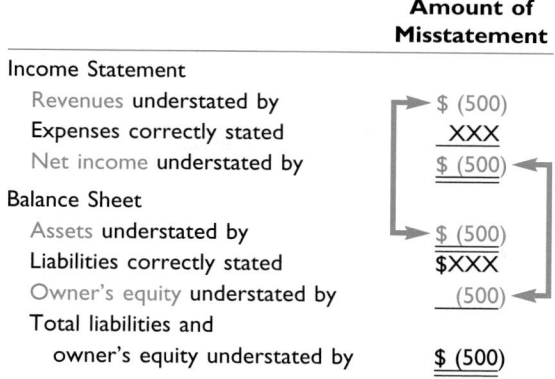

	Amount of Misstatement
Income Statement	
Revenues understated by	$ (500)
Expenses correctly stated	XXX
Net income understated by	$ (500)
Balance Sheet	
Assets understated by	$ (500)
Liabilities correctly stated	$XXX
Owner's equity understated by	(500)
Total liabilities and owner's equity understated by	$ (500)

Fixed Assets

Physical resources that are owned and used by a business and are permanent or have a long life are called **fixed assets** or **plant assets**. In a sense, fixed assets are a type of long-term deferred expense. However, because of their nature and long life, they are discussed separately from other deferred expenses, such as supplies and prepaid insurance.

Computer King's fixed assets include office equipment that is used much like the supplies are used to generate revenue. Unlike supplies, however, there is no visible reduction in the quantity of the equipment. Instead, as time passes, the equipment loses its ability to provide useful services. This decrease in usefulness is called **depreciation**.

All fixed assets, except land, lose their usefulness. Decreases in the usefulness of assets that are used in generating revenue are recorded as expenses. However, such decreases for fixed assets are difficult to measure. For this reason, a portion of the cost of a fixed asset is recorded as an expense each year of its useful life. This periodic expense is called **depreciation expense**. Methods of computing depreciation expense are discussed and illustrated in a later chapter.

The adjusting entry to record depreciation is similar to the adjusting entry for supplies used. The account debited is a depreciation expense account. However, the asset account Office Equipment is not credited because both the original cost of a fixed asset and the amount of depreciation recorded since its purchase are normally reported on the balance sheet. The account credited is an **accumulated depreciation** account. Accumulated depreciation accounts are called **contra accounts** or **contra asset accounts** because they are deducted from the related asset accounts on the balance sheet.

Normal titles for fixed asset accounts and their related contra asset accounts are as follows:

Lowe's Companies, Inc. and Subsidiaries reported land, buildings, and store equipment at a cost of over $2.3 billion and accumulated depreciation of over $460 million.

Fixed Asset	Contra Asset
Land	None—Land is not depreciated.
Buildings	Accumulated Depreciation—Buildings
Store Equipment	Accumulated Depreciation—Store Equipment
Office Equipment	Accumulated Depreciation—Office Equipment

The adjusting entry to record depreciation for December for Computer King is illustrated in the following journal entry and T accounts. The estimated amount of depreciation for the month is assumed to be $50.

		31	Depreciation Expense	53		5 0 00			17
18			Accumulated Depreciation—						18
19			Office Equipment	19			5 0 00	19

Office Equipment		**Accumulated Depreciation**	
Bal.	1,800	Dec. 31	50

	Depreciation Expense	
Dec. 31	50	

Q&A

If equipment cost $5,000 and the related accumulated depreciation is $3,000, what is the book value?

$2,000 ($5,000 − $3,000)

The $50 increase in the accumulated depreciation account is subtracted from the $1,800 cost recorded in the related fixed asset account. The difference between the two balances is the cost of $1,750 that has not yet been depreciated. This amount ($1,750) is called the **book value of the asset**, which may be presented on the balance sheet in the following manner:

Office equipment	$1,800	
Less accumulated depreciation	50	$1,750

You should note that the market value of a fixed asset normally differs from its book value. This is because depreciation is an *allocation* method, not a *valuation* method. That is, depreciation allocates the cost of a fixed asset to expense over its estimated life. Depreciation does not attempt to measure changes in market values, which may vary significantly from year to year.

If the previous adjustment for depreciation ($50) is not recorded, Depreciation Expense on the income statement will be understated by $50, and the net income will be overstated by $50. On the balance sheet, the book value of Office Equipment and Pat King, Capital will be overstated by $50. The effects of omitting the adjustment for depreciation are shown below.

	Amount of Misstatement
Income Statement	
Revenues correctly stated	$XX
Expenses understated by	(50)
Net income overstated by	$ 50
Balance Sheet	
Assets overstated by	$ 50
Liabilities correctly stated	$XX
Owner's equity overstated by	50
Total liabilities and owner's equity overstated by	$ 50

OBJECTIVE 4

Summary *of Adjustment Process*

Summarize the adjustment process and prepare an adjusted trial balance.

We have described and illustrated the basic types of adjusting entries in the preceding section. A summary of these basic adjustments, including the type of adjustment, the adjusting entry, and the effect of omitting an adjustment on the financial statements, is shown in Exhibit 5.

EXHIBIT 5   Summary of Basic Adjustments

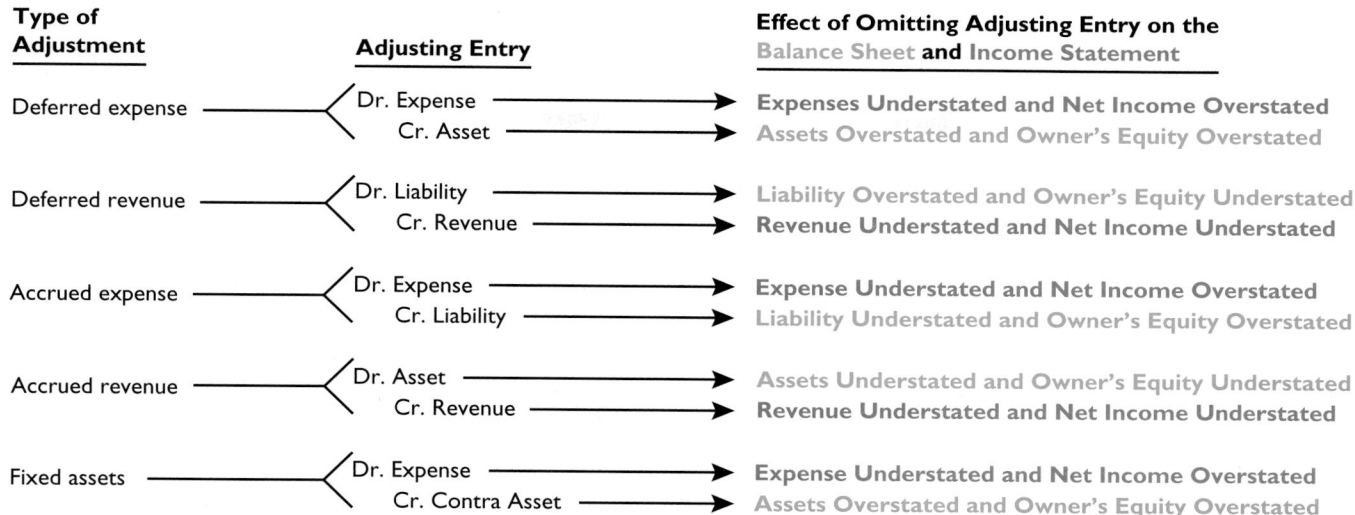

Type of Adjustment	Adjusting Entry	Effect of Omitting Adjusting Entry on the Balance Sheet and Income Statement
Deferred expense	Dr. Expense	Expenses Understated and Net Income Overstated
	Cr. Asset	Assets Overstated and Owner's Equity Overstated
Deferred revenue	Dr. Liability	Liability Overstated and Owner's Equity Understated
	Cr. Revenue	Revenue Understated and Net Income Understated
Accrued expense	Dr. Expense	Expense Understated and Net Income Overstated
	Cr. Liability	Liability Understated and Owner's Equity Overstated
Accrued revenue	Dr. Asset	Assets Understated and Owner's Equity Understated
	Cr. Revenue	Revenue Understated and Net Income Understated
Fixed assets	Dr. Expense	Expense Understated and Net Income Overstated
	Cr. Contra Asset	Assets Overstated and Owner's Equity Overstated

 *Which of the accounts—Fees Earned, Miscellaneous Expense, Cash, Wages Expense, Supplies, Accounts Receivable, Drawing, Equipment, Accumulated Depreciation—would normally require an adjusting entry?*

Fees Earned; Wages Expense; Supplies; Accounts Receivable; Accumulated Depreciation.

The adjusting entries for Computer King that we illustrated in this chapter are shown in Exhibit 6. The adjusting entries are dated as of the last day of the period, even though they are usually recorded at a later date. Each entry may be supported by an explanation, but a caption above the first adjusting entry is acceptable.

These adjusting entries have been posted to the ledger for Computer King, and are shown in color in Exhibit 7. You should note that in the posting process the Post. Ref. column of the journal indicates the account number to which the entry was posted. The corresponding Post. Ref. column of the account indicates the journal page from which the entry was posted.

EXHIBIT 6   Adjusting Entries—Computer King

	Date		Description	Post. Ref.	Debit	Credit	
1			Adjusting Entries				1
2	1999 Dec.	31	Supplies Expense	55	1 2 4 0 00		2
3			Supplies	14		1 2 4 0 00	3
4							4
5		31	Insurance Expense	56	1 0 0 00		5
6			Prepaid Insurance	15		1 0 0 00	6
7							7
8		31	Unearned Rent	23	1 2 0 00		8
9			Rent Revenue	42		1 2 0 00	9
10							10
11		31	Wages Expense	51	2 5 0 00		11
12			Wages Payable	22		2 5 0 00	12
13							13
14		31	Accounts Receivable	12	5 0 0 00		14
15			Fees Earned	41		5 0 0 00	15
16							16
17		31	Depreciation Expense	53	5 0 00		17
18			Accumulated Depreciation—				18
19			Office Equipment	19		5 0 00	19

JOURNAL   PAGE 5

EXHIBIT 7
Ledger with Adjusting Entries—Computer King

ACCOUNT *Cash*   **ACCOUNT NO. 11**

Date	Item	Post. Ref.	Debit	Credit	Balance Debit	Balance Credit
1999 Nov. 1		1	15,000		15,000	
5		1		10,000	5,000	
18		1	7,500		12,500	
30		1		3,650	8,850	
30		1		950	7,900	
30		2		2,000	5,900	
Dec. 1		2		2,400	3,500	
1		2		800	2,700	
1		2	360		3,060	
6		2		180	2,880	
11		2		400	2,480	
13		3		950	1,530	
16		3	3,100		4,630	
20		3		900	3,730	
21		3	650		4,380	
23		3		1,450	2,930	
27		3		1,200	1,730	
31		3		310	1,420	
31		4		225	1,195	
31		4	2,870		4,065	
31		4		2,000	2,065	

ACCOUNT *Accounts Receivable*   **ACCOUNT NO. 12**

Date	Item	Post. Ref.	Debit	Credit	Balance Debit	Balance Credit
1999 Dec. 16		3	1,750		1,750	
21		3		650	1,100	
31		4	1,120		2,220	
31	Adjusting	5	500		2,720	

ACCOUNT *Supplies*   **ACCOUNT NO. 14**

Date	Item	Post. Ref.	Debit	Credit	Balance Debit	Balance Credit
1999 Nov. 10		1	1,350		1,350	
30		1		800	550	
Dec. 23		3	1,450		2,000	
31	Adjusting	5		1,240	760	

ACCOUNT *Prepaid Insurance*   **ACCOUNT NO. 15**

Date	Item	Post. Ref.	Debit	Credit	Balance Debit	Balance Credit
1999 Dec. 1		2	2,400		2,400	
31	Adjusting	5		100	2,300	

ACCOUNT *Land*   **ACCOUNT NO. 17**

Date	Item	Post. Ref.	Debit	Credit	Balance Debit	Balance Credit
1999 Nov. 5		1	10,000		10,000	

ACCOUNT *Office Equipment*   **ACCOUNT NO. 18**

Date	Item	Post. Ref.	Debit	Credit	Balance Debit	Balance Credit
1999 Dec. 4		2	1,800		1,800	

ACCOUNT *Accumulated Depreciation*   **ACCOUNT NO. 19**

Date	Item	Post. Ref.	Debit	Credit	Balance Debit	Balance Credit
1999 Dec. 31	Adjusting	5		50		50

ACCOUNT *Accounts Payable*   **ACCOUNT NO. 21**

Date	Item	Post. Ref.	Debit	Credit	Balance Debit	Balance Credit
1999 Nov. 10		1		1,350		1,350
30		1	950			400
Dec. 4		2		1,800		2,200
11		2	400			1,800
20		3	900			900

ACCOUNT *Wages Payable*   **ACCOUNT NO. 22**

Date	Item	Post. Ref.	Debit	Credit	Balance Debit	Balance Credit
1999 Dec. 31	Adjusting	5		250		250

ACCOUNT *Unearned Rent*   **ACCOUNT NO. 23**

Date	Item	Post. Ref.	Debit	Credit	Balance Debit	Balance Credit
1999 Dec. 1		2		360		360
31	Adjusting	5	120			240

ACCOUNT *Pat King, Capital*   **ACCOUNT NO. 31**

Date	Item	Post. Ref.	Debit	Credit	Balance Debit	Balance Credit
1999 Nov. 1		1		15,000		15,000

ACCOUNT *Pat King, Drawing*   **ACCOUNT NO. 32**

Date	Item	Post. Ref.	Debit	Credit	Balance Debit	Balance Credit
1999 Nov. 30		2	2,000		2,000	
Dec. 31		4	2,000		4,000	

ACCOUNT *Fees Earned*   **ACCOUNT NO. 41**

Date	Item	Post. Ref.	Debit	Credit	Balance Debit	Balance Credit
1999 Nov. 18		1		7,500		7,500
Dec. 16		3		3,100		10,600
16		3		1,750		12,350
31		4		2,870		15,220
31		4		1,120		16,340
31	Adjusting	5		500		16,840

ACCOUNT *Rent Revenue*   **ACCOUNT NO. 42**

Date	Item	Post. Ref.	Debit	Credit	Balance Debit	Balance Credit
1999 Dec. 31	Adjusting	5		120		120

ACCOUNT *Wages Expense*   **ACCOUNT NO. 51**

Date	Item	Post. Ref.	Debit	Credit	Balance Debit	Balance Credit
1999 Nov. 30		1	2,125		2,125	
Dec. 13		3	950		3,075	
27		3	1,200		4,275	
31	Adjusting	5	250		4,525	

ACCOUNT *Rent Expense*   **ACCOUNT NO. 52**

Date	Item	Post. Ref.	Debit	Credit	Balance Debit	Balance Credit
1999 Nov. 30		1	800		800	
Dec. 1		2	800		1,600	

ACCOUNT *Depreciation Expense*   **ACCOUNT NO. 53**

Date	Item	Post. Ref.	Debit	Credit	Balance Debit	Balance Credit
1999 Dec. 31	Adjusting	5	50		50	

ACCOUNT *Utilities Expense*   **ACCOUNT NO. 54**

Date	Item	Post. Ref.	Debit	Credit	Balance Debit	Balance Credit
1999 Nov. 30		1	450		450	
Dec. 31		3	310		760	
31		4	225		985	

ACCOUNT *Supplies Expense*   **ACCOUNT NO. 55**

Date	Item	Post. Ref.	Debit	Credit	Balance Debit	Balance Credit
1999 Nov. 30		1	800		800	
Dec. 31	Adjusting	5	1,240		2,040	

ACCOUNT *Insurance Expense*   **ACCOUNT NO. 56**

Date	Item	Post. Ref.	Debit	Credit	Balance Debit	Balance Credit
1999 Dec. 31	Adjusting	5	100		100	

ACCOUNT *Miscellaneous Expense*   **ACCOUNT NO. 59**

Date	Item	Post. Ref.	Debit	Credit	Balance Debit	Balance Credit
1999 Nov. 30		1	275		275	
Dec. 6		2	180		455	

EXHIBIT 7
(concluded)

Point of INTEREST

One way for an accountant to check whether all adjustments have been made is to compare the current period's adjustments with those of the prior period.

After all the adjusting entries have been posted, another trial balance, called the **adjusted trial balance,** is prepared. The purpose of the adjusted trial balance is to verify the equality of the total debit balances and total credit balances before we prepare the financial statements. If the adjusted trial balance does not balance, an error has occurred. However, as we discussed in Chapter 2, errors may have occurred even though the adjusted trial balance totals agree. For example, the adjusted trial balance totals would agree if an adjusting entry has been omitted.

To highlight the effect of the adjustments on the accounts, Exhibit 8 shows the unadjusted trial balance, the accounts affected by the adjustments, and the adjusted trial balance. In Chapter 4, we discuss how financial statements, including a classified balance sheet, can be prepared from an adjusted trial balance. We also discuss

	Computer King Unadjusted Trial Balance December 31, 1999				Effect of Adjusting Entry			Computer King Adjusted Trial Balance December 31, 1999		
1	Cash	2,065		1			1	Cash	2,065		1
2	Accounts Receivable	2,220		2	+ 500		2	Accounts Receivable	2,720		2
3	Supplies	2,000		3	−1,240		3	Supplies	760		3
4	Prepaid Insurance	2,400		4	− 100		4	Prepaid Insurance	2,300		4
5	Land	10,000		5			5	Land	10,000		5
6	Office Equipment	1,800		6			6	Office Equipment	1,800		6
7	Accumulated Depreciation			7	+ 50		7	Accumulated Depreciation		50	7
8	Accounts Payable		900	8			8	Accounts Payable		900	8
9	Wages Payable			9	+ 250		9	Wages Payable		250	9
10	Unearned Rent		360	10	− 120		10	Unearned Rent		240	10
11	Pat King, Capital		15,000	11			11	Pat King, Capital		15,000	11
12	Pat King, Drawing	4,000		12			12	Pat King, Drawing	4,000		12
13	Fees Earned		16,340	13	+ 500		13	Fees Earned		16,840	13
14	Rent Revenue			14	+ 120		14	Rent Revenue		120	14
15	Wages Expense	4,275		15	+ 250		15	Wages Expense	4,525		15
16	Rent Expense	1,600		16			16	Rent Expense	1,600		16
17	Depreciation Expense			17	+ 50		17	Depreciation Expense	50		17
18	Utilities Expense	985		18			18	Utilities Expense	985		18
19	Supplies Expense	800		19	+1,240		19	Supplies Expense	2,040		19
20	Insurance Expense			20	+ 100		20	Insurance Expense	100		20
21	Miscellaneous Expense	455		21			21	Miscellaneous Expense	455		21
22		32,600	32,600	22			22		33,400	33,400	22

EXHIBIT 8
Trial Balances

the use of a work sheet as an aid to summarizing the data for preparing adjusting entries and financial statements.

FINANCIAL ANALYSIS AND INTERPRETATION

OBJECTIVE 5

Use vertical analysis to compare financial statement items with each other and with industry averages.

Comparing each item in a current statement with a total amount within that same statement can be useful in highlighting significant relationships within a financial statement. **Vertical analysis** is the term used to describe such comparisons.

In vertical analysis of a balance sheet, each asset item is stated as a percent of the total assets. Each liability and owner's equity item is stated as a percent of the total liabilities and owner's equity. In vertical analysis of an income statement, each item is stated as a percent of revenues or fees earned.

Vertical analysis may also be prepared for several periods to highlight changes in relationships over time. Vertical analysis of two years of income statements for J. Holmes, Attorney-at-Law, is shown in Exhibit 9.

Exhibit 9 indicates both favorable and unfavorable trends affecting the income statement of J. Holmes, Attorney-at-Law. The increase in wages expenses of 2% (32% − 30%) is an unfavorable trend, as is the increase in utilities expense of 0.7% (6.7% − 6.0%). A favorable trend is the decrease in supplies expense of 0.6% (2.0% − 1.4%). Rent expense and miscellaneous expense as a percent of fees earned were constant. The net result of these trends was that net income decreased as a percent of fees earned from 52.8% to 50.7%.

EXHIBIT 9
Vertical Analysis of Income
Statements

	2001		2000	
J. Holmes, Attorney-at-Law **Income Statements** **For the Years Ended December 31, 2000 and 2001**				
	Amount	Percent	Amount	Percent
Fees earned	$187,500	100.0%	$150,000	100.0%
Operating expenses:				
Wages expense	$60,000	32.0%	$45,000	30.0%
Rent expense	15,000	8.0%	12,000	8.0%
Utilities expense	12,500	6.7%	9,000	6.0%
Supplies expense	2,700	1.4%	3,000	2.0%
Miscellaneous expense	2,300	1.2%	1,800	1.2%
Total operating expenses	$92,500	49.3%	$70,800	47.2%
Net income	$95,000	50.7%	$79,200	52.8%

The analysis of the various percentages shown for J. Holmes, Attorney-at-Law, can be enhanced by comparisons with industry averages published by trade associations and financial information services. Any major differences between industry averages should be investigated.

ENCORE

Intel Corporation develops and produces microprocessors for personal computers. In the ten years ending in 1995, Intel's net revenues grew at an annual growth rate of 33%. Likewise, Intel's earnings have grown from a $195 million loss in 1986 to over $5 billion of operating income in 1995. Intel's success has been driven by its ability to design, develop, and produce newer and faster microprocessors. This ability has been a result of a strong research and development effort in which spending has increased at an annual rate of 21% over the past ten years. Intel's current microprocessor is so tiny that it would take 500 of them placed end to end to be as large as a human hair!

Intel's microprocessors have become well-known, beginning with the 8086 processor and continuing with the 286, 386, and 486 processors. Rather than name its next generation of microprocessor the 586, Intel named its new chip the "Pentium" and registered it as a trademark. This prevented Intel's competitors from selling their products as "Pentiums," which they had been able to do with the numbers 386 and 486. In addition, Intel began a promotional campaign to identify its microprocessor as unique. Intel did this by entering into a cooperative program with computer manufacturers and distributors to label personal computers with the slogan "Intel Inside" or "Pentium Inside."

Intel has been highly successful. However, technology companies such as Intel are subject to significant risks that their products will become out of date as technology changes. This is why Intel has invested so heavily in research and development over the years. In addition, Intel has the poten-tial risk for faulty product designs or production of faulty processors due to poor quality control. For example, in 1994, Intel discovered an error related to the divide function in the floating point unit of its Pentium microprocessor. This error required an adjusting entry for replacement processors and inventory write-downs, which cost Intel approximately $475 million. ■

"Intel Inside"

KEY POINTS

1 Explain how the matching concept relates to the accrual basis of accounting.

The accrual basis of accounting requires the use of an adjusting process at the end of the accounting period to match revenues and expenses properly. Revenues are reported in the period in which they are earned, and expenses are matched with the revenues they generate.

2 Explain why adjustments are necessary and list the characteristics of adjusting entries.

At the end of an accounting period, some of the amounts listed on the trial balance are not necessarily current balances. For example, amounts listed for prepaid expenses are normally overstated because the use of these assets has not been recorded on a daily basis. A delay in recognizing an expense already paid or a revenue already received is called a deferral.

Some revenues and expenses related to a period may not be recorded at the end of the period, since these items are normally recorded only when cash has been received or paid. A revenue or expense that has not been paid or recorded is called an accrual.

The entries required at the end of an accounting period to bring accounts up to date and to ensure the proper matching of revenues and expenses are called adjusting entries. Adjusting entries require a debit or a credit to a revenue or an expense account and an offsetting debit or credit to an asset or a liability account.

Adjusting entries affect amounts reported in the income statement and the balance sheet. Thus, if an adjusting entry is not recorded, these financial statements will be incorrect (misstated).

3 Journalize entries for accounts requiring adjustment.

Adjusting entries illustrated in this chapter include deferred (prepaid) expenses, deferred (unearned) revenues, accrued expenses (accrued liabilities), and accrued revenues (accrued assets). In addition, the adjusting entry necessary to record depreciation on fixed assets was illustrated.

4 Summarize the adjustment process and prepare an adjusted trial balance.

A summary of adjustments, including the type of adjustment, the adjusting entry, and the effect of omitting an adjustment on the financial statements, is shown in Exhibit 5. After all the adjusting entries have been posted, the equality of the total debit balances and total credit balances is verified by an adjusted trial balance.

5 Use vertical analysis to compare financial statement items with each other and with industry averages.

Comparing each item in a current statement with a total amount within the same statement is called vertical analysis. In vertical analysis of a balance sheet, each asset item is stated as a percent of the total assets. Each liability and owner's equity item is stated as a percent of the total liabilities and owner's equity. In vertical analysis of an income statement, each item is stated as a percent of revenues or fees earned.

ILLUSTRATIVE PROBLEM

Three years ago, T. Roderick organized Harbor Realty. At July 31, 2000, the end of the current year, the unadjusted trial balance of Harbor Realty appears as shown at the top of the following page. The data needed to determine year-end adjustments are as follows:

a.   Supplies on hand at July 31, 2000, $380.
b.   Insurance premiums expired during the year, $315.
c.   Depreciation of equipment during the year, $4,950.
d.   Wages accrued but not paid at July 31, 2000, $440.
e.   Accrued fees earned but not recorded at July 31, 2000, $1,000.
f.   Unearned fees on July 31, 2000, $750.

Harbor Realty
Trial Balance
July 31, 2000

	Debit	Credit
Cash	3 4 2 5 00	
Accounts Receivable	7 0 0 0 00	
Supplies	1 2 7 0 00	
Prepaid Insurance	6 2 0 00	
Office Equipment	51 6 5 0 00	
Accumulated Depreciation		9 7 0 0 00
Accounts Payable		9 2 5 00
Wages Payable		0 00
Unearned Fees		1 2 5 0 00
T. Roderick, Capital		29 0 0 0 00
T. Roderick, Drawing	5 2 0 0 00	
Fees Earned		59 1 2 5 00
Wages Expense	22 4 1 5 00	
Depreciation Expense	0 00	
Rent Expense	4 2 0 0 00	
Utilities Expense	2 7 1 5 00	
Supplies Expense	0 00	
Insurance Expense	0 00	
Miscellaneous Expense	1 5 0 5 00	
	100 0 0 0 00	100 0 0 0 00

Instructions

1. Prepare the necessary adjusting journal entries.
2. Determine the balance of the accounts affected by the adjusting entries and prepare an adjusted trial balance.

Solution

1.

JOURNAL

	Date		Description	Post. Ref.	Debit	Credit	
1	2000 July	31	Supplies Expense		8 9 0 00		1
2			Supplies			8 9 0 00	2
3							3
4		31	Insurance Expense		3 1 5 00		4
5			Prepaid Insurance			3 1 5 00	5
6							6
7		31	Depreciation Expense		4 9 5 0 00		7
8			Accumulated Depreciation			4 9 5 0 00	8
9							9
10		31	Wages Expense		4 4 0 00		10
11			Wages Payable			4 4 0 00	11
12							12
13		31	Accounts Receivable		1 0 0 0 00		13
14			Fees Earned			1 0 0 0 00	14
15							15
16		31	Unearned Fees		5 0 0 00		16
17			Fees Earned			5 0 0 00	17

2.

Harbor Realty Adjusted Trial Balance July 31, 2000		
Cash	3 4 2 5 00	
Accounts Receivable	8 0 0 0 00	
Supplies	3 8 0 00	
Prepaid Insurance	3 0 5 00	
Office Equipment	51 6 5 0 00	
Accumulated Depreciation		14 6 5 0 00
Accounts Payable		9 2 5 00
Wages Payable		4 4 0 00
Unearned Fees		7 5 0 00
T. Roderick, Capital		29 0 0 0 00
T. Roderick, Drawing	5 2 0 0 00	
Fees Earned		60 6 2 5 00
Wages Expense	22 8 5 5 00	
Depreciation Expense	4 9 5 0 00	
Rent Expense	4 2 0 0 00	
Utilities Expense	2 7 1 5 00	
Supplies Expense	8 9 0 00	
Insurance Expense	3 1 5 00	
Miscellaneous Expense	1 5 0 5 00	
	106 3 9 0 00	106 3 9 0 00

SELF-EXAMINATION QUESTIONS   Answers at End of Chapter

Matching

Match each of the following statements with its proper term. Some terms may not be used.

A.	**accounting period concept**
B.	**accrual basis**
C.	**accrued expenses**
D.	**accrued revenues**
E.	**accumulated depreciation**
F.	**adjusted trial balance**
G.	**adjusting entries**
H.	**adjusting process**
I.	**book value of the asset**
J.	**cash basis**
K.	**closing entries**
L.	**contra account**
M.	**deferred expenses**
N.	**deferred revenues**
O.	**depreciation**

___ 1. The accounting concept that assumes that the economic life of the business can be divided into time periods.

___ 2. Under this basis of accounting, revenues and expenses are reported in the income statement in the period in which cash is received or paid.

___ 3. Under this basis of accounting, revenues are reported in the income statement in the period in which they are earned.

___ 4. The accounting concept that supports reporting revenues when the services are provided to customers.

___ 5. The accounting concept that supports reporting revenues and the related expenses in the same period.

___ 6. An analysis and updating of the accounts when financial statements are prepared.

___ 7. The journal entries that bring the accounts up to date at the end of the accounting period.

___ 8. Items that have been initially recorded as assets but are expected to become expenses over time or through the normal operations of the business.

___ 9. Items that have been initially recorded as liabilities but are expected to become revenues over time or through the normal operations of the business.

___ 10. Expenses that have been incurred *but not recorded* in the accounts.

P.	**depreciation expense**
Q.	**final trial balance**
R.	**fixed assets**
S.	**horizontal analysis**
T.	**matching concept**
U.	**objectivity concept**
V.	**post-closing trial balance**
W.	**revenue recognition concept**
X.	**vertical analysis**

___ 11. Revenues that have been earned *but not recorded* in the accounts.

___ 12. Physical resources that are owned and used by a business and are permanent or have a long life.

___ 13. The decrease in the ability of a fixed asset to provide useful services.

___ 14. The portion of the cost of a fixed asset that is recorded as an expense each year of its useful life.

___ 15. The asset account credited when recording the depreciation of a fixed asset.

___ 16. The difference between the cost of a fixed asset and its accumulated depreciation.

___ 17. The trial balance prepared after all the adjusting entries have been posted.

___ 18. An analysis that compares each item in a current statement with a total amount within the same statement.

___ 19. An account offset against another account.

Multiple Choice

1. Which of the following items represents a deferral?
   A. Prepaid insurance
   B. Wages payable
   C. Fees earned
   D. Accumulated depreciation

2. If the supplies account, before adjustment on May 31, indicated a balance of $2,250, and supplies on hand at May 31 totaled $950, the adjusting entry would be:
   A. debit Supplies, $950; credit Supplies Expense, $950
   B. debit Supplies, $1,300; credit Supplies Expense, $1,300
   C. debit Supplies Expense, $950; credit Supplies, $950
   D. debit Supplies Expense, $1,300; credit Supplies, $1,300

3. The balance in the unearned rent account for Jones Co. as of December 31 is $1,200. If Jones Co. failed to record the adjusting entry for $600 of rent earned during December, the effect on the balance sheet and income statement for December is:
   A. assets understated $600; net income overstated $600

   B. liabilities understated $600; net income understated $600
   C. liabilities overstated $600; net income understated $600
   D. liabilities overstated $600; net income overstated $600

4. If the estimated amount of depreciation on equipment for a period is $2,000, the adjusting entry to record depreciation would be:
   A. debit Depreciation Expense, $2,000; credit Equipment, $2,000
   B. debit Equipment, $2,000; credit Depreciation Expense, $2,000
   C. debit Depreciation Expense, $2,000; credit Accumulated Depreciation, $2,000
   D. debit Accumulated Depreciation, $2,000; credit Depreciation Expense, $2,000

5. If the equipment account has a balance of $22,500 and its accumulated depreciation account has a balance of $14,000, the book value of the equipment is:
   A. $36,500   C. $14,000
   B. $22,500   D. $8,500

CLASS DISCUSSION QUESTIONS

1. How are revenues and expenses reported on the income statement under (a) the cash basis of accounting and (b) the accrual basis of accounting?
2. Fees for services provided are billed to a customer during 1999. The customer remits the amount owed in 2000. During which year would the revenues be reported on the income statement under (a) the cash basis? (b) the accrual basis?
3. Employees performed services in 1999, but the wages were not paid until 2000. During which year would the wages expense be reported on the income statement under (a) the cash basis? (b) the accrual basis?
4. Is the matching concept related to (a) the cash basis of accounting or (b) the accrual basis of accounting?
5. Is the balance listed for cash on the trial balance, before the accounts have been adjusted, the amount that should normally be reported on the balance sheet? Explain.

6. Is the balance listed for supplies on the trial balance, before the accounts have been adjusted, the amount that should normally be reported on the balance sheet? Explain.
7. Why are adjusting entries needed at the end of an accounting period?
8. Are adjusting entries in the journal dated as of the last day of the fiscal period or as of the day the entries are actually made? Explain.
9. What is the difference between *adjusting entries* and *correcting entries?*
10. Identify the five different categories of adjusting entries frequently required at the end of an accounting period.
11. If the effect of the credit portion of an adjusting entry is to increase the balance of a liability account, which of the following statements describes the effect of the debit portion of the entry?
    a. Increases the balance of a revenue account.
    b. Increases the balance of an expense account.
    c. Increases the balance of an asset account.
12. Does every adjusting entry have an effect on determining the amount of net income for a period? Explain.
13. What is the nature of the balance in the prepaid insurance account at the end of the accounting period (a) before adjustment? (b) after adjustment?
14. On May 1 of the current year, a business paid the May rent on the building that it occupies. (a) Do the rights acquired at May 1 represent an asset or an expense? (b) What is the justification for debiting Rent Expense at the time of payment?
15. In accounting for depreciation on equipment, what is the name of the contra asset account?
16. (a) Explain the purpose of the two accounts: Depreciation Expense and Accumulated Depreciation. (b) What is the normal balance of each account? (c) Is it customary for the balances of the two accounts to be equal in amount? (d) In what financial statements, if any, will each account appear?

Resources for Your Success On-Line at warren.swcollege.com
Remember! If you need additional help, visit South-Western's Web site. See page 26 for a description of the online and printed materials that are available.

EXERCISES

Exercise 3–1
Classify accruals and deferrals

Objectives 2, 3

Classify the following items as (a) deferred expense (prepaid expense), (b) deferred revenue (unearned revenue), (c) accrued expense (accrued liability), or (d) accrued revenue (accrued asset).

1. Supplies on hand.
2. Fees received but not yet earned.
3. Utilities owed but not yet paid.
4. A two-year premium paid on a fire insurance policy.
5. Fees earned but not yet received.
6. Taxes owed but payable in the following period.
7. Salary owed but not yet paid.
8. Subscriptions received in advance by a magazine.

Exercise 3–2
Classify adjusting entries

Objectives 2, 3

The following accounts were taken from the unadjusted trial balance of O'Dell Co., a congressional lobbying firm. Indicate whether or not each account would normally require an adjusting entry. If the account normally requires an adjusting entry, use the following notation to indicate the type of adjustment:

AE—Accrued Expense
AR—Accrued Revenue
DR—Deferred Revenue
DE—Deferred Expense

To illustrate, the answers for the first two accounts are shown below:

Account	Answer
George Lee, Drawing	Does not normally require adjustment.
Accounts Receivable	Normally requires adjustment (AR).
Accumulated Depreciation	
Cash	
Interest Payable	
Interest Receivable	
Land	
Office Equipment	
Prepaid Insurance	
Supplies Expense	
Unearned Fees	
Wages Expense	

Exercise 3–3
Adjusting entry for supplies

Objective 3

✓ Amount of entry: $1,445

The balance in the supplies account, before adjustment at the end of the year, is $1,820. Journalize the adjusting entry required if the amount of supplies on hand at the end of the year is $375.

Exercise 3–4
Determine supplies purchased

Objective 3

✓ $1,300

The supplies and supplies expense accounts at December 31, after adjusting entries have been posted at the end of the first year of operations, are shown in the following T accounts:

Supplies			Supplies Expense		
Bal.	280		Bal.	1,020	

Determine the amount of supplies purchased during the year.

Exercise 3–5
Effect of omitting adjusting entry

Objective 3

At December 31, the end of the first month of operations, the usual adjusting entry transferring supplies used to an expense account is omitted. Which items will be incorrectly stated, because of the error, on (a) the income statement for December and (b) the balance sheet as of December 31? Also indicate whether the items in error will be overstated or understated.

Exercise 3–6
Adjusting entries for prepaid insurance

Objective 3

✓ Amount of entry: $1,140

The balance in the prepaid insurance account, before adjustment at the end of the year, is $3,780. Journalize the adjusting entry required under each of the following *alternatives* for determining the amount of the adjustment: (a) the amount of insurance expired during the year is $1,140; (b) the amount of unexpired insurance applicable to future periods is $2,640.

Exercise 3–7
Adjusting entries for prepaid insurance

Objective 3

✓ a. Amount of entry: $1,400

The prepaid insurance account had a balance of $2,400 at the beginning of the year. The account was debited for $1,800 for premiums on policies purchased during the year. Journalize the adjusting entry required at the end of the year for each of the following situations: (a) the amount of unexpired insurance applicable to future periods is $2,800; (b) the amount of insurance expired during the year is $1,650.

Exercise 3–8
Adjusting entries for unearned fees

Objective 3

✓ Amount of entry: $5,500

The balance in the unearned fees account, before adjustment at the end of the year, is $7,000. Journalize the adjusting entry required if the amount of unearned fees at the end of the year is $1,500.

Exercise 3–9
Effect of omitting adjusting entry

Objective 3

At the end of January, the first month of the year, the usual adjusting entry transferring rent earned to a revenue account from the unearned rent account was omitted. Indicate which items will be incorrectly stated, because of the error, on (a) the income statement for January and (b) the balance sheet as of January 31. Also indicate whether the items in error will be overstated or understated.

Exercise 3–10
Adjusting entries for accrued salaries

Objective 3

✓ a. $4,200

River Realty Co. pays weekly salaries of $10,500 on Friday for a five-day week ending on that day. Journalize the necessary adjusting entry at the end of the accounting period, assuming that the period ends (a) on Tuesday, (b) on Wednesday.

Exercise 3–11
Determine wages paid

Objective 3

✓ $52,520

The wages payable and wages expense accounts at December 31, after adjusting entries have been posted at the end of the first year of operations, are shown in the following T accounts:

Wages Payable			**Wages Expense**		
	Bal.	1,010	Bal.	53,530	

Determine the amount of wages paid during the year.

Exercise 3–12
Effect of omitting adjusting entry

Objective 3

Accrued salaries of $2,500 owed to employees for December 30 and 31 are not considered in preparing the financial statements for the year ended December 31. Indicate which items will be erroneously stated, because of the error, on (a) the income statement for the year and (b) the balance sheet as of December 31. Also indicate whether the items in error will be overstated or understated.

Exercise 3–13
Effect of omitting adjusting entry

Objective 3

Assume that the error in Exercise 3–12 was not corrected and that the $2,500 of accrued salaries was included in the first salary payment in January. Indicate which items will be erroneously stated, because of failure to correct the initial error, on (a) the income statement for the month of January and (b) the balance sheet as of January 31.

Exercise 3–14
Adjusting entries for prepaid and accrued taxes

Objective 3

✓ b. $8,572

Edwards Financial Planning Co. was organized on April 1 of the current year. On April 2, Edwards prepaid $1,296 to the city for taxes (license fees) for the *next* 12 months and debited the prepaid taxes account. Edwards is also required to pay in January an annual tax (on property) for the *previous* calendar year. The estimated amount of the property tax for the current year (April 1 to December 31) is $7,600. (a) Journalize the two adjusting entries required to bring the accounts affected by the two taxes up to date as of December 31, the end of the current year. (b) What is the amount of tax expense for the current year?

Exercise 3–15

Effects of errors on financial statements

Objective 3

✓ a. $534,000,000

The balance sheet for **The Quaker Oats Company** as of December 31, 1996, includes the following accrued expenses as liabilities:

Accrued payroll, benefits, bonus	$111,300,000
Accrued advertising and merchandising	130,200,000
Other accrued liabilities	292,500,000

The net income for The Quaker Oats Company for the year ended December 31, 1996, was $247,900,000. (a) If the accruals had not been recorded at December 31, 1996, by how much would net income have been misstated for the fiscal year ended December 31, 1996? (b) What is the percentage of the misstatement in (a) to the reported net income of $247,900,000?

Exercise 3–16

Effects of errors on financial statements

Objective 3

✓ 1. Revenue understated, $6,800

The accountant for Baskin Medical Co., a medical services consulting firm, mistakenly omitted adjusting entries for (a) unearned revenue ($6,800) and (b) accrued wages ($1,050). Indicate the effect of each error, considered individually, on the income statement for the current year ended December 31. Also indicate the effect of each error on the December 31 balance sheet. Set up a table similar to the following, and record your answers by inserting the dollar amount in the appropriate spaces. Insert a zero if the error does not affect the item.

	Error (a)		Error (b)	
	Over-stated	Under-stated	Over-stated	Under-stated
1. Revenue for the year would be	$	$	$	$
2. Expenses for the year would be	$	$	$	$
3. Net income for the year would be	$	$	$	$
4. Assets at December 31 would be	$	$	$	$
5. Liabilities at December 31 would be	$	$	$	$
6. Owner's equity at December 31 would be	$	$	$	$

Exercise 3–17

Effects of errors on financial statements

Objective 3

✓ $121,050

If the net income for the current year had been $115,300 in Exercise 3–16, what would be the correct net income if the proper adjusting entries had been made?

Exercise 3–18

Adjusting entry for accrued fees

Objective 3

At the end of the current year, $3,390 of fees have been earned but have not been billed to clients.

a. Journalize the adjusting entry to record the accrued fees.

b. ◄▬▬► If the cash basis rather than the accrual basis had been used, would an adjusting entry have been necessary? Explain.

Exercise 3–19

Adjusting entries for unearned and accrued fees

Objective 3

The balance in the unearned fees account, before adjustment at the end of the year, is $31,700. Of these fees, $21,500 have been earned. In addition, $9,100 of fees have been earned but have not been billed. Journalize the adjusting entries (a) to adjust the unearned fees account and (b) to record the accrued fees.

Exercise 3–20

Effect on financial statements of omitting adjusting entry

Objective 3

The adjusting entry for accrued fees was omitted at December 31, the end of the current year. Indicate which items will be in error, because of the omission, on (a) the income statement for the current year and (b) the balance sheet as of December 31. Also indicate whether the items in error will be overstated or understated.

Exercise 3–21
Adjusting entry for depreciation

Objective 3

The estimated amount of depreciation on equipment for the current year is $4,400. Journalize the adjusting entry to record the depreciation.

Exercise 3–22
Determine fixed asset's book value

Objective 3

✓ a. $263,800

The balance in the equipment account is $379,200, and the balance in the accumulated depreciation—equipment account is $115,400.

a.   What is the book value of the equipment?
b.   ◄█████► Does the balance in the accumulated depreciation account mean that the equipment's loss of value is $115,400? Explain.

Exercise 3–23
Book value of fixed assets

Objective 3

Microsoft Corporation reported *Property, Plant, and Equipment* of $2,777 million and *Accumulated Depreciation* of $1,312 million at June 30, 1997.

a.   What was the book value of the fixed assets at June 30, 1997?
b.   ◄█████► Would the book value of Microsoft Corporation's fixed assets normally approximate their fair market values?

Exercise 3–24
Adjusting entries for depreciation; effect of error

Objective 3

On December 31, a business estimates depreciation on equipment used during the first year of operations to be $4,300. (a) Journalize the adjusting entry required as of December 31. (b) If the adjusting entry in (a) were omitted, which items would be erroneously stated on (1) the income statement for the year and (2) the balance sheet as of December 31?

Exercise 3–25
Adjusting entries from trial balances

Objectives 3, 4

The unadjusted and adjusted trial balances for Surgical Services Co. on December 31, 1999, are shown below.

Surgical Services Co.
Trial Balance
December 31, 1999

	Unadjusted		Adjusted	
Cash	6		6	
Accounts Receivable	18		21	
Supplies	6		2	
Prepaid Insurance	10		6	
Land	12		12	
Equipment	20		20	
Accumulated Depr.—Equip.		3		5
Accounts Payable		13		13
Wages Payable		0		1
Randy Reese, Capital		44		44
Randy Reese, Drawing	4		4	
Fees Earned		36		39
Wages Expense	12		13	
Rent Expense	4		4	
Insurance Expense	0		4	
Utilities Expense	2		2	
Depreciation Expense	0		2	
Supplies Expense	0		4	
Miscellaneous Expense	2		2	
Totals	96	96	102	102

Journalize the five entries that adjusted the accounts at December 31, 1999. None of the accounts were affected by more than one adjusting entry.

Exercise 3–26

Adjusting entries from trial balances

Objective 3, 4

What's Wrong WITH THIS?

✓ Corrected trial balance totals, $177,520

The accountant for Homestead Laundry prepared the following unadjusted and adjusted trial balances. Assume that all balances in the unadjusted trial balance and the amounts of the adjustments are correct. How many errors can you find in the accountant's adjusting entries?

Homestead Laundry
Trial Balance
August 31, 1999

	Unadjusted		Adjusted	
Cash	7,790		7,790	
Accounts Receivable	10,000		12,500	
Laundry Supplies	4,750		8,660	
Prepaid Insurance*	2,825		1,325	
Laundry Equipment	85,600		79,880	
Accumulated Depreciation		55,700		55,700
Accounts Payable		4,950		5,800
Wages Payable				850
Kim Momin, Capital		30,900		30,900
Kim Momin, Drawing	8,000		8,000	
Laundry Revenue		76,900		76,900
Wages Expense	24,500		24,500	
Rent Expense	15,575		15,575	
Utilities Expense	8,500		8,500	
Depreciation Expense			5,720	
Laundry Supplies Expense			3,910	
Insurance Expense			500	
Miscellaneous Expense	910		910	
	168,450	168,450	177,770	170,150

*$1,500 of insurance expired during the year.

Exercise 3–27

Vertical analysis of income statement

Objective 5

REAL WORLD

The financial statements for **Hershey Foods Corporation** are presented in Appendix G at the end of the text.

a. Determine for Hershey Foods Corporation:
   1. The amount of the change and percent of change in net income for the year ended December 31, 1996.
   2. The percentage relationship between net income and net sales (net income divided by net sales) for the years ended December 31, 1996 and 1995.
b. ▬▬▬▶ What conclusions can you draw from your analysis?

PROBLEMS SERIES A

Problem 3–1A

Adjusting entries

Objective 3

HAT

On December 31, the end of the current year, the following data were accumulated to assist the accountant in preparing the adjusting entries for Lakeview Realty:

a. Fees accrued but unbilled at December 31 are $3,750.
b. The supplies account balance on December 31 is $3,100. The supplies on hand at December 31 are $720.
c. Wages accrued but not paid at December 31 are $1,100.
d. The unearned rent account balance at December 31 is $4,800, representing the receipt of an advance payment on December 1 of four months' rent from tenants.
e. Depreciation of office equipment for the year is $2,100.

Instructions

1. Journalize the adjusting entries required at December 31.
2. 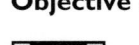► Briefly explain the difference between adjusting entries and entries that would be made to correct errors.

Problem 3–2A
Adjusting entries
Objective 3

HAT

Selected account balances before adjustment for Claremont Realty at October 31, the end of the current year, are as follows:

	Debits	Credits		Debits	Credits
Accounts Receivable	$ 9,250		Unearned Fees		$ 6,500
Supplies	2,700		Fees Earned		99,850
Prepaid Rent	21,000		Wages Expense	$40,750	
Equipment	50,500		Rent Expense	—	
Accumulated Depreciation		$16,900	Depreciation Expense	—	
Wages Payable		—	Supplies Expense	—	

Data needed for year-end adjustments are as follows:

a. Supplies on hand at Oct. 31, $1,030.
b. Depreciation of equipment during year, $1,800.
c. Rent expired during year, $18,000.
d. Wages accrued but not paid at Oct. 31, $990.
e. Unearned fees at Oct. 31, $2,500.
f. Unbilled fees at Oct. 31, $6,790.

Instructions

Journalize the six adjusting entries required at October 31, based upon the data presented.

Problem 3–3A
Adjusting entries
Objectives 3, 4

SPREADSHEET

Shelby Company specializes in the maintenance and repair of signs, such as billboards. On August 31, the end of the current year, the accountant for Shelby Company prepared a trial balance and an adjusted trial balance. The two trial balances are as follows:

Shelby Company
Trial Balance
August 31, 20—

	Unadjusted		Adjusted	
Cash	9,750		9,750	
Accounts Receivable	20,400		20,400	
Supplies	7,880		2,030	
Prepaid Insurance	2,700		1,100	
Land	47,500		47,500	
Buildings	107,480		107,480	
Accumulated Depreciation—Buildings		79,600		85,100
Trucks	72,000		72,000	
Accumulated Depreciation—Trucks		32,800		43,900
Accounts Payable		8,920		9,720
Salaries Payable		—		1,300
Unearned Service Fees		7,500		1,500
Angela Scanlon, Capital		93,890		93,890
Angela Scanlon, Drawing	8,000		8,000	
Service Fees Earned		152,680		158,680
Salary Expense	81,200		82,500	
Depreciation Expense—Trucks	—		11,100	
Rent Expense	9,600		9,600	
Supplies Expense	—		5,850	
Utilities Expense	6,200		7,000	
Depreciation Expense—Buildings	—		5,500	
Taxes Expense	1,720		1,720	
Insurance Expense	—		1,600	
Miscellaneous Expense	960		960	
	375,390	375,390	394,090	394,090

Instructions

Journalize the seven entries that adjusted the accounts at August 31. None of the accounts were affected by more than one adjusting entry.

Problem 3–4A

Adjusting entries

Objective 3

HAT

GENERAL LEDGER

Rainbow Trout Co., an outfitter store for fishing treks, prepared the following trial balance at the end of its first year of operations:

Rainbow Trout Co.
Trial Balance
April 30, 20—

Cash	1,150	
Accounts Receivable	3,500	
Supplies	1,300	
Equipment	9,900	
Accounts Payable		750
Unearned Fees		2,000
Lee Wulff, Capital		10,500
Lee Wulff, Drawing	1,000	
Fees Earned		36,750
Wages Expense	19,500	
Rent Expense	9,000	
Utilities Expense	3,750	
Miscellaneous Expense	900	
	50,000	50,000

For preparing the adjusting entries, the following data were assembled:

a.   Supplies on hand on April 30 were $175.
b.   Fees earned but unbilled on April 30 were $1,380.
c.   Depreciation of equipment was estimated to be $800 for the year.
d.   Unpaid wages accrued on April 30 were $450.
e.   The balance in unearned fees represented the Jan. 1 receipt in advance for services to be provided. Only $750 of the services were provided between Jan. 1 and April 30.

Instructions

Journalize the adjusting entries necessary on April 30.

Problem 3–5A

Adjusting entries and
adjusted trial balances

Objectives 3, 4

HAT

SPREADSHEET

GENERAL LEDGER

✓ 2. Total of Debit Column:
$469,900

Atwater Service Co., which specializes in appliance repair services, is owned and operated by Carri Atwater. Atwater Service Co.'s accounting clerk prepared the following trial balance at December 31, the end of the current year:

Atwater Service Co.
Trial Balance
December 31, 20—

Cash	3,200	
Accounts Receivable	17,200	
Prepaid Insurance	3,900	
Supplies	2,450	
Land	50,000	
Building	141,500	
Accumulated Depreciation—Building		95,700
Equipment	90,100	
Accumulated Depreciation—Equipment		65,300
Accounts Payable		7,500
Unearned Rent		4,000
Carri Atwater, Capital		65,900
Carri Atwater, Drawing	5,000	
Fees Earned		218,400
Salaries and Wages Expense	78,700	
Utilities Expense	28,200	
Advertising Expense	19,000	
Repairs Expense	13,500	
Miscellaneous Expense	4,050	
	456,800	456,800

The data needed to determine year-end adjustments are as follows:

a. Depreciation of building for the year, $1,500.
b. Depreciation of equipment for the year, $5,500.
c. Accrued salaries and wages at December 31, $1,150.
d. Unexpired insurance at December 31, $1,100.
e. Fees earned but unbilled on December 31, $4,950.
f. Supplies on hand at December 31, $500.
g. Rent unearned at December 31, $1,500.

Instructions

1. Journalize the adjusting entries. Add additional accounts as needed.
2. Determine the balances of the accounts affected by the adjusting entries and prepare an adjusted trial balance.

Problem 3–6A

Adjusting entries and errors

Objective 3

✓ Corrected Net Income:

$222,350

At the end of July, the first month of operations, the following selected data were taken from the financial statements of John Stuedemann, III, an attorney:

Net income for July	$213,500
Total assets at July 31	177,250
Total liabilities at July 31	36,500
Total owner's equity at July 31	140,750

In preparing the financial statements, adjustments for the following data were overlooked:

a. Unbilled fees earned at July 31, $16,900.
b. Depreciation of equipment for July, $4,000.
c. Accrued wages at July 31, $1,100.
d. Supplies used during July, $2,950.

Instructions

1. Journalize the entries to record the omitted adjustments.
2. Determine the correct amount of net income for July and the total assets, liabilities, and owner's equity at July 31. In addition to indicating the corrected amounts, indicate the effect of each omitted adjustment by setting up and completing a columnar table similar to the following. Adjustment (a) is presented as an example.

	Net Income	Total Assets	Total Liabilities	Total Owner's Equity
Reported amounts	$213,500	$177,250	$36,500	$140,750
Corrections:				
Adjustment (a)	+16,900	+16,900	0	+16,900
Adjustment (b)	_____	_____	_____	_____
Adjustment (c)	_____	_____	_____	_____
Adjustment (d)	_____	_____	_____	_____
Corrected amounts	_____	_____	_____	_____

PROBLEMS SERIES B

Problem 3–1B

Adjusting entries

Objective 3

On December 31, the end of the current year, the following data were accumulated to assist the accountant in preparing the adjusting entries for Simkin Realty:

a. The supplies account balance on December 31 is $1,450. The supplies on hand on December 31 are $315.
b. The unearned rent account balance on December 31 is $3,600, representing the receipt of an advance payment on December 1 of three months' rent from tenants.
c. Wages accrued but not paid at December 31 are $850.

d. Fees accrued but unbilled at December 31 are $11,500.
e. Depreciation of office equipment for the year is $1,500.

Instructions

1. Journalize the adjusting entries required at December 31.
2. ◀▬ Briefly explain the difference between adjusting entries and entries that would be made to correct errors.

Problem 3–2B
Adjusting entries

Objective 3

Selected account balances before adjustment for Ocean City Realty at December 31, the end of the current year, are as follows:

	Debits	Credits		Debits	Credits
Accounts Receivable	$11,250		Unearned Fees		$ 5,000
Supplies	4,750		Fees Earned		87,950
Prepaid Rent	27,000		Wages Expense	$29,400	
Equipment	42,500		Rent Expense	—	
Accumulated Depreciation		$10,900	Depreciation Expense	—	
Wages Payable		—	Supplies Expense	—	

Data needed for year-end adjustments are as follows:

a. Unbilled fees at December 31, $4,150.
b. Supplies on hand at December 31, $980.
c. Rent expired during year, $24,000.
d. Depreciation of equipment during year, $3,050.
e. Unearned fees at December 31, $3,750.
f. Wages accrued but not paid at December 31, $920.

Instructions

Journalize the six adjusting entries required at December 31, based upon the data presented.

Problem 3–3B
Adjusting entries

Objectives 3, 4

SPREADSHEET

Somerset Company specializes in the repair of music equipment and is owned and operated by Deana Perot. On April 30, 2000, the end of the current year, the accountant for Somerset Company prepared a trial balance and an adjusted trial balance. The two trial balances are as follows:

Somerset Company
Trial Balance
April 30, 2000

	Unadjusted		Adjusted	
Cash	11,825		11,825	
Accounts Receivable	29,500		29,500	
Supplies	6,950		1,340	
Prepaid Insurance	3,750		2,500	
Equipment	92,150		92,150	
Accumulated Depreciation—Equipment		53,480		61,270
Automobiles	36,500		36,500	
Accumulated Depreciation—Automobiles		18,250		22,900
Accounts Payable		8,310		9,890
Salaries Payable		—		1,800
Unearned Service Fees		5,000		2,500
Deana Perot, Capital		55,470		55,470
Deana Perot, Drawing	5,000		5,000	
Service Fees Earned		244,600		247,100
Salary Expense	172,300		174,100	
Rent Expense	18,000		18,000	
Supplies Expense	—		5,610	
Depreciation Expense—Equipment	—		7,790	
Depreciation Expense—Automobiles ...	—		4,650	
Utilities Expense	4,700		6,280	
Taxes Expense	2,725		2,725	
Insurance Expense	—		1,250	
Miscellaneous Expense	1,710		1,710	
	385,110	385,110	400,930	400,930

Instructions

Journalize the seven entries that adjusted the accounts at April 30. None of the accounts were affected by more than one adjusting entry.

Problem 3–4B

Adjusting entries

Objective 3

GENERAL LEDGER

Icarus Company, an electronics repair store, prepared the following trial balance at the end of its first year of operations:

Icarus Company
Trial Balance
June 30, 20—

Cash	1,150	
Accounts Receivable	5,500	
Supplies	1,800	
Equipment	17,900	
Accounts Payable		750
Unearned Fees		2,000
Sonja Ash, Capital		10,000
Sonja Ash, Drawing	1,500	
Fees Earned		35,250
Wages Expense	8,500	
Rent Expense	8,000	
Utilities Expense	2,750	
Miscellaneous Expense	900	
	48,000	48,000

For preparing the adjusting entries, the following data were assembled:

a. Fees earned but unbilled on June 30 were $1,200.
b. Supplies on hand on June 30 were $290.
c. Depreciation of equipment was estimated to be $1,000 for the year.
d. The balance in unearned fees represented the April 1 receipt in advance for services to be provided. Only $700 of the services was provided between April 1 and June 30.
e. Unpaid wages accrued on June 30 were $140.

Instructions

Journalize the adjusting entries necessary on June 30.

Problem 3–5B

Adjusting entries and adjusted trial balances

Objectives 3, 4

SPREADSHEET
GENERAL LEDGER

✓ 2. Total of Debit Column:
$482,570

Zornes Company is a small editorial services company owned and operated by Valerie Spann. Zornes Company's accounting clerk prepared the trial balance shown at the top of the next page on December 31, the end of the current year.

The data needed to determine year-end adjustments are as follows:

a. Unexpired insurance at December 31, $1,200.
b. Supplies on hand at December 31, $500.
c. Depreciation of building for the year, $1,620.
d. Depreciation of equipment for the year, $5,500.
e. Rent unearned at December 31, $2,000.
f. Accrued salaries and wages at December 31, $1,300.
g. Fees earned but unbilled on December 31, $3,750.

Instructions

1. Journalize the adjusting entries. Add additional accounts as needed.
2. Determine the balances of the accounts affected by the adjusting entries and prepare an adjusted trial balance.

Zornes Company
Trial Balance
December 31, 20—

Cash	6,700	
Accounts Receivable	23,800	
Prepaid Insurance	3,400	
Supplies	1,950	
Land	50,000	
Building	141,500	
Accumulated Depreciation—Building		91,700
Equipment	90,100	
Accumulated Depreciation—Equipment		65,300
Accounts Payable		7,500
Unearned Rent		6,000
Valerie Spann, Capital		81,500
Valerie Spann, Drawing	10,000	
Fees Earned		218,400
Salaries and Wages Expense	80,200	
Utilities Expense	28,200	
Advertising Expense	19,000	
Repairs Expense	11,500	
Miscellaneous Expense	4,050	
	470,400	470,400

Problem 3–6B

Adjusting entries and errors

Objective 3

✓ Corrected Net Income:

$133,700

At the end of June, the first month of operations, the following selected data were taken from the financial statements of E. Swindle, an attorney:

Net income for June	$132,750
Total assets at June 30	189,700
Total liabilities at June 30	20,200
Total owner's equity at June 30	169,500

In preparing the financial statements, adjustments for the following data were overlooked:

a. Supplies used during June, $1,600.
b. Unbilled fees earned at June 30, $5,000.
c. Depreciation of equipment for June, $1,500.
d. Accrued wages at June 30, $950.

Instructions

1. Journalize the entries to record the omitted adjustments.
2. Determine the correct amount of net income for June and the total assets, liabilities, and owner's equity at June 30. In addition to indicating the corrected amounts, indicate the effect of each omitted adjustment by setting up and completing a columnar table similar to the following. Adjustment (a) is presented as an example.

	Net Income	Total Assets	Total Liabilities	Total Owner's Equity
Reported amounts	$132,750	$189,700	$20,200	$169,500
Corrections:				
Adjustment (a)	−1,600	−1,600	0	−1,600
Adjustment (b)	___	___	___	___
Adjustment (c)	___	___	___	___
Adjustment (d)	___	___	___	___
Corrected amounts	═══	═══	═══	═══

CONTINUING PROBLEM

HAT

✓ 2. Total of Debit Column:
$13,725

The trial balance that you prepared for Music Today at the end of Chapter 2 should appear as follows:

Music Today
Trial Balance
December 31, 1999

Cash	3,285	
Accounts Receivable	880	
Supplies	535	
Prepaid Insurance	1,680	
Office Equipment	2,500	
Accounts Payable		2,875
Unearned Revenue		1,500
Chris Stipe, Capital		4,000
Chris Stipe, Drawing	550	
Fees Earned		4,780
Wages Expense	910	
Office Rent Expense	970	
Equipment Rent Expense	575	
Utilities Expense	380	
Music Expense	340	
Advertising Expense	225	
Supplies Expense	90	
Miscellaneous Expense	235	
	13,155	13,155

The data needed to determine adjustments for the two-month period ending December 31, 1999, are as follows:

a. During December, Music Today provided guest disc jockeys for KPRG for a total of 70 hours. For information on the amount of the accrued revenue to be billed to KPRG, see the contract described in the December 3, 1999 transaction at the end of Chapter 2.
b. Supplies on hand at December 31, $340.
c. The balance of the prepaid insurance account relates to the December 1, 1999 transaction at the end of Chapter 2.
d. Depreciation of the office equipment is $45.
e. The balance of the unearned revenue account relates to the contract between Music Today and KPRG, described in the December 3, 1999 transaction at the end of Chapter 2.
f. Accrued wages as of December 31, 1999, were $75.

Instructions

1. Prepare adjusting journal entries. You will need the following additional accounts:

   18 Accumulated Depreciation—Office Equipment
   22 Wages Payable
   57 Insurance Expense
   58 Depreciation Expense

2. Post the adjusting entries, inserting balances in the accounts affected.
3. Prepare an adjusted trial balance.

SPECIAL ACTIVITIES

Activity 3–1
Flora Real Estate Co.
Ethics and professional conduct in business

Martha Clark opened Flora Real Estate Co. on January 1, 1998. At the end of the first year, the business needed additional capital. On behalf of Flora Real Estate, Martha applied to First City Bank for a loan of $30,000. Based on Flora Real Estate's financial statements, which had been prepared on a cash basis, the First City Bank loan officer rejected the loan as too risky.

After receiving the rejection notice, Martha instructed her accountant to prepare the financial statements on an accrual basis. These statements included $24,000 in accounts receivable and $3,000 in accounts payable. Martha then instructed her accountant to record an additional $12,000 of accounts receivable for commissions on property for which a contract had been signed on December 27, 1998, but which would not be formally "closed" and the title transferred until January 20, 1999.

Martha then applied for a $30,000 loan from Second City Bank, using the revised financial statements. On this application, Martha indicated that she had not previously been rejected for credit.

Discuss the ethical and professional conduct of Martha Clark in applying for the loan from Second City Bank.

Activity 3–2
Ford Motor Co.
Accrued expense

On December 30, 1999, you buy a Ford Expedition. It comes with a three-year, 36,000-mile warranty. On January 21, 2000, you return the Expedition to the dealership for some basic repairs covered under the warranty. The cost of the repairs to the dealership is $180. In what year, 1999 or 2000, should Ford Motor Co. recognize the cost of the warranty repairs as an expense?

Activity 3–3
United Airlines
Accrued revenue

The following is an excerpt from a conversation between Max Liu and Ethel Stern just before they boarded a flight to Puerto Rico on United Airlines. They are going to Puerto Rico to attend their company's annual sales conference.

Max: Ethel, aren't you taking an introductory accounting course at City College?
Ethel: Yes, I decided it's about time I learned something about accounting. You know, our annual bonuses are based upon the sales figures that come from the accounting department.
Max: I guess I never really thought about it.
Ethel: You should think about it! Last year, I placed a $100,000 order on December 21. But when I got my bonus, the $100,000 sale wasn't included. They said it hadn't been shipped until January 3, so it would have to count in next year's bonus.
Max: A real bummer!
Ethel: Right! I was counting on that bonus including the $100,000 sale.
Max: Did you complain?
Ethel: Yes, but it didn't do any good. Tracy, the head accountant, said something about matching revenues and expenses. Also, something about not recording revenues until the sale is final. I figure I'd take the accounting course and find out whether she's just jerking me around.
Max: I never really thought about it. When do you think United Airlines will record its revenues from this flight?
Ethel: Mmm . . . I guess it could record the revenue when it sells the ticket . . . or . . . when the boarding passes are taken at the door . . . or . . . when we get off the plane . . . or when our company pays for the tickets . . . or . . . I don't know. I'll ask my accounting instructor.

Discuss when United Airlines should recognize the revenue from ticket sales to properly match revenues and expenses.

Activity 3–4
Quick Television Repair
Adjustments and financial statements

Several years ago, your father opened Quick Television Repair. He made a small initial investment and added money from his personal bank account as needed. He withdrew money for living expenses at irregular intervals. As the business grew, he hired an assistant. He is now considering adding more employees, purchasing additional service trucks, and purchasing the building he now rents. To secure funds for the expansion, your father submitted a loan application to the bank and included the most recent financial statements (shown below) prepared from accounts maintained by a part-time bookkeeper.

Quick Television Repair
Income Statement
For the Year Ended December 31, 20—

Service revenue		$66,900
Less: Rent paid	$18,000	
Wages paid	16,500	
Supplies paid	7,000	
Utilities paid	3,100	
Insurance paid	3,000	
Miscellaneous payments	2,150	49,750
Net income		$17,150

Quick Television Repair
Balance Sheet
December 31, 20—

Assets

Cash	$ 3,750
Amounts due from customers	2,100
Truck	25,000
Total assets	$30,850

Equities

Owner's capital	$30,850

After reviewing the financial statements, the loan officer at the bank asked your father if he used the accrual basis of accounting for revenues and expenses. Your father responded that he did and that is why he included an account for "Amounts Due from Customers." The loan officer then asked whether or not the accounts were adjusted prior to the preparation of the statements. Your father answered that they had not been adjusted.

a.   ✏ Why do you think the loan officer suspected that the accounts had not been adjusted prior to the preparation of the statements?
b.   Indicate possible accounts that might need to be adjusted before an accurate set of financial statements could be prepared.

Activity 3–5
Into the Real World
Codes of ethics

Obtain a copy of your college or university's student code of conduct. In groups of three or four, answer the following questions.

1.   Compare this code of conduct with the accountant's Codes of Professional Conduct in Appendix B at the end of this text. What are the similarities and differences between the two codes of conduct?
2.   One of your classmates asks you for permission to copy your homework, which your instructor will be collecting and grading for part of your overall term grade. Although your instructor has not stated whether one student may or may not copy another student's homework, is it ethical for you to allow your classmate to copy your homework? Is it ethical for your classmate to copy your homework?

ANSWERS TO SELF-EXAMINATION QUESTIONS

Matching

1. A	4. W	7. G	10. C	12. R	14. P	16. I	18. X
2. J	5. T	8. M	11. D	13. O	15. E	17. F	19. L
3. B	6. H	9. N					

Multiple Choice

1. **A** A deferral is the delay in recording an expense already paid, such as prepaid insurance (answer A). Wages payable (answer B) is considered an accrued expense or accrued liability. Fees earned (answer C) is a revenue item. Accumulated depreciation (answer D) is a contra account to a fixed asset.

2. **D** The balance in the supplies account, before adjustment, represents the amount of supplies available. From this amount ($2,250) is subtracted the amount of supplies on hand ($950) to determine the supplies used ($1,300). Since increases in expense accounts are recorded by debits and decreases in asset accounts are recorded by credits, answer D is the correct entry.

3. **C** The failure to record the adjusting entry debiting unearned rent, $600, and crediting rent revenue, $600, would have the effect of overstating liabilities by $600 and understating net income by $600 (answer C).

4. **C** Since increases in expense accounts (such as depreciation expense) are recorded by debits and it is customary to record the decreases in usefulness of fixed assets as credits to accumulated depreciation accounts, answer C is the correct entry.

5. **D** The book value of a fixed asset is the difference between the balance in the asset account and the balance in the related accumulated depreciation account, or $22,500 − $14,000, as indicated by answer D ($8,500).

4

Completing the Accounting Cycle

Setting the STAGE

Have you ever ridden in a taxicab? When you get in, you tell the driver where you want to go, and the driver lowers the meter lever (flag) to start the meter running. At the end of the trip, the driver stops the meter. You then pay the driver for the amount indicated on the meter. As the next passenger is picked up, the driver lowers the lever, and the cycle starts all over again.

Businesses also go through a cycle of activities. At the beginning of the cycle, management plans where it wants the business to go and begins the necessary actions to achieve its operating goals. Throughout the cycle, which is normally one year, the accountant records the operating activities (transactions) of the business. At the end of the cycle, the accountant prepares financial statements that summarize the operating activities for the year. The accountant then prepares the accounts for recording the operating activities in the next cycle.

As we saw in Chapter 1, the initial cycle for Computer King began with Pat King's investment in the business on November 1, 1999. The cycle continued with recording Computer King's transactions for November and December, as we discussed in Chapters 1 and 2. In Chapter 3, the cycle continued and we recorded the adjusting entries for the two months ending December 31, 1999. Now, in this chapter, we discuss the flow of the adjustment data into the accounts and into the financial statements. We show this process by using a work sheet. We conclude this chapter by discussing how the accounting records are prepared for the next period.

objectives

After studying this chapter, you should be able to:

1 Prepare a work sheet.

2 Prepare financial statements from a work sheet.

3 Prepare the adjusting and closing entries from a work sheet.

4 Explain what is meant by the fiscal year and the natural business year.

5 Review the seven basic steps of the accounting cycle.

6 Analyze and interpret the financial solvency of a business by computing the working capital and the current ratio.

Work Sheet

OBJECTIVE I

Prepare a work sheet.

Accountants often use **working papers** for collecting and summarizing data they need for preparing various analyses and reports. Such working papers are useful tools, but they are not considered a part of the formal accounting records. This is in contrast to the chart of accounts, the journal, and the ledger, which are essential parts of the accounting system. Working papers are usually prepared by using a spreadsheet program on a computer.

 Common spreadsheet programs used in business include Microsoft Excel® and Lotus 1-2-3®.

The **work sheet** is a working paper that accountants may use to summarize adjusting entries and the account balances for the financial statements. In small companies with few accounts and adjustments, a work sheet may not be necessary. For example, the financial statements for Computer King may be prepared directly from the adjusted trial balance illustrated in Chapter 3. In a computerized accounting system, a work sheet may not be necessary because the software program automatically posts entries to the accounts and prepares financial statements.

The work sheet is a useful device for understanding the flow of the accounting data from the unadjusted trial balance to the financial statements. This flow of data is the same in either a manual or a computerized accounting system. Because it is important that you understand this flow of data, we illustrate the preparation of the work sheet.

The work sheet is a useful device for understanding the flow of the accounting data from the unadjusted trial balance to the financial statements.

Unadjusted Trial Balance Columns

To begin the work sheet, list at the top the name of the business, the type of working paper (work sheet), and the period of time, as shown in Exhibit 1. Next, enter the unadjusted trial balance directly on the work sheet. The work sheet in Exhibit 1 shows the unadjusted trial balance for Computer King at December 31, 1999.

Adjustments Columns

The adjustments that we explained and illustrated for Computer King in Chapter 3 are entered in the Adjustments columns as shown in Exhibit 2. Cross-referencing (by letters) the debit and credit of each adjustment is useful in reviewing the work sheet. It is also helpful for identifying the adjusting entries that need to be recorded in the journal.

The order in which the adjustments are entered on the work sheet is not important. Most accountants enter the adjustments in the order in which the data are assembled. If the titles of some of the accounts to be adjusted do not appear in the trial balance, they should be inserted in the Account Title column, below the trial balance totals, as needed.

To review, the entries in the Adjustments columns of the work sheet are:

(a) **Supplies.** The supplies account has a debit balance of $2,000. The cost of the supplies on hand at the end of the period is $760. Therefore, the supplies expense for December is the difference between the two amounts, or $1,240. Enter the adjustment by writing (1) $1,240 in the Adjustments Debit column on the same line as Supplies Expense and (2) $1,240 in the Adjustments Credit column on the same line as Supplies.

(b) **Prepaid Insurance.** The prepaid insurance account has a debit balance of $2,400, which represents the prepayment of insurance for 24 months beginning December 1. Thus, the insurance expense for December is $100 ($2,400/24). Enter the adjustment by writing (1) $100 in the Adjustments Debit column on the same line as Insurance Expense and (2) $100 in the Adjustments Credit column on the same line as Prepaid Insurance.

(c) **Unearned Rent.** The unearned rent account has a credit balance of $360, which represents the receipt of three months' rent, beginning with December. Thus, the rent revenue for December is $120. Enter the adjustment by writing (1) $120 in the Adjustments Debit column on the same line as Unearned Rent and (2) $120 in the Adjustments Credit column on the same line as Rent Revenue.

(d) **Wages.** Wages accrued but not paid at the end of December total $250. This amount is an increase in expenses and an increase in liabilities. Enter the adjustment by writing (1) $250 in the Adjustments Debit column on the same line as Wages Expense and (2) $250 in the Adjustments Credit column on the same line as Wages Payable.

(e) **Accrued Fees.** Fees accrued at the end of December but not recorded total $500. This amount is an increase in an asset and an increase in revenue. Enter the adjustment by writing (1) $500 in the Adjustments Debit column on the same line as Accounts Receivable and (2) $500 in the Adjustments Credit column on the same line as Fees Earned.

(f) **Depreciation.** Depreciation of the office equipment is $50 for December. Enter the adjustment by writing (1) $50 in the Adjustments Debit column on the same line as Depreciation Expense and (2) $50 in the Adjustments Credit column on the same line as Accumulated Depreciation.

Total the Adjustments columns to verify the mathematical accuracy of the adjustment data. The total of the Debit column must equal the total of the Credit column.

Adjusted Trial Balance Columns

The adjustment data are added to or subtracted from the amounts in the unadjusted Trial Balance columns. The adjusted amounts are then extended to (placed in) the Adjusted Trial Balance columns, as shown in Exhibit 2. For example, the cash amount of $2,065 is extended to the Adjusted Trial Balance Debit column, since no adjustments affected Cash. Accounts Receivable has an initial balance of $2,220 and a debit adjustment (increase) of $500. The amount to write in the Adjusted Trial Balance Debit column is the debit balance of $2,720. The same procedure continues until all account balances are extended to the Adjusted Trial Balance columns. Total the columns of the Adjusted Trial Balance to verify the equality of debits and credits.

Income Statement and Balance Sheet Columns

The work sheet is completed by extending the adjusted trial balance amounts to the Income Statement and Balance Sheet columns. The amounts for revenues and

EXHIBIT 1
Work Sheet with Unadjusted Trial Balance Entered

Computer King
Work Sheet
For the Two Months Ended December 31, 1999

	Account Title	Trial Balance Dr.	Trial Balance Cr.	Adjustments Dr.	Adjustments Cr.	Adjusted Trial Balance Dr.	Adjusted Trial Balance Cr.	Income Statement Dr.	Income Statement Cr.	Balance Sheet Dr.	Balance Sheet Cr.	
1	Cash	2,065										1
2	Accounts Receivable	2,220										2
3	Supplies	2,000										3
4	Prepaid Insurance	2,400										4
5	Land	10,000										5
6	Office Equipment	1,800										6
7	Accounts Payable		900									7
8	Unearned Rent		360									8
9	Pat King, Capital		15,000									9
10	Pat King, Drawing	4,000										10
11	Fees Earned		16,340										11
12	Wages Expense	4,275										12
13	Rent Expense	1,600										13
14	Utilities Expense	985										14
15	Supplies Expense	800										15
16	Miscellaneous Expense	455										16
17		32,600	32,600									17
18												18
19												19
20												20
21												21
22												22
23												23
24												24
25												25

The work sheet is used for summarizing the effects of adjusting entries. It also aids in preparing financial statements.

EXHIBIT 5
Financial Statements Prepared from Work Sheet

Computer King
Income Statement
For the Two Months Ended December 31, 1999

Fees earned	$16 84 0 00	
Rent revenue	1 20 00	
Total revenues		$16 96 0 00
Expenses:		
Wages expense	$ 4 52 5 00	
Supplies expense	2 04 0 00	
Rent expense	1 60 0 00	
Utilities expense	9 85 00	
Insurance expense	1 00 00	
Depreciation expense	5 0 00	
Miscellaneous expense	4 55 00	
Total expenses		9 75 5 00
Net income		$ 7 20 5 00

Computer King
Statement of Owner's Equity
For the Two Months Ended December 31, 1999

Pat King, capital, November 1, 1999		$ 0
Investment on November 1, 1999	$15 00 0 00	
Net income for November and December	7 20 5 00	
	$22 20 5 00	
Less withdrawals	4 00 0 00	
Increase in owner's equity		18 20 5 00
Pat King, capital, December 31, 1999		$18 20 5 00

Computer King
Balance Sheet
December 31, 1999

Assets			Liabilities		
Current assets:			Current liabilities:		
Cash	$ 2 06 5 00		Accounts payable	$ 9 00 00	
Accounts receivable	2 72 0 00		Wages payable	2 50 00	
Supplies	7 60 00		Unearned rent	2 40 00	
Prepaid insurance	2 30 0 00		Total liabilities		$ 1 39 0 00
Total current assets		$ 7 84 5 00			
Property, plant, and equipment:					
Land	$10 00 0 00				
Office equipment $1,800					
Less accum. depr. 50	1 75 0 00		Owner's Equity		
Total property, plant,			Pat King, capital		18 20 5 00
and equipment		11 75 0 00	Total liabilities and		
Total assets		$19 59 5 00	owner's equity		$19 59 5 00

expenses are extended to the Income Statement columns. The amounts for assets, liabilities, owner's capital, and drawing are extended to the Balance Sheet columns.[1]

In the Computer King work sheet, the first account listed is Cash and the balance appearing in the Adjusted Trial Balance Debit column is $2,065. Cash is an asset, it is listed on the balance sheet, and it has a debit balance. Therefore, $2,065 is extended to the Balance Sheet Debit column. The balance of Fees Earned of $16,840 is extended to the Income Statement Credit column. The same procedure continues until all account balances have been extended to the proper columns, as shown in Exhibit 3.

After all of the balances have been extended to the four statement columns, total each of these columns, as shown in Exhibit 4. The difference between the two Income Statement column totals is the amount of the net income or the net loss for the period. Likewise, the difference between the two Balance Sheet column totals is also the amount of the net income or net loss for the period.

If the Income Statement Credit column total (representing total revenue) is greater than the Income Statement Debit column total (representing total expenses), the difference is the net income. If the Income Statement Debit column total is greater than the Income Statement Credit column total, the difference is a net loss. For Computer King, the computation of net income is as follows:

Total of Credit column (revenues)	$16,960
Total of Debit column (expenses)	9,755
Net income (excess of revenues over expenses)	$ 7,205

If the total of the Balance Sheet Debit column of the work sheet is $350,000 and the total of the Balance Sheet Credit column is $400,000, what is the net income or net loss?

$50,000 net loss ($350,000 − $400,000)

As shown in Exhibit 4, write the amount of the net income, $7,205, in the Income Statement Debit column and the Balance Sheet Credit column. Write the term *Net income* in the Account Title column. If there were a net loss instead of net income, you would write the amount in the Income Statement Credit column and the Balance Sheet Debit column and the term *Net loss* in the Account Title column. Inserting the net income or net loss in the statement columns on the work sheet shows the effect of transferring the net balance of the revenue and expense accounts to the owner's capital account. Later in this chapter, we explain how to journalize this transfer.

After the net income or net loss has been entered on the work sheet, again total each of the four statement columns. The totals of the two Income Statement columns must now be equal. The totals of the two Balance Sheet columns must also be equal.

Financial Statements

OBJECTIVE 2

Prepare financial statements from a work sheet.

The work sheet is an aid in preparing the income statement, the statement of owner's equity, and the balance sheet, which are presented in Exhibit 5. In the following paragraphs, we discuss these financial statements for Computer King, prepared from the completed work sheet in Exhibit 4. The statements are similar in form to those presented in Chapter 1.

Income Statement

The income statement is normally prepared directly from the work sheet. However, the order of the expenses may be changed. As we did in Chapter 1, we list the ex-

----

[1] The balances of the capital and drawing accounts are also extended to the Balance Sheet columns because this work sheet does not provide for separate Statement of Owner's Equity columns.

penses in the income statement in Exhibit 5 in order of size, beginning with the larger items. Miscellaneous expense is the last item, regardless of its amount.

Statement of Owner's Equity

The first item normally presented on the statement of owner's equity is the balance of the proprietor's capital account at the beginning of the period. On the work sheet, however, the amount listed as capital is not always the account balance at the beginning of the period. The proprietor may have invested additional assets in the business during the period. Hence, for the beginning balance and any additional investments, it is necessary to refer to the capital account in the ledger. These amounts, along with the net income (or net loss) and the drawing amount shown in the work sheet, are used to determine the ending capital account balance.

The basic form of the statement of owner's equity is shown in Exhibit 5. For Computer King, the amount of drawings by the owner was less than the net income. If the owner's withdrawals had exceeded the net income, the order of the net income and the withdrawals would have been reversed. The difference between the two items would then be deducted from the beginning capital account balance. Other factors, such as additional investments or a net loss, also require some change in the form, as shown in the following example:

Allan Johnson, capital, January 1, 20—	$39,000	
Additional investment during the year	6,000	
Total		$45,000
Net loss for the year	$ 5,600	
Withdrawals	9,500	
Decrease in owner's equity		15,100
Allan Johnson, capital, December 31, 20—		$29,900

Balance Sheet

The balance sheet in Exhibit 5 was expanded by adding subsections for current assets, property, plant, and equipment, and current liabilities. Such a balance sheet is a *classified* balance sheet. In the following paragraphs, we describe some of the sections and subsections that may be used in a balance sheet. We will introduce additional sections in later chapters.

Assets

Assets are commonly divided into classes for presentation on the balance sheet. Two of these classes are (1) current assets and (2) property, plant, and equipment.

Current Assets. Cash and other assets that are expected to be converted to cash or sold or used up usually within one year or less, through the normal operations of the business, are called current assets. In addition to cash, the current assets usually owned by a service business are notes receivable, accounts receivable, supplies, and other prepaid expenses.

> Two common classes of assets are current assets and property, plant, and equipment.

Notes receivable are amounts customers owe. They are written promises to pay the amount of the note and possibly interest at an agreed rate. Accounts receivable are also amounts customers owe, but they are less formal than notes and do not provide for interest. Accounts receivable normally result from providing services or selling merchandise on account. Notes receivable and accounts receivable are current assets because they will usually be converted to cash within one year or less.

The operations of a manufacturing business involve the purchase of raw materials (purchasing activity), the conversion of the raw materials into a product through the use of labor and machinery (production activity), the sale and distribution of the products to customers (sales activity), and the receipt of cash from customers (collection activity). This overall process is referred to as the *operating cycle*. Thus, the operating cycle begins with spending cash and it ends with receiving cash from customers. The operating cycle for a manufacturing business is shown below.

The Operating Cycle

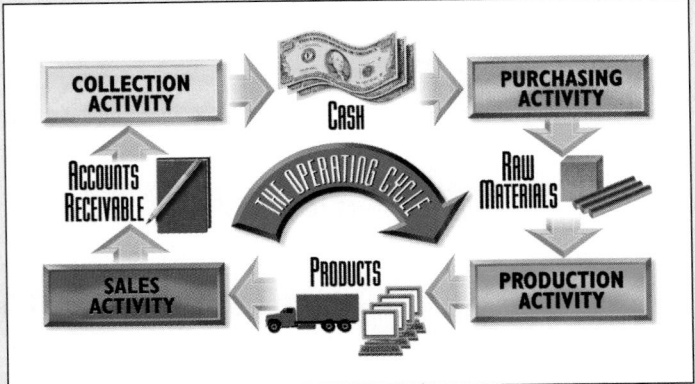

Operating cycles differ, depending upon the nature of the business and its operations. For example, the operating cycles for tobacco, distillery, and lumber industries are much longer than the operating cycles of the automobile, consumer electronics, and home furnishings industries. Likewise, the operating cycles for retailers are normally shorter than for manufacturers because retailers purchase goods in a form ready for sale to the customer. Of course, some retailers will have shorter operating cycles than others because of the nature of their products. For example, a jewelry store or an automobile dealer normally has a longer operating cycle than a consumer electronics store or a grocery store.

Businesses with longer operating cycles normally have higher profit margins on their products than businesses with shorter operating cycles. For example, it is not unusual for jewelry stores to price their jewelry at 30%–50% above cost. In contrast, grocery stores operate on very small profit margins, often below 5%. Grocery stores make up the difference by selling their products more quickly. ■

Property, Plant, and Equipment. The property, plant, and equipment section may also be described as **fixed assets** or **plant assets**. These assets include equipment, machinery, buildings, and land. With the exception of land, as we discussed in Chapter 3, fixed assets depreciate over a period of time. The cost, accumulated depreciation, and book value of each major type of fixed asset is normally reported on the balance sheet or in accompanying notes.

Liabilities

Liabilities are the amounts the business owes to creditors. The two most common classes of liabilities are (1) current liabilities and (2) long-term liabilities.

> **Two common classes of liabilities are current liabilities and long-term liabilities.**

Current Liabilities. Liabilities that will be due within a short time (usually one year or less) and that are to be paid out of current assets are called current liabilities. The most common liabilities in this group are notes payable and accounts payable. Other current liability accounts commonly found in the ledger are Wages Payable, Interest Payable, Taxes Payable, and Unearned Fees.

Long-Term Liabilities. Liabilities that will not be due for a long time (usually more than one year) are called long-term liabilities. If Computer King had long-term liabilities, they would be reported below the current liabilities. As long-term liabilities come due and are to be paid within one year, they are classified as current liabilities. If they are to be renewed rather than paid, they would continue to be classified as long-term. When an asset is pledged as security for a liability, the obligation may be called a *mortgage note payable* or a *mortgage payable*.

Owner's Equity

The owner's right to the assets of the business is presented on the balance sheet below the liabilities section. The owner's equity is added to the total liabilities, and this total must be equal to the total assets.

Adjusting and Closing Entries

OBJECTIVE 3

Prepare the adjusting and closing entries from a work sheet.

As we discussed in Chapter 3, the adjusting entries are recorded in the journal at the end of the accounting period. If a work sheet has been prepared, the data for these entries are in the Adjustments columns. For Computer King, the adjusting entries prepared from the work sheet are shown in Exhibit 6.

EXHIBIT 6
Adjusting Entries for Computer King

									JOURNAL										PAGE 5				
		Date		Description	Post. Ref.		Debit						Credit					
1				Adjusting Entries															1
2	1999 Dec.	31	Supplies Expense	55	1 2 4 0 00					2
3			Supplies	14			1 2 4 0 00	3
4								4
5		31	Insurance Expense	56	1 0 0 00				5
6			Prepaid Insurance	15			1 0 0 00	6
7								7
8		31	Unearned Rent	23	1 2 0 00				8
9			Rent Revenue	42			1 2 0 00	9
10								10
11		31	Wages Expense	51	2 5 0 00				11
12			Wages Payable	22			2 5 0 00	12
13								13
14		31	Accounts Receivable	12	5 0 0 00				14
15			Fees Earned	41			5 0 0 00	15
16								16
17		31	Depreciation Expense	53	5 0 00				17
18			Accumulated Depreciation—					18
19			Office Equipment	19			5 0 00	19

After the adjusting entries have been posted to Computer King's ledger, shown in Exhibit 10, the ledger is in agreement with the data reported on the financial statements. The balances of the accounts reported on the balance sheet are carried forward from year to year. Because they are relatively permanent, these accounts are called **real accounts**. The balances of the accounts reported on the income statement are *not* carried forward from year to year. Likewise, the balance of the owner's withdrawal account, which is reported on the statement of owner's equity, is not carried forward. Because these accounts report amounts for only one period, they are called **temporary accounts** or **nominal accounts**.

Closing entries transfer the balances of temporary accounts to the owner's capital account.

To report amounts for only one period, temporary accounts should have zero balances at the beginning of a period. How are these balances converted to zero? The revenue and expense account balances are transferred to an account called **Income Summary**. The balance of Income Summary is then transferred to the owner's capital account. The balance of the owner's drawing account is also transferred to the owner's capital account. The entries that transfer these balances are called **closing entries**. The transfer process is called the **closing process**. Exhibit 7 is a diagram of this process.

EXHIBIT 7
The Closing Process

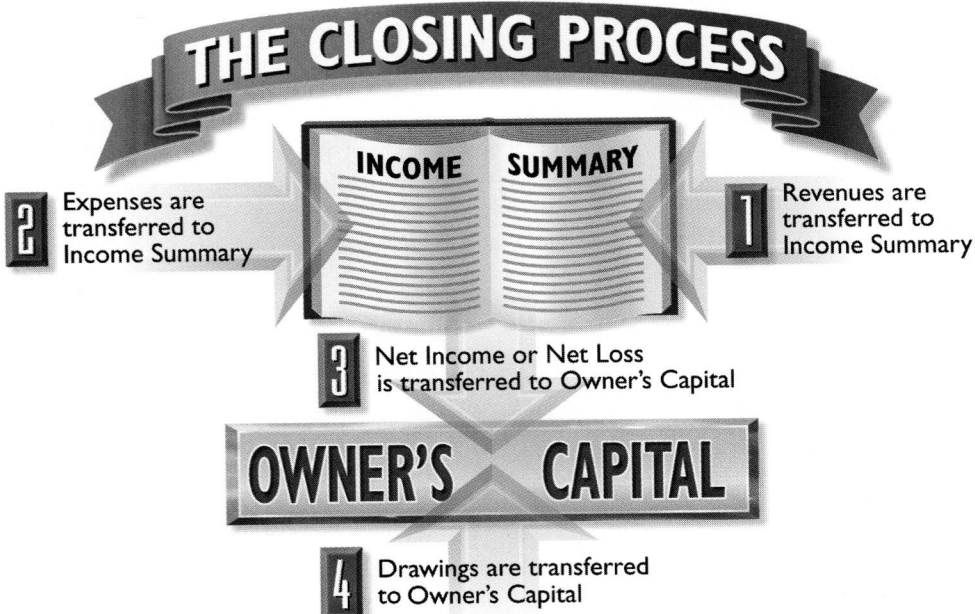

The income summary account does *not* appear on the financial statements.

You should note that Income Summary is used only at the end of the period. At the beginning of the closing process, Income Summary has no balance. During the closing process, Income Summary will be debited and credited for various amounts. At the end of the closing process, Income Summary will again have no balance. Because Income Summary has the effect of clearing the revenue and expense accounts of their balances, it is sometimes called a **clearing account**. Other titles used for this account include Revenue and Expense Summary, Profit and Loss Summary, and Income and Expense Summary.

It is possible to close the temporary revenue and expense accounts without using a clearing account such as Income Summary. In this case, the balances of the revenue and expense accounts are closed directly to the owner's capital account. This process is automatic in a computerized accounting system. In a manual system, the use of an income summary account aids in detecting and correcting errors.

Journalizing and Posting Closing Entries

Four closing entries are required at the end of an accounting period, as outlined in Exhibit 7. The account titles and balances needed in preparing these entries may be obtained from the work sheet, the income statement and the statement of owner's equity, or the ledger. If a work sheet is used, the data for the first two entries appear in the Income Statement columns. The amount for the third entry is the net income or net loss appearing at the bottom of the work sheet. The amount for the fourth entry is the drawing account balance that appears in the Balance Sheet Debit column of the work sheet.

A flowchart of the closing entries for Computer King is shown in Exhibit 8. The balances in the accounts are those shown in the Adjusted Trial Balance columns of the work sheet in Exhibit 2.

The closing entries for Computer King are shown in Exhibit 9. After the closing entries have been posted to the ledger, as shown in Exhibit 10, the balance in the capital account will agree with the amount reported on the statement of owner's equity and the balance sheet. In addition, the revenue, expense, and drawing accounts will have zero balances.

EXHIBIT 8 Flowchart of Closing Entries for Computer King

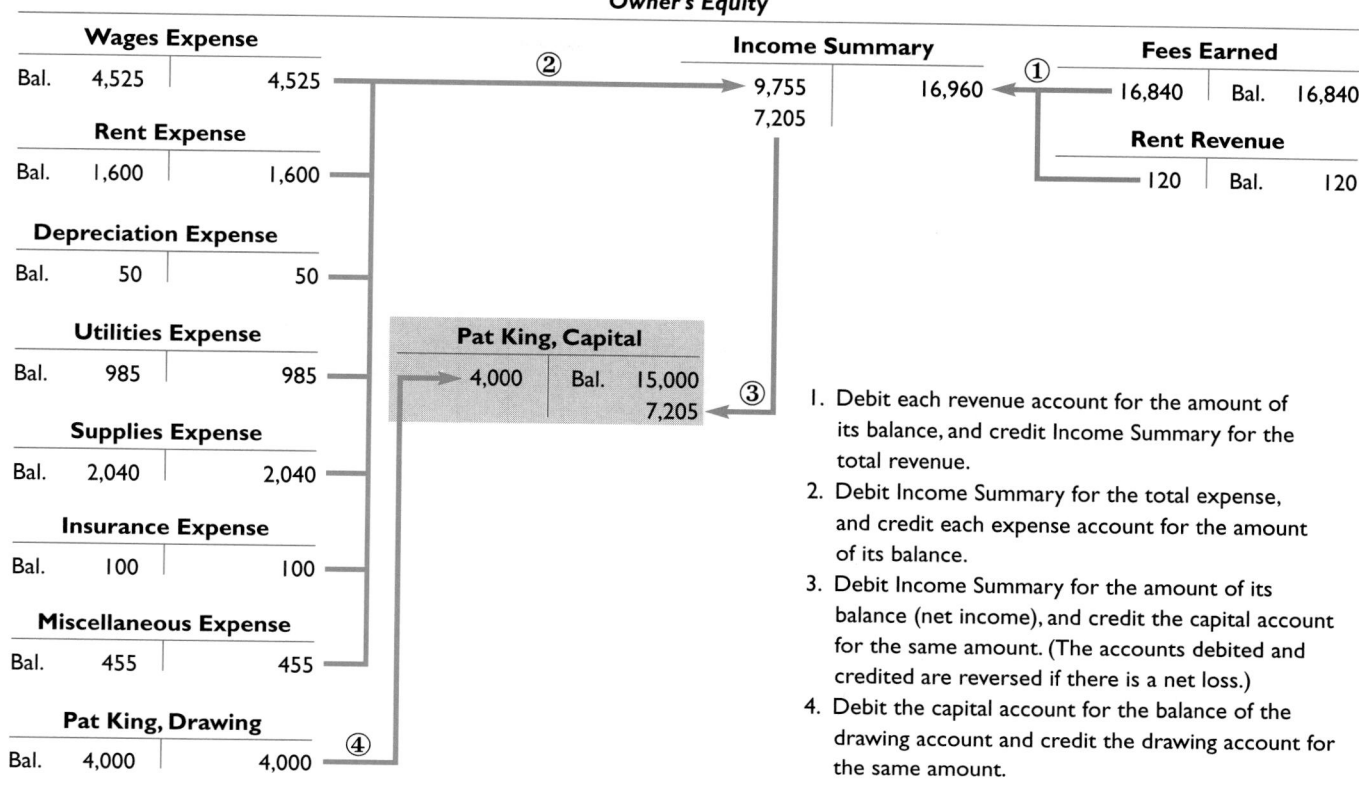

1. Debit each revenue account for the amount of its balance, and credit Income Summary for the total revenue.
2. Debit Income Summary for the total expense, and credit each expense account for the amount of its balance.
3. Debit Income Summary for the amount of its balance (net income), and credit the capital account for the same amount. (The accounts debited and credited are reversed if there is a net loss.)
4. Debit the capital account for the balance of the drawing account and credit the drawing account for the same amount.

EXHIBIT 9
Closing Entries for Computer King

	Date		Description	Post. Ref.	Debit	Credit	
1			Closing Entries				1
2	1999 Dec.	31	Fees Earned	41	16 8 4 0 00		2
3			Rent Revenue	42	1 2 0 00		3
4			Income Summary	33		16 9 6 0 00	4
5							5
6		31	Income Summary	33	9 7 5 5 00		6
7			Wages Expense	51		4 5 2 5 00	7
8			Rent Expense	52		1 6 0 0 00	8
9			Depreciation Expense	53		5 0 00	9
10			Utilities Expense	54		9 8 5 00	10
11			Supplies Expense	55		2 0 4 0 00	11
12			Insurance Expense	56		1 0 0 00	12
13			Miscellaneous Expense	59		4 5 5 00	13
14							14
15		31	Income Summary	33	7 2 0 5 00		15
16			Pat King, Capital	31		7 2 0 5 00	16
17							17
18		31	Pat King, Capital	31	4 0 0 0 00		18
19			Pat King, Drawing	32		4 0 0 0 00	19

JOURNAL PAGE 6

EXHIBIT 10
Ledger for Computer King

LEDGER

ACCOUNT Cash   ACCOUNT NO. 11

Date		Item	Post. Ref.	Debit	Credit	Balance Debit	Balance Credit
1999 Nov.	1		1	15000 00		15000 00	
	5		1		10000 00	5000 00	
	18		1	7500 00		12500 00	
	30		1		3650 00	8850 00	
	30		1		950 00	7900 00	
	30		2		2000 00	5900 00	
Dec.	1		2		2400 00	3500 00	
	1		2		800 00	2700 00	
	1		2	360 00		3060 00	
	6		2		180 00	2880 00	
	11		2		400 00	2480 00	
	13		3		950 00	1530 00	
	16		3	3100 00		4630 00	
	20		3		900 00	3730 00	
	21		3	650 00		4380 00	
	23		3		1450 00	2930 00	
	27		3		1200 00	1730 00	
	31		3		310 00	1420 00	
	31		4		225 00	1195 00	
	31		4	2870 00		4065 00	
	31		4		2000 00	2065 00	

ACCOUNT Accounts Receivable   ACCOUNT NO. 12

Date		Item	Post. Ref.	Debit	Credit	Balance Debit	Balance Credit
1999 Dec.	16		3	1750 00		1750 00	
	21		3		650 00	1100 00	
	31		4	1120 00		2220 00	
	31	Adjusting	5	500 00		2720 00	

ACCOUNT Supplies   ACCOUNT NO. 14

Date		Item	Post. Ref.	Debit	Credit	Balance Debit	Balance Credit
1999 Nov.	10		1	1350 00		1350 00	
	30		1		800 00	550 00	
Dec.	23		3	1450 00		2000 00	
	31	Adjusting	5		1240 00	760 00	

ACCOUNT Prepaid Insurance   ACCOUNT NO. 15

Date		Item	Post. Ref.	Debit	Credit	Balance Debit	Balance Credit
1999 Dec.	1		2	2400 00		2400 00	
	31	Adjusting	5		100 00	2300 00	

EXHIBIT 10
(*continued*)

ACCOUNT *Land*   **ACCOUNT NO.** *17*

Date	Item	Post. Ref.	Debit	Credit	Balance Debit	Balance Credit
1999 Nov. 5		1	10 0 0 0 00		10 0 0 0 00	

ACCOUNT *Office Equipment*   **ACCOUNT NO.** *18*

Date	Item	Post. Ref.	Debit	Credit	Balance Debit	Balance Credit
1999 Dec. 4		2	1 8 0 0 00		1 8 0 0 00	

ACCOUNT *Accumulated Depreciation*   **ACCOUNT NO.** *19*

Date	Item	Post. Ref.	Debit	Credit	Balance Debit	Balance Credit
1999 Dec. 31	Adjusting	5		5 0 00		5 0 00

ACCOUNT *Accounts Payable*   **ACCOUNT NO.** *21*

Date	Item	Post. Ref.	Debit	Credit	Balance Debit	Balance Credit
1999 Nov. 10		1		1 3 5 0 00		1 3 5 0 00
30		1	9 5 0 00			4 0 0 00
Dec. 4		2		1 8 0 0 00		2 2 0 0 00
11		2	4 0 0 00			1 8 0 0 00
20		3	9 0 0 00			9 0 0 00

ACCOUNT *Wages Payable*   **ACCOUNT NO.** *22*

Date	Item	Post. Ref.	Debit	Credit	Balance Debit	Balance Credit
1999 Dec. 31	Adjusting	5		2 5 0 00		2 5 0 00

ACCOUNT *Unearned Rent*   **ACCOUNT NO.** *23*

Date	Item	Post. Ref.	Debit	Credit	Balance Debit	Balance Credit
1999 Dec. 1		2		3 6 0 00		3 6 0 00
31	Adjusting	5	1 2 0 00			2 4 0 00

ACCOUNT *Pat King, Capital*   **ACCOUNT NO.** *31*

Date	Item	Post. Ref.	Debit	Credit	Balance Debit	Balance Credit
1999 Nov. 1		1		15 0 0 0 00		15 0 0 0 00
Dec. 31	Closing	6		7 2 0 5 00		22 2 0 5 00
31	Closing	6	4 0 0 0 00			18 2 0 5 00

EXHIBIT 10
(continued)

ACCOUNT Pat King, Drawing — ACCOUNT NO. 32

Date		Item	Post. Ref.	Debit	Credit	Balance Debit	Balance Credit
1999 Nov.	30		2	2 0 0 0 00		2 0 0 0 00	
Dec.	31		4	2 0 0 0 00		4 0 0 0 00	
	31	Closing	6		4 0 0 0 00	—	—

ACCOUNT Income Summary — ACCOUNT NO. 33

Date		Item	Post. Ref.	Debit	Credit	Balance Debit	Balance Credit
1999 Dec.	31	Closing	6		16 9 6 0 00		16 9 6 0 00
	31	Closing	6	9 7 5 5 00			7 2 0 5 00
	31	Closing	6	7 2 0 5 00		—	—

ACCOUNT Fees Earned — ACCOUNT NO. 41

Date		Item	Post. Ref.	Debit	Credit	Balance Debit	Balance Credit
1999 Nov.	18		1		7 5 0 0 00		7 5 0 0 00
Dec.	16		3		3 1 0 0 00		10 6 0 0 00
	16		3		1 7 5 0 00		12 3 5 0 00
	31		4		2 8 7 0 00		15 2 2 0 00
	31		4		1 1 2 0 00		16 3 4 0 00
	31	Adjusting	5		5 0 0 00		16 8 4 0 00
	31	Closing	6	16 8 4 0 00		—	—

ACCOUNT Rent Revenue — ACCOUNT NO. 42

Date		Item	Post. Ref.	Debit	Credit	Balance Debit	Balance Credit
1999 Dec.	31	Adjusting	5		1 2 0 00		1 2 0 00
	31	Closing	6	1 2 0 00		—	—

ACCOUNT Wages Expense — ACCOUNT NO. 51

Date		Item	Post. Ref.	Debit	Credit	Balance Debit	Balance Credit
1999 Nov.	30		1	2 1 2 5 00		2 1 2 5 00	
Dec.	13		3	9 5 0 00		3 0 7 5 00	
	27		3	1 2 0 0 00		4 2 7 5 00	
	31	Adjusting	5	2 5 0 00		4 5 2 5 00	
	31	Closing	6		4 5 2 5 00	—	—

EXHIBIT 10
(*concluded*)

ACCOUNT Rent Expense — ACCOUNT NO. 52

Date		Item	Post. Ref.	Debit	Credit	Balance Debit	Balance Credit
1999 Nov.	30		1	8 0 0 00		8 0 0 00	
Dec.	1		2	8 0 0 00		1 6 0 0 00	
	31	Closing	6		1 6 0 0 00	—	—

ACCOUNT Depreciation Expense — ACCOUNT NO. 53

Date		Item	Post. Ref.	Debit	Credit	Balance Debit	Balance Credit
1999 Dec.	31	Adjusting	5	5 0 00		5 0 00	
	31	Closing	6		5 0 00	—	—

ACCOUNT Utilities Expense — ACCOUNT NO. 54

Date		Item	Post. Ref.	Debit	Credit	Balance Debit	Balance Credit
1999 Nov.	30		1	4 5 0 00		4 5 0 00	
Dec.	31		3	3 1 0 00		7 6 0 00	
	31		4	2 2 5 00		9 8 5 00	
	31	Closing	6		9 8 5 00	—	—

ACCOUNT Supplies Expense — ACCOUNT NO. 55

Date		Item	Post. Ref.	Debit	Credit	Balance Debit	Balance Credit
1999 Nov.	30		1	8 0 0 00		8 0 0 00	
Dec.	31	Adjusting	5	1 2 4 0 00		2 0 4 0 00	
	31	Closing	6		2 0 4 0 00	—	—

ACCOUNT Insurance Expense — ACCOUNT NO. 56

Date		Item	Post. Ref.	Debit	Credit	Balance Debit	Balance Credit
1999 Dec.	31	Adjusting	5	1 0 0 00		1 0 0 00	
	31	Closing	6		1 0 0 00	—	—

ACCOUNT Miscellaneous Expense — ACCOUNT NO. 59

Date		Item	Post. Ref.	Debit	Credit	Balance Debit	Balance Credit
1999 Nov.	30		1	2 7 5 00		2 7 5 00	
Dec.	6		2	1 8 0 00		4 5 5 00	
	31	Closing	6		4 5 5 00	—	—

After the entry to close an account has been posted, a line should be inserted in both balance columns opposite the final entry. The next period's transactions for the revenue, expense, and drawing accounts will be posted directly below the closing entry.

Post-Closing Trial Balance

The last accounting procedure for a period is to prepare a trial balance after the closing entries have been posted. The purpose of the **post-closing** (after closing) **trial balance** is to make sure that the ledger is in balance at the beginning of the next period. The accounts and amounts should agree exactly with the accounts and amounts listed on the balance sheet at the end of the period. The post-closing trial balance for Computer King is shown in Exhibit 11.

If total revenues are $600,000, total expenses are $525,000, and drawing is $50,000, what is the balance of the income summary account that is closed to the owner's capital?

$75,000 ($600,000 − $525,000). The drawing account balance is closed directly to the owner's capital, rather than to Income Summary.

EXHIBIT 11
Post-Closing Trial Balance

Computer King Post-Closing Trial Balance December 31, 1999		
Cash	2 0 6 5 00	
Accounts Receivable	2 7 2 0 00	
Supplies	7 6 0 00	
Prepaid Insurance	2 3 0 0 00	
Land	10 0 0 0 00	
Office Equipment	1 8 0 0 00	
Accumulated Depreciation		5 0 00
Accounts Payable		9 0 0 00
Wages Payable		2 5 0 00
Unearned Rent		2 4 0 00
Pat King, Capital		18 2 0 5 00
	19 6 4 5 00	19 6 4 5 00

Instead of preparing a formal post-closing trial balance, it is possible to list the accounts directly from the ledger, using a computer. The computer printout, in effect, becomes the post-closing trial balance. Without such a printout, there is no efficient means of determining the cause of unequal trial balance totals.

Fiscal Year

OBJECTIVE 4

Explain what is meant by the fiscal year and the natural business year.

In the Computer King illustration, operations began on November 1 and the accounting period was for two months, November and December. A proprietorship is required by the federal income tax law, except in rare cases, to maintain the same accounting period as its owner. Since Pat King maintains a calendar-year accounting period for tax purposes, Computer King must also close its accounts on December 31, 1999. In future years, the financial statements for Computer King will be prepared for twelve months ending on December 31 each year.

Circuit City's 1997 fiscal year-end was February 28, 1997. This should not surprise you, since you would expect that Circuit City experiences a high volume of sales around the December holiday season, followed by relatively low sales in January and February.

During its 1997 fiscal year, Circuit City reported the following net sales and operating revenues:

Net Sales and Operating Revenue
(in thousands of dollars)

First quarter	$1,615,266
Second quarter	1,767,043
Third quarter	1,863,947
Fourth quarter	2,417,555

The annual accounting period adopted by a business is known as its **fiscal year**. Fiscal years begin with the first day of the month selected and end on the last day of the following twelfth month. The period most commonly used is the calendar year. Other periods are not unusual, especially for businesses organized as corporations. For example, a corporation may adopt a fiscal year that ends when business activities have reached the lowest point in its annual operating cycle. Such a fiscal year is called the **natural business year**. At the low point in its operating cycle, a business has more time to analyze the results of operations and to prepare financial statements.

Because companies with fiscal years often have highly seasonal operations, investors and others should be careful in interpreting partial-year reports for such companies. That is, you should expect the results of operations for these companies to vary significantly throughout the fiscal year.

The financial history of a business may be shown by a series of balance sheets and income statements for several fiscal years. If the life of a business is expressed by a line moving from left to right, the series of balance sheets and income statements may be graphed as follows:

The 1996 edition of *Accounting Trends & Techniques,* published by the American Institute of Certified Public Accountants, reported the following results of a survey concerning the month of the fiscal year-end of 600 industrial and merchandising companies:

Percentage of Companies with Fiscal Years Ending in the Month of:

January	4%	July	2%
February	2	August	2
March	2	September	6
April	1	October	4
May	3	November	3
June	10	December	61

FINANCIAL HISTORY OF A BUSINESS

Income statement for the year ended Dec. 31, 1998 — DECEMBER **31** 1998 — Balance sheet Dec. 31, 1998

Income statement for the year ended Dec. 31, 1999 — DECEMBER **31** 1999 — Balance sheet Dec. 31, 1999

Income statement for the year ended Dec. 31, 2000 — DECEMBER **31** 2000 — Balance sheet Dec. 31, 2000

You may think of the income statements, balance sheets, and financial history of a business as similar to the record of a college football team. The final score of each football game is similar to the net income reported on the income statement of a business. The team's season record after each game is similar to the balance sheet. At the end of the season, the final record of the team measures its success or failure. Likewise, at the end of a life of a business, its final balance sheet is a measure of its financial success or failure.

OBJECTIVE 5

Review the seven basic steps of the accounting cycle.

Accounting Cycle

The process that begins with analyzing and journalizing transactions and ends with the post-closing trial balance is called the **accounting cycle**. The most important output of the accounting cycle is the financial statements.

Understanding the steps of the accounting cycle is essential for further study of accounting. The basic steps of the cycle are shown, by number, in the flowchart in Exhibit 12.

 In a computerized accounting system, the software automatically records and posts transactions. The ledger and supporting records are maintained in computerized master files. In addition, a work sheet is normally not prepared.

EXHIBIT 12   Accounting Cycle

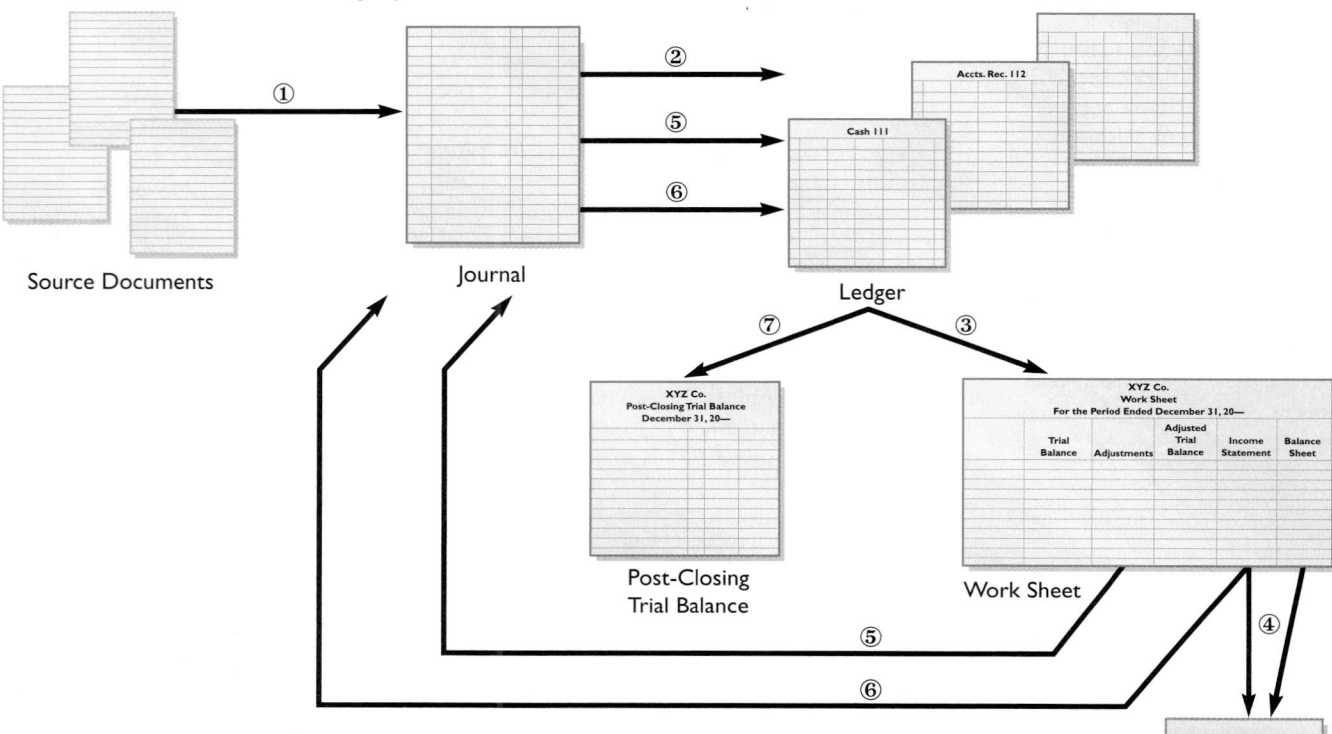

Source Documents

Journal

Ledger

Post-Closing Trial Balance

Work Sheet

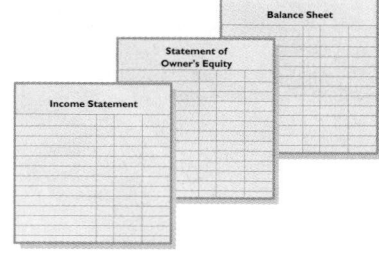

Financial Statements

① Transactions are analyzed and recorded in the journal.
② Transactions are posted to the ledger.
③ A trial balance is prepared, adjustment data are assembled, and the work sheet is completed.
④ Financial statements are prepared.
⑤ Adjusting entries are journalized and posted to the ledger.
⑥ Closing entries are journalized and posted to the ledger.
⑦ A post-closing trial balance is prepared.

FINANCIAL ANALYSIS AND INTERPRETATION

OBJECTIVE 6

Analyze and interpret the financial solvency of a business by computing the working capital and the current ratio.

The ability of a business to pays its debts is called **solvency**. Two financial measures for evaluating a business's short-term solvency are working capital and the current ratio. **Working capital** is the excess of the current assets of a business over its current liabilities, as shown below.

Working capital = Current assets − Current liabilities

An excess of the current assets over the current liabilities implies that the business is able to pay its current liabilities. If the current liabilities are greater than the current assets, the business may not be able to pay its debts and continue in business.

To illustrate, Computer King's working capital at the end of 1999 is $6,455, as computed below. This amount of working capital implies that Computer King can pay its current liabilities.

Working capital = Current assets − Current liabilities
Working capital = $7,845 − $1,390
Working capital = $6,455

The current ratio is another means of expressing the relationship between current assets and current liabilities. The current ratio is computed by dividing current assets by current liabilities, as shown below.

Current ratio = Current assets/Current liabilities

To illustrate, the current ratio for Computer King at the end of 1999 is 5.6, computed as follows:

Current ratio = Current assets/Current liabilities
Current ratio = $7,845/$1,390 = 5.6

The current ratio is useful in making comparisons across companies and with industry averages. To illustrate, assume that as of December 31, 1999, the working capital of a company that competes with Computer King is much greater than $6,455, but its current ratio is only 1.3. Considering these facts alone, Computer King is in a more favorable position to obtain short-term credit, even though the competing company has a greater amount of working capital.

ENCORE

Financial statements prepared under accounting practices in other countries often differ from those prepared under generally accepted accounting principles found in the United States. This is to be expected, since cultures and market structures differ from country to country.

To illustrate, **Bayerische Motoren Werke Aktiengesellschaft** (better known as **BMW!**) prepares its financial statements under German law and German accounting principles. In doing so, BMW's balance sheet reports fixed assets first, followed by current assets. It also reports owner's equity before the liabilities. In contrast, balance sheets prepared under U.S. accounting principles report current assets followed by fixed assets and current liabilities followed by long-term liabilities and owner's equity. The U.S. form of balance sheet is organized to emphasize creditor interpretation and analysis. For example, current assets and current liabilities are presented first, so that working capital and the current ratio can be easily computed. Likewise, to emphasize their importance, liabilities are reported before owner's equity.

Regardless of these differences, the basic principles underlying the accounting equation and the double-entry accounting system are the same in Germany and the United States.

Even though differences in recording and reporting exist, the accounting equation holds true: the total assets still equal the total liabilities and owner's equity. ■

APPENDIX: REVERSING ENTRIES

COMPUTER KING

Some of the adjusting entries recorded at the end of an accounting period have an important effect on otherwise routine transactions that occur in the following period. A typical example is accrued wages owed to employees at the end of a period. If there has been an adjusting entry for accrued wages expense, the first payment of wages in the following period will include the accrual. In the absence of some special provision, Wages Payable must be debited for the amount owed for the earlier period, and Wages Expense must be debited for the portion of the payroll that represents expense for the later period. However, an *optional* entry—the reversing entry—may be used to simplify the analysis and recording of this first payroll entry in a period. As the term implies, a **reversing entry** is the exact opposite of the adjusting entry to which it relates. The amounts and accounts are the same as the adjusting entry; the debits and credits are reversed.

We will illustrate the use of reversing entries by using the data for Computer King's accrued wages, which were presented in Chapter 3. These data are summarized in Exhibit 13.

EXHIBIT 13
Accrued Wages

1. Wages are paid on the second and fourth Fridays for the two-week periods ending on those Fridays.

2. The wages accrued for Monday and Tuesday, December 30 and 31, are $250.

3. Wages paid on Friday, January 10, total $1,275.

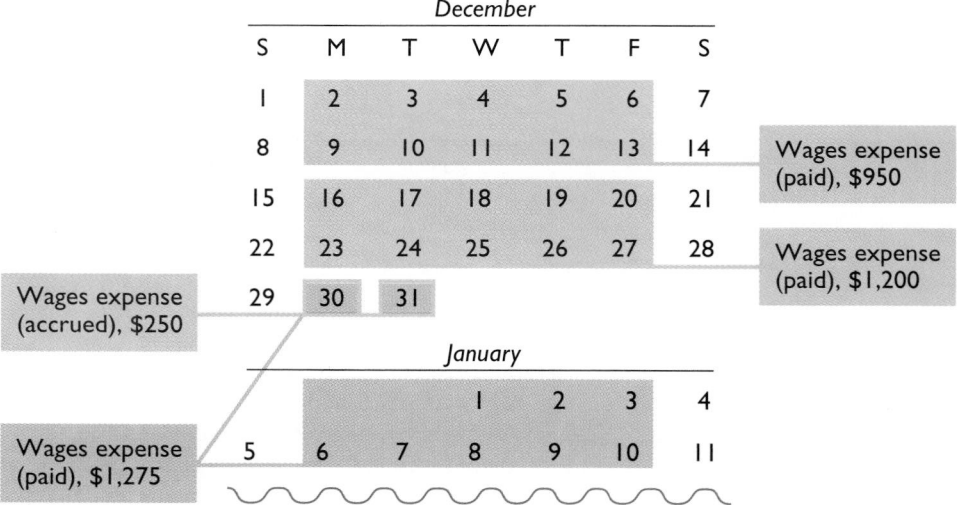

The adjusting entry for the accrued wages of December 30 and 31 is as follows:

Dec.	31	Wages Expense	51	2 5 0 00				
		Wages Payable	22			2 5 0 00		

After the adjusting entry has been posted, Wages Expense will have a debit balance of $4,525 ($4,275 + $250), and Wages Payable will have a credit balance of $250. After the closing process is completed, Wages Expense will have a zero balance and will be ready for entries in the next period. Wages Payable, on the other hand, has a balance of $250. Without a reversing entry, it is necessary to record the $1,275 payroll on January 10 as follows:

2000					
Jan.	10	Wages Payable	22	2 5 0 00	
		Wages Expense	51	1 0 2 5 00	
		Cash	11		1 2 7 5 00

The employee who records the January 10th entry must refer to the prior period's adjusting entry to determine the amount of the debits to Wages Payable and Wages Expense. Because the January 10th payroll is not recorded in the usual manner, there is a greater chance that an error may occur. This chance of error is reduced by recording a reversing entry as of the first day of the fiscal period. For example, the reversing entry for the accrued wages expense is as follows:

2000					
Jan.	1	Wages Payable	22	2 5 0 00	
		Wages Expense	51		2 5 0 00

The reversing entry transfers the $250 liability from Wages Payable to the credit side of Wages Expense. The nature of the $250 is unchanged—it is still a liability. When the payroll is paid on January 10, the following entry is recorded:

Jan.	10	Wages Expense	51	1 2 7 5 00	
		Cash	11		1 2 7 5 00

After this entry is posted, Wages Expense has a debit balance of $1,025. This amount is the wages expense for the period January 1–10. The sequence of entries, including adjusting, closing, and reversing entries, is illustrated in the following accounts:

ACCOUNT Wages Payable					ACCOUNT NO. 22		
		Post.				Balance	
Date	Item	Ref.	Debit	Credit	Debit	Credit	
1999 Dec. 31	Adjusting	5		2 5 0 00		2 5 0 00	
2000 Jan. 1	Reversing	7	2 5 0 00		—	—	

ACCOUNT Wages Expense					ACCOUNT NO. 51		
		Post.				Balance	
Date	Item	Ref.	Debit	Credit	Debit	Credit	
1999 Nov. 30		1	2 1 2 5 00		2 1 2 5 00		
Dec. 13		3	9 5 0 00		3 0 7 5 00		
27		3	1 2 0 0 00		4 2 7 5 00		
31	Adjusting	5	2 5 0 00		4 5 2 5 00		
31	Closing	6		4 5 2 5 00	—	—	
2000 Jan. 1	Reversing	7		2 5 0 00		2 5 0 00	
10		7	1 2 7 5 00		1 0 2 5 00		

In addition to accrued expenses (accrued liabilities), reversing entries may be journalized for accrued revenues (accrued assets). For example, the following reversing entry could be recorded for Computer King's accrued fees earned:

Jan.	1	Fees Earned	41		5	0	0	00						
		Accounts Receivable	12							5	0	0	00	

Reversing entries may also be journalized for prepaid expenses that are initially recorded as expenses and unearned revenues that are initially recorded as revenues. These situations are described and illustrated in Appendix C.

As we mentioned, the use of reversing entries is optional. However, with the increased use of computerized accounting systems, data entry personnel may be inputting routine accounting entries. In such an environment, reversing entries may be useful, since these individuals may not recognize the impact of adjusting entries on the related transactions in the following period.

KEY POINTS

1 Prepare a work sheet.

The work sheet is prepared by first entering a trial balance in the Trial Balance columns. The adjustments are then entered in the Adjustments Debit and Credit columns. The Trial Balance amounts plus or minus the adjustments are extended to the Adjusted Trial Balance columns. The work sheet is completed by extending the Adjusted Trial Balance amounts of assets, liabilities, owner's capital, and drawing to the Balance Sheet columns. The Adjusted Trial Balance amounts of revenues and expenses are extended to the Income Statement columns. The net income (or net loss) for the period is entered on the work sheet in the Income Statement Debit (or Credit) column and the Balance Sheet Credit (or Debit) column. Each of the four statement columns is then totaled.

2 Prepare financial statements from a work sheet.

The income statement is normally prepared directly from the work sheet. On the income statement, the expenses are normally presented in the order of size, from largest to smallest.

The basic form of the statement of owner's equity is prepared by listing the beginning balance of owner's equity, adding investments in the business and net income during the period, and deducting the owner's withdrawals. The amount listed on the work sheet as capital does not always represent the account balance at the beginning of the accounting period. The proprietor may have invested additional assets in the business during the period. Hence, for the beginning balance and any additional investments, it is necessary to refer to the capital account.

Various sections and subsections are often used in preparing a balance sheet. Two common classes of assets are current assets and fixed assets. Cash and other assets that are normally expected to be converted to cash or sold or used up within one year or less are called current assets. Property, plant, and equipment may also be called fixed assets or plant assets. The cost, accumulated depreciation, and book value of each major type of fixed asset are normally reported on the balance sheet.

Two common classes of liabilities are current liabilities and long-term liabilities. Liabilities that will be due within a short time (usually one year or less) and that are to be paid out of current assets are called current liabilities. Liabilities that will not be due for a long time (usually more than one year) are called long-term liabilities.

The owner's claim against the assets is presented below the liabilities section and added to the total liabilities. The total liabilities and total owner's equity must equal the total assets.

3 Prepare the adjusting and closing entries from a work sheet.

The data for journalizing the adjusting entries are in the Adjustments columns of the work sheet. The four entries required in closing the temporary accounts are:

1. Debit each revenue account for the amount of its balance, and credit Income Summary for the total revenue.
2. Debit Income Summary for the total expense, and credit each expense account for the amount of its balance.
3. Debit Income Summary for the amount of its balance (net income), and credit the capital account for the same amount. (Debit and credit are reversed if there is a net loss.)

4. Debit the capital account for the balance of the drawing account and credit the drawing account for the same amount.

After the closing entries have been posted to the ledger, the balance in the capital account will agree with the amount reported on the statement of owner's equity and balance sheet. In addition, the revenue, expense, and drawing accounts will have zero balances.

The last step of the accounting cycle is to prepare a post-closing trial balance. The purpose of the post-closing trial balance is to make sure that the ledger is in balance at the beginning of the next period.

4 Explain what is meant by the fiscal year and the natural business year.

The annual accounting period adopted by a business is known as its fiscal year. A corporation may adopt a fiscal year that ends when business activities have reached the lowest point in its annual operating cycle. Such a fiscal year is called the natural business year.

5 Review the seven basic steps of the accounting cycle.

The basic steps of the accounting cycle are:

1. Transactions are analyzed and recorded in a journal.
2. Transactions are posted to the ledger.
3. A trial balance is prepared, adjustment data are assembled, and the work sheet is completed.
4. Financial statements are prepared.
5. Adjusting entries are journalized and posted to the ledger.
6. Closing entries are journalized and posted to the ledger.
7. A post-closing trial balance is prepared.

6 Analyze and interpret the financial solvency of a business by computing the working capital and the current ratio.

The ability of a business to pay its debts is called solvency. Two financial measures for evaluating a business's short-term solvency are working capital and the current ratio. Working capital is the excess of the current assets of a business over its current liabilities. The current ratio is computed by dividing current assets by current liabilities.

ILLUSTRATIVE PROBLEM

Three years ago, T. Roderick organized Harbor Realty. At July 31, 2000, the end of the current fiscal year, the trial balance of Harbor Realty is as follows:

Harbor Realty
Trial Balance
July 31, 2000

Cash	3 4 2 5 00	
Accounts Receivable	7 0 0 0 00	
Supplies	1 2 7 0 00	
Prepaid Insurance	6 2 0 00	
Office Equipment	51 6 5 0 00	
Accumulated Depreciation		9 7 0 0 00
Accounts Payable		9 2 5 00
Unearned Fees		1 2 5 0 00
T. Roderick, Capital		29 0 0 0 00
T. Roderick, Drawing	5 2 0 0 00	
Fees Earned		59 1 2 5 00
Wages Expense	22 4 1 5 00	
Rent Expense	4 2 0 0 00	
Utilities Expense	2 7 1 5 00	
Miscellaneous Expense	1 5 0 5 00	
	100 0 0 0 00	100 0 0 0 00

The data needed to determine year-end adjustments are as follows:

a. Supplies on hand at July 31, 2000, are $380.
b. Insurance premiums expired during the year are $315.
c. Depreciation of equipment during the year is $4,950.
d. Wages accrued but not paid at July 31, 2000, are $440.
e. Accrued fees earned but not recorded at July 31, 2000, are $1,000.
f. Unearned fees on July 31, 2000, are $750.

Instructions

1. Enter the trial balance on a ten-column work sheet and complete the work sheet.
2. Prepare an income statement, a statement of owner's equity (no additional investments were made during the year), and a balance sheet.
3. On the basis of the data in the work sheet, journalize the closing entries.

Solution

1.

Harbor Realty
Work Sheet
For the Year Ended July 31, 2000

Account Title	Trial Balance Dr.	Trial Balance Cr.	Adjustments Dr.	Adjustments Cr.	Adjusted Trial Balance Dr.	Adjusted Trial Balance Cr.	Income Statement Dr.	Income Statement Cr.	Balance Sheet Dr.	Balance Sheet Cr.
1 Cash	3 4 2 5				3 4 2 5				3 4 2 5	
2 Accounts Receivable	7 0 0 0		(e)1 0 0 0		8 0 0 0				8 0 0 0	
3 Supplies	1 2 7 0			(a) 8 9 0	3 8 0				3 8 0	
4 Prepaid Insurance	6 2 0			(b) 3 1 5	3 0 5				3 0 5	
5 Office Equipment	51 6 5 0				51 6 5 0				51 6 5 0	
6 Accum. Depreciation		9 7 0 0		(c)4 9 5 0		14 6 5 0				14 6 5 0
7 Accounts Payable		9 2 5				9 2 5				9 2 5
8 Unearned Fees		1 2 5 0	(f) 5 0 0			7 5 0				7 5 0
9 T. Roderick, Capital		29 0 0 0				29 0 0 0				29 0 0 0
10 T. Roderick, Drawing	5 2 0 0				5 2 0 0				5 2 0 0	
11 Fees Earned		59 1 2 5		(e)1 0 0 0		60 6 2 5		60 6 2 5		
12				(f) 5 0 0						
13 Wages Expense	22 4 1 5		(d) 4 4 0		22 8 5 5		22 8 5 5			
14 Rent Expense	4 2 0 0				4 2 0 0		4 2 0 0			
15 Utilities Expense	2 7 1 5				2 7 1 5		2 7 1 5			
16 Miscellaneous Expense	1 5 0 5				1 5 0 5		1 5 0 5			
17	100 0 0 0	100 0 0 0								
18 Supplies Expense			(a) 8 9 0		8 9 0		8 9 0			
19 Insurance Expense			(b) 3 1 5		3 1 5		3 1 5			
20 Depreciation Expense			(c)4 9 5 0		4 9 5 0		4 9 5 0			
21 Wages Payable				(d) 4 4 0		4 4 0				4 4 0
22			8 0 9 5	8 0 9 5	106 3 9 0	106 3 9 0	37 4 3 0	60 6 2 5	68 9 6 0	45 7 6 5
23 Net income							23 1 9 5			23 1 9 5
24							60 6 2 5	60 6 2 5	68 9 6 0	68 9 6 0

2.

Harbor Realty
Income Statement
For the Year Ended July 31, 2000

Fees earned		$60 625 00
Operating expenses:		
Wages expense	$22 855 00	
Depreciation expense	4 950 00	
Rent expense	4 200 00	
Utilities expense	2 715 00	
Supplies expense	890 00	
Insurance expense	315 00	
Miscellaneous expense	1 505 00	
Total operating expenses		37 430 00
Net income		$23 195 00

Harbor Realty
Statement of Owner's Equity
For the Year Ended July 31, 2000

T. Roderick, capital, August 1, 1999		$29 000 00
Net income for the year	$23 195 00	
Less withdrawals	5 200 00	
Increase in owner's equity		17 995 00
T. Roderick, capital, July 31, 2000		$46 995 00

Harbor Realty
Balance Sheet
July 31, 2000

Assets			Liabilities		
Current assets:			Current liabilities:		
Cash	$ 3 425 00		Accounts payable	$ 925 00	
Accounts receivable	8 000 00		Unearned fees	750 00	
Supplies	380 00		Wages payable	440 00	
Prepaid insurance	305 00		Total liabilities		$ 2 115 00
Total current assets		$12 110 00			
Property, plant, and equipment:			**Owner's Equity**		
Office equipment	$51 650 00		T. Roderick, capital		46 995 00
Less accumulated depr.	14 650 00	37 000 00	Total liabilities and		
Total assets		$49 110 00	owner's equity		$49 110 00

3.

	Date		Description	Post. Ref.	Debit	Credit	
1			Closing Entries				1
2	2000 July	31	Fees Earned		60 6 2 5 00		2
3			Income Summary			60 6 2 5 00	3
4							4
5		31	Income Summary		37 4 3 0 00		5
6			Wages Expense			22 8 5 5 00	6
7			Rent Expense			4 2 0 0 00	7
8			Utilities Expense			2 7 1 5 00	8
9			Miscellaneous Expense			1 5 0 5 00	9
10			Supplies Expense			8 9 0 00	10
11			Insurance Expense			3 1 5 00	11
12			Depreciation Expense			4 9 5 0 00	12
13							13
14		31	Income Summary		23 1 9 5 00		14
15			T. Roderick, Capital			23 1 9 5 00	15
16							16
17		31	T. Roderick, Capital		5 2 0 0 00		17
18			T. Roderick, Drawing			5 2 0 0 00	18

JOURNAL — PAGE

SELF-EXAMINATION QUESTIONS   Answers at End of Chapter

Matching

Match each of the following statements with its proper term. Some terms may not be used.

A. accounting cycle
B. adjusted trial balance
C. adjusting entries
D. closing entries
E. current assets
F. current liabilities
G. current ratio
H. fiscal year
I. Income Summary
J. long-term liabilities
K. natural business year
L. notes receivable
M. owner's equity
N. permanent assets
O. post-closing trial balance

____ 1. A working paper that accountants may use to summarize adjusting entries and the account balances for the financial statements.

____ 2. Cash and other assets that are expected to be converted to cash or sold or used up, usually within one year or less, through the normal operations of the business.

____ 3. A customer's written promise to pay an amount and possibly interest at an agreed rate.

____ 4. Liabilities that will be due within a short time (usually one year or less) and that are to be paid out of current assets.

____ 5. Liabilities that will not be due for usually more than one year.

____ 6. An account to which the revenue and expense account balances are transferred at the end of a period.

____ 7. The trial balance prepared after the closing entries have been posted.

____ 8. The annual accounting period adopted by a business.

____ 9. A fiscal year that ends when business activities have reached the lowest point in an annual operating cycle.

____ 10. The process that begins with analyzing and journalizing transactions and ends with the post-closing trial balance.

P.	property, plant, and equipment
Q.	real accounts
R.	solvency
S.	temporary accounts
T.	work sheet
U.	working capital

___ 11. The ability of a business to pays its debts.

___ 12. The excess of the current assets of a business over its current liabilities.

___ 13. A financial ratio that is computed by dividing current assets by current liabilities.

___ 14. The entries that transfer the balances of the revenue, expense, and drawing accounts to the owner's capital account.

___ 15. The section of the balance sheet that includes equipment, machinery, buildings, and land.

___ 16. Accounts that report amounts for only one period.

Multiple Choice

1. Which of the following accounts in the Adjusted Trial Balance columns of the work sheet would be extended to the Balance Sheet columns?
   A. Utilities Expense   C. M. E. Jones, Drawing
   B. Rent Revenue   D. Miscellaneous Expense

2. Which of the following accounts would be classified as a current asset on the balance sheet?
   A. Office Equipment
   B. Land
   C. Accumulated Depreciation
   D. Accounts Receivable

3. Which of the following entries closes the owner's drawing account at the end of the period?
   A. Debit the drawing account, credit the income summary account.
   B. Debit the owner's capital account, credit the drawing account.
   C. Debit the income summary account, credit the drawing account.
   D. Debit the drawing account, credit the owner's capital account.

4. Which of the following accounts would not be closed to the income summary account at the end of a period?
   A. Fees Earned
   B. Wages Expense
   C. Rent Expense
   D. Accumulated Depreciation

5. Which of the following accounts would not be included in a post-closing trial balance?
   A. Cash
   B. Fees Earned
   C. Accumulated Depreciation
   D. J. C. Smith, Capital

CLASS DISCUSSION QUESTIONS

1. Is the work sheet a substitute for the financial statements? Discuss.
2. In the Income Statement columns of the work sheet, the Debit column total is greater than the Credit column total before the amount for the net income or net loss has been included. Would the income statement report a net income or a net loss? Explain.
3. In the Balance Sheet columns of the work sheet for Jones Co. for the current year, the Debit column total is $120,000 greater than the Credit column total before the amount for net income or net loss has been included. Would the income statement report a net income or a net loss? Explain.
4. Describe the nature of the assets that compose the following sections of a balance sheet: (a) current assets, (b) property, plant, and equipment.
5. What is the difference between a current liability and a long-term liability?
6. What types of accounts are referred to as temporary accounts?
7. Why are closing entries required at the end of an accounting period?
8. What is the difference between adjusting entries and closing entries?
9. Describe the four entries that close the temporary accounts.
10. What type of accounts are closed by transferring their balances (a) as a debit to Income Summary, (b) as a credit to Income Summary?
11. To what account is the income summary account closed?
12. To what account is the owner's drawing account closed?
13. What is the purpose of the post-closing trial balance?
14. What is the natural business year?

15. Why might a department store select a fiscal year ending January 31, rather than a fiscal year ending December 31?

16. The fiscal years for several well-known companies were as follows:

Company	Fiscal Year Ending
Kmart	January 30
J.C. Penney	January 26
Zayre Corp.	January 26
Toys "R" Us, Inc.	February 3
Federated Department Stores	February 3
The Limited, Inc.	February 2

What general characteristic shared by these companies explains why they do not have fiscal years ending December 31?

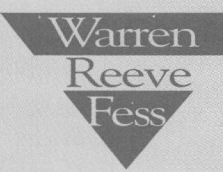

Resources for Your Success On-Line at **warren.swcollege.com**
Remember! If you need additional help, visit South-Western's Web site. See page 26 for a description of the online and printed materials that are available.

EXERCISES

Exercise 4–1
Place account balances in a work sheet

Objective 1

The balances for the accounts listed below appear in the Adjusted Trial Balance columns of the work sheet. Indicate whether each balance should be extended to (a) an Income Statement column or (b) a Balance Sheet column.

1. Accounts Payable
2. Wages Expense
3. Pete Parham, Capital
4. Fees Earned
5. Supplies
6. Unearned Fees
7. Utilities Expense
8. Pete Parham, Drawing
9. Wages Payable
10. Accounts Receivable

Exercise 4–2
Classify accounts

Objective 1

Balances for each of the following accounts appear in the Adjusted Trial Balance columns of the work sheet. Identify each as (a) asset, (b) liability, (c) revenue, or (d) expense.

1. Prepaid Advertising
2. Supplies
3. Unearned Rent
4. Rent Revenue
5. Salary Expense
6. Insurance Expense
7. Accounts Receivable
8. Land
9. Salary Payable
10. Fees Earned
11. Supplies Expense
12. Prepaid Insurance

Exercise 4–3
Steps in completing a work sheet

Objective 1

The steps performed in completing a work sheet are listed below in random order.

a. Add the Debit and Credit columns of the Balance Sheet and Income Statement columns of the work sheet to determine the amount of net income or net loss for the period.

b. Enter the unadjusted account balances from the general ledger into the unadjusted Trial Balance columns of the work sheet.

c. Enter the amount of net income or net loss for the period in the proper Income Statement column and Balance Sheet column.

d. Add the Debit and Credit columns of the Balance Sheet and Income Statement columns of the work sheet to verify that the totals are equal.

e. Extend the adjusted trial balance amounts to the Income Statement columns and the Balance Sheet columns.

f. Add the Debit and Credit columns of the Adjusted Trial Balance columns of the work sheet to verify that the totals are equal.

g. Add or deduct adjusting entry data to trial balance amounts and extend amounts to the Adjusted Trial Balance columns.

h. Add the Debit and Credit columns of the unadjusted Trial Balance columns of the work sheet to verify that the totals are equal.

i. Add the Debit and Credit columns of the Adjustments columns of the work sheet to verify that the totals are equal.

j. Enter the adjusting entries into the work sheet, based upon the adjustment data.

Indicate the order in which the preceding steps would be performed in preparing and completing a work sheet.

Exercise 4–4
Adjustments data on work sheet

Objective 1

✓ Total debits of Adjustments column: $14

Betty's Sanitize Services Co. offers cleaning services to business clients. The trial balance for Betty's Sanitize Services Co. has been prepared on the following work sheet for the year ended December 31, 1999:

Betty's Sanitize Services Co.
Work Sheet
For the Year Ended December 31, 1999

Account Title	Trial Balance Dr.	Trial Balance Cr.	Adjustments Dr.	Adjustments Cr.	Adjusted Trial Balance Dr.	Adjusted Trial Balance Cr.
Cash	6					
Accounts Receivable	25					
Supplies	4					
Prepaid Insurance	6					
Land	10					
Equipment	14					
Accumulated Depr.—Equip.		1				
Accounts Payable		13				
Wages Payable		0				
Betty Ratcliff, Capital		41				
Betty Ratcliff, Drawing	4					
Fees Earned		30				
Wages Expense	8					
Rent Expense	4					
Insurance Expense	0					
Utilities Expense	2					
Depreciation Expense	0					
Supplies Expense	0					
Miscellaneous Expense	2					
Totals	85	85				

The data for year-end adjustments are as follows:

a. Fees earned, but not yet billed, $4.
b. Supplies on hand, $2.
c. Insurance premiums expired, $4.
d. Depreciation expense, $2.
e. Wages accrued, but not paid, $2.

Enter the adjustments data, and place the balances in the Adjusted Trial Balance columns.

Exercise 4–5
Complete a work sheet

Objective 1

✓ Net income: $8

Betty's Sanitize Services Co. offers cleaning services to business clients. The following is a partially completed work sheet for Betty's Sanitize Services Co.:

Betty's Sanitize Services Co.
Work Sheet
For the Year Ended December 31, 1999

Account Title	Adjusted Trial Balance		Income Statement		Balance Sheet	
	Dr.	Cr.	Dr.	Cr.	Dr.	Cr.
Cash	6					
Accounts Receivable	29					
Supplies	2					
Prepaid Insurance	2					
Land	10					
Equipment	14					
Accumulated Depr.—Equip.		3				
Accounts Payable		13				
Wages Payable		2				
Betty Ratcliff, Capital		41				
Betty Ratcliff, Drawing	4					
Fees Earned		34				
Wages Expense	10					
Rent Expense	4					
Insurance Expense	4					
Utilities Expense	2					
Depreciation Expense	2					
Supplies Expense	2					
Miscellaneous Expense	2					
Totals	93	93				
Net income (loss)						

Complete the work sheet.

Exercise 4–6
Financial statements

Objective 2

✓ Betty Ratcliff, capital, Dec. 31, 1999: $45

Based upon the data in Exercise 4–5, prepare an income statement, statement of owner's equity, and balance sheet for Betty's Sanitize Services Co.

Exercise 4–7
Adjusting entries

Objective 3

Based upon the data in Exercise 4–4, prepare the adjusting entries for Betty's Sanitize Services Co.

Exercise 4–8
Closing entries

Objective 3

Based upon the data in Exercise 4–5, prepare the closing entries for Betty's Sanitize Services Co.

Exercise 4–9
Income statement

Objective 2

✓ Net income: $99,950

The following account balances were taken from the Adjusted Trial Balance columns of the work sheet for The Messenger Co., a delivery service firm, for the current fiscal year ended June 30:

Fees Earned	$183,700
Salaries Expense	47,100
Rent Expense	18,000
Utilities Expense	7,500
Supplies Expense	3,100
Miscellaneous Expense	1,350
Insurance Expense	1,500
Depreciation Expense	5,200

Prepare an income statement.

Exercise 4–10
Income statement; net loss

Objective 2

✓ Net loss: $(4,150)

The following revenue and expense account balances were taken from the ledger of Reimer Services Co. after the accounts had been adjusted on March 31, the end of the current fiscal year:

Depreciation Expense	$ 7,500
Insurance Expense	3,900
Miscellaneous Expense	2,250
Rent Expense	36,000
Service Revenue	113,900
Supplies Expense	3,100
Utilities Expense	8,500
Wages Expense	56,800

Prepare an income statement.

Exercise 4–11
Statement of owner's equity

Objective 2

✓ Marion Weaver, capital, Dec. 31: $167,000

Neophyte Services Co. offers its services to new arrivals in the Evanston area. Selected accounts from the ledger of Neophyte Services Co. for the current fiscal year ended December 31 are as follows:

Marion Weaver, Capital				Marion Weaver, Drawing			
Dec. 31	10,000	Jan. 1	143,750	Mar. 31	2,500	Dec. 31	10,000
		Dec. 31	33,250	June 30	2,500		
				Sep. 30	2,500		
				Dec. 31	2,500		

Income Summary			
Dec. 31	578,150	Dec. 31	611,400
31	33,250		

Prepare a statement of owner's equity for the year.

Exercise 4–12
Statement of owner's equity; net loss

Objective 2

✓ Casey Martin, capital, July 31: $309,800

Selected accounts from the ledger of Casey Sports Services Co. for the current fiscal year ended July 31 are as follows:

Casey Martin, Capital				Casey Martin, Drawing			
July 31	40,000	Aug. 1	410,300	Oct. 31	10,000	July 31	40,000
31	60,500			Jan. 31	10,000		
				Apr. 30	10,000		
				July 31	10,000		

Income Summary			
July 31	723,400	July 31	662,900
		31	60,500

Prepare a statement of owner's equity for the year.

Exercise 4–13
Classify assets

Objective 2

Identify each of the following as (a) a current asset or (b) property, plant, and equipment:

1. Accounts receivable
2. Building
3. Cash
4. Equipment
5. Land
6. Supplies

Exercise 4–14
Balance sheet classification

Objective 2

At the balance sheet date, a business owes a mortgage note payable of $450,000, the terms of which provide for monthly payments of $15,000.

➤ Explain how the liability should be classified on the balance sheet.

Exercise 4–15
Balance sheet
Objective 2

✓ Total assets: $116,820

Looking Good Co. offers personal weight reduction consulting services to individuals. After all the accounts have been closed on April 30, the end of the current fiscal year, the balances of selected accounts from the ledger of Looking Good Co. are as follows:

Accounts Payable	$12,750	Prepaid Insurance	$4,100
Accounts Receivable	28,920	Prepaid Rent	2,400
Accumulated Depreciation—Equipment	21,100	Salaries Payable	3,750
Cash	7,150	Supplies	4,750
Equipment	90,600	Unearned Fees	2,500
M. Monroe, Capital	97,820		

Prepare a classified balance sheet.

Exercise 4–16
Balance sheet
Objective 2

What's Wrong WITH THIS?

✓ Corrected balance sheet, total assets: $132,500

List the errors you find in the following balance sheet. Prepare a corrected balance sheet.

SPA Services Co.
Balance Sheet
For the Year Ended August 31, 1999

Assets			Liabilities		
Current assets:			Current liabilities:		
Cash	$ 5,170		Accounts receivable		$ 5,390
Accounts payable	4,390		Accum. depr.—building		23,000
Supplies	590		Accum. depr.—equipment		16,000
Prepaid insurance	1,600		Net loss		15,500
Land	75,000		Total liabilities		$ 59,890
Total current assets		$ 86,750			
Property, plant,			**Owner's Equity**		
and equipment:			Wages payable		$ 975
Building	$ 55,500		S. Elby, capital		127,135
Equipment	28,250		Total owner's equity		$128,110
Total property, plant,			Total liabilities and		
and equipment		$101,250	owner's equity		$188,000
Total assets		$188,000			

Exercise 4–17
Adjusting entries from work sheet
Objective 3

Air Clean Purifier Co. is a consulting firm specializing in pollution control. The entries in the Adjustments columns of the work sheet for Air Clean Purifier Co. are shown below.

	Adjustments	
	Dr.	Cr.
Accounts Receivable	2,100	
Supplies		1,025
Prepaid Insurance		1,100
Accumulated Depreciation—Equipment		800
Wages Payable		636
Unearned Rent	3,500	
Fees Earned		2,100
Wages Expense	636	
Supplies Expense	1,025	
Rent Revenue		3,500
Insurance Expense	1,100	
Depreciation Expense	800	

Prepare the adjusting journal entries.

Exercise 4–18
Identify accounts to be closed
Objective 3

From the following list, identify the accounts that should be closed to Income Summary at the end of the fiscal year:

a. Accounts Payable
b. Accumulated Depreciation—
    Buildings
c. Depreciation Expense—Buildings
d. Donna Taff, Capital
e. Donna Taff, Drawing
f. Equipment

g. Fees Earned
h. Land
i. Salaries Expense
j. Salaries Payable
k. Supplies
l. Supplies Expense

Exercise 4–19
Closing entries

Objective 3

Prior to its closing, Income Summary had total debits of $417,500 and total credits of $520,000.

➤ Briefly explain the purpose served by the income summary account and the nature of the entries that resulted in the $417,500 and the $520,000.

Exercise 4–20
Closing entries

Objective 3

✓ b. $438,000

After all revenue and expense accounts have been closed at the end of the fiscal year, Income Summary has a debit of $695,500 and a credit of $839,000. At the same date, Shawn Marsh, Capital has a credit balance of $319,500, and Shawn Marsh, Drawing has a balance of $25,000. (a) Journalize the entries required to complete the closing of the accounts. (b) Determine the amount of Shawn Marsh, Capital at the end of the period.

Exercise 4–21
Closing entries

Objective 3

Minish Services Co. offers its services to individuals desiring to improve their personal images. After the accounts have been adjusted at October 31, the end of the fiscal year, the following balances were taken from the ledger of Minish Services Co.

B. J. Galis, Capital	$298,500	Rent Expense	$74,000
B. J. Galis, Drawing	30,000	Supplies Expense	15,500
Fees Earned	355,000	Miscellaneous Expense	5,500
Wages Expense	197,300		

Journalize the four entries required to close the accounts.

Exercise 4–22
Identify permanent accounts

Objective 3

Which of the following accounts will usually appear in the post-closing trial balance?

a. Accounts Receivable
b. Accumulated Depreciation
c. Cash
d. Depreciation Expense
e. Equipment
f. Erik Geering, Capital
g. Erik Geering, Drawing
h. Fees Earned
i. Supplies
j. Wages Expense
k. Wages Payable

Exercise 4–23
Post-closing trial balance

Objective 3

What's Wrong WITH THIS?

✓ Correct column totals, $67,000

An accountant prepared the following post-closing trial balance:

Uptown Repairs Co.
Post-Closing Trial Balance
March 31, 20—

Cash	7,400	
Accounts Receivable	18,500	
Supplies		1,100
Equipment		40,000
Accumulated Depreciation—Equipment	11,100	
Accounts Payable	7,250	
Salaries Payable		1,500
Unearned Rent	4,000	
Lorraine Penn, Capital	43,150	
	91,400	42,600

Prepare a corrected post-closing trial balance. Assume that all accounts have normal balances and that the amounts shown are correct.

Exercise 4–24
Steps in the accounting cycle

Rearrange the following steps in the accounting cycle in proper sequence:

a. Adjusting entries are journalized and posted to the ledger.
b. Closing entries are journalized and posted to the ledger.
c. Financial statements are prepared.
d. A post-closing trial balance is prepared.
e. Transactions are analyzed and recorded in the journal.
f. Transactions are posted to the ledger.
g. A trial balance is prepared, adjustment data are assembled, and the work sheet is completed.

Exercise 4–25
Working capital and current ratio

Objective 6

The financial statements for Hershey Foods Corporation are presented in Appendix G at the end of the text.

a.   Determine the working capital and the current ratio for Hershey Foods Corporation as of December 31, 1996 and 1995.
b.   ➤ What conclusions concerning the company's ability to meets its financial obligations can you draw from these data?

Appendix Exercise 4–26
Adjusting and reversing entries

On the basis of the following data, (a) journalize the adjusting entries at December 31, 1999, the end of the current fiscal year, and (b) journalize the reversing entries on January 1, 2000, the first day of the following year.

1.   Sales salaries are uniformly $7,500 for a five-day workweek, ending on Friday. The last payday of the year was Friday, December 26.
2.   Accrued fees earned but not recorded at December 31, $13,200.

Appendix Exercise 4–27
Entries posted to the wages expense account

Portions of the wages expense account of a business are as follows:

ACCOUNT Wages Expense					ACCOUNT NO. 53		
		Post.				**Balance**	
Date	Item	Ref.	Dr.	Cr.	Dr.	Cr.
1999							
Dec. 26	(1)	51	30,000		1,560,000	
31	(2)	52	18,000		1,578,000	
31	(3)	53		1,578,000	—	—
2000							
Jan. 1	(4)	54		18,000		18,000
2	(5)	55	30,000		12,000	

a.   Indicate the nature of the entry (payment, adjusting, closing, reversing) from which each numbered posting was made.
b.   Journalize the complete entry from which each numbered posting was made.

PROBLEMS SERIES A

Problem 4–1A
Work sheet and related items

Objectives 1, 2, 3

HAT
SPREADSHEET
GENERAL LEDGER

✓ 2. Net income: $21,340

The trial balance of Wonder Wash Laundry at August 31, 2000, the end of the current fiscal year, and the data needed to determine year-end adjustments are as follows:

Wonder Wash Laundry
Trial Balance
August 31, 2000

Cash	13,100	
Laundry Supplies	6,560	
Prepaid Insurance	4,490	
Laundry Equipment	95,100	
Accumulated Depreciation		40,200
Accounts Payable		6,100
Louis Krupman, Capital		37,800
Louis Krupman, Drawing	2,000	
Laundry Revenue		140,900
Wages Expense	51,400	
Rent Expense	36,000	
Utilities Expense	13,650	
Miscellaneous Expense	2,700	
	225,000	225,000

a. Wages accrued but not paid at August 31 are $1,350.
b. Depreciation of equipment during the year is $6,600.
c. Laundry supplies on hand at August 31 are $1,500.
d. Insurance premiums expired during the year are $2,800.

Instructions

1. Enter the trial balance on a ten-column work sheet and complete the work sheet. Add accounts as needed.
2. Prepare an income statement, a statement of owner's equity (no additional investments were made during the year), and a balance sheet.
3. On the basis of the adjustment data in the work sheet, journalize the adjusting entries.
4. On the basis of the data in the work sheet, journalize the closing entries.

Problem 4–2A

Adjusting and closing entries; statement of owner's equity

Objectives 2, 3

HAT

SPREADSHEET

✓ 2. K. Roemmich, capital, Dec. 31: $126,060

Roemmich Company is a financial planning services firm owned and operated by K. Roemmich. As of December 31, 1999, the end of the current fiscal year, the accountant for Roemmich Company prepared a work sheet, part of which is shown below.

Roemmich Company
Trial Balance
December 31, 1999

	Income Statement		Balance Sheet	
Cash			3,650	
Accounts Receivable			23,960	
Supplies			2,790	
Prepaid Insurance			1,000	
Land			42,500	
Buildings			116,000	
Accumulated Depreciation—Buildings ..				82,400
Equipment			82,000	
Accumulated Depreciation—Equipment				50,900
Accounts Payable				7,870
Salaries Payable				1,450
Taxes Payable				2,920
Unearned Rent				300
K. Roemmich, Capital				114,900
K. Roemmich, Drawing			10,000	
Service Fees Earned		144,260		
Rent Revenue		1,600		
Salary Expense	72,650			
Depreciation Expense—Equipment	18,100			
Rent Expense	9,000			
Supplies Expense	8,970			
Utilities Expense	5,300			
Depreciation Expense—Buildings	4,800			
Taxes Expense	3,520			
Insurance Expense	1,400			
Miscellaneous Expense	960			
	124,700	145,860	281,900	260,740
Net income	21,160			21,160
	145,860	145,860	281,900	281,900

Instructions

1. Journalize the entries that were required to close the accounts at December 31.
2. Prepare a statement of owner's equity for the fiscal year ended December 31. There were no additional investments during the year.
3. If the balance of K. Roemmich, Capital decreased $15,000 after the closing entries were posted, what was the amount of net income or net loss?

If the working papers correlating with this textbook are not used, omit Problem 4–3A.

Problem 4–3A
Ledger accounts and work sheet, and related items

Objectives 1, 2, 3

✓ 2. Net income: $4,033

The ledger and trial balance of Grisham Company as of January 31, 2000, the end of the first month of its current fiscal year, are presented in the working papers.

Instructions

1. Complete the ten-column work sheet. Data needed to determine the necessary adjusting entries are as follows:
   a. Service revenue accrued at January 31 is $750.
   b. Supplies on hand at January 31 are $500.
   c. Insurance premiums expired during January are $90.
   d. Depreciation of the building during January is $125.
   e. Depreciation of equipment during January is $95.
   f. Unearned rent at January 31 is $100.
   g. Wages accrued but not paid at January 31 are $600.
2. Prepare an income statement, a statement of owner's equity, and a balance sheet. (Note: The owner made an additional investment during the period.)
3. Journalize and post the adjusting entries, inserting balances in the accounts affected.
4. Journalize and post the closing entries. Indicate closed accounts by inserting a line in both Balance columns opposite the closing entry. Insert the new balance of the capital account.
5. Prepare a post-closing trial balance.

Problem 4–4A
Work sheet and financial statements

Objectives 1, 2

GENERAL LEDGER

HAT

✓ 2. Net income: $39,680

Last Chance Company offers legal consulting advice to death-row inmates. Last Chance Company prepared the following trial balance at April 30, 2000, the end of the current fiscal year:

Last Chance Company
Trial Balance
April 30, 2000

Cash	3,200	
Accounts Receivable	10,500	
Prepaid Insurance	3,800	
Supplies	1,950	
Land	50,000	
Building	137,500	
Accumulated Depreciation—Building		51,700
Equipment	90,100	
Accumulated Depreciation—Equipment		35,300
Accounts Payable		7,500
Unearned Rent		3,000
Jason Soroka, Capital		164,100
Jason Soroka, Drawing	10,000	
Fees Revenue		198,400
Salaries and Wages Expense	80,200	
Advertising Expense	38,200	
Utilities Expense	19,000	
Repairs Expense	11,500	
Miscellaneous Expense	4,050	
	460,000	460,000

The data needed to determine year-end adjustments are as follows:

a. Accrued fees revenue at April 30 are $3,800.
b. Insurance expired during the year is $2,900.
c. Supplies on hand at April 30 are $450.
d. Depreciation of building for the year is $1,620.
e. Depreciation of equipment for the year is $3,500.

f. Accrued salaries and wages at April 30 are $2,050.
g. Unearned rent at April 30 is $1,000.

Instructions

1. Enter the trial balance on a ten-column work sheet and complete the work sheet. Add accounts as needed.
2. Prepare an income statement for the year ended April 30.
3. Prepare a statement of owner's equity for the year ended April 30. No additional investments were made during the year.
4. Prepare a balance sheet as of April 30.
5. Compute the percent of net income to total revenue for the year.

Problem 4–5A

Ledger accounts, work sheet, and related items

Objectives 1, 2, 3

GENERAL LEDGER

HAT

✓ 2. Net income: $16,895

The trial balance of Avery Repairs at December 31, 2000, the end of the current year, and the data needed to determine year-end adjustments are as follows:

Avery Repairs
Trial Balance
December 31, 2000

11	Cash	6,825	
13	Supplies	4,820	
14	Prepaid Insurance	3,500	
16	Equipment	42,200	
17	Accumulated Depreciation—Equipment		9,050
18	Trucks	45,000	
19	Accumulated Depreciation—Trucks		27,100
21	Accounts Payable		4,015
31	Steve Galvine, Capital		29,885
32	Steve Galvine, Drawing	3,000	
41	Service Revenue		99,950
51	Wages Expense	42,010	
53	Rent Expense	10,100	
55	Truck Expense	9,350	
59	Miscellaneous Expense	3,195	
		170,000	170,000

a. Supplies on hand at December 31 are $1,100.
b. Insurance premiums expired during year are $2,500.
c. Depreciation of equipment during year is $6,080.
d. Depreciation of trucks during year is $5,500.
e. Wages accrued but not paid at December 31 are $600.

Instructions

1. For each account listed in the trial balance, enter the balance in the appropriate Balance column of a four-column account and place a check mark (✓) in the Posting Reference column.
2. Enter the trial balance on a ten-column work sheet and complete the work sheet. Add accounts as needed.
3. Prepare an income statement, a statement of owner's equity (no additional investments were made during the year), and a balance sheet.
4. Journalize and post the adjusting entries, inserting balances in the accounts affected. The following additional accounts from Avery's chart of accounts should be used: Wages Payable, 22; Supplies Expense, 52; Depreciation Expense—Equipment, 54; Depreciation Expense—Trucks, 56; Insurance Expense, 57.
5. Journalize and post the closing entries. (Income Summary is account #33 in the chart of accounts.) Indicate closed accounts by inserting a line in both Balance columns opposite the closing entry.
6. Prepare a post-closing trial balance.

PROBLEMS SERIES B

Problem 4–1B
Work sheet and related items

Objectives 1, 2, 3

SPREADSHEET
GENERAL LEDGER

✓ 2. Net income: $7,630

The trial balance of The Wash and Dry Laundromat at July 31, 2000, the end of the current fiscal year, and the data needed to determine year-end adjustments are as follows:

The Wash and Dry Laundromat
Trial Balance
July 31, 2000

Cash	6,290	
Laundry Supplies	5,850	
Prepaid Insurance	2,400	
Laundry Equipment	99,750	
Accumulated Depreciation		52,700
Accounts Payable		6,950
Nikki Weiss, Capital		37,450
Nikki Weiss, Drawing	4,000	
Laundry Revenue		67,900
Wages Expense	22,900	
Rent Expense	14,400	
Utilities Expense	8,500	
Miscellaneous Expense	910	
	165,000	165,000

a. Laundry supplies on hand at March 31 are $1,240.
b. Insurance premiums expired during the year are $1,700.
c. Depreciation of equipment during the year is $6,200.
d. Wages accrued but not paid at March 31 are $1,050.

Instructions

1. Enter the trial balance on a ten-column work sheet and complete the work sheet. Add accounts as needed.
2. Prepare an income statement, a statement of owner's equity (no additional investments were made during the year), and a balance sheet.
3. On the basis of the adjustment data in the work sheet, journalize the adjusting entries.
4. On the basis of the data in the work sheet, journalize the closing entries.

Problem 4–2B
Adjusting and closing entries; statement of owner's equity

Objectives 2, 3

SPREADSHEET

✓ 2. S. Holmes, capital, Nov. 30: $55,230

Holmes Company is an investigative services firm that is owned and operated by S. Holmes. On November 30, 1999, the end of the current fiscal year, the accountant for Holmes Company prepared a work sheet, a part of which is shown at the top of the next page.

Instructions

1. Journalize the entries that were required to close the accounts at November 30.
2. Prepare a statement of owner's equity for the fiscal year ended November 30, 1999. There were no additional investments during the year.
3. If S. Holmes, Capital decreased $10,000 after the closing entries were posted, what was the amount of net income or net loss?

Holmes Company
Work Sheet (Partial)
November 30, 1999

	Income Statement		Balance Sheet	
Cash			7,325	
Accounts Receivable			21,600	
Supplies			1,610	
Prepaid Insurance			1,350	
Equipment			69,750	
Accumulated Depreciation—Equipment				33,995
Accounts Payable				5,230
Salaries Payable				3,480
Taxes Payable				2,200
Unearned Rent				1,500
S. Holmes, Capital				31,345
S. Holmes, Drawing			7,500	
Service Fees Earned		185,900		
Rent Revenue		2,250		
Salary Expense	119,865			
Rent Expense	15,600			
Supplies Expense	5,310			
Depreciation Expense—Equipment	4,600			
Utilities Expense	3,640			
Taxes Expense	3,115			
Insurance Expense	2,925			
Miscellaneous Expense	1,710			
	156,765	188,150	109,135	77,750
Net income	31,385			31,385
	188,150	188,150	109,135	109,135

If the working papers correlating with this textbook are not used, omit Problem 4–3B.

Problem 4–3B

Ledger accounts, work sheet, and related items

Objectives 1, 2, 3

✓ 2. Net income: $4,617

The ledger and trial balance of Grisham Company as of January 31, 2000, the end of the first month of its current fiscal year, are presented in the working papers.

Instructions

1. Complete the ten-column work sheet. Data needed to determine the necessary adjusting entries are as follows:
   a. Service revenue accrued at January 31 is $1,100.
   b. Supplies on hand at January 31 are $449.
   c. Insurance premiums expired during January are $100.
   d. Depreciation of the building during January is $110.
   e. Depreciation of equipment during January is $115.
   f. Unearned rent at January 31 is $100.
   g. Wages accrued at January 31 are $300.
2. Prepare an income statement, a statement of owner's equity, and a balance sheet. (Note: The owner made an additional investment during the period.)
3. Journalize and post the adjusting entries, inserting balances in the accounts affected.
4. Journalize and post the closing entries. Indicate closed accounts by inserting a line in both Balance columns opposite the closing entry.
5. Prepare a post-closing trial balance.

Problem 4–4B

Work sheet and financial statements

Objectives 1, 2

GENERAL LEDGER

✓ 2. Net income: $46,670

Koontz Company maintains and repairs warning lights, such as those found on radio towers and lighthouses. Koontz Company prepared the following trial balance at May 31, 2000, the end of the current fiscal year:

Koontz Company
Trial Balance
May 31, 2000

Cash	7,500	
Accounts Receivable	16,500	
Prepaid Insurance	2,600	
Supplies	1,950	
Land	60,000	
Building	100,500	
Accumulated Depreciation—Building		81,700
Equipment	72,400	
Accumulated Depreciation—Equipment		63,800
Accounts Payable		6,100
Unearned Rent		1,500
Joe Carpenter, Capital		60,700
Joe Carpenter, Drawing	4,000	
Fees Revenue		161,200
Salaries and Wages Expense	60,200	
Advertising Expense	19,000	
Utilities Expense	18,200	
Repairs Expense	8,100	
Miscellaneous Expense	4,050	
	375,000	375,000

The data needed to determine year-end adjustments are as follows:

a. Fees revenue accrued at May 31 is $3,500.
b. Insurance expired during the year is $1,000.
c. Supplies on hand at May 31 are $450.
d. Depreciation of building for the year is $1,620.
e. Depreciation of equipment for the year is $3,160.
f. Accrued salaries and wages at May 31 are $1,700.
g. Unearned rent at May 31 is $1,000.

Instructions

1. Enter the trial balance on a ten-column work sheet and complete the work sheet. Add accounts as needed.
2. Prepare an income statement for the year ended May 31.
3. Prepare a statement of owner's equity for the year ended May 31. No additional investments were made during the year.
4. Prepare a balance sheet as of May 31.
5. Compute the percent of net income to total revenue for the year.

Problem 4–5B

Ledger accounts, work sheet, and related items

Objectives 1, 2, 3

GENERAL LEDGER

✓ 3. Net income: $23,275

The trial balance of Quick Repairs at March 31, 2000, the end of the current year, is shown at the top of the next page. The data needed to determine year-end adjustments are as follows:

a. Supplies on hand at March 31 are $1,205.
b. Insurance premiums expired during year are $935.
c. Depreciation of equipment during year is $3,380.
d. Depreciation of trucks during year is $4,400.
e. Wages accrued but not paid at March 31 are $800.

Quick Repairs
Trial Balance
March 31, 2000

11	Cash	6,950	
13	Supplies	4,295	
14	Prepaid Insurance	2,735	
16	Equipment	40,650	
17	Accumulated Depreciation—Equipment		11,209
18	Trucks	36,300	
19	Accumulated Depreciation—Trucks		6,400
21	Accounts Payable		2,015
31	Renee Dills, Capital		40,426
32	Renee Dills, Drawing	5,000	
41	Service Revenue		89,950
51	Wages Expense	33,925	
53	Rent Expense	9,600	
55	Truck Expense	8,350	
59	Miscellaneous Expense	2,195	
		150,000	150,000

Instructions

1. For each account listed in the trial balance, enter the balance in the appropriate Balance column of a four-column account and place a check mark (✓) in the Posting Reference column.
2. Enter the trial balance on a ten-column work sheet and complete the work sheet. Add accounts as needed.
3. Prepare an income statement, a statement of owner's equity (no additional investments were made during the year), and a balance sheet.
4. Journalize and post the adjusting entries, inserting balances in the accounts affected. The following additional accounts from Quick's chart of accounts should be used: Wages Payable, 22; Supplies Expense, 52; Depreciation Expense—Equipment, 54; Depreciation Expense—Trucks, 56; Insurance Expense, 57.
5. Journalize and post the closing entries. (Income Summary is account #33 in the chart of accounts.) Indicate closed accounts by inserting a line in both Balance columns opposite the closing entry.
6. Prepare a post-closing trial balance.

CONTINUING PROBLEM

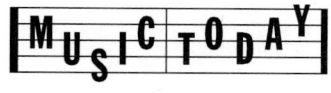

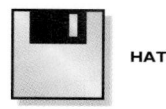

HAT

✓ 2. Net income: $1,620

The unadjusted trial balance of Music Today as of December 31, 1999, along with the adjustment data for the two months ended December 31, 1999, are shown in Chapter 3.

Instructions

1. Prepare a ten-column work sheet.
2. Prepare an income statement, a statement of owner's equity, and a balance sheet. (Note: Chris Stipe made investments in Music Today on November 1 and December 1, 1999.)
3. Journalize and post the closing entries. The income summary account is #33 in the ledger of Music Today. Indicate closed accounts by inserting a line in both Balance columns opposite the closing entry.
4. Prepare a post-closing trial balance.

COMPREHENSIVE PROBLEM 1

GENERAL LEDGER

HAT

QUICKBOOKS

✓ 4. Net income: $6,775

For the past several years, Angie Mills has operated a part-time consulting business from her home. As of September 1, 2000, Angie decided to move to rented quarters and to operate the business, which was to be known as Interactive Consulting, on a full-time basis. Interactive Consulting entered into the following transactions during September:

Sept. 1. The following assets were received from Angie Mills: cash, $7,050; accounts receivable, $1,500; supplies, $1,250; and office equipment, $7,200. There were no liabilities received.
   2. Paid three months' rent on a lease rental contract, $3,600.
   2. Paid the premiums on property and casualty insurance policies, $1,500.
   4. Received cash from clients as an advance payment for services to be provided and recorded it as unearned fees, $3,500.
   5. Purchased additional office equipment on account from Payne Company, $1,800.
   6. Received cash from clients on account, $800.
   10. Paid cash for a newspaper advertisement, $120.
   12. Paid Payne Company for part of the debt incurred on September 5, $800.
   12. Recorded services provided on account for the period September 1–12, $1,200.
   13. Paid part-time receptionist for two weeks' salary, $400.
   17. Recorded cash from cash clients for fees earned during the first half of September, $2,100.
   18. Paid cash for supplies, $750.
   20. Recorded services provided on account for the period September 13–20, $1,100.
   24. Recorded cash from cash clients for fees earned for the period September 17–24, $1,850.
   25. Received cash from clients on account, $1,300.
   27. Paid part-time receptionist for two weeks' salary, $400.
   29. Paid telephone bill for September, $130.
   30. Paid electricity bill for September, $200.
   30. Recorded cash from cash clients for fees earned for the period September 25–30, $1,050.
   30. Recorded services provided on account for the remainder of September, $500.
   30. Angie withdrew $1,500 for personal use.

Instructions

1. Journalize each transaction in a two-column journal, referring to the following chart of accounts in selecting the accounts to be debited and credited. (Do not insert the account numbers in the journal at this time.)

11 Cash	31 Angie Mills, Capital
12 Accounts Receivable	32 Angie Mills, Drawing
14 Supplies	41 Fees Earned
15 Prepaid Rent	51 Salary Expense
16 Prepaid Insurance	52 Rent Expense
18 Office Equipment	53 Supplies Expense
19 Accumulated Depreciation	54 Depreciation Expense
21 Accounts Payable	55 Insurance Expense
22 Salaries Payable	59 Miscellaneous Expense
23 Unearned Fees	

2. Post the journal to a ledger of four-column accounts.
3. Prepare a trial balance as of September 30, 2000, on a ten-column work sheet, listing all the accounts in the order given in the ledger. Complete the work sheet, using the following adjustment data:
   a. Insurance expired during September is $125.
   b. Supplies on hand on September 30 are $1,220.

    c.   Depreciation of office equipment for September is $250.

    d.   Accrued receptionist salary on September 30 is $120.

    e.   Rent expired during September is $800.

    f.   Unearned fees on September 30 are $1,200.

4.   Prepare an income statement, a statement of owner's equity, and a balance sheet.

5.   Journalize and post the adjusting entries.

6.   Journalize and post the closing entries. (Income Summary is account #33 in the chart of accounts.) Indicate closed accounts by inserting a line in both Balance columns opposite the closing entry.

7.   Prepare a post-closing trial balance.

QuickBooks Instructions:

QuickBooks® is accounting software designed especially for small businesses. To launch the program, double click on the QuickBooks icon within the QuickBooks program group on your computer screen.

    Select "New Company" from the File menu.

    Note: When a window appears for which no specific instructions are given below, read the information in the window and then click "Next."

- *Welcome* window: After clicking on the "Next" button to begin the General section, click "No, I'm not upgrading." Then click "Next."
- *Your company name* window: Enter the company name as indicated in the problem. The legal name will be the same.
- *Your company address* window: Enter your address as the address of the company.
- *Other company information* window: Enter your I.D. number or Social Security number. Change the first month of the income tax year and the fiscal year from January if the company in your problem is just starting in business or is not on a calendar year.
- *Your company income tax form* window: Select <Other/None> for the Tax Form. In the message box that then appears, click "Do not display this message in the future." Then click OK."
- *Select your type of business* window: Select the type of business (e.g., service) as indicated in the problem.
- *Save As* window: Click "OK" when the file name is displayed (unless you want to change it). The file name displayed is based on the company name you entered.
- *Your income and expense accounts* window: Click "No, I'd like to create my own."
- *Sales tax* window: Click "No."
- *Your invoice format* window: Click "Service."
- *Employees* window: Enter "0" for zero.
- *Estimates* window: Click "No."
- *Time tracking* window: Click "No."
- *Tracking reimbursable expenses* window: Click "No."
- *Classifying transactions* window: Click "No."
- *Two ways to handle bills and payments* window: Click "Enter the bills first and then enter the payments later."
- *Reminders list* window: Click "When I ask for it."
- *Accrual- or cash-based reporting* window: Click "Accrual-based reports."
- *Choose your QuickBooks start date* window: Enter the date of the first transaction in the problem, in MM/DD/YY format.
- *Adding an income account* window: Enter the name of an income account shown in the problem chart of accounts.
- *Add another income account* window: Click "Yes" and continue to add necessary income accounts, or Click "No."
- *Expense accounts* window: Click "No thank you."
- *No accounts set up* window: Click "Yes."
- *Adding an expense account* window: Enter the name of an expense account shown in the problem chart of accounts.

- *Add another expense account* window: Click "Yes" and continue to add necessary expense accounts, or Click "No."
- *Receipt of payment* window: Click "Sometimes."
- *Statement charges* window: Click "No."
- *Service items* window: Click "No."
- *Non-inventory parts* window: Click "No."
- *Other charges* window: Click "No."
- *Income Details: Inventory* window: Click "Skip inventory items."
- *Enter customers* window: Click "No."
- *Adding vendors with open balances* window: Click "No."
- *Credit card accounts* window: Click "No."
- *Adding lines of credit* window: Click "No."
- *Loans and notes payable* window: Click "No."
- *Bank accounts* window: Click "Yes."
- *Adding a bank account* window: Enter "Cash" as the name of your bank account.
- *Last statement date and balance* window: Enter the date of the first transaction. Enter the opening balance (if any) of the cash account.
- *Adding another bank account* window: Click "No."
- *Asset accounts* window: Click "Yes."
- *Adding an asset account* window: Enter the name of an asset account (except for "Cash") shown in the problem chart of accounts. Identify the type of asset from the pull-down menu. Enter the opening balance (if any) of the asset account.
- *Adding another asset* window: Click "Yes" if other asset accounts need to be added. Otherwise, click "No." If the asset is a fixed asset, click "Yes" in response to the question: "Do you track depreciation for this fixed asset?" In the *Fixed asset cost and depreciation* window, enter "0."
- *Enabling payroll* window: Click "Skip payroll."
- *Employees* window: Click "No."
- *To Do List* window: Click "No."
- *Finance charges* window: Click "No."
- *Budgets* window: Click "No." Continue clicking the "Next" button to advance to the end of the EasyStep Interview. Then click the "Leave" button.

Before you begin recording transactions, you need to edit the chart of accounts to fit the form of business (proprietorship or corporation) in your problem. Select "Chart of Accounts" from the "Lists" pull-down menu. If you are working a proprietorship problem, select "Retained Earnings" from the Chart of Accounts window. From the pull-down "Edit" menu, choose "Delete Account." Click "OK" to confirm that you want to delete this account. Next, to add the problem's equity accounts, click "New" in the Account window. Choose the account type from the "Type" drop-down list. Enter the account's name. (The account description and bank number are optional.) Enter the account's opening balance (if any) and the start date in the "as of" field. If you need to add other asset or liability accounts, click "Next" to create another new account. When the chart of accounts for your problem is complete, click "OK" to close the window. Then click "X" to close the Chart of Accounts window.

You are now ready to begin recording your problem's first transaction. Click on the "Activities" pull-down menu. Then select the type of transaction you want to enter. For example, select "Make Journal Entry." Then, in the "General Journal Entry" window, change the date. Enter "1" as the Entry No., and Enter "Cash" in the Account column. Then press the Tab key and enter "7050" in the Debit column. Press the Tab key several times to move down to the next row and then enter "Accounts Receivable" in the Account column. Press the Tab key and enter "1500" in the Debit column. Press the Tab key several times to move down to the next row and then enter "Supplies" in the Account column. Press the Tab key and enter "1250" in the Debit column. Press the Tab key several times to move down to the next row and then enter "Office Equipment" in the Account column. Press the Tab key and enter "7200" in the debit column. Press the Tab key several times to move down to the next row and then enter "Angie Mills, Capital" in the Account column. The entry in the Credit column will display automatically. Click on "OK."

SPECIAL ACTIVITIES

Activity 4–1
VisCo Co.
Ethics and professional conduct in business

VisCo Co. is a graphics arts design consulting firm. Hugh Lowder, its treasurer and vice president of finance, has prepared a classified balance sheet as of March 31, 2000, the end of its fiscal year. This balance sheet will be submitted with VisCo's loan application to National Trust & Savings Bank.

In the Current Assets section of the balance sheet, Hugh reported a $40,000 receivable from Jill Reamy, the president of VisCo, as a trade account receivable. Jill borrowed the money from VisCo in February 1999 for a down payment on a new home. She has orally assured Hugh that she will pay off the account receivable within the next year. Hugh reported the $40,000 in the same manner on the preceding year's balance sheet.

➤ Evaluate whether it is acceptable for Hugh Lowder to prepare the March 31, 2000 balance sheet in the manner indicated above.

Activity 4–2
Compadres Supplies Co.
Financial statements

The following is an excerpt from a telephone conversation between Janice Cato, president of Compadres Supplies Co., and Mike Metz, who is owner of Temp Employment Co.

Janice: Mike, you're going to have to do a better job of finding me a new computer programmer. That last guy was great at programming, but he didn't have any common sense.

Mike: What do you mean? The guy had a master's degree with straight A's.

Janice: Yes, well, last month he developed a new financial reporting system. He said we could do away with manually preparing a work sheet and financial statements. The computer would automatically generate our financial statements with "a push of a button."

Mike: So what's the big deal? Sounds to me like it would save you time and effort.

Janice: Right! The balance sheet showed a minus for supplies!

Mike: Minus supplies? How can that be?

Janice: That's what I asked.

Mike: So, what did he say?

Janice: Well, after he checked the program, he said that it must be right. The minuses were greater than the pluses . . .

Mike: Didn't he know that supplies can't have a credit balance—it must have a debit balance?

Janice: He asked me what a debit and credit were.

Mike: I see your point.

1. ➤ Comment on (a) the desirability of computerizing Compadres Supplies Co.'s financial reporting system, (b) the elimination of the work sheet in a computerized accounting system, and (c) the computer programmer's lack of accounting knowledge.

2. ➤ Explain to the programmer why supplies could not have a credit balance.

Activity 4–3
Bug Out
Financial statements

Assume that you recently accepted a position with the First National Bank as an assistant loan officer. As one of your first duties, you have been assigned the responsibility of evaluating a loan request for $60,000 from Bug Out, a small proprietorship. In support of the loan application, Linda Abney, owner, submitted a "Statement of Accounts" (trial balance) for the first year of operations ended December 31, 2000.

1. ➤ Explain to Linda Abney why a set of financial statements (income statement, statement of owner's equity, and balance sheet) would be useful to you in evaluating the loan request.

2. In discussing the "Statement of Accounts" with Linda Abney, you discovered that the accounts had not been adjusted at December 31. Analyze the "Statement of Accounts" (shown on the next page) and indicate possible adjusting entries that might be necessary before an accurate set of financial statements could be prepared.

3. ➤ Assuming that an accurate set of financial statements will be submitted by Linda Abney in a few days, what other considerations or information would you require before making a decision on the loan request?

Bug Out
Statement of Accounts
December 31, 2000

Cash	4,120	
Billings Due from Others	8,740	
Supplies (chemicals, etc.)	14,950	
Trucks	32,750	
Equipment	26,150	
Amounts Owed to Others		5,700
Investment in Business		47,500
Service Revenue		107,650
Wages Expense	60,100	
Utilities Expense	6,900	
Rent Expense	4,800	
Insurance Expense	1,400	
Other Expenses	940	
	160,850	160,850

Activity 4–4
Into the Real World
Compare balance sheets

In groups of three or four, compare the balance sheets of two different companies, and present to the class a summary of the similarities and differences of the two companies. You may obtain the balance sheets you need from one of the following sources:

1. Your school or local library.
2. The investor relations department of each company.
3. The company's Web site on the Internet.
4. EDGAR (Electronic Data Gathering, Analysis, and Retrieval), the electronic archives of financial statements filed with the Securities and Exchange Commission. The EDGAR address is **www.sec.gov/edgarhp.htm**

   To obtain annual report information, type in a company name on the "Search EDGAR Archives" form. EDGAR will list the reports available for the selected company. A company's annual report (along with other information) is provided in its annual 10-K report to the SEC. Click on the 10-K (or 10-K405) report for the year you wish to download. If you wish, you can save the whole 10-K report to a file and then open it with your word processor.

ANSWERS TO SELF-EXAMINATION QUESTIONS

Matching

1. T	3. L	5. J	7. O	9. K	11. R	13. G	15. P
2. E	4. F	6. I	8. H	10. A	12. U	14. D	16. S

Multiple Choice

1. **C** The drawing account, M. E. Jones, Drawing (answer C), would be extended to the Balance Sheet columns of the work sheet. Utilities Expense (answer A), Rent Revenue (answer B), and Miscellaneous Expense (answer D) would all be extended to the Income Statement columns of the work sheet.

2. **D** Cash or other assets that are expected to be converted to cash or sold or used up within one year or less, through the normal operations of the business, are classified as current assets on the balance sheet. Accounts Receivable (answer D) is a current asset, since it will normally be converted to cash within one year. Office Equipment (answer A), Land (answer B), and Accumulated Depreciation (answer C) are all reported in the property, plant, and equipment section of the balance sheet.

3. **B** The entry to close the owner's drawing account is

to debit the owner's capital account and credit the drawing account (answer B).

4. **D** Since all revenue and expense accounts are closed at the end of the period, Fees Earned (answer A), Wages Expense (answer B), and Rent Expense (answer C) would all be closed to Income Summary. Accumulated Depreciation (answer D) is a contra asset account that is not closed.

5. **B** Since the post-closing trial balance includes only balance sheet accounts (all of the revenue, expense, and drawing accounts are closed), Cash (answer A), Accumulated Depreciation (answer C), and J. C. Smith, Capital (answer D) would appear on the post-closing trial balance. Fees Earned (answer B) is a temporary account that is closed prior to preparing the post-closing trial balance.

5

Accounting Systems and Internal Controls

Setting *the* STAGE

Controls are a part of your everyday life. At one extreme, laws are used to govern your behavior. For example, the speed limit is a control on your driving, designed for traffic safety. In addition, you are also affected by many nonlegal controls. For example, you can keep credit card receipts in order to compare your transactions to the monthly credit card statement. Comparing receipts to the monthly statement is a control designed to catch mistakes made by the credit card company. Likewise, recording checks in your checkbook is a control that you can use at the end of the month to verify the accuracy of your bank statement. In addition, banks give you a personal identification number (**PIN**) as a control against unauthorized access to your cash if you lose your automated teller machine (**ATM**) card. Dairies use freshness dating on their milk containers as a control to prevent the purchase or sale of soured milk. As you can see, you use and encounter controls every day.

Just as there are many examples of controls throughout society, businesses must also implement controls to help guide the behavior of their employees toward business objectives. For example, some businesses require you to punch a time card when you enter and leave the workplace. This is a control used to verify that you get paid for the actual hours you worked.

In this chapter, we will discuss controls that can be included in accounting systems to provide reasonable assurance that the financial statements are reliable. We will apply the principles of accounting systems design to manual systems as well as computerized accounting systems.

1 Define an accounting system and describe its implementation.

2 List the three objectives of internal control and define and give examples of the five elements of internal control.

3 Journalize and post transactions in a manual accounting system that uses subsidiary ledgers and special journals.

4 Describe and give examples of additional subsidiary ledgers and modified special journals.

5 Describe the components of a computer system and apply computerized accounting to the revenue and collection cycle.

B *asic Accounting Systems*

OBJECTIVE 1

Define an accounting system and describe its implementation.

The **Internal Revenue Service (IRS)** learned the hard way that the *analysis* stage is very important. The IRS spent $3 billion on a widely criticized computer modernization program that had no clear outlines or goals. After spending this amount, the agency unveiled a blueprint for the project. Deputy Treasury Secretary Lawrence Summers declared that the IRS would begin more careful planning for the project. "We're [now] planning before we build, rather than building before we plan," he stated.

In the four previous chapters, we developed an accounting system for Computer King. An **accounting system** is the methods and procedures for collecting, classifying, summarizing, and reporting a business's financial and operating information. The accounting system for most businesses, however, is more complex than Computer King's. Accounting systems for large businesses must be able to collect, accumulate, and report many types of transactions. For example, **United Airlines'** accounting system collects and maintains information on ticket reservations, credit card collections, aircraft maintenance, employee hours, frequent-flier mileage balances, fuel consumption, and travel agent commissions, just to name a few. As you might expect, United Airlines' accounting system has evolved as the company has grown.

Accounting systems evolve through a three-step process as a business grows and changes. The first step in this process is **analysis**, which consists of (1) identifying the needs of those who use the business's financial information and (2) determining how the system should provide this information. For Computer King, we determined that Pat King would need financial statements for the new business. In the second step, the system is **designed** so that it will meet the users' needs. For Computer King, a very basic manual system was designed. This system included a chart of accounts, a two-column journal, and a general ledger. Finally, the system is **implemented** and used. For Computer King, the system was used to record transactions and prepare financial statements.

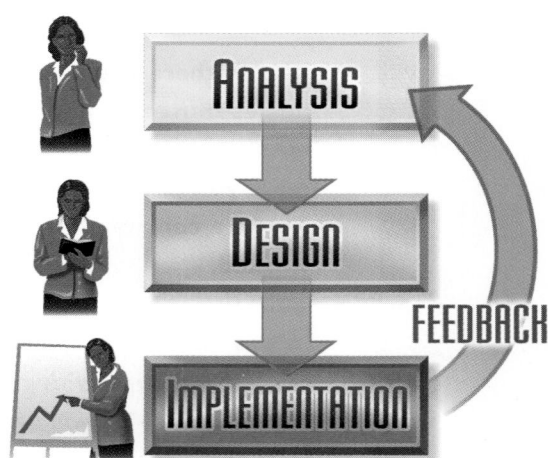

Once a system has been implemented, **feedback** or input from the users of the information can be used to analyze and improve the system. For example, in later chapters we will see that Computer King will expand its chart of accounts as it becomes a more complex business.

Internal controls protect assets, ensure that business information is accurate, and ensure that regulations are being followed.

Internal controls and information processing methods are essential in an accounting system. Internal controls are the policies and procedures that protect assets from misuse, ensure that business information is accurate, and ensure that laws and regulations are being followed. **Processing methods** are the means by which the system collects, summarizes, and reports accounting information. These methods may be either *manual* or *computerized*. In the following sections, we will discuss internal controls, manual accounting systems that use special journals, and computerized accounting systems.

I *nternal Control*

OBJECTIVE 2

List the three objectives of internal control and define and give examples of the five elements of internal control.

Businesses use internal controls to guide their operations and prevent abuses of their systems. For example, assume that you own and manage a lawn care service. Your business uses several employee teams, and you provide each team with a vehicle and lawn equipment. What are some of the issues you would face as a manager in controlling the operations of this business? Below are some examples.

- Lawn care must be provided on time.
- The quality of lawn care services must meet customer expectations.
- Employees must provide work for the hours they are paid.
- Lawn care equipment should be used for business purposes only.
- Vehicles should be used for business purposes only.
- Customers must be billed and bills collected for services rendered.

How would you address some of these issues? You could, for example, develop a schedule at the beginning of each day and then inspect the work at the end of the day to verify that it was completed according to quality standards. You could have "surprise" inspections by arriving on site at random times to verify that the teams are working according to schedule. You could require employees to "clock in" at the beginning of the day and "clock out" at the end of the day, to make sure that they are paid for hours worked. You could require the work teams to return the vehicles and equipment to a central location to prevent unauthorized use. You could keep a log of odometer readings at the end of each day to verify that the vehicle has not been used for "joy riding." You could bill customers after you have inspected the work, and then you could monitor the collection of all receivables. All of these are examples of internal control.

 A 1996 survey by **KPMG**, an international accounting firm, identified expense account manipulation, receiving payments from suppliers for favorable purchase treatment (kickbacks), purchases for personal use, and misappropriation of cash as the most typical methods of employee fraud. Based on a 1995 survey by the **Association of Fraud Examiners**, annual fraud losses are estimated to be $400 billion in the United States, which for the average organization would be 6% of revenues or $9 per day per employee.

Objectives of Internal Control

Internal control provides reasonable assurance that:

1. assets are safeguarded and used for business purposes.
2. business information is accurate.
3. employees comply with laws and regulations.

Internal control can safeguard assets by preventing theft, fraud, misuse, or misplacement. One of the most serious breaches of internal control is employee fraud. Employee fraud is the intentional act of deceiving an employer for personal gain. Such deception may range from purposely overstating expenses on a travel expense report in order to receive a higher reimbursement to embezzling millions of dollars through complex schemes.

Micky Monus, co-founder of the **Phar-Mor** drug store chain, overstated inventories by $9.4 million in order to finance the now defunct World Basketball League. The accounting records were falsified, which caused the chain to appear profitable when it was actually losing millions of dollars.

Accurate business information is necessary for operating a business successfully. The safeguarding of assets and accurate information often go hand-in-hand. The reason is that employees attempting to defraud a business will also need to adjust the accounting records in order to hide the fraud.

Businesses must comply with applicable laws and regulations and financial reporting standards. Examples of such standards and laws include environmental regulations, contract terms, safety regulations, and generally accepted accounting principles (GAAP).

Elements of Internal Control

How does management achieve its internal control objectives? Management is responsible for designing and applying five **elements of internal control** to meet the three internal control objectives. These elements are:[1]

1. the control environment
2. risk assessment
3. control procedures
4. monitoring
5. information and communication

The elements of internal control are illustrated in Exhibit 1. In this exhibit, the elements of internal control form an umbrella over the business to protect it from control threats. The business's control environment is represented by the size of the umbrella. Risk assessment, control procedures, and monitoring are the fabric that keeps the umbrella from leaking. Information and communication links the umbrella to management. In the following paragraphs, we discuss each of these elements.

Control Environment

A business's control environment is the overall attitude of management and employees about the importance of controls. One of the factors that influences the control environment is *management's philosophy and operating style*. A management that overemphasizes operating goals and deviates from control policies may indirectly encourage employees to ignore controls. For example, if management rou-

EXHIBIT I
Elements of Internal Control

---

[1] *Internal Control—Integrated Framework by the Committee of Sponsoring Organizations* of the Treadway Commission (COSO), pp. 12–14. This document provides a professionally sponsored framework for internal control.

An employee of J.C. Penney Co. was convicted of taking $1 million in bribes and kickbacks from suppliers in exchange for information about competitors' bids. One of the prosecuting attorneys told the court, "This case will be discussed in corporate boardrooms. . . . The message ought to be sent out that there's a consequence to corporate fraud."

tinely ignores a policy requiring that safety glasses be worn in the plant, it may cause other employees to interpret the policy as "optional," thereby creating an unsafe work environment. On the other hand, a management that emphasizes the importance of controls and encourages adherence to control policies will create an effective control environment.

The business's *organizational structure,* which is the framework for planning and controlling operations, also influences the control environment. For example, a department store chain might organize each of its stores as separate business units. Each store manager has full authority over pricing and other operating activities. In such a structure, each store manager has the responsibility for establishing an effective control environment.

Personnel policies also affect the control environment. Personnel policies involve the hiring, training, evaluating, compensating, and promoting of employees. In addition, job descriptions, employee codes of ethics, and conflict-of-interest policies are part of the personnel policies. Such policies and procedures can enhance the internal control environment if they provide reasonable assurance that only competent, honest employees are hired and retained.

In the early 1990s, Sears had a policy of paying bonuses to its automobile department managers, based on the amount of service provided. This arrangement created incentives for managers to overstate the amount of work required by customers. Thus, customers were being charged for work that they did not need.

Allstate Corporation, an insurance company, used a risk-based internal control framework to develop its internal auditing process. The internal auditors looked for *potential* control weaknesses. They evaluated risk on the probability that it would occur and its significance if it should occur.

Risk Assessment

All organizations face risks. Examples of risk include changes in customer requirements, competitive threats, regulatory changes, changes in economic factors such as interest rates, and employee violations of company policies and procedures. Management should assess these risks and take necessary actions to control them, so that the objectives of internal control can be achieved.

Once risks are identified, they can be analyzed to estimate their significance, to assess their likelihood of occurring, and to determine actions that will minimize them. For example, the manager of a warehouse operation may analyze the risk of employee back injuries, which might give rise to lawsuits. If the manager determines that the risk is significant, the company may take action by purchasing back support braces for its warehouse employees and requiring them to wear the braces.

Control Procedures

Control procedures are established to provide reasonable assurance that business goals will be achieved, including the prevention of fraud. In the following paragraphs, we will briefly discuss control procedures that can be integrated throughout the accounting system. These procedures are listed in Exhibit 2.

An accounting clerk for the Grant County (Washington) Alcoholism Program was in charge of collecting money, making deposits, and keeping the records. While the clerk was away on maternity leave, the replacement clerk discovered a fraud: $17,800 in fees had been collected but had been hidden for personal gain.

Competent Personnel, Rotating Duties, and Mandatory Vacations.
The successful operation of an accounting system requires procedures to ensure that people are able to perform the duties to which they are assigned. Hence, it is necessary that all accounting employees be adequately trained and supervised in performing their jobs. It may also be advisable to rotate duties of clerical personnel and mandate vacations for nonclerical personnel. These policies encourage employees to adhere to prescribed procedures. In addition, existing errors or fraud may be detected.

Separating Responsibilities for Related Operations.
To decrease the possibility of inefficiency, errors, and fraud, the responsibility for related operations should be divided among two or more persons. For example, the responsibilities

EXHIBIT 2
Internal Control Procedures

for purchasing, receiving, and paying for computer supplies should be divided among three persons or departments. If the same person orders supplies, verifies the receipt of the supplies, and pays the supplier, the following abuses are possible:

1. Orders may be placed on the basis of friendship with a supplier, rather than on price, quality, and other objective factors.
2. The quantity and quality of supplies received may not be verified, thus causing payment for supplies not received or poor-quality supplies.
3. Supplies may be stolen by the employee.
4. The validity and accuracy of invoices may be verified carelessly, thus causing the payment of false or inaccurate invoices.

 It has been estimated that the typical company pays one out of every one hundred invoices more than once.

Source: Checkers, Simon, and Rosner— *Client Report,* Spring 1994 (Issue 3).

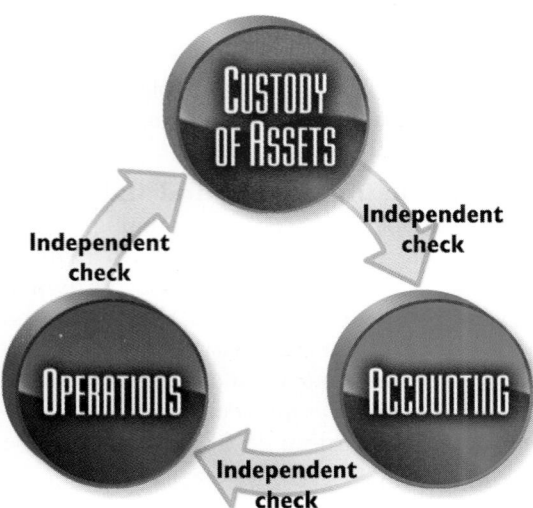

The "checks and balances" provided by dividing responsibilities among various departments requires no duplication of effort. The business documents prepared by one department are designed to coordinate with and support those prepared by other departments.

Separating Operations, Custody of Assets, and Accounting. Control policies should establish the responsibilities for various business activities. To reduce the possibility of errors and fraud, the responsibilities for operations, custody of assets, and accounting should be separated. The accounting records then serve as an independent check on the individuals who have custody of the assets and who engage in the business operations. For example, the employees entrusted with handling cash receipts from credit customers should not record cash receipts in the accounting records. To do so would allow employees to borrow or steal cash and hide the theft in the records. Likewise, if those engaged in operating activities also record the results of operations, they could distort the accounting reports to show favorable results. For example, a store manager whose year-end bonus is based upon operating profits might be tempted to record fictitious sales in order to receive a larger bonus.

One of the largest fraud losses in history involved a securities trader for the Singapore office of **Barings Bank**, a British merchant bank. The trader established an unauthorized account number that was used to hide $1.4 billion in losses. Even after Barings' internal auditors noted that the trader both executed trades and recorded them, management did not take action. As a result, a lone individual in a remote office, combined with weak controls, bankrupted an internationally recognized firm.

Proofs and Security Measures. Proofs and security measures should be used to safeguard assets and ensure reliable accounting data. This control procedure applies to many different techniques, such as authorization, approval, and reconciliation procedures. For example, employees who travel on company business may be required to obtain a department manager's approval on a travel request form.

Other examples of control procedures include the use of bank accounts and other measures to ensure the safety of cash and valuable documents. Using a cash register that displays the amount recorded for each sale and provides for the customer a printed receipt can be an effective part of the internal control structure. An all-night convenience store could use the following security measures to deter robberies:

Why is separation of duties considered a control procedure?

Internal control is enhanced by separating the control of a transaction from the record-keeping function. Fraud is more easily committed when a single individual controls both the transaction and the accounting for the transaction.

1. Locating the cash register near the door, so that it is fully visible from outside the store; having two employees work late hours; employing a security guard.
2. Depositing cash in the bank daily, before 5 p.m.
3. Keeping only small amounts of cash on hand after 5 p.m. by depositing excess cash in a store safe that can't be opened by employees on duty.
4. Installing cameras and alarm systems.

Monitoring

Monitoring the internal control system locates weaknesses and improves control effectiveness. The internal control system may be monitored through either ongoing efforts by management or by separate evaluations. Ongoing monitoring efforts may include observing both employee behavior and warning signs from the accounting system.[2] The indicators shown in Exhibit 3 may be clues to internal control problems.

Separate monitoring evaluations are generally performed when there are major changes in strategy, senior management, business structure, or operations. In large businesses, internal auditors who are independent of operations normally are responsible for monitoring the internal control system. In addition, external auditors also evaluate internal control as a normal part of their annual financial statement audit.

Information and Communication

Information and communication are essential elements of internal control. Information about the control environment, risk assessment, control procedures, and monitoring are needed by management to guide operations and ensure compliance with reporting, legal, and regulatory requirements.

Auditors for Bremerton, Washington, discovered a shortage of over $4,000 in traffic citation receipts collected as cash or checks by the municipal court cashier. The cashier was able to embezzle the cash because (1) there were no receipts issued for cash received, (2) bank deposits were not reconciled with total receipts, and (3) total tickets issued by the police were not reconciled with cash

In one of the largest frauds ever committed against a university, a former financial aid officer for **New York University** was charged with stealing $4.1 million from the state of New York. The aid officer allegedly falsified over a thousand tuition assistance checks to students who were not entitled to receive aid and who did not know about the checks. The aid officer deposited the bogus checks for personal use. The initial evidence of the fraud was the officer's spending of $785,000 on expensive jewelry.

---

[2] Edwin C. Bliss, "Employee Theft," *Boardroom Reports*, July 15, 1994, pp. 5–6.

EXHIBIT 3
Indicators of Internal
Control Problems

CLUES TO POTENTIAL PROBLEMS

Warning signs with regard to people

1. Abrupt change in lifestyle (without winning the lottery).
2. Close social relationships with suppliers.
3. Refusing to take a vacation.
4. Frequent borrowing from other employees.
5. Excessive use of alcohol or drugs.

Warning signs from the accounting system

1. Missing documents or gaps in transaction numbers (could mean documents are being used for fraudulent transactions).
2. An unusual increase in customer refunds (refunds may be phony).
3. Differences between daily cash receipts and bank deposits (could mean receipts are pocketed before being deposited).
4. Sudden increase in slow payments (employee may be pocketing the payment).
5. Backlog in recording transactions (possibly an attempt to delay detection of fraud).

Management can also use external information to assess events and conditions that impact decision making and external reporting. For example, management uses information from the Financial Accounting Standards Board (FASB) to assess the impact of possible changes in reporting standards.

M anual Accounting Systems

OBJECTIVE 3

Journalize and post transactions in a manual accounting system that uses subsidiary ledgers and special journals.

After the internal control procedures have been developed, the basic processing method must be selected. Accounting systems may be either manual or computerized. Since an understanding of manual accounting systems assists managers in recognizing the relationships that exist between accounting data and accounting reports, we illustrate manual systems first.

In preceding chapters, all transactions for Computer King were manually recorded in an all-purpose (two-column) journal. The journal entries were then posted individually to the accounts in the ledger. Such manual accounting systems are simple to use and easy to understand. Manually kept records may serve a business reasonably well when the amount of data collected, stored, and used is relatively small. For a large business with a large database, however, such manual processing is too costly and too time-consuming. For example, a large company such as **AT&T** has millions of long-distance telephone fees earned on account with millions of customers daily. Each telephone fee on account requires an entry debiting Accounts Receivable and crediting Fees Earned. In addition, a record of each customer's receivable must be kept. Clearly, a simple manual system would not serve the business needs of AT&T.

When a business has a large number of similar transactions, using an all-purpose journal is inefficient and impractical. In such cases, subsidiary ledgers and spe-

Accounting Systems and Profit Measurement

A Greek restaurant owner in Canada had his own system of accounting. He kept his accounts payable in a cigar box on the left-hand side of his cash register, his daily cash returns in the cash register, and his receipts for paid bills in another cigar box on the right. A truly "manual" system.

When his youngest son graduated as an accountant, he was appalled by his father's primitive methods. "I don't know how you can run a business that way," he said. "How do you know what your profits are?"

"Well, son," the father replied, "when I got off the boat from Greece, I had nothing but the pants I was wearing. Today, your brother is a doctor. You are an accountant. Your sister is a speech therapist. Your mother and I have a nice car, a city house, and a country home. We have a good business, and everything is paid for...."

"So, you add all that together, subtract the pants, and there's your profit!" ■

cial journals are useful. In addition, the manual system can be supplemented or replaced by a computerized system. Although we will illustrate the manual use of subsidiary ledgers and special journals, the basic principles described in the following paragraphs also apply to a computerized accounting system.

Subsidiary Ledgers

An accounting system should be designed to provide information on the amounts due from various customers (accounts receivable) and amounts owed to various creditors (accounts payable). A separate account for each customer and creditor could be added to the ledger. However, as the number of customers and creditors increases, the ledger becomes awkward to use when it includes many customers and creditors.

A large number of individual accounts with a common characteristic can be grouped together in a separate ledger called a **subsidiary ledger**. The primary ledger, which contains all of the balance sheet and income statement accounts, is then called the **general ledger**. Each subsidiary ledger is represented in the general ledger by a summarizing account, called a **controlling account**. The sum of the balances of the accounts in a subsidiary ledger must equal the balance of the related controlling account. Thus, you may think of a subsidiary ledger as a secondary ledger that supports a controlling account in the general ledger.

The individual accounts with customers are arranged in alphabetical order in a subsidiary ledger called the **accounts receivable subsidiary ledger** or **customers ledger**. The controlling account in the general ledger that summarizes the debits and credits to the individual customer accounts is *Accounts Receivable*. The individual accounts with creditors are arranged in alphabetical order in a subsidiary ledger called the **accounts payable subsidiary ledger** or **creditors ledger**. The related controlling account in the general ledger is *Accounts Payable*. The relationship between the general ledger and these subsidiary ledgers is illustrated in Exhibit 4.

The sum of the balances of the subsidiary ledger accounts must equal the balance of the related controlling account.

Special Journals

One method of processing data more efficiently in a manual accounting system is to expand the all-purpose two-column journal to a multicolumn journal. Each column in a multicolumn journal is used only for recording transactions that affect a certain account. For example, a special column could be used only for recording debits to the cash account, and another special column could be used only for recording credits to the cash account. The addition of the two special columns would eliminate the writing of *Cash* in the journal for every receipt and every payment of cash. Also, there would be no need to post each individual debit and credit to the cash account. Instead, the *Cash Dr.* and *Cash Cr.* columns could be totaled periodically and only the totals posted. In a similar way, special columns could be added for recording credits to Fees Earned, debits and credits to Accounts Receivable and Accounts Payable, and for other entries that are often repeated.

EXHIBIT 4   General Ledger and Subsidiary Ledgers

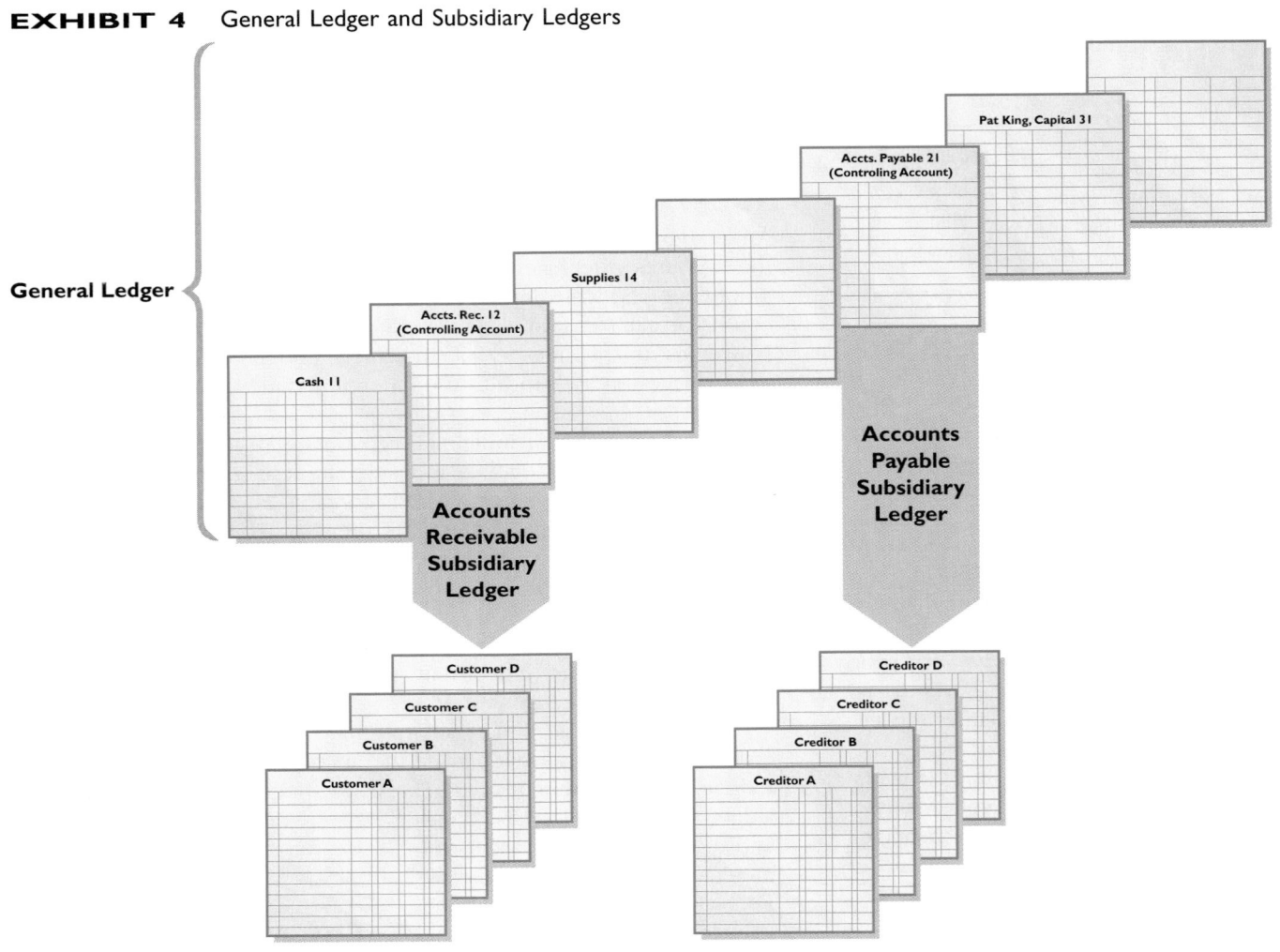

An all-purpose multicolumn journal may be adequate for a small business that has many transactions of a similar nature. However, a journal that has many columns for recording many different types of transactions is impractical for larger businesses.

The next logical extension of the accounting system is to replace the single multicolumn journal with several **special journals**. Each special journal is designed to be used for recording a single kind of transaction that occurs frequently. For example, since most businesses have many transactions in which cash is paid out, they will likely use a special journal for recording cash payments. Likewise, they will use another special journal for recording cash receipts. Special journals are a method of summarizing transactions, which is a basic feature of any accounting system.

> **Special journals are a method of summarizing transactions.**

The format and number of special journals that a business uses depends upon the nature of the business. A business that gives credit might use a special journal designed for recording only revenue from services provided on credit. On the other hand, a business that does not give credit would have no need for such a journal. In other cases, record-keeping costs may be reduced by using supporting documents as special journals.

The transactions that occur most often in a small- to medium-size service business and the special journals in which they are recorded are as follows:

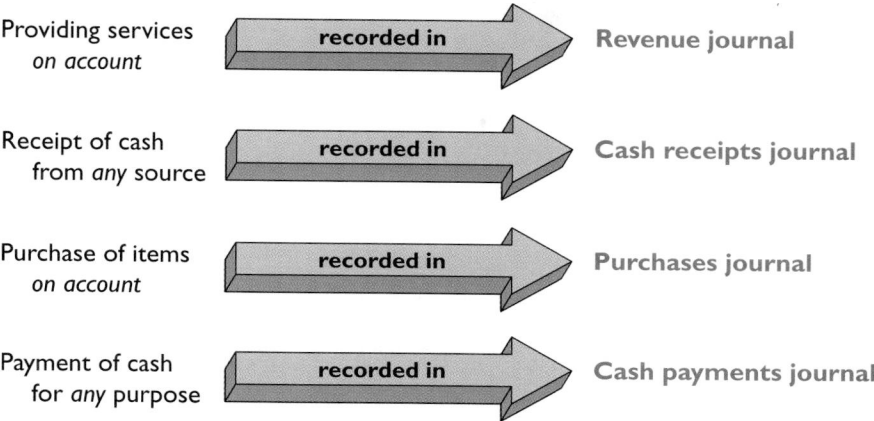

	recorded in	
Providing services *on account*	→	**Revenue journal**
Receipt of cash from *any* source	→	**Cash receipts journal**
Purchase of items *on account*	→	**Purchases journal**
Payment of cash for *any* purpose	→	**Cash payments journal**

The all-purpose two-column journal, called the **general journal** or simply the **journal**, can be used for entries that do not fit into any of the special journals. For example, adjusting and closing entries are recorded in the general journal.

In the following paragraphs, we illustrate special journals and subsidiary ledgers in a manual accounting system for Computer King. To simplify the illustration, we will use a minimum number of transactions. We will focus our discussion on two common operating cycles: (1) the revenue and cash receipts cycle and (2) the purchase and payment cycle. We will assume that Computer King had the following selected general ledger balances on March 1, 2000:

Account Number	Account	Balance
11	Cash	$6,200
12	Accounts Receivable	3,400
14	Supplies	2,500
18	Office Equipment	2,500
21	Accounts Payable	1,230

Manual Accounting System: The Revenue and Collection Cycle

The **revenue and collection cycle** for Computer King consists of providing services on account and collecting cash from customers. Revenues earned on account create a customer receivable and will be recorded in a revenue journal. Customers' accounts receivable are collected and will be recorded in a cash receipts journal.

Internal control is enhanced by separating the function of recording revenue transactions in the revenue journal from recording cash collections in the cash receipts journal. For example, if these duties are separated, it is more difficult for one person to steal cash collections and manipulate the accounting records.

Revenue Journal

The **revenue journal** is used only for recording **fees earned on account**. *Cash fees earned would be recorded in the cash receipts journal.* The sale of products is recorded in a **sales journal**, which is similar to the revenue journal. We will compare the efficiency of using a revenue journal with a general journal by assuming that Computer King recorded the following revenue transactions in a general journal:

2000 Mar.	2	Accounts Receivable—Handler Co.	12/✔	2 2 0 0 00	
		Fees Earned	41		2 2 0 0 00
	6	Accounts Receivable—Jordan Co.	12/✔	1 7 5 0 00	
		Fees Earned	41		1 7 5 0 00
	18	Accounts Receivable—Kenner Co.	12/✔	2 6 5 0 00	
		Fees Earned	41		2 6 5 0 00
	27	Accounts Receivable—Handler Co.	12/✔	3 0 0 0 00	
		Fees Earned	41		3 0 0 0 00

The general journal entry on March 2 is posted as a $2,200 debit to Accounts Receivable in the general ledger, a $2,200 debit to Handler Co. in the accounts receivable subsidiary ledger, and a $2,200 credit to Fees Earned in the general ledger.

For these four transactions, Computer King recorded eight account titles and eight amounts. In addition, Computer King made 12 postings to the ledgers—four to Accounts Receivable in the general ledger, four to the accounts receivable subsidiary ledger (indicated by each check mark), and four to Fees Earned in the general ledger. These transactions could be recorded more efficiently in a revenue journal, as shown in Exhibit 5. In each revenue transaction, the amount of the debit to Accounts Receivable is the same as the amount of the credit to Fees Earned. Therefore, only a single amount column is necessary. The date, invoice number, customer name, and amount are entered separately for each transaction.

EXHIBIT 5
Revenue Journal

			REVENUE JOURNAL		PAGE 35	
	Date	Invoice No.	Account Debited	Post. Ref.	Accts. Rec. Dr. Fees Earned Cr.	
1	2000 Mar. 2	615	Handler Co.		2 2 0 0 00	1
2	6	616	Jordan Co.		1 7 5 0 00	2
3	18	617	Kenner Co.		2 6 5 0 00	3
4	27	618	Handler Co.		3 0 0 0 00	4
5	31				9 6 0 0 00	5

The basic procedure of posting from a revenue journal is shown in Exhibit 6. A single monthly total is posted to Accounts Receivable and Fees Earned in the general ledger. Each transaction, such as the $2,200 debit to Handler Co., must also be posted individually to a customer account in the accounts receivable subsidiary ledger. These postings to customer accounts should be made frequently. In this way, management has information on the current balance of each customer's account. Since the balances in the customer accounts are usually debit balances, the three-column account form shown in the exhibit is often used.

EXHIBIT 6
Revenue Journal Postings to
Ledgers

REVENUE JOURNAL   PAGE 35

	Date	Invoice No.	Account Debited	Post. Ref.	Accts. Rec. Dr. Fees Earned Cr.	
1	2000 March 2	615	Handler Co.	✔	2,200	1
2	6	616	Jordan Co.	✔	1,750	2
3	18	617	Kenner Co.	✔	2,650	3
4	27	618	Handler Co.	✔	3,000	4
5	31				9,600	5
6					(12) (41)	6

GENERAL LEDGER

ACCOUNT Accounts Receivable — Account No. 12

Date	Item	Post. Ref.	Dr.	Cr.	Balance Dr.	Balance Cr.
2000 March 1	Balance	✔				3,400
31		R35	9,600			13,000

ACCOUNT Fees Earned — Account No. 41

Date	Item	Post. Ref.	Dr.	Cr.	Balance Dr.	Balance Cr.
2000 March 31		R35		9,600		9,600

ACCOUNTS RECEIVABLE SUBSIDIARY LEDGER

NAME: Handler Co.

Date	Item	Post. Ref.	Dr.	Cr.	Balance
2000 March 2		R35	2,200		2,200
27		R35	3,000		5,200

NAME: Jordan Co.

Date	Item	Post. Ref.	Dr.	Cr.	Balance
2000 March 6		R35	1,750		1,750

NAME: Kenner Co.

Date	Item	Post. Ref.	Dr.	Cr.	Balance
2000 March 1	Balance	✔			3,400
18		R35	2,650		6,050

What is the relationship between the revenue journal and the ledger accounts?

Revenue transactions are recorded and summarized in the revenue journal. Thus, the revenue journal is the source of postings to the subsidiary and general ledger accounts. The fees earned from services provided on account to individual customers are posted from the revenue journal to the customer subsidiary ledger accounts. At the end of the period, the total of the revenue journal column is then posted as a debit to the accounts receivable controlling account and a credit to the revenue account.

To provide a trail of the entries posted to the subsidiary ledger, the source of these entries is indicated in the *Posting Reference* column of each account by inserting the letter *R* (for revenue journal) and the page number of the revenue journal. A check mark (✔) instead of a number is then inserted in the *Posting Reference* column of the revenue journal, as shown in Exhibit 6.

If a customer's account has a credit balance, that fact should be indicated by an asterisk or parentheses in the *Balance* column. When an account's balance is zero, a line may be drawn in the *Balance* column.

At the end of each month, the amount column of the revenue journal is totaled. This total is equal to the sum of the month's debits to the individual accounts in the subsidiary ledger. It is posted in the general ledger as a debit to Accounts Receivable and a credit to Fees Earned, as shown in Exhibit 6. The respective account numbers (12 and 41) are then inserted below the total in the revenue journal to indicate that the posting is completed, as shown in Exhibit 6. In this way, all of the transactions for fees earned during the month are posted to the general ledger only once—at the end of the month—greatly simplifying the posting process.

Cash Receipts Journal

All transactions that involve the receipt of cash are recorded in a **cash receipts journal**. Thus, the cash receipts journal has a column entitled *Cash Dr.,* as shown in Exhibit 7. All transactions recorded in the cash receipts journal will involve an entry in the *Cash Dr.* column. For example, on March 28 Computer King received cash of $2,200 from Handler Co. and entered that amount in the *Cash Dr.* column.

The kinds of transactions in which cash is received and how often they occur determine the titles of the other columns. For Computer King, the most frequent source of cash is collections from customers. Thus, the cash receipts journal in Exhibit 7 has an *Accounts Receivable Cr.* column. On March 28, when Handler Co. made a payment on its account, Computer King entered *Handler Co.* in the *Account Credited* column and entered *2,200* in the *Accounts Receivable Cr.* column.

The *Other Accounts Cr.* column in Exhibit 7 is used for recording credits to any account for which there is no special credit column. For example, Computer King received cash on March 1 for rent. Since no special column exists for Rent Revenue, Computer King entered *Rent Revenue* in the *Account Credited* column and entered *400* in the *Other Accounts Cr.* column.

Postings from the cash receipts journal to the ledgers of Computer King are also shown in Exhibit 7. This posting process is similar to that of the revenue journal. At regular intervals, each amount in the *Other Accounts Cr.* column is posted to the proper account in the general ledger. The posting is indicated by inserting the account number in the *Posting Reference* column of the cash receipts journal. The posting reference *CR* (for cash receipts journal) and the proper page number are inserted in the *Posting Reference* columns of the accounts.

The amounts in the *Accounts Receivable Cr.* column are posted individually to the customer accounts in the accounts receivable subsidiary ledger. These postings should be made frequently. The posting reference *CR* and the proper page number are inserted in the *Posting Reference* column of each customer's account. A check mark is placed in the *Posting Reference* column of the cash receipts journal to show that each amount has been posted. None of the individual amounts in the *Cash Dr.* column is posted separately.

At the end of the month, all of the amount columns are totaled. The debits should equal the credits. Because each amount in the *Other Accounts Cr.* column has been posted individually to a general ledger account, a check mark is inserted below the column total to indicate that no further action is needed. The totals of the *Accounts Receivable Cr.* and *Cash Dr.* columns are posted to the proper accounts in the general ledger, and their account numbers are inserted below the totals to show that the postings have been completed.

Accounts Receivable Control and Subsidiary Ledger

After all posting has been completed for the month, the sum of the balances in the accounts receivable subsidiary ledger should be compared with the balance of the accounts receivable controlling account in the general ledger. If the controlling account and the subsidiary ledger do not agree, the error or errors must be located and corrected. The balances of the individual customer accounts may be summarized in a schedule. The total of Computer King's schedule of accounts receivable, $5,650, agrees with the balance of its accounts receivable controlling account on March 31, 2000, as shown below.

Accounts Receivable—(Controlling)		Computer King Schedule of Accounts Receivable March 31, 2000	
Balance, March 31, 2000	$5,650	Handler Co.	$3,000
		Kenner Co.	2,650
		Jordan Co.	0
		Total accounts receivable	$5,650

EXHIBIT 7
Cash Receipts Journal and
Postings

CASH RECEIPTS JOURNAL — PAGE 14

	Date	Account Credited	Post. Ref.	Other Accounts Cr.	Accounts Receivable Cr.	Cash Dr.	
1	2000 March 1	Rent Revenue	42	400		400	1
2	19	Kenner Co.	✔		3,400	3,400	2
3	28	Handler Co.	✔		2,200	2,200	3
4	30	Jordan Co.	✔		1,750	1,750	4
5	31			400	7,350	7,750	5
6				(✔)	(12)	(11)	6

GENERAL LEDGER

ACCOUNT Rent Revenue — Account No. 42

Date	Item	Post. Ref.	Dr.	Cr.	Balance Dr.	Balance Cr.
2000 March 1		CR14		400		400

ACCOUNT Accounts Receivable — Account No. 12

Date	Item	Post. Ref.	Dr.	Cr.	Balance Dr.	Balance Cr.
2000 March 1	Balance	✔			3,400	
31		R35	9,600		13,000	
31		CR14		7,350	5,650	

ACCOUNT Cash — Account No. 11

Date	Item	Post. Ref.	Dr.	Cr.	Balance Dr.	Balance Cr.
2000 March 1	Balance	✔			6,200	
31		CR14	7,750		13,950	

ACCOUNTS RECEIVABLE SUBSIDIARY LEDGER

NAME: Handler Co.

Date	Item	Post. Ref.	Dr.	Cr.	Balance
2000 March 2		R35	2,200		2,200
27		R35	3,000		5,200
28		CR14		2,200	3,000

NAME: Jordan Co.

Date	Item	Post. Ref.	Dr.	Cr.	Balance
2000 March 6		R35	1,750		1,750
30		CR14		1,750	—

NAME: Kenner Co.

Date	Item	Post. Ref.	Dr.	Cr.	Balance
2000 March 1	Balance	✔			3,400
18		R35	2,650		6,050
19		CR14		3,400	2,650

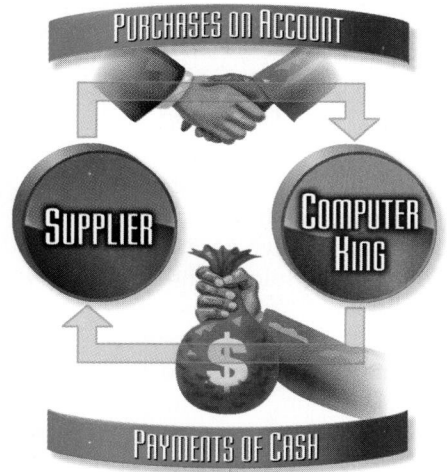

PURCHASES ON ACCOUNT

SUPPLIER

COMPUTER KING

$

PAYMENTS OF CASH

Manual Accounting System: The Purchase and Payment Cycle

The **purchase and payment cycle** for Computer King consists of purchases on account and payments of cash to suppliers. To make purchases of supplies and other items on account requires establishing a supplier account payable. These transactions will be recorded in a purchases journal. The payments of suppliers' accounts payable will be recorded in the cash payments journal.

Internal control is enhanced by separating the function of recording purchases in the purchases journal from recording cash payments in the cash payments journal. Separating duties in this way prevents an individual from establishing a fictitious supplier and then collecting payments for fictitious purchases from this supplier.

Purchases Journal

The **purchases journal** is designed for recording all **purchases on account**. *Cash purchases would be recorded in the cash payments journal.* The purchases journal has a column entitled *Accounts Payable Cr.* The purchases journal also has special columns for recording debits to the accounts most often affected. Since Computer King makes frequent debits to its supplies account, a *Supplies Dr.* column is included for these transactions. For example, as shown in Exhibit 8, Computer King recorded the purchase of supplies on March 3 by entering *600* in the *Supplies Dr.* column, *600* in the *Accounts Payable Cr.* column, and *Howard Supplies* in the *Account Credited* column.

The *Other Accounts Dr.* column in Exhibit 8 is used to record purchases, on account, of any item for which there is no special debit column. The title of the account to be debited is entered in the *Other Accounts* column, and the amount is entered in the *Amount* column. For example, Computer King recorded the purchase of office equipment on account on March 12 by entering *Office Equipment* in the *Other Accounts Dr.* column, *2,800* in the *Amount* column, *2,800* in the *Accounts Payable Cr.* column, and *Jewett Business Systems* in the *Account Credited* column.

Postings from the purchases journal to the ledgers of Computer King are also shown in Exhibit 8. The principles used in posting the purchases journal are similar to those used in posting the revenue and cash receipts journals. The source of the entries posted to the subsidiary and general ledgers is indicated in the *Posting Reference* column of each account by inserting the letter *P* (for purchases journal) and the page number of the purchases journal. A check mark (✓) is inserted in the *Posting Reference* column of the purchases journal after each credit is posted to a creditor's account in the accounts payable subsidiary ledger.

At regular intervals, the amounts in the *Other Accounts Dr.* column are posted to the accounts in the general ledger. As each amount is posted, the related general ledger account number is inserted in the *Posting Reference* column of the *Other Accounts* section.

At the end of each month, the amount columns in the purchases journal are totaled. The sum of the two debit column totals should equal the sum of the credit column.

The totals of the *Accounts Payable Cr.* and *Supplies Dr.* columns are posted to the appropriate general ledger accounts in the usual manner, with the related account numbers inserted below the column totals. Because each amount in the *Other Accounts Dr.* column was posted individually, a check mark is placed below the $2,800 total to show that no further action is needed.

Cash Payments Journal

The special columns for the **cash payments journal** are determined in the same manner as for the revenue, cash receipts, and purchases journals. The determining factors are the kinds of transactions to be recorded and how often they occur.

The cash payments journal has a *Cash Cr.* column, as shown in Exhibit 9. All transactions recorded in the cash payments journal will involve an entry in this column. Payments to creditors on account happen often enough to require an *Accounts Payable Dr.* column. Debits to creditor accounts for invoices paid are recorded in the *Accounts Payable Dr.* column. For example, on March 15 Computer King paid $1,230 on its account with Grayco Supplies. Computer King recorded this transaction by entering *1,230* in the *Accounts Payable Dr.* column, *1,230* in the *Cash Cr.* column, and *Grayco Supplies* in the *Account Debited* column.

EXHIBIT 8 Purchases Journal and Postings

PURCHASES JOURNAL   PAGE 11

Date	Account Credited	Post. Ref.	Accounts Payable Cr.	Supplies Dr.	Other Accounts Dr.	Post. Ref.	Amount	
2000								
March 3	Howard Supplies	✔	600	600				1
7	Donnelly Supplies	✔	420	420				2
12	Jewett Business Systems	✔	2,800		Office Equipment	18	2,800	3
19	Donnelly Supplies	✔	1,450	1,450				4
27	Howard Supplies	✔	960	960				5
31			6,230	3,430			2,800	6
			(21)	(14)			(✔)	7

GENERAL LEDGER

ACCOUNT Accounts Payable   Account No. 21

Date	Item	Post. Ref.	Dr.	Cr.	Balance
2000					
March 1	Balance	✔			1,230
31		P11		6,230	7,460

ACCOUNT Supplies   Account No. 14

Date	Item	Post. Ref.	Dr.	Cr.	Balance
2000					
March 1	Balance	✔			2,500
31		P11	3,430		5,930

ACCOUNT Office Equipment   Account No. 18

Date	Item	Post. Ref.	Dr.	Cr.	Balance
2000					
March 1	Balance	✔			2,500
12		P11	2,800		5,300

ACCOUNTS PAYABLE SUBSIDIARY LEDGER

NAME: Donnelly Supplies

Date	Item	Post. Ref.	Dr.	Cr.	Balance
2000					
March 7		P11		420	420
19		P11		1,450	1,870

NAME: Grayco Supplies

Date	Item	Post. Ref.	Dr.	Cr.	Balance
2000					
March 1	Balance	✔			1,230

NAME: Howard Supplies

Date	Item	Post. Ref.	Dr.	Cr.	Balance
2000					
March 3		P11		600	600
27		P11		960	1,560

NAME: Jewett Business Systems

Date	Item	Post. Ref.	Dr.	Cr.	Balance
2000					
March 12		P11		2,800	2,800

Computer King makes all payments by check. As each transaction is recorded in the cash payments journal, the related check number is entered in the column at the right of the *Date* column. The check numbers are helpful in controlling cash payments, and they provide a useful cross-reference.

The *Other Accounts Dr.* column is used for recording debits to any account for which there is no special column. For example, Computer King paid $1,600 on March 2 for rent. The transaction was recorded by entering *Rent Expense* in the space provided and *1,600* in the *Other Accounts Dr.* and *Cash Cr.* columns.

Postings from the cash payments journal to the ledgers of Computer King are also shown in Exhibit 9. The amounts entered in the *Accounts Payable Dr.* column

EXHIBIT 9
Cash Payments Journal and
Postings

CASH PAYMENTS JOURNAL   PAGE 7

	Date	Ck. No.	Account Debited	Post. Ref.	Other Accounts Dr.	Accounts Payable Dr.	Cash Cr.	
	2000							
1	March 2	150	Rent Expense	52	1,600		1,600	1
2	15	151	Grayco Supplies	✔		1,230	1,230	2
3	21	152	Jewett Business Systems	✔		2,800	2,800	3
4	22	153	Donnelly Supplies	✔		420	420	4
5	30	154	Utilities Expense	54	1,050		1,050	5
6	31	155	Howard Supplies	✔		600	600	6
7	31				2,650	5,050	7,700	7
8					(✔)	(21)	(11)	8

GENERAL LEDGER

ACCOUNT Accounts Payable   Account No. 21

Date	Item	Post. Ref.	Dr.	Cr.	Balance
2000					
March 1	Balance	✔			1,230
31		P11		6,230	7,460
31		CP7	5,050		2,410

ACCOUNT Cash   Account No. 11

Date	Item	Post. Ref.	Dr.	Cr.	Balance
2000					
March 1	Balance	✔			6,200
31		CR14	7,750		13,950
31		CP7		7,700	6,250

ACCOUNT Rent Expense   Account No. 52

Date	Item	Post. Ref.	Dr.	Cr.	Balance
2000					
March 2		CP7	1,600		1,600

ACCOUNT Utilities Expense   Account No. 54

Date	Item	Post. Ref.	Dr.	Cr.	Balance
2000					
March 30		CP7	1,050		1,050

ACCOUNTS PAYABLE SUBSIDIARY LEDGER

NAME: Donnelly Supplies

Date	Item	Post. Ref.	Dr.	Cr.	Balance
2000					
March 7		P11		420	420
19		P11		1,450	1,870
22		CP7	420		1,450

NAME: Grayco Supplies

Date	Item	Post. Ref.	Dr.	Cr.	Balance
2000					
March 1	Balance	✔			1,230
15		CP7	1,230		—

NAME: Howard Supplies

Date	Item	Post. Ref.	Dr.	Cr.	Balance
2000					
March 3		P11		600	600
27		P11		960	1,560
31		CP7	600		960

NAME: Jewett Business Systems

Date	Item	Post. Ref.	Dr.	Cr.	Balance
2000					
March 12		P11		2,800	2,800
21		CP7	2,800		—

are posted to the individual creditor accounts in the accounts payable subsidiary ledger. These postings should be made frequently. After each posting, *CP* (for cash payments journal) and the page number of the journal are inserted in the *Posting Reference* column of the account. A check mark is placed in the *Posting Reference* column of the cash payments journal to indicate that each amount has been posted.

At regular intervals, each item in the *Other Accounts Dr.* column is also posted individually to an account in the general ledger. The posting is indicated by writing the account number in the *Posting Reference* column of the cash payments journal.

At the end of the month, each of the amount columns in the cash payments journal is totaled. The sum of the two debit totals is compared with the credit total to determine their equality. A check mark is placed below the total of the *Other Accounts Dr.* column to indicate that no further action is needed. When each of the totals of the other two columns is posted to the general ledger, an account number is inserted below each column total.

Accounts Payable Control and Subsidiary Ledger

After all posting has been completed for the month, the sum of the balances in the accounts payable subsidiary ledger should be compared with the balance of the accounts payable controlling account in the general ledger. If the controlling account and the subsidiary ledger do not agree, the error or errors must be located and corrected. The balances of the individual supplier accounts may be summarized in a schedule. The total of Computer King's schedule of accounts payable, $2,410, agrees with the balance of the accounts payable controlling account on March 31, 2000, as shown below.

Accounts Payable— (Controlling)		Computer King Schedule of Accounts Payable March 31, 2000	
Balance, March 31, 2000	$2,410	Donnelly Supplies	$1,450
		Grayco Supplies	0
		Howard Supplies	960
		Jewett Business Systems	0
		Total	$2,410

Adapting Manual Accounting Systems

OBJECTIVE 4

Describe and give examples of additional subsidiary ledgers and modified special journals.

The preceding sections of this chapter illustrate subsidiary ledgers and special journals that are common for a medium-size business. Many businesses use subsidiary ledgers for other accounts, in addition to Accounts Receivable and Accounts Payable. Also, special journals are often adapted or modified in practice to meet the specific needs of a business. In the following paragraphs, we describe other subsidiary ledgers and modified special journals.

Additional Subsidiary Ledgers

Generally, subsidiary ledgers are used for accounts that consist of a large number of individual items, each of which has unique characteristics. For example, businesses may use a subsidiary equipment ledger to keep track of each item of equipment purchased, its cost, location, and other data. Such ledgers are similar to the accounts receivable and accounts payable subsidiary ledgers that we illustrated in this chapter.

Modified Special Journals

A business may modify its special journals by adding one or more columns for recording transactions that occur frequently. For example, a business may collect sales taxes that must be remitted periodically to the taxing authorities. Thus, the business may add a special column for *Sales Taxes Payable* in its revenue journal, as shown below.

	Date	Invoice No.	Account Debited	Post. Ref.	Accts. Rec. Dr.	Fees Earned Cr.	Sales Taxes Payable Cr.	
			REVENUE JOURNAL				**PAGE 40**	
1	2000 Nov. 2	842	Litten Co.	✔	4 7 7 0 00	4 5 0 0 00	2 7 0 00	1
2	3	843	Kauffman Supply Co.	✔	1 1 6 6 00	1 1 0 0 00	6 6 00	2

Some other examples of how special journals may be modified for a variety of different types of businesses are:

- **Farm**—The purchases journal may be modified to include columns for various types of seeds (corn, wheat), livestock (cows, hogs, sheep), fertilizer, and fuel.
- **Automobile Repair Shop**—The revenue journal may be modified to include columns for each major type of repair service. In addition, columns for warranty repairs, credit card charges, and sales taxes may be added.
- **Hospital**—The cash receipts journal may be modified to include columns for receipts from patients on account, from Blue Cross/Blue Shield or other major insurance reimbursers, and Medicare.
- **Movie Theater**—The cash receipts journal may be modified to include columns for revenues from admissions, gift certificates, and concession sales.
- **Restaurant**—The purchases journal may be modified to include columns for food, linen, silverware and glassware, and kitchen supplies.

Regardless of how a special journal is modified, the basic principles and procedures discussed in this chapter apply. For example, the columns in special journals are normally totaled at periodic intervals. The totals of the debit and credit columns are then compared to verify their equality before the totals are posted to the general ledger accounts.

Computerized Accounting Systems

OBJECTIVE 5

Describe the components of a computer system and apply computerized accounting to the revenue and collection cycle.

Computerized accounting systems have become more widely used as the cost of hardware and software has declined. We will begin with an introduction to basic computer terms and then illustrate the revenue and collection cycle in a computerized system.

Computer Hardware Basics

You may own a computer or be familiar with its basic elements. However, if you are not familiar with computer systems, we provide a brief overview in the following sections. A computerized accounting system requires **hardware**, which includes a computer, its components, and related equipment. The basic external hardware elements of a microcomputer are illustrated in Exhibit 10. These hardware elements provide for user input, data input, and data output.

The computer receives **user input** from the keyboard or the mouse. The computer receives **data input** from either a floppy disk or through a CD (compact disk) drive. Many computers have the floppy disk and CD drives built into the computer.

Data output from the computer may be displayed on the monitor or printed by a printer. Data input or output may also travel over a **network**, which is a method of connecting the computer to another user or data storage location. For example, telephone lines may serve as a data network.

EXHIBIT 10
External Hardware Elements of a Computer

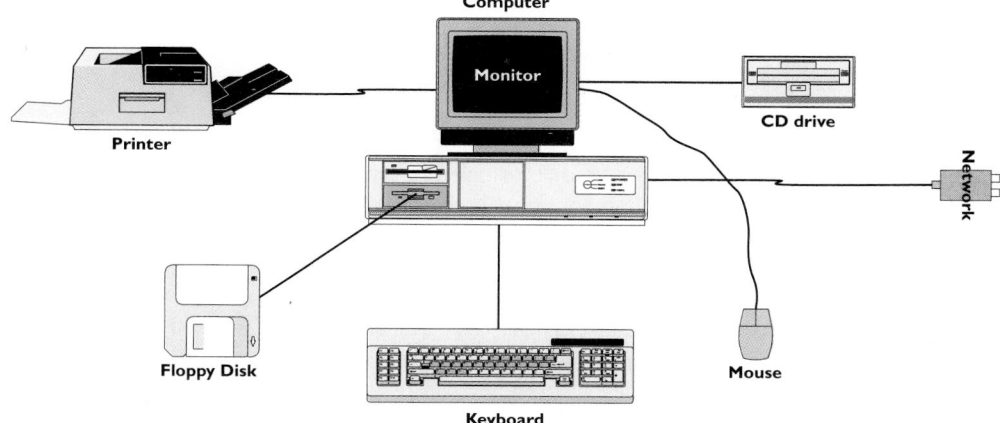

Computer Software Basics

The instructions used by the computer are provided by programs, or **software**. There are two major types of computer software: operating systems and applications. The **operating system** provides the instructions for the basic operations of the computer. The operating system also provides the underlying interface between the user and the computer. Every computer needs an operating system. An example of a popular operating system is Windows®. An **application** is software that performs a particular task. Examples of applications include word processing, spreadsheets, and accounting. There are thousands of applications available to perform many different tasks for users, from games to highly sophisticated mathematical analysis. Some common applications are listed below.

Applications

Type	Example
Word processing	Word, WordPerfect®
Spreadsheet	Excel, Lotus 1-2-3®
Presentation	PowerPoint®
Accounting	QuickBooks®, Peachtree®
Web browser	Netscape® Navigator

Point of **INTEREST**

Gordon Moore, chairman of Intel, once stated: "If the auto industry had moved at the same speed as our [computer] industry, your car today would cruise comfortably at a million miles an hour and probably get a half a million miles per gallon of gasoline. But it would be cheaper to throw your Rolls Royce away than to park it downtown for an evening."

Computerized System: An Illustration of the Revenue and Collection Cycle

Computerized accounting systems have three main advantages over manual systems. First, computerized systems simplify the record-keeping process. Transactions are recorded in electronic forms and, at the same time, posted electronically to general and subsidiary ledger accounts. Second, computerized systems are generally more accurate than manual systems. Third, computerized systems provide management current account balance information to support decision making, since account balances are posted as the transactions occur.

How do computerized accounting systems work? We will illustrate the revenue and collection cycle of Computer King by using a popular accounting application called

COMPUTER KING

BUSINESS ON STAGE

Computers are being used today in virtually every area of business. In the not-too-distant future, it is difficult to imagine how any business could be successful without integrating computers into its operations and management.

Computers!
Computers!
Computers!

What are some of the ways that computers are being used in manufacturing, management, marketing, accounting, and finance? Computer-aided design (CAD) and computer-aided manufacturing (CAM) are being used by manufacturing companies. CAD is used heavily by automobile companies to design and engineer new cars and trucks. The use of CAD speeds up the design process and allows manufacturers to deliver new products to the market sooner. CAM uses computers to control the production process and monitor the quality of the products. CAM is used heavily in chemical, oil refining, and other industries that involve volume processing of materials.

Many applications of computers exist in the management of businesses. For example, computers can facilitate training by providing an interactive medium that allows employees to obtain instant feedback on their performance and progress. One of the most exciting areas in which computers are affecting management is in communications. Electronic mail (e-mail) provides a very fast and inexpensive way of communicating written messages. In addition, the Internet and the World Wide Web allow rapid access to an almost infinite amount of information of potential usefulness to the managers of a business. Finally, teleconferencing and videoconferencing allow groups of managers to confer simultaneously over long distances, with significant savings in time, energy, and money.

Computers have allowed businesses to develop large databases from warranty cards, sweepstakes entries, coupons, promotions, and other sources. Such databases allow businesses insight into customer habits and preferences. This in turn allows businesses to target specific categories of customers for their marketing efforts. It also allows businesses to respond more quickly to changing customer preferences and needs.

In most businesses, the accounting area was the first to adopt computer technology for processing transactions and preparing management reports. Computers allow transactions to be processed almost instantaneously, with related reports available for immediate use by managers. In addition, computers can be used to plan for the future by modeling business operations and conducting "what if" analyses, using various assumptions and alternative decisions by management. ■

QuickBooks®. As shown in Exhibit 11, the first step is to enter information onto an electronic invoice form, as illustrated for the March 2 Handler Company invoice (No. 615). When the form is completed, it may be printed out and mailed to the customer. In addition, upon completing the invoice form the software automatically records the fees earned and posts the $2,200 to the Handler Co. account receivable.

In step two, the collection from the customer is received. Upon collection, the "receive payment" electronic form is opened and completed. In Exhibit 11, this form indicates that a $2,200 payment was collected from Handler Co. on March 28. This amount was applied to invoice 615, as shown by the check mark next to the March 2 date at the bottom of the form. The March 27 invoice of $3,000 remains uncollected, as shown at the bottom of the form. When this screen is completed, the cash account is automatically updated to reflect the increase in cash, and the Handler Company accounts receivable balance is automatically reduced from $5,200 to $3,000.

At any time, managers may request reports from the software. In step three, three such reports are illustrated in Exhibit 11: (1) the customer balance summary, (2) the income by customer summary, and (3) the check register. The reports are shown for March 31, 2000. Notice that the customer balance summary lists the outstanding accounts receivable balances by customer. This is essentially a report providing the details of the accounts receivable subsidiary ledger. It shows essentially the same information as Computer King's Schedule of Accounts Receivable on p. 190. The income by customer summary provides a listing of revenue by customer, which is similar to information provided by the revenue journal in a manual system. This listing is created from the electronic invoice form used in the first step of the cycle. The check register (First National Bank) lists the explanations for changes in the cash balance due to receipts and payments. Since receipts are only illustrated in this example, this report is similar to the cash receipts journal under the manual system. This listing is created from the "receive payment form" used in Step 2.

At the end of the month the manual system posted revenue journal and cash collection totals to the accounts receivable controlling ac-

EXHIBIT 11 The Revenue and Collection Cycle in QuickBooks®

1. **Record fee by filling out an electronic invoice form.**

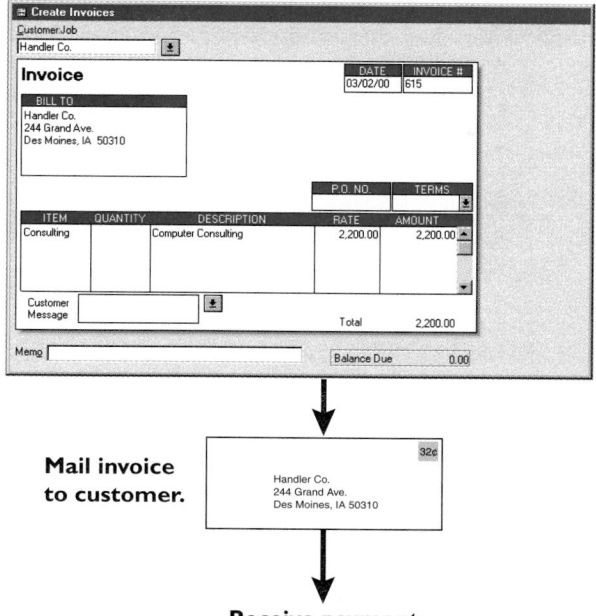

Mail invoice to customer.

Receive payment

2. **Record collection of payment by filling out "receive payment" form.**

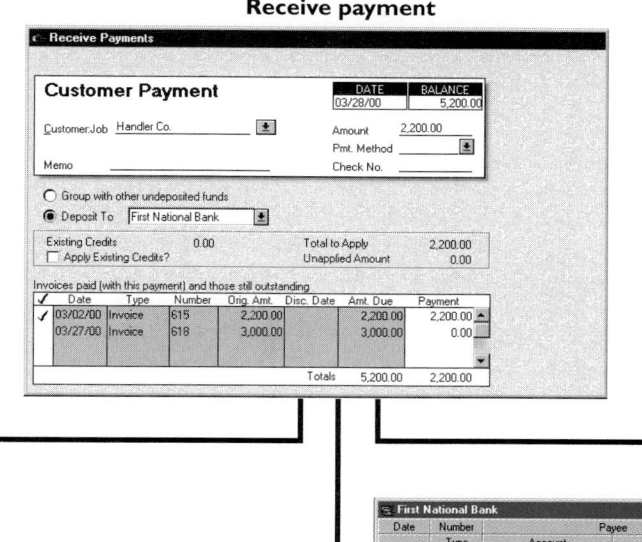

3. **Prepare reports.**

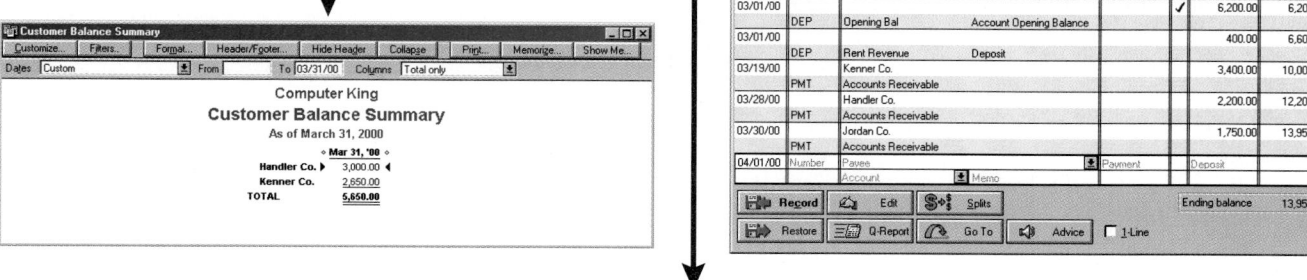

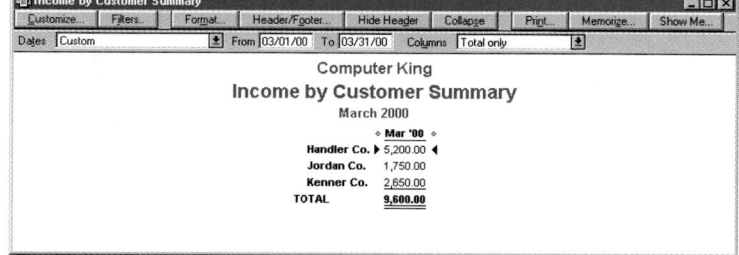

Most Windows-based accounting software uses electronic forms. An electronic form is a window that appears like a paper form. The form has spaces, or fields, in which to input information about a particular type of transaction. Many of the information spaces have pull-down lists for easy data entry. The most common electronic forms used by QuickBooks® are invoices, checks, bills, and receipts of payments.

count. In a computerized system, special journals typically are not used. Instead, transactions are recorded in electronic forms, which are automatically posted to affected accounts at the time the form is completed. In a manual system, the controlling account balance can be reconciled to the sum of the individual customer account balances to identify any posting and mathematical errors. The computer, however, does not make posting and mathematical errors. Thus, there are no month-end postings to controlling accounts. Controlling accounts are simply the sum of the balances of any individual subsidiary account balances.

We have illustrated the revenue and collection cycle to help you understand how a portion of a computerized accounting system works. A similar description could be provided for the purchases and payments cycle. A description of a complete computerized accounting system is beyond our scope. However, a thorough understanding of this chapter provides a solid foundation for applying the accounting system concepts in either a manual or a computerized system.

ENCORE

At the age of 16, Barry Minkow began a carpet cleaning company out of his parents' garage. Minkow aggressively promoted his company to Wall Street and attracted many outside investors. During this time, Minkow was considered a teenage tycoon. The story of his company, called **ZZZZ Best**, ended abruptly when Minkow, at the age of 21, was sentenced to 25 years for defrauding investors out of $26 million by falsely claiming his company was profitable and successful. Seven years later, upon his release from prison, Minkow claimed to be a changed man.

Minkow said his experience taught him the symptoms of personal corruption, and the lack of business controls.

Lessons From ZZZZ Best

- **Small compromises may lead to larger ones.** Minkow says for him it started with a $200 money order theft from a local liquor store. This escalated to overcharging customers' credit cards, and then eventually to investor fraud. Minkow says the

fraudulent behavior becomes easy to rationalize: "If I can get away with it the first time, I can probably do it again with the same result."

- **An unhealthy obsession with what others think about you.** Minkow states that he felt insecure because he lived in an area where classmates were driven to school in Mercedes, and this led to an obsession for personal wealth and prestige.

- **Taking shortcuts, or the easy way out.** Minkow tells the story of completing a carpet cleaning job and selling the customer an additional $100 Scotchguard application. When returning to his truck, he found that there was no Scotchguard left. Minkow sprayed the customer's carpet with water, rather than going back to the shop and picking up more Scotchguard.

- **Pride.** Minkow says his mother came to his office during the height of his fame and asked whether he knew God. Minkow responded, "God. How much is He? I'll buy Him."

Minkow has written a book, is conducting Bible studies, has earned degrees in theology, is a radio talk-show host, and is providing lectures on his experiences. He states that any money from these efforts will go toward paying back the investors who lost their savings in ZZZZ Best. To those that say it's just another scam, his response is that "authenticity is confirmed by consistency." Minkow's defrauded investors will wait and see. ■

Sources: Los Angeles Times staff interview, March 31, 1995; Barry Minkow, "My Million-Dollar Lesson About Compromise," *New Man* (January–February 1996), pp. 34–37.

KEY POINTS

1 Define an accounting system and describe its implementation.

An accounting system is the methods and procedures for collecting, classifying, summarizing, and reporting a business's financial information. The three steps through which an accounting system evolves are (1) analysis of information needs, (2) design of the system, and (3) implementation of the systems design.

2 List the three objectives of internal control and define and give examples of the five elements of internal control.

Internal control provides reasonable assurance that (1) assets are safeguarded and used for business purposes, (2) business information is accurate, and (3) laws and regulations are complied with. The five elements of internal control are the control environment, risk assessment, control procedures, monitoring, and information and communication.

3 Journalize and post transactions in a manual accounting system that uses subsidiary ledgers and special journals.

Subsidiary ledgers may be used to maintain separate records for each customer (the accounts receivable subsidiary ledger) and creditor (the accounts payable subsidiary ledger). Each subsidiary ledger is represented in the general ledger by a summarizing account, called a controlling account. The sum of the balances of the accounts in a subsidiary ledger must agree with the balance of the related controlling account.

Special journals may be used to reduce the processing time and expense of recording a large number of similar transactions. The revenue journal is used to record the sale of services on account. The cash receipts journal is used to record all receipts of cash. The purchases journal is used to record purchases on account. The cash payments journal is used to record all payments of cash. The general journal is used for recording transactions that do not fit in any of the special journals. The use of each special journal and the accounts receivable and accounts payable subsidiary ledgers is illustrated in the chapter.

4 Describe and give examples of additional subsidiary ledgers and modified special journals.

Subsidiary ledgers may be maintained for a variety of accounts, such as fixed assets, as well as accounts receivable and accounts payable. Special journals may be modified by adding columns in which to record frequently occurring transactions. For example, an additional column is often added to the revenue journal for recording the collection of sales taxes payable.

5 Describe the components of a computer system and apply computerized accounting to the revenue and collection cycle.

Computers consist of both hardware and software. Hardware provides the data input/output functions as well as internal data management and processing. Software provides the instructions for the computer. The operating system provides the computer with basic instructions, while applications are software that perform a particular task. Computerized accounting systems are similar to manual accounting systems. The main advantages of a computerized accounting system are the simultaneous recording and posting of transactions, the high degree of accuracy, and the timeliness of reporting. An example of the revenue and collection cycle using QuickBooks® is provided in the chapter.

ILLUSTRATIVE PROBLEM

Selected transactions of O'Malley Co. for the month of May are as follows:

a. May 1 Issued Check No. 1001 in payment of rent for May, $1,200.

b. 2 Purchased office supplies on account from McMillan Co., $3,600.

c. 4 Issued Check No. 1003 in payment of transportation charges on the supplies purchased on May 2, $320.

d. 8 Rendered services on account to Waller Co., Invoice No. 51, $4,500.

e. 9 Issued Check No. 1005 for office supplies purchased, $450.

f. 10 Received cash for office supplies sold to employees at cost, $120.

g. 11 Purchased office equipment on account from Fender Office Products, $15,000.

h. 12 Issued Check No. 1010 in payment of the supplies purchased from McMillan Co. on May 2, $3,600.

i. 16 Rendered services on account to Riese Co., Invoice No. 58, $8,000.

j. May 18 Received $4,500 from Waller Co. in payment of May 8 invoice.
k.   20 Invested additional cash in the business, $10,000.
l.   25 Rendered services for cash, $15,900.
m.   30 Issued Check No. 1040 for withdrawal of cash for personal use, $1,000.
n.   30 Issued Check No. 1041 in payment of electricity and water bills, $690.
o.   30 Issued Check No. 1042 in payment of office and sales salaries for May, $15,800.
p.   31 Journalized adjusting entries from the work sheet prepared for the fiscal
          year ended May 31.

O'Malley Co. maintains a revenue journal, a cash receipts journal, a purchases journal, a cash payments journal, and a general journal. In addition, accounts receivable and accounts payable subsidiary ledgers are used.

Instructions

1. Indicate the journal in which each of the preceding transactions, (a) through (p), would be recorded.
2. Indicate whether an account in the accounts receivable or accounts payable subsidiary ledgers would be affected for each of the preceding transactions.
3. Journalize transactions (b), (c), (d), (h), and (j) in the appropriate journals.

Solution

1.	**Journal**	**2.**	**Subsidiary Ledger**
a.	Cash payments journal		
b.	Purchases journal		Accounts payable ledger
c.	Cash payments journal		
d.	Revenue journal		Accounts receivable ledger
e.	Cash payments journal		
f.	Cash receipts journal		
g.	Purchases journal		Accounts payable ledger
h.	Cash payments journal		Accounts payable ledger
i.	Revenue journal		Accounts receivable ledger
j.	Cash receipts journal		Accounts receivable ledger
k.	Cash receipts journal		
l.	Cash receipts journal		
m.	Cash payments journal		
n.	Cash payments journal		
o.	Cash payments journal		
p.	General journal		

3.
Transaction (b):

PURCHASES JOURNAL

Date	Account Credited	Post. Ref.	Accounts Payable Cr.	Office Supplies Dr.	Other Accounts Dr.	Post. Ref.	Amount
May 2	McMillan Co.		3 6 0 0 00	3 6 0 0 00			

Transactions (c) and (h):

CASH PAYMENTS JOURNAL

Date	Ck. No.	Account Debited	Post. Ref.	Other Accounts Dr.	Accounts Payable Dr.	Cash Cr.
May 4	1003	Transportation In		3 2 0 00		3 2 0 00
12	1010	McMillan Co.			3 6 0 0 00	3 6 0 0 00

Transaction (d):

REVENUE JOURNAL

Date	Invoice No.	Account Debited	Post. Ref.	Accts. Rec. Dr. Fees Earned Cr.
May 8	51	Waller Co.		4 5 0 0 00

Transaction (j):

CASH RECEIPTS JOURNAL

Date	Account Credited	Post. Ref.	Other Accounts Cr.	Accounts Receivable Cr.	Cash Dr.
May 18	Waller Co.			4 5 0 0 00	4 5 0 0 00

SELF-EXAMINATION QUESTIONS   Answers at End of Chapter

Matching

Match each of the following statements with its proper term. Some terms may not be used.

A. accounting system	___ 1. The journal in which all cash payments are recorded.
B. accounts payable subsidiary ledger	___ 2. The journal in which all cash receipts are recorded.
C. accounts receivable subsidiary ledger	___ 3. The intentional act of deceiving an employer for personal gain.
	___ 4. The subsidiary ledger containing the individual accounts with customers (debtors).

D. application

E. cash payments journal

F. cash receipts journal

G. controlling account

H. elements of internal control

I. employee fraud

J. general journal

K. general ledger

L. hardware

M. internal controls

N. operating system

O. purchases journal

P. revenue journal

Q. software

R. special journals

S. subsidiary ledger

___ 5. Computer equipment used for data input/output and internal data management and processing.

___ 6. Journals designed to be used for recording a single type of transaction.

___ 7. The methods and procedures used by a business to collect, classify, summarize, and report financial data for use by management and external users.

___ 8. The policies and procedures used to safeguard assets, ensure accurate business information, and ensure compliance with laws and regulations.

___ 9. The subsidiary ledger containing the individual accounts with suppliers (creditors).

___ 10. Software that performs a specific task, such as word processing or spreadsheet.

___ 11. The control environment, risk assessment, control activities, information and communication, and monitoring.

___ 12. The journal in which all sales of services on account are recorded.

___ 13. The account in the general ledger that summarizes the balances of the accounts in a subsidiary ledger.

___ 14. The journal in which all items purchased on account are recorded.

___ 15. Computer software that provides the basic instructions to the computer and serves as the interface between the user and the computer.

___ 16. The two-column form used for entries that do not "fit" in any of the special journals.

___ 17. The primary ledger, when used in conjunction with subsidiary ledgers, that contains all of the balance sheet and income statement accounts.

___ 18. A ledger containing individual accounts with a common characteristic.

Multiple Choice

1. The initial step in the process of developing an accounting system is called:
   A. analysis
   B. design
   C. implementation
   D. feedback

2. The policies and procedures used by management to protect assets from misuse, ensure accurate business information, and assure compliance with laws and regulations are called:
   A. internal controls
   B. systems analysis
   C. systems design
   D. systems implementation

3. A payment of cash for the purchase of services should be recorded in the:
   A. purchases journal
   B. cash payments journal
   C. revenue journal
   D. cash receipts journal

4. When there are a large number of individual accounts with a common characteristic, it is common to place them in a separate ledger called:
   A. a subsidiary ledger
   B. a creditors ledger
   C. an accounts payable ledger
   D. an accounts receivable ledger

5. Which of the following would be used in a computerized accounting system?
   A. Revenue journal
   B. Cash receipts journal
   C. Electronic invoice form
   D. Month-end postings to the general ledger

CLASS DISCUSSION QUESTIONS

1. Why is the accounting system of a business an information system?
2. What is the three-step process of systems evolution?
3. What are the three objectives of internal control?
4. Name and describe the five elements of internal control.
5. How does a policy of rotating clerical employees from job to job aid in strengthening the control procedures within the control environment?
6. Why should the responsibility for a sequence of related operations be divided among different persons?

7. Why should the employee who handles cash receipts not have the responsibility for maintaining the accounts receivable records?
8. In an attempt to improve operating efficiency, one employee was made responsible for all purchasing, receiving, and storing of supplies. Is this organizational change wise from an internal control standpoint? Explain.
9. The ticket seller at a movie theater doubles as a ticket taker for a few minutes each day while the ticket taker is on a break. Which control procedure of a business's system of internal control is violated in this situation?
10. Why should the responsibility for maintaining the accounting records be separated from the responsibility for operations?
11. What is the term applied (a) to the ledger containing the individual customer accounts and (b) to the single account summarizing accounts receivable?
12. What are the major advantages of the use of special journals?
13. Environmental Services Co. uses the special journals described in this chapter. Which journal will be used to record fees earned (a) for cash, (b) on account?
14. In recording 250 fees earned on account during a single month, how many times will it be necessary to write Fees Earned (a) if each transaction, including fees earned, is recorded individually in a two-column general journal; (b) if each transaction for fees earned is recorded in a revenue journal?
15. How many individual postings to Fees Earned for the month would be needed in Question 14 if the procedure described in (a) had been used; if the procedure described in (b) had been used?
16. During the current month, the following errors occurred in recording transactions in the purchases journal or in posting from it.
    a. An invoice for $900 of supplies from Hoffman Co. was recorded as having been received from Hoffer Co., another supplier.
    b. A credit of $840 to JPC Company was posted as $480 in the subsidiary ledger.
    c. An invoice for equipment of $6,500 was recorded as $5,500.
    d. The Accounts Payable column of the purchases journal was overstated by $2,000. How will each error come to the bookkeeper's attention, other than by chance discovery?
17. The Accounts Payable and Cash columns in the cash payments journal were unknowingly overstated by $100 at the end of the month. (a) Assuming no other errors in recording or posting, will the error cause the trial balance totals to be unequal? (b) Will the creditors ledger agree with the accounts payable controlling account?
18. Assuming the use of a two-column general journal, a purchases journal, and a cash payments journal as illustrated in this chapter, indicate the journal in which each of the following transactions should be recorded:
    a. Purchase of supplies for cash.
    b. Purchase of office supplies on account.
    c. Payment of cash on account to creditor.
    d. Purchase of store equipment on account.
    e. Payment of cash for office supplies.
19. List five common computer hardware elements used for data input and output.
20. What is the difference between application software and the operating system?
21. What is an electronic form and how is it used in a computerized accounting system?
22. In the **Equity Funding** fraud, approximately $2 billion of insurance policies that were claimed to have been sold by the company were bogus. The bogus policies, which were supported by falsified policy applications, were listed along with real policies on Equity Funding's computer tapes (records). Equity Funding personnel, including the computer programmers, kept these tapes in a separate room where they were easily accessible. In addition, computer programmers and other company personnel had access to the computer. What general weaknesses in Equity Funding's internal controls contributed to the occurrence and the size of the fraud?

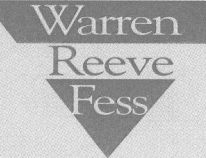

Resources for Your Success On-Line at warren.swcollege.com
Remember! If you need additional help, visit South-Western's Web site. See page 26 for a description of the online and printed materials that are available.

EXERCISES

Exercise 5–1
Internal controls

Objective 2

Debbie Byers has recently been hired as the manager of Long Island Deli. Long Island Deli is a national chain of franchised delicatessens. During her first month as store manager, Debbie encountered the following internal control situations:

a. Long Island Deli has one cash register. Prior to Debbie's joining the deli, each employee working on a shift would take a customer order, accept payment, and then prepare the order. Debbie made one employee on each shift responsible for taking orders and accepting the customer's payment. Other employees prepare the orders.

b. Since only one employee uses the cash register, that employee is responsible for counting the cash at the end of the shift and verifying that the cash in the drawer matches the amount of cash sales recorded by the cash register. Debbie expects each cashier to balance the drawer to the penny *every* time—no exceptions.

c. Debbie caught an employee putting a box of 100 single-serving bags of potato chips in his car. Not wanting to create a scene, Debbie smiled and said, "I don't think you're putting those chips on the right shelf. Don't they belong inside the deli?" The employee returned the chips to the stockroom.

State whether you agree or disagree with Debbie's method of handling each situation and explain your answer.

Exercise 5–2
Internal controls

Objective 2

Gypsy Fashions is a retail store specializing in women's clothing. The store has established a liberal return policy for the holiday season in order to encourage gift purchases. Any item purchased during November and December may be returned through January 31, with a receipt, for cash or exchange. If the customer does not have a receipt, cash will still be refunded for any item under $25. If the item is more than $25, a check is mailed to the customer.

Whenever an item is returned, a store clerk completes a return slip, which the customer signs. The return slip is placed in a special box. The store manager visits the return counter approximately once every two hours to authorize the return slips. Clerks are instructed to place the returned merchandise on the proper rack on the selling floor as soon as possible.

This year, returns at Gypsy Fashions have reached an all-time high. There are a large number of returns under $25 without receipts.

a. How can sales clerks employed at Gypsy Fashions use the store's return policy to steal money from the cash register?

b. 1. What internal control weaknesses do you see in the return policy that make cash thefts easier?

2. Would issuing a store credit in place of a cash refund for all merchandise returned without a receipt reduce the possibility of theft? List some advantages and disadvantages of issuing a store credit in place of a cash refund.

3. Assume that Gypsy Fashions is committed to the current policy of issuing cash refunds without a receipt. What changes could be made in the store's procedures regarding customer refunds in order to improve internal control?

Exercise 5–3
Internal controls for bank lending

Objective 2

Las Cruz Bank provides loans to businesses in the community through its Commercial Lending Department. Small loans (less than $100,000) may be approved by an individual loan officer, while larger loans (greater than $100,000) must be approved by a board of loan officers. Once a loan is approved, the funds are made available to the loan applicant under agreed terms. The president of Las Cruz Bank has instituted a policy whereby she has the individual authority to approve loans up to $5,000,000. The president believes that this policy will allow flexibility to approve loans to valued clients much quicker than under the previous policy.

As an internal auditor of Las Cruz Bank, how would you respond to this change in policy?

Exercise 5–4
Identify postings from revenue journal
Objective 3

Using the following revenue journal for J. A. Bach Co., identify each of the posting references, indicated by a letter, as representing (1) a posting to a general ledger account, (2) a posting to a subsidiary ledger account, or (3) a posting to two general ledger accounts.

REVENUE JOURNAL

Date	Invoice No.	Account Debited	Post. Ref.	
Nov. 1	772	Environmental Safety Co.	(a)	$2,465
10	773	Greenberg Co.	(b)	580
20	774	Smith and Smith	(c)	1,520
27	775	Envirolab	(d)	965
30				$5,530
				(e)

Exercise 5–5
Accounts receivable ledger
Objective 3

✓ d. Total accounts receivable, $5,965

Based upon the data presented in Exercise 5–4, assume that the beginning balances for the customer accounts were zero, except for Envirolab, which had a $435 beginning balance. In addition, there were no collections during the period.

a. Set up a T account for Accounts Receivable and T accounts for the four accounts needed in the customer ledger.
b. Post to the T accounts.
c. Determine the balance in the accounts, if necessary.
d. Prepare a schedule of accounts receivable at November 30.

Exercise 5–6
Identify journals
Objective 3

Assuming the use of a two-column (all-purpose) general journal, a revenue journal, and a cash receipts journal as illustrated in this chapter, indicate the journal in which each of the following transactions should be recorded:

a. Receipt of cash for rent.
b. Closing of drawing account at the end of the year.
c. Adjustment to record accrued salaries at the end of the year.
d. Sale of office supplies on account, at cost, to a neighboring business.
e. Receipt of cash on account from a customer.
f. Receipt of cash from sale of office equipment.
g. Providing services on account.
h. Providing services for cash.
i. Investment of additional cash in the business by the owner.
j. Receipt of cash refund from overpayment of taxes.

Exercise 5–7
Identify journals
Objective 3

Assuming the use of a two-column (all-purpose) general journal, a purchases journal, and a cash payments journal as illustrated in this chapter, indicate the journal in which each of the following transactions should be recorded:

a. Purchase of office equipment for cash.
b. Purchase of services on account.
c. Adjustment to prepaid insurance at the end of the month.
d. Adjustment to record depreciation at the end of the month.
e. Adjustment to prepaid rent at the end of the month.
f. Adjustment to record accrued salaries at the end of the period.
g. Purchase of office supplies for cash.
h. Advance payment of a one-year fire insurance policy on the office.
i. Purchase of office supplies on account.
j. Purchase of an office computer on account.
k. Payment of six months' rent in advance.

Exercise 5–8
Identify transactions in accounts receivable ledger
Objective 3

The debits and credits from three related transactions are presented in the following customer's account taken from the accounts receivable subsidiary ledger.
Describe each transaction, and identify the source of each posting.

NAME   *Good Times Catering*
ADDRESS   *1319 Maple Street*

Date	Item	Post. Ref.	Debit	Credit	Balance
2000					
Sep. 3		R50	450		450
9		J9		60	390
13		CR38		390	—

Exercise 5–9

Identify postings from purchases journal

Objective 3

Using the following purchases journal, identify each of the posting references, indicated by a letter, as representing (1) a posting to a general ledger account, (2) a posting to a subsidiary ledger account, or (3) that no posting is required.

PURCHASES JOURNAL   **PAGE 49**

Date	Account Credited	Post. Ref.	Accounts Payable Cr.	Store Supplies Dr.	Office Supplies Dr.	Other Accounts Dr. Account	Other Accounts Dr. Post. Ref.	Other Accounts Dr. Amount
20—								
June 4	Coastal Insurance Co.	(a)	4,525			Prepaid Insurance	(b)	4,525
6	Porter Supply Co.	(c)	3,000			Office Equipment	(d)	3,000
11	Baker Products	(e)	1,950	1,500	450			
13	Wilson and Wilson	(f)	6,800		6,800			
20	Cowen Supply	(g)	3,775	3,775				
27	Porter Suppply Co.	(h)	9,100			Store Equipment	(i)	9,100
30			29,150	5,275	7,250			16,625
			(j)	(k)	(l)			(m)

Exercise 5–10

Identify postings from cash payments journal

Objective 3

Using the following cash payments journal, identify each of the posting references, indicated by a letter, as representing (1) a posting to a general ledger account, (2) a posting to a subsidiary ledger account, or (3) that no posting is required.

CASH PAYMENTS JOURNAL   **PAGE 46**

Date	Ck. No.	Account Debited	Post. Ref.	Other Accounts Dr.	Accounts Payable Dr.	Cash Cr.
20—						
July 3	611	Aquatic Systems Co.	(a)		4,000	4,000
5	612	Utilities Expense	(b)	325		325
10	613	Prepaid Rent	(c)	3,200		3,200
17	614	Coe Bros.	(d)		2,500	2,500
20	615	Office Equipment	(e)	2,100		2,100
22	616	Advertising Expense	(f)	400		400
25	617	Office Supplies	(g)	250		250
27	618	Evans Co.	(h)		5,500	5,500
31	619	Salaries Expense	(i)	1,750		1,750
31				8,025	12,000	20,025
				(j)	(k)	(l)

Exercise 5–11

Identify transactions in accounts payable ledger account

Objective 3

The debits and credits from three related transactions are presented in the following creditor's account taken from the accounts payable ledger.

Describe each transaction, and identify the source of each posting.

NAME   *Echo Co.*
ADDRESS   *1717 Kirby Street*

Date	Item	Post. Ref.	Debit	Credit	Balance
2000					
July 6		P34		10,500	10,500
10		J10	500		10,000
16		CP37	10,000		—

Exercise 5–12

Error in accounts payable ledger and schedule of accounts payable

Objective 3

What's Wrong WITH THIS?

✓ b. Total accounts payable, $34,250

After Assurance Testing Services Inc. had completed all postings for October in the current year (2000), the sum of the balances in the following accounts payable ledger did not agree with the balance of the appropriate controlling account in the general ledger.

NAME   *Martinez Mining Co.*
ADDRESS   *1240 W. Main Street*

Date	Item	Post. Ref.	Debit	Credit	Balance
2000					
Oct. 1	Balance	(✓)			4,750
10		CP22	4,750		—
17		P30		4,400	4,400
25		J7	350		3,050

NAME   *Cutler and Powell*
ADDRESS   *717 Elm Street*

Date	Item	Post. Ref.	Debit	Credit	Balance
2000					
Oct. 1	Balance	(✓)			6,100
18		CP23	6,100		—
29		P31		7,500	7,500

NAME   *C. D. Greer and Son*
ADDRESS   *972 S. Tenth Street*

Date	Item	Post. Ref.	Debit	Credit	Balance
2000					
Oct. 17		P30		3,750	3,750
27		P31		9,000	12,750

NAME   *Donnelly Minerals Inc.*
ADDRESS   *1170 Mattis Avenue*

Date	Item	Post. Ref.	Debit	Credit	Balance
2000					
Oct. 1	Balance	(✓)			8,300
7		P30		4,900	13,300
12		J7	300		13,000
20		CP23	5,700		7,300

NAME   *L. L. Weiss Co.*
ADDRESS   *915 E. Walnut Street*

Date	Item	Post. Ref.	Debit	Credit	Balance
2000					
Oct. 5		P30		2,750	2,750

Assuming that the controlling account balance of $34,250 has been verified as correct, (a) determine the error(s) in the preceding accounts and (b) prepare a schedule of accounts payable from the corrected accounts payable subsidiary ledger.

Exercise 5–13
Identify postings from special journals

Objective 3

Albright Consulting Company makes most of its sales and purchases on credit. It uses the five journals described in this chapter (revenue, cash receipts, purchases, cash payments, and general journals). Identify the journal most likely used in recording the postings for selected transactions indicated by letter in the following T accounts:

	Cash				**Prepaid Rent**		
a.	10,000	b.	8,750			f.	400

	Accounts Receivable				**Accounts Payable**		
c.	10,950	d.	9,200	g.	7,600	h.	7,790

	Office Supplies				**Fees Earned**		
e.	6,500					i.	10,950

	Rent Expense	
j.	400	

Exercise 5–14
Cash receipts journal

Objective 3

What's Wrong WITH THIS?

The following cash receipts journal headings have been suggested for a small service firm. How many errors can you find in the headings?

	CASH RECEIPTS JOURNAL					PAGE
Date	Account Credited	Post. Ref.	Fees Earned Cr.	Accounts Rec. Cr.	Cash Cr.	Other Accounts Dr.

Exercise 5–15
Modified special journals

Objectives 3, 4

Wellguard Health Clinic was established on June 15 of the current year. The clients for whom Wellguard provided health services during the remainder of June are listed below. These clients pay Wellguard the amount indicated plus a 5% sales tax.

June 16. A. Sommerfeld on account, Invoice No. 1, $200 plus tax.
   19. B. Lin, Invoice No. 2, $80 plus tax.
   21. J. Koss, Invoice No. 3, $60 plus tax.
   22. D. Jeffries, Invoice No. 4, $100 plus tax.
   24. K. Sallinger, in exchange for medical supplies having a value of $160, plus tax.
   26. J. Koss, Invoice No. 5, $120 plus tax.
   28. B. Lin, Invoice No. 6, $40 plus tax.
   30. D. Finnigan, Invoice No. 7, $260 plus tax.

a. Journalize the transactions for June, using a three-column revenue journal and a two-column general journal. Post the customer accounts in the accounts receivable subsidiary ledger and insert the balance immediately after recording each entry.
b. Post the general journal and the revenue journal to the following general ledger accounts, inserting account balances only after the last postings:

   12   Accounts Receivable
   14   Medical Supplies
   22   Sales Tax Payable
   41   Fees Earned

c. 1. What is the sum of the balances in the accounts receivable subsidiary ledger at June 30?
   2. What is the balance of the controlling account at June 30?

Exercise 5–16
Computer components

Objective 5

Which of the following items are used for computer data input or output?

a. Keyboard
b. Monitor
c. Operating system
d. RAM
e. Modem

f. CD Drive
g. Hard Drive
h. Network
i. Application
j. Printer

Exercise 5–17
Computerized accounting systems

Objective 5

Most computerized accounting systems use electronic forms to record transaction information, as illustrated in Exhibit 11.

a. Identify the key input fields (spaces) to an electronic invoice form.
b. What accounts are posted from an electronic invoice form?
c. Why aren't special journal totals posted to control accounts at the end of the month in an electronic accounting system?

PROBLEMS SERIES A

Problem 5–1A
Revenue journal; accounts receivable and general ledgers

Objective 3

HAT

✓ I. Revenue journal, total fees earned, $9,880

Worthy Accounting Services was established on May 15, 2000, to provide accounting and tax services. The clients for whom Worthy provided services during the remainder of May are listed below.

May 18. Jacob Co., Invoice No. 1, $970 on account.
   20. Ro-Gain Co., Invoice No. 2, $650 on account.
   22. Innis Co., Invoice No. 3, $2,600 on account.
   27. D. L. Victor Co., Invoice No. 4, $1,870 on account.
   28. Bower Co., Invoice No. 5, $1,200 on account.
   28. Ro-Gain Co., $700 in exchange for supplies.
   30. Ro-Gain Co., Invoice No. 6, $2,150 on account.
   31. Innis Co., Invoice No. 7, $440 on account.

Instructions

1. Journalize the transactions for May, using a single-column revenue journal and a two-column general journal. Post to the following customer accounts in the accounts receivable ledger, and insert the balance immediately after recording each entry: Bower Co.; D. L. Victor Co.; Innis Co.; Jacob Co.; Ro-Gain Co.
2. Post the revenue journal to the following accounts in the general ledger, inserting the account balances only after the last postings:

   12   Accounts Receivable
   14   Supplies
   41   Fees Earned

3. a. What is the sum of the balances of the accounts in the subsidiary ledger at May 31?
   b. What is the balance of the controlling account at May 31?
4. Assume that on June 1, the state in which Worthy operates begins requiring that sales tax be collected on accounting services. Briefly explain how the revenue journal may be modified to accommodate sales of services on account requiring the collection of a state sales tax.

Problem 5–2A
Revenue and cash receipts journals; accounts receivable and general ledgers

Objective 3

Transactions related to revenue and cash receipts completed by Elite Engineering Services during the period November 15–30 of the current year are as follows:

Nov. 15. Issued Invoice No. 717 to Yamura Co., $9,450.
   16. Received cash from AGI Co. for the balance owed on its account.
   17. Issued Invoice No. 718 to Hardy Co., $2,400.
   18. Issued Invoice No. 719 to Ross and Son, $9,600.
      Post all journals to the accounts receivable ledger.

HAT

✓ 3. Total cash receipts, $98,880

Nov. 21. Received cash from Hardy Co. for the balance owed on November 15.
24. Issued Invoice No. 720 to Hardy Co., $11,400.
Post all journals to the accounts receivable ledger.
25. Received cash from Yamura Co. for the balance due on invoice of November 15.
26. Received cash from Hardy Co. for invoice of November 17.
27. Issued Invoice No. 721 to AGI Co., $9,540.
29. Recorded fees earned for the second half of the month, $14,300.
30. Received office equipment in settlement of balance due on the Ross and Son account.
Post all journals to the accounts receivable ledger.

Instructions

1. Insert the following balances in the general ledger as of November 1:

11	Cash	$ 9,450
12	Accounts Receivable	14,750
18	Office Equipment	4,500
41	Fees Earned	—

2. Insert the following balances in the accounts receivable subsidiary ledger as of November 15:

AGI Co.	$8,700
Hardy Co.	5,400
Ross and Son	—
Yamura Co.	—

3. In a single-column revenue journal and a cash receipts journal, insert *November 15 Total(s) Forwarded* on the left side of the first line of the journal. Use the following column headings for the cash receipts journal: Other Accounts, Fees Earned, Accounts Receivable, and Cash. The Fees Earned column is used to record cash fees. Insert a check mark (✓) in the Post. Ref. Column. The following dollar figures show the totals forwarded as of November 15 for their respective amount columns:

   Revenue journal: 38,750
   Cash receipts journal: 6,780; 12,450; 39,400; 58,630

   These amounts have not been posted, but represent the totals of the November 1–15 transactions.
4. Using the two special journals and the two-column general journal, journalize the transactions for the remainder of November. Post to the accounts receivable ledger, and insert the balances at the points indicated in the narrative of transactions. Determine the balance in the customer's account before recording a cash receipt.
5. Total each of the columns of the special journals, and post the individual entries and totals to the general ledger. Insert account balances after the last posting.
6. Determine that the subsidiary ledger agrees with the controlling account in the general ledger.

Problem 5–3A
Purchases, accounts payable account, and accounts payable ledger

Objective 3

HAT

Robbins Surveyors provides survey work for construction projects. The office staff use office supplies, while surveying crews use field supplies. Purchases on account completed by Robbins Surveyors during May 2000 are as follows:

May 1. Purchased field supplies on account from Wendell Co., $2,460.
3. Purchased office supplies on account from Lassiter Co., $1,670.
8. Purchased field supplies on account from Trent Supply, $950.
12. Purchased field supplies on account from Wendell Co., $1,050.
13. Purchased office equipment on account from Gore Computers Co., $8,600.
15. Purchased office supplies on account from J-Mart Co., $1,300.
19. Purchased office equipment on account from Eskew Co., $6,300.

✓ 3. Total accounts payable credit, $28,770

May 23. Purchased field supplies on account from Trent Supply, $1,400.
26. Purchased office supplies on account from J-Mart Co., $840.
30. Purchased field supplies on account from Trent Supply, $4,200.

Instructions

1. Insert the following balances in the general ledger as of May 1:

14	Field Supplies	$ 3,215
15	Office Supplies	1,400
18	Office Equipment	15,400
21	Accounts Payable	7,720

2. Insert the following balances in the accounts payable subsidiary ledger as of May 1:

Eskew Co.	$4,300
Gore Computers Co.	—
J-Mart Co.	970
Lassiter Co.	2,450
Trent Supply	—
Wendell Co.	—

3. Journalize the transactions for May, using a purchases journal similar to the one illustrated in this chapter. Prepare the purchases journal with columns for Accounts Payable, Field Supplies, Office Supplies, and Other Accounts. Post to the creditor accounts in the accounts payable ledger immediately after each entry.
4. Post the purchases journal to the accounts in the general ledger.
5. a. What is the sum of the balances in the subsidiary ledger at May 31?
   b. What is the balance of the controlling account at May 31?

Problem 5–4A
Purchases and cash payments journals; accounts payable and general ledgers

Objective 3

HAT
SPREADSHEET

✓ 1. Total cash payments, $60,150

Black Gold Exploration Co. was established on March 15, 2000, to provide oil-drilling services. Black Gold uses field equipment (rigs and pipe) and field supplies (drill bits and lubricants) in its operations. Transactions related to purchases and cash payments during the remainder of March are as follows:

Mar. 16. Issued Check No. 1 in payment of rent for the remainder of March, $1,000.
16. Purchased field equipment on account from Harper Equipment Co., $20,000.
17. Purchased field supplies on account from Culver Supply Co., $6,200.
18. Issued Check No. 2 in payment of field supplies, $1,200, and office supplies, $120.
19. Purchased office equipment on account from Lacy Co., $12,400.
20. Purchased office supplies on account from Ange Supply Co., $230.
    Post the journals to the accounts payable ledger.
24. Issued Check No. 3 to Harper Equipment Co. in payment of invoice, $20,000.
26. Issued Check No. 4 to Culver Supply Co. in payment of invoice, $6,200.
28. Issued Check No. 5 to purchase land from the owner, $10,000.
28. Issued Check No. 6 to Lacy Co. in payment of the balance owed.
28. Purchased office supplies on account from Ange Supply Co., $630.
    Post the journals to the accounts payable ledger.
30. Purchased the following from Harper Equipment Co. on account: field supplies, $2,300, and office equipment, $4,400.
30. Issued Check No. 7 to Ange Supply Co. in payment of invoice, $230.
30. Purchased field supplies on account from Culver Supply Co., $1,900.
31. Issued Check No. 8 in payment of salaries, $9,000.
31. Acquired land in exchange for field equipment having a cost of $6,000.
    Post the journals to the accounts payable ledger.

Instructions

1. Journalize the transactions for March. Use a purchases journal and a cash payments journal, similar to those illustrated in this chapter, and a two-column general journal. Refer to the following partial chart of accounts:

11	Cash	19	Land
14	Field Supplies	21	Accounts Payable
15	Office Supplies	61	Salary Expense
17	Field Equipment	71	Rent Expense
18	Office Equipment		

At the points indicated in the narrative of transactions, post to the following accounts in the accounts payable ledger:

Ange Supply Co.
Culver Supply Co.
Harper Equipment Co.
Lacy Co.

2.   Post the individual entries (Other Accounts columns of the purchases journal and the cash payments journal; both columns of the general journal) to the appropriate general ledger accounts.
3.   Total each of the columns of the purchases journal and the cash payments journal, and post the appropriate totals to the general ledger. (Because the problem does not include transactions related to cash receipts, the cash account in the ledger will have a credit balance.)
4.   Prepare a schedule of accounts payable.

Problem 5–5A
All journals and general ledger; trial balance

Objective 3

GENERAL LEDGER

✓ 2. Total cash receipts, $50,250

The transactions completed by Same-Day Courier Company during May, the first month of the fiscal year, were as follows:

May 1. Issued Check No. 205 for May rent, $1,000.
    2. Purchased a vehicle on account from Bunting Co., $24,500.
    3. Purchased office equipment on account from Gill Computer Co., $4,600.
    5. Issued Invoice No. 91 to Carlton Co., $1,600.
    6. Received check for $4,200 from Pease Co. in payment of invoice.
    6. Issued Check No. 206 for fuel expense, $800.
    9. Issued Invoice No. 92 to Collins Co., $2,340.
   10. Received check for $8,150 from Sing Co. in payment of invoice.
   10. Issued Check No. 207 to Haber Enterprises in payment of $3,160 invoice.
   10. Issued Check No. 208 to Bastille Co. in payment of $2,000 invoice.
   11. Issued Invoice No. 93 to Joy Co., $950.
   11. Issued Check No. 209 to Porter Co. in payment of $910 invoice.
   12. Received check for $1,600 from Carlton Co. in payment of invoice.
   13. Issued Check No. 210 to Bunting Co. in payment of $24,500 invoice.
   16. Cash fees earned for May 1–16, $14,450.
   16. Issued Check No. 211 for purchase of a vehicle, $12,000.
   17. Purchased maintenance supplies on account from Bastille Co., $3,150.
   18. Issued Check No. 212 for miscellaneous administrative expenses, $1,900.
   18. Received check for rent revenue on office space, $1,100.
   19. Purchased the following on account from Master Co.: maintenance supplies, $1,500, and office supplies, $2,500.
   20. Issued Check No. 213 in payment of advertising expense, $1,350.
   20. Used maintenance supplies with a cost of $3,900 to overhaul vehicle engines.
   23. Issued Invoice No. 94 to Sing Co., $4,200.
   24. Purchased office supplies on account from Haber Enterprises, $700.
   25. Received check for $2,150 from Pease Co. in payment of invoice.
   25. Issued Invoice No. 95 to Collins Co., $6,700.
   26. Issued Check No. 214 to Gill Computer Co. in payment of $4,600 invoice.
   27. Issued Check No. 215 to C. Davis as a personal withdrawal, $3,200.
   30. Issued Check No. 216 in payment of driver salaries, $14,600.
   31. Issued Check No. 217 in payment of office salaries, $6,700.
   31. Issued Check No. 218 for office supplies, $720.
   31. Cash fees earned for May 17–31, $18,600.

Instructions

1.   Enter the following account balances in the general ledger as of May 1:

11	Cash	$ 28,400	32	C. Davis, Drawing	—
12	Accounts Receivable	14,500	41	Fees Earned	—
14	Maintenance Supplies	5,200	42	Rent Revenue	—
15	Office Supplies	3,400	51	Driver Salaries Expense	—
16	Office Equipment	16,800	52	Maintenance Supplies	
17	Accumulated Depreciation			Expense	—
	—Office Equipment	4,100	53	Fuel Expense	—
18	Vehicles	82,000	61	Office Salaries Expense	—
19	Accumulated Depreciation		62	Rent Expense	—
	—Vehicles	16,300	63	Advertising Expense	—
21	Accounts Payable	6,070	64	Miscellaneous Adminis-	
31	C. Davis, Capital	123,830		trative Expense	—

2. Journalize the transactions for May 2000 using the following journals similar to those illustrated in this chapter: single-column revenue journal, cash receipts journal, purchases journal (with columns for Accounts Payable, Maintenance Supplies, Office Supplies, and Other Accounts), cash payments journal, and two-column general journal. You do not need to make daily postings to the individual accounts in the accounts payable ledger and the accounts receivable ledger.

3. Post the appropriate individual entries to the general ledger.

4. Total each of the columns of the special journals, and post the appropriate totals to the general ledger; insert the account balances.

5. Prepare a trial balance.

6. Verify the agreement of each subsidiary ledger with its controlling account. The sum of the balances of the accounts in the subsidiary ledgers as of May 31 are as follows:

Accounts receivable $14,190
Accounts payable   7,850

PROBLEMS SERIES B

Problem 5–1B
Revenue journal; accounts receivable and general ledgers

Objective 3

✓ 1. Revenue journal, total fees earned, $950

Head Start Reading Labs was established on May 20, 2000, to provide educational services. The clients for whom Head Start provided services on account during the remainder of the month are as follows:

May 21. J. Dunlop, Invoice No. 1, $90 on account.
　　22. L. Stanley, Invoice No. 2, $140 on account.
　　24. T. Morris, Invoice No. 3, $65 on account.
　　25. L. Stanley, $140 in exchange for educational supplies.
　　27. F. Mintz, Invoice No. 4, $245 on account.
　　28. D. Bennett, Invoice No. 5, $120 on account.
　　30. L. Stanley, Invoice No. 6, $210 on account.
　　31. T. Morris, Invoice No. 7, $80 on account.

Instructions

1. Journalize the transactions for May, using a single-column revenue journal and a two-column general journal. Post to the following customer accounts in the accounts receivable ledger, and insert the balance immediately after recording each entry: D. Bennett; J. Dunlop; F. Mintz; T. Morris; L. Stanley.

2. Post the revenue journal and the general journal to the following accounts in the general ledger, inserting the account balances only after the last postings:

　　12　Accounts Receivable
　　13　Supplies
　　41　Fees Earned

3. a. What is the sum of the balances of the accounts in the subsidiary ledger at May 31?
　　b. What is the balance of the controlling account at May 31?

4. ⬛️ ➤ Assume that on June 1, the state in which Head Start Reading Labs operates begins requiring that sales tax be collected on educational services. Briefly explain how the revenue journal may be modified to accommodate sales of services on account that require the collection of a state sales tax.

Problem 5–2B

Revenue and cash receipts journals; accounts receivable and general ledgers

Objective 3

✓ 3. Total cash receipts, $83,990

Transactions related to revenue and cash receipts completed by Continental Architects Co. during the period June 15–30, 2000, are as follows:

June 15. Issued Invoice No. 793 to Ping Co., $6,500.
　16. Received cash from Morton Co. for the balance owed on its account.
　19. Issued Invoice No. 794 to Quest Co., $5,570.
　20. Issued Invoice No. 795 to Mendez Co., $6,780.
　　　Post all journals to the accounts receivable ledger.
　23. Received cash from Quest Co. for the balance owed on June 15.
　24. Issued Invoice No. 796 to Quest Co., $2,430.
　　　Post all journals to the accounts receivable ledger.
　25. Received cash from Ping Co. for the balance due on invoice of June 15.
　28. Received cash from Quest Co. for invoice of June 19.
　28. Issued Invoice No. 797 to Morton Co., $3,460.
　30. Received $6,780 notes receivable in settlement of the balance due on the Mendez Co. account.
　30. Recorded cash fees received for the second half of the month, $8,500.
　　　Post all journals to the accounts receivable ledger.

Instructions

1. Insert the following balances in the general ledger as of June 1:

11	Cash	$10,550
12	Accounts Receivable	12,650
14	Notes Receivable	4,000
41	Fees Earned	—

2. Insert the following balances in the accounts receivable ledger as of June 15:

Mendez Co.	—
Morton Co.	$14,500
Ping Co.	—
Quest Co.	8,350

3. In a single-column revenue journal and a cash receipts journal, insert *June 15 Total(s) Forwarded* on the left side of the first line of the journal. Use the following column headings for the cash receipts journal: Other Accounts, Fees Earned, Accounts Receivable, and Cash. The Fees Earned column is used to record cash fees. Insert a check mark (✓) in the Post. Ref. Column. The following dollar figures show the totals forwarded as of June 15 for their respective amount columns:

Revenue journal: 32,650
Cash receipts journal: 4,560; 13,560; 22,450; 40,570

These amounts have not been posted, but represent the totals of the June 1–15 transactions.

4. Using the two special journals and the two-column general journal, journalize the transactions for the remainder of June. Post to the accounts receivable ledger, and insert the balances at the points indicated in the narrative of transactions. Determine the balance in the customer's account before recording a cash receipt.

5. Total each of the columns of the special journals, and post the individual entries and totals to the general ledger. Insert account balances after the last posting.

6. Determine that the subsidiary ledger agrees with the controlling account in the general ledger.

Problem 5–3B
Purchases, accounts payable account, and accounts payable ledger
Objective 3

✓ 3. Total accounts payable credit, $27,330

Lee Landscaping Services designs and installs landscaping. The landscape designers and office staff use office supplies, while field supplies (rock, bark, etc.) are used in the actual landscaping. Purchases on account completed by Lee Landscaping during July 2000 are as follows:

July 1. Purchased office equipment on account from Emerald Computers Co., $4,700.
 5. Purchased office supplies on account from Lapp Co., $3,400.
 9. Purchased office supplies on account from Lang Supplies Co., $2,400.
 13. Purchased field supplies on account from Yin Co., $1,460.
 14. Purchased field supplies on account from Yin Co., $2,340.
 17. Purchased field supplies on account from Nelson Co., $950.
 20. Purchased office equipment on account from Cencor Co., $7,530.
 24. Purchased field supplies on account from Nelson Co., $3,210.
 29. Purchased office supplies on account from Lang Supplies Co., $840.
 31. Purchased field supplies on account from Nelson Co., $500.

Instructions

1. Insert the following balances in the general ledger as of July 1:

14	Field Supplies	$ 4,670
15	Office Supplies	850
18	Office Equipment	12,500
21	Accounts Payable	9,080

2. Insert the following balances in the accounts payable ledger as of July 1:

Cencor Co.	$5,670	Lapp Co.	$960
Emerald Computers Co.	—	Nelson Co.	—
Lang Supplies Co.	2,450	Yin Co.	—

3. Journalize the transactions for July, using a purchases journal similar to the one illustrated in this chapter. Prepare the purchases journal with columns for Accounts Payable, Field Supplies, Office Supplies, and Other Accounts. Post to the creditor accounts in the accounts payable ledger immediately after each entry.
4. Post the purchases journal to the accounts in the general ledger.
5. a. What is the sum of the balances in the subsidiary ledger at July 31?
 b. What is the balance of the controlling account at July 31?

Problem 5–4B
Purchases and cash payments journals; accounts payable and general ledgers
Objective 3

SPREADSHEET

✓ 1. Total cash payments, $57,030

Purity Water Testing Service was established on June 16, 2000. Purity uses field equipment and field supplies (chemicals and other supplies) to analyze water for unsafe contaminants in streams, lakes, and ponds. Transactions related to purchases and cash payments during the remainder of June are as follows:

June 16. Issued Check No. 1 in payment of rent for the remainder of June, $900.
 16. Purchased field supplies on account from Heath Supply Co., $4,200.
 16. Purchased field equipment on account from Juan Equipment Co., $13,000.
 17. Purchased office supplies on account from Aztec Supply Co., $530.
 18. Purchased office equipment on account from Chavez Co., $3,800.
 19. Issued Check No. 2 in payment of field supplies, $2,200, and office supplies, $400.
 Post the journals to the accounts payable ledger.
 23. Purchased office supplies on account from Aztec Supply Co., $900.
 23. Issued Check No. 3 to purchase land from the owner, $20,000.
 24. Issued Check No. 4 to Heath Supply Co. in payment of invoice, $4,200.
 25. Issued Check No. 5 to Chavez Co. in payment of the balance owed.
 26. Issued Check No. 6 to Juan Equipment Co. in payment of invoice, $13,000.
 Post the journals to the accounts payable ledger.
 30. Acquired land in exchange for field equipment having a cost of $8,000.
 30. Purchased field supplies on account from Heath Supply Co., $6,400.
 30. Issued Check No. 7 to Aztec Supply Co. in payment of invoice, $530.

June 30. Purchased the following from Juan Equipment Co. on account: field supplies, $3,400, and field equipment, $5,000.

30. Issued Check No. 8 in payment of salaries, $12,000.

Post the journals to the accounts payable ledger.

Instructions

1. Journalize the transactions for June. Use a purchases journal and a cash payments journal, similar to those illustrated in this chapter, and a two-column general journal. Refer to the following partial chart of accounts:

11	Cash	19	Land
14	Field Supplies	21	Accounts Payable
15	Office Supplies	61	Salary Expense
17	Field Equipment	71	Rent Expense
18	Office Equipment		

   At the points indicated in the narrative of transactions, post to the following accounts in the accounts payable ledger:

   Aztec Supply Co.
   Chavez Co.
   Heath Supply Co.
   Juan Equipment Co.

2. Post the individual entries (Other Accounts columns of the purchases journal and the cash payments journal and both columns of the general journal) to the appropriate general ledger accounts.
3. Total each of the columns of the purchases journal and the cash payments journal and post the appropriate totals to the general ledger. (Because the problem does not include transactions related to cash receipts, the cash account in the ledger will have a credit balance.)
4. Prepare a schedule of accounts payable.

Problem 5–5B

All journals and general ledger; trial balance

Objective 3

GENERAL LEDGER

✓ 2. Total cash receipts, $38,800

The transactions completed by Speedy Delivery Company during July, the first month of the fiscal year, were as follows:

July 1. Issued Check No. 610 for July rent, $1,000.
2. Issued Invoice No. 940 to Capps Co., $2,000.
3. Received check for $6,700 from Pease Co. in payment of invoice.
5. Purchased a vehicle on account from Browning Transportation, $21,300.
6. Purchased office equipment on account from Gunter Computer Co., $4,200.
6. Issued Invoice No. 941 to Collins Co., $3,500.
9. Issued Check No. 611 for fuel expense, $900.
10. Received check from Sokol Co. in payment of $4,400 invoice.
10. Issued Check No. 612 for $4,200 to Hoy Co. in payment of invoice.
10. Issued Invoice No. 942 to Joy Co., $6,600.
11. Issued Check No. 613 to Burks Co. in payment of $2,300 invoice.
11. Issued Check No. 614 for $1,500 to Porter Co. in payment of account.
12. Received check from Capps Co. in payment of $2,000 invoice.
13. Issued Check No. 615 to Browning Transportation in payment of $21,300 balance.
16. Issued Check No. 616 for $9,000 for cash purchase of a vehicle.
16. Cash fees earned for July 1–16, $10,600.
17. Issued Check No. 617 for miscellaneous administrative expense, $1,200.
18. Purchased maintenance supplies on account from Burks Co., $1,200.
19. Purchased the following on account from McClain Co.: maintenance supplies, $1,450; office supplies, $1,750.
20. Issued Check No. 618 in payment of advertising expense, $1,400.
20. Used $3,200 maintenance supplies to repair delivery vehicles.
23. Purchased office supplies on account from Hoy Co., $500.
24. Issued Invoice No. 943 to Sokol Co., $5,700.

July 24. Issued Check No. 619 to D. D. Miles as a personal withdrawal, $4,000.
25. Issued Invoice No. 944 to Collins Co., $9,300.
25. Received check for $7,200 from Pease Co. in payment of balance.
26. Issued Check No. 620 to Gunter Computer Co. in payment of $4,200 invoice of July 3.
30. Issued Check No. 621 for monthly salaries as follows: driver salaries, $12,000; office salaries, $8,000.
31. Cash fees earned for July 17–31, $7,400.
31. Issued Check No. 622 in payment for office supplies, $700.
31. Received check for rent revenue on office space, $500.

Instructions

1. Enter the following account balances in the general ledger as of July 1:

11	Cash	$ 36,800	32	D. D. Miles, Drawing	—
12	Accounts Receivable	18,300	41	Fees Earned	—
14	Maintenance Supplies	5,400	42	Rent Revenue	—
15	Office Supplies	3,600	51	Driver Salaries Expense	—
16	Office Equipment	18,900	52	Maintenance Supplies Expense	—
17	Accumulated Depreciation —Office Equipment	2,200	53	Fuel Expense	—
18	Vehicles	56,000	61	Office Salaries Expense	—
19	Accumulated Depreciation —Vehicles	8,800	62	Rent Expense	—
21	Accounts Payable	8,000	63	Advertising Expense	—
31	D. D. Miles, Capital	120,000	64	Miscellaneous Administrative Expense	—

2. Journalize the transactions for July 2000 using the following journals similar to those illustrated in this chapter: cash receipts journal, purchases journal (with columns for Accounts Payable, Maintenance Supplies, Office Supplies, and Other Accounts), single-column revenue journal, cash payments journal, and two-column general journal. You do not need to make daily postings to the individual accounts in the accounts payable ledger and the accounts receivable ledger.
3. Post the appropriate individual entries to the general ledger.
4. Total each of the columns of the special journals and post the appropriate totals to the general ledger; insert the account balances.
5. Prepare a trial balance.
6. Verify the agreement of each subsidiary ledger with its controlling account. The sum of the balances of the accounts in the subsidiary ledgers as of July 31 are:

Accounts receivable $25,100
Accounts payable   4,900

QUICKBOOKS PROBLEM 1

The Revenue and Collection Cycle

This problem uses the Larry's Landscaping sample company provided with QuickBooks® 5.0. Begin by first copying *sample.qbw* into another file name, **revcol.qbw,** so that the original sample.qbw file will not be changed. You must copy the file using the copy and paste commands in your operating system. This is an important step, since we will be using the unchanged sample.qbw file later in the text. If you do not first copy sample.qbw into another file name, you will automatically change sample.qbw. We will be assuming that you have an unchanged version in future QuickBooks problems in this text.

Retrieve Larry's Landscaping by opening the file that you just created. The first time you open Larry's Landscaping you will be in QuickBooks Navigator®. You may wish to use the Navigator to review the forms used for "Sales and Customers." This problem will use these forms.

Larry's Landscaping has been in business since October of the current year. We will add some additional transactions to those that have already been recorded and saved in the company file. The following additional jobs were invoiced to customers:

Invoice No.	Customer	Class	Terms	Item(s)	Quantity	Rate	Amount	Sales Tax Rate
34	Desai, Ashmi	Design	Net 30	Custom design (nontaxable)	40 hrs.	$55	$2,200	San Dom. (7.75%)
35	Crenshaw, Bob	Land-scaping	Net 15	Rock fountain with $400 of concrete	Various	Various	960	San Thom. (8.25%)
36	Middlefield Elementary School	Land-scaping	Net 30	Gardening Plants/trees	20 bushes	$90	110 1,800	San Thom. (8.25%)
37	Paxton, Drew	Land-scaping	Net 30	Installation Garden rocks Garden lighting	50 hrs. 80 lbs. 1	$35 $9.75 $300	1,750 780 300	San Thom. (8.25%)

The following collections were made on account:

Customer	Amount	Applied to Invoice No.
Ecker Design	$4,107.22	28
Middlefield Elementary School	665.00	30
Benson Family Store	695.00	5

Instructions

1. Enter invoice nos. 34–37 on the electronic invoice forms in QuickBooks. To open the electronic invoice, click on the Invoice button or select the Invoice submenu item under "Activities."
2. Enter the three collections on the electronic "receive payment" forms of QuickBooks. To open the receive payment forms, select the submenu item under "Activities."
3. Print the following reports (submenu item under Reports in parentheses):
   a. Customer Balance Summary Report (A/R reports)
   b. Income by Customer Summary for December 1–15 (Sales reports)
   c. Income detail of Paxton Consulting for December 1–15. (Double-click on Paxton Consulting sales total on Customer Summary Report.)
   d. Deposit detail for December 1–15. (Other reports)

QUICKBOOKS PROBLEM 2

The Purchase and Payment Cycle

This problem uses the Larry's Landscaping sample company provided with QuickBooks® 5.0. Begin by first copying *sample.qbw* into another file name, **purpay.qbw,** so that the original sample.qbw file will not be changed. You must copy the file using the copy and paste commands in your operating system. This is an important step, since we will be using the unchanged sample.qbw file later in the text. If you do not first copy sample.qbw into another file name, you will automatically change sample.qbw. We will be assuming that you have an unchanged version in future QuickBooks problems in this text.

Retrieve Larry's Landscaping by opening the file that you just created. The first time you open Larry's Landscaping, you will be in QuickBooks Navigator. You may wish to use the Navigator to review the forms used for "Purchases and Vendors." This problem will use these forms.

Larry's Landscaping has been in business since October of the current year. We will add some additional transactions to those that have already been recorded and saved in the company file. The following bills were received from vendors:

Vendor	Amount	Expense Account	Amount	Customer: Job	Class
Denk's Nursery	$ 560	Job materials: fountain and garden lighting	$ 560	Wallace, Ralph	Landscaping
Doherty Patio & Deck Designs	2,500	Job expenses: subcontractor	2,500	Mills, Richard	Landscaping
Sena Lumber and Building Materials	550	Delivery fee Materials: decks and patio	50 500	Hughes, David	Landscaping

The following payments were made to satisfy vendor accounts:

Conner Garden Supplies	$ 210
Middlefield Nursery	240
Sena Lumber and Building Materials	1,400

Instructions

1. Enter the three vendor bills into the electronic bills in QuickBooks. To open the electronic bill, click on the Bill button or select the Bill submenu item under "Activities."
2. Enter the three payments on the "pay bills" forms by checking the appropriate bill for payments. Deselect the "to be printed" option for checks. "Pay bills" is a submenu item under "Activities."
3. Print the following reports (submenu item under Reports in parentheses):
   a. Vendor Balance Summary. (A/P Reports)
   b. Vendor Balance Detail for Sena Lumber and Building Materials. (Double-click Sena Lumber and Building Materials balance on the summary report.)
   c. Expenses by Vendor Summary for Oct. 1–Dec. 15. (Profit & Loss)
   d. Expenses by Vendor Detail for Denk's Nursery for Oct. 1–Dec. 15. (Double-click Denk's Nursery expense balance on the Expenses by Vendor Summary Report.)

SPECIAL ACTIVITIES

**Activity 5–1
Armor Security Co.**
Ethics and professional conduct in business

Lee Baskin sells security systems for Armor Security Co. Baskin has a monthly sales quota of $40,000. If Baskin exceeds this quota, he is awarded a bonus. In measuring the quota, a sale is credited to the salesperson when a customer signs a contract for installation of a security system. Through the 25th of the current month, Baskin has sold $30,000 in security systems.

Vortex Co., a business rumored to be on the verge of bankruptcy, contacted Baskin on the 26th of the month about having a security system installed. Baskin estimates that the contract would yield about $14,000 worth of business for Armor Security Co. In addition, this contract would be large enough to put Baskin "over the top" for a bonus in the current month. However, Baskin is concerned that Vortex Co. will not be able to make the contract payment after the security system is installed. In fact, Baskin has heard rumors that a competing security services company refused to install a system for Vortex Co. because of these concerns.

Upon further consideration, Baskin concluded that his job is to sell security systems and that it's someone else's problem to collect the resulting accounts receivable. Thus, Baskin wrote the contract with Vortex Co. and received a bonus for the month.

Discuss whether Lee Baskin was acting in an ethical manner. How might Armor Security Co. use internal controls to prevent this scenario from occurring?

**Activity 5–2
Blacktop Pavement Co.**
Manual vs. computerized accounting systems

The following conversation took place between Blacktop Pavement Co.'s bookkeeper, Gerry Monroe, and the accounting supervisor, Lyn Hargrove.

Lyn: Gerry, I'm thinking about bringing in a new computerized accounting system to replace our manual system. I guess this will mean that you will need to learn how to do computerized accounting.

Gerry: What does computerized accounting mean?

Lyn: I'm not sure, but you'll need to prepare for this new way of doing business.

Gerry: I'm not so sure we need a computerized system. I've been looking at some of the sample reports from the software vendor. It looks to me like the computer will not add much to what we are already doing.

Lyn: What do you mean?

Gerry: Well, look at these reports. This Sales by Customer Report looks like our revenue journal, and the Deposit Detail Report looks like our cash receipts journal. Granted, the computer types them, so they look much neater than my special journals, but I don't see that we're gaining much from this change.

Lyn: Well, surely there's more to it than nice-looking reports. I've got to believe that a computerized system will save us time and effort someplace.

Gerry: I don't see how. We still need to key in transactions into the computer. If anything, there may be more work when it's all said and done.

➤ Do you agree with Gerry? Why might a computerized environment be preferred over the manual system?

Activity 5–3
Windsor Company
Internal controls

Like most businesses, when Windsor Company renders services to another business, it is typical that the service is rendered "on account," rather than as a cash transaction. As a result, Windsor Company has an account receivable for the service provided. Likewise, the company receiving the service has an account payable for the amount owed for services received. At a later date, Windsor Company will receive cash from the customer to satisfy the accounts receivable balance. However, when individuals conduct transactions with each other, it is common for the transaction to be for cash. For example, when you buy a pizza, you often pay with cash.

➤ Why is it unusual for businesses such as Windsor Company to engage in cash transactions, while for individuals it is more common?

Activity 5–4
Hershey Foods
Corporation
Internal controls and the annual report

Corporations generally issue annual reports to their stockholders and other interested parties. These annual reports include a Management Responsibility (or Management Report) section as well as financial statements. The Management Responsibility section discusses responsibility for the financial statements and normally includes an assessment of the company's internal control system.

➤ What does the annual report for **Hershey Foods Corporation** (in Appendix G) indicate about the internal control system?

Activity 5–5
Ragsdale Medical
Group
Design of accounting systems

For the past few years, your client, Ragsdale Medical Group (RMG), has operated a small medical practice. RMG's current annual revenues are $420,000. Because the accountant has been spending more and more time each month recording all transactions in a two-column journal and preparing the financial statements, RMG is considering improving the accounting system by adding special journals and subsidiary ledgers. RMG has asked you to help with this project and has compiled the following information:

Type of Transaction	Estimated Frequency per Month
Fees earned on account	240
Purchase of medical supplies on account	190
Cash receipts from patients on account	175
Cash payments on account	160
Cash receipts from patients at time services provided	120
Purchase of office supplies on account	35
Purchase of magazine subscriptions on account	5
Purchase of medical equipment on account	4
Cash payments for office salaries	3
Cash payments for utilities expense	3

A local sales tax is collected on all patient bills, and monthly financial statements are prepared.

1. ◄ Briefly discuss the circumstances under which special journals would be used in place of a two-column (all-purpose) journal. Include in your answer your recommendations for RMG's medical practice.
2. Assume that RMG has decided to use a revenue journal and a purchases journal. Design the format for each journal, giving special consideration to the needs of the medical practice.
3. Which subsidiary ledgers would you recommend for the medical practice?

Activity 5–6
Into the Real World

Shopping for a microcomputer

Obtain a copy of a recent computer magazine (such as *PC Week*) from the library or magazine stand. In this magazine, select an ad by a company that offers a variety of microcomputer systems—from a basic system to a top-of-the-line system. Some good examples would be **Dell**, **Micron**, **Compaq**, or **Gateway 2000**. Alternatively, go to the web page of one of the computer companies to obtain product information. Divide responsibilities among your team so that you can accomplish the following tasks:

1. Bring to class one of the ads or a printout of web pages with product specifications. The Internet sites of the companies mentioned above are:

   www.dell.com
   www.micron.com
   www.compaq.com
   www.gateway.com

2. List and briefly explain each feature of the top-of-the-line computer identified in the ad or web page. Compare the features of the top-of-the-line system and the basic entry-level system. How do they differ? How do the prices differ?
3. Try to discover the purpose of the features that are not familiar to you by talking to others in your group or to friends.

ANSWERS TO SELF-EXAMINATION QUESTIONS

Matching

1. E	4. C	7. A	9. B	11. H	13. G	15. N	17. K
2. F	5. L	8. M	10. D	12. P	14. O	16. J	18. S
3. I	6. R					

Multiple Choice

1. **A** Analysis (answer A) is the initial step of determining the informational needs and how the system provides this information. Design (answer B) is the step in which proposals for changes are developed. Implementation (answer C) is the final step involving carrying out or implementing the proposals for changes. Feedback (answer D) is not a separate step but is considered part of the systems implementation.

2. **A** The policies and procedures that are established to safeguard assets, ensure accurate business information, and ensure compliance with laws and regulations are called internal controls (answer A). The three steps in setting up an accounting system are (1) analysis (answer B), (2) design (answer C), and (3) implementation (answer D).

3. **B** All payments of cash for any purpose are recorded in the cash payments journal (answer B). Only purchases of services or other items on account are recorded in the purchases journal (answer A). All sales of services on account are recorded in the revenue journal (answer C), and all receipts of cash are recorded in the cash receipts journal (answer D).

4. **A** The general term used to describe the type of separate ledger that contains a large number of individual accounts with a common characteristic is a subsidiary ledger (answer A). The creditors ledger (answer B), sometimes called the accounts payable ledger (answer C), is a specific subsidiary ledger containing only individual accounts with creditors. Likewise, the accounts receivable ledger (answer D), also called the customers ledger, is a specific subsidiary ledger containing only individual accounts with customers.

5. **C** Both the revenue journal (answer A) and the cash receipts journal (answer B) are generally not used in a computerized accounting system. Rather, electronic forms, such as an electronic invoice form (answer C), are used to record original transactions. The computer automatically posts transactions from electronic forms to the general ledger and individual accounts at the time the transactions are recorded. Therefore, month-end postings to the general ledger are not necessary (answer D) in a computerized accounting system.

Accounting for Merchandising Businesses

Setting *the* STAGE

Assume that you bought groceries at a store and received the receipt shown here. This receipt indicates that you purchased three items totaling $5.28, the sales tax was $.32 (6%), the total due was $5.60, you gave the clerk $10.00, and you received change of $4.40. The receipt also indicates that the sale was made by Store #426 of the Ingles chain, located in Athens, Georgia. The date and time of the sale and other data used internally by the store are also indicated.

```
INGLES #426
ATHENS GA

                           10/02/99
GROCERY                      2.99L
GROCERY                      1.00L
FZ FOOD                      1.29L
SUBTOTAL                     5.28
TAX                           .32
TOTAL                        5.60

CASH                        10.00

CHANGE                       4.40

# ITEMS     3

   THANK YOU C123 R03 T12:38
```

When you buy groceries, textbooks, school supplies, or an automobile, you are doing business with a retail or merchandising business. The accounting for a merchandising business is more complex than for a service business. For example, the accounting system for a merchandiser must be designed to record the receipt of goods for resale, keep track of the goods available for sale, and record the sale and cost of the merchandise sold.

In this chapter, we will focus on the accounting principles and concepts for merchandising businesses. We begin our discussion by highlighting the basic differences in the activities of merchandise and service businesses. We then describe and illustrate purchases and sales transactions and financial statements for merchandising businesses.

1 Distinguish the activities of a service business from those of a merchandising business.

2 Journalize the entries for merchandise transactions, including:
  a. Merchandise purchases
  b. Merchandise sales
  c. Merchandise transportation costs
  d. Transactions for both the buyer and the seller

3 Prepare a chart of accounts for a merchandising business.

4 Prepare an income statement for a merchandising business.

5 Describe the accounting cycle for a merchandising business.

6 Compute the ratio of net sales to assets as a measure of how effectively a business is using its assets.

Nature of Merchandising Businesses

OBJECTIVE 1

Distinguish the activities of a service business from those of a merchandising business.

How do the activities of Computer King, an attorney, and an architect, which are service businesses, differ from those of **Wal-Mart** or **Kmart**, which are merchandising businesses? These differences are best illustrated by focusing on the revenues and expenses in the following condensed income statements:

Service Business		Merchandising Business	
Fees earned	$XXX	Sales	$XXX
Operating expenses	−XXX	Cost of merchandise sold	−XXX
Net income	$XXX	Gross profit	$XXX
		Operating expenses	−XXX
		Net income	$XXX

The revenue activities of a service business involve providing services to customers. On the income statement for a service business, the revenues from services are reported as *fees earned*. The operating expenses incurred in providing the services are subtracted from the fees earned to arrive at *net income*.

In contrast, the revenue activities of a merchandising business involve the buying and selling of merchandise. A merchandising business must first purchase merchandise to sell to its customers. When this merchandise is sold, the revenue is reported as sales, and its cost is recognized as an expense called the **cost of merchandise sold**. The cost of merchandise sold is subtracted from sales to arrive at gross profit. This amount is called **gross profit** because it is the profit *before* deducting operating expenses.

 For many merchandising businesses, the cost of merchandise sold is usually the largest expense. For example, the approximate percentage of cost of merchandise sold to sales is 70% for **J.C. Penney Company** and 75% for **Lowe's Companies**.

Merchandise on hand (not sold) at the end of an accounting period is called **merchandise inventory**. Merchandise inventory is reported as a current asset on the balance sheet.

In the remainder of this chapter, we illustrate transactions that affect the income statement (sales, cost of merchandise sold, and gross profit) and the balance sheet (merchandise inventory). We will assume that Computer King opened a retail store in January 2001.

$$\text{Sales} - \frac{\text{Cost of}}{\text{Merchandise Sold}} = \frac{\text{Gross}}{\text{Profit}}$$

$$\frac{\text{Gross}}{\text{Profit}} - \frac{\text{Operating}}{\text{Expenses}} = \frac{\text{Net}}{\text{Income}}$$

Merchandise transactions are recorded in the accounts, using the rules of debit and credit that we described and illustrated in earlier chapters. Special journals may be used, or transactions may be entered, recorded, and posted to the accounts electronically. Although journal entries may not be manually prepared, we will use a two-column general journal format in this chapter in order to simplify the discussion.[1]

Accounting for Purchases

OBJECTIVE 2a

Journalize the entries for merchandise purchases.

Retailers, such as **Kmart**, **Sears**, and **Wal-Mart**, and grocery store chains, such as **Winn-Dixie** and **Kroger**, use bar codes and optical scanners as part of their computerized inventory systems.

There are two systems for accounting for merchandise: perpetual and periodic. In the **perpetual inventory system**, each purchase and sale of merchandise is recorded in an inventory account. As a result, the amount of merchandise available for sale and the amount sold are continuously (perpetually) disclosed in the inventory records. In the **periodic inventory system**, the inventory records do not show the amount available for sale or sold during the period. Instead, a detailed listing of the merchandise for sale (called a **physical inventory**) at the end of the accounting period is prepared. This physical inventory is used to determine the cost of the merchandise on hand at the end of the period and the cost of the merchandise sold during the period.

In a perpetual inventory system, each purchase is debited to Merchandise Inventory, and the cost of each sale is credited to Merchandise Inventory.

Large retailers and many small merchandising businesses use computerized perpetual inventory systems. Such systems normally use bar codes, such as the one on the back of this textbook. An optical scanner reads the bar code to record merchandise purchased and sold.

Because the perpetual inventory system is widely used, we illustrate it in this chapter. We describe and illustrate the periodic inventory system in a later chapter and in an appendix at the end of the text.

Under the perpetual inventory system, cash purchases of merchandise are recorded as follows:

	Date		Description	Post. Ref.	Debit	Credit	
	JOURNAL					**PAGE 24**	
1	20— Jan.	3	Merchandise Inventory		2 5 1 0 00		1
2			Cash			2 5 1 0 00	2
3			Purchased inventory from Bowen Co.				3

Purchases of merchandise on account are recorded as follows:

	Date		Description	Post. Ref.	Debit	Credit	
5	Jan.	4	Merchandise Inventory		9 2 5 0 00		5
6			Accounts Payable—Thomas Corporation			9 2 5 0 00	6
7			Purchased inventory on account.				7

[1] Special journals and computerized accounting systems for merchandising businesses are described in Appendix 1 at the end of this chapter.

Purchases Discounts

The terms of a purchase are normally indicated on the **invoice** or bill that the seller sends to the buyer. An example of such an invoice is shown in Exhibit 1.

EXHIBIT 1
Invoice

Wallace Electronics	3800 Mission Street San Francisco, CA 94110-1732		
			Made in U.S.A.
SOLD TO Computer King 1000 Peachtree Street Atlanta, GA 30309-1000		**CUSTOMER'S ORDER NO. & DATE** 412 Jan. 10, 2001 **REFER TO INVOICE NO.** 106-8	
DATE SHIPPED Jan. 12, 2001	**HOW SHIPPED AND ROUTE** Western Trucking Co.	**TERMS** 2/10, n/30	**INVOICE DATE** Jan. 12, 2001
FROM San Francisco	**F.O.B.** Atlanta	**PREPAID OR COLLECT?** Prepaid	
QUANTITY 20	**DESCRIPTION** 392E Monitors	**UNIT PRICE** 75.00	**AMOUNT** 1,500.00

Q&A *If an invoice dated August 13 has terms n/30, what is the due date of the invoice?*

September 12 [30 days = 18 days in August (31 days − 13 days) + 12 days in September]

The terms for when payments for merchandise are to be made, agreed on by the buyer and the seller, are called the **credit terms**. If payment is required on delivery, the terms are *cash* or *net cash*. Otherwise, the buyer is allowed an amount of time, known as the **credit period**, in which to pay.

The credit period usually begins with the date of the sale as shown on the invoice. If payment is due within a stated number of days after the date of the invoice, such as 30 days, the terms are *net 30 days*. These terms may be written as *n/30*.[2] If payment is due by the end of the month in which the sale was made, the terms are written as *n/eom*.

As a means of encouraging the buyer to pay before the end of the credit period, the seller may offer a discount. For example, a seller may offer a 2% discount if the buyer pays within 10 days of the invoice date. If the buyer does not take the discount, the total amount is due within 30 days. These terms are expressed as *2/10, n/30* and are read as *2% discount if paid within 10 days, net amount due within 30 days*. The credit terms of 2/10, n/30 are summarized in Exhibit 2, using the information from the invoice in Exhibit 1.

EXHIBIT 2
Credit Terms

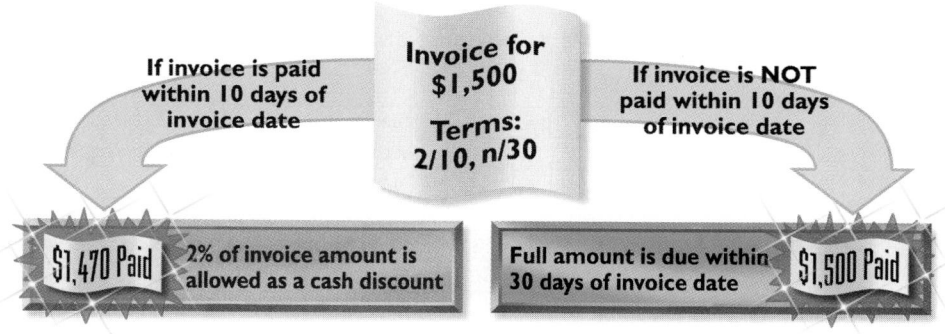

[2] The word *net* as used here does not have the usual meaning of a number after deductions have been subtracted, as in *net income*.

Q&A *If an invoice dated November 22 has credit terms 2/10, n/30, what is (a) the last day the invoice may be paid within the discount period and (b) the last day of the credit period if the discount is not taken?*

(a) December 2 [10 days = 8 days in November (30 days − 22 days) + 2 days in December]; (b) December 22 [30 days = 8 days in November (30 days − 22 days) + 22 days in December]

Discounts taken by the buyer for early payment of an invoice are called **purchases discounts**. These discounts reduce the cost of the merchandise purchased. Most businesses design their accounting systems so that all available discounts are taken. Even if the buyer has to borrow to make the payment within a discount period, it is normally to the buyer's advantage to do so. To illustrate, assume that Computer King borrows money to pay the invoice for $1,500, shown in Exhibit 1. The last day of the discount period in which the $30 discount can be taken is January 22, 2001. The money is borrowed for the remaining 20 days of the credit period. If we assume an annual interest rate of 12% and a 360-day year, the interest on the loan of $1,470 ($1,500 − $30) is $9.80 ($1,470 × 12% × 20/360). The net savings to Computer King is $20.20, computed as follows:

Discount of 2% on $1,500	$30.00
Interest for 20 days at rate of 12% on $1,470	− 9.80
Savings from borrowing	$20.20

The savings can also be seen by comparing the interest rate on the money saved by taking the discount and the interest rate on the money borrowed to take the discount. For Computer King, the interest rate on the money saved in this example is estimated by converting 2% for 20 days to a yearly rate, as follows:

$$2\% \times \frac{360 \text{ days}}{20 \text{ days}} = 2\% \times 18 = 36\%$$

If Computer King borrows the money to take the discount, it *pays* interest of 12%. If Computer King does not take the discount, it *pays* estimated interest of 36% for using the $30 for an additional 20 days.

Under the perpetual inventory system, the buyer initially debits the merchandise inventory account for the amount of the invoice. When paying the invoice, the buyer credits the merchandise inventory account for the amount of the discount. In this way, the merchandise inventory shows the *net* cost to the buyer. For example, Computer King would record the invoice in Exhibit 1 and its payment at the end of the discount period as follows:

 Businesses often program their accounting systems to pay bills automatically at the right time.

 **Point of INTEREST**

Should you pay your bills, such as utility bills and credit card bills, as soon as they are received? Probably not. Most bills that you receive do not offer discounts for early payment. Rather, the bills normally indicate only a due date and perhaps a penalty for late payment. Many times you receive bills weeks before their due date. In such cases, it is to your advantage to file the bill by its due date in a folder or other organizer, such as a desk calendar, and mail the payment a few days before it is due. This way, you can use your money to earn interest in your checking or savings account.

Jan.	12	Merchandise Inventory		1 5 0 0 00			
		Accounts Payable—Wallace Electronics				1 5 0 0 00	
		Invoice 106-8.					
	22	Accounts Payable—Wallace Electronics		1 5 0 0 00			
		Cash				1 4 7 0 00	
		Merchandise Inventory				3 0 00	
		Paid Invoice 106-8.					

If Computer King does not take the discount because it does not pay Invoice 106-8 until February 11, it would record the payment as follows:

Feb.	11	Accounts Payable—Wallace Electronics				1	5	0	0	00							
		Cash										1	5	0	0	00	
		Paid Invoice 106-8 after discount															
		period.															

Purchases Returns and Allowances

When merchandise is returned (**purchases return**) or a price adjustment is requested (**purchases allowance**), the buyer (debtor) usually sends the seller a letter or a debit memorandum. A **debit memorandum**, shown in Exhibit 3, informs the seller of the amount the buyer proposes to *debit* to the account payable due the seller. It also states the reasons for the return or the request for a price reduction.

EXHIBIT 3
Debit Memorandum

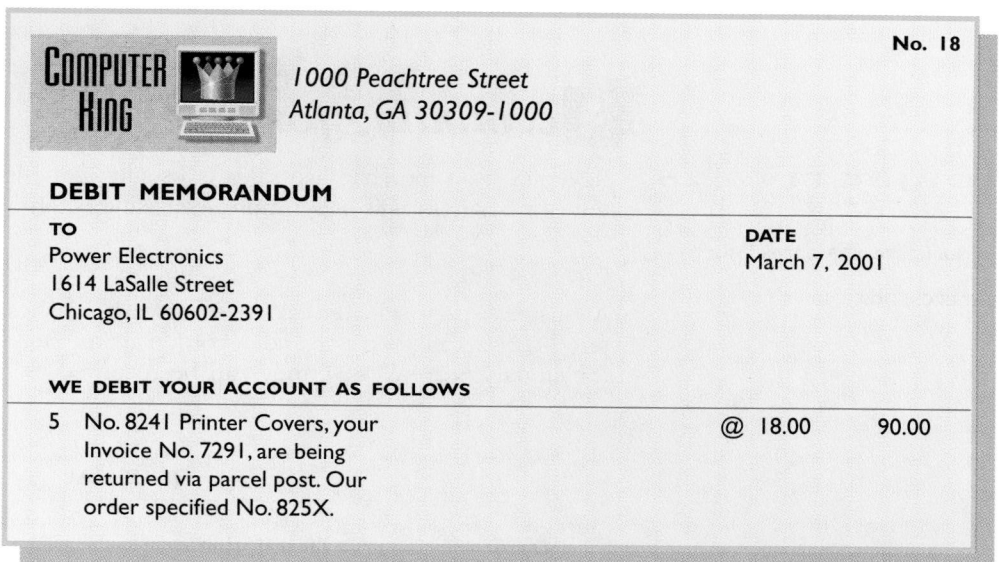

The buyer may use a copy of the debit memorandum as the basis for recording the return or allowance, or wait for approval from the seller (creditor). In either case, the buyer must debit Accounts Payable and credit Merchandise Inventory. To illustrate, Computer King records the return of the merchandise indicated in the debit memo in Exhibit 3 as follows:

Mar.	7	Accounts Payable—Power Electronics					9	0	00								
		Merchandise Inventory											9	0	00		
		Debit Memo No. 18.															

When a buyer returns merchandise or has been granted an allowance prior to paying the invoice, the amount of the debit memorandum is deducted from the invoice amount. The amount is deducted before the purchase discount is computed. For example, assume that on May 2, Computer King purchases $5,000 of merchandise from Computer Maker, subject to terms 2/10, n/30. On May 4, Computer King returns $3,000 of the merchandise, and on May 12, Computer King pays the original invoice less the return. Computer King would record these transactions as follows:

May	2	Merchandise Inventory			5 0 0 0 00		
		Accounts Payable—Computer Maker				5 0 0 0 00	
		Purchased merchandise.					
	4	Accounts Payable—Computer Maker			3 0 0 0 00		
		Merchandise Inventory				3 0 0 0 00	
		Returned portion of merchandise					
		purchased.					
	12	Accounts Payable—Computer Maker			2 0 0 0 00		
		Cash				1 9 6 0 00	
		Merchandise Inventory				4 0 00	
		Paid invoice [($5,000 − $3,000) × 2%					
		= $40; $2,000 − $40 = $1,960].					

Q&A

Ennis Co. purchases merchandise of $8,000 on terms 2/10, n/30. Ennis pays the original invoice, less a return of $2,500, within the discount period. How much did Ennis Co. pay?

$5,390 [($8,000 − $2,500) × 2% = $110 discount; $8,000 − $2,500 − $110 = $5,390]

Accounting for Sales

OBJECTIVE 2b

Journalize the entries for merchandise sales.

Revenue from merchandise sales is usually identified in the ledger as *Sales*. Sometimes a business will use a more exact title, such as *Sales of Merchandise*.

Cash Sales

A business may sell merchandise for cash. Cash sales are normally rung up (entered) on a cash register and recorded in the accounts. To illustrate, if cash sales for January 3 are $1,800, they can be recorded as follows:

		JOURNAL				PAGE 25	
	Date	**Description**	**Post. Ref.**	**Debit**		**Credit**	
1	20— Jan. 3	Cash		1 8 0 0 00			1
2		Sales				1 8 0 0 00	2
3		To record cash sales.					3

Under the perpetual inventory system, the cost of merchandise sold and the reduction in merchandise inventory should also be recorded. In this way, the merchandise inventory account will indicate the amount of merchandise on hand (not sold). On the income statement at the end of the period, the balance of the cost of merchandise sold account is subtracted from the related sales for the period in order to determine the gross profit. To illustrate, assume that the cost of merchandise sold on January 3 was $1,200. The entry to record the cost of merchandise sold and the reduction in the merchandise inventory is as follows:

Jan.	3	Cost of Merchandise Sold			1 2 0 0 00		
		Merchandise Inventory				1 2 0 0 00	
		To record the cost of merchandise					
		sold.					

How do retailers record sales made with the use of credit cards? Sales made to customers using credit cards issued by banks, such as **MasterCard** or **VISA**, are recorded as *cash sales*. The seller deposits the credit card receipts for these sales directly into its bank account.

Normally, banks charge service fees for handling credit card sales. The seller debits these service fees to an expense account. An entry at the end of a month to record the payment of service charges on bank credit card sales is shown below.

Jan.	31	Credit Card Expense		4 8 00	
		Cash			4 8 00
		To record service charges on credit			
		card sales for the month.			

Sales on Account

A business may sell merchandise on account. The seller records such sales as a debit to Accounts Receivable and a credit to Sales. An example of an entry for a sale on account of $510 follows. The cost of merchandise sold was $280.

Jan.	12	Accounts Receivable—Sims Co.		5 1 0 00	
		Sales			5 1 0 00
		Invoice No. 7172.			
	12	Cost of Merchandise Sold		2 8 0 00	
		Merchandise Inventory			2 8 0 00
		Cost of merchandise sold on Invoice			
		No. 7172.			

Sales may also be made to customers using nonbank credit cards. An example of a nonbank credit card is the **American Express** card. Nonbank credit card sales must first be reported to the card company before cash is received. Therefore, such sales create a *receivable* with the card company. Before the card company pays cash, it normally deducts a service fee. For example, assume that American Express card sales of $1,000 are made and reported to the card company on January 20. The cost of the merchandise sold was $550. On January 27, the card company deducts a service fee of $50 and sends $950 to the seller. These transactions are recorded by the seller as follows:

Jan.	20	Accounts Receivable—American Express		1 0 0 0 00	
		Sales			1 0 0 0 00
		American Express (nonbank) credit card			
		sales.			
	20	Cost of Merchandise Sold		5 5 0 00	
		Merchandise Inventory			5 5 0 00
		Cost of merchandise sold on American			
		Express credit card sales.			
	27	Cash		9 5 0 00	
		Credit Card Expense		5 0 00	
		Accounts Receivable—American Express			1 0 0 0 00
		Received cash from American Express for			
		sales reported on January 20.			

A retailer may accept **Master-Card** or **VISA** but not **American Express**. Why? The service fees that credit card companies charge retailers are the primary reason that some businesses do not accept all credit cards. For example, American Express Co.'s service fees are normally higher than Master-Card's or VISA's. As a result, some retailers choose not to accept American Express cards. The disadvantage of this practice is that the retailer may lose customers to competitors who do accept American Express cards.

Sales Discounts

As we mentioned in our discussion of purchase transactions, a seller may offer the buyer credit terms that include a discount for early payment. The seller refers to such discounts as **sales discounts**, which reduce sales revenue.

To reduce sales, the sales account could be debited. However, managers may want to know the amount of the sales discounts for a period in deciding whether to change credit terms. For this reason, the seller records the sales discounts in a separate account. The sales discounts account is a *contra* (or *offsetting*) account to Sales. To illustrate, assume that cash is received within the discount period (10 days) from the credit sale of $1,500, shown on the invoice in Exhibit 1. Wallace Electronics Supply would record the receipt of the cash as follows:

Jan.	22	Cash	1 4 7 0 00		
		Sales Discounts	3 0 00		
		Accounts Receivable—Computer King		1 5 0 0 00	
		Collection on Invoice No. 106-8, less			
		2% discount.			

Sales Returns and Allowances

Merchandise sold may be returned to the seller (**sales return**). In addition, because of defects or for other reasons, the seller may reduce the initial price at which the goods were sold (**sales allowance**). If the return or allowance is for a sale on account, the seller usually issues the buyer a **credit memorandum**. This memorandum shows the amount of and the reason for the seller's credit to an account receivable. A credit memorandum is illustrated in Exhibit 4.

EXHIBIT 4
Credit Memorandum

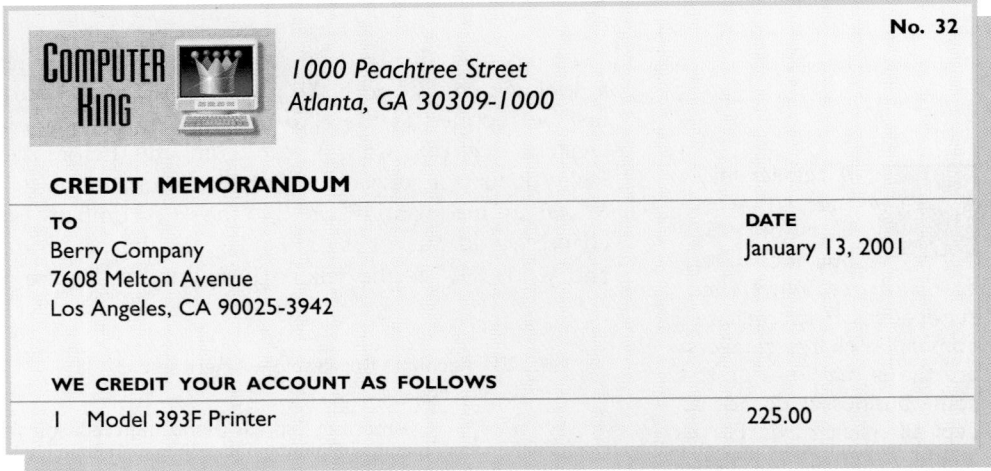

Like sales discounts, sales returns and allowances reduce sales revenue. They also result in additional shipping and other expenses. Since managers often want to know the amount of returns and allowances for a period, the seller records sales returns and allowances in a separate account. Sales Returns and Allowances is a *contra* (or *offsetting*) account to Sales.

The seller debits Sales Returns and Allowances for the amount of the return or allowance. If the original sale was on account, the seller credits Accounts Receivable. Since the merchandise inventory is kept up to date in a perpetual system, the seller adds the cost of the returned merchandise to the merchandise inventory account. The seller must also credit the cost of returned merchandise to the cost of

Book publishers often experience large returns if a book is not immediately successful. For example, 35% of adult hardcover books shipped to retailers are returned to publishers, according to the Association of American Publishers.

merchandise sold account, since this account was debited when the original sale was recorded. To illustrate, assume that the cost of the merchandise returned in Exhibit 4 was $140. Computer King records the credit memo in Exhibit 4 as follows:

Jan.	13	Sales Returns and Allowances				2	2	5	00					
		Accounts Receivable—Berry Company									2	2	5	00
		Credit Memo No. 32.												
	13	Merchandise Inventory				1	4	0	00					
		Cost of Merchandise Sold									1	4	0	00
		Cost of merchandise returned, Credit												
		Memo No. 32.												

What if the buyer pays for the merchandise and the merchandise is later returned? In this case, the seller may issue a credit and apply it against other accounts receivable owed by the buyer, or the cash may be refunded. If the credit is applied against the buyer's other receivables, the seller records entries similar to those preceding. If cash is refunded for merchandise returned or for an allowance, the seller debits Sales Returns and Allowances and credits Cash.

Sales Taxes

Almost all states and many other taxing units levy a tax on sales of merchandise.[3] The liability for the sales tax is incurred when the sale is made.

At the time of a cash sale, the seller collects the sales tax. When a sale is made on account, the seller charges the tax to the buyer by debiting Accounts Receivable. The seller credits the sales account for the amount of the sale and credits the tax to Sales Tax Payable.

 The five states with the highest sales tax are Illinois, Minnesota, Nevada, Texas, and Washington. Some states have no sales tax, including Alaska, Delaware, Montana, New Hampshire, and Oregon.

For example, the seller would record a sale of $100 on account, subject to a tax of 6%, as follows:

Aug.	12	Accounts Receivable				1	0	6	00					
		Sales									1	0	0	00
		Sales Tax Payable											6	00
		Invoice No. 339.												

Business collects sales tax from customers

Business remits sales tax to state

Normally on a regular basis, the seller pays to the taxing unit the amount of the sales tax collected. The seller records such a payment as follows:

Sept.	15	Sales Tax Payable				2	9	0	0	00				
		Cash									2	9	0	0	00
		Payment for sales taxes collected												
		during August.												

---

[3] Businesses that purchase merchandise for resale to others are normally exempt from paying sales taxes on their purchases. Only final buyers of merchandise normally pay sales taxes.

Trade Discounts

Wholesalers are businesses that sell merchandise to other businesses rather than to the general public. Many wholesalers publish catalogs. Rather than updating their catalogs frequently, wholesalers often publish price updates, which may involve large discounts from the list prices in their catalogs. In addition, wholesalers may offer special discounts to certain classes of buyers, such as government agencies or businesses that order large quantities. Such discounts are called **trade discounts**.

Sellers and buyers do not normally record the list prices of merchandise and the related trade discounts in their accounts. For example, assume that an item has a list price of $1,000 and a 40% trade discount. The seller records the sale of the item at $600 [$1,000 less the trade discount of $400 ($1,000 × 40%)]. Likewise, the buyer records the purchase at $600.

Transportation Costs

OBJECTIVE 2c

Journalize the entries for merchandise transportation costs.

The terms of a sale should indicate when the ownership (title) of the merchandise passes to the buyer. This point determines which party, the buyer or the seller, must pay the transportation costs.[4]

The ownership of the merchandise may pass to the buyer when the seller delivers the merchandise to the transportation company or freight carrier. For example, **Chrysler Corp.** records the sale and the transfer of ownership of its vehicles to dealers when the vehicles are shipped. In this case, the terms are said to be **FOB (free on board) shipping point**. This term means that Chrysler is responsible for the transportation charges to the shipping point, which is where the shipment originates. The dealer then pays the transportation costs to the final destination. Such costs are part of the dealer's total cost of purchasing inventory and should be added to the cost of the inventory by debiting Merchandise Inventory.

The buyer bears the transportation costs if the shipping terms are FOB shipping point.

To illustrate, assume that on June 10, Computer King buys merchandise from Reese Company on account, $900, terms FOB shipping point, and pays the transportation cost of $50. Computer King records these two transactions as follows:

June	10	Merchandise Inventory	9 0 0 00		
		Accounts Payable—Reese Company		9 0 0 00	
		Purchased merchandise, terms FOB			
		shipping point.			
	10	Merchandise Inventory	5 0 00		
		Cash		5 0 00	
		Paid shipping cost on merchandise			
		purchased.			

The ownership of the merchandise may pass to the buyer when the buyer receives the merchandise. In this case, the terms are said to be **FOB (free on board)**

---

[4] The passage of title also determines whether the buyer or seller must pay other costs, such as the cost of insurance, while the merchandise is in transit.

destination. This term means that the seller delivers the merchandise to the buyer's final destination, free of transportation charges to the buyer. The seller thus pays the transportation costs to the final destination. The seller debits Transportation Out or Delivery Expense, which is reported on the seller's income statement as an expense.

To illustrate, assume that on June 15, Computer King sells merchandise to Kranz Company on account, $700, terms FOB destination. The cost of the merchandise sold is $480, and Computer King pays the transportation cost of $40. Computer King records the sale, the cost of the sale, and the transportation cost as follows:

> The seller bears the transportation costs if the shipping terms are FOB destination.

 Sometimes FOB shipping point and FOB destination are expressed in terms of the location at which the title to the merchandise passes to the buyer. For example, if **Toyota Motor Co.'s** assembly plant in Osaka, Japan, sells automobiles to a dealer in Chicago, FOB shipping point could be expressed as FOB Osaka. Likewise, FOB destination could be expressed as FOB Chicago.

June	15	Accounts Receivable—Kranz Company	7 0 0 00	
		Sales		7 0 0 00
		Sold merchandise, terms FOB		
		destination.		
	15	Cost of Goods Sold	4 8 0 00	
		Merchandise Inventory		4 8 0 00
		Recorded cost of merchandise sold to		
		Kranz Company.		
	15	Transportation Out	4 0 00	
		Cash		4 0 00
		Paid shipping cost on merchandise sold.		

Shipping terms, the passage of title, and whether the buyer or seller is to pay the transportation costs are summarized in Exhibit 5.

EXHIBIT 5 Transportation Terms

As a convenience to the buyer, the seller may prepay the transportation costs, even though the terms are FOB shipping point. The seller will then add the transportation costs to the invoice. The buyer will debit Merchandise Inventory for the total amount of the invoice, including the transportation costs.

To illustrate, assume that on June 20, Computer King sells merchandise to Planter Company on account, $800, terms FOB shipping point. Computer King pays the transportation cost of $45 and adds it to the invoice. The cost of the merchandise sold is $360. Computer King records these transactions as follows:

June	20	Accounts Receivable—Planter Company		8 0 0 00	
		Sales			8 0 0 00
		Sold merchandise, terms FOB shipping			
		point.			
	20	Cost of Merchandise Sold		3 6 0 00	
		Merchandise Inventory			3 6 0 00
		Recorded cost of merchandise sold to			
		Planter Company.			
	20	Accounts Receivable—Planter Company		4 5 00	
		Cash			4 5 00
		Prepaid shipping cost on merchandise			
		sold.			

Illustration of Accounting for Merchandise Transactions

OBJECTIVE 2d

Journalize the entries for merchandise transactions for both the buyer and the seller.

Each merchandising transaction affects a buyer and a seller. In the following illustration, we show how the same transactions would be recorded by both the seller and the buyer. In this example, the seller is Scully Company and the buyer is Burton Co.

Transaction	Scully Company (Seller)			Burton Co. (Buyer)		

July 1. Scully Company sold merchandise on account to Burton Co., $7,500, terms FOB shipping point, n/45. The cost of the merchandise sold was $4,500.	Accounts Receivable—Burton Co.
	    Sales
	Cost of Merchandise Sold
	    Merchandise Inventory
		7,500
		
		4,500
			7,500
			
			4,500
				Merchandise Inventory
				    Accounts Payable—Scully Co.
					7,500	7,500

July 2. Burton Co. paid transportation charges of $150 on July 1 purchase from Scully Company.	No entry.			Merchandise Inventory Cash	150	150

Transaction	Scully Company (Seller)			Burton Co. (Buyer)		
July 5. Scully Company sold merchandise on account to Burton Co., $5,000, terms FOB destination, n/30. The cost of the merchandise sold was $3,500.	Accounts Receivable—Burton Co. Sales	5,000	5,000	Merchandise Inventory Accounts Payable—Scully Co.	5,000	5,000
	Cost of Merchandise Sold Merchandise Inventory	3,500	3,500			
July 7. Scully Company paid transportation costs of $250 for delivery of merchandise sold to Burton Co. on July 5.	Transportation Out Cash	250	250	No entry.		
July 13. Scully Company issued Burton Co. a credit memorandum for merchandise returned, $1,000. The merchandise had been purchased by Burton Co. on account on July 5. The cost of the merchandise returned was $700.	Sales Returns & Allowances Accounts Receivable—Burton Co.	1,000	1,000	Accounts Payable—Scully Co. Merchandise Inventory	1,000	1,000
	Merchandise Inventory Cost of Merchandise Sold	700	700			
July 15. Scully Company received payment from Burton Co. for purchase of July 5.	Cash Accounts Receivable—Burton Co.	4,000	4,000	Accounts Payable—Scully Co. Cash	4,000	4,000
July 18. Scully Company sold merchandise on account to Burton Co., $12,000, terms FOB shipping point, 2/10, n/eom. Scully Company prepaid transportation costs of $500, which were added to the invoice. The cost of the merchandise sold was $7,200.	Accounts Receivable—Burton Co. Sales	12,000	12,000	Merchandise Inventory Accounts Payable—Scully Co.	12,500	12,500
	Accounts Receivable—Burton Co. Cash	500	500			
	Cost of Merchandise Sold Merchandise Inventory	7,200	7,200			
July 28. Scully Company received payment from Burton Co. for purchase of July 18, less discount (2% × $12,000).	Cash Sales Discounts Accounts Receivable—Burton Co.	12,260 240	12,500	Accounts Payable—Scully Co. Merchandise Inventory Cash	12,500	240 12,260

Chart of Accounts for a Merchandising Business

OBJECTIVE 3

Prepare a chart of accounts for a merchandising business.

The chart of accounts for a merchandising business should reflect the types of merchandising transactions we have described in this chapter. As a basis for illustration, we use Computer King.

On January 1, 2001, when Computer King opened a merchandising outlet selling microcomputers and software, it stopped providing con-

sulting services. As a result, Computer King's chart of accounts changed from that of a service business to that of a merchandiser. A new chart of accounts for Computer King is shown in Exhibit 6. The accounts related to merchandising transactions are shown in color.

EXHIBIT 6

Chart of Accounts for Computer King, Merchandising Business

Balance Sheet Accounts		Income Statement Accounts	
	100 Assets		400 Revenues
110	Cash	410	Sales
111	Notes Receivable	411	Sales Returns and Allowances
112	Accounts Receivable	412	Sales Discounts
113	Interest Receivable		500 Costs and Expenses
115	Merchandise Inventory	510	Cost of Merchandise Sold
116	Office Supplies	520	Sales Salaries Expense
117	Prepaid Insurance	521	Advertising Expense
120	Land	522	Depreciation Expense—Store Equipment
123	Store Equipment	523	Transportation Out
124	Accumulated Depreciation— Store Equipment	529	Miscellaneous Selling Expense
125	Office Equipment	530	Office Salaries Expense
126	Accumulated Depreciation— Office Equipment	531	Rent Expense
		532	Depreciation Expense—Office Equipment
	200 Liabilities	533	Insurance Expense
210	Accounts Payable	534	Office Supplies Expense
211	Salaries Payable	539	Misc. Administrative Expense
212	Unearned Rent		600 Other Income
215	Notes Payable	610	Rent Revenue
	300 Owner's Equity	611	Interest Revenue
310	Pat King, Capital		700 Other Expense
311	Pat King, Drawing	710	Interest Expense
312	Income Summary		

Computer King is now using three-digit account numbers, which permits it to add new accounts as they are needed. The first digit indicates the major financial statement classification (1 for assets, 2 for liabilities, and so on). The second digit indicates the subclassification (e.g., 11 for current assets, 12 for noncurrent assets). The third digit identifies the specific account (e.g., 110 for Cash, 123 for Store Equipment).

Computer King is using a more complex numbering system because it has a greater variety of transactions. In addition, its growth creates a need for more detailed information for use in managing it. For example, a wages expense account was adequate for Computer King when it was a small service business with few employees. However, as a merchandising business, Computer King now uses two payroll accounts, one for Sales Salaries Expense and one for Office Salaries Expense.

I ncome Statement for a Merchandising Business

OBJECTIVE 4

Prepare an income statement for a merchandising business.

Although merchandising transactions affect the balance sheet in reporting inventory, they primarily affect the income statement. There are two widely used formats for preparing an income statement for a merchandising business: multiple step and single step.

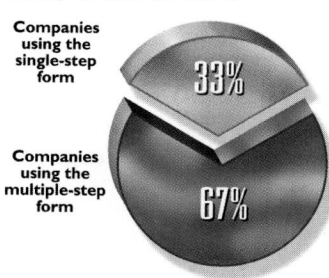
Multiple-Step Form

The **multiple-step income statement** contains several sections, subsections, and subtotals. We use Computer King's income statement, shown in Exhibit 7, as a basis for illustrating this form of statement.

EXHIBIT 7   Multiple-Step Income Statement

Computer King
Income Statement
For the Year Ended December 31, 2001

Revenue from sales:			
Sales		$720 185 00	
Less: Sales returns and allowances	$ 6 140 00		
Sales discounts	5 790 00	11 930 00	
Net sales			$708 255 00
Cost of merchandise sold			525 305 00
Gross profit			$182 950 00
Operating expenses:			
Selling expenses:			
Sales salaries expense	$60 030 00		
Advertising expense	10 860 00		
Depr. expense—store equipment	3 100 00		
Miscellaneous selling expense	630 00		
Total selling expense		$ 74 620 00	
Administrative expenses:			
Office salaries expense	$21 020 00		
Rent expense	8 100 00		
Depr. expense—office equipment	2 490 00		
Insurance expense	1 910 00		
Office supplies expense	610 00		
Misc. administrative expense	760 00		
Total administrative expenses		34 890 00	
Total operating expenses			⁓109 510 00
Income from operations			$ 73 440 00
Other income:			
Interest revenue	$ 3 800 00		
Rent revenue	600 00		
Total other income		$ 4 400 00	
Other expense:			
Interest expense		⁓2 440 00	1 960 00
Net income			$ 75 400 00

The amount of detail presented in the various sections varies from company to company. For example, instead of reporting gross sales, sales returns and allowances, and sales discounts, some companies just report net sales.

Retail operations can be classified as either (1) in-store retailing or (2) nonstore retailing. There are eleven general types of in-store retailing and three general types of nonstore retailing. Each type is briefly described below.

In-Store Retailing	Description	Examples
Department	Offers a variety of merchandise in many departments under one roof; each department is a separate buying and selling center	Sears, Rich's, J.C. Penney, Bloomingdale's
Specialty store	Offers a specific type of merchandise and carries a complete assortment	Toys R Us, Radio Shack, Zales Jewelers, Circuit City
Variety store	Offers a variety of inexpensive goods	Dollar General, Ben Franklin
Convenience store	Offers convenience goods, with long store hours	Circle K, 7 Eleven
Supermarket	Offers a wide variety of food, with self-service	Safeway, Kroger, Publix
Discount store	Offers low prices and high turnover of merchandise	Target, Kmart, Wal-Mart
Off-price retailer	Offers merchandise at prices 25% or more below normal prices with low service	T.J. Maxx, Ross
Factory outlet store	Offers close-outs and factory seconds; usually owned by the manufacturer	Levi Strauss, Bass, Polo, Lenox
Wholesale club	Offers food and general merchandise at deeply discounted prices to members	Sam's, Costco
Catalog store	Offers merchandise in showrooms where customers order from catalogs	Service Merchandise, Best, Lurias
Hypermart	Offers food and general merchandise at very low prices; sometimes called a "mall without a wall"	Hypermart USA, American Fare
Nonstore Retailing		
Vending machine	Offers merchandise for sale from machines	Canteen
Direct selling	Salesperson sells merchandise in customer's home	Avon, Amway
Direct response marketing	Offers merchandise for sale through catalogs, direct mail, and advertising	Lands' End, J. Crew, L.L. Bean

Revenue from Sales

The total amount charged customers for merchandise sold, for cash and on account, is reported in this section. Sales returns and allowances and sales discounts are deducted from this total to yield *net sales*.

Cost of Merchandise Sold

The cost of merchandise sold during the period may also be called the **cost of goods sold** or the **cost of sales**.

Gross Profit

The excess of net sales over the cost of merchandise sold is called the **gross profit**. It is sometimes called **gross profit on sales** or **gross margin**.

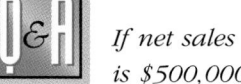

If net sales is $500,000 and gross profit is $180,000, what is the cost of merchandise sold?

$320,000

Operating Expenses

Most merchandising businesses classify operating expenses as either selling expenses or administrative expenses. Expenses that are incurred directly in the selling of merchandise are **selling expenses**. They include such expenses as salespersons' salaries, store supplies used, depreciation of store equipment, and advertising. Expenses incurred in the administration or general operations of the business are **administrative expenses** or **general expenses**. Examples of these expenses are office salaries, depreciation of office equipment, and office supplies used. Credit card expense is also normally classified as an administrative expense.

Expenses that are related to both selling and administration may be divided between the two classifications. In small businesses, however, such expenses as rent, insurance, and taxes are commonly reported as administrative expenses. Transactions for small, infrequent expenses are often reported as Miscellaneous Selling Expense or Miscellaneous Administrative Expense.

Income from Operations

The excess of gross profit over total operating expenses is called **income from operations** or **operating income**. The relationships of income from operations to total assets and to net sales are important factors in judging the efficiency and profitability of operations. If operating expenses are greater than the gross profit, the excess is called a **loss from operations**.

Other Income and Other Expense

Revenue from sources other than the primary operating activity of a business is classified as other income. In a merchandising business, these items include income from interest, rent, and gains resulting from the sale of fixed assets.

Expenses that cannot be traced directly to operations are identified as other expense. Interest expense that results from financing activities and losses incurred in the disposal of fixed assets are examples of these items.

Other income and other expense are offset against each other on the income statement. If the total of other income exceeds the total of other expense, the difference is added to income from operations. If the reverse is true, the difference is subtracted from income from operations.

Net Income

The final figure on the income statement is called **net income** (or **net loss**). It is the net increase (or net decrease) in the owner's equity as a result of the period's profit-making activities.

Single-Step Form

In the single-step income statement, the total of all expenses is deducted *in one step* from the total of all revenues. Such a statement is shown in Exhibit 8 for Computer King. The statement has been condensed to focus on its primary features.

EXHIBIT 8
Single-Step Income Statement

Computer King
Income Statement
For the Year Ended December 31, 2001

Revenues:		
Net sales		$708 2 5 5 00
Interest revenue		3 8 0 0 00
Rent revenue		6 0 0 00
Total revenues		$712 6 5 5 00
Expenses:		
Cost of merchandise sold	$525 3 0 5 00	
Selling expenses	74 6 2 0 00	
Administrative expenses	34 8 9 0 00	
Interest expense	2 4 4 0 00	
Total expenses		637 2 5 5 00
Net income		$ 75 4 0 0 00

The single-step form emphasizes total revenues and total expenses as the factors that determine net income. A criticism of the single-step form is that such amounts as gross profit and income from operations are not readily available for analysis.

OBJECTIVE 5

Describe the accounting cycle for a merchandising business.

The Accounting Cycle for a Merchandising Business

Earlier in this chapter, we described and illustrated the chart of accounts and the analysis and recording of transactions for a merchandising business. We also illustrated the preparation of an income statement for a merchandiser, Computer King,

at the end of an accounting cycle. In the remainder of this chapter, we describe the other elements of the accounting cycle for a merchandising business. In this discussion, we will focus primarily on the elements of this cycle that are likely to differ from those of a service business.

Merchandise Inventory Shrinkage

Under the perpetual inventory system, a separate merchandise inventory account is maintained in the ledger. During the accounting period, this account shows the amount of merchandise for sale at any time. However, merchandising businesses may experience some loss of inventory due to shoplifting, employee theft, or errors in recording or counting inventory. As a result, the physical inventory taken at the end of the accounting period may differ from the amount of inventory shown in the inventory records. Normally, the amount of merchandise for sale, as indicated by the balance of the merchandise inventory account, is larger than the total amount of merchandise counted during the physical inventory. For this reason, the difference is often called **inventory shrinkage** or **inventory shortage**.

To illustrate, Computer King's inventory records indicate that $63,950 of merchandise should be available for sale on December 31, 2001. The physical inventory taken on December 31, 2001, however, indicates that only $62,150 of merchandise is actually available. Thus, the inventory shrinkage for the year ending December 31, 2001, is $1,800 ($63,950 − $62,150), as shown at the left. This amount is recorded by the following adjusting entry:

 *If the inventory account has a balance of $280,000 and the physical inventory indicates merchandise on hand of $265,000, what is the amount of inventory shrinkage?*

$15,000 ($280,000 − $265,000)

		Adjusting Entry							
Dec.	31	Cost of Merchandise Sold		1	8	0	0	00	
		Merchandise Inventory							1 8 0 0 00

After this entry has been recorded, the accounting records agree with the actual physical inventory at the end of the period. Since no system of procedures and safeguards can totally eliminate it, inventory shrinkage is often considered a normal cost of operations. If the amount of the shrinkage is abnormally large, it may be disclosed separately on the income statement. In such cases, the shrinkage may be recorded in a separate account, such as Loss From Merchandise Inventory Shrinkage.

Work Sheet

Merchandising businesses that use a perpetual inventory system are also likely to use a computerized accounting system. In a computerized system, the adjusting entries are recorded and financial statements prepared without using a work sheet. For this reason, we illustrate the work sheet and the adjusting entries for Computer King in the appendix at the end of this chapter.

Statement of Owner's Equity

The statement of owner's equity for Computer King is shown in Exhibit 9. This statement is prepared in the same manner that we described previously for a service business.

EXHIBIT 9
Statement of Owner's Equity
for Merchandising Business

EXHIBIT 9
Statement of Owner's Equity
for Merchandising Business

Computer King Statement of Owner's Equity For the Year Ended December 31, 2001			
Pat King, capital, January 1, 2001			$153 8 0 0 00
Net income for year	$75 4 0 0 00		
Less withdrawals	18 0 0 0 00		
Increase in owner's equity			57 4 0 0 00
Pat King, capital, December 31, 2001			$211 2 0 0 00

Balance Sheet

As we discussed and illustrated in previous chapters, the balance sheet may be presented with assets on the left-hand side and the liabilities and owner's equity on the right-hand side. This form of the balance sheet is called the **account form**. The balance sheet may also be presented in a downward sequence in three sections. This form of balance sheet is called the **report form**. The report form of balance sheet for Computer King is shown in Exhibit 10. In this balance sheet, note that

EXHIBIT 10
Report Form of Balance
Sheet

Computer King Balance Sheet December 31, 2001			
Assets			
Current assets:			
Cash		$52 9 5 0 00	
Notes receivable		40 0 0 0 00	
Accounts receivable		60 8 8 0 00	
Interest receivable		2 0 0 00	
Merchandise inventory		62 1 5 0 00	
Office supplies		4 8 0 00	
Prepaid insurance		2 6 5 0 00	
Total current assets			$219 3 1 0 00
Property, plant, and equipment:			
Land		$10 0 0 0 00	
Store equipment	$27 1 0 0 00		
Less accumulated depreciation	5 7 0 0 00	21 4 0 0 00	
Office equipment	$15 5 7 0 00		
Less accumulated depreciation	4 7 2 0 00	10 8 5 0 00	
Total property, plant, and equipment			42 2 5 0 00
Total assets			$261 5 6 0 00
Liabilities			
Current liabilities:			
Accounts payable		$22 4 2 0 00	
Note payable (current portion)		5 0 0 0 00	
Salaries payable		1 1 4 0 00	
Unearned rent		1 8 0 0 00	
Total current liabilities			$ 30 3 6 0 00
Long-term liabilities:			
Note payable (final payment due 2004)			20 0 0 0 00
Total liabilities			$ 50 3 6 0 00
Owner's Equity			
Pat King, capital			211 2 0 0 00
Total liabilities and owner's equity			$261 5 6 0 00

merchandise inventory at the end of the period is reported as a current asset and that the current portion of the note payable is $5,000.

Closing Entries

The closing entries for a merchandising business are similar to those for a service business. The first entry closes the temporary accounts with credit balances, such as Sales, to the income summary account. The second entry closes the temporary accounts with debit balances, including Sales Returns and Allowances, Sales Discounts, and Cost of Merchandise Sold, to the income summary account. The third entry closes the balance of the income summary account to the owner's capital account. The fourth entry closes the owner's drawing account to the owner's capital account.

In a computerized accounting system, the closing entries are prepared automatically. For this reason, we illustrate the closing entries for Computer King in the appendix at the end of this chapter.

FINANCIAL ANALYSIS AND INTERPRETATION

OBJECTIVE 6

Compute the ratio of net sales to assets as a measure of how effectively a business is using its assets.

The ratio of net sales to assets measures how effectively a business is using its assets to generate sales. A high ratio indicates an effective use of assets. The assets used in computing the ratio may be the total assets at the end of the year, the average of the total assets at the beginning and end of the year, or the average of the monthly assets. For our purposes, we will use the average of the total assets at the beginning and end of the year. The ratio is computed as follows:

$$\text{Ratio of net sales to assets} = \frac{\text{Net sales}}{\text{Average total assets}}$$

To illustrate the use of this ratio, the following data are taken from the 1996 annual reports of **Sears** and **J.C. Penney**:

	Sears	J.C. Penney
Net sales (in millions)	$38,236	$23,649
Total assets (in millions):		
Beginning of year	33,130	17,102
End of year	36,137	22,088

The ratio of net sales to assets for each company is as follows:

	Sears	J.C. Penney
Ratio of net sales to assets:	1.10*	1.21**

*$38,236/[($33,130 + $36,137)/2]
**$23,649/[($17,102 + $22,088)/2]

Based on these ratios, J.C. Penney appears better than Sears in utilizing its assets to generate sales. Comparing this ratio over time for both Sears and J.C. Penney, as well as comparing it with industry averages, would provide a better basis for interpreting the financial performance of each company.

ENCORE

Sam Walton

As a young man just out of the Army, Sam Walton wanted to go into retailing and operate his own business. With $5,000 of his own money and a loan of $20,000 from his father-in-law, he opened his first store in Newport, Arkansas, on September 1, 1945. This first store was a Ben Franklin variety store. Within five years, this store was the No. 1 Ben Franklin store—for sales and profit—not only in Arkansas, but in a six-state region. Unfortunately, Sam forgot to include a renewal clause in the lease for his store building. His landlord decided not to renew Sam's lease, but instead offered to buy the business, including fixtures and inventory. The landlord wanted to purchase the profitable store for his son to own and operate. Without any other suitable location in town, Sam had to sell.

Unwilling to quit, Sam purchased a new store in Bentonville, Arkansas, and opened Walton's Five and Dime on August 1, 1951. By 1960, Sam had opened fifteen variety stores, with revenues of $1.4 million. Sam realized the potential of discounting when a regional discounter moved into Arkansas. So Sam opened his first Wal-Mart on July 2, 1962, choosing the name Wal-Mart because it didn't have many letters, which would make it cheaper to build and maintain the store signs. To avoid competing with Kmart, Sam initially expanded into small towns of less than 10,000 people.

The rest of the story is history. Wal-Mart grew from 32 stores and $31 million in sales in 1970 to 276 stores and $1.2 billion in sales in 1980. Today it has over 2,000 stores and $70 billion in sales. During that time, Wal-Mart issued stock, opened Sam's Clubs, and Sam Walton became one of the richest men in America. ■

APPENDIX 1: ACCOUNTING SYSTEMS FOR MERCHANDISERS

Merchandising companies may use either manual or computerized accounting systems, similar to those used by service businesses. In this appendix, we describe and illustrate special journals and electronic forms that merchandise businesses may use in these systems.

Manual Accounting System

In a manual accounting system, a merchandise business normally uses four special journals: sales journal (for sales on account), purchases journal (for purchases on account), cash receipts journal, and cash payments journal. These journals can be adapted from the special journals that we illustrated earlier for a service business.

Exhibit 11 illustrates Computer King's sales journal, which is modified from a revenue journal. In a sales journal, each transaction is recorded by entering the sales amount in the *Accounts Receivable Dr./Sales Cr.* column and entering the cost of the merchandise sold amount in the *Cost of Merchandise Sold Dr./Merchandise Inventory Cr.* column. The totals of the two columns would be

posted to the four general ledger accounts. The inventory and accounts receivable subsidiary ledgers would be updated when each transaction is recorded.

EXHIBIT 11

Sales Journal for a Merchandising Business

				SALES JOURNAL			PAGE 35
	Date	Invoice No.	Account Debited	Post. Ref.	Accts. Rec. Dr. Sales Cr.	Cost of Merchandise Sold Dr. Merchandise Inventory Cr.	
1	2001 Mar. 2	810	Berry Co.	✔	2 7 5 0 00	2 0 0 0 00	1
2	14	811	Handler Co.	✔	4 2 6 0 00	3 4 7 0 00	2
3	19	812	Jordan Co.	✔	5 8 0 0 00	4 6 5 0 00	3
4	26	813	Kenner Co.	✔	4 5 0 0 00	3 8 4 0 00	4
5					17 3 1 0 00	13 9 6 0 00	5
6					(112) (410)	(510) (115)	6

Exhibit 12 illustrates a purchases journal for Computer King's merchandising business. This journal is similar to the purchases journal for Computer King's service business that we illustrated previously. It includes an *Accounts Payable Cr.* column and a *Merchandise Inventory Dr.* column, rather than a *Supplies Dr.* column. At the end of the month, these two column totals would be posted to the general ledger controlling accounts, Accounts Payable and Merchandise Inventory. The amounts in *Other Amounts Dr.* would be posted individually. The inventory and accounts payable subsidiary ledgers would be updated when each transaction is recorded.

EXHIBIT 12   Purchases Journal for a Merchandising Business

				PURCHASES JOURNAL					PAGE 11	
	Date	Account Credited	Post. Ref.	Accounts Payable Cr.	Merchandise Inventory Dr.	Other Accounts Dr.	Post. Ref.	Amount		
1	2001 Mar. 4	Compu-Tek	✔	13 8 8 0 00	13 8 8 0 00					1
2	7	Wallace Electronics Supply	✔	4 6 5 0 00	4 6 5 0 00					2
3	15	Dale Furniture Co.	✔	5 7 0 0 00		Store Equipment	123	5 7 0 0 00		3
4	22	Boss Computers	✔	3 8 4 0 00	3 8 4 0 00					4
5	29	Power Electronics	✔	3 2 0 0 00	3 2 0 0 00					5
6				31 2 7 0 00	25 5 7 0 00			5 7 0 0 00		6
7				(210)	(115)			(✔)		7

Exhibit 13 illustrates a portion of Computer King's cash receipts journal. In this journal, cash sales are recorded in a *Sales Cr.* column rather than a *Fees Earned Cr.* column. In addition, the cost of merchandise sold for cash is recorded in a *Cost of Merchandise Sold Dr./Merchandise Inventory Cr.* column. Each entry in this column is posted to the inventory subsidiary ledger at the time the transaction is recorded. Sales discounts are recorded in a *Sales Discounts Dr.* column. At the end of the month, all the column totals except for *Other Accounts Cr.* are posted to the general ledger.

EXHIBIT 13   Cash Receipts Journal for Merchandising Business

	Date	Account Credited	Post. Ref.	Other Accounts Cr.	Cost of Merchandise Sold Dr. Merchandise Inventory Cr.	Sales Cr.	Accounts Receivable Cr.	Sales Discounts Dr.	Cash Dr.	
	2001 Mar. 3	Sales	✔		4 0 0 00	6 0 0 00			6 0 0 00	1
2	12	Berry Co.	✔				2 7 5 0 00	5 5 00	2 6 9 5 00	2

CASH RECEIPTS JOURNAL — PAGE 14

Exhibit 14 illustrates a portion of the cash payments journal for Computer King. This journal is modified for a merchandising business by adding a *Merchandise Inventory Cr.* column for recording discounts on purchases paid within the discount period. Each entry in this column is posted to the inventory subsidiary ledger at the time the transaction is recorded. At the end of the month, all the column totals except for *Other Accounts Dr.* are posted to the general ledger.

EXHIBIT 14   Cash Payments Journal for Merchandising Business

CASH PAYMENTS JOURNAL — PAGE 7

	Date	Ck. No.	Account Debited	Post. Ref.	Other Accounts Dr.	Accounts Payable Dr.	Merchandise Inventory Cr.	Cash Cr.	
	2001 Mar. 14	210	Compu-Tek	✔		13 8 8 0 00		13 8 8 0 00	1
2	17	211	Wallace Electronics Supply	✔		4 6 5 0 00	9 3 00	4 5 5 7 00	2

Computerized Accounting Systems

In a computerized accounting system, special journals may be replaced by electronic forms that capture the necessary information. The software then uses this information as the basis for making entries automatically. In QuickBooks, for example, the inventory items to be purchased and sold must first be identified, using an "Edit Item" form. The software will later record each item's purchase or sale, using information from this form. The Edit Item form in Exhibit 15 shows this information

EXHIBIT 15
Edit Item Form

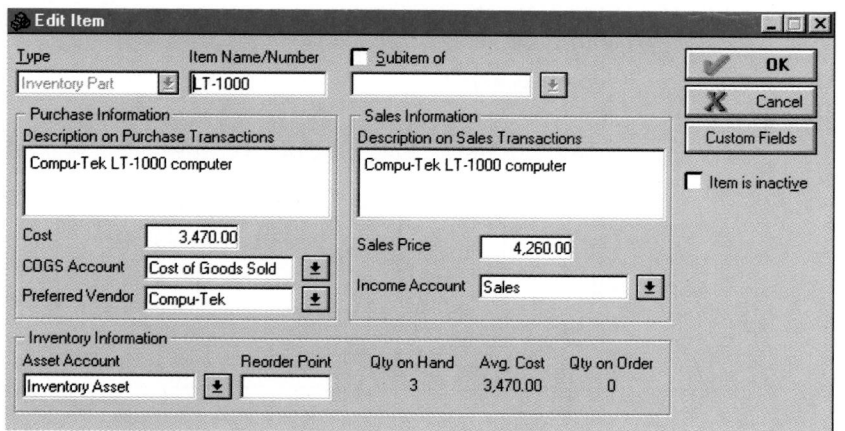

for Computer King's purchase of LT-1000 computers from Compu-Tek. Each computer cost $3,470 per unit and will be sold for $4,260 per unit.

After inventory items have been described inside QuickBooks, transaction data can be entered. We will begin with Computer King's March 4, 2001 purchase from Compu-Tek, which we illustrated previously in the purchases journal in Exhibit 12. We will use the "Enter Bills" form, shown in Exhibit 16, to record the purchase of four LT-1000's from Compu-Tek.

EXHIBIT 16
Enter Bills Form

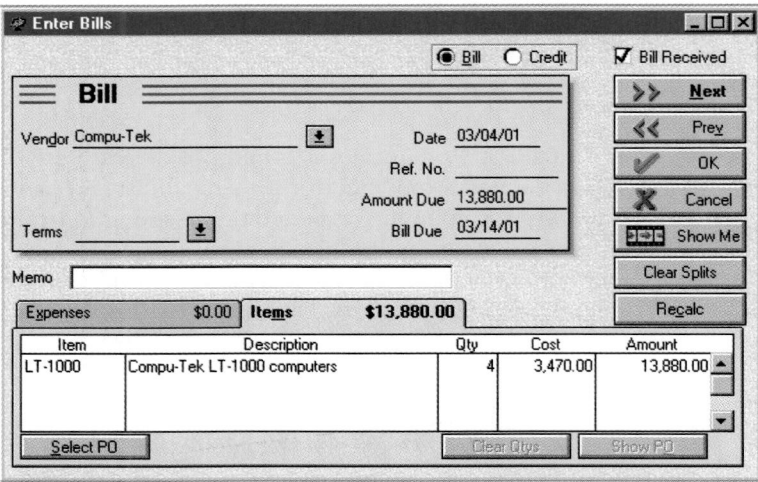

After the Enter Bills form has been completed, the software adds the cost of four LT-1000s to Computer King's inventory. At the same time, it establishes an account payable to Compu-Tek for $13,880.

Now, assume that on March 14 Computer King bills Handler Co. for one of these computers, as illustrated in the sales journal in Exhibit 11. Using the "Create Invoices" form in QuickBooks, as shown in Exhibit 17, we enter the sale and the software establishes an account receivable for Handler Co. In addition, the software reduces the inventory stock level of the LT-1000 by $3,470 and records the cost of goods sold. This latter transaction is recorded automatically and is not shown on the Create Invoices form.

EXHIBIT 17
Create Invoices Form

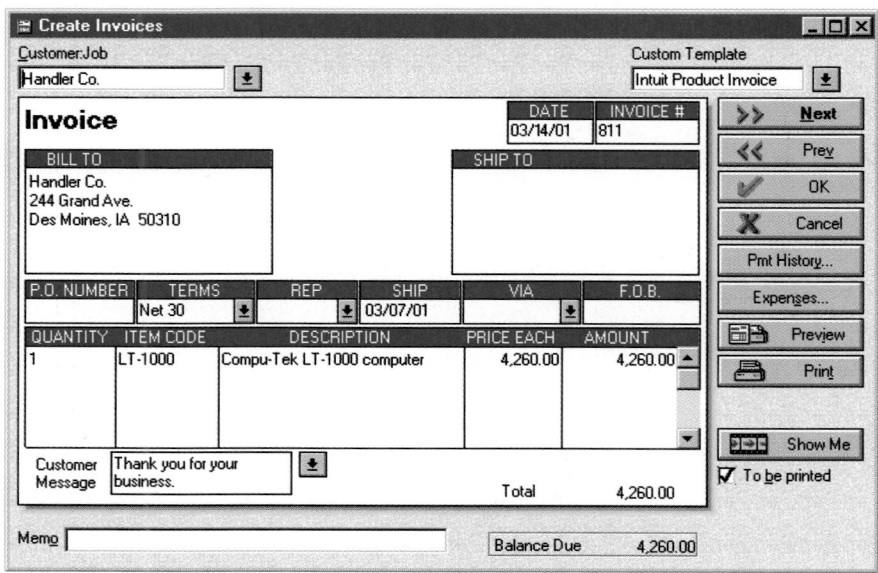

An income statement prepared after these forms have been completed would show sales of $4,260, cost of goods sold of $3,470, and gross profit of $790. A balance sheet would show accounts receivable of $4,260, inventory of $10,410 (3 × $3,470), and accounts payable of $13,880.

APPENDIX 2: WORK SHEET AND ADJUSTING AND CLOSING ENTRIES FOR A MERCHANDISING BUSINESS

A merchandising business that does not use a computerized accounting system may use a work sheet in assembling the data for preparing financial statements and adjusting and closing entries. In this appendix, we illustrate such a work sheet, along with the adjusting and closing entries for a merchandising business.

The work sheet in Exhibit 18 is for Computer King on December 31, 2001, the end of its first year of operations as a merchandiser. In this work sheet, we list all of the accounts, including the accounts that have no balances, in the order that they appear in Computer King's ledger.

The data needed for adjusting the accounts of Computer King are as follows:

Interest accrued on notes receivable on December 31, 2001		$ 200
Physical merchandise inventory on December 31, 2001		62,150
Office supplies on hand on December 31, 2001		480
Insurance expired during 2001		1,910
Depreciation during 2001 on: Store equipment		3,100
Office equipment		2,490
Salaries accrued on December 31, 2001: Sales salaries	$780	
Office salaries	360	1,140
Rent earned during 2001		600

There is no specific order in which to analyze the accounts in the work sheet, assemble the adjustment data, and make the adjusting entries. However, you can normally save time by selecting the accounts in the order in which they appear on the trial balance. Using this approach, the adjustment for accrued interest is listed first {entry (a) on the work sheet}, followed by the adjustment for merchandise inventory shrinkage {entry (b) on the work sheet}, and so on.

After all the adjustments have been entered on the work sheet, the Adjustments columns are totaled to prove the equality of debits and credits. As we illustrated in previous chapters, the adjusted amounts of the balances in the Trial Balance columns are extended to the Adjusted Trial Balance columns.[5] The Adjusted Trial Balance columns are then totaled to prove the equality of debits and credits.

The balances, as adjusted, are then extended to the statement columns. The four statement columns are totaled, and the net income or net loss is determined. For Computer King, the difference between the credit and debit columns of the Income Statement section is $75,400, the amount of the net income. The difference between the debit and credit columns of the Balance Sheet section is also $75,400, which is the increase in owner's equity as a result of the net income. Agreement between the two balancing amounts is evidence of debit-credit equality and mathematical accuracy.

The income statement, statement of owner's equity, and balance sheet are prepared from the work sheet in a manner similar to that of a service business. The

[5] Some accountants prefer to eliminate the Adjusted Trial Balance columns and to extend the adjusted balances directly to the statement columns. Such a work sheet is often used if there are only a few adjustment items.

EXHIBIT 18   Work Sheet for Merchandising Business

Computer King
Work Sheet
For the Year Ended December 31, 2001

	Account Title	Trial Balance Dr.	Trial Balance Cr.	Adjustments Dr.	Adjustments Cr.	Adjusted Trial Balance Dr.	Adjusted Trial Balance Cr.	Income Statement Dr.	Income Statement Cr.	Balance Sheet Dr.	Balance Sheet Cr.	
1	Cash	52,950				52,950				52,950		1
2	Notes Receivable	40,000				40,000				40,000		2
3	Accounts Receivable	60,880				60,880				60,880		3
4	Interest Receivable			(a) 200		200				200		4
5	Merchandise Inventory	63,950			(b)1,800	62,150				62,150		5
6	Office Supplies	1,090			(c) 610	480				480		6
7	Prepaid Insurance	4,560			(d)1,910	2,650				2,650		7
8	Land	10,000				10,000				10,000		8
9	Store Equipment	27,100				27,100				27,100		9
10	Accum. Depr.—Store Equip.		2,600		(e)3,100		5,700				5,700	10
11	Office Equipment	15,570				15,570				15,570		11
12	Accum. Depr.—Office Equip.		2,230		(f) 2,490		4,720				4,720	12
13	Accounts Payable		22,420				22,420				22,420	13
14	Salaries Payable				(g)1,140		1,140				1,140	14
15	Unearned Rent		2,400	(h) 600			1,800				1,800	15
16	Notes Payable											16
17	(final payment due 2008)		25,000				25,000				25,000	17
18	Pat King, Capital		153,800				153,800				153,800	18
19	Pat King, Drawing	18,000				18,000				18,000		19
20	Sales		720,185				720,185		720,185			20
21	Sales Returns and Allowances	6,140				6,140		6,140				21
22	Sales Discounts	5,790				5,790		5,790				22
23	Cost of Merchandise Sold	523,505		(b)1,800		525,305		525,305				23
24	Sales Salaries Expense	59,250		(g) 780		60,030		60,030				24
25	Advertising Expense	10,860				10,860		10,860				25
26	Depr. Exp.—Store Equip.			(e)3,100		3,100		3,100				26
27	Miscellaneous Selling Expense	630				630		630				27
28	Office Salaries Expense	20,660		(g) 360		21,020		21,020				28
29	Rent Expense	8,100				8,100		8,100				29
30	Depr. Exp.—Office Equip.			(f)2,490		2,490		2,490				30
31	Insurance Expense			(d)1,910		1,910		1,910				31
32	Office Supplies Expense			(c) 610		610		610				32
33	Misc. Administrative Expense	760				760		760				33
34	Rent Revenue				(h) 600		600		600			34
35	Interest Revenue		3,600		(a) 200		3,800		3,800			35
36	Interest Expense	2,440				2,440		2,440				36
37		932,235	932,235	11,850	11,850	939,165	939,165	649,185	724,585	289,980	214,580	37
38	Net income							75,400			75,400	38
39								724,585	724,585	289,980	289,980	39

(a) Interest earned but not received on notes receivable, $200.

(b) Merchandise inventory shrinkage for period, $1,800 ($63,950 − $62,150).

(c) Office supplies used, $610 ($1,090 − $480).

(d) Insurance expired, $1,910.

(e) Depreciation of store equipment, $3,100.

(f) Depreciation of office equipment, $2,490.

(g) Salaries accrued but not paid
(sales salaries, $780; office salaries, $360), $1,140.

(h) Rent earned from amount received in advance, $600.

Adjustments columns in the work sheet provide the data for journalizing the adjusting entries. Computer King's adjusting entries at the end of 2001 are as follows:

	Date		Description	Post. Ref.	Debit	Credit	
1	2001		Adjusting Entries				1
2	Dec.	31	Interest Receivable	113	2 0 0 00		2
3			Interest Revenue	611		2 0 0 00	3
4							4
5		31	Cost of Merchandise Sold	510	1 8 0 0 00		5
6			Merchandise Inventory	115		1 8 0 0 00	6
7							7
8		31	Office Supplies Expense	534	6 1 0 00		8
9			Office Supplies	116		6 1 0 00	9
10							10
11		31	Insurance Expense	533	1 9 1 0 00		11
12			Prepaid Insurance	117		1 9 1 0 00	12
13							13
14		31	Depreciation Expense—				14
15			Store Equipment	522	3 1 0 0 00		15
16			Accumulated Depreciation—				16
17			Store Equipment	124		3 1 0 0 00	17
18							18
19		31	Depreciation Expense—				19
20			Office Equipment	532	2 4 9 0 00		20
21			Accumulated Depreciation—				21
22			Office Equipment	126		2 4 9 0 00	22
23							23
24		31	Sales Salaries Expense	520	7 8 0 00		24
25			Office Salaries Expense	530	3 6 0 00		25
26			Salaries Payable	211		1 1 4 0 00	26
27							27
28		31	Unearned Rent	212	6 0 0 00		28
29			Rent Revenue	610		6 0 0 00	29

JOURNAL — **PAGE 28**

The Income Statement columns of the work sheet provide the data for preparing the closing entries. The closing entries for Computer King at the end of 2001 are as follows:

	Date		Description	Post. Ref.	Debit	Credit	
1	2001		Closing Entries				1
2	Dec.	31	Sales	410	720 1 8 5 00		2
3			Rent Revenue	610	6 0 0 00		3
4			Interest Revenue	611	3 8 0 0 00		4
5			Income Summary	312		724 5 8 5 00	5

JOURNAL — **PAGE 29**

	Date		Description	Post. Ref.	Debit	Credit	
			JOURNAL			**PAGE 29**	
7	Dec.	31	Income Summary	312	649 1 8 5 00		7
8			Sales Returns and Allowances	411		6 1 4 0 00	8
9			Sales Discounts	412		5 7 9 0 00	9
10			Cost of Merchandise Sold	510		525 3 0 5 00	10
11			Sales Salaries Expense	520		60 0 3 0 00	11
12			Advertising Expense	521		10 8 6 0 00	12
13			Depr. Expense—Store Equipment	522		3 1 0 0 00	13
14			Miscellaneous Selling Expense	529		6 3 0 00	14
15			Office Salaries Expense	530		21 0 2 0 00	15
16			Rent Expense	531		8 1 0 0 00	16
17			Depr. Expense—Office Equipment	532		2 4 9 0 00	17
18			Insurance Expense	533		1 9 1 0 00	18
19			Office Supplies Expense	534		6 1 0 00	19
20			Misc. Administrative Expense	539		7 6 0 00	20
21			Interest Expense	710		2 4 4 0 00	21
22							22
23		31	Income Summary	312	75 4 0 0 00		23
24			Pat King, Capital	310		75 4 0 0 00	24
25							25
26		31	Pat King, Capital	310	18 0 0 0 00		26
27			Pat King, Drawing	311		18 0 0 0 00	27

The balance of Income Summary, after the first two closing entries have been posted, is the net income or net loss for the period. The third closing entry transfers this balance to the owner's capital account. Computer King's income summary account after the closing entries have been posted is as follows:

	Date		Item	Post. Ref.	Debit	Credit	Balance Debit	Balance Credit
			ACCOUNT *Income Summary*				**ACCOUNT NO. 312**	
	2001 Dec.	31	Revenues	29		724 5 8 5 00		724 5 8 5 00
		31	Expenses	29	649 1 8 5 00			75 4 0 0 00
		31	Net income	29	75 4 0 0 00		—	—

After the closing entries have been prepared and posted to the accounts, a post-closing trial balance may be prepared to verify the debit-credit equality. The only accounts that should appear on the post-closing trial balance are the asset, contra asset, liability, and owner's capital accounts with balances. These are the same accounts that appear on the end-of-period balance sheet.

KEY POINTS

1 Distinguish the activities of a service business from those of a merchandising business.

The primary differences between a service business and a merchandising business relate to revenue activities. Merchandising businesses purchase merchandise for selling to customers.

On a merchandising business's income statement, revenue from selling merchandise is reported as sales. The cost of the merchandise sold is subtracted from sales to arrive at gross profit. The operating expenses are subtracted from gross profit to arrive at net income.

Merchandise inventory, which is merchandise not sold, is reported as a current asset on the balance sheet.

2a Journalize the entries for merchandise purchases.

Purchases of merchandise for cash or on account are recorded by debiting Merchandise Inventory. For purchases of merchandise on account, the credit terms may allow cash discounts for early payment. Such purchases discounts are viewed as a reduction in the cost of the merchandise purchased. When merchandise is returned or a price adjustment is granted, the buyer credits Merchandise Inventory.

2b Journalize the entries for merchandise sales.

Sales of merchandise for cash or on account are recorded by crediting Sales. The cost of merchandise sold and the reduction in merchandise inventory are also recorded for the sale.

For sales of merchandise on account, the credit terms may allow sales discounts for early payment. Such discounts

are recorded by the seller as a debit to Sales Discounts. Sales discounts are reported as a deduction from the amount initially recorded in Sales. Likewise, when merchandise is returned or a price adjustment is granted, the seller debits Sales Returns and Allowances.

The liability for sales tax is incurred when the sale is made and is recorded by the seller as a credit to the sales tax payable account. When the amount of the sales tax is paid to the taxing unit, Sales Tax Payable is debited and Cash is credited.

Many wholesalers offer trade discounts, which are discounts off the list prices of merchandise. Normally, neither the seller or the buyer records the list price and the related trade discount in the accounts.

2c Journalize the entries for merchandise transportation costs.

When merchandise is shipped FOB shipping point, the buyer pays the transportation costs and debits Merchandise Inventory. When merchandise is shipped FOB destination, the seller pays the transportation costs and debits Transportation Out or Delivery Expense. If the seller prepays transportation costs as a convenience to the buyer, the seller debits Accounts Receivable for the costs.

2d Journalize the entries for merchandise transactions for both the buyer and the seller.

The illustration in this chapter summarizes the entries that the seller and the buyer of merchandise would record.

3 Prepare a chart of accounts for a merchandising business.

The chart of accounts for a merchandising business is more

complex than that for a service business and normally includes accounts such as Sales, Sales Discounts, Sales Returns and Allowances, Cost of Merchandise Sold, and Merchandise Inventory.

4 Prepare an income statement for a merchandising business.

The income statement for a merchandising business reports sales, cost of merchandise sold, and gross profit. The income statement can be prepared in either the multiple-step form or the single-step form.

5 Describe the accounting cycle for a merchandising business.

The accounting cycle for a merchandising business is similar to that of a service business. However, a merchandiser is likely to experience inventory shrinkage, which must be recorded. The normal adjusting entry is to debit Cost of Merchandise Sold and credit Merchandise Inventory for the amount of the shrinkage.

The balance sheet may be prepared in either the account form or the report form. Merchandise inventory should be reported as a current asset.

6 Compute the ratio of net sales to assets as a measure of how effectively a business is using its assets.

The assets used in computing the ratio of net sales to assets may be total assets at the end of the year, the average of the total assets at the beginning and end of the year, or the average of the monthly assets. A high ratio of net sales to assets indicates an effective use of assets.

ILLUSTRATIVE PROBLEM

The following transactions were completed by Montrose Company during May of the current year. Montrose Company uses a perpetual inventory system.

May 3. Purchased merchandise on account from Floyd Co., $4,000, terms FOB shipping point, 2/10, n/30, with prepaid transportation costs of $120 added to the invoice.

    5. Purchased merchandise on account from Kramer Co., $8,500, terms FOB destination, 1/10, n/30.

    6. Sold merchandise on account to C. F. Howell Co., list price $4,000, trade discount 30%, terms 2/10, n/30. The cost of the merchandise sold was $1,125.

    8. Purchased office supplies for cash, $150.

    10. Returned merchandise purchased on May 5 from Kramer Co., $1,300.

    13. Paid Floyd Co. on account for purchase of May 3, less discount.

    14. Purchased merchandise for cash, $10,500.

    15. Paid Kramer Co. on account for purchase of May 5, less return of May 10 and discount.

    16. Received cash on account from sale of May 6 to C. F. Howell Co., less discount.

    19. Sold merchandise on nonbank credit cards and reported accounts to the card company, American Express, $2,450. The cost of the merchandise sold was $980.

    22. Sold merchandise on account to Comer Co., $3,480, terms 2/10, n/30. The cost of the merchandise sold was $1,400.

    24. Sold merchandise for cash, $4,350. The cost of the merchandise sold was $1,750.

    25. Received merchandise returned by Comer Co. from sale on May 22, $1,480. The cost of the returned merchandise was $600.

    31. Received cash from card company for nonbank credit card sales of May 19, less $140 service fee.

Instructions

1. Journalize the preceding transactions.
2. Journalize the adjusting entry for merchandise inventory shrinkage, $3,750.

Solution

1.

May	3	Merchandise Inventory	4,120	
		Accounts Payable—Floyd Co.		4,120
	5	Merchandise Inventory	8,500	
		Accounts Payable—Kramer Co.		8,500
	6	Accounts Receivable—C. F. Howell Co.	2,800	
		Sales		2,800
		[$4,000 − (30% × $4,000)]		
	6	Cost of Merchandise Sold	1,125	
		Merchandise Inventory		1,125
	8	Office Supplies	150	
		Cash		150
	10	Accounts Payable—Kramer Co.	1,300	
		Merchandise Inventory		1,300
	13	Accounts Payable—Floyd Co.	4,120	
		Merchandise Inventory		80
		Cash		4,040
		[$4,000 − (2% × $4,000) + $120]		

May 14	Merchandise Inventory	10,500	
	Cash		10,500
15	Accounts Payable—Kramer Co.	7,200	
	Merchandise Inventory		72
	Cash		7,128
	[($8,500 − $1,300) × 1% = $72;		
	$8,500 − $1,300 − $72 = $7,128]		
16	Cash	2,744	
	Sales Discounts	56	
	Accounts Receivable—C. F. Howell Co.		2,800
19	Accounts Receivable—American Express	2,450	
	Sales		2,450
19	Cost of Merchandise Sold	980	
	Merchandise Inventory		980
22	Accounts Receivable—Comer Co.	3,480	
	Sales		3,480
22	Cost of Merchandise Sold	1,400	
	Merchandise Inventory		1,400
24	Cash	4,350	
	Sales		4,350
24	Cost of Merchandise Sold	1,750	
	Merchandise Inventory		1,750
25	Sales Returns and Allowances	1,480	
	Accounts Receivable—Comer Co.		1,480
25	Merchandise Inventory	600	
	Cost of Merchandise Sold		600
31	Cash	2,310	
	Credit Card Expense	140	
	Accounts Receivable—American Express		2,450

2.

| May 31 | Cost of Merchandise Sold | 3,750 | |
| | Merchandise Inventory | | 3,750 |

SELF-EXAMINATION QUESTIONS

Answers at End of Chapter

Matching

Match each of the following statements with its proper term. Some terms may not be used.

A. account form	___ 1. The cost that is reported as an expense when merchandise is sold.
B. administrative expenses (general expenses)	___ 2. Sales minus the cost of merchandise sold.
	___ 3. Merchandise on hand (not sold) at the end of an accounting period.
C. cost of merchandise sold	___ 4. The inventory system in which each purchase and sale of merchandise is recorded in an inventory account.
D. credit memorandum	___ 5. The inventory system in which the inventory records do not show the amount available for sale or sold during the period.
E. debit memorandum	
	___ 6. A detailed listing of the merchandise for sale at the end of an accounting period.

(continues)

F. FOB (free on board) destination

G. FOB (free on board) shipping point

H. gross profit

I. income from operations (operating income)

J. inventory shrinkage

K. invoice

L. loss from operations

M. merchandise inventory

N. multiple-step income statement

O. other expense

P. other income

Q. periodic inventory system

R. perpetual inventory system

S. physical inventory

T. purchase return or allowance

U. purchases discounts

V. report form

W. sales discounts

X. sales return or allowance

Y. selling expenses

Z. single-step income statement

AA. trade discounts

___ 7. The bill that the seller sends to the buyer.

___ 8. Discounts taken by the buyer for early payment of an invoice.

___ 9. From the buyer's perspective, returned merchandise or an adjustment for defective merchandise.

___ 10. A form used by a buyer to inform the seller of the amount the buyer proposes to debit to the account payable due the seller.

___ 11. From the seller's perspective, discounts that a seller may offer the buyer for early payment.

___ 12. From the seller's perspective, returned merchandise or an adjustment for defective merchandise.

___ 13. A form used by a seller to inform the buyer of the amount the seller proposes to credit to the account receivable due from the buyer.

___ 14. Discounts from the list prices in published catalogs or special discounts offered to certain classes of buyers.

___ 15. Freight terms in which the buyer pays the transportation costs from the shipping point to the final destination.

___ 16. Freight terms in which the seller pays the transportation costs from the shipping point to the final destination.

___ 17. A form of income statement that contains several sections, subsections, and subtotals.

___ 18. Expenses that are incurred directly in the selling of merchandise.

___ 19. Expenses incurred in the administration or general operations of the business.

___ 20. The excess of gross profit over total operating expenses.

___ 21. The excess of operating expenses over gross profit.

___ 22. Revenue from sources other than the primary operating activity of a business.

___ 23. Expenses that cannot be traced directly to operations.

___ 24. A form of income statement in which the total of all expenses is deducted from the total of all revenues.

___ 25. The amount by which the merchandise for sale, as indicated by the balance of the merchandise inventory account, is larger than the total amount of merchandise counted during the physical inventory.

___ 26. The form of balance sheet in which assets are reported on the left-hand side and the liabilities and owner's equity on the right-hand side.

___ 27. The form of balance sheet in which assets, liabilities, and owner's equity are reported in a downward sequence.

Multiple Choice

1. If merchandise purchased on account is returned, the buyer may inform the seller of the details by issuing:
    A. a debit memorandum
    B. a credit memorandum
    C. an invoice
    D. a bill

2. If merchandise is sold on account to a customer for $1,000, terms FOB shipping point, 1/10, n/30, and the seller prepays $50 in transportation costs, the amount of the discount for early payment would be:
    A. $0   C. $10.00
    B. $5.00   D. $10.50

3. The income statement in which the total of all expenses is deducted from the total of all revenues is termed:

    A. multiple-step form   C. account form
    B. single-step form   D. report form

4. On a multiple-step income statement, the excess of net sales over the cost of merchandise sold is called:
    A. operating income
    B. income from operations
    C. gross profit
    D. net income

5. Which of the following expenses would normally be classified as Other expense on a multiple-step income statement?
    A. Depreciation expense—office equipment
    B. Sales salaries expense
    C. Insurance expense
    D. Interest expense

CLASS DISCUSSION QUESTIONS

1. What distinguishes a merchandising business from a service business?
2. Can a business earn a gross profit but incur a net loss? Explain.
3. What is the name of the account in which purchases of merchandise are recorded in a perpetual inventory system?
4. What is the name of the account in which sales of merchandise are recorded?
5. How does the accounting for sales to customers using bank credit cards, such as MasterCard and VISA, differ from accounting for sales to customers using nonbank credit cards, such as American Express?
6. The credit period during which the buyer of merchandise is allowed to pay usually begins with what date?
7. What is the meaning of (a) 1/10, n/60; (b) n/30; (c) n/eom?

8. It is not unusual for a customer to drive into some **Texaco**, **Mobil**, or **BP** gasoline stations and discover that the cash price per gallon is 3 or 4 cents less than the credit price per gallon. As a result, many customers pay cash rather than use their credit cards. Why would a gasoline station owner establish such a policy?
9. What is the nature of (a) a credit memorandum issued by the seller of merchandise, (b) a debit memorandum issued by the buyer of merchandise?
10. Who bears the transportation costs when the terms of sale are (a) FOB shipping point, (b) FOB destination?
11. Name at least three accounts that would normally appear in the chart of accounts of a merchandising business but would not appear in the chart of accounts of a service business.
12. Differentiate between the multiple-step and the single-step forms of the income statement.
13. What are the major advantages and disadvantages of the single-step form of income statement compared to the multiple-step statement?
14. What type of revenue is reported in the Other income section of the multiple-step income statement?
15. The Furniture Co., which uses a perpetual inventory system, experienced a normal inventory shrinkage of $32,000. What accounts would be debited and credited to record the adjustment for the inventory shrinkage at the end of the accounting period?
16. Assume that The Furniture Co. in Question 15 experienced an abnormal inventory shrinkage of $178,000. The Furniture Co. has decided to record the abnormal inventory shrinkage so that it would be separately disclosed on the income statement. What account would be debited for the abnormal inventory shrinkage?

Warren
Reeve
Fess

Resources for Your Success On-Line at warren.swcollege.com
Remember! If you need additional help, visit South-Western's Web site. See page 26 for a description of the online and printed materials that are available.

EXERCISES

Exercise 6–1
Determining gross profit

Objective 1

 a. $280,000

During the current year, merchandise is sold for $180,000 cash and for $520,000 on account. The cost of the merchandise sold is $420,000.

a. What is the amount of the gross profit?
b. Will the income statement necessarily report a net income? Explain.

Exercise 6–2
Determining cost of merchandise sold

Objective 1

✓ $330,000

Sales were $415,000, and the gross profit was $85,000. What was the amount of the cost of merchandise sold?

Exercise 6–3
Purchase-related transaction

Objective 2

✓ a. $2,940

Gupta Company purchased merchandise on account from a supplier for $4,000, terms 2/10, n/30. Gupta Company returned $1,000 of the merchandise and received full credit.

a. If Gupta Company pays the invoice within the discount period, what is the amount of cash required for the payment?
b. Under a perpetual inventory system, what account is credited by Gupta Company to record the return?

Exercise 6–4
Determining amounts to be paid on invoices

Objective 2

✓ a. $3,762

Determine the amount to be paid in full settlement of each of the following invoices, assuming that credit for returns and allowances was received prior to payment and that all invoices were paid within the discount period.

	Merchandise	Transportation Paid by Seller		Returns and Allowances
a.	$5,000	—	FOB shipping point, 1/10, n/30	$1,200
b.	1,000	$50	FOB shipping point, 2/10, n/30	600
c.	9,500	—	FOB destination, n/30	400
d.	3,000	75	FOB shipping point, 1/10, n/30	500
e.	5,000	—	FOB destination, 2/10, n/30	—

Exercise 6–5
Purchase-related transactions

Objective 2

✓ B: $7,227

A retailer is considering the purchase of ten units of a specific item from either of two suppliers. Their offers are as follows:

A: $700 a unit, total of $7,000, 2/10, n/30, plus transportation costs of $375.
B: $730 a unit, total of $7,300, 1/10, n/30, no charge for transportation.

Which of the two offers, A or B, yields the lower price?

Exercise 6–6
Purchase-related transactions

Objective 2

The debits and credits from four related transactions are presented in the following T accounts. Describe each transaction.

Cash				Accounts Payable			
	(2)	150	(3)	500	(1)		6,000
	(4)	5,445	(4)	5,500			

Merchandise Inventory			
(1)	6,000	(3)	500
(2)	150	(4)	55

Exercise 6–7
Purchase-related transactions

Objective 2

✓ (c) Cash, cr. $11,270

Elissa Co., a women's clothing store, purchased $14,000 of merchandise from a supplier on account, terms FOB destination, 2/10, n/30. Elissa Co. returned $2,500 of the merchandise, receiving a credit memorandum, and then paid the amount due within the discount period. Journalize Elissa Co.'s entries to record (a) the purchase, (b) the merchandise return, and (c) the payment.

Exercise 6–8
Purchase-related transactions

Objective 2

✓ (e) Cash, dr. $920

Journalize entries for the following related transactions of Restoration Company:

a. Purchased $10,000 of merchandise from Veneer Co. on account, terms 2/10, n/30.
b. Paid the amount owed on the invoice within the discount period.
c. Discovered that $4,000 of the merchandise was defective and returned items, receiving credit.
d. Purchased $3,000 of merchandise from Veneer Co. on account, terms n/30.
e. Received a check for the balance owed from the return in (c), after deducting for the purchase in (d).

Exercise 6–9
Sales-related transactions, including the use of credit cards

Objective 2

Journalize the entries for the following transactions:

a. Sold merchandise for cash, $12,800. The cost of the merchandise sold was $7,500.
b. Sold merchandise on account, $9,500. The cost of the merchandise sold was $6,000.
c. Sold merchandise to customers who used MasterCard and VISA, $6,750. The cost of the merchandise sold was $3,850.
d. Sold merchandise to customers who used American Express, $5,100. The cost of the merchandise sold was $2,860.
e. Paid an invoice from First National Bank for $350, representing a service fee for processing MasterCard and VISA sales.
f. Received $4,845 from American Express Company after a $255 collection fee had been deducted.

Exercise 6–10
Sales returns and allowances

Objective 2

What's Wrong WITH THIS?

During the year, sales returns and allowances totaled $212,150. The cost of the merchandise returned was $167,300. The accountant recorded all the returns and allowances by debiting the sales account and crediting Cost of Merchandise Sold for $212,150.

➤ Was the accountant's method of recording returns acceptable? Explain. In your explanation, include the advantages of using a sales returns and allowances account.

Exercise 6–11
Sales-related transactions

Objective 2

✓ a. $7,350

After the amount due on a sale of $7,500, terms 2/10, n/eom, is received from a customer within the discount period, the seller consents to the return of the entire shipment. The cost of the merchandise returned was $4,380. (a) What is the amount of the refund owed to the customer? (b) Journalize the entries made by the seller to record the return and the refund.

Exercise 6–12
Sales-related transactions

Objective 2

The debits and credits for three related transactions are presented in the following T accounts. Describe each transaction.

Cash		
(5)	7,920	

Sales		
		(1) 9,000

Accounts Receivable		
(1)	9,000	(3) 1,000
		(5) 8,000

Sales Discounts		
(5)	80	

Merchandise Inventory		
(4)	550	(2) 6,000

Sales Returns and Allowances		
(3)	1,000	

Cost of Merchandise Sold		
(2)	6,000	(4) 550

Exercise 6–13
Sales-related transactions
Objective 2

✓ d. $10,225

Merchandise is sold on account to a customer for $10,000, terms FOB shipping point, 3/10, n/30. The seller paid the transportation costs of $525. Determine the following: (a) amount of the sale, (b) amount debited to Accounts Receivable, (c) amount of the discount for early payment, and (d) amount due within the discount period.

Exercise 6–14
Sales tax
Objective 2

✓ c. $1,365

A sale of merchandise on account for $1,300 is subject to a 5% sales tax. (a) Should the sales tax be recorded at the time of sale or when payment is received? (b) What is the amount of the sale? (c) What is the amount debited to Accounts Receivable? (d) What is the title of the account to which the $65 is credited?

Exercise 6–15
Sales tax transactions
Objective 2

Journalize the entries to record the following selected transactions:

a.   Sold $12,000 of merchandise on account, subject to a sales tax of 4%. The cost of the merchandise sold was $7,000.
b.   Paid $2,380 to the state sales tax department for taxes collected.

Exercise 6–16
Sales-related transactions
Objective 2

Sauls Co., a furniture wholesaler, sells merchandise to Bayer Co. on account, $7,000, terms 2/15, n/30. The cost of the merchandise sold is $3,900. Sauls Co. issues a credit memorandum for $800 for merchandise returned and subsequently receives the amount due within the discount period. The cost of the merchandise returned is $410. Journalize Sauls Co.'s entries for (a) the sale, including the cost of the merchandise sold, (b) the credit memorandum, including the cost of the returned merchandise, and (c) the receipt of the check for the amount due from Bayer Co.

Exercise 6–17
Purchase-related transactions
Objective 2

Based on the data presented in Exercise 6–16, journalize Bayer Co.'s entries for (a) the purchase, (b) the return of the merchandise for credit, and (c) the payment of the invoice within the discount period.

Exercise 6–18
Normal balances of merchandise accounts
Objective 2

What is the normal balance of the following accounts: (a) Sales Returns and Allowances, (b) Merchandise Inventory, (c) Sales Discounts, (d) Transportation Out, (e) Sales, (f) Cost of Merchandise Sold?

Exercise 6–19
Chart of accounts
Objective 3

Hurley Co. is a newly organized business with the following list of accounts, arranged in alphabetical order:

Accounts Payable	Miscellaneous Selling Expense
Accounts Receivable	Notes Payable (short-term)
Accumulated Depreciation—Office Equipment	Notes Receivable (short-term)
Accumulated Depreciation—Store Equipment	Office Equipment
Advertising Expense	Office Salaries Expense
Cash	Office Supplies
Cost of Merchandise Sold	Office Supplies Expense
Depreciation Expense—Office Equipment	Prepaid Insurance
Depreciation Expense—Store Equipment	Rent Expense
Income Summary	Salaries Payable
Insurance Expense	Sales
Interest Expense	Sales Discounts
Interest Receivable	Sales Returns and Allowances
Interest Revenue	Sales Salaries Expense
J. Hurley, Capital	Store Equipment
J. Hurley, Drawing	Store Supplies
Land	Store Supplies Expense
Merchandise Inventory	Transportation Out
Miscellaneous Administrative Expense	

Construct a chart of accounts, assigning account numbers and arranging the accounts in balance sheet and income statement order, as illustrated in Exhibit 6. Each account number is three digits: the first digit is to indicate the major classification ("1" for assets, and so on); the second digit is to indicate the subclassification ("11" for current assets, and so on); and the third digit is to identify the specific account ("110" for Cash, and so on).

Exercise 6–20

Income statement for merchandiser

Objective 4

✓ Gross profit: $1,130,000

For the fiscal year, sales were $3,230,000, sales discounts were $120,000, sales returns and allowances were $280,000, and the cost of merchandise sold was $1,700,000. What was the amount of net sales and gross profit?

Exercise 6–21

Income statement for merchandiser

Objective 4

The following expenses were incurred by a merchandising business during the year. In which expense section of the income statement should each be reported: (a) selling, (b) administrative, or (c) other?

1. Interest expense on notes payable.
2. Salaries of office personnel.
3. Advertising expense.
4. Insurance expense on store equipment.
5. Rent expense on office building.
6. Depreciation expense on office equipment.
7. Office supplies used.
8. Salary of sales manager.

Exercise 6–22

Determining amounts for items omitted from income statement

Objective 4

✓ a. $298,000
✓ h. $690,000

Two items are omitted in each of the following four lists of income statement data. Determine the amounts of the missing items, identifying them by letter.

Sales	$ (a)	$600,000	$800,000	$757,500
Sales returns and allowances	10,000	10,000	(e)	30,500
Sales discounts	8,000	5,000	10,000	(g)
Net sales	280,000	(c)	765,000	(h)
Cost of merchandise sold	150,000	345,000	(f)	540,000
Gross profit	(b)	(d)	300,000	150,000

Exercise 6–23

Multiple-step income statement

Objective 4

What's Wrong WITH THIS?

How many errors can you find in the following income statement?

The Platinum Company
Income Statement
For the Year Ended December 31, 20—

Revenue from sales:			
Sales		$1,000,000	
Add: Sales returns and allowances	$18,000		
Sales discounts	4,500	22,500	
Gross sales			$1,022,500
Cost of merchandise sold			495,000
Income from operations			$ 527,500
Operating expenses:			
Selling expenses		$ 145,000	
Transportation out		5,300	
Administrative expenses		87,200	
Total operating expenses			237,500
			$ 290,000
Other expense:			
Interest revenue			27,500
Gross profit			$ 262,500

Exercise 6–24
Single-step income statement

Objective 4

✓ Net income: $412,500

Summary operating data for McNeely Company during the current year ended June 30, 2000, are as follows: cost of merchandise sold, $900,000; administrative expenses, $125,000; interest expense, $17,500; rent revenue, $30,000; net sales, $1,600,000; and selling expenses, $175,000. Prepare a single-step income statement.

Exercise 6–25
Multiple-step income statement

Objective 4

 SPREADSHEET

✓ Net income: $57,500

At the end of the year, the balances of the accounts appearing in the ledger of Satellite Company, a furniture wholesaler, are as follows:

Administrative Expenses	$ 70,000	Salaries Payable	$ 3,220
Building	512,500	Sales	975,000
Cash	48,500	Sales Discounts	10,000
Cost of Merchandise Sold	650,000	Sales Returns and Allowances	45,000
Interest Expense	7,500	Selling Expenses	135,000
Merchandise Inventory	130,000	Store Supplies	7,700
Notes Payable	25,000	T. Turner, Capital	638,580
Office Supplies	10,600	T. Turner, Drawing	15,000

a. Prepare a multiple-step income statement for the year ended December 31.
b. ◀━━▶ Compare the major advantages and disadvantages of the multiple-step and single-step forms of income statements.

Exercise 6–26
Adjusting entry for merchandise inventory shrinkage

Objective 5

Widmer Inc. perpetual inventory records indicate that $317,200 of merchandise should be on hand on December 31, 2000. The physical inventory indicates that $298,700 of merchandise is actually on hand. Journalize the adjusting entry for the inventory shrinkage for Widmer Inc. for the year ended December 31, 2000.

Exercise 6–27
Closing the accounts of a merchandiser

Objective 5

From the following list, identify the accounts that should be closed to Income Summary at the end of the fiscal year: (a) Accounts Receivable, (b) Cost of Merchandise Sold, (c) Merchandise Inventory, (d) Sales, (e) Sales Discounts, (f) Sales Returns and Allowances, (g) Supplies, (h) Supplies Expense, (i) Salaries Expense, (j) Salaries Payable.

Exercise 6–28
Ratio of net sales to total assets

Objective 6

  HAT

The financial statements for **Hershey Foods Corporation** are presented in Appendix G at the end of the text.

a. Determine the ratio of net sales to average total assets for Hershey Foods Corporation for the years ended December 31, 1996 and 1995.
b. ◀━━▶ What conclusions can be drawn from these ratios concerning the trend in the ability of Hershey to effectively use its assets to generate sales?

Note: Hershey's total assets at the end of 1994 were $2,890,981,000.

Appendix 1
Exercise 6–29
Merchandising special journals

Castle Rug Company had the following credit sales transactions during May:

Date	Customer	Quantity	Rug Style	Sales
May 3	H. Harding	1	9 by 6 Chinese	$ 5,000
8	K. Thomas	1	8 by 10 Persian	8,000
19	L. Lao	1	8 by 10 Indian	9,000
26	F. Lopez	1	9 by 12 Persian	12,000

The May 1 inventory was $13,000, consisting of:

Quantity	Style	Cost per Rug	Total Cost
2	9 by 6 Chinese	$3,000	$6,000
2	8 by 10 Persian	3,500	7,000

During May, Castle Rug Company purchased the following rugs from Hadiz Rug Importers:

Date	Quantity	Rug Style	Cost per Rug	Amount
May 10	2	8 by 10 Indian	$4,000	$ 8,000
12	1	9 by 6 Chinese	3,500	3,500
21	3	9 by 12 Persian	6,000	18,000

The general ledger includes the following accounts:

Account Number	Account
11	Accounts Receivable
12	Merchandise Inventory
21	Accounts Payable
41	Sales
51	Cost of Merchandise Sold

a. Record the sales in a two-column sales journal. Use the sales journal form shown in the appendix at the end of this chapter. Begin with Invoice Number 60.
b. Record the purchases in a purchases journal. Use the purchases journal form shown in the appendix at the end of this chapter.
c. Assume that you have posted the journal entries to the appropriate ledgers. Insert the correct posting references in the sales and purchases journals.
d. Determine the May 31 balance of Merchandise Inventory.

Appendix 2
Exercise 6–30
Closing entries

Based on the data presented in Exercise 6–25, journalize the closing entries.

PROBLEMS SERIES A

Problem 6–1A
Purchase-related transactions

Objective 2

The following selected transactions were completed by Bartow Co. during August of the current year:

Aug. 1. Purchased merchandise from Jones Co., $8,000, terms FOB shipping point, 2/10, n/eom. Prepaid transportation costs of $250 were added to the invoice.
  4. Purchased merchandise from Guthrie Co., $9,200, terms FOB destination, n/30.
  10. Paid Jones Co. for invoice of August 1, less discount.
  12. Purchased merchandise from Dobbs Co., $5,000, terms FOB destination, 1/10, n/30.
  14. Issued debit memorandum to Dobbs Co. for $1,500 of merchandise returned from purchase on August 12.
  18. Purchased merchandise from Aschor Company, $11,500, terms FOB shipping point, n/eom.
  18. Paid transportation charges of $200 on August 18 purchase from Aschor Company.
  19. Purchased merchandise from Hatcher Co., $7,500, terms FOB destination, 2/10, n/30.
  22. Paid Dobbs Co. for invoice of August 12, less debit memorandum of August 14 and discount.
  29. Paid Hatcher Co. for invoice of August 19, less discount.
  31. Paid Aschor Company for invoice of August 18.
  31. Paid Guthrie Co. for invoice of August 4.

Instructions
Journalize the entries to record the transactions of Bartow Co. for August.

Problem 6–2A
Sales-related transactions

Objective 2

The following selected transactions were completed by Cohen Supplies Co., which sells electrical supplies primarily to wholesalers and occasionally to retail customers.

May 1. Sold merchandise on account to Fox Co., $2,500, terms FOB shipping point, n/eom. The cost of merchandise sold was $1,300.

2. Sold merchandise for $3,000 plus 6% sales tax to cash customers. The cost of merchandise sold was $1,750.

5. Sold merchandise on account to Baldwin Company, $13,000, terms FOB destination, 1/10, n/30. The cost of merchandise sold was $9,200.

7. Sold merchandise for $2,150 plus 6% sales tax to customers who used VISA cards. Deposited credit card receipts into the bank. The cost of merchandise sold was $1,800.

13. Sold merchandise to customers who used American Express cards, $4,500. The cost of merchandise sold was $2,600.

14. Sold merchandise on account to Blech Co., $7,500, terms FOB shipping point, 1/10, n/30. The cost of merchandise sold was $4,000.

15. Received check for amount due from Baldwin Company for sale on May 5.

16. Issued credit memorandum for $800 to Blech Co. for merchandise returned from sale on May 14. The cost of the merchandise returned was $360.

18. Sold merchandise on account to Stockton Company, $9,000, terms FOB shipping point, 1/10, n/30. Paid $210 for transportation costs and added them to the invoice. The cost of merchandise sold was $5,000.

24. Received check for amount due from Blech Co. for sale on May 14 less credit memorandum of May 16 and discount.

27. Received $7,680 from American Express for $8,000 of sales reported during the week of May 12–18.

28. Received check for amount due from Stockton Company for sale of May 18.

31. Paid Anywhere Delivery Service $1,200 for merchandise delivered during May to customers under shipping terms of FOB destination.

31. Received check for amount due from Fox Co. for sale of May 1.

June 3. Paid First National Bank $325 for service fees for handling MasterCard sales during May.

10. Paid $1,100 to state sales tax division for taxes owed on May sales.

Instructions
Journalize the entries to record the transactions of Cohen Supplies Co.

Problem 6–3A
Sales-related and purchase-related transactions

Objective 2

GENERAL LEDGER

The following were selected from among the transactions completed by Taxel Company during March of the current year:

Mar. 2. Purchased merchandise on account from Queen Co., list price $25,000, trade discount 30%, terms FOB shipping point, 2/10, n/30, with prepaid transportation costs of $720 added to the invoice.

4. Purchased merchandise on account from Rossi Co., $6,000, terms FOB destination, 1/10, n/30.

6. Sold merchandise on account to C. F. Howell Co., list price $7,500, trade discount 40%, terms 2/10, n/30. The cost of the merchandise sold was $1,850.

9. Returned $1,300 of merchandise purchased on March 4 from Rossi Co.

12. Paid Queen Co. on account for purchase of March 2, less discount.

14. Paid Rossi Co. on account for purchase of March 4, less return of March 9 and discount.

16. Received cash on account from sale of March 6 to C. F. Howell Co., less discount.

19. Sold merchandise on nonbank credit cards and reported accounts to the card company, American Express, $4,450. The cost of the merchandise sold was $2,950.

22. Sold merchandise on account to Vantage Co., $3,480, terms 2/10, n/30. The cost of the merchandise sold was $1,400.

24. Sold merchandise for cash, $4,350. The cost of the merchandise sold was $1,750.

25. Received merchandise returned by Vantage Co. from sale on March 22, $1,480. The cost of the returned merchandise was $600.

31. Received cash from American Express for nonbank credit card sales of March 19, less $290 service fee.

Instructions

Journalize the transactions.

Problem 6–4A

Sales-related and purchase-related transactions for seller and buyer

Objective 2

The following selected transactions were completed during November between Singh Company and Bristol Company:

Nov. 3. Singh Company sold merchandise on account to Bristol Company, $11,200, terms FOB shipping point, 2/10, n/30. Singh Company paid transportation costs of $600, which were added to the invoice. The cost of the merchandise sold was $7,500.

8. Singh Company sold merchandise on account to Bristol Company, $13,500, terms FOB destination, 1/15, n/eom. The cost of the merchandise sold was $9,500.

8. Singh Company paid transportation costs of $750 for delivery of merchandise sold to Bristol Company on November 8.

12. Bristol Company returned $3,000 of merchandise purchased on account on November 8 from Singh Company. The cost of the merchandise returned was $1,600.

13. Bristol Company paid Singh Company for purchase of November 3, less discount.

23. Bristol Company paid Singh Company for purchase of November 8, less discount and less return of November 12.

24. Singh Company sold merchandise on account to Bristol Company, $7,100, terms FOB shipping point, n/eom. The cost of the merchandise sold was $4,000.

27. Bristol Company paid transportation charges of $150 on November 24 purchase from Singh Company.

30. Bristol Company paid Singh Company on account for purchase of November 24.

Instructions

Journalize the November transactions for (1) Singh Company and (2) Bristol Company.

Problem 6–5A

Multiple-step income statement and report form of balance sheet

Objective 5

✓ 1. Net income: $160,000

The following selected accounts and their normal balances appear in the ledger of Maxilla Co. for the fiscal year ended June 30, 2000:

Cash	$ 36,500	Sales Returns and Allowances	$ 19,000	
Notes Receivable	50,000	Sales Discounts	11,000	
Accounts Receivable	62,000	Cost of Merchandise Sold	870,000	
Merchandise Inventory	100,000	Sales Salaries Expense	110,000	Selling Exp.
Office Supplies	1,600	Advertising Expense	28,300	
Prepaid Insurance	6,800	Depreciation Expense—		
Office Equipment	54,000	Store Equipment	4,600	
Accumulated Depreciation—		Miscellaneous Selling Expense	1,100	
Office Equipment	10,800	Office Salaries Expense	51,000	Admin Expense
Store Equipment	107,500	Rent Expense	22,150	
Accumulated Depreciation—		Insurance Expense	12,750	
Store Equipment	48,600	Depreciation Expense—		
Accounts Payable	27,000	Office Equipment	9,000	
Salaries Payable	2,000	Office Supplies Expense	900	
Note Payable		Miscellaneous Administrative		
(final payment due 2010)	30,000	Expense	1,200	
T. Zeller, Capital	200,000	Interest Revenue	5,000	Other
T. Zeller, Drawing	60,000	Interest Expense	4,000	
Sales	1,300,000			

Instructions

1. Prepare a multiple-step income statement.
2. Prepare a statement of owner's equity.
3. Prepare a report form of balance sheet, assuming that the current portion of the note payable is $5,000.

(continues)

4.   ▬▬▶ Briefly explain (a) how multiple-step and single-step income statements differ and (b) how report-form and account-form balance sheets differ.

Problem 6–6A
Single-step income statement and account form of balance sheet

Objective 5

✓ 1. Net income: $160,000

Selected accounts and related amounts for Maxilla Co. for the fiscal year ended June 30, 2000, are presented in Problem 6–5A.

Instructions

1. Prepare a single-step income statement in the format shown in Exhibit 8.
2. Prepare a statement of owner's equity.
3. Prepare an account form of balance sheet, assuming that the current portion of the note payable is $5,000.

Appendix 2
Problem 6–7A
Work sheet, financial statements, and adjusting and closing entries

✓ 2. Net income: $153,865

The accounts and their balances in the ledger of The Wash Co. on December 31 of the current year are as follows:

Cash	$ 51,165	Sales	$1,007,500
Accounts Receivable	116,100	Sales Returns and Allowances	15,500
Merchandise Inventory	235,000	Sales Discounts	6,000
Prepaid Insurance	10,600	Cost of Merchandise Sold	571,200
Store Supplies	3,750	Sales Salaries Expense	86,400
Office Supplies	1,700	Advertising Expense	29,450
Store Equipment	125,000	Depreciation Expense—	
Accumulated Depreciation—		Store Equipment	—
Store Equipment	40,300	Store Supplies Expense	—
Office Equipment	62,000	Miscellaneous Selling Expense	1,885
Accumulated Depreciation—		Office Salaries Expense	60,000
Office Equipment	17,200	Rent Expense	30,000
Accounts Payable	66,700	Insurance Expense	—
Salaries Payable	—	Depreciation Expense—	
Unearned Rent	1,200	Office Equipment	—
Note Payable		Office Supplies Expense	—
(final payment due 2010)	105,000	Miscellaneous Administrative	
M. Tag, Capital	222,100	Expense	1,650
M. Tag, Drawing	40,000	Rent Revenue	—
Income Summary	—	Interest Expense	12,600

The data needed for year-end adjustments on December 31 are as follows:

Physical merchandise inventory on December 31		$225,000
Insurance expired during the year		7,100
Supplies on hand on December 31:		
Store supplies		1,050
Office supplies		750
Depreciation for the year:		
Store equipment		8,500
Office equipment		4,500
Salaries payable on December 31:		
Sales salaries	$3,450	
Office salaries	2,550	6,000
Unearned rent on December 31		400

Instructions

1. Prepare a work sheet for the fiscal year ended December 31. List all accounts in the order given.
2. Prepare a multiple-step income statement.
3. Prepare a statement of owner's equity.

4. Prepare a report form of balance sheet, assuming that the current portion of the note payable is $15,000.
5. Journalize the adjusting entries.
6. Journalize the closing entries.

PROBLEMS SERIES B

Problem 6–1B
Purchase-related transactions

Objective 2

The following selected transactions were completed by Bolton Company during March of the current year:

Mar. 1. Purchased merchandise from Duke Co., $7,500, terms FOB destination, n/30.
  4. Purchased merchandise from Laufer Co., $8,000, terms FOB shipping point, 2/10, n/eom. Prepaid transportation costs of $150 were added to the invoice.
  5. Purchased merchandise from Harmon Co., $5,000, terms FOB destination, 2/10, n/30.
  8. Issued debit memorandum to Harmon Co. for $1,000 of merchandise returned from purchase on March 5.
  14. Paid Laufer Co. for invoice of March 4, less discount.
  15. Paid Harmon Co. for invoice of March 5, less debit memorandum of March 8 and discount.
  19. Purchased merchandise from Ivy Co., $5,000, terms FOB shipping point, n/eom.
  19. Paid transportation charges of $120 on March 19 purchase from Ivy Co.
  20. Purchased merchandise from Hatcher Co., $12,000, terms FOB destination, 1/10, n/30.
  30. Paid Hatcher Co. for invoice of March 20, less discount.
  31. Paid Duke Co. for invoice of March 1.
  31. Paid Ivy Co. for invoice of March 19.

Instructions
Journalize the entries to record the transactions of Bolton Company for March.

Problem 6–2B
Sales-related transactions

Objective 2

The following selected transactions were completed by Greenley Supply Co., which sells office supplies primarily to wholesalers and occasionally to retail customers.

Oct. 1. Sold merchandise on account to Beck Co., $3,500, terms FOB destination, 2/10, n/30. The cost of the merchandise sold was $1,800.
  2. Sold merchandise for $2,000 plus 5% sales tax to cash customers. The cost of merchandise sold was $1,100.
  4. Sold merchandise on account to Atlas Co., $2,400, terms FOB shipping point, n/eom. The cost of merchandise sold was $1,800.
  5. Sold merchandise for $1,400 plus 5% sales tax to customers who used Master-Card. Deposited credit card receipts into the bank. The cost of merchandise sold was $750.
  11. Received check for amount due from Beck Co. for sale on October 1.
  14. Sold merchandise to customers who used American Express cards, $6,600. The cost of merchandise sold was $4,200.
  15. Sold merchandise on account to Monroe Co., $6,500, terms FOB shipping point, 1/10, n/30. The cost of merchandise sold was $3,900.
  17. Issued credit memorandum for $1,500 to Monroe Co. for merchandise returned from sale on October 15. The cost of the merchandise returned was $650.
  18. Sold merchandise on account to Hempel Co., $7,500, terms FOB shipping point, 1/10, n/30. Added $85 to the invoice for transportation costs prepaid. The cost of merchandise sold was $4,500.
  25. Received check for amount due from Monroe Co. for sale on October 15 less credit memorandum of October 17 and discount.

Oct. 26. Received $9,410 from American Express for $10,000 of sales reported during the week of October 11–17.

28. Received check for amount due from Hempel Co. for sale of October 18.

31. Received check for amount due from Atlas Co. for sale of October 4.

31. Paid Fast Delivery Service $850 for merchandise delivered during October to customers under shipping terms of FOB destination.

Nov. 4. Paid First National Bank $390 for service fees for handling MasterCard sales during October.

10. Paid $1,050 to state sales tax division for taxes owed on October sales.

Instructions
Journalize the entries to record the transactions of Greenley Supply Co.

Problem 6–3B
Sales-related and purchase-related transactions

Objective 2

GENERAL LEDGER

The following were selected from among the transactions completed by The Document Company during April of the current year:

Apr. 4. Purchased merchandise on account from Vela Co., list price $20,000, trade discount 40%, terms FOB destination, 2/10, n/30.

5. Sold merchandise for cash, $4,100. The cost of the merchandise sold was $2,450.

7. Purchased merchandise on account from Summit Co., $7,500, terms FOB shipping point, 2/10, n/30, with prepaid transportation costs of $200 added to the invoice.

7. Returned $2,500 of merchandise purchased on April 4 from Vela Co.

11. Sold merchandise on account to Bowles Co., list price $2,250, trade discount 20%, terms 1/10, n/30. The cost of the merchandise sold was $1,050.

14. Paid Vela Co. on account for purchase of April 4, less return of April 7 and discount.

15. Sold merchandise on nonbank credit cards and reported accounts to the card company, American Express, $5,850. The cost of the merchandise sold was $3,900.

17. Paid Summit Co. on account for purchase of April 7, less discount.

21. Received cash on account from sale of April 11 to Bowles Co., less discount.

25. Sold merchandise on account to Clemons Co., $3,200, terms 1/10, n/30. The cost of the merchandise sold was $2,025.

28. Received cash from American Express for nonbank credit card sales of April 15, less $280 service fee.

30. Received merchandise returned by Clemons Co. from sale on April 25, $1,700. The cost of the returned merchandise was $810.

Instructions
Journalize the transactions.

Problem 6–4B
Sales-related and purchase-related transactions for seller and buyer

Objective 2

The following selected transactions were completed during July between Servco Company and Barkey Co.:

July 3. Servco Company sold merchandise on account to Barkey Co., $10,500, terms FOB destination, 2/15, n/eom. The cost of the merchandise sold was $6,000.

3. Servco Company paid transportation costs of $450 for delivery of merchandise sold to Barkey Co. on July 3.

10. Servco Company sold merchandise on account to Barkey Co., $12,000, terms FOB shipping point, n/eom. The cost of the merchandise sold was $9,000.

11. Barkey Co. returned $2,000 of merchandise purchased on account on July 3 from Servco Company. The cost of the merchandise returned was $1,200.

14. Barkey Co. paid transportation charges of $200 on July 10 purchase from Servco Company.

17. Servco Company sold merchandise on account to Barkey Co., $20,000, terms FOB shipping point, 1/10, n/30. Servco Company paid transportation costs of $1,750, which were added to the invoice. The cost of the merchandise sold was $12,000.

July 18. Barkey Co. paid Servco Company for purchase of July 3, less discount and less return of July 11.

27. Barkey Co. paid Servco Company on account for purchase of July 17, less discount.

31. Barkey Co. paid Servco Company on account for purchase of July 10.

Instructions

Journalize the July transactions for (1) Servco Company and (2) Barkey Co.

Problem 6–5B

Multiple-step income statement and report form of balance sheet

Objective 5

✓ 1. Net income: $230,000

The following selected accounts and their normal balances appear in the ledger of The Shirt Co. for the fiscal year ended March 31, 2000:

Cash	$ 23,000	Sales Returns and Allowances	$ 13,100 ✓
Notes Receivable	120,000	Sales Discounts	11,900 ✓
Accounts Receivable	141,000	Cost of Merchandise Sold	1,000,000 ✓
Merchandise Inventory	200,000	Sales Salaries Expense	113,200 ✓
Office Supplies	5,600	Advertising Expense	33,800 ✓
Prepaid Insurance	3,400	Depreciation Expense—	
Office Equipment	85,000	Store Equipment	6,400 ✓
Accumulated Depreciation—		Miscellaneous Selling Expense	1,600
Office Equipment	12,800	Office Salaries Expense	54,150 ✓
Store Equipment	113,000	Rent Expense	21,350 ✓
Accumulated Depreciation—		Depreciation Expense—	
Store Equipment	24,200	Office Equipment	12,700 ✓
Accounts Payable	45,600	Insurance Expense	3,900 ✓
Salaries Payable	2,400	Office Supplies Expense	1,300 ✓
Note Payable		Miscellaneous Administrative	
(final payment due 2010)	56,000	Expense	1,600 ✓
J. Peterman, Capital	370,000	Interest Revenue	11,000
J. Peterman, Drawing	50,000	Interest Expense	6,000
Sales	1,500,000 ✓		

Instructions

1. Prepare a multiple-step income statement.
2. Prepare a statement of owner's equity.
3. Prepare a report form of balance sheet, assuming that the current portion of the note payable is $15,000.
4. ▬▬▶ Briefly explain (a) how multiple-step and single-step income statements differ and (b) how report-form and account-form balance sheets differ.

Problem 6–6B

Single-step income statement and account form of balance sheet

Objective 5

✓ 1. Net income: $230,000

Selected accounts and related amounts for The Shirt Co. for the fiscal year ended March 31, 2000, are presented in Problem 6–5B.

Instructions

1. Prepare a single-step income statement in the format shown in Exhibit 8.
2. Prepare a statement of owner's equity.
3. Prepare an account form of balance sheet, assuming that the current portion of the note payable is $15,000.

Appendix 2
Problem 6–7B

Work sheet, financial statements, and adjusting and closing entries

✓ 2. Net income: $169,250

The accounts and their balances in the ledger of The Shoe Co. on December 31 of the current year are as follows:

Cash	$ 38,000	Store Supplies	$ 4,250
Accounts Receivable	112,500	Office Supplies	2,100
Merchandise Inventory	230,000	Store Equipment	132,000
Prepaid Insurance	9,700		

Accumulated Depreciation—Store Equipment	$ 40,300	Sales Salaries Expense	$ 76,400	
Office Equipment	50,000	Advertising Expense	25,000	
Accumulated Depreciation—Office Equipment	17,200	Depreciation Expense—Store Equipment	—	
Accounts Payable	66,700	Store Supplies Expense	—	
Salaries Payable	—	Miscellaneous Selling Expense	1,600	
Unearned Rent	1,200	Office Salaries Expense	44,000	
Note Payable (final payment due 2010)	105,000	Rent Expense	26,000	
		Insurance Expense	—	
J. Oxford, Capital	174,600	Depreciation Expense—Office Equipment	—	
J. Oxford, Drawing	40,000	Office Supplies Expense	—	
Income Summary	—	Miscellaneous Administrative Expense	1,650	
Sales	895,000			
Sales Returns and Allowances	11,900	Rent Revenue	—	
Sales Discounts	7,100	Interest Expense	11,600	
Cost of Merchandise Sold	476,200			

The data needed for year-end adjustments on December 31 are as follows:

Physical merchandise inventory on December 31		$212,000
Insurance expired during the year		6,500
Supplies on hand on December 31:		
Store supplies		1,300
Office supplies		750
Depreciation for the year:		
Store equipment		7,500
Office equipment		3,800
Salaries payable on December 31:		
Sales salaries	$3,850	
Office salaries	1,150	5,000
Unearned rent on December 31		400

Instructions

1. Prepare a work sheet for the fiscal year ended December 31. List all accounts in the order given.
2. Prepare a multiple-step income statement.
3. Prepare a statement of owner's equity.
4. Prepare a report form of balance sheet, assuming that the current portion of the note payable is $15,000.
5. Journalize the adjusting entries.
6. Journalize the closing entries.

QUICKBOOKS PROBLEM [APPENDIX 1]

Buying and Selling Inventory

This problem uses the Larry's Landscaping sample company provided with QuickBooks® 5.0. Begin by first copying *sample.qbw* into another file name, **invent.qbw**, so that the original sample.qbw file will not be changed. You must copy the file using the copy and paste commands in your operating system. This is an important step, since we will be using the unchanged sample.qbw file later in the text. If you do not first copy sample.qbw into another file name, you will automatically change sample.qbw. We will be assuming that you have an unchanged version in future QuickBooks problems in this text.

Retrieve Larry's Landscaping by opening the file that you just created. The first time you open Larry's Landscaping, you will be in QuickBooks Navigator®. You may wish to use the Navigator to review the forms used for "Purchases and Vendors." This problem will use these forms.

Begin by opening the "Item List" window and reviewing Larry's Landscaping's inventory items—pumps, lighting, soil, sprinkler pipes, and sprinkler heads, for example. There are currently seven fountain pumps in inventory.

Instructions

1. Enter a new item of inventory by selecting the "Edit Item" button at the bottom of the "Item List" window. The new item is an inventory part, "iron fountain." Its cost is $110, and its selling price is $150. The income account is "Fountains and Garden" (under job materials for landscaping services). The preferred vendor is Harper Metal Works. Set the descriptions as "Iron garden fountain" for both purchase and sale transactions.

2. Larry's Landscaping has received a bill from Harper Metal Works for the purchase of five iron fountains. Record this purchase, using the "Enter Bills" form. Use the "Items" tab to record the five fountains.

3. Prepare an invoice to Erica Pretell for landscaping services, using the "Create Invoices" form (invoice #34). The invoice should include three lines. The first line is for 40 hours of installation labor. The second line is for two iron fountains. The third line is for two fountain pumps.

4. Prepare a QuickBooks report showing the following:
   a. Inventory stock status by item.
   b. Summary sales by item for inventory items (showing sales, cost of goods sold, and gross margin) for December. Use the filter to report inventory items only.

COMPREHENSIVE PROBLEM 2

GENERAL LEDGER

QUICKBOOKS

✓ 5. Net income: $67,415

The Cycle Co. is a merchandising business. The account balances for The Cycle Co. as of May 1, 2000 (unless otherwise indicated) are as follows:

110	Cash	$ 29,160
111	Notes Receivable	—
112	Accounts Receivable	56,220
113	Interest Receivable	—
115	Merchandise Inventory	123,900
116	Prepaid Insurance	3,750
117	Store Supplies	2,550
123	Store Equipment	54,300
124	Accumulated Depreciation—Store Equipment	12,600
210	Accounts Payable	38,500
211	Salaries Payable	—
310	F. R. Schwinn, Capital, June 1, 1999	179,270
311	F. R. Schwinn, Drawing	25,000
312	Income Summary	—
410	Sales	731,600
411	Sales Returns and Allowances	13,600
412	Sales Discounts	5,200

510	Cost of Merchandise Sold	$497,540
520	Sales Salaries Expense	74,400
521	Advertising Expense	18,000
522	Depreciation Expense	—
523	Store Supplies Expense	—
529	Miscellaneous Selling Expense	2,800
530	Office Salaries Expense	29,400
531	Rent Expense	24,500
532	Insurance Expense	—
539	Miscellaneous Administrative Expense	1,650
611	Interest Revenue	—

During May, the last month of the fiscal year, the following transactions were completed:

May 1. Paid rent for May, $2,400.
1. Received a $7,500 note receivable from Holmes Co. on account.
2. Purchased merchandise on account from Lindsey Co., terms 2/10, n/30, FOB shipping point, $25,000.
3. Paid transportation charges on purchase of May 2, $750.
5. Sold merchandise on account to Richards Co., terms 2/10, n/30, FOB shipping point, $8,500. The cost of the merchandise sold was $5,000.
7. Received $16,900 cash from Vasquez Co. on account, no discount.
10. Sold merchandise for cash, $18,300. The cost of the merchandise sold was $11,000.
12. Paid for merchandise purchased on May 2, less discount.
13. Received merchandise returned on sale of May 5, $1,500. The cost of the merchandise returned was $900.
14. Paid advertising expense for last half of May, $2,500.
15. Received cash from sale of May 5, less return of May 13 and discount.
19. Purchased merchandise for cash, $7,400.
19. Paid $25,950 to Chang Co. on account, no discount.
20. Sold merchandise on account to Petroski Co., terms 1/10, n/30, FOB shipping point, $16,000. The cost of the merchandise sold was $9,600.
21. For the convenience of the customer, paid shipping charges on sale of May 20, $600.
21. Received $31,000 cash from Sinnett Co. on account, no discount.
21. Purchased merchandise on account from Hummer Co., terms 1/10, n/30, FOB destination, $15,000.
24. Returned $2,500 of damaged merchandise purchased on May 21, receiving credit from the seller.
25. Refunded cash on sales made for cash, $750. The cost of the merchandise returned was $480.
27. Paid sales salaries of $2,700 and office salaries of $900.
29. Purchased store supplies for cash, $350.
30. Sold merchandise on account to Brown Co., terms 2/10, n/30, FOB shipping point, $43,100. The cost of the merchandise sold was $25,000.
30. Received cash from sale of May 20, less discount, plus transportation paid on May 21.
31. Paid for purchase of May 21, less return of May 24 and discount.

Instructions

(*Note:* If the work sheet described in the appendix is used, follow the alternative instructions.)

1. Enter the balances of each of the accounts in the appropriate balance column of a four-column account. Write *Balance* in the item section, and place a check mark (✓) in the Posting Reference column.
2. Journalize the transactions for May.

3. Post the journal to the general ledger, extending the month-end balances to the appropriate balance columns after all posting is completed. In this problem, you are not required to update or post to the accounts receivable and accounts payable subsidiary ledgers.
4. Journalize and post the adjusting entries, using the following adjustment data:

a.	Interest accrued on notes receivable on May 31		$ 100
b.	Merchandise inventory on May 31		110,000
c.	Insurance expired during the year		1,250
d.	Store supplies on hand on May 31		1,050
e.	Depreciation for the current year		8,860
f.	Accrued salaries on May 31:		
	Sales salaries	$400	
	Office salaries	140	540

5. Prepare a multiple-step income statement, a statement of owner's equity, and a report form of balance sheet.
6. Journalize and post the closing entries. Indicate closed accounts by inserting a line in both balance columns opposite the closing entry. Insert the new balance in the owner's capital account.
7. Prepare a post-closing trial balance.

Alternative Instructions

1. Enter the balances of each of the accounts in the appropriate balance column of a four-column account. Write *Balance* in the item section, and place a check mark (✓) in the Posting Reference column.
2. Journalize the transactions for May.
3. Post the journal to the general ledger, extending the month-end balances to the appropriate balance columns after all posting is completed. In this problem, you are not required to update or post to the accounts receivable and accounts payable subsidiary ledgers.
4. Prepare a trial balance as of May 31 on a ten-column work sheet, listing all accounts in the order given in the ledger. Complete the work sheet for the fiscal year ended May 31, using the following adjustment data:

a.	Interest accrued on notes receivable on May 31		$ 100
b.	Merchandise inventory on May 31		110,000
c.	Insurance expired during the year		1,250
d.	Store supplies on hand on May 31		1,050
e.	Depreciation for the current year		8,860
f.	Accrued salaries on May 31:		
	Sales salaries	$400	
	Office salaries	140	540

5. Prepare a multiple-step income statement, a statement of owner's equity, and a report form of balance sheet.
6. Journalize and post the adjusting entries.
7. Journalize and post the closing entries. Indicate closed accounts by inserting a line in both balance columns opposite the closing entry. Insert the new balance in the owner's capital account.
8. Prepare a post-closing trial balance.

QuickBooks Instructions

To set up the company file, follow the QuickBooks instructions for Comprehensive Problem 1 at the end of Chapter 4.

SPECIAL ACTIVITIES

Activity 6–1
Druck Company
Ethics and professional conduct in business

On August 1, 2000, Druck Company, a garden retailer, purchased $10,000 of corn seed, terms 2/10, n/30, from Dynacorn Co. Even though the discount period had expired, Wing Yu subtracted the discount of $200 when he processed the documents for payment on August 15, 2000.

➤ Discuss whether Wing Yu behaved in a professional manner by subtracting the discount, even though the discount period had expired.

Actvity 6–2
The Video Store Co.
Purchases discounts and accounts payable

The Video Store Co. is owned and operated by Gerry Crosby. The following is an excerpt from a conversation between Gerry Crosby and JoAnn Sims, the chief accountant for The Video Store.

Gerry: JoAnn, I've got a question about this recent balance sheet.
JoAnn: Sure, what's your question?
Gerry: Well, as you know, I'm applying for a bank loan to finance our new store in Albion, and I noticed that the accounts payable are listed as $150,000.
JoAnn: That's right. Approximately $120,000 of that represents amounts due our suppliers, and the remainder is miscellaneous payables to creditors for utilities, office equipment, supplies, etc.
Gerry: That's what I thought. But as you know, we normally receive a 2% discount from our suppliers for earlier payment, and we always try to take the discount.
JoAnn: That's right. I can't remember the last time we missed a discount.
Gerry: Well, in that case, it seems to me the accounts payable should be listed minus the 2% discount. Let's list the accounts payable due suppliers as $117,600, rather than $120,000. Every little bit helps. You never know. It might make the difference between getting the loan and not.

➤ How would you respond to Gerry Crosby's request?

Activity 6–3
Mega Sound versus Ultra-Sound Electronics
Determining cost of purchase

The following is an excerpt from a conversation between Jill Mandel and Kim Kenwood. Jill is debating whether to buy a stereo system from Mega Sound, a locally owned electronics store, or Ultra-Sound Electronics, a mail-order electronics company.

Jill: Kim, I don't know what to do about buying my new stereo.
Kim: What's the problem?
Jill: Well, I can buy it locally at Mega Sound for $689.95. However, Ultra-Sound Electronics has the same system listed for $699.99.
Kim: So what's the big deal? Buy it from Mega Sound.
Jill: It's not quite that simple. Ultra-Sound said something about not having to pay sales tax, since I was out-of-state.
Kim: Yes, that's a good point. If you buy it at Mega Sound, they'll charge you 5% sales tax.
Jill: But Ultra-Sound Electronics charges $15 for shipping and handling. If I have them send it next-day air, it'll cost $35 for shipping and handling.
Kim: I guess it is a little confusing.
Jill: That's not all. Mega Sound will give an additional 1% discount if I pay cash. Otherwise, they will let me use my MasterCard, or I can pay it off in three monthly installments.
Kim: Anything else???
Jill: Well . . . Ultra-Sound says I have to charge it on my MasterCard. They don't accept checks.
Kim: I am not surprised. Many mail-order houses don't accept checks.
Jill: I give up. What would you do?

1. Assuming that Ultra-Sound Electronics doesn't charge sales tax on the sale to Jill, which company is offering the best buy?
2. ➤ What might be some considerations other than price that might influence Jill's decision on where to buy the stereo system?

Activity 6–4
Escapade Boat Company
Sales discounts

Your sister operates Escapade Boat Company, a mail-order boat parts distributorship that is in its third year of operation. The following income statement was recently prepared for the year ended October 31, 2000:

Escapade Boat Company
Income Statement
For the Year Ended October 31, 2000

Revenues:		
Net sales		$500,000
Interest revenue		2,500
Total revenues		$502,500
Expenses:		
Cost of merchandise sold	$350,000	
Selling expenses	46,000	
Administrative expenses	24,000	
Interest expense	5,000	
Total expenses		425,000
Net income		$ 77,500

Your sister is considering a proposal to increase net income by offering sales discounts of 2/15, n/30, and by shipping all merchandise FOB shipping point. Currently, no sales discounts are allowed and merchandise is shipped FOB destination. It is estimated that these credit terms will increase net sales by 10%. The ratio of the cost of merchandise sold to net sales is expected to be 70%. All selling and administrative expenses are expected to remain unchanged, except for store supplies, miscellaneous selling, office supplies, and miscellaneous administrative expenses, which are expected to increase proportionately with increased net sales. The amounts of these preceding items for the year ended October 31, 2000, were as follows:

Store supplies expense	$2,000
Miscellaneous selling expense	1,000
Office supplies expense	800
Miscellaneous administrative expense	1,500

The other income and other expense items will remain unchanged. The shipment of all merchandise FOB shipping point will eliminate all transportation-out expenses, which for the year ended October 31, 2000, were $18,000.

1. Prepare a projected single-step income statement for the year ending October 31, 2001, based on the proposal.
2. a. Based on the projected income statement in (1), would you recommend the implementation of the proposed changes?
    b. Describe any possible concerns you may have related to the proposed changes described in (1).

Activity 6–5
Into the Real World
Shopping for a television

Assume that you are planning to purchase a 32-inch Sony television. In groups of three or four, determine the lowest cost for the television, considering the available alternatives and the advantages and disadvantages of each alternative. For example, you could purchase locally, through mail order, or through an Internet shopping service. Consider such factors as delivery charges, interest-free financing, discounts, coupons, and availability of warranty services. Prepare a report for presentation to the class.

ANSWERS TO SELF-EXAMINATION QUESTIONS

Matching

1. C	5. Q	9. T	13. D	16. F	19. B	22. P	25. J
2. H	6. S	10. E	14. AA	17. N	20. I	23. O	26. A
3. M	7. K	11. W	15. G	18. Y	21. L	24. Z	27. V
4. R	8. U	12. X					

Multiple Choice

1. **A** A debit memorandum (answer A), issued by the buyer, indicates the amount the buyer proposes to debit to the accounts payable account. A credit memorandum (answer B), issued by the seller, indicates the amount the seller proposes to credit to the accounts receivable account. An invoice (answer C) or a bill (answer D), issued by the seller, indicates the amount and terms of the sale.

2. **C** The amount of discount for early payment is $10 (answer C), or 1% of $1,000. Although the $50 of transportation costs paid by the seller is debited to the customer's account, the customer is not entitled to a discount on that amount.

3. **B** The single-step form of income statement (answer B) is so named because the total of all expenses is deducted in one step from the total of all revenues. The multiple-step form (answer A) includes numerous sections and subsections with several subtotals. The account form (answer C) and the report form (answer D) are two common forms of the balance sheet.

4. **C** Gross profit (answer C) is the excess of net sales over the cost of merchandise sold. Operating income (answer A) or income from operations (answer B) is the excess of gross profit over operating expenses. Net income (answer D) is the final figure on the income statement after all revenues and expenses have been reported.

5. **D** Expenses such as interest expense (answer D) that cannot be associated directly with operations are identified as *Other expense* or *Nonoperating expense*. Depreciation expense—office equipment (answer A) is an administrative expense. Sales salaries expense (answer B) is a selling expense. Insurance expense (answer C) is a mixed expense with elements of both selling expense and administrative expense. For small businesses, insurance expense is usually reported as an administrative expense.

7

Cash

Setting the STAGE

If your bank returns checks it has paid from your account, along with your monthly bank statement, you may have noticed a magnetic coding in the bottom right-hand corner of each check. This coding indicates the amount of the check. In the past, you may have accepted this coding, as well as the bank statement, as correct. However, a clerk may have entered the magnetic coding incorrectly, which causes the check to be processed for the wrong amount. For example, the following check written for $25 was incorrectly processed as $250:

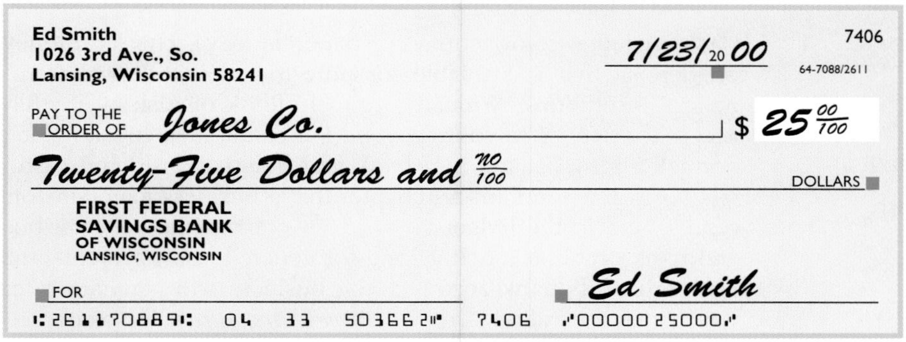
Ed Smith
1026 3rd Ave., So.
Lansing, Wisconsin 58241
7406
7/23/20 00
64-7088/2611
PAY TO THE ORDER OF
Jones Co.
$ 25 00/100
Twenty-Five Dollars and no/100
DOLLARS
FIRST FEDERAL SAVINGS BANK OF WISCONSIN
LANSING, WISCONSIN
FOR
Ed Smith
⑆2611708891⑆ 04 33 5036621⑈ 7406 ⑈0000025000⑈

We are all concerned about our cash. Likewise, businesses are concerned about safeguarding and controlling cash. Inadequate controls can and often do lead to theft, misuse of funds, or otherwise embarrassing situations. For example, in one of the biggest errors in banking history, Chemical Bank incorrectly deducted customer automated teller machine (ATM) withdrawals twice from each customer's account. For instance, if a customer withdrew $100 from an account, the customer actually had $200 deducted from the account balance. Before the error was discovered, Chemical Bank mistakenly deducted about $15 million from more than 100,000 customer accounts. The error was caused by inadequate controls over the changing of the bank's computer programs.[1]

To detect errors, control procedures should be used by both you and the bank. In this chapter, we will apply basic internal control concepts and procedures to the control of cash.

[1] Saul Hansell, "Cash Machines Getting Greedy At a Big Bank," *The Wall Street Journal,* February 18, 1994.

After studying this chapter, you should be able to:

1 Describe the nature of cash and the importance of internal control over cash.

2 Summarize basic procedures for achieving internal control over cash receipts.

3 Summarize basic procedures for achieving internal control over cash payments, including the use of a voucher system.

4 Describe the nature of a bank account and its use in controlling cash.

5 Prepare a bank reconciliation and journalize any necessary entries.

6 Account for small cash transactions, using a petty cash fund.

7 Summarize how cash is presented on the balance sheet.

8 Compute and interpret the ratio of cash to current liabilities.

Nature of Cash and the Importance of Controls Over Cash

Cash includes coins, currency (paper money), checks, money orders, and money on deposit that is available for unrestricted withdrawal from banks and other financial institutions. Normally, you can think of cash as anything that a bank would accept for deposit in your account. For example, a check made payable to you could normally be deposited in a bank and thus is considered cash.

We will assume in this chapter that a business maintains only *one* bank account, represented in the ledger as *Cash*. In practice, however, a business may have several bank accounts, such as one for general cash payments and another for payroll. For each of its bank accounts, the business will maintain a ledger account, one of which may be called *Cash in Bank—First Bank*, for example. It will also maintain separate ledger accounts for cash that it does not keep in the bank, such as cash for small payments, and cash used for special purposes, such as travel reimbursements. We will introduce some of these other cash accounts in the chapter.

Because of the ease with which money can be transferred, cash is the asset most likely to be diverted and used improperly by employees. In addition, many transactions either directly or indirectly affect the receipt or the payment of cash. Businesses must therefore design and use controls that safeguard cash and control the authorization of cash transactions. In the following paragraphs, we will discuss these controls.

Control of Cash Receipts

To protect cash from theft and misuse, a business must control cash from the time it is received until it is deposited in a bank. Such procedures are called **preventive controls**. Procedures that are designed to detect theft or misuse of cash are called **detective controls**. In a sense, detective controls are also preventive in nature, since employees are less likely to steal or misuse cash if they know there is a good chance they will be discovered.

Retail businesses normally receive cash from two main sources: (1) cash receipts from customers and (2) mail receipts from customers making payments on account. These two sources of cash are shown in Exhibit 1.

EXHIBIT 1 Retailers' Sources of Cash

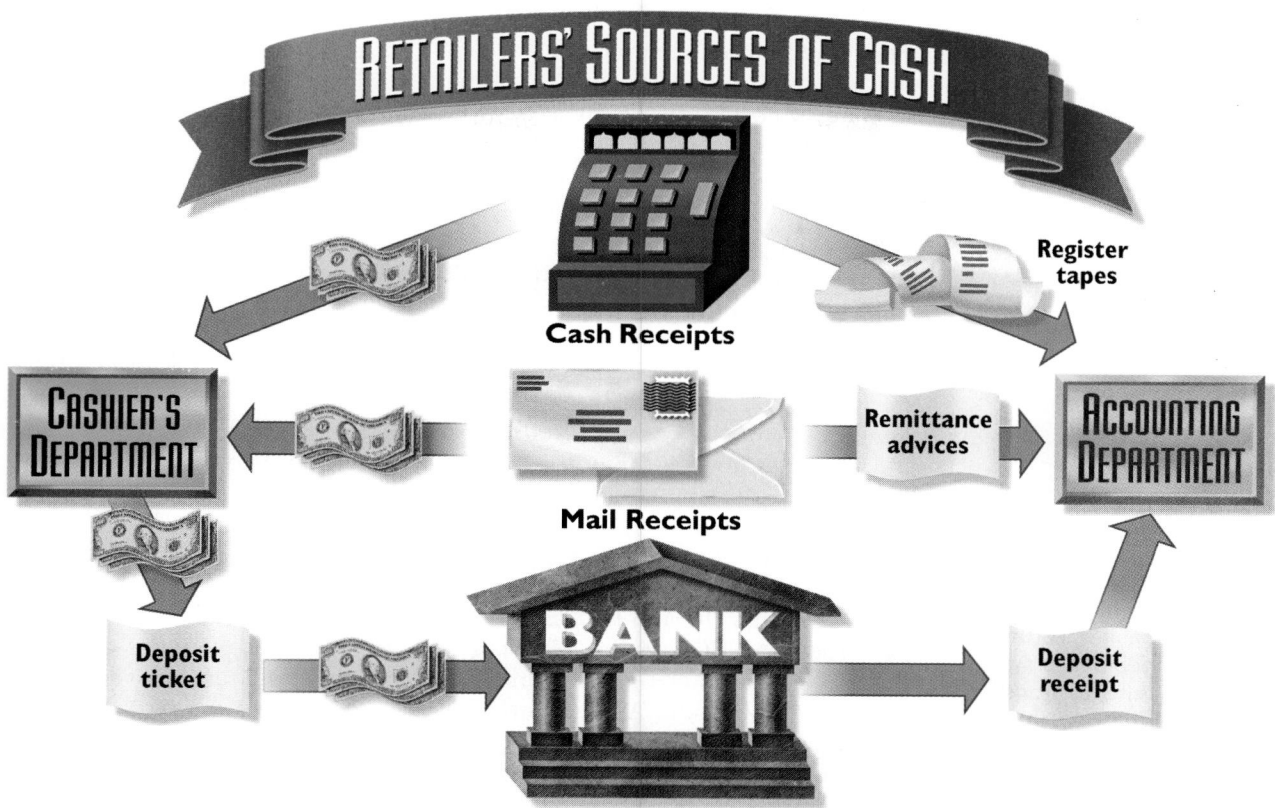

Controlling Cash Received from Cash Sales

 Fast-food restaurants, such as **McDonald's**, **Wendy's**, and **Burger King**, receive cash primarily from over-the-counter sales to customers. Mail-order retailers, such as **Lands' End**, **Orvis**, and **L.L. Bean**, receive cash primarily through the mail and from credit card companies.

Regardless of the source of cash receipts, every business must properly safeguard and record its cash receipts. One of the most important controls to protect cash received in over-the-counter sales is a cash register. You may have noticed that when a clerk (cashier) enters the amount of a sale, the cash register normally displays the amount. This is a control to ensure that the clerk has charged you the correct amount. You also receive a receipt to verify the accuracy of the amount.

At the beginning of a work shift, each cash register clerk is given a cash drawer that contains a predetermined amount of cash for making change for customers. The amount in each drawer is sometimes called a **change fund**. At the end of the work shift, each clerk and the supervisor count the cash in the clerk's cash drawer. The amount of cash in each drawer should equal the beginning amount of cash plus the cash sales for the day. However, errors in recording cash sales or errors in making change cause the amount of actual cash on hand to differ from this amount. Such differences are recorded in a cash short and over account. For example, the following entry records a clerk's cash sales of $3,150 when the actual cash on hand is $3,142:

Cash		3	1	4	2	00			
Cash Short and Over					8	00			
Sales							3	1 5 0	00
To record cash sales and actual cash									
on hand.									

At the end of the accounting period, a debit balance in the cash short and over account is included in Miscellaneous Administrative Expense in the income statement. A credit balance is included in the Other Income section. If a clerk consistently has significant cash short and over amounts, the supervisor may require the clerk to take additional training.

After a cash register clerk's cash has been counted and recorded on a memorandum form, the cash is then placed in a store safe in the Cashier's Department until it can be deposited in the bank. The supervisor forwards the clerk's cash register tapes to the Accounting Department, where they become the basis for recording the transactions for the day.

Controlling Cash Received in the Mail

Cash is received in the mail when customers pay their bills. This cash is usually in the form of checks and money orders. Most companies' invoices are designed so that customers return a portion of the invoice, called a **remittance advice**, with their payment. The employee who opens the incoming mail should initially compare the amount of cash received with the amount shown on the remittance advice. If a customer does not return a remittance advice, an employee prepares one. Like the cash register, the remittance advice serves as a record of cash initially received. It also helps ensure that the posting to the customer's account is accurate. Finally, as a preventive control, the employee opening the mail normally also stamps checks and money orders "For Deposit Only" in the bank account of the business.

All cash received in the mail is sent to the Cashier's Department. An employee there combines it with the receipts from cash sales and prepares a bank deposit ticket. The remittance advices and their summary totals are delivered to the Accounting Department. An accounting clerk then prepares the records of the transactions and posts them to the customer accounts.

When cash is deposited in the bank, the bank normally stamps a duplicate copy of the deposit ticket with the amount received. This bank receipt is returned to the Accounting Department, where a clerk then compares the receipt with the total amount that should have been deposited. This control helps ensure that all the cash is deposited and that no cash is lost or stolen on the way to the bank. Any shortages are thus promptly detected.

The separation of the duties of the Cashier's Department, which handles cash, and the Accounting Department, which records cash, is a preventive control. If Accounting Department employees both handled and recorded cash, an employee could steal cash and change the accounting records to hide the theft.

 Some retail companies are using debit card systems to transfer and record the receipt of cash. In a debit card system, a customer pays for goods at the time of purchase by presenting a plastic card. The card authorizes the electronic transfer of cash from the customer's checking account to the retailer's bank account at the time of the sale.

Internal Control of Cash Payments

Summarize basic procedures for achieving internal control over cash payments, including the use of a voucher system.

Internal control of cash payments should provide reasonable assurance that payments are made for only authorized transactions. In addition, controls should ensure that cash is used efficiently. For example, controls should ensure that all available discounts, such as purchase and trade discounts, are taken.

In a small business, an owner/manager may sign all checks, based upon personal knowledge of goods and services purchased. In a large business, however, checks are often prepared by employees who do not have such a complete knowledge of the transactions. In a large business, for example, the duties of pur-

 **Howard Schultz & Associates (HS&A)** specializes in reviewing cash payments for its clients. HS&A searches for errors, such as duplicate payments, failures to take discounts, and inaccurate computations. The typical amount recovered for a client is about one-tenth of 1 percent (0.1%) of the total payments reviewed. This averages to about $300,000 per client. In one case, HS&A recovered over $4.5 million for a client.

Source: Thomas Buell, Jr., "Demand Grows for Auditor," *The Naples Daily News,* January 12, 1992, p. 14E.

chasing goods, inspecting the goods received, and verifying the invoices are usually performed by different employees. These duties must be coordinated to ensure that checks for proper amounts are issued to creditors. One system used for this purpose is the voucher system.

Basic Features of the Voucher System

A **voucher system** is a set of procedures for authorizing and recording liabilities and cash payments. A voucher system normally uses (1) vouchers, (2) a file for unpaid vouchers, and (3) a file for paid vouchers. Generally, a voucher is any document that serves as proof of authority to pay cash. For example, an invoice properly approved for payment could be considered a voucher. In many businesses, however, a **voucher** is a special form for recording relevant data about a liability and the details of its payment. An example of such a form is shown in Exhibit 2.

EXHIBIT 2 Voucher

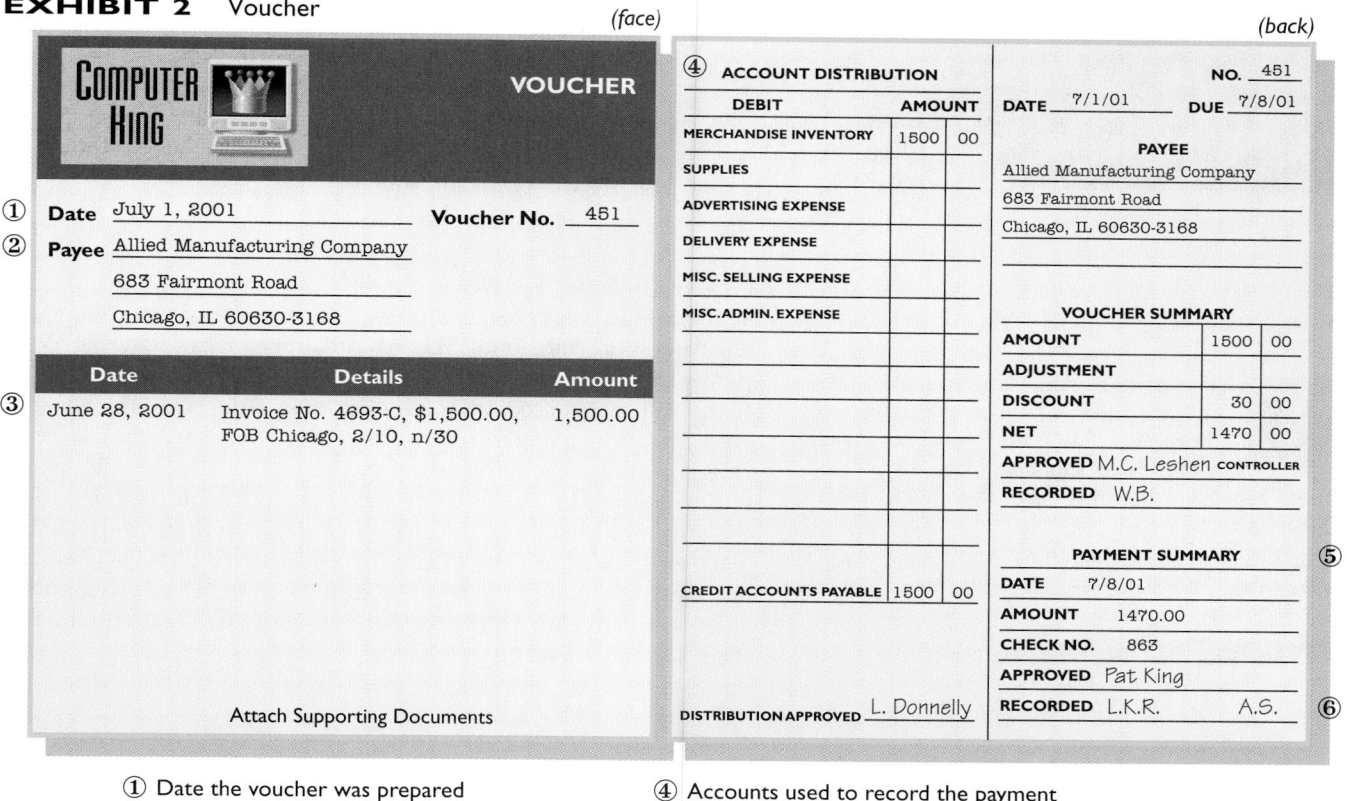

① Date the voucher was prepared
② Name and address of the creditor
③ Description of the supporting documents
④ Accounts used to record the payment
⑤ Details of payment
⑥ Spaces for signature or initials of approving employees

Each voucher includes the creditor's invoice number and the amount and terms of the invoice. The accounts used in recording the payment are listed in the *account distribution.*

A voucher is normally prepared in the Accounting Department, after all necessary supporting documents have been received. For example, when a voucher is prepared for the purchase of goods, the voucher should be supported by the supplier's invoice, a purchase order, and a receiving report. In preparing the voucher, an accounts payable clerk verifies the quantity, price, and mathematical accuracy of the supporting documents. This provides assurance that the payment is for goods that were properly ordered and received.

After a voucher is prepared, the voucher and its supporting documents are given to the proper official for approval. After it has been approved, the voucher is returned to the Accounting Department, where it is recorded in the accounts. It is then filed in an unpaid voucher file by its due date so that all available purchase discounts are taken.[2]

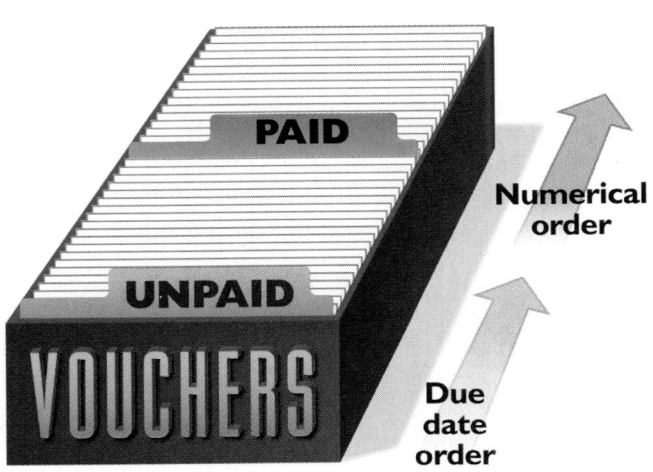

On its due date, the voucher is removed from the unpaid voucher file. The date, the number, and the amount of the check written in payment are listed on the back of the voucher. The payment of the voucher is recorded in the same manner as the payment of an account payable.

After payment, vouchers are marked "Paid" and are usually filed in numerical order in a paid voucher file. They are then readily available for examination by employees needing information about past payments.

A voucher system may be either manual or computerized. In a computerized system, properly approved supporting documents would be entered directly into computer files. At the due date, the checks would be automatically generated and mailed to creditors. At that time, the voucher would be automatically transferred to a paid voucher file. In some cases, payments may be made electronically rather than by check.

Electronic Funds Transfer

With rapidly changing technology, new systems are being devised to more efficiently record and transfer cash among companies. Such systems often use **electronic funds transfer (EFT)**. In an EFT system, computers rather than paper (money, checks, etc.) are used to effect cash transactions. For example, a business may pay its employees by means of EFT. Under such a system, employees may authorize the deposit of their payroll checks directly into checking accounts. Each pay period, the business electronically transfers the employees' net pay to their checking accounts through the use of computer systems and telephone lines. Likewise, many companies are using EFT systems to pay their suppliers and other vendors.

 The treasurer for **Chevron U.S.A.** reported that Chevron is making more than 5,800 electronic payments a month to suppliers. These payments represent nearly 14% of the checks that Chevron once wrote.

Source: Fred R. Bleakley, "Fast Money: Electronic Payments Now Supplant Checks at More Large Firms," *The Wall Street Journal,* April 3, 1994.

Bank Accounts: Their Nature and Use as a Control Over Cash

OBJECTIVE 4

Describe the nature of a bank account and its use in controlling cash.

Most of you are already familiar with bank accounts. You have a checking account at a local bank, credit union, savings and loan association, or other financial institution. In this section, we discuss the nature of a bank account used by a business. The features of such accounts will be similar to your own bank account. We then discuss the use of bank accounts as an additional control over cash.

---

[2] Occasionally, a purchase discount is missed. Some companies record the amounts of missed discounts in an account titled Discounts Lost. Doing so allows managers to monitor the significance of discounts lost. Since most companies design controls to take all purchase discounts, we do not illustrate the use of a discounts lost account.

Business Bank Accounts

A business often maintains several bank accounts. The forms used with each bank account are a signature card, deposit ticket, check, and record of checks drawn.

When you open a checking account, you sign a **signature card**. This card is used by the bank to verify the signature on checks that are submitted for payment. Also, when you open an account, the bank assigns an identifying number to the account.

The details of a deposit are listed by the depositor on a printed **deposit ticket** supplied by the bank. These forms are often prepared in duplicate. The bank teller stamps or initials a copy of the deposit ticket and gives it to the depositor as a receipt. Other types of receipts may also be used to give the depositor written proof of the date and the total amount of the deposit.

A **check** is a written document signed by the depositor, ordering the bank to pay a sum of money to an individual or entity. There are three parties to a check—the drawer, the drawee, and the payee. The **drawer** is the one who signs the check, ordering payment by the bank. The **drawee** is the bank on which the check is drawn. The **payee** is the party to whom payment is to be made.

The name and address of the depositor are usually printed on each check. In addition, checks are prenumbered, so that they can easily be kept track of by both the issuer and the bank. Banks encode their identification number and the depositor's account number in magnetic ink on each check. These numbers make it possible for the bank to sort and post checks automatically. When a check is presented for payment, the amount for which it is drawn is inserted, next to the account number, in magnetic ink. The processed check shown at the beginning of this chapter illustrated these features.

A record of each check should be prepared at the time a check is written. A small booklet called a **transactions register** is often used by both businesses and individuals for this purpose.

Point of INTEREST

You may order checks from your bank, which will debit your account for a check printing charge. It is usually less costly, however, to order checks directly from a printer. If you use electronic banking services, you will use fewer checks, but you will probably pay a fee for each electronic transaction.

The purpose of a check may be written in space provided on the check or on an attachment to the check. Normally, checks issued to a creditor on account are sent with a form that identifies the specific invoice that is being paid. The purpose of this **remittance advice** is to make sure that proper credit is recorded in the accounts of the creditor. In this way, mistakes are less likely to occur. A check and remittance advice is shown in Exhibit 3.

EXHIBIT 3
Check and Remittance
Advice

MONROE COMPANY				363
813 Greenwood Street	Detroit, MI 48206-4070		July 12 20 00	9-42 / 720

Pay to the
Order of _____ Hammond Office Products _____ $ 921.20

Nine hundred twenty-one 20/100 ---------------------------------- **Dollars**

AMERICAN NATIONAL BANK OF DETROIT
DETROIT, MI 48201-2500   (313)933-8547   MEMBER FDIC

K.R. Simons   **Treasurer**
Earl M. Hartman   **Vice President**

⑆072000423⑆ 1627042 363⑈

DETACH THIS PORTION BEFORE CASHING

Date	Description	Gross Amount	Deductions	Net Amount
7/12/00	Invoice No. 529482	940.00	18.80	921.20

MONROE COMPANY

Before depositing the check, the payee removes the remittance advice. The payee may then use the remittance advice as written proof of the details of the cash receipt.

Bank Statement

Banks usually maintain a record of all checking account transactions. A summary of all transactions, called a **statement of account**, is mailed to the depositor, usually each month. Like any account with a customer or a creditor, the bank statement shows the beginning balance, additions, deductions, and the balance at the end of the period. A typical bank statement is shown in Exhibit 4.

The depositor's checks received by the bank during the period may accompany the bank statement, arranged in the order of payment. The paid checks are stamped "Paid," together with the date of payment. Other entries that the bank has made in the depositor's account may be described in debit or credit memorandums enclosed with the statement.

You should note that a depositor's checking account balance *in the bank's records* is a liability with a credit balance. Debit memorandums issued by the bank on a depositor's account therefore decrease the depositor's balance. Likewise, credit memorandums increase the depositor's balance. A bank issues a debit memorandum to charge (decrease) a depositor's account for service charges or for deposited checks returned because of insufficient funds. Likewise, a bank issues a credit memorandum when it increases the depositor's account for collecting a note receivable for the depositor, making a loan to the depositor, or adding interest to the depositor's account.[3]

---

[3] Although interest-bearing checking accounts are common for individuals, Federal Reserve Regulation Q prohibits the paying of interest on corporate checking accounts.

EXHIBIT 4
Bank Statement

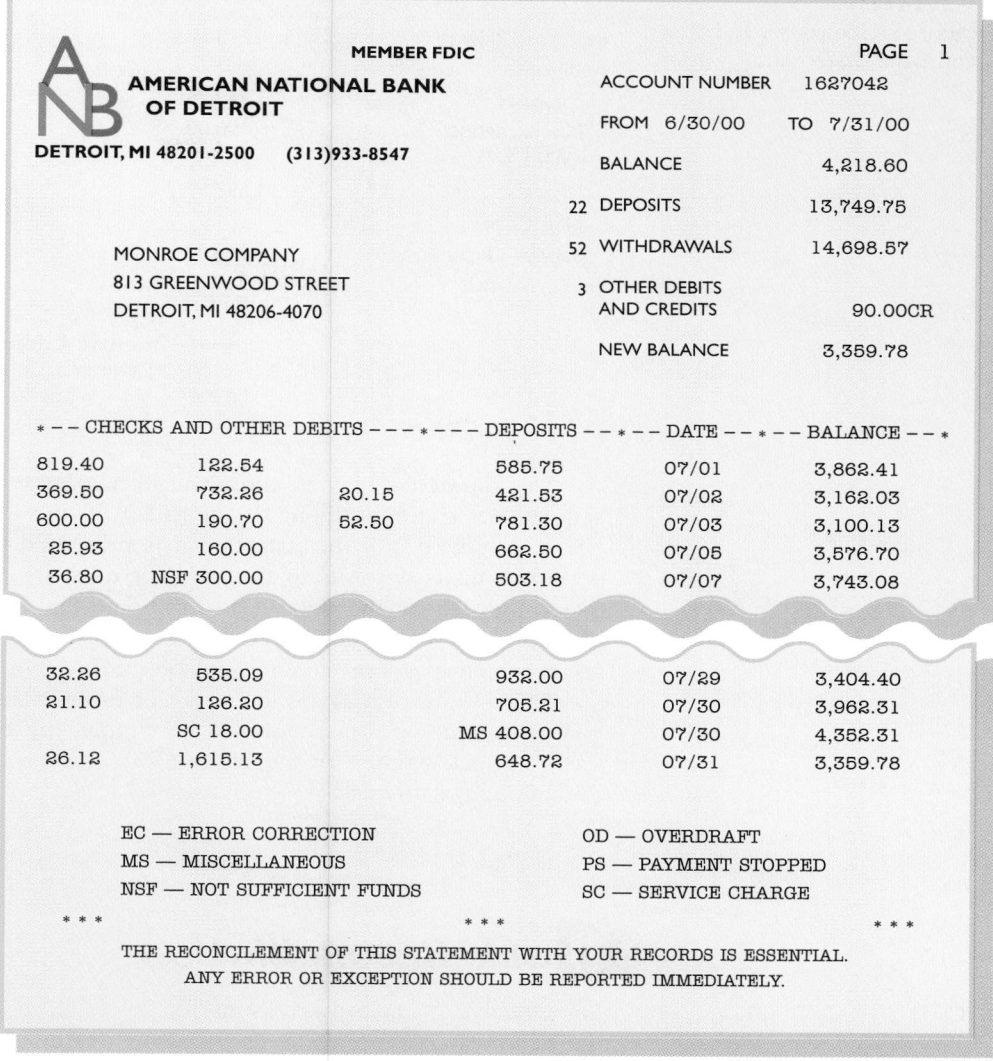

*–– CHECKS AND OTHER DEBITS ––– *			*–– DEPOSITS –– *	*–– DATE –– *	*–– BALANCE –– *
819.40	122.54		585.75	07/01	3,862.41
369.50	732.26	20.15	421.53	07/02	3,162.03
600.00	190.70	52.50	781.30	07/03	3,100.13
25.93	160.00		662.50	07/05	3,576.70
36.80	NSF 300.00		503.18	07/07	3,743.08
32.26	535.09		932.00	07/29	3,404.40
21.10	126.20		705.21	07/30	3,962.31
	SC 18.00		MS 408.00	07/30	4,352.31
26.12	1,615.13		648.72	07/31	3,359.78

EC — ERROR CORRECTION   OD — OVERDRAFT
MS — MISCELLANEOUS   PS — PAYMENT STOPPED
NSF — NOT SUFFICIENT FUNDS   SC — SERVICE CHARGE

* * *   * * *   * * *

THE RECONCILEMENT OF THIS STATEMENT WITH YOUR RECORDS IS ESSENTIAL.
ANY ERROR OR EXCEPTION SHOULD BE REPORTED IMMEDIATELY.

Bank Accounts as a Control Over Cash

A bank account is one of the primary tools a business uses to control cash. For example, businesses often require that all cash receipts be initially deposited in a bank account. Likewise, businesses usually use checks to make all cash payments, except for very small amounts. When such a system is used, there is a double record of cash transactions—one by the business and the other by the bank.

A business can use a bank statement to compare the cash transactions recorded in its accounting records to those recorded by the bank. The cash balance shown by a bank statement is usually different from the cash balance shown in the accounting records of the business, as shown in Exhibit 5.

A bank account and a business's records provide a double record of cash transactions.

EXHIBIT 5
Monroe Company's Records
and Bank Statement

Bank Statement			Monroe Company Records	
Beginning Balance . .		$ 4,218.60	Beginning Balance . .	$ 4,227.60
Additions:				
Deposits		13,749.75	Deposits	14,565.95
Miscellaneous . . .		408.00		
Deductions:				
Checks		14,698.57	Checks	16,243.56
NSF Check	$300			
Service Charge . .	18	318.00		
Ending Balance		$ 3,359.78	Ending Balance	$ 2,549.99

Monroe Company should determine
the reason for the difference in
these two amounts.

This difference may be the result of a delay by either party in recording transactions. For example, there is a time lag of one day or more between the date a check is written and the date that it is presented to the bank for payment. If the depositor mails deposits to the bank or uses the night depository, a time lag between the date of the deposit and the date that it is recorded by the bank is also probable. The bank may also debit or credit the depositor's account for transactions about which the depositor will not be informed until later.

The difference may be the result of errors made by either the business or the bank in recording transactions. For example, the business may incorrectly post to Cash a check written for $4,500 as $450. Likewise, a bank may incorrectly record the amount of a check, as we illustrated at the beginning of this chapter.

Bank Reconciliation

OBJECTIVE 5

Prepare a bank reconciliation and journalize any necessary entries.

For effective control, the reasons for the difference between the cash balance on the bank statement and the cash balance in the accounting records should be determined by preparing a bank reconciliation. A **bank reconciliation** is a listing of the items and amounts that cause the cash balance reported in the bank statement to differ from the balance of the cash account in the ledger.

A bank reconciliation is usually divided into two sections. The first section begins with the cash balance according to the bank statement and ends with the adjusted balance. The second section begins with the cash balance according to the depositor's records and ends with the adjusted balance. The two amounts designated as the adjusted balance must be equal. The content of the bank reconciliation is shown below.

Cash balance according to bank statement . . .		$XXX	Cash balance according to depositor's records		$XXX
Add: Additions by depositor not on			Add: Additions by bank not recorded by		
bank statement	$XX		depositor	$XX	
Bank errors	XX	XX	Depositor errors	XX	XX
		$XXX			$XXX
Deduct: Deductions by depositor not on			Deduct: Deductions by bank not recorded		
bank statement	$XX		by depositor	$XX	
Bank errors	XX	XX	Depositor errors	XX	XX
Adjusted balance		$XXX	Adjusted balance		$XXX

must be equal

The Federal Reserve System

One of the most powerful financial institutions in the United States is the *Federal Reserve System,* often referred to as the *Fed.* The Federal Reserve System consists of twelve district banks located in the following cities: Boston, New York, Philadelphia, Cleveland, Charlotte, Atlanta, St. Louis, Chicago, Minneapolis, Kansas City, Dallas, and San Francisco. The Fed's overall operations are coordinated by a seven-member Board of Governors headquartered in Washington, D.C. Four key activities of the Fed are (1) carrying out monetary policy, (2) setting rules on credit, (3) distributing currency, and (4) clearing checks.

The Fed carries out monetary policy in three ways. First, the Fed's open-market operations involve the purchase and sale of government securities. For example, when the Fed buys U.S. securities in the open market, it puts money into the economy. Second, the Fed sets the requirements for reserves that member banks must maintain on deposit. These reserves are unavailable for loans or other investments. Current reserve requirements range from 3% to 10% of a bank's deposits. Third, the Fed sets the discount rate. This rate is the interest rate that the Fed charges member banks for loans. The discount rate is often quoted in the financial press. It indirectly affects the interest rates that member banks charge customers on credit card balances, home mortgages, and other types of loans.

The Fed sets rules on credit in various ways. For example, the Fed sets minimum down payments and maximum repayment periods on consumer loans of member banks. The Fed also sets margin requirements for purchasing securities such as stocks. For example, if the margin requirement is 40%, then an investor who purchases stocks worth $20,000 must pay at least $8,000. The remaining $12,000 can be financed.

The Fed distributes to member banks the coins minted and the paper money printed by the U.S. Treasury. Almost all paper money is in the form of Federal Reserve Notes. For example, if you look at a dollar bill, you will see the words *Federal Reserve Note* above the picture of George Washington. The large letter in the seal to the left of the picture indicates which Federal Reserve Bank issued the Note.

Finally, the Fed helps banks clear checks. The Fed's check-clearing system lets banks quickly convert checks drawn on other banks into cash. ■

The following steps are useful in finding the reconciling items and determining the adjusted balance of Cash:

1. Compare each deposit listed on the bank statement with unrecorded deposits appearing in the preceding period's reconciliation and with deposit receipts or other records of deposits. *Add deposits not recorded by the bank to the balance according to the bank statement.*

2. Compare paid checks with outstanding checks appearing on the preceding period's reconciliation and with recorded checks. *Deduct checks outstanding that have not been paid by the bank from the balance according to the bank statement.*

3. Compare bank credit memorandums to entries in the journal. For example, a bank would issue a credit memorandum for a note receivable and interest that it collected for a depositor. *Add credit memorandums that have not been recorded to the balance according to the depositor's records.*

4. Compare bank debit memorandums to entries recording cash payments. For example, a bank normally issues debit memorandums for service charges and check printing charges. A bank also issues debit memorandums for not-sufficient-funds checks. A *not-sufficient-funds (NSF) check* is a customer's check that was recorded and deposited but was not paid when it was presented to the customer's bank for payment. NSF checks are normally charged back to the customer as an account receivable. *Deduct debit memorandums that have not been recorded from the balance according to the depositor's records.*

5. List any errors discovered during the preceding steps. For example, if an amount has been recorded incorrectly by the depositor, the amount of the error should be added to or deducted from the cash balance according to the depositor's records. Similarly, errors by the bank should be added to or deducted from the cash balance according to the bank statement.

To illustrate a bank reconciliation, we will use the bank statement for Monroe Company in Exhibit 4. This bank statement shows a balance of $3,359.78 as of July 31. The cash balance in Monroe Company's ledger as of the same date is $2,549.99. The following reconciling items are revealed by using the steps outlined above:

Deposit of July 31 not recorded on bank statement . . . . $ 816.20
Checks outstanding: No. 812, $1,061.00; No. 878, $435.39; No. 883, $48.60 . . . . . .   1,544.99
Note plus interest of $8 collected by bank (credit memorandum), not recorded
    in the journal 408.00
Check from customer (Thomas Ivey) returned by bank because of insufficient
    funds (NSF) 300.00
Bank service charges (debit memorandum) not recorded in the journal 18.00
Check No. 879 for $732.26 to Taylor Co. on account, recorded in the journal
    as $723.26 . . . .   9.00

EXHIBIT 6
Bank Reconciliation for
Monroe Company

The bank reconciliation based on the bank statement and the reconciling items is shown in Exhibit 6.

Monroe Company Bank Reconciliation July 31, 2000					
Cash balance according to bank statement		$3 3 5 9 78	Cash balance according to depositor's records		$2 5 4 9 99
Add deposit of July 31, not recorded by bank		8 1 6 20	Add note and interest collected by bank		4 0 8 00
		$4 1 7 5 98			$2 9 5 7 99
			Deduct: Check returned because		
Deduct outstanding checks:			of insufficient funds	$ 3 0 0 00	
No. 812	$1 0 6 1 00		Bank service charges	1 8 00	
No. 878	4 3 5 39		Error in recording		
No. 883	4 8 60	1 5 4 4 99	Check No. 879	9 00	3 2 7 00
Adjusted balance		$2 6 3 0 99	Adjusted balance		$2 6 3 0 99

Entries must be made in the depositor's accounts for any items that affect the business's record of cash.

No entries are necessary on the depositor's records as a result of the information included in the first section of the bank reconciliation. This section begins with the cash balance according to the bank statement. However, the bank should be notified of any errors that need to be corrected on its records.

Any items in the second section of the bank reconciliation must be recorded in the depositor's accounts. This section begins with the cash balance according to the depositor's records. For example, journal entries should be made for any unrecorded bank memorandums and any depositor's errors.

The journal entries for Monroe Company, based on the bank reconciliation above, are as follows:

1	July	31	Cash	4 0 8 00		1
2			Notes Receivable		4 0 0 00	2
3			Interest Revenue		8 00	3
4			Note collected by bank.			4
5						5
6		31	Accounts Receivable—Thomas Ivey	3 0 0 00		6
7			Miscellaneous Administrative Expense	1 8 00		7
8			Accounts Payable—Taylor Co.	9 00		8
9			Cash		3 2 7 00	9
10			NSF check, bank service charges, and error			10
11			in recording Check No. 879.			11

Q & A *Assume that the bank recorded a deposit of $4,100 as $1,400. How would this bank error be shown on the bank reconciliation?*

The error of $2,700 would be added to the cash balance according to the bank statement.

After these entries have been posted, the cash account will have a debit balance of $2,630.99. This balance agrees with the adjusted cash balance shown on the bank reconciliation. This is the amount of cash available as of July 31 and the amount that would be reported on Monroe Company's July 31 balance sheet.

Although businesses may reconcile their bank accounts in a slightly different format from what we described above, the objective is the same: to control cash by reconciling the company's records to the records of an independent outside source, the bank. In doing so, any errors or misuse of cash may be detected.

For effective control, the bank reconciliation should be prepared by an employee who does not take part in or record cash transactions. When these duties are not properly separated, mistakes are likely to occur, and it is more likely that cash will be stolen or otherwise misapplied. For example, an employee who takes part in all of these duties could prepare and cash an unauthorized check, omit it from the accounts, and omit it from the reconciliation.

Point of INTEREST

Many of you reconcile your bank account each month after you receive your bank statements. First you scan the bank statement for any bank entries that you have not yet recorded. Examples of such entries include service charges (a debit entry) and interest earned (a credit entry). You then enter these amounts in your checkbook (register) and determine the balance of your account. If you stop at this point, you are assuming that the bank hasn't made any errors. This may not be a good assumption.

If you fully reconcile your account, you should also scan your checkbook for items that the bank has not yet recorded: (1) deposits in transit and (2) outstanding checks. Deposits in transit should be added to the bank balance, and outstanding checks should be subtracted from the bank balance. The result is an adjusted bank balance which should agree with the balance of your checkbook. If the two are not equal, either you or the bank has made an error.

Petty Cash

OBJECTIVE 6

Account for small cash transactions, using a petty cash fund.

As in your own day-to-day life, it is usually not practical for a business to write checks to pay small amounts, such as postage. Yet, these small payments may occur often enough to add up to a significant total amount. Thus, it is desirable to control such payments. For this purpose, a special cash fund, called a **petty cash fund**, is used.

A petty cash fund is established by first estimating the amount of cash needed for payments from the fund during a period, such as a week or a month. After necessary approvals, a check is written and cashed for this amount.

 Businesses often use other cash funds to meet their special needs, such as travel expenses for salespersons. For example, each salesperson might be given $1,000 for travel-related expenses. Periodically, the salesperson submits a detailed expense report and their travel funds are replenished.

The money obtained from cashing the check is then given to an employee, called the petty cash custodian, who is authorized to disburse monies from the fund. For control purposes, the company may place restrictions on the maximum amount and the types of payments that may be made from the fund.

Each time monies are paid from petty cash, the custodian records the details of the payment on a petty cash receipt form. A typical petty cash receipt is illustrated in Exhibit 7.

EXHIBIT 7
Petty Cash Receipt

```
                    PETTY CASH RECEIPT

No. _____121_____              Date ___August 1, 2001___

Paid to _____Metropolitan Times_____      Amount
                                              ┌─────────┐
For _____Daily newspaper_____     │  3 │ 00 │
                                              └─────────┘
Charge to ___Miscellaneous Administrative Expense___

Payment received:

_____S.O. Hall_____   Approved by ____N.E.R.____
```

The petty cash fund is normally replenished at periodic intervals or when it is depleted or reaches a minimum amount. When a petty cash fund is replenished, the accounts debited are determined by summarizing the petty cash receipts. A check is then written for this amount, payable to the petty cash custodian.

To illustrate normal petty cash fund entries, assume that a petty cash fund of $100 is established on August 1. The entry to record this transaction is as follows:

13	Aug.	1	Petty Cash	1 0 0 00		13
14			Cash		1 0 0 00	14
15			Established petty cash fund.			15

At the end of August, the petty cash receipts indicate expenditures for the following items: office supplies, $28; postage (office supplies), $22; store supplies, $35; and daily newspapers (miscellaneous administrative expense), $3. The entry to replenish the petty cash fund on August 31 is as follows:

17	Aug.	31	Office Supplies	5 0 00		17
18			Store Supplies	3 5 00		18
19			Miscellaneous Administrative Expense	3 00		19
20			Cash		8 8 00	20
21			Replenished petty cash fund.			21

> **Q&A**
>
> *If the petty cash account has a balance of $200, the cash in the fund totals $20, and the petty cash receipts total $180 at the end of a period, what account is credited and what is the amount of the credit in the entry to replenish the fund?*
>
> ----------------------
>
> Cash is credited for $180.

Replenishing the petty cash fund restores it to its original amount of $100. You should note that there is no entry in Petty Cash when the fund is replenished. Petty Cash is debited only when the fund is initially set up or when the amount of the fund is increased at a later time. Petty Cash is credited if it is being decreased.

Petty Cash is debited only when the fund is set up or the amount of the fund is increased.

Presentation of Cash on the Balance Sheet

OBJECTIVE 7

Summarize how cash is presented on the balance sheet.

Cash is the most liquid asset, and therefore it is listed as the first asset in the Current Assets section of the balance sheet. Most companies present only a single cash amount on the balance sheet by combining all their bank and cash fund accounts.

A company may have cash in excess of its operating needs. In such cases, the company normally invests in highly liquid investments in order to earn interest. These investments are called **cash equivalents**.[4] Examples of cash equivalents include U.S. Treasury Bills, notes issued by major corporations (referred to as commercial paper), and money market funds. Companies that have invested excess cash in cash equivalents usually report *Cash and cash equivalents* as one amount on the balance sheet.

Banks may require depositors to maintain minimum cash balances in their bank accounts. Such a balance is called a **compensating balance**. This requirement is often imposed by the bank as a part of a loan agreement or line of credit. A *line of credit* is a preapproved amount the bank is willing to lend to a customer upon request. Compensating balance requirements should be disclosed in notes to the financial statements.

The following note discloses compensating balance requirements for **Kmart Corporation**: . . . *In support of lines of credit, it is expected that compensating balances will be maintained on deposit with the banks, which will average 10% of the line to the extent that it is not in use and an additional 10% on the portion in use. . . .*

FINANCIAL ANALYSIS AND INTERPRETATION

OBJECTIVE 8

Compute and interpret the ratio of cash to current liabilities.

In an earlier chapter, we discussed the use of working capital and the current ratio in evaluating a company's ability to pay its current liabilities (short-term solvency). Both of these measures assume that the noncash current assets will be converted to cash in time to pay the current liabilities. For most companies, these measures are useful for assessing short-term solvency. However, a company that is in financial distress may have difficulty converting its receivables, inventory, and prepaid assets to cash on a timely basis. In these cases, the ratio of cash to current liabilities may be useful in assessing the ability of creditors to collect what they are owed. Because this ratio is most relevant for companies in financial distress, it is called the **doomsday ratio**.[5] Its name comes from the worst case assumption that the business ceases to exist and only the cash on hand is available to meet creditor obligations.

In computing the ratio of cash to current liabilities, cash and cash equivalents are used in the numerator, as shown below.

$$\text{Doomsday ratio} = \frac{\textbf{Cash and cash equivalents}}{\textbf{Current liabilities}}$$

To illustrate, assume the following data for Laettner Co. and Oakley Co. for the current year:

---

[4] To be classified as a cash equivalent, according to *FASB Statement 95*, the investment is expected to be converted to cash within 90 days.
[5] This ratio is discussed more fully in *101 Business Ratios* by Sheldon Gates, McLane Publications, Scottsdale, Arizona, 1993.

	Laettner Co.	Oakley Co.
Cash and cash equivalents	$100,000	$ 120,000
Current liabilities	400,000	1,500,000

The doomsday ratio for each company is computed as follows. In this case, Oakley Co. is more risky to creditors than is Laettner.

	Doomsday Ratio	
Laettner Co.	0.25	($100,000/$400,000)
Oakley Co.	0.08	($120,000/$1,500,000)

Because most businesses maintain cash and cash equivalents at amounts substantially less than their current liabilities, the doomsday ratio is almost always less than one. For example, the doomsday ratio for **Tandy Corporation** is 0.15. For **La-Z-Boy Chair Company**, it is 0.28.

Differences among companies will occur because of differences in management philosophy and operating styles. Nevertheless, a comparison over time that indicates a decreasing ratio generally indicates more risk for creditors.

ENCORE

The Theft at Perini Corporation

The financial vice-president of **Perini Corporation** received a disturbing call from one of the company's banks. The bank reported that Perini's bank account was substantially overdrawn. Perini, a large construction company based near Boston, had never overdrawn any of its bank accounts in over twenty-five years. Shortly thereafter, another of Perini's banks called and reported that its Perini account was also overdrawn. A review of the recent bank statements, which had been lying around unreconciled for two weeks, revealed canceled checks of more than $1.1 million that had not been recorded.

Perini kept its unused checks in an unlocked room. Perini also kept its supply of coffee cups in the same room, where every clerk and secretary had access to them. A quick review revealed two missing boxes of checks.

Perini used a checkwriting machine that automatically signed the vice-president's name. Unfortunately, Perini didn't implement the controls suggested by its auditor. Instead, the machine-processed checks were placed in an unlocked box, there was no reconciliation of the counter on the machine with the number of checks that should have been written, and the keys to lock the machine were not carefully safeguarded. The vice-president said that such controls were "too much trouble."

The rest of the story involves a possible suspect who is killed in a lovers' feud involving a neurosurgeon; a bizarre arson in Perini's financial offices; a hit-and-run accident involving a boat; and a quiet, $22,000-a-year accountant who purchased a new Continental, moved to Las Vegas, bought an $85,000 house, and began running sex shows in casinos. Even though the FBI assigned one of its best agents to the case, the money was never recovered and the perpetrator of the theft remains a mystery. ■

1 Describe the nature of cash and the importance of internal control over cash.

Cash includes coins, currency (paper money), checks, money orders, and money on deposit that is available for unrestricted withdrawal from banks and other financial institutions. Because of the ease with which money can be transferred, businesses should design and use controls that safeguard cash and authorize cash transactions.

2 Summarize basic procedures for achieving internal control over cash receipts.

One of the most important controls to protect cash received in over-the-counter sales is a cash register. A remittance advice is a preventive control for cash received through the mail. Separating the duties of handling cash and recording cash is also a preventive control.

3 Summarize basic procedures for achieving internal control over cash payments, including the use of a voucher system.

A voucher system is a set of procedures for authorizing and recording liabilities and cash payments. A voucher system uses vouchers, a file for unpaid vouchers, and a file for paid vouchers.

4 Describe the nature of a bank account and its use in controlling cash.

The forms used with bank accounts are a signature card, deposit ticket, check, and record of checks drawn. Each month, the bank usually sends a bank statement to the depositor, summarizing all of the transactions for the month. The bank statement allows a business to compare the cash transactions recorded in the accounting records to those recorded by the bank.

5 Prepare a bank reconciliation and journalize any necessary entries.

The first section of the bank reconciliation begins with the cash balance according to the bank statement. This balance is adjusted for the depositor's changes in cash that do not appear on the bank statement and for any bank errors. The second section begins with the cash balance according to the depositor's records. This balance is adjusted for the bank's changes in cash that do not appear on the depositor's records and for any depositor errors. The adjusted balances for the two sections must be equal.

No entries are necessary on the depositor's records as a result of the information included in the first section of the bank reconciliation. However, the items in the second section must be

journalized on the depositor's records.

6 Account for small cash transactions, using a petty cash fund.

A petty cash fund may be used by a business to make small payments that occur frequently. The money in a petty cash fund is placed in the custody of a specific employee, who authorizes payments from the fund. Periodically or when the amount of money in the fund is depleted or reduced to a minimum amount, the fund is replenished.

7 Summarize how cash is presented on the balance sheet.

Cash is listed as the first asset in the Current Assets section of the balance sheet. Companies that have invested excess cash in highly liquid investments usually report *Cash and cash equivalents* on the balance sheet.

8 Compute and interpret the ratio of cash to current liabilities.

A company that is in financial distress may have difficulty converting its receivables, inventory, and prepaid assets to cash on a timely basis. In these cases, the ratio of cash to current liabilities, called the doomsday ratio, may be useful in assessing the ability of creditors to collect what they are owed.

The bank statement for Urethane Company for June 30 indicates a balance of $9,143.11. All cash receipts are deposited each evening in a night depository, after banking hours. The accounting records indicate the following summary data for cash receipts and payments for June:

Cash balance as of June 1	$ 3,943.50
Total cash receipts for June	28,971.60
Total amount of checks issued in June	28,388.85

Comparing the bank statement and the accompanying canceled checks and memorandums with the records reveals the following reconciling items:

a. The bank had collected for Urethane Company $1,030 on a note left for collection. The face of the note was $1,000.
b. A deposit of $1,852.21, representing receipts of June 30, had been made too late to appear on the bank statement.
c. Checks outstanding totaled $5,265.27.
d. A check drawn for $139 had been incorrectly charged by the bank as $157.
e. A check for $30 returned with the statement had been recorded in the depositor's records as $240. The check was for the payment of an obligation to Avery Equipment Company for the purchase of office supplies on account.
f. Bank service charges for June amounted to $18.20.

Instructions

1. Prepare a bank reconciliation for June.
2. Journalize the entries that should be made by Urethane Company.

Solution

1.

Urethane Company
Bank Reconciliation
June 30, 20—

Cash balance according to bank statement		$ 9,143.11
Add: Deposit of June 30 not recorded by bank	$1,852.21	
Bank error in charging check as $157 instead of $139 . . .	18.00	1,870.21
		$11,013.32
Deduct: Outstanding checks		5,265.27
Adjusted balance		$ 5,748.05
Cash balance according to depositor's records		$ 4,526.25*
Add: Proceeds of note collected by bank, including $30 interest	$1,030.00	
Error in recording check	210.00	1,240.00
		$ 5,766.25
Deduct: Bank service charges		18.20
Adjusted balance		$ 5,748.05

*$3,943.50 + $28,971.60 − $28,388.85

2.

Cash	1,240.00	
Notes Receivable		1,000.00
Interest Revenue		30.00
Accounts Payable		210.00
Miscellaneous Administrative Expense	18.20	
Cash		18.20

SELF-EXAMINATION QUESTIONS   Answers at End of Chapter

Matching

Match each of the following statements with its proper term. Some terms may not be used.

A. bank reconciliation	___ 1. Coins, currency (paper money), checks, money orders, and money on deposit that is available for unrestricted withdrawal from banks and other financial institutions.
B. bank statement	
C. cash	___ 2. A set of procedures for authorizing and recording liabilities and cash payments.

D. **cash equivalents**
E. **cash receipts journal**
F. **cash short and over**
G. **doomsday ratio**
H. **electronic funds transfer (EFT)**
I. **notes receivable**
J. **petty cash fund**
K. **voucher**
L. **voucher system**
M. **working capital ratio**

___ 3. A special form for recording relevant data about a liability and the details of its payment.

___ 4. A system in which computers rather than paper (money, checks, etc.) are used to effect cash transactions.

___ 5. A special cash fund to pay relatively small amounts.

___ 6. The analysis that details the items responsible for the difference between the cash balance reported in the bank statement and the balance of the cash account in the ledger.

___ 7. Highly liquid investments that are usually reported with cash on the balance sheet.

___ 8. The ratio of cash and cash equivalents to current liabilities.

Multiple Choice

1. The bank erroneously charged Tropical Services' account for $450.50 for a check that was correctly written and recorded by Tropical Services as $540.50. To reconcile the bank account of Tropical Services at the end of the month, you would:
   A. add $90 to the cash balance according to the bank statement.
   B. add $90 to the cash balance according to Tropical Services' records.
   C. deduct $90 from the cash balance according to the bank statement.
   D. deduct $90 from the cash balance according to Tropical Services' records.

2. In preparing a bank reconciliation, the amount of checks outstanding would be:
   A. added to the cash balance according to the bank statement.
   B. deducted from the cash balance according to the bank statement.
   C. added to the cash balance according to the depositor's records.
   D. deducted from the cash balance according to the depositor's records.

3. Journal entries based on the bank reconciliation are required for:
   A. additions to the cash balance according to the depositor's records.
   B. deductions from the cash balance according to the depositor's records.
   C. both A and B.
   D. neither A nor B.

4. A petty cash fund is:
   A. used to pay relatively small amounts.
   B. established by estimating the amount of cash needed for disbursements of relatively small amounts during a specified period.
   C. reimbursed when the amount of money in the fund is reduced to a predetermined minimum amount.
   D. all of the above.

5. Which of the following is the correct entry to replenish a petty cash fund?
   A. Debit Petty Cash; credit Cash
   B. Debit various expense accounts; credit Petty Cash
   C. Debit various expense accounts; credit Cash
   D. Debit Cash; credit Petty Cash

CLASS DISCUSSION QUESTIONS

1. Why is cash the asset that often warrants the most attention in the design of an effective internal control structure?

2. The combined cash count of all cash registers at the close of business is $14 less than the cash sales indicated by the cash register tapes. (a) In what account is the cash shortage recorded? (b) Are cash shortages debited or credited to this account?

3. In which section of the income statement would a credit balance in Cash Short and Over be reported?

4. Before a voucher for the purchase of merchandise is approved for payment, supporting documents should be compared to verify the accuracy of the liability. Name an example of a supporting document for the purchase of merchandise.

5. When is a voucher recorded?

6. The accounting clerk pays all obligations by prenumbered checks. What are the strengths and weaknesses in the internal control over cash payments in this situation?

7. In what order are vouchers ordinarily filed (a) in the unpaid voucher file and (b) in the paid voucher file? Give reasons for the answers.

8. The balance of Cash is likely to differ from the bank statement balance. What two factors are likely to be responsible for the difference?

9. What is the purpose of preparing a bank reconciliation?

10. Do items reported on the bank statement as credits represent (a) additions made by the bank to the depositor's balance, or (b) deductions made by the bank from the depositor's balance?

11. What entry should be made if a check received from a customer and deposited is returned by the bank for lack of sufficient funds (an NSF check)?

12. Explain why some cash payments are made in coins and currency from a petty cash fund.

13. What account or accounts are debited when (a) establishing a petty cash fund and (b) replenishing a petty cash fund?

14. The petty cash account has a debit balance of $500. At the end of the accounting period, there is $93 in the petty cash fund, along with petty cash receipts totaling $407. Should the fund be replenished as of the last day of the period? Discuss.

15. How are cash equivalents reported in the financial statements?

16. How is a compensating balance reported in the financial statements?

Resources for Your Success On-Line at warren.swcollege.com
Remember! If you need additional help, visit South-Western's Web site. See page 26 for a description of the online and printed materials that are available.

EXERCISES

Exercise 7–1
Internal control of cash receipts

Objective 2

The procedures used for over-the-counter receipts are as follows. At the close of each day's business, the sales clerks count the cash in their respective cash drawers, after which they determine the amount recorded by the cash register and prepare the memorandum cash form, noting any discrepancies. An employee from the cashier's office counts the cash, compares the total with the memorandum, and takes the cash to the cashier's office.

a. ▄▄▄▶ Indicate the weak link in internal control.
b. ▄▄▄▶ How can the weakness be corrected?

Exercise 7–2
Internal control of cash receipts

Objective 2

Don Carey works at the drive-through window of Bob's Burgers. Occasionally, when a drive-through customer orders, Don fills the order and pockets the customer's money. He does not ring up the order on the cash register.
▄▄▄▶ Identify the internal control weaknesses that exist at Bob's Burgers, and discuss what can be done to prevent this theft.

Exercise 7–3
Internal control of cash receipts

Objective 2

The mailroom employees send all remittances and remittance advices to the cashier. The cashier deposits the cash in the bank and forwards the remittance advices and duplicate deposit slips to the Accounting Department.

a. ▄▄▄▶ Indicate the weak link in internal control in the handling of cash receipts.
b. ▄▄▄▶ How can the weakness be corrected?

Exercise 7–4
Entry for cash sales; cash short

Objective 2

The actual cash received from cash sales was $11,940.50, and the amount indicated by the cash register total was $11,965.75. Journalize the entry to record the cash receipts and cash sales.

Exercise 7–5
Entry for cash sales; cash over

The actual cash received from cash sales was $13,189.20, and the amount indicated by the cash register total was $13,180.70. Journalize the entry to record the cash receipts and cash sales.

Exercise 7–6
Internal control of cash payments

Objective 3

Panatone Co. is a medium-size merchandising company. An investigation revealed that in spite of a sufficient bank balance, a significant amount of available cash discounts had been lost because of failure to make timely payments. In addition, it was discovered that several purchases invoices had been paid twice.

➤ Outline procedures for the payment of vendors' invoices, so that the possibilities of losing available cash discounts and of paying an invoice a second time will be minimized.

Exercise 7–7
Internal control of cash payments

Objective 3

Comm3 Company, a communications equipment manufacturer, recently fell victim to an embezzlement scheme masterminded by one of its employees. To understand the scheme, it is necessary to review Comm3's procedures for the purchase of services.

The purchasing agent is responsible for ordering services (such as repairs to a photocopy machine or office cleaning) after receiving a service requisition from an authorized manager. However, since no tangible goods are delivered, a receiving report is not prepared. When the Accounting Department receives an invoice billing Comm3 for a service call, the accounts payable clerk calls the manager who requested the service in order to verify that it was performed.

The embezzlement scheme involves Kim Mira, the manager of plant and facilities. Kim arranged for her uncle's company, Gear Industrial Supply and Service, to be placed on Comm3's approved vendor list. Kim did not disclose the family relationship.

On several occasions, Kim would submit a requisition for services to be provided by Gear's Industrial Supply and Service. However, the service requested was really not needed, and it was never performed. Gear would bill Comm3 for the service and then split the cash payment with Kim.

➤ Explain what changes should be made to Comm3's procedures for ordering and paying for services in order to prevent such occurrences in the future.

Exercise 7–8
Bank reconciliation

Objective 5

Identify each of the following reconciling items as: (a) an addition to the cash balance according to the bank statement, (b) a deduction from the cash balance according to the bank statement, (c) an addition to the cash balance according to the depositor's records, or (d) a deduction from the cash balance according to the depositor's records. (None of the transactions reported by bank debit and credit memorandums have been recorded by the depositor.)

1. Check for $37 charged by bank as $73.
2. Check drawn by depositor for $150 but recorded as $1,500.
3. Outstanding checks, $8,512.30.
4. Deposit in transit, $12,300.
5. Note collected by bank, $5,200.00.
6. Check of a customer returned by bank to depositor because of insufficient funds, $650.
7. Bank service charges, $30.

Exercise 7–9
Entries based on bank reconciliation

Objective 5

Which of the reconciling items listed in Exercise 7–8 require an entry in the depositor's accounts?

Exercise 7–10
Bank reconciliation

Objective 5

SPREADSHEET

✓ Adjusted balance: $12,604.70

The following data were accumulated for use in reconciling the bank account of The Skin Saver Co. for October:

a. Cash balance according to the depositor's records at October 31, $12,530.20.
b. Cash balance according to the bank statement at October 31, $11,100.50.
c. Checks outstanding, $3,276.20.
d. Deposit in transit, not recorded by bank, $4,780.40.
e. A check for $340 in payment of an account was erroneously recorded in the check register as $430.
f. Bank debit memorandum for service charges, $15.50.

Prepare a bank reconciliation, using the format shown in Exhibit 6.

Exercise 7–11
Entries for bank reconciliation

Objective 5

Using the data presented in Exercise 7–10, journalize the entry or entries that should be made by the depositor.

Exercise 7–12
Entries for note collected by bank

Objective 5

Accompanying a bank statement for Profumeria Company is a credit memorandum for $13,900, representing the principal ($13,000) and interest ($900) on a note that had been collected by the bank. The depositor had been notified by the bank at the time of the collection, but had made no entries. Journalize the entry that should be made by the depositor to bring the accounting records up to date.

Exercise 7–13
Bank reconciliation

Objective 5

✓ Adjusted balance: $13,055.15

An accounting clerk for The Zhanay Co. prepared the following bank reconciliation:

The Zhanay Co.
Bank Reconciliation
January 31, 2000

Cash balance according to depositor's records		$11,100.75
Add: Outstanding checks	$5,557.12	
Error by The Zhanay Co. in recording Check No. 345 as $2,510 instead of $2,150	360.00	
Note for $1,500 collected by bank, including interest	1,620.00	7,537.12
		$18,637.87
Deduct: Deposit in transit on January 31	$1,150.00	
Bank service charges	25.60	1,175.60
Cash balance according to bank statement		$17,462.27

a. From the data in the above bank reconciliation, prepare a new bank reconciliation for The Zhanay Co. using the format shown in the illustrative problem.
b. If a balance sheet were prepared for The Zhanay Co. on January 31, 2000, what amount should be reported for cash?

Exercise 7–14
Using bank reconciliation to determine cash receipts stolen

Objective 5

✓ a. $238.36

Monarch Co. records all cash receipts on the basis of its cash register tapes. Monarch Co. discovered during June 2000 that one of its sales clerks had stolen an undetermined amount of cash receipts when he took the daily deposits to the bank. The following data have been gathered for June:

Cash in bank according to the general ledger	$ 9,573.22
Cash according to the June 30, 2000 bank statement	12,271.14
Outstanding checks as of June 30, 2000	1,901.38
Bank service charge for June	25.10
Note receivable, including interest collected by bank in June	1,060.00

No deposits were in transit on June 30, which fell on a Sunday.

a. Determine the amount of cash receipts stolen by the sales clerk.
b. ◄▬▬► What accounting controls would have prevented or detected this theft?

Exercise 7–15
Bank reconciliation

Objective 5

What's Wrong
WITH THIS?

✓ Corrected adjusted balance: $11,998.02

How many errors can you find in the following bank reconciliation prepared as of the end of the current month?

Enrico Co.
Bank Reconciliation
For the Month Ended June 30, 20—

Cash balance according to bank statement			$12,767.76
Add outstanding checks:			
No. 3721		$ 545.95	
3739		172.75	
3743		459.60	
3744		601.50	1,779.80
			$14,547.56
Deduct deposit of June 30, not recorded by bank			1,010.06
Adjusted balance			$12,537.50
Cash balance according to depositor's records . .			$ 9,048.72
Add: Proceeds of note collected by bank:			
Principal	$3,000.00		
Interest	150.00	$3,150.00	
Service charges		19.50	3,169.50
			$12,218.22
Deduct: Check returned because of			
insufficient funds.		$ 451.20	
Error in recording May 15			
deposit of $1,859 as $1,589		270.00	721.20
Adjusted balance			$11,497.02

Exercise 7–16
Petty cash fund entries

Objective 6

Journalize the entries to record the following:

a. Check No. 2511 is issued to establish a petty cash fund of $500.
b. The amount of cash in the petty cash fund is now $79.30. Check No. 2555 is issued to replenish the fund, based on the following summary of petty cash receipts: office supplies, $215.83; miscellaneous selling expense, $125.60; miscellaneous administrative expense, $68.10. (Since the amount of the check to replenish the fund plus the balance in the fund do not equal $500, record the discrepancy in the cash short and over account.)

Exercise 7–17
Doomsday ratio

Objective 8

  **HAT**

The financial statements for **Hershey Foods Corporation** are presented in Appendix G at the end of the text.

a. Compute the doomsday ratio for Hershey Foods Corporation for 1996 and 1995.
b. What conclusions can be drawn from comparing the ratios for 1996 and 1995?

PROBLEMS SERIES A

Problem 7–1A
Evaluate internal control of cash

Objectives 1, 2, 3

The following procedures were recently installed by Sixto Company:

a. Each cashier is assigned a separate cash register drawer to which no other cashier has access.
b. All sales are rung up on the cash register, and a receipt is given to the customer. All sales are recorded on a tape locked inside the cash register.

c. At the end of a shift, each cashier counts the cash in his or her cash register, unlocks the tape, and compares the amount of cash with the amount on the tape to determine cash shortages and overages.

d. Checks received through the mail are given daily to the accounts receivable clerk for recording collections on account and for depositing in the bank.

e. The bank reconciliation is prepared by the accountant.

f. Disbursements are made from the petty cash fund only after a petty cash receipt has been completed and signed by the payee.

g. Vouchers and all supporting documents are perforated with a PAID designation after being paid by the treasurer.

Instructions

■━━► Indicate whether each of the procedures of internal control over cash represents (1) a strength or (2) a weakness. For each weakness, indicate why it exists.

Problem 7–2A
Transactions for petty cash, cash short and over

Objectives 2, 6

HAT

Levine Company completed the following selected transactions during April of the current year:

April 1. Established a petty cash fund of $1,000.
15. The cash sales for the day, according to the cash register tapes, totaled $9,995.60. The actual cash received from cash sales was $10,008.15.
26. Petty cash on hand was $342.15. Replenished the petty cash fund for the following disbursements, each evidenced by a petty cash receipt:

April 4. Store supplies, $210.75.
6. Express charges on merchandise purchased, $60.50 (Merchandise Inventory).
8. Office supplies, $94.30.
9. Office supplies, $35.20.
12. Postage stamps, $52.00 (Office Supplies).
16. Repair to adding machine, $39.50 (Miscellaneous Administrative Expense).
20. Repair to typewriter, $31.50 (Miscellaneous Administrative Expense).
22. Postage due on special delivery letter, $1.05 (Miscellaneous Administrative Expense).
24. Express charges on merchandise purchased, $115.60 (Merchandise Inventory).

30. The cash sales for the day, according to the cash register tapes, totaled $12,009.50. The actual cash received from cash sales was $11,998.90.
30. Decreased the petty cash fund by $250.

Instructions
Journalize the transactions.

Problem 7–3A
Bank reconciliation and entries

Objective 5

SPREADSHEET

✓ 1. Adjusted balance: $29,393.00

The cash account for Universal Systems at March 31 of the current year indicated a balance of $26,740.50. The bank statement indicated a balance of $33,391.40 on March 31. Comparing the bank statement and the accompanying canceled checks and memorandums with the records reveals the following reconciling items:

a. Checks outstanding totaled $4,943.90.

b. A deposit of $1,215.50, representing receipts of March 31, had been made too late to appear on the bank statement.

c. The bank had collected $2,600 on a note left for collection. The face of the note was $2,500.

d. A check for $675 returned with the statement had been incorrectly recorded by Universal Systems as $765. The check was for the payment of an obligation to Jones Co. for the purchase of office supplies on account.

e. A check drawn for $1,300 had been incorrectly charged by the bank as $1,030.

f. Bank service charges for March amounted to $37.50.

Instructions

1. Prepare a bank reconciliation.
2. Journalize the necessary entries. The accounts have not been closed.

Problem 7–4A

Bank reconciliation and entries

Objective 5

✓ 1. Adjusted balance: $10,131.88

The cash account for Etra Co. at June 1 of the current year indicated a balance of $5,911.95. During June, the total cash deposited was $40,500.40, and checks written totaled $38,850.47. The bank statement indicated a balance of $13,880.45 on June 30. Comparing the bank statement, the canceled checks, and the accompanying memorandums with the records revealed the following reconciling items:

a. Checks outstanding totaled $7,180.27.
b. A deposit of $3,481.70, representing receipts of June 30, had been made too late to appear on the bank statement.
c. A check for $450 had been incorrectly charged by the bank as $400.
d. A check for $136.75 returned with the statement had been recorded by Etra Co. as $316.75. The check was for the payment of an obligation to Scott and Son on account.
e. The bank had collected for Etra Co. $2,400 on a note left for collection. The face of the note was $2,000.
f. Bank service charges for June amounted to $10.

Instructions

1. Prepare a bank reconciliation as of June 30.
2. Journalize the necessary entries. The accounts have not been closed.

Problem 7–5A

Bank reconciliation and entries

Objective 5

✓ 1. Adjusted balance: $13,096.09

Elisha Interiors deposits all cash receipts each Wednesday and Friday in a night depository, after banking hours. The data required to reconcile the bank statement as of August 31 have been taken from various documents and records and are reproduced as follows. The sources of the data are printed in capital letters. All checks were written for payments on account.

CASH ACCOUNT:

Balance as of August 1	$10,578.00

CASH RECEIPTS FOR MONTH OF AUGUST	6,582.60

DUPLICATE DEPOSIT TICKETS:

Date and amount of each deposit in August:

Date	Amount	Date	Amount	Date	Amount
Aug. 2	$869.50	Aug. 12	$780.70	Aug. 23	$731.45
5	701.80	16	600.10	26	601.50
9	819.24	19	701.26	31	777.05

CHECKS WRITTEN:

Number and amount of each check issued in August:

Check No.	Amount	Check No.	Amount	Check No.	Amount
614	$243.50	621	$409.50	628	$ 737.70
615	650.10	622	Void	629	329.90
616	279.90	623	Void	630	882.80
617	395.50	624	770.01	631	1,081.56
618	535.40	625	658.63	632	62.40
619	320.10	626	550.03	633	310.08
620	238.87	627	318.73	634	203.30

Total amount of checks issued in August	$8,978.01

```
                              MEMBER FDIC                              PAGE   1

         AMERICAN NATIONAL BANK         ACCOUNT NUMBER
            OF DETROIT
                                        FROM  8/01/20–    TO  8/31/20–
DETROIT, MI 48201-2500    (313)933-8547
                                        BALANCE        10,422.80

                                     9  DEPOSITS        6,586.35

                                    20  WITHDRAWALS     8,514.11

         ELISHA INTERIORS            4  OTHER DEBITS
                                        AND CREDITS     4,850.50CR

                                        NEW BALANCE    13,345.54
```

* – – – – –CHECKS AND OTHER DEBITS – – – – – – – *			– DEPOSITS –	* – DATE – *	– BALANCE – *
No.580	310.10	No.612	92.50	780.80	08/01	10,801.00
No.613	137.50	No.614	243.50	869.50	08/03	11,289.50
No.615	650.10	No.616	279.90	701.80	08/06	11,061.30
No.617	395.50	No.618	535.40	819.24	08/11	10,949.64
No.619	320.10	No.620	238.87	780.70	08/13	11,171.37
No.621	409.50	No.624	707.01	MS 5,000.00	08/14	15,054.86
No.625	658.63	No.626	550.03	MS 100.00	08/14	13,946.20
No.627	318.73	No.629	329.90	600.10	08/17	13,897.67
No.630	882.80	No.631	1,081.56 NSF 225.40		08/20	11,707.91
No.632	62.40	No.633	310.08	701.26	08/21	12,036.69
				731.45	08/24	12,768.14
				601.50	08/28	13,369.64
		SC	24.10		08/31	13,345.54

```
         EC — ERROR CORRECTION              OD — OVERDRAFT
         MS — MISCELLANEOUS                 PS — PAYMENT STOPPED
         NSF — NOT SUFFICIENT FUNDS         SC — SERVICE CHARGE

  * * *                              * * *                          * * *

         THE RECONCILEMENT OF THIS STATEMENT WITH YOUR RECORDS IS ESSENTIAL.
           ANY ERROR OR EXCEPTION SHOULD BE REPORTED IMMEDIATELY.
```

BANK RECONCILIATION FOR PRECEDING MONTH:

Elisha Interiors
Bank Reconciliation
July 31, 20—

Cash balance according to bank statement		$10,422.80
Add deposit of July 31, not recorded by bank		780.80
		$11,203.60
Deduct outstanding checks:		
No. 580	$310.10	
No. 602	85.50	
No. 612	92.50	
No. 613	137.50	625.60
Adjusted balance		$10,578.00
Cash balance according to depositor's records		$10,605.70
Deduct service charges		27.70
Adjusted balance		$10,578.00

Instructions

1. Prepare a bank reconciliation as of August 31. If errors in recording deposits or checks are discovered, assume that the errors were made by the company. Assume that all deposits are from cash sales. All checks are written to satisfy accounts payable.
2. Journalize the necessary entries. The accounts have not been closed.
3. What is the amount of Cash that should appear on the balance sheet as of August 31?
4. ✏️ If in preparing the bank reconciliation you note that a canceled check for $180 has been incorrectly recorded by the bank as $810, briefly explain how the error would be included in the bank reconciliation and how it should be corrected.

PROBLEMS SERIES B

Problem 7–1B
Evaluating internal control of cash

Objectives 1, 2, 3

The following procedures were recently installed by Epic Company:

a. All mail is opened by the mail clerk, who forwards all cash remittances to the cashier. The cashier prepares a listing of the cash receipts and forwards a copy of the list to the accounts receivable clerk for recording in the accounts.
b. At the end of each day, an accounting clerk compares the duplicate copy of the daily cash deposit slip with the deposit receipt obtained from the bank.
c. The bank reconciliation is prepared by the cashier, who works under the supervision of the treasurer.
d. At the end of each day, any deposited cash receipts are placed in the bank's night depository.
e. At the end of the day, cash register clerks are required to use their own funds to make up any cash shortages in their registers.
f. The accounts payable clerk prepares a voucher for each disbursement. The voucher along with the supporting documentation is forwarded to the treasurer's office for approval.
g. After necessary approvals have been obtained for the payment of a voucher, the treasurer signs and mails the check. The treasurer then stamps the voucher and supporting documentation as paid and returns the voucher and supporting documentation to the accounts payable clerk for filing.
h. Along with petty cash expense receipts for postage, office supplies, etc., several post-dated employee checks are in the petty cash fund.

Instructions
✏️ Indicate whether each of the procedures of internal control over cash represents (1) a strength or (2) a weakness. For each weakness, indicate why it exists.

Problem 7–2B
Transactions for petty cash; cash short and over

Objectives 2, 6

Boron Company completed the following selected transactions during August of the current year:

Aug. 2. Established a petty cash fund of $600.
  17. The cash sales for the day, according to the cash register tapes, totaled $3,970.60. The actual cash received from cash sales was $4,001.75.
  29. Petty cash on hand was $73.80. Replenished the petty cash fund for the following disbursements, each evidenced by a petty cash receipt:
  Aug. 3. Store supplies, $151.50.
    5. Express charges on merchandise sold, $76 (Transportation Out).
    8. Office supplies, $12.75.
    11. Office supplies, $29.30.
    17. Postage stamps, $52 (Office Supplies).
    19. Repair to office calculator, $37.50 (Miscellaneous Administrative Expense).
    22. Postage due on special delivery letter, $1.05 (Miscellaneous Administrative Expense).
    23. Express charges on merchandise sold, $105 (Transportation Out).
    27. Office supplies, $41.15.

Aug. 30. The cash sales for the day, according to the cash register tapes, totaled $3,055.50.
The actual cash received from cash sales was $3,049.10.
31. Increased the petty cash fund by $150.

Instructions

Journalize the transactions.

Problem 7–3B
Bank reconciliation and entries

Objective 5

SPREADSHEET

✓ 1. Adjusted balance: $27,854.30

The cash account for Astoria Carpets at November 30 of the current year indicated a balance of $25,640.30. The bank statement indicated a balance of $31,016.30 on November 30. Comparing the bank statement and the accompanying canceled checks and memorandums with the records revealed the following reconciling items:

a. Checks outstanding totaled $6,169.75.
b. A deposit of $2,917.75, representing receipts of November 30, had been made too late to appear on the bank statement.
c. The bank had collected $3,150 on a note left for collection. The face of the note was $3,000.
d. A check for $2,100 returned with the statement had been incorrectly recorded by Astoria Carpets as $1,200. The check was for the payment of an obligation to Ace Co. for the purchase of office equipment on account.
e. A check drawn for $1,780 had been erroneously charged by the bank as $1,870.
f. Bank service charges for November amounted to $36.00.

Instructions

1. Prepare a bank reconciliation.
2. Journalize the necessary entries. The accounts have not been closed.

Problem 7–4B
Bank reconciliation and entries

Objective 5

✓ 1. Adjusted balance: $15,119.87

The cash account for Ambos Co. at August 1 of the current year indicated a balance of $12,705.37. During August, the total cash deposited was $30,650.75, and checks written totaled $31,770.25. The bank statement indicated a balance of $16,465.50 on August 31. Comparing the bank statement, the canceled checks, and the accompanying memorandums with the records revealed the following reconciling items:

a. Checks outstanding totaled $8,003.84.
b. A deposit of $3,148.21, representing receipts of August 31, had been made too late to appear on the bank statement.
c. The bank had collected for Ambos Co. $3,650 on a note left for collection. The face of the note was $3,500.
d. A check for $390 returned with the statement had been incorrectly charged by the bank as $3,900.
e. A check for $210 returned with the statement had been recorded by Ambos Co. as $120. The check was for the payment of an obligation to Bartles Co. on account.
f. Bank service charges for August amounted to $26.

Instructions

1. Prepare a bank reconciliation as of August 31.
2. Journalize the necessary entries. The accounts have not been closed.

Problem 7–5B
Bank reconciliation and entries

Objective 5

✓ 1. Adjusted balance: $10,022.02

Merrick Company deposits all cash receipts each Wednesday and Friday in a night depository, after banking hours. The data required to reconcile the bank statement as of June 30 have been taken from various documents and records and are reproduced as follows. The sources of the data are printed in capital letters. All checks were written for payments on account.

CASH ACCOUNT:
Balance as of June 1 $7,317.40

CASH RECEIPTS FOR MONTH OF JUNE $8,151.58

DUPLICATE DEPOSIT TICKETS:

Date and amount of each deposit in June:

Date	Amount		Date	Amount		Date	Amount
June 1	$1,080.50		June 10	$ 896.61		June 22	$897.34
3	854.17		15	882.95		24	942.71
8	840.50		17	1,246.74		29	510.06

CHECKS WRITTEN:

Number and amount of each check issued in June:

Check No.	Amount		Check No.	Amount		Check No.	Amount
740	$237.50		747	Void		754	$249.75
741	495.15		748	$450.90		755	172.75
742	501.90		749	640.13		756	113.95
743	671.30		750	276.77		757	407.95
744	506.88		751	299.37		758	359.60
745	117.25		752	537.01		759	701.50
746	298.66		753	380.95		760	486.39

Total amount of checks issued in June $7,905.66

JUNE BANK STATEMENT:

AB AMERICAN NATIONAL BANK OF DETROIT			**MEMBER FDIC**		**PAGE 1**	

DETROIT, MI 48201-2500   (313)933-8547

ACCOUNT NUMBER	
FROM 6/01/20–	TO 6/30/20–
BALANCE	7,447.20
9 DEPOSITS	8,691.77
20 WITHDRAWALS	7,345.91
4 OTHER DEBITS AND CREDITS	2,298.70CR
NEW BALANCE	11,091.76

MERRICK COMPANY

* – – – –CHECKS AND OTHER DEBITS – – – – – –				* – – DEPOSITS – – *	– DATE –	* – – BALANCE– – *
No.731	162.15	No.738	251.40	690.25	06/01	7,723.90
No.739	60.55	No.740	237.50	1,080.50	06/02	8,506.35
No.741	495.15	No.742	501.90	854.17	06/04	8,363.47
No.743	671.30	No.744	506.88	840.50	06/09	8,025.79
No.745	117.25	No.746	298.66	MS 2,500.00	06/09	10,109.88
No.748	450.90	No.749	640.13	MS 125.00	06/09	9,143.85
No.750	276.77	No.751	299.37	896.61	06/11	9,464.32
No.752	537.01	No.753	380.95	882.95	06/16	9,429.31
No.754	449.75	No.756	113.95	1,606.74	06/18	10,472.35
No.757	407.95	No.760	486.39	897.34	06/23	10,475.35
				942.71	06/25	11,418.06
		NSF	291.90		06/28	11,126.16
		SC	34.40		06/30	11,091.76

EC — ERROR CORRECTION	OD — OVERDRAFT
MS — MISCELLANEOUS	PS — PAYMENT STOPPED
NSF — NOT SUFFICIENT FUNDS	SC — SERVICE CHARGE

* * *   * * *   * * *

THE RECONCILEMENT OF THIS STATEMENT WITH YOUR RECORDS IS ESSENTIAL.
ANY ERROR OR EXCEPTION SHOULD BE REPORTED IMMEDIATELY.

BANK RECONCILIATION FOR PRECEDING MONTH:

Merrick Company
Bank Reconciliation
May 31, 20—

Cash balance according to bank statement		$7,447.20
Add deposit for May 31, not recorded by bank		690.25
		$8,137.45
Deduct outstanding checks:		
No. 731	$162.15	
736	345.95	
738	251.40	
739	60.55	820.05
Adjusted balance		$7,317.40
Cash balance according to depositor's records		$7,352.50
Deduct service charges		35.10
Adjusted balance		$7,317.40

Instructions

1. Prepare a bank reconciliation as of June 30. If errors in recording deposits or checks are discovered, assume that the errors were made by the company. Assume that all deposits are from cash sales. All checks are written to satisfy accounts payable.
2. Journalize the necessary entries. The accounts have not been closed.
3. What is the amount of Cash that should appear on the balance sheet as of June 30?
4. ▬▬► If in preparing the bank reconciliation you note that a canceled check for $350 has been incorrectly recorded by the bank as $530, briefly explain how the error would be included in the bank reconciliation and how it should be corrected.

SPECIAL ACTIVITIES

Activity 7–1
The Beeper Co.
Ethics and professional conduct in business

During the preparation of the bank reconciliation for The Beeper Co., Bob Beck, the assistant controller, discovered that State National Bank incorrectly recorded a $1,350 check written by The Beeper Co. as $350. Bob has decided not to notify the bank, but to wait for the bank to detect the error. Bob plans to record the $1,000 error as Other Income if the bank fails to detect the error within the next three months.

▬▬► Discuss whether Bob is behaving in a professional manner.

Activity 7–2
Up Down Electronics
Internal controls

The following is an excerpt from a conversation between two sales clerks, Carol Chern and Will Williams. Both Carol and Will are employed by Up Down Electronics, a locally owned and operated computer retail store.

Carol: Did you hear the news?

Will: What news?

Carol: Agatha and Bailey were both arrested this morning.

Will: What? Arrested? You're putting me on!

Carol: No, really! The police arrested them first thing this morning. Put them in handcuffs, read them their rights—the whole works. It was unreal!

Will: What did they do?

Carol: Well, apparently they were filling out merchandise refund forms for fictitious customers and then taking the cash.

Will: I guess I never thought of that. How did they catch them?

Carol: The store manager noticed that returns were twice that of last year and seemed to be increasing. When he confronted Agatha, she became flustered and admitted to taking the cash, apparently over $4,000 in just three months. They're going over the last six months' transactions to try to determine how much Bailey stole. He apparently started stealing first.

➤ Suggest appropriate control procedures that would have prevented or detected the theft of cash.

Activity 7–3
Healthy Grocery Stores
Internal controls

The following is an excerpt from a conversation between the store manager of Healthy Grocery Stores, Kim Hsu, and Myles Jacobson, president of Healthy Grocery Stores.

Myles: Kim, I'm concerned about this new scanning system.
Kim: What's the problem?
Myles: Well, how do we know the clerks are ringing up all the merchandise?
Kim: That's one of the strong points about the system. The scanner automatically rings up each item, based on its bar code. We update the prices daily, so we're sure that the sale is rung up for the right price.
Myles: That's not my concern. What keeps a clerk from pretending to scan items and then simply not charging his friends? If his friends were buying 10–15 items, it would be easy for the clerk to pass through several items with his finger over the bar code or just pass the merchandise through the scanner with the wrong side showing. It would look normal for anyone observing. In the old days, we at least could hear the cash register ringing up each sale.
Kim: I see your point.

➤ Suggest ways that Healthy Grocery Stores could prevent or detect the theft of merchandise as described.

Activity 7–4
Two by Four Markets
Ethics and professional conduct in business

Leo Peltz and Deborah Ferris are both cash register clerks for Two by Four Markets. Jo Calloway is the store manager for Two by Four Markets. The following is an excerpt of a conversation between Leo and Deborah:

Leo: Debbie, how long have you been working for Two by Four Markets?
Deborah: Almost five years this October. You just started two weeks ago . . . right?
Leo: Yes. Do you mind if I ask you a question?
Deborah: No, go ahead.
Leo: What I want to know is, have they always had this rule that if your cash register is short at the end of the day you have to make up the shortage out of your own pocket?
Deborah: Yes, as long as I've been working here.
Leo: Well, it's the pits. Last week I had to pay in almost $30.
Deborah: It's not that big a deal. I just make sure that I'm not short at the end of the day.
Leo: How do you do that?
Deborah: I just short-change a few customers early in the day. There are a few jerks that deserve it anyway. Most of the time, their attention is elsewhere and they don't think to check their change.
Leo: What happens if you're over at the end of the day?
Deborah: Jo lets me keep it as long as it doesn't get to be too large. I've not been short in over a year. I usually clear about $10 to $20 extra per day.

➤ Discuss this case from the viewpoint of proper controls and professional behavior.

Activity 7–5
Tofel Company
Bank reconciliation and internal control

The records of Tofel Company indicate an August 31 cash balance of $20,806.05, which includes undeposited receipts for August 30 and 31. The cash balance on the bank statement as of August 31 is $18,004.95. This balance includes a note of $3,000 plus $150 interest collected by the bank but not recorded in the journal. Checks outstanding on August 31 were as follows: No. 470, $1,050.20; No. 479, $510; No. 490, $616.50; No. 796, $127.40; No. 797, $520; and No. 799, $851.50.

On August 3, the cashier resigned, effective at the end of the month. Before leaving on August 31, the cashier prepared the following bank reconciliation:

Cash balance per books, August 31		$20,806.05
Add outstanding checks:		
No. 796	$127.40	
797	520.00	
799	851.50	1,198.90
		$22,004.95
Less undeposited receipts		4,000.00
Cash balance per bank, August 31		$18,004.95
Deduct unrecorded note with interest		3,150.00
True cash, August 31		$14,854.95

Calculator Tape of Outstanding Checks:

```
   0.00 *
 127.40 +
 520.00 +
 851.50 +
1,198.90 *
```

Subsequently, the owner of Tofel Company discovered that the cashier had stolen all undeposited receipts in excess of the $4,000 on hand on August 31. The owner, a close family friend, has asked your help in determining the amount that the former cashier has stolen.

1. Determine the amount the cashier stole from Tofel Company. Show your computations in good form.
2. How did the cashier attempt to conceal the theft?
3. a. Identify two major weaknesses in internal controls, which allowed the cashier to steal the undeposited cash receipts.
   b. ●▬▬► Recommend improvements in internal controls, so that similar types of thefts of undeposited cash receipts can be prevented.

Activity 7–6
Into the Real World
Observe internal controls over cash

Select a business in your community and observe its internal controls over cash receipts and cash payments. The business could be a bank or a bookstore, restaurant, department store, or other retailer. In groups of three or four, identify and discuss the similarities and differences in each business's cash internal controls.

Activity 7–7
Into the Real World
Invest excess cash

You have $10,000 cash. Go to the Web site of (or visit) a local bank and collect information about the savings and checking options that are available. Identify the option that is best for you and why it is best.

ANSWERS TO SELF-EXAMINATION QUESTIONS

Matching

1. C   2. L   3. K   4. H   5. J   6. A   7. D   8. G

Multiple Choice

1. **C** The error was made by the bank, so the cash balance according to the bank statement needs to be adjusted. Since the bank deducted $90 ($540.50 − $450.50) too little, the error of $90 should be deducted from the cash balance according to the bank statement (answer C).

2. **B** On any specific date, the cash account in a depositor's ledger may not agree with the account in the bank's ledger because of delays and/or errors by either party in recording transactions. The purpose of a bank reconciliation, therefore, is to determine the reasons for any differences between the two account balances. All errors should then be corrected by the depositor or the bank, as appropriate. In arriving at the adjusted (correct) cash balance according to the bank statement, outstanding checks must be deducted (answer B) to adjust for checks that have been written by the depositor but that have not yet been presented to the bank for payment.

3. **C** All reconciling items that are added to and deducted from the cash balance according to the depositor's records on the bank reconciliation (answer C) require that journal entries be made by the depositor to correct errors made in recording transactions or to bring the cash account up to date for delays in recording transactions.

4. **D** To avoid the delay, annoyance, and expense that is associated with paying all obligations by check, relatively small amounts (answer A) are paid from a petty cash fund. The fund is established by estimating the amount of cash needed to pay these small amounts during a specified period (answer B), and it is then reimbursed when the amount of money in the fund is reduced to a predetermined minimum amount (answer C).

5. **C** The journal entry to replenish the petty cash account debits the various expense accounts for which funds were disbursed and credits Cash (answer C). A petty cash account is established or increased by debiting Petty Cash and crediting Cash (answer A). A petty cash account is decreased or done away with by debiting Cash and crediting Petty Cash (answer D). Entry B is not a normal entry involving petty cash.

8

Receivables

Setting the STAGE

Assume that you have decided to sell your car to a neighbor for $7,500. Your neighbor agrees to pay you $1,500 immediately and the remaining $6,000 in a year. How much should you charge your neighbor for interest?

You could determine an appropriate interest rate by asking some financial institutions what they currently charge their customers. Using this information as a starting point, you could then negotiate with your neighbor and agree upon a rate. Assuming that the agreed-upon rate is 8%, you will receive interest totaling $480 for the one-year loan.

In this chapter, we will describe and illustrate how interest is computed. In addition, we will discuss the accounting for receivables, including uncollectible receivables. Most of these receivables result from a business rendering services or selling merchandise on account.

After studying this chapter, you should be able to:

1 List the common classifications of receivables.

2 Summarize and provide examples of internal control procedures that apply to receivables.

3 Describe the nature of and the accounting for uncollectible receivables.

4 Journalize the entries for the allowance method of accounting for uncollectibles, and estimate uncollectible receivables based on sales and on an analysis of receivables.

5 Journalize the entries for the direct write-off of uncollectible receivables.

6 Describe the nature and characteristics of promissory notes.

7 Journalize the entries for notes receivable transactions.

8 Prepare the Current Assets presentation of receivables on the balance sheet.

9 Compute and interpret the accounts receivable turnover and the number of days' sales in receivables.

Classification of Receivables

OBJECTIVE 1

List the common classifications of receivables.

Many companies sell on credit in order to sell more services or products. The receivables that result from such sales are normally classified as accounts receivable or notes receivable. The term **receivables** includes all money claims against other entities, including people, business firms, and other organizations. These receivables are usually a significant portion of the total current assets.

 The 1996 annual report of **La-Z-Boy Chair Company** reported that receivables made up over 60% of La-Z-Boy's current assets.

Accounts Receivable

The most common transaction creating a receivable is selling merchandise or services on credit. The receivable is recorded as a debit to the accounts receivable account. Such **accounts receivable** are normally expected to be collected within a relatively short period, such as 30 or 60 days. They are classified on the balance sheet as a current asset.

Notes Receivable

As long as notes receivable are expected to be collected within a year, they are normally classified on the balance sheet as a current asset. **Notes receivable** are amounts that customers owe, for which a formal, written instrument of credit has been issued.

Notes are often used for credit periods of more than sixty days. For example, a dealer in automobiles or furniture may require a down payment at the time of sale and accept a note or a series of notes for the remainder. Such arrangements usually provide for monthly payments.

Notes may be used to settle a customer's account receivable. Notes and accounts receivable that result from sales transactions are sometimes called **trade receivables**. Unless we indicate otherwise, we will assume that all notes and accounts receivable in this chapter are from sales transactions.

Point of INTEREST

If you have purchased an automobile on credit, you probably signed a note. From your viewpoint, the note is a note payable. From the creditor's viewpoint, the note is a note receivable.

Other Receivables

Other receivables are normally listed separately on the balance sheet. If they are expected to be collected within one year, they are classified as a current asset. If collection is expected beyond one year, they are classified as a noncurrent asset and reported under the caption *Investments*. **Other receivables** include interest receivable, taxes receivable, and receivables from officers or employees.

OBJECTIVE 2

Summarize and provide examples of internal control procedures that apply to receivables.

Internal Control of Receivables

The principles of internal control that we discussed in prior chapters can be used to establish controls to safeguard receivables. For example, the four functions of credit approval, sales, accounting, and collections should be separated, as shown in Exhibit 1.

EXHIBIT 1
Separating the
Receivable Functions

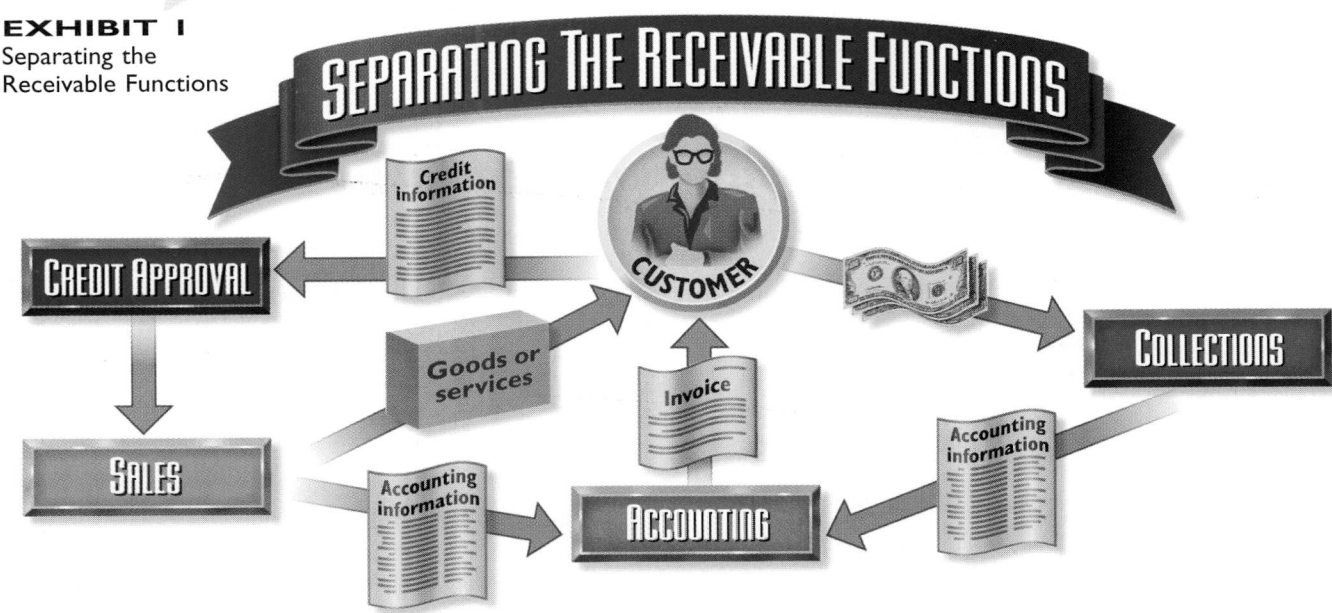

The individuals responsible for sales should be separate from the individuals accounting for the receivables and approving credit. By doing so, the accounting and credit approval functions serve as independent checks on sales. The employee who handles the accounting for receivables should not be involved with collecting receivables. Separating these functions reduces the possibility of errors and misuse of funds.

To illustrate the need to separate functions, assume that the accounts receivable billing clerk has access to cash receipts from customer collections. The clerk can steal a customer's cash payment and then alter the customer's monthly statement to indicate that the payment was received. The customer would not complain and the theft could go undetected.

To further illustrate the need for internal control of receivables, assume that salespersons have authority to approve credit. If the salespersons are paid commissions, say 10% of sales, they can increase their commissions by approving poor credit risks. Thus, the credit approval function is normally assigned to individuals outside the sales area.

Credit standards are used by businesses to decide which customers should receive credit and how much credit they should receive. Setting credit standards requires businesses to assess the customer's "creditworthiness" or credit "quality." Traditionally, assessing creditworthiness involves considering the five Cs of credit. Each of these five Cs is briefly described below.

The Five "Cs"

1. *Character* refers to the probability that the customer will honor an obligation. Many credit managers insist that this is the most important of the Cs. It reflects on the honesty of the customer and the customer's feeling of moral responsibility to honor debts. Credit managers often seek information on a customer's character by making inquiries within the business community. Such inquiries may be made with local bankers, attorneys, other creditors, and even competitors.

2. *Capacity* refers to a customer's ability to pay. Credit managers assess this factor by reviewing the customer's past payment history, a general knowledge of the customer's business, and perhaps even a physical observation of the customer's operations.

3. *Capital* refers to the general condition of the customer's business as assessed from the financial statements. Credit managers usually place special emphasis on solvency and liquidity measures and ratios such as working capital and the current ratio.

4. *Collateral* refers to assets that the customer may be willing to pledge as security for the credit. Financial institutions usually require collateral for major loans to businesses. The collateral may take the form of any asset, such as land, buildings, or inventory.

5. *Conditions* refers to the national and regional economic trends that may affect a customer's ability to pay. For example, during economic downturns credit managers usually tighten credit standards, with the anticipation that more customers will not be able to pay. ■

Uncollectible Receivables

OBJECTIVE 3

Describe the nature of and the accounting for uncollectible receivables.

In prior chapters, we described and illustrated the accounting for transactions involving sales of merchandise or services on credit. A major issue that we have not yet discussed is uncollectible receivables from these transactions.

Businesses attempt to limit the number and amount of uncollectible receivables by using various controls. The primary controls in this area involve the credit-granting function. These controls normally involve investigating customer creditworthiness, using references and background checks. For example, most of us have completed credit application forms requiring such information. Companies may also impose credit limits on new customers. For example, you may have been limited to a maximum of $500 or $1,000 when your credit card was first issued to you.

 In addition to their own credit departments, many businesses use external credit agencies, such as **Dun and Bradstreet**, to evaluate credit customers.

Once a receivable is past due, companies should use procedures to maximize the collection of an account. After repeated attempts at collection, such procedures may include turning an account over to a collection agency.

Retail businesses often attempt to shift the risk of uncollectible receivables to other companies. For example, some retailers do not accept sales on account, but will only accept cash or credit cards. Such policies effectively shift the risk to the credit card companies. Other retailers, such as **Macy's**, **Sears**, and **J.C. Penney's**, have issued their own credit cards.

Companies often sell their receivables to other companies. This transaction is called **factoring** the receivables, and the buyer of the receivables is called a **factor**. An advantage of factoring is that the company selling its receivables receives immediate cash for operating and other needs. In addition, depending upon the factoring agreement, some of the risk of uncollectible accounts may be shifted to the factor.[1]

---

[1] The accounting for the factoring of accounts receivable is discussed in advanced accounting texts.

Regardless of the care used in granting credit and the collection procedures used, a part of the credit sales will not be collectible. The operating expense incurred because of the failure to collect receivables is called **uncollectible accounts expense**, **bad debts expense**, or **doubtful accounts expense**.[2]

When does an account or a note become uncollectible? There is no general rule for determining when an account becomes uncollectible. The fact that a debtor fails to pay an account according to a sales contract or fails to pay a note on the due date does not necessarily mean that the account will be uncollectible. The debtor's bankruptcy is one of the most significant indications of partial or complete uncollectibility. Other indications include the closing of the customer's business and the failure of repeated attempts to collect.

There are two methods of accounting for receivables that appear to be uncollectible. The **allowance method** provides an expense for uncollectible receivables in advance of their write-off.[3] The other procedure, called the **direct write-off method**, recognizes the expense only when accounts are judged to be worthless. We will discuss each of these methods next.

Allowance Method of Accounting for Uncollectibles

OBJECTIVE 4

Journalize the entries for the allowance method of accounting for uncollectibles, and estimate uncollectible receivables based on sales and on an analysis of receivables.

Most large businesses use the allowance method to estimate the uncollectible portion of their trade receivables. To illustrate this method, we will use assumed data for Richards Company. This new business began in August and chose to use the calendar year as its fiscal year. The accounts receivable account has a balance of $105,000 at the end of December.

The customer accounts making up the $105,000 balance in Accounts Receivable include some that are past due. However, Richards doesn't know which specific accounts will be uncollectible at this time. It is likely that some accounts will be collected only in part and that others will become worthless. Based on a careful study, Richards estimates that a total of $4,000 will eventually be uncollectible. The following adjusting entry at the end of the fiscal period records this estimate:

		Adjusting Entry			
Dec.	31	Uncollectible Accounts Expense	4 0 0 0 00		
		Allowance for Doubtful Accounts		4 0 0 0 00	

The adjusting entry reduces receivables to their net realizable value and matches the uncollectible expense with revenues.

Because the $4,000 reduction in accounts receivable is an estimate, it cannot be credited to specific customer accounts or to the accounts receivable controlling account. Instead, a **contra asset** account entitled *Allowance for Doubtful Accounts* is credited.

As with all periodic adjustments, the entry above serves two purposes. First, it reduces the value of the receivables to the amount of cash expected to be realized in the future. This amount, which is $101,000 ($105,000 − $4,000), is called the **net realizable value** of the receivables. Second, the adjusting entry matches the $4,000 expense of uncollectible accounts with the related revenues of the period.

---

[2] If both notes and accounts are involved, both may be included in the expense account title, as in Uncollectible Notes and Accounts Expense, or Uncollectible Receivables Expense.

[3] The allowance method is not acceptable for determining the federal income tax of most taxpayers.

If the balance of accounts receivable is $380,000 and the balance of the allowance for doubtful accounts is $56,000, what is the net realizable value of the receivables?

$324,000 ($380,000 − $56,000)

After the adjusting entry has been posted, as shown in the following T accounts, Accounts Receivable still has a debit balance of $105,000. This balance is the amount of the total claims against customers on account. The credit balance of $4,000 in Allowance for Doubtful Accounts is the amount to be deducted from Accounts Receivable to determine the net realizable value. The balance of the Uncollectible Accounts Expense is reported in the current period income statement, normally as an administrative expense. This classification is used because the credit-granting and collection duties are the responsibilities of departments within the administrative area.

Accounts Receivable			
Aug. 31	20,000	Sept. 30	15,000
Sept. 30	25,000	Oct. 31	25,000
Oct. 31	40,000	Nov. 30	23,000
Nov. 30	38,000	Dec. 31	30,000
Dec. 31	75,000		93,000
Bal. 105,000	198,000		

Allowance for Doubtful Accounts	
	Dec. 31 Adj. 4,000

Uncollectible Accounts Expense	
Dec. 31 Adj. 4,000	

Write-Offs to the Allowance Account

When a customer's account is identified as uncollectible, it is written off against the allowance account as follows:

Jan.	21	Allowance for Doubtful Accounts	6 1 0 00		
		Accounts Receivable—John Parker		6 1 0 00
		To write off the uncollectible		
		account.		

(Fills the bucket)

(Empties the bucket)

The authorization to support this entry should come from a designated manager. It should normally be in writing.

The total amount written off against the allowance account during a period will rarely be equal to the amount in the account at the beginning of the period. The allowance account will have a credit balance at the end of the period if the write-offs during the period are less than the beginning balance. It will have a debit balance if the write-offs exceed the beginning balance. However, after the year-end adjusting entry is recorded, the allowance account should have a credit balance. The flow into and out of the allowance account can be shown as in the illustration at the left.

An account receivable that has been written off against the allowance account may later be collected. In such cases, the account should be reinstated by an entry that reverses the write-off entry. The cash received in payment should then be recorded as a receipt on account. For example, assume that the account of $610 written off in the preceding entry is later collected on June 10. The entry to reinstate the account and the entry to record its collection are as follows:

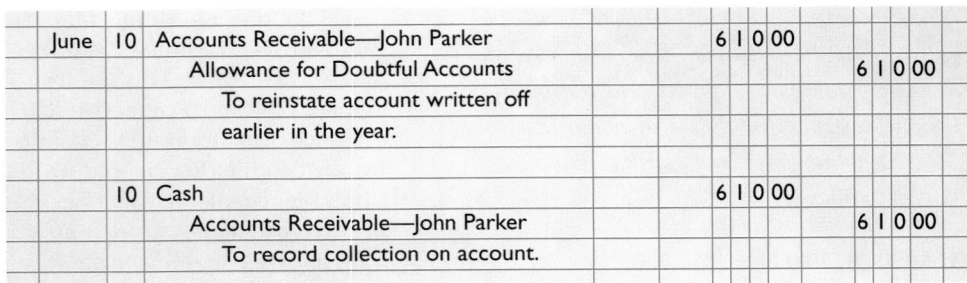

June	10	Accounts Receivable—John Parker		6 1 0 00	
		Allowance for Doubtful Accounts			6 1 0 00
		To reinstate account written off			
		earlier in the year.			
	10	Cash		6 1 0 00	
		Accounts Receivable—John Parker			6 1 0 00
		To record collection on account.			

The percentage of uncollectible accounts will vary across companies and industries. For example, in their annual reports, **J.C. Penney** reported 2.1% of its receivables as uncollectible, **Deere & Company** (manufacturer of John Deere tractors, etc.) reported only 1.2% of its dealer receivables as uncollectible, and **Columbia Healthcare Corporation** reported 31.6% of its receivables as uncollectible.

The two preceding entries can be combined. However, recording two separate entries in the customer's account, with proper notation of the write-off and reinstatement, provides useful credit information.

Estimating Uncollectibles

How is the amount of uncollectible accounts estimated? The estimate of uncollectibles at the end of a fiscal period is based on past experience and forecasts of the future. When the general economy is doing well, the amount of uncollectible expense is normally less than it would be when the economy is doing poorly. The estimate of uncollectibles is usually based on either (1) the amount of sales, as shown on the income statement for the period, or (2) the amount of the receivables, as shown on the balance sheet at the end of the period, and the age of the receivable accounts.

Estimate Based on Sales

Accounts receivable are created by credit sales. The amount of credit sales during the period may therefore be used to estimate the amount of uncollectible accounts expense. The amount of this estimate is added to whatever balance exists in Allowance for Doubtful Accounts. For example, assume that the allowance account has a credit balance of $700 before adjustment. It is estimated from past experience that 1% of credit sales will be uncollectible. If credit sales for the period are $300,000, the adjusting entry for uncollectible accounts at the end of the period is as follows:

The estimate based on sales is *added* to any balance in Allowance for Doubtful Accounts.

		Adjusting Entry			
Dec.	31	Uncollectible Accounts Expense		3 0 0 0 00	
		Allowance for Doubtful Accounts			3 0 0 0 00

Before the year-end adjustment, Allowance for Doubtful Accounts has a credit balance of $45,000. Uncollectible accounts are estimated as 2% of credit sales of $1,200,000. The accounts receivable balance before adjustment is $290,000. What are (1) the uncollectible expense for the period, (2) the balance of Allowance for Doubtful Accounts after adjustment, and (3) the net realizable value of the receivables after adjustment?

----

(1) $24,000 (2% × $1,200,000); (2) $69,000 ($24,000 + $45,000); and (3) $221,000 ($290,000 − $69,000)

After the adjusting entry has been posted, the balance of the allowance account is $3,700. If there had been a debit balance of $200 in the allowance account before the year-end adjustment, the amount of the adjustment would still have been $3,000. The balance in the allowance account would have been $2,800 ($3,000 − $200).

The estimate-based-on-sales method *emphasizes the matching of uncollectible accounts expense with the related sales of the period.* Thus, this method places more emphasis on the income statement than on the balance sheet.

Estimate Based on Analysis of Receivables

The longer an account receivable remains outstanding, the less likely that it will be collected. Thus, we can base the estimate of uncollectible accounts on how long the accounts have been outstanding. For this purpose, we can use a process called **aging the receivables**.

The *Annual Collectibility Survey* conducted by the Commercial Collection Agency Section of the Commercial Law League of America reported the following collection rates:

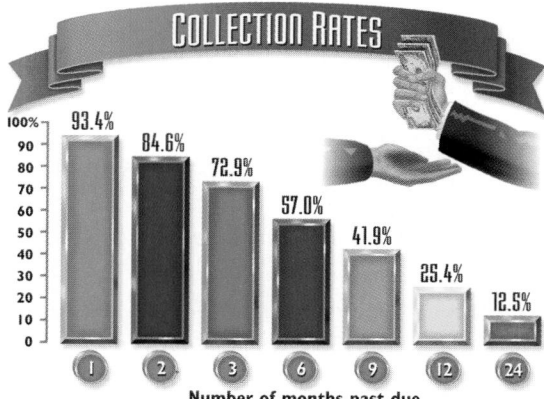

COLLECTION RATES

93.4% 84.6% 72.9% 57.0% 41.9% 25.4% 12.5%

Number of months past due
① ② ③ ⑥ ⑨ ⑫ ㉔

Source: *Boardroom Reports*, May 1994, p. 12.

The beginning point for determining the age of a receivable is its due date. Exhibit 2 shows an example of a typical aging of accounts receivable.

The aging schedule is completed by adding the columns to determine the total amount of receivables in each age group. A sliding scale of percentages, based on industry or company experience, is used to estimate the amount of uncollectibles in each group, as shown in Exhibit 3.

Based on Exhibit 3, the desired balance for the Allowance for Doubtful Accounts is estimated as $3,390. Comparing this estimate with the unadjusted balance of the allowance account determines the amount of the adjusting entry for uncollectible accounts expense. For example, assume that the unadjusted balance

> **The estimate based on receivables is compared to the balance in the allowance account to determine the amount of the adjusting entry.**

EXHIBIT 2
Aging of Accounts Receivable

| Customer | Balance | Not Past Due | Days Past Due | | | | | |
			1–30	31–60	61–90	91–180	181–365	over 365
Ashby & Co.	$ 150			$ 150				
B.T. Barr	610					$ 350	$260	
Brock Co.	470	$ 470						
J. Zimmer Co.	160							160
Total	$86,300	$75,000	$4,000	$3,100	$1,900	$1,200	$800	$300

EXHIBIT 3
Estimate of Uncollectible Accounts

| Age Interval | Balance | Estimated Uncollectible Accounts | |
		Percent	Amount
Not past due	$75,000	2%	$1,500
1–30 days past due	4,000	5	200
31–60 days past due	3,100	10	310
61–90 days past due	1,900	20	380
91–180 days past due	1,200	30	360
181–365 days past due	800	50	400
Over 365 days past due	300	80	240
Total	$86,300		$3,390

of the allowance account is a credit balance of $510. The amount to be added to this balance is therefore $2,880 ($3,390 − $510). The adjusting entry is as follows:

		Adjusting Entry				
Dec.	31	Uncollectible Accounts Expense		2 8 8 0 00		
		Allowance for Doubtful Accounts				2 8 8 0 00

After the adjusting entry has been posted, the credit balance in the allowance account is $3,390, the desired amount. The net realizable value of the receivables is $82,910 ($86,300 − $3,390). If the unadjusted balance of the allowance account had been a debit balance of $300, the amount of the adjustment would have been $3,690 ($3,390 + $300).

Estimates of the uncollectible accounts expense based on the analysis of receivables *emphasizes the current net realizable value of the receivables*. Thus, this method places more emphasis on the balance sheet than on the income statement.

Before the year-end adjustment, Allowance for Doubtful Accounts has a debit balance of $3,000. Using the aging of receivables method, the desired balance of the allowance for doubtful accounts is estimated as $55,000. The accounts receivable balance before adjustment is $290,000. What are (1) the uncollectible expense for the period, (2) the balance of Allowance for Doubtful Accounts after adjustment, and (3) the net realizable value of the receivables after adjustment?

---

(1) $58,000 ($3,000 + $55,000); (2) $55,000; and (3) $235,000 ($290,000 − $55,000)

Direct Write-Off Method of Accounting for Uncollectibles

OBJECTIVE 5

Journalize the entries for the direct write-off of uncollectible receivables.

The allowance method emphasizes reporting uncollectible accounts expense in the period in which the related sales occur. This emphasis on matching expenses with related revenue is the preferred method of accounting for uncollectible receivables.

There are situations, however, where it is impossible to estimate, with reasonable accuracy, the uncollectibles at the end of the period. Also, if a business sells most of its goods or services on a cash basis, the amount of its expense from uncollectible accounts is usually small. In such cases, the amount of receivables is also likely to represent a small part of the current assets. Examples of such a business are a physician's office, an attorney's office, and a small retail store such as a hardware store. In such cases, the direct write-off method of recording uncollectible expense may be used.

Under the direct write-off method, uncollectible accounts expense is not recorded until an account has been determined to be worthless. Thus, an allowance account and an adjusting entry are not needed at the end of the period. The entry to write off an account that has been determined to be uncollectible is as follows:

May	10	Uncollectible Accounts Expense		4 2 0 00		
		Accounts Receivable—D. L. Ross				4 2 0 00
		To write off uncollectible account.				

What if a customer later pays on an account that has been written off? If this happens, the account should be reinstated. The account is reinstated by reversing the earlier write-off entry. For example, assume that the account written off in the May 10 entry is collected in November of the same fiscal year.[4] The entry to reinstate the account is as follows:

Nov.	21	Accounts Receivable—D. L. Ross		4 2 0 00	
		Uncollectible Accounts Expense			4 2 0 00
		To reinstate account written off			
		earlier in the year.			

Cash received in payment of the reinstated amount is recorded in the usual manner. That is, Cash is debited and Accounts Receivable is credited for $420.

Characteristics of Notes Receivable

OBJECTIVE 6

Describe the nature and characteristics of promissory notes.

A claim supported by a note has some advantages over a claim in the form of an account receivable. By signing a note, the debtor recognizes the debt and agrees to pay it according to the terms listed. A note is therefore a stronger legal claim if there is a court action.

A **promissory note** is a written promise to pay a sum of money on demand or at a definite time. It is payable to the order of a person or firm or to the bearer or holder of the note. It is signed by the person or firm that makes the promise. The one to whose order the note is payable is called the **payee**, and the one making the promise is called the **maker**. In the example in Exhibit 4, Pearland Company is the payee and Selig Company is the maker.

EXHIBIT 4
Promissory Note

$ ___2,500.00___   Fresno, California ___March 16___ 20 _00_

___Ninety days___   **AFTER DATE** ___We___ **PROMISE TO PAY TO**

THE ORDER OF ___Pearland Company___

Two thousand five hundred 00/100 - **DOLLARS**

PAYABLE AT ___First National Bank___

VALUE RECEIVED WITH INTEREST AT ___10%___

NO. ___14___ **DUE** ___June 14, 2000___   *H. B. Lane*

                          TREASURER, *SELIG COMPANY*

Notes have several characteristics that affect how they are recorded and reported in the financial statements. We describe these characteristics next.

---

[4] As a practical matter, the entries to record the collection on an account previously written off are the same, regardless of whether the collection occurs in the current period or in a later fiscal period.

Due Date

The date a note is to be paid is called the **due date** or **maturity date**. The period of time between the issuance date and the due date of a short-term note may be stated in either days or months. When the term of a note is stated in days, the due date is the specified number of days after its issuance. To illustrate, the due date of the 90-day note in Exhibit 4 is determined as follows:

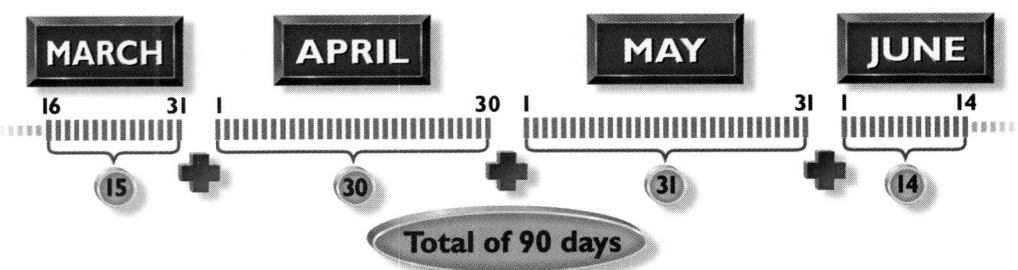

The term of a note may be stated as a certain number of months after the issuance date. In such cases, the due date is determined by counting the number of months from the issuance date. For example, a three-month note dated June 5 would be due on September 5. A two-month note dated July 31 would be due on September 30.

What is the due date of a 120-day note receivable dated September 9?

January 7 [21 days in September (30 days − 9 days) + 31 days in October + 30 days in November + 31 days in December + 7 days in January = 120 days]

Interest

A note normally specifies that interest be paid for the period between the issuance date and the due date.[5] Notes covering a period of time longer than one year normally provide that the interest be paid semiannually, quarterly, or at some other stated interval. When the term of the note is less than one year, the interest is usually payable at the time the note is paid.

The interest rate on notes is normally stated in terms of a year, regardless of the actual period of time involved. Thus, the interest on $2,000 for one year at 12% is $240 (12% of $2,000). The interest on $2,000 for one-fourth of one year at 12% is $60 (1/4 of $240).

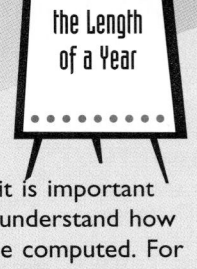

BUSINESS ON STAGE

Whenever a business borrows money or enters into a credit agreement that requires the payment of interest, it is important that the business understand how the interest will be computed. For example, the difference in 180 days' interest computed on the basis of a 365-day year versus a 360-day year is shown below for a loan of $40,000 at an interest rate of 12%.

$40,000 × 0.12 × 180/365 = $2,367.12
$40,000 × 0.12 × 180/360 = $2,400.00

The difference of $32.88 may seem small, but for a business that might enter into thousands of such transactions for millions of dollars, the difference between computing interest on a 360-day year versus a 365-day year can be significant. ∎

Interest and the Length of a Year

Point of INTEREST

Your credit card balances that are not paid at the end of the month incur an interest charge expressed as a percent per month. Interest charges of 1½% per month are common. Such charges approximate an annual interest rate of 18% per year (1½% × 12). Thus, if you can borrow money at less than 18%, you are better off borrowing the money to pay off the credit card balance.

---

[5] You may occasionally see references to non-interest-bearing notes receivable. Such notes, which are not widely used, normally include an implicit interest rate.

The basic formula for computing interest is as follows:

Face Amount (or Principal) × Rate × Time = Interest

To illustrate the formula, the interest on the note in Exhibit 4 is computed as follows:

$$\$2,500 \times 0.10 \times \frac{90}{360} = \$62.50 \text{ interest}$$

 *What is the maturity value of a $15,000, 90-day, 12% note?*

$15,450 [$15,000 + ($15,000 × 0.12 × 90/360)]

In computing interest for a period of less than one year, agencies of the federal government and many financial institutions use the actual number of days in the year, 365. In the preceding computation, for example, the time would have been stated as 90/365 of one year. To simplify computations, however, we will use 360 days.

Maturity Value

The amount that is due at the maturity or due date is called the **maturity value**. The maturity value of a note is the sum of the face amount and the interest. In the note in Exhibit 4, the maturity value is $2,562.50 ($2,500 face amount plus $62.50 interest).

Accounting for Notes Receivable

OBJECTIVE 7

Journalize the entries for notes receivable transactions.

As we mentioned earlier, a note may be received from a customer to replace an account receivable. To illustrate, assume that a 30-day, 12% note dated November 21, 2000, is accepted in settlement of the account of W. A. Bunn Co., which is past due and has a balance of $6,000. The entry to record the transaction is as follows:

Nov.	21	Notes Receivable	6 0 0 0 00	
		Accounts Receivable—W. A. Bunn Co.		6 0 0 0 00
		Received 30-day, 12% note dated		
		November 21, 2000.		

When the note matures, the entry to record the receipt of $6,060 ($6,000 principal plus $60 interest) is as follows:

Dec.	21	Cash	6 0 6 0 00	
		Notes Receivable		6 0 0 0 00
		Interest Revenue		6 0 00
		Received principal and interest on		
		matured note.		

If the maker of a note fails to pay the debt on the due date, the note is a **dishonored note receivable**. When a note is dishonored, the face value of the note plus any interest due is transferred to the accounts receivable account. For example, assume that the $6,000, 30-day, 12% note received from W. A. Bunn Co. and recorded on November 21 is dishonored at maturity. The entry to transfer the note and the interest back to the customer's account is as follows:

Dec.	21	Accounts Receivable—W. A. Bunn Co.	6 0 6 0 00			
		Notes Receivable			6 0 0 0 00	
		Interest Revenue			6 0 00	
		To record dishonored note and				
		interest.				

The interest of $60 has been earned, even though the note has been dishonored. If the account receivable is uncollectible, the amount of $6,060 will be part of the uncollectible accounts expense.

If a note matures in a later fiscal period, the interest accrued in the period in which the note is received must be recorded by an adjusting entry. For example, assume that a 90-day, 12% note dated December 1, 2000, is received from Crawford Company to settle its account, which has a balance of $4,000. Assuming that the accounting period ends on December 31, the entries to record the receipt of the note, accrued interest, and payment of the note at maturity are shown below.

2000 Dec.	1	Notes Receivable	4 0 0 0 00			
		Accounts Receivable—Crawford				
		Company			4 0 0 0 00	
		Received note in settlement of				
		account.				
	31	Interest Receivable	4 0 00			
		Interest Revenue			4 0 00	
		Adjusting entry for accrued				
		interest, $4,000 × 0.12 × 30/360.				
2001 Mar.						
	1	Cash	4 1 2 0 00			
		Notes Receivable			4 0 0 0 00	
		Interest Receivable			4 0 00	
		Interest Revenue			8 0 00	
		Received payment of note and				
		interest; maturity value, $4,000 ×				
		0.12 × 90/360.				

The interest revenue account is closed at the end of each accounting period. The amount of interest revenue is normally reported in the Other Income section of the income statement.

OBJECTIVE 8

Prepare the Current Assets presentation of receivables on the balance sheet.

Receivables on the Balance Sheet

All receivables that are expected to be realized in cash within a year are presented in the Current Assets section of the balance sheet. It is normal to list the assets in the order of their liquidity. This is the order in which they are expected to be converted to cash during normal operations. An example of the presentation of receivables is shown in the partial balance sheet for Crabtree Co. in Exhibit 5.

EXHIBIT 5
Receivables in Balance Sheet

Crabtree Co. Balance Sheet December 31, 20—				
Assets				
Current assets:				
Cash				$119 5 0 0 00
Notes receivable				250 0 0 0 00
Accounts receivable		$445 0 0 0 00		
Less allowance for doubtful accounts		15 0 0 0 00	430 0 0 0 00	
Interest receivable			14 5 0 0 00	

The following credit risk disclosure appeared in the financial statements of **Deere & Company**:

Credit receivables have significant concentrations of credit risk in the agricultural, industrial, lawn and grounds care, and recreational (non-Deere equipment) business sectors. . . . The portions of credit receivables related to the agricultural equipment business were 60 percent and 56 percent; those related to the industrial equipment business were 12 percent and 14 percent; those related to the lawn and grounds care equipment business were seven percent and eight percent; and those related to the recreational equipment business were 21 percent and 22 percent, respectively. On a geographic basis, there is not a disproportionate concentration of credit risk in any area. . . .

The balance of Crabtree's notes receivable, accounts receivable, and interest receivable accounts are reported in Exhibit 5. The allowance for doubtful accounts is subtracted from the accounts receivable. Alternatively, the accounts receivable may be listed on the balance sheet at its net realizable value of $430,000, with a note showing the amount of the allowance. If the allowance account includes provisions for doubtful notes as well as accounts, it should be deducted from the total of Notes Receivable and Accounts Receivable.

Other disclosures related to receivables are presented either on the face of the financial statements or in the accompanying notes. Such disclosures include the market (fair) value of the receivables.[6] In addition, if unusual credit risks exist within the receivables, the nature of the risks should be disclosed. For example, if the majority of the receivables are due from one customer or are due from customers located in one area of the country or one industry, these facts should be disclosed.[7]

FINANCIAL ANALYSIS AND INTERPRETATION

OBJECTIVE 9

Compute and interpret the accounts receivable turnover and the number of days' sales in receivables.

Businesses that grant long credit terms tend to have relatively greater amounts tied up in accounts receivable than those granting short credit terms. In either case, it is desirable to collect receivables as promptly as possible. The cash collected from receivables improves solvency and lessens the risk of loss from uncollectible accounts. Two financial measures that are especially useful in evaluating the efficiency in collecting receivables are (1) the accounts receivable turnover and (2) the number of days' sales in receivables.

The **accounts receivable turnover** measures how frequently during the year the accounts receivable are being converted to cash. For example, with credit terms of 2/10, n/30 days, the accounts receivable should turn over slightly more than twelve times per year. The accounts receivable turnover is computed as follows:

---

[6] *Statement of Financial Accounting Standards, No. 107,* "Disclosures about Fair Value of Financial Instruments," Financial Accounting Standards Board, Norwalk, 1991, pars. 10 and 19.

[7] *Statement of Financial Accounting Standards, No. 105,* "Disclosure of Information about Financial Instruments with Off-Balance Sheet Risk and Financial Instruments with Concentrations of Credit Risk," Financial Accounting Standards Board, Norwalk, 1990, par. 20, and *Statement of Financial Accounting Standards, No. 107, op.cit.,* par. 13.

$$\text{Accounts receivable turnover} = \frac{\text{Net sales on account}}{\text{Average accounts receivable}}$$

The average accounts receivable can be determined by using monthly data or by simply adding the beginning and ending accounts receivable balances and dividing by two. For example, assume that Sidner Company has net sales on account of $36,000,000 and beginning and ending accounts receivable balances of $1,080,000 and $1,220,000. The accounts receivable turnover is 31.3, as shown below:

$$\text{Accounts receivable turnover} = \frac{\text{Net sales on account}}{\text{Average accounts receivable}}$$

$$= \frac{\$36,000,000}{(\$1,080,000 + \$1,220,000)/2} = 31.3$$

The **number of days' sales in receivables** is an estimate of the length of time the accounts receivable have been outstanding. With credit terms of 2/10, n/30 days, the number of days' sales in receivables should be less than 30 days. It is computed as follows:

$$\text{Number of days' sales in receivables} = \frac{\text{Accounts receivable, end of year}}{\text{Average daily sales on account}}$$

Average daily sales on account is determined by dividing net sales on account by 365 days. For example, using the preceding data for Sidner Company, the number of days' sales in receivables is 12.4, as shown below:

$$\text{Number of days' sales in receivables} = \frac{\text{Accounts receivable, end of year}}{\text{Average daily sales on account}}$$

$$= \frac{\$1,220,000}{(\$36,000,000/365 \text{ days})} = 12.4$$

For these measures to be meaningful, a company should compare its current measures with those from prior periods and with industry figures. An improvement in the efficiency in collecting accounts receivable is indicated when the accounts receivable turnover increases and the number of days' sales in receivables decreases.

ENCORE

Need a Friendly Loan?

If you are approached by a stranger and offered a quick loan to help you out of a financial bind, you should probably think twice. A young police officer in Hong Kong wishes he had.

Sergeant Li Chi-lok went to a local casino on a Friday night to play pai kau (Chinese dominoes). By 4 a.m. Saturday, he had lost his $9,000 gambling stake. Tired and out of

money, he watched other gamblers until a young man approached him. "Did you win or lose? If you need money, we have some," the loan shark said. Sergeant Li yielded to temptation and borrowed $10,000, but was only given $9,000—$1,000 was taken as a service charge. When he stopped gambling, he had borrowed $20,000 and owed $25,000.

The loan sharks took Sergeant Li to an apartment, where he was told to call relatives to pay off his debt. However, the interest accumulated rapidly. By midday on Saturday, the amount owed had risen to $33,000. Twelve hours later, it rose to $44,000, and by lunchtime on Sunday it had risen to $60,000. Sergeant Li was allowed to go after his mother deposited $20,000 in a bank account and he signed an IOU for the remaining debt. During his ordeal, Sergeant Li was tied up and severely beaten. His injuries included a punctured lung and a broken leg, arm, and finger.

Loan sharks aren't confined to Hong Kong. In the United Kingdom, there are more than 27,000 legal moneylenders, who charge annual interest rates up to 500%. In the United States, most states have usury laws restricting the amount of interest that a creditor may charge. However, illegal loan sharking still exists. For example, a Boston loan shark and gambling bookie recently pleaded guilty to charging 100 customers interest rates ranging from 100% to

500%. In New York, a restaurant owner testified that he had paid $60,000 on a $20,000 loan, but that it was still not enough to satisfy a Buffalo loan shark. In another case, a woman embezzled more than $100,000 from a doctor she worked for in order to pay her husband's loan shark. She escaped prosecution by cooperating with the FBI's case against the loan shark. ■

APPENDIX: DISCOUNTING NOTES RECEIVABLE

Although it is not a common transaction, a company may endorse its notes receivable and transfer them to a bank. The bank transfers cash (the **proceeds**) to the company, after deducting a **discount** (interest) that is computed on the maturity value of the note for the discount period. The discount period is the time that the bank must hold the note before it becomes due.

To illustrate, assume that a 90-day, 12%, $1,800 note receivable from Pryor & Co., dated April 8, is discounted at the payee's bank on May 3 at the rate of 14%. The data used in determining the effect of the transaction are as follows:

Face value of note dated April 8	$1,800.00
Interest on note (90 days at 12%)	54.00
Maturity value of note due July 7	$1,854.00
Discount on maturity value (65 days from May 3 to July 7, at 14%)	46.87
Proceeds	$1,807.13

The endorser records as interest revenue the excess of the proceeds from discounting the note, $1,807.13, over its face value, $1,800, as follows:

May	3	Cash		1 80 7 13	
		Notes Receivable			1 80 0 00
		Interest Revenue			7 13
		Discounted $1,800, 90-day, 12% note			
		at 14%.			

What if the proceeds from discounting a note receivable are less than the face value? When this situation occurs, the endorser records the excess of the face value over the proceeds as interest expense. The length of the discount period and the difference between the interest rate and the discount rate determine whether interest expense or interest revenue will result from discounting.

Without a statement limiting responsibility, the endorser of a note is committed to paying the note if the maker defaults. This potential liability is called a **contingent liability**. Thus, the endorser of a note that has been discounted has a contingent liability until the due date. If the maker pays the promised amount at maturity, the contingent liability is removed without any action on the part of the endorser. If, on the other hand, the maker dishonors the note and the endorser is notified according to legal requirements, the endorser's liability becomes an actual one.

When a discounted note receivable is dishonored, the bank notifies the endorser and asks for payment. In some cases, the bank may charge a **protest fee** for notifying the endorser that a note has been dishonored. The entire amount paid to the bank by the endorser, including the interest and protest fee, should be debited to the account receivable of the maker. For example, assume that the $1,800, 90-day, 12% note discounted on May 3 is dishonored at maturity by the maker, Pryor & Co. The bank charges a protest fee of $12. The endorser's entry to record the payment to the bank is as follows:

July	7	Accounts Receivable—Pryor & Co.	1 866 00	
		Cash		1 866 00
		Paid dishonored, discounted note		
		(maturity value of $1,854 plus protest		
		fee of $12).		

KEY POINTS

1 List the common classifications of receivables.

The term receivables includes all money claims against other entities, including people, business firms, and other organizations. They are normally classified as accounts receivable, notes receivable, or other receivables.

2 Summarize and provide examples of internal control procedures that apply to receivables.

The internal controls that apply to receivables include the separation of responsibilities for related functions. In this way, the work of one employee can serve as a check on the work of another employee.

3 Describe the nature of and the accounting for uncollectible receivables.

The two methods of accounting for uncollectible receivables are the allowance method and the direct write-off method. The allowance method provides in advance for uncollectible receivables. The direct write-off

method recognizes the expense only when the account is judged to be uncollectible.

4 Journalize the entries for the allowance method of accounting for uncollectibles, and estimate uncollectible receivables based on sales and on an analysis of receivables.

A year-end adjusting entry provides for (1) the reduction of the value of the receivables to the amount of cash expected to be realized from them in the future and (2) the allocation to the current period of the expected expense resulting from such reduction. The adjusting entry debits Uncollectible Accounts Expense and credits Allowance for Doubtful Accounts. When an account is believed to be uncollectible, it is written off against the allowance account.

When the estimate of uncollectibles is based on the amount of sales for the fiscal period, the adjusting entry is made without regard to the balance of the allowance account. When the esti-

mate of uncollectibles is based on the amount and the age of the receivable accounts at the end of the period, the adjusting entry is recorded so that the balance of the allowance account will equal the estimated uncollectibles at the end of the period.

The allowance account, which will have a credit balance after the adjusting entry has been posted, is a contra asset account. The uncollectible accounts expense is generally reported on the income statement as an administrative expense.

5 Journalize the entries for the direct write-off of uncollectible receivables.

Under the direct write-off method, the entry to write off an account debits Uncollectible Accounts Expense and credits Accounts Receivable. Neither an allowance account nor an adjusting entry is needed at the end of the period.

6 Describe the nature and characteristics of promissory notes.

A note is a written promise to pay a sum of money on demand or at a definite time. Characteristics of notes that affect how they are recorded and reported include the due date, interest rate, and maturity value. The basic formula for computing interest on a note is: Principal × Rate × Time = Interest. The due date is the date a note is to be paid, and the period of time between the issuance date and the due date is normally stated in either days or months. The maturity value of a note is the sum of the face amount and the interest.

7 Journalize the entries for notes receivable transactions.

A note received in settlement of an account receivable is recorded as a debit to Notes Receivable and a credit to Accounts Receivable. When a note matures, Cash is debited, Notes Receivable is credited, and Interest Revenue is credited. If the maker of a note fails to pay the debt on the due date, the note is said to be dishonored. When the holder of a dishonored note has been paid by the endorser, the amount of the endorser's claim against the maker of the note is debited to an accounts receivable account.

8 Prepare the Current Assets presentation of receivables on the balance sheet.

All receivables that are expected to be realized in cash within a year are presented in the Current Assets section of the balance sheet. It is normal to list the assets in the order of their liquidity, which is the order in which they can be converted to cash in normal operations.

9 Compute and interpret the accounts receivable turnover and the number of days' sales in receivables.

The accounts receivable turnover is net sales on account divided by average accounts receivable. It measures how frequently accounts receivable are being converted into cash. The number of days' sales in receivables is the end-of-year accounts receivable divided by the average daily sales on account. It measures the length of time the accounts receivable have been outstanding.

ILLUSTRATIVE PROBLEM

Ditzler Company, a construction supply company, uses the allowance method of accounting for uncollectible accounts receivable. Selected transactions completed by Ditzler Company are as follows:

Feb. 1. Sold merchandise on account to Ames Co., $8,000. The cost of the merchandise sold was $4,500.

Mar. 15. Accepted a 60-day, 12% note for $8,000 from Ames Co. on account.

Apr. 9. Wrote off a $2,500 account from Dorset Co. as uncollectible.

21. Loaned $7,500 cash to Jill Klein, receiving a 90-day, 14% note.

May 14. Received the interest due from Ames Co. and a new 90-day, 14% note as a renewal of the loan. (Record both the debit and the credit to the notes receivable account.)

June 13. Reinstated the account of Dorset Co., written off on April 9, and received $2,500 in full payment.

July 20. Jill Klein dishonored her note.

Aug. 12. Received from Ames Co. the amount due on its note of May 14.

19. Received from Jill Klein the amount owed on the dishonored note, plus interest for 30 days at 15%, computed on the maturity value of the note.

Dec. 16. Accepted a 60-day, 12% note for $12,000 from Global Company on account.

31. It is estimated that 3% of the credit sales of $1,375,000 for the year ended December 31 will be uncollectible.

Instructions

1. Journalize the transactions. Omit explanations.
2. Journalize the adjusting entry to record the accrued interest on December 31 on the Global Company note.

Solution

1.

Feb.	1	Accounts Receivable—Ames Co.	8 0 0 0 00		
		Sales		8 0 0 0 00	
	1	Cost of Merchandise Sold	4 5 0 0 00		
		Merchandise Inventory		4 5 0 0 00	
Mar.	15	Notes Receivable—Ames Co.	8 0 0 0 00		
		Accounts Receivable—Ames Co.		8 0 0 0 00	
Apr.	9	Allowance for Doubtful Accounts	2 5 0 0 00		
		Accounts Receivable—Dorset Co.		2 5 0 0 00	
	21	Notes Receivable—Jill Klein	7 5 0 0 00		
		Cash		7 5 0 0 00	
May	14	Notes Receivable—Ames Co.	8 0 0 0 00		
		Cash	1 6 0 00		
		Notes Receivable—Ames Co.		8 0 0 0 00	
		Interest Revenue		1 6 0 00	
June	13	Accounts Receivable—Dorset Co.	2 5 0 0 00		
		Allowance for Doubtful Accounts		2 5 0 0 00	
	13	Cash	2 5 0 0 00		
		Accounts Receivable—Dorset Co.		2 5 0 0 00	
July	20	Accounts Receivable—Jill Klein	7 7 6 2 50		
		Notes Receivable—Jill Klein		5 0 0 0 00	
		Interest Revenue		2 6 2 50	
Aug.	12	Cash	8 2 8 0 00		
		Notes Receivable—Ames Co.		8 0 0 0 00	
		Interest Revenue		2 8 0 00	
	19	Cash	7 8 5 9 53		
		Accounts Receivable—Jill Klein		7 7 6 2 50	
		Interest Revenue		9 7 03	
		($7,762.50 × 15% × 30/360)			
Dec.	16	Notes Receivable—Global Company	12 0 0 0 00		
		Accounts Receivable—Global Company		12 0 0 0 00	
	31	Uncollectible Accounts Expense	41 2 5 0 00		
		Allowance for Doubtful Accounts		41 2 5 0 00	

2.

Dec.	31	Interest Receivable	6 0 00		
		Interest Revenue		6 0 00	
		($12,000 × 12% × 15/360)			

Matching

Match each of the following statements with its proper term. Some terms may not be used.

A.	**accounts receivable**
B.	**accounts receivable turnover**
C.	**aging the receivables**
D.	**allowance method**
E.	**contra asset**
F.	**direct write-off method**
G.	**dishonored note receivable**
H.	**maturity value**
I.	**notes receivable**
J.	**number of days' sales in receivables**
K.	**promissory note**
L.	**receivables**
M.	**uncollectible accounts expense**

____ 1. All money claims against other entities, including people, business firms, and other organizations.

____ 2. A receivable created by selling merchandise or services on credit.

____ 3. Amounts customers owe, for which a formal, written instrument of credit has been issued.

____ 4. The operating expense incurred because of the failure to collect receivables.

____ 5. The method of accounting for uncollectible accounts that provides an expense for uncollectible receivables in advance of their write-off.

____ 6. The method of accounting for uncollectible accounts that recognizes the expense only when accounts are judged to be worthless.

____ 7. The process of analyzing the accounts receivable and classifying them according to various age groupings, with the due date being the base point for determining age.

____ 8. The amount that is due at the maturity or due date of a note.

____ 9. A note that the maker fails to pay on the due date.

____ 10. An estimate of the length of time the accounts receivable have been outstanding.

____ 11. Measures how frequently during the year the accounts receivable are being converted to cash.

____ 12. A written promise to pay a sum of money on demand or at a definite time.

Multiple Choice

1. At the end of the fiscal year, before the accounts are adjusted, Accounts Receivable has a balance of $200,000 and Allowance for Doubtful Accounts has a credit balance of $2,500. If the estimate of uncollectible accounts determined by aging the receivables is $8,500, the amount of uncollectible accounts expense is:
   A. $2,500   C. $8,500
   B. $6,000   D. $11,000

2. At the end of the fiscal year, Accounts Receivable has a balance of $100,000 and Allowance for Doubtful Accounts has a balance of $7,000. The expected net realizable value of the accounts receivable is:
   A. $7,000   C. $100,000
   B. $93,000   D. $107,000

3. What is the maturity value of a 90-day, 12% note for $10,000?

   A. $8,800   C. $10,300
   B. $10,000   D. $11,200

4. What is the due date of a $12,000, 90-day, 8% note receivable dated August 5?
   A. October 31   C. November 3
   B. November 2   D. November 4

5. When a note receivable is dishonored, Accounts Receivable is debited for what amount?
   A. The face value of the note
   B. The maturity value of the note
   C. The maturity value of the note less accrued interest
   D. The maturity value of the note plus accrued interest

CLASS DISCUSSION QUESTIONS

1. What are the three classifications of receivables?
2. What types of transactions give rise to accounts receivable?
3. In what section of the balance sheet should a note receivable be listed if its term is (a) 90 days, (b) 5 years?
4. Give two examples of other receivables.

5. The accounts receivable clerk is also responsible for handling cash receipts. Which principle of internal control is violated in this situation?

6. Which of the two methods of accounting for uncollectible accounts provides for the recognition of the expense at the earlier date?

7. What kind of an account (asset, liability, etc.) is Allowance for Doubtful Accounts, and is its normal balance a debit or a credit?

8. After the accounts are adjusted and closed at the end of the fiscal year, Accounts Receivable has a balance of $601,250 and Allowance for Doubtful Accounts has a balance of $32,250. Describe how the accounts receivable and the allowance for doubtful accounts are reported on the balance sheet.

9. A firm has consistently adjusted its allowance account at the end of the fiscal year by adding a fixed percent of the period's net sales on account. After five years, the balance in Allowance for Doubtful Accounts has become very large in relationship to the balance in Accounts Receivable. Give two possible explanations.

10. Which of the two methods of estimating uncollectibles provides for the most accurate estimate of the current net realizable value of the receivables?

11. For a business, what are the advantages of a note receivable in comparison to an account receivable?

12. Stamm Company issued a promissory note to Blair Company. (a) Who is the payee? (b) What is the title of the account used by Blair Company in recording the note?

13. If a note provides for payment of principal of $20,000 and interest at the rate of 10%, will the interest amount to $2,000? Explain.

14. The maker of a $6,000, 8%, 90-day note receivable failed to pay the note on the due date of June 30. What accounts should be debited and credited by the payee to record the dishonored note receivable?

15. The note receivable dishonored in Question 14 is paid on July 30 by the maker, plus interest for 30 days, 9%. What entry should be made to record the receipt of the payment?

16. Under what caption should accounts receivable be reported on the balance sheet?

Resources for Your Success On-Line at warren.swcollege.com
Remember! If you need additional help, visit South-Western's Web site. See page 26 for a description of the online and printed materials that are available.

EXERCISES

Exercise 8–1
Internal control procedures

Objective 2

Cardinal Company sells carpeting. Over 75% of all carpet sales are on credit. The following procedures are used by Cardinal to process this large number of credit sales and the subsequent collections.

a. All credit sales to a first-time customer must be approved by the Credit Department. Salespersons will assist the customer in filling out a credit application, but an employee in the Credit Department is responsible for verifying employment and checking the customer's credit history before granting credit.

b. Cardinal's standard credit period is 45 days. The Credit Department may approve an extension of this repayment period of up to one year. Whenever an extension is granted, the customer signs a promissory note. Up to 30% of the credit sales in any one year are for repayment periods exceeding 45 days.

c. A formal ledger is not maintained for customers who sign promissory notes. Cardinal simply keeps a copy of each signed note in a file cabinet. These unpaid notes are filed by due date.

d. Cardinal employs an accounts receivable clerk. The clerk is responsible for recording customer credit sales (based on sales tickets), receiving cash from customers, giving customers credit for their payments, and handling all customer billing complaints.

e. The general ledger control account for Accounts Receivable is maintained by the General Accounting Department at Cardinal. This department records total credit sales, based on credit sale information from the store's electronic cash register, and total customer receipts, based on the bank deposit slip.

State whether each of these procedures is appropriate or inappropriate, considering the principles of internal control. If inappropriate, state which internal control procedure is violated.

Exercise 8–2
Nature of uncollectible accounts

Objective 3

✓ a. 4.3%
✓ b. 25.3%

Hilton Hotels Corporation owns and operates casinos at several of its hotels, located primarily in Nevada. At the end of a recent fiscal year, the following accounts and notes receivable were reported (in thousands):

Hotel accounts and notes receivable	$75,796	
Less: Allowance for doubtful accounts	3,256	
		$72,540
Casino accounts receivable	$26,334	
Less: Allowance for doubtful accounts	6,654	
		19,680

a. Compute the percentage of allowance for doubtful accounts to the gross hotel accounts and notes receivable for the end of the fiscal year.

b. Compute the percentage of the allowance for doubtful accounts to the gross casino accounts receivable for the end of the fiscal year.

c. Discuss possible reasons for the difference in the two ratios computed in (a) and (b).

Exercise 8–3
Estimating doubtful accounts

Objective 4

✓ $20,685

Swenson Co. is a wholesaler of office supplies. An aging of the company's accounts receivable on December 31, 2000, and a historical analysis of the percentage of uncollectible accounts in each age category are as follows:

Age Interval	Balance	Percent Uncollectible
Not past due	$325,000	2%
1–30 days past due	86,000	4
31–60 days past due	17,000	9
61–90 days past due	12,000	15
91–180 days past due	7,400	60
Over 180 days past due	3,500	85
	$450,900	

Estimate what the proper balance of the allowance for doubtful accounts should be as of December 31, 2000.

Exercise 8–4
Entry for uncollectible accounts

Objective 4

Using the data in Exercise 8–3, assume that the allowance for doubtful accounts for Swenson Co. had a debit balance of $3,050 as of December 31, 2000.

Journalize the adjusting entry for uncollectible accounts as of December 31, 2000.

Exercise 8–5
Providing for doubtful accounts

Objective 4

✓ a. $10,000
✓ b. $35,600

At the end of the current year, the accounts receivable account has a debit balance of $575,000, and net sales for the year total $4,000,000. Determine the amount of the adjusting entry to provide for doubtful accounts under each of the following assumptions:

a. The allowance account before adjustment has a credit balance of $2,750. Uncollectible accounts expense is estimated at 1/4 of 1% of net sales.
b. The allowance account before adjustment has a credit balance of $2,750. Analysis of the accounts in the customer's ledger indicates doubtful accounts of $38,350.
c. The allowance account before adjustment has a debit balance of $1,050. Uncollectible accounts expense is estimated at 1/2 of 1% of net sales.
d. The allowance account before adjustment has a debit balance of $1,050. Analysis of the accounts in the customer's ledger indicates doubtful accounts of $31,400.

Exercise 8–6
Entries to write off accounts receivable

Objectives 4, 5

Aspen Company, a computer consulting firm, has decided to write off the $2,800 balance of an account owed by a customer. Journalize the entry to record the write-off, (a) assuming that the allowance method is used, and (b) assuming that the direct write-off method is used.

Exercise 8–7
Entries for uncollectible receivables, using allowance method

Objective 4

Journalize the following transactions in the accounts of Alpine Company, a restaurant supply company that uses the allowance method of accounting for uncollectible receivables:

Feb. 20. Sold merchandise on account to J. Renner, $5,500. The cost of the merchandise sold was $3,400.
May 19. Received $3,000 from J. Renner and wrote off the remainder owed on the sale of February 20 as uncollectible.
Sept. 30. Reinstated the account of J. Renner that had been written off on May 19 and received $2,500 cash in full payment.

Exercise 8–8
Entries for uncollectible accounts, using direct write-off method

Objective 5

Journalize the following transactions in the accounts of MedCo Co., a hospital supply company that uses the direct write-off method of accounting for uncollectible receivables:

Mar. 11. Sold merchandise on account to E. Hayes, $6,200. The cost of the merchandise sold was $4,250.
May 1. Received $1,800 from E. Hayes and wrote off the remainder owed on the sale of March 11 as uncollectible.
Aug. 15. Reinstated the account of E. Hayes that had been written off on May 1 and received $4,400 cash in full payment.

Exercise 8–9
Effect of doubtful accounts on net income

Objectives 4, 5

✓ $53,400

During its first year of operations, Klondike Automotive Supply Co. had net sales of $1,050,000, wrote off $32,800 of accounts as uncollectible, using the direct write-off method, and reported net income of $62,600. If the allowance method of accounting for uncollectibles had been used, 4% of net sales would have been estimated as uncollectible. Determine what the net income would have been if the allowance method had been used.

Exercise 8–10
Effect of doubtful accounts on net income

Objectives 4, 5

✓ a. $94,800
✓ b. $26,700

Using the data in Exercise 8–9, assume that during the second year of operations Klondike Automotive Supply Co. had net sales of $1,800,000, wrote off $54,500 of accounts as uncollectible, using the direct write-off method, and reported net income of $112,300.

a. Determine what net income would have been in the second year if the allowance method (using 4% of net sales) had been used in both the first and second years.
b. Determine what the balance of the allowance for doubtful accounts would have been at the end of the second year if the allowance method had been used in both the first and second years.

Exercise 8–11
Determine due date and interest on notes

Objective 6

Determine the due date and the amount of interest due at maturity on the following notes:

✓ a. May 18; $100

	Date of Note	Face Amount	Term of Note	Interest Rate
a.	April 3	$10,000	45 days	8%
b.	May 20	6,000	60 days	10%
c.	August 31	8,000	90 days	14%
d.	June 9	15,000	90 days	10%
e.	October 1	12,500	120 days	12%

Exercise 8–12

Entries for notes receivable

Objectives 6, 7

SPREADSHEET

✓ b. $15,450

Gier Interior Decorators issued a 120-day, 9% note for $15,000, dated March 3, to Everson Furniture Company on account.

a. Determine the due date of the note.
b. Determine the maturity value of the note.
c. Journalize the entries to record the following: (1) receipt of the note by the payee, and (2) receipt by the payee of payment of the note at maturity.

Exercise 8–13

Entries for notes receivable

Objective 7

The series of seven transactions recorded in the following T accounts were related to a sale to a customer on account and the receipt of the amount owed. Briefly describe each transaction.

Cash			
(7)	28,300	(7)	28,000

Sales			
		(1)	30,000

Notes Receivable			
(5)	27,500	(6)	27,500

Sales Returns and Allowances			
(3)	2,500		

Accounts Receivable			
(1)	30,000	(3)	2,500
(6)	28,000	(5)	27,500
		(7)	28,000

Cost of Merchandise Sold			
(2)	18,000	(4)	1,500

Merchandise Inventory			
(4)	1,500	(2)	18,000

Interest Revenue			
		(6)	500
		(7)	300

Exercise 8–14

Entries for notes receivable, including year-end entries

Objective 7

The following selected transactions were completed by Frith Co., a supplier of elastic bands for clothing:

1999
Dec. 15. Received from Acker Co., on account, a $27,000, 90-day, 10% note dated December 15.
　　31. Recorded an adjusting entry for accrued interest on the note of December 15.
　　31. Closed the interest revenue account. The only entry in this account originated from the December 31 adjustment.
2000
Mar. 14. Received payment of note and interest from Acker Co.

Journalize the transactions.

Exercise 8–15

Entries for receipt and dishonor of note receivable

Objective 7

Journalize the following transactions of Iris Theater Productions:

Aug. 1. Received a $60,000, 90-day, 10% note dated August 1 from Broadway Company on account.
Oct. 30. The note is dishonored by Broadway Company.
Nov. 29. Received the amount due on the dishonored note plus interest for 30 days at 15% on the total amount charged to Broadway Company on October 30.

Exercise 8–16
Entries for receipt and dishonor of notes receivable

Objectives 4, 7

Journalize the following transactions in the accounts of Clinton Co., which operates a riverboat casino:

Mar. 1. Received an $8,000, 30-day, 12% note dated March 1 from Adams Co. on account.

      21. Received a $15,000, 60-day, 10% note dated March 21 from Murphy Co. on account.

      31. The note dated March 1 from Adams Co. is dishonored, and the customer's account is charged for the note, including interest.

May 20. The note dated March 21 from Murphy Co. is dishonored, and the customer's account is charged for the note, including interest.

June 29. Cash is received for the amount due on the dishonored note dated March 1 plus interest for 90 days at 15% on the total amount debited to Adams Co. on March 31.

Aug. 31. Wrote off against the allowance account the amount charged to Murphy Co. on May 20 for the dishonored note dated March 21.

Exercise 8–17
Receivables in the balance sheet

Objective 8

What's Wrong WITH THIS?

List any errors you can find in the following partial balance sheet.

James Company
Balance Sheet
December 31, 20—

Assets

Current assets:

Cash		$ 95,000
Notes receivable	$250,000	
Less interest receivable	9,000	241,000
Accounts receivable	$445,000	
Plus allowance for doubtful accounts	15,000	460,000

Exercise 8–18
Accounts receivable turnover; number of days' sales in receivables

Objective 9

HAT

The financial statements for **Hershey Foods Corporation** are presented in Appendix G at the end of the text. Assume that all sales are credit sales and that the accounts receivable were $331,670,000 at December 31, 1994.

a. Compute the accounts receivable turnover for 1995 and 1996.

b. Compute the number of days' sales in receivables at December 31, 1995 and 1996.

c.   ➤ What conclusions can be drawn from these analyses regarding Hershey's efficiency in collecting receivables?

Appendix Exercise 8–19
Discounting notes receivable

Hathaway Co., a building construction company, holds a 90-day, 8% note for $35,000, dated August 18, which was received from a customer on account. On September 17, the note is discounted at the bank at the rate of 12%.

a. Determine the maturity value of the note.

b. Determine the number of days in the discount period.

c. Determine the amount of the discount.

d. Determine the amount of the proceeds.

e. Journalize the entry to record the discounting of the note on September 17.

Appendix Exercise 8–20
Entries for receipt and discounting of note receivable and dishonored notes

Journalize the following transactions in the accounts of Big Time Theater Productions:

May. 1. Received a $100,000, 90-day, 10% note dated May 1 from Johns Company on account.

June 1. Discounted the note at City National Bank at 12%.

July 30. The note is dishonored by Johns Company; paid the bank the amount due on the note, plus a protest fee of $250.

Aug. 29. Received the amount due on the dishonored note plus interest for 30 days at 16% on the total amount charged to Johns Company on July 30.

PROBLEMS SERIES A

Problem 8–1A
Entries related to uncollectible accounts

Objective 4

✓ 3. $572,300

The following transactions, adjusting entries, and closing entries were completed by Runnels Contractors Co. during the current fiscal year ended December 31:

Feb. 10. Received 75% of the $18,000 balance owed by Sackett Co., a bankrupt business, and wrote off the remainder as uncollectible.

May 3. Reinstated the account of B. Pilon, which had been written off in the preceding year as uncollectible. Journalized the receipt of $2,050 cash in full payment of Pilon's account.

Sept. 19. Wrote off the $6,250 balance owed by Larkin Co., which has no assets.

Nov. 30. Reinstated the account of Giles Co., which had been written off in the preceding year as uncollectible. Journalized the receipt of $4,500 cash in full payment of the account.

Dec. 31. Wrote off the following accounts as uncollectible (compound entry): Huang Co., $2,950; Nance Co., $1,600; Powell Distributors, $6,500; J. J. Stevens, $3,200.

31. Based on an analysis of the $595,000 of accounts receivable, it was estimated that $22,700 will be uncollectible. Journalized the adjusting entry.

31. Journalized the entry to close the appropriate account to Income Summary.

Instructions

1. Record the January 1 credit balance of $20,050 in Allowance for Doubtful Accounts.
2. Journalize the transactions and the adjusting and closing entries. Post each entry that affects the following three selected accounts and determine the new balances:

115	Allowance for Doubtful Accounts
313	Income Summary
718	Uncollectible Accounts Expense

3. Determine the expected net realizable value of the accounts receivable as of December 31.
4. Assuming that instead of basing the provision for uncollectible accounts on an analysis of receivables, the adjusting entry on December 31 had been based on an estimated expense of 3/4 of 1% of the net sales of $4,100,000 for the year, determine the following:
   a. Uncollectible accounts expense for the year.
   b. Balance in the allowance account after the adjustment of December 31.
   c. Expected net realizable value of the accounts receivable as of December 31.

Problem 8–2A
Compare two methods of accounting for uncollectible receivables

Objectives 4, 5

SPREADSHEET

✓ 1. Year 4: Balance of allowance account, end of year, $9,650.

Telco Company, a telephone service and supply company, has just completed its fourth year of operations. The direct write-off method of recording uncollectible accounts expense has been used during the entire period. Because of substantial increases in sales volume and amount of uncollectible accounts, the firm is considering changing to the allowance method. Information is requested as to the effect that an annual provision of 1% of sales would have had on the amount of uncollectible accounts expense reported for each of the past four years. It is also considered desirable to know what the balance of Allowance for Doubtful Accounts would have been at the end of each year. The following data have been obtained from the accounts:

Year	Sales	Uncollectible Accounts Written Off	Year of Origin of Accounts Receivable Written Off as Uncollectible			
			1st	2nd	3rd	4th
1st	$ 450,000	$2,500	$2,500			
2nd	660,000	3,950	1,900	$2,050		
3rd	850,000	6,700	700	2,600	$3,400	
4th	1,200,000	8,800		2,200	2,550	$4,050

Instructions

1. Assemble the desired data, using the following column headings:

	Uncollectible Accounts Expense			Balance of
Year	Expense Actually Reported	Expense Based on Estimate	Increase (Decrease) in Amount of Expense	Allowance Account, End of Year

2. ◖▬▬► Experience during the first four years of operations indicated that the receivables were either collected within two years or had to be written off as uncollectible. Does the estimate of 1% of sales appear to be reasonably close to the actual experience with uncollectible accounts originating during the first two years? Explain.

Problem 8–3A
Details of notes receivable and related entries

Objectives 6, 7

SPREADSHEET

✔ 1. Note 2: Due date, July 11; Interest due at maturity, $150.

During the current fiscal year, Nehls Co. received the following notes. Nehls Co. wholesales bathroom fixtures.

	Date	Face Amount	Term	Interest Rate
1.	March 11	$24,000	60 days	8%
2.	June 11	15,000	30 days	12%
3.	Aug. 20	9,200	90 days	7%
4.	Oct. 31	12,000	60 days	9%
5.	Nov. 28	15,000	60 days	8%
6.	Dec. 26	18,000	30 days	12%

Instructions

1. Determine for each note (a) the due date and (b) the amount of interest due at maturity, identifying each note by number.
2. Journalize the entry to record the dishonor of Note (3) on its due date.
3. Journalize the adjusting entry to record the accrued interest on Notes (5) and (6) on December 31.
4. Journalize the entries to record the receipt of the amounts due on Notes (5) and (6) in January.

Problem 8–4A
Notes receivable entries

Objective 7

HAT

The following data relate to notes receivable and interest for Fiber Optic Co., a cable manufacturer and supplier. (All notes are dated as of the day they are received.)

July   1. Received a $12,000, 9%, 60-day note on account.
Aug. 16. Received a $30,000, 10%, 120-day note on account.
     30. Received $12,180 on note of July 1.
Sept. 1. Received a $25,000, 9%, 60-day note on account.
Oct. 31. Received $25,375 on note of September 1.
Nov. 8. Received a $24,000, 7%, 30-day note on account.
     30. Received a $15,000, 10%, 30-day note on account.
Dec. 8. Received $24,140 on note of November 8.
     14. Received $31,000 on note of August 16.
     30. Received $15,125 on note of November 30.

Instructions
Journalize entries to record the transactions.

Problem 8–5A
Sales and notes receivable transactions

Objective 7

The following were selected from among the transactions completed by Wurtz Co. during the current year. Wurtz Co. sells and installs home and business security systems.

Jan. 10. Loaned $25,000 cash to Joyce Yang, receiving a 90-day, 8% note.
Feb. 1. Sold merchandise on account to Spencer and Son, $12,000. The cost of the merchandise sold was $8,800.

GENERAL LEDGER

HAT

Feb. 10. Sold merchandise on account to Roper Co., $40,000. The cost of merchandise sold was $30,000.

Mar. 3. Accepted a 60-day, 10% note for $12,000 from Spencer and Son on account.

11. Accepted a 60-day, 12% note for $40,000 from Roper Co. on account.

Apr. 10. Received the interest due from Joyce Yang and a new 90-day, 12% note as a renewal of the loan of January 10. (Record both the debit and the credit to the notes receivable account.)

May 2. Received from Spencer and Son the amount due on the note of March 3.

10. Roper Co. dishonored its note dated March 11.

June 9. Received from Roper Co. the amount owed on the dishonored note, plus interest for 30 days at 15% computed on the maturity value of the note.

July 9. Received from Joyce Yang the amount due on her note of April 10.

Aug. 23. Sold merchandise on account to C. D. Connors Co., $8,000. The cost of the merchandise sold was $5,000.

Sep. 2. Received from C. D. Connors Co. the amount of the invoice of August 23, less 1% discount.

Instructions

Journalize the transactions.

PROBLEMS SERIES B

Problem 8–1B

Entries related to uncollectible accounts

Objective 4

✓ 3. $493,500

The following transactions, adjusting entries, and closing entries were completed by The Art Gallery during the current fiscal year ended December 31:

Jan. 21. Reinstated the account of Jill Luce, which had been written off in the preceding year as uncollectible. Journalized the receipt of $3,025 cash in full payment of Luce's account.

28. Wrote off the $7,500 balance owed by Oasis Co., which is bankrupt.

Mar. 7. Received 40% of the $8,000 balance owed by Primrose Co., a bankrupt business, and wrote off the remainder as uncollectible.

Aug. 29. Reinstated the account of Louis Sabo, which had been written off two years earlier as uncollectible. Recorded the receipt of $1,200 cash in full payment.

Dec. 30. Wrote off the following accounts as uncollectible (compound entry): Channel Co., $11,050; Engel Co., $6,260; Loach Furniture, $4,775; Briana Parker, $1,820.

31. Based on an analysis of the $535,500 of accounts receivable, it was estimated that $42,000 will be uncollectible. Journalized the adjusting entry.

31. Journalized the entry to close the appropriate account to Income Summary.

Instructions

1. Record the January 1 credit balance of $28,955 in Allowance for Doubtful Accounts.
2. Journalize the transactions and the adjusting and closing entries. Post each entry that affects the following three selected accounts and determine the new balances:

115	Allowance for Doubtful Accounts
313	Income Summary
718	Uncollectible Accounts Expense

3. Determine the expected net realizable value of the accounts receivable as of December 31.
4. Assuming that, instead of basing the provision for uncollectible accounts on an analysis of receivables, the adjusting entry on December 31 had been based on an estimated expense of 3/4 of 1% of the net sales of $5,500,000 for the year, determine the following:

a. Uncollectible accounts expense for the year.
b. Balance in the allowance account after the adjustment of December 31.
c. Expected net realizable value of the accounts receivable as of December 31.

Problem 8–2B

Compare two methods of accounting for uncollectible receivables

Objectives 4, 5

SPREADSHEET

✓ 1. Year 4: Balance of allowance account, end of year, $8,450

Baldwin Company, which operates a chain of 30 electronics supply stores, has just completed its fourth year of operations. The direct write-off method of recording uncollectible accounts expense has been used during the entire period. Because of substantial increases in sales volume and amount of uncollectible accounts, the firm is considering changing to the allowance method. Information is requested as to the effect that an annual provision of 1% of sales would have had on the amount of uncollectible accounts expense reported for each of the past four years. It is also considered desirable to know what the balance of Allowance for Doubtful Accounts would have been at the end of each year. The following data have been obtained from the accounts:

Year	Sales	Uncollectible Accounts Written Off	Year of Origin of Accounts Receivable Written Off as Uncollectible			
			1st	2nd	3rd	4th
1st	$ 650,000	$ 2,600	$2,600			
2nd	720,000	3,500	1,950	$1,550		
3rd	950,000	9,600	2,200	3,400	$4,000	
4th	1,250,000	11,550		2,300	2,950	$6,300

Instructions

1. Assemble the desired data, using the following column headings:

	Uncollectible Accounts Expense			Balance of
Year	Expense Actually Reported	Expense Based on Estimate	Increase (Decrease) in Amount of Expense	Allowance Account, End of Year

2.  Experience during the first four years of operations indicated that the receivables were either collected within two years or had to be written off as uncollectible. Does the estimate of 1% of sales appear to be reasonably close to the actual experience with uncollectible accounts originating during the first two years? Explain.

Problem 8–3B

Details of notes receivable and related entries

Objectives 6, 7

SPREADSHEET

✓ 1. Note 2: Due date, Aug. 9; Interest due at maturity, $600

During the last six months of the current fiscal year, Norby Co. received the following notes. Norby Co. produces advertising videos.

	Date	Face Amount	Term	Interest Rate
1.	Apr. 1	$15,000	120 days	8%
2.	June 10	30,000	60 days	12%
3.	Aug. 11	18,000	90 days	8%
4.	Sept. 1	20,000	90 days	7%
5.	Nov. 1	24,000	90 days	9%
6.	Dec. 16	36,000	30 days	13%

Instructions

1. Determine for each note (a) the due date and (b) the amount of interest due at maturity, identifying each note by number.
2. Journalize the entry to record the dishonor of Note (3) on its due date.
3. Journalize the adjusting entry to record the accrued interest on Notes (5) and (6) on December 31.
4. Journalize the entries to record the receipt of the amounts due on Notes (5) and (6) in January.

Problem 8–4B
Notes receivable entries
Objective 7

The following data relate to notes receivable and interest for Robbins Co., a financial services company. (All notes are dated as of the day they are received.)

Mar. 1. Received a $30,000, 9%, 60-day note on account.
21. Received an $18,000, 9%, 90-day note on account.
Apr. 30. Received $30,450 on note of March 1.
May 16. Received a $48,000, 12%, 90-day note on account.
31. Received a $7,500, 8%, 30-day note on account.
June 19. Received $18,405 on note of March 21.
30. Received $7,550 on note of May 31.
July 1. Received a $5,000, 12%, 30-day note on account.
31. Received $5,050 on note of July 1.
Aug. 14. Received $49,440 on note of May 16.

Instructions
Journalize the entries to record the transactions.

Problem 8–5B
Sales and notes receivable transactions
Objective 7

GENERAL LEDGER

The following were selected from among the transactions completed during the current year by Cady Co., an appliance wholesale company:

Jan. 11. Sold merchandise on account to Hayden Co., $18,000. The cost of merchandise sold was $12,000.
Mar.   3. Accepted a 60-day, 10% note for $18,000 from Hayden Co. on account.
May   2. Received from Hayden Co. the amount due on the note of March 3.
June 1. Sold merchandise on account to Kohl's for $5,000. The cost of merchandise sold was $3,500.
5. Loaned $9,000 cash to Frank Scharf, receiving a 30-day, 12% note.
11. Received from Kohl's the amount due on the invoice of June 1, less 2% discount.
July 5. Received the interest due from Frank Scharf and a new 60-day, 14% note as a renewal of the loan of June 5. (Record both the debit and the credit to the notes receivable account.)
Sept. 3. Received from Frank Scharf the amount due on his note of July 5.
4. Sold merchandise on account to Nugent Co., $5,000. The cost of merchandise sold was $3,500.
Oct. 4. Accepted a 60-day, 12% note for $5,000 from Nugent Co. on account.
Dec. 3. Nugent Co. dishonored the note dated October 4.
23. Received from Nugent Co. the amount owed on the dishonored note, plus interest for 20 days at 12% computed on the maturity value of the note.

Instructions
Journalize the transactions.

QUICKBOOKS PROBLEM

Aging of Accounts Receivable

Open the *sample.qbw* file (Larry's Landscaping) in QuickBooks for this problem.

1. Print the "A/R Aging Summary" report for Larry's Landscaping.
2. Print the detailed invoices that are 1–30 days past due for Richard Mills. (Use the QuickZoom feature.)
3. Interpret the A/R Aging Summary report.

SPECIAL ACTIVITIES

Activity 8–1
Belgrade National Bank
Ethics and professional conduct in business

Kay Levitt, vice-president of operations for Belgrade National Bank, has instructed the bank's computer programmer to use a 365-day year to compute interest on depository accounts (payables). Kay also instructed the programmer to use a 360-day year to compute interest on loans (receivables).

➤ Discuss whether Kay is behaving in a professional manner.

Activity 8–2
Itana Construction Supplies Co.
Collecting accounts receivable

The following is an excerpt from a conversation between the office manager, Jeremy Nevin, and the president of Itana Construction Supplies Co., Melinda Kirk. Itana sells building supplies to local contractors.

Jeremy: Melinda, we're going to have to do something about these overdue accounts receivable. One-third of our accounts are over 60 days past due, and I've had accounts that have stayed open for almost a year!

Melinda: I didn't realize it was that bad. Any ideas?

Jeremy: Well, we could stop giving credit. Make everyone pay with cash or a credit card. We accept MasterCard and Visa already, but only the walk-in customers use them. Almost all of the contractors put purchases on their bills.

Melinda: Yes, but we've been allowing credit for years. As far as I know, all of our competitors allow contractors credit. If we stopped giving credit, we'd lose many of our contractors. They'd just go elsewhere. You know, some of these guys run up bills as high as $40,000 or $50,000. There's no way they could put that kind of money on a credit card.

Jeremy: That's a good point. But we've got to do something.

Melinda: How many of the contractor accounts do you actually end up writing off as uncollectible?

Jeremy: Not many. Almost all eventually pay. It's just that they take so long!

➤ Suggest one or more solutions to Itana Construction Supplies Co.'s problem concerning the collection of accounts receivable.

Activity 8–3
Costello Wholesale Co.
Value of receivables

The following is an excerpt from a conversation between Bryan Eastman, the president and owner of Costello Wholesale Co., and Michele Joiner, Costello's controller. The conversation took place on January 4, 2000, shortly after Michele began preparing the financial statements for the year ending December 31, 1999.

Michele: Bryan, I've completed my analysis of the collectibility of our accounts receivable. My staff and I estimate that the allowance for doubtful accounts should be somewhere between $50,000 and $80,000. Right now, the balance of the allowance account is $12,000.

Bryan: Oh, no! We are already below the estimated earnings projection I gave the bank last year. We used that as a basis for convincing the bank to loan us $100,000. They're going to be upset! Is there any way we can increase the allowance without the adjustment increasing expenses?

Michele: I'm afraid not. The allowance can only be increased by debiting the uncollectible accounts expense account.

Bryan: Well, I guess we're stuck. The bank will just have to live with it. But let's increase the allowance by only $38,000. That gets us into our range of estimates with the minimum expense increase.

Michele: Bryan, there is one more thing we need to discuss.

Bryan: What now?

Michele: Jim, my staff accountant, noticed that you haven't made any payments on your receivable for over a year. Also, it has increased from $25,000 last year to $75,000. Jim thinks we ought to reclassify it as a noncurrent asset and report it as an "other receivable."

Bryan: What's the problem? Didn't we just include it in accounts receivable last year?

Michele: Yes, but last year it was immaterial.

Bryan: Look, I'll make a $50,000 payment next week. So let's report it like we did last year.

➤ If you were Michele, how would you address Bryan's suggestions?

Activity 8–4
Quick Rehab Co.
Estimate uncollectible accounts

For several years, sales have been on a "cash only" basis. On January 1, 1996, however, Quick Rehab Co. began offering credit on terms of n/30. The amount of the adjusting entry to record the estimated uncollectible receivables at the end of each year has been 1/2 of 1% of credit sales, which is the rate reported as the average for the industry. Credit sales and the year-end credit balances in Allowance for Doubtful Accounts for the past four years are as follows:

Year	Credit Sales	Allowance for Doubtful Accounts
1996	$5,800,000	$ 6,800
1997	6,000,000	7,200
1998	6,100,000	10,000
1999	6,250,000	13,000

LeRoy Tyson, president of Quick Rehab Co., is concerned that the method used to account for and write off uncollectible receivables is unsatisfactory. He has asked for your advice in the analysis of past operations in this area and for recommendations for change.

1. Determine the amount of (a) the addition to Allowance for Doubtful Accounts and (b) the accounts written off for each of the four years.
2. a. ✏️➤ Advise LeRoy Tyson as to whether the estimate of 1/2 of 1% of credit sales appears reasonable.
   b. ✏️➤ Assume that after discussing (a) with LeRoy Tyson, he asked you what action might be taken to determine what the balance of Allowance for Doubtful Accounts should be at December 31, 1999, and what possible changes, if any, you might recommend in accounting for uncollectible receivables. How would you respond?

Activity 8–5
Into the Real World
Granting credit

In groups of three or four, determine how credit is typically granted to customers. Interview an individual responsible for granting credit for a bank, a department store, an automobile dealer, or other business in your community. You should ask such questions as the following:

1. What procedures are used to decide whether to grant credit to a customer?
2. What procedures are used to try to collect from customers who are delinquent in their payments?
3. Approximately what percentage of customers' accounts are written off as uncollectible in a year?

Summarize your findings in a report to the class.

Activity 8–6
Into the Real World
Collection of receivables

Go to the Web page of two department store chains, **Federated Department Stores Inc.** and **Mercantile Stores Co. Inc.** The Internet sites for these companies are:

www.federated-fds.com
www.rootsstore.com

Using the financial information provided at each site, calculate the most recent accounts receivable turnover for each company, and identify which company is collecting its receivables faster.

ANSWERS TO SELF-EXAMINATION QUESTIONS

Matching

1. L	3. I	5. D	7. C	9. G	11. B
2. A	4. M	6. F	8. H	10. J	12. K

Multiple Choice

1. **B** The estimate of uncollectible accounts, $8,500 (answer C), is the amount of the desired balance of Allowance for Doubtful Accounts after adjustment. The amount of the current provision to be made for uncollectible accounts expense is thus $6,000 (answer B), which is the amount that must be added to the Allowance for Doubtful Accounts credit balance of $2,500 (answer A), so that the account will have the desired balance of $8,500.

2. **B** The amount expected to be realized from accounts receivable is the balance of Accounts Receivable, $100,000, less the balance of Allowance for Doubtful Accounts, $7,000, or $93,000 (answer B).

3. **C** Maturity value is the amount that is due at the maturity or due date. The maturity value of $10,300 (answer C) is determined as follows:

Face amount of note	$10,000
Plus interest ($10,000 × 0.12 × 90/360)	300
Maturity value of note	$10,300

4. **C** November 3 is the due date of a $12,000, 90-day, 8% note receivable dated August 5 [26 days in August (31 days − 5 days) + 30 days in September + 31 days in October + 3 days in November].

5. **B** If a note is dishonored, Accounts Receivable is debited for the maturity value of the note (answer B). The maturity value of the note is its face value (answer A) plus the accrued interest. The maturity value of the note less accrued interest (answer C) is equal to the face value of the note. The maturity value of the note plus accrued interest (answer D) is incorrect, since the interest would be added twice.

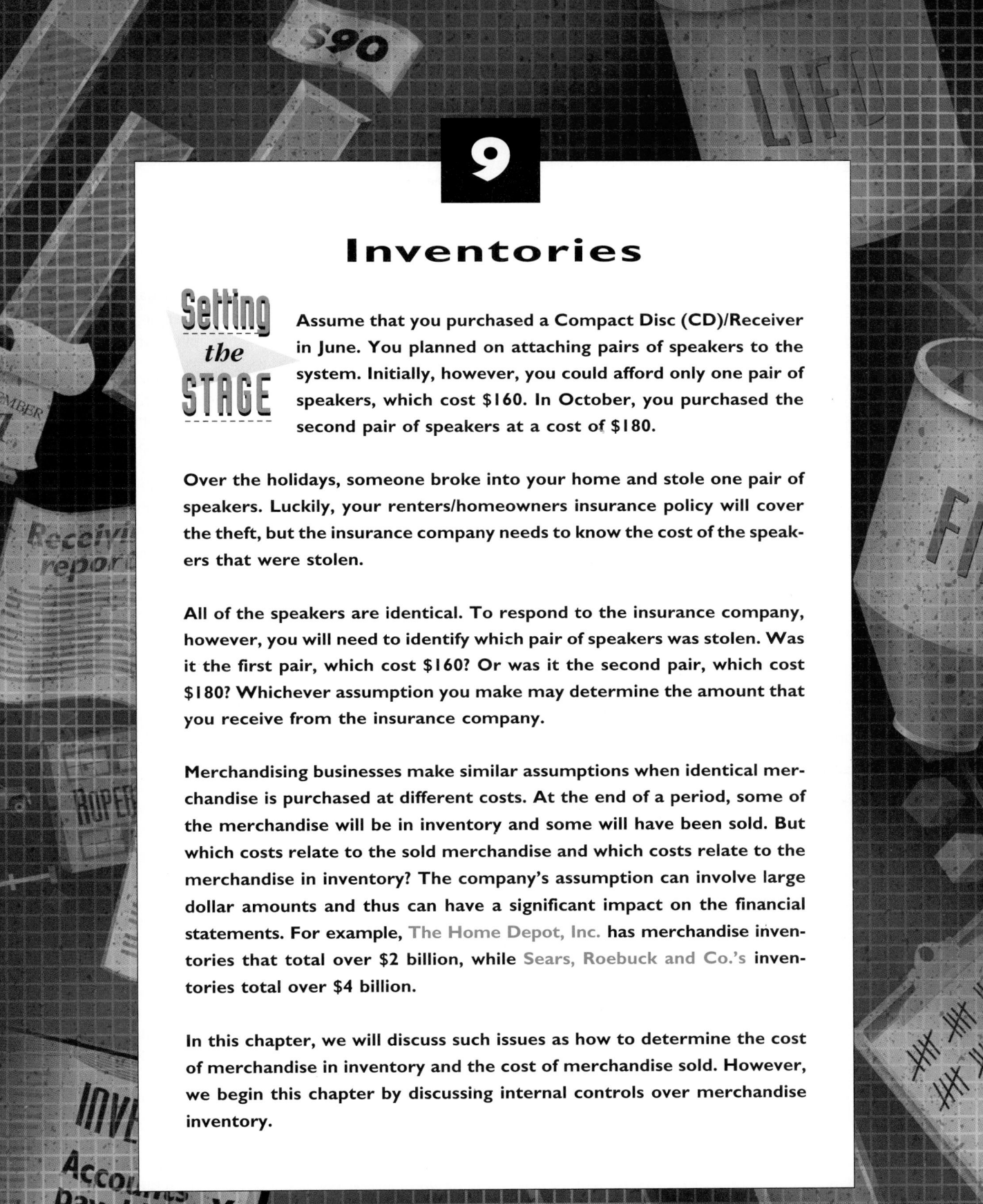

9

Inventories

Assume that you purchased a Compact Disc (CD)/Receiver in June. You planned on attaching pairs of speakers to the system. Initially, however, you could afford only one pair of speakers, which cost $160. In October, you purchased the second pair of speakers at a cost of $180.

Over the holidays, someone broke into your home and stole one pair of speakers. Luckily, your renters/homeowners insurance policy will cover the theft, but the insurance company needs to know the cost of the speakers that were stolen.

All of the speakers are identical. To respond to the insurance company, however, you will need to identify which pair of speakers was stolen. Was it the first pair, which cost $160? Or was it the second pair, which cost $180? Whichever assumption you make may determine the amount that you receive from the insurance company.

Merchandising businesses make similar assumptions when identical merchandise is purchased at different costs. At the end of a period, some of the merchandise will be in inventory and some will have been sold. But which costs relate to the sold merchandise and which costs relate to the merchandise in inventory? The company's assumption can involve large dollar amounts and thus can have a significant impact on the financial statements. For example, The Home Depot, Inc. has merchandise inventories that total over $2 billion, while Sears, Roebuck and Co.'s inventories total over $4 billion.

In this chapter, we will discuss such issues as how to determine the cost of merchandise in inventory and the cost of merchandise sold. However, we begin this chapter by discussing internal controls over merchandise inventory.

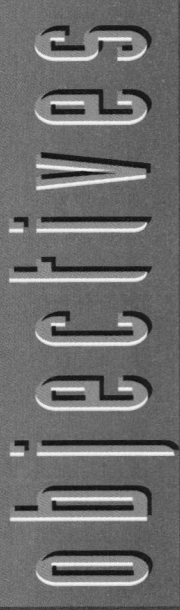

1 Summarize and provide examples of internal control procedures that apply to inventories.

2 Describe the effect of inventory errors on the financial statements.

3 Describe three inventory cost flow assumptions and how they impact the income statement and balance sheet.

4 Compute the cost of inventory under the perpetual inventory system, using the following costing methods:

First-in, first-out
Last-in, first-out
Average cost

5 Compute the cost of inventory under the periodic inventory system, using the following costing methods:
First-in, first-out
Last-in, first-out
Average cost

6 Compare and contrast the use of the three inventory costing methods.

7 Compute the proper valuation of inventory at other than cost, using the lower-of-cost-or-market and net realizable value concepts.

8 Prepare a balance sheet presentation of merchandise inventory.

9 Estimate the cost of inventory, using the retail method and the gross profit method.

10 Compute and interpret the inventory turnover ratio and the number of days' sales in inventory.

Internal Control of Inventories

OBJECTIVE I

Summarize and provide examples of internal control procedures that apply to inventories.

The cost of inventory is a significant item in many businesses' financial statements. What do we mean by the term inventory? **Inventory** is used to indicate (1) merchandise held for sale in the normal course of business and (2) materials in the process of production or held for production. In this chapter, we focus primarily on inventory of merchandise purchased for resale.

Circuit City's inventory represents over 75% of its current assets and over 50% of its total assets. Circuit City's cost of merchandise sold represents over 70% of its net sales.

What costs should be included in inventory? As we have illustrated in earlier chapters, the cost of merchandise is its purchase price, less any purchases discounts. These costs are usually the largest portion of the inventory cost. Merchandise inventory also includes other costs, such as transportation, import duties, and insurance against losses in transit.

For companies such as Circuit City, good internal control over inventory must be maintained. Two primary objectives of internal control over inventory are safeguarding the inventory and properly reporting it in the financial statements. These internal controls can be either preventive or detective in nature. A preventive control is designed to prevent errors or misstatements from occurring. A detective control is designed to detect an error or misstatement after it has occurred.

Control over inventory should begin as soon as the inventory is received. Prenumbered receiving reports should be completed by the company's receiving department in order to establish the initial accountability for the inventory. To make sure the inventory received is what was ordered, each receiving report should agree with the company's original purchase order for the merchandise. Likewise, the price at which the inventory was ordered, as shown on the purchase order, should be compared to the price at which the vendor billed the company, as shown on the vendor's invoice. After the receiving report, purchase order, and vendor's invoice have

Jewelry stores normally keep diamond rings, bracelets, and other items in a locked glass case. Is this a preventive or a detective control?

This is a preventive control to protect against theft (shoplifting).

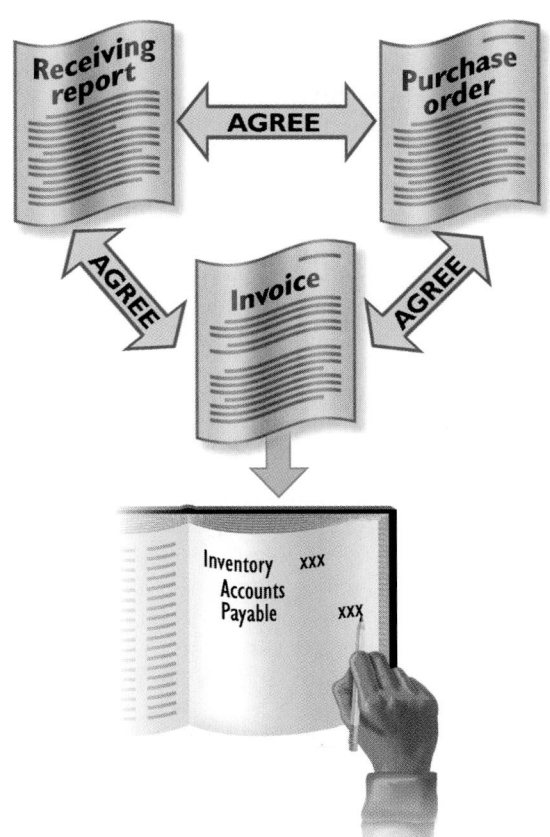

been reconciled, the company should record the inventory and related account payable in the accounting records.

Controls for safeguarding inventory include developing and using security measures to prevent inventory damage or employee theft. For example, inventory should be stored in a warehouse or other area to which access is restricted to authorized employees. The removal of merchandise from the warehouse should be controlled by using requisition forms, which should be properly authorized. The storage area should also be climate controlled to prevent damage from heat or cold. Further, when the business is not operating or is not open, the storage area should be locked.

When shopping, you may have noticed how retail stores protect inventory from customer theft. Retail stores often use such devices as two-way mirrors, cameras, and security guards. High-priced items are often displayed in locked cabinets. Retail clothing stores often place plastic alarm tags on valuable items such as leather coats. Sensors at the exit doors set off alarms if the tags have not been removed by the clerk. These controls are designed to prevent customers from shoplifting.

 **Sam's Club** and **Wal-Mart** stores use a greeter at the entry of each store to welcome customers. The greeter also serves as a preventive control by asking customers not to bring packages or other bags into the store, which could be used for shoplifting.

Using a perpetual inventory system for merchandise also provides an effective means of control over inventory. The amount of each type of merchandise is always readily available in a subsidiary **inventory ledger**. In addition, the subsidiary ledger can be an aid in maintaining inventory quantities at proper levels. Frequently comparing balances with predetermined maximum and minimum levels allows for the timely reordering of merchandise and prevents the ordering of excess inventory.

To ensure the accuracy of the amount of inventory reported in the financial statements, a merchandising business should take a **physical inventory** (i.e., count the merchandise). In a perpetual inventory system, the physical inventory is compared to the recorded inventory in order to determine the amount of shrinkage or shortage. If the inventory shrinkage is unusually large, management can investigate further and take any necessary corrective action. Knowledge that a physical inventory will be taken also helps prevent employee thefts or misuses of inventory.

How does a business "take" a physical inventory? The first step in this process is to determine the quantity of each kind of merchandise owned by the business. A common practice is to use teams of two persons. One person determines the quantity, and the other lists the quantity and description on inventory count sheets. Quantities of high-cost items are usually verified by supervisors or a second count team.

 Most companies take their physical inventories when their inventory levels are the lowest. For example, most retailers take their physical inventory in late January or early February, which is after the holiday selling season but before restocking for spring.

What merchandise should be included in inventory? All the merchandise *owned* by the business on the inventory date should be included. For merchandise in transit, the party (the seller or the buyer) who has title to the merchandise on the inventory date is the owner. To determine who has title, it may be necessary to examine purchases and sales invoices of the last few days of the current pe-

All merchandise *owned* by a business should be included in the business's inventory.

BUSINESS ON STAGE

What Does It Cost to Have an Inventory?

Inventories are essential for merchandising and manufacturing businesses. Inventories are necessary in order to generate sales, and sales are necessary in order to generate profits.

The primary benefit of carrying inventory is that it provides protection against unexpected events and disruptions in business operations. For example, an unexpected strike by a supplier's employees can halt production for a manufacturer or cause lost sales for a merchandiser. Businesses that rely upon foreign suppliers are particularly affected by disruptions caused by international crises and events. Carrying inventory also allows a business to meet unexpected increases in the demand for its product. Thus, you can think of inventories as a buffer or cushion against the unexpected.

Inventory is not free, however. The costs of carrying inventory are classified as (1) holding costs, (2) ordering costs, and (3) stockout costs. *Holding costs* include the costs of handling, storage, insurance, property taxes, and depreciation. In addition, holding costs for a merchandising business include losses that occur when customer preferences and tastes change unexpectedly and inventory is marked down. Finally, holding costs include the cost of funds that could be used for other purposes if they were not tied up in inventory. For example, if a business must borrow $100,000 at 10% to finance its inventories, then the interest of $10,000 per year is part of the cost of holding inventory.

Ordering costs are the costs of placing and processing orders with suppliers. Ordering costs also include the cost of investigating possible suppliers and negotiating contracts with suppliers.

Stockout costs include the costs of failing to meet customer demands—the cost of lost sales and lost profits, as well as lost customer goodwill. For a manufacturer, stockout costs include the costs of production delays and downtime, as well as the related costs of restarting production.

Inventory management involves the difficult task of balancing the benefits of carrying inventory against the related costs. In a merchandise business, inventory management is normally the responsibility of a merchandising manager or buyer. ■

riod and the first few days of the following period.

As we discussed in an earlier chapter, shipping terms determine when title passes. When goods are purchased or sold **FOB shipping point**, title passes to the buyer when the goods are shipped. When the terms are **FOB destination**, title passes to the buyer when the goods are delivered.

To illustrate, assume that Roper Co. orders $25,000 of merchandise on December 28, 2000. The merchandise is shipped FOB shipping point by the seller on December 30 and arrives at Roper Co.'s warehouse on January 4, 2001. As a result, the merchandise is not counted by the inventory crew on December 31, the end of Roper Co.'s fiscal year. However, the $25,000 of merchandise should be included in Roper's inventory because title has passed. Roper Co. should record the merchandise in transit on December 31, debiting Merchandise Inventory and crediting Accounts Payable for $25,000.

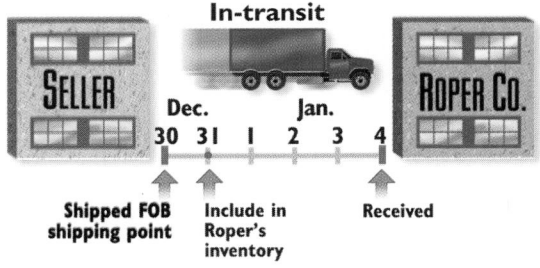

Manufacturers sometimes ship merchandise to retailers who act as the manufacturer's agent when selling the merchandise. The manufacturer retains title until the goods are sold. Such merchandise is said to be shipped *on consignment* to the retailers. The unsold merchandise is a part of the manufacturer's (consignor's) inventory, even though the merchandise is in the hands of the retailers. The consigned merchandise should not be included in the retailer's (consignee's) inventory.

OBJECTIVE 2

Describe the effect of inventory errors on the financial statements.

Effect of Inventory Errors on Financial Statements

Any errors in the inventory count will affect both the balance sheet and the income statement. For example, an error in the physical inventory will misstate the ending inventory, current assets, and total assets on the balance sheet. This is because the

Crazy Eddie Inc., which operated electronics stores, defrauded investors by misstating inventory. The company reported rapid gains in sales and earnings due to what the company said was store expansion, adept sales-floor techniques, and catchy commercials. However, Crazy Eddie had overstated inventory counts at one warehouse by $10 million, drafted phony inventory count sheets, and included in inventory $4 million of merchandise that, in fact, was being returned to suppliers. As a result, income was overstated. The apparent purpose of the scheme was to "artificially inflate the net worth of the company" and the value of stock owned by the store's founder, Eddie Antar, and others.

Source: Jeffrey A. Tannenbaum, "Filings by Crazy Eddie Suggest Founder Led Scheme to Inflate Company's Value," *The Wall Street Journal,* May 31, 1988, p. 28.

physical inventory is the basis for recording the adjusting entry for inventory shrinkage. Also, an error in taking the physical inventory misstates the cost of goods sold, gross profit, and net income on the income statement. In addition, because net income is closed to the owner's equity at the end of the period, owner's equity will also be misstated on the balance sheet. This misstatement of owner's equity will equal the misstatement of the ending inventory, current assets, and total assets.

To illustrate, assume that in taking the physical inventory on December 31, 2000, Sapra Company incorrectly recorded its physical inventory as $115,000 instead of the correct amount of $125,000. As a result, the merchandise inventory, current assets, and total assets reported on the December 31, 2000, balance sheet would be understated by $10,000 ($125,000 − $115,000). Because the ending physical inventory is understated, the inventory shrinkage and the cost of merchandise sold will be overstated by $10,000. Thus, the gross profit and the net income for the year will be understated by $10,000. Since the net income is closed to owner's equity at the end of the period, the owner's equity on the December 31, 2000 balance sheet will also be understated by $10,000. The effects on Sapra Company's financial statements are summarized as follows:

	Amount of Misstatement
Balance Sheet:	
Merchandise inventory understated	$(10,000)
Current assets understated	(10,000)
Total assets understated	(10,000)
Owner's equity understated	(10,000)
Income Statement:	
Cost of merchandise sold overstated	$ 10,000
Gross profit understated	(10,000)
Net income understated	(10,000)

At the end of 1999, the physical ending inventory of Melchor Co. was overstated by $25,000. What is the effect of this error on the financial statements (balance sheet and income statement) prepared at the end of 1999?

On the balance sheet, the merchandise inventory, current assets, total assets, and owner's equity are overstated by $25,000. On the income statement, the cost of merchandise sold is understated by $25,000, and the gross profit and net income are overstated by $25,000.

Now assume that in the preceding example the physical inventory had been *overstated* on December 31, 2000, by $10,000. That is, Sapra Company erroneously recorded its inventory as $135,000. In this case, the effects on the balance sheet and income statement would be just the *opposite* of those indicated above.

Errors in the physical inventory are normally detected in the period after they occur. In such cases, the financial statements of the prior year must be corrected. We will discuss such corrections in a later chapter.

OBJECTIVE 3

Describe three inventory cost flow assumptions and how they impact the income statement and balance sheet.

Inventory Cost Flow Assumptions

A major accounting issue arises when identical units of merchandise are acquired at different unit costs during a period. In such cases, when an item is sold, it is necessary to determine its unit cost so that the proper accounting entry can be recorded. To illustrate, assume that three identical units of Item X are purchased during May, as shown below.

Item X		Units	Cost
May 10	Purchase	1	$ 9
18	Purchase	1	13
24	Purchase	1	14
Total		3	$36
Average cost per unit			$12

Assume that one unit is sold on May 30 for $20. If this unit can be identified with a specific purchase, the **specific identification method** can be used to determine the cost of the unit sold. For example, if the unit sold was purchased on May 18, the cost assigned to the unit is $13 and the gross profit is $7 ($20 − $13). If, however, the unit sold was purchased on May 10, the cost assigned to the unit is $9 and the gross profit is $11 ($20 − $9).

 The specific identification method is normally used by jewelry stores and art galleries.

The specific identification method is not practical unless each unit can be identified accurately. An automobile dealer, for example, may be able to use this method, since each automobile has a unique serial number. For many businesses, however, identical units cannot be separately identified, and a cost flow must be assumed. That is, which units have been sold and which units are still in inventory must be assumed.

There are three common cost flow assumptions used in business. Each of these assumptions is identified with an inventory costing method, as shown below.

Cost Flow Assumption	1. Cost flow is in the order in which the costs were incurred.	2. Cost flow is in the reverse order in which the costs were incurred.	3. Cost flow is an average of the costs.
Inventory Costing Method	First-in, first-out (fifo)	Last-in, first-out (lifo)	Average cost

When the **first-in, first-out (fifo) method** is used, the ending inventory is made up of the most recent costs. When the **last-in, first-out (lifo) method** is used, the ending inventory is made up of the earliest costs. When the **average cost method** is used, the cost of the units in inventory is an average of the purchase costs.

To illustrate, we use the preceding example to prepare the income statement for May and the balance sheet as of May 31 for each of the cost flow methods. These financial statements are shown in Exhibit 1.

As you can see, the selection of an inventory costing method can have a significant impact on the financial statements. For this reason, the selection has important implications for managers and others in analyzing and interpreting the financial statements. The chart in Exhibit 2 shows the frequency with which fifo, lifo, and the average methods are used in practice.

EXHIBIT 1
Effect of Inventory Costing
Methods on Financial State-
ments

Fifo Method

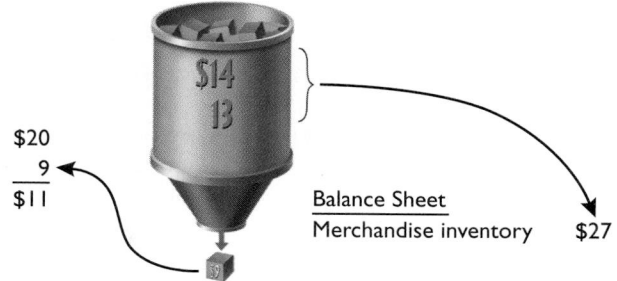

Income Statement
Sales $20
Cost of merchandise sold   9
Gross profit $11

Balance Sheet
Merchandise inventory $27

Lifo Method

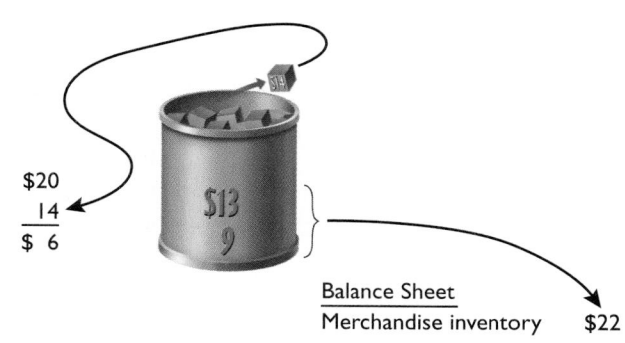

Income Statement
Sales $20
Cost of merchandise sold   14
Gross profit $ 6

Balance Sheet
Merchandise inventory $22

Average Cost Method

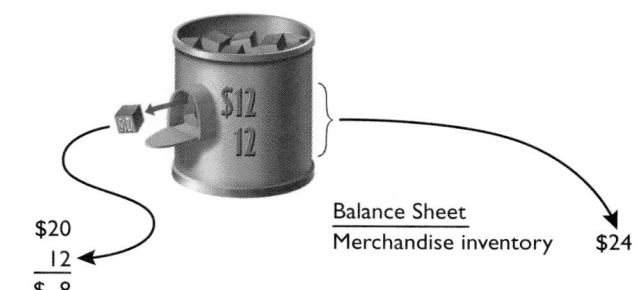

Income Statement
Sales $20
Cost of merchandise sold   12
Gross profit $ 8

Balance Sheet
Merchandise inventory $24

EXHIBIT 2
Inventory Costing Methods

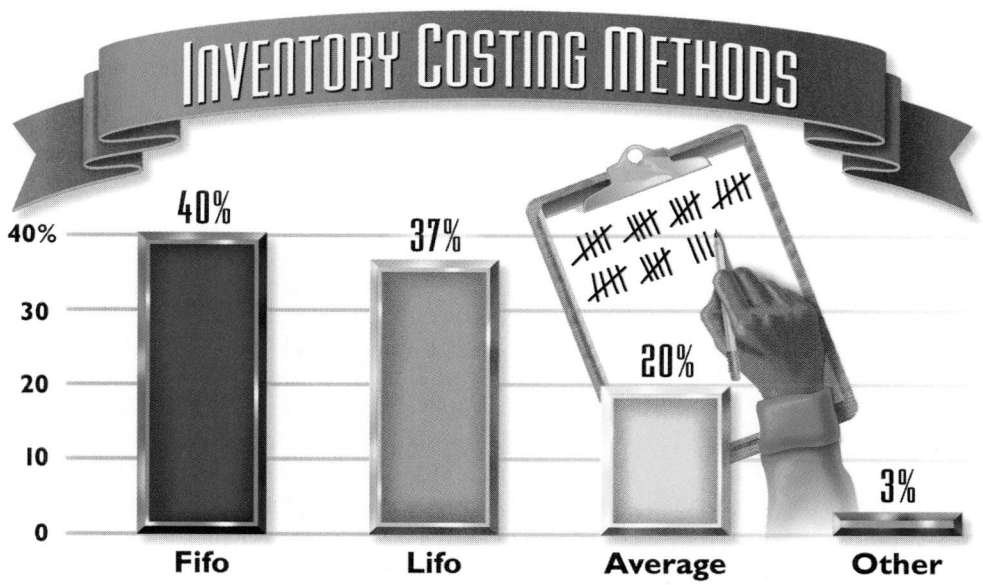

Source: Accounting Trends & Techniques, 50th ed., American Institute of Certified Public Accountants, New York, 1996.

Inventory Costing Methods Under a Perpetual Inventory System

OBJECTIVE 4

Compute the cost of inventory under the perpetual inventory system, using the following costing methods:

First-in, first-out

Last-in, first-out

Average cost

In a perpetual inventory system, all merchandise increases and decreases are recorded in a manner similar to the recording of increases and decreases in cash. The merchandise inventory account at the beginning of an accounting period indicates the merchandise in stock on that date. Purchases are recorded by debiting *Merchandise Inventory* and crediting *Cash* or *Accounts Payable.* On the date of each sale, the cost of the merchandise sold is recorded by debiting *Cost of Merchandise Sold* and crediting *Merchandise Inventory.*

As we illustrated in the preceding section, when identical units of an item are purchased at different unit costs during a period, a cost flow must be assumed. In such cases, the fifo, lifo, or average cost method is used. We illustrate each of these methods, using the following data for Item 127B:

	Item 127B	Units	Cost
Jan. 1	Inventory	10	$20
4	Sale	7	
10	Purchase	8	21
22	Sale	4	
28	Sale	2	
30	Purchase	10	22

First-In, First-Out Method

Most businesses dispose of goods in the order in which the goods are purchased. This would be especially true of perishables and goods whose styles or models often change. For example, grocery stores shelve their milk products by expiration dates. Likewise, men's and women's clothing stores display clothes by season. At the end of a season, they often have sales to clear their stores of off-season or out-of-style clothing. Thus, the fifo method is often consistent with the *physical flow* or movement of merchandise. To the extent that this is the case, the fifo method provides results that are about the same as those obtained by identifying the specific costs of each item sold and in inventory.

When the fifo method of costing inventory is used, costs are included in the cost of merchandise sold in the order in which they were incurred. To illustrate, Exhibit 3 shows the journal entries for purchases and sales and the inventory subsidiary ledger account for Item 127B. The number of units in inventory after each transaction, together with total costs and unit costs, are shown in the account. We assume that the units are sold for $30 each on account.

Using fifo, costs are included in the merchandise sold in the order in which they were incurred.

You should note that after the 7 units were sold on January 4, there was an inventory of 3 units at $20 each. The 8 units purchased on January 10 were acquired at a unit cost of $21, instead of $20. Therefore, the inventory after the January 10 purchase is reported on two lines, 3 units at $20 each and 8 units at $21 each. Next, note that the $81 cost of the 4 units sold on January 22 is made up of the remaining 3 units at $20 each and 1 unit at $21. At this point, 7 units are in inventory at a cost of $21 per unit. The remainder of the illustration is explained in a similar manner.

EXHIBIT 3
Entries and Perpetual Inventory Account (Fifo)

Jan. 4	Accounts Receivable	210	
	Sales		210
4	Cost of Merchandise Sold	140	
	Merchandise Inventory		140
10	Merchandise Inventory	168	
	Accounts Payable		168
22	Accounts Receivable	120	
	Sales		120
22	Cost of Merchandise Sold	81	
	Merchandise Inventory		81
28	Accounts Receivable	60	
	Sales		60
28	Cost of Merchandise Sold	42	
	Merchandise Inventory		42
30	Merchandise Inventory	220	
	Accounts Payable		220

Item 127B

| Date | Purchases | | | Cost of Merchandise Sold | | | Inventory | | |
	Quantity	Unit Cost	Total Cost	Quantity	Unit Cost	Total Cost	Quantity	Unit Cost	Total Cost
Jan. 1							10	20	200
4				7	20	140	3	20	60
10	8	21	168				3	20	60
							8	21	168
22				3	20	60			
				1	21	21	7	21	147
28				2	21	42	5	21	105
30	10	22	220				5	21	105
							10	22	220

Last-In, First-Out Method

When the lifo method is used in a perpetual inventory system, the cost of the units sold is the cost of the most recent purchases. To illustrate, Exhibit 4 shows the journal entries for purchases and sales and the subsidiary ledger account for Item 127B, prepared on a lifo basis.

Using lifo, the cost of units sold is the cost of the most recent purchases.

EXHIBIT 4
Entries and Perpetual Inventory Account (Lifo)

Jan. 4	Accounts Receivable	210	
	Sales		210
4	Cost of Merchandise Sold	140	
	Merchandise Inventory		140
10	Merchandise Inventory	168	
	Accounts Payable		168
22	Accounts Receivable	120	
	Sales		120
22	Cost of Merchandise Sold	84	
	Merchandise Inventory		84
28	Accounts Receivable	60	
	Sales		60
28	Cost of Merchandise Sold	42	
	Merchandise Inventory		42
30	Merchandise Inventory	220	
	Accounts Payable		220

Item 127B

| Date | Purchases | | | Cost of Merchandise Sold | | | Inventory | | |
	Quantity	Unit Cost	Total Cost	Quantity	Unit Cost	Total Cost	Quantity	Unit Cost	Total Cost
Jan. 1							10	20	200
4				7	20	140	3	20	60
10	8	21	168				3	20	60
							8	21	168
22				4	21	84	3	20	60
							4	21	84
28				2	21	42	3	20	60
							2	21	42
30	10	22	220				3	20	60
							2	21	42
							10	22	220

If you compare the ledger accounts for the fifo perpetual system and the lifo perpetual system, you should discover that the accounts are the same through the January 10 purchase. Using lifo, however, the cost of the 4 units sold on January 22 is the cost of the units from the January 10 purchase ($21 per unit). The cost of the 7 units in inventory after the sale on January 22 is the cost of the 3 units remaining from the beginning inventory and the cost of the 4 units remaining from the January 10 purchase. The remainder of the lifo illustration is explained in a similar manner.

When the lifo method is used, the inventory ledger is sometimes maintained in units only. The units are converted to dollars when the financial statements are prepared at the end of the period.

The use of the lifo method was originally limited to rare situations in which the units sold were taken from the most recently acquired goods. For tax reasons, which we will discuss later, its use has greatly increased during the past few decades. Lifo is now often used even when it does not represent the physical flow of goods.

Average Cost Method

When the average cost method is used in a perpetual inventory system, an average unit cost for each type of item is computed each time a purchase is made. This unit cost is then used to determine the cost of each sale until another purchase is made and a new average is computed. This averaging technique is called a *moving average*. Since the average cost method is not often used in a perpetual inventory system, we do not illustrate it in this chapter.

Computerized Perpetual Inventory Systems

The records for a perpetual inventory system may be maintained manually. However, such a system is costly and time consuming for businesses with a large number of inventory items with many purchase and sales transactions. In most cases, the record keeping for perpetual inventory systems is computerized.

An example of using computers in maintaining perpetual inventory records for retail stores is described below:

1. The relevant details for each inventory item, such as a description, quantity, and unit size, are stored in an inventory record. The individual inventory records make up the computerized inventory file, the total of which agrees with the balance of the inventory ledger account.
2. Each time an item is purchased or returned by a customer, the inventory data are entered into the computer's inventory records and files.
3. Each time an item is sold, a salesclerk scans the item's bar code with an optical scanner. The scanner reads the magnetic code and rings up the sale on the cash register. The inventory records and files are then updated.
4. After a physical inventory is taken, the inventory count data are entered into the computer. These data are compared with the current balances, and a listing of the overages and shortages is printed. The inventory balances are then adjusted to the quantities determined by the physical count.

 **Wal-Mart, Kmart, Sears,** and other retailers use bar code scanners as part of their perpetual inventory systems.

Such systems can be extended to aid managers in controlling and managing inventory quantities. For example, items that are selling fast can be reordered before the stock is depleted. Past sales patterns can be analyzed to determine when to mark down merchandise for sales and when to restock seasonal merchandise. In addition, such systems can provide managers with data for developing and fine-tuning their marketing strategies. For example, such data can be used to evaluate the effectiveness of advertising campaigns and sales promotions.

The fifo, lifo, and average cost flow assumptions also apply to other areas of business. For example, individuals and businesses often purchase marketable securities at different costs per share. When such investments are sold, the investor must either specifically identify which shares are sold or use the fifo cost flow assumption. To illustrate, assume that a business purchased 100 shares of Microsoft Corporation at $85 and 100 shares at $95. If the business later sells 100 shares for $100, which shares did it sell? The business must determine the cost of the shares sold so that it can report a gain or loss on the sale for tax purposes. In addition, it must report the gain or loss on its income statement.

Inventory Costing Methods Under a Periodic Inventory System

When the periodic inventory system is used, only revenue is recorded each time a sale is made. No entry is made at the time of the sale to record the cost of the merchandise sold. At the end of the accounting period, a physical inventory is taken to determine the cost of the inventory and the cost of the merchandise sold.

For merchandising businesses that use the periodic system, the cost of merchandise sold during a period is reported in a separate section in the income statement. To illustrate, assume that Computer King opened a merchandising outlet selling personal computers and software. During 2001, Computer King purchased $340,000 of merchandise. If the inventory at December 31, 2001, the end of the year, is $59,700, the cost of merchandise sold during 2001 would be reported as follows:

Cost of merchandise sold:

Purchases	$340,000	
Less merchandise inventory, December 31, 2001	59,700	
Cost of merchandise sold		$280,300

To continue the illustration, assume that during 2002 Computer King purchased additional merchandise of $521,980. It received credit for purchases returns and allowances of $9,100, took purchases discounts of $2,525, and paid transportation costs of $17,400. The purchases returns and allowances and the purchases discounts are deducted from the total purchases to yield the *net purchases*. The transportation costs are added to the net purchases to yield the *cost of merchandise purchased*. These amounts would be reported in the cost of merchandise sold section of Computer King's income statement for 2002 as follows:

Purchases		$521,980	
Less: Purchases returns and allowances	$9,100		
Purchases discounts	2,525	11,625	
Net purchases		$510,355	
Add transportation in		17,400	
Cost of merchandise purchased			$527,755

The ending inventory of Computer King on December 31, 2001, $59,700, becomes the beginning inventory for 2002. In the cost of merchandise sold section of the income statement for 2002, this beginning inventory is added to the cost of merchandise purchased to yield the *merchandise available for sale*. The ending inventory, which is assumed to be $62,150, is then subtracted from the merchandise available for sale to yield the cost of merchandise sold. The cost of merchandise sold during 2002 would be reported as follows:

Cost of merchandise sold:

Merchandise inventory, January 1, 2002			$ 59,700
Purchases		$521,980	
Less: Purchases returns and allowances	$9,100		
Purchases discounts	2,525	11,625	
Net purchases		$510,355	
Add transportation in		17,400	
Cost of merchandise purchased			527,755
Merchandise available for sale			$587,455
Less merchandise inventory, December 31, 2002			62,150
Cost of merchandise sold			$525,305

Q&A *What is the cost of merchandise sold if the beginning inventory is $50,000, the ending inventory is $65,000, the net purchases are $400,000, and the transportation in is $12,000?*

$397,000 ($50,000 + $400,000 + $12,000 − $65,000)

Like the perpetual inventory system, a cost flow assumption must be made when identical units are acquired at different unit costs during a period. In such cases, the fifo, lifo, or average cost method is used.

First-In, First-Out Method

To illustrate the use of the fifo method in a periodic inventory system, we assume the following data:

Jan. 1	Inventory:	200 units at	$ 9	$ 1,800
Mar. 10	Purchase:	300 units at	10	3,000
Sept. 21	Purchase:	400 units at	11	4,400
Nov. 18	Purchase:	100 units at	12	1,200
Available for sale during year		1,000		$10,400

The physical count on December 31 shows that 300 units have not been sold. Using the fifo method, the cost of the 700 units sold is determined as follows:

Earliest costs, Jan. 1:	200 units at	$ 9	$1,800
Next earliest costs, Mar. 10:	300 units at	10	3,000
Next earliest costs, Sept. 21:	200 units at	11	2,200
Cost of merchandise sold:	700		$7,000

Deducting the cost of merchandise sold of $7,000 from the $10,400 of merchandise available for sale yields $3,400 as the cost of the inventory at December 31. The $3,400 inventory is made up of the most recent costs incurred for this item. Exhibit 5 shows the relationship of the cost of merchandise sold during the year and the inventory at December 31.

EXHIBIT 5
First-In, First-Out Flow of Costs

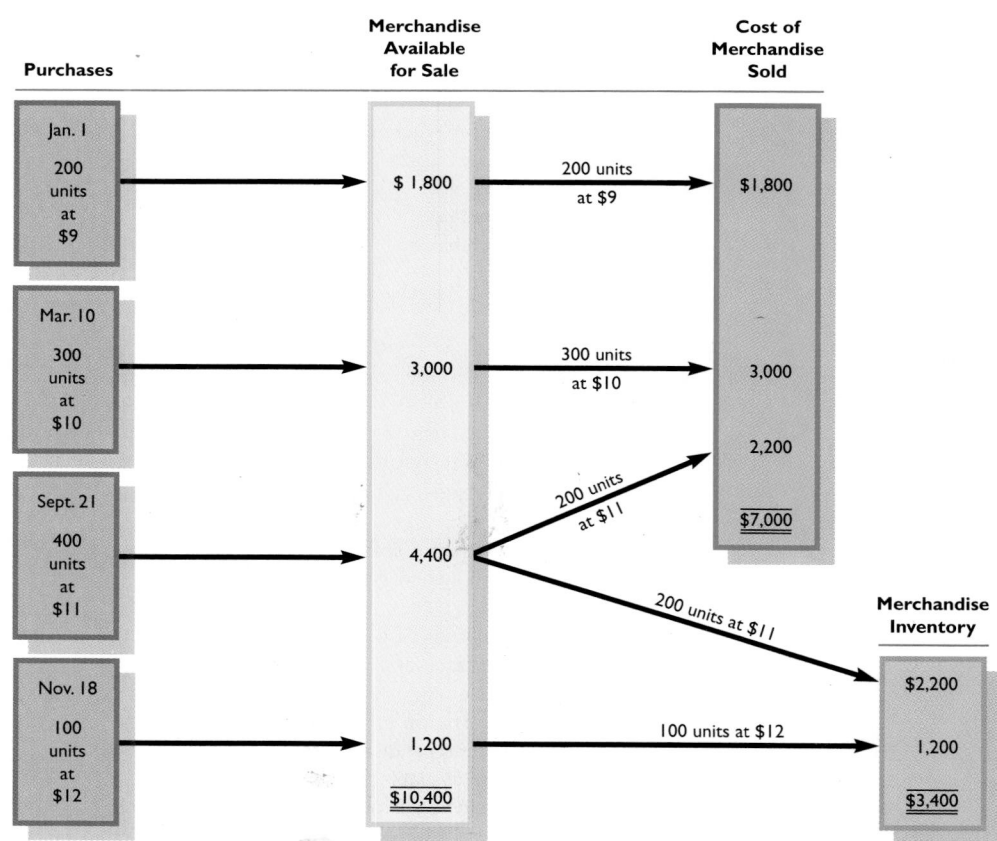

Last-In, First-Out Method

When the lifo method is used, the cost of merchandise sold is made up of the most recent costs. Based on the data in the fifo example, the cost of the 700 units of inventory is determined as follows:

Most recent costs, Nov. 18:	100 units at $12	$1,200
Next most recent costs, Sept. 21:	400 units at 11	4,400
Next most recent costs, Mar. 10:	200 units at 10	2,000
Cost of merchandise sold:	700	$7,600

Deducting the cost of merchandise sold of $7,600 from the $10,400 of merchandise available for sale yields $2,800 as the cost of the inventory at December 31. The $2,800 inventory is made up of the earliest costs incurred for this item. Exhibit 6 shows the relationship of the cost of merchandise sold during the year and the inventory at December 31.

EXHIBIT 6
Last-In, First-Out Flow of Costs

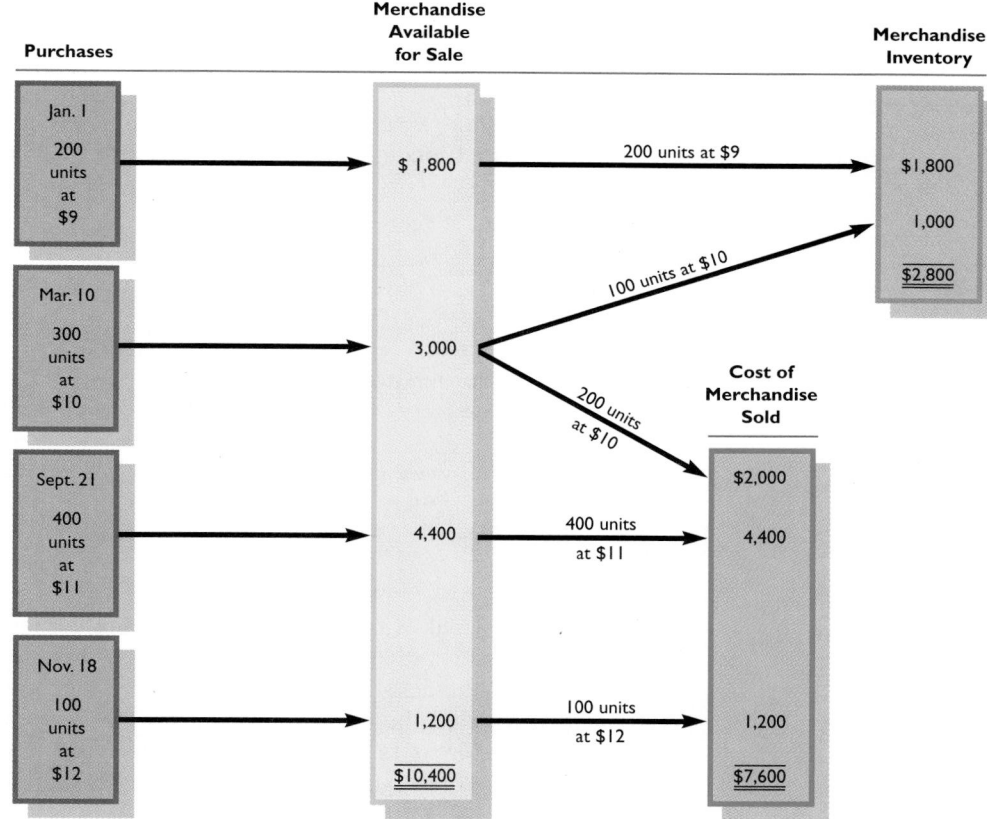

Average Cost Method

The average cost method is sometimes called the **weighted average method**. When this method is used, costs are matched against revenue according to an average of the unit costs of the goods sold. The same weighted average unit costs are used in determining the cost of the merchandise inventory at the end of the period. For businesses in which merchandise sales may be made up of various purchases of identical units, the average method approximates the physical flow of goods.

The weighted average unit cost is determined by dividing the total cost of the units of each item available for sale during the period by the related number of units of that item. Using the same cost data as in the fifo and lifo examples, the average cost of the 1,000 units, $10.40, and the cost of the 700 units, $7,280, are determined as follows:

Average unit cost: $10,400/1,000 units = $10.40
Cost of merchandise sold: 700 units at $10.40 = $7,280

Deducting the cost of merchandise sold of $7,280 from the $10,400 of merchandise available for sale yields $3,120 as the cost of the inventory at December 31.

Comparing Inventory Costing Methods

OBJECTIVE 6

Compare and contrast the use of the three inventory costing methods.

As we have illustrated, a different cost flow is assumed for each of the three alternative methods of costing inventories. You should note that if the cost of units had remained stable, all three methods would have yielded the same results. Since prices do change, however, the three methods will normally yield different amounts for (1) the cost of the merchandise sold for the period, (2) the gross profit (and net income) for the period, and (3) the ending inventory. Using the preceding examples for the periodic inventory system and assuming that net sales were $15,000, the following partial income statements indicate the effects of each method when prices are rising:[1]

Partial Income Statements

	First-In, First-Out		Average Cost		Last-In, First-Out	
Net sales		$15,000		$15,000		$15,000
Cost of merchandise sold:						
Beginning inventory	$ 1,800		$ 1,800		$ 1,800	
Purchases	8,600		8,600		8,600	
Merchandise available for sale	$10,400		$10,400		$10,400	
Less ending inventory	3,400		3,120		2,800	
Cost of merchandise sold		7,000		7,280		7,600
Gross profit		$ 8,000		$ 7,720		$ 7,400

As shown above, the fifo method yielded the lowest amount for the cost of merchandise sold and the highest amount for gross profit (and net income). It also yielded the highest amount for the ending inventory. On the other hand, the lifo method yielded the highest amount for the cost of merchandise sold, the lowest amount for gross profit (and net income), and the lowest amount for ending inventory. The average cost method yielded results that were between those of fifo and lifo.

Use of the First-In, First-Out Method

When the fifo method is used during a period of inflation or rising prices, the earlier unit costs are lower than the more recent unit costs, as shown in the preceding fifo example. Much of the benefit of the larger amount of gross profit is lost, however, because the inventory must be replaced at ever higher prices. In fact, the

---

[1] Similar results would also occur when comparing inventory costing methods under a perpetual inventory system.

balance sheet will report the ending merchandise inventory at an amount that is about the same as its current replacement cost. When the rate of inflation reaches double digits, as it did during the 1970s, the larger gross profits that result from the fifo method are often called *inventory profits* or *illusory profits*. You should note that in a period of deflation or declining prices, the effect is just the opposite.

Use of the Last-In, First-Out Method

When the lifo method is used during a period of inflation or rising prices, the results are opposite those of the other two methods. As shown in the preceding example, the lifo method will yield a higher amount of cost of merchandise sold, a lower amount of gross profit, and a lower amount of inventory at the end of the period than the other two methods. The reason for these effects is that the cost of the most recently acquired units is about the same as the cost of their replacement. In a period of inflation, the more recent unit costs are higher than the earlier unit costs. Thus, it can be argued that the lifo method more nearly matches current costs with current revenues.

 **Chrysler Corporation's** reason for changing from the fifo method to the lifo method was stated in the following footnote that accompanied its financial statements: *Chrysler changed its method of accounting from first-in, first-out (fifo) to last-in, first-out (lifo) for substantially all of its domestic productive inventories. The change to lifo was made to more accurately match current costs with current revenues.*

During periods of rising prices, using lifo offers an income tax savings. The income tax savings results because lifo reports the lowest amount of net income of the three methods. During the double-digit inflationary period of the 1970s, many businesses changed from fifo to lifo for the tax savings. However, the ending inventory on the balance sheet may be quite different from its current replacement cost. In such cases, the financial statements normally include a note that states the estimated difference between the lifo inventory and the inventory if fifo had been used. Again, you should note that in a period of deflation or falling price levels, the effects are just the opposite.

 In the following note, **Sears, Roebuck and Co.** reported the difference in its inventory if fifo had been used instead of lifo: *Inventories would have been $730 million higher if valued on the first-in, first-out, or FIFO, method.*

Use of the Average Cost Method

As you might have already reasoned, the average cost method of inventory costing is, in a sense, a compromise between fifo and lifo. The effect of price trends is averaged in determining the cost of merchandise sold and the ending inventory. For a series of purchases, the average cost will be the same, regardless of the direction of price trends. For example, a complete reversal of the sequence of unit costs presented in the preceding illustration would not affect the reported cost of merchandise sold, gross profit, or ending inventory.

OBJECTIVE 7

Compute the proper valuation of inventory at other than cost, using the lower-of-cost-or-market and net realizable value concepts.

Valuation of Inventory at Other Than Cost

As we indicated earlier, cost is the primary basis for valuing inventories. In some cases, however, inventory is valued at other than cost. Two such cases arise when (1) the cost of replacing items in inventory is below the recorded cost and (2) the inventory is not salable at normal sales prices. This latter case may be due to imperfections, shop wear, style changes, or other causes.

Valuation at Lower of Cost or Market

If the cost of replacing an item in inventory is lower than the original purchase cost, the **lower-of-cost-or-market (LCM) method** is used to value the inventory. *Market,* as used in *lower of cost or market,* is the cost to replace the merchandise on the inventory date. This market value is based on quantities normally purchased from the usual source of supply. In businesses where inflation is the norm, market prices rarely decline. In businesses where technology changes rapidly (e.g., microcomputers and televisions), market declines are common. The primary advantage of the lower-of-cost-or-market method is that gross profit (and net income) is reduced in the period in which the market decline occurred.

 During 1994, **Dell Computer Company** recorded over $39.3 million of charges (expenses) in writing down its inventory of computer notebooks. The remaining inventories of notebooks were then sold at significantly reduced prices.

 *If the cost of an item is $410, its current replacement cost is $400, and its selling price is $525, at what amount should the item be included in the inventory according to the LCM method?*

$400

In applying the lower-of-cost-or-market method, the cost and replacement cost can be determined in one of three ways. Cost and replacement cost can be determined for (1) each item in the inventory, (2) major classes or categories of inventory, or (3) the inventory as a whole. In practice, the cost and replacement cost of each item are usually determined.

To illustrate, assume that there are 400 identical units of Item A in inventory, acquired at a unit cost of $10.25 each. If at the inventory date the item would cost $10.50 to replace, the cost price of $10.25 would be multiplied by 400 to determine the inventory value. On the other hand, if the item could be replaced at $9.50 a unit, the replacement cost of $9.50 would be used for valuation purposes.

Exhibit 7 illustrates a method of organizing inventory data and applying the lower-of-cost-or-market method to each inventory item. The amount of the market decline, $450 ($15,520 − $15,070), may be reported as a separate item on the income statement or included in the cost of merchandise sold. Regardless, net income will be reduced by the amount of the market decline.

EXHIBIT 7
Determining Inventory at Lower of Cost or Market

Commodity	Inventory Quantity	Unit Cost Price	Unit Market Price	Total Cost	Total Market	Total Lower of C or M
A	400	$10.25	$ 9.50	$ 4,100	$ 3,800	$ 3,800
B	120	22.50	24.10	2,700	2,892	2,700
C	600	8.00	7.75	4,800	4,650	4,650
D	280	14.00	14.75	3,920	4,130	3,920
Total				$15,520	$15,472	$15,070

 Out-of-date merchandise is a major problem for many types of retailers. For example, you may have noticed the shelf-life dates of grocery products, such as milk, eggs, canned goods, and meat. Grocery stores often mark down the prices of products nearing the end of their shelf life to avoid having to dispose of the products as waste.

Valuation at Net Realizable Value

As you would expect, merchandise that is out of date, spoiled, or damaged or that can be sold only at prices below cost should be written down. Such merchandise should be valued at net realizable value. **Net realizable value** is the estimated selling price less any direct cost of disposal, such as sales commissions. For example, assume that damaged merchandise costing $1,000 can be sold for only $800, and direct selling expenses are estimated to be $150. This inventory should be valued at $650 ($800 − $150), which is its net realizable value.

Presentation of Merchandise Inventory on the Balance Sheet

OBJECTIVE 8

Prepare a balance sheet presentation of merchandise inventory.

Merchandise inventory is usually presented in the Current Assets section of the balance sheet, following receivables. Both the method of determining the cost of the inventory (fifo, lifo, or average) and the method of valuing the inventory (cost or the lower of cost or market) should be shown. It is not unusual for large businesses with varied activities to use different costing methods for different segments of their inventories. The details may be disclosed in parentheses on the balance sheet or in a footnote to the financial statements. Exhibit 8 shows how parentheses may be used.

 The following note was taken from the financial statements of Chrysler Corporation: *Automotive inventories are valued at the lower of cost or market. The cost of substantially all domestic automotive inventories is recorded on a Last-In, First-Out (LIFO) basis. Aerospace inventories are stated at the lower of cost or market, with cost recognized on a First-In, First-Out (FIFO) basis.*

EXHIBIT 8
Merchandise Inventory on the Balance Sheet

Afro-Arts Balance Sheet December 31, 2001		
Assets		
Current assets:		
Cash		$ 19 400 00
Accounts receivable	$80 000 00	
Less allowance for doubtful accounts	3 000 00	77 000 00
Merchandise inventory—at lower of cost (first-in, first-out method) or market		216 300 00

A company may change its inventory costing methods for a valid reason. In such cases, the effect of the change and the reason for the change should be disclosed in the financial statements for the period in which the change occurred.

Estimating Inventory Cost

OBJECTIVE 9

Estimate the cost of inventory, using the retail method and the gross profit method.

It may be necessary for a business to know the amount of inventory when perpetual inventory records are not maintained and it is impractical to take a physical inventory. For example, a business that uses a periodic inventory system may need monthly income statements, but taking a physical inventory each month may be too costly. Moreover, when a disaster such as a fire has destroyed the inventory, the amount of the loss must be determined. In this case, taking a physical inventory is impossible, and even if perpetual inventory records have been kept, the accounting records may also have been destroyed. In such cases, the inventory cost can be estimated by using (1) the retail method or (2) the gross profit method.

Retail Method of Inventory Costing

The **retail inventory method** of estimating inventory cost is based on the relationship of the cost of merchandise available for sale to the retail price of the same merchandise. To use this method, the retail prices of all merchandise are maintained and totaled. Next, the inventory at retail is determined by deducting sales for the period from the retail price of the goods that were available for sale during the period. The estimated inventory cost is then computed by multiplying the inventory at retail by the ratio of cost to selling (retail) price for the merchandise available for sale, as illustrated in Exhibit 9.

EXHIBIT 9
Determining Inventory by
the Retail Method

	Cost	Retail
Merchandise inventory, January 1	$ 19,400	$ 36,000
Purchases in January (net)	42,600	64,000
Merchandise available for sale	$ 62,000	$100,000
Ratio of cost to retail price: $\frac{\$62,000}{\$100,000} = 62\%$		
Sales for January (net)		70,000
Merchandise inventory, January 31, at retail		$ 30,000
Merchandise inventory, January 31, at estimated cost ($30,000 × 62%)		$ 18,600

When estimating the percent of cost to selling price, we assume that the mix of the items in the ending inventory is the same as the entire stock of merchandise available for sale. In Exhibit 9, for example, it is unlikely that the retail price of every item was made up of exactly 62% cost and 38% gross profit. We assume, however, that the weighted average of the cost percentages of the merchandise in the inventory ($30,000) is the same as in the merchandise available for sale ($100,000). When the inventory is made up of different classes of merchandise with very different gross profit rates, the cost percentages and the inventory should be developed for each class of inventory.

One of the major advantages of the retail method is that it provides inventory figures for use in preparing monthly or quarterly statements when the periodic system is used. Department stores and similar merchandisers like to determine gross profit and operating income each month but may take a physical inventory only once a year. In addition, comparing the estimated ending inventory with the physical ending inventory, both at retail prices, will help identify inventory shortages resulting from shoplifting and other causes. Management can then take appropriate actions.

The retail method may also be used as an aid to taking a physical inventory. In this case, the items counted are recorded on the inventory sheets at their retail (selling) prices instead of their cost prices. The physical inventory at selling price is then converted to cost by applying the ratio of cost to selling (retail) price for the merchandise available for sale.

To illustrate, assume that the data in Exhibit 9 are for an entire fiscal year rather than for only January. If the physical inventory taken at the end of the year totaled $29,000, priced at retail, this amount rather than the $30,000 would be converted to cost. Thus, the inventory at cost would be $17,980 ($29,000 × 62%) instead of $18,600 ($30,000 × 62%). The $17,980 would be used for the year-end financial statements and for income tax purposes.

Gross Profit Method of Estimating Inventories

The **gross profit method** uses the estimated gross profit for the period to estimate the inventory at the end of the period. The gross profit is usually estimated from the actual rate for the preceding year, adjusted for any changes made in the cost

If the ratio of cost to retail is 70% and the ending inventory at retail is $100,000, what is the estimated ending inventory at cost?

- -

$70,000 (70% × $100,000)

and sales prices during the current period. By using the gross profit rate, the dollar amount of sales for a period can be divided into its two components: (1) gross profit and (2) cost of merchandise sold. The latter amount may then be deducted from the cost of merchandise available for sale to yield the estimated cost of the inventory.

Exhibit 10 illustrates the gross profit method for estimating a company's inventory on January 31. In this example, the inventory on January 1 is assumed to be $57,000, the net purchases during the month are $180,000, and the net sales during the month are $250,000. In addition, the historical gross profit was 30% of net sales.

EXHIBIT 10   Estimating Inventory by Gross Profit Method

Merchandise inventory, January 1		$ 57,000
Purchases in January (net)		180,000
Merchandise available for sale		$237,000
Sales in January (net)	$250,000	
Less estimated gross profit ($250,000 × 30%)	75,000	
Estimated cost of merchandise sold		175,000
Estimated merchandise inventory, January 31		$ 62,000

What is the estimated cost of the ending inventory if the merchandise available for sale is $350,000, sales are $500,000, and the gross profit percentage is 40%?

$50,000 [$350,000 − (60% × $500,000)]

The gross profit method is useful for estimating inventories for monthly or quarterly financial statements in a periodic inventory system. It is also useful in estimating the cost of merchandise destroyed by fire or other disasters.

FINANCIAL ANALYSIS AND INTERPRETATION

OBJECTIVE 10

Compute and interpret the inventory turnover ratio and the number of days' sales in inventory.

A merchandising business should keep enough inventory on hand to meet the needs of its customers. A failure to do so may result in lost sales. At the same time, too much inventory reduces solvency by tying up funds that could be better used to expand or improve operations. In addition, excess inventory increases expenses such as storage, insurance, and property taxes. Finally, excess inventory increases the risk of losses due to price declines, damage, or changes in customers' buying patterns.

As with many types of financial analyses, it is possible to use more than one measure to analyze the efficiency and effectiveness by which a business manages its inventory. Two such measures are the inventory turnover and the number of days' sales in inventory.

Inventory turnover measures the relationship between the volume of goods (merchandise) sold and the amount of inventory carried during the period. It is computed as follows:

$$\text{Inventory turnover} = \frac{\textbf{Cost of merchandise sold}}{\textbf{Average inventory}}$$

The average inventory can be computed using weekly, monthly, or yearly figures. To simplify, we determine the average inventory by dividing the sum of the inventories at the beginning and end of the year by 2. As long as the amount of inventory carried throughout the year remains stable, this average will be accurate enough for our analysis.

To illustrate, the following data have been taken from recent annual reports for **SUPERVALU INC.** and **La-Z-Boy Chair Company**:

	SUPERVALU	La-Z-Boy
Cost of merchandise sold	$15,040,117,000	$705,379,000
Inventories:		
Beginning of year	$1,113,937,000	$81,091,000
End of year	$1,109,791,000	$79,192,000
Average	$1,111,864,000	$80,141,500
Inventory turnover	13.5	8.8

The inventory turnover for SUPERVALU is 13.5 and 8.8 for La-Z-Boy. Generally, the larger the inventory turnover, the more efficient and effective the management of inventory. However, differences in companies and industries are too great to allow specific statements as to what is a good inventory turnover. For example, SUPERVALU is a leading food distributor and the twelfth largest food retailer in the United States. Because SUPERVALU's inventory is perishable, we would expect it to have a high inventory turnover. In contrast, La-Z-Boy is the largest reclining chair manufacturer in the United States. Thus, we would expect La-Z-Boy to have a lower inventory turnover than SUPERVALU. As with other financial measures we have discussed, a comparison of a company's inventory turnover over time and with industry averages will provide useful insights into the management of its inventory.

The **number of days' sales in inventory** is a rough measure of the length of time it takes to acquire, sell, and replace the inventory. It is computed as follows:

$$\text{Number of days' sales in inventory} = \frac{\text{Inventory, end of year}}{\text{Average daily cost of merchandise sold}}$$

The average daily cost of merchandise sold is determined by dividing the cost of merchandise sold by 365. The number of days' sales in inventory for SUPERVALU and La-Z-Boy is computed as shown below.

	SUPERVALU	La-Z-Boy
Average daily cost of merchandise sold:		
$15,040,117,000/365	$41,205,800	
$705,379,000/365		$1,932,545
Ending inventory	$1,109,791,000	$79,192,000
Number of days' sales in inventory	26.9 days	41 days

Generally, the lower the number of days' sales in inventory, the better. As with inventory turnover, we should expect differences among industries, such as those for SUPERVALU and La-Z-Boy.

ENCORE

We usually think of inventory in terms of retail stores such as grocery stores, department stores, and convenience stores. In the following paragraphs, however, we describe what you might think of as unusual inventories.

Unusual Inventories— The Strange but True

• **Studio Props.** Theaters periodically have sales to clear out items from past shows. The Studio Theatre in Washington, D.C., included the following items in one of its sales: patio furniture from "Together, Teeth Apart;" restaurant equipment from the ultra-real diner in "The Wash;" "Goblin Market's" giant rocking horse, doll house, quilt, and toy chest; an evening gown from "Death and the Maiden;" and stuffed bunnies from "The Baltimore Waltz."

- **Movie Vehicles.** The mudspattered 1930 Ford Model A pickup sat in a huge, heated garage. Although it looked like just an old truck, this Model A was a star of "The Untouchables." Pierre Laginess is the owner of Antique and Classic Rental Service, a Michigan-based business that provides used collector cars, trucks, and bicycles to film studios. The business began in the early 1970s when Laginess provided a stately, but menacing, 1928 Buick sedan for the original "Godfather." Since then, the business has provided vehicles for "Billy Bathgate," "Hoffa," "Lost in Yonkers," and the television series, "The Young Indiana Jones Chronicles." The business sells many of the cars that have been used in films. Laginess says producers shy away from a vehicle that has had too much exposure.

Eagle-eyed fans recognize them, he said. So they go on sale.

- **Real Used Jeans.** While some jeans makers prewash, "stonewash," or even shotgun their garments to achieve the popular used look, at Whiskey Dust in New York City, you can get the sweaty cowboy finish the old-fashioned way: with real cowboy scent. Whiskey Dust's customers, which include rock stars Jon Bon Jovi and Eric Clapton, pay $65 for Montana Broke jeans that the store says were worn by genuine cowboys. Each well-used pair comes with a guarantee of authenticity and a "Montana Broke Tracking Guide," explaining the origin of each rip, splotch, and frayed hem. The store's customers enthusiastically embrace its unusual inventory. "It's wonderful value. You get a lot of history." Several thousand miles away, Judy McFarlane, a 55-year-old Montana homemaker and a

used jeans supplier, has little problem getting her inventory. "I don't even bother to advertise. People call me all the time." The cowboys "think it's a riot," says Ms. McFarlane.

- **Unwanted Ashes.** The merger of two funeral homes has caused an unusual inventory problem: the unwanted, unclaimed ashes of 1,500 people who were cremated. The remains are those of eastern Washington residents who died between 1917 and 1972. A lot of remains come from the Great Depression era of the 1930s and include doctors, lawyers, and people from all walks of life. For various reasons, relatives didn't claim the ashes. The state law provides that a funeral home can dispose of unclaimed remains after a two-year holding period. The funeral home plans to pack the urns into caskets and bury them at a local cemetery. ■

KEY POINTS

1 **Summarize and provide examples of internal control procedures that apply to inventories.**
Internal control procedures for inventories include those developed to protect the inventories from damage, employee theft, and customer theft. In addition, a physical inventory count should be taken periodically to detect shortages as well as to deter employee thefts.

2 **Describe the effect of inventory errors on the financial statements.**
Any errors in reporting inventory based upon the physical inventory will misstate the ending inventory, current assets, total assets, and owner's equity on the balance sheet. In addition, the cost of goods sold, gross profit,

and net income will be misstated on the income statement.

3 **Describe three inventory cost flow assumptions and how they impact the income statement and balance sheet.**
The three common cost flow assumptions used in business are the (1) first-in, first-out method, (2) last-in, first-out method, and (3) average cost method. Each method normally yields different amounts for the cost of merchandise sold and the ending merchandise inventory. Thus, the choice of a cost flow assumption directly affects the income statement and balance sheet.

4 **Compute the cost of inventory under the perpetual inventory system, using**

the following costing methods:
First-in, first-out
Last-in, first-out
Average cost
In a perpetual inventory system, the number of units and the cost of each type of merchandise are recorded in a subsidiary inventory ledger, with a separate account for each type of merchandise. Inventory costs and the amounts charged against revenue are illustrated using the fifo and lifo methods.

5 **Compute the cost of inventory under the periodic inventory system, using the following costing methods:**
First-in, first-out
Last-in, first-out
Average cost

In a periodic inventory system, a physical inventory is taken to determine the cost of the inventory and the cost of merchandise sold. Inventory costs and the amounts charged against revenue are illustrated using fifo, lifo, and average cost methods.

6 Compare and contrast the use of the three inventory costing methods.

The three inventory costing methods will normally yield different amounts for (1) the ending inventory, (2) the cost of the merchandise sold for the period, and (3) the gross profit (and net income) for the period. During periods of inflation, the fifo method yields the lowest amount for the cost of merchandise sold, the highest amount for gross profit (and net income), and the highest amount for the ending inventory. The lifo method yields the opposite results. During periods of deflation, the preceding effects are reversed. The average cost method yields results that are between those of fifo and lifo.

7 Compute the proper valuation of inventory at other than cost, using the lower-of-cost-or-market and net realizable value concepts.

If the market price of an item of inventory is lower than its cost,

the lower market price is used to compute the value of the item. Market price is the cost to replace the merchandise on the inventory date. It is possible to apply the lower of cost or market to each item in the inventory, to major classes or categories, or to the inventory as a whole.

Merchandise that can be sold only at prices below cost should be valued at net realizable value, which is the estimated selling price less any direct cost of disposal.

8 Prepare a balance sheet presentation of merchandise inventory.

Merchandise inventory is usually presented in the Current Assets section of the balance sheet, following receivables. Both the method of determining the cost of the inventory (fifo, lifo, or average) and the method of valuing the inventory (cost or the lower of cost or market) should be shown.

9 Estimate the cost of inventory, using the retail method and the gross profit method.

In using the retail method to estimate inventory, the retail prices of all merchandise acquired are accumulated. The inventory at retail is determined by deducting

sales for the period from the retail price of the goods that were available for sale during the period. The inventory at retail is then converted to cost on the basis of the ratio of cost to selling (retail) price for the merchandise available for sale.

In using the gross profit method to estimate inventory, the estimated gross profit is deducted from the sales to determine the estimated cost of merchandise sold. This amount is then deducted from the cost of merchandise available for sale to determine the estimated ending inventory.

10 Compute and interpret the inventory turnover ratio and the number of days' sales in inventory.

The inventory turnover ratio, computed as the cost of merchandise sold divided by the average inventory, measures the relationship between the volume of goods (merchandise) sold and the amount of inventory carried during the period. The number of days' sales in inventory, computed as the ending inventory divided by the average daily cost of merchandise sold, measures the length of time it takes to acquire, sell, and replace the inventory.

ILLUSTRATIVE PROBLEM

Stewart Co.'s beginning inventory and purchases during the year ended December 31, 2001, were as follows:

		Units	Unit Cost	Total Cost
January 1	Inventory	1,000	$50.00	$ 50,000
March 10	Purchase	1,200	52.50	63,000
June 25	Sold 800 units			
August 30	Purchase	800	55.00	44,000
October 5	Sold 1,500 units			
November 26	Purchase	2,000	56.00	112,000
December 31	Sold 1,000 units			
Total		5,000		$269,000

Instructions

1. Determine the cost of inventory on December 31, 2001, using the perpetual inventory system and each of the following inventory costing methods:

  a. first-in, first-out
  b. last-in, first-out
2. Determine the cost of inventory on December 31, 2001, using the periodic inventory system and each of the following inventory costing methods:
  a. first-in, first-out
  b. last-in, first-out
  c. average cost
3. Assume that during the fiscal year ended December 31, 2001, sales were $290,000 and the estimated gross profit rate was 40%. Estimate the ending inventory at December 31, 2001, using the gross profit method.

Solution

1. a. First-in, first-out method: $95,200

Date	Purchases Quantity	Purchases Unit Cost	Purchases Total Cost	Cost of Merchandise Sold Quantity	Cost of Merchandise Sold Unit Cost	Cost of Merchandise Sold Total Cost	Inventory Quantity	Inventory Unit Cost	Inventory Total Cost
2001 Jan. 1							1,000	50.00	50,000
Mar. 10	1,200	52.50	63,000				1,000	50.00	50,000
							1,200	52.50	63,000
June 25				800	50.00	40,000	200	50.00	10,000
							1,200	52.50	63,000
Aug. 30	800	55.00	44,000				200	50.00	10,000
							1,200	52.50	63,000
							800	55.00	44,000
Oct. 5				200	50.00	10,000	700	55.00	38,500
				1,200	52.50	63,000			
				100	55.00	5,500			
Nov. 26	2,000	56.00	112,000				700	55.00	38,500
							2,000	56.00	112,000
Dec. 31				700	55.00	38,500	1,700	56.00	95,200
				300	56.00	16,800			

  b. Last-in, first-out method: $91,000 ($35,000 + $56,000)

Date	Purchases Quantity	Purchases Unit Cost	Purchases Total Cost	Cost of Merchandise Sold Quantity	Cost of Merchandise Sold Unit Cost	Cost of Merchandise Sold Total Cost	Inventory Quantity	Inventory Unit Cost	Inventory Total Cost
2001 Jan. 1							1,000	50.00	50,000
Mar. 10	1,200	52.50	63,000				1,000	50.00	50,000
							1,200	52.50	63,000
June 25				800	52.50	42,000	1,000	50.00	50,000
							400	52.50	21,000
Aug. 30	800	55.00	44,000				1,000	50.00	50,000
							400	52.50	21,000
							800	55.00	44,000
Oct. 5				800	55.00	44,000	700	50.00	35,000
				400	52.50	21,000			
				300	50.00	15,000			
Nov. 26	2,000	56.00	112,000				700	50.00	35,000
							2,000	56.00	112,000
Dec. 31				1,000	56.00	56,000	700	50.00	35,000
							1,000	56.00	56,000

2. a. First-in, first-out method:
1,700 units at $56 = $95,200

b. Last-in, first-out method:

1,000 units at $50.00	$50,000
700 units at $52.50	36,750
1,700 units	$86,750

c. Average cost method:

Average cost per unit: $269,000 ÷ 5,000 units = $53.80
Inventory, December 31, 2001:   1,700 units at $53.80 = $91,460

3.

Merchandise inventory, January 1, 2001		$ 50,000
Purchases (net)		219,000
Merchandise available for sale		$269,000
Sales (net)	$290,000	
Less estimated gross profit ($290,000 × 40%)	116,000	
Estimated cost of merchandise sold		174,000
Estimated merchandise inventory, December 31, 2001		$ 95,000

SELF-EXAMINATION QUESTIONS   Answers at End of Chapter

Matching

Match each of the following statements with its proper term. Some terms may not be used.

A. average cost method

B. first-in, first-out (fifo) method

C. gross profit method

D. inventory turnover

E. last-in, first-out (lifo) method

F. lower-of-cost-or-market (LCM) method

G. net realizable value

H. number of days' sales in inventory

I. physical inventory

J. retail inventory method

____ 1. A detailed listing of merchandise on hand.

____ 2. A method of inventory costing based on the assumption that the costs of merchandise sold should be charged against revenue in the order in which the costs were incurred.

____ 3. A method of inventory costing based on the assumption that the most recent merchandise inventory costs should be charged against revenue.

____ 4. The method of inventory costing that is based upon the assumption that costs should be charged against revenue by using the weighted average unit cost of the items sold.

____ 5. A method of valuing inventory that reports the inventory at the lower of its cost or current market value (replacement cost).

____ 6. The estimated selling price of an item of inventory less any direct costs of disposal, such as sales commissions.

____ 7. A method of estimating inventory cost that is based on the relationship of the cost of merchandise available for sale to the retail price of the same merchandise.

____ 8. A method of estimating inventory cost that is based on the relationship of gross profit to sales.

____ 9. A ratio that measures the relationship between the volume of goods (merchandise) sold and the amount of inventory carried during the period.

____ 10. A measure of the length of time it takes to acquire, sell, and replace the inventory.

Multiple Choice

1. If the inventory shrinkage at the end of the year is overstated by $7,500, the error will cause an:
   A. understatement of cost of merchandise sold for the year by $7,500.
   B. overstatement of gross profit for the year by $7,500.
   C. overstatement of merchandise inventory for the year by $7,500.
   D. understatement of net income for the year by $7,500.

2. The inventory costing method that is based on the assumption that costs should be charged against revenue in the order in which they were incurred is:
   A. fifo
   B. lifo
   C. average cost
   D. perpetual inventory

3. The following units of a particular item were purchased and sold during the period:

Beginning inventory	40 units at $20
First purchase	50 units at $21
Second purchase	50 units at $22
First sale	110 units
Third purchase	50 units at $23
Second sale	45 units

   What is the cost of the 35 units on hand at the end of the period as determined under the perpetual inventory system by the lifo costing method?
   A. $715
   B. $705
   C. $700
   D. $805

4. The following units of a particular item were available for sale during the period:

Beginning inventory	40 units at $20
First purchase	50 units at $21
Second purchase	50 units at $22
Third purchase	50 units at $23

   What is the unit cost of the 35 units on hand at the end of the period, as determined under the periodic inventory system by the fifo costing method?
   A. $20
   B. $21
   C. $22
   D. $23

5. If merchandise inventory is being valued at cost and the price level is steadily rising, the method of costing that will yield the highest net income is:
   A. lifo
   B. fifo
   C. average
   D. periodic

CLASS DISCUSSION QUESTIONS

1. What security measures may be used by retailers to protect merchandise inventory from customer theft?

2. Which inventory system provides the more effective means of controlling inventories (perpetual or periodic)? Why?

3. Before inventory purchases are recorded, the receiving report should be reconciled to what documents?

4. What document should be presented by an employee requesting inventory items to be released from the company's warehouse?

5. Why is it important to periodically take a physical inventory if the perpetual system is used?

6. The inventory shrinkage at the end of the year was understated by $10,000. (a) Did the error cause an overstatement or an understatement of the gross profit for the year? (b) Which items on the balance sheet at the end of the year were overstated or understated as a result of the error?

7. Ober Co. sold merchandise to Nunley Company on December 31, FOB shipping point. If the merchandise is in transit on December 31, the end of the fiscal year, which company would report it in its financial statements? Explain.

8. A manufacturer shipped merchandise to a retailer on a consignment basis. If the merchandise is unsold at the end of the period, in whose inventory should the merchandise be included?

9. Do the terms *fifo* and *lifo* refer to techniques used in determining quantities of the various classes of merchandise on hand? Explain.

10. Does the term *last-in* in the lifo method mean that the items in the inventory are assumed to be the most recent (last) acquisitions? Explain.

11. If merchandise inventory is being valued at cost and the price level is steadily rising, which of the three methods of costing—fifo, lifo, or average cost—will yield (a) the highest inventory cost, (b) the lowest inventory cost, (c) the highest gross profit, (d) the lowest gross profit?

12. Which of the three methods of inventory costing—fifo, lifo, or average cost—will in general yield an inventory cost most nearly approximating current replacement cost?

13. If inventory is being valued at cost and the price level is steadily rising, which of the three methods of costing—fifo, lifo, or average cost—will yield the lowest annual income tax expense? Explain.

14. Can a company change its method of costing inventory? Explain.

15. Because of imperfections, an item of merchandise cannot be sold at its normal selling price. How should this item be valued for financial statement purposes?
16. How is the method of determining the cost of the inventory and the method of valuing it disclosed in the financial statements?
17. What uses can be made of the estimate of the cost of inventory determined by the gross profit method?

Resources for Your Success On-Line at warren.swcollege.com
Remember! If you need additional help, visit South-Western's Web site. See page 26 for a description of the online and printed materials that are available.

EXERCISES

Exercise 9–1
Internal control of inventories

Objective 1

Duce Hardware Store currently uses a periodic inventory system. Robin Templin, the owner, is considering the purchase of a computer system that would make it feasible to switch to a perpetual inventory system.

Robin is unhappy with the periodic inventory system because it does not provide timely information on inventory levels. Robin has noticed on several occasions that the store runs out of good-selling items, while too many poor-selling items are on hand.

Robin is also concerned about lost sales while a physical inventory is being taken. Duce Hardware currently takes a physical inventory twice a year. To minimize distractions, the store is closed on the day inventory is taken. Robin believes that closing the store is the only way to get an accurate inventory count.

Will switching to a perpetual inventory system strengthen Duce Hardware's control over inventory items? Will switching to a perpetual inventory system eliminate the need for a physical inventory count? Explain.

Exercise 9–2
Internal control of inventories

Objective 1

Bryers Luggage Shop is a small retail establishment located in a large shopping mall. This shop has implemented the following procedures regarding inventory items:

a. Whenever Bryers receives a shipment of new inventory, the items are taken directly to the stockroom. Bryers' accountant uses the vendor's invoice to record the amount of inventory received.
b. Since the display area of the store is limited, only a sample of each piece of luggage is kept on the selling floor. Whenever a customer selects a piece of luggage, the salesclerk gets the appropriate piece from the store's stockroom. Since all salesclerks need access to the stockroom, it is not locked. The stockroom is adjacent to the break room used by all mall employees.
c. Since the shop carries mostly high-quality, designer luggage, all inventory items are tagged with a control device that activates an alarm if a tagged item is removed from the store.

State whether each of these procedures is appropriate or inappropriate, considering the principles of internal control. If it is inappropriate, state which internal control procedure is violated.

Exercise 9–3
Identifying items to be included in inventory

Objective 1

Tobiason Co., which is located in Camanche, Iowa, has identified the following items for possible inclusion in its December 31, 1999 year-end inventory.

a. Tobiason has segregated $15,800 of merchandise ordered by one of its customers for shipment on January 3, 2000.

b. Tobiason has in its warehouse $21,000 of merchandise on consignment from Stovall Co.

c. Merchandise Tobiason shipped FOB shipping point on December 31, 1999, was picked up by the freight company at 11:50 p.m.

d. Merchandise Tobiason shipped to a customer FOB shipping point was picked up by the freight company on December 26, 1999, but had still not arrived at its destination as of December 31, 1999.

e. Tobiason has $35,000 of merchandise on hand, which was sold to customers earlier in the year, but which has been returned by customers to Tobiason for various warranty repairs.

f. Tobiason has sent $100,000 of merchandise to various retailers on a consignment basis.

g. On December 21, 1999, Tobiason ordered $85,000 of merchandise, FOB Camanche. The merchandise was shipped from the supplier on December 28, 1999, but had not been received by December 31, 1999.

h. On December 27, 1999, Tobiason ordered $15,000 of merchandise from a supplier in Des Moines. The merchandise was shipped FOB Des Moines on December 30, 1999, but had not been received by December 31, 1999.

i. On December 31, 1999, Tobiason received $28,000 of merchandise that had been returned by customers because the wrong merchandise had been shipped. The replacement order is to be shipped overnight on January 3, 2000.

Indicate which items should be included (I) and which should be excluded (E) from the inventory.

Exercise 9–4
Effect of errors in physical inventory

Objective 2

✓ a. Owner's equity, $13,800 understated

The River Bottom sells canoes, kayaks, whitewater rafts, and other boating supplies. During the taking of its physical inventory on December 31, 2000, The River Bottom incorrectly counted its inventory as $82,500 instead of the correct amount of $96,300.

a. State the effect of the error on the December 31, 2000 balance sheet of The River Bottom.

b. State the effect of the error on the income statement of The River Bottom for the year ended December 31, 2000.

Exercise 9–5
Effect of errors in physical inventory

Objective 2

✓ b. Net income, $6,100 overstated

Thema's Motorcycle Shop sells motorcycles, jet skis, and other related supplies and accessories. During the taking of its physical inventory on December 31, 2000, Thema's Motorcycle Shop incorrectly counted its inventory as $102,800 instead of the correct amount of $96,700.

a. State the effect of the error on the December 31, 2000 balance sheet of Thema's Motorcycle Shop.

b. State the effect of the error on the income statement of Thema's Motorcycle Shop for the year ended December 31, 2000.

Exercise 9–6
Error in inventory shrinkage

Objective 2

What's Wrong WITH THIS?

During 2000, the accountant discovered that the physical inventory at the end of 1999 had been understated by $45,000. Instead of correcting the error, however, the accountant assumed that a $45,000 overstatement of the physical inventory in 2000 would balance out the error.

➤ Are there any flaws in the accountant's assumption? Explain.

Exercise 9–7
Perpetual inventory using fifo

Objectives 3, 4

✓ Inventory balance, April 30, $892

Beginning inventory, purchases, and sales data for Commodity MCX are as follows:

Apr.	1	Inventory	25 units at $40
	7	Sale	15 units
	12	Purchase	18 units at $42
	20	Sale	14 units
	22	Sale	3 units
	30	Purchase	10 units at $43

The business maintains a perpetual inventory system, costing by the first-in, first-out method. Determine the cost of the merchandise sold for each sale and the inventory balance after each sale, presenting the data in the form illustrated in Exhibit 3.

Exercise 9–8
Perpetual inventory using lifo
Objectives 3, 4

✓ Inventory balance, April 30, $872

Assume that the business in Exercise 9–7 maintains a perpetual inventory system, costing by the last-in, first-out method. Determine the cost of merchandise sold for each sale and the inventory balance after each sale, presenting the data in the form illustrated in Exhibit 4.

Exercise 9–9
Perpetual inventory using lifo
Objectives 3, 4

✓ Inventory balance, March 31, $238

Beginning inventory, purchases, and sales data for Commodity SKM for March are as follows:

Inventory		Purchases		Sales	
Mar. 1	30 units at $15	Mar. 8	10 units at $18	Mar. 11	9 units
		21	15 units at $19	17	24 units
				29	8 units

Assuming that the perpetual inventory system is used, costing by the lifo method, determine the cost of the inventory balance at March 31, presenting data in the form illustrated in Exhibit 4.

Exercise 9–10
Perpetual inventory using fifo
Objectives 3, 4

✓ Inventory balance, March 31, $266

Assume that the business in Exercise 9–9 maintains a perpetual inventory system, costing by the first-in, first-out method. Determine the cost of the inventory balance at March 31, presenting the data in the form illustrated in Exhibit 3.

Exercise 9–11
Fifo, lifo costs under perpetual inventory system
Objectives 3, 4

✓ a. $840

The following units of a particular item were available for sale during the year:

Beginning inventory	20 units at $45
Sale	15 units at $90
First purchase	30 units at $50
Sale	25 units at $90
Second purchase	40 units at $56
Sale	35 units at $90

The firm uses the perpetual inventory system, and there are 15 units of the item on hand at the end of the year. What is the total cost of the ending inventory according to (a) fifo, (b) lifo?

Exercise 9–12
Identify items missing in determining cost of merchandise sold
Objective 5

For (a) through (d), identify the items designated by "X."

a. Purchases − (X + X) = Net purchases.
b. Net purchases + X = Cost of merchandise purchased.
c. Merchandise inventory (beginning) + Cost of merchandise purchased = X.
d. Merchandise available for sale − X = Cost of merchandise sold.

Exercise 9–13
Cost of merchandise sold and related items
Objective 5

✓ a. Cost of merchandise sold, $536,500

The following data were extracted from the accounting records of C. L. Williams Company for the year ended April 30, 1999:

Merchandise Inventory, May 1, 1998 . . .	$115,000
Merchandise Inventory, April 30, 1999 . .	125,000
Purchases	550,000
Purchases Returns and Allowances	4,500
Purchases Discounts	2,950
Sales	670,625
Transportation In	3,950

a. Prepare the cost of merchandise sold section of the income statement for the year ended April 30, 1999.

b. Determine the gross profit to be reported on the income statement for the year ended April 30, 1999.

Exercise 9–14
Cost of merchandise sold

Objective 5

What's Wrong WITH THIS?

✓ Correct cost of merchandise sold, $489,700

How many errors can you find in the following schedule of cost of merchandise sold for the current year ended December 31?

Cost of merchandise sold:

Merchandise inventory, December 31			$105,000
Purchases		$500,000	
Plus: Purchases returns and allowances	$12,500		
Purchases discounts	6,500	19,000	
Gross purchases		$519,000	
Less transportation in		2,400	
Cost of merchandise purchased			516,600
Merchandise available for sale			$621,600
Less merchandise inventory, January 1			111,300
Cost of merchandise sold			$510,300

Exercise 9–15
Periodic inventory by three methods

Objectives 3, 5

SPREADSHEET

✓ b. $1,055

The units of an item available for sale during the year were as follows:

Jan.	1	Inventory	35 units at $23
Mar.	4	Purchase	10 units at $25
Aug.	20	Purchase	30 units at $28
Nov.	30	Purchase	25 units at $30

There are 45 units of the item in the physical inventory at December 31. The periodic inventory system is used. Determine the inventory cost by (a) the first-in, first-out method, (b) the last-in, first-out method, and (c) the average cost method.

Exercise 9–16
Periodic inventory by three methods; cost of merchandise sold

Objectives 3, 5

SPREADSHEET

✓ a. Inventory, $1,390

The units of an item available for sale during the year were as follows:

Jan.	1	Inventory	25 units at $60
Mar.	4	Purchase	30 units at $65
Aug.	7	Purchase	10 units at $68
Nov.	15	Purchase	15 units at $70

There are 20 units of the item in the physical inventory at December 31. The periodic inventory system is used. Determine the inventory cost and the cost of merchandise sold by three methods, presenting your answers in the following form:

		Cost	
Inventory Method		Merchandise Inventory	Merchandise Sold
a.	First-in, first-out	$	$
b.	Last-in, first-out		
c.	Average cost		

Exercise 9–17
Lower-of-cost-or-market inventory

Objective 7

✓ LCM: $11,715

On the basis of the following data, determine the value of the inventory at the lower of cost or market. Assemble the data in the form illustrated in Exhibit 7.

Commodity	Inventory Quantity	Unit Cost Price	Unit Market Price
4HU	10	$325	$320
153T	17	110	115
Z10	12	275	260
SAW1	15	51	45
SAW2	30	95	100

Exercise 9–18
Merchandise inventory on the balance sheet

Objective 8

Based on the data in Exercise 9–17 and assuming that cost was determined by the fifo method, show how the merchandise inventory would appear on the balance sheet.

Exercise 9–19
Retail inventory method

Objective 9

✓ Inventory: $228,000

A business using the retail method of inventory costing determines that merchandise inventory at retail is $380,000. If the ratio of cost to retail price is 60%, what is the amount of inventory to be reported on the financial statements?

Exercise 9–20
Retail inventory method

Objective 9

✓ Inventory, June 30: $307,200

On the basis of the following data, estimate the cost of the merchandise inventory at June 30 by the retail method:

		Cost	Retail
June 1	Merchandise inventory	$428,300	$ 670,500
June 1–30	Purchases (net)	608,500	949,500
June 1–30	Sales (net)		1,140,000

Exercise 9–21
Gross profit inventory method

Objective 9

✓ a. $318,800

The merchandise inventory was destroyed by fire on October 20. The following data were obtained from the accounting records:

Jan. 1	Merchandise inventory	$ 160,000
Jan. 1–Oct. 20	Purchases (net)	850,000
	Sales (net)	1,080,000
	Estimated gross profit rate	36%

a. Estimate the cost of the merchandise destroyed.
b. Briefly describe the situations in which the gross profit method is useful.

Exercise 9–22
Inventory turnover and number of days' sales in inventory

Objective 10

HAT

The financial statements for **Hershey Foods Corporation** are presented in Appendix G at the end of the text. Hershey Foods Corporation has inventories of $445,702,000 at December 31, 1994.

a. For the years ended December 31, 1996 and 1995, determine: (1) the inventory turnover, and (2) the number of days' sales in inventory.
b. ▬▬▶ What conclusions can be drawn from these analyses concerning Hershey's efficiency in managing inventory?

PROBLEMS SERIES A

Problem 9–1A
Fifo perpetual inventory

Objectives 3, 4

✓ 3. $6,500

The beginning inventory of Commodity PAC315 at Saunders Co. and data on purchases and sales for a three-month period are as follows:

Date	Transaction	Number of Units	Per Unit	Total
April 1	Inventory	15	$220	$3,300
7	Purchase	25	225	5,625
18	Sale	10	300	3,000
22	Sale	13	300	3,900
May 4	Purchase	15	230	3,450
10	Sale	10	310	3,100
21	Sale	5	310	1,550
31	Purchase	20	235	4,700
June 5	Sale	15	315	4,725
13	Sale	12	315	3,780
21	Purchase	20	240	4,800
28	Sale	14	320	4,480

Instructions

1. Record the inventory, purchases, and cost of merchandise sold data in a perpetual inventory record similar to the one illustrated in Exhibit 3, using the first-in, first-out method.
2. Determine the total sales and the total cost of Commodity PAC315 sold for the period. Journalize the entries in the sales and cost of merchandise sold accounts. Assume that all sales were on account.
3. Determine the gross profit from sales of Commodity PAC315 for the period.
4. Determine the ending inventory cost.

Problem 9–2A

Lifo perpetual inventory

Objectives 3, 4

✓ 2. Gross profit, $6,300

The beginning inventory of Commodity PAC315 and data on purchases and sales for a three-month period are shown in Problem 9–1A.

Instructions

1. Record the inventory, purchases, and cost of merchandise sold data in a perpetual inventory record similar to the one illustrated in Exhibit 4, using the last-in, first-out method.
2. Determine the total sales, the total cost of Commodity PAC315 sold, and the gross profit from sales for the period.
3. Determine the ending inventory cost.

Problem 9–3A

Periodic inventory by three methods

Objectives 3, 5

SPREADSHEET

✓ 1. $10,847

Three Rivers Television uses the periodic inventory system. Details regarding the inventory of television sets at January 1, purchases invoices during the year, and the inventory count at December 31 are summarized as follows:

| Model | Inventory, January 1 | Purchases Invoices | | | Inventory Count, December 31 |
		1st	2nd	3rd	
B91	4 at $149	6 at $151	8 at $157	7 at $156	6
F10	3 at 208	3 at 212	5 at 213	4 at 225	4
H21	2 at 520	2 at 527	2 at 530	2 at 535	3
J39	6 at 520	8 at 531	4 at 549	6 at 542	7
P80	9 at 213	7 at 215	6 at 222	6 at 225	8
T15	6 at 305	3 at 310	3 at 316	4 at 317	5
V11	—	4 at 222	4 at 232	—	1

Instructions

1. Determine the cost of the inventory on December 31 by the first-in, first-out method. Present data in columnar form, using the following headings:

Model	Quantity	Unit Cost	Total Cost

If the inventory of a particular model comprises one entire purchase plus a portion of another purchase acquired at a different unit cost, use a separate line for each purchase.
2. Determine the cost of the inventory on December 31 by the last-in, first-out method, following the procedures indicated in (1).
3. Determine the cost of the inventory on December 31 by the average cost method, using the columnar headings indicated in (1).
4. ✏➤ Discuss which method (fifo or lifo) would be preferred for income tax purposes in periods of (a) rising prices and (b) declining prices.

Problem 9–4A

Lower-of-cost-or-market inventory

Objective 7

SPREADSHEET

✓ Total LCM, $54,272

If the working papers correlating with this textbook are not used, omit Problem 9–4A.

Data on the physical inventory of Tyner Co. as of December 31, the end of the current fiscal year, are presented in the working papers. The quantity of each commodity on hand has been determined and recorded on the inventory sheet. Unit market prices have also been determined as of December 31 and recorded on the sheet. The inventory is to be determined at cost and also at the lower of cost or market, using the first-in, first-out method. Quantity and cost data from the last purchases invoice of the year and the next-to-the-last purchases invoice are summarized as follows:

Description	Last Purchases Invoice		Next-to-the-Last Purchases Invoice	
	Quantity Purchased	Unit Cost	Quantity Purchased	Unit Cost
F71	30	$ 60	40	$ 58
C22	25	190	15	190
D82	18	143	15	142
E34	150	25	100	27
F17	6	550	15	540
J19	75	14	100	13
K41	8	400	5	398
M21	500	6	500	7
R72	70	17	50	16
T15	5	250	4	260
V55	500	9	500	8
AC2	100	45	100	46
BB7	5	410	5	400
BD1	120	19	100	17
DD1	50	15	40	16
EB2	50	28	50	27
FF7	55	28	50	28
GE4	6	701	5	699

Instructions

Record the appropriate unit costs on the inventory sheet, and complete the pricing of the inventory. When there are two different unit costs applicable to an item, proceed as follows:

1. Draw a line through the quantity, and insert the quantity and unit cost of the last purchase.
2. On the following line, insert the quantity and unit cost of the next-to-the-last purchase. The first item on the inventory sheet has been completed as an example.

Problem 9–5A

Retail method; gross profit method

Objective 9

SPREADSHEET

✓ 1. $98,800
✓ 2. a. $246,000

Selected data on merchandise inventory, purchases, and sales for Bozeman Co. and Gallatin Co. are as follows:

	Cost	Retail
Bozeman Co.		
Merchandise inventory, February 1	$ 177,100	$ 227,000
Transactions during February:		
Purchases (net)	903,200	1,435,000
Sales		1,550,000
Sales returns and allowances		40,000
Gallatin Co.		
Merchandise inventory, July 1	$ 317,900	
Transactions during July and August:		
Purchases (net)	1,432,100	
Sales	2,475,000	
Sales returns and allowances	125,000	
Estimated gross profit rate	36%	

Instructions

1. Determine the estimated cost of the merchandise inventory of Bozeman Co. on February 28 by the retail method, presenting details of the computations.
2. a. Estimate the cost of the merchandise inventory of Gallatin Co. on August 31 by the gross profit method, presenting details of the computations.
   b. Assume that Gallatin Co. took a physical inventory on August 31 and discovered that $212,900 of merchandise was on hand. What was the estimated loss of inventory due to theft or damage during July and August?

Problem 9–1B
Fifo perpetual inventory

Objectives 3, 4

✓ 3. $214,750

The beginning inventory of ZIP910 at Marks Co. and data on purchases and sales for a three-month period are as follows:

Date		Transaction	Number of Units	Per Unit	Total
July	1	Inventory	25,000	$6.10	$152,500
	8	Purchase	75,000	6.15	461,250
	20	Sale	45,000	7.00	315,000
	31	Sale	35,000	7.00	245,000
Aug.	8	Sale	5,000	7.10	35,500
	10	Purchase	50,000	6.20	310,000
	27	Sale	40,000	7.20	288,000
	30	Sale	20,000	7.15	143,000
Sept.	5	Purchase	60,000	6.05	363,000
	13	Sale	30,000	7.00	210,000
	22	Purchase	35,000	6.00	210,000
	30	Sale	55,000	7.00	385,000

Instructions

1. Record the inventory, purchases, and cost of merchandise sold data in a perpetual inventory record similar to the one illustrated in Exhibit 3, using the first-in, first-out method.
2. Determine the total sales and the total cost of Commodity ZIP910 sold for the period. Journalize the entries in the sales and cost of merchandise sold accounts. Assume that all sales were on account.
3. Determine the gross profit from sales for the period.
4. Determine the ending inventory cost.

Problem 9–2B
Lifo perpetual inventory

Objectives 3, 4

✓ 2. Gross profit, $215,750

The beginning inventory of ZIP910 at Marks Co. and data on purchases and sales for a three-month period are shown in Problem 9–1B.

Instructions

1. Record the inventory, purchases, and cost of merchandise sold data in a perpetual inventory record similar to the one illustrated in Exhibit 4, using the last-in, first-out method.
2. Determine the total sales, the total cost of Commodity ZIP910 sold, and the gross profit from sales for the period.
3. Determine the ending inventory cost.

Problem 9–3B
Periodic inventory by three methods

Objectives 3, 5

SPREADSHEET

✓ 1. $8,951

Martel Television uses the periodic inventory system. Details regarding the inventory of television sets at July 1, 1999, purchases invoices during the year, and the inventory count at June 30, 2000, are summarized as follows:

Model	Inventory, July 1	Purchases Invoices			Inventory Count, June 30
		1st	2nd	3rd	
A37	6 at $240	4 at $250	8 at $260	10 at $262	14
E15	6 at 80	5 at 82	8 at 89	8 at 90	8
L10	2 at 108	2 at 110	3 at 128	3 at 130	3
O18	8 at 88	4 at 79	3 at 85	6 at 92	8
K72	2 at 250	2 at 260	4 at 271	4 at 272	3
S91	5 at 160	4 at 170	4 at 175	7 at 180	8
V17	—	4 at 150	4 at 200	4 at 202	6

Instructions

1. Determine the cost of the inventory on June 30, 2000, by the first-in, first-out method. Present data in columnar form, using the following headings:

Model	Quantity	Unit Cost	Total Cost

If the inventory of a particular model comprises one entire purchase plus a portion of another purchase acquired at a different unit cost, use a separate line for each purchase.

2. Determine the cost of the inventory on June 30, 2000, by the last-in, first-out method, following the procedures indicated in (1).

3. Determine the cost of the inventory on June 30, 2000, by the average cost method, using the columnar headings indicated in (1).

4. ◖▬▬▬▶ Discuss which method (fifo or lifo) would be preferred for income tax purposes in periods of (a) rising prices and (b) declining prices.

Problem 9–4B

Lower-of-cost-or-market inventory

Objective 7

SPREADSHEET

✓ Total LCM, $54,951

If the working papers correlating with this textbook are not used, omit Problem 9–4B.

Data on the physical inventory of Minish Company as of December 31, the end of the current fiscal year, are presented in the working papers. The quantity of each commodity on hand has been determined and recorded on the inventory sheet. Unit market prices have also been determined as of December 31 and recorded on the sheet. The inventory is to be determined at cost and also at the lower of cost or market, using the first-in, first-out method. Quantity and cost data from the last purchases invoice of the year and the next-to-the-last purchases invoice are summarized as follows:

Description	Last Purchases Invoice Quantity Purchased	Last Purchases Invoice Unit Cost	Next-to-the-Last Purchases Invoice Quantity Purchased	Next-to-the-Last Purchases Invoice Unit Cost
F71	30	$ 60	30	$ 58
C22	25	208	20	205
D82	10	145	25	142
E34	150	25	100	24
F17	10	560	10	570
J19	100	15	100	14
K41	10	387	5	384
M21	500	6	500	6
R72	80	19	50	18
T15	5	255	4	260
V55	700	9	500	9
AC2	100	47	50	46
BB7	5	420	5	424
BD1	100	20	75	19
DD1	60	17	40	16
EB2	50	29	25	28
FF7	75	27	60	25
GE4	5	702	5	699

Instructions

Record the appropriate unit costs on the inventory sheet, and complete the pricing of the inventory. When there are two different unit costs applicable to an item, proceed as follows:

1. Draw a line through the quantity, and insert the quantity and unit cost of the last purchase.

2. On the following line, insert the quantity and unit cost of the next-to-the-last purchase. The first item on the inventory sheet has been completed as an example.

Problem 9–5B
Retail method; gross profit method

Objective 9

SPREADSHEET

✓ 1. $226,300

✓ 2. a. $128,440

Selected data on merchandise inventory, purchases, and sales for Hefron Co. and Cummins Co. are as follows:

	Cost	Retail
Hefron Co.		
Merchandise inventory, August 1	$ 137,980	$270,000
Transactions during August:		
Purchases (net)	658,450	821,000
Sales		790,000
Sales returns and allowances		9,000
Cummins Co.		
Merchandise inventory, April 1	$ 117,500	
Transactions during April and May:		
Purchases (net)	825,000	
Sales	1,325,000	
Sales returns and allowances	12,000	
Estimated gross profit rate	38%	

Instructions

1. Determine the estimated cost of the merchandise inventory of Hefron Co. on August 31 by the retail method, presenting details of the computations.
2. a. Estimate the cost of the merchandise inventory of Cummins Co. on May 31 by the gross profit method, presenting details of the computations.
   b. Assume that Cummins Co. took a physical inventory on May 31 and discovered that $118,000 of merchandise was on hand. What was the estimated loss of inventory due to theft or damage during April and May?

SPECIAL ACTIVITIES

Activity 9–1
Torres Co.
Ethics and professional conduct in business

Torres Co. is experiencing a decrease in sales and operating income for the fiscal year ending December 31, 2000. Jess Jaeger, controller of Torres Co., has suggested that all orders received before the end of the fiscal year be shipped by midnight, December 31, 2000, even if the shipping department must work overtime. Since Torres Co. ships all merchandise FOB shipping point, it would record all such shipments as sales for the year ending December 31, 2000, thereby offsetting some of the decreases in sales and operating income.

➤ Discuss whether Jess Jaeger is behaving in a professional manner.

Activity 9–2
Walgreen Co.
Fifo vs. lifo

The following footnote was taken from the 1996 financial statements of **Walgreen Co.**:

Inventories are valued on a . . . last-in, first-out (LIFO) cost . . . basis. At August 31, 1996 and 1995, inventories would have been greater by $427,767,000 and $415,015,000 respectively, if they had been valued on a lower of first-in, first-out (FIFO) cost or market basis.

Additional data are as follows:

Earnings before income taxes, 1996	$ 606,937,000
Total lifo inventories, August 31, 1996	1,631,974,000

Based on the preceding data, determine (a) what the total inventories at August 31, 1996, would have been, using the fifo method, and (b) what the earnings before income taxes for the year ended August 31, 1996, would have been if fifo had been used instead of lifo.

Activity 9–3
Essex Wholesale Co.
Lifo and inventory flow

The following is an excerpt from a conversation between Jessica Erbert, the warehouse manager for Essex Wholesale Co., and its accountant, Tara Dowell. Essex Wholesale operates a large regional warehouse that supplies produce and other grocery products to grocery stores in smaller communities.

Jessica: Tara, can you explain what's going on here with these monthly statements?
Tara: Sure, Jessica. How can I help you?
Jessica: I don't understand this last-in, first-out inventory procedure. It just doesn't make sense.
Tara: Well, what it means is that we assume that the last goods we receive are the first ones sold. So the inventory is made up of the items we purchased first.
Jessica: Yes, but that's my problem. It doesn't work that way! We always distribute the oldest produce first. Some of that produce is perishable! We can't keep any of it very long or it'll spoil.
Tara: Jessica, you don't understand. We only *assume* that the products we distribute are the last ones received. We don't actually have to distribute the goods in this way.
Jessica: I always thought that accounting was supposed to show what really happened. It all sounds like "make believe" to me! Why not report what really happens?

✏️➤ Respond to Jessica's concerns.

Activity 9–4
Ritter Company
Costing inventory

Ritter Company began operations in 1999 by selling a single product. Data on purchases and sales for the year were as follows:

Purchases:

Date	Units Purchased	Unit Cost	Total Cost
April 8	4,875	$12.20	$ 59,475
May 10	5,125	13.00	66,625
June 4	5,000	13.20	66,000
July 10	5,000	14.00	70,000
August	3,400	14.25	48,450
October 5	1,600	14.50	23,200
November 1	1,000	14.75	14,750
December 10	1,000	16.00	16,000
	27,000		$364,500

Sales:

April	2,000 units
May	2,000
June	3,500
July	4,000
August	3,500
September	3,500
October	2,250
November	1,250
December	1,000
Total units	23,000
Total sales	$552,000

On January 3, 2000, the president of the company, Stuart Ritter, asked for your advice on costing the 4,000-unit physical inventory that was taken on December 31, 1999. Moreover, since the firm plans to expand its product line, he asked for your advice on the use of a perpetual inventory system in the future.

1. Determine the cost of the December 31, 1999 inventory under the periodic system, using the (a) first-in, first-out method, (b) last-in, first-out method, and (c) average cost method.
2. Determine the gross profit for the year under each of the three methods in (1).

3. a.  Explain varying viewpoints why each of the three inventory costing methods may best reflect the results of operations for 1999.

   b.  Which of the three inventory costing methods may best reflect the replacement cost of the inventory on the balance sheet as of December 31, 1999?

   c.  Which inventory costing method would you choose to use for income tax purposes? Why?

   d.  Discuss the advantages and disadvantages of using a perpetual inventory system. From the data presented in this case, is there any indication of the adequacy of inventory levels during the year?

Activity 9–5
Into the Real World
Observe internal controls over inventory

Select a business in your community and observe its internal controls over inventory. In groups of three or four, identify and discuss the similarities and differences in each business's inventory controls. Prepare a written summary of your findings.

Activity 9–6
Into the Real World
Compare inventory cost flow assumptions

In groups of three or four, examine the financial statements of a well-known retailing business. You may obtain the financial statements you need from one of the following sources:

1. Your school or local library.
2. The investor relations department of the company.
3. The company's Web site on the Internet.
4. EDGAR (Electronic Data Gathering, Analysis, and Retrieval), the electronic archives of financial statements filed with the Securities and Exchange Commission. The Edgar address is:

   www.sec.gov/edgarhp.htm

   To obtain annual report information, type in a company name on the "Search EDGAR Archives" form. EDGAR will list the reports available for the selected company. A company's annual report (along with other information) is provided in its annual 10-K report to the SEC. Click on the 10-K (or 10-K405) report for the year you wish to download. If you wish, you can save the whole 10-K report to a file, then open it with your word processor.

Determine the cost flow assumption(s) that the company is using for its inventory, and determine whether the company is using the lower-of-cost-or-market rule. Prepare a written summary of your findings.

ANSWERS TO SELF-EXAMINATION QUESTIONS

Matching

1. I	3. E	5. F	7. J	9. D
2. B	4. A	6. G	8. C	10. H

Multiple Choice

1. **D** The overstatement of inventory shrinkage by $7,500 at the end of the year will cause the cost of merchandise sold for the year to be overstated by $7,500, the gross profit for the year to be understated by $7,500, the merchandise inventory to be understated by $7,500, and the net income for the year to be understated by $7,500 (answer D).

2. **A** The fifo method (answer A) is based on the assumption that costs are charged against revenue in the order in which they were incurred. The lifo method (answer B) charges the most recent costs incurred against revenue, and the average cost method (answer C) charges a weighted average of unit costs of items sold against revenue. The perpetual inventory system (answer D) is a system and not a method of costing.

3. **A**   The lifo method of costing is based on the assumption that costs should be charged against revenue in the reverse order in which costs were incurred. Thus, the oldest costs are assigned to inventory. Thirty of the 35 units would be assigned a unit cost of $20 (since 110 of the beginning inventory units were sold on the first sale), and the remaining 5 units would be assigned a cost of $23, for a total of $715 (answer A).

4. **D**   The fifo method of costing is based on the assumption that costs should be charged against revenue in the order in which they were incurred (first-in, first-out). Thus, the most recent costs are assigned to inventory. The 35 units would be assigned a unit cost of $23 (answer D).

5. **B**   When the price level is steadily rising, the earlier unit costs are lower than recent unit costs. Under the fifo method (answer B), these earlier costs are matched against revenue to yield the highest possible net income. The periodic inventory system (answer D) is a system and not a method of costing.

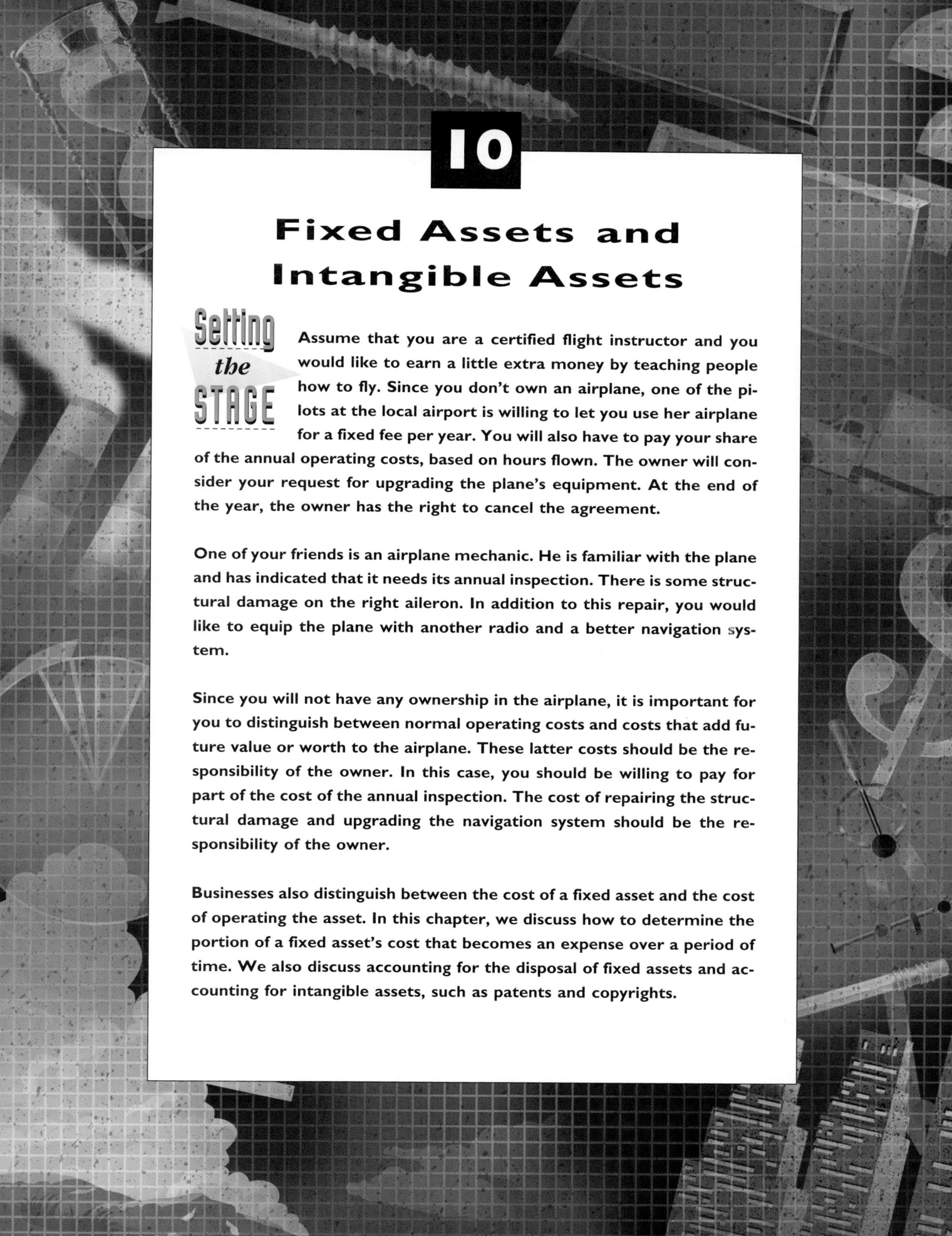

10

Fixed Assets and Intangible Assets

Setting the STAGE

Assume that you are a certified flight instructor and you would like to earn a little extra money by teaching people how to fly. Since you don't own an airplane, one of the pilots at the local airport is willing to let you use her airplane for a fixed fee per year. You will also have to pay your share of the annual operating costs, based on hours flown. The owner will consider your request for upgrading the plane's equipment. At the end of the year, the owner has the right to cancel the agreement.

One of your friends is an airplane mechanic. He is familiar with the plane and has indicated that it needs its annual inspection. There is some structural damage on the right aileron. In addition to this repair, you would like to equip the plane with another radio and a better navigation system.

Since you will not have any ownership in the airplane, it is important for you to distinguish between normal operating costs and costs that add future value or worth to the airplane. These latter costs should be the responsibility of the owner. In this case, you should be willing to pay for part of the cost of the annual inspection. The cost of repairing the structural damage and upgrading the navigation system should be the responsibility of the owner.

Businesses also distinguish between the cost of a fixed asset and the cost of operating the asset. In this chapter, we discuss how to determine the portion of a fixed asset's cost that becomes an expense over a period of time. We also discuss accounting for the disposal of fixed assets and accounting for intangible assets, such as patents and copyrights.

After studying this chapter, you should be able to:

1 Define fixed assets and describe the accounting for their cost.

2 Compute depreciation, using the following methods: straight-line method, units-of-production method, and declining-balance method.

3 Classify fixed asset costs as either capital expenditures or revenue expenditures.

4 Journalize entries for the disposal of fixed assets.

5 Define a lease and summarize the accounting rules related to the leasing of fixed assets.

6 Describe internal controls over fixed assets.

7 Compute depletion and journalize the entry for depletion.

8 Journalize the entries for acquiring and amortizing intangible assets, such as patents, copyrights, and goodwill.

9 Describe how depreciation expense is reported in an income statement and prepare a balance sheet that includes fixed assets and intangible assets.

10 Compute and interpret the ratio of fixed assets to long-term liabilities.

Nature of Fixed Assets

OBJECTIVE 1

Define fixed assets and describe the accounting for their cost.

Businesses use a variety of fixed assets, such as equipment, furniture, tools, machinery, buildings, and land. **Fixed assets** are long-term or relatively permanent assets. They are **tangible assets** because they exist physically. They are owned and used by the business and are not offered for sale as part of normal operations. Other descriptive titles for these assets are **plant assets** or **property, plant, and equipment**.

There is no standard rule for the minimum length of life necessary for an asset to be classified as a fixed asset. Such assets must be capable of providing repeated use or benefit and are normally expected to last more than a year. However, an asset need not actually be used on an ongoing basis or even often. For example, standby equipment for use in the event of a breakdown of regular equipment or for use only during peak periods is included in fixed assets.

Long-term assets acquired for resale in the normal course of business are not classified as fixed assets, regardless of their permanent nature or the length of time they are held. For example, undeveloped land or other real estate acquired as an investment for resale should be listed on the balance sheet in the asset section entitled *Investments*.

Q&A *St. Mary's Hospital maintains an auxiliary generator for use in electrical outages. Such outages are rare, and the generator has not been used for the past two years. Should the generator be included as a fixed asset in St. Mary's ledger?*

Yes. Even though the generator has not been used recently, it should be included as a fixed asset.

The normal costs of using or operating a fixed asset are reported as expenses on a company's income statement. The costs of acquiring a fixed asset become expenses over a period of time. In the next section, we discuss these latter costs and their recognition as expenses.

Costs of Acquiring Fixed Assets

The cost of acquiring a fixed asset includes all amounts spent to get it in place and ready for use. For example, freight costs and the costs of installing equipment are included as part of the asset's total cost. Exhibit 1 summarizes some of the common costs of acquiring fixed assets. These costs should be recorded by debiting the re-

EXHIBIT 1
Costs of Acquiring Fixed
Assets

LAND

- Purchase price
- Sales taxes
- Permits from government agencies
- Broker's commissions
- Title fees
- Surveying fees
- Delinquent real estate taxes
- Razing or removing unwanted buildings, less any salvage
- Grading and leveling
- Paving a public street bordering the land

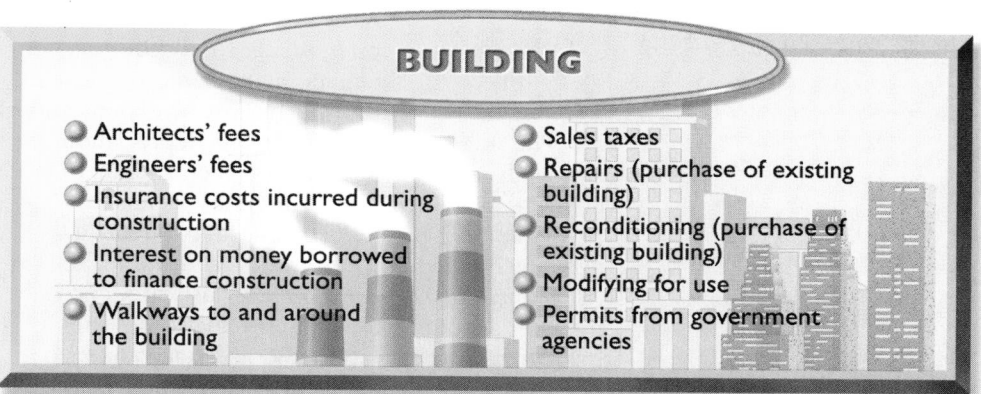

BUILDING

- Architects' fees
- Engineers' fees
- Insurance costs incurred during construction
- Interest on money borrowed to finance construction
- Walkways to and around the building
- Sales taxes
- Repairs (purchase of existing building)
- Reconditioning (purchase of existing building)
- Modifying for use
- Permits from government agencies

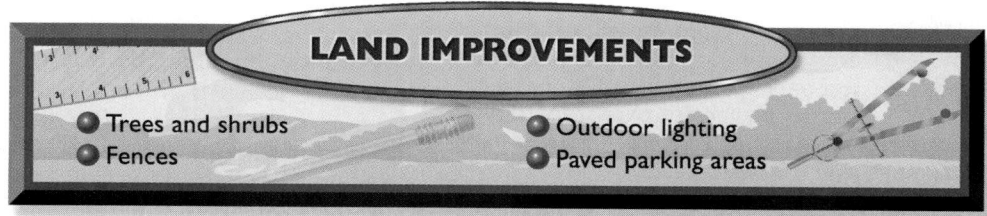

LAND IMPROVEMENTS

- Trees and shrubs
- Fences
- Outdoor lighting
- Paved parking areas

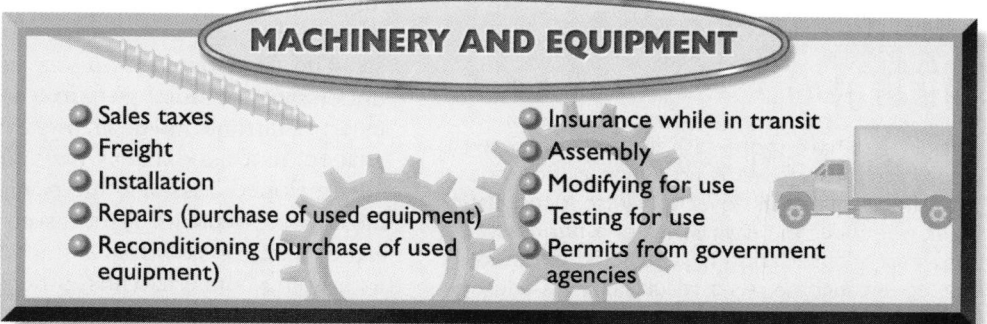

MACHINERY AND EQUIPMENT

- Sales taxes
- Freight
- Installation
- Repairs (purchase of used equipment)
- Reconditioning (purchase of used equipment)
- Insurance while in transit
- Assembly
- Modifying for use
- Testing for use
- Permits from government agencies

lated fixed asset account, such as Land,[1] Building, Land Improvements, or Machinery and Equipment.

Costs *not necessary* for getting a fixed asset ready for use do not increase the asset's usefulness. Such costs should not be included as part of the asset's total cost. For example, the following costs should be debited to an expense account:

[1] As discussed here, land is assumed to be used only as a location or site. Land acquired for its mineral deposits or other natural resources will be considered later in the chapter.

Q&A *Glacier Co. is purchasing property (building and land) for use as a warehouse. In purchasing the land, Glacier has agreed to pay the prior owner's delinquent property taxes. Should the cost of paying the delinquent property taxes be included as part of the cost of the property?*

Yes. All costs of acquiring the property, including the delinquent property taxes, should be included as part of the total cost of the property.

- Vandalism
- Mistakes in installation
- Uninsured theft
- Damage during unpacking and installing
- Fines for not obtaining proper permits from government agencies

Nature of Depreciation

As we have discussed in earlier chapters, land has an unlimited life and therefore can provide unlimited services. On the other hand, other fixed assets such as equipment, buildings, and land improvements lose their ability, over time, to provide services. As a result, the costs of equipment, buildings, and land improvements should be transferred to expense accounts in a systematic manner during their expected useful lives. This periodic transfer of cost to expense is called **depreciation**.

The adjusting entry to record depreciation is usually made at the end of each month or at the end of the year. This entry debits *Depreciation Expense* and credits a *contra asset* account entitled *Accumulated Depreciation* or *Allowance for Depreciation*. The use of a contra asset account allows the original cost to remain unchanged in the fixed asset account.

Factors that cause a decline in the ability of a fixed asset to provide services may be identified as physical depreciation or functional depreciation. **Physical depreciation** occurs from wear and tear while in use and from the action of the weather. **Functional depreciation** occurs when a fixed asset is no longer able to provide services at the level for which it was intended. For example, a personal computer made in the 1980s would not be able to provide an Internet connection. Such advances in technology during this century have made functional depreciation an increasingly important cause of depreciation.

> **The adjusting entry to record depreciation debits *Depreciation Expense* and credits *Accumulated Depreciation*.**

 Companies often use different useful lives for similar assets. For example, **Sears, Roebuck and Co.** depreciates its equipment over 5 to 10 years, while **J.C. Penney Co.** depreciates its equipment over 10 to 20 years.

The term *depreciation* as used in accounting is often misunderstood because the same term is also used in business to mean a decline in the market value of an asset. However, the amount of a fixed asset's unexpired cost reported in the balance sheet usually does not agree with the amount that could be realized from its sale. Fixed assets are held for use in a business rather than for sale. It is assumed that the business will continue as a going concern. Thus, a decision to dispose of a fixed asset is based mainly on the usefulness of the asset to the business and not on its market value.

 **Point of INTEREST**

Would you have more cash if you depreciated your car? The answer is no. Depreciation does not affect your cash flows. Likewise, depreciation does not affect the cash flows of a business. However, depreciation is subtracted in determining net income. As a result, analysts add depreciation back to a company's net income, so that they can estimate the cash generated from current operations. In the long run, however, fixed assets need to be replaced, and their replacement requires the outlay of cash. Thus, in considering the long-run, cash-generating ability of a business, the cash needed for replacement of fixed assets should be considered.

Another common misunderstanding is that accounting for depreciation provides cash needed to replace fixed assets as they wear out. This misunderstanding probably occurs because depreciation, unlike most expenses, does not require an outlay of cash in the period in which it is recorded. The cash account is neither increased nor decreased by the periodic entries that transfer the cost of fixed assets to depreciation expense accounts.

Accounting for Depreciation

OBJECTIVE 2

Compute depreciation, using the following methods: straight-line method, units-of-production method, and declining-balance method.

Three factors are considered in determining the amount of depreciation expense to be recognized each period. These three factors are (a) the fixed asset's initial cost, (b) its expected useful life, and (c) its estimated value at the end of its useful life. This third factor is called the **residual value**, **scrap value**, **salvage value**, or **trade-in value**. Exhibit 2 shows the relationship among the three factors and the periodic depreciation expense.

EXHIBIT 2   Factors that Determine Depreciation Expense

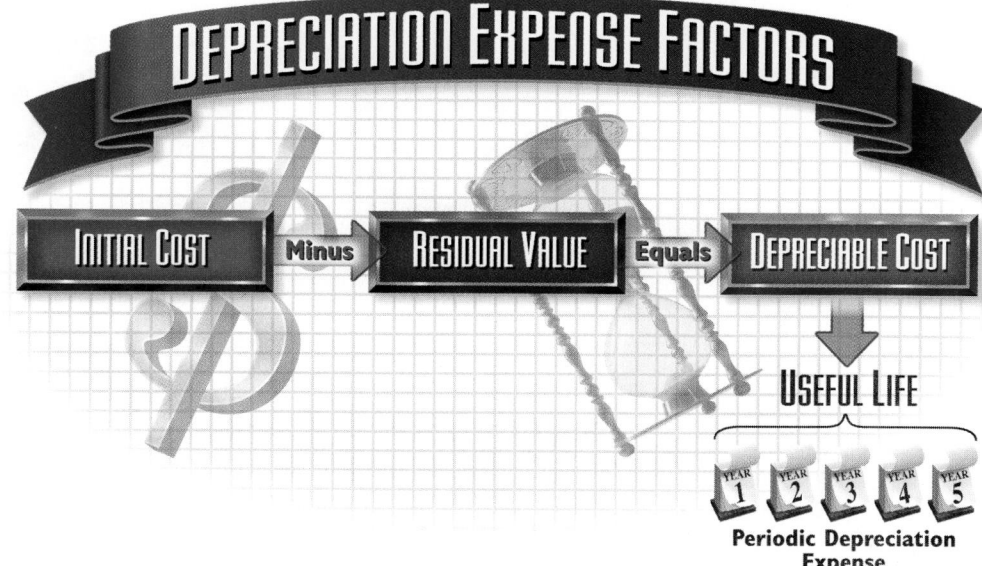

Periodic Depreciation Expense

A fixed asset's **residual value** at the end of its expected useful life must be estimated at the time the asset is placed in service. If a fixed asset is expected to have little or no residual value when it is taken out of service, then its initial cost should be spread over its expected useful life as depreciation expense. If, however, a fixed asset is expected to have a significant residual value, the difference between its initial cost and its residual value, called the asset's **depreciable cost**, is the amount that is spread over the asset's useful life as depreciation expense.

A fixed asset's **expected useful life** must also be estimated at the time the asset is placed in service. Estimates of expected useful lives are available from various trade associations and other publications. For federal income tax purposes, the Internal Revenue Service has established guidelines for useful lives. These guidelines may also be helpful in determining depreciation for financial reporting purposes.

 The Internal Revenue Service guideline for the useful life of automobiles and light-duty trucks is 5 years, while the designated life for most machinery and equipment is 7 years.

In practice, many businesses use the guideline that all assets placed in or taken out of service during the first half of a month are treated as if the event occurred on the first day of *that* month. That is, these businesses compute depreciation on these assets for the entire month. Likewise, all fixed asset additions and deductions during the second half of a month are treated as if the event occurred on the first day of the *next* month. We will follow this practice in this chapter.

It is not necessary that a business use a single method of computing depreciation for all its depreciable assets. The methods used in the accounts and financial statements may also differ from the methods used in determining income taxes and property taxes. The three methods used most often are (1) straight-line, (2) units-of-production, and (3) declining-balance.[2] Exhibit 3 shows the extent of the use of these methods in financial statements.

EXHIBIT 3
Use of Depreciation Methods

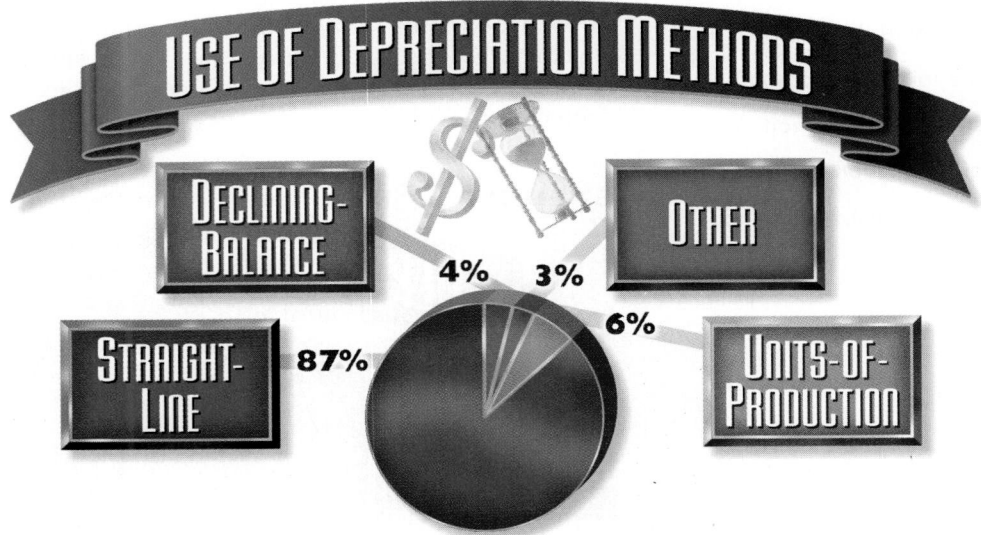

Source: Accounting Trends & Techniques, 50th ed., American Institute of Certified Public Accountants, New York, 1996.

Straight-Line Method

The **straight-line method** provides for the same amount of depreciation expense for each year of the asset's useful life. For example, assume that the cost of a depreciable asset is $24,000, its estimated residual value is $2,000, and its estimated life is 5 years. The annual depreciation is computed as follows:

A truck that cost $35,000 has a residual value of $5,000 and a useful life of 12 years. What are (a) the depreciable cost, (b) the straight-line rate, and (c) the annual straight-line depreciation?

- - - - - - - - - - - - - - - - - - - -

(a) $30,000 ($35,000 − $5,000), (b) 8⅓% (¹/₁₂), (c) $2,500 ($30,000 × 8⅓%).

$$\frac{\$24,000 \text{ cost} - \$2,000 \text{ estimated residual value}}{5 \text{ years estimated life}} = \frac{\$4,400 \text{ annual}}{\text{depreciation}}$$

When an asset is used for only part of a year, the annual depreciation is prorated. For example, assume that the fiscal year ends on December 31 and that the asset in the above example is placed in service on October 1. The depreciation for the first fiscal year of use would be $1,100 ($4,400 × ³/₁₂).

For ease in applying the straight-line method, the annual depreciation may be converted to a percentage of the depreciable cost. This percentage is determined by dividing 100% by the number of years of useful life. For example, a useful life of 20 years converts to a 5% rate (100%/20), 8 years converts to a 12.5% rate (100%/8), and so on.[3] In the above example, the annual depreciation of $4,400 can be computed by multiplying the depreciable cost of $22,000 by 20% (100%/5).

The straight-line method is simple and is widely used. It provides a reasonable transfer of costs to periodic expense when the asset's use and the related revenues from its use are about the same from period to period.

Units-of-Production Method

How would you depreciate a fixed asset when its service is related to use rather than time? When the amount of use of a fixed asset varies from year to year, the units-of-production method is more appropriate than the straight-line method. In

---

[2] Another method not often used today, called the *sum-of-the-years-digits method,* is described and illustrated in the appendix at the end of this chapter.

[3] The depreciation rate may also be expressed as a fraction. For example, the annual straight-line rate for an asset with a 3-year useful life is ⅓.

such cases, the units-of-production method better matches the depreciation expense with the related revenue.

The **units-of-production method** provides for the same amount of depreciation expense for each unit produced or each unit of capacity used by the asset. To apply this method, the useful life of the asset is expressed in terms of units of productive capacity such as hours or miles. The total depreciation expense for each accounting period is then determined by multiplying the unit depreciation by the number of units produced or used during the period. For example, assume that a machine with a cost of $24,000 and an estimated residual value of $2,000 is expected to have an estimated life of 10,000 operating hours. The depreciation for a unit of one hour is computed as follows:

$$\frac{\$24,000 \text{ cost} - \$2,000 \text{ estimated residual value}}{10,000 \text{ estimated hours}} = \frac{\$2.20 \text{ hourly}}{\text{depreciation}}$$

Assuming that the machine was in operation for 2,100 hours during a year, the depreciation for that year would be $4,620 ($2.20 × 2,100 hours).

Declining-Balance Method

The **declining-balance method** provides for a declining periodic expense over the estimated useful life of the asset. To apply this method, the annual straight-line depreciation rate is doubled. For example, the declining-balance rate for an asset with an estimated life of 5 years is 40%, which is double the straight-line rate of 20% (100%/5).

For the first year of use, the cost of the asset is multiplied by the declining-balance rate. After the first year, the declining **book value** (cost minus accumulated depreciation) of the asset is multiplied by this rate. To illustrate, the annual declining-balance depreciation for an asset with an estimated 5-year life and a cost of $24,000 is shown below.

Year	Cost	Accum. Depr. at Beginning of Year	Book Value at Beginning of Year	Rate	Depreciation for Year	Book Value at End of Year
1	$24,000		$24,000.00	40%	$9,600.00	$14,400.00
2	24,000	$ 9,600.00	14,400.00	40%	5,760.00	8,640.00
3	24,000	15,360.00	8,640.00	40%	3,456.00	5,184.00
4	24,000	18,816.00	5,184.00	40%	2,073.60	3,110.40
5	24,000	20,889.60	3,110.40	—	1,110.40	2,000.00

You should note that when the declining-balance method is used, the estimated residual value is *not* considered in determining the depreciation rate. It is also ignored in computing the periodic depreciation. However, the asset should not be depreciated below its estimated residual value. In the above example the estimated residual value was $2,000. Therefore, the depreciation for the fifth year is $1,110.40 ($3,110.40 − $2,000.00) instead of $1,244.16 (40% × $3,110.40).

In the example above, we assumed that the first use of the asset occurred at the beginning of the fiscal year. This is normally not the case in practice, however, and depreciation for the first partial year of use must be computed. For example, assume that the asset above was in service at the end of the *third* month of the fiscal year. In this case, only a portion (³⁄₁₂) of the first full year's depreciation of $9,600 is allocated to the first fiscal year. Thus, depreciation of $7,200 (³⁄₁₂ × $9,600) is allocated to the first partial year of use. The depreciation for the second fiscal year would then be $6,720 [40% × ($24,000 − $7,200)].

Comparing Depreciation Methods

The straight-line method provides for the same periodic amounts of depreciation expense over the life of the asset. The units-of-production method provides for periodic amounts of depreciation expense that vary, depending upon the amount the asset is used.

The declining-balance method provides for a higher depreciation amount in the first year of the asset's use, followed by a gradually declining amount. For this reason, the declining-balance method is called an **accelerated depreciation method**. It is most appropriate when the decline in an asset's productivity or earning power is greater in the early years of its use than in later years. Further, using this method is often justified because repairs tend to increase with the age of an asset. The reduced amounts of depreciation in later years are thus offset to some extent by increased repair expenses.

The periodic depreciation amounts for the straight-line method and the declining-balance method are compared in Exhibit 4. This comparison is based on an asset cost of $24,000, an estimated life of 5 years, and an estimated residual value of $2,000.

EXHIBIT 4
Comparing Depreciation Methods

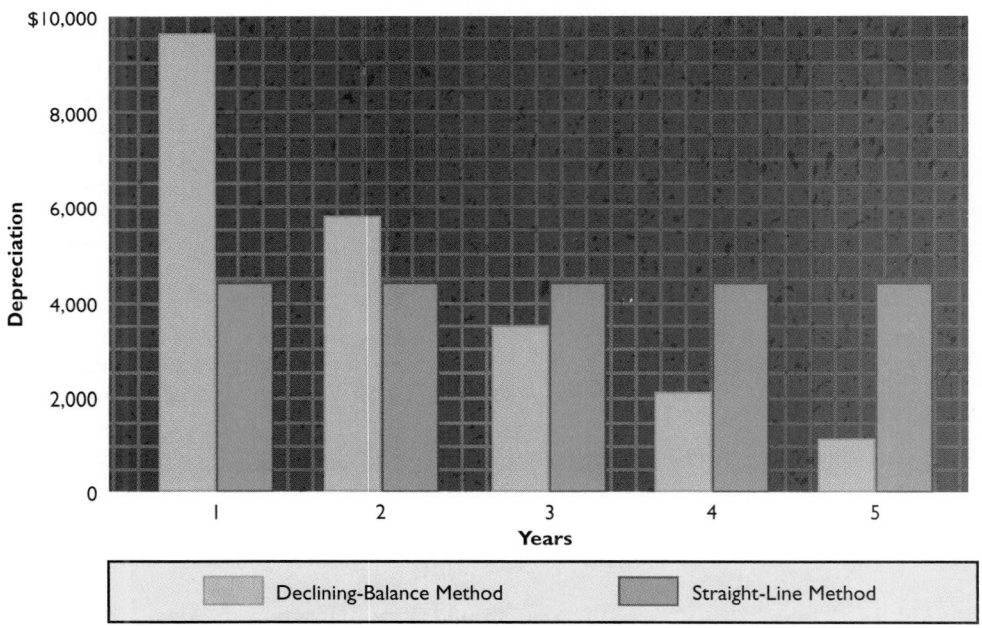

Depreciation for Federal Income Tax

The Internal Revenue Code specifies the *Modified Accelerated Cost Recovery System (MACRS)* for use by businesses in computing depreciation for tax purposes.[4] MACRS specifies eight classes of useful life and depreciation rates for each class. The two most common classes, other than real estate, are the 5-year class and the 7-year class.[5] The 5-year class includes automobiles and light-duty trucks, and the 7-year class includes most machinery and equipment. The depreciation deduction for these two classes is similar to that computed using the declining-balance method.

In using the MACRS rates, residual value is ignored, and all fixed assets are assumed to be put in and taken out of service in the middle of the year. For the

---

[4] Fixed assets that were acquired before 1987 are allowed to use depreciation methods other than MACRS. These are discussed in tax accounting texts.

[5] Real estate is in 27½-year classes and 31½-year classes and is depreciated by the straight-line method.

5-year-class assets, depreciation is spread over six years, as shown in the following MACRS schedule of depreciation rates:

Year	5-Year-Class Depreciation Rates
1	20.0%
2	32.0
3	19.2
4	11.5
5	11.5
6	5.8
	100.0%

To simplify its record keeping, a business will sometimes use the MACRS method for both financial statement and tax purposes. This is acceptable if MACRS does not result in significantly different amounts than would have been reported using one of the three depreciation methods discussed earlier in this chapter.

Using MACRS for both financial statement and tax purposes may, however, hurt a business. In one case, a business that had used MACRS depreciation for its financial statements lost a $1 million order because its fixed assets had low book values. The bank viewed these low book values as inadequate, so it would not loan the business the amount needed to produce the order.[6]

What is the third year MACRS depreciation for an automobile that cost $26,000 and has a residual value of $6,500?

$4,992 ($26,000 × 19.2%)

Revising Depreciation Estimates

Revising the estimates of the residual value and the useful life is normal. When these estimates are revised, they are used to determine the depreciation expense in future periods. They do not affect the amounts of depreciation expense recorded in earlier years.

To illustrate, assume that a fixed asset purchased for $130,000 was originally estimated to have a useful life of 30 years and a residual value of $10,000. The asset has been depreciated for 10 years by the straight-line method. At the end of ten years, the asset's book value (undepreciated cost) is $90,000, determined as follows:

Asset cost	$130,000
Less accumulated depreciation ($4,000 per year × 10 years)	40,000
Book value (undepreciated cost), end of tenth year	$ 90,000

During the eleventh year, it is estimated that the remaining useful life is 25 years (instead of 20) and that the residual value is $5,000 (instead of $10,000). The depreciation expense for each of the remaining 25 years is $3,400, computed as follows:

Book value (undepreciated cost), end of tenth year	$90,000
Less revised estimated residual value	5,000
Revised remaining depreciable cost	$85,000
Revised annual depreciation expense ($85,000/25)	$ 3,400

For the $130,000 asset in the example on this page, assume that after 10 more years (20 years in total) its remaining useful life is estimated at 5 years with no residual value. What is the revised depreciation for the twenty-first year?

$11,200 ($130,000 − $40,000 depreciation for years 1–10 = $90,000; $90,000 − $34,000 depreciation for years 11–20 = $56,000; $56,000 divided by 5 years = $11,200)

[6] Lee Berton, "Do's and Don'ts," *The Wall Street Journal,* June 10, 1988, p. 34R.

BUSINESS ON STAGE

Running Like a Top

Businesses that use equipment to provide goods or services must maintain that equipment. These businesses usually follow one of three maintenance philosophies: (1) corrective maintenance, (2) preventive maintenance, and (3) predictive maintenance.

- **Corrective maintenance.** Under this philosophy, equipment is fixed when the equipment breaks down. It would be similar to you changing the oil in your car when your engine freezes up. Companies that use corrective maintenance don't want to waste time performing maintenance until there is an actual failure. Unfortunately, an unplanned machine failure can cause significant disruptions. Such disruptions include unplanned stops in production, delays in waiting for replacement parts, and additional repair due to broken machine components. Because of this, many consider corrective maintenance a poor philosophy.

- **Preventive maintenance.** Under this philosophy, equipment is repaired under a planned schedule. It would be similar to you changing your car's oil every 6,000 miles. Preventive maintenance is considered superior to corrective maintenance because the maintenance is planned. Therefore, employees can be trained, multiple machines can be repaired, or housekeeping can be performed during the scheduled maintenance. In addition, replacement parts can be ordered ahead of time, minimizing delays caused by emergencies. Lastly, preventive maintenance may reduce the overall maintenance expenditures, because actual machine failures are minimized.

- **Predictive maintenance.** Under this new maintenance philosophy, equipment is repaired at the exact time it needs to be repaired prior to actual failure. It would be similar to you changing your car's oil when a sensor in the car indicated that the oil had reached a given level of impurity. Predictive maintenance is considered superior to preventive maintenance because maintenance is only performed when it is actually needed. This may reduce the total amount of time that equipment spends in maintenance during its life, compared to preventive maintenance. At the same time, however, predictive maintenance may still be planned, once it is indicated—so it has the same advantages as preventive maintenance. New sensors and computers are being developed to support predictive maintenance. Vibration sensors are one example. These sensors are placed on machines to measure vibration, which indicates bearing wear. When the vibration levels reach a certain point, bearings are replaced, which is just prior to their failing. ■

Composite-Rate Method

Assets may be grouped according to common traits, such as similar useful lives. For example, a group might include all delivery trucks with useful lives of less than 8 years. Likewise, a group might include all office equipment or all store fixtures. Depreciation may be determined for each group of assets, using a single *composite rate,* rather than a rate for each individual asset. The depreciation computations are similar for groups of assets as for individual assets.

Capital and Revenue Expenditures

OBJECTIVE 3

Classify fixed asset costs as either capital expenditures or revenue expenditures.

The costs of acquiring fixed assets, adding to a fixed asset, improving a fixed asset, or extending a fixed asset's useful life are called **capital expenditures**. Such expenditures are recorded by either debiting the asset account or its related accumulated depreciation account. Costs that benefit only the current period or costs incurred for normal maintenance and repairs are called **revenue expenditures**. Such expenditures are debited to expense accounts. For example, the cost of replacing spark plugs in an automobile or the cost of repainting a building should be debited to an expense account.

To properly match revenues and expenses, it is important to distinguish between capital and revenue expenditures. Capital expenditures will affect the depreciation expense of more than one period, while revenue expenditures will affect the expenses of only the current period.

Types of Capital Expenditures

We have discussed accounting for the initial costs of acquiring fixed assets. Capital expenditures on assets after they have been acquired may be either (a) additions, (b) betterments, or (c) extraordinary repairs.

Additions to Fixed Assets

The cost of an addition to a fixed asset should be debited to the related fixed asset account.

For example, the cost of adding a new wing to a building should be debited to the building account. This cost should then be depreciated over its estimated useful life or the remaining useful life of the building, whichever is shorter.

Betterments

An expenditure that improves a fixed asset's operating efficiency or capacity for its remaining useful life is called a **betterment**. Such expenditures should be debited to the related fixed asset account. For example, if the power unit attached to a machine is replaced by one of greater capacity, its cost should be debited to the machine account. Also, the cost and the accumulated depreciation related to the old power unit should be removed from the accounts. The cost of the new power unit should then be depreciated over its estimated useful life or the remaining useful life of the machine, whichever is shorter.

Extraordinary Repairs

An expenditure that increases the useful life of an asset beyond its original estimate is called an **extraordinary repair**. Such expenditures should be debited to the related accumulated depreciation account. In such cases, the repairs are said to *restore* or *make good* a portion of the depreciation recorded in prior years. The depreciation for future periods should be computed on the basis of the revised book value of the asset and the revised estimate of the remaining useful life.

To illustrate, assume that a machine costing $50,000 has no estimated residual value and an estimated useful life of 10 years. Assume also that the machine has been depreciated for 6 years by the straight-line method ($5,000 annual depreciation). At the beginning of the seventh year, an $11,500 extraordinary repair increases the remaining useful life of the machine to 7 years (instead of 4). The repair of $11,500 should be debited to Accumulated Depreciation. The annual depreciation for the remaining 7 years of use would be $4,500, computed as follows:

Q&A *Identify each of the items related to a truck as an addition, a betterment, or an extraordinary repair: (a) a snowplow attachment that allows the truck to be used for snow removal, (b) a new transmission, (c) a hydraulic hitch to replace a manual hitch.*

(a) addition, (b) extraordinary repair, (c) betterment.

Cost of machine		$50,000
Less Accumulated Depreciation balance:		
Depreciation for first 6 years ($5,000 × 6)	$30,000	
Deduct debit for extraordinary repairs	11,500	
Balance of Accumulated Depreciation		18,500
Revised book value of machine after extraordinary repair		$31,500
Annual depreciation ($31,500/7 years remaining useful life)		$ 4,500

Summary of Capital and Revenue Expenditures

Exhibit 5 summarizes the accounting for capital and revenue expenditures related to fixed assets.

EXHIBIT 5
Capital and Revenue Expenditures

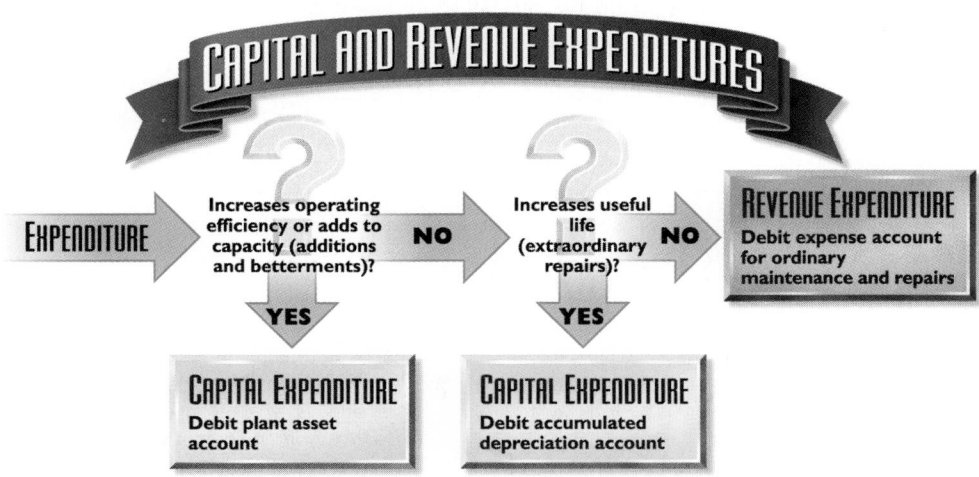

Disposal of Fixed Assets

Fixed assets that are no longer useful may be discarded, sold, or traded for other fixed assets. The details of the entry to record a disposal will vary. In all cases, however, the book value of the asset must be removed from the accounts. The entry for this purpose debits the asset's accumulated depreciation account for its balance on the date of disposal and credits the asset account for the cost of the asset.

A fixed asset should not be removed from the accounts only because it has been fully depreciated. If the asset is still used by the business, the cost and accumulated depreciation should remain in the ledger. This maintains accountability for the asset in the ledger. If the book value of the asset was removed from the ledger, the accounts would contain no evidence of the continued existence of the asset. In addition, the cost and the accumulated depreciation data on such assets are often needed for property tax and income tax reports.

The entry to record the disposal of a fixed asset removes the cost of the asset and its accumulated depreciation from the accounts.

Discarding Fixed Assets

When fixed assets are no longer useful to the business and have no residual or market value, they are discarded. To illustrate, assume that an item of equipment acquired at a cost of $25,000 is fully depreciated at December 31, the end of the preceding fiscal year. On February 14, the equipment is discarded. The entry to record this is as follows:

Feb.	14	Accumulated Depreciation—Equipment	25 0 0 0 00	
		Equipment		25 0 0 0 00
		To write off equipment discarded.		

If an asset has not been fully depreciated, depreciation should be recorded prior to removing it from service and from the accounting records. To illustrate, assume that equipment costing $6,000 is depreciated at an annual straight-line rate of 10%. In addition, assume that on December 31 of the preceding fiscal year, the accumulated depreciation balance, after adjusting entries, is $4,750. Finally, assume that the asset is removed from service on the following March 24. The entry to record the depreciation for the three months of the current period prior to the asset's removal from service is as follows:

Mar.	24	Depreciation Expense—Equipment	1 5 0 00	
		Accumulated Depreciation—Equipment		1 5 0 00
		To record current depreciation on		
		equipment discarded ($600 × $3/_{12}$).		

The discarding of the equipment is then recorded by the following entry:

Mar.	24	Accumulated Depreciation—Equipment	4 9 0 0 00	
		Loss on Disposal of Fixed Assets	1 1 0 0 00	
		Equipment		6 0 0 0 00
		To write off equipment discarded.		

The loss of $1,100 is recorded because the balance of the accumulated depreciation account ($4,900) is less than the balance in the equipment account ($6,000). Losses on the discarding of fixed assets are nonoperating items and are normally reported in the Other Expense section of the income statement.

Selling Fixed Assets

The entry to record the sale of a fixed asset is similar to the entries illustrated above, except that the cash or other asset received must also be recorded. If the selling price is more than the book value of the asset, the transaction results in a gain. If the selling price is less than the book value, there is a loss.

To illustrate, assume that equipment is acquired at a cost of $10,000 and is depreciated at an annual straight-line rate of 10%. The equipment is sold for cash on October 12 of the eighth year of its use. The balance of the accumulated depreciation account as of the preceding December 31 is $7,000. The entry to update the depreciation for the nine months of the current year is as follows:

Oct.	12	Depreciation Expense—Equipment	7 5 0 00	
		Accumulated Depreciation—Equipment		7 5 0 00
		To record current depreciation on		
		equipment sold ($10,000 × 3/4 × 10%).		

After the current depreciation is recorded, the book value of the asset is $2,250 ($10,000 − $7,750). The entries to record the sale, assuming three different selling prices, are as follows:

Sold at book value, for $2,250. No gain or loss.

Oct.	12	Cash	2 2 5 0 00	
		Accumulated Depreciation—Equipment	7 7 5 0 00	
		Equipment		10 0 0 0 00

Sold below book value, for $1,000. Loss of $1,250.

Oct.	12	Cash	1 0 0 0 00	
		Accumulated Depreciation—Equipment	7 7 5 0 00	
		Loss on Disposal of Fixed Assets	1 2 5 0 00	
		Equipment		10 0 0 0 00

Sold above book value, for $2,800. Gain of $550.

Oct.	12	Cash	2 8 0 0 00	
		Accumulated Depreciation—Equipment	7 7 5 0 00	
		Equipment		10 0 0 0 00
		Gain on Disposal of Fixed Assets		5 5 0 00

Exchanging Similar Fixed Assets

Old equipment is often traded in for new equipment having a similar use. In such cases, the seller allows the buyer an amount for the old equipment traded in. This amount, called the **trade-in allowance**, may be either greater or less than the book value of the old equipment. The remaining balance—the amount owed—is either paid in cash or a liability is recorded. It is normally called **boot**, which is its tax name.

Gains on exchanges of similar fixed assets are also not recognized for federal income tax purposes.

Gains on Exchanges

Gains on exchanges of similar fixed assets are not recognized for financial reporting purposes.[7] This is based on the theory that revenue occurs from the production and sale of goods produced by fixed assets and not from the exchange of similar fixed assets.

When the trade-in allowance exceeds the book value of an asset traded in and no gain is recognized, the cost recorded for the new asset can be determined in either of two ways:

> 1. **Cost of new asset = List price of new asset − Unrecognized gain**
>
> *or*
>
> 2. **Cost of new asset = Cash given (or liability assumed) + Book value of old asset**

To illustrate, assume the following exchange:

Similar equipment acquired (new):

List price of new equipment.	$5,000
Trade-in allowance on old equipment.	1,100
Cash paid at June 19, date of exchange.	$3,900

Equipment traded in (old):

Cost of old equipment.	$4,000
Accumulated depreciation at date of exchange	3,200
Book value at June 19, date of exchange.	$ 800

Recorded cost of new equipment:

Method One:

List price of new equipment.		$5,000
Trade-in allowance	$1,100	
Book value of old equipment	800	
Unrecognized gain on exchange		(300)
Cost of new equipment.		$4,700

Method Two:

Book value of old equipment	$ 800
Cash paid at date of exchange	3,900
Cost of new equipment.	$4,700

The entry to record this exchange and the payment of cash is as follows:

June	19	Accumulated Depreciation—Equipment	3 2 0 0 00		
		Equipment (new equipment)	4 7 0 0 00		
		Equipment (old equipment)		4 0 0 0 00	
		Cash		3 9 0 0 00	
		To record exchange of equipment.			

Not recognizing the $300 gain ($1,100 trade-in allowance minus $800 book value) at the time of the exchange reduces future depreciation expense. That is, the depreciation expense for the new asset is based on a cost of $4,700 rather than on the list price of $5,000. In effect, the unrecognized gain of $300 reduces the total amount of depreciation taken during the life of the equipment by $300.

Equipment with a book value of $14,000 is traded in for similar equipment with a list price of $50,000. A trade-in allowance of $15,000 was allowed on the old equipment. What is the cost of the new equipment to be recorded in the accounts?

- - - - - - - - - - - - - - - - -

$49,000 ($50,000 − $1,000 gain, or $14,000 + $35,000 boot)

---

[7] Gains on exchanges of similar fixed assets are recognized if cash (boot) is received. This topic is discussed in advanced accounting texts.

Losses on Exchanges

For financial reporting purposes, losses are recognized on exchanges of similar fixed assets if the trade-in allowance is less than the book value of the old equipment. When there is a loss, the cost recorded for the new asset should be the market (list) price. To illustrate, assume the following exchange:

Similar equipment acquired (new):	
List price of new equipment	$10,000
Trade-in allowance on old equipment	2,000
Cash paid at September 7, date of exchange	$ 8,000
Equipment traded in (old):	
Cost of old equipment	$ 7,000
Accumulated depreciation at date of exchange	4,600
Book value at September 7, date of exchange	$ 2,400
Trade-in allowance on old equipment	2,000
Loss on exchange	$ 400

The entry to record the exchange is as follows:

Sept.	7	Accumulated Depreciation—Equipment		4 6 0 0 00	
		Equipment		10 0 0 0 00	
		Loss on Disposal of Fixed Assets		4 0 0 00	
		Equipment			7 0 0 0 00
		Cash			8 0 0 0 00
		To record exchange of equipment,			
		with loss.			

Review of Accounting for Exchanges of Similar Fixed Assets

Exhibit 6 reviews the accounting for exchanges of similar fixed assets, using the following data:

List price of new equipment acquired	$15,000
Cost of old equipment traded in	$12,500
Accumulated depreciation at date of exchange	10,100
Book value at date of exchange	$ 2,400

EXHIBIT 6

Summary Illustration—Accounting for Exchanges of Similar Fixed Assets

CASE ONE (GAIN): Trade-in allowance is more than book value of asset traded in.		
Trade-in allowance, $3,000; cash paid, $12,000 ($15,000 − $3,000)		
Cost of new asset	List price of new asset acquired, less unrecognized gain: $14,400 ($15,000 − $600) **or** Cash paid plus book value of asset traded in: $14,400 ($12,000 + $2,400)	
Gain recognized	None	
Entry	Equipment	14,400
	Accumulated Depreciation	10,100
	Equipment	12,500
	Cash	12,000

EXHIBIT 6 (concluded)

CASE TWO (LOSS): Trade-in allowance is less than book value of asset traded in.			
Trade-in allowance, $2,000; cash paid, $13,000 ($15,000 − $2,000)			
Cost of new asset	List price of new asset acquired: $15,000		
Loss recognized	$400		
Entry	Equipment	15,000	
	Accumulated Depreciation	10,100	
	Loss on Disposal of Fixed Assets	400	
	Equipment		12,500
	Cash		13,000

Leasing Fixed Assets

OBJECTIVE 5

Define a lease and summarize the accounting rules related to the leasing of fixed assets.

You are probably familiar with leases. A *lease* is a contract for the use of an asset for a stated period of time. Leases are frequently used in business. For example, automobiles, computers, medical equipment, buildings, and airplanes are often leased.

 Of the companies surveyed in the 1996 edition of *Accounting Trends & Techniques*, 91% reported leases.

The two parties to a lease contract are the lessor and the lessee. The *lessor* is the party who owns the asset. The *lessee* is the party to whom the rights to use the asset are granted by the lessor. The lessee is obligated to make periodic rent payments for the lease term. All leases are classified by the lessee as either capital leases or operating leases.

A **capital lease** is accounted for as if the lessee has, in fact, purchased the asset. The lessee debits an asset account for the fair market value of the asset and credits a long-term lease liability account. The accounting for capital leases and the criteria that a capital lease must satisfy are discussed in more advanced accounting texts.

A lease that is not classified as a capital lease for accounting purposes is classified as an **operating lease**. The lessee records the payments under an operating lease by debiting *Rent Expense* and crediting *Cash*. Neither future lease obligations nor the future rights to use the leased asset are recognized in the accounts. However, the lessee must disclose future lease commitments in footnotes to the financial statements.

The asset rentals described in earlier chapters of this text were accounted for as operating leases. To simplify, we will continue to treat asset leases as operating leases.

Internal Control of Fixed Assets

OBJECTIVE 6

Describe internal controls over fixed assets.

Because of their dollar value and long-term nature, it is important to design and apply effective internal controls over fixed assets. Such controls should begin with authorization and approval procedures for the purchase of fixed assets. Controls should also exist to ensure that fixed assets are acquired at the lowest possible costs. One procedure to achieve this objective is to require competitive bids from preapproved vendors.

As soon as a fixed asset is received, it should be inspected and tagged for control purposes and recorded in a subsidiary ledger. This establishes the initial accountability for the asset. Subsidiary ledgers for fixed assets are also useful in determining depreciation expense and recording disposals. Operating data that may be recorded in the subsidiary ledger, such as number of breakdowns, length of time out of service, and cost of repairs, are useful in deciding whether to replace the asset. A company that maintains a computerized subsidiary ledger may use bar-coded tags, similar to the one on the back of this textbook, so that fixed asset data can be directly scanned into computer records.

Fixed assets should be insured against theft, fire, flooding, or other disasters. They should also be safeguarded from theft, misuse, or other damage. For example, fixed assets that are highly open to theft, such as computers, should be locked or otherwise protected when not in use. For computers, safeguarding also includes climate controls and special fire-extinguishing equipment. Procedures should also exist for training employees to properly operate fixed assets such as equipment and machinery.

A physical inventory of fixed assets should be taken periodically in order to verify the accuracy of the accounting records. Such an inventory would detect missing, obsolete, or idle fixed assets. In addition, fixed assets should be inspected periodically in order to determine their condition.

Careful control should also be exercised over the disposal of fixed assets. All disposals should be properly authorized and approved. Fully depreciated assets should be retained in the accounting records until disposal has been authorized and they are removed from service.

Natural Resources

OBJECTIVE 7

Compute depletion and journalize the entry for depletion.

The fixed assets of some businesses include timber, metal ores, minerals, or other natural resources. As these businesses harvest or mine and then sell these resources, a portion of the cost of acquiring them must be debited to an expense account. This process of transferring the cost of natural resources to an expense account is called **depletion**. The amount of depletion is determined by multiplying the quantity extracted during the period by the depletion rate. This rate is computed by dividing the cost of the mineral deposit by its estimated size.

Computing depletion is similar to computing units-of-production depreciation. To illustrate, assume that a business paid $400,000 for the mining rights to a mineral deposit estimated at 1,000,000 tons of ore. The depletion rate is $0.40 per ton ($400,000/1,000,000 tons). If 90,000 tons are mined during the year, the periodic depletion is $36,000 (90,000 tons × $0.40). The entry to record the depletion is shown below.

 *A business purchased mineral rights to 250,000 tons of ore for $1,500,000. If 35,000 tons of ore were mined in the first year, what are (a) the depletion rate per ton and (2) the depletion expense for the first year?*

(a) $6 per ton ($1,500,000/250,000 tons); (b) $210,000 (35,000 tons × $6)

		Adjusting Entry								
Dec.	31	Depletion Expense		36 0 0 0 00					
		Accumulated Depletion				36 0 0 0 00	

Like the accumulated depreciation account, Accumulated Depletion is a *contra asset* account. It is reported on the balance sheet as a deduction from the cost of the mineral deposit.

Intangible Assets

OBJECTIVE 8

Journalize the entries for acquiring and amortizing intangible assets, such as patents, copyrights, and goodwill.

Patents, copyrights, trademarks, and goodwill are long-term assets that are useful in the operations of a business and are not held for sale. These assets are called **intangible assets** because they do not exist physically.

The basic principles of accounting for intangible assets are like those described earlier for fixed assets. The major concerns are determining (1) the initial cost and (2) the **amortization**—the amount of cost to transfer to expense. Amortization results from the passage of time or a decline in the usefulness of the intangible asset.

Patents

Manufacturers may acquire exclusive rights to produce and sell goods with one or more unique features. Such rights are granted by **patents**, which the federal government issues to inventors. These rights continue in effect for 20 years. A business may purchase patent rights from others, or it may obtain patents developed by its own research and development efforts.

The initial cost of a purchased patent, including any related legal fees, should be debited to an asset account. This cost should be written off, or amortized, over the years of the patent's expected usefulness. This period of time may be less than the remaining legal life of the patent. The estimated useful life of the patent may also change as technology or consumer tastes change.

The straight-line method is normally used to determine the periodic amortization. When the amortization is recorded, it is debited to an expense account and credited directly to the patents account. Not using a separate contra asset account is common for all intangible assets.

To illustrate, assume that at the beginning of its fiscal year a business acquires patent rights for $100,000. The patent had been granted 6 years earlier by the Federal Patent Office. Although the patent will not expire for 14 years, its remaining useful life is estimated as 5 years. The entry to amortize the patent at the end of the fiscal year is as follows:

		Adjusting Entry		
Dec.	31	Amortization Expense—Patents	20 0 0 0 00	
		Patents		20 0 0 0 00

Rather than purchase patent rights, a business may incur significant costs in developing patents through its own research and development efforts. Such **research and development costs** are usually accounted for as current operating expenses in the period in which they are incurred.

Expensing research and development costs in the period they are incurred is justified for two reasons. First, the future benefits from research and development efforts are highly uncertain. In fact, most research and development efforts do not result in patents. Second, even if a patent is granted, it may be difficult to objectively estimate its cost. If many research projects are in process at the same time, for example, it is difficult to separate the costs of one project from another.

Copyrights and Trademarks

The exclusive right to publish and sell a literary, artistic, or musical composition is granted by a **copyright**. Copyrights are issued by the federal government and extend for 50 years beyond the author's death. The costs of a copyright include all costs of creating the work plus any administrative or legal costs of obtaining the copyright. A copyright that is purchased from another should be recorded at the

Coke® is one of the world's most recognizable trademarks. As stated in *LIFE*, "Two-thirds of the earth is covered by water; the rest is covered by Coke. If the French are known for wine and the Germans for beer, America achieved global beverage dominance with fizzy water and caramel color."

price paid for it. Because of the uncertainty regarding the useful life of a copyright, it is normally amortized over a short period of time. For example, the copyright costs of this text are amortized over 3 years.

A **trademark** is a name, term, or symbol used to identify a business and its products. For example, the distinctive red-and-white Coca Cola logo is an example of a trademark. Most businesses identify their trademarks with ® in their advertisements and on their products. Under federal law, businesses can protect against others using their trademarks by registering them for 10 years and renewing the registration for 10-year periods thereafter. Like a copyright, the legal costs of registering a trademark with the federal government should be recorded as an asset. Also, if a trademark is purchased from another business, the cost of its purchase would be recorded as an asset. The cost of a trademark should be amortized over its estimated useful life, but not more than 40 years.

Goodwill

In business, **goodwill** refers to an intangible asset of a business that is created from such favorable factors as location, product quality, reputation, and managerial skill. Goodwill allows a business to earn a rate of return on its investment that is often in excess of the normal rate for other firms in the same business.

Generally accepted accounting principles permit the recording of goodwill in the accounts only if it is objectively determined by a transaction. An example of a transaction that may justify recording goodwill is the purchase or sale of a business. Goodwill must be amortized over its estimated useful life, which cannot exceed 40 years.

In its 1996 annual report, **La-Z-Boy Chair Company** reported goodwill from acquired companies. La-Z-Boy amortizes this goodwill over a period of 30 years.

Financial Reporting for Fixed Assets and Intangible Assets

OBJECTIVE 9

Describe how depreciation expense is reported in an income statement and prepare a balance sheet that includes fixed assets and intangible assets.

How should fixed assets and intangible assets be reported in the financial statements? The amount of depreciation and amortization expense of a period should be reported separately in the income statement or disclosed in a footnote. A general description of the method or methods used in computing depreciation should also be reported.

The amount of each major class of fixed assets should be disclosed in the balance sheet or in footnotes. The related accumulated depreciation should also be disclosed, either by major class or in total. If there are too many classes of fixed assets, a single amount may be presented in the balance sheet, supported by a separate detailed listing. Fixed assets are normally presented under the more descriptive caption of **property, plant, and equipment**.

The cost of mineral rights or ore deposits is normally shown as part of the fixed assets section of the balance sheet. The related accumulated depletion should also be disclosed. In some cases, the mineral rights are shown net of depletion on the face of the balance sheet, accompanied by a footnote that discloses the amount of the accumulated depletion.

Intangible assets are usually reported in the balance sheet in a separate section immediately following fixed assets. The balance of each major class of intangible assets should be disclosed at an amount net of amortization taken to date. Exhibit 7 is a partial balance sheet that shows the reporting of fixed assets and intangible assets.

EXHIBIT 7
Fixed Assets and Intangible
Assets in the Balance Sheet

Discovery Mining Co.
Balance Sheet
December 31, 20—

Assets

Total current assets				$ 462,500

Property, plant, and equipment:	Cost	Accum. Depr.	Book Value	
Land	$ 30,000	—	$ 30,000	
Buildings	110,000	$ 26,000	84,000	
Factory equipment	650,000	192,000	458,000	
Office equipment	120,000	13,000	107,000	
	$ 910,000	$ 231,000		$679,000

Mineral deposits:	Cost	Accum. Depl.	Book Value	
Alaska deposit	$1,200,000	$ 800,000	$ 400,000	
Wyoming deposit	750,000	200,000	550,000	
	$1,950,000	$1,000,000		950,000

Total property, plant, and equipment		1,629,000
Intangible assets:		
Patents	$ 75,000	
Goodwill	50,000	
Total intangible assets		125,000

FINANCIAL ANALYSIS AND INTERPRETATION

OBJECTIVE 10

Compute and interpret the
ratio of fixed assets to long-
term liabilities.

Long-term liabilities are often secured by fixed assets. The ratio of total fixed assets to long-term liabilities provides a solvency measure that indicates the margin of safety to creditors. It also gives an indication of the potential ability of the business to borrow additional funds on a long-term basis. The **ratio of fixed assets to long-term liabilities** is computed as follows:

$$\text{Ratio of fixed assets to long-term liabilities (debt)} = \frac{\text{Fixed assets (net)}}{\text{Long-term liabilities (debt)}}$$

To illustrate, the following data were taken from the 1996 and 1995 financial statements of **Procter & Gamble**:

	(in millions)	
	1996	**1995**
Property, plant, and equipment (net)	$11,118	$11,026
Long-term debt	4,670	5,161

The ratio of fixed assets to long-term liabilities (debt) is 2.4 ($11,118/$4,670) for 1996 and 2.1 ($11,026/$5,161) for 1995. The increase in the ratio from 1995 to 1996 indicates more of a margin of safety for creditors. As with other financial measures, the interpretation and analysis is enhanced by comparisons over time and with industry averages.

ENCORE

The Ultimate Inventor

Would you like to become an inventor and own patents worth millions? Yoshiro Nakamatsu, who bills himself as the Thomas Edison of Japan, hopes to open a school that will teach people how to create new products. Yoshiro Nakamatsu is the president of Tokyo's **Hi-Tech Innovation Institute** and claims to have 3,042 patents over his inventing career. Nakamatsu's net worth from royalties from his inventions is estimated at $75 million.

At the age of 5, with encouragement from his grandfather, Nakamatsu invented a stabilizer to make planes fly better. He was granted his first patent at age 14. Since then, he has licensed 16 patents to **IBM**, including one for his 1952 invention of the floppy disk for personal computers. Some of Nakamatsu's other inventions and what he claims they do include the following:

- **Yummy TV.** A snack food designed to relieve eye strain caused by watching too much TV.
- **Enerex.** An engine that produces energy from water.
- **Cerebrex Chair.** A chair that uses electronic impulses to both sharpen the mind and rest the body.
- **Nakamatsu Golf Putter.** A putter that has an oversized vibrating handle to make putting 93 percent accurate within 10 feet.
- **Anti-Gravity Floating Vibrating Three-Dimensional Sonic System.** A speaker system for stereo compact disc players and other electronic products.
- **Magnetic Eyeglasses.** Eyeglasses that have magnets attached to them for improving the blood circulation of the eyes.
- **Dr. Nakamatsu's Yummi Nutri Brain Biscuits.** Food for your brain.
- **Nakamatsu's Engine.** An engine that is far more efficient than gasoline or electric engines because it runs on "cosmic" power.

In his lectures, Nakamatsu offers the following advice on how to become a genius and excel at inventing: (1) swim, (2) lift weights, (3) sleep less than six hours a night, (4) work between the hours of midnight and 4 a.m., and (5) never have sex before the age of 24. ■

Source: Dean Takahashi, "Japanese Inventor Nearly Triples Edison's Output," *The Austin American-Statesman,* May 17, 1996.

APPENDIX: SUM-OF-THE-YEARS-DIGITS DEPRECIATION

The 1996 edition of *Accounting Trends & Techniques* reported that only 1%–2% of the surveyed companies now use this method for financial reporting purposes.

At one time, the sum-of-the-years-digits method of depreciation was used by many businesses. However, the tax law changes of the 1980s limited its use for tax purposes.

Under the **sum-of-the-years-digits method**, depreciation expense is determined by multiplying the original cost of the asset less its estimated residual value by a smaller fraction each year. Thus, the sum-of-the-years-digits method is similar to the declining-balance method, in that the depreciation expense declines each year.

The denominator of the fraction used in determining the depreciation expense is the sum of the digits of the years of the asset's useful life. For example, an asset with a useful life of 5 years would have a denominator of 15 (5 + 4 + 3 + 2 + 1).[8] The numerator of the fraction is the number of years of useful life remaining at the beginning of each year for which depreciation is being computed. Thus, the numerator decreases each year by 1. For a useful life of 5 years, the numerator is 5 the first year, 4 the second year, 3 the third year, and so on.

The following depreciation schedule illustrates the sum-of-the-years-digits method for an asset with a cost of $24,000, an estimated residual value of $2,000, and an estimated useful life of 5 years:

Year	Cost Less Residual Value	Rate	Depreciation for Year	Accum. Depr. at End of Year	Book Value at End of Year
1	$22,000	$5/15$	$7,333.33	$ 7,333.33	$16,666.67
2	22,000	$4/15$	5,866.67	13,200.00	10,800.00
3	22,000	$3/15$	4,400.00	17,600.00	6,400.00
4	22,000	$2/15$	2,933.33	20,533.33	3,466.67
5	22,000	$1/15$	1,466.67	22,000.00	2,000.00

What if the fixed asset is not placed in service at the beginning of the year? When the date an asset is first put into service is not the beginning of a fiscal year, each full year's depreciation must be allocated between the two fiscal years benefited. To illustrate, assume that the asset in the above example was put into service at the beginning of the fourth month of the first fiscal year. The depreciation for that year would be $5,500 ($9/12 \times 5/15 \times $22,000$). The depreciation for the second year would be $6,233.33, computed as follows:

$3/12 \times 5/15 \times$ $22,000	$1,833.33
$9/12 \times 4/15 \times$ $22,000	4,400.00
Total depreciation for second fiscal year	$6,233.33

KEY POINTS

1 Define fixed assets and describe the accounting for their cost.

Fixed assets are long-term tangible assets that are owned by the business and are used in the normal operations of the business. Examples of fixed assets are equipment, buildings, and land. The initial cost of a fixed asset includes all amounts spent to get the asset in place and ready for use. For example, sales tax, freight, insurance in transit, and installation costs are all included in the cost of a fixed asset. As time passes, all fixed assets except land lose their ability to provide services. As a result, the cost of a fixed asset should be transferred to an expense ac-

count, in a systematic manner, during the asset's expected useful life. This periodic transfer of cost to expense is called depreciation.

2 Compute depreciation, using the following methods: straight-line method, units-of-production method, and declining-balance method.

In computing depreciation, three factors need to be considered: (1) the fixed asset's initial cost, (2) the useful life of the asset, and (3) the residual value of the asset.

The straight-line method spreads the initial cost less the residual value equally over the useful life. The units-of-production method spreads the initial

cost less the residual value equally over the units expected to be produced by the asset during its useful life. The declining-balance method is applied by multiplying the declining book value of the asset by twice the straight-line rate.

3 Classify fixed asset costs as either capital expenditures or revenue expenditures.

Costs for additions to fixed assets and other costs related to improving efficiency or capacity are classified as capital expenditures. Costs for additions to an asset and costs that add to the usefulness of the asset for more than one period (called betterments) are also classified as capital ex-

---

[8] The denominator can also be determined from the following formula: S = N[(N + 1)/2], where S = sum of the digits and N = number of years of estimated life.

penditures. Costs that increase the useful life of an asset beyond the original estimate are a capital expenditure and are called extra-ordinary repairs. Expenditures that benefit only the current period or that maintain normal operating efficiency are debited to expense accounts and are classified as revenue expenditures.

4 Journalize entries for the disposal of fixed assets.

The journal entries to record disposals of fixed assets will vary. In all cases, however, any depreciation for the current period should be recorded, and the book value of the asset is then removed from the accounts. The entry to remove the book value from the accounts is a debit to the asset's accumulated depreciation account and a credit to the asset account for the cost of the asset. For assets retired from service, a loss may be recorded for any remaining book value of the asset.

When a fixed asset is sold, the book value is removed and the cash or other asset received is also recorded. If the selling price is more than the book value of the asset, the transaction results in a gain. If the selling price is less than the book value, there is a loss.

When a fixed asset is exchanged for another of similar nature, no gain is recognized on the exchange. The acquired asset's cost is adjusted for any gains. A loss on an exchange of similar assets is recorded.

5 Define a lease and summarize the accounting rules

related to the leasing of fixed assets.

A lease is a contract for the use of an asset for a period of time. A capital lease is accounted for as if the lessee has purchased the asset. The lease payments under an operating lease are accounted for as rent expense for the lessee.

6 Describe internal controls over fixed assets.

Internal controls over fixed assets should include procedures for authorizing the purchase of assets. Once acquired, fixed assets should be safeguarded from theft, misuse, or damage. A physical inventory of fixed assets should be taken periodically.

7 Compute depletion and journalize the entry for depletion.

The amount of periodic depletion is computed by multiplying the quantity of minerals extracted during the period by a depletion rate. The depletion rate is computed by dividing the cost of the mineral deposit by its estimated size. The entry to record depletion debits a depletion expense account and credits an accumulated depletion account.

8 Journalize the entries for acquiring and amortizing intangible assets, such as patents, copyrights, and goodwill.

Long-term assets that are without physical attributes but are used in the business are classified as

intangible assets. Examples of intangible assets are patents, copyrights, trademarks, and goodwill. The initial cost of an intangible asset should be debited to an asset account. This cost should be written off, or amortized, over the years of the asset's expected usefulness by debiting an expense account and crediting the intangible asset account.

9 Describe how depreciation expense is reported in an income statement and prepare a balance sheet that includes fixed assets and intangible assets.

The amount of depreciation expense and the method or methods used in computing depreciation should be disclosed in the financial statements. In addition, each major class of fixed assets should be disclosed, along with the related accumulated depreciation. Intangible assets are usually presented in the balance sheet in a separate section immediately following fixed assets. Each major class of intangible assets should be disclosed at an amount net of the amortization recorded to date.

10 Compute and interpret the ratio of fixed assets to long-term liabilities.

The ratio of fixed assets to long-term liabilities is a solvency measure that indicates the margin of safety to creditors. It also provides an indication of the ability of a company to borrow additional funds on a long-term basis.

ILLUSTRATIVE PROBLEM

McCollum Company, a furniture wholesaler, acquired new equipment at a cost of $150,000 at the beginning of the fiscal year. The equipment has an estimated life of 5 years and an estimated residual value of $12,000. Ellen McCollum, the president, has requested information regarding alternative depreciation methods.

Instructions

1. Determine the annual depreciation for each of the five years of estimated useful life of the equipment, the accumulated depreciation at the end of each year, and the

book value of the equipment at the end of each year by (a) the straight-line method and (b) the declining-balance method (at twice the straight-line rate).

2. Assume that the equipment was depreciated under the declining-balance method. In the first week of the fifth year, the equipment was traded in for similar equipment priced at $175,000. The trade-in allowance on the old equipment was $10,000, and cash was paid for the balance. Journalize the entry to record the exchange.

Solution

1.

	Year	Depreciation Expense	Accumulated Depreciation, End of Year	Book Value, End of Year
a.	1	$27,600*	$ 27,600	$122,400
	2	27,600	55,200	94,800
	3	27,600	82,800	67,200
	4	27,600	110,400	39,600
	5	27,600	138,000	12,000

*$27,600 = ($150,000 − $12,000) ÷ 5

	Year	Depreciation Expense	Accumulated Depreciation, End of Year	Book Value, End of Year
b.	1	$60,000**	$ 60,000	$ 90,000
	2	36,000	96,000	54,000
	3	21,600	117,600	32,400
	4	12,960	130,560	19,440
	5	7,440***	138,000	12,000

**$60,000 = $150,000 × 40%
***The asset is not depreciated below the estimated residual value of $12,000.

2.

Accumulated Depreciation—Equipment	130 5 6 0 00			
Equipment	175 0 0 0 00			
Loss on Disposal of Fixed Assets	9 4 4 0 00			
Equipment			150 0 0 0 00	
Cash			165 0 0 0 00	

SELF-EXAMINATION QUESTIONS   Answers at End of Chapter

Matching

Match each of the following statements with its proper term. Some terms may not be used.

A.	**accelerated depreciation method**
B.	**amortization**
C.	**betterment**
D.	**book value**
E.	**boot**
F.	**capital expenditures**
G.	**capital leases**
H.	**copyright**
I.	**declining-balance method**
J.	**depletion**

___ 1. Long-term or relatively permanent tangible assets that are used in the normal business operations.

___ 2. The systematic periodic transfer of the cost of a fixed asset to an expense account during its expected useful life.

___ 3. The estimated value of a fixed asset at the end of its useful life.

___ 4. A method of depreciation that provides for equal periodic depreciation expense over the estimated life of a fixed asset.

___ 5. A method of depreciation that provides for depreciation expense based on the expected productive capacity of a fixed asset.

___ 6. A method of depreciation that provides declining periodic depreciation expense over the estimated life of a fixed asset.

___ 7. The cost of a fixed asset minus accumulated depreciation on the asset.

___ 8. A depreciation method that provides for a higher depreciation amount in the first year of the asset's use, followed by a gradually declining amount of depreciation.

K. depreciation

L. extraordinary repair

M. fixed assets

N. goodwill

O. intangible assets

P. operating leases

Q. patents

R. ratio of fixed assets to long-term liabilities

S. ratio of fixed assets to total assets

T. residual value

U. revenue expenditures

V. straight-line method

W. trade-in allowance

X. trademark

Y. units-of-production method

____ 9. The costs of acquiring fixed assets, adding to a fixed asset, improving a fixed asset, or extending a fixed asset's useful life.

____ 10. Costs that benefit only the current period or costs incurred for normal maintenance and repairs of fixed assets.

____ 11. An expenditure that improves a fixed asset's operating efficiency or capacity for its remaining useful life.

____ 12. An expenditure that increases the useful life of an asset beyond its original estimate.

____ 13. The amount a seller allows a buyer for a fixed asset that is traded in for a similar asset.

____ 14. The amount a buyer owes a seller when a fixed asset is traded in on a similar asset.

____ 15. Leases that include one or more provisions that result in treating the leased assets as purchased assets in the accounts.

____ 16. Leases that do not meet the criteria for capital leases and thus are accounted for as operating expenses.

____ 17. The process of transferring the cost of natural resources to an expense account.

____ 18. Long-term assets that are useful in the operations of a business, are not held for sale, and are without physical qualities.

____ 19. The periodic transfer of the cost of an intangible asset to expense.

____ 20. An intangible asset that is created from such favorable factors as location, product quality, reputation, and managerial skill.

____ 21. Exclusive rights to produce and sell goods with one or more unique features.

____ 22. An exclusive right to publish and sell a literary, artistic, or musical composition.

____ 23. A name, term, or symbol used to identify a business and its products.

____ 24. A financial ratio that provides a measure indicating the margin of safety to creditors.

Multiple Choice

1. Which of the following expenditures incurred in connection with acquiring machinery is a proper charge to the asset account?
    A. Freight   C. Both A and B
    B. Installation costs   D. Neither A nor B

2. What is the amount of depreciation, using the declining-balance method (twice the straight-line rate) for the second year of use for equipment costing $9,000, with an estimated residual value of $600 and an estimated life of 3 years?
    A. $6,000   C. $2,000
    B. $3,000   D. $400

3. An example of an accelerated depreciation method is:

    A. Straight-line   C. Units-of-production
    B. Declining-balance   D. Depletion

4. A fixed asset priced at $100,000 is acquired by trading in a similar asset that has a book value of $25,000. Assuming that the trade-in allowance is $30,000 and that $70,000 cash is paid for the new asset, what is the cost of the new asset for financial reporting purposes?
    A. $100,000   C. $70,000
    B. $95,000   D. $30,000

5. Which of the following is an example of an intangible asset?
    A. Patents   C. Copyrights
    B. Goodwill   D. All of the above

CLASS DISCUSSION QUESTIONS

1. Which of the following qualities are characteristic of fixed assets? (a) tangible, (b) capable of repeated use in the operations of the business, (c) held for sale in the normal course of business, (d) used continuously in the operations of the business, (e) long-lived.

2. Gregg Office Equipment Co. has a fleet of automobiles and trucks for use by salespersons and for delivery of office supplies and equipment. Bridger Auto Sales Co. has automobiles and trucks for sale. Under what caption would the automobiles and trucks be reported on the balance sheet of (a) Gregg Office Equipment Co., (b) Bridger Auto Sales Co.?

3. Jolliff Co. acquired an adjacent vacant lot with the hope of selling it in the future at a gain. The lot is not intended to be used in Jolliff's business operations. Where should such real estate be listed in the balance sheet?

4. Parish Company solicited bids from several contractors to construct an addition to its office building. The lowest bid received was for $240,000. Parish Company decided to construct the addition itself at a cost of $225,000. What amount should be recorded in the building account?

5. Are the amounts at which fixed assets are reported in the balance sheet their approximate market values as of the balance sheet date? Discuss.

6. a. Does the recognition of depreciation in the accounts provide a special cash fund for the replacement of fixed assets? Explain.
   b. Describe the nature of depreciation as the term is used in accounting.

7. Name the three factors that need to be considered in determining the amount of periodic depreciation.

8. Wilkie Company purchased a machine that has a manufacturer's suggested life of 12 years. The company plans to use the machine on a special project that will last 8 years. At the completion of the project, the machine will be sold. Over how many years should the machine be depreciated?

9. Is it necessary for a business to use the same method of computing depreciation (a) for all classes of its depreciable assets, (b) in the financial statements and in determining income taxes?

10. Of the three common depreciation methods, which is most widely used?

11. a. Under what conditions is the use of an accelerated depreciation method most appropriate?
    b. Why is an accelerated depreciation method often used for income tax purposes?
    c. What is the Modified Accelerated Cost Recovery System (MACRS), and under what conditions is it used?

12. A revision of depreciable fixed asset lives resulted in an increase in the remaining lives of certain fixed assets. The company would like to include, as income of the current period, the cumulative effect of the changes, which reduces the depreciation expense of past periods. Is this in accordance with generally accepted accounting principles? Discuss.

Source: "Q's and A's Technical Hotline," *Journal of Accountancy,* December 1991, p. 89.

13. Differentiate between capital expenditures and revenue expenditures.

14. Immediately after a used truck is acquired, a new motor is installed and the tires are replaced at a total cost of $2,750. Is this a capital expenditure or a revenue expenditure?

15. For some of the fixed assets of a business, the balance in Accumulated Depreciation is exactly equal to the cost of the asset. (a) Is it permissible to record additional depreciation on the assets if they are still useful to the business? Explain. (b) When should an entry be made to remove the cost and the accumulated depreciation from the accounts?

16. In what sections of the income statement are gains and losses from the disposal of fixed assets presented?

17. Differentiate between a capital lease and an operating lease.

18. The financial statements of **La-Z-Boy Chair Company** contain the following footnote:

The Company has several long-term leases covering manufacturing facilities. The lease agreements require the Company to insure and maintain the facilities and provide for annual payments, which include interest. These leases give the Company the option to purchase the facilities for nominal amounts, or in some instances to renew the leases for extended periods at nominal annual rentals.

Would these leases be classified as operating or capital leases? Discuss.

19. Describe the internal controls for acquiring fixed assets.

20. Why is a physical count of fixed assets necessary?
21. What is the term applied to the periodic charge for (a) ore removed from a mine, (b) the use of an intangible asset?
22. a. Over what period of time should the cost of a patent acquired by purchase be amortized?
    b. In general, what is the required treatment for research and development costs?
23. How should (a) fixed assets and (b) intangible assets be reported in the balance sheet?

Resources for Your Success On-Line at **warren.swcollege.com**
Remember! If you need additional help, visit South-Western's Web site. See page 26 for a description of the online and printed materials that are available.

EXERCISES

Exercise 10–1
Costs of acquiring fixed assets
Objective 1

Eileen Larkin owns and operates First Run Print Co. During July, First Run Print Co. incurred the following costs in acquiring two printing presses. One printing press was new, and the other was used by a business that recently filed for bankruptcy.

Costs related to new printing press:

1. Special foundation
2. Sales tax on purchase price
3. Insurance while in transit
4. Freight
5. New parts to replace those damaged in unloading
6. Fee paid to factory representative for installation

Costs related to secondhand printing press:

7. Freight
8. Installation
9. Repair of vandalism during installation
10. Replacement of worn-out parts
11. Repair of damage incurred in reconditioning the press
12. Fees paid to attorney to review purchase agreement
    a. Indicate which costs incurred in acquiring the new printing press should be debited to the asset account.
    b. Indicate which costs incurred in acquiring the secondhand printing press should be debited to the asset account.

Exercise 10–2
Determine cost of land
Objective 1

A company has developed a tract of land into a ski resort. The company has cut the trees, cleared and graded the land and hills, and constructed ski lifts. (a) Should the tree cutting, land clearing, and grading costs of constructing the ski slopes be debited to the land account? (b) If such costs are debited to Land, should they be depreciated?

Source: "Technical Issues Feature," *Journal of Accountancy,* December 1987, p. 82.

Exercise 10–3
Determine cost of land

Objective 1

✓ $136,200

Langley Delivery Company acquired an adjacent lot to construct a new warehouse, paying $30,000 and giving a short-term note for $90,000. Legal fees paid were $3,500, delinquent taxes assumed were $7,500, and fees paid to remove an old building from the land were $7,200. Materials salvaged from the demolition of the building were sold for $2,000. A contractor was paid $312,500 to construct a new warehouse. Determine the cost of the land to be reported on the balance sheet.

Exercise 10–4
Nature of depreciation

Objective 1

Sheehan Metal Casting Co. reported $625,000 for equipment and $310,000 for accumulated depreciation—equipment on its balance sheet.

Does this mean (a) that the replacement cost of the equipment is $625,000 and (b) that $310,000 is set aside in a special fund for the replacement of the equipment? Explain.

Exercise 10–5
Straight-line depreciation rates

Objective 2

✓ a. 25%

Convert each of the following estimates of useful life to a straight-line depreciation rate, stated as a percentage, assuming that the residual value of the fixed asset is to be ignored: (a) 4 years, (b) 5 years, (c) 10 years, (d) 20 years, (e) 25 years, (f) 40 years, (g) 50 years.

Exercise 10–6
Straight-line depreciation

Objective 2

✓ $12,800

A refrigerator used by a meat processor has a cost of $138,000, an estimated residual value of $10,000, and an estimated useful life of 10 years. What is the amount of the annual depreciation computed by the straight-line method?

Exercise 10–7
Depreciation by units-of-production method

Objective 2

✓ $54,750

A diesel-powered generator with a cost of $475,000 and estimated residual value of $25,000 is expected to have a useful operating life of 60,000 hours. During July, the generator was operated 7,300 hours. Determine the depreciation for the month.

Exercise 10–8
Depreciation by units-of-production method

Objective 2

✓ a. Truck #1, credit Accumulated Depreciation, $4,320

Prior to adjustment at the end of the year, the balance in Trucks is $150,000, and the balance in Accumulated Depreciation—Trucks is $62,800. Details of the subsidiary ledger are as follows:

Truck No.	Cost	Estimated Residual Value	Estimated Useful Life	Accumulated Depreciation at Beginning of Year	Miles Operated During Year
1	$65,000	$5,000	250,000 miles	$22,500	18,000 miles
2	38,600	3,600	200,000	32,000	20,000
3	28,000	3,000	100,000	9,300	34,500
4	18,400	1,000	120,000	—	12,000

a. Determine the depreciation rates per mile and the amount to be credited to the accumulated depreciation section of each of the subsidiary accounts for the miles operated during the current year.
b. Journalize the entry to record depreciation for the year.

Exercise 10–9
Depreciation by two methods

Objective 2

✓ a. $27,500

A backhoe acquired on January 2 at a cost of $220,000 has an estimated useful life of 8 years. Assuming that it will have no residual value, determine the depreciation for each of the first two years (a) by the straight-line method and (b) by the declining-balance method, using twice the straight-line rate.

Exercise 10–10
Depreciation by two methods

Objective 2

✓ a. $5,200

A dairy storage tank acquired at the beginning of the fiscal year at a cost of $60,000 has an estimated residual value of $8,000 and an estimated useful life of 10 years. Determine the following: (a) the amount of annual depreciation by the straight-line method and (b) the amount of depreciation for the first and second year computed by the declining-balance method (at twice the straight-line rate).

Exercise 10–11
Partial-year depreciation

Objective 2

✓ a. First year, $18,000
   Second year, $24,000

Sandblasting equipment acquired at a cost of $125,000 has an estimated residual value of $5,000 and an estimated useful life of 5 years. It was placed in service on April 1 of the current fiscal year, which ends on December 31. Determine the depreciation for the current fiscal year and for the following fiscal year by (a) the straight-line method and (b) the declining-balance method, at twice the straight-line rate.

Exercise 10–12
Revision of depreciation

Objective 2

✓ a. $8,500

X-ray equipment with a cost of $360,000 has an estimated residual value of $20,000, an estimated useful life of 40 years, and is depreciated by the straight-line method. (a) What is the amount of the annual depreciation? (b) What is the book value at the end of the twentieth year of use? (c) If at the start of the twenty-first year it is estimated that the remaining life is 15 years and that the residual value is $10,000, what is the depreciation expense for each of the remaining 15 years?

Exercise 10–13
Revision of depreciation

Objective 2

✓ $10,000

Mobile communications equipment acquired on January 5, 1997, at a cost of $112,500, has an estimated residual value of $11,700 and an estimated useful life of 12 years. Depreciation has been recorded for the first four years ended December 31, 2000, by the straight-line method. Determine the amount of depreciation for the current year ended December 31, 2001, if the revised estimated residual value is $8,900 and the revised estimated remaining useful life (including the current year) is 7 years.

Exercise 10–14
Capital and revenue expenditures

Objective 3

Absaroka Co. incurred the following costs related to trucks and vans used in operating its delivery service:

1. Overhauled the engine on one of the trucks that had been purchased four years ago.
2. Removed a two-way radio from one of the trucks and installed a new radio with greater range of communication.
3. Installed a hydraulic lift to a van.
4. Changed the oil and greased the joints of all the trucks and vans.
5. Replaced two of the trucks' shock absorbers with new shock absorbers that allow for the delivery of heavier loads.
6. Replaced the brakes and alternator on a truck that had been in service for the past 5 years.
7. Installed security systems on three of the newer trucks.
8. Repaired a flat tire on one of the vans.
9. Rebuilt the transmission on one of the vans that had been driven only 25,000 miles. The van was no longer under warranty.
10. Tinted the back and side windows of one of the vans to discourage theft of contents.

Classify each of the costs as a capital expenditure or a revenue expenditure. For those costs identified as capital expenditures, classify each as an addition, a betterment, or an extraordinary repair.

Exercise 10–15
Capital and revenue expenditures

Objective 3

Mark Lemke Co. owns and operates Second to None Transport Co. During the past year, Mark incurred the following costs related to his 18-wheel truck.

1. Overhauled the engine.
2. Removed the old CB radio and replaced it with a newer model with greater range.
3. Replaced a headlight that had burned out.
4. Replaced the hydraulic brake system that had begun to fail during his latest trip through the Smoky Mountains.
5. Replaced a shock absorber that had worn out.
6. Installed fog lights.

7. Installed a wind deflector on top of the cab to increase fuel mileage.
8. Modified the factory-installed turbo charger with a special-order kit designed to add 30 more horsepower to the engine performance.
9. Replaced the old radar detector with a newer model that detects the KA frequencies now used by many of the state patrol radar guns. The detector is wired directly into the cab, so that it is partially hidden. In addition, Mark fastened the detector to the truck with a locking device that prevents its removal.
10. Installed a television in the sleeping compartment of the truck.

Classify each of the costs as a capital expenditure or a revenue expenditure. For those costs identified as capital expenditures, classify each as an addition, a betterment, or an extraordinary repair.

Exercise 10–16
Major repair to fixed asset

Objective 3

✓ a. $30,000
✓ d. $25,000

A number of major structural repairs on a building were completed at the beginning of the current fiscal year at a cost of $80,000. The repairs are expected to extend the life of the building 6 years beyond the original estimate. The original cost of the building was $750,000, and it is being depreciated by the straight-line method for 25 years. The residual value is expected to be negligible and has been ignored. The balance of the related accumulated depreciation account after the depreciation adjustment at the end of the preceding year is $330,000.

a. What has the amount of annual depreciation been in past years?
b. To what account should the cost of repairs ($80,000) be debited?
c. What is the book value of the building after the repairs have been recorded?
d. What is the amount of depreciation for the current year, using the straight-line method (assuming that the repairs were completed at the very beginning of the year)?

Exercise 10–17
Entries for sale of fixed asset

Objective 4

✓ a. $46,500

Metal recycling equipment acquired on January 3, 1997, at a cost of $87,500, has an estimated useful life of 8 years, an estimated residual value of $5,500, and is depreciated by the straight-line method.

a. What was the book value of the equipment at December 31, 2000, the end of the fiscal year?
b. Assuming that the equipment was sold on July 1, 2001, for $40,000, journalize the entries to record (1) depreciation for the six months of the current year ending December 31, 2001, and (2) the sale of the equipment.

Exercise 10–18
Disposal of fixed asset

Objective 4

✓ b. $15,500

Equipment acquired on January 3, 1997, at a cost of $51,500, has an estimated useful life of 4 years and an estimated residual value of $3,500.

a. What was the annual amount of depreciation for the years 1997, 1998, and 1999, using the straight-line method of depreciation?
b. What was the book value of the equipment on January 1, 2000?
c. Assuming that the equipment was sold on January 2, 2000, for $13,000, journalize the entry to record the sale.
d. Assuming that the equipment had been sold on January 2, 2000, for $17,000 instead of $13,000, journalize the entry to record the sale.

Exercise 10–19
Asset traded for similar asset

Objective 4

✓ a. $139,000

A printing press priced at $170,000 is acquired by trading in a similar press and paying cash for the difference between the trade-in allowance and the price of the new press. (a) Assuming that the trade-in allowance is $31,000, what is the amount of cash given? (b) Assuming that the book value of the press traded in is $23,800, what is the cost of the new press for financial reporting purposes?

Exercise 10–20
Asset traded for similar asset

Objective 4

✓ b. $170,000

Assume the same facts as in Exercise 10–19, except that the book value of the press traded in is $35,000. (a) What is the amount of cash given? (b) What is the cost of the new press for financial reporting purposes?

Exercise 10–21
Entries for trade of fixed asset

Objective 4

On April 1, Cougar Co., a water distiller, acquired new bottling equipment with a list price of $315,000. Cougar received a trade-in allowance of $50,000 on the old equipment of a similar type, paid cash of $30,000, and gave a series of five notes payable for the remainder. The following information about the old equipment is obtained from the account in the equipment ledger: cost, $212,500; accumulated depreciation on December 31, the end of the preceding fiscal year, $135,000; annual depreciation, $9,000. Journalize the entries to record (a) the current depreciation of the old equipment to the date of trade-in and (b) the transaction on April 1 for financial reporting purposes.

Exercise 10–22
Entries for trade of fixed asset

Objective 4

On October 1, Weissman Co. acquired a new truck with a list price of $125,000. Weissman received a trade-in allowance of $22,000 on an old truck of similar type, paid cash of $15,000, and gave a series of five notes payable for the remainder. The following information about the old truck is obtained from the account in the equipment ledger: cost, $82,500; accumulated depreciation on December 31, the end of the preceding fiscal year, $57,500; annual depreciation, $7,500. Journalize the entries to record (a) the current depreciation of the old truck to the date of trade-in and (b) the transaction on October 1 for financial reporting purposes.

Exercise 10–23
Depreciable cost of asset acquired by exchange

Objective 4

✓ a. $50,000

On the first day of the fiscal year, a delivery truck with a list price of $50,000 was acquired in exchange for an old delivery truck and $38,000 cash. The old truck had a book value of $14,000 at the date of the exchange.

a. Determine the depreciable cost for financial reporting purposes.
b. Assuming that the book value of the old delivery truck was $9,000, determine the depreciable cost for financial reporting purposes.

Exercise 10–24
Internal control of fixed assets

Objective 6

AllNet Co. is a computer software company marketing products in the United States and Canada. While AllNet Co. has over 90 sales offices, all accounting is handled at the company's headquarters in Cleveland, Ohio.

AllNet Co. keeps all its fixed asset records on a computerized system. The computer maintains a subsidiary ledger of all fixed assets owned by the company and calculates depreciation automatically. Whenever a manager at one of the ninety sales offices wants to purchase a fixed asset, a purchase request is submitted to headquarters for approval. Upon approval, the fixed asset is purchased and the invoice is sent back to headquarters so that the asset can be entered into the fixed asset system.

A manager who wants to dispose of a fixed asset simply sells or disposes of the asset and notifies headquarters to remove the asset from the system. Company cars and personal computers are frequently purchased by employees when they are disposed of. Most pieces of office equipment are traded in when new assets are acquired.

What internal control weakness exists in the procedures used to acquire and dispose of fixed assets at AllNet Co.?

Exercise 10–25
Depletion entries

Objective 7

✓ a. $5,100,000

Boxer Co. acquired mineral rights for $18,000,000. The mineral deposit is estimated at 30,000,000 tons. During the current year, 8,500,000 tons were mined and sold for $6,500,000.

a. Determine the amount of depletion expense for the current year.
b. Journalize the adjusting entry to recognize the expense.

Exercise 10–26
Amortization entries

Objective 8

✓ a. $56,750

Nitro Company acquired patent rights on January 3, 1997, for $935,000. The patent has a useful life equal to its legal life of 20 years. On January 5, 2000, Nitro successfully defended the patent in a lawsuit at a cost of $170,000.

a. Determine the patent amortization expense for the current year ended December 31, 2000.
b. Journalize the adjusting entry to recognize the amortization.

Exercise 10–27
Balance sheet presentation

Objective 9

What's Wrong
WITH THIS?

How many errors can you find in the following partial balance sheet?

Gazette Company
Balance Sheet
December 31, 20—

Assets

Total current assets $297,500

	Replacement Cost	Accumulated Depreciation	Book Value	
Property, plant, and equipment:				
Land	$ 65,000	$ 20,000	$ 45,000	
Buildings	160,000	76,000	84,000	
Factory equipment	450,000	192,000	258,000	
Office equipment	120,000	77,000	43,000	
Patents	60,000	—	60,000	
Goodwill	45,000	—	45,000	
Total property, plant, and equipment	$900,000	$365,000		535,000

Exercise 10–28
Ratio of fixed assets to long-term liabilities

Objective 10

HAT

The financial statements of **Hershey Foods Corporation** are presented in Appendix G at the end of the text.

a. Compute the ratio of fixed assets (property, plant, and equipment) to long-term liabilities (long-term debt) as of December 31, 1996 and 1995.

b. ━━━▶ What conclusions can be drawn from these ratios concerning Hershey's ability to borrow additional funds on a long-term basis?

Appendix Exercise 10–29
Sum-of-the-years-digits depreciation

✓ First year: $48,889

Based on the data in Exercise 10–9, determine the depreciation for the backhoe for each of the first two years, using the sum-of-the-years-digits depreciation method.

Appendix Exercise 10–30
Sum-of-the-years-digits depreciation

✓ First year: $9,455

Based on the data in Exercise 10–10, determine the depreciation for the dairy storage tank for each of the first two years, using the sum-of-the-years-digits depreciation method.

Appendix Exercise 10–31
Partial-year depreciation

✓ First year: $30,000

Based on the data in Exercise 10–11, determine the depreciation for the sandblasting equipment for each of the first two years, using the sum-of-the-years-digits depreciation method.

PROBLEMS SERIES A

Problem 10–1A
Allocate payments and receipts to fixed asset accounts

Objective 1

SPREADSHEET

The following payments and receipts are related to land, land improvements, and buildings acquired for use in a wholesale apparel business. The receipts are identified by an asterisk.

a.	Finder's fee paid to real estate agency	$ 15,000
b.	Cost of real estate acquired as a plant site: Land	250,000
	Building	50,000
c.	Fee paid to attorney for title search.	1,000
d.	Delinquent real estate taxes on property, assumed by purchaser. . . .	18,500
e.	Cost of razing and removing building	21,250
f.	Proceeds from sale of salvage materials from old building.	3,500*
g.	Cost of filling and grading land.	15,500
h.	Special assessment paid to city for extension of water main to the property	9,000
i.	Architect's and engineer's fees for plans and supervision	75,000
j.	Premium on 1-year insurance policy during construction	5,700
k.	Cost of repairing windstorm damage during construction.	3,500
l.	Cost of repairing vandalism damage during construction	800
m.	Cost of paving parking lot to be used by customers	17,500
n.	Cost of trees and shrubbery planted	20,000
o.	Proceeds from insurance company for windstorm and vandalism damage	4,300*
p.	Interest incurred on building loan during construction	85,000
q.	Money borrowed to pay building contractor	1,000,000*
r.	Payment to building contractor for new building	1,250,000
s.	Refund of premium on insurance policy (j) canceled after 10 months	950*

Instructions

1. Assign each payment and receipt to Land (unlimited life), Land Improvements (limited life), Building, or Other Accounts. Indicate receipts by an asterisk. Identify each item by letter and list the amounts in columnar form, as follows:

Item	Land	Land Improvements	Building	Other Accounts

2. ➡ The costs assigned to the land, which is used as a plant site, will not be depreciated, while the costs assigned to land improvements will be depreciated. Explain this seemingly contradictory application of the concept of depreciation.

Problem 10–2A
Compare three depreciation methods

Objective 2

✓ 1999: straight-line depreciation, $45,000

Roche Company purchased waterproofing equipment on January 2, 1999, for $195,000. The equipment was expected to have a useful life of 4 years, or 45,000 operating hours, and a residual value of $15,000. The equipment was used for 8,900 hours during 1999, 13,100 hours in 2000, 14,500 hours in 2001, and 8,500 hours in 2002.

Instructions

Determine the amount of depreciation expense for the years ended December 31, 1999, 2000, 2001, and 2002, by (a) the straight-line method, (b) the units-of-production method, and (c) the declining-balance method, using twice the straight-line rate. Also determine the total depreciation expense for the four years by each method. The following columnar headings are suggested for recording the depreciation expense amounts:

	Depreciation Expense		
Year	Straight-Line Method	Units-of-Production Method	Declining-Balance Method

Problem 10–3A
Depreciation by three methods; partial years

Objective 2

✓ a. 1999, $20,400

Afco Company purchased tool sharpening equipment on July 1, 1999, for $129,600. The equipment was expected to have a useful life of 3 years, or 13,600 operating hours, and a residual value of $7,200. The equipment was used for 2,400 hours during 1999, 7,600 hours in 2000, 3,000 hours in 2001, and 600 hours in 2002.

Instructions
Determine the amount of depreciation expense for the years ended December 31, 1999, 2000, 2001, and 2002, by (a) the straight-line method, (b) the units-of-production method, and (c) the declining-balance method, using twice the straight-line rate.

Problem 10–4A
Depreciation by two methods; trade of fixed asset

Objectives 2, 4

SPREADSHEET

✓ 1. b. Year 1, $100,000 depreciation expense
✓ 2. $245,000

New tire retreading equipment, acquired at a cost of $200,000 at the beginning of a fiscal year, has an estimated useful life of 4 years and an estimated residual value of $15,000. The manager requested information regarding the effect of alternative methods on the amount of depreciation expense each year. On the basis of the data presented to the manager, the declining-balance method was selected.

In the first week of the fourth year, the equipment was traded in for similar equipment priced at $250,000. The trade-in allowance on the old equipment was $30,000, cash of $20,000 was paid, and a note payable was issued for the balance.

Instructions
1. Determine the annual depreciation expense for each of the estimated 4 years of use, the accumulated depreciation at the end of each year, and the book value of the equipment at the end of each year by (a) the straight-line method and (b) the declining-balance method (at twice the straight-line rate). The following columnar headings are suggested for each schedule:

Year	Depreciation Expense	Accumulated Depreciation, End of Year	Book Value, End of Year

2. For financial reporting purposes, determine the cost of the new equipment acquired in the exchange.
3. Journalize the entry to record the exchange.
4. Journalize the entry to record the exchange, assuming that the trade-in allowance was $18,000 instead of $30,000.

Problem 10–5A
Transactions for fixed assets, including trade

Objectives 1, 3, 4

HAT

The following transactions, adjusting entries, and closing entries were completed by New World Furniture Co. during a 3-year period. All are related to the use of delivery equipment. The declining-balance method (at twice the straight-line rate) of depreciation is used.

1998
Jan. 2. Purchased a used delivery truck for $15,000, paying cash.
      5. Paid $3,000 to replace the automatic transmission and install new brakes on the truck. (Debit Delivery Equipment.)
June 7. Paid garage $125 for changing the oil, replacing the oil filter, and tuning the engine on the delivery truck.
Dec. 31. Recorded depreciation on the truck for the fiscal year. The estimated useful life of the truck is 8 years, with a residual value of $4,000.
     31. Closed the appropriate accounts to the income summary account.

1999
Mar. 19. Paid garage $310 to tune the engine and make other minor repairs on the truck.
Apr. 30. Traded in the used truck for a new truck priced at $40,000, receiving a trade-in allowance of $13,375 and paying the balance in cash. (Record depreciation to date in 1999.)
Dec. 31. Recorded depreciation on the truck. It has an estimated trade-in value of $3,000 and an estimated life of 10 years.
     31. Closed the appropriate accounts to the income summary account.

2000

Oct. 1. Purchased a new truck for $42,000, paying cash.

2. Sold the truck purchased April 30, 1999, for $30,000. (Record depreciation for the year.)

Dec. 31. Recorded depreciation on the remaining truck. It has an estimated residual value of $4,500 and an estimated useful life of 10 years.

31. Closed the appropriate accounts to the income summary account.

Instructions

Journalize the transactions and the adjusting and closing entries. Post to the following accounts in the ledger and determine the balances after each posting:

122	Delivery Equipment
123	Accumulated Depreciation—Delivery Equipment
616	Depreciation Expense—Delivery Equipment
617	Truck Repair Expense
812	Gain on Disposal of Fixed Assets

Problem 10–6A

Amortization and depletion entries

Objectives 7, 8

✓ a. $30,000

Data related to the acquisition of timber rights and intangible assets during the current year ended December 31 are as follows:

a. Goodwill in the amount of $1,200,000 was purchased on January 4. It is decided to amortize over the maximum period allowable.

b. Governmental and legal costs of $112,800 were incurred on July 3 in obtaining a patent with an estimated economic life of 8 years. Amortization is to be for one-half year.

c. Timber rights on a tract of land were purchased for $480,000 on July 3. The stand of timber is estimated at 1,600,000 board feet. During the current year, 350,000 board feet of timber were cut.

Instructions

1. Determine the amount of the amortization or depletion expense for the current year for each of the foregoing items.

2. Journalize the adjusting entries to record the amortization or depletion expense for each item.

PROBLEMS SERIES B

Problem 10–1B

Allocate payments and receipts to fixed asset accounts

Objective 1

SPREADSHEET

The following payments and receipts are related to land, land improvements, and buildings acquired for use in a wholesale ceramic business. The receipts are identified by an asterisk.

a.	Fee paid to attorney for title search	$ 1,500
b.	Cost of real estate acquired as a plant site: Land	300,000
	Building	125,000
c.	Delinquent real estate taxes on property, assumed by purchaser	18,750
d.	Cost of razing and removing building	5,800
e.	Proceeds from sale of salvage materials from old building	2,100*
f.	Special assessment paid to city for extension of water main to the property	5,000
g.	Premium on 1-year insurance policy during construction	6,600
h.	Cost of filling and grading land	29,700
i.	Cost of repairing windstorm damage during construction	1,500
j.	Cost of paving parking lot to be used by customers	12,500
k.	Cost of trees and shrubbery planted	15,000
l.	Architect's and engineer's fees for plans and supervision	60,000
m.	Cost of repairing vandalism damage during construction	500

n.   Interest incurred on building loan during construction. . . . . $ 48,000
o.   Cost of floodlights installed on parking lot   13,500
p.   Money borrowed to pay building contractor 600,000*
q.   Payment to building contractor for new building   850,000
r.   Proceeds from insurance company for windstorm and
     vandalism damage 2,000*
s.   Refund of premium on insurance policy (g) canceled after 11 months .   550*

Instructions

1.   Assign each payment and receipt to Land (unlimited life), Land Improvements (limited life), Building, or Other Accounts. Indicate receipts by an asterisk. Identify each item by letter and list the amounts in columnar form, as follows:

Item	Land	Land Improvements	Building	Other Accounts

2.   ▬▬▶ The costs assigned to the land, which is used as a plant site, will not be depreciated, while the costs assigned to land improvements will be depreciated. Explain this seemingly contradictory application of the concept of depreciation.

Problem 10–2B
Compare three depreciation methods

Objective 2

✓ 1999: straight-line depreciation, $120,000

Westby Company purchased packaging equipment on January 3, 1999, for $375,000. The equipment was expected to have a useful life of 3 years, or 24,000 operating hours, and a residual value of $15,000. The equipment was used for 6,500 hours during 1999, 11,600 hours in 2000, and 5,900 hours in 2001.

Instructions

Determine the amount of depreciation expense for the years ended December 31, 1999, 2000, and 2001, by (a) the straight-line method, (b) the units-of-production method, and (c) the declining-balance method, using twice the straight-line rate. Also determine the total depreciation expense for the three years by each method. The following columnar headings are suggested for recording the depreciation expense amounts:

	Depreciation Expense		
Year	Straight- Line Method	Units-of- Production Method	Declining- Balance Method

Problem 10–3B
Depreciation by three methods; partial years

Objective 2

✓ a. 2002: $34,000

Newbauer Company purchased plastic laminating equipment on July 1, 1999, for $216,000. The equipment was expected to have a useful life of 3 years, or 34,000 operating hours, and a residual value of $12,000. The equipment was used for 4,800 hours during 1999, 15,200 hours in 2000, 9,600 hours in 2001, and 4,400 hours in 2002.

Instructions

Determine the amount of depreciation expense for the years ended December 31, 1999, 2000, 2001, and 2002, by (a) the straight-line method, (b) the units-of-production method, and (c) the declining-balance method, using twice the straight-line rate.

Problem 10–4B
Depreciation by two methods; trade of fixed asset

Objectives 2, 4

SPREADSHEET

✓ 1. b. Year 1: $100,000 depreciation expense
✓ 2. $292,400

New lithographic equipment, acquired at a cost of $250,000 at the beginning of a fiscal year, has an estimated useful life of 5 years and an estimated residual value of $20,000. The manager requested information regarding the effect of alternative methods on the amount of depreciation expense each year. On the basis of the data presented to the manager, the declining-balance method was selected.

In the first week of the fifth year, the equipment was traded in for similar equipment priced at $300,000. The trade-in allowance on the old equipment was $40,000, cash of $30,000 was paid, and a note payable was issued for the balance.

Instructions

1.   Determine the annual depreciation expense for each of the estimated 5 years of use, the accumulated depreciation at the end of each year, and the book value of the

equipment at the end of each year by (a) the straight-line method and (b) the declining-balance method (at twice the straight-line rate). The following columnar headings are suggested for each schedule:

Year	Depreciation Expense	Accumulated Depreciation, End of Year	Book Value End of Year

2. For financial reporting purposes, determine the cost of the new equipment acquired in the exchange.
3. Journalize the entry to record the exchange.
4. Journalize the entry to record the exchange, assuming that the trade-in allowance was $25,000 instead of $40,000.

Problem 10–5B
Transactions for fixed assets, including trade

Objectives 1, 3, 4

The following transactions, adjusting entries, and closing entries were completed by Oak Furniture Co. during a 3-year period. All are related to the use of delivery equipment. The declining-balance method (at twice the straight-line rate) of depreciation is used.

1998
Jan.   3. Purchased a used delivery truck for $22,300, paying cash.
         6. Paid $1,700 for a new transmission for the truck. (Debit Delivery Equipment.)
Sep. 17. Paid garage $415 for miscellaneous repairs to the truck.
Dec. 31. Recorded depreciation on the truck for the fiscal year. The estimated useful life of the truck is 4 years, with a residual value of $5,000.
        31. Closed the appropriate accounts to the income summary account.

1999
June 30. Traded in the used truck for a new truck priced at $34,000, receiving a trade-in allowance of $11,000 and paying the balance in cash. (Record depreciation to date in 1999.)
Oct.   9. Paid garage $305 for miscellaneous repairs to the truck.
Dec. 31. Recorded depreciation on the truck. It has an estimated trade-in value of $8,000 and an estimated life of 5 years.
        31. Closed the appropriate accounts to the income summary account.

2000
Oct.   1. Purchased a new truck for $40,000, paying cash.
         2. Sold the truck purchased June 30, 1999, for $20,000. (Record depreciation for the year.)
Dec. 31. Recorded depreciation on the remaining truck. It has an estimated residual value of $5,000 and an estimated useful life of 8 years.
        31. Closed the appropriate accounts to the income summary account.

Instructions
Journalize the transactions and the adjusting and closing entries. Post to the following accounts in the ledger and determine the balances after each posting:

122   Delivery Equipment
123   Accumulated Depreciation—Delivery Equipment
616   Depreciation Expense—Delivery Equipment
617   Truck Repair Expense
812   Gain on Disposal of Fixed Assets

Problem 10–6B
Amortization and depletion entries

Objectives 7, 8

✓ a. $108,000

Data related to the acquisition of timber rights and intangible assets during the current year ended December 31 are as follows:

a. Timber rights on a tract of land were purchased for $270,000 on May 5. The stand of timber is estimated at 1,500,000 board feet. During the current year, 600,000 board feet of timber were cut.
b. Goodwill in the amount of $3,000,000 was purchased on January 3. It is decided to amortize over the maximum period allowable.

c.   Governmental and legal costs of $125,000 were incurred on July 1 in obtaining a patent with an estimated economic life of 10 years. Amortization is to be for one-half year.

Instructions

1.   Determine the amount of the amortization or depletion expense for the current year for each of the foregoing items.
2.   Journalize the adjusting entries required to record the amortization or depletion for each item.

SPECIAL ACTIVITIES

Activity 10–1
Fallon Co.
Ethics and professional conduct in business

Irene Stucky, CPA, is an assistant to the controller of Fallon Co. In her spare time, Irene also prepares tax returns and performs general accounting services for clients. Frequently, Irene performs these services after her normal working hours, using Fallon Co.'s computers and laser printers. Occasionally, Irene's clients will call her at the office during regular working hours.

➤ Discuss whether Irene is performing in a professional manner.

Activity 10–2
Cascade Co.
Financial vs. tax depreciation

The following is an excerpt from a conversation between two employees of Cascade Co., Wendy Delaney and Alan Bentley. Wendy is the accounts payable clerk, and Alan is the cashier.

Wendy: Alan, could I get your opinion on something?
Alan: Sure, Wendy.
Wendy: Do you know Maggie, the fixed assets clerk?
Alan: I know who she is, but I don't know her real well. Why?
Wendy: Well, I was talking to her at lunch last Monday about how she liked her job, etc. You know, the usual . . . and she mentioned something about having to keep two sets of books . . . one for taxes and one for the financial statements. That can't be good accounting, can it? What do you think?
Alan: Two sets of books? It doesn't sound right.
Wendy: It doesn't seem right to me either. I was always taught that you had to use generally accepted accounting principles. How can there be two sets of books? What can be the difference between the two?

➤ How would you respond to Alan and Wendy if you were Maggie?

Activity 10–3
Caddis Construction Co.
Effect of depreciation on net income

Caddis Construction Co. specializes in building replicas of historic houses. Jill Trout, president of Caddis, is considering the purchase of various items of equipment on July 1, 1997, for $300,000. The equipment would have a useful life of 5 years and no residual value. In the past, all equipment has been leased. For tax purposes, Jill is considering depreciating the equipment by the straight-line method. She discussed the matter with her CPA and learned that, although the straight-line method could be elected, it was to her advantage to use the modified accelerated cost recovery system (MACRS) for tax purposes. She asked for your advice as to which method to use for tax purposes.

1.   Compute depreciation for each of the years (1997, 1998, 1999, 2000, 2001, and 2002) of useful life by (a) the straight-line method and (b) MACRS. In using the straight-line method, one-half year's depreciation should be computed for 1997 and 2002. Use the MACRS rates presented in the chapter.
2.   Assuming that income before depreciation and income tax is estimated to be $300,000 uniformly per year and that the income tax rate is 30%, compute the net income for each of the years 1997, 1998, 1999, 2000, 2001, and 2002, if (a) the straight-line method is used and (b) MACRS is used.
3.   ➤ What factors would you present for Jill's consideration in the selection of a depreciation method?

Activity 10–4
Into the Real World
Shopping for a delivery

You are planning to acquire a delivery truck for use in your business for three years. In groups of three or four, explore a local dealer's purchase and leasing options for the truck. Summarize the costs of purchasing versus leasing, and list other factors that might help you decide whether to buy or lease the truck.

Activity 10–5
Into the Real World
Applying for patents, copyrights, and trademarks

Go to the Internet and review the procedures for applying for a patent, a copyright, and a trademark. One Internet site that is useful for this purpose is:

www.idresearch.com

Prepare a written summary of these procedures.

ANSWERS TO SELF-EXAMINATION QUESTIONS

Matching

1. M	4. V	7. D	10. U	13. W	16. P	19. B	22. H
2. K	5. Y	8. A	11. C	14. E	17. J	20. N	23. X
3. T	6. I	9. F	12. L	15. G	18. O	21. Q	24. R

Multiple Choice

1. **C** All amounts spent to get a fixed asset (such as machinery) in place and ready for use are proper charges to the asset account. In the case of machinery acquired, the freight (answer A) and the installation costs (answer B) are both (answer C) proper charges to the machinery account.

2. **C** The periodic charge for depreciation under the declining-balance method (twice the straight-line rate) for the second year is determined by first computing the depreciation charge for the first year. The depreciation for the first year of $6,000 (answer A) is computed by multiplying the cost of the equipment, $9,000, by ²/₃ (the straight-line rate of ¹/₃ multiplied by 2). The depreciation for the second year of $2,000 (answer C) is then determined by multiplying the book value at the end of the first year, $3,000 (the cost of $9,000 minus the first-year depreciation of $6,000), by ²/₃ . The third year's depreciation is $400 (answer D). It is determined by multiplying the book value at the end of the second year, $1,000, by ²/₃, thus yielding $667. However, the equipment cannot be depreciated below its residual value of $600; thus, the third-year depreciation is $400 ($1,000 − $600).

3. **B** A depreciation method that provides for a higher depreciation amount in the first year of the use of an asset and a gradually declining periodic amount thereafter is called an accelerated depreciation method. The declining-balance method (answer B) is an example of such a method.

4. **B** The acceptable method of accounting for an exchange of similar assets in which the trade-in allowance ($30,000) exceeds the book value of the old asset ($25,000) requires that the cost of the new asset be determined by adding the amount of cash given ($70,000) to the book value of the old asset ($25,000), which totals $95,000. Alternatively, the unrecognized gain ($5,000) can be subtracted from the list price ($100,000).

5. **D** Long-lived assets that are useful in operations, not held for sale, and without physical qualities are called intangible assets. Patents, goodwill, and copyrights are examples of intangible assets (answer D).

Current Liabilities

If you are employed, you know that your paycheck is normally less than the total amount you earned because your employer deducted amounts for such items as federal income tax and social security tax. For example, if you worked 20 hours last week at $10 per hour and you are paid weekly, your payroll check could appear as follows:

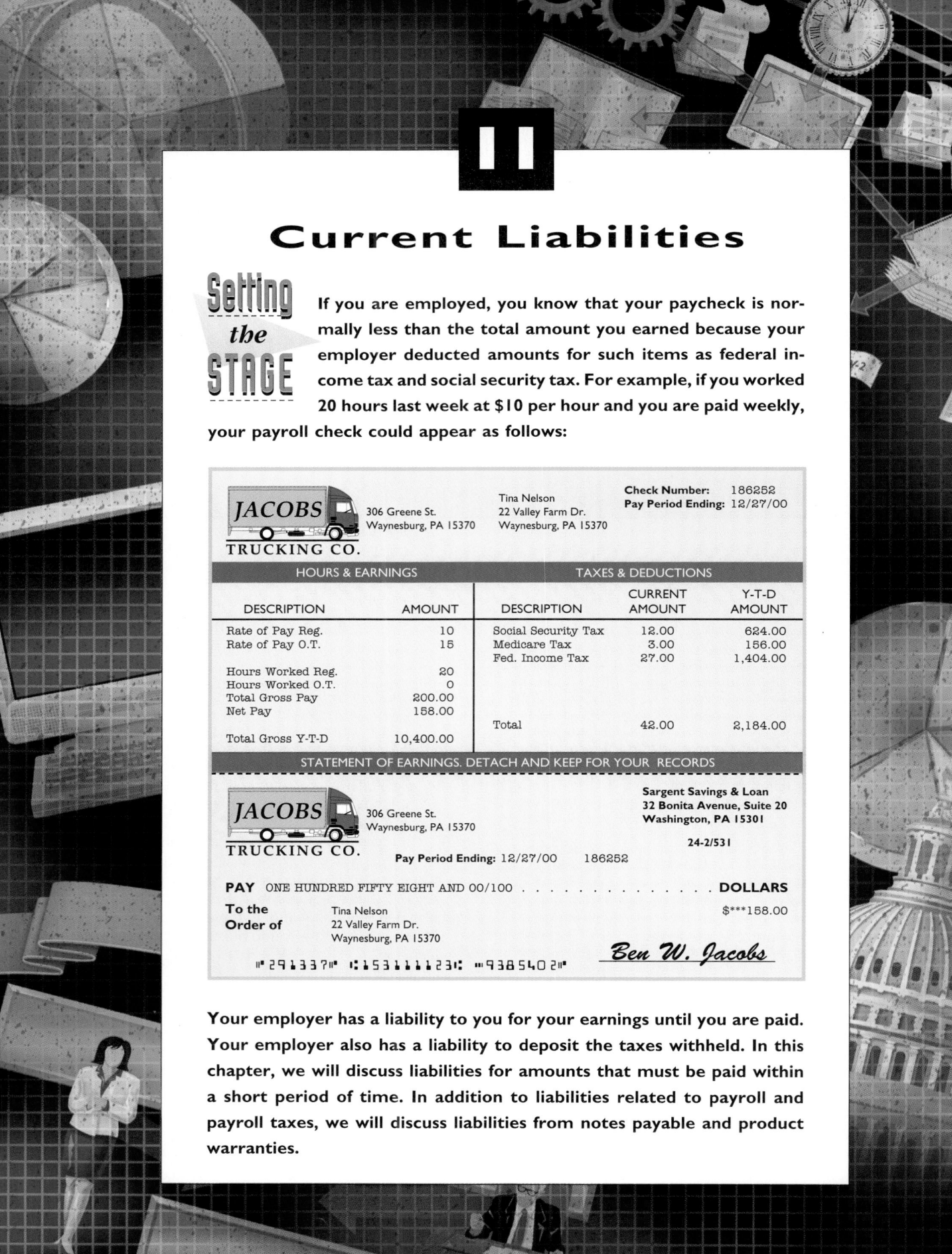

| JACOBS TRUCKING CO. | 306 Greene St. Waynesburg, PA 15370 | Tina Nelson 22 Valley Farm Dr. Waynesburg, PA 15370 | Check Number: 186252 Pay Period Ending: 12/27/00 |

HOURS & EARNINGS		TAXES & DEDUCTIONS		
DESCRIPTION	AMOUNT	DESCRIPTION	CURRENT AMOUNT	Y-T-D AMOUNT
Rate of Pay Reg.	10	Social Security Tax	12.00	624.00
Rate of Pay O.T.	15	Medicare Tax	3.00	156.00
		Fed. Income Tax	27.00	1,404.00
Hours Worked Reg.	20			
Hours Worked O.T.	0			
Total Gross Pay	200.00			
Net Pay	158.00			
		Total	42.00	2,184.00
Total Gross Y-T-D	10,400.00			

STATEMENT OF EARNINGS. DETACH AND KEEP FOR YOUR RECORDS

- -

| JACOBS TRUCKING CO. | 306 Greene St. Waynesburg, PA 15370 | Sargent Savings & Loan 32 Bonita Avenue, Suite 20 Washington, PA 15301 |

Pay Period Ending: 12/27/00   186252

24-2/531

PAY ONE HUNDRED FIFTY EIGHT AND 00/100 . . . . **DOLLARS**

To the Order of Tina Nelson
22 Valley Farm Dr.
Waynesburg, PA 15370

$***158.00

Ben W. Jacobs

⑾ 291337⑾ ⑆153111123⑆ ⑾9385402⑾

Your employer has a liability to you for your earnings until you are paid. Your employer also has a liability to deposit the taxes withheld. In this chapter, we will discuss liabilities for amounts that must be paid within a short period of time. In addition to liabilities related to payroll and payroll taxes, we will discuss liabilities from notes payable and product warranties.

After studying this chapter, you should be able to:

1 Define and give examples of current liabilities.

2 Journalize entries for short-term notes payable.

3 Describe the accounting treatment for contingent liabilities and journalize entries for product warranties.

4 Determine employer liabilities for payroll, including liabilities arising from employee earnings and deductions from earnings.

5 Describe payroll accounting systems that use a payroll register, employee earnings records, and a general journal.

6 Journalize entries for employee fringe benefits, including vacation pay and pensions.

7 Use the quick ratio to analyze the ability of a business to pay its current liabilities.

The Nature of Current Liabilities

OBJECTIVE 1

Define and give examples of current liabilities.

Your credit card balance is probably due within a short time, such as 30 days. Such liabilities that are to be paid out of current assets and are due within a short time, usually within one year, are called **current liabilities**. Most current liabilities arise from two basic transactions:

1. Receiving goods or services prior to making payment.
2. Receiving payment prior to delivering goods or services.

An example of the first type of transaction is **accounts payable** arising from purchases of merchandise for resale. An example of the second type of transaction is **unearned rent** arising from the receipt of rent in advance. Some additional examples of current liabilities that we discussed in previous chapters are:

- Taxes payable—the amount of taxes owed to governmental units
- Interest payable—the amount of interest owed on borrowed funds
- Wages payable—the amount owed to employees

In this chapter, we will introduce some other common current liabilities. These include short-term notes payable, contingencies, payroll liabilities, and employee fringe benefits.

Short-Term Notes Payable

OBJECTIVE 2

Journalize entries for short-term notes payable.

Notes may be issued when merchandise or other assets are purchased. They may also be issued to creditors to temporarily satisfy an account payable created earlier. For example, assume that a business issues a 90-day, 12% note for $1,000, dated August 1, 2000, to Murray Co. for a $1,000 overdue account. The entry to record the issuance of the note is as follows:

Aug.	1	Accounts Payable—Murray Co.	1 0 0 0 00	
		Notes Payable		1 0 0 0 00
		Issued a 90-day, 12% note on account.		

When the note matures, the entry to record the payment of $1,000 principal plus $30 interest ($1,000 × 12% × 90/360) is as follows:

Oct.	30	Notes Payable		1 0 0 0 00		
		Interest Expense		3 0 00		
		Cash			1 0 3 0 00	
		Paid principal and interest due on note.				

The interest expense is reported in the Other Expense section of the income statement for the year ended December 31, 2000. The interest expense account is closed at December 31.

The preceding entries for notes payable are similar to those we discussed in an earlier chapter for notes receivable. Notes payable entries are presented from the viewpoint of the borrower, while notes receivable entries are presented from the viewpoint of the creditor or lender. To illustrate, the following entries are journalized for a borrower (Bowden Co.), who issues a note payable to a creditor (Coker Co.):

	Bowden Co. (Borrower)			Coker Co. (Creditor)		
May 1. Bowden Co. purchased merchandise on account from Coker Co., $10,000, 2/10, n/30. The merchandise cost Coker Co. $7,500.	Merchandise Inventory Accounts Payable	10,000	10,000	Accounts Receivable Sales Cost of Merchandise Sold Merchandise Inventory	10,000 7,500	10,000 7,500
May 31. Bowden Co. issued a 60-day, 12% note for $10,000 to Coker Co. on account.	Accounts Payable Notes Payable	10,000	10,000	Notes Receivable Accounts Receivable	10,000	10,000
July 30. Bowden Co. paid Coker Co. the amount due on the note of May 31. Interest: $10,000 × 12% × 60/360.	Notes Payable Interest Expense Cash	10,000 200	10,200	Cash Interest Revenue Notes Receivable	10,200	200 10,000

Notes may also be issued when money is borrowed from banks. Although the terms may vary, many banks would accept from the borrower an interest-bearing note for the amount of the loan. For example, assume that on September 19 a firm borrows $4,000 from First National Bank by giving the bank a 90-day, 15% note. The entry to record the receipt of cash and the issuance of the note is as follows:

Sep.	19	Cash		4 0 0 0 00		
		Notes Payable			4 0 0 0 00	
		Issued a 90-day, 15% note to the bank.				

On the due date of the note (December 18), the borrower owes $4,000, the principal of the note, plus interest of $150 ($4,000 × 15% × 90/360). The entry to record the payment of the note is as follows:

Dec.	18	Notes Payable		4 0 0 0 00		
		Interest Expense		1 5 0 00		
		Cash			4 1 5 0 00	
		Paid principal and interest due on note.				

Sometimes a borrower will issue to a creditor a discounted note rather than an interest-bearing note. Although such a note does not specify an interest rate, the creditor sets a rate of interest and deducts the interest from the face amount of the note. This interest is called the discount. The rate used in computing the discount is called the discount rate. The borrower is given the remainder, called the proceeds.

To illustrate, assume that on August 10, Cary Company issues a $20,000, 90-day note to Seinfeld Company in exchange for inventory. Seinfeld discounts the note at a rate of 15%. The amount of the discount, $750, is debited to *Interest Expense*. The proceeds, $19,250, are debited to *Merchandise Inventory. Notes Payable* is credited for the face amount of the note, which is also its maturity value. This entry is shown below.

In buying a used delivery truck, a business issues an $8,000, 60-day note dated July 15, which the truck's seller discounts at 12%. What is the cost of the truck (the proceeds)?

$7,840 [$8,000 − ($8,000 × 12% × 60/360)]

Aug.	10	Merchandise Inventory	19 2 5 0 00		
		Interest Expense	7 5 0 00		
		Notes Payable		20 0 0 0 00	
		Issued a 90-day note to Seinfeld Co.,			
		discounted at 15%.			

When the note is paid, the following entry is recorded:[1]

Nov.	8	Notes Payable	20 0 0 0 00		
		Cash		20 0 0 0 00	
		Paid note due.			

Contingent Liabilities

OBJECTIVE 3

Describe the accounting treatment for contingent liabilities and journalize entries for product warranties.

Some past transactions will result in liabilities if certain events occur in the future. These potential obligations are called **contingent liabilities**. For example, **Ford Motor Company** would have a contingent liability for the estimated costs associated with warranty work. The obligation is contingent upon a *future event,* namely, a customer requiring warranty work on a vehicle. The obligation is the result of a *past transaction,* which is the original sale of the vehicle.

If a contingent liability is *probable* and the amount of the liability can be *reasonably estimated,* it should be recorded in the accounts. **Ford Motor Company's** vehicle warranty costs are an example of a *recordable* contingent liability. The warranty costs are *probable*

Saturn Corporation has marketed itself as "A Different Kind of Car Company." One way Saturn acted "differently" was its response to a defective coolant placed in the radiators in some of its new cars. Instead of just replacing the coolant, Saturn replaced the cars! Saturn even gave customers a selection of free additional options on their replacement cars to compensate for the inconvenience. Saturn focuses on reducing warranty defects and has been consistently ranked in the top three of J.D. Power and Associates' customer satisfaction ratings.

---

[1] If the accounting period ends before a discounted note is paid, an adjusting entry should record the prepaid (deferred) interest that is not yet an expense. This deferred interest would be deducted from Notes Payable in the Current Liabilities section of the balance sheet.

because it is known that warranty repairs will be required on some vehicles. In addition, the costs can be *estimated* from past warranty experience.

To illustrate, assume that during June a company sells a product for $60,000 on which there is a 36-month warranty for repairing defects. Past experience indicates that the average cost to repair defects is 5% of the sales price. The entry to record the estimated product warranty expense for June is as follows:

A business sells to a customer $120,000 of commercial audio equipment with a one-year repair and replacement warranty. Historically, the average cost to repair or replace is 2% of sales. How is this contingent liability recorded?

June	30	Product Warranty Expense	3 0 0 0 00	
		Product Warranty Payable		3 0 0 0 00
		Warranty expense for June, 5% × $60,000.		

Product Warranty Expense	2,400	
Product Warranty Payable		2,400

This transaction matches revenues and expenses properly by recording warranty costs in the same period in which the sale is recorded. When the defective product is repaired, the repair costs are recorded by debiting *Product Warranty Payable* and crediting *Cash, Supplies,* or other appropriate accounts. Thus, if a customer required a $200 part replacement on August 16, the entry would be:

Aug.	16	Product Warranty Payable	2 0 0 00	
		Supplies		2 0 0 00
		Replaced defective part under warranty.		

If a contingent liability is probable but cannot be *reasonably estimated* or is only *possible,* then the nature of the contingent liability should be disclosed in the footnotes to the financial statements. Professional judgment is required in distinguishing between contingent liabilities that are probable versus those that are only possible.

Common examples of contingent liabilities disclosed in notes to the financial statements are litigation, environmental matters, guarantees, and sale of receivables. The following example of a contingency disclosure, related to tobacco litigation, was taken from an annual report of **Philip Morris Companies, Inc.**: *". . . Pending claims related to tobacco products generally fall within three categories: (i) smoking and health cases alleging personal injury brought on behalf of individual smokers, (ii) smoking and health cases alleging personal injury and purporting to be brought on behalf of a class of plaintiffs, and (iii) health care cost recovery actions brought primarily by states and local governments seeking reimbursement for Medicaid and other health care expenditures allegedly caused by cigarette smoking. . . ."*

The accounting treatment of contingent liabilities is summarized in Exhibit 1.

The 1996 edition of *Accounting Trends & Techniques* indicates that 70% of the surveyed companies disclosed contingencies for litigation, 49% for environmental matters, 34% for guarantees, and 13% for sale of receivables.

EXHIBIT 1
Accounting Treatment of Contingent Liabilities

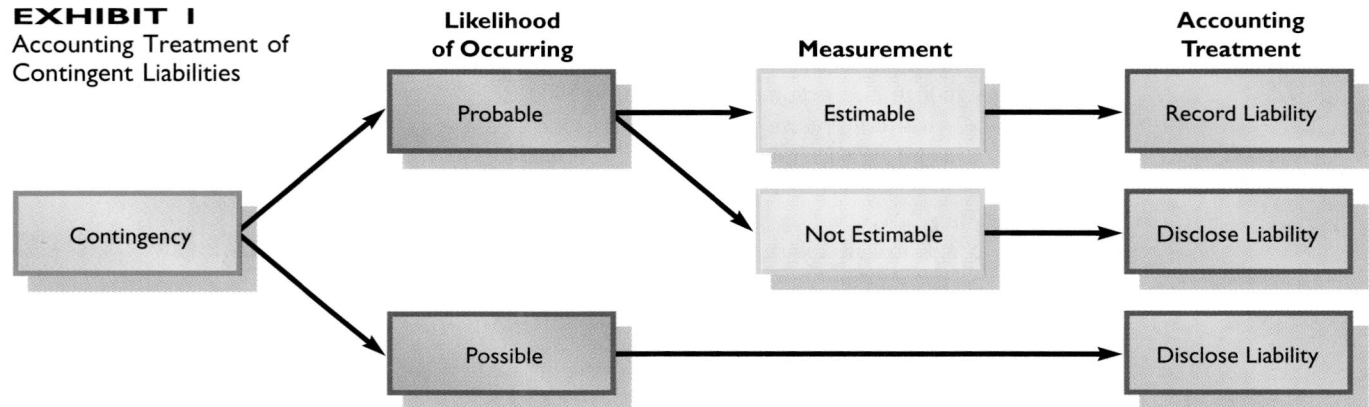

BUSINESS ON STAGE

Teaming up for High Performance

Picture a factory in your mind. Do you see employees working alone, performing mind-numbing repetitive work? Fortunately, this picture is fast disappearing from the employment landscape. Many companies, such as **Procter & Gamble**, **Hewlett-Packard**, and **Federal Express**, are using teams. Teams typically consist of between 8 to 15 full-time employees. Often team members represent different functions, such as marketing, manufacturing, and finance.

Why are companies using teams? Teams have the following advantages over individual employees:

- Teams are able to put employees' skills together to solve problems, complete projects, and combine tasks that form a process.
- Teams perform the coordination and communication tasks formerly performed by middle management.
- Empowered teams are more creative and more satisfied in their work.
- Teams take on expanded responsibilities, such as ordering materials, conducting quality checks, making team hiring and firing decisions, developing work schedules, and jointly establishing performance targets with management.

One area of challenge is in the area of team compensation and rewards. Popular plans develop individual base pay rates on the basis of skills obtained, rather than just seniority. A recent survey noted that 85% of companies using teams set base pay rates above the industry average. Additional bonuses are available based on achieving team goals. The same survey noted such bonuses averaged around 10% of base pay.

Team-based management assigns responsibility and authority to the team members and provides rewards for this added work. As one team member put it, "It's a real mind shift. You're used to the expectation that it's your job to have the best idea. But no individual is going to have the best idea. That's not how it works—the best ideas come from the collective intelligence of the team. If you accept that, you're in for a big change in how you think about yourself." ∎

Employee salaries and wages are expenses to an employer.

Payroll and Payroll Taxes

OBJECTIVE 4

Determine employer liabilities for payroll, including liabilities arising from employee earnings and deductions from earnings.

We are all familiar with the term payroll. In accounting, the term **payroll** refers to the amount paid to employees for the services they provide during a period. A business's payroll is usually significant for several reasons. First, employees are sensitive to payroll errors and irregularities. Maintaining good employee morale requires that the payroll be paid on a timely, accurate basis. Second, the payroll is subject to various federal and state regulations. Finally, the payroll and related payroll taxes have a significant effect on the net income of most businesses. Although the amount of such expenses varies widely, it is not unusual for a business's payroll and payroll-related expenses to equal nearly one-third of its revenue.

Point of **INTEREST**

Information on average salaries for a variety of professions can be found at the *Economic Research Institute's* Web site at **www.erieri.com**.

Liability for Employee Earnings

Salaries and wages paid to employees are an employer's labor expenses. The term **salary** usually refers to payment for managerial, administrative, or similar services. The rate of salary is normally expressed in terms of a month or a year. The term **wages** usually refers to payment for manual labor, both skilled and unskilled. The rate of wages is normally stated on an hourly or weekly basis. In practice, the terms salary and wages are often used interchangeably.

The basic salary or wage of an employee may be increased by commissions, profit sharing, or cost-of-living adjustments. Many businesses pay managers an annual bonus in addition to a basic salary. The amount of the bonus is often based on some measure of productivity, such as income or profit of the business. Although payment is usually made by check or in cash, it may be in the form of securities, notes, lodging, or other property or services. Generally, the form of

INTERMISSION

Your Social Security Taxes—Then and Now

In its 1936 publication, *Security in Your Old Age*, the Social Security Board set forth the following explanation of how the social security tax would affect a worker's paycheck:

The taxes called for in this law will be paid both by your employer and by you. For the next 3 years you will pay maybe 15 cents a week, maybe 25 cents a week, maybe 30 cents or more, according to what you earn. That is to say, during the next 3 years, beginning January 1, 1937, you will pay 1 cent for every dollar you earn, and at the same time your employer will pay 1 cent for every dollar you earn, up to $3,000 a year. Twenty-six million other workers and their employers will be paying at the same time.

After the first 3 years—that is to say, beginning in 1940—you will pay, and your employer will pay, 1½ cents for each dollar you earn, up to $3,000 a year. This will be the tax for 3 years, and then beginning in 1943, you will pay 2 cents, and so will your employer, for every dollar you earn for the next three years. After that, you and your employer will each pay half a cent more for 3 years, and finally, beginning in 1949, twelve years from now, you and your employer will each pay 3 cents on each dollar you earn, up to $3,000 a year. That is the most you will ever pay.

The rate on January 1, 1998, was 7.65 cents per dollar earned (7.65%). The social security portion was 6.20% on the first $68,400 of earnings. The Medicare portion was 1.45% on all earnings. ■

Source: Arthur Lodge, "That Is the Most You Will Ever Pay," *Journal of Accountancy,* October 1985, p. 44.

payment has no effect on how salaries and wages are treated by either the employer or the employee.

Salary and wage rates are determined by agreement between the employer and the employees. Businesses engaged in interstate commerce must follow the requirements of the Fair Labor Standards Act. Employers covered by this legislation, which is commonly called the Federal Wage and Hour Law, are required to pay a minimum rate of 1½ times the regular rate for all hours worked in excess of 40 hours per week. Exemptions are provided for executive, administrative, and certain supervisory positions. Premium rates for overtime or for working at night, holidays, or other less desirable times are fairly common, even when not required by law. In some cases, the premium rates may be as much as twice the base rate.

To illustrate computing an employee's earnings, assume that John T. McGrath is employed by McDermott Supply Co. at the rate of $25 per hour. Any hours in excess of 40 hours per week are paid at a rate of 1½ times the normal rate, or $37.50 ($25 + $12.50) per hour. For the week ended December 27, McGrath's time card indicates that he worked 44 hours. His earnings for that week are computed as follows:

Earnings at base rate (40 × $25)	$1,000
Earnings at overtime rate (4 × $37.50)	150
Total earnings	$1,150

Deductions from Employee Earnings

The total earnings of an employee for a payroll period, including bonuses and overtime pay, are called **gross pay**. From this amount is subtracted one or more **deductions** to arrive at the net pay. **Net pay** is the amount the employer must pay the employee. The deductions for federal taxes are usually the largest deduction. Deductions may also be required for state or local income taxes. Other deductions may be made for medical insurance, contributions to pensions, and for items authorized by individual employees.

FICA Tax

Most of us have FICA tax withheld from our payroll checks by our employers. Employers are required by the Federal Insurance Contributions Act (FICA) to withhold a portion of the earnings of each of the employees. The amount of **FICA tax** withheld is the employees' contribution to two federal programs. Tax is withheld separately under each program. The first program, called **social security**, is for old age, survivors, and disability insurance (OASDI). The second program, called **Medicare**, is health insurance for senior citizens.

The amount of tax that employers are required to withhold from each employee is normally based on the amount of earnings paid in the *calendar* year. Although both the schedule of future tax rates and the maximum amount subject to tax are revised often by Congress, such changes have little effect on the basic payroll system. In this text, we will use a social security rate of 6% on the first $70,000 of annual earnings and a Medicare rate of 1.5% on all annual earnings.

 Tables are available from the Internal Revenue Service for determining social security and Medicare withholding.

To illustrate, assume that John T. McGrath's annual earnings prior to the

If an employee earns $6,000 per month and has been employed since January 1 of the current year, what is the total FICA tax deducted from the employee's December paycheck?

Social security tax ($4,000 × 6%) $240
Medicare tax ($6,000 × 1.5%)   90
    Total FICA tax $330

current payroll period total $69,150. Assume also that the current period earnings are $1,150. The total FICA tax of $68.25 is determined as follows:

Earnings subject to 6% social security tax ($70,000 − $69,150)	$ 850
Social security tax rate	× 6%
Social security tax	$51.00
Earnings subject to 1.5% Medicare tax	$1,150
Medicare tax rate	× 1.5%
Medicare tax	17.25
Total FICA tax	$68.25

Income Taxes

Except for certain types of employment, all employers must withhold a portion of employee earnings for payment of the employees' federal income tax. As a basis for determining the amount to be withheld, each employee completes and submits to the employer an "Employee's Withholding Allowance Certificate," often called a W-4. Exhibit 2 is an example of a completed W-4 form.

EXHIBIT 2
Employee's Withholding Allowance Certificate (W-4 Form)

-------- Cut here and give the certificate to your employer. Keep the top portion for your records. --------

| Form **W-4** Department of the Treasury Internal Revenue Service | **Employee's Withholding Allowance Certificate** ▶ For Privacy Act and Paperwork Reduction Act Notice, see reverse. | OMB No. 1545-0010 **1999** |

1 Type or print your first name and middle initial   John   T.   McGrath   Last name
2 Your social security number   381 48 9120

Home address (number and street or rural route)   1830 4th Street
3 ☒ Single ☐ Married ☐ Married, but withhold at higher Single rate.
Note: if married, but legally separated, or spouse is a nonresident alien, check the Single box.

City or town, state, and ZIP code   Clinton, Iowa 52732-6142
4 If your last name differs from that on your social security card, check here and call 1-800-772-1213 for a new card . . . . . ▶ ☐

5 Total number of allowances you are claiming (from line G above or from the worksheets on page 2 if they apply) .   **5** 1
6 Additional amount, if any, you want withheld from each paycheck . . . .   **6** $
7 I claim exemption from withholding for 1997, and I certify that I meet BOTH of the following conditions for exemption:
● Last year I had a right to a refund of ALL Federal income tax withheld because I had NO tax liability; AND
● This year I expect a refund of ALL Federal income tax withheld because I expect to have NO tax liability.
If you meet both conditions, enter "EXEMPT" here . . . . ▶ **7**

Under penalties of perjury, I certify that I am entitled to the number of withholding allowances claimed on this certificate or entitled to claim exempt status.

Employee's signature ▶ *John T. McGrath*   Date ▶ June 2 , 19 99

8 Employer's name and address (Employer: Complete 8 and 10 only if sending to the IRS)
9 Office code (optional)
10 Employer identification number

You may recall filling out a W-4 form. On the W-4, an employee indicates marital status, the number of withholding allowances, and whether any additional withholdings are authorized. A single employee may claim one withholding allowance. A married employee may claim an additional allowance for a spouse. An employee may also claim an allowance for each dependent other than a spouse. Each allowance claimed reduces the amount of federal income tax withheld from the employee's check.

The amount that must be withheld for income tax differs, depending upon each employee's gross pay and completed W-4. Most employers use wage bracket withholding tables furnished by the Internal Revenue Service to determine the amount to be withheld.

 Federal income tax withholding tables are available from the Internal Revenue Service as part of *Circular E,* "Employer's Tax Guide."

Exhibit 3 is an example of a wage bracket withholding table. This table is for a single employee who is paid weekly. Other tables are used for employees who are married or who are paid biweekly, semimonthly, monthly, or at other time periods. Unlike social security tax, there is no ceiling on the amount of employee earnings subject to federal income tax withholding.

EXHIBIT 3
Wage Bracket Withholding
Table

SINGLE Persons—WEEKLY Payroll Period

If the wages are—		And the number of withholding allowances claimed is—										
At least	But less than	0	1	2	3	4	5	6	7	8	9	10
		The amount of income tax to be withheld is—										
900	910	180	166	152	138	123	109	95	80	67	59	52
910	920	183	169	155	140	126	112	98	83	69	61	53
920	930	186	172	157	143	129	115	100	86	72	62	55
930	940	189	175	160	146	132	117	103	89	75	64	56
940	950	192	177	163	149	135	120	106	92	77	65	58
950	960	194	180	166	152	137	123	109	94	80	67	59
960	970	197	183	169	154	140	126	112	97	83	69	61
970	980	200	186	171	157	143	129	114	100	86	72	62
980	990	203	189	174	160	146	131	117	103	89	74	64
990	1,000	206	191	177	163	149	134	120	106	91	77	65
1,000	1,010	208	194	180	166	151	137	123	108	94	80	67
1,010	1,020	211	197	183	168	154	140	126	111	97	83	68
1,020	1,030	214	200	185	171	157	143	128	114	100	86	71
1,030	1,040	217	203	188	174	160	145	131	117	103	88	74
1,040	1,050	220	205	191	177	163	148	134	120	105	91	77
1,050	1,060	222	208	194	180	165	151	137	122	108	94	80
1,060	1,070	225	211	197	182	168	154	140	125	111	97	82
1,070	1,080	228	214	199	185	171	157	142	128	114	100	85
1,080	1,090	231	217	202	188	174	159	145	131	117	102	88
1,090	1,100	235	219	205	191	177	162	148	134	119	105	91
1,100	1,110	238	222	208	194	179	165	151	136	122	108	94
1,110	1,120	241	225	211	196	182	168	154	139	125	111	96
1,120	1,130	244	228	213	199	185	171	156	142	128	114	99
1,130	1,140	247	231	216	202	188	173	159	145	131	116	102
1,140	1,150	250	234	219	205	191	176	162	148	133	119	105
1,150	1,160	253	237	222	208	193	179	165	150	136	122	108
1,160	1,170	256	240	225	210	196	182	168	153	139	125	110
1,170	1,180	259	244	228	213	199	185	170	156	142	128	113
1,180	1,190	262	247	231	216	202	187	173	159	145	130	116
1,190	1,200	266	250	234	219	205	190	176	162	147	133	119
1,200	1,210	269	253	237	222	207	193	179	164	150	136	122
1,210	1,220	272	256	240	224	210	196	182	167	153	139	124
1,220	1,230	275	259	243	227	213	199	184	170	156	142	127
1,230	1,240	278	262	246	231	216	201	187	173	159	144	130
1,240	1,250	281	265	249	234	219	204	190	176	161	147	133

In using the withholding table, the amount of federal income tax withheld each pay period is indicated where the row showing the employee's wage bracket intersects the column showing the employee's withholding allowances. For example, assume that John T. McGrath, who is single and has declared one withholding allowance, made $1,150 for the week ended December 27. Using the withholding table in Exhibit 3, the amount of federal income tax withheld is $237.

In addition to the federal income tax, employees may also be required to pay a state income tax and a city income tax. State and city taxes are withheld from employees' earnings and paid to state and city governments.

Professional athletes must pay local taxes in each location in which they play their sport.

Other Deductions

Neither the employer nor the employee has any choice in deducting taxes from gross earnings. However, employees may choose to have additional amounts deducted for other purposes. For example, you as an employee may authorize deductions for retirement savings, for contributions to charitable organizations, or for premiums on employee insurance. A union contract may also require the deduction of union dues.

Computing Employee Net Pay

Gross earnings less payroll deductions equals the amount to be paid to an employee for the payroll period. This amount is the *net pay*, which is often called the *take-home pay*. Assuming that John T. McGrath authorized deductions for retirement savings and for a United Way contribution, the amount to be paid McGrath for the week ended December 27 is $819.75, as shown below.

Gross earnings for the week		$1,150.00
Deductions:		
Social security tax	$ 51.00	
Medicare tax	17.25	
Federal income tax	237.00	
Retirement savings	20.00	
United Way	5.00	
Total deductions		330.25
Net pay		$ 819.75

Liability for Employer's Payroll Taxes

So far, we have discussed the payroll taxes that are withheld from the employees' earnings. Most employers are also subject to federal and state payroll taxes based on the amount paid their employees. Such taxes are an operating expense of the business. Exhibit 4 summarizes the responsibility for employee and employer payroll taxes.

EXHIBIT 4   Responsibility for Tax Payments

FICA Tax

Employers are required to contribute to the social security and Medicare programs for each employee. The employer must match the employee's contribution to each program.

The U.S. Government receives money from various taxes, fees, and borrowing. This money is spent on a variety of government services. The relative sizes of these sources and outlays for fiscal 1995 are shown below.

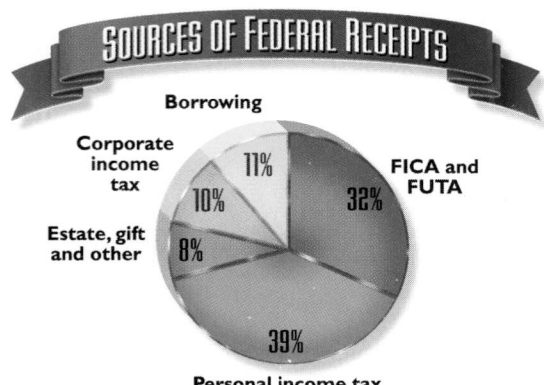

SOURCES OF FEDERAL RECEIPTS

Borrowing

Corporate income tax 10%

11%

FICA and FUTA 32%

Estate, gift and other 8%

Personal income tax 39%

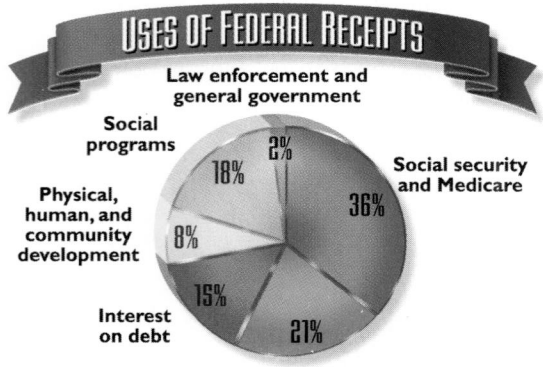

USES OF FEDERAL RECEIPTS

Law enforcement and general government 2%

Social programs 18%

Social security and Medicare 36%

Physical, human, and community development 8%

Interest on debt 15%

National defense 21%

Source: Internal Revenue Service

Federal Unemployment Compensation Tax

The Federal Unemployment Tax Act (FUTA) provides for temporary payments to those who become unemployed as a result of layoffs due to economic causes beyond their control. Types of employment subject to this program are similar to those covered by FICA taxes. A tax of 6.2% is levied on employers only, rather than on both employers and employees.[2] It is applied to only the first $7,000 of the earnings of each covered employee during a calendar year. Congress often revises the rate and maximum earnings subject to federal unemployment compensation tax. The funds collected by the federal government are not paid directly to the unemployed, but are allocated among the states for use in state programs.

State Unemployment Compensation Tax

State Unemployment Tax Acts (SUTA) also provide for payments to unemployed workers. The amounts paid as benefits are obtained, for the most part, from a tax levied upon employers only. A few states require employee contributions also. The rates of tax and the tax bases vary. In most states, employers who provide stable employment for their employees are granted reduced rates. The employment experience and the status of each employer's tax account are reviewed annually, and the tax rates are adjusted accordingly.[3]

Accounting Systems for Payroll and Payroll Taxes

OBJECTIVE 5

Describe payroll accounting systems that use a payroll register, employee earnings records, and a general journal.

In designing payroll systems, the requirements of various federal, state, and local agencies for payroll data are considered. Payroll data must also be maintained accurately for each payroll period and for each employee. Periodic reports using payroll data must be submitted to government agencies. The payroll data itself must be retained for possible inspection by the various agencies.

Payroll systems must be designed to pay employees on a timely basis. Payroll systems should also be designed to provide useful data for management decision-making needs. Such needs might include settling employee grievances and negotiating retirement or other benefits with employees.

Although payroll systems differ among businesses, the major elements common to most payroll systems are the payroll register, employee's earnings record, and payroll checks. We discuss and illustrate each of these elements next. We have kept

---

[2] This rate may be reduced to 0.8% for credits for state unemployment compensation tax.

[3] As of January 1, 1998, the maximum state rate credited against the federal unemployment rate was 5.4% of the first $7,000 of each employee's earnings during a calendar year.

the illustrations relatively simple, and they may be modified in practice to meet the needs of each individual business.

Payroll Register

The **payroll register** is a multicolumn form used in assembling and summarizing the data needed for each payroll period. Its design varies according to the number and classes of employees and the extent to which computers are used. Exhibit 5 shows a form suitable for a small number of employees.

The nature of the data appearing in the payroll register is evident from the column headings. The number of hours worked and the earnings and deduction data are inserted in their proper columns. The sum of the deductions for each employee is then subtracted from the total earnings to yield the amount to be paid. The check numbers are recorded in the payroll register as evidence of payment.

The last two columns of the payroll register are used to accumulate the total wages or salaries to be debited to the various expense accounts. This process is usually called **payroll distribution**.

The format of the payroll register in Exhibit 5 aids in determining the mathematical accuracy of the payroll before checks are issued to employees. All column totals should be verified, as shown below.

Earnings:		
Regular	$13,328.00	
Overtime	574.00	
Total		$13,902.00
Deductions:		
Social security tax	$ 643.07	
Medicare tax	208.53	
Federal income tax	3,332.00	
Retirement savings	680.00	
United Way	470.00	
Accounts receivable	50.00	
Total		5,383.60
Paid—net amount		$ 8,518.40
Accounts debited:		
Sales Salaries Expense		$11,122.00
Office Salaries Expense		2,780.00
Total (as above)		$13,902.00

Recording Employees' Earnings

Amounts in the payroll register may be posted directly to the accounts. An alternative is to use the payroll register as a supporting record for a journal entry. The entry based on the payroll register in Exhibit 5 follows.

Dec.	27	Sales Salaries Expense		11 1 2 2 00	
		Office Salaries Expense		2 7 8 0 00	
		Social Security Tax Payable			6 4 3 07
		Medicare Tax Payable			2 0 8 53
		Employees Federal Income Tax Payable			3 3 3 2 00
		Retirement Savings Deductions Payable			6 8 0 00
		United Way Deductions Payable			4 7 0 00
		Accounts Receivable—Fred G. Elrod			5 0 00
		Salaries Payable			8 5 1 8 40
		Payroll for week ended December 27.			

EXHIBIT 5
Payroll Register

	Employee Name	Total Hours	Earnings			
			Regular	Overtime	Total	
1	Abrams, Julie S.	40	500.00		500.00	1
2	Elrod, Fred G.	44	392.00	58.80	450.80	2
3	Gomez, Jose C.	40	840.00		840.00	3
4	McGrath, John T.	44	1,000.00	150.00	1,150.00	4
25	Wilkes, Glenn K.	40	480.00		480.00	25
26	Zumpano, Michael W.	40	600.00		600.00	26
27	Total		13,328.00	574.00	13,902.00	27
28						28

Recording and Paying Payroll Taxes

Payroll taxes become a liability to the employer when the payroll is paid.

The employer's payroll taxes become liabilities when the related payroll is *paid* to employees. In addition, employers are required to compute and report payroll taxes on a *calendar-year* basis, even if a different fiscal year is used for financial reporting and income tax purposes.

To illustrate, assume that Everson Company's fiscal year ends on April 30. Also, assume that Everson Company owes its employees $26,000 of wages on December 31. The following portions of the $26,000 of wages are subject to payroll taxes on December 31:

	Earnings Subject to Payroll Taxes
Social Security Tax (6.0%)	$18,000
Medicare Tax (1.5%)	26,000
State and Federal Unemployment Compensation Tax	1,000

If the payroll is paid on December 31, the payroll taxes will be based on the preceding amounts. If the payroll is paid on January 2, however, the *entire* $26,000 will be subject to *all* payroll taxes.

The payroll register in Exhibit 5 indicates that the amount of social security tax withheld is $643.07 and Medicare tax withheld is $208.53. Since the employer must match the employees' FICA contributions, the employer's social security payroll tax will also be $643.07, and the Medicare tax will be $208.53. Further, assume that the earnings subject to state and federal unemployment compensation taxes are $2,710. Multiplying this amount by the state (5.4%) and federal (0.8%) rates yields the unemployment compensation taxes shown in the payroll tax computation on the next page.

 Social security contributions (both the employees' and employer's amounts) and federal income taxes must be deposited quarterly in a federal depository bank. An "Employer's Quarterly Federal Tax Return" (Form 941) must also be filed. Unemployment compensation tax returns and payments are required annually by the federal government and most state governments.

	Deductions							Paid		Accounts Debited		
	Social Security Tax	Medicare Tax	Federal Income Tax	Retirement Savings	Misc.		Total	Net Amount	Check No.	Sales Salaries Expense	Office Salaries Expense	
1	30.00	7.50	74.00	20.00	UW	10.00	141.50	358.50	6857	500.00		1
2	27.05	6.76	62.00		AR	50.00	145.81	304.99	6858		450.80	2
3	50.40	12.60	173.00	25.00	UW	10.00	271.00	569.00	6859	840.00		3
4	51.00	17.25	237.00	20.00	UW	5.00	330.25	819.75	6860	1,150.00		4
25	28.80	7.20	69.00	10.00			115.00	365.00	6880	480.00		25
26	36.00	9.00	71.00	5.00	UW	2.00	123.00	477.00	6881		600.00	26
27	643.07	208.53	3,332.00	680.00	UW	470.00	5,383.60	8,518.40		11,122.00	2,780.00	27
28					AR	50.00						28

Miscellaneous Deductions: UW—United Way; AR—Accounts Receivable

EXHIBIT 5
(concluded)

Social security tax	$ 643.07
Medicare tax	208.53
State unemployment compensation tax (5.4% × $2,710)	146.34
Federal unemployment compensation tax (0.8% × $2,710)	21.68
Total payroll tax expense	$1,019.62

The entry to journalize the payroll tax expense for the week and the liability for the taxes accrued is shown below.

Dec.	27	Payroll Tax Expense	1 0 1 9 62		
		Social Security Tax Payable		6 4 3 07	
		Medicare Tax Payable		2 0 8 53	
		State Unemployment Tax Payable		1 4 6 34	
		Federal Unemployment Tax Payable		2 1 68	
		Payroll taxes for week ended			
		December 27.			

Employee's Earnings Record

The amount of each employee's earnings to date must be available at the end of each payroll period. This cumulative amount is required in order to compute each employee's social security and Medicare tax withholding and the employer's payroll taxes. It is essential, therefore, that a detailed payroll record be maintained for each employee. This record is called an **employee's earnings record**.

Exhibit 6 shows a portion of the employee's earnings record for John T. Mc-Grath. The relationship between this record and the payroll register can be seen by tracing the amounts entered on McGrath's earnings record for December 27 back to its source—the fourth line of the payroll register in Exhibit 5.

In addition to spaces for recording data for each payroll period and the cumulative total of earnings, the employee's earnings record has spaces for quarterly totals and the yearly total. These totals are used in various reports for tax, insurance, and other purposes. One such report is the Wage and Tax Statement, commonly called a **Form W-2**. You may recall receiving a W-2 form for use in preparing your individual tax return. This form must be provided annually to each employee as well as to

EXHIBIT 6
Employee's Earnings Record

John T. McGrath
1830 4th Street
Clinton, IA 52732-6142   PHONE: 555-3148

| MARRIED | NUMBER OF WITHHOLDING ALLOWANCES: 1 | PAY RATE: | $1,000.00 Per Week |
| OCCUPATION: | Salesperson | EQUIVALENT HOURLY RATE: $25 | |

			Earnings			
	Period Ending	Total Hours	Regular Earnings	Overtime Earnings	Total Earnings	Cumulative Total
42	SEP. 27	51	1,000.00	412.50	1,412.50	52,800.00	42
43	THIRD QUARTER		13,000.00	4,800.00	17,800.00		43
44	OCT. 4	50	1,000.00	375.00	1,375.00	54,175.00	44
50	NOV. 15	48	1,000.00	300.00	1,300.00	62,200.00	50
51	NOV. 22	50	1,000.00	375.00	1,375.00	63,575.00	51
52	NOV. 29	52	1,000.00	450.00	1,450.00	65,025.00	52
53	DEC. 6	50	1,000.00	375.00	1,375.00	66,400.00	53
54	DEC. 13	48	1,000.00	300.00	1,300.00	67,700.00	54
55	DEC. 20	52	1,000.00	450.00	1,450.00	69,150.00	55
56	DEC. 27	44	1,000.00	150.00	1,150.00	70,300.00	56
57	FOURTH QUARTER		13,000.00	4,500.00	17,500.00		57
58	YEARLY TOTAL		52,000.00	18,300.00	70,300.00		58

the Social Security Administration. The amounts reported in the Form W-2 shown below were taken from McGrath's employee's earnings record.

a Control number	22222	Void ☐	For Official Use Only ► OMB No. 1545-0008		
b Employer's identification number 61-8436524			1 Wages, tips, other compensation 70,300.00		2 Federal income tax withheld 16,772.00
c Employer's name, address, and ZIP code McDermott Supply Co. 415 5th Ave. So. Dubuque, IA 52736-0142			3 Social security wages 70,000.00		4 Social security tax withheld 4,200.00
			5 Medicare wages and tips 70,300.00		6 Medicare tax withheld 1,054.50
			7 Social security tips		8 Allocated tips
d Employee's social security number 381-48-9120			9 Advance EIC payment		10 Dependent care benefits
e Employee's name (first, middle initial, last) John T. McGrath 1830 4th St. Clinton, IA 52732-6142			11 Nonqualified plans		12 Benefits included in box 1
			13 See Instrs. for box 13		14 Other
			15 Statutory employee ☐ Deceased ☐ Pension plan ☐ Legal rep. ☐ Hshld. emp. ☐ Subtotal ☐ Deferred compensation ☐		
f Employee's address and ZIP code					
16 State IA	Employer's state I.D. No.	17 State wages, tips, etc.	18 State income tax	19 Locality name Dubuque	20 Local wages, tips, etc.	21 Local income tax

Cat. No. 10134D   Department of the Treasury—Internal Revenue Service

Form **W-2** Wage and Tax Statement

Copy A For Social Security Administration

For Paperwork Reduction Act Notice, see separate instructions.

SOC. SEC. NO.: 381-48-9120

EMPLOYEE NO.: 814

DATE OF BIRTH: February 15, 1974

DATE EMPLOYMENT TERMINATED:

	Social Security Tax	Medicare Tax	Federal Income Tax	Retirement Savings	Other		Total	Net Amount	Check No.	
42	84.75	21.19	339.00	20.00			464.94	947.56	6175	42
43	1,068.00	267.00	4,296.00	260.00	UW	40.00	5,931.00	11,869.00		43
44	82.50	20.63	330.00	20.00			453.13	921.87	6225	44
50	78.00	19.50	312.00	20.00			429.50	870.50	6530	50
51	82.50	20.63	330.00	20.00			453.13	921.87	6582	51
52	87.00	21.75	348.00	20.00			476.75	973.25	6640	52
53	82.50	20.63	330.00	20.00	UW	5.00	458.13	916.87	6688	53
54	78.00	19.50	312.00	20.00			429.50	870.50	6743	54
55	87.00	21.75	348.00	20.00			476.75	973.25	6801	55
56	51.00	17.25	237.00	20.00	UW	5.00	330.25	819.75	6860	56
57	1,032.00	262.50	4,100.00	260.00	UW	10.00	5,664.50	11,835.50		57
58	4,200.00	1,054.50	16,772.00	1,040.00	UW	100.00	23,166.50	47,133.50		58

(Column group headers: **Deductions** spans Social Security Tax through Total; **Paid** spans Net Amount and Check No.)

EXHIBIT 6
(*concluded*)

Payroll Checks

At the end of each pay period, **payroll checks** are prepared. Each check includes a detachable statement showing the details of how the net pay was computed. Exhibit 7 is a payroll check for John T. McGrath.

The amount paid to employees is normally recorded as a single amount, regardless of the number of employees. There is no need to record each payroll check separately in the journal, since all of the details are available in the payroll register.

For paying their payroll, most employers use payroll checks drawn on a special bank account. After the data for the payroll period have been recorded and summarized in the payroll register, a single check for the total amount to be paid is written on the firm's regular bank account. This check is then deposited in the special payroll bank account. Individual payroll checks are written from the payroll account, and the numbers of the payroll checks are inserted in the payroll register.

An advantage of using a separate payroll bank account is that the task of reconciling the bank statements is simplified. In addition, a payroll bank account establishes control over payroll checks by preventing the theft or misuse of uncashed payroll checks.

EXHIBIT 7
Payroll Check

HOURS & EARNINGS		TAXES & DEDUCTIONS		

McDermott Supply Co.
415 5th Ave. So.
Dubuque, IA 52736-0142

John T. McGrath
1830 4th St.
Clinton, IA 52732-6142

Check Number: 6860
Pay Period Ending: 12/27/99

DESCRIPTION	AMOUNT	DESCRIPTION	CURRENT AMOUNT	Y-T-D AMOUNT
Rate of Pay Reg.	25	Social Security Tax	51.00	4,200.00
Rate of Pay O.T.	37.50	Medicare Tax	17.25	1,054.50
Hours Worked Reg.	40	Fed. Income Tax	237.00	16,772.00
Hours Worked O.T.	4	U.S. Savings Bonds	20.00	1,040.00
		United Fund	5.00	100.00
Net Pay	819.75			
Total Gross Pay	1,150.00	Total	330.25	23,166.50
Total Gross Y-T-D	70,300.00			

STATEMENT OF EARNINGS. DETACH AND KEEP FOR YOUR RECORDS

McDermott Supply Co.
415 5th Ave. So.
Dubuque, IA 52736-0142

LaGesse Savings & Loan
33 Katie Avenue, Suite 33
Clinton, IA 52736-3581

24-2/531

Pay Period Ending: 12/27/99   6860

PAY EIGHT HUNDRED NINETEEN AND 75/100 . . . . **DOLLARS**

To the Order of   JOHN T. MCGRATH
1830 4TH ST.
CLINTON, IA 52732-6142

$***819.75

Franklin D. McDermott

⑥⑧⑥⓪ ⑤③①①①①②③ ⑨③⑧⑤④⓪②

Currency may be used to pay payroll. However, many employees have their net pay deposited directly in a bank. In these cases, funds are transferred electronically.

Payroll System Diagram

You may find Exhibit 8 useful in following the flow of data within the payroll segment of an accounting system. The diagram indicates the relationships among the primary components of the payroll system we described in this chapter.

Our focus in the preceding discussion has been on the outputs of a payroll system: the payroll register, payroll checks, the employee's earnings record, and tax and other reports. As shown in the diagram in Exhibit 8, the inputs into a payroll system may be classified as either constants or variables.

Constants are data that remain unchanged from payroll to payroll and thus do not need to be entered into the system each pay period. Examples of constants include such data as each employee's name and social security number, marital status, number of income tax withholding allowances, rate of pay, payroll category (office, sales, etc.), and department where employed. The FICA tax rates and various tax tables are also constants that apply to all employees. In a computerized accounting system, constants are stored within a payroll file.

Variables are data that change from payroll to payroll and thus must be entered into the system each pay period. Examples of variables include such data as the number of hours or days worked for each employee during the payroll period, days of sick leave with pay, vacation credits, and cumulative earnings and taxes withheld. If salespersons are paid commissions, the amount of their sales would also vary from period to period.

EXHIBIT 8   Flow of Data in a Payroll System

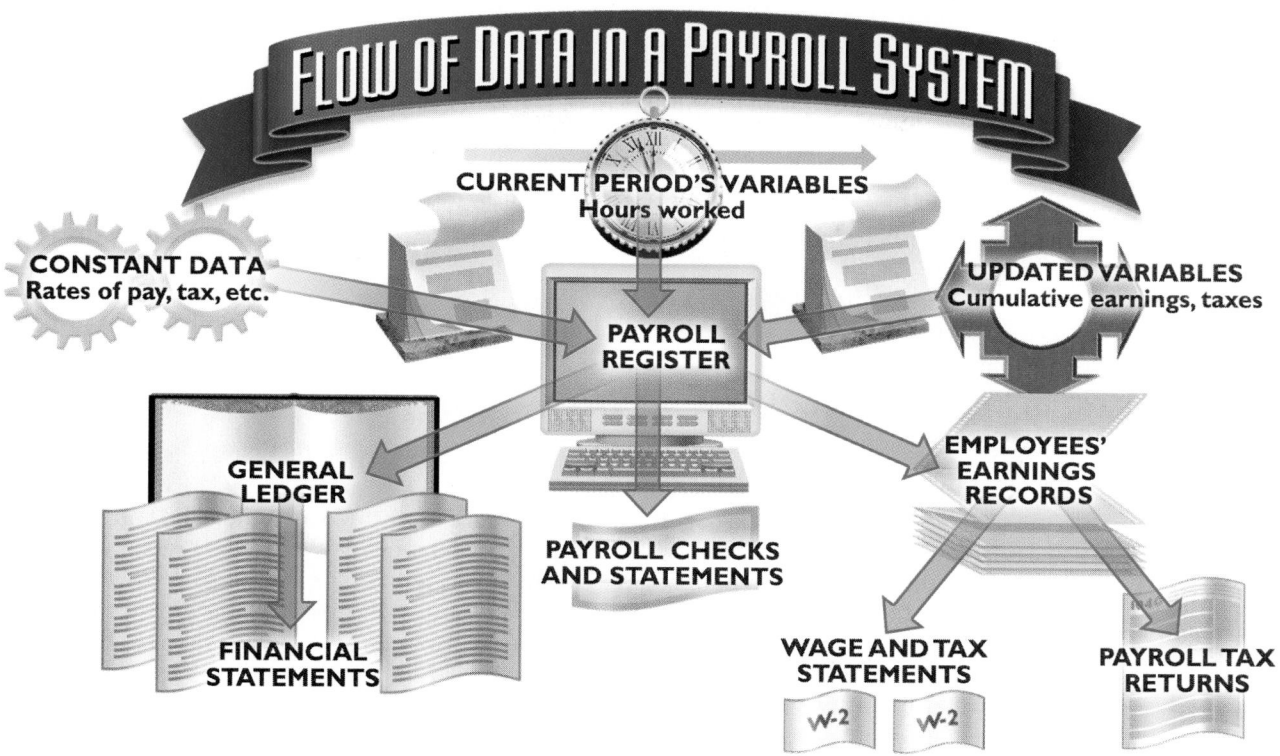

Internal Controls for Payroll Systems

Payroll processing, as we discussed above, requires the input of a large amount of data, along with numerous and sometimes complex computations. These factors, combined with the large dollar amounts involved, require controls to ensure that payroll payments are timely and accurate. In addition, the system must also provide adequate safeguards against theft or other misuse of funds.

The cash payment controls we discussed in the cash chapter also apply to payrolls. Thus, it is normally desirable to use a system that includes procedures for proper authorization and approval of payroll. When a check-signing machine is used, it is important that blank payroll checks and access to the machine be carefully controlled to prevent the theft or misuse of payroll funds.

It is especially important to authorize and approve in writing employee additions and deletions and changes in pay rates. For example, numerous payroll frauds have involved a supervisor adding fictitious employees to the payroll. The supervisor then cashes the fictitious employees' checks. Similar frauds have occurred where employees have been fired but the Payroll Department is not notified. As a result, payroll checks to the fired employees are prepared and cashed by a supervisor.

To prevent or detect frauds such as those we described above, employees' attendance records should be controlled. For example, you may have used an "In and Out" card on which your time of arrival to and departure from work was recorded when you inserted the card into a time clock. A Payroll Department employee may be stationed near

Point of INTEREST

In the movie *Superman III,* Gus Gorman embezzled payroll funds by programming the computer to round down each employee's payroll amount to the nearest penny. He then added the amount "rounded out" to his own payroll check. For example, if an employee's total pay was $458.533, the payroll program would pay the employee $458.53 and add the $.003 to a special account. The total in this special account would be transferred to Gus's paycheck at the end of the processing of the payroll. In this way, Gus's check increased from $143.80 to $85,000 in one pay period!

A Chicago politician, Ambrosio Medrano, was convicted of fraud involving fictitious employees (ghost employees). Medrano admitted placing two individuals, both supporters of his campaign, on the Cook County payroll. Neither of these people, also convicted of theft, was required to perform any services for their $48,000 in wages and benefits.

the time clock during normal arrival and departure times in order to verify that employees "clock in" only once and only for themselves. Employee identification cards or badges may also be used to verify that only authorized employees are clocking in and are permitted to enter work areas. When payroll checks are distributed, employee identification cards may be used to deter one employee from picking up another's check.

Other controls include verifying and approving all payroll rate changes. In addition, in a computerized system, all program changes should be properly approved and tested by employees who are independent of the payroll system. The use of a special payroll bank account, as we discussed earlier in the chapter, also enhances control over payroll.

Employees' Fringe Benefits

OBJECTIVE 6

Journalize entries for employee fringe benefits, including vacation pay and pensions.

Many companies provide their employees a variety of benefits in addition to salary and wages earned. Such **fringe benefits** may take many forms, including vacations, pension plans, and health, life, and disability insurance. When the employer pays part or all of the cost of the fringe benefits, these costs must be recognized as expenses. To properly match revenues and expenses, the estimated cost of these benefits should be recorded as an expense during the period in which the employee earns the benefit.

Exhibit 9 shows benefit dollars as a percent of total benefits for 864 companies surveyed by the U.S. Chamber of Commerce.

EXHIBIT 9
Benefit Dollars as a Percent of Total

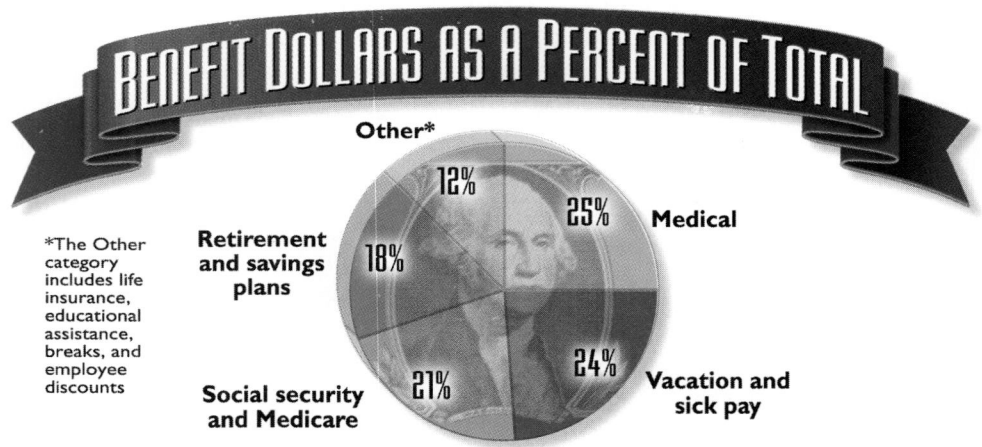

Source: U.S. Chamber of Commerce survey of employer benefits, 1996.

Vacation Pay

Most employers grant vacation rights, sometimes called **compensated absences**, to their employees. Such rights give rise to a recordable contingent liability. The liability for employees' vacation pay should be accrued as a liability as the vacation rights are earned. The entry to accrue vacation pay may be recorded in total at the end of each fiscal year, or it may be recorded at the end of each pay period. To illustrate this latter case, assume that employees earn one day of vacation for each month worked during the year. Assume also that the estimated vacation pay for the payroll period ending May 5 is $2,000. The entry to record the accrued vacation pay for this pay period is shown as follows.

Vacation pay becomes the employer's liability as the employee earns vacation rights.

May	5	Vacation Pay Expense	2 0 0 0 00	
		Vacation Pay Payable		2 0 0 0 00
		Vacation pay for week ended May 5.		

If employees are required to take all their vacation time within one year, the vacation pay payable is reported on the balance sheet as a current liability. If employees are allowed to accumulate their vacation time, the estimated vacation pay liability that is applicable to time that will *not* be taken within one year is a long-term liability.

When payroll is prepared for the period in which employees have taken vacations, the vacation pay payable is reduced. The entry debits *Vacation Pay Payable* and credits *Salaries Payable* and the other related accounts for taxes and withholdings.

Pensions

Studies indicate that 57% of all civilian employees work for companies that sponsor pension plans. However, of this amount, only about 75% of the workers actually participate in these plans.

A **pension** represents a cash payment to retired employees. Rights to pension payments are earned by employees during their working years, based on the pension plan established by the employer. One of the fundamental characteristics of such a plan is whether it is a defined contribution plan or a defined benefit plan.

Defined Contribution Plan

A **defined contribution plan** requires that a fixed amount of money be invested for the employee's behalf during the employee's working years. In a defined contribution plan, the employer is required to make annual pension contributions. There is no promise of future pension payments, however, so the employee bears the investment risk in a defined contribution plan. The employer's cost is debited to *Pension Expense*. To illustrate, assume that the pension plan of Flossmoor Industries requires a contribution equal to 10% of employee annual salaries. The entry to record the transaction, assuming $500,000 of annual salaries, is as follows:

Dec.	31	Pension Expense	50 0 0 0 00	
		Cash		50 0 0 0 00
		Contributed 10% of annual salaries to		
		pension plan.		

One of the more popular defined contribution pension plans is the *401K plan*. Under this plan, employees may contribute a limited part of their income to investments, such as mutual funds. A 401K plan offers employees two advantages: (1) the tax on the contribution is deferred (within limits), and (2) future investment earnings are tax deferred until withdrawn at retirement. In addition, for approximately 90% of the 401K plans, the employer matches some portion of the employee's contribution. For example, if the plan has a 50% matching feature, then each $1 contributed by the employee will be matched with a $0.50 contribution by the employer. Many financial planners advise employees to contribute to a 401K plan because of these benefits.

Once Flossmoor makes the annual contribution to the pension fund, its obligation is completed. The employee's final pension will depend on the investment results earned by the pension fund on the contributed balances.

Defined Benefit Plan

Employers may choose to promise employees a fixed annual pension benefit at retirement, based on years of service and compensation levels. An example would be a promise to pay an annual pension based on a formula, such as the following:

1.5% × years of service × average salary for most recent 3 years prior to retirement

Pension benefits based on a formula are termed a **defined benefit plan**. Unlike a defined contribution plan, the employer bears the investment risk in funding a future retirement income benefit. As a result, many companies are replacing their defined benefit plans with defined contribution plans.

The number of defined contribution plans has been increasing, while defined benefit plans have been declining. In 1996, 83% of all plans were structured as defined contribution plans. This was up from 67% three years earlier.

The accounting for defined benefit plans is usually very complex due to the uncertainties of projecting future pension obligations. These obligations depend upon such factors as employee life expectancies, employee turnover, expected employee compensation levels, and investment income on pension contributions.

The pension cost of a defined benefit plan is debited to *Pension Expense*. The amount funded is credited to *Cash*. Any unfunded amount is credited to *Unfunded Pension Liability*. For example, assume that the pension plan of Hinkle Co. requires an annual pension cost of $80,000, based on an estimate of the future benefit obligation. Further assume that Hinkle Co. pays $60,000 to the pension fund. The entry to record this transaction is as follows:

Dec.	31	Pension Expense	80 0 0 0 00	
		Cash		60 0 0 0 00
		Unfunded Pension Liability		20 0 0 0 00
		To record annual pension cost and		
		contribution to pension plan.		

Many companies have underfunded defined benefit pension plans. The following companies have a large unfunded pension liability:

Company	Unfunded Pension Liability (in millions)
General Motors	$2,677
Bethlehem Steel	1,907
LTV Corporation	1,245
Navistar	960
Sears, Roebuck & Co.	446

Source: Pension Benefit Guarantee Corporation, 1996 Watch List.

If the unfunded pension liability is to be paid within one year, it will be classified as a current liability. That portion of the liability to be paid beyond one year is a long-term liability.

Postretirement Benefits Other than Pensions

In addition to the pension benefits described above, employees may earn rights to other **postretirement benefits** from their employer. Such benefits may include dental care, eye care, medical care, life insurance, tuition assistance, tax services, and legal services for employees or their dependents. The amount of the annual benefits expense is based upon health statistics of the workforce. This amount is recorded by debiting *Postretirement Benefits Expense. Cash* is credited for the same amount if the benefits are fully funded. If the benefits are not fully funded, a postretirement benefits plan liability account is credited. Thus, the accounting for postretirement health benefits is very similar to that of defined benefit pension plans.

A business's financial statements should fully disclose the nature of its postretirement benefit obligations. These disclosures are usually included as footnotes to the financial statements. The complex nature of accounting for postretirement benefits is described in more advanced accounting courses.

FINANCIAL ANALYSIS AND INTERPRETATION

OBJECTIVE 7

Use the quick ratio to analyze the ability of a business to pay its current liabilities.

A business must be able to pay its current liabilities within a short period of time, usually one year. One measure of its ability to make these payments is the **quick ratio** or **acid-test ratio**. The quick ratio is computed as follows:

$$\text{Quick Ratio} = \frac{\text{Quick Assets}}{\text{Current Liabilities}}$$

The quick ratio measures the "instant" debt-paying ability of a company, using quick assets. Quick assets are cash, cash equivalents, and receivables that can quickly be converted into cash. It is often considered desirable to have a quick ratio exceeding 1. A ratio less than 1 would indicate that current liabilities cannot be covered by cash and "near cash" assets.

To illustrate, assume that Noble Co. and Hart Co. have the following quick assets, current liabilities, and quick ratios:

	Noble Co.	Hart Co.
Quick assets:		
Cash	$100,000	$ 55,000
Cash equivalents	47,000	65,000
Accounts receivable (net)	84,000	472,000
Total	$231,000	$592,000
Current liabilities:		
Accounts payable	$125,000	$427,000
Wages payable	65,000	120,000
Employees federal income tax payable	18,000	36,000
Social security tax payable	3,025	7,200
Medicare tax payable	975	1,800
Notes payable	8,000	148,000
Total	$220,000	$740,000
Quick ratio	1.05	0.8

As you can see, Noble Co. has quick assets in excess of current liabilities, or a quick ratio of 1.05. The ratio exceeds 1, indicating that the quick assets should be sufficient to meet current liabilities. Hart Co., however, has a quick ratio of 0.8. Its quick assets will not be sufficient to cover the current liabilities. Hart could solve this problem by working with a bank to convert its short-term debt of $148,000 into a long-term obligation. This would remove the notes payable from current liabilities. If Hart did this, then its quick ratio would improve to 1 ($592,000 ÷ $592,000), which would be just sufficient for quick assets to cover current liabilities.

ENCORE

How to Become a Millionaire

A recent survey found that 66% of individuals believe that their standard of living at retirement will be the same or higher than during their current working years. Yet, a third of these respondents don't have a formal savings plan for retirement. One-fourth of these respondents believe that they will need to save only $100,000 in order to maintain their lifestyle in retirement. However, experts believe that today's 25-year-old will need savings of $750,000 to $1 million to support a basic retirement, given increased life expectancies and inflation. How do you save this much money? The two keys to savings success are (1) save regularly, such as monthly or quarterly, even if it's a small amount, and (2) start early. For example, to have the same retirement income as a 25-year-old saving $100 per month, a 30-year-old would need to save $200 per month. Waiting until you are 35 years old would require saving $400 per month. Every five years of delay requires doubling the necessary contribution. This is the power of compound interest. Therefore, the worst strategy is to begin retirement saving at middle age. Unfortunately, according to one survey, 41% of workers age 25 to 34 who are eligible for defined contribution pension plans, such as a 401K, do not take advantage of them.

So how much would a 25-year-old need to save monthly to reach the $1 million mark? There are many assumptions that go into such a calculation. Let's assume that an individual begins saving $150 per month at the age of 25, earns 8% on these savings, increases the amount contributed by 5% per year (to match salary increases), and retires at the age of 65. Under these assumptions, the individual would accumulate $975,000 by age 65. What would be the retirement savings if the assumptions were changed so that the savings plan began at age 35, 45, or 55? The graph at the right shows what happens to the savings amount. As you can see, time is money. Beginning just 10 years later at age 35 reduces the accumulated savings by over 60%, to approximately $374,000.

Retirement planning work sheets are available from a number of mutual fund companies on the Internet. One easy-to-use work sheet is provided at the Web site of **T. Rowe Price, www.troweprice.com.** ■

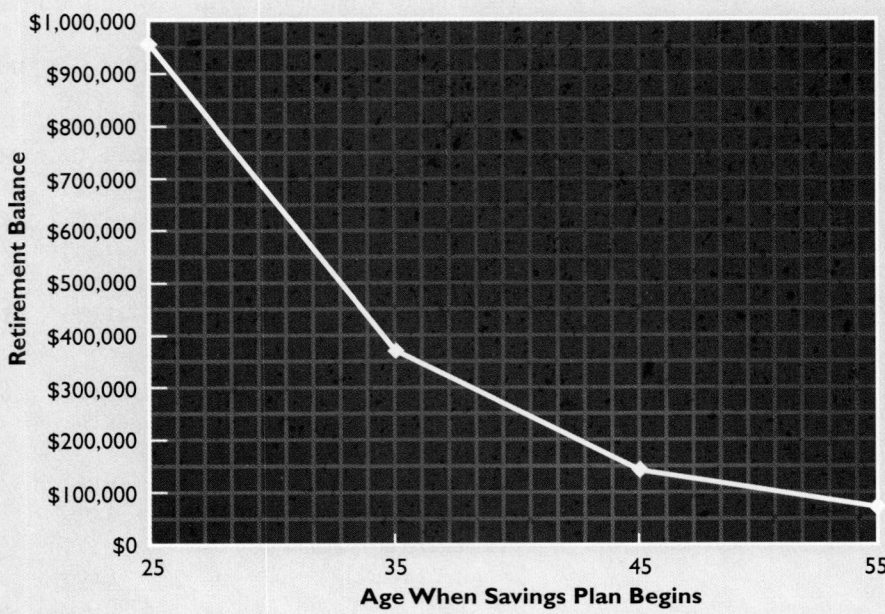

Retirement Balance Under Different Savings Scenarios

Age When Savings Plan Begins

HEY POINTS

1 Define and give examples of current liabilities.

Current liabilities are obligations that are to be paid out of current assets and are due within a short time, usually within one year. Current liabilities arise from either (1) receiving goods or services prior to making payment or (2) receiving payment prior to delivering goods or services.

2 Journalize entries for short-term notes payable.

A note issued to a creditor to temporarily satisfy an account payable is recorded as a debit to *Accounts Payable* and a credit to *Notes Payable*. At the time the note is paid, *Notes Payable* and *Interest Expense* are debited and *Cash* is credited. Notes may also be issued to purchase merchandise or other assets or to borrow money from a bank. When a discounted note is issued, *Interest Expense* is debited for the interest deduction at the time of is-

suance, an asset account is debited for the proceeds, and *Notes Payable* is credited for the face value of the note. The face value and the maturity value of a discounted note are equal.

3 Describe the accounting treatment for contingent liabilities and journalize entries for product warranties.

A contingent liability is a potential obligation that results from a past transaction but depends on a future event. If the contingent liability is both probable and estimable, the liability should be recorded. If the contingent liability is reasonably possible or is not estimable, it should be disclosed in the footnotes to the financial statements. An example of a recordable contingent liability is product warranties. If a company grants a warranty on a product, an estimated warranty expense and liability should be recorded

in the period of the sale. The expense and the liability are recorded by debiting *Product Warranty Expense* and crediting *Product Warranty Payable*.

4 Determine employer liabilities for payroll, including liabilities arising from employee earnings and deductions from earnings.

An employer's liability for payroll is calculated by determining employees' total earnings for a payroll period, including overtime pay. From this amount employee deductions are subtracted to arrive at the net pay to be paid each employee. The employer's liabilities for employee deductions are recognized at the time the payroll is recorded. Most employers also incur liabilities for payroll taxes, such as social security tax, Medicare tax, federal unemployment compensation tax, and state unemployment compensation tax.

5 **Describe payroll accounting systems that use a payroll register, employee earnings records, and a general journal.**

The payroll register is used in assembling and summarizing the data needed for each payroll period. The data recorded in the payroll register include the number of hours worked and the earnings and deduction data for each employee. The payroll register also includes columns for accumulating total wages or salaries to be debited to the various expense accounts. It is supported by a detailed payroll record for each employee, called an employee's earnings record.

6 **Journalize entries for employee fringe benefits, including vacation pay and pensions.**

Fringe benefits are expenses of the period in which the employees earn the benefits. Fringe benefits are recorded by debiting an expense account and crediting a liability account. For example, the entry to record accrued vacation pay debits *Vacation Pay Expense* and credits *Vacation Pay Payable*.

7 **Use the quick ratio to analyze the ability of a business to pay its current liabilities.**

The quick ratio or acid-test ratio is a measure of a business's ability to pay current liabilities within a short period of time. The quick ratio is quick assets divided by current liabilities. A quick ratio exceeding 1 is usually desirable.

ILLUSTRATIVE PROBLEM

Selected transactions of Taylor Company, completed during the fiscal year ended December 31, are as follows:

Mar. 1. Purchased merchandise on account from Kelvin Co., $20,000.
Apr. 10. Issued a 60-day, 12% note for $20,000 to Kelvin Co. on account.
June 9. Paid Kelvin Co. the amount owed on the note of April 10.
Aug. 1. Issued a $50,000, 90-day note to Harold Co. in exchange for a building. Harold Co. discounted the note at 15%.
Oct. 30. Paid Harold Co. the amount due on the note of August 1.
Dec. 27. Journalized the entry to record the biweekly payroll. A summary of the payroll record follows:

Salary distribution:		
Sales	$63,400	
Officers	36,600	
Office	10,000	$110,000
Deductions:		
Social security tax	$ 5,050	
Medicare tax	1,650	
Federal income tax withheld	17,600	
State income tax withheld	4,950	
Savings bond deductions	850	
Medical insurance deductions	1,120	31,220
Net amount		$ 78,780

30. Issued a check in payment of liabilities for employees' federal income tax of $17,600, social security tax of $10,100, and Medicare tax of $3,300.
31. Issued a check for $9,500 to the pension fund trustee to fully fund the pension cost for December.
31. Journalized an entry to record the employees' accrued vacation pay, $36,100.
31. Journalized an entry to record the estimated accrued product warranty liability, $37,240.

Instructions

Journalize the preceding transactions.

Solution

				Debit	Credit
Mar.	1	Merchandise Inventory		20 0 0 0 00	
		Accounts Payable—Kelvin Co.			20 0 0 0 00
Apr.	10	Accounts Payable—Kelvin Co.		20 0 0 0 00	
		Notes Payable			20 0 0 0 00
June	9	Notes Payable		20 0 0 0 00	
		Interest Expense		4 0 0 00	
		Cash			20 4 0 0 00
Aug.	1	Building		48 1 2 5 00	
		Interest Expense		1 8 7 5 00	
		Notes Payable			50 0 0 0 00
Oct.	30	Notes Payable		50 0 0 0 00	
		Cash			50 0 0 0 00
Dec.	27	Sales Salaries Expense		63 4 0 0 00	
		Officers Salaries Expense		36 6 0 0 00	
		Office Salaries Expense		10 0 0 0 00	
		Social Security Tax Payable			5 0 5 0 00
		Medicare Tax Payable			1 6 5 0 00
		Employees Federal Income Tax Payable			17 6 0 0 00
		Employees State Income Tax Payable			4 9 5 0 00
		Bond Deductions Payable			8 5 0 00
		Medical Insurance Payable			1 1 2 0 00
		Salaries Payable			78 7 8 0 00
	30	Employees Federal Income Tax Payable		17 6 0 0 00	
		Social Security Income Payable		10 1 0 0 00	
		Medicare Tax Payable		3 3 0 0 00	
		Cash			31 0 0 0 00
	31	Pension Expense		9 5 0 0 00	
		Cash			9 5 0 0 00
	31	Vacation Pay Expense		36 1 0 0 00	
		Vacation Pay Payable			36 1 0 0 00
	31	Product Warranty Expense		37 2 4 0 00	
		Product Warranty Payable			37 2 4 0 00

SELF-EXAMINATION QUESTIONS   Answers at End of Chapter

Matching

Match each of the following statements with its proper term. Some terms may not be used.

A.	**defined benefit plan**
B.	**defined contribution plan**

____ 1. A detailed record of each employee's earnings.

____ 2. A multicolumn form used to assemble and summarize payroll data at the end of each payroll period.

C. discount

D. discount rate

E. employee's earnings record

F. FICA tax

G. fringe benefit

H. gross pay

I. net pay

J. payroll

K. payroll register

L. postretirement benefits

M. proceeds

N. quick ratio

___ 3. A pension plan that promises employees a fixed annual pension benefit at retirement, based on years of service and compensation levels.

___ 4. Gross pay less payroll deductions; the amount the employer is obligated to pay the employee.

___ 5. The net amount available from discounting a note payable.

___ 6. A pension plan that requires a fixed amount of money to be invested for the employee's behalf during the employee's working years.

___ 7. Benefits provided to employees in addition to wages and salaries.

___ 8. The rate used in computing the interest to be deducted from the maturity value of a note.

___ 9. The total earnings of an employee for a payroll period.

___ 10. Rights to benefits that employees earn during their term of employment, for themselves and their dependents, after they retire.

___ 11. The total amount paid to employees for a certain period.

___ 12. Federal Insurance Contributions Act tax used to finance federal programs for old-age and disability benefits (social security) and health insurance for the aged (Medicare).

___ 13. A financial ratio that measures the ability to pay current liabilities within a short period of time.

___ 14. The interest deducted from the maturity value of a note.

Multiple Choice

1. A business issued a $5,000, 60-day, 12% note to the bank. The amount due at maturity is:
   A. $4,900   C. $5,100
   B. $5,000   D. $5,600

2. A business issued a $5,000, 60-day note to a supplier, which discounted the note at 12%. The proceeds are:
   A. $4,400   C. $5,000
   B. $4,900   D. $5,100

3. An employee's rate of pay is $20 per hour, with time and a half for all hours worked in excess of 40 during a week. The social security rate is 6.0% on the first $70,000 of annual earnings, and the Medicare rate is 1.5% on all earnings. The following additional data are available:

Hours worked during current week	45
Year's cumulative earnings prior to current week	$69,400
Federal income tax withheld	$212

Based on these data, the amount of the employee's net pay for the current week is:
   A. $620.50   C. $666.75
   B. $641.50   D. $687.75

4. Which of the following taxes are employers usually not required to withhold from employees?
   A. Federal income tax
   B. Federal unemployment compensation tax
   C. Medicare tax
   D. State and local income tax

5. Within limitations on the maximum earnings subject to the tax, employers do not incur operating costs for which of the following payroll taxes?
   A. Social security tax
   B. Federal unemployment compensation tax
   C. State unemployment compensation tax
   D. Employees' federal income tax

CLASS DISCUSSION QUESTIONS

1. What two types of transactions cause most current liabilities?
2. When are short-term notes payable issued?
3. When should the liability associated with a product warranty be recorded? Discuss.
4. **Compaq Computer Corporation** reported $469 million of product warranties in the current liabilities section of its December 31, 1996 balance sheet. How would costs of repairing a defective product be recorded?

5. The "Questions and Answers Technical Hotline" in the *Journal of Accountancy* included the following question:

   Several years ago, Company B instituted legal action against Company A. Under a memorandum of settlement and agreement, Company A agreed to pay Company B a total of $17,500 in three installments—$5,000 on March 1, $7,500 on July 1, and the remaining $5,000 on December 31. Company A paid the first two installments during its fiscal year ended September 30. Should the unpaid amount of $5,000 be presented as a current liability at September 30?

   How would you answer this question?
6. What programs are funded by the FICA (Federal Insurance Contributions Act) tax?
7. a. Identify the federal taxes that most employers are required to withhold from employees.
    b. Give the titles of the accounts to which the amounts withheld are credited.
8. For each of the following payroll-related taxes, indicate whether there is a ceiling on the annual earnings subject to the tax: (a) social security tax, (b) Medicare tax, (c) federal income tax, (d) federal unemployment compensation tax.
9. Why are deductions from employees' earnings classified as liabilities for the employer?
10. Do payroll taxes levied against employers become liabilities at the time the liabilities for wages are incurred or at the time the wages are paid?
11. Taylor Company, with 20 employees, is expanding operations. It is trying to decide whether to hire one employee full-time for $25,000 or two employees part-time for a total of $25,000. Would any of the employer's payroll taxes discussed in this chapter have a bearing on this decision? Explain.
12. For each of the following payroll-related taxes, indicate whether they generally apply to (a) employees only, (b) employers only, (c) both employees and employers:
    1. Social security tax
    2. Medicare tax
    3. Federal income tax
    4. Federal unemployment compensation tax
    5. State unemployment compensation tax
13. What are the principal reasons for using a special payroll checking account?
14. In a payroll system, what type of input data are referred to as (a) constants, (b) variables?
15. To strengthen internal controls, what department should provide written authorizations for the addition of names to the payroll?
16. Explain how a payroll system that is properly designed and operated tends to ensure that (a) wages paid are based on hours actually worked and (b) payroll checks are not issued to fictitious employees.
17. To match revenues and expenses properly, should the expense for employee vacation pay be recorded in the period during which the vacation privilege is earned or during the period in which the vacation is taken? Discuss.
18. Identify several factors that influence the future pension obligation of an employer under a defined benefit pension plan.
19. Where should the unfunded pension liability from a defined benefit pension plan be reported on the balance sheet?
20. What are some examples of postretirement benefits other than pensions that employees may earn for themselves and their dependents?

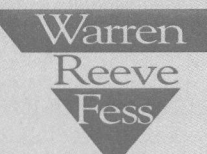

Resources for Your Success On-Line at warren.swcollege.com
Remember! If you need additional help, visit South-Western's Web site. See page 26 for a description of the online and printed materials that are available.

EXERCISES

Exercise 11–1
Current liabilities

Objective 1

✓ Total current liabilities, $130,150

Tech World Magazine Inc. sold 3,200 annual subscriptions of *Tech World* for $36 during December 2000. These new subscribers will receive monthly issues, beginning in January 2001. In addition, the business had taxable income of $125,000 during the first calendar quarter of 2001. The federal tax rate is 35%. A quarterly tax payment will be made on April 7, 2001.

Prepare the current liabilities section of the balance sheet for Tech World Magazine Inc. on March 31, 2001.

Exercise 11–2
Entries for discounting notes payable

Objective 2

Star Bright Lighting Co. issues a 60-day note for $300,000 to Builtwell Wholesale Supply Co. for merchandise inventory. Builtwell discounts the note at 9%.

a. Journalize the borrower's entries to record:
  1. the issuance of the note.
  2. the payment of the note at maturity.
b. Journalize the creditor's entries to record:
  1. the receipt of the note.
  2. the receipt of the payment of the note at maturity.

Exercise 11–3
Evaluate alternative notes

Objective 2

✓ a. $2,000

A borrower has two alternatives for a loan: (1) issue an $80,000, 90-day, 10% note or (2) issue an $80,000, 90-day note that the creditor discounts at 10%.

a. Calculate the amount of the interest expense for each option.
b. Determine the proceeds received by the borrower in each situation.
c. ▬▬► Which alternative is more favorable to the borrower? Explain.

Exercise 11–4
Entries for notes payable

Objective 2

A business issued a 60-day, 12% note for $25,000 to a creditor on account. Journalize the entries to record (a) the issuance of the note and (b) the payment of the note at maturity, including interest.

Exercise 11–5
Fixed asset purchases with note

Objective 2

On June 30, Mario Game Company purchased land for $250,000 and a building for $730,000, paying $280,000 cash and issuing an 8% note for the balance, secured by a mortgage on the property. The terms of the note provide for 20 semiannual payments of $35,000 on the principal plus the interest accrued from the date of the preceding payment. Journalize the entry to record (a) the transaction on June 30, (b) the payment of the first installment on December 31, and (c) the payment of the second installment the following June 30.

Exercise 11–6
Accrued product warranty

Objective 3

Precision Audio Company warrants its products for one year. The estimated product warranty is 3% of sales. Assume that sales were $400,000 for January. In February, a customer received warranty repairs requiring $200 of parts and $600 of labor.

a. Journalize the adjusting entry required at January 31, the end of the first month of the current year, to record the accrued product warranty.
b. Journalize the entry to record the warranty work provided in February.

Exercise 11–7
Contingent liabilities

Objective 3

Several months ago, Endurance Battery Company experienced a hazardous materials spill at one of its plants. As a result, the Environmental Protection Agency (EPA) fined the company $150,000. The company is contesting the fine. In addition, an employee is seeking $600,000 damages related to the spill. Lastly, a homeowner has sued the company for $100,000. The homeowner lives 20 miles from the plant, but believes that the incident has reduced the home's resale value by $100,000.

Endurance Battery's legal counsel believes that it is probable that the EPA fine will stand. In addition, counsel indicates that an out-of-court settlement of $300,000 has recently been reached with the employee. The final papers will be signed next week. Counsel believes that the homeowner's case is much weaker and will be decided in favor of Endurance. Other litigation related to the spill is possible, but the damage amounts are uncertain.

a. Journalize the contingent liabilities associated with the hazardous materials spill.
b. ▬▬► Prepare a footnote disclosure relating to this incident.

Exercise 11–8
Calculate payroll

Objective 4

✓ b. Net pay, $786.50

An employee earns $20 per hour and 1½ times that rate for all hours in excess of 40 hours per week. Assume that the employee worked 50 hours during the week, and that the gross pay prior to the current week totaled $59,760. Assume further that the social security tax rate was 6.0% (on earnings up to $70,000), the Medicare tax rate was 1.5%, and federal income tax to be withheld was $231.

a. Determine the gross pay for the week.
b. Determine the net pay for the week.

Exercise 11–9
Calculate payroll

Objective 4

✓ Administrator net pay, $853.20

Prism Business Consultants has three employees—a consultant, a computer programmer, and an administrator. The following payroll information is available for each employee:

	Consultant	Computer Programmer	Administrator
Regular earnings rate	$3,000 per week	$28 per hour	$22 per hour
Overtime earnings rate	Not applicable	1½ times hourly rate	1½ times hourly rate
Gross pay prior to current pay period	$108,700	$69,100	$39,100
Number of withholding allowances	1	0	3

For the current pay period, the computer programmer worked 43 hours and the administrator worked 48 hours. For the current pay period, the federal income tax withheld for the consultant was $840. The federal income tax withheld for the computer programmer and the administrator can be determined from the wage bracket withholding table in Exhibit 3 in the chapter. Assume further that the social security tax rate was 6.0% on the first $70,000 of annual earnings, and the Medicare tax rate was 1.5%.

Determine the gross pay and the net pay for each of the three employees for the current pay period.

Exercise 11–10
Summary payroll data

Objectives 4, 5

✓ a. (3) Total earnings, $200,000

In the following summary of data for a payroll period, some amounts have been intentionally omitted:

Earnings:
1. At regular rate   ?
2. At overtime rate $ 28,500
3. Total earnings   ?

Deductions:
4. Social security tax   11,500
5. Medicare tax   3,000
6. Income tax withheld   28,200
7. Medical insurance   1,050
8. Union dues   ?
9. Total deductions   45,000
10. Net amount paid   155,000

Accounts debited:
11. Factory Wages   124,300
12. Sales Salaries   ?
13. Office Salaries   34,300

a. Calculate the amounts omitted in lines (1), (3), (8), and (12).
b. Journalize the entry to record the payroll accrual.
c. Journalize the entry to record the payment of the payroll.
d.   ► From the data given in this exercise and your answer to (a), would you conclude that this payroll was paid sometime during the first few weeks of the calendar year? Explain.

Exercise 11–11
Payroll internal control procedures

Objective 5

Memphis Sounds is a retail store specializing in the sale of jazz compact discs and cassettes. The store employs 3 full-time and 10 part-time workers. The store's weekly payroll averages $1,800 for all 13 workers.

Memphis Sounds uses a personal computer to assist in preparing paychecks. Each week, the store's accountant collects employee time cards and enters the hours worked into the payroll program. The payroll program calculates each employee's pay and prints a paycheck. The accountant uses a check-signing machine to sign the paychecks. Next, the store's owner authorizes the transfer of funds from the store's regular bank account to the payroll account.

For the week of May 10, the accountant accidentally recorded 400 hours worked instead of 40 hours for one of the full-time employees.

✏️ ▶ Does Memphis Sounds have internal controls in place to catch this error? If so, how will this error be detected?

Exercise 11–12
Internal control procedures

Objective 5

Sure-Grip Tools is a small manufacturer of home workshop power tools. The company employs 30 production workers and 10 administrative persons. The following procedures are used to process the company's weekly payroll:

a. Whenever a salaried employee is terminated, Personnel authorizes Payroll to remove the employee from the payroll system. However, this procedure is not required when an hourly worker is terminated. Hourly employees only receive a paycheck if their time cards show hours worked. The computer automatically drops an employee from the payroll system when that employee has six consecutive weeks with no hours worked.

b. Whenever an employee receives a pay raise, the supervisor must fill out a wage adjustment form, which is signed by the company president. This form is used to change the employee's wage rate in the payroll system.

c. All employees are required to record their hours worked by clocking in and out on a time clock. Employees must clock out for lunch break. Due to congestion around the time clock area at lunch time, management has not objected to having one employee clock in and out for an entire department.

d. Paychecks are signed by using a check-signing machine. This machine is located in the main office, so that it can be easily accessed by anyone needing a check signed.

e. Sure-Grip maintains a separate checking account for payroll checks. Each week, the total net pay for all employees is transferred from the company's regular bank account to the payroll account.

✏️ ▶ State whether each of the procedures is appropriate or inappropriate after considering the principles of internal control. If a procedure is inappropriate, describe the appropriate procedure.

Exercise 11–13
Payroll tax entries

Objective 5

✓ a. $36,015

According to a summary of the payroll of Tender Heart Publishing Co., $460,000 was subject to the 6.0% social security tax and $510,000 was subject to the 1.5% Medicare tax. Also, $15,000 was subject to state and federal unemployment taxes.

a. Calculate the employer's payroll taxes, using the following rates: state unemployment, 4.3%; federal unemployment, 0.8%.

b. Journalize the entry to record the accrual of payroll taxes.

Exercise 11–14
Payroll procedures

Objective 5

What's Wrong WITH THIS?

The fiscal year for Homestead Stores Inc. ends on June 30. In addition, the company computes and reports payroll taxes on a fiscal-year basis. Thus, social security and FUTA maximum earnings limitations apply to the fiscal-year payroll.

✏️ ▶ What is wrong with these procedures for accounting for payroll taxes?

Exercise 11–15
Accrued vacation pay

Objective 6

A business provides its employees with varying amounts of vacation per year, depending on the length of employment. The estimated amount of the current year's vacation pay is $187,200. Journalize the adjusting entry required on January 31, the end of the first month of the current year, to record the accrued vacation pay.

Exercise 11–16
Pension plan entries

Objective 6

Forever Memories Inc. operates a chain of photography stores. The company maintains a defined contribution pension plan for its employees. The plan requires quarterly installments to be paid to the funding agent, Interstate Insurance Company, by the fifteenth of the month following the end of each quarter. Assuming that the pension cost is $175,000 for the quarter ended December 31, journalize entries to record (a) the accrued pension liability on December 31 and (b) the payment to the funding agent on January 15.

Exercise 11–17
Quick ratio

Objective 7

HAT

The financial statements for **Hershey Foods Corporation** are presented in Appendix G at the end of the text.

a. Compute the quick ratio as of December 31, 1995 and 1996.
b. ✎➤ What conclusions can be drawn from these data as to Hershey's ability to meet its current liabilities?

PROBLEMS SERIES A

Problem 11–1A
Liability transactions

Objectives 2, 3

HAT
GENERAL LEDGER

The following items were selected from among the transactions completed by Renaissance Products Co. during the current year:

Feb. 15. Purchased merchandise on account from Ranier Co., $14,000, terms n/30.
Mar. 17. Issued a 30-day, 9% note for $14,000 to Ranier Co., on account.
Apr. 16. Paid Ranier Co. the amount owed on the note of March 17.
July 15. Borrowed $20,000 from Security Bank, issuing a 90-day, 12% note.
        25. Purchased tools by issuing a $60,000, 120-day note to Sun Supply Co., which discounted the note at the rate of 13%.
Oct. 13. Paid Security Bank the interest due on the note of July 15 and renewed the loan by issuing a new 30-day, 15% note for $20,000. (Journalize both the debit and credit to the notes payable account.)
Nov. 12. Paid Security Bank the amount due on the note of October 13.
        22. Paid Sun Supply Co. the amount due on the note of July 25.
Dec. 1. Purchased office equipment from Valley Equipment Co. for $75,000, paying $15,000 and issuing a series of ten 12% notes for $6,000 each, coming due at 30-day intervals.
        17. Settled a product liability lawsuit with a customer for $35,000, payable in January. Renaissance accrued the loss in a litigation claims payable account.
        31. Paid the amount due Valley Equipment Co. on the first note in the series issued on December 1.

Instructions

1. Journalize the transactions.
2. Journalize the adjusting entry for each of the following accrued expenses at the end of the current year: (a) product warranty cost, $15,450; (b) interest on the nine remaining notes owed to Valley Equipment Co.

Problem 11–2A
Entries for payroll and payroll taxes

Objectives 4, 5

✓ 1. (b) Dr. Payroll Taxes Expense, $22,950

The following information about the payroll for the week ended December 30 was obtained from the records of Wallace Co.:

Salaries:		Deductions:	
Sales salaries	$185,000	Income tax withheld	$66,000
Warehouse salaries	36,800	Social security tax withheld	17,400
Office salaries	108,200	Medicare tax withheld	4,950
	$330,000	U.S. savings bonds	19,300
		Group insurance	28,700

Tax rates assumed:
  Social security, 6% on first $70,000 of employee annual earnings
  Medicare, 1.5%
  State unemployment (employer only), 4.2%
  Federal unemployment (employer only), 0.8%

Instructions

1. Assuming that the payroll for the last week of the year is to be paid on December 31, journalize the following entries:
   a. December 30, to record the payroll.
   b. December 30, to record the employer's payroll taxes on the payroll to be paid on December 31. Of the total payroll for the last week of the year, $12,000 is subject to unemployment compensation taxes.
2. Assuming that the payroll for the last week of the year is to be paid on January 5 of the following fiscal year, journalize the following entries:
   a. December 30, to record the payroll.
   b. January 5, to record the employer's payroll taxes on the payroll to be paid on January 5.

Problem 11–3A
Wage and tax statement data on employer FICA tax

Objectives 4, 5

SPREADSHEET

✓ 2. (e) $23,160

Sunrise Bread Company began business on January 2 of last year. Salaries were paid to employees on the last day of each month, and social security tax, Medicare tax, and federal income tax were withheld in the required amounts. An employee who is hired in the middle of the month receives half the monthly salary for that month. All required payroll tax reports were filed, and the correct amount of payroll taxes was remitted by the company for the calendar year. Before the Wage and Tax Statements (Form W-2) could be prepared for distribution to employees and for filing with the Social Security Administration, the employees' earnings records were inadvertently destroyed.

None of the employees resigned or were discharged during the year, and there were no changes in salary rates. The social security tax was withheld at the rate of 6.0% on the first $70,000 of salary and Medicare tax at the rate of 1.5% on salary. Data on dates of employment, salary rates, and employees' income taxes withheld, which are summarized as follows, were obtained from personnel records and payroll records.

Employee	Date First Employed	Monthly Salary	Monthly Income Tax Withheld
Alvarez	Jan. 16	$6,400	$1,376.00
Conrad	Nov. 1	3,000	544.20
Felix	Jan. 2	2,500	447.25
Lydall	July 16	4,200	783.30
Porter	Jan. 2	6,700	1,497.45
Soong	May 1	2,800	463.40
Walker	Feb. 16	5,000	1,027.00

Instructions

1. Calculate the amounts to be reported on each employee's Wage and Tax Statement (Form W-2) for the year, arranging the data in the following form:

Employee	Gross Earnings	Federal Income Tax Withheld	Social Security Tax Withheld	Medicare Tax Withheld

2. Calculate the following employer payroll taxes for the year: (a) social security; (b) Medicare; (c) state unemployment compensation at 4.2% on the first $7,000 of each employee's earnings; (d) federal unemployment compensation at 0.8% on the first $7,000 of each employee's earnings; (e) total.

If the working papers correlating with this textbook are not used, omit Problem 11–4A.

Problem 11–4A
Payroll register

Objectives 4, 5

✓ 3. Dr. Payroll Taxes Expense, $643.75

The payroll register for Argentina Leather Goods Co. for the week ended December 12, 2000, is presented in the working papers.

Instructions

1. Journalize the entry to record the payroll for the week.
2. Journalize the entry to record the issuance of the checks to employees.

3. Journalize the entry to record the employer's payroll taxes for the week. Assume the following tax rates: state unemployment, 3.6%; federal unemployment, 0.8%. Of the earnings, $1,250 is subject to unemployment taxes.
4. Journalize the entry to record a check issued on Dec. 15 to Second National Bank in payment of employees' income taxes, $1,422.18, social security taxes, $942.00, and Medicare taxes, $235.50.

Problem 11–5A
Payroll register

Objectives 4, 5

SPREADSHEET

✓ 1. Total net amount paid, $6,745.68

The following data for Grimsley Electrical Supplies Inc. relate to the payroll for the week ended December 7, 2000:

Employee	Hours Worked	Hourly Rate	Weekly Salary	Federal Income Tax	U.S. Savings Bonds	Accumulated Earnings, Nov. 30
M	48.00	$28.00		$321.00	$35.00	$61,100.00
N	20.00	21.00		65.00		12,600.00
O			$1,500.00	337.00	50.00	70,500.00
P	40.00	18.00		140.00	15.00	33,840.00
Q	42.00	20.00		112.00	10.00	37,600.00
R	45.00	19.50		168.00		42,300.00
S	40.00	16.00		110.00	15.00	30,080.00
T			1,000.00	217.00		47,000.00
U	50.00	32.00		401.00	40.00	73,100.00

Employees O and T are office staff, and all of the other employees are sales personnel. All sales personnel are paid 1½ times the regular rate for all hours in excess of 40 hours per week. The social security tax rate is 6.0% on the first $70,000 of each employee's annual earnings, and Medicare tax is 1.5% of each employee's annual earnings. The next payroll check to be used is No. 818.

Instructions

1. Prepare a payroll register for Grimsley Electrical Supplies Inc. for the week ended December 7, 2000.
2. Journalize the entry to record the payroll for the week.

Problem 11–6A
Payroll accounts and year-end entries

Objectives 4, 5, 6

HAT
GENERAL LEDGER

The following accounts, with the balances indicated, appear in the ledger of Mid States CableView Co. on December 1 of the current year:

211	Salaries Payable	—
212	Social Security Tax Payable	$ 7,784
213	Medicare Tax Payable	2,048
214	Employees Federal Income Tax Payable	12,632
215	Employees State Income Tax Payable	12,291
216	State Unemployment Tax Payable	1,240
217	Federal Unemployment Tax Payable	325
218	Bond Deductions Payable	1,400
219	Medical Insurance Payable	4,500
611	Operations Salaries Expense	915,200
711	Officers Salaries Expense	365,300
712	Office Salaries Expense	221,700
719	Payroll Taxes Expense	119,566

The following transactions relating to payroll, payroll deductions, and payroll taxes occurred during December:

Dec. 2. Issued Check No. 728 for $1,400 to First National Bank to purchase U.S. savings bonds for employees.
    3. Issued Check No. 729 to First National Bank for $22,464, in payment of $7,784 of social security tax, $2,048 of Medicare tax, and $12,632 of employees' federal income tax due.

Dec. 14. Journalized the entry to record the biweekly payroll. A summary of the payroll record follows:

Salary distribution:		
Operations	$42,400	
Officers	16,220	
Office	10,450	$69,070
Deductions:		
Social security tax	$ 3,799	
Medicare tax	1,036	
Federal income tax withheld	12,294	
State income tax withheld	3,108	
Savings bond deductions	700	
Medical insurance deductions	750	21,687
Net amount		$47,383

14. Issued Check No. 738 in payment of the net amount of the biweekly payroll.
14. Journalized the entry to record payroll taxes on employees' earnings of December 14: social security tax, $3,799; Medicare tax, $1,036; state unemployment tax, $286; federal unemployment tax, $77.
17. Issued Check No. 744 to First National Bank for $21,964, in payment of $7,598 of social security tax, $2,072 of Medicare tax, and $12,294 of employees' federal income tax due.
18. Issued Check No. 750 to Pico Insurance Company for $4,500, in payment of the semiannual premium on the group medical insurance policy.
28. Journalized the entry to record the biweekly payroll. A summary of the payroll record follows:

Salary distribution:		
Operations	$40,800	
Officers	16,350	
Office	10,580	$67,730
Deductions:		
Social security tax	$ 3,657	
Medicare tax	1,016	
Federal income tax withheld	12,056	
State income tax withheld	3,048	
Savings bond deduction	700	20,477
Net amount		$47,253

28. Issued Check No. 782 in payment of the net amount of the biweekly payroll.
28. Journalized the entry to record payroll taxes on employees' earnings of December 28: social security tax, $3,657; Medicare tax, $1,016; state unemployment tax, $174; federal unemployment tax, $38.
30. Issued Check No. 791 to First National Bank for $1,400 to purchase U.S. savings bonds for employees.
30. Issued Check No. 792 for $18,447 to First National Bank in payment of employees' state income tax due on December 31.
31. Paid $46,000 of the annual pension cost of $50,000. (Record both the payment and unfunded pension liability.)

Instructions

1. Journalize the transactions.
2. Journalize the following adjusting entries on December 31:
   a. Salaries accrued: operations salaries, $4,080; officers salaries, $1,635; office salaries, $1,058. The payroll taxes are immaterial and are not accrued.
   b. Vacation pay, $12,500.

PROBLEMS SERIES B

Problem 11–1B
Liability transactions

Objectives 2, 3

GENERAL LEDGER

The following items were selected from among the transactions completed by Pride Polymers during the current year:

Apr.   7. Borrowed $12,000 from First Financial Corporation, issuing a 60-day, 12% note for that amount.

May 10. Purchased equipment by issuing a $60,000, 120-day note to Milford Equipment Co., which discounted the note at the rate of 10%.

June   6. Paid First Financial Corporation the interest due on the note of April 7 and renewed the loan by issuing a new 30-day, 16% note for $12,000. (Record both the debit and credit to the notes payable account.)

July   6. Paid First Financial Corporation the amount due on the note of June 6.

Aug.   3. Purchased merchandise on account from Hamilton Co., $25,000, terms, n/30.

Sep.   2. Issued a 60-day, 15% note for $25,000 to Hamilton Co., on account.

       7. Paid Milford Equipment Co. the amount due on the note of May 10.

Nov.   1. Paid Hamilton Co. the amount owed on the note of September 2.

      15. Purchased store equipment from Shingo Equipment Co. for $80,000, paying $17,000 and issuing a series of seven 12% notes for $9,000 each, coming due at 30-day intervals.

Dec. 15. Paid the amount due Shingo Equipment Co. on the first note in the series issued on November 15.

      21. Settled a product liability lawsuit with a customer for $50,000, to be paid in January. Pride Polymers accrued the loss in a litigation claims payable account.

Instructions

1. Journalize the transactions.
2. Journalize the adjusting entry for each of the following accrued expenses at the end of the current year:
   a. Product warranty cost, $9,500.
   b. Interest on the six remaining notes owed to Shingo Equipment Co.

Problem 11–2B
Entries for payroll and payroll taxes

Objectives 4, 5

✓ 1. (b) Dr. Payroll Taxes Expense, $32,280

The following information about the payroll for the week ended December 30 was obtained from the records of Hannah Co.:

Salaries:		Deductions:	
Sales salaries	$245,000	Income tax withheld	$104,500
Warehouse salaries	87,400	Social security tax withheld	24,120
Office salaries	165,600	Medicare tax withheld	7,470
	$498,000	U.S. savings bonds	24,400
		Group insurance	32,800

Tax rates assumed:
   Social security, 6% on first $70,000 of employee annual earnings
   Medicare, 1.5%
   State unemployment (employer only), 3.8%
   Federal unemployment (employer only), 0.8%

Instructions

1. Assuming that the payroll for the last week of the year is to be paid on December 31, journalize the following entries:
   a. December 30, to record the payroll.
   b. December 30, to record the employer's payroll taxes on the payroll to be paid on December 31. Of the total payroll for the last week of the year, $15,000 is subject to unemployment compensation taxes.
2. Assuming that the payroll for the last week of the year is to be paid on January 4 of the following fiscal year, journalize the following entries:

a. December 30, to record the payroll.
b. January 4, to record the employer's payroll taxes on the payroll to be paid on January 4.

Problem 11–3B
Wage and tax statement data and employer FICA tax

Objectives 4, 5

SPREADSHEET

✓ 2. (e) $24,701.70

Sanchez Company began business on January 2 of last year. Salaries were paid to employees on the last day of each month, and social security tax, Medicare tax, and federal income tax were withheld in the required amounts. An employee who is hired in the middle of the month receives half the monthly salary for that month. All required payroll tax reports were filed, and the correct amount of payroll taxes was remitted by the company for the calendar year. Before the Wage and Tax Statements (Form W-2) could be prepared for distribution to employees and for filing with the Social Security Administration, the employees' earnings records were inadvertently destroyed.

None of the employees resigned or were discharged during the year, and there were no changes in salary rates. The social security tax was withheld at the rate of 6.0% on the first $70,000 of salary and Medicare tax at the rate of 1.5% on salary. Data on dates of employment, salary rates, and employees' income taxes withheld, which are summarized as follows, were obtained from personnel records and payroll records.

Employee	Date First Employed	Monthly Salary	Monthly Income Tax Withheld
Albright	June 2	$5,400	$1,137.00
Charles	Jan. 2	6,500	1,426.25
Given	Mar. 1	3,700	686.35
Nelson	Jan. 2	4,200	783.30
Quinn	Nov. 15	3,800	722.00
Ramsey	Apr. 15	3,000	535.50
Wu	Jan. 16	7,000	1,564.50

Instructions

1. Calculate the amounts to be reported on each employee's Wage and Tax Statement (Form W-2) for the year, arranging the data in the following form:

Employee	Gross Earnings	Federal Income Tax Withheld	Social Security Tax Withheld	Medicare Tax Withheld

2. Calculate the following employer payroll taxes for the year: (a) social security; (b) Medicare; (c) state unemployment compensation at 3.8% on the first $7,000 of each employee's earnings; (d) federal unemployment compensation at 0.8% on the first $7,000 of each employee's earnings; (e) total.

If the working papers correlating with this textbook are not used, omit Problem 11–4B.

Problem 11–4B
Payroll register

Objectives 4, 5

✓ 3. Dr. Payroll Taxes Expense, $618.75

The payroll register for Chopin Piano Co. for the week ended December 12, 2000, is presented in the working papers.

Instructions

1. Journalize the entry to record the payroll for the week.
2. Journalize the entry to record the issuance of the checks to employees.
3. Journalize the entry to record the employer's payroll taxes for the week. Assume the following tax rates: state unemployment, 3.2%; federal unemployment, 0.8%. Of the earnings, $750 is subject to unemployment taxes.
4. Journalize the entry to record a check issued on Dec. 15 to Second National Bank in payment of employees' income taxes, $1,422.18, social security taxes, $942.00, and Medicare taxes, $235.50.

Problem 11–5B
Payroll register

Objectives 4, 5

SPREADSHEET

✓ 1. Total net amount paid,
$5,545.09

The following data for Industrial Solvents Inc. relate to the payroll for the week ended December 7, 2000:

Employee	Hours Worked	Hourly Rate	Weekly Salary	Federal Income Tax	U.S. Savings Bonds	Accumulated Earnings, Nov. 30
A	46.00	$26.00		$247.00	$15.00	$51,640.00
B	40.00	18.00		136.00		38,880.00
C			$1,450.00	325.00	70.00	69,600.00
D	42.00	22.00		165.00	10.00	36,000.00
E	40.00	16.00		112.00		30,000.00
F	45.00	18.50		162.00	20.00	15,300.00
G	40.00	14.00		92.00	25.00	24,000.00
H			900.00	182.00		3,600.00
I	20.00	14.00		17.00	15.00	3,000.00

Employees C and H are office staff, and all of the other employees are sales personnel. All sales personnel are paid 1½ times the regular rate for all hours in excess of 40 hours per week. The social security tax rate is 6.0% on the first $70,000 of each employee's annual earnings, and Medicare tax is 1.5% of each employee's annual earnings. The next payroll check to be used is No. 981.

Instructions

1. Prepare a payroll register for Industrial Solvents Inc. for the week ended December 7, 2000.
2. Journalize the entry to record the payroll for the week.

Problem 11–6B
Payroll accounts and year-end entries

Objectives 4, 5, 6

GENERAL LEDGER

The following accounts, with the balances indicated, appear in the ledger of Teton Outdoor Equipment Company on December 1 of the current year:

211	Salaries Payable	—
212	Social Security Tax Payable	$ 6,232
213	Medicare Tax Payable	1,640
214	Employees Federal Income Tax Payable	10,113
215	Employees State Income Tax Payable	9,839
216	State Unemployment Tax Payable	1,104
217	Federal Unemployment Tax Payable	288
218	Bond Deductions Payable	1,050
219	Medical Insurance Payable	3,800
611	Sales Salaries Expense	784,600
711	Officers Salaries Expense	296,700
712	Office Salaries Expense	121,300
719	Payroll Taxes Expense	96,343

The following transactions relating to payroll, payroll deductions, and payroll taxes occurred during December:

Dec. 1 Issued Check No. 728 to Pico Insurance Company for $3,800, in payment of the semiannual premium on the group medical insurance policy.
2. Issued Check No. 729 to First National Bank for $17,985, in payment for $6,232 of social security tax, $1,640 of Medicare tax, and $10,113 of employees' federal income tax due.
3. Issued Check No. 730 for $1,050 to First National Bank to purchase U.S. savings bonds for employees.
14. Journalized the entry to record the biweekly payroll. A summary of the payroll record follows:

Salary distribution:

Sales	$36,110	
Officers	13,672	
Office	5,675	$55,457

Deductions:

Social security tax	$ 3,050	
Medicare tax	832	
Federal income tax withheld	9,871	
State income tax withheld	2,496	
Savings bond deductions	525	
Medical insurance deductions	633	17,407
Net amount		$38,050

Dec. 14. Issued Check No. 738 in payment of the net amount of the biweekly payroll.

14. Journalized the entry to record payroll taxes on employees' earnings of December 14: social security tax, $3,050; Medicare tax, $832; state unemployment tax, $242; federal unemployment tax, $65.

17. Issued Check No. 744 to First National Bank for $17,635, in payment for $6,100 of social security tax, $1,664 of Medicare tax, and $9,871 of employees' federal income tax due.

28. Journalized the entry to record the biweekly payroll. A summary of the payroll record follows:

Salary distribution:

Sales	$37,450	
Officers	13,600	
Office	5,820	$56,870

Deductions:

Social security tax	$ 3,071	
Medicare tax	853	
Federal income tax withheld	10,123	
State income tax withheld	2,559	
Savings bond deduction	525	17,131
Net amount		$39,739

28. Issued Check No. 782 for the net amount of the biweekly payroll.

28. Journalized the entry to record payroll taxes on employees' earnings of December 28: social security tax, $3,071; Medicare tax, $853; state unemployment tax, $196; federal unemployment tax, $44.

30. Issued Check No. 791 for $14,894 to First National Bank, in payment of employees' state income tax due on December 31.

30. Issued Check No. 792 to First National Bank for $1,050 to purchase U.S. savings bonds for employees.

31. Paid $57,700 of the annual pension cost of $65,000. (Record both the payment and the unfunded pension liability.)

Instructions

1. Journalize the transactions.
2. Journalize the following adjusting entries on December 31:
   a. Salaries accrued: sales salaries, $3,745; officers salaries, $1,360; office salaries, $582. The payroll taxes are immaterial and are not accrued.
   b. Vacation pay, $14,200.

QUICHBOOHS PROBLEM

Payroll

This problem uses the Larry's Landscaping sample company provided with QuickBooks® 5.0. Begin by first copying *sample.qbw* into another file name, **payroll.qbw,** so that the original sample.qbw file will not be changed. You can copy the file using the copy and paste commands in your operating system. This is an important step, since we will be using the unchanged sample.qbw file later in the text.

Retrieve Larry's Landscaping by opening the file that you just created. The first time you open Larry's Landscaping, you will be in QuickBooks Navigator®. You may wish to use the Navigator to review the forms used for "Payroll and Employees." This problem will use some of these forms.

Larry's Landscaping has been in business since October of the current year. We will add some payroll transactions to those that have already been recorded and saved in the company file.

We will begin by adding a new employee. Under the "lists" menu item, select "employees." This window displays the list of present employees. Use the "employee" drop-down list in the list window to add a "new" employee. A form for employee information is opened. Fill in the form with the following information:

Address Information:

Mr. Tyrone K. Highwater
216 Bridge Road
Bayshore, CA 94326
(415) 555-2335
SS #: 432-56-1234

Payroll Information:

Regular pay, $10 per hour; overtime pay, $15 per hour (enter as two separate lines under "earnings").

Set "class" at "landscaping" from the drop-down list. Set the "pay period" to weekly from the drop-down list. Mr. Highwater is single and claims one deduction for federal and state tax purposes.

Vacation and sick pay are set at default values. Health insurance is $25 per pay period (−25 in the amount column) up to a limit of $600 for the calendar year (−600 in the limit column), and there is no employer training tax (delete line by using edit menu).

Create Payroll Check:

We will now create a payroll check for Mr. Highwater. Begin by selecting the activity "payroll," then "pay employees" (or clicking the "payroll" button on the menu bar). Deselect the "to be printed" check box. Select Tyrone K. Highwater by clicking a check mark next to his name. Change the payroll period ending and check date to December 20. Select the button "enter hours and preview check before creating." We are now ready to create the payroll check. Select "create."

The "create" window collects the payroll information needed for Mr. Highwater. Enter 40 hours of regular pay and 8 hours for overtime pay. All hours were for work performed for David Hughes (from drop-down list). The health insurance rate of $25 per pay period is automatically inserted from the payroll information entered previously. Notice how the software automatically calculates federal withholding tax, California withholding tax, social security tax, and Medicare tax.

Instructions

Open the payroll report "payroll summary by employee" from the "reports" menu item. Change the beginning and ending dates for the report from December 15 to December 20. Print the report for Tyrone Highwater. Notice that QuickBooks automatically calculates a summary of Highwater's gross pay, deductions, and net pay. In addition, all the employer payroll taxes, including social security tax (employer's portion), Medicare tax (employer's portion), FUTA, and SUTA are shown on the report. QuickBooks uses this information to prepare a check to satisfy federal payroll tax liabilities, along with automatically filling out Form 941.

COMPREHENSIVE PROBLEM 3

GENERAL LEDGER

Selected transactions completed by Wacker Co. during its first fiscal year ending December 31 were as follows:

Jan. 2. Issued a check to establish a petty cash fund of $400.

Mar. 1. Replenished the petty cash fund, based on the following summary of petty cash receipts: office supplies, $144; miscellaneous selling expense, $97; miscellaneous administrative expense, $138.

Apr. 5. Purchased $8,000 of merchandise on account, terms 1/10, n/30. The perpetual inventory system is used to account for inventory.

May 5. Paid the invoice of April 5 after the discount period had passed.

     10. Received cash from daily cash sales for $8,710. The amount indicated by the cash register was $8,750.

June 2. Received a 60-day, 12% note for $40,000 on account.

Aug. 1. Received amount owed on June 2 note, plus interest at the maturity date.

      3. Received $700 on account and wrote off the remainder owed on a $1,000 accounts receivable balance. (The allowance method is used in accounting for uncollectible receivables.)

     28. Reinstated the account written off on August 3 and received $300 cash in full payment.

Sep. 2. Purchased land by issuing a $30,000, 90-day note to Ace Development Co., which discounted it at 12%.

Oct. 1. Traded office equipment for new equipment with a list price of $140,000. A trade-in allowance of $25,000 was received on the old equipment that had cost $80,000 and had accumulated depreciation of $50,000 as of October 1. A 120-day, 12% note was issued for the balance owed.

Nov. 30. Journalized the monthly payroll for November, based on the following data:

Salaries:		Deductions:	
Sales salaries	$15,500	Income tax withheld	$3,885
Office salaries	5,500	Social security tax withheld	1,260
	$21,000	Medicare tax withheld	315

Unemployment tax rates:	
State unemployment	3.8%
Federal unemployment	0.8%
Amount subject to unemployment taxes:	
State unemployment	$500
Federal unemployment	500

     30. Journalized the employer's payroll taxes on the payroll.

Dec. 1. Journalized the payment of the September 2 note at maturity.

     30. The pension cost for the year was $40,000, of which $36,000 was paid to the pension plan trustee.

Instructions

1. Journalize the selected transactions.
2. Based on the following data, prepare a bank reconciliation for December of the current year:
    a. Balance according to the bank statement at December 31, $89,560.
    b. Balance according to the ledger at December 31, $69,685.
    c. Checks outstanding at December 31, $34,310.
    d. Deposit in transit, not recorded by bank, $14,200.
    e. Bank debit memorandum for service charges, $55.
    f. A check for $200 in payment of an invoice was incorrectly recorded in the accounts as $20.
3. Based on the bank reconciliation prepared in (2), journalize the entry or entries to be made by Wacker Co.
4. Based on the following selected data, journalize the adjusting entries as of December 31 of the current year:
    a. Estimated uncollectible accounts at December 31, $4,220. The balance of Allowance for Doubtful Accounts at December 31 was $800 (debit).
    b. The physical inventory on December 31 indicated an inventory shrinkage of $2,600.

c. Prepaid insurance expired during the year, $14,400.
d. Office supplies used during the year, $3,900.
e. Depreciation is computed as follows:

Asset	Cost	Residual Value	Acquisition Date	Useful Life in Years	Depreciation Method Used
Buildings	$290,000	$ 0	January 2	50	Straight-line
Office Equip.	140,000	12,000	July 1	5	Straight-line
Store Equip.	90,000	10,000	January 3	8	Declining-balance (at twice the straight-line rate)

f. A patent costing $36,000 when acquired on January 2 has a remaining legal life of 9 years and is expected to have value for 6 years.
g. The cost of mineral rights was $80,000. Of the estimated deposit of 25,000 tons of ore, 4,000 tons were mined during the year.
h. Total vacation pay expense for the year, $6,000.
i. A product warranty was granted beginning December 1 and covering a one-year period. The estimated cost is 3% of sales, which totaled $390,000 in December.

5. Based on the following post-closing trial balance and other data, prepare a balance sheet in report form at December 31 of the current year.

Wacker Co.
Post-Closing Trial Balance
December 31, 2000

Petty Cash	400	
Cash	69,450	
Notes Receivable	50,000	
Accounts Receivable	194,300	
Allowance for Doubtful Accounts		4,220
Merchandise Inventory	40,250	
Prepaid Insurance	28,800	
Office Supplies	6,300	
Land	50,000	
Buildings	290,000	
Accumulated Depreciation—Buildings		5,800
Office Equipment	140,000	
Accumulated Depreciation—Office Equipment		12,800
Store Equipment	90,000	
Accumulated Depreciation—Store Equipment		22,500
Mineral Rights	80,000	
Accumulated Depletion		12,800
Patents	30,000	
Social Security Tax Payable		2,640
Medicare Tax Payable		660
Employees Federal Income Tax Payable		4,100
State Unemployment Tax Payable		45
Federal Unemployment Tax Payable		20
Salaries Payable		16,000
Accounts Payable		94,000
Product Warranty Payable		11,700
Vacation Pay Payable		6,000
Unfunded Pension Liability		4,000
Notes Payable		450,000
B. Wacker, Capital		422,215
	1,069,500	1,069,500

The following information relating to the balance sheet accounts at December 31 is obtained from supplementary records:

Notes receivable is a current asset.
The merchandise inventory is stated at cost by the LIFO method.
The product warranty payable is a current liability.
Vacation pay payable:

Current liability	$ 5,000
Long-term liability	1,000

The unfunded pension liability is a long-term liability.
Notes payable:

Current liability	$115,000
Long-term liability	335,000

6. On February 7 of the following year, the merchandise inventory was destroyed by fire. Based on the following data obtained from the accounting records, estimate the cost of the merchandise destroyed:

Jan. 1 Merchandise inventory	$ 40,250
Jan. 1–Feb. 7 Purchases (net)	235,250
Jan. 1–Feb. 7 Sales (net)	420,000
Estimated gross profit rate	40%

SPECIAL ACTIVITIES

Activity 11–1
Bennett and Barns, CPAs
Ethics and professional conduct in business

Ellen Thomson is a certified public accountant (CPA) and staff assistant for Bennett and Barns, a local CPA firm. It had been the policy of the firm to provide a holiday bonus equal to two weeks' salary to all employees. The firm's new management team announced on November 25 that a bonus equal to only one week's salary would be made available to employees this year. Ellen thought that this policy was unfair because she and her co-workers planned on the full two-week bonus. The two-week bonus had been given for ten straight years, so it seemed as though the firm had breached an implied commitment. Thus, Ellen decided that she would make up the lost bonus week by working an extra six hours of overtime per week over the next five weeks until the end of the year. Bennett and Barns' policy is to pay overtime at 150% of straight time.

Ellen's supervisor was surprised to see overtime being reported, since there is generally very little additional or unusual client service demands at the end of the calendar year. However, the overtime was not questioned, since firm employees are on the "honor system" in reporting their overtime.

➤ Discuss whether the firm is acting in an ethical manner by changing the bonus. Is Ellen behaving in an ethical manner?

Activity 11–2
Tri-America Company
Recognizing pension expense

What do you THINK?

The annual examination of Tri-America Company's financial statements by its external public accounting firm (auditors) is nearing completion. The following conversation took place between the controller of Tri-America Company (Donald) and the audit manager from the public accounting firm (Cathy).

Cathy: You know, Donald, we are about to wrap up our audit for this fiscal year. Yet, there is one item still to be resolved.
Donald: What's that?
Cathy: Well, as you know, at the beginning of the year, Tri-America began a defined benefit pension plan. This plan promises your employees an annual payment when they retire, using a formula based on their salaries at retirement and their years of service. I believe that a pension expense should be recognized this year, equal to the amount of pension earned by your employees.

Donald: Wait a minute. I think you have it all wrong. The company doesn't have a pension expense until it actually pays the pension in cash when the employee retires. After all, some of these employees may not reach retirement, and if they don't, the company doesn't owe them anything.

Cathy: You're not really seeing this the right way. The pension is earned by your employees during their working years. You actually make the payment much later—when they retire. It's like one long accrual—much like incurring wages in one period and paying them in the next. Thus, I think that you should recognize the expense in the period the pension is earned by the employees.

Donald: Let me see if I've got this straight. I should recognize an expense this period for something that may or may not be paid to the employees in 20 or 30 years, when they finally retire. How am I supposed to determine what the expense is for the current year? The amount of the final retirement depends on many uncertainties: salary levels, employee longevity, mortality rates, and interest earned on investments to fund the pension. I don't think that an amount can be determined, even if I accepted your arguments.

> Evaluate Cathy's position. Is she right or is Donald correct?

Activity 11–3
Bolton's Trucking Company
Executive bonuses and accounting methods

Chris Bolton, the owner of Bolton Trucking Company, initiated an executive bonus plan for his chief executive officer (CEO). The new plan provides a bonus to the CEO equal to 3% of the income before taxes. Upon learning of the new bonus arrangement, the CEO issued instructions to change the company's accounting for trucks. The CEO has asked the controller to make the following two changes:

a.   Change from the double-declining-balance method to the straight-line method of depreciation.

b.   Add 50% to the useful lives of all trucks.

> Why did the CEO ask for these changes? How would you respond to the CEO's request?

Activity 11–4
Into the Real World
Salary survey

Several Internet services provide career guidance, classified employment ads, placement services, resumé posting, career questionnaires, and salary surveys. Select one of the following Internet sites to determine current average salary levels for one of your career options:

www.cfstaffing.com/salary.html	Accounting salary information
www.tripod.com/work	General career guidance, career profiles, and salary information
www.espan.com/salary	Computer, engineering, finance, and accounting salary information
www.occ.com	Online Career Center

Activity 11–5
Into the Real World
Payroll forms

Payroll accounting involves the use of government-supplied forms to account for payroll taxes. Three common forms are the W-2, Form 940, and Form 941. Form a team with several of your classmates and retrieve copies of each of these forms. They may be obtained from a local IRS office, a library, or downloaded from the Internet at **www.irs.treas.gov** (go to forms and publications). Alternatively, these forms can also be retrieved from QuickBooks® accounting software.

a.   Briefly describe the purpose of each of the three forms.

b.   Fill in the forms using the information provided (leaving blanks where there is no information provided). Assume that your group began a business, called Audit-Proof Tax Service, on November 1 of the current year. Each of you makes a salary of $2,000 per month and claims a single exemption. Salaries were paid on November 30 and December 31. Assume that the withholding tax was $234 per month for each person in the group.

ANSWERS TO SELF-EXAMINATION QUESTIONS

Matching

1.	E	3.	A	5.	M	7.	G	9.	H	11.	J	13.	N	14.	C
2.	K	4.	I	6.	B	8.	D	10.	L	12.	F		

Multiple Choice

1. **C**   The maturity value is $5,100, determined as follows:

Face amount of note	$5,000
Plus interest ($5,000 × 12% × 60/360)	100
Maturity value	$5,100

2. **B**   The net amount available to a borrower from discounting a note payable is called the proceeds. The proceeds of $4,900 (answer B) is determined as follows:

Face amount of note	$5,000
Less discount ($5,000 × 12% × 60/360)	100
Proceeds	$4,900

3. **D**   The amount of net pay of $687.75 (answer D) is determined as follows:

Gross pay:			
40 hours at $20.	$800.00		
5 hours at $30.	150.00	$950.00	
Deductions:			
Federal income			
tax withheld.		$212.00	
FICA:			
Social security			
tax ($600 × .06)	$36.00		
Medicare tax ($950 × .015)	14.25	50.25	262.25
			$687.75

4. **B**   Employers are usually required to withhold a portion of their employees' earnings for payment of federal income taxes (answer A), Medicare tax (answer C), and state and local income taxes (answer D). Generally, federal unemployment compensation taxes (answer B) are levied against the employer only and thus are not deducted from employee earnings.

5. **D**   The employer incurs operating costs for social security tax (answer A), federal unemployment compensation tax (answer B), and state unemployment compensation tax (answer C). The employees' federal income tax (answer D) is not an operating cost of the employer. It is withheld from the employees' earnings.

12

Corporations: Organization, Capital Stock Transactions, and Dividends

Setting
the
STAGE

If you own stock in a corporation, you are interested in how the stock is doing in the market. If you are considering buying stocks, you are interested in your rights as a stockholder and returns that you can expect from the stock. In either case, you should be able to interpret stock market quotations, such as the following:

39½	22	WalMart	WMT	.27	.7	25	24165	36⅛	35⅜	36 1/16	+	⅝
29 15/16	18⅛	Walgreen	WAG	.24	.9	32	6482	28⅛	27⅜	28 1/16	+	9/16
39½	25⅝	WallaceCS	WCS	.621	1.6	20	1808	38 3/16	37	38 1/16	+	⅝
35 9/16	22	Warnaco	WAC	.32	1.0	26	1017	30¾	30 11/16	30 11/16	...	
147¼	61⅞	WarnerLamb	WLA	1.52	1.0	53	11305	147 13/16	145½	147⅛	+	2 1/16
27 1/16	20⅞	WashGasLt	WGL	1.18	4.5	15	689	26⅜	25⅞	26⅛	−	1/16
5	3⅝	WashHomes	WHI	.15	3.3	dd	53	4½	4 7/16	4½	+	1/16

Although you may not own any stocks, you probably buy services or products from corporations, and you may work for a corporation. Understanding the corporate form of organization will help you in your role as a stockholder, a consumer, or an employee. In this chapter, we discuss the characteristics of corporations, as well as how corporations account for stocks.

After studying this chapter, you should be able to:

1 Describe the nature of the corporate form of organization.

2 List the two main sources of stockholders' equity.

3 List the major sources of paid-in capital, including the various classes of stock.

4 Journalize the entries for issuing stock.

5 Journalize the entries for treasury stock transactions.

6 State the effect of stock splits on corporate financial statements.

7 Journalize the entries for cash dividends and stock dividends.

8 Compute and interpret the dividend yield on common stock.

Nature of a Corporation

OBJECTIVE 1

Describe the nature of the corporate form of organization.

In the preceding chapters, we used the proprietorship in illustrations. As we mentioned in a previous chapter, more than 70% of all businesses are proprietorships and 10% are partnerships. Most of these businesses are small businesses. The remaining 20% of businesses are corporations. Many corporations are large and, as a result, they generate more than 90% of the total business dollars in the United States.

Characteristics of a Corporation

A **corporation** is a legal entity, distinct and separate from the individuals who create and operate it. As a legal entity, a corporation may acquire, own, and dispose of property in its own name. It may also incur liabilities and enter into contracts.

Because a corporation is a legal entity, it can sell shares of ownership, called **stock**, without affecting its operations or continued existence. The **stockholders** or **shareholders** who own the stock own the corporation. Corporations whose shares of stock are traded in public markets are called **public corporations**. Corporations whose shares are not traded publicly are usually owned by a small group of investors and are called **nonpublic** or **private corporations**.

 A corporation was defined in the Dartmouth College case of 1819, in which Chief Justice Marshall of the United States Supreme Court stated: "A corporation is an artificial being, invisible, intangible, and existing only in contemplation of the law."

 The **Coca-Cola Corporation** is a well-known public corporation. The **Mars Candy Company**, which is owned by family members, is a well-known private corporation.

Corporations can be large because they have the ability to raise large amounts of capital by selling stock. In contrast, a proprietorship's ability to raise capital is limited because it has only one owner. A **partnership** is similar to a proprietorship, except that it has more than one owner. Like a proprietorship, a partnership's ability to raise capital is limited because ownership is not easily transferred.[1]

Stockholders can buy and sell stock without affecting the corporation. In contrast, a proprietorship or a partnership ceases to exist whenever the owner or a partner leaves the business. Likewise, if a new partner is admitted, a new partnership must be formed.

 **Point of INTEREST**

If you invest in a public corporation, the most you can lose is the amount of your investment, regardless of actions of the corporation.

The stockholders of a corporation have **limited liability**. This means that a corporation's creditors usually may not go beyond the assets of the corporation to satisfy their claims. Thus, the financial loss that a stockholder may suffer is limited to the amount invested. This feature has contributed to the rapid growth of the corporate form of business.

[1] The accounting for partnerships is discussed in Appendix F.

Point of INTEREST

If you start a business as a proprietorship or as a partnership with others, your personal assets are at risk for any debts incurred by the business. For example, you could be personally liable for damages awarded in a lawsuit against the business.

In contrast, the owner of a proprietorship and the partners of a partnership have **unlimited liability**. They are individually liable to creditors for debts incurred by the business. Thus, if a proprietorship or a partnership is not able to pay its debts, the owner or the partners must contribute personal assets to settle the business debts. This characteristic is significant for partnerships because partners are **mutual agents**, which means that the actions of one partner bind the entire partnership.[2]

A proprietorship is controlled directly by its owner. A partnership is controlled by the partners according to a contract, called the *articles of partnership* or *partnership agreement*. In contrast, the stockholders control a corporation by electing a **board of directors**. This board meets periodically to establish corporate policies. It also selects the chief executive officer (CEO) and other major officers to manage the corporation's day-to-day affairs. Exhibit 1 shows the organizational structure of a corporation.

EXHIBIT 1
Organizational Structure of a Corporation

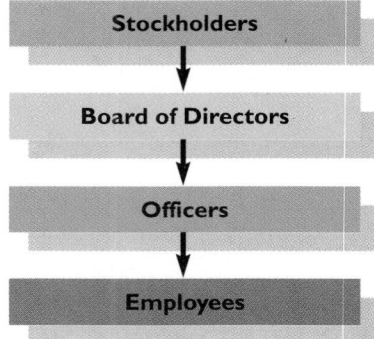

Corporations have a separate legal existence, transferable units of ownership, and limited stockholder liability.

As a separate entity, a corporation is subject to taxes. For example, corporations must pay federal income taxes on their income.[3] Thus, corporate income that is distributed to stockholders in the form of **dividends** has already been taxed. In turn, stockholders must pay income taxes on the dividends they receive. This *double taxation* of corporate earnings is a major disadvantage of the corporate form.[4] In contrast, proprietorships and partnerships are not required to pay federal income taxes. Instead, the owner or partners report their share of the business's income on their personal tax returns.

Forming a Corporation

The first step in forming a corporation is to file an **application of incorporation** with the state. State incorporation laws differ, and corporations often organize in those states with the more favorable laws. For example, more than half of the largest companies are incorporated in Delaware. Exhibit 2 lists some corporations that you may be familiar with, their states of incorporation, and the location of their headquarters.

After the application of incorporation has been approved, the state grants a **charter** or **articles of incorporation**. The articles

Corporations may be organized for nonprofit reasons, such as recreational, educational, charitable, or humanitarian purposes. Such corporations are not required to pay federal taxes. Examples of nonprofit corporations include the Sierra Club and the National Audubon Society. However, most corporations are organized to earn a profit and a fair rate of return for their stockholders. Examples of for-profit corporations include Pepsi-Co, General Motors, and Microsoft.

[2] Some states permit limited partnerships, in which the liability of some partners is limited to the amount of their capital investment. However, a limited partnership must have at least one partner who has unlimited liability.

[3] Some states also require corporations to pay income taxes.

[4] Under the *Internal Revenue Code,* a corporation with a few stockholders may elect to be treated like a partnership for income tax purposes. Such corporations are known as Subchapter S corporations.

EXHIBIT 2
Examples of Corporations and Their States of Incorporation

Corporation	State of Incorporation	Headquarters
Borden, Inc.	New Jersey	New York, N.Y.
Caterpillar, Inc.	Delaware	Peoria, Ill.
Delta Air Lines, Inc.	Delaware	Atlanta, Ga.
Dow Chemical Company	Delaware	Midland, Mich.
General Electric Company	New York	Fairfield, Conn.
The Home Depot	Delaware	Atlanta, Ga.
Kellogg Company	Delaware	Battle Creek, Mich.
3M	Delaware	St. Paul, Minn.
May Department Stores	New York	St. Louis, Mo.
RJR Nabisco	Delaware	New York, N.Y.
Tandy Corporation	Delaware	Ft. Worth, Tex.
The Washington Post Company	Delaware	Washington, D.C.
Whirlpool Corporation	Delaware	Benton Harbor, Mich.

of incorporation formally create the corporation.[5] The corporate management and board of directors then prepare a set of **bylaws**, which are the rules and procedures for conducting the corporation's affairs.

Significant costs may be incurred in organizing a corporation. These costs include legal fees, taxes, state incorporation fees, license fees, and promotional costs. Such costs are debited to an intangible asset account entitled *Organization Costs* and are normally amortized over a five-year period.

The following entries illustrate the recording of a corporation's organization costs of $8,500 on January 5 and the amortization of those costs on December 31, the end of the first year of operations:

Jan.	5	Organization Costs	8 5 0 0 00	
		Cash		8 5 0 0 00
		Paid costs of organizing the corporation.		
Dec.	31	Amortization Expense—Organization Costs	1 7 0 0 00	
		Organization Costs		1 7 0 0 00
		Amortized organization costs at end of		
		first year ($8,500/5 years = $1,700).		

Stockholders' Equity

OBJECTIVE 2

List the two main sources of stockholders' equity.

The owners' equity in a corporation is commonly called **stockholders' equity**, **shareholders' equity**, **shareholders' investment**, or **capital**. In a corporation balance sheet, the Stockholders' Equity section reports the amount of each of the two main sources of stockholders' equity. The first source is capital contributed to the corporation by the stockholders and others, called **paid-in capital** or **contributed capital**. The second source is net income retained in the business, called **retained earnings**.

An example of a Stockholders' Equity section of a corporation balance sheet is shown below.

[5] The articles of incorporation may also restrict a corporation's activities in certain areas, such as owning certain types of real estate, conducting certain types of business activities, or purchasing its own stock.

PAID-IN CAPITAL

Stockholder investments

RETAINED EARNINGS

Reinvested earnings

Stockholders' Equity

Paid-in capital:

Common stock	$330,000	
Retained earnings	80,000	
Total stockholders' equity		$410,000

The paid-in capital contributed by the stockholders is recorded in separate accounts for each class of stock. If there is only one class of stock, the account is entitled *Common Stock* or *Capital Stock.*

Retained earnings are generated from operations. Net income increases retained earnings while dividends decrease retained earnings. Thus, retained earnings represents a corporation's accumulated net income that has not been distributed to stockholders as dividends.

> **The two main sources of stockholders' equity are paid-in capital and retained earnings.**

The balance of the retained earnings account at the end of the fiscal year is created by closing entries. First, the balance in the income summary account (the net income or net loss) is transferred to Retained Earnings. Second, the balance of the dividends account, which is similar to the drawing account for a proprietorship, is transferred to Retained Earnings.

Other terms that may be used to identify retained earnings in the financial statements include *earnings retained for use in the business* and *earnings reinvested in the business.* A debit balance in Retained Earnings is called a **deficit**. Such a balance results from accumulated net losses. In the Stockholders' Equity section, a deficit is deducted from paid-in capital in determining total stockholders' equity.

The balance of retained earnings should not be interpreted as representing surplus cash or cash left over for dividends. The reason for this is that earnings retained in the business and the related cash generated from these earnings are normally used by management to improve or expand operations. As cash is used to expand or improve operations, its balance decreases. However, the balance of the retained earnings account is unaffected. As a result, over time the balance of the retained earnings account normally becomes less and less related to the balance of the cash account.

Sources of Paid-In Capital

OBJECTIVE 3

List the major sources of paid-in capital, including the various classes of stock.

As we mentioned in the preceding section, the two main sources of stockholders' equity are paid-in capital (or contributed capital) and retained earnings. The main source of paid-in capital is from issuing stock. In the following paragraphs, we discuss the characteristics of the various classes of stock. We conclude this section with a brief discussion of other sources of paid-in capital.

Stock

The number of shares of stock that a corporation is *authorized* to issue is stated in its charter. The term *issued* refers to the shares issued to the stockholders. A corporation may, under circumstances we discuss later in this chapter, reacquire some of the stock that it has issued. The stock remaining in the hands of stockholders is then called **outstanding stock**. The relationship between authorized, issued, and outstanding stock is shown in the graphic at the top of the next page.

Shares of stock are often assigned a monetary amount, called **par**. Corporations may issue **stock certificates** to stockholders to document their ownership. Printed

Number of shares authorized, issued, and outstanding

 Some corporations have stopped issuing stock certificates except on special request. In these cases, the corporation maintains records of ownership by using electronic media.

on a stock certificate is the par value of the stock, the name of the stockholder, and the number of shares owned. Stock may also be issued without par, in which case it is called **no-par stock**. Some states require the board of directors to assign a **stated value** to no-par stock.

Because corporations have limited liability, creditors have no claim against the personal assets of stockholders. However, some state laws require that corporations maintain a minimum **stockholder** contribution to protect creditors. This minimum amount is called *legal capital*. The amount of required legal capital varies among the states, but it usually includes the amount of par or stated value of the shares of stock issued.

The major rights that accompany ownership of a share of stock are as follows:

1. The right to vote in matters concerning the corporation.
2. The right to share in distributions of earnings.
3. The right to share in assets on liquidation.

When only one class of stock is issued, it is called **common stock**. In this case, each share of common stock has equal rights. To appeal to a broader investment market, a corporation may issue one or more classes of stock with various preference rights. A common example of such a right is the preference to dividends. Such a stock is generally called a **preferred stock**.

Q&A *On its balance sheet, a corporation reports the following three numbers related to its common stock: 200,000 shares; 150,000 shares; and 138,000 shares. What is the number of shares authorized, issued, outstanding, and reacquired?*

200,000 shares authorized; 150,000 shares issued; 138,000 shares outstanding; 12,000 (150,000 − 138,000) shares reacquired.

The two primary classes of paid-in capital are common stock and preferred stock.

The dividend rights of preferred stock are usually stated in monetary terms or as a percent of par. For example, *$4 preferred stock* has a right to an annual $4 per share dividend. If the par value of the preferred stock were $50, the same right to dividends could be stated as *8% ($4/$50) preferred stock*.

The board of directors of a corporation has the sole authority to distribute dividends to the stockholders. When such action is taken, the directors are said to *declare* a dividend. Since dividends are normally based on earnings, a corporation cannot guarantee dividends even to preferred stockholders. However, because they have first rights to any dividends, the preferred stockholders have a greater chance of receiving regular dividends than do the common stockholders.

Nonparticipating Preferred Stock
Preferred stockholders' dividend rights are usually limited to a certain amount. Such stock is said to be **nonparticipating preferred stock**.[6] To continue our preced-

---

[6] In some cases, preferred stock may receive additional dividends if certain conditions are met. Such stock is called *participating preferred stock*. It is rarely used in today's financial markets.

ing example, assume that a corporation has 1,000 shares of $4 nonparticipating preferred stock and 4,000 shares of common stock outstanding. Also assume that the net income, amount of earnings retained, and the amount of earnings distributed by the board of directors for the first three years of operations are as follows:

	1999	2000	2001
Net income	$20,000	$55,000	$62,000
Amount retained	10,000	20,000	40,000
Amount distributed	$10,000	$35,000	$22,000

Exhibit 3 shows the earnings distributed each year to the preferred stock and the common stock. In this example, the preferred stockholders received an annual dividend of $4 per share, compared to the common stockholders' dividends of $1.50, $7.75, and $4.50 per share. You should note that although preferred stockholders have a greater chance of receiving a regular dividend, common stockholders have a greater chance of receiving larger dividends than do the preferred stockholders.

EXHIBIT 3
Dividends to Nonparticipating Preferred Stock

	1999	2000	2001
Amount distributed	$10,000	$35,000	$22,000
Preferred dividend (1,000 shares)	4,000	4,000	4,000
Common dividend (4,000 shares)	$ 6,000	$31,000	$18,000
Dividends per share:			
Preferred	$ 4.00	$ 4.00	$ 4.00
Common	$ 1.50	$ 7.75	$ 4.50

With an investment objective of earning dividends, cumulative preferred stock is a safer investment than noncumulative preferred stock, and both types of preferred stock are a safer investment than common stock.

Cumulative Preferred Stock

Cumulative preferred stock has a right to receive regular dividends that have been passed (not declared) before any common stock dividends are paid. Noncumulative preferred stock does not have this right.

Dividends that have been passed are said to be **in arrears**. Such dividends should be disclosed, normally in a footnote to the financial statements.

To illustrate how dividends on cumulative preferred stock are calculated, assume that the preferred stock in Exhibit 3 is cumulative, and that no dividends were paid in 1999 and 2000. In 2001, the board of directors declares dividends of $22,000. Exhibit 4 shows how the dividends paid in 2001 are distributed between the preferred and common stockholders.

Other Preferential Rights

In addition to dividend preference, preferred stock may be given preferences to assets if the corporation goes out of business and is liquidated. However, claims of creditors must be satisfied first. Preferred stockholders are next in line to receive any remaining assets, followed by the common stockholders.

Romer Corporation has 50,000 shares of $2, $100 par cumulative preferred stock outstanding. Preferred dividends are three years in arrears (not including the current year). What amount of preferred dividends must be paid before any dividends on common shares can be paid?

$400,000 [3 years in arrears (50,000 × $2 × 3) plus the current year's dividend of $100,000]

EXHIBIT 4
Dividends to Cumulative
Preferred Stock

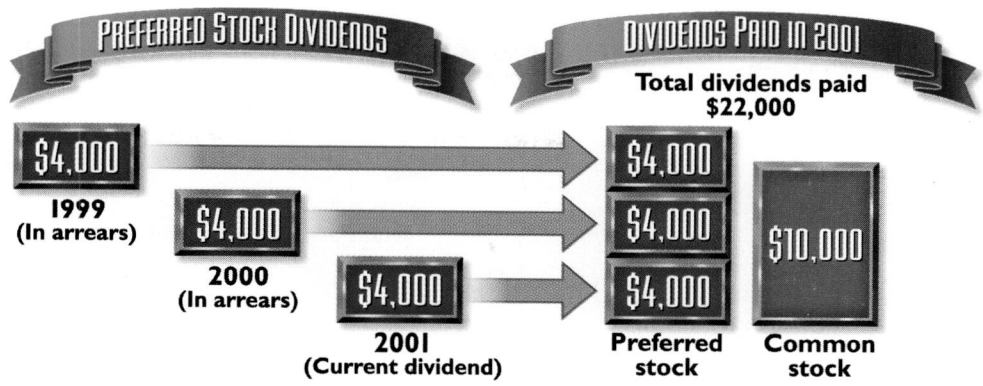

Amount distributed		$22,000
Preferred dividend (1,000 shares):		
1999 dividend in arrears	$4,000	
2000 dividend in arrears	4,000	
2001 dividend	4,000	12,000
Common dividend (4,000 shares)		$10,000
Dividends per share:		
Preferred		$ 12.00
Common		$ 2.50

Other Sources of Paid-In Capital

In addition to arising from the issuance of stock, paid-in capital may arise from receiving donations of real estate or other assets. Civic groups and municipalities sometimes give land or buildings to a corporation as an incentive to locate or remain in a community. In such cases, the corporation debits the assets for their fair market value and credits *Donated Capital.*

To illustrate, assume that on April 20 the city of Moraine donated land to Merrick Corporation as an incentive for it to relocate its headquarters to Moraine. The land was valued at $500,000. Merrick Corporation would record the land as follows:

Apr.	20	Land		500 0 0 0 00	
		Donated Capital			500 0 0 0 00
		Recorded land donated by the city			
		of Moraine.			

Paid-in capital may also arise when a corporation buys and sells its own stock in the marketplace. Later in this chapter, we will discuss the recording of such transactions.

OBJECTIVE 4 # Issuing Stock

Journalize the entries for issuing stock.

A separate account is used for recording the amount of each class of stock issued to investors in a corporation. For example, assume that a corporation is authorized to issue 10,000 shares of preferred stock, $100 par, and 100,000 shares of common stock, $20 par. One-half of each class of authorized shares is issued at par for cash. The corporation's entry to record the stock issue is as follows:[7]

	Cash		1,500 0 0 0 00			
	Preferred Stock				500 0 0 0 00	
	Common Stock				1,000 0 0 0 00	
	Issued preferred stock and common					
	stock at par for cash.					

INTERMISSION

Preferred stocks shield shareholders somewhat from the lows of corporate fortunes. If dividend payments must be reduced, preferred stockholders receive dividends before common shareholders. However, preferred stockholders often miss out on the highs of corporate fortunes. Because preferred shareholders receive a fixed dividend, and the bulk of any large dividends goes to common shareholders, most preferred stock is nonparticipating. These "safe-but-stodgy" equities can offer dramatic profits, however, as described in the following excerpt from an article in *Business Week*:

"Safe but Stodgy" Preferred Stock

. . . In times of grave financial trouble, dividends on preferreds are often suspended and placed in arrears. . . . If and when the company reinstates dividends, current shareholders are entitled to all the back payments, whether or not they owned stock during the arrearage period—if the preferred is cumulative. . . .

The gains [from purchasing preferred stock with dividends in arrears] can be impressive. **Bethlehem Steel** announced in April that it would pay $22.5 million in arrears and resume the regular quarterly dividend on its two classes of preferred stock. Because Bethlehem had missed four payments, investors receive an extra year's worth of dividends: One class that usually pays $1.25 quarterly will return $6.25—not bad on a stock that traded in the low 30s just a few months ago.

Playing preferreds in arrears requires patience. **Long Island Lighting**, for instance, recently announced that it would try to resume paying dividends next year after a four-year hiatus. But the larger concern lies in the fact that you're betting on a turnaround. And all bets are off if the company goes bankrupt: You not only lose arrearages but you're also sure to see the share price plummet. On the repayment totem pole, preferreds occupy the second-lowest notch—before the common shareholders but after the creditors and bondholders. . . . ■

Source: Troy Segal, "Preferred Stock: The Risky Hunt for Hidden Rewards," *Business Week,* June 13, 1988, p. 114.

Stock is often issued by a corporation at a price other than its par. This is because the par value of a stock is simply its legal capital. The price at which stock can be sold by a corporation depends on a variety of factors, such as:

1. The financial condition, earnings record, and dividend record of the corporation.
2. Investor expectations of the corporation's potential earning power.
3. General business and economic conditions and prospects.

When stock is issued for a price that is more than its par, the stock has sold at a **premium**. When stock is issued for a price that is less than its par, the stock has sold at a **discount**. Thus, if stock with a par of $50 is issued for a price of $60, the stock has sold at a premium of $10. If the same stock is issued for a price of $45, the stock has sold at a discount of $5. Many states do not permit stock to be issued at a discount. In others, it may be done only under unusual conditions. Since issuing stock at a discount is rare, we will not illustrate it.

A corporation issuing stock must maintain records of the stockholders in order to issue dividend checks and distribute financial statements and other reports. Large public corporations normally use a financial institution, such as a bank, for this purpose.[8] In such cases, the financial institution is referred to as a *transfer agent* or *registrar*. For example, the transfer agent and registrar for **Coca-Cola Enterprises** is **First Chicago Trust Company of New York**.

---

[7] The accounting for investments in stocks from the point of view of the investor is discussed in a later chapter.

[8] Small corporations may use a subsidiary ledger, called a *stockholders ledger*. In this case, the stock accounts (Preferred Stock and Common Stock) are controlling accounts for the subsidiary ledger.

The following stock quotation for **Wal-Mart Corporation** is taken from *The Wall Street Journal*:

NEW YORK STOCK EXCHANGE

52 Weeks Hi	Lo	Stock	Sym	Div	Yld %	PE	Vol 100s	Hi	Lo	Close	Net Chg
39½	22	WalMart	WMT	.27	.7	25	24165	36⅛	35⅜	36¹/₁₆	+ ⅚

The preceding quotation is interpreted as follows:

Hi	Highest price during the past 52 weeks
Lo	Lowest price during the past 52 weeks
Stock	Name of the company
Sym	Stock exchange symbol (WMT for Wal-Mart)
Div	Dividends paid per share during the past year
Yld %	Annual dividend yield per share based on the closing price (Wal-Mart's 0.7% yield on common stock is computed as $0.27/$36¹/₁₆)
PE	Price-earnings ratio on common stock (price ÷ earnings per share)
Vol	The volume of stock traded in 100s
Hi	Highest price for the day
Lo	Lowest price for the day
Close	Closing price for the day
Net Chg	The net change in price from the previous day

Premium on Stock

When stock is issued at a premium, Cash or other asset accounts are debited for the amount received. Common Stock or Preferred Stock is then credited for the par amount. The excess of the amount paid over par is a part of the total investment of the stockholders in the corporation. Therefore, such an amount in excess of par should be classified as a part of the paid-in capital. An account entitled *Paid-In Capital in Excess of Par* is usually credited for this amount.

To illustrate, assume that Caldwell Company issues 2,000 shares of $50 par preferred stock for cash at $55. The entry to record this transaction is as follows:

Cash	110 000 00	
Preferred Stock		100 000 00
Paid-In Capital in Excess of		
Par—Preferred Stock		10 000 00
Issued $50 par preferred stock at $55.		

When stock is issued in exchange for assets other than cash, such as land, buildings, and equipment, the assets acquired should be recorded at their fair market value. If this value cannot be objectively determined, the fair market price of the stock issued may be used.

To illustrate, assume that a corporation acquired land for which the fair market value cannot be determined. In exchange, the corporation issued 10,000 shares of its $10 par common. Assuming that the stock has a current market price of $12 per share, this transaction is recorded as follows:

Land	120 000 00	
Common Stock		100 000 00
Paid-In Capital in Excess of Par		20 000 00
Issued $10 par common stock, valued at $12 per share, for land.		

No-Par Stock

In most states, both preferred and common stock may be issued without a par value. When no-par stock is issued, the entire proceeds are credited to the stock account. This is true even though the issue price varies from time to time. For example, assume that a corporation issues 10,000 shares of no-par common stock at $40 a share and at a later date issues 1,000 additional shares at $36. The entries to record the no-par stock are as follows:

Cash	400 000 00	
Common Stock		400 000 00
Issued 10,000 shares of no-par common at $40.		
Cash	36 000 00	
Common Stock		36 000 00
Issued 1,000 shares of no-par common at $36.		

Some states require that the entire proceeds from the issue of no-par stock be recorded as legal capital. In this case, the preceding entries would be proper. In other states, no-par stock may be assigned a *stated value per share*. The stated value is recorded like a par value, and the excess of the proceeds over the stated value is recorded as follows:

Cash	400 0 0 0 00				
Common Stock			250 0 0 0 00		
Paid-In Capital in Excess of Stated Value			150 0 0 0 00		
Issued 10,000 shares of no-par common					
at $40; stated value, $25.					
Cash	36 0 0 0 00				
Common Stock			25 0 0 0 00		
Paid-In Capital in Excess of Stated Value			11 0 0 0 00		
Issued 1,000 shares of no-par common					
at $36; stated value, $25.					

Treasury Stock Transactions

A corporation may buy its own stock to provide shares for resale to employees, for reissuing as a bonus to employees, or for supporting the market price of the stock. For example, **General Motors** bought back its common stock and stated that two primary uses of this stock would be for incentive compensation plans and employee savings plans. Such stock that a corporation has once issued and then reacquires is called **treasury stock**.

 The 1996 edition of *Accounting Trends & Techniques* indicated that over 64% of the companies surveyed reported treasury stock.

A commonly used method of accounting for the purchase and resale of treasury stock is the **cost method**.[9] When the stock is purchased by the corporation, the account *Treasury Stock* is debited for its cost (the price paid for it). The par value and the price at which the stock was originally issued are ignored. When the stock is resold, Treasury Stock is credited for its cost, and any difference between the cost and the selling price is normally debited or credited to *Paid-In Capital from Sale of Treasury Stock.*

To illustrate, assume that the paid-in capital of a corporation is as follows:

Common stock, $25 par (20,000 shares authorized
 and issued) $500,000
Excess of issue price over par   150,000 $650,000

The purchase and sale of the treasury stock are recorded as follows:

Treasury Stock	45 0 0 0 00				
Cash			45 0 0 0 00		
Purchased 1,000 shares of treasury					
stock at $45.					

---

[9] Another method that is infrequently used, called the *par value method*, is discussed in advanced accounting texts.

	Cash		12 0 0 0 00		
	Treasury Stock			9 0 0 0 00	
	Paid-In Capital from Sale of Treasury Stock			3 0 0 0 00	
	Sold 200 shares of treasury stock at $60.				
	Cash		8 0 0 0 00		
	Paid-In Capital from Sale of Treasury Stock		1 0 0 0 00		
	Treasury Stock			9 0 0 0 00	
	Sold 200 shares of treasury stock at $40.				

(handwritten margin notes: "Premium →", "Discount →")

As shown above, a sale of treasury stock may result in a decrease in paid-in capital. To the extent that Paid-In Capital from Sale of Treasury Stock has a credit balance, it should be debited for any decrease. Any remaining decrease should then be debited to the retained earnings account.

At the end of the period, the balance in the treasury stock account is reported as a deduction from the total of the paid-in capital and retained earnings. The balance of Paid-In Capital from Sale of Treasury Stock is reported as part of the paid-in capital, as shown in Exhibit 5.

EXHIBIT 5
Stockholders' Equity Section
with Treasury Stock

Stockholders' Equity

Paid-in capital:		
Common stock, $25 par (20,000 shares authorized and issued)	$500,000	
Excess of issue price over par	150,000	
From sale of treasury stock	2,000	
Total paid-in capital		$652,000
Retained earnings		130,000
Total		$782,000
Deduct treasury stock (600 shares at cost) . .		27,000
Total stockholders' equity		$755,000

(handwritten margin notes: "Diff in what gained + lost")

Stock Splits

OBJECTIVE 6

State the effect of stock splits on corporate financial statements.

Corporations sometimes reduce the par or stated value of their common stock and issue a proportionate number of additional shares. When this is done, a corporation is said to have *split* its stock, and the process is called a **stock split**. *(handwritten: — Makes more shares avail.)*

When stock is split, the reduction in par or stated value applies to all shares, including the unissued, issued, and treasury shares. A major objective of a stock split is to reduce the market price per share of the stock. This, in turn, should attract more investors to enter the market for the stock and broaden the types and numbers of stockholders.

To illustrate a stock split, assume that Rojek Corporation has 10,000 shares of $100 par common stock outstanding with a current market price of $150 per share. The board of directors declares a 5-for-1 stock split, reduces the par to $20, and increases the number of shares to 50,000. The amount of common stock outstanding is $1,000,000

When **Nature's Sunshine Products Inc.** declared a two-for-one stock split, the company president said:

We believe the split will place our stock price in a range attractive to both individual and institutional investors, broadening the market for the stock.

4 shares, $100 par

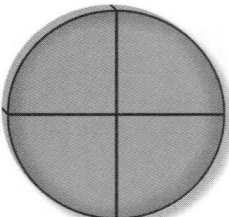

$400 total par value

20 shares, $20 par

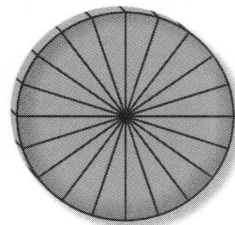

$400 total par value

both before and after the stock split. Only the number of shares and the par per share are changed. Each Rojek Corporation shareholder owns the same total par amount of stock before and after the stock split. For example, a stockholder who owned 4 shares of $100 par stock before the split (total par of $400) would own 20 shares of $20 par stock after the split (total par of $400).

Since there are more shares outstanding after the stock split, we would expect that the market price of the stock would fall. For example, in the preceding example, there would be 5 times as many shares outstanding after the split. Thus, we would expect the market price of the stock to fall from $150 to approximately $30 ($150/5).

Since a stock split changes only the par or stated value and the number of shares outstanding, it is not recorded by a journal entry. Although the accounts are not affected, the details of stock splits are normally disclosed in the notes to the financial statements.

LTM Corporation announced a 4-for-1 stock split of its $50 par value common stock, which is currently trading for $120 per share. What is the new par value and the estimated market price of the stock after the split?

$12.50 ($50/4) par value; $30 ($120/4) estimated market price.

A stock split does not change the balance of any corporation accounts.

Not Recorded as a Journal Entry

OBJECTIVE 7

Journalize the entries for cash dividends and stock dividends.

Accounting for Dividends

When a board of directors declares a cash dividend, it authorizes the distribution of a portion of the corporation's cash to stockholders. When a board of directors declares a stock dividend, it authorizes the distribution of a portion of its stock. In both cases, the declaration of a dividend reduces the retained earnings of the corporation.[10]

Cash Dividends

A cash distribution of earnings by a corporation to its shareholders is called a **cash dividend**. Although dividends may be paid in the form of other assets, cash dividends are the most common form.

There are usually three conditions that a corporation must meet to pay a cash dividend:

1. Sufficient retained earnings
2. Sufficient cash
3. Formal action by the board of directors

A large amount of retained earnings does not always mean that a corporation is able to pay dividends. As we indicated earlier in the chapter, the balance of the cash and retained earnings account are often unrelated. Thus, a large retained earnings account does not mean that there is cash available to pay dividends.

A corporation's board of directors is not required by law to declare dividends. This is true even if both retained earnings and cash are large enough to justify a dividend. However, most corporations try to maintain a stable dividend record in

---

[10] In rare cases, when a corporation is reducing its operations or going out of business, a dividend may be a distribution of paid-in capital. Such a dividend is called a *liquidating dividend*.

BUSINESS ON STAGE

Stock Exchanges

Stocks are bought and sold through stock exchanges. The New York Stock Exchange and the American Stock Exchange are the two national exchanges. In addition, regional exchanges and the over-the-counter market serve important roles in the trading of stocks.

New York Stock Exchange. This exchange, founded in 1792, is located on Wall Street in New York City. It consists of over 1,366 members who own "seats" on the exchange and who are allowed to trade securities. Only stocks listed on the exchange (the "Big Board") can be traded. Currently, stocks of over 3,000 generally older, well-established, larger companies are listed. To qualify for listing, a company must have over 1 million shares outstanding and $2.5 million of pretax profits. Examples of such companies include General Motors and Conrail.

American Stock Exchange. This exchange is similar to the New York Stock Exchange, except that the companies are generally small to medium-size companies. To qualify for listing, a company must have over 500,000 shares outstanding and $750,000 of pretax profits. Currently, about 800 stocks are listed on the American Stock Exchange. As a company grows, it may move from the American Stock Exchange to the New York Stock Exchange. Examples of American Stock Exchange companies include El Paso Electric and Amdahl.

Regional Exchanges. There are several regional exchanges, including Chicago, Boston, Cincinnati, Philadelphia, and San Francisco. Initially, such exchanges traded mostly in stocks of local firms. Today, many firms, such as Sears, are traded on both regional and national exchanges.

Over-the-Counter Market. This market refers to a network of brokers who communicate with each other to set prices and trade securities. This system is referred to as the *National Association of Securities Dealers Automated Quotation* system, or more simply by its abbreviation, *Nasdaq.* Larger, actively traded issues are referred to as Nasdaq National Market issues, while less active issues are referred to as Nasdaq Small-Cap issues. Approximately, 30,000 stocks are traded on Nasdaq. Examples of Nasdaq companies include Apple Computer, Intel, and Microsoft. ■

order to make their stock attractive to investors. Although dividends may be paid once a year or semiannually, most corporations pay dividends quarterly. In years of high profits, a corporation may declare a *special* or *extra* dividend.

You may have seen announcements of dividend declarations in financial newspapers or investor services. An example of such an announcement is shown below.

*On June 26, the board of directors of **Campbell Soup Co.** declared a quarterly cash dividend of $0.33 per common share to stockholders of record as of the close of business on July 8, payable on July 31.*

This announcement includes three important dates: the *date of declaration* (June 26), the *date of record* (July 8), and the *date of payment* (July 31). During the period of time between the record date and the payment date, the stock price is usually quoted as selling *ex-dividends*. This means that since the date of record has passed, a new investor will not receive the dividend.

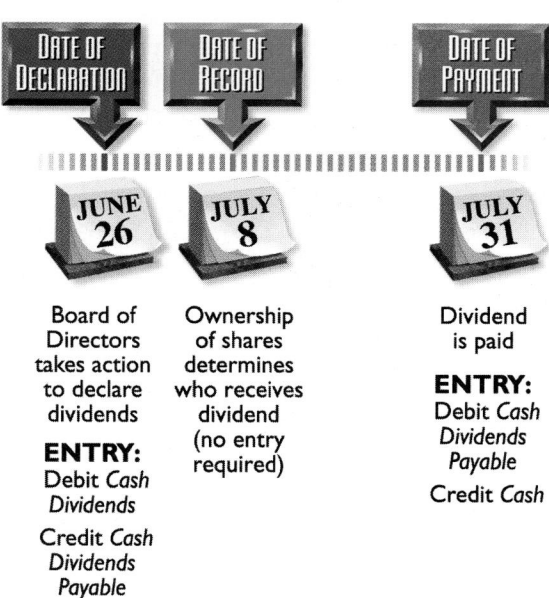

DATE OF DECLARATION	DATE OF RECORD	DATE OF PAYMENT
JUNE 26	JULY 8	JULY 31
Board of Directors takes action to declare dividends	Ownership of shares determines who receives dividend (no entry required)	Dividend is paid
ENTRY: Debit *Cash Dividends* Credit *Cash Dividends Payable*		**ENTRY:** Debit *Cash Dividends Payable* Credit *Cash*

To illustrate, assume that on *December 1* the board of directors of Hiber Corporation declares the following quarterly cash dividends. The date of record is *December 10*, and the date of payment is *January 2.*

	Dividend per Share	Total Dividends
Preferred stock, $100 par, 5,000 shares outstanding	$2.50	$12,500
Common stock, $10 par, 100,000 shares outstanding	$0.30	30,000
Total		$42,500

Hiber Corporation records the $42,500 liability for the dividends on December 1, the declaration date, as follows:

Dec.	1	Cash Dividends		42 5 0 0 00	
		Cash Dividends Payable			42 5 0 0 00
		Declared cash dividend.			

No entry is required on the date of record, December 10, since this date merely determines which stockholders will receive the dividend. On the date of payment, January 2, the corporation records the $42,500 payment of the dividends as follows:

Jan.	2	Cash Dividends Payable		42 5 0 0 00	
		Cash			42 5 0 0 00
		Paid cash dividend.			

If Hiber Corporation's fiscal year ends December 31, the balance in Cash Dividends will be transferred to Retained Earnings as a part of the closing process by debiting Retained Earnings and crediting Cash Dividends. Cash Dividends Payable will be listed on the December 31 balance sheet as a current liability.

If a corporation that holds treasury stock declares a cash dividend, the dividends are not paid on the treasury shares. To do so would place the corporation in the position of earning income through dealing with itself. For example, if Hiber Corporation in the preceding illustration had held 5,000 shares of its own common stock, the cash dividends on the common stock would have been $28,500 [(100,000 − 5,000) × $0.30] instead of $30,000.

Stock Dividends

A distribution of shares of stock to stockholders is called a **stock dividend**. Usually, such distributions are in common stock and are issued to holders of common stock. Stock dividends are different from cash dividends in that there is no distribution of cash or other assets to stockholders.

The effect of a stock dividend on the stockholders' equity of the issuing corporation is to transfer retained earnings to paid-in capital. For public corporations, the amount transferred from retained earnings to paid-in capital is normally the *fair value* (market price) of the shares issued in the stock dividend.[11] To illustrate, assume that the stockholders' equity accounts of Hendrix Corporation as of December 15 are as follows:

Common Stock, $20 par (2,000,000 shares issued)	$40,000,000
Paid-In Capital in Excess of Par—Common Stock	9,000,000
Retained Earnings	26,600,000

On December 15, the board of directors declares a stock dividend of 5% or 100,000 shares (2,000,000 shares × 5%) to be issued on January 10 to stockholders of record on December 31. The market price of the stock on the declaration date is $31 a share. The entry to record the declaration is as follows:

[11] The use of fair market value is justified as long as the number of shares issued for the stock dividend is small (less than 25% of the shares outstanding).

Dec.	15	Stock Dividends (100,000 × $31 market price)	3,100 0 0 0 00		
		Stock Dividends Distributable			
		(100,000 × $20 Par)		2,000 0 0 0 00	
		Paid-In Capital in Excess of			
		Par—Common Stock		1,100 0 0 0 00	
		Declared stock dividend.			

The $3,100,000 balance in Stock Dividends is closed to Retained Earnings on December 31. The stock dividends distributable account is listed in the Paid-In Capital section of the balance sheet. Thus, the effect of the stock dividend is to transfer $3,100,000 of retained earnings to paid-in capital.

On January 10, the number of shares outstanding is increased by 100,000 by the following entry to record the issue of the stock:

Jan.	10	Stock Dividends Distributable	2,000 0 0 0 00	
		Common Stock		2,000 0 0 0 00
		Issued stock for the stock dividend.		

A stock dividend does not change the assets, liabilities, or total stockholders' equity of the corporation. Likewise, it does not change a stockholder's proportionate interest (equity) in the corporation. For example, if a stockholder owned 1,000 of a corporation's 10,000 shares outstanding, the stockholder owns 10% (1,000/10,000) of the corporation. After declaring a 6% stock dividend, the corporation will issue 600 additional shares (10,000 shares × 6%), and the total shares outstanding will be 10,600. The stockholder of 1,000 shares will receive 60 additional shares and will now own 1,060 shares, which is still a 10% equity.

FINANCIAL ANALYSIS AND INTERPRETATION

OBJECTIVE 8

Compute and interpret the dividend yield on common stock.

The dividend yield indicates the rate of return to stockholders in terms of cash dividend distributions. Although the dividend yield can be computed for both preferred and common stock, it is most often computed for common stock. This is because most preferred stock has a stated dividend rate or amount. In contrast, the amount of common stock dividends normally varies with the profitability of the corporation.

The dividend yield is computed by dividing the annual dividends paid per share of common stock by the market price per share at a specific date, as shown below:

$$\text{Dividend Yield} = \frac{\textbf{Dividends per Share of Common Stock}}{\textbf{Market Price per Share of Common Stock}}$$

To illustrate, the market price of **Coca-Cola's** common stock was $61 as of the close of business, February 14, 1997. During the past year, Coca-Cola had paid dividends of $0.50 per share. Thus, the dividend yield of Coca-Cola's common stock is 0.8% ($0.50/$61). Because the market price of a corporation's stock will vary from day to day, its dividend yield will also vary from day to day.

The dividend yield on common stock is of special interest to investors whose main objective is to receive a current dividend return on their investment. This is in contrast to investors whose main objective is a rapid increase in the market price of their investments. For example, technology companies often do not pay dividends, but reinvest their earnings in research and development. The main attraction of such stocks, such as **Microsoft's** common stock, is the expectation of the market price of the stock rising. Since many factors affect stock prices, an investment strategy relying solely on market price increases is more risky than a strategy based on dividend yields.

ENCORE

The **Florida Panthers**, a National League Hockey team based in Fort Lauderdale, sold its common stock to the public. At an initial offering price of $10 per share, the stock appeared to be a bargain compared to some of the Panthers' official merchandise. For example, a Panthers' playoff cap is $19, a replica air-knit jersey is $79, and a hockey stick puck holder is $29.

Like many sports teams, the Panthers are facing some difficult financial issues. For example, the team's margins are being squeezed by players' salaries, which have more than doubled in two years. In addition, the Panthers must share the Miami Arena and some of its revenues with the **Miami Heat** basketball team. Until the Panthers move into a new arena for the 1998–99 season,

> **Would You Like to Own a Sports Team?**

they expect net losses of up to $20 million a year. The prospectus distributed to potential investors indicates that the Panthers have no plans to pay a dividend "in the foreseeable future."

But what about the thrill of owning a team and voting on draft picks, hiring and firing coaches, and attending games in the owner's box? Not likely. The stock offering is structured so that the current owner, H. Wayne Huizenga, will receive 250,000 shares of Class B common stock. While 7.3 million shares of Class A common stock will be issued to the public, each share of Class B stock has 10,000 times more voting power than 1 share of Class A stock.

So, are you interested? With no dividend, projected losses for the next two years, and no voting power, do you think that buying a share of Panthers stock would be a good in-

vestment or just end up being a piece of sports memorabilia? In November 1996 the Panthers did issue their stock at $10 per share. The stock is traded on the NYSE under the symbol *PAW*. At the end of trading on December 26, 1997, it was at $18.125 per share. ■

Source: Tim Carvell, "So You Want to Own a Team?" *Fortune*, November 11, 1996, pp. 46–48.

KEY POINTS

1 Describe the nature of the corporate form of organization.

Corporations have a separate legal existence, transferable units of stock, and limited stockholders' liability. Corporations may be either public or private corporations, and they are subject to federal income taxes.

The documents included in forming a corporation include an application of incorporation, articles of incorporation, and by-laws. Costs often incurred in organizing a corporation include legal fees, taxes, state incorporation fees, and promotional costs. Such costs are debited to an intangible asset account entitled

Organization Costs. They are normally amortized to expense over five years.

2 List the two main sources of stockholders' equity.

The two main sources of stockholders' equity are (1) capital contributed by the stockholders and others, called paid-in capital, and (2) net income retained in the business, called retained earnings. Stockholders' equity is reported in a corporation balance sheet according to these two sources.

3 List the major sources of paid-in capital, including the various classes of stock.

The main source of paid-in capital is from issuing stock. The two primary classes of stock are common stock and preferred stock. Preferred stock is normally nonparticipating and may be cumulative or noncumulative. In addition to the issuance of stock, paid-in capital may arise from donations of assets and from treasury stock transactions.

4 Journalize the entries for issuing stock.

When a corporation issues stock at par for cash, the cash account is debited and the class of stock issued is credited for its par amount. When a corporation issues stock at more than par, Paid-In Capital in Excess of Par is credited for the difference between the cash received and the par value of the stock. When stock is issued in exchange for assets other than cash, the assets acquired should be recorded at their fair market value.

When no-par stock is issued, the entire proceeds are credited to the stock account. No-par stock may be assigned a stated value per share, and the excess of the proceeds over the stated value may be credited to Paid-In Capital in Excess of Stated Value.

5 Journalize the entries for treasury stock transactions.

When a corporation buys its own stock, the cost method of accounting is normally used. Treasury Stock is debited for its cost, and Cash is credited. If the stock is resold, Treasury Stock is credited for its cost and any difference between the cost and the selling price is normally debited or credited to Paid-In Capital from Sale of Treasury Stock.

6 State the effect of stock splits on corporate financial statements.

When a corporation reduces the par or stated value of its common stock and issues a proportionate number of additional shares, a stock split has occurred. There are no changes in the balances of any corporation accounts, and no entry is required for a stock split.

7 Journalize the entries for cash dividends and stock dividends.

The entry to record a declaration of cash dividends debits Divi-

dends and credits Dividends Payable for each class of stock. The payment of dividends is recorded in the normal manner. When a stock dividend is declared, Stock Dividends is debited for the fair value of the stock to be issued. Stock Dividends Distributable is credited for the par or stated value of the common stock to be issued. The difference between the fair value of the stock and its par or stated value is credited to Paid-In Capital in Excess of Par—Common Stock. When the stock is issued on the date of payment, Stock Dividends Distributable is debited and Common Stock is credited for the par or stated value of the stock issued.

8 Compute and interpret the dividend yield on common stock.

The dividend yield indicates the rate of return to stockholders in terms of cash dividend distributions. It is computed by dividing the annual dividends paid per share of common stock by the market price per share at a specific date. This ratio is of special interest to investors whose main objective is to receive a current dividend return on their investment.

ILLUSTRATIVE PROBLEM

Altenburg Inc. is a lighting fixture wholesaler located in Arizona. During its current fiscal year, ended December 31, 2000, Altenburg Inc. completed the following selected transactions:

Feb. 3. Purchased 2,500 shares of its own common stock at $26, recording the stock at cost. (Prior to the purchase, there were 40,000 shares of $20 par common stock outstanding.)

May 1. Declared a semiannual dividend of $1 on the 10,000 shares of preferred stock and a 30¢ dividend on the common stock to stockholders of record on May 31, payable on June 15.

June 15. Paid the cash dividends.

Sep. 23. Sold 1,000 shares of treasury stock at $28, receiving cash.

Nov. 1. Declared semiannual dividends of $1 on the preferred stock and 30¢ on the common stock. In addition, a 5% common stock dividend was declared on the common stock outstanding, to be capitalized at the fair market value of the common stock, which is estimated at $30.

Dec. 1. Paid the cash dividends and issued the certificates for the common stock dividend.

Instructions

Journalize the entries to record the transactions for Altenburg Inc.

Solution

2000					
Feb.	3	Treasury Stock	65 0 0 0 00	
		Cash		65 0 0 0 00
May	1	Cash Dividends	21 2 5 0 00	
		Cash Dividends Payable		21 2 5 0 00*
		*(10,000 × $1) + [(40,000 − 2,500)		
		× $0.30]		
June	15	Cash Dividends Payable	21 2 5 0 00	
		Cash		21 2 5 0 00
Sep.	23	Cash	28 0 0 0 00	
		Treasury Stock		26 0 0 0 00
		Paid-In Capital from Sale of Treasury Stock		2 0 0 0 00
Nov.	1	Cash Dividends	21 5 5 0 00*	
		Cash Dividends Payable		21 5 5 0 00
		*(10,000 × $1) + [(40,000 − 1,500)		
		× $0.30]		
	1	Stock Dividends	57 7 5 0 00*	
		Stock Dividends Distributable		38 5 0 0 00
		Paid-In Capital in Excess of		
		Par—Common Stock		19 2 5 0 00
		*(40,000 − 1,500) × 5% × $30		
Dec.	1	Cash Dividends Payable	21 5 5 0 00	
		Stock Dividends Distributable	38 5 0 0 00	
		Cash		21 5 5 0 00
		Common Stock		38 5 0 0 00

Matching

Match each of the following statements with its proper term. Some terms may not be used.

A. cash dividend

B. common stock

C. cumulative preferred stock

D. deficit

____ 1. Shares of ownership of a corporation.

____ 2. The owners of a corporation.

____ 3. The owners' equity in a corporation.

____ 4. Capital contributed to a corporation by the stockholders and others.

____ 5. Net income retained in a corporation.

____ 6. A debit balance in the retained earnings account.

E.   discount

F.   dividend yield

G.   nonparticipating preferred stock

H.   outstanding stock

I.   paid-in capital

J.   par

K.   preferred stock

L.   premium

M.   retained earnings

N.   stated value

O.   stock

P.   stock dividend

Q.   stock split

R.   stockholders

S.   stockholders' equity

T.   treasury stock

____ 7.   The stock in the hands of stockholders.

____ 8.   A value, similar to par value, approved by the board of directors of a corporation for no-par stock.

____ 9.   The stock outstanding when a corporation has issued only one class of stock.

____ 10. A class of stock with preferential rights over common stock.

____ 11. A class of preferred stock whose dividend rights are usually limited to a certain amount.

____ 12. A class of preferred stock that has a right to receive regular dividends that have been passed (not declared) before any common stock dividends are paid.

____ 13. The excess of the issue price of a stock over its par value.

____ 14. The excess of the par value of a stock over its issue price.

____ 15. Stock that a corporation has once issued and then reacquires.

____ 16. A reduction in the par or stated value of a common stock and the issuance of a proportionate number of additional shares.

____ 17. A cash distribution of earnings by a corporation to its shareholders.

____ 18. A distribution of shares of stock to its stockholders.

____ 19. A ratio, computed by dividing the annual dividends paid per share of common stock by the market price per share at a specific date, that indicates the rate of return to stockholders in terms of cash dividend distributions.

____ 20. The monetary amount printed on a stock certificate.

Multiple Choice

1. If a corporation has outstanding 1,000 shares of $9 cumulative preferred stock of $100 par and dividends have been passed for the preceding three years, what is the amount of preferred dividends that must be declared in the current year before a dividend can be declared on common stock?
    A. $ 9,000   C. $36,000
    B. $27,000   D. $45,000

2. Paid-in capital for a corporation may arise from which of the following sources?
    A. Issuing cumulative preferred stock
    B. Receiving donations of real estate
    C. Selling the corporation's treasury stock
    D. All of the above

3. The Stockholders' Equity section of the balance sheet may include:

A. Common Stock   C. Preferred Stock
B. Donated Capital   D. All of the above

4. If a corporation reacquires its own stock, the stock is listed on the balance sheet in the:
    A. Current Assets section.
    B. Long-Term Liabilities section.
    C. Stockholders' Equity section.
    D. Investments section.

5. A corporation has issued 25,000 shares of $100 par common stock and holds 3,000 of these shares as treasury stock. If the corporation declares a $2 per share cash dividend, what amount will be recorded as cash dividends?
    A. $22,000   C. $44,000
    B. $25,000   D. $50,000

CLASS DISCUSSION QUESTIONS

1. Contrast the owners' liability to creditors of (a) a partnership (partners) and (b) a corporation (stockholders).
2. Why is it said that the earnings of a corporation are subject to *double taxation?* Discuss.
3. Why are most large businesses organized as corporations?
4. a. What type of expenditure is charged to the organization costs account?
    b. Give examples of such expenditures.
    c. In what section of the balance sheet is the balance of Organization Costs listed?
5. Distinguish between paid-in capital and retained earnings of a corporation.
6. The retained earnings account of a corporation at the beginning of the year had a

credit balance of $175,000. The only other entry in the account during the year was a debit of $200,000 transferred from the income summary account at the end of the year. (a) What is the term applied to the $200,000 debit? (b) What is the term applied to the debit balance of retained earnings at the end of the year, after all closing entries have been posted?

7. Of two corporations organized at approximately the same time and engaged in competing businesses, one issued $100 par common stock, and the other issued $25 par common stock. Do the par designations provide any indication as to which stock is preferable as an investment? Explain.

8. What are the three basic rights that accompany ownership of a share of common stock?

9. a. Differentiate between common stock and preferred stock.
   b. Describe briefly (1) nonparticipating preferred stock and (2) cumulative preferred stock.

10. A stockbroker advises a client to "buy cumulative preferred stock. . . . With that type of stock, . . .[you] will never have to worry about losing the dividends." Is the broker right?

11. What are some sources of paid-in capital other than the issuance of stock?

12. If a corporation is given land as an inducement to locate in a particular community, (a) how should the amount of the debit to the land account be determined, and (b) what is the title of the account that should be credited for the same amount?

13. If common stock of $50 par is sold for $70, what is the $20 difference between the issue price and par called?

14. What are some of the factors that influence the market price of a corporation's stock?

15. When a corporation issues stock at a premium, is the premium income? Explain.

16. Land is acquired by a corporation for 5,000 shares of its $50 par common stock, which is currently selling for $65 per share on a national stock exchange. What accounts should be credited to record the transaction?

17. Indicate which of the following accounts would be reported as part of paid-in capital on the balance sheet:
    a. Retained Earnings
    b. Common Stock
    c. Donated Capital
    d. Preferred Stock

18. a. In what respect does treasury stock differ from unissued stock?
    b. How should treasury stock be presented on the balance sheet?

19. A corporation reacquires 7,500 shares of its own $25 par common stock for $225,000, recording it at cost. (a) What effect does this transaction have on revenue or expense of the period? (b) What effect does it have on stockholders' equity?

20. The treasury stock in Question 19 is resold for $280,000. (a) What is the effect on the corporation's revenue of the period? (b) What is the effect on stockholders' equity?

21. What is the primary purpose of a stock split?

22. What are the three conditions for the declaration and the payment of a cash dividend?

23. The dates in connection with the declaration of a cash dividend are April 1, May 15, and May 30. Identify each date.

24. A corporation with both cumulative preferred stock and common stock outstanding has a substantial credit balance in its retained earnings account at the beginning of the current fiscal year. Although net income for the current year is sufficient to pay the preferred dividend of $50,000 each quarter and a common dividend of $200,000 each quarter, the board of directors declares dividends only on the preferred stock. Suggest possible reasons for passing the dividends on the common stock.

25. An owner of 200 shares of Dunston Company common stock receives a stock dividend of 4 shares. (a) What is the effect of the stock dividend on the stockholder's proportionate interest (equity) in the corporation? (b) How does the total equity of 204 shares compare with the total equity of 200 shares before the stock dividend?

26. a. Where should a declared but unpaid cash dividend be reported on the balance sheet?
    b. Where should a declared but unissued stock dividend be reported on the balance sheet?

Warren
Reeve
Fess

Resources for Your Success On-Line at **warren.swcollege.com**

Remember! If you need additional help, visit South-Western's Web site. See page 26 for a description of the online and printed materials that are available.

EXERCISES

Exercise 12–1
Dividends per share
Objective 3

✓ Preferred stock, 3rd year: $4.00

Davenport Inc., a developer of radiology equipment, has stock outstanding as follows: 15,000 shares of $4 (4%) nonparticipating, noncumulative preferred stock of $100 par, and 250,000 shares of $75 par common. During its first five years of operations, the following amounts were distributed as dividends: first year, none; second year, $45,000; third year, $90,000; fourth year, $200,000; fifth year, $240,000. Calculate the dividends per share on each class of stock for each of the five years.

Exercise 12–2
Dividends per share
Objective 3

✓ Preferred stock, 4th year: $8.00

Taft Inc., a computer software development firm, has stock outstanding as follows: 25,000 shares of $3 (3%) cumulative, nonparticipating preferred stock of $100 par, and 100,000 shares of $50 par common. During its first five years of operations, the following amounts were distributed as dividends: first year, none; second year, $20,000; third year, $80,000; fourth year, $220,000; fifth year, $180,000. Calculate the dividends per share on each class of stock for each of the five years.

Exercise 12–3
Entries for issuing par stock
Objective 4

✓ b. $420,000

On June 5, Szabo Inc., a marble contractor, issued for cash 15,000 shares of $18 par common stock at $24, and on August 7, it issued for cash 5,000 shares of $10 par preferred stock at $12.

a. Journalize the entries for June 5 and August 7.
b. What is the total amount invested (total paid-in capital) by all stockholders as of August 7?

Exercise 12–4
Entries for issuing no-par stock
Objective 4

✓ b. $175,500

On January 3, Elco Corp., a carpet wholesaler, issued for cash 2,500 shares of no-par common stock (with a stated value of $50) at $65, and on May 15, it issued for cash 1,000 shares of $10 par preferred stock at $13.

a. Journalize the entries for January 3 and May 15, assuming that the common stock is to be credited with the stated value.
b. What is the total amount invested (total paid-in capital) by all stockholders as of May 15?

Exercise 12–5
Issuing stock for assets other than cash
Objective 4

On April 10, Morriss Corporation, a wholesaler of hydraulic lifts, acquired land in exchange for 1,500 shares of $50 par common stock with a current market price of $82. Journalize the entry to record the transaction.

Exercise 12–6
Selected stock transactions
Objective 4

The Guitar Corp., an electric guitar retailer, was organized by Patty Hilderbrand, Ed Petty, and Kathy Yan. The charter authorized 50,000 shares of common stock with a par of $10. The following transactions affecting stockholders' equity were completed during the first year of operations:

a. Issued 800 shares of stock at par to Petty for cash.
b. Issued 100 shares of stock at par to Hilderbrand for promotional services rendered in connection with the organization of the corporation, and issued 900 shares of stock at par to Hilderbrand for cash.

c. Purchased land and a building from Yan. The building is mortgaged for $25,000 for 22 years at 9%, and there is accrued interest of $500 on the mortgage note at the time of the purchase. It is agreed that the land is to be priced at $30,000 and the building at $40,000, and that Yan's equity will be exchanged for stock at par. The corporation agreed to assume responsibility for paying the mortgage note and the accrued interest.

Journalize the entries to record the transactions.

Exercise 12–7
Issuing stock

Objective 4

Biomed Inc., with an authorization of 20,000 shares of preferred stock and 100,000 shares of common stock, completed several transactions involving its stock on July 1, the first day of operations. The trial balance at the close of the day follows:

Cash	450,000	
Land	90,000	
Buildings	60,000	
Preferred $5 Stock, $100 par		100,000
Paid-In Capital in Excess of Par—Preferred Stock ..		50,000
Common Stock, $50 par		320,000
Paid-In Capital in Excess of Par—Common Stock ..		130,000
	600,000	600,000

All shares within each class of stock were sold at the same price. The preferred stock was issued in exchange for the land and buildings.

Journalize the two entries to record the transactions summarized in the trial balance.

Exercise 12–8
Issuing stock

Objective 4

Office Products Inc., a wholesaler of office products, was organized on January 7 of the current year, with an authorization of 50,000 shares of $3 noncumulative preferred stock, $100 par and 250,000 shares of $20 par common stock. The following selected transactions were completed during the first year of operations:

Jan. 7. Issued 30,000 shares of common stock at par for cash.
     9. Issued 900 shares of common stock at par to an attorney in payment of legal fees for organizing the corporation.
Feb. 4. Issued 8,500 shares of common stock in exchange for land, buildings, and equipment with fair market prices of $60,000, $120,000, and $12,000, respectively.
Mar. 15. Issued 5,000 shares of preferred stock at $101 for cash.

Journalize the transactions.

Exercise 12–9
Treasury stock transactions

Objective 5

✓ b. $3,000 credit

Heavenly Inc. bottles and distributes spring water. On July 1 of the current year, Heavenly Inc. reacquired 3,000 shares of its common stock at $40 per share. On August 10, Heavenly Inc. sold 1,500 of the reacquired shares at $43 per share. The remaining 1,500 shares were sold at $39 per share on December 19.

a. Journalize the transactions of July 1, August 10, and December 19.
b. What is the balance in Paid-In Capital from Sale of Treasury Stock on December 31 of the current year?
c. Where will the balance in Paid-In Capital from Sale of Treasury Stock be reported on the balance sheet?
d. ▰▰▰➤ For what reasons might Heavenly Inc. have purchased the treasury stock?

Exercise 12–10
Treasury stock transactions

Objective 5

✓ b. $44,000 credit

Spray Inc. develops and produces spraying equipment for lawn maintenance and industrial uses. On October 1 of the current year, Spray Inc. reacquired 7,500 shares of its common stock at $89 per share. On November 15, 2,000 of the reacquired shares were sold at $93 per share, and on December 28, 4,000 of the reacquired shares were sold at $98.

a. Journalize the transactions of October 1, November 15, and December 28.
b. What is the balance in Paid-In Capital from Sale of Treasury Stock on December 31 of the current year?

c.   What is the balance in Treasury Stock on December 31 of the current year?

d.   How will the balance in Treasury Stock be reported on the balance sheet?

Exercise 12–11
Effect of stock split

Objective 6

✓ a. 75,000 shares

Flanagan Corporation wholesales ovens and ranges to restaurants throughout the Northeast. Flanagan Corporation, which had 15,000 shares of common stock outstanding, declared a 5-for-1 stock split (4 additional shares for each share issued).

a.   What will be the number of shares outstanding after the split?

b.   If the common stock had a market price of $175 per share before the stock split, what would be an approximate market price per share after the split?

Exercise 12–12
Effect of cash dividend and stock split

Objectives 6, 7

Indicate whether the following actions would (+) increase, (−) decrease, or (0) not affect Collier Inc.'s total assets, liabilities, and stockholders' equity:

		Assets	Liabilities	Stockholders' Equity
(1)	Declaring a cash dividend	_____	_____	_____
(2)	Paying the cash dividend declared in (1)	_____	_____	_____
(3)	Declaring a stock dividend	_____	_____	_____
(4)	Issuing stock certificates for the stock dividend declared in (3)	_____	_____	_____
(5)	Authorizing and issuing stock certificates in a stock split	_____	_____	_____

Exercise 12–13
Entries for cash dividends

Objective 7

The dates of importance in connection with a cash dividend of $60,000 on a corporation's common stock are January 3, January 27, and February 15. Journalize the entries required on each date.

Exercise 12–14
Entries for stock dividends

Objective 7

✓ b. (1) $342,500
   (3) $642,000

Quick-Fix Inc. is an HMO for twelve businesses in the Cincinnati area. The following account balances appear on the balance sheet of Quick-Fix Inc.: Common stock (50,000 shares authorized), $10 par, $300,000; Paid-in capital in excess of par—common stock, $42,500; and Retained earnings, $299,500. The board of directors declared a 2% stock dividend when the market price of the stock was $16 a share. Quick-Fix Inc. reported no income or loss for the current year.

a.   Journalize the entries to record (1) the declaration of the dividend, capitalizing an amount equal to market value, and (2) the issuance of the stock certificates.

b.   Determine the following amounts before the stock dividend was declared: (1) total paid-in capital, (2) total retained earnings, and (3) total stockholders' equity.

c.   Determine the following amounts after the stock dividend was declared and closing entries were recorded at the end of the year: (1) total paid-in capital, (2) total retained earnings, and (3) total stockholders' equity.

Exercise 12–15
Selected stock and dividend transactions

Objectives 4, 6, 7

Selected transactions completed by SWAT Boating Supply Corporation during the current fiscal year are as follows:

Jan.   9. Split the common stock 3 for 1 and reduced the par from $75 to $25 per share. After the split, there were 150,000 common shares outstanding.

Mar.   1. Declared semiannual dividends of $2 on 5,000 shares of preferred stock and $0.50 on the common stock to stockholders of record on March 25, payable on April 15.

Apr.   15. Paid the cash dividends.

Nov.   30. Declared semiannual dividends of $2 on the preferred stock and $0.80 on the common stock (before the stock dividend). In addition, a 2% common stock dividend was declared on the common stock outstanding. The fair market value of the common stock is estimated at $51.

Dec.   30. Paid the cash dividends and issued the certificates for the common stock dividend.

Journalize the transactions.

Exercise 12–16
Dividend yield

Objective 8

  HAT

The finincial statements for **Hershey Foods Corporation** are presented in Appendix G at the end of this text.

a. Determine Hershey's dividend yield as of December 31, 1996 and 1995 on common stock (exclude Class B Common Stock).
Note: Hershey's common stock price was $43.75 and $32.50 on December 31, 1996 and 1995, respectively.

b. What conclusions can you reach from an analysis of these data?

PROBLEMS SERIES A

Problem 12–1A
Dividends on preferred and common stock

Objective 3

SPREADSHEET

✓ I. Common dividends in 1996: $5,000

Gallatin Corp. manufactures mountain bikes and distributes them through retail outlets in Colorado and Montana. Gallatin Corp. has declared the following annual dividends over a six-year period: 1996, $25,000; 1997, $8,000; 1998, $10,000; 1999, $4,000; 2000, $50,000; and 2001, $75,500. During the entire period, the outstanding stock of the company was composed of 10,000 shares of cumulative, nonparticipating, $2 preferred stock, $50 par, and 25,000 shares of common stock, $10 par.

Instructions

1. Calculate the total dividends and the per-share dividends declared on each class of stock for each of the six years. There were no dividends in arrears on January 1, 1996. Summarize the data in tabular form, using the following column headings:

Year	Total Dividends	Preferred Dividends Total	Per Share	Common Dividends Total	Per Share
1996	$25,000				
1997	8,000				
1998	10,000				
1999	4,000				
2000	50,000				
2001	75,500				

2. Calculate the average annual dividend per share for each class of stock for the six-year period.
3. Assuming that the preferred stock was sold at par and common stock was sold at $10 at the beginning of the six-year period, calculate the percentage return on initial shareholders' investment, based on the average annual dividend per share (a) for preferred stock and (b) for common stock.

Problem 12–2A
Stock transaction for corporate expansion

Objective 4

VXT Corp. produces medical lasers for use in hospitals. The following accounts and their balances appear in the ledger of VXT Corp. on April 30 of the current year:

Preferred $9 Stock, $100 par (20,000 shares authorized, 8,000 shares issued)	$ 800,000
Paid-In Capital in Excess of Par—Preferred Stock	86,000
Common Stock, $20 par (100,000 shares authorized, 75,000 shares issued)	1,500,000
Paid-In Capital in Excess of Par—Common Stock	210,000
Retained Earnings	715,000

At the annual stockholders' meeting on May 12, the board of directors presented a plan for modernizing and expanding plant operations at a cost of approximately $1,000,000. The plan provided (a) that the corporation borrow $220,000, (b) that 3,000 shares of the unissued preferred stock be issued through an underwriter, and (c) that a building, valued at $355,000, and the land on which it is located, valued at $100,000, be acquired in accordance with preliminary negotiations by the issuance of 16,000 shares of common stock. The plan was approved by the stockholders and accomplished by the following transactions:

June 2. Borrowed $220,000 from Palmer National Bank, giving a 10% mortgage note.
     10. Issued 3,000 shares of preferred stock, receiving $108 per share in cash from the underwriter.
     30. Issued 16,000 shares of common stock in exchange for land and a building, according to the plan.

No other transactions occurred during June.

Instructions
Journalize the entries to record the foregoing transactions.

Problem 12–3A
Selected stock transactions

Objectives 4, 5, 7

GENERAL LEDGER
HAT

Robin Corporation sells and services pipe welding equipment in Texas. The following selected accounts appear in the ledger of Robin Corporation on January 1, 2000, the beginning of the current fiscal year:

Preferred 3% Stock, $100 par (20,000 shares authorized, 12,500 shares issued)	$1,250,000
Paid-In Capital in Excess of Par—Preferred Stock	112,500
Common Stock, $10 par (600,000 shares authorized, 400,000 shares issued)	4,000,000
Paid-In Capital in Excess of Par—Common Stock	600,000
Retained Earnings	1,450,000

During the year, the corporation completed a number of transactions affecting the stockholders' equity. They are summarized as follows:

a. Purchased 20,000 shares of treasury common for $380,000.
b. Sold 5,000 shares of treasury common for $135,000.
c. Sold 3,000 shares of preferred 3% stock at $110.
d. Issued 50,000 shares of common stock at $32, receiving cash.
e. Sold 10,000 shares of treasury common for $170,000.
f. Declared cash dividends of $3 per share on preferred stock and $0.25 per share on common stock.
g. Paid the cash dividends.

Instructions
Journalize the entries to record the transactions. Identify each entry by letter.

Problem 12–4A
Entries for selected corporate transactions

Objectives 4, 5, 7

GENERAL LEDGER
HAT

✓ 3. $1,850,470

GPS Enterprises Inc. produces aeronautical navigation equipment. The stockholders' equity accounts of GPS Enterprises Inc., with balances on January 1 of the current fiscal year, are as follows:

Common Stock, $10 stated value (100,000 shares authorized, 80,000 shares issued)	$800,000
Paid-In Capital in Excess of Stated Value	180,000
Retained Earnings	497,750
Treasury Stock (4,000 shares, at cost)	60,000

The following selected transactions occurred during the year:

Jan. 31. Paid cash dividends of $1 per share on the common stock. The dividend had been properly recorded when declared on December 28 of the preceding fiscal year for $76,000.
Mar. 7. Sold all of the treasury stock for $81,000.
May 5. Issued 10,000 shares of common stock for $210,000.
June 11. Received land from the Olinville City Council as a donation. The land had an estimated fair market value of $75,000.
July 30. Declared a 4% stock dividend on common stock, to be capitalized at the market price of the stock, which is $22 a share.

Aug. 27. Issued the certificates for the dividend declared on July 30.

Oct. 8. Purchased 2,000 shares of treasury stock for $42,500.

Dec. 20. Declared an $0.80-per-share dividend on common stock.

     31. Closed the credit balance of the income summary account, $182,500.

     31. Closed the two dividends accounts to Retained Earnings.

Instructions

1. Enter the January 1 balances in T accounts for the stockholders' equity accounts listed. Also prepare T accounts for the following: Paid-In Capital from Sale of Treasury Stock; Donated Capital; Stock Dividends Distributable; Stock Dividends; Cash Dividends.

2. Journalize the entries to record the transactions, and post to the nine selected accounts.

3. Determine the total stockholders' equity on December 31.

Problem 12–5A

Entries for selected corporate transactions

Objectives 4, 5, 6, 7

GENERAL LEDGER

HAT

Ocean Pacific Corporation manufactures and distributes leisure clothing. Selected transactions completed by Ocean Pacific during the current fiscal year are as follows:

Jan. 2. Split the common stock 5 for 1 and reduced the par from $50 to $10 per share. After the split, there were 75,000 common shares outstanding.

Mar. 3. Declared semiannual dividends of $4 on 10,000 shares of preferred stock and $0.60 on the 75,000 shares of $10 par common stock to stockholders of record on March 28, payable on April 15.

Apr. 15. Paid the cash dividends.

     30. Purchased 8,000 shares of the corporation's own common stock at $17, recording the stock at cost.

July 10. Sold 3,000 shares of treasury stock at $20, receiving cash.

     23. Declared semiannual dividends of $4 on the preferred stock and $0.75 on the common stock (before the stock dividend). In addition, a 2% common stock dividend was declared on the common stock outstanding, to be capitalized at the fair market value of the common stock, which is estimated at $21.

Aug. 25. Paid the cash dividends and issued the certificates for the common stock dividend.

Instructions

Journalize the transactions.

PROBLEMS SERIES B

Problem 12–1B

Dividends on preferred and common stock

Objective 3

SPREADSHEET

✓ 1. Common dividends in 1998: $31,000

TCX Inc. owns and operates movie theaters throughout Georgia and Alabama. TCX Inc. has declared the following annual dividends over a six-year period: 1996, $32,000; 1997, $65,000; 1998, $84,000; 1999, $60,000; 2000, $72,000; and 2001, $95,000. During the entire period, the outstanding stock of the company was composed of 5,000 shares of cumulative, nonparticipating, $10 preferred stock, $100 par, and 20,000 shares of common stock, $10 par.

Instructions

1. Calculate the total dividends and the per-share dividends declared on each class of stock for each of the six years. There were no dividends in arrears on January 1, 1996. Summarize the data in tabular form, using the following column headings:

Year	Total Dividends	Preferred Dividends		Common Dividends	
		Total	Per Share	Total	Per Share
1996	$32,000				
1997	65,000				
1998	84,000				
1999	60,000				
2000	72,000				
2001	95,000				

2. Calculate the average annual dividend per share for each class of stock for the six-year period.

3. Assuming that the preferred stock was sold at par and common stock was sold at $15 at the beginning of the six-year period, calculate the percentage return on initial shareholders' investment, based on the average annual dividend per share (a) for preferred stock and (b) for common stock.

Problem 12–2B

Stock transactions for corporate expansion

Objective 4

On January 1 of the current year, the following accounts and their balances appear in the ledger of Teca Corp., a meat processor:

Preferred $9 Stock, $100 par (10,000 shares authorized, 5,000 shares issued)	$ 500,000
Paid-In Capital in Excess of Par—Preferred Stock	80,000
Common Stock, $20 par (100,000 shares authorized, 75,000 shares issued)	1,500,000
Paid-In Capital in Excess of Par—Common Stock	125,000
Retained Earnings	505,000

At the annual stockholders' meeting on February 11, the board of directors presented a plan for modernizing and expanding plant operations at a cost of approximately $800,000. The plan provided (a) that a building, valued at $280,000, and the land on which it is located, valued at $50,000, be acquired in accordance with preliminary negotiations by the issuance of 12,000 shares of common stock, (b) that 2,500 shares of the unissued preferred stock be issued through an underwriter, and (c) that the corporation borrow $200,000. The plan was approved by the stockholders and accomplished by the following transactions:

Mar. 3. Issued 12,000 shares of common stock in exchange for land and a building, according to the plan.

  15. Issued 2,500 shares of preferred stock, receiving $104 per share in cash from the underwriter.

  31. Borrowed $200,000 from Highland National Bank, giving a 9% mortgage note.

No other transactions occurred during March.

Instructions

Journalize the entries to record the foregoing transactions.

Problem 12–3B

Selected stock transactions

Objectives 4, 5, 7

GENERAL LEDGER

The following selected accounts appear in the ledger of KWR Environmental Corporation on July 1, 1999, the beginning of the current fiscal year:

Preferred 4% Stock, $50 par (10,000 shares authorized, 7,000 shares issued)	$350,000
Paid-In Capital in Excess of Par—Preferred Stock	28,000
Common Stock, $20 par (50,000 shares authorized, 25,000 shares issued)	500,000
Paid-In Capital in Excess of Par—Common Stock	90,000
Retained Earnings	537,000

During the year, the corporation completed a number of transactions affecting the stockholders' equity. They are summarized as follows:

a. Issued 5,000 shares of common stock at $30, receiving cash.

b. Sold 1,000 shares of preferred 4% stock at $53.

c. Purchased 2,500 shares of treasury common for $60,000.

d. Sold 1,500 shares of treasury common for $45,000.

e. Sold 500 shares of treasury common for $11,500.

f. Declared cash dividends of $2 per share on preferred stock and $1 per share on common stock.

g. Paid the cash dividends.

Instructions

Journalize the entries to record the transactions. Identify each entry by letter.

Problem 12–4B

Entries for selected corporate transactions

Objectives 4, 5, 7

GENERAL LEDGER

✓ 3. $2,692,090

Pittard Enterprises Inc. manufactures bathroom fixtures. The stockholders' equity accounts of Pittard Enterprises Inc., with balances on January 1 of the current fiscal year, are as follows:

Common Stock, $25 stated value (100,000 shares authorized, 50,000 shares issued)	$1,250,000
Paid-In Capital in Excess of Stated Value	250,000
Retained Earnings	725,000
Treasury Stock (2,500 shares, at cost)	80,000

The following selected transactions occurred during the year:

Jan. 20. Received land from the city as a donation. The land had an estimated fair market value of $150,000.
29. Paid cash dividends of $1 per share on the common stock. The dividend had been properly recorded when declared on December 30 of the preceding fiscal year for $47,500.
Mar. 3. Issued 6,000 shares of common stock for $240,000.
Apr. 1. Sold all of the treasury stock for $105,000.
July 1. Declared a 2% stock dividend on common stock, to be capitalized at the market price of the stock, which is $42 a share.
Aug. 11. Issued the certificates for the dividend declared on July 1.
Nov. 20. Purchased 2,500 shares of treasury stock for $90,000.
Dec. 21. Declared a $0.50-per-share dividend on common stock.
31. Closed the credit balance of the income summary account, $169,400.
31. Closed the two dividends accounts to Retained Earnings.

Instructions

1. Enter the January 1 balances in T accounts for the stockholders' equity accounts listed. Also prepare T accounts for the following: Paid-In Capital from Sale of Treasury Stock; Donated Capital; Stock Dividends Distributable; Stock Dividends; Cash Dividends.
2. Journalize the entries to record the transactions, and post to the nine selected accounts.
3. Determine the total stockholders' equity on December 31.

Problem 12–5B

Entries for selected corporate transactions

Objectives 4, 5, 6, 7

GENERAL LEDGER

Selected transactions completed by CSB Boating Supply Corporation during the current fiscal year are as follows:

Jan. 9. Split the common stock 4 for 1 and reduced the par from $100 to $25 per share. After the split, there were 100,000 common shares outstanding.
Feb. 10. Purchased 5,000 shares of the corporation's own common stock at $38, recording the stock at cost.
May 1. Declared semiannual dividends of $3 on 5,000 shares of preferred stock and $0.80 on the common stock to stockholders of record on May 20, payable on July 15.
July 15. Paid the cash dividends.
Aug. 22. Sold 2,500 shares of treasury stock at $44, receiving cash.
Nov. 30. Declared semiannual dividends of $3 on the preferred stock and $0.90 on the common stock (before the stock dividend). In addition, a 2% common stock dividend was declared on the common stock outstanding. The fair market value of the common stock is estimated at $51.
Dec. 30. Paid the cash dividends and issued the certificates for the common stock dividend.

Instructions

Journalize the transactions.

SPECIAL ACTIVITIES

**Activity 12–1
Resources Unlimited
Inc.**

*Ethics and professional
conduct in business*

Aubrey Stone and Karl Murray are organizing Resources Unlimited Inc. to undertake a high-risk gold-mining venture in Mexico. Aubrey and Karl tentatively plan to request authorization for 100,000,000 shares of common stock to be sold to the general public. Aubrey and Karl have decided to establish par of $0.10 per share in order to appeal to a wide variety of potential investors. Aubrey and Karl feel that investors would be more willing to invest in the company if they received a large quantity of shares for what might appear to be a "bargain" price.

➤ Discuss whether Aubrey and Karl are behaving in a professional manner.

**Activity 12–2
Wellness Inc.**

Issuing stock

**What do you
THINK?**

Wellness Inc. began operations on January 3, 2000, with the issuance of 50,000 shares of $100 par common stock. The sole stockholders of Wellness Inc. are Neal Barnes and Dr. Donna Elfand, who organized Wellness Inc. with the objective of developing a new flu vaccine. Dr. Elfand claims that the flu vaccine, which is nearing the final development stage, will protect individuals against 98% of the flu types that have been medically identified. To complete the project, Wellness Inc. needs $3,000,000 of additional funds. The local banks have been unwilling to loan the funds because of the lack of sufficient collateral and the riskiness of the business.

The following is a conversation between Neal Barnes, the chief executive officer of Wellness Inc., and Dr. Donna Elfand, the leading researcher.

Barnes: What are we going to do? The banks won't loan us any more money, and we've got to have $3 million to complete the project. We are so close! It would be a disaster to quit now. The only thing I can think of is to issue additional stock. Do you have any suggestions?

Elfand: I guess you're right. But if the banks won't loan us any more money, how do you think we can find any investors to buy stock?

Barnes: I've been thinking about that. What if we promise the investors that we will pay them 2% of net sales until they have received an amount equal to what they paid for the stock?

Elfand: What happens when we pay back the $3 million? Do the investors get to keep the stock? If they do, it'll dilute our ownership.

Barnes: How about, if after we pay back the $3 million, we make them turn in their stock for $200 per share? That's twice what they paid for it, plus they would have already gotten all their money back. That's a $200 profit per share for the investors.

Elfand: It could work. We get our money, but don't have to pay any interest, dividends, or the $200 until we start generating net sales. At the same time, the investors could get their money back plus $200 per share.

Barnes: We'll need current financial statements for the new investors. I'll get our accountant working on them and contact our attorney to draw up a legally binding contract for the new investors. Yes, this could work.

In late 2000, the attorney and the various regulatory authorities approved the new stock offering, and 30,000 shares of common stock were privately sold to new investors at the stock's par of $100.

In preparing financial statements for 2000, Neal Barnes and Chris Thaxton, the controller for Wellness Inc., have the following conversation.

Thaxton: Neal, I've got a problem.
Barnes: What's that, Chris?
Thaxton: Issuing common stock to raise that additional $3 million was a great idea. But . . .
Barnes: But what?
Thaxton: I've got to prepare the 2000 annual financial statements, and I am not sure how to classify the common stock.
Barnes: What do you mean? It's common stock.

Thaxton: I'm not so sure. I called the auditor and explained how we are contractually obligated to pay the new stockholders 2% of net sales until $100 per share is paid. Then, we may be obligated to pay them $200 per share.

Barnes: So . . .

Thaxton: So the auditor thinks that we should classify the additional issuance of $3 million as debt, not stock! And, if we put the $3 million on the balance sheet as debt, we will violate our other loan agreements with the banks. And, if these agreements are violated, the banks may call in all our debt immediately. If they do that, we are in deep trouble. We'll probably have to file for bankruptcy. We just don't have the cash to pay off the banks.

1. ▰▬▶ Discuss the arguments for and against classifying the issuance of the $3 million of stock as debt.

2. ▰▬▶ What do you think might be a practical solution to this classification problem?

Activity 12–3
Tidmore Inc.
Dividends

Tidmore Inc. has paid quarterly cash dividends since 1990. These dividends have steadily increased from $0.20 per share to the latest dividend declaration of $0.50 per share. The board of directors would like to continue this trend and is hesitant to suspend or decrease the amount of quarterly dividends. Unfortunately, sales dropped sharply in the fourth quarter of 2000 because of worsening economic conditions and increased competition. As a result, the board is uncertain as to whether it should declare a dividend for the last quarter of 2000.

On November 1, 2000, Tidmore Inc. borrowed $500,000 from Second National Bank to use in modernizing its retail stores and to expand its product line in reaction to its competition. The terms of the 10-year, 12% loan require Tidmore Inc. to:

a. Pay monthly interest on last day of month.
b. Pay $50,000 of the principal each November 1, beginning in 2001.
c. Maintain a current ratio (current assets ÷ current liabilities) of 2.
d. Maintain a minimum balance (a compensating balance) of $25,000 in its Second National Bank account.

On December 31, 2000, the $500,000 loan had been disbursed in modernization of the retail stores and in expansion of the product line. Tidmore Inc.'s balance sheet as of December 31, 2000, is as follows:

Tidmore Inc.
Balance Sheet
December 31, 2000

Assets			
Current assets:			
Cash		$ 40,000	
Accounts receivable	$ 91,500		
Less allowance for doubtful accounts	6,500	85,000	
Merchandise inventory		500,000	
Prepaid expenses		4,500	
Total current assets			$ 629,500
Property, plant, and equipment:			
Land		$150,000	
Buildings	$950,000		
Less accumulated depreciation	215,000	735,000	
Equipment	$460,000		
Less accumulated depreciation	110,000	350,000	
Total property, plant, and equipment			1,235,000
Total assets			$1,864,500

(continues)

Liabilities

Current liabilities:

Accounts payable	$ 71,800		
Notes payable (Second National Bank)	50,000		
Salaries payable	3,200		
Total current liabilities		$125,000	
Long-term liabilities:			
Notes payable (Second National Bank)		450,000	
Total liabilities			$ 575,000

Stockholders' Equity

Paid-in capital:

Common stock, $20 par (50,000 shares authorized, 25,000 shares issued)	$500,000		
Excess of issue price over par	40,000		
Total paid-in capital		$540,000	
Retained earnings		749,500	
Total stockholders' equity			1,289,500
Total liabilities and stockholders' equity			$1,864,500

The board of directors is scheduled to meet January 10, 2001, to discuss the results of operations for 2000 and to consider the declaration of dividends for the fourth quarter of 2000. The chairman of the board has asked for your advice on the declaration of dividends.

1.   ◖■▬ What factors should the board consider in deciding whether to declare a cash dividend?
2.   ◖■▬ The board is considering the declaration of a stock dividend instead of a cash dividend. Discuss the issuance of a stock dividend from the point of view of (a) a stockholder and (b) the board of directors.

Activity 12–4
Into the Real World
Profiling a corporation

Select a public corporation you are familiar with or which interests you. Using the Internet, your school library, and other sources, develop a short (2 to 5 pages) profile of the corporation. Include in your profile the following information:

1. Name of the corporation.
2. State of incorporation.
3. Nature of its operations.
4. Total assets for the most recent balance sheet.
5. Total revenues for the most recent income statement.
6. Net income for the most recent income statement.
7. Classes of stock outstanding.
8. Market price of the stock outstanding.
9. High and low price of the stock for the past year.
10. Dividends paid for each share of stock during the past year.

In groups of three or four, discuss each corporate profile. Select one of the corporations, assuming that your group has $100,000 to invest in its stock. Summarize why your group selected the corporation it did and how financial accounting information may have affected your decision. Keep track of the performance of your corporation's stock for the remainder of the term.

Note: Most major corporations maintain "home pages" on the Internet. This home page provides a variety of information on the corporation and often includes the corporation's financial statements. In addition, the New York Stock Exchange Web site (**www.nyse.com**) includes links to the home pages of many listed companies. Financial statements can also be accessed using EDGAR, the electronic archives of financial statements filed with the Securities and Exchange Commission (SEC). The EDGAR Internet address is **www.sec.gov/edgarhp.htm.**

To obtain annual report information, type in a company name on the "Search EDGAR Archives" form. EDGAR will list the reports available for the selected company. A company's annual report (along with other information) is provided in its annual 10-K report to the SEC. Click on the 10-K (or 10-K405) report for the year you wish to download. If you wish, you can save the whole 10-K report to a file, then open it with your word processor.

ANSWERS TO SELF-EXAMINATION QUESTIONS

Matching

1.	O	4.	I	7.	H	10.	K	13.	L	15.	T	17.	A	19.	F
2.	R	5.	M	8.	N	11.	G	14.	E	16.	Q	18.	P	20.	J
3.	S	6.	D	9.	B	12.	C								

Multiple Choice

1. **C** If a corporation has cumulative preferred stock outstanding, dividends that have been passed for prior years plus the dividend for the current year must be paid before dividends may be declared on common stock. In this case, dividends of $27,000 ($9,000 × 3) have been passed for the preceding three years, and the current year's dividends are $9,000, making a total of $36,000 (answer C) that must be paid to preferred stockholders before dividends can be declared on common stock.

2. **D** Paid-in capital is one of the two major subdivisions of the stockholders' equity of a corporation. It may result from many sources, including the issuance of cumulative preferred stock (answer A), the receipt of donated real estate (answer B), or the sale of a corporation's treasury stock (answer C).

3. **D** The Stockholders' Equity section of corporate balance sheets is divided into two principal subsections: (1) investments contributed by the stockholders and others and (2) net income retained in the business. Included as part of the investments by stockholders and others is the par of common stock (answer A), donated capital (answer B), and the par of preferred stock (answer C).

4. **C** Reacquired stock, known as treasury stock, should be listed in the Stockholders' Equity section (answer C) of the balance sheet. The price paid for the treasury stock is deducted from the total of all the stockholders' equity accounts.

5. **C** If a corporation that holds treasury stock declares a cash dividend, the dividends are not paid on the treasury shares. To do so would place the corporation in the position of earning income through dealing with itself. Thus, the corporation will record $44,000 (answer C) as cash dividends [(25,000 shares issued less 3,000 shares held as treasury stock) × $2 per share dividend].

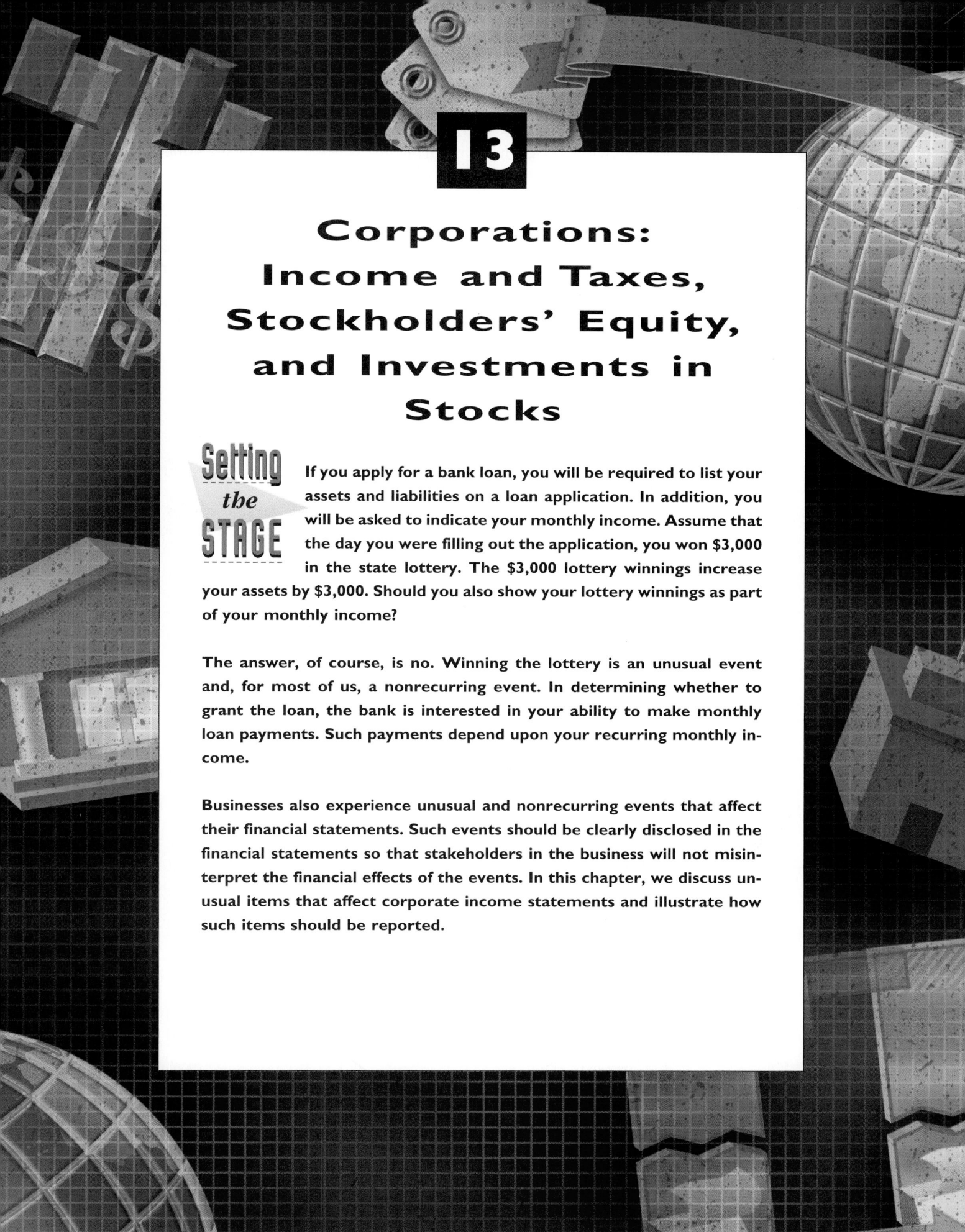

13

Corporations: Income and Taxes, Stockholders' Equity, and Investments in Stocks

Setting the STAGE

If you apply for a bank loan, you will be required to list your assets and liabilities on a loan application. In addition, you will be asked to indicate your monthly income. Assume that the day you were filling out the application, you won $3,000 in the state lottery. The $3,000 lottery winnings increase your assets by $3,000. Should you also show your lottery winnings as part of your monthly income?

The answer, of course, is no. Winning the lottery is an unusual event and, for most of us, a nonrecurring event. In determining whether to grant the loan, the bank is interested in your ability to make monthly loan payments. Such payments depend upon your recurring monthly income.

Businesses also experience unusual and nonrecurring events that affect their financial statements. Such events should be clearly disclosed in the financial statements so that stakeholders in the business will not misinterpret the financial effects of the events. In this chapter, we discuss unusual items that affect corporate income statements and illustrate how such items should be reported.

1 Journalize the entries for corporate income taxes, including deferred income taxes.

2 Prepare an income statement reporting the following unusual items: discontinued operations, extraordinary items, and changes in accounting principles.

3 Prepare an income statement reporting earnings per share data.

4 Prepare financial statement presentations of stockholders' equity.

5 Describe the concept and the reporting of comprehensive income.

6 Describe the accounting for investments in stocks.

7 Describe alternative methods of combining businesses and how consolidated financial statements are prepared.

8 Compute and interpret the price-earnings ratio.

Corporate Income Taxes

OBJECTIVE 1

Journalize the entries for corporate income taxes, including deferred income taxes.

Under the United States tax code, corporations are taxable entities that must pay federal income taxes. Depending upon where it is located, a corporation may also be required to pay state and local income taxes. Although we limit our discussion to federal income taxes, the basic concepts also apply to other income taxes.

Payment of Income Taxes

Most corporations are required to pay estimated federal income taxes in four installments throughout the year. For example, assume that a corporation with a calendar-year accounting period estimates its income tax expense for the year as $84,000. The entry to record the first of the four estimated tax payments of $21,000 (1/4 of $84,000) is as follows:

Point of INTEREST

Individuals must pay estimated taxes (on the 15th of January, April, June, and September) if the amount of tax withholding is not sufficient to pay their taxes at the end of the year. This usually occurs when a significant portion of an individual's income is from rent, dividends, or interest.

April	15	Income Tax Expense					21	0	0	0	00						
		Cash											21	0	0	0	00
		To record quarterly payment of															
		estimated income tax.															

At year end, the actual taxable income and the related tax are determined.[1] If additional taxes are owed, the additional liability is recorded. If the total estimated tax payments are greater than the tax liability based on actual taxable income, the overpayment should be debited to a receivable account and credited to *Income Tax Expense.*

---

[1] A corporation's income tax returns and supporting records are subject to audits by taxing authorities, who may assess additional taxes. Because of this possibility, the liability for income taxes is sometimes described in the balance sheet as *Estimated income tax payable.*

Because income taxes are often a significant amount, they are normally reported on the income statement as a special deduction, as shown below in an excerpt from an income statement for **The Procter & Gamble Company**.

Years Ended June 30	1997
Net Sales	**$35,764**
Cost of products sold	20,316
Marketing, research, and administrative expenses	9,960
Operating Income	**5,488**
Interest expense	457
Other income, net	218
Earnings Before Income Taxes	**5,249**
Income taxes	1,834
Net Earnings	**$ 3,415**

Allocation of Income Taxes

The **taxable income** of a corporation is determined according to the tax laws. It is often different from the income before income taxes reported in the income statement according to generally accepted accounting principles. As a result, the *income tax based on taxable income* usually differs from the *income tax based on income before taxes*. This difference may need to be allocated between various financial statement periods, depending on the nature of the items causing the differences.

Some differences between taxable income and income before income taxes are created because items are recognized in one period for tax purposes and in another period for income statement purposes. Such differences, called **temporary differences**, reverse or turn around in later years. Some examples of items that create temporary differences are listed below.

1. *Revenues or gains are taxed* **after** *they are reported in the income statement.* Example: In some cases, companies who make sales under an installment plan recognize revenue for financial reporting purposes when a sale is made, but defer recognizing revenue for tax purposes until cash is collected.
2. *Expenses or losses are deducted in determining taxable income* **after** *they are reported in the income statement.* Example: Product warranty expense estimated and reported in the year of the sale for financial statement reporting is deducted for tax reporting when paid.
3. *Revenues or gains are taxed* **before** *they are reported in the income statement.* Example: Cash received in advance for magazine subscriptions is included in taxable income when received, but included in the income statement only when earned in a future period.
4. *Expenses or losses are deducted in determining taxable income* **before** *they are reported in the income statement.* Example: MACRS depreciation is used for tax purposes, and the straight-line method is used for financial reporting purposes.

Since temporary differences reverse in later years, they do not change or reduce the total amount of taxable income over the life of a business. Exhibit 1 illustrates the reversing nature of temporary differences in which a business uses MACRS depreciation for tax purposes and straight-line depreciation for financial statement purposes. MACRS recognizes more depreciation in the early years, but less depreciation in the later years. The total depreciation expense is the same for both methods over the life of the asset.

EXHIBIT 1
Temporary Differences

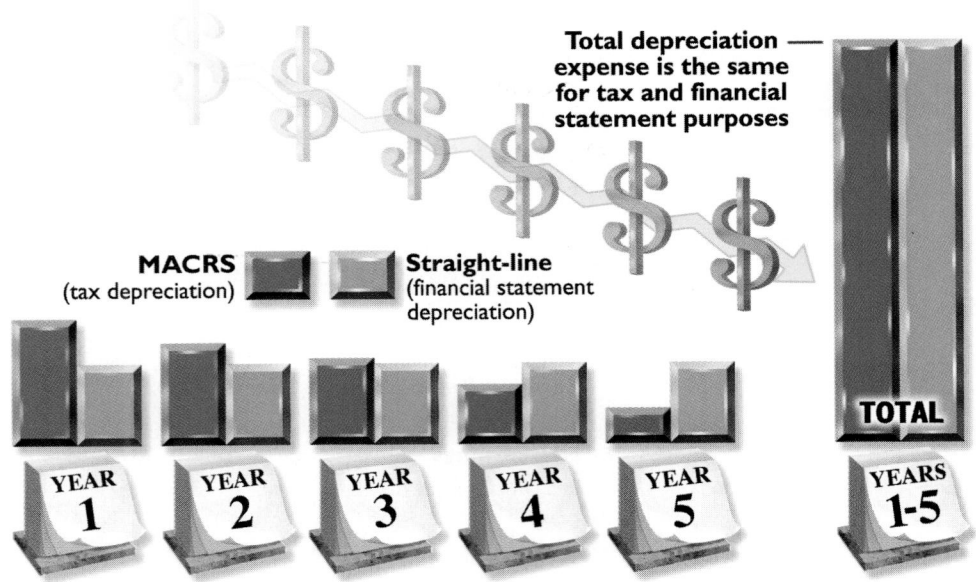

As Exhibit 1 illustrates, temporary differences affect only the timing of when revenues and expenses are recognized for tax purposes. As a result, the total amount of taxes paid does not change. Only the timing of the payment of taxes is affected. In most cases, managers use tax-planning techniques so that temporary differences delay or defer the payment of taxes to later years. As a result, at the end of each year, the amount of the current tax liability and the postponed (deferred) liability must be recorded.

To illustrate, assume that at the end of the first year of operations a corporation reports $300,000 income before income taxes on its income statement. If we assume an income tax rate of 40%, the income tax expense reported on the income statement is $120,000 ($300,000 × 40%).[2] However, to reduce the amount owed for current income taxes, the corporation uses tax planning to reduce the taxable income to $100,000. Thus, the income tax actually due for the year is only $40,000 ($100,000 × 40%). The $80,000 ($120,000 − $40,000) difference between the two tax amounts is created by timing differences in recognizing revenue. This amount is deferred to future years. The example is summarized below.

Income tax based on $300,000 reported income at 40%	$120,000
Income tax based on $100,000 taxable income at 40%	40,000
Income tax deferred to future years	$ 80,000

To match the current year's expenses (including income tax) against the current year's revenue on the income statement, income tax is allocated between periods, using the following journal entry:

Income Tax Expense		120 0 0 0 00	
Income Tax Payable			40 0 0 0 00
Deferred Income Tax Payable			80 0 0 0 00
To record income tax for the year.			

A corporation has $300,000 income before income taxes and $130,000 taxable income. What is the amount of deferred income tax?

$68,000 [($300,000 × 40%) − ($130,000 × 40%)]

---

[2] For purposes of illustration, the 40% rate is assumed to include all federal, state, and local income taxes.

The income tax expense reported on the income statement is the total tax, $120,000, expected to be paid on the income for the year. In future years, the $80,000 in *Deferred Income Tax Payable* will be transferred to *Income Tax Payable* as the timing differences reverse and the taxes become due. For example, if $48,000 of the deferred tax reverses and becomes due in the second year, the following journal entry would be made in the second year:

	Deferred Income Tax Payable		48 0 0 0 00	
	Income Tax Payable			48 0 0 0 00
	To record current liability for			
	deferred tax.			

The balance of *Deferred Income Tax Payable* at the end of a year is reported as a liability. The amount due within one year is classified as a current liability. The remainder is classified as a long-term liability or reported in a Deferred Credits section following the Long-Term Liabilities section.[3]

Differences between taxable income and income (before taxes) reported on the income statement may also arise because certain revenues are exempt from tax and certain expenses are not deductible in determining taxable income.[4] For example, interest income on municipal bonds may be exempt from taxation. Such differences create no special financial reporting problems, since the amount of income tax determined according to the tax laws is the *same* amount reported on the income statement.

Point of INTEREST

Interest from investments in municipal bonds is also tax exempt for individual tax purposes.

Unusual Items that Affect the Income Statement

OBJECTIVE 2

Prepare an income statement reporting the following unusual items: discontinued operations, extraordinary items, and changes in accounting principles.

Three types of unusual items that may affect the current year's net income are:

1. The results of discontinued operations.
2. Extraordinary items that result in a gain or loss.
3. A change from one generally accepted accounting principle to another.

These items are reported separately in the income statement, as shown in the income statement for Jones Corporation in Exhibit 2. Many different terms and formats may be used. For example, the related tax effects of unusual items may be reported with the item with which they are associated or in the notes to the statement.

In the following paragraphs, we briefly discuss each of the three types of unusual items. We assume that these items are material to the financial statements. Immaterial items would not affect the normal financial statement presentation.

---

[3] In some cases, a deferred tax asset may arise for tax benefits to be received in the future. Such deferred tax assets are reported as either a current or a long-term asset, depending on when the benefits are expected to be realized.

[4] Such differences, which will not reverse with the passage of time, are sometimes called *permanent differences*.

EXHIBIT 2
Unusual Items in Income
Statement

Jones Corporation
Income Statement
For the Year Ended December 31, 2000

Net sales	$9,600,000
Cost of merchandise sold	5,800,000
Gross profit	$3,800,000
Operating expenses	2,490,000
Income from continuing operations before income tax	$1,310,000
Income tax expense	620,000
Income from continuing operations	$ 690,000
Loss on discontinued operations (Note A)	100,000
Income before extraordinary items and cumulative effect of a change in accounting principle	$ 590,000
Extraordinary item:	
Gain on condemnation of land, net of applicable income tax of $65,000	150,000
Cumulative effect on prior years of changing to a different depreciation method (Note B)	92,000
Net income	$ 832,000

Note A.

On July 1 of the current year, the electrical products division of the corporation was sold at a loss of $100,000, net of applicable income tax of $50,000. The net sales of the division for the current year were $2,900,000. The assets sold were composed of inventories, equipment, and plant totaling $2,100,000. The purchaser assumed liabilities of $600,000.

Note B.

Depreciation of all property, plant, and equipment has been computed by the straight-line method in 2000. Prior to 2000, depreciation of equipment for one of the divisions had been computed on the double-declining-balance method. In 2000, the straight-line method was adopted for this division in order to achieve uniformity and to better match depreciation charges with the estimated economic utility of such assets. Consistent with APB Opinion No. 20, this change in depreciation has been applied to prior years. The effect of the change was to increase income by $30,000 before extraordinary items for 2000. The adjustment of $92,000 (after reduction for income tax of $88,000) to apply the new method to prior years is also included in income for 2000.

Discontinued Operations

A gain or loss from disposing of a business segment is reported on the income statement as a gain or loss from **discontinued operations**. The term **business segment** refers to a major line of business for a company, such as a division or a department or a certain class of customer. For example, assume that Jones Corporation has separate divisions that produce electrical products, hardware supplies, and lawn equipment. Jones sells its electrical products division at a loss. As shown in Exhibit 2, this loss is deducted from Jones's income from continuing operations (income from its hardware and lawn equipment divisions). In addition, Note A discloses the identity of the segment sold, the disposal date, a description of the segment's assets and liabilities, and the manner of disposal.

Extraordinary Items

Extraordinary items result from events and transactions that (1) are significantly different (unusual) from the typical or the normal operating activities of the business and (2) occur infrequently. The gains and losses that result from natural disasters which occur infrequently, such as floods, earthquakes, and fires, are extraordinary items. Gains or losses from condemning land or buildings for public use are also extraordinary. Such gains and losses, other than those from disposing of a business segment, should be reported in the income statement as extraordinary items, as shown in Exhibit 2.

Events that are both unusual and infrequent are uncommon. For example, the 1996 edition of *Accounting Trends & Techniques* indicated that only 81 of 600 companies surveyed reported extraordinary items.

Sometimes extraordinary items result in unusual financial results. For example, **Delta Air Lines** once reported an extraordinary gain of over $5.5 million as the result of the crash of one of its 727s. The plane that crashed was insured for $6.5 million, but its book value in Delta's accounting records was $962,000.

Gains and losses on the disposal of fixed assets are *not* extraordinary items. This is because (1) they are not unusual and (2) they recur from time to time in the normal operations of a business. Likewise, gains and losses from the sale of investments are usual and recurring for most businesses.

Changes in Accounting Principles

Businesses are often required to change their accounting principles when the Financial Accounting Standards Board (FASB) issues a new accounting standard. In addition, a business may voluntarily change from one generally accepted accounting principle to another. For example, a corporation may change from the fifo to the lifo method of costing inventory to better match revenues and expenses. Changes in generally accepted accounting principles should be disclosed in the financial statements (or in notes to the statements) of the period in which they occur. This disclosure should include the following:

1. The nature of the change.
2. The justification for the change.
3. The effect on the current year's net income.
4. The cumulative effect of the change on the net income of prior periods.

To illustrate, assume that one of Jones Corporation's divisions changes from the double-declining-balance method to the straight-line method of depreciation. As shown in Exhibit 2, the cumulative effect of this change is reported after the extraordinary items. The effect on the prior period is explained in Note B. If financial statements for prior periods are also presented, they should be restated as if the change had been made in the prior periods, and the effect of the restatement should be reported either on the face of the statements or in a note.

 **Sears, Roebuck and Co.** reported net income of $1,801 million in 1995, $1,454 million in 1994, and $2,374 million in 1993. However, Sears also reported gains from discontinued operations of $776 million in 1995, $402 million in 1994, and $1,960 million in 1993. These gains reflect Sears' decision to refocus its efforts on its retail operations. So, for example, Sears spun off (discontinued) its **Allstate** insurance operations in 1995 at a gain of $776 million. Thus, the income from continuing operations for 1995 was $1,025 ($1,801 − $776) million. Without adequate disclosure and reporting of such unusual items, a reasonable prediction of future earnings and cash flows would be impaired.

 The 1996 edition of *Accounting Trends & Techniques* indicated that the majority of accounting changes were due to adopting a new accounting standard issued by the Financial Accounting Standards Board.

Reporting unusual items separately on the income statement allows investors to isolate the effects of these items on income and cash flows. By reporting such items, investors and other users of the financial statements can consider such factors in assessing a business's future income and cash flows.

Earnings per Common Share

OBJECTIVE 3

Prepare an income statement reporting earnings per share data.

The amount of net income is often used by investors and creditors in evaluating a company's profitability. However, net income by itself is difficult to use in comparing companies of different sizes. Also, trends in net income may be difficult to evaluate, using only net income, if there have been significant changes in a company's stockholders' equity. Thus, the profitability of companies is often expressed as earnings per share. **Earnings per common share (EPS)**, sometimes called **basic earnings per share**, is the net income per share of common stock outstanding during a period.

Because of its importance, earnings per share is reported in the financial press and by various investor services, such as **Moody's** and **Standard & Poor's**. Changes in earnings per share can lead to significant changes in the price of a corporation's stock in the marketplace. For example, **Ben & Jerry's Homemade Inc.** stock dropped to its lowest point in three years ($13.375 per share) after the company announced earnings per share of 10 cents. The premium ice cream company had earned 34 cents per share a year earlier, and Wall Street analysts had been expecting earnings of 27 cents per share. In contrast, during the same time, the stock of **Scientific-Atlanta Inc.** surged by over 13 percent to $39 per share, after the company announced earnings per share of 53 cents as compared to 25 cents per share a year earlier. Wall Street analysts had been expecting earnings per share of 41 cents.

Corporations whose stock is traded in a public market must report earnings per common share on their income statements.[5] If no preferred stock is outstanding, the earnings per common share is calculated as follows:

$$\text{Earnings per common share} = \frac{\text{Net income}}{\text{Number of common shares outstanding}}$$

When the number of common shares outstanding has changed during the period, a weighted average number of shares outstanding is used. If a company has preferred stock outstanding, the net income must be reduced by the amount of any preferred dividends, as shown below.

$$\text{Earnings per common share} = \frac{\text{Net income} - \text{Preferred stock dividends}}{\text{Number of common shares outstanding}}$$

Comparing the earnings per share of two or more years, based on only the net incomes of those years, could be misleading. For example, assume that Jones Corporation, whose partial income statement was presented in Exhibit 2, reported $700,000 net income for 1999. Also assume that no extraordinary or other unusual items were reported in 1999. Jones has no preferred stock outstanding and has 200,000 common shares outstanding in 1999 and 2000. The earnings per common share is $3.50 ($700,000/200,000 shares) for 1999 and $4.16 ($832,000/200,000 shares) for 2000. Comparing the two earnings per share amounts suggests that operations have improved. However, the 2000 earnings per share comparable to the $3.50 is $3.45, which is the income from continuing operations of $690,000 divided by 200,000 shares. The latter amount indicates a slight downturn in normal earnings.

When unusual items exist, earnings per common share should be reported for those items. To illustrate, a partial income statement for Jones Corporation, showing earnings per common share, is shown in Exhibit 3. In this income statement, Jones reports all the earnings per common share amounts on the face of the income statement. However, only earnings per share amounts for income from continuing opera-

EXHIBIT 3
Income Statement with Earnings per Share

Jones Corporation
Income Statement
For the Year Ended December 31, 2000

Earnings per common share:	
Income from continuing operations	$3.45
Loss on discontinued operations (Note A)	0.50
Income before extraordinary items and cumulative effect	
of a change in accounting principle	$2.95
Extraordinary item:	
Gain on condemnation of land, net of applicable income	
tax of $65,000	0.75
Cumulative effect on prior years of changing to a different	
depreciation method (Note B)	0.46
Net income	$4.16

[5] *Statement of Financial Accounting Standards No. 128,* "Earnings per Share," Financial Accounting Standards Board (Norwalk, Connecticut: 1997).

tions and net income are required to be presented on the face of the statement. The other per share amounts may be presented in the notes to the financial statements.[6]

In the preceding paragraphs, we have assumed a simple capital structure with only common stock or common stock and preferred stock outstanding. Often, however, corporations have complex capital structures with various types of securities outstanding, such as convertible preferred stock, options, warrants, and contingently issuable shares. In such cases, the possible effects of converting such securities to common stock must be calculated and reported in the financial statements.[7] Such effects are often reported as *earnings per common share assuming dilution* or *diluted earnings per share*. Considering the effect of such securities on earnings per share is discussed in advanced accounting texts.

Reporting Stockholders' Equity

OBJECTIVE 4

Prepare financial statement presentations of stockholders' equity.

As with other sections of the balance sheet, alternative terms and formats may be used in reporting stockholders' equity. In addition, the significant changes in the sources of stockholders' equity—paid-in capital and retained earnings—may be reported in separate statements or notes that support the balance sheet presentation.

Reporting Paid-In Capital

Two alternatives for reporting paid-in capital in the balance sheet are shown in Exhibit 4. In the first example, each class of stock is listed first, followed by its related paid-in capital accounts. In the second example, the stock accounts are listed first. The other paid-in capital accounts are listed as a single item described as *Addi-*

EXHIBIT 4
Paid-In Capital Section of Stockholders' Equity

Stockholders' Equity			
Paid-in capital:			
Preferred $5 stock, cumulative, $50 par (2,000 shares authorized and issued)	$100,000		
Excess of issue price over par	10,000	$ 110,000	
Common stock, $20 par (50,000 shares authorized, 45,000 shares issued)	$900,000		
Excess of issue price over par	132,000	1,032,000	
From donated land		60,000	
Total paid-in capital			$1,202,000

Shareholders' Equity	
Contributed capital:	
Preferred 10% stock, cumulative, $50 par (2,000 shares authorized and issued)	$100,000
Common stock, $20 par (50,000 shares authorized, 45,000 shares issued)	900,000
Additional paid-in capital	202,000
Total contributed capital	$1,202,000

[6] Ibid., pars. 36 & 37.
[7] Ibid., pars. 11–39.

tional paid-in capital. These combined accounts could also be described as *Capital in excess of par (or stated value) of shares* or a similar title.

Significant changes in paid-in capital during a period may be presented either in a *statement of stockholders' equity* or in notes to the financial statements. We describe and illustrate the statement of stockholders' equity later in this section. In addition, relevant rights and privileges of the various classes of stock outstanding must be disclosed.[8] Examples of types of information that must be disclosed include dividend and liquidation preferences, rights to participate in earnings, conversion rights, and redemption rights. Such information may be disclosed on the face of the balance sheet or in the accompanying notes.

 The 1996 edition of *Accounting Trends & Techniques* reported that over 80% of the companies surveyed presented a statement of stockholders' equity.

Reporting Retained Earnings

A corporation may report changes in retained earnings by preparing a separate retained earnings statement, a combined income and retained earnings statement, or a statement of stockholders' equity.

When a separate retained earnings statement is prepared, the beginning balance of retained earnings is reported. The net income is then added (or net loss is subtracted) and any dividends are subtracted to arrive at the ending retained earnings for the period. An example of a such a statement for Adang Corporation is shown in Exhibit 5.

 The 1996 edition of *Accounting Trends & Techniques* indicated that 6% of the companies surveyed presented a separate statement of retained earnings, 3% presented a combined income and retained earnings statement, and 9% presented changes in retained earnings in the notes to the financial statements. The other 82% of the companies presented changes in retained earnings in a statement of stockholders' equity.

EXHIBIT 5
Retained Earnings Statement

Adang Corporation **Retained Earnings Statement** **For the Year Ended June 30, 2000**		
Retained earnings, July 1, 1999		$350,000
Net income	$280,000	
Less dividends declared	75,000	
Increase in retained earnings		205,000
Retained earnings, June 30, 2000		$555,000

An alternative format for presenting the retained earnings statement is to combine it with the income statement. An advantage of the combined format is that it emphasizes net income as the connecting link between the income statement and the retained earnings portion of stockholders' equity. Since the combined form is not often used, we do not illustrate it.

Appropriations

The retained earnings available for use as dividends may be restricted by action of a corporation's board of directors. The amount restricted, called an **appropriation**, remains part of the retained earnings. However, it must be disclosed, usually in the notes to the financial statements.

Appropriations may be classified as either legal, contractual, or discretionary. The board of directors may be legally required to restrict retained earnings because

The 1996 edition of *Accounting Trends & Techniques* reported that 356 of the 600 companies surveyed disclosed dividend restrictions in notes to their financial statements.

---

[8] *Statement of Financial Accounting Standards No. 129,* "Disclosure Information about Capital Structure," Financial Accounting Standards Board (Norwalk, Connecticut: 1997).

of state laws. For example, some state laws require that retained earnings be restricted by the amount of treasury stock purchased, so that legal capital will not be used for dividends. The board may also be required to restrict retained earnings because of contractual requirements. For example, the terms of a bank loan may require restrictions, so that money for repaying the loan will not be used for dividends. Finally, the board may restrict retained earnings voluntarily. For example, the board may limit dividend distributions so that more money is available for expanding the business.

Prior Period Adjustments

Material errors in a prior period's net income may arise from mathematical mistakes and from mistakes in applying accounting principles. The effect of material errors that are not discovered within the same fiscal period in which they occurred should not be included in determining net income for the current period. Instead, corrections of such errors, called **prior period adjustments**, are reported in the retained earnings statement. These adjustments are reported as an adjustment to the retained earnings balance at the beginning of the period in which the error is discovered and corrected. Because prior period adjustments are rare, we do not illustrate their reporting.

Statement of Stockholders' Equity

Significant changes in stockholders' equity should be reported for the period in which they occur. These changes may be reported in a **statement of stockholders' equity**. This statement is often prepared in a columnar format, where each column represents a major stockholders' equity classification. Changes in each classification are then described in the left-hand column. Exhibit 6 is a statement of stockholders' equity for Telex Inc.

EXHIBIT 6   Statement of Stockholders' Equity

<table>
<tr><td colspan="7" align="center">Telex Inc.
Statement of Stockholders' Equity
For the Year Ended December 31, 2000</td></tr>
<tr><td></td><td>Preferred
Stock</td><td>Common
Stock</td><td>Paid-In
Capital in
Excess of Par—
Common Stock</td><td>Retained
Earnings</td><td>Treasury
(Common)
Stock</td><td>Total</td></tr>
<tr><td>Balance, January 1</td><td>$5,000,000</td><td>$10,000,000</td><td>$3,000,000</td><td>$2,000,000</td><td>$(500,000)</td><td>$19,500,000</td></tr>
<tr><td>Net income</td><td></td><td></td><td></td><td>850,000</td><td></td><td>850,000</td></tr>
<tr><td>Dividends on preferred stock</td><td></td><td></td><td></td><td>(250,000)</td><td></td><td>(250,000)</td></tr>
<tr><td>Dividends on common stock</td><td></td><td></td><td></td><td>(400,000)</td><td></td><td>(400,000)</td></tr>
<tr><td>Issuance of additional
  common stock</td><td></td><td>500,000</td><td>50,000</td><td></td><td></td><td>550,000</td></tr>
<tr><td>Purchase of treasury stock</td><td></td><td></td><td></td><td></td><td>(30,000)</td><td>(30,000)</td></tr>
<tr><td>Balance, December 31</td><td>$5,000,000</td><td>$10,500,000</td><td>$3,050,000</td><td>$2,200,000</td><td>$(530,000)</td><td>$20,220,000</td></tr>
</table>

Comprehensive Income

OBJECTIVE 5

Describe the concept and the reporting of comprehensive income.

In 1997, the Financial Accounting Standards Board issued an accounting standard that required the reporting concept referred to as *comprehensive income*.[9] This new standard defines **comprehensive income** as all changes in stockholders' equity

[9] *Statement of Financial Accounting Standards No. 130,* "Reporting Comprehensive Income," Financial Accounting Standards Board (Norwalk, Connecticut: 1997).

during a period except those resulting from dividends and stockholders' investments. Under this standard, companies must report traditional net income plus or minus other comprehensive income items to arrive at comprehensive income. *Other comprehensive income items* include foreign currency items, pension liability adjustments, and unrealized gains and losses on investments.

To the extent that other comprehensive income items give rise to tax effects, the taxes should be allocated to these items as we illustrated earlier in this chapter. The cumulative effects of other comprehensive income items must be reported separately from retained earnings and paid-in capital on the balance sheet. When other comprehensive income items are not present, the income statement and balance sheet formats are similar to those we have illustrated in this and preceding chapters.

Companies may report comprehensive income on the income statement, in a separate statement of comprehensive income, or in the statement of stockholders' equity. In addition, companies may use terms other than comprehensive income, such as *total nonowner changes in equity.*

You should note that comprehensive income does not affect the determination of net income or retained earnings as we have discussed and illustrated. In the next section, we will illustrate the reporting of unrealized gains and losses on investments as part of other comprehensive income.

Accounting for Investments in Stocks

OBJECTIVE 6

Describe the accounting for investments in stocks.

Corporations not only issue stock, but they also purchase stocks of other companies for investment purposes. Like individuals, businesses have a variety of reasons for investing in stocks, called **equity securities**. A business may purchase stocks as a means of earning a return (income) on excess cash that it does not need for its normal operations. Such investments are usually for a short period of time. In other cases, a business may purchase the stock of another company as a means of developing or maintaining business relationships with the other company. A business may also purchase common stock as a means of gaining control of another company's operations. In these two latter cases, the business usually intends to hold the investment for a long period of time.

The equity securities in which a business

 Warren Buffett became one of the wealthiest men in the world through wise and patient investing. Buffett invests through a public company called **Berkshire Hathaway Inc.**, of which he owns 40%. Berkshire Hathaway started as an old-line textile company. Today, however, it has over $27 billion of equity investment holdings, listed on its balance sheet as "available-for-sale" securities. Some of these investments include **Coca-Cola Company**, **Gillette Company**, and **McDonald's Corporation**.

invests may be classified as trading securities or available-for-sale securities. **Trading securities** are securities that management intends to actively trade for profit. Businesses holding trading securities are those whose normal operations involve buying and selling securities. Examples of such businesses include banks and insurance companies. **Available-for-sale securities** are securities that management expects to sell in the future, but which are not actively traded for profit. In this section, we describe and illustrate the accounting for available-for-sale equity securities. The accounting for trading securities is described and illustrated in advanced accounting texts.

Short-Term Investments in Stocks

Rather than allow excess cash to be idle until it is needed, a business may invest all or part of it in income-yielding securities. Since these investments can be quickly sold and converted to cash as needed, they are called **temporary investments** or

marketable securities. Although such investments may be retained for several years, they continue to be classified as temporary, provided they meet two conditions. First, the securities are readily marketable and can be sold for cash at any time. Second, management intends to sell the securities when the business needs cash for operations.

Temporary investments are recorded in a current asset account, *Marketable Securities,* at their cost. This cost includes all amounts spent to acquire the securities, such as broker's commissions. Any dividends received on the investment are recorded as a debit to *Cash* and a credit to *Dividend Revenue.*

To illustrate, assume that on June 1 Crabtree Co. purchased 2,000 shares of Inis Corporation common stock at $89.75 per share plus a brokerage fee of $500. On October 1, Inis declared a $0.90 per share cash dividend payable on November 30. Crabtree's entries to record the stock purchase and the receipt of the dividend are as follows:

June	1	Marketable Securities	180 0 0 0 00	
		Cash		180 0 0 0 00
		Purchased 2,000 shares of Inis		
		Corporation common stock		
		($89.75 × 2,000 shares = $179,500;		
		$179,500 + $500 = $180,000).		
Nov.	30	Cash	1 8 0 0 00	
		Dividend Revenue		1 8 0 0 00
		Received dividend on Inis Corporation		
		common stock		
		(2,000 shares × $0.90 = $1,800).		

Point of INTEREST

You may monitor market values of stocks on a continuous basis throughout the day through brokers or the major stock exchanges, such as **www.NYSE.com** or **www.Nasdaq.com**.

On the balance sheet, temporary investments are reported at their fair market value. Market values are normally available from stock quotations in financial newspapers, such as *The Wall Street Journal*. Any difference between the fair market values of the securities and their cost is an **unrealized holding gain or loss**. This gain or loss is termed "unrealized" because a transaction (the sale of the securities) is necessary before a gain or loss becomes real (realized).

To illustrate, assume that Crabtree Co.'s portfolio of temporary investments has the following fair market values and unrealized gains and losses on December 31, 2000:

Common Stock	Cost	Market	Unrealized Gain (Loss)
Edwards Inc.	$150,000	$190,000	$40,000
SWS Corp.	200,000	200,000	—
Inis Corporation	180,000	210,000	30,000
Bass Co.	160,000	150,000	(10,000)
Total	$690,000	$750,000	$60,000

If income taxes of $18,000 are allocated to the unrealized gain, Crabtree's temporary investments should be reported at their total cost of $690,000, plus the unrealized gain (net of applicable income tax) of $42,000 ($60,000 − $18,000), as shown in Exhibit 7.

EXHIBIT 7
Temporary Investments on
the Balance Sheet

Crabtree Co. Balance Sheet December 31, 2000		
Assets		
Current assets:		
Cash		$119,500
Temporary investments in marketable securities at cost	$690,000	
Plus unrealized gain (net of applicable income tax of $18,000)	42,000	732,000

The unrealized gain (net of applicable taxes) of $42,000 should also be reported as an *other comprehensive income* item, as we mentioned in the preceding section. For example, assume that Crabtree Co. has net income of $720,000 for the year ended December 31, 2000. Crabtree elects to report net income and comprehensive income on one financial statement, *Statement of Income and Comprehensive Income,* as shown in Exhibit 8.

EXHIBIT 8
Statement of Income and
Comprehensive Income

Crabtree Co. Statement of Income and Comprehensive Income For the Year Ended December 31, 2000	
Net income	$720,000
Other comprehensive income:	
Unrealized gain on temporary investments in marketable securities (net of applicable income tax of $18,000)	42,000
Comprehensive income	$762,000

Unrealized losses are reported in a similar manner. Unrealized gains and losses are reported as other comprehensive income items until the related securities are sold. When temporary securities are sold, the unrealized gains or losses become realized and are included in determining net income.[10]

Long-Term Investments in Stocks

Long-term investments in stocks are not intended as a source of cash in the normal operations of the business. They are reported in the balance sheet under the caption **Investments**, which usually follows the Current Assets section.

There are two methods of accounting for long-term investments in stock: (1) the cost method and (2) the equity method. The method used depends on whether the investor (the buyer of the stock) has a significant influence over the operating and financing activities of the company (the investee) whose stock is owned. If the investor does not have a significant influence, the cost method is used. If the investor has a significant influence, the equity method is used. Evidence of such in-

---

[10]To avoid double-counting, realized gains and losses must be removed from comprehensive income. These adjustments are discussed in advanced accounting texts.

fluence includes the percentage of ownership, the existence of intercompany transactions, and the interchange of managerial personnel. Generally, if the investor owns 20% or more of the voting stock of the investee, it is assumed that the investor has significant influence over the investee.

Cost Method

Under the **cost method**, the accounting for long-term investments in stocks is similar to that for short-term investments in stocks, which we illustrated in the preceding section. The cost of the stocks is debited to an investment (asset) account. Cash dividends received on the stock are recorded as a debit to *Cash* and a credit to *Dividend Revenue*. On the balance sheet, the stocks are reported at their fair market value net of any applicable income tax effects. In addition, the unrealized gains and losses are reported as part of the comprehensive income.[11]

To illustrate the purchase of stock and the receipt of dividends under the cost method, assume that on March 1, Makowski Corporation purchases 100 shares of Compton Corporation common stock at 59 plus a brokerage fee of $40. On April 30, Compton Corporation declares a $2-per-share dividend, payable on June 15. Makowski's entries to record the investment and the dividend are as follows:

Mar.	1	Investment in Compton Corp. Stock	5 9 4 0 00	
		Cash		5 9 4 0 00
		Purchased 100 shares of Compton		
		Corp. common stock at 59 plus		
		brokerage fee of $40.		
June	15	Cash	2 0 0 00	
		Dividend Revenue		2 0 0 00
		Received dividend of $2 per share on		
		Compton Corp. common stock.		

> The 1996 edition of *Accounting Trends & Techniques* indicated that 17% of the companies surveyed used the cost method to account for investments.

Equity Method

Under the **equity method**, a stock purchase is recorded in the same manner as if the cost method were used. The equity method, however, is different from the cost method in the way in which net income and cash dividends of the investee are recorded. The equity method of recording these items is summarized as follows:

1. The investor's share of the periodic net income of the investee is recorded as an *increase in the investment account* and as *revenue for the period*. Likewise, the investor's share of an investee's net loss is recorded as a *decrease in the investment account* and as a *loss for the period*.
2. The investor's share of cash dividends from the investee is recorded as an *increase in the cash account* and a *decrease in the investment account*.

> The 1996 edition of *Accounting Trends & Techniques* indicated that over 40% of the companies surveyed used the equity method to account for investments.

To illustrate, assume that on January 2, Hally Inc. pays cash of $350,000 for 40% of the common stock and net assets of Brock Corporation. Assume also that, for the year ending December 31, Brock Corporation reports net income of $105,000 and

---

[11] An exception to reporting unrealized gains and losses as part of comprehensive income is made if the decrease in the market value for a stock is considered permanent. In this case, the cost of the individual stock is written down (decreased), and the amount of the write-down is included in net income.

declares and pays $45,000 in dividends. Using the equity method, Hally Inc. (the investor) records these transactions as follows:

Jan.	2	Investment in Brock Corp. Stock		350 0 0 0 00	
		Cash			350 0 0 0 00
		Purchased 40% of Brock Corp.			
		common stock.			
Dec.	31	Investment in Brock Corp. Stock		42 0 0 0 00	
		Income of Brock Corp.			42 0 0 0 00
		Recorded share (40%) of Brock Corp.			
		net income of $105,000.			
Dec.	31	Cash		18 0 0 0 00	
		Investment in Brock Corp. Stock			18 0 0 0 00
		Recorded share (40%) of dividends of			
		$45,000 paid by Brock Corp.			

The combined effect of recording 40% of Brock Corporation's net income and dividends is to increase Hally's interest in the net assets of Brock by $24,000 ($42,000 − $18,000), as shown below.

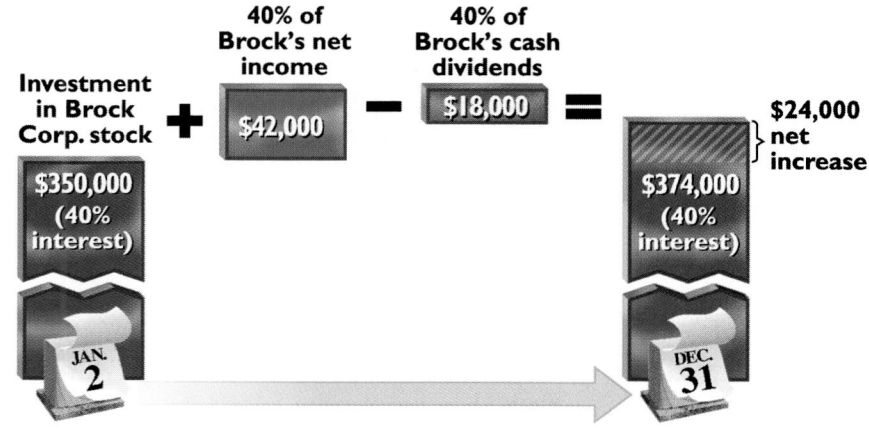

Assume that Hally Inc. increased its ownership in Brock Corporation to 60% at the beginning of the next year. If Brock Corporation reported net income of $80,000 and declared dividends of $50,000, how much would Hally Inc. debit Investment in Brock Corp. Stock?

$18,000 [($80,000 × 60%) − ($50,000 × 60%)]

Sale of Investments in Stocks

The accounting for the sale of stock is the same for both short-term and long-term investments. When shares of stock are sold, the investment account is credited for the carrying amount (book value) of the shares sold. The cash or receivables account is debited for the proceeds (sales price less commission and other selling costs). Any difference between the proceeds and the carrying amount is recorded as a gain or loss on the sale and is included in the determination of net income.

To illustrate, assume that an investment in Drey Inc. stock has a carrying amount of $15,700 when it is sold on March 1. If the proceeds from the sale of the stock are $17,500, the entry to record the transaction is as follows:

Mar.	1	Cash		17 5 0 0 00	
		Investment in Drey Inc. Stock			15 7 0 0 00
		Gain on Sale of Investments			1 8 0 0 00
		Sold investment in Drey Inc. stock.			

Business Combinations

OBJECTIVE 7

Describe alternative methods of combining businesses and how consolidated financial statements are prepared.

Each year, many businesses combine in order to produce more efficiently or to diversify product lines. Business combinations often involve complex accounting principles and terminology. Our objective in this section is to introduce you to some of the unique terminology and concepts related to business combinations. We also briefly describe the use and preparation of consolidated financial statements.

Mergers and Consolidations

One corporation may acquire all the assets and liabilities of another corporation, which is then dissolved. This joining of two corporations is called a merger. The acquiring company may use cash, debt, or its own stock as the payment. Whatever the form of payment, the amount received by the dissolving corporation is distributed to its stockholders in final liquidation.

Boeing Co. acquired **McDonnell Douglas Corporation** for $15 billion in mid-1997. The merged company will become the United States' biggest aerospace company, with projected sales of more than $38 billion. Under the merger, McDonnell Douglas will no longer exist as a separate company.

A new corporation may be created, and the assets and liabilities of two or more existing corporations transferred to it. This type of combination is called a **consolidation**. The new corporation usually issues its own stock in exchange for the net assets acquired. The original corporations are then dissolved.

Parent and Subsidiary Corporations

Business combinations may also occur when one corporation buys a controlling share of the outstanding voting stock of one or more other corporations. In this case, none of the corporations dissolve. The corporations continue as separate legal entities in a parent-subsidiary relationship. The corporation owning all or a majority of the voting stock of the other corporation is called the **parent company**. The corporation that is controlled is called the **subsidiary company**. Two or more corporations closely related through stock ownership are sometimes called **affiliated** companies. An example of an affiliated company is **Waldenbooks**, a subsidiary of **Kmart**.

A corporation may acquire the controlling share of the voting common stock of another corporation by paying cash, exchanging other assets, issuing debt, or using some combination of these methods. The stockholders of the acquired company, in turn, transfer their stock to the parent corporation. In such cases, the transaction is recorded like a normal purchase of assets, and the combination is accounted for by the **purchase method**.

A parent-subsidiary relationship may be created by exchanging the voting common stock of the acquiring corporation (the parent) for the common stock of the acquired corporation (the subsidiary). If at least 90% of the stock of the subsidiary is acquired in this way, the transaction is a pooling of interests, and the combination is accounted for by the **pooling-of-interests method**. In a pooling of interests, the stockholders of the acquired company (the subsidiary) become stockholders of the acquiring company (the parent).

The 1996 edition of *Accounting Trends & Techniques* reported that 88% of the business combinations surveyed were accounted for by the purchase method.

The accounting for a purchase and a pooling of interests are significantly different. A purchase is accounted for as a *sale-purchase transaction,* whereas a pooling of interests is accounted for as a *joining of ownership interests.* Because businesses must meet very strict criteria to use the pooling-of-interests method, the vast majority of business combinations are accounted for by using the purchase method.

BUSINESS ON STAGE

Buying and Selling Stocks

After you have evaluated a business and identified companies in which you would like to make an investment, how would you go about making the purchase? The most common method is to purchase common stock through a stockbroker, or account representative. A *stockbroker* is a person who executes trades on the major stock exchanges on your behalf. Stockbrokers can be associated with large "full-service" firms, such as **Merrill Lynch**; "discount" brokerage firms, such as **OLDE Discount Brokers**; or regional and local firms.

Once you've selected your stockbroker, you begin by opening an account. This usually involves placing money in the account. After your account is opened, you can place an order for the purchase of your selected stocks. There are two basic types of purchase orders—a market order and a limit order.

A *market order* instructs the broker to buy the stock at the best possible price. If the stock is actively traded, the buy price will usually be close to the last traded price prior to the order. Stockbrokers usually execute trades within minutes of taking an order. A *limit order* instructs the broker to buy the stock at a specified price or lower. An example of a limit order would be to buy 50 shares of **Coca-Cola** common stock at $60 or lower. The limit order prohibits the broker from purchasing the stock at a price higher than $60.

When you decide to sell, you can place a stop-loss order. With a *stop-loss order,* you set a selling market price below the current price. If the market price drops to your limit, then the sale is executed, thus limiting your loss. After your trade is executed, you will receive a statement confirming your trade, which shows your investment, the number of shares bought or sold, the dollar value, and the stockbroker's commission. These statements should be kept for tax purposes.

Recently, an alternative method of trading stocks has emerged on the Internet. Internet trading is just beginning, but it appears to be a promising alternative to using a stockbroker. For more information, see E*TRADE's home page at **www.etrade.com**. ■

REAL WORLD The 1996 edition of *Accounting Trends & Techniques* indicates that most of the companies surveyed reported minority interest in the long-term liabilities (noncurrent) section of the consolidated balance sheet.

Consolidated Financial Statements

Although parent and subsidiary corporations may operate as a single economic unit, they continue to maintain separate accounting records and prepare their own periodic financial statements. At the end of the year, the financial statements of the parent and subsidiary are combined and reported as a single company. These combined financial statements are called **consolidated financial statements**. Such statements are usually identified by adding "and subsidiary(ies)" to the name of the parent corporation or by adding "consolidated" to the statement title.

To the stockholders of the parent company, consolidated financial statements are more meaningful than separate statements for each corporation. This is because the parent company, in substance, controls the subsidiaries, even though the parent and its subsidiaries are separate entities.

When a business combination is accounted for as a purchase, the subsidiary's net assets are reported in the consolidated balance sheet at their fair market value at the time of the purchase. In some cases, a parent may pay more than the fair market value of a subsidiary's net assets because the subsidiary has prospects for high future earnings. The difference between the amount paid by the parent and the fair market value of the subsidiary's net assets is reported on the consolidated balance sheet as an intangible asset. This asset is identified as **Goodwill** or **Excess of cost of business acquired over related net assets.**

When a consolidated balance sheet is prepared, the ownership interest of the parent in the subsidiary's stock, which is the balance in the parent's investment in subsidiary account, must be eliminated. This is done by eliminating the parent's investment in subsidiary account against the balances of the subsidiary's stockholders' equity accounts.

If the parent owns less than 100% of the subsidiary stock, the subsidiary stock owned by outsiders is *not* eliminated but is normally reported immediately preceding the consolidated stockholders' equity. This amount is described as the **minority interest**.

When the data on the financial statements of the parent and its subsidiaries are combined to form the consolidated statements, intercompany transactions are given special attention. An example of such a transaction is the parent purchasing goods from the subsidiary or the subsidiary loaning money to the parent.

These transactions affect the individual accounts of the parent and subsidiary and thus the financial statements of both companies.[12] To illustrate, assume that P Inc. (the parent) sold merchandise to S Inc. (the subsidiary) for $90,000. The merchandise cost P $50,000. In turn, S Inc. sold the merchandise to a customer for $120,000.

The individual income statements for P Inc. and S Inc. are shown in Exhibit 9. The consolidated (combined) income statement is shown in Exhibit 10. The consolidated income statement presents the income statements for P Inc. and S Inc. as if they were one operating entity. Thus, the $90,000 sale and the $90,000 cost of merchandise sold are eliminated. This is because the consolidated entity cannot sell to itself or buy from itself.

EXHIBIT 9
Income Statements for P Inc. and S Inc.

	P Inc.		S Inc.	
Sales		$950,000		$400,000
Cost of merchandise sold		625,000		240,000
Gross profit		$325,000		$160,000
Operating expenses:				
Selling expenses	$155,000		$55,000	
Administrative expenses	85,000	240,000	35,000	90,000
Net income		$ 85,000		$ 70,000

EXHIBIT 10
Consolidated Income Statement for P Inc. and S Inc.

Sales		$1,260,000*
Cost of merchandise sold		775,000**
Gross profit		$ 485,000
Operating expenses:		
Selling expenses	$210,000	
Administrative expenses	120,000	330,000
Net income		$ 155,000

*$950,000 − $90,000 + $400,000
**$625,000 + $240,000 − $90,000

General Motors Corporation is a multinational company that consolidates its foreign subsidiaries, such as the European *Opel* division, into U.S. dollars.

Many U.S. corporations own subsidiaries in foreign countries. Such corporations are often called *multinational corporations*. The financial statements of the foreign subsidiary are usually prepared in the foreign currency. Before the financial statements of foreign subsidiaries are consolidated with their domestic parent's financial statements, the amounts shown on the statements for the foreign companies must be converted to U.S. dollars.

FINANCIAL ANALYSIS AND INTERPRETATION

OBJECTIVE 8

Compute and interpret the price-earnings ratio.

The assessment of a firm's growth potential and future earnings prospects is indicated by how much the market is willing to pay per dollar of a company's earnings. This ratio, called the **price-earnings ratio**, or **P/E ratio**, is commonly included

---

[12]Examples of accounts often affected by intercompany transactions include *Accounts Receivable* and *Accounts Payable*, *Interest Receivable* and *Interest Payable*, and *Interest Expense* and *Interest Revenue*.

in stock market quotations reported by the financial press. A high P/E ratio indicates that the market expects high growth and earnings in the future. Likewise, a low P/E ratio indicates lower growth and earnings expectations.

The price-earnings ratio on common stock is computed by dividing the stock's market price per share at a specific date by the company's annual earnings per share, as shown below:

$$\text{Price-earnings ratio} = \frac{\textbf{Market price per share of common stock}}{\textbf{Earnings per share of common stock}}$$

To illustrate, assume that Harper Inc. reported earnings per share of $1.64 in 2000 and $1.35 in 1999. The market prices per common share are $20.50 at the end of 2000 and $13.50 at the end of 1999. The price-earnings ratio on this stock is computed as follows:

	Price-Earnings Ratio
Year 2000	12.5 ($20.50/$1.64)
Year 1999	10.0 ($13.50/$1.35)

The price-earnings ratio indicates that a share of Harper Inc.'s common stock was selling for 10 times the amount of earnings per share at the end of 1999. At the end of 2000, the common stock was selling for 12.5 times the amount of earnings per share. These results would indicate a generally improving expectation of growth and earnings for Harper Inc. However, a prospective investor should also consider the price-earnings ratios for competing firms in the same industry.

ENCORE

Mattell Inc., one of the largest toy makers in the world, is best known for its Barbie dolls, Fisher-Price infant and preschool toys, Hot Wheels die-cast cars, and its Cabbage Patch dolls. It is estimated that over 80 million Cabbage Patch dolls have been sold since they were introduced in 1983.

In the fall of 1996, Mattell decided to introduce a new version of the Cabbage Patch dolls, called Snacktime Kids. The Snacktime Kids come with pieces of plastic shaped carrots, pretzels, biscuits, and licorice that can be put into the doll's mechanical mouth. Once in the doll's mouth, a battery-driven motor "chews" them

Monster Eats into Mattell's Profits

and ejects them into a pack on the doll's back.

Unfortunately, the dolls cannot discern between the plastic snacks and other small objects provided by its owner, such as hair and fingers. One young father demonstrated how he was forced to decapitate a Snacktime Kid after it "attacked" his daughter. Evidently, the doll began devouring the little girl's hair as if it were spaghetti. Fearing the worst, the father terminated the ravenous toy *with extreme prejudice*. Similar hair-gobbling incidents were reported across the country.

In early January 1997, Mattell announced a refund program for the dolls, offering to buy back Snacktime Kids from parents for $40 a doll. Mat-

tell estimated that 500,000 Snacktime Kids had been sold and another 200,000 dolls were still on the shelves. The buyback of the monster dolls cost Mattell $10 million in sales and $8 million in after-tax earnings. In addition, at least one lawsuit claiming grievous psychological trauma was filed against Mattell. The lawsuit asked for $25 million in punitive damages.

Although Mattell hopes that the buyback program will have a nonrecurring impact on its profits, it isn't the first time that Mattell has had to pull a toy from the market. In 1992, Mattell pulled Teacher Barbie from

stores after the talking doll was criticized by educators, who said it set a bad example with comments like, "Math class is tough." Teacher Barbie was "reeducated," however, and put back on the market. ■

KEY POINTS

1 Journalize the entries for corporate income taxes, including deferred income taxes.

Corporations are subject to federal income tax and are required to make estimated payments throughout the year. To record the payment of estimated tax, Income Tax is debited and Cash is credited. If additional taxes are owed at the end of the year, Income Tax is debited and Income Tax Payable is credited for the amount owed. If the estimated tax payments are greater than the actual tax liability, a receivable account is debited and Income Tax is credited.

The tax effects of temporary differences between taxable income and income before income taxes must be allocated between periods. The journal entry for such allocations normally debits Income Tax and credits Income Tax Payable and Deferred Income Tax Payable.

2 Prepare an income statement reporting the following unusual items: discontinued operations, extraordinary items, and changes in accounting principles.

A gain or loss resulting from the disposal of a business segment should be identified on the income statement, net of related income tax. The results of continuing operations should also be identified.

Gains and losses may result from events and transactions that are unusual and occur infrequently. Such extraordinary items, net of related income tax, should be identified on the income statement.

A change in an accounting principle results from the adoption of a generally accepted accounting principle different from the one used previously for reporting purposes. The effect of the change in principle on net income in the current period, as well as the cumulative effect on income of prior periods, should be disclosed in the financial statements. The effects of a change in an accounting principle should be reported net of related income tax.

3 Prepare an income statement reporting earnings per share data.

Earnings per share is reported on the income statements of public corporations. If there are unusual items on the income statement, the per share amount should be presented for each of these items as well as net income.

4 Prepare financial statement presentations of stockholders' equity.

Significant changes in the sources of stockholders' equity—paid-in capital and retained earnings—may be reported in separate statements or notes that support the balance sheet presentation.

Changes in retained earnings may be reported by preparing a separate retained earnings statement, a combined income and retained earnings statement, or a statement of stockholders' equity. Restrictions to retained earnings, called appropriations, must be disclosed, usually in the notes to the financial statements. Material errors in a prior period's net income, called prior-period adjustments, are reported in the retained earnings statement. Significant changes in stockholders' equity may also be reported in a statement of stockholders' equity.

5 Describe the concept and the reporting of comprehensive income.

Comprehensive income is all changes in stockholders' equity during a period except those resulting from dividends and stockholders' investments. Companies must report traditional net income plus or minus other comprehensive income items to arrive at comprehensive income. Other comprehensive income items include transactions and events that are excluded from net income, such as unrealized gains and losses on certain investments in debt and equity securities.

6 Describe the accounting for investments in stocks.

A business may purchase stocks as a means of earning a return (income) on excess cash that it does not need for its normal operations. Such investments are recorded in a marketable securities account. Their cost includes all amounts spent to acquire the securities. Any dividends received on an investment are recorded as a debit to Cash and a credit to Dividend Revenue. On the balance sheet, temporary investments are reported at their fair market values. Any difference between the fair market values of the securities and their cost is an unrealized holding gain or loss (net of applicable taxes) that is reported as an other comprehensive income item.

Long-term investments in stocks are not intended as a source of cash in the normal operations of the business. They are reported in the balance sheet under the caption Investments. Two methods of accounting for long-term investments in stock are (1) the cost method and (2) the equity method.

The accounting for the sale of stock is the same for both short-term and long-term investments. The investment account is credited for the carrying amount (book value) of the shares sold, the cash or receivables account is debited for the proceeds, and any difference between the proceeds and the carrying amount is recorded as a gain or loss on the sale.

7 Describe alternative methods of combining businesses and how consolidated financial statements are prepared.

Businesses may combine in a merger or a consolidation. Business combinations may also occur when one corporation acquires a controlling share of the outstanding voting stock of another corporation. In this case, a parent-subsidiary relationship exists, and the companies are called affiliated or associated companies.

Although the corporations that make up a parent-subsidiary affiliation may operate as a single economic unit, they usually continue to maintain separate accounting records and prepare their own periodic financial statements. The financial statements prepared by combining the parent and subsidiary statements are called consolidated financial statements.

When a parent corporation purchases less than 100% of the subsidiary's stock, the remaining stockholders' equity is identified as minority interest. The minority interest is reported on the consolidated balance sheet, usually preceding stockholders' equity.

In preparing consolidated income statements for a parent and its subsidiary, all amounts from intercompany transactions, such as intercompany sales of merchandise and cost of merchandise sold, are eliminated.

8 Compute and interpret the price-earnings ratio.

The assessment of a firm's growth potential and future earnings prospects is indicated by the price-earnings ratio, or P/E ratio. It is computed by dividing the stock's market price per share at a specific date by the company's annual earnings per share.

ILLUSTRATIVE PROBLEM

The following data were selected from the records of Botanica Greenhouses Inc. for the current fiscal year ended August 31:

Administrative expenses	$ 82,200
Cost of merchandise sold	750,000
Gain on condemnation of land	25,000
Income tax:	
Applicable to continuing operations	27,200
Applicable to gain on condemnation of land ...	10,000
Applicable to loss from disposal of a segment	
of the business (reduction)	24,000
Interest expense	15,200
Loss from disposal of a segment of the business ..	60,200
Sales	1,097,500
Selling expenses	182,100

Instructions

Prepare a multiple-step income statement, concluding with a section for earnings per share in the form illustrated in this chapter. There were 10,000 shares of common stock (no preferred) outstanding throughout the year. Assume that the gain on condemnation of land is an extraordinary item.

Solution

Botanica Greenhouses Inc.
Income Statement
For the Year Ended August 31, 20—

Sales			$1,097,500
Cost of merchandise sold			750,000
Gross profit			$ 347,500
Operating expenses:			
Selling expenses		$182,100	
Administrative expenses		82,200	
Total operating expenses			264,300
Income from operations			$ 83,200
Other expense:			
Interest expense			15,200
Income from continuing operations before income tax			$ 68,000
Income tax expense			27,200
Income from continuing operations			$ 40,800
Loss from disposal of a segment of the business		$ 60,200	
Less applicable income tax		24,000	36,200
Income before extraordinary item			$ 4,600
Extraordinary item:			
Gain on condemnation of land		$ 25,000	
Less applicable income tax		10,000	15,000
Net income			$ 19,600
Earnings per share:			
Income from continuing operations			$4.08
Loss on discontinued operations			3.62
Income before extraordinary item			$0.46
Extraordinary item			1.50
Net income			$1.96

SELF-EXAMINATION QUESTIONS   Answers at End of Chapter

Matching

Match each of the following statements with its proper term. Some terms may not be used.

A. appropriation

B. available-for-sale securities

C. balance sheet

D. comprehensive income

E. consolidated financial statements

F. consolidation

____ 1. The income according to the tax laws that is used as a base for determining the amount of taxes owed.

____ 2. Differences between taxable income and income before income taxes, created because items are recognized in one period for tax purposes and in another period for income statement purposes. Such differences reverse or turn around in later years.

____ 3. Operations of a major line of business for a company, such as a division, a department, or a certain class of customer, that have been disposed of.

____ 4. Events and transactions that (1) are significantly different (unusual) from the typical or the normal operating activities of a business and (2) occur infrequently.

____ 5. Net income per share of common stock outstanding during a period.

(continues)

G. cost method

H. discontinued operations

I. earnings per common share (EPS)

J. equity method

K. equity per share

L. equity security

M. extraordinary items

N. investments

O. merger

P. minority interest

Q. parent company

R. permanent differences

S. pooling-of-interests method

T. price-earnings ratio

U. prior period adjustments

V. purchase method

W. statement of cash flows

X. statement of stockholders' equity

Y. subsidiary company

Z. taxable income

AA. temporary differences

BB. temporary investments

CC. trading securities

DD. unrealized holding gain or loss

____ 6. The amount of retained earnings that has been restricted and therefore is unavailable for use as dividends.

____ 7. Errors in a prior period's net income that arise from mathematical mistakes or from mistakes in applying accounting principles.

____ 8. A statement summarizing significant changes in stockholders' equity that have occured during a period.

____ 9. All changes in stockholders' equity during a period, except those resulting from dividends and stockholders' investments.

____ 10. Preferred or common stock.

____ 11. Securities that management intends to actively trade for profit.

____ 12. Securities that management expects to sell in the future but which are not actively traded for profit.

____ 13. The balance sheet caption used to report investments in income-yielding securities that can be quickly sold and converted to cash as needed.

____ 14. The difference between the fair market values of the securities and their cost.

____ 15. The balance sheet caption used to report long-term investments in stocks not intended as a source of cash in the normal operations of the business.

____ 16. A method of accounting for an investment in common stock by which the investor recognizes as income its share of cash dividends of the investee.

____ 17. A method of accounting for an investment in common stock by which the investment account is adjusted for the investor's share of periodic net income and cash dividends of the investee.

____ 18. The joining of two corporations in which one company acquires all the assets and liabilities of another corporation, which is then dissolved.

____ 19. The creation of a new corporation by the transfer of assets and liabilities of two or more existing corporations, which are then dissolved.

____ 20. The corporation owning all or a majority of the voting stock of the other corporation.

____ 21. The corporation that is controlled by a parent company.

____ 22. The accounting method used when a corporation acquires the controlling share of the voting common stock of another corporation by paying cash, exchanging other assets, issuing debt, or some combination of these methods.

____ 23. The accounting method used when a corporation acquires the controlling share of the voting common stock of another corporation by exchanging the voting common stock of the acquiring corporation for the common stock of the acquired corporation.

____ 24. Financial statements resulting from combining parent and subsidiary statements.

____ 25. The portion of a subsidiary corporation's stock owned by outsiders.

____ 26. The ratio computed by dividing a corporation's stock market price per share at a specific date by the company's annual earnings per share.

Multiple Choice

1. During its first year of operations, a corporation elected to use the straight-line method of depreciation for financial reporting purposes and MACRS in determining taxable income. If the income tax is 40% and the amount of depreciation expense is $60,000 under the straight-line method and $100,000 under MACRS, what is the amount of income tax deferred to future years?

   A. $16,000   C. $40,000
   B. $24,000   D. $60,000

2. A material gain resulting from condemning land for public use would be reported on the income statement as:
   A. an extraordinary item
   B. an other income item
   C. revenue from sales
   D. a change in estimate

3. An appropriation for plant expansion would normally be reported in the financial statements in the:

A. Property, plant, and equipment section
B. Long-term liabilities section
C. Stockholders' equity section
D. Notes to the statements

4. An item treated as a prior period adjustment should be reported in the financial statements as:
A. an extraordinary item
B. an other expense item
C. an adjustment of the beginning balance of Retained Earnings
D. a change in estimate

5. Cisneros Corporation owns 75% of Harrell Inc. During the current year, Harrell Inc. reported net income of $150,000 and declared dividends of $40,000. How much would Cisneros Corporation increase Investment in Harrell Inc. Stock for the current year?
A. $0
B. $30,000
C. $82,500
D. $112,500

CLASS DISCUSSION QUESTIONS

1. A corporation has paid estimated federal income tax during the year on the basis of its estimated income. Indicate the accounts that would be debited and credited at the end of the year if the corporation (a) owes an additional tax; (b) overpaid its tax.
2. How would the amount of deferred income tax payable be reported in the balance sheet if (a) it is payable within one year and (b) it is payable beyond one year?
3. What two criteria must be met to classify an item as an extraordinary item on the income statement?
4. During the current year, 20 acres of land that cost $150,000 were condemned for construction of an interstate highway. Assuming that an award of $180,000 in cash was received and that the applicable income tax on this transaction is 30%, how would this information be presented in the income statement?
5. Corporation X realized a material gain when its facilities at a designated floodway were acquired by the urban renewal agency. How should the gain be reported in the income statement?

   Source: "Technical Hotline," *Journal of Accountancy,* June 1989, p. 32.

6. The annual report of **Sears, Roebuck and Co.** disclosed the discontinuance of several business segments, including **Coldwell Banker Residential Services**. The estimated loss on disposal of these operations was $64 million, including $22 million of tax expense. Indicate how the loss from discontinued operations should be reported by Sears, Roebuck and Co. on its income statement.
7. If significant changes are made in the accounting principles applied from one period to the next, why should the effect of these changes be disclosed in the financial statements?
8. A corporation reports earnings per share of $1.12 for the most recent year and $1.00 for the preceding year. The $1.12 includes a $0.17-per-share gain from a sale of the only investment owned since the business was organized in 1940. (a) Should the composition of the $1.12 be disclosed in the financial reports? (b) On the basis of the limited information presented, would you conclude that operations had improved or declined?
9. What is the primary advantage of combining the retained earnings statement with the income statement?
10. What are the three classifications of appropriations and how are appropriations normally reported in the financial statements?
11. Indicate how prior period adjustments would be reported on the financial statements presented only for the current period.
12. Describe the format of the statement of stockholders' equity.
13. How is comprehensive income determined?
14. a. List some examples of other comprehensive income items.
    b. Does the reporting of comprehensive income affect the determination of net income and retained earnings?

15. Why might a business invest in another company's stock?

16. How are temporary investments in marketable securities reported on the balance sheet?

17. How are unrealized gains and losses on temporary investments in marketable securities reported on the statement of income and comprehensive income?

18. a. What are two methods of accounting for long-term investments in stock?
    b. Under what caption are long-term investments in stock reported on the balance sheet?

19. Rosetta Inc. received a $0.25-per-share cash dividend on 40,000 shares of MGS Corporation common stock, which Rosetta Inc. carries as a long-term investment. (a) Assuming that Rosetta Inc. uses the cost method of accounting for its investment in MGS Corporation, what account would be credited for the receipt of the $10,000 dividend? (b) Assuming that Rosetta Inc. uses the equity method of accounting for its investment in MGS Corporation, what account would be credited for the receipt of the $10,000 dividend?

20. Which method of accounting for long-term investments in stock (cost or equity) should be used by the parent company in accounting for its investments in stock of subsidiaries?

21. What are the two methods of accounting for the creation of a parent-subsidiary relationship?

22. P Company purchases the entire common stock of S Corporation for $18,000,000. What accounts on S's balance sheet are represented in the investment account on P's balance sheet?

23. Parent Corporation owns 85% of the outstanding common stock of Subsidiary Corporation, which has no preferred stock. (a) What is the term applied to the remaining 15% interest? (b) On the consolidated balance sheet, where is the amount of Subsidiary's book equity allocable to outsiders reported?

24. An annual report of **The Campbell Soup Company** reported on its income statement $2.4 million as "equity in earnings of affiliates." Journalize the entry that Campbell would have made to record this equity in earnings of affiliates.

Resources for Your Success On-Line at warren.swcollege.com
Remember! If you need additional help, visit South-Western's Web site. See page 26 for a description of the online and printed materials that are available.

EXERCISES

Exercise 13–1
Income tax entries

Objective 1

Journalize the entries to record the following selected transactions of Masters Grave Markers Inc.:

Apr. 15. Paid the first installment of the estimated income tax for the current fiscal year ending December 31, $60,000. No entry had been made to record the liability.

June 15. Paid the second installment of $60,000.

Sep. 15. Paid the third installment of $60,000.

Dec. 31. Recorded the estimated income tax liability for the year just ended and the deferred income tax liability, based on the transactions above and the following data:

Income tax rate	40%
Income before income tax	$850,000
Taxable income according to tax return	700,000

Jan. 15. Paid the fourth installment of $100,000.

Exercise 13–2
Extraordinary item
Objective 2

A company received life insurance proceeds on the death of its president before the end of its fiscal year. It intends to report the amount in its income statement as an extraordinary item.

    → Would this be in conformity with generally accepted accounting principles? Discuss.

Source: "Technical Hotline," *Journal of Accountancy,* June 1989, p. 31.

Exercise 13–3
Extraordinary item
Objective 2

On May 11, 1996, **ValuJet** tragically lost its Flight 592 en route from Miami to Atlanta. One hundred and ten people lost their lives. The crash cost ValuJet millions of dollars, including $2 million the company paid to the Federal Aviation Administration (FAA) to compensate it for the costs of the special inspections that were conducted. Do you believe that the costs related to this crash should be reported as an extraordinary item on the 1996 income statement of ValuJet?

Exercise 13–4
Identifying extraordinary items
Objective 2

Assume that the amount of each of the following items is material to the financial statements. Classify each item as either normally recurring (NR) or extraordinary (E).

a. Salaries of corporate officers.
b. Gain on sale of land condemned for public use.
c. Uncollectible accounts expense.
d. Interest revenue on notes receivable.
e. Uninsured flood loss. (Flood insurance is unavailable because of periodic flooding in the area.)
f. Loss on sale of fixed assets.
g. Uninsured loss on building due to hurricane damage. The firm was organized in 1920 and had not previously incurred hurricane damage.
h. Loss on disposal of equipment considered to be obsolete because of development of new technology.

Exercise 13–5
Income statement
Objectives 2, 3

✓ Net income, $87,000

Ocean-Way Inc. produces and distributes equipment for sailboats. On the basis of the following data for the current fiscal year ended April 30, prepare a multiple-step income statement for Ocean-Way Inc., including an analysis of earnings per share in the form illustrated in this chapter. There were 20,000 shares of $100 par common stock outstanding throughout the year.

Administrative expenses	$ 36,750
Cost of merchandise sold	620,000
Cumulative effect on prior years of changing to a different depreciation method (decrease in income)	50,000
Gain on condemnation of land (extraordinary item)	37,750
Income tax reduction applicable to change in depreciation method	18,200
Income tax applicable to gain on condemnation of land	7,750
Income tax reduction applicable to loss from discontinued operations	45,500
Income tax applicable to ordinary income	105,200
Loss on discontinued operations	114,500
Sales	985,500
Selling expenses	65,750

Exercise 13–6
Income statement

Objectives 2, 3

What's Wrong WITH THIS?

✓ Correct EPS for net income, $13.55

Ultra Sound Inc. sells automotive and home stereo equipment. It has 50,000 shares of $100 par common stock and 10,000 shares of $2, $100 par cumulative preferred stock outstanding as of December 31, 2000. It also holds 10,000 shares of common stock as treasury stock as of December 31, 2000. How many errors can you find in the following income statement for the year ended December 31, 2000?

Ultra Sound Inc.
Income Statement
For the Year Ended December 31, 2000

Net sales		$8,450,000
Cost of merchandise sold		6,100,000
Gross profit		$2,350,000
Operating expenses:		
Selling expenses	$1,020,000	
Administrative expenses	280,000	1,300,000
Income from continuing operations before income tax		$1,050,000
Income tax expense		420,000
Income from continuing operations		$ 530,000
Cumulative effect on prior years' income (decrease) of changing to a different depreciation method (net of applicable income tax of $36,000)		(92,000)
Correction of error (understatement) in December 31, 1999 physical inventory (net of applicable income tax of $20,000)		30,000
Income before condemnation of land and discontinued operations		$ 468,000
Extraordinary item:		
Gain on condemnation of land, net of applicable income tax of $80,000		120,000
Loss on discontinued operations (net of applicable income tax of $64,000)		(96,000)
Net income		$ 492,000
Earnings per common share:		
Income from continuing operations		$10.60
Cumulative effect on prior years' income (decrease) of changing to a different depreciation method		(1.84)
Correction of error (understatement) in December 31, 1999 physical inventory		0.60
Income before extraordinary item and discontinued operations		$ 9.36
Extraordinary item		2.40
Loss on discontinued operations		(1.92)
Net income		$ 9.84

Exercise 13–7
Reporting paid-in capital

Objective 4

✓ Total paid-in capital, $1,628,000

The following accounts and their balances were selected from the unadjusted trial balance of FastCo Inc., a freight forwarder, at December 31, the end of the current fiscal year:

Preferred $1 Stock, $50 par	$ 500,000
Paid-In Capital in Excess of Par—Preferred Stock	75,000
Common Stock, no par, $10 stated value	750,000
Paid-In Capital in Excess of Par—Common Stock	140,000
Paid-In Capital from Sale of Treasury Stock	13,000
Donated Capital	150,000
Retained Earnings	1,230,000

Prepare the Paid-In Capital portion of the Stockholders' Equity section of the balance sheet. There are 100,000 shares of common stock authorized and 50,000 shares of preferred stock authorized.

Exercise 13–8
Stockholders' equity section of balance sheet

Objective 4

✓ Total stockholders' equity, $582,000

The following accounts and their balances appear in the ledger of McCopy Inc. on September 30 of the current year:

Common Stock, $10 par	$250,000
Paid-In Capital in Excess of Par	40,000
Paid-In Capital from Sale of Treasury Stock	7,000
Retained Earnings	310,000
Treasury Stock	25,000

Prepare the Stockholders' Equity section of the balance sheet as of September 30. Thirty thousand shares of common stock are authorized, and 2,500 shares have been reacquired.

Exercise 13–9
Stockholders' equity section of balance sheet

Objective 4

✓ Total stockholders' equity, $2,637,500

Le'Car Inc. retails racing products for BMWs, Porsches, and Ferraris. The following accounts and their balances appear in the ledger of Le'Car Inc. on December 31, the end of the current year:

Common Stock, $10 par	$ 800,000
Paid-In Capital in Excess of Par—Common Stock	127,500
Paid-In Capital in Excess of Par—Preferred Stock	37,500
Paid-In Capital from Sale of Treasury Stock—Common	15,000
Preferred $2 Stock, $100 par	500,000
Retained Earnings	1,252,500
Treasury Stock—Common	95,000

Ten thousand shares of preferred and 150,000 shares of common stock are authorized. There are 5,000 shares of common stock held as treasury stock.
   Prepare the Stockholders' Equity section of the balance sheet as of December 31, the end of the current year.

Exercise 13–10
Retained earnings statement

Objective 4

McArthur Corporation, a manufacturer of industrial pumps, reports the following results for the year ending August 31, 2000:

Retained earnings, September 1, 1999	$1,356,800
Net income	472,000
Cash dividends declared	100,000
Stock dividends declared	85,000

Prepare a retained earnings statement for the fiscal year ended August 31, 2000.

Exercise 13–11
Stockholders' equity section of balance sheet

Objective 4

What's Wrong WITH THIS?

✓ Corrected total stockholders' equity, $1,435,000

How many errors can you find in the following Stockholders' Equity section of the balance sheet prepared as of the end of the current year?

Stockholders' Equity

Paid-in capital:		
Preferred $2 stock, cumulative, $100 par		
(2,500 shares authorized and issued)	$250,000	
Excess of issue price over par	60,000	$ 310,000
Retained earnings		340,000
Treasury stock (4,000 shares at cost)		75,000
Dividends payable		60,000
Total paid-in capital		$ 785,000
Common stock, $15 par (50,000 shares		
authorized, 40,000 shares issued)	$810,000	
Donated capital	50,000	
Organization costs	120,000	980,000
Total stockholders' equity		$1,765,000

Exercise 13–12
Statement of stockholders' equity

Objective 4

✓ Total stockholders' equity, Dec. 31, $1,787,000

The stockholders' equity accounts of Monique Corporation for the current fiscal year ended December 31 are as follows:

ACCOUNT Common Stock, $1 Par

Date		Item	Debit	Credit	Balance Debit	Balance Credit
20—						
Jan.	1	Balance				100,000
May	20	Issued 40,000 shares		40,000		140,000

ACCOUNT Paid-In Capital in Excess of Par

Date		Item	Debit	Credit	Balance Debit	Balance Credit
20—						
Jan.	1	Balance				400,000
May	20	Issued 40,000 shares		24,000		424,000

ACCOUNT Treasury Stock

Date		Item	Debit	Credit	Balance Debit	Balance Credit
20—						
Nov.	30	Purchased 5,000 shares	7,000		7,000	

ACCOUNT Retained Earnings

Date		Item	Debit	Credit	Balance Debit	Balance Credit
20—						
Jan.	1	Balance				925,000
Dec.	31	Income summary		320,000		1,245,000
	31	Cash dividends	15,000			1,230,000

ACCOUNT Cash Dividends

Date		Item	Debit	Credit	Balance Debit	Balance Credit
20—						
Mar.	12		10,000		10,000	
June	17		5,000		15,000	
Dec.	31	Closing		15,000	—	—

Prepare a statement of stockholders' equity for the fiscal year ended December 31.

Exercise 13–13
Temporary investments in marketable securities

Objective 6

During its first year of operations, Loran Corporation purchased the following securities as a temporary investment:

Security	Shares Purchased	Cost	Cash Dividends Received
Geer Inc.	5,000	$18,000	$1,500
Jones Corp.	3,000	24,000	600

a. Journalize the purchase of the temporary investments for cash.
b. Journalize the receipt of the dividends.

Exercise 13–14
Financial statement reporting of temporary investments

Objectives 5, 6

✓ b. Comprehensive income, $127,800

Using the data for Loran Corporation in Exercise 13–13, assume that as of December 31, 2000, the Geer Inc. stock had a market value of $5 per share and the Jones Corp. stock had a market value of $10 per share. For the year ending December 31, 2000, Loran Corporation had net income of $120,000. Its tax rate is 40%.

a. Prepare the balance sheet presentation for the temporary investments.
b. Prepare a statement of income and comprehensive income presentation for the temporary investments.

Exercise 13–15
Entries for investment in stock, receipt of dividends, and sale of shares

Objective 6

On February 3, Adair Corporation acquired 1,500 shares of the 40,000 outstanding shares of TZ Co. common stock at 60½ plus commission charges of $510. On August 13, a cash dividend of $1 per share and a 4% stock dividend were received. On November 15, 500 shares were sold at 62, less commission charges of $275. Journalize the entries to record (a) the purchase of the stock, (b) the receipt of dividends, and (c) the sale of the 500 shares.

Exercise 13–16
Equity method

Objective 6

The following note to the consolidated financial statements for **The Goodyear Tire and Rubber Co.** relates to the principles of consolidation used in preparing the financial statements:

The Company's investments in 20% to 50% owned companies in which it has the ability to exercise significant influence over operating and financial policies are accounted for by the equity method. Accordingly, the Company's share of the earnings of these companies is included in consolidated net income.

Is it a requirement that Goodyear use the equity method in this situation? Explain.

Exercise 13–17
Entries using equity method for stock investment

Objective 6

At a total cost of $9,000,000, Eastern Corporation acquired 75,000 shares of Southern Corp. common stock as a long-term investment. Eastern Corporation uses the equity method of accounting for this investment. Southern Corp. has 250,000 shares of common stock outstanding, including the shares acquired by Eastern Corporation. Journalize the entries by Eastern Corporation to record the following information:

a. Southern Corp. reports net income of $500,000 for the current period.
b. A cash dividend of $1.20 per common share is paid by Southern Corp. during the current period.

Exercise 13–18
Eliminations for consolidated income statement

Objective 7

✓ a. (1) $100,000
✓ b. $1,285,000

For the current year ended June 30, the results of operations of Montana Corporation and its wholly owned subsidiary, Blue Sky Enterprises, are as follows:

	Montana Corporation		Blue Sky Enterprises	
Sales		$2,150,000		$650,000
Cost of merchandise sold	$725,000		$340,000	
Selling expenses	255,000		75,000	
Administrative expenses	85,000		35,000	
Interest expense (revenue)	(12,000)	1,053,000	12,000	462,000
Net income		$1,097,000		$188,000

During the year, Montana sold merchandise to Blue Sky for $100,000. The merchandise was sold by Blue Sky to nonaffiliated companies for $150,000. Montana's interest revenue was realized from a long-term loan to Blue Sky.

a. Determine the amounts to be eliminated from the following items in preparing a consolidated income statement for the current year: (1) sales and (2) cost of merchandise sold.
b. Determine the consolidated net income.

Exercise 13–19
Price-earnings ratio

Objective 8

HAT

The financial statements for **Hershey Foods Corporation** are presented in Appendix G at the end of the text.

a. Determine the price-earnings ratio for Hershey Foods Corporation for 1996 and 1995. The market price of Hershey Foods common stock was 43¾ and 32½ on December 31, 1996 and 1995, respectively. (Use only the Class A common stock.)

b. What conclusions can you reach by considering the price-earnings ratio?

PROBLEMS SERIES A

Problem 13–1A
Income tax allocation

Objective 1

SPREADSHEET

✓ 1. Year-end balance, 3rd year, $51,500

Differences between the accounting methods applied to accounts and financial reports and those used in determining taxable income yielded the following amounts for the first four years of a corporation's operations:

	First Year	Second Year	Third Year	Fourth Year
Income before income taxes	$250,000	$340,000	$420,000	$495,000
Taxable income	170,000	282,500	428,750	510,000

The income tax rate for each of the four years was 40% of taxable income, and each year's taxes were promptly paid.

Instructions

1. Determine for each year the amounts described by the following captions, presenting the information in the form indicated:

Year	Income Tax Deducted on Income Statement	Income Tax Payments for the Year	Deferred Income Tax Payable Year's Addition (Deduction)	Deferred Income Tax Payable Year-End Balance

2. Total the first three amount columns.

Problem 13–2A
Income tax; income statement

Objectives 1, 2

SPREADSHEET

✓ Net income, $98,800

Off-Road Inc. produces and sells off-road motorcycles and jeeps. The following data were selected from the records of Off-Road Inc. for the current fiscal year ended March 31:

Advertising expense	$ 42,900
Cost of merchandise sold	395,000
Depreciation expense—office equipment	6,000
Depreciation expense—store equipment	21,500
Gain on condemnation of land	40,000
Income tax:	
Applicable to continuing operations	63,200
Applicable to loss from disposal of a segment of the business (reduction)	5,000
Applicable to gain on condemnation of land	16,000
Interest revenue	13,200
Loss from disposal of a segment of the business . .	26,000
Miscellaneous administrative expense	9,900
Miscellaneous selling expense	3,500
Office salaries expense	68,000

Rent expense	$ 20,000
Sales	835,000
Sales salaries expense	119,800
Store supplies expense	2,600

Instructions

Prepare a multiple-step income statement, concluding with a section for earnings per share (rounded to the nearest cent) in the form illustrated in this chapter. There were 30,000 shares of common stock (no preferred) outstanding throughout the year. Assume that the gain on condemnation of land is an extraordinary item.

Problem 13–3A
Income statement, retained earnings statement, balance sheet

Objectives 1, 2, 3, 4

✓ Net income, $400,950

The following data were taken from the records of Masuda Corporation for the year ended March 31, 2000:

Income statement data:

Administrative expenses	$ 130,000
Cost of merchandise sold	4,000,000
Gain on condemnation of land	6,100
Income tax:	
Applicable to continuing operations	308,975
Applicable to loss from disposal of a	
segment of the business	21,100
Applicable to gain on condemnation of land	1,150
Interest expense	68,500
Interest revenue	675
Loss from disposal of a segment of the business	80,500
Sales	5,500,000
Selling expenses	537,800

Retained earnings and balance sheet data:

Accounts payable	$ 149,500
Accounts receivable	329,050
Accumulated depreciation	3,050,000
Allowance for doubtful accounts	11,500
Cash	125,500
Common stock, $25 par (400,000 shares authorized;	
104,900 shares issued)	2,622,500
Deferred income taxes payable (current portion, $4,700)	25,700
Dividends:	
Cash dividends for common stock	100,000
Cash dividends for preferred stock	110,000
Stock dividends for common stock	150,900
Dividends payable	25,000
Equipment	11,064,050
Income tax payable	55,900
Interest receivable	2,500
Merchandise inventory (March 31, 2000), at lower of	
cost (fifo) or market	522,500
Organization costs	55,000
Paid-in capital from sale of treasury stock	5,000
Paid-in capital in excess of par—common stock	325,000
Paid-in capital in excess of par—preferred stock	240,000
Preferred 8% stock, $100 par (30,000 shares authorized;	
15,000 shares issued)	1,500,000
Prepaid expenses	15,900
Retained earnings, April 1, 1999	4,104,350
Treasury stock (1,000 shares of common stock at cost	
of $40 per share)	40,000

Instructions

1. Prepare a multiple-step income statement for the year ended March 31, 2000, concluding with earnings per share. In computing earnings per share, assume that the average number of common shares outstanding was 100,000 and preferred dividends were $110,000. Round to nearest cent. Assume that the gain on condemnation of land is an extraordinary item.
2. Prepare a retained earnings statement for the year ended March 31, 2000.
3. Prepare a balance sheet in report form as of March 31, 2000.

Problem 13–4A

Entries for investments in stock

Objective 6

HAT

Vaughn Company produces and sells theater costumes. The following transactions relate to certain securities acquired by Vaughn Company, whose fiscal year ends on December 31:

1997

Mar. 20. Purchased 3,000 shares of the 40,000 outstanding common shares of Cruise Corporation at 27½ plus commission and other costs of $975.

June 15. Received the regular cash dividend of $1 a share on Cruise Corporation stock.

Dec. 15. Received the regular cash dividend of $1 a share plus an extra dividend of $0.20 a share on Cruise Corporation stock.

(Assume that all intervening transactions have been recorded properly and that the number of shares of stock owned have not changed from December 31, 1997, to December 31, 2000.)

2001

Jan. 3. Purchased controlling interest in Minish Inc. for $350,000 by purchasing 40,000 shares directly from the estate of the founder of Minish. There are 60,000 shares of Minish Inc. stock outstanding.

Mar. 20. Received the regular cash dividend of $1 a share and a 5% stock dividend on the Cruise Corporation stock.

July 20. Sold 750 shares of Cruise Corporation stock at 30. The broker deducted commission and other costs of $200, remitting the balance.

Dec. 18. Received a cash dividend at the new rate of $1.08 a share on the Cruise Corporation stock.

31. Received $48,000 of cash dividends on Minish Inc. stock. Minish Inc. reported net income of $120,000 in 2001. Vaughn uses the equity method of accounting for its investment in Minish Inc.

Instructions
Journalize the entries for the preceding transactions.

PROBLEMS SERIES B

Problem 13–1B

Income tax allocation

Objective 1

SPREADSHEET

✓ 1. Year-end balance, 3rd year, $70,500

Differences between the accounting methods applied to accounts and financial reports and those used in determining taxable income yielded the following amounts for the first four years of a corporation's operations:

	First Year	Second Year	Third Year	Fourth Year
Income before income taxes	$320,000	$450,000	$400,000	$649,000
Taxable income	250,000	360,000	383,750	678,750

The income tax rate for each of the four years was 40% of taxable income, and each year's taxes were promptly paid.

Instructions

1. Determine for each year the amounts described by the following captions, presenting the information in the form indicated:

Year	Income Tax Deducted on Income Statement	Income Tax Payments for the Year	Deferred Income Tax Payable	
			Year's Addition (Deduction)	Year-End Balance

2. Total the first three amount columns.

Problem 13–2B
Income tax; income statement

Objectives 1, 2

SPREADSHEET

✓ Net income, $33,500

The following data were selected from the records of Sunny Greenhouses Inc. for the current fiscal year ended July 31:

Advertising expense	$ 47,000
Cost of merchandise sold	750,000
Depreciation expense—office equipment	5,200
Depreciation expense—store equipment	29,000
Gain from disposal of a segment of the business	60,200
Income tax:	
Applicable to continuing operations	8,200
Applicable to gain from disposal of a segment of the business	24,000
Applicable to loss on condemnation of land (reduction)	10,000
Insurance expense	8,000
Interest expense	15,200
Loss on condemnation of land	25,000
Miscellaneous administrative expense	5,250
Miscellaneous selling expense	10,100
Office salaries expense	42,750
Rent expense	21,000
Sales	1,100,000
Sales commissions expense	146,000

Instructions

Prepare a multiple-step income statement, concluding with a section for earnings per share in the form illustrated in this chapter. There were 5,000 shares of common stock (no preferred) outstanding throughout the year. Assume that the loss on condemnation of land is an extraordinary item.

Problem 13–3B
Income statement, retained earnings statement, balance sheet

Objectives 1, 2, 3, 4

✓ Net income, $314,600

The following data were taken from the records of Aarstol Corporation for the year ended July 31, 2000:

Income statement data:

Administrative expenses	$ 130,000
Cost of merchandise sold	3,850,000
Gain on condemnation of land	1,900
Income tax:	
Applicable to continuing operations	254,775
Applicable to loss from disposal of a segment of the business	21,100
Applicable to gain on condemnation of land	500
Interest expense	68,500
Interest revenue	3,675
Loss from disposal of a segment of the business	80,500
Sales	5,100,000
Selling expenses	427,800

Retained earnings and balance sheet data:

Accounts payable	$ 149,500
Accounts receivable	309,050

Accumulated depreciation	$ 3,050,000
Allowance for doubtful accounts	21,500
Cash	145,500
Common stock, $25 par (400,000 shares authorized; 104,850 shares issued)	2,621,250
Deferred income taxes payable (current portion, $4,700)	25,700
Dividends:	
Cash dividends for common stock	120,000
Cash dividends for preferred stock	105,000
Stock dividends for common stock	198,850
Dividends payable	30,000
Equipment	11,014,050
Income tax payable	55,900
Interest receivable	2,500
Merchandise inventory (July 31, 2000), at lower of cost (fifo) or market	425,000
Notes receivable	77,500
Organization costs	55,000
Paid-in capital from sale of treasury stock	16,000
Paid-in capital in excess of par—common stock	325,000
Paid-in capital in excess of par—preferred stock	240,000
Preferred 8% stock, $100 par (30,000 shares authorized; 15,000 shares issued)	1,500,000
Prepaid expenses	15,900
Retained earnings, August 1, 1999	4,158,900
Treasury stock (1,000 shares of common stock at cost of $40 per share)	40,000

Instructions

1. Prepare a multiple-step income statement for the year ended July 31, 2000, concluding with earnings per share. In computing earnings per share, assume that the average number of common shares outstanding was 100,000 and preferred dividends were $105,000. Round to nearest cent. Assume that the gain on condemnation of land is an extraordinary item.
2. Prepare a retained earnings statement for the year ended July 31, 2000.
3. Prepare a balance sheet in report form as of July 31, 2000.

Problem 13–4B

Entries for investments in stock

Objective 6

Killian Company is a wholesaler of men's hair products. The following transactions relate to certain securities acquired by Killian Company, whose fiscal year ends on December 31:

1997

Jan. 11. Purchased 2,500 shares of the 40,000 outstanding common shares of Burnell Corporation at 23¼ plus commission and other costs of $375.

July 5. Received the regular cash dividend of $1 a share on Burnell Corporation stock.

Dec. 5. Received the regular cash dividend of $1 a share plus an extra dividend of $0.15 a share on Burnell Corporation stock.
    (Assume that all intervening transactions have been recorded properly and that the number of shares of stock owned have not changed from December 31, 1997, to December 31, 2000.)

2001

Jan. 2. Purchased controlling interest in Nelda Inc. for $500,000 by purchasing 30,000 shares directly from the estate of the founder of Nelda. There are 50,000 shares of Nelda Inc. stock outstanding.

July 7. Received the regular cash dividend of $1 a share and a 4% stock dividend on the Burnell Corporation stock.

Aug. 20. Sold 500 shares of Burnell Corporation stock at 24. The broker deducted commission and other costs of $125, remitting the balance.

Dec. 9. Received a cash dividend at the new rate of $1.10 a share on the Burnell Corporation stock.

 31. Received $36,000 of cash dividends on Nelda Inc. stock. Nelda Inc. reported net income of $90,000 in 2001. Killian uses the equity method of accounting for its investment in Nelda Inc.

Instructions
Journalize the entries for the preceding transactions.

SPECIAL ACTIVITIES

Activity 13–1
Lindquest Inc.
Ethics and professional conduct in business

At a recent dinner party, you met Fred Proctor, the controller for Lindquest Inc. Fred has worked for Lindquest for the past six years. During your conversation, you complained about having to pay your third-quarter estimated taxes on Monday, September 15. In response, Fred indicated that he always *underpays* his estimated taxes. That way, he can use his money as long as possible. Is it appropriate to deliberately underpay your estimated taxes?

Activity 13–2
Wasley Corporation
Ethics and professional conduct in business

Joel Wasley is the president and chief operating officer of Wasley Corporation, a developer of personal financial planning software. During the past year, Wasley Corporation was forced to sell three acres of land to the city of Dallas for expansion of a freeway exit. The corporation fought the sale, but after condemnation hearings, a judge ordered it to sell the land. Because of the location of the land and the fact that Wasley Corporation had purchased the land over 15 years ago, the corporation recorded a $0.75-per-share gain on the sale. Always looking to turn a negative into a positive, Joel Wasley has decided to announce the corporation's earnings per share of $2.20, without identifying the $0.75 impact of selling the land. Although he will retain majority ownership, Joel plans on selling 10,000 of his shares in the corporation sometime within the next month. Are Joel's plans to announce earnings per share of $2.20 without mentioning the $0.75 impact of selling the land ethical and professional?

Activity 13–3
Oranges Inc.
Reporting extraordinary item

Oranges Inc. is in the process of preparing its annual financial statements. Oranges Inc. is a large citrus grower located in central Florida. The following is a discussion between Gene Pierno, the controller, and Judith Reimers, the chief executive officer and president of Oranges Inc.

Judith: Gene, I've got a question about your rough draft of this year's income statement.

Gene: Sure, Judith. What's your question?

Judith: Well, your draft shows a net loss of $1.5 million.

Gene: That's right. We'd have had a profit, except for this year's frost damage. I figured that the frost destroyed over 25 percent of our crop. We had a good year otherwise.

Judith: That's my concern. I estimated that if we eliminate the frost damage, we'd show a profit of . . . let's see . . . about $500,000.

Gene: That sounds about right.

Judith: This income statement seems misleading. Why can't we show the loss on the frost damage separately? That way the bank and our outside investors will be able to see that this year's loss is just temporary. I'd hate to get them upset over nothing.

Gene: Maybe we can do something. I recall from my accounting courses something about showing unusual items separately. Let's see . . . yes, I remember. They're called extraordinary items.

Judith: Well, we haven't had any frost damage in over five years. This year's damage is certainly extraordinary. Let's do it!

> Discuss the appropriateness of revising Oranges Inc.'s income statement to report the frost damage separately as an extraordinary item.

Activity 13–4
Geraldine Icerman
Consolidated financial statements

Your grandmother recently retired, sold her home in Boston, and moved to a retirement community in Arizona. With some of the proceeds from the sale of her home, she is considering investing $350,000 in the stock market.

In the process of selecting among alternative stock investments, your grandmother collected annual reports from twenty different companies. In reviewing these reports, however, she has become confused and has questions concerning several items that appear in the financial reports. She has asked for your help and has written down the following questions for you to answer:

a. *In reviewing the annual reports, I noticed many references to "consolidated financial statements." What are consolidated financial statements?*
b. *"Excess of cost of business acquired over related net assets" appears on the consolidated balance sheets in several annual reports. What does this mean? Is it an asset (it appears with other assets)?*
c. *What is minority interest?*
d. *A footnote to one of the consolidated statements indicated interest and the amount of a loan from one company to another had been eliminated. Is this good accounting? A loan is a loan. How can a company just eliminate a loan that hasn't been paid off?*
e. *How can financial statements for an American company (in dollars) be combined with a British subsidiary (in pounds)?*

1. ◖▬▶ Briefly respond to each of your grandmother's questions.
2. ◖▬▶ While discussing the items in (1) with your grandmother, she asked for your advice on whether she should limit her investment to one stock. What would you advise?

Activity 13–5
Into the Real World
Extraordinary items and discontinued operations

In groups of three or four students, search company annual reports, news releases, or the Internet for extraordinary items and announcements of discontinued operations. Identify the most unusual extraordinary item in your group. Also, select a discontinued operation of a well-known company that might be familiar to other students or might interest them.

Prepare a brief analysis of the earnings per share impact of both the extraordinary item and the discontinued operation. Estimate the *potential* impact on the company's market price by multiplying the current price-earnings ratio by the earnings per share amount of each item.

One Internet site that has annual reports is EDGAR (Electronic Data Gathering, Analysis, and Retrieval), the electronic archives of financial statements filed with the Securities and Exchange Commission. The EDGAR address is:

www.sec.gov/edgarhp.htm

To obtain annual report information, type in a company name on the "Search EDGAR Archives" form. EDGAR will list the reports available for the selected company. A company's annual report (along with other information) is provided in its annual 10-K report to the SEC. Click on the 10-K (or 10-K405) report for the year you wish to download. If you wish, you can save the whole 10-K report to a file and then open it with your word processor.

ANSWERS TO SELF-EXAMINATION QUESTIONS

Matching

1. Z	5. I	9. D	12. B	15. N	18. O	21. Y	24. E
2. AA	6. A	10. L	13. BB	16. G	19. F	22. V	25. P
3. H	7. U	11. CC	14. DD	17. J	20. Q	23. S	26. T
4. M	8. X						

Multiple Choice

1. **A** The amount of income tax deferred to future years is $16,000 (answer A), determined as follows:

Depreciation expense, MACRS	$100,000
Depreciation expense, straight-line method . . .	60,000
Excess expense in determining taxable income	$ 40,000
Income tax rate	× 40%
Income tax deferred to future years	$ 16,000

2. **A** Events and transactions that are distinguished by their unusual nature and by the infrequency of their occurrence, such as a gain on condemning land for public use, are reported in the income statement as extraordinary items (answer A).

3. **D** Appropriations are normally reported in the notes to the financial statements.

4. **C** The correction of a material error related to a prior period should be excluded from the determination of net income of the current period and reported as an adjustment of the balance of retained earnings at the beginning of the current period (answer C).

5. **C** Under the equity method of accounting for investments in stocks, Cisneros Corporation records its share of both net income and dividends of Harrell Inc. in Investment in Harrell Inc. Stock. Thus, Investment in Harrell Inc. Stock would increase by $82,500 [($150,000 × 75%) − ($40,000 × 75%)] for the current year. $30,000 (answer B) is only Cisneros Corporation's share of Harrell's dividends for the current year. $112,500 (answer D) is only Cisneros Corporation's share of Harrell's net income for the year.

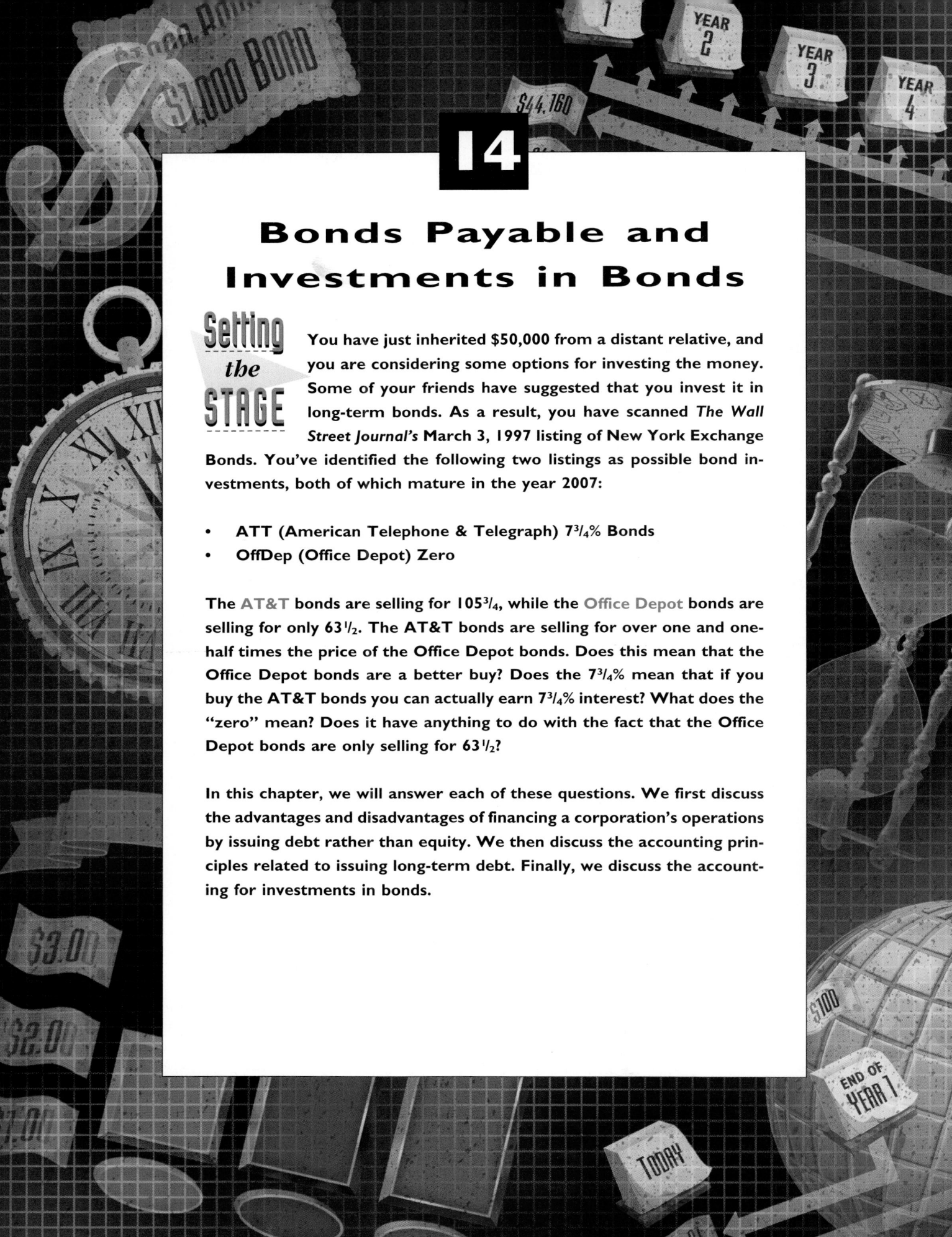

14

Bonds Payable and Investments in Bonds

Setting the STAGE

You have just inherited $50,000 from a distant relative, and you are considering some options for investing the money. Some of your friends have suggested that you invest it in long-term bonds. As a result, you have scanned *The Wall Street Journal's* March 3, 1997 listing of New York Exchange Bonds. You've identified the following two listings as possible bond investments, both of which mature in the year 2007:

- ATT (American Telephone & Telegraph) 7³/₄% Bonds
- OffDep (Office Depot) Zero

The AT&T bonds are selling for 105³/₄, while the Office Depot bonds are selling for only 63¹/₂. The AT&T bonds are selling for over one and one-half times the price of the Office Depot bonds. Does this mean that the Office Depot bonds are a better buy? Does the 7³/₄% mean that if you buy the AT&T bonds you can actually earn 7³/₄% interest? What does the "zero" mean? Does it have anything to do with the fact that the Office Depot bonds are only selling for 63¹/₂?

In this chapter, we will answer each of these questions. We first discuss the advantages and disadvantages of financing a corporation's operations by issuing debt rather than equity. We then discuss the accounting principles related to issuing long-term debt. Finally, we discuss the accounting for investments in bonds.

objectives

After studying this chapter, you should be able to:

1 Compute the potential impact of long-term borrowing on the earnings per share of a corporation.

2 Describe the characteristics of bonds.

3 Compute the present value of bonds payable.

4 Journalize entries for bonds payable.

5 Describe bond sinking funds.

6 Journalize entries for bond redemptions.

7 Journalize entries for the purchase, interest, discount and premium amortization, and sale of bond investments.

8 Prepare a corporation balance sheet.

9 Compute and interpret the number of times interest charges earned.

Financing Corporations

OBJECTIVE 1

Compute the potential impact of long-term borrowing on the earnings per share of a corporation.

Most of you have financed (purchased on credit) an automobile, a home, or a computer. Similarly, corporations often finance their operations by purchasing on credit and issuing notes or bonds. We have discussed accounts payable and notes payable in earlier chapters. A **bond** is simply a form of an interest-bearing note. Like a note, a bond requires periodic interest payments, and the face amount must be repaid at the maturity date. Bondholders are creditors of the issuing corporation, and their claims on the assets of the corporation rank ahead of stockholders.

Point of INTEREST

Bonds of major corporations are actively traded on bond exchanges. You can purchase bonds through a financial services firm, such as **Merrill Lynch** or **A. G. Edwards & Sons**.

One of the many factors that influence the decision to issue debt or equity is the effect of each alternative on earnings per share. To illustrate the possible effects, assume that a corporation's board of directors is considering the following alternative plans for financing a $4,000,000 company:

Plan 1: 100% financing from issuing common stock, $10 par

Plan 2: 50% financing from issuing preferred 9% stock, $50 par
50% financing from issuing common stock, $10 par

Plan 3: 50% financing from issuing 12% bonds
25% financing from issuing preferred 9% stock, $50 par
25% financing from issuing common stock, $10 par

In each case, we assume that the stocks or bonds are issued at their par or face amount. The corporation is expecting to earn $800,000 annually, before deducting interest on the bonds and income taxes estimated at 40% of income. Exhibit 1 shows the effect of the three plans on the income of the corporation and the earnings per share on common stock.

Exhibit 1 indicates that Plan 3 yields the highest earnings per share on common stock and is thus the most attractive for common stockholders. If the estimated earnings are more than $800,000, the difference between the earnings per share to

EXHIBIT 1

Effect of Alternative Financing Plans—$800,000 Earnings

	Plan 1	Plan 2	Plan 3
12% bonds	—	—	$2,000,000
Preferred 9% stock, $50 par	—	$2,000,000	1,000,000
Common stock, $10 par	$4,000,000	2,000,000	1,000,000
Total	$4,000,000	$4,000,000	$4,000,000
Earnings before interest and income tax	$ 800,000	$ 800,000	$ 800,000
Deduct interest on bonds	—	—	240,000
Income before income tax	$ 800,000	$ 800,000	$ 560,000
Deduct income tax	320,000	320,000	224,000
Net income	$ 480,000	$ 480,000	$ 336,000
Dividends on preferred stock	—	180,000	90,000
Available for dividends on common stock	$ 480,000	$ 300,000	$ 246,000
Shares of common stock outstanding	÷ 400,000	÷ 200,000	÷ 100,000
Earnings per share on common stock	$ 1.20	$ 1.50	$ 2.46

common stockholders under Plan 1 and Plan 3 is even greater.[1] However, if smaller earnings occur, Plans 2 and 3 become less attractive to common stockholders. To illustrate, the effect of earnings of $440,000 rather than $800,000 is shown in Exhibit 2.

EXHIBIT 2

Effect of Alternative Financing Plans—$440,000 Earnings

	Plan 1	Plan 2	Plan 3
12% bonds	—	—	$2,000,000
Preferred 9% stock, $50 par	—	$2,000,000	1,000,000
Common stock, $10 par	$4,000,000	2,000,000	1,000,000
Total	$4,000,000	$4,000,000	$4,000,000
Earnings before interest and income tax	$ 440,000	$ 440,000	$ 440,000
Deduct interest on bonds	—	—	240,000
Income before income tax	$ 440,000	$ 440,000	$ 200,000
Deduct income tax	176,000	176,000	80,000
Net income	$ 264,000	$ 264,000	$ 120,000
Dividends on preferred stock	—	180,000	90,000
Available for dividends on common stock	$ 264,000	$ 84,000	$ 30,000
Shares of common stock outstanding	÷ 400,000	÷ 200,000	÷ 100,000
Earnings per share on common stock	$ 0.66	$ 0.42	$ 0.30

In addition to the effect on earnings per share, the board of directors should consider other factors in deciding whether to issue debt or equity. For example, once bonds are issued, periodic interest payments and repayment of the face value of the bonds are beyond the control of the corporation. That is, if these payments are not made, the bondholders could seek court action and could force the company into bankruptcy. In contrast, a corporation is not legally obligated to pay dividends.

When interest rates are low, corporations usually finance their operations with debt. For example, as interest rates fell in the early 1990s, corporations rushed to issue new debt. In one day alone, more than $4.5 billion of debt was issued.

---

[1] The higher earnings per share under Plan 1 is due to a finance concept known as **leverage**. This concept is discussed further in a later chapter.

Characteristics of Bonds Payable

OBJECTIVE 2

Describe the characteristics of bonds.

A corporation that issues bonds enters into a contract, called a **bond indenture** or **trust indenture**, with the bondholders. A bond issue is normally divided into a number of individual bonds. Usually the face value of each bond, called the **principal**, is $1,000 or a multiple of $1,000. The interest on bonds may be payable annually, semiannually, or quarterly. Most bonds pay interest semiannually.

The prices of bonds are quoted as a percentage of the bonds' face value. Thus, investors could purchase or sell **Whirlpool** bonds quoted at 106¼

AT&T 7½% bonds maturing in 2006 were listed as selling for 106⅞ on October 7, 1997.

for $1,062.50. Likewise, bonds quoted at 109 could be purchased or sold for $1,090.

When all bonds of an issue mature at the same time, they are called **term bonds**. If the maturities are spread over several dates, they are called **serial bonds**. For example, one-tenth of an issue of $1,000,000 bonds, or $100,000, may mature 16 years from the issue date, another $100,000 in the 17th year, and so on until the final $100,000 matures in the 25th year.

Bonds that may be exchanged for other securities, such as common stock, are called **convertible bonds**. Bonds that a corporation reserves the right to redeem before their maturity are called **callable bonds**. Bonds issued on the basis of the general credit of the corporation are called **debenture bonds**.

INTERMISSION

Good Debt/ Bad Debt

Some of the same factors that influence a corporation's decision on financing are also considered when a company refinances, or changes the structure of its debt and stockholders' equity. These concerns are described in the following excerpt from an article in *USA TODAY*.

When a major company like **Allegis Corp.** announces that it is "recapitalizing" [refinancing], many shareholders may be baffled.... Recapitalization plans aren't as complicated as they seem, however.... How companies balance equity and debt is up to them. At **IBM Corp.**, only 11% of total capital is debt. **Sears, Roebuck and Co.** has 46% debt. The level of debt a company keeps depends on the risk its managers are willing to assume.

What does risk have to do with it?

It's no different for a company than for an individual. The more debt you have, the greater the risk. Reason: Any profit you earn first must go to meet interest payments. If earnings aren't sufficient to cover the interest owed, you'll have to deplete your savings—or sell something—to raise the needed cash.

What happens in a recapitalization?

A company decides to borrow heavily to raise cash for a large, one-time cash ... payment to shareholders.... [In addition,] ... shareholders also receive new shares to replace their old shares in the company.... [In] the process, the company generally [reduces its equity]. It's replaced with debt.

How can the company afford the debt load?

The company is forced to operate more efficiently than ever. It will have to slash expenses to keep earnings up in the face of higher interest expenses. **Owens-Corning Fiberglas Corp.**, for example, pared its research costs significantly after its recapitalization last year....

Is there any advantage in being so heavily in debt?

Debt does have a good side. By borrowing, you gain "leverage"—the ability to control more assets by using someone else's money. That can magnify the return to shareholders, if business is good and the firm operates efficiently.... ■

Source: Neil Budde, "How Company Recapitalization Plans Work," USA TODAY, June 8, 1987.

The Present-Value Concept and Bonds Payable

OBJECTIVE 3

Compute the present value of bonds payable.

When a corporation issues bonds, the price that buyers are willing to pay for the bonds depends upon the following three factors:

1. The face amount of the bonds, which is the amount due at the maturity date.
2. The periodic interest to be paid on the bonds.
3. The market rate of interest.

The face amount and the periodic interest to be paid on the bonds is identified in the bond indenture. The periodic interest is expressed as a percentage of the face amount of the bond. This percentage or rate of interest is called the **contract rate** or **coupon rate**.

The **market** or **effective rate of interest** is determined by transactions between buyers and sellers of similar bonds. The market rate of interest is affected by a variety of factors, including investors' assessment of current economic conditions as well as future expectations.

If the contract rate of interest equals the market rate of interest, the bonds will sell at their face amount. If the market rate is higher than the contract rate, the bonds will sell at a **discount**, or less than their face amount. Why is this the case? Buyers are not willing to pay the face amount for bonds whose contract rate is lower than the market rate. The discount, in effect, represents the amount necessary to make up for the difference in the market and the contract interest rates. In contrast, if the market rate is lower than the contract rate, the bonds will sell at a **premium**, or more than their face amount. In this case, buyers are willing to pay more than the face amount for bonds whose contract rate is higher than the market rate.

The face amount of the bonds and the periodic interest on the bonds represent cash to be received by the buyer in the future. The buyer determines how much to pay for the bonds by computing the present value of these future cash receipts, using the market rate of interest. The concept of present value is based on the time value of money.

If IBM 7¼% bonds maturing in 2002 are listed as selling for 104⅜, is the market rate of interest higher or lower than that for similar bonds?

Lower

What is the time value of money? An amount of cash to be received at some date in the future is worth less than the same amount of cash held today. For example, what would you rather have: $100 today or $100 one year from now? You would rather have the $100 today because it could be invested to earn income. For example, if the $100 could be invested to earn 10% per year, the $100 will accumulate to $110 ($100 plus $10 earnings) in one year. In this sense, you can think of the $100 in hand today as the **present value** of $110 to be received a year from today. This present value is illustrated in the following time line:

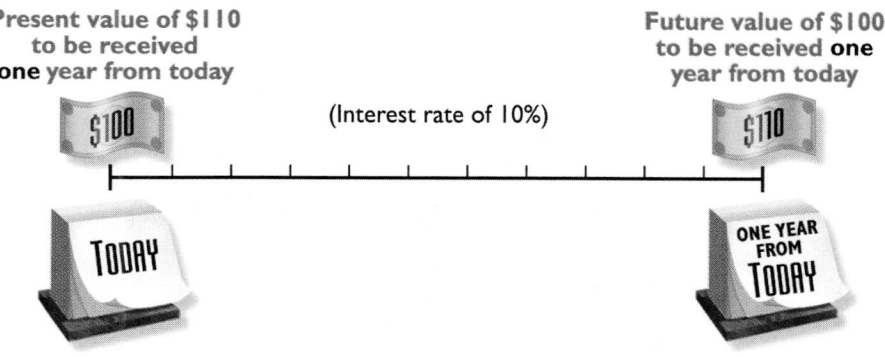

What is the future value of $100 to be received in two years, assuming an interest rate of 10%?

$121 ($100 × 1.10 × 1.10)

A related concept to present value is **future value**. In the preceding illustration, the $110 to be received a year from today is the future value of $100 today, assuming an interest rate of 10%.

Present Value of the Face Amount of Bonds

The present value of the face amount of bonds is the value today of the amount to be received at a future maturity date. For example, assume that you are to receive the face value of a $1,000 bond in one year. If the market rate of interest is 10%, the present value of the face value of the $1,000 bond is $909.09 ($1,000/1.10). This present value is illustrated in the following time line:

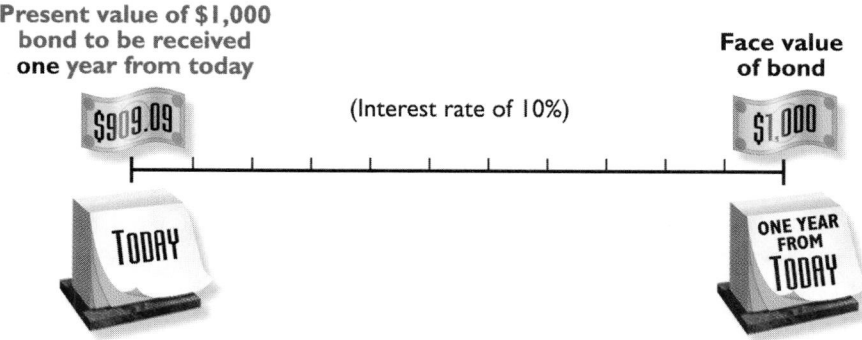

If you are to receive the face value of a $1,000 bond in two years, with interest of 10% compounded at the end of the first year, the present value is $826.45 ($909.09/1.10).[2] We illustrate this present value in the following time line:

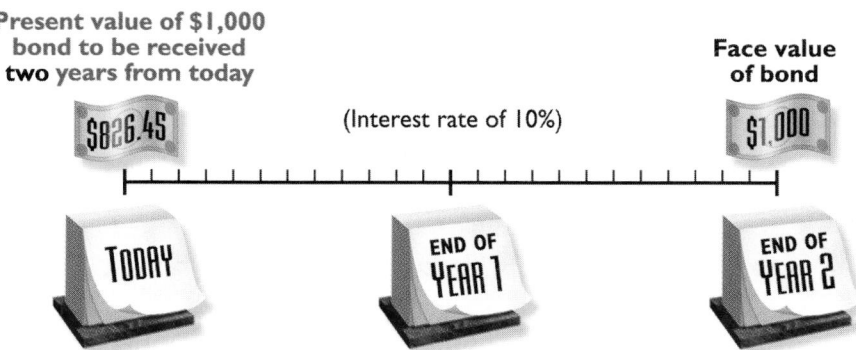

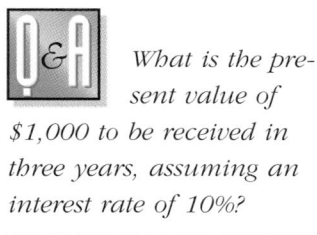

What is the present value of $1,000 to be received in three years, assuming an interest rate of 10%?

$751.32 ($826.45/1.10)

You can determine the present value of the face amount of bonds to be received in the future by a time line and a series of divisions. In practice, however, it is easier to use a table of present values. The *present value of $1 table* can be used to find the present-value factor for $1 to be received after a number of periods in the future. The face amount of the bonds is then multiplied by this factor to determine its present value. Exhibit 3 is a partial table of the present value of $1.[3]

Point of INTEREST

Spreadsheet software with built-in present value functions can be used to calculate present values.

---

[2] Note that the future value of $826.45 in two years, at an interest rate of 10% compounded annually, is $1,000.
[3] To simplify the illustrations and homework assignments, the tables presented in this chapter are limited to 10 periods for a small number of interest rates, and the amounts are carried to only five decimal places. Computer programs are available for determining present value factors for any number of interest rates, decimal places, or periods. More complete interest tables, including future value tables, are presented in Appendix A.

EXHIBIT 3   Present Value of $1 at Compound Interest

Periods	5%	5½%	6%	6½%	7%	10%	11%	12%	13%	14%
1	0.95238	0.94787	0.94340	0.93897	0.93458	0.90909	0.90090	0.89286	0.88496	0.87719
2	0.90703	0.89845	0.89000	0.88166	0.87344	0.82645	0.81162	0.79719	0.78315	0.76947
3	0.86384	0.85161	0.83962	0.82785	0.81630	0.75132	0.73119	0.71178	0.69305	0.67497
4	0.82270	0.80722	0.79209	0.77732	0.76290	0.68301	0.65873	0.63552	0.61332	0.59208
5	0.78353	0.76513	0.74726	0.72988	0.71299	0.62092	0.59345	0.56743	0.54276	0.51937
6	0.74622	0.72525	0.70496	0.68533	0.66634	0.56447	0.53464	0.50663	0.48032	0.45559
7	0.71068	0.68744	0.66506	0.64351	0.62275	0.51316	0.48166	0.45235	0.42506	0.39964
8	0.67684	0.65160	0.62741	0.60423	0.58201	0.46651	0.43393	0.40388	0.37616	0.35056
9	0.64461	0.61763	0.59190	0.56735	0.54393	0.42410	0.39092	0.36061	0.33288	0.30751
10	0.61391	0.58543	0.55840	0.53273	0.50835	0.38554	0.35218	0.32197	0.29459	0.26974

What is the present value of $3,000 to be received in 5 years at a market rate of interest of 14% compounded annually?

$1,558.11 ($3,000 × 0.51937)

Exhibit 3 indicates that the present value of $1 to be received in two years with a market rate of interest of 10% a year is 0.82645. Multiplying the $1,000 face amount of the bond in the preceding example by 0.82645 yields $826.45.

In Exhibit 3, the Periods column represents the number of compounding periods, and the percentage columns represent the compound interest rate per period. For example, 10% for two years compounded *annually,* as in the preceding example, is 10% for two periods. Likewise, 10% for two years compounded *semiannually* would be 5% (10% per year/2 semiannual periods) for four periods (2 years × 2 semiannual periods). Similarly, 10% for three years compounded semiannually would be 5% (10%/2) for six periods (3 years × 2 semiannual periods).

Present Value of the Periodic Bond Interest Payments

The present value of the periodic bond interest payments is the value today of the amount of interest to be received at the end of each interest period. Such a series of equal cash payments at fixed intervals is called an **annuity**.

The **present value of an annuity** is the sum of the present values of each cash flow. To illustrate, assume that the $1,000 bond in the preceding example pays interest of 10% annually and that the market rate of interest is also 10%. In addition, assume that the bond matures at the end of two years. The present value of the two interest payments of $100 ($1,000 × 10%) is $173.56, as shown in the time line at the left. It can be determined by using the present value table shown in Exhibit 3.

Instead of using present value of amount tables, such as Exhibit 3, separate present value tables are normally used for annuities. Exhibit 4 is a partial table of the *present value of an annuity of $1* at compound interest. It shows the present value of $1 to be received at the end of each period for various compound

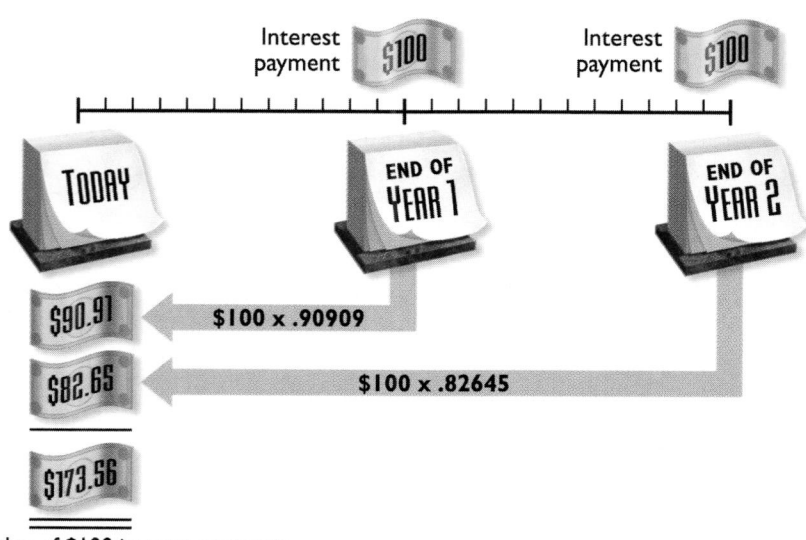

Present value of $100 interest payments to be received each year for 2 years (rounded to the nearest cent)

rates of interest. For example, the present value of $100 to be received at the end of each of the next two years at 10% compound interest per period is $173.55 ($100 × 1.73554). This amount is the same amount that we computed previously, except for rounding.

EXHIBIT 4 Present Value of Annuity of $1 at Compound Interest

Periods	5%	5½%	6%	6½%	7%	10%	11%	12%	13%	14%
1	0.95238	0.94787	0.94340	0.93897	0.93458	0.90909	0.90090	0.89286	0.88496	0.87719
2	1.85941	1.84632	1.83339	1.82063	1.80802	1.73554	1.71252	1.69015	1.66810	1.64666
3	2.72325	2.69793	2.67301	2.64848	2.62432	2.48685	2.44371	2.40183	2.36115	2.32163
4	3.54595	3.50515	3.46511	3.42580	3.38721	3.16987	3.10245	3.03735	2.97447	2.91371
5	4.32948	4.27028	4.21236	4.15568	4.10020	3.79079	3.69590	3.60478	3.51723	3.43308
6	5.07569	4.99553	4.91732	4.84101	4.76654	4.35526	4.23054	4.11141	3.99755	3.88867
7	5.78637	5.68297	5.58238	5.48452	5.38929	4.86842	4.71220	4.56376	4.42261	4.28830
8	6.46321	6.33457	6.20979	6.08875	5.97130	5.33493	5.14612	4.96764	4.79677	4.63886
9	7.10782	6.95220	6.80169	6.65610	6.51523	5.75902	5.53705	5.32825	5.13166	4.94637
10	7.72174	7.53763	7.36009	7.18883	7.02358	6.14457	5.88923	5.65022	5.42624	5.21612

What is the present value of a $10,000, 7%, 5-year bond that pays interest annually, assuming a market rate of interest of 7%?

$10,000 [($10,000 × 0.71299) + ($700 × 4.10020)]

As we stated earlier, the amount buyers are willing to pay for a bond is the sum of the present value of the face value and the periodic interest payments, calculated by using the market rate of interest. In our example, this calculation is as follows:

Present value of face value of $1,000 due in 2 years at 10% compounded annually: $1,000 × 0.82645 (present value factor of $1 for 2 periods at 10%)	$ 826.45
Present value of 2 annual interest payments of $100 at 10% compounded annually: $100 × 1.73554 (present value of annuity of $1 for 2 periods at 10%)	173.55
Total present value of bonds	$1,000.00

In this example, the market rate and the contract rate of interest are the same. Thus, the present value is the same as the face value.

Accounting for Bonds Payable

OBJECTIVE 4
- - - - - - - - - - - - - - - - - - - -

Journalize entries for bonds payable.

In the preceding section, we described and illustrated how present value concepts are used in determining how much buyers are willing to pay for bonds. In this section, we describe and illustrate how corporations record the issuance of bonds and the payment of bond interest.

Bonds Issued at Face Amount

To illustrate the journal entries for issuing bonds, assume that on January 1, 1999, a corporation issues for cash $100,000 of 12%, five-year bonds, with interest of $6,000 payable *semiannually*. The market rate of interest at the time the bonds are issued is 12%. Since the contract rate and the market rate of interest are the same, the bonds will sell at their face amount. This amount is the sum of (1) the present value of the face amount of $100,000 to be repaid in five years and (2) the present value of ten *semiannual* interest payments of $6,000 each. This computation and a time line are shown below.

Present value of face amount of $100,000 due in 5 years,
   at 12% compounded semiannually: $100,000 × 0.55840
   (present value of $1 for 10 periods at 6%) .... $ 55,840
Present value of 10 semiannual interest payments of $6,000,
   at 12% compounded semiannually: $6,000 × 7.36009 (present
   value of annuity of $1 for 10 periods at 6%) 44,160*
Total present value of bonds $100,000

* Because the present-value tables are rounded to five decimal places, minor rounding differences may appear in the illustrations.

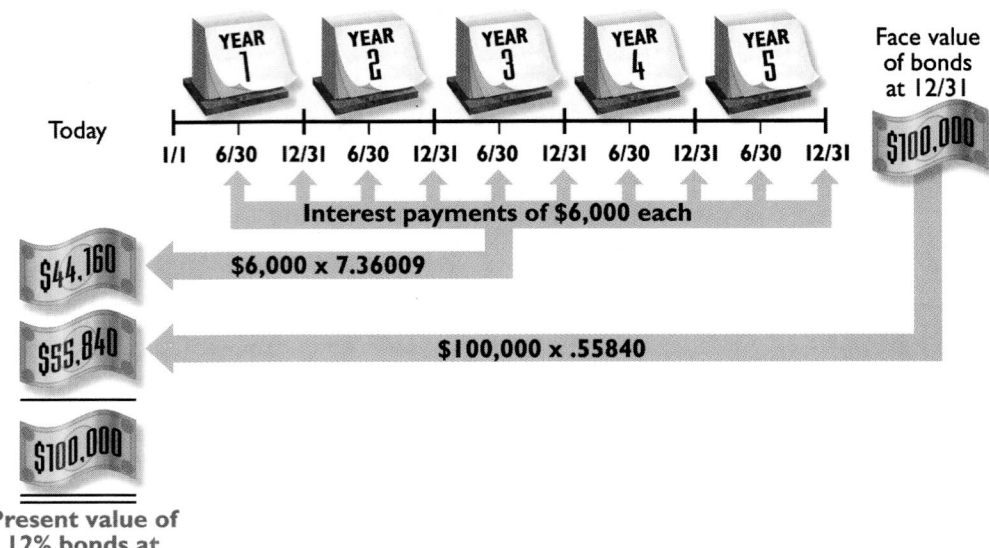

The following entry records the issuing of the $100,000 bonds at their face amount:

	1999					
	Jan.	1	Cash	100 0 0 0 00		
			Bonds Payable		100 0 0 0 00	
			Issued $100,000 bonds payable at			
			face amount.			

Every six months after the bonds have been issued, interest payments of $6,000 are made. The first interest payment is recorded as shown below.

	June	30	Interest Expense	6 0 0 0 00		
			Cash		6 0 0 0 00	
			Paid six months' interest on bonds.			

At the maturity date, the payment of the principal of $100,000 is recorded as follows:

	2003					
	Dec.	31	Bonds Payable	100 0 0 0 00		
			Cash		100 0 0 0 00	
			Paid bond principal at maturity			
			date.			

Bonds Issued at a Discount

Bonds will sell at a discount when the market rate of interest is higher than the contract rate.

What if the market rate of interest is higher than the contract rate of interest? If the market rate of interest is 13% and the contract rate is 12% on the five-year, $100,000 bonds, the bonds will sell at a discount. The present value of these bonds is calculated as follows:

Present value of face amount of $100,000 due in
  5 years, at 13% compounded semiannually: $100,000
    × 0.53273 (present value of $1 for 10 periods at 6½%) $53,273
Present value of 10 semiannual interest payments of $6,000,
  at 13% compounded semiannually: $6,000 × 7.18883 (present
  value of an annuity of $1 for 10 periods at 6½%)   43,133
Total present value of bonds $96,406

The two present values that make up the total are both less than the related amounts in the preceding example. This is because the market rate of interest was 12% in the first example, while the market rate of interest is 13% in this example. The present value of a future amount becomes less and less as the interest rate used to compute the present value increases.

The entry to record the issuing of the $100,000 bonds at a discount is shown below.

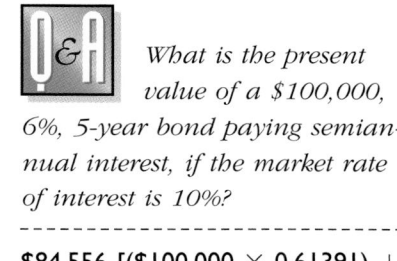

What is the present value of a $100,000, 6%, 5-year bond paying semiannual interest, if the market rate of interest is 10%?

$84,556 [($100,000 × 0.61391) + ($3,000 × 7.72174)]

	1999					
	Jan.	1	Cash	96 4 0 6 00		
			Discount on Bonds Payable	3 5 9 4 00		
			Bonds Payable		100 0 0 0 00	
			Issued $100,000 bonds at discount.			

The $3,594 discount may be viewed as the amount that is needed to entice investors to accept a contract rate of interest that is below the market rate. You may think of the discount as the market's way of adjusting a bond's contract rate of interest to the higher market rate of interest. Using this logic, generally accepted accounting principles require that bond discounts be amortized as interest expense over the life of the bond.

Amortizing a Bond Discount

There are two methods of amortizing a bond discount: (1) the **straight-line method** and (2) the **effective interest rate method**, often called the **interest method**. Both methods amortize the same total amount of discount over the life of the bonds. The interest method is required by generally accepted accounting principles. However, the straight-line method is acceptable if the results obtained do not materially differ from the results that would be obtained by using the interest method. Because the straight-line method illustrates the basic concept of amortizing discounts and is sim-

If the amount of a bond discount on a newly issued 6%, 5-year, $100,000 bond is $28,092, what are (a) the semiannual straight-line amortization of the discount and (b) the annual interest expense?

(a) $2,809.20, (b) $11,618.40 ($2,809.20 + $2,809.20 + $6,000)

pler, we will use it in this chapter. We illustrate the interest method in an appendix to this chapter.

The straight-line method of amortizing a bond discount provides for amortization in equal periodic amounts. Applying this method to the preceding example yields amortization of $\frac{1}{10}$ of $3,594, or $359.40, each half year. The amount of the interest expense on the bonds is the same, $6,359.40 ($6,000 + $359.40) for each half year. The entry to record the first interest payment and the amortization of the related discount is shown below.

1999 June	30	Interest Expense	6 3 5 9 40		
		Discount on Bonds Payable		3 5 9 40	
		Cash		6 0 0 0 00	
		Paid semiannual interest and			
		amortized $\frac{1}{10}$ of bond discount.			

Bonds Issued at a Premium

Bonds will sell at a premium when the market rate of interest is less than the contract rate.

If the market rate of interest is 11% and the contract rate is 12% on the five-year, $100,000 bonds, the bonds will sell at a premium. The present value of these bonds is computed as follows:

Present value of face amount of $100,000 due in 5 years,
  at 11% compounded semiannually: $100,000 × 0.58543
  (present value of $1 for 10 periods at 5½%) . . . . $ 58,543
Present value of 10 semiannual interest payments of $6,000,
  at 11% compounded semiannually: $6,000 × 7.53763
  (present value of an annuity of $1 for 10 periods at 5½%)   45,226
Total present value of bonds $103,769

The entry to record the issuing of the bonds is as follows:

1999 Jan.	1	Cash	103 7 6 9 00		
		Bonds Payable		100 0 0 0 00	
		Premium on Bonds Payable		3 7 6 9 00	
		Issued $100,000 bonds at a			
		premium.			

Amortizing a Bond Premium

If the amount of a bond premium on a newly issued 13%, 5-year, $100,000 bond is $11,581, what are (a) the semiannual straight-line amortization of the premium and (b) the annual interest expense?

(a) $1,158.10, (b) $10,683.80 ($13,000 − $1,158.10 − $1,158.10)

The amortization of bond premiums is basically the same as that for bond discounts, except that interest expense is decreased. In the above example, the straight-line method yields amortization of $\frac{1}{10}$ of $3,769, or $376.90, each half year. The entry to record the first interest payment and the amortization of the related premium is as follows:

1999 June	30	Interest Expense	5 6 2 3 10		
		Premium on Bonds Payable	3 7 6 90		
		Cash		6 0 0 0 00	
		Paid semiannual interest and			
		amortized $\frac{1}{10}$ of bond premium.			

Zero-Coupon Bonds

Some corporations issue bonds that provide for only the payment of the face amount at the maturity date. Such bonds are called **zero-coupon bonds**. Because they do not provide for interest payments, these bonds sell at a large discount. For example, **Office Depot's** zero-coupon bonds maturing in 2007 were selling for $63\frac{1}{2}$ on March 3, 1997.

The issuing price of zero-coupon bonds is the present value of their face amount. To illustrate, if the market rate of interest is 13%, the present value of $100,000 zero-coupon, five-year bonds is calculated as follows:

 Some bonds with high contract rates, as well as some zero-coupon bonds, are issued by weak companies. Because such bonds are high-risk bonds, they are called **junk bonds**.

Present value of $100,000 due in 5 years, at 13%
   compounded semiannually: $100,000 × 0.53273
   (present value of $1 for 10 periods at $6\frac{1}{2}$%) $53,273

The accounting for zero-coupon bonds is similar to that for interest-bearing bonds that have been sold at a discount. The discount is amortized as interest expense over the life of the bonds. The entry to record the issuing of the bonds is as follows:

1999					
Jan.	1	Cash		53 273 00	
		Discount on Bonds Payable		46 727 00	
		Bonds Payable			100 000 00
		Issued $100,000 zero-coupon			
		bonds.			

Bond Sinking Funds

OBJECTIVE 5

Describe bond sinking funds.

A bond indenture may restrict dividend payments to stockholders as a means of increasing the likelihood that the bonds will be paid at maturity. In addition to or instead of this restriction, the bond indenture may require that funds for the payment of the face value of the bonds at maturity be set aside over the life of the bond issue. The amounts set aside are kept separate from other assets in a special fund called a **sinking fund**.

When cash is transferred to the sinking fund, it is recorded in an account called *Sinking Fund Cash*. When investments are purchased with the sinking fund cash, they are recorded in an account called *Sinking Fund Investments*. As income (interest or dividends) is received, it is recorded in an account called *Sinking Fund Revenue*.

Sinking fund revenue represents earnings of the corporation and is reported in the income statement as Other Income. The cash and the securities making up the sinking fund are reported in the balance sheet as Investments, immediately below the Current Assets section.

BUSINESS ON STAGE

Bonds are rated as to their riskiness as investments by such independent financial reporting services as **Moody's** and **Standard and Poor's**. These services rely heavily on analysis of the financial statements and the terms of the bond indenture in setting the credit rating. This credit rating, in turn, influences how much the bonds will sell for in the marketplace. Moody's and Standard and Poor's rate bonds slightly differently. The following table shows each rating and its accompanying interpretation.

Moody's Rating	Standard and Poor's Rating	Interpretation
AAA	Aaa	Highest rating; ability to pay interest and principal is very secure.
AA	Aa	High quality; differs from highest-rated bonds only to a small degree.
A	A	Upper-medium quality; interest and principal may be in jeopardy if a long, deep economic downturn (recession) occurs.
BBB	Baa	Medium grade; adequate ability to pay interest and principal in normal economic conditions.
BB	Ba	Quite risky; modest ability to pay interest and principal.
B	B	Poor investment; highly speculative; ability to pay interest and principal over a long period is small.
CCC	Caa	Poor standing; may be in default; purchase for speculative purposes only.
CC	Ca	Highly speculative; often in default on current payments.
C	C	Very poor prospects for ever being a good investment.
D	—	In default; little chance of ever receiving interest or principal.

Moody's classifies bonds of BBB or greater as "Investment Grade" bonds. In addition, Moody's will use a "+" sign or "−" sign to indicate the relative strength of a bond within a general rating category. For example, AAA+ indicates that a bond is at the high end of the AAA category.

Standard & Poor's classifies bonds of Baa or greater as "Investment Grade." Instead of using a "+" or "−" sign to indicate relative strength within a rating category, Standard & Poor's uses 1, 2, and 3. For example, Aaa1 indicates that a bond is in the upper third of the Aaa category, while Aaa3 indicates that a bond is in the bottom third. ■

Bond Redemption

OBJECTIVE 6

Journalize entries for bond redemptions.

A corporation may call or redeem bonds before they mature. This is often done if the market rate of interest declines significantly after the bonds have been issued. In this situation, the corporation may sell new bonds at a lower interest rate and use the funds to redeem the original bond issue. The corporation can thus save on future interest expenses.

A corporation often issues callable bonds to protect itself against significant declines in future interest rates. However, callable bonds are more risky for investors, who may not be able to replace the called bonds with investments paying an equal amount of interest.

Callable bonds can be redeemed by the issuing corporation within the period of time and at the price stated in the bond indenture. Normally, the call price is above the face value. A corporation may also redeem its bonds by purchasing them on the open market.

A corporation usually redeems its bonds at a price

 **Indo Rayon** issued 5-year, 10% bonds, callable after 3 years.

different from that of the carrying amount (or book value) of the bonds. The **carrying amount** of bonds payable is the balance of the bonds payable account (face amount of the bonds) less any unamortized discount or plus any unamortized premium. If the price paid for redemption is below the bond carrying amount, the difference in these two amounts is recorded as a gain. If the price paid for the redemption is above the carrying amount, a loss is recorded. Gains and losses on the redemption of bonds are reported as an extraordinary item on the income statement.

To illustrate, assume that on June 30 a corporation has a bond issue of $100,000 outstanding, on which there is an unamortized premium of $4,000. Assuming that the corporation purchases one-fourth ($25,000) of the bonds for $24,000 on June 30, the entry to record the redemption is as follows:

	1999 June	30	Bonds Payable	25 0 0 0 00		
			Premium on Bonds Payable	1 0 0 0 00		
			Cash		24 0 0 0 00	
			Gain on Redemption of Bonds		2 0 0 0 00	
			Redeemed $25,000 bonds for			
			$24,000.			

Q&A *A $250,000 bond issue on which there is an unamortized discount of $20,000 is redeemed for $235,000. What is the gain or loss on the redemption of the bonds?*

$5,000 loss ($250,000 − $20,000 − $235,000)

In the preceding entry, only a portion of the premium relating to the redeemed bonds is written off. The difference between the carrying amount of the bonds purchased, $26,000 ($25,000 + $1,000), and the price paid for the redemption, $24,000, is recorded as a gain.

If the corporation calls the entire bond issue for $105,000 on June 30, the entry to record the redemption is as follows:

	1999 June	30	Bonds Payable	100 0 0 0 00		
			Premium on Bonds Payable	4 0 0 0 00		
			Loss on Redemption of Bonds	1 0 0 0 00		
			Cash		105 0 0 0 00	
			Redeemed $100,000 bonds for			
			$105,000.			

Investments in Bonds

OBJECTIVE 7

Journalize entries for the purchase, interest, discount and premium amortization, and sale of bond investments.

Throughout this chapter, we have discussed bonds and the related transactions of the issuing corporation (the debtor). However, these transactions also affect investors. In this section, we discuss the accounting for bonds from the point of view of investors.

Accounting for Bond Investments—Purchase, Interest, and Amortization

Bonds may be purchased either directly from the issuing corporation or through an organized bond exchange. Bond exchanges publish daily bond quotations. These quotations normally include the bond interest rate, maturity date, volume of sales, and the high, low, and closing prices for each corporation's bonds traded during the day. Prices for bonds are quoted as a percentage of the face amount. Thus, the price of a $1,000 bond quoted at 99½ would be $995, while the price of a bond quoted at 104¼ would be $1,042.50.

 **REAL WORLD** IBM's 7⅛% bonds maturing in 2096 were listed as selling for 98⅛ on October 8, 1997.

As with other assets, the cost of a bond investment includes all costs related to the purchase. For example, for bonds purchased through an exchange, the amount paid as a broker's commission should be included as part of the cost of the investment.

When bonds are purchased between interest dates, the buyer normally pays the seller the interest accrued from the last interest payment date to the date of purchase. The amount of the interest paid is normally debited to *Interest Revenue*, since it is an offset against the amount that will be received at the next interest date.

To illustrate, assume that an investor purchases a $1,000 bond at 102 plus a brokerage fee of $5.30 and accrued interest of $10.20. The investor records the transaction as follows:

1999					
Apr.	2	Investment in Lewis Co. Bonds	1 0 2 5 30		
		Interest Revenue	1 0 20		
		Cash			1 0 3 5 50

The cost of the bond is recorded in a single investment account. The face amount of the bond and the premium (or discount) are normally not recorded in separate accounts. This is different from the accounting for bonds payable. Separate premium and discount accounts are usually not used by investors, because they usually do not hold bond investments until the bonds mature.

When bonds held as long-term investments are purchased at a price other than the face amount, the premium or discount should be amortized over the remaining life of the bonds. The amortization of premiums and discounts affects the investment and interest accounts as shown below.

> **A premium or discount on a bond investment is recorded in the investment account and is amortized over the remaining life of the bonds.**

Premium Amortization:			Discount Amortization:		
Interest Revenue	XXX		Investment in Bonds	XXX	
Investment in Bonds		XXX	Interest Revenue		XXX

The amount of the amortization can be determined by using either the straight-line or interest methods. Unlike bonds payable, the amortization of premiums and discounts on bond investments is usually recorded at the end of the period, rather than when interest is received.

To illustrate the accounting for bond investments, assume that on July 1, 1999, Crenshaw Inc. purchases $50,000 of 8% bonds of Deitz Corporation, due in $8\frac{3}{4}$ years. Crenshaw Inc. purchases the bonds directly from Deitz Corporation to yield an effective interest rate of 11%. The purchase price is $41,706 plus interest of $1,000 ($50,000 × 8% × $\frac{3}{12}$) accrued from April 1, 1999, the date of the last semiannual interest payment. Entries in the accounts of Crenshaw Inc. at the time of purchase and for the remainder of the fiscal period ending December 31, 1999, are as follows:

1999					
July	1	Investment in Deitz Corp. Bonds	41 7 0 6 00		
		Interest Revenue	1 0 0 0 00		
		Cash			42 7 0 6 00
		Purchased investment in bonds,			
		plus accrued interest:			
		Cost of $50,000 of Deitz			
		Corp. bonds $41,706			
		Interest accrued ($50,000			
		× 8% × $\frac{3}{12}$) 1,000			
		Total $42,706			

Oct.	1	Cash		2 0 0 0 00		
		Interest Revenue			2 0 0 0 00	
		Received semiannual interest for				
		April 1 to October 1 ($50,000 ×				
		8% × $^6/_{12}$).				
Dec.	31	Interest Receivable		1 0 0 0 00		
		Interest Revenue			1 0 0 0 00	
		Adjusting entry for interest				
		accrued from October 1 to				
		December 31 ($50,000 ×				
		8% × $^3/_{12}$).				
	31	Investment in Deitz Corp. Bonds		4 7 4 00		
		Interest Revenue			4 7 4 00	
		Adjusting entry for amortization of				
		discount for July 1 to December 31:				
		Face value of bonds $50,000				
		Cost of bond				
		investment 41,706				
		Discount on bond				
		investment $ 8,294				
		Number of months to				
		maturity (8 $^3/_4$ years				
		× 12) 105 months				
		Monthly amortization				
		($8,294/105 months,				
		rounded to nearest				
		dollar) $79 per mo.				
		Amortization for 6				
		months ($79 × 6) $474				

The effect of these entries on the interest revenue account is shown below.

Interest Revenue

July 1	1,000	Oct. 1	2,000
		Dec. 31	1,000
		31	474
		Bal. 2,474	3,474

Accounting for Bond Investments—Sale

Many long-term investments in bonds are sold before their maturity date. When this occurs, the seller receives the sales price (less commissions and other selling costs) plus any accrued interest since the last interest payment date. Before recording the cash proceeds, the seller should amortize any discount or premium for the current period up to the date of sale. Any gain or loss on the sale is then recorded when the cash proceeds are recorded. Such gains and losses are normally reported in the Other Income section of the income statement.

To illustrate, assume that the Deitz Corporation bonds in the above example are sold for $47,350 plus accrued interest on June 30, 2006. The *carrying amount* of the bonds (cost plus amortized discount) as of January 1, 2006 (78 months after their purchase) is $47,868 [$41,706 + ($79 per mo. × 78 months)]. The entries to amortize the discount for the current year and to record the sale of the bonds are as follows:

2006						
June	30	Investment in Deitz Corp. Bonds		474 00		
		Interest Revenue				474 00
		Amortized discount for current				
		year ($79 × 6 months).				
	30	Cash		48 350 00		
		Loss on Sale of Investments		992 00		
		Interest Revenue				1 000 00
		Investment in Deitz Corp. Bonds				48 342 00
		Received interest and proceeds				
		from sale of bonds.				
		Interest for April 1 to June 30 =				
		$50,000 × 8% × ³/₁₂ = $1,000				
		Carrying amount of				
		bonds on Jan. 1, 2006 $47,868				
		Discount amortized,				
		Jan. 1 to June 30, 2006 474				
		Carrying amount of				
		bonds on June 30, 2006 $48,342				
		Proceeds of sale 47,350				
		Loss on sale $ 992				

Q&A *If the Deitz Corporation bonds had been sold on September 30 instead of June 30, what would have been the amount of the loss?*

$1,229 {$47,350 − [$48,342 + ($79 × 3 months)]}

Corporation Balance Sheet

OBJECTIVE 8

Prepare a corporation balance sheet.

In previous chapters, we illustrated the income statement and retained earnings statement for a corporation. The consolidated balance sheet in Exhibit 5 illustrates the presentation of many of the items discussed in this and preceding chapters. These items include bond sinking funds, investments in bonds, goodwill, deferred income taxes, bonds payable and unamortized discount, and minority interest in subsidiaries.

Balance Sheet Presentation of Bonds Payable

In Exhibit 5, Escoe Corporation's bonds payable are reported as long-term liabilities. If there were two or more bond issues, the details of each would be reported on the balance sheet or in a supporting schedule or note. Separate accounts are normally maintained for each bond issue.

When the balance sheet date is within one year of the maturity date of the bonds, the bonds may be classified as a current liability. This would be the case if the bonds are to be paid out of current assets. If the bonds are to be paid from a sinking fund or if they are to be refinanced with another bond issue, they should remain in the noncurrent category. In this case, the details of the retirement of the bonds are normally disclosed in a note to the financial statements.

The balance in Escoe's discount on bonds payable account is reported as a *deduction* from the bonds payable. Conversely, the balance in a bond premium ac-

EXHIBIT 5   Balance Sheet of a Corporation

Escoe Corporation and Subsidiaries
Consolidated Balance Sheet
December 31, 2000

Assets

Current assets:

Cash		$ 255,000	
Marketable securities	$ 160,000		
Less unrealized loss	7,500	152,500	
Accounts and notes receivable	$ 722,000		
Less allowance for doubtful receivables	37,000	685,000	
Inventories, at lower of cost (first-in, first-out) or market		917,500	
Prepaid expenses		70,000	
Total current assets			$2,080,000

Investments:

Bond sinking fund (market value, $473,000)		$ 422,500	
Investment in bonds of Dalton Company (market value, $231,000)		240,000	
Total investments			662,500

	Cost	Accumulated Depreciation	Book Value	
Property, plant, and equipment (depreciated by the straight-line method):				
Land	$ 250,000	—	$ 250,000	
Buildings	920,000	$ 379,955	540,045	
Machinery and equipment	2,764,400	766,200	1,998,200	
Total property, plant, and equipment	$3,934,400	$1,146,155		2,788,245
Intangible assets:				
Goodwill			$ 300,000	
Organization costs			50,000	
Total intangible assets				350,000
Total assets				$5,880,745

Liabilities

Current liabilities:

Accounts payable		$ 508,810	
Income tax payable		120,500	
Dividends payable		94,000	
Accrued liabilities		81,400	
Deferred income tax payable		10,000	
Total current liabilities			$ 814,710

Long-term liabilities:

Debenture 8% bonds payable, due December 31, 2015 (market value, $950,000)	$1,000,000		
Less unamortized discount	60,000	$ 940,000	
Minority interest in subsidiaries		115,000	
Total long-term liabilities			1,055,000

Deferred credits:

Deferred income tax payable			85,500
Total liabilities			$1,955,210

Stockholders' Equity

Paid-in capital:

Common stock, $20 par (250,000 shares authorized, 100,000 shares issued)		$2,000,000	
Excess of issue price over par		320,000	
Total paid-in capital		$2,320,000	
Retained earnings		1,605,535	
Total stockholders' equity			3,925,535
Total liabilities and stockholders' equity			$5,880,745

count would be reported as an *addition* to the related bonds payable. Either on the face of the financial statements or in accompanying notes, a description of the bonds (terms, due date, and effective interest rate) and other relevant information such as sinking fund requirements should be disclosed.[4] Finally, the market (fair) value of the bonds payable should also be disclosed.

Balance Sheet Presentation of Bond Investments

Investments in bonds or other debt securities that management intends to hold to their maturity are called **held-to-maturity securities.** Such securities are classified as long-term investments under the caption Investments. These investments are reported at their cost less any amortized premium or plus any amortized discount. In addition, the market (fair) value of the bond investments should be disclosed, either on the face of the balance sheet or in an accompanying note.

FINANCIAL ANALYSIS AND INTERPRETATION

OBJECTIVE 9

Compute and interpret the number of times interest charges earned.

Some corporations, such as railroads and public utilities, have a high ratio of debt to stockholders' equity. For such corporations, analysts often assess the relative risk of the debtholders in terms of the **number of times the interest charges are earned** during the year. The higher the ratio, the greater the chance that interest payments will continue to be made if earnings decrease.[5]

The amount available to make interest payments is not affected by taxes on income. This is because interest is deductible in determining taxable income. To illustrate, the following data were taken from the 1996 annual report of **Briggs & Stratton Corporation**:

Interest expense	$10,060,000
Income before income tax	$149,052,000

The number of times interest charges are earned, 15.8, is calculated below.

$$\text{Number of times interest charges earned} = \frac{\text{Income before income tax} + \text{Interest expense}}{\text{Interest expense}}$$

$$\text{Number of times interest charges earned} = \frac{\$149,052,000 + \$10,060,000}{\$10,060,000} = 15.8$$

The number of times interest charges are earned indicates that the debtholders of Briggs & Stratton have adequate protection against a potential drop in earnings jeopardizing their receipt of interest payments. However, a final assessment should include a review of trends of past years and a comparison with industry averages.

---

[4] *Statement of Financial Accounting Standards No. 129,* "Disclosure Information About Capital Structure," Financial Accounting Standards Board (Norwalk, Connecticut: 1997).

[5] A similar analysis can also be applied to dividends on preferred stock. In such cases, net income would be divided by the amount of preferred dividends to yield the number of times preferred dividends were earned. This measure gives an indication of the relative assurance of continued dividend payments to preferred stockholders.

ENCORE

Let's Dance— A Bond with a Tune

How would you like to tune into some of the royalties from David Bowie's hit song, *Let's Dance*? Recently, the British rock star offered bonds backed by future royalties from his hit songs and albums recorded prior to 1990. In addition to *Let's Dance*, other songs include *Jean Genie, A Space Oddity, Changes, Diamond Dogs,* and *Rebel*.

Bowie's bonds, which have an average maturity of 10 years, pay 7.9% annual interest. Such asset-backed bonds have grown in popularity. However, this is the first time that a popular artist has made use of future royalties as asset backing. The Bowie Bonds, which are officially called Class-A royalty-backed securities, were rated AAA—the highest rating—by **Moody's Investors Service**.

The 50-year-old Bowie is one of the most financially savvy rock stars in the world, with a well-chosen art collection and an appreciation for market trends. Bowie's principal residence is a $3.4 million, 640-acre estate in County Wicklow, Ireland, a noted tax haven. He lives there with his second wife, the supermodel and actress Iman. Still, Bowie's business manager said that when he approached him with the bond idea, "he [Bowie] kind of looked at me cross-eyed and said, 'What?'"

Potential investors were reassured by the fact that Bowie never sells fewer than a million albums a year. At the time of the offering, Bowie's latest album, "Earthling," was near the top of the European charts. In addition, the month before the offering, he performed for a sold-out concert at New York's Madison Square Garden.

Prudential Insurance Co. isn't kidding when it says you can own a piece of the *rock*. In a private placement in early 1997, Prudential purchased all of David Bowie's $55 million bonds for its general investment fund, where the money of life insurance policyholders is invested. ■

APPENDIX—EFFECTIVE INTEREST RATE METHOD OF AMORTIZATION

The effective interest rate method of amortizing discounts and premiums provides for a constant rate of interest on the carrying amount of the bonds at the beginning of each period. This is in contrast to the straight-line method, which provides for a constant amount of interest expense.

The interest rate used in the interest method of amortization is the market rate on the date the bonds are issued. The carrying amount of the bonds to which the interest rate is applied is the face amount of the bonds minus any unamortized discount or plus any unamortized premium. Under the interest method, the interest expense to be reported on the income statement is computed by multiplying the effective interest rate by the carrying amount of the bonds. The difference between the interest expense computed in this way and the periodic interest payment is the amount of discount or premium to be amortized for the period.

Amortization of Discount by the Interest Method

To illustrate the interest method for amortizing bond discounts, we assume the following data from the chapter illustration of issuing $100,000 bonds at a discount:

Face value of 12%, 5-year bonds, interest compounded semiannually	$100,000
Present value of bonds at effective (market) rate of interest of 13%	96,406
Discount on bonds payable	$ 3,594

Applying the interest method to these data yields the amortization table in Exhibit 6. You should note the following items in this table:

1. The interest paid (Column A) remains constant at 6% of $100,000, the face amount of the bonds.
2. The interest expense (Column B) is computed at 6½% of the bond carrying amount at the beginning of each period. This results in an increasing interest expense each period.
3. The excess of the interest expense over the interest payment of $6,000 is the amount of discount to be amortized (Column C).
4. The unamortized discount (Column D) decreases from the initial balance, $3,594, to a zero balance at the maturity date of the bonds.
5. The carrying amount (Column E) increases from $96,406, the amount received for the bonds, to $100,000 at maturity.

EXHIBIT 6   Amortization of Discount on Bonds Payable

Interest Payment	A Interest Paid (6% of Face Amount)	B Interest Expense (6½% of Bond Carrying Amount)	C Discount Amortization (B − A)	D Unamortized Discount (D − C)	E Bond Carrying Amount ($100,000 − D)
				$3,594	$ 96,406
1	$6,000	$6,266 (6½% of $96,406)	$266	3,328	96,672
2	6,000	6,284 (6½% of $96,672)	284	3,044	96,956
3	6,000	6,302 (6½% of $96,956)	302	2,742	97,258
4	6,000	6,322 (6½% of $97,258)	322	2,420	97,580
5	6,000	6,343 (6½% of $97,580)	343	2,077	97,923
6	6,000	6,365 (6½% of $97,923)	365	1,712	98,288
7	6,000	6,389 (6½% of $98,288)	389	1,323	98,677
8	6,000	6,414 (6½% of $98,677)	414	909	99,091
9	6,000	6,441 (6½% of $99,091)	441	468	99,532
10	6,000	6,470 (6½% of $99,532)	468*	—	100,000

*Cannot exceed unamortized discount.

The entry to record the first interest payment on June 30, 1999, and the related discount amortization is as follows:

1999 June	30	Interest Expense	6 2 6 6 00		
		Discount on Bonds Payable		2 6 6 00	
		Cash		6 0 0 0 00	
		Paid semiannual interest and			
		amortized bond discount for			
		one-half year.			

If the amortization is recorded only at the end of the year, the amount of the discount amortized on December 31 would be $550. This is the sum of the first two semiannual amortization amounts ($266 and $284) from Exhibit 6.

Amortization of Premium by the Interest Method

To illustrate the interest method for amortizing bond premiums, we assume the following data from the chapter illustration of issuing $100,000 bonds at a premium:

Present value of bonds at effective (market) rate of interest of 11%	$103,769
Face value of 12%, 5-year bonds, interest compounded semiannually	100,000
Premium on bonds payable	$ 3,769

Using the interest method to amortize the above premium yields the amortization table in Exhibit 7. You should note the following items in this table:

1. The interest paid (Column A) remains constant at 6% of $100,000, the face amount of the bonds.
2. The interest expense (Column B) is computed at 5½% of the bond carrying amount at the beginning of each period. This results in a decreasing interest expense each period.
3. The excess of the periodic interest payment of $6,000 over the interest expense is the amount of premium to be amortized (Column C).
4. The unamortized premium (Column D) decreases from the initial balance, $3,769, to a zero balance at the maturity date of the bonds.
5. The carrying amount (Column E) decreases from $103,769, the amount received for the bonds, to $100,000 at maturity.

EXHIBIT 7   Amortization of Premium on Bonds Payable

Interest Payment	A Interest Paid (6% of Face Amount)	B Interest Expense (5½% of Bond Carrying Amount)	C Premium Amortization (A − B)	D Unamortized Premium (D − C)	E Bond Carry- ing Amount ($100,000 + D)
				$3,769	$103,769
1	$6,000	$5,707 (5½% of $103,769)	$293	3,476	103,476
2	6,000	5,691 (5½% of $103,476)	309	3,167	103,167
3	6,000	5,674 (5½% of $103,167)	326	2,841	102,841
4	6,000	5,656 (5½% of $102,841)	344	2,497	102,497
5	6,000	5,637 (5½% of $102,497)	363	2,134	102,134
6	6,000	5,617 (5½% of $102,134)	383	1,751	101,751
7	6,000	5,596 (5½% of $101,751)	404	1,347	101,347
8	6,000	5,574 (5½% of $101,347)	426	921	100,921
9	6,000	5,551 (5½% of $100,921)	449	472	100,472
10	6,000	5,526 (5½% of $100,472)	472*	—	100,000

*Cannot exceed unamortized premium.

The entry to record the first interest payment on June 30, 1999, and the related premium amortization is as follows:

	1999							
	June	30	Interest Expense		5 7 0 7 00			
			Premium on Bonds Payable		2 9 3 00			
			Cash				6 0 0 0 00	
			Paid semiannual interest and					
			amortized bond premium for					
			one-half year.					

If the amortization is recorded only at the end of the year, the amount of the premium amortized on December 31, 1999, would be $602. This is the sum of the first two semiannual amortization amounts ($293 and $309) from Exhibit 7.

KEY POINTS

1 Compute the potential impact of long-term borrowing on the earnings per share of a corporation.
Three alternative plans for financing a corporation by issuing common stock, preferred stock, or bonds are illustrated in Exhibits 1 and 2. The effects of alternative financing on the earnings per share vary significantly, depending upon the level of earnings.

2 Describe the characteristics of bonds.
The characteristics of bonds depend upon the type of bonds issued by a corporation. Bonds that may be issued include term bonds, serial bonds, convertible bonds, callable bonds, and debenture bonds.

3 Compute the present value of bonds payable.
The concept of present value is based on the time value of money. That is, an amount of cash to be received at some date in the future is worth less than the same amount of cash held today. For example, if $100 cash today can be invested to earn 10% per year, the $100 today is referred to as the present value amount that is equal to $110 to be received a year from today.
A price that a buyer is willing to pay for a bond is the sum

of (1) the present value of the face amount of the bonds at the maturity date and (2) the present value of the periodic interest payments.

4 Journalize entries for bonds payable.
The journal entry for issuing bonds payable debits Cash for the proceeds received and credits Bonds Payable for the face amount of the bonds. Any difference between the face amount of the bonds and the proceeds is debited to Discount on Bonds Payable or credited to Premium on Bonds Payable.
A discount or premium on bonds payable is amortized to interest expense over the life of the bonds. The entry to amortize a discount debits Interest Expense and credits Discount on Bonds Payable. The entry to amortize a premium debits Premium on Bonds Payable and credits Interest Expense.

5 Describe bond sinking funds.
A bond indenture may require that funds for the payment of the bonds at maturity be set aside over the life of the bonds. The amounts set aside are kept separate from other assets in a special fund called a sinking fund. A sinking fund is reported as an Investment on the balance sheet.

Income from a sinking fund is reported as Other Income on the income statement.

6 Journalize entries for bond redemptions.
When a corporation redeems bonds, Bonds Payable is debited for the face amount of the bonds, the premium (discount) on bonds account is debited (credited) for its balance, Cash is credited, and any gain or loss on the redemption is recorded.

7 Journalize entries for the purchase, interest, discount and premium amortization, and sale of bond investments.
A long-term investment in bonds is recorded by debiting Investment in Bonds. When bonds are purchased between interest dates, the amount of the interest paid should be debited to Interest Revenue. Any discount or premium on bond investments should be amortized, using the straight-line or effective interest rate methods. The amortization of a discount is recorded by debiting Investment in Bonds and crediting Interest Revenue. The amortization of a premium is recorded by debiting Interest Revenue and crediting Investment in Bonds.
When bonds held as long-term investments are sold, any

discount or premium for the current period should first be amortized. Cash is then debited for the proceeds of the sale, Investment in Bonds is credited for its balance, and any gain or loss is recorded.

Prepare a corporation balance sheet.

The corporation balance sheet may include bond sinking funds, investments in bonds, goodwill, deferred income taxes, bonds payable and unamortized pre-

mium or discount, and minority interest in subsidiaries.

Bonds payable are usually reported as long-term liabilities. A discount on bonds should be reported as a deduction from the related bonds payable. A premium on bonds should be reported as an addition to the related bonds payable. Investments in bonds that are held-to-maturity securities are reported as Investments at cost less any amortized premium or plus any amortized discount.

Compute and interpret the number of times interest charges earned.

The number of times interest charges are earned during the year is a measure of the risk that interest payments to debtholders will continue to be made if earnings decrease. It is computed by dividing income before income tax plus interest expense by interest expense.

ILLUSTRATIVE PROBLEM

The fiscal year of Russell Inc., a manufacturer of acoustical supplies, ends December 31. Selected transactions for the period 1999 through 2006, involving bonds payable issued by Russell Inc., are as follows:

1999
June 30. Issued $2,000,000 of 25-year, 7% callable bonds dated June 30, 1999, for cash of $1,920,000. Interest is payable semiannually on June 30 and December 31.
Dec. 31. Paid the semiannual interest on the bonds.
    31. Recorded straight-line amortization of $1,600 of discount on the bonds.
    31. Closed the interest expense account.
2000
June 30. Paid the semiannual interest on the bonds.
Dec. 31. Paid the semiannual interest on the bonds.
    31. Recorded straight-line amortization of $3,200 of discount on the bonds.
    31. Closed the interest expense account.
2006
June 30. Recorded the redemption of the bonds, which were called at 101½. The balance in the bond discount account is $57,600 after the payment of interest and amortization of discount have been recorded. (Record the redemption only.)

Instructions

1. Journalize entries to record the preceding transactions.
2. Determine the amount of interest expense for 1999 and 2000.
3. Estimate the effective annual interest rate by dividing the interest expense for 1999 by the bond carrying amount at the time of issuance and multiplying by 2.
4. Determine the carrying amount of the bonds as of December 31, 2000.

Solution

1.

1999					
June	30	Cash	1,920 0 0 0 00		
		Discount on Bonds Payable	80 0 0 0 00		
		Bonds Payable		2,000 0 0 0 00	
Dec.	31	Interest Expense	70 0 0 0 00		
		Cash		70 0 0 0 00	
	31	Interest Expense	1 6 0 0 00		
		Discount on Bonds Payable		1 6 0 0 00	

Dec.	31	Income Summary	71 6 0 0 00	
		Interest Expense		71 6 0 0 00
2000 June	30	Interest Expense	70 0 0 0 00	
		Cash		70 0 0 0 00
Dec.	31	Interest Expense	70 0 0 0 00	
		Cash		70 0 0 0 00
	31	Interest Expense	3 2 0 0 00	
		Discount on Bonds Payable		3 2 0 0 00
	31	Income Summary	143 2 0 0 00	
		Interest Expense		143 2 0 0 00
2006 June	30	Bonds Payable	2,000 0 0 0 00	
		Loss on Redemption of Bonds Payable	87 6 0 0 00	
		Discount on Bonds Payable		57 6 0 0 00
		Cash		2,030 0 0 0 00

2. a. 1999—$71,600
   b. 2000—$143,200

3. $71,600 ÷ $1,920,000 = 3.73% rate for six months of a year
   3.73% × 2 = 7.46% annual rate

4.
Initial carrying amount of bonds	$1,920,000
Discount amortized on December 31, 1999	1,600
Discount amortized on December 31, 2000	3,200
Carrying amount of bonds, December 31, 2000	$1,924,800

SELF-EXAMINATION QUESTIONS
Answers at End of Chapter

Matching
Match each of the following statements with its proper term. Some terms may not be used.

A.	annuity
B.	available-for-sale securities
C.	bond
D.	bond fund
E.	bond indenture
F.	carrying amount
G.	contract rate
H.	discount
I.	dividend yield
J.	effective interest rate method
K.	effective rate of interest
L.	future value
M.	held-to-maturity securities

___ 1. A form of an interest-bearing note used by corporations to borrow on a long-term basis.

___ 2. The contract between a corporation issuing bonds and the bondholders.

___ 3. The periodic interest to be paid on the bonds that is identified in the bond indenture; expressed as a percentage of the face amount of the bond.

___ 4. A series of equal cash flows at fixed intervals.

___ 5. The sum of the present values of a series of equal cash flows to be received at fixed intervals.

___ 6. The estimated worth today of an amount of cash to be received (or paid) in the future.

___ 7. The estimated worth in the future of an amount of cash on hand today invested at a fixed rate of interest.

___ 8. The excess of the face amount of bonds over their issue price.

___ 9. The excess of the issue price of bonds over their face amount.

___ 10. A fund in which cash or assets are set aside for the purpose of paying the face amount of the bonds at maturity.

N.	**number of times interest charges earned**
O.	**premium**
P.	**present value**
Q.	**present value of an annuity**
R.	**sinking fund**

___ 11. The balance of the bonds payable account (face amount of the bonds) less any unamortized discount or plus any unamortized premium.

___ 12. Investments in bonds or other debt securities that management intends to hold to their maturity.

___ 13. A ratio that measures the risk that interest payments to debtholders will continue to be made if earnings decrease.

___ 14. The market rate of interest at the time bonds are issued.

Multiple Choice

1. If a corporation plans to issue $1,000,000 of 12% bonds at a time when the market rate for similar bonds is 10%, the bonds can be expected to sell at:
   A. their face amount
   B. a premium
   C. a discount
   D. a price below their face amount

2. If the bonds payable account has a balance of $500,000 and the discount on bonds payable account has a balance of $40,000, what is the carrying amount of the bonds?
   A. $460,000   C. $540,000
   B. $500,000   D. $580,000

3. The cash and securities that make up the sinking fund established for the payment of bonds at maturity are classified on the balance sheet as:

   A. current assets   C. long-term liabilities
   B. investments   D. current liabilities

4. If a firm purchases $100,000 of bonds of X Company at 101 plus accrued interest of $2,000 and pays broker's commissions of $50, the amount debited to Investment in X Company Bonds would be:
   A. $100,000   C. $103,000
   B. $101,050   D. $103,050

5. The balance in the discount on bonds payable account would usually be reported in the balance sheet in the:
   A. Current Assets section
   B. Current Liabilities section
   C. Long-Term Liabilities section
   D. Investments section

CLASS DISCUSSION QUESTIONS

1. Describe the two distinct obligations incurred by a corporation when issuing bonds.
2. Explain the meaning of each of the following terms as they relate to a bond issue: (a) convertible, (b) callable, and (c) debenture.
3. What is meant by the "time value of money?"
4. What has the higher present value: (a) $3,000 to be received at the end of two years, or (b) $1,500 to be received at the end of each of the next two years?
5. If you asked your broker to purchase for you an 8% bond when the market interest rate for such bonds was 9%, would you expect to pay more or less than the face amount for the bond? Explain.
6. A corporation issues $7,500,000 of 7% bonds to yield interest at the rate of 6%. (a) Was the amount of cash received from the sale of the bonds greater or less than $7,500,000? (b) Identify the following terms related to the bond issue: (1) face amount, (2) market or effective rate of interest, (3) contract rate of interest, and (4) maturity amount.
7. If bonds issued by a corporation are sold at a premium, is the market rate of interest greater or less than the contract rate?
8. The following data relate to a $500,000, 8% bond issue for a selected semiannual interest period:

Bond carrying amount at beginning of period	$525,000
Interest paid at end of period	20,000
Interest expense allocable to the period	18,750

   (a) Were the bonds issued at a discount or at a premium? (b) What is the unamortized amount of the discount or premium account at the beginning of the period? (c) What account was debited to amortize the discount or premium?

9. Assume that Koffee Co. amortizes premiums and discounts on bonds payable at the end of the year rather than when interest is paid. What accounts would be debited and credited to record (a) the amortization of a discount on bonds payable and (b) the amortization of a premium on bonds payable?

10. Would a zero-coupon bond ever sell for its face amount?

11. What is the purpose of a bond sinking fund?

12. How are earnings from investments in a sinking fund reported on the income statement?

13. How are cash and securities comprising a sinking fund classified on the balance sheet?

14. Assume that two 10-year, 8% bond issues are identical, except that one bond issue is callable at its face amount at the end of 6 years. Which of the two bond issues do you think will sell for a higher value?

15. Bonds Payable has a balance of $800,000, and Premium on Bonds Payable has a balance of $15,000. If the issuing corporation redeems the bonds at 102, is there a gain or loss on the bond redemption?

16. How are gains or losses on bond redemptions reported on the income statement?

17. Assume that a company purchases bonds between interest dates. What accounts would normally be debited?

18. Indicate how the following accounts should be reported on the balance sheet: (a) Premium on Bonds Payable and (b) Discount on Bonds Payable.

19. Where are investments in bonds that are classified as held-to-maturity securities reported on the balance sheet?

20. At what amount are held-to-maturity investments in bonds reported on the balance sheet?

Resources for Your Success On-Line at **warren.swcollege.com**
Remember! If you need additional help, visit South-Western's Web site. See page 26 for a description of the online and printed materials that are available.

EXERCISES

Exercise 14–1
Effect of financing on earnings per share

Objective 1

SPREADSHEET

✓ a. $0.30

Nevin Co., which produces and sells skiing equipment, is financed as follows:

Bonds payable, 10% (issued at face amount)	$2,000,000
Preferred $9 stock (nonparticipating), $100 par	2,000,000
Common stock, $10 par	2,000,000

Income tax is estimated at 40% of income.

Determine the earnings per share of common stock, assuming that the income before bond interest and income tax is (a) $600,000, (b) $1,000,000, and (c) $2,500,000.

Exercise 14–2
Evaluate alternative financing plans

Objective 1

➤ Based upon the data in Exercise 14–1, discuss factors other than earnings per share that should be considered in evaluating such financing plans.

Exercise 14–3
Present value of amounts due

Objective 3

✓ a. $8,164

Determine the present value of $10,000 to be received in three years, using an interest rate of 7%, compounded annually, as follows:

a. By successive divisions. (Round to the nearest dollar.)
b. By using the present value table in Exhibit 3.

Exercise 14–4
Present value of annuity

Objective 3

✓ a. $17,129

Determine the present value of $5,000 to be received at the end of each of four years, using an interest rate of 6½%, compounded annually, as follows:

a. By successive computations, using the present value table in Exhibit 3.
b. By using the present value table in Exhibit 4.

Exercise 14–5
Present value of an annuity

Objective 3

✓ $511,334.40

On January 1, 2000, you win $1,000,000 in the state lottery. The $1,000,000 prize will be paid in equal installments of $40,000 over 25 years. The payments will be made on December 31 of each year, beginning on December 31, 2000. If the current interest rate is 6%, determine the present value of your winnings. Use the present value tables in Appendix A.

Exercise 14–6
Present value of an annuity

Objective 3

Assume the same data as in Exercise 14–5, except that the current interest rate is 12%. Will the present value of your winnings using an interest rate of 12% be one-half the present value of your winnings using an interest rate of 6%? Why or why not?

Exercise 14–7
Present value of bonds payable; discount

Objectives 3, 4

✓ $9,227,796

Beall Co. produces and sells bottle capping equipment for soft drink and spring water bottlers. To finance its operations, Beall Co. issued $10,000,000 of five-year, 8% bonds with interest payable semiannually at an effective interest rate of 10%. Determine the present value of the bonds payable, using the present value tables in Exhibits 3 and 4.

Exercise 14–8
Present value of bonds payable; premium

Objectives 3, 4

✓ $5,188,439

Whitsell Automotive Alarms Co. issued $5,000,000 of five-year, 12% bonds with interest payable semiannually, at an effective interest rate of 11%. Determine the present value of the bonds payable, using the present value tables in Exhibits 3 and 4.

Exercise 14–9
Bond price

Objectives 3, 4

IBM Corporation 8⅜% bonds due in 2019 were reported in *The Wall Street Journal* as selling for 115 on October 7, 1997.
    Were the bonds selling at a premium or at a discount on October 7, 1997? Explain.

Exercise 14–10
Entries for issuing bonds

Objective 4

Wilmer Co. produces and distributes fiber optic cable for use by telecommunications companies. Wilmer Co. issued $7,500,000 of 20-year, 8% bonds on April 1 of the current year, with interest payable on April 1 and October 1. The fiscal year of the company is the calendar year. Journalize the entries to record the following selected transactions for the current year:

Apr. 1. Issued the bonds for cash at their face amount.
Oct. 1. Paid the interest on the bonds.
Dec. 31. Recorded accrued interest for three months.

Exercise 14–11
Entries for issuing bonds and amortizing discount by straight-line method

Objective 4

✓ b. $917,753

On the first day of its fiscal year, Ryland Company issued $8,000,000 of five-year, 10% bonds to finance its operations of producing and selling home electronics equipment. Interest is payable semiannually. The bonds were issued at an effective interest rate of 12%, resulting in Ryland Company receiving cash of $7,411,236.

a.   Journalize the entries to record the following:
  1.   Sale of the bonds.
  2.   First semiannual interest payment. (Amortization of discount is to be recorded annually.)
  3.   Second semiannual interest payment.
  4.   Amortization of discount at the end of the first year, using the straight-line method. (Round to the nearest dollar.)
b.   Determine the amount of the bond interest expense for the first year.

Exercise 14–12
Computing bond proceeds, entries for bond issuing, and amortizing premium by straight-line method

Objectives 3, 4

Markle Corporation wholesales oil and grease products to equipment manufacturers. On March 1, 2000, Markle Corporation issued $5,000,000 of five-year, 12% bonds at an effective interest rate of 10%. Interest is payable semiannually on March 1 and September 1. Journalize the entries to record the following:

a.   Sale of bonds on March 1, 2000. (Use the tables of present values in Exhibits 3 and 4 to determine the bond proceeds.)
b.   First interest payment on September 1, 2000, and amortization of bond premium for six months, using the straight-line method. (Round to the nearest dollar.)

Exercise 14–13
Entries for issuing and calling bonds; loss

Objectives 4, 6

Gier Corp., a wholesaler of office furniture, issued $9,000,000 of 20-year, 8% callable bonds on March 1, 2000, with interest payable on March 1 and September 1. The fiscal year of the company is the calendar year. Journalize the entries to record the following selected transactions:

2000
Mar. 1. Issued the bonds for cash at their face amount.
Sep. 1. Paid the interest on the bonds.
2004
Sep. 1. Called the bond issue at 101½, the rate provided in the bond indenture. (Omit entry for payment of interest.)

Exercise 14–14
Entries for issuing and calling bonds; gain

Objectives 4, 6

Mosser Corp. produces and sells automotive and aircraft safety belts. To finance its operations, Mosser Corp. issued $12,000,000 of 30-year, 7% callable bonds on June 1, 1999, with interest payable on June 1 and December 1. The fiscal year of the company is the calendar year. Journalize the entries to record the following selected transactions:

1999
June 1. Issued the bonds for cash at their face amount.
Dec. 1. Paid the interest on the bonds.
2005
Dec. 1. Called the bond issue at 99, the rate provided in the bond indenture. (Omit entry for payment of interest.)

Exercise 14–15
Reporting bonds

Objectives 5, 6, 8

What's Wrong WITH THIS?

At the beginning of the current year, two bond issues (MM and QQ) were outstanding. During the year, bond issue MM was redeemed and a significant loss on the redemption of bonds was reported as Other Expense on the income statement. At the end of the year, bond issue QQ was reported as a current liability because its maturity date was early in the following year. A sinking fund of cash and securities sufficient to pay the series QQ bonds was reported in the balance sheet as *Investments*.
  Can you find any flaws in the reporting practices related to the two bond issues?

Exercise 14–16
Amortizing discount on bond investment

Objective 7

A company purchased a $1,000, 20-year zero-coupon bond for $189 to yield 8.5% to maturity. How is the interest revenue computed?
Source: "Technical Hotline," *Journal of Accountancy,* January 1989, p. 100.

Exercise 14–17

Entries for purchase and sale of investment in bonds; loss

Objective 7

Crone Co. sells optical supplies to opticians and ophthalmologists. Journalize the entries to record the following selected transactions of Crone Co.:

a. Purchased for cash $200,000 of Lambert Co. 6% bonds at 103 plus accrued interest of $2,000.
b. Received first semiannual interest.
c. At the end of the first year, amortized $250 of the bond premium.
d. Sold the bonds at 99 plus accrued interest of $4,000. The bonds were carried at $203,500 at the time of the sale.

Exercise 14–18

Entries for purchase and sale of investment in bonds; gain

Objective 7

Rockne Company develops and sells graphics software for use by architects. Journalize the entries to record the following selected transactions of Rockne Company:

a. Purchased for cash $150,000 of Culp Co. 6% bonds at 97 plus accrued interest of $1,500.
b. Received first semiannual interest.
c. Amortized $200 on the bond investment at the end of the first year.
d. Sold the bonds at 99 plus accrued interest of $3,000. The bonds were carried at $148,000 at the time of the sale.

Exercise 14–19

Number of times interest charges earned

Objective 9

HAT

The financial statements for **Hershey Foods Corporation** are presented in Appendix G at the end of the text.

a. Determine the number of times interest charges were earned for the years ended December 31, 1996 and 1995. (The makeup of "interest expense, net" as reported on the income statement is described in Note 6 to the statements. Use only the interest on long-term and lease obligations and short-term debt in your computation.)
b. ➤ What conclusions can be drawn from the data concerning the risk of the debtholders for the interest payments and the general financial strength of Hershey?

Appendix Exercise 14–20

Amortize discount by interest method

✓ b. $892,029

On the first day of its fiscal year, Ryland Company issued $8,000,000 of five-year, 10% bonds to finance its operations of producing and selling home electronics equipment. Interest is payable semiannually. The bonds were issued at an effective interest rate of 12%, resulting in Ryland Company receiving cash of $7,411,236.

a. Journalize the entries to record the following:
    1. Sale of the bonds.
    2. First semiannual interest payment. (Amortization of discount is to be recorded annually.)
    3. Second semiannual interest payment.
    4. Amortization of discount at the end of the first year, using the interest method. (Round to the nearest dollar.)
b. Compute the amount of the bond interest expense for the first year.

Appendix Exercise 14–21

Amortize premium by interest method

✓ b. $537,073

Markle Corporation wholesales oil and grease products to equipment manufacturers. On March 1, 2000, Markle Corporation issued $5,000,000 of five-year, 12% bonds at an effective interest rate of 10%, receiving cash of $5,386,072. Interest is payable semiannually on March 1 and September 1. Markle Corporation's fiscal year begins on March 1.

a. Journalize the entries to record the following:
    1. First interest payment on September 1, 2000. (Amortization of premium is to be recorded annually.)
    2. Second interest payment on March 1, 2001.
    3. Amortization of premium at the end of the first year, using the interest method. (Round to the nearest dollar.)
b. Determine the bond interest expense for the first year.

Appendix Exercise 14–22

Compute bond proceeds, amortizing premium by interest method, and interest expense

Fabian Co. produces and sells spray painting equipment for construction contractors. On the first day of its fiscal year, Fabian Co. issued $10,000,000 of five-year, 11% bonds at an effective interest rate of 10%, with interest payable semiannually. Compute the following, presenting figures used in your computations.

✓ a. $10,386,057

✓ b. $30,697

a. The amount of cash proceeds from the sale of the bonds. (Use the tables of present values in Exhibits 3 and 4.)

b. The amount of premium to be amortized for the first semiannual interest payment period, using the interest method. (Round to the nearest dollar.)

c. The amount of premium to be amortized for the second semiannual interest payment period, using the interest method. (Round to the nearest dollar.)

d. The amount of the bond interest expense for the first year.

Appendix Exercise 14–23
Compute bond proceeds, amortizing discount by interest method, and interest expense

✓ a. $3,705,618

✓ b. $22,337

Leland Co. produces and sells concrete mixing equipment. On the first day of its fiscal year, Leland Co. issued $4,000,000 of five-year, 10% bonds at an effective interest rate of 12%, with interest payable semiannually. Compute the following, presenting figures used in your computations.

a. The amount of cash proceeds from the sale of the bonds. (Use the tables of present values in Exhibits 3 and 4.)

b. The amount of discount to be amortized for the first semiannual interest payment period, using the interest method. (Round to the nearest dollar.)

c. The amount of discount to be amortized for the second semiannual interest payment period, using the interest method. (Round to the nearest dollar.)

d. The amount of the bond interest expense for the first year.

PROBLEMS SERIES A

Problem 14–1A
Effect of financing on earnings per share

Objective 1

SPREADSHEET

✓ 1. Plan 3: $7.36

Three different plans for financing a $10,000,000 corporation are under consideration by its organizers. Under each of the following plans, the securities will be issued at their par or face amount, and the income tax rate is estimated at 40% of income.

	Plan 1	Plan 2	Plan 3
12% bonds			$ 5,000,000
Preferred 8% stock, $100 par		$ 5,000,000	2,500,000
Common stock, $10 par	$10,000,000	5,000,000	2,500,000
Total	$10,000,000	$10,000,000	$10,000,000

Instructions

1. Determine for each plan the earnings per share of common stock, assuming that the income before bond interest and income tax is $4,000,000.

2. Determine for each plan the earnings per share of common stock, assuming that the income before bond interest and income tax is $1,000,000.

3. ➤ Discuss the advantages and disadvantages of each plan.

Problem 14–2A
Present value; bond premium; entries for bonds payable transactions

Objectives 3, 4

✓ 3. $268,844

Willard Corporation produces and sells burial vaults. On July 1, 2000, Willard Corporation issued $5,000,000 of ten-year, 12% bonds at an effective interest rate of 10%. Interest on the bonds is payable semiannually on December 31 and June 30. The fiscal year of the company is the calendar year.

Instructions

1. Journalize the entry to record the amount of the cash proceeds from the sale of the bonds. Use the tables of present values in Appendix A to compute the cash proceeds, rounding to the nearest dollar.

2. Journalize the entries to record the following:
   a. The first semiannual interest payment on December 31, 2000, and the amortization of the bond premium, using the straight-line method. (Round to the nearest dollar.)
   b. The interest payment on June 30, 2001, and the amortization of the bond premium, using the straight-line method.

3. Determine the total interest expense for 2000.

4. ◄▬▬► Will the bond proceeds always be greater than the face amount of the bonds when the contract rate is greater than the market rate of interest? Explain.

Problem 14–3A
Present value; bond discount; entries for bonds payable transactions

Objectives 3, 4

✓ 3. $694,407

On July 1, 1999, Geyser Corporation, a wholesaler of used robotic equipment, issued $12,000,000 of ten-year, 11% bonds at an effective interest rate of 12%. Interest on the bonds is payable semiannually on December 31 and June 30. The fiscal year of the company is the calendar year.

Instructions

1. Journalize the entry to record the amount of the cash proceeds from the sale of the bonds. Use the tables of present values in Appendix A to compute the cash proceeds, rounding to the nearest dollar.
2. Journalize the entries to record the following:
   a. The first semiannual interest payment on December 31, 1999, and the amortization of the bond discount, using the straight-line method. (Round to the nearest dollar.)
   b. The interest payment on June 30, 2000, and the amortization of the bond discount, using the straight-line method.
3. Determine the total interest expense for 1999.
4. ◄▬▬► Will the bond proceeds always be less than the face amount of the bonds when the contract rate is less than the market rate of interest? Explain.

Problem 14–4A
Entries for bonds payable transactions

Objectives 4, 6

HAT

✓ 2. a. $240,578

The following transactions were completed by Stucco Inc., whose fiscal year is the calendar year:

1999
July   1. Issued $5,000,000 of 10-year, 9% callable bonds dated July 1, 1999, at an effective rate of 10%, receiving cash of $4,688,442. Interest is payable semiannually on December 31 and June 30.
Dec. 31. Paid the semiannual interest on the bonds.
     31. Recorded bond discount amortization of $15,578, which was determined by using the straight-line method.
     31. Closed the interest expense account.
2000
June 30. Paid the semiannual interest on the bonds.
Dec. 31. Paid the semiannual interest on the bonds.
     31. Recorded bond discount amortization of $31,156, which was determined by using the straight-line method.
     31. Closed the interest expense account.
2007
June 30. Recorded the redemption of the bonds, which were called at 99. The balance in the bond discount account is $62,310 after payment of interest and amortization of discount have been recorded. (Record the redemption only.)

Instructions

1. Journalize the entries to record the foregoing transactions.
2. Indicate the amount of the interest expense in (a) 1999 and (b) 2000.
3. Determine the carrying amount of the bonds as of December 31, 2000.

Problem 14–5A
Entries for bond investments

Objective 7

HAT

Finney Inc. develops and leases databases of publicly available information. The following selected transactions relate to certain securities acquired as a long-term investment by Finney Inc., whose fiscal year ends on December 31:

1999
Sep.   1. Purchased $300,000 of Miller Company 10-year, 10% bonds dated July 1, 1999, directly from the issuing company, for $308,850 plus accrued interest of $5,000.
Dec. 31. Received the semiannual interest on the Miller Company bonds.
     31. Recorded bond premium amortization of $300 on the Miller Company bonds. The amortization amount was determined by using the straight-line method.

(Assume that all intervening transactions and adjustments have been properly recorded and that the number of bonds owned has not changed from Dec. 31, 1999, to Dec. 31, 2004.)

2005

June 30. Received the semiannual interest on the Miller Company bonds.

Aug. 31. Sold one-half of the Miller Company bonds at 102 plus accrued interest. The broker deducted $700 for commission, etc., remitting the balance. Prior to the sale, $300 of premium on one-half of the bonds is to be amortized, reducing the carrying amount of those bonds to $151,725.

Dec. 31. Received the semiannual interest on the Miller Company bonds.

31. Recorded bond premium amortization of $450 on the Miller Company bonds.

Instructions

Journalize the entries to record the foregoing transactions.

Appendix
Problem 14–6A

Entries for bonds payable transactions; interest method of amortizing bond premium

✓ 2. $281,156

Willard Corporation produces and sells burial vaults. On July 1, 2000, Willard Corporation issued $5,000,000 of ten-year, 12% bonds at an effective interest rate of 10%, receiving proceeds of $5,623,113. Interest on the bonds is payable semiannually on December 31 and June 30. The fiscal year of the company is the calendar year.

Instructions

1. Journalize the entries to record the following:
   a. The first semiannual interest payment on December 31, 2000, and the amortization of the bond premium, using the interest method. (Round to nearest dollar.)
   b. The interest payment on June 30, 2001, and the amortization of the bond premium, using the interest method. (Round to nearest dollar.)
2. Determine the total interest expense for 2000.

Appendix
Problem 14–7A

Entries for bonds payable transactions; interest method of amortizing bond discount

✓ 2. $678,712

On July 1, 1999, Geyser Corporation, a wholesaler of used robotic equipment, issued $12,000,000 of ten-year, 11% bonds at an effective interest rate of 12%, receiving proceeds of $11,311,867. Interest on the bonds is payable semiannually on December 31 and June 30. The fiscal year of the company is the calendar year.

Instructions

1. Journalize the entries to record the following:
   a. The first semiannual interest payment on December 31, 1999, and the amortization of the bond discount, using the interest method. (Round to nearest dollar.)
   b. The interest payment on June 30, 2000, and the amortization of the bond discount, using the interest method. (Round to nearest dollar.)
2. Determine the total interest expense for 1999.

PROBLEMS SERIES B

Problem 14–1B

Effect of financing on earnings per share

Objective 1

SPREADSHEET

✓ 1. Plan 3: $7.60

Three different plans for financing a $15,000,000 corporation are under consideration by its organizers. Under each of the following plans, the securities will be issued at their par or face amount, and the income tax rate is estimated at 40% of income.

	Plan 1	Plan 2	Plan 3
12% bonds			$ 6,250,000
Preferred $4 stock, $50 par		$ 7,500,000	5,000,000
Common stock, $30 par	$15,000,000	7,500,000	3,750,000
Total	$15,000,000	$15,000,000	$15,000,000

Instructions

1. Determine for each plan the earnings per share of common stock, assuming that the income before bond interest and income tax is $3,000,000.
2. Determine for each plan the earnings per share of common stock, assuming that the income before bond interest and income tax is $1,450,000.
3. ◀▬▬▶ Discuss the advantages and disadvantages of each plan.

Problem 14–2B
Present value; bond premium; entries for bonds payable transactions

Objectives 3, 4

✓ 3. $509,422

Leibee Inc. produces and sells voltage regulators. On July 1, 1999, Leibee Inc. issued $10,000,000 of ten-year, $10\frac{1}{2}\%$ bonds at an effective interest rate of 10%. Interest on the bonds is payable semiannually on December 31 and June 30. The fiscal year of the company is the calendar year.

Instructions

1. Journalize the entry to record the amount of the cash proceeds from the sale of the bonds. Use the tables of present values in Appendix A to compute the cash proceeds, rounding to the nearest dollar.
2. Journalize the entries to record the following:
   a. The first semiannual interest payment on December 31, 1999, including the amortization of the bond premium, using the straight-line method.
   b. The interest payment on June 30, 2000, and the amortization of the bond premium, using the straight-line method.
3. Determine the total interest expense for 1999.
4. ◀▬▬▶ Will the bond proceeds always be greater than the face amount of the bonds when the contract rate is greater than the market rate of interest? Explain.

Problem 14–3B
Present value; bond discount; entries for bonds payable transactions

Objectives 3, 4

✓ 3. $346,733

On July 1, 1999, Cyrano Communications Equipment Inc. issued $7,500,000 of ten-year, 8% bonds at an effective interest rate of 10%. Interest on the bonds is payable semiannually on December 31 and June 30. The fiscal year of the company is the calendar year.

Instructions

1. Journalize the entry to record the amount of the cash proceeds from the sale of the bonds. Use the tables of present values in Appendix A to compute the cash proceeds, rounding to the nearest dollar.
2. Journalize the entries to record the following:
   a. The first semiannual interest payment on December 31, 1999, and the amortization of the bond discount, using the straight-line method. (Round to the nearest dollar.)
   b. The interest payment on June 30, 2000, and the amortization of the bond discount, using the straight-line method.
3. Determine the total interest expense for 1999.
4. ◀▬▬▶ Will the bond proceeds always be less than the face amount of the bonds when the contract rate is less than the market rate of interest? Explain.

Problem 14–4B
Entries for bonds payable transactions

Objectives 4, 6

✓ 2. a. $621,325

Coquette Co. produces and sells synthetic string for tennis rackets. The following transactions were completed by Coquette Co., whose fiscal year is the calendar year:

1999
July   1. Issued $10,000,000 of 10-year, 13% callable bonds dated July 1, 1999, at an effective rate of 12%, receiving cash of $10,573,500. Interest is payable semiannually on December 31 and June 30.
Dec. 31. Paid the semiannual interest on the bonds.
      31. Recorded bond premium amortization of $28,675, which was determined by using the straight-line method.
      31. Closed the interest expense account.
2000
June 30. Paid the semiannual interest on the bonds.
Dec. 31. Paid the semiannual interest on the bonds.
      31. Recorded bond premium amortization of $57,350, which was determined by using the straight-line method.
      31. Closed the interest expense account.

2005
July 1. Recorded the redemption of the bonds, which were called at 101. The balance in the bond premium account is $229,400 after the payment of interest and amortization of premium have been recorded. (Record the redemption only.)

Instructions

1. Journalize the entries to record the foregoing transactions.
2. Indicate the amount of the interest expense in (a) 1999 and (b) 2000.
3. Determine the carrying amount of the bonds as of December 31, 2000.

Problem 14–5B

Entries for bond investments

Objective 7

The following selected transactions relate to certain securities acquired by McFeters Blueprints Inc., whose fiscal year ends on December 31:

1999
Sep.   1. Purchased $1,000,000 of Buday Company 20-year, 9% bonds dated July 1, 1999, directly from the issuing company, for $964,300 plus accrued interest of $15,000.
Dec. 31. Received the semiannual interest on the Buday Company bonds.
       31. Recorded bond discount amortization of $600 on the Buday Company bonds. The amortization amount was determined by using the straight-line method.

(Assume that all intervening transactions and adjustments have been properly recorded and that the number of bonds owned has not changed from December 31, 1999, to December 31, 2003.)

2004
June 30. Received the semiannual interest on the Buday Company bonds.
Oct. 31. Sold one-half of the Buday Company bonds at 97 plus accrued interest. The broker deducted $850 for commission, etc., remitting the balance. Prior to the sale, $750 of discount on one-half of the bonds was amortized, reducing the carrying amount of those bonds to $486,800.
Dec. 31. Received the semiannual interest on the Buday Company bonds.
       31. Recorded bond discount amortization of $900 on the Buday Company bonds.

Instructions

Journalize the entries to record the foregoing transactions.

**Appendix
Problem 14–6B**

Entries for bonds payable transactions; interest method of amortizing bond premium

✓ 2. $515,578

Leibee Inc. produces and sells voltage regulators. On July 1, 1999, Leibee Inc. issued $10,000,000 of ten-year, $10\frac{1}{2}$% bonds at an effective interest rate of 10%, receiving proceeds of $10,311,560. Interest on the bonds is payable semiannually on December 31 and June 30. The fiscal year of the company is the calendar year.

Instructions

1. Journalize the entries to record the following:
    a. The first semiannual interest payment on December 31, 1999, and the amortization of the bond premium, using the interest method. (Round to nearest dollar.)
    b. The interest payment on June 30, 2000, and the amortization of the bond premium, using the interest method. (Round to nearest dollar.)
2. Determine the total interest expense for 1999.

**Appendix
Problem 14–7B**

Entries for bonds payable transactions; interest method of amortizing bond discount

✓ 2. $328,267

On July 1, 1999, Cyrano Communications Equipment Inc. issued $7,500,000 of ten-year, 8% bonds at an effective interest rate of 10%, receiving proceeds of $6,565,338. Interest on the bonds is payable semiannually on December 31 and June 30. The fiscal year of the company is the calendar year.

Instructions

1. Journalize the entries to record the following:
    a. The first semiannual interest payment on December 31, 1999, and the amortization of the bond discount, using the interest method.

b. The interest payment on June 30, 2000, and the amortization of the bond discount, using the interest method.

2. Determine the total interest expense for 1999.

COMPREHENSIVE PROBLEM 4

GENERAL LEDGER

Selected transactions completed by Stryker Products Inc. during the fiscal year ending July 31, 2000, were as follows:

a. Issued 10,000 shares of $25 par common stock at $45, receiving cash.

b. Issued 7,500 shares of $100 par preferred 8% stock at $120, receiving cash.

c. Issued $2,000,000 of 10-year, 10½% bonds at an effective interest rate of 10%, with interest payable semiannually. Use the present value tables in Appendix A to determine the bond proceeds. Round to the nearest dollar.

d. Declared a dividend of $0.40 per share on common stock and $2 per share on preferred stock. On the date of record, 100,000 shares of common stock were outstanding, no treasury shares were held, and 15,000 shares of preferred stock were outstanding.

e. Paid the cash dividends declared in (d).

f. Redeemed $300,000 of 8-year, 12% bonds at 101. The balance in the bond premium account is $7,900 after the payment of interest and amortization of premium have been recorded. (Record only the redemption of the bonds payable.)

g. Purchased 3,000 shares of treasury common stock at $42 per share.

h. Declared a 5% stock dividend on common stock and a $2 cash dividend per share on preferred stock. On the date of declaration, the market value of the common stock was $41 per share. On the date of record, 100,000 shares of common stock had been issued, 3,000 shares of treasury common stock were held, and 15,000 shares of preferred stock had been issued.

i. Issued the stock certificates for the stock dividends declared in (h) and paid the cash dividends to the preferred stockholders.

j. Purchased $100,000 of Dilmore Inc. 10-year, 15% bonds, directly from the issuing company, for $97,000 plus accrued interest of $3,750.

k. Sold, at $48 per share, 2,000 shares of treasury common stock purchased in (g).

l. Recorded the payment of semiannual interest on the bonds issued in (c) and the amortization of the premium for six months. The amortization was determined using the straight-line method. (Round the amortization to the nearest dollar.)

m. Accrued interest for four months on the Dilmore Inc. bonds purchased in (j). Also recorded amortization of $100.

Instructions

1. Journalize the selected transactions.

2. After all of the transactions for the year ended July 31, 2000, had been posted (including the transactions recorded in (1) and all adjusting entries), the following data were taken from the records of Stryker Products Inc.:

Income statement data:

Advertising expense	$ 75,000
Cost of merchandise sold	3,850,000
Delivery expense	17,000
Depreciation expense—office equipment	13,100
Depreciation expense—store equipment	45,000
Gain on redemption of bonds	4,900
Income tax:	
Applicable to continuing operations	254,775
Applicable to loss from disposal of a segment of the business	21,100
Applicable to gain from redemption of bonds	1,000

Interest expense	$ 101,884
Interest revenue	1,350
Loss from disposal of a segment of the business	80,500
Miscellaneous administrative expenses	1,600
Miscellaneous selling expenses	6,300
Office rent expense	25,000
Office salaries expense	85,000
Office supplies expense	5,300
Sales	5,100,000
Sales commissions	95,000
Sales salaries expense	180,000
Store supplies expense	9,500

Retained earnings and balance sheet data:

Accounts payable	$ 149,500
Accounts receivable	280,500
Accumulated depreciation—office equipment	835,250
Accumulated depreciation—store equipment	2,214,750
Allowance for doubtful accounts	21,500
Bonds payable, $10\frac{1}{2}$%, due 2010	2,000,000
Cash	125,500
Common stock, $25 par (400,000 shares authorized; 104,850 shares outstanding)	2,621,250
Deferred income tax payable (current portion, $4,700)	25,700
Dividends:	
Cash dividends for common stock	120,000
Cash dividends for preferred stock	105,000
Stock dividends for common stock	198,850
Dividends payable	30,000
Income tax payable	55,900
Interest receivable	5,000
Investment in Dilmore Inc. bonds (long-term)	97,100
Merchandise inventory (July 31, 2000), at lower of cost (fifo) or market	425,000
Notes receivable	77,500
Office equipment	2,410,100
Organization costs	55,000
Paid-in capital from sale of treasury stock	12,000
Paid-in capital in excess of par—common stock	325,000
Paid-in capital in excess of par—preferred stock	240,000
Preferred 8% stock, $100 par (30,000 shares authorized; 15,000 shares issued)	1,500,000
Premium on bonds payable	59,196
Prepaid expenses	15,900
Retained earnings, August 1, 1999	2,868,684
Store equipment	9,282,671
Treasury stock (1,000 shares of common stock at cost of $42 per share)	42,000

a.   Prepare a multiple-step income statement for the year ended July 31, 2000, concluding with earnings per share. In computing earnings per share, assume that the average number of common shares outstanding was 100,000 and preferred dividends were $105,000. Round to nearest cent.

b.   Prepare a retained earnings statement for the year ended July 31, 2000.

c.   Prepare a balance sheet in report form as of July 31, 2000.

SPECIAL ACTIVITIES

Activity 14–1
SlideCo
Ethics and professional conduct in business

SlideCo produces and sells water slides for theme parks. SlideCo has outstanding a $40,000,000, 25-year, 10% debenture bond issue dated July 1, 1991. The bond issue is due June 30, 2016. The bond indenture requires a sinking fund, which has a balance of $10,000,000 as of July 1, 2000. SlideCo is currently experiencing a shortage of funds due to a recent plant expansion. Eli Cronin, treasurer of SlideCo, has suggested using the sinking fund cash to temporarily relieve the shortage of funds. Cronin's brother-in-law, who is trustee of the sinking fund, is willing to loan SlideCo the necessary funds from the sinking fund.

➤ Discuss whether Eli Cronin is behaving in a professional manner.

Activity 14–2
Ludwig Distributors Inc.
Present values

Ludwig Distributors Inc. is a wholesaler of oriental rugs. The following is a luncheon conversation between Jennifer Sabel, the assistant controller, and Clancy Bishop, an assistant financial analyst for Ludwig.

Clancy: Jenny, do you mind if I spoil your lunch and ask you an accounting question?
Jennifer: No, go ahead. This chicken salad sandwich is pretty bad. It smells like it's three days old, and I've already picked three bones out of it.
Clancy: Well, as you know, in finance we use present values for capital budgeting analysis, assessing financing alternatives, etc. It's probably the most important concept that I learned in school that I actually use.
Jennifer: So . . . ?
Clancy: I was just wondering why accountants don't use present values more.
Jennifer: What do you mean?
Clancy: Well, it seems to me that you ought to value all the balance sheet liabilities at their present values.

➤ How would you respond if you were Jennifer?

Activity 14–3
Playmill Inc.
Preferred stock vs. bonds

Playmill Inc. has decided to expand its operations to owning and operating theme parks. The following is an excerpt from a conversation between the chief executive officer, JoAnn Robison, and the vice-president of finance, Pat Coffey.

JoAnn: Pat, have you given any thought to how we're going to finance the acquisition of WaterWave Corporation?
Pat: Well, the two basic options, as I see it, are to issue either preferred stock or bonds. The equity market is a little depressed right now. The rumor is that the Federal Reserve Bank's going to increase the interest rates either this month or next.
JoAnn: Yes, I've heard the rumor. The problem is that we can't wait around to see what's going to happen. We'll have to move on this next week if we want any chance to complete the acquisition of WaterWave.
Pat: Well, the bond market is strong right now. Maybe we should issue debt this time around.
JoAnn: That's what I would have guessed as well. WaterWave's financial statements look pretty good, except for the volatility of their income and cash flows. But that's characteristic of their industry.

➤ Discuss the advantages and disadvantages of issuing preferred stock versus bonds.

Activity 14–4
Shea Bottling Co.
Financing business expansion

You hold a 25% common stock interest in the family-owned business, a soft drink bottling distributorship. Your sister, who is the manager, has proposed an expansion of plant facilities at an expected cost of $2,500,000. Two alternative plans have been suggested as methods of financing the expansion. Each plan is briefly described as follows:

Plan 1. Issue $2,500,000 of 20-year, 8% notes at face amount.
Plan 2. Issue an additional 35,000 shares of $20 par common stock at $25 per share, and $1,625,000 of 20-year, 8% notes at face amount.

The balance sheet as of the end of the previous fiscal year is as follows:

Shea Bottling Co.
Balance Sheet
December 31, 20—

Assets

Current assets	$2,350,000
Property, plant, and equipment	5,150,000
Total assets	$7,500,000

Liabilities and Stockholders' Equity

Liabilities	$2,000,000
Common stock, $20	800,000
Paid-in capital in excess of par	80,000
Retained earnings	4,620,000
Total liabilities and stockholders' equity	$7,500,000

Net income has remained relatively constant over the past several years. The expansion program is expected to increase yearly income before bond interest and income tax from $500,000 in the previous year to $600,000 for this year. Your sister has asked you, as the company treasurer, to prepare an analysis of each financing plan.

1. Prepare a table indicating the expected earnings per share on the common stock under each plan. Assume an income tax rate of 40%.
2. a. ▬▶ Discuss the factors that should be considered in evaluating the two plans.
    b. ▬▶ Which plan offers the greater benefit to the present stockholders? Give reasons for your opinion.

Activity 14–5
Into the Real World
Investing in bonds

Select a bond from listings that appear daily in *The Wall Street Journal,* and summarize the information related to the bond you select. Include the following information in your summary:

1. Contract rate of interest
2. Year when the bond matures
3. Current yield (effective rate of interest)
4. Closing price of bond (indicate date)
5. Other information noted about the bond, such as whether it is a zero-coupon bond (see the Explanatory Notes to the listings)

In groups of three or four, share the information you developed about the bond you selected. As a group, select one bond to invest $100,000 in and prepare a justification for your choice for presentation to the class. For example, your justification should include a consideration of risk and return.

Activity 14–6
Into the Real World
Bond ratings

Moody's Investors Service maintains a Web site at **www.Moodys.com.** One of the services offered at this site is a listing of announcements of recent bond rating changes. Visit this site and read over some of these announcements. Write down several of the reasons provided for rating downgrades and upgrades. If you were a bond investor or bond issuer, would you care if Moody's changed the rating on your bonds? Why or why not?

ANSWERS TO SELF-EXAMINATION QUESTIONS

Matching

1. C	3. G	5. Q	7. L	9. O	11. F	13. N	14. K
2. E	4. A	6. P	8. H	10. R	12. M		

Multiple Choice

1. **B** Since the contract rate on the bonds is higher than the prevailing market rate, a rational investor would be willing to pay more than the face amount, or a premium (answer B), for the bonds. If the contract rate and the market rate were equal, the bonds could be expected to sell at their face amount (answer A). Likewise, if the market rate is higher than the contract rate, the bonds would sell at a price below their face amount (answer D) or at a discount (answer C).

2. **A** The bond carrying amount is the face amount plus unamortized premium or less unamortized discount. For this question, the carrying amount is $500,000 less $40,000, or $460,000 (answer A).

3. **B** Although the sinking fund may consist of cash as well as securities, the fund is listed on the balance sheet as an investment (answer B) because it is to be used to pay the long-term liability at maturity.

4. **B** The amount debited to the investment account is the cost of the bonds, which includes the amount paid to the seller for the bonds (101% × $100,000) plus broker's commissions ($50), or $101,050 (answer B). The $2,000 of accrued interest that is paid to the seller should be debited to Interest Revenue, since it is an offset against the amount that will be received as interest at the next interest date.

5. **C** The balance of Discount on Bonds Payable is usually reported as a deduction from Bonds Payable in the Long-Term Liabilities section (answer C) of the balance sheet. Likewise, a balance in a premium on bonds payable account would usually be reported as an addition to Bonds Payable in the Long-Term Liabilities section of the balance sheet.

15

Statement of Cash Flows

Setting the STAGE

How much cash do you have in the bank or in your wallet or purse? How much cash did you have at the beginning of the month? The difference between these two amounts is the net change in your cash during the month. Knowing the reasons for the change in cash may be useful in evaluating whether your financial position has improved and whether you will be able to pay your bills in the future.

For example, assume that you had $200 at the beginning of the month and $550 at the end of the month. The net change in cash is $350. Based on this net change, it appears that your financial position has improved. However, this conclusion may or may not be valid, depending upon how the change of $350 was created. If you borrowed $1,000 during the month and spent $650 on living expenses, your cash would have increased by $350 by living off of borrowed funds. On the other hand, if you earned $1,000 and spent $650 on living expenses, your cash would have also increased by $350, but your financial position is improved compared to the first scenario.

In previous chapters, we have used the income statement, balance sheet, and retained earnings statement and other information to analyze the effects of management decisions on a business's financial position and operating performance. In this chapter, we present how to prepare and use the statement of cash flows.

After studying this chapter, you should be able to:

1 Explain why the statement of cash flows is one of the basic financial statements.

2 Summarize the types of cash flow activities reported in the statement of cash flows.

3 Prepare a statement of cash flows, using the indirect method.

4 Prepare a statement of cash flows, using the direct method.

5 Calculate and interpret the free cash flow.

Purpose of the Statement of Cash Flows

OBJECTIVE 1

Explain why the statement
of cash flows is one of the
basic financial statements.

The statement of cash flows reports a firm's major cash inflows and outflows for a period.[1] It provides useful information about a firm's ability to generate cash from operations, maintain and expand its operating capacity, meet its financial obligations, and pay dividends.

The statement of cash flows is one of the basic financial statements. It is useful to managers in evaluating past operations and in planning future investing and financing activities. It is useful to investors, creditors, and others in assessing a firm's profit potential. In addition, it provides a basis for assessing the ability of a firm to pay its maturing debt.

The statement of cash flows is one of the basic financial statements.

Reporting Cash Flows

OBJECTIVE 2

Summarize the types of cash
flow activities reported in
the statement of cash flows.

The statement of cash flows reports cash flows by three types of activities:

1. **Cash flows from operating activities** are cash flows from transactions that affect net income. Examples of such transactions include the purchase and sale of merchandise by a retailer.
2. **Cash flows from investing activities** are cash flows from transactions that affect the investments in noncurrent assets. Examples of such transactions include the sale and purchase of fixed assets, such as equipment and buildings.
3. **Cash flows from financing activities** are cash flows from transactions that affect the equity and debt of the business. Examples of such transactions include issuing or retiring equity and debt securities.

The cash flows from operating activities is normally presented first, followed by the cash flows from investing activities and financing activities. The total of the net cash flow from these activities is the net increase or decrease in cash for the period. The cash balance at the beginning of the period is added to the net

The statement of cash flows reports cash flows from operating, investing, and financing activities.

---

[1] As used in this chapter, cash refers to cash and cash equivalents. Examples of cash equivalents include marketable securities, certificates of deposit, U.S. Treasury bills, and money market funds.

Focus on Cash Flow

In the past, investors and creditors have relied heavily on a company's earnings information in judging the company's performance. Now, more and more investors and creditors are also focusing on cash flows for providing additional information, as described below.

As the term suggests, cash flow is basically a measure of the money flowing into—or out of—a business. If large companies were run, like lemonade stands, on a cash basis, earnings and cash flow would be identical.

Every major corporation, however, keeps its books on an accrual basis. . . . [This] can give a truer picture of corporate profitability, but sometimes it obscures important developments.

Take a company that spent $140 million on new machinery last year. If it depreciates the equipment over a seven-year period, it will be subtracting $20 million from reported profits each year.

But if the machines will stay up to date and useful for 25 years, the company's reported earnings may understate its true strength. . . .

Sometimes the reverse is true. If a company has been neglecting capital spending, its earnings may look good. But on a cash-flow basis, it will look no better . . . than its competitors. ∎

Source: John R. Dorfman, "Stock Analysts Increase Focus on Cash Flow," *The Wall Street Journal,* February 17, 1987, Section 2, p. 1.

increase or decrease in cash, and the cash balance at the end of the period is reported. The ending cash balance on the statement of cash flows equals the cash reported on the balance sheet.

Exhibit 1 shows common cash flow transactions reported in each of the three sections of the statement of cash flows. By reporting cash flows by operating, investing, and financing activities, significant relationships within and among the activities can be evaluated. For example, the cash receipts from issuing bonds can be related to repayments of borrowings when both are reported as financing activities. Also, the impact of each of the three activities (operating, investing, and financing) on cash flows can be identified. This allows investors and creditors to evaluate the effects of cash flows on a firm's profits and ability to pay debt.

EXHIBIT I   Cash Flows

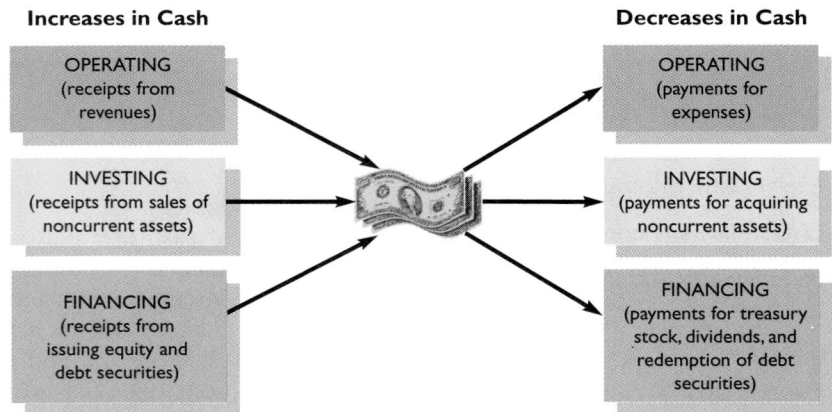

Cash Flows from Operating Activities

The most frequent and often the most important cash flows of a business relate to operating activities. There are two alternative methods for reporting cash flows from operating activities in the statement of cash flows. These methods are (1) the direct method and (2) the indirect method.

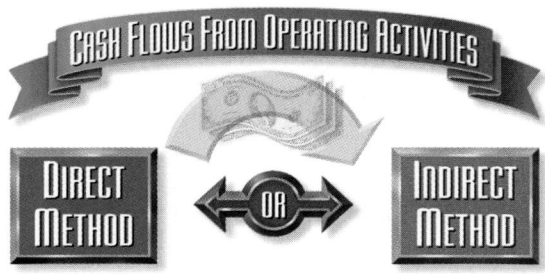

The **direct method** reports the sources of operating cash and the uses of operating cash. The major source of operating cash is cash received from customers. The major uses of operating cash include cash paid to suppliers for merchandise and services and cash paid to employees for wages. The difference between these operating cash receipts and cash payments is the net cash flow from operating activities.

Which U.S. manufacturing companies have the largest cash balances? The list from 1996 fiscal year-end balance sheets is as follows:

	In millions
General Motors	$14,063
IBM	7,687
Microsoft	6,940
Chrysler	5,158
Boeing	4,375
General Electric	4,191
Intel	4,165

These companies have had substantial cash flows from operations over the past 3–5 years, and as a result, have been able to build large cash balances (in the billions!). These balances can be used to cushion future business downturns, as would be the case for businesses subject to boom and bust cycles, such as GM, Chrysler, and Boeing. Alternatively, the cash can be used to expand the business or move into new markets, as would be the case for technology companies, such as Microsoft, Intel, IBM, and GE.

The primary advantage of the direct method is that it reports the sources and uses of cash in the statement of cash flows. Its primary disadvantage is that the necessary data may not be readily available and may be costly to gather.

The **indirect method** reports the operating cash flows by beginning with net income and adjusting it for revenues and expenses that do not involve the receipt or payment of cash. In other words, accrual net income is adjusted to determine the net amount of cash flows from operating activities.

A major advantage of the indirect method is that it focuses on the differences between net income and cash flows from operations. In this sense, it shows the relationship between the income statement, the balance sheet, and the statement of cash flows. Because the data are readily available, the indirect method is normally less costly to use than the direct method.

Exhibit 2 illustrates the cash flow from operating activities section of the statement of cash flows under the direct and indirect methods. Both statements are for Computer King for the month ended November 1999. Both methods show the same amount of net cash flow from operating activities, regardless of the method. We will illustrate both methods in detail later in this chapter.

EXHIBIT 2 Cash Flow from Operations: Direct and Indirect Methods

Direct Method	
Cash flows from operating activities:	
Cash received from customers	$7,500
Deduct cash payments for expenses and payments to creditors	4,600
Net cash flow from operating activities	$2,900

Indirect Method	
Cash flows from operating activities:	
Net income, per income statement	$3,050
Add increase in accounts payable	400
	$3,450
Deduct increase in supplies	550
Net cash flow from operating activities	$2,900

Over the next five years, **Chrysler** plans to spend $23 billion in new product development, while **General Motors** plans to invest $3 billion overseas.

Cash Flows from Investing Activities

Cash inflows from investing activities normally arise from selling fixed assets, investments, and intangible assets. Cash outflows normally include payments to acquire fixed assets, investments, and intangible assets.

Cash flows from investing activities are reported on the statement of cash flows by first listing the cash inflows. The cash outflows are then presented. If the inflows are greater than the outflows, **net cash flow provided by investing activities** is reported. If the cash inflows are less than the cash outflows, **net cash flow used for investing activities** is reported.

The cash flows from investing activities section in the statement of cash flows for Computer King is shown below.

Cash flows from investing activities:
Cash payments for acquiring land . . . . $(10,000)

BUSINESS ON STAGE

A business must manage its cash position so that there is enough cash on hand to pay bills and other liabilities. Cash management is particularly important for seasonal businesses, which use cash in one part of the year and generate it in another. For example, consider this assumed cash position from operations for Smart Toys, Inc., a toy retailer:

> Seasonal
> Cash
> Management

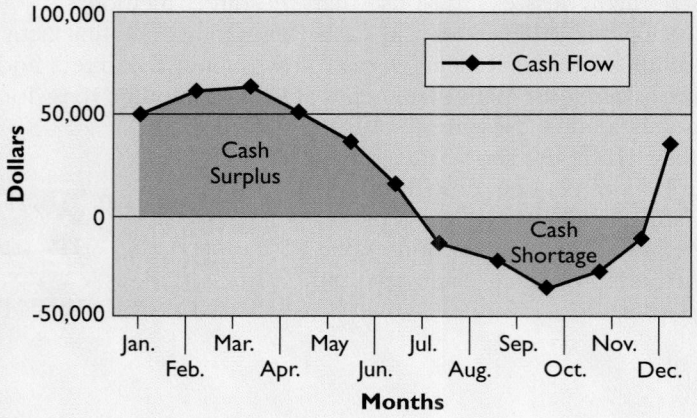

Smart Toys uses cash to purchase inventory prior to the winter holiday season. It is able to generate surplus cash by selling its inventory throughout the holiday season and into the early part of the calendar year.

If the cash required to purchase inventory exceeds Smart Toys' ability to generate operating cash flow, it may experience a cash shortage. In such a case, it must obtain short-term credit, which may be structured as a line of credit from a bank. A line of credit is an agreement that allows the business to borrow an unsecured amount of money up to some stated limit. For example, Smart Toys has a line of credit of $60,000, of which $40,000 was used during the year. Amounts drawn on a line of credit must usually be paid back within a year.

Seasonal businesses must be careful to avoid overextending their cash position during the "down cycle." For example, if Smart Toys purchases items that do not sell, a cash surplus will not be generated during the selling season. ■

Cash Flows from Financing Activities

Cash inflows from financing activities normally arise from issuing debt or equity securities. Examples of such inflows include issuing bonds, notes payable, and preferred and common stocks. Cash outflows from financing activities include paying cash dividends, repaying debt, and acquiring treasury stock.

Intel Corp. plans to keep enough cash on hand to build two computer chip factories. What happens when you have twice that amount on hand? Intel used its excess cash in 1996 ($1.3 billion) to repurchase common stock (treasury stock).

Cash flows from financing activities are reported on the statement of cash flows by first listing the cash inflows. The cash outflows are then presented. If the inflows are greater than the outflows, **net cash flow provided by financing activities** is reported. If the cash inflows are less than the cash outflows, **net cash flow used for financing activities** is reported.

The cash flows from financing activities section in the statement of cash flows for Computer King is shown below.

Cash flows from financing activities:	
Cash received as owner's investment . .	$15,000
Deduct cash withdrawal by owner	2,000
Net cash flow from financing activities . .	$13,000

Noncash Investing and Financing Activities

A business may enter into investing and financing activities that do not directly involve cash. For example, it may issue common stock to retire long-term debt. Such a transaction does not have a direct effect on cash. However, the transaction does eliminate the need for future cash payments to pay interest and retire the bonds. Thus, because of their future effect on cash flows, such transactions should be reported to readers of the financial statements.

When noncash investing and financing transactions occur during a period, their effect is reported in a separate schedule. This schedule usually appears at the bottom of the statement of cash flows. Other examples of noncash investing and financing transactions include acquiring fixed assets by issuing bonds or capital stock and issuing common stock in exchange for convertible preferred stock.

No Cash Flow per Share

The term *cash flow per share* is sometimes reported in the financial press. Often, the term is used to mean "cash flow from operations per share." Such reporting may be misleading to users of the financial statements. For example, users might interpret cash flow per share as the amount available for dividends. This would not be the case if most of the cash generated by operations is required for repaying loans or for reinvesting in the business. Users might also think that cash flow per share is equivalent or perhaps superior to earnings per share. For these reasons, the financial statements, including the statement of cash flows, should not report cash flow per share.

Statement of Cash Flows— The Indirect Method

OBJECTIVE 3

Prepare a statement of cash flows, using the indirect method.

The indirect method of reporting cash flows from operating activities is normally less costly and more efficient than the direct method. In addition, when the direct method is used, the indirect method must also be used in preparing a supplemental reconciliation of net income with cash flows from operations. The 1996 edition of *Accounting Trends & Techniques* reported that 98% of the companies surveyed used the indirect method. For these reasons, we will discuss first the indirect method of preparing the statement of cash flows.

To collect the data for the statement of cash flows, all the cash receipts and cash payments for a period could be analyzed. However, this procedure is expensive and time-consuming. A more efficient approach is to analyze the changes in the noncash balance sheet accounts. The logic of this approach is that a change in any balance sheet account (including cash) can be analyzed in terms of changes in the other balance sheet accounts. To illustrate, the accounting equation is rewritten below to focus on the cash account:

$$\textbf{Assets = Liabilities + Stockholders' Equity}$$
$$\textbf{Cash + Noncash Assets = Liabilities + Stockholders' Equity}$$
$$\textbf{Cash = Liabilities + Stockholders' Equity − Noncash Assets}$$

Any change in the cash account results in a change in one or more noncash balance sheet accounts. That is, if the cash account changes, then a liability, stockholders' equity, or noncash asset account must also change.

Additional data are also obtained by analyzing the income statement accounts and supporting records. For example, since the net income or net loss for the period is closed to *Retained Earnings,* a change in the retained earnings account can be partially explained by the net income or net loss reported on the income statement.

There is no order in which the noncash balance sheet accounts must be analyzed. However, it is usually more efficient to analyze the accounts in the reverse order in which they appear on the balance sheet. Thus, the analysis of retained earnings provides the starting point for determining the cash flows from operating activities, which is the first section of the statement of cash flows.

The comparative balance sheet for Rundell Inc. on December 31, 2000 and 1999, is used to illustrate the indirect method. This balance sheet is shown in Exhibit 3. Selected ledger accounts and other data are presented as needed.[2]

---

[2] An appendix that discusses using a work sheet as an aid in assembling data for the statement of cash flows is presented at the end of this chapter. This appendix illustrates a work sheet that can be used with the indirect method and a work sheet that can be used with the direct method of reporting cash flows from operating activities.

EXHIBIT 3
Comparative Balance Sheet

Rundell Inc.
Comparative Balance Sheet
December 31, 2000 and 1999

Assets	2000	1999	Increase Decrease*
Cash	$ 97,500	$ 26,000	$71,500
Accounts receivable (net)	74,000	65,000	9,000
Inventories	172,000	180,000	8,000*
Land	80,000	125,000	45,000*
Building	260,000	200,000	60,000
Accumulated depreciation—building	(65,300)	(58,300)	(7,000)
Total assets	$618,200	$537,700	$80,500
Liabilities			
Accounts payable (merchandise creditors)	$ 43,500	$ 46,700	$ 3,200*
Accrued expenses payable (operating expenses)..........	26,500	24,300	2,200
Income taxes payable	7,900	8,400	500*
Dividends payable	14,000	10,000	4,000
Bonds payable	100,000	150,000	50,000*
Total liabilities	$191,900	$239,400	$47,500*
Stockholders' Equity			
Common stock ($2 par)	$ 24,000	$ 16,000	$ 8,000
Paid-in capital in excess of par	120,000	80,000	40,000
Retained earnings	282,300	202,300	80,000
Total stockholders' equity	$426,300	$298,300	$128,000
Total liabilities and stockholders' equity	$618,200	$537,700	$ 80,500

Retained Earnings

The comparative balance sheet for Rundell Inc. shows that retained earnings increased $80,000 during the year. Analyzing the entries posted to the retained earnings account indicates how this change occurred. The retained earnings account for Rundell Inc. is shown below.

ACCOUNT *Retained Earnings*					ACCOUNT NO.		
						Balance	
Date		**Item**	**Debit**	**Credit**	**Debit**	**Credit**	
2000 Jan.	1	Balance				202,300	
Dec.	31	Net income		108,000		310,300	
	31	Cash dividends	28,000			282,300	

The retained earnings account must be carefully analyzed because some of the entries to retained earnings may not affect cash. For example, a decrease in retained earnings resulting from issuing a stock dividend does not affect cash. Such transactions are not reported on the statement of cash flows.

For Rundell Inc., the retained earnings account indicates that the $80,000 change resulted from net income of $108,000 and cash dividends declared of $28,000. The effect of each of these items on cash flows is discussed below.

Cash Flows from Operating Activities

The net income of $108,000 reported by Rundell Inc. normally is not equal to the amount of cash generated from operations during the period. This is because net income is determined using the accrual method of accounting.

Under the accrual method of accounting, the time when revenues and expenses are recorded often differs from when cash is received or paid. For example, merchandise may be sold on account and the cash received at a later date.

Likewise, insurance expense represents the amount of insurance expired during the period. The premiums for the insurance may have been paid in a prior period. Thus, the net income reported on the income statement must be adjusted in determining cash flows from operating activities. The typical adjustments to net income are summarized in Exhibit 4.[3]

EXHIBIT 4

Adjustments to Net Income—Indirect Method

Net income, per income statement		$XX
Add: Depreciation of fixed assets and amortization of intangible assets ...	$XX	
Decreases in current assets (receivables, inventories, prepaid expenses)	XX	
Increases in current liabilities (accounts and notes payable, accrued liabilities)	XX	
Losses on disposal of assets	XX	XX
Deduct: Increases in current assets (receivables, inventories, prepaid expenses)	$XX	
Decreases in current liabilities (accounts and notes payable, accrued liabilities)	XX	
Gains on disposal of assets	XX	XX
Net cash flow from operating activities		$XX

Some of the adjustment items in Exhibit 4 are for expenses that affect noncurrent accounts but not cash. For example, depreciation of fixed assets and amortization of intangible assets are deducted from revenue but do not affect cash.

Some of the adjustment items in Exhibit 4 are for revenues and expenses that affect current assets and current liabilities but not cash flows. For example, a sale of $10,000 on account increases accounts receivable by $10,000. However, cash is not affected. Thus, the increase in accounts receivable of $10,000 between two balance sheet dates is deducted from net income in arriving at cash flows from operating activities.

Cash flows from operating activities should not include investing or financing transactions. For example, assume that land costing $50,000 was sold for $90,000 (a gain of $40,000). The sale should be reported as an investing activity: "Cash receipts from the sale of land, $90,000." However, the $40,000 gain on the sale of the land is included in net income on the income statement. Thus, the $40,000 gain is deducted from net income in determining cash flows from operations in order to avoid "double counting" the cash flow from the gain. Losses from the sale of fixed assets are added to net income in determining cash flows from operations.

The effect of dividends payable on cash flows from operating activities is omitted from Exhibit 4. Dividends payable is omitted because dividends do not affect net income. Later in the chapter, we will discuss the reporting of dividends in the statement of cash flows. In the following paragraphs, we will discuss the adjustment of Rundell Inc.'s net income to "Cash flows from operating activities."

---

[3] Other items that also require adjustments to net income to obtain cash flow from operating activities include amortization of bonds payable discounts (add), losses on debt retirement (add), amortization of bonds payable premium (deduct), and gains on retirement of debt (deduct).

Depreciation

The comparative balance sheet in Exhibit 3 indicates that Accumulated Depreciation—Building increased by $7,000. As shown below, this account indicates that depreciation for the year was $7,000 for the building.

ACCOUNT *Accumulated Depreciation—Building*				ACCOUNT NO.		
					Balance	
Date		**Item**	**Debit**	**Credit**	**Debit**	**Credit**
2000 Jan.	1	Balance				58,300
Dec.	31	Depreciation for year		7,000		65,300

Net income was $45,000 for the year. The accumulated depreciation balance increased by $15,000 over the year. There were no sales of fixed assets or changes in noncash current assets or liabilities. What is the cash flow from operations?

- -

$60,000 ($45,000 + $15,000)

The $7,000 of depreciation expense reduced net income but did not require an outflow of cash. Thus, the $7,000 is added to net income in determining cash flows from operating activities, as follows:

Cash flows from operating activities:
Net income	$108,000	
Add depreciation	7,000	$115,000

Current Assets and Current Liabilities

As shown in Exhibit 4, decreases in noncash current assets and increases in current liabilities are added to net income. In contrast, increases in noncash current assets and decreases in current liabilities are deducted from net income. The current asset and current liability accounts of Rundell Inc. are as follows:

Accounts	December 31		Increase Decrease*
	2000	**1999**	
Accounts receivable (net)	$ 74,000	$ 65,000	$9,000
Inventories	172,000	180,000	8,000*
Accounts payable (merchandise creditors)	43,500	46,700	3,200*
Accrued expenses payable (operating expenses)	26,500	24,300	2,200
Income taxes payable	7,900	8,400	500*

The $9,000 increase in **accounts receivable** indicates that the sales on account during the year are $9,000 more than collections from customers on account. The amount reported as sales on the income statement therefore includes $9,000 that did not result in a cash inflow during the year. Thus, $9,000 is deducted from net income.

The $8,000 decrease in **inventories** indicates that the merchandise sold exceeds the cost of the merchandise purchased by $8,000. The amount deducted as cost of merchandise sold on the income statement therefore includes $8,000 that did not require a cash outflow during the year. Thus, $8,000 is added to net income.

The $3,200 decrease in **accounts payable** indicates that the amount of cash payments for merchandise exceeds the merchandise purchased on account by $3,200. The amount reported on the income statement for cost of mer-

Apple Computer had a loss of $816 million in 1996, but a positive cash flow from operations of $519 million. This is a difference of approximately $1.3 billion. Most of this difference was explained by a $1.1 billion reduction in inventory balances.

The Chief Financial Officer (CFO) of **Honeywell Corporation** put all managers through a financial training course. The CFO wanted the managers to understand how cash can be tied up in such things as receivables and inventory and that growth can be achieved without significant working capital requirements. As a result, Honeywell generated cash by reducing its working capital needs from $2.2 billion to $1.6 billion.

chandise sold therefore excludes $3,200 that required a cash outflow during the year. Thus, $3,200 is deducted from net income.

The $2,200 increase in **accrued expenses payable** indicates that the amount incurred during the year for operating expenses exceeds the cash payments by $2,200. The amount reported on the income statement for operating expenses therefore includes $2,200 that did not require a cash outflow during the year. Thus, $2,200 is added to net income.

The $500 decrease in **income taxes payable** indicates that the amount paid for taxes exceeds the amount incurred during the year by $500. The amount reported on the income statement for income tax therefore is less than the amount paid by $500. Thus, $500 is deducted from net income.

Net income was $36,000 for the year. Accounts receivable increased $3,000 and accounts payable increased $5,000. What is the cash flow from operations?

$38,000 ($36,000 − $3,000 + $5,000)

Gain on Sale of Land

The ledger or income statement of Rundell Inc. indicates that the sale of land resulted in a gain of $12,000. As we discussed previously, the sale proceeds, which include the gain and the carrying value of the land, are included in cash flows from investing activities.[4] The gain is also included in net income. Thus, to avoid double reporting, the gain of $12,000 is deducted from net income in determining cash flows from operating activities, as shown below.

Cash flows from operating activities:
Net income	$108,000
Deduct gain on sale of land	12,000

Reporting Cash Flows from Operating Activities

We have now presented all the necessary adjustments to convert the net income to cash flows from operating activities for Rundell Inc. These adjustments are summarized in Exhibit 5 in a format suitable for the statement of cash flows.

EXHIBIT 5
Cash Flows from Operating
Activities—Indirect Method

Cash flows from operating activities:			
Net income			$108,000
Add: Depreciation	$ 7,000		
Decrease in inventories	8,000		
Increase in accrued expenses	2,200	17,200	
			$125,200
Deduct: Increase in accounts receivable	$ 9,000		
Decrease in accounts payable	3,200		
Decrease in income taxes payable	500		
Gain on sale of land	12,000	24,700	
Net cash flow from operating activities			$100,500

Cash Flows Used for Payment of Dividends

According to the retained earnings account of Rundell Inc., shown earlier in the chapter, cash dividends of $28,000 were declared during the year. However, the dividends payable account, shown below, indicates that dividends of only $24,000 were paid during the year.

---

[4] The reporting of the proceeds (cash flows) from the sale of land as part of investing activities is discussed later in this chapter.

ACCOUNT *Dividends Payable*					ACCOUNT NO.		
						Balance	
Date		Item	Debit	Credit	Debit	Credit	
2000 Jan.	1	Balance				10,000	
	10	Cash paid	10,000		—	—	
June	20	Dividends declared		14,000		14,000	
July	10	Cash paid	14,000		—	—	
Dec.	20	Dividends declared		14,000		14,000	

The $24,000 of dividend payments represents a cash outflow that is reported in the financing activities section as follows:

Cash flows from financing activities:
    Cash paid for dividends $24,000

Common Stock

The common stock account increased by $8,000, and the paid-in capital in excess of par—common stock account increased by $40,000, as shown below. These increases result from issuing 4,000 shares of common stock for $12 per share.

ACCOUNT *Common Stock*					ACCOUNT NO.		
						Balance	
Date		Item	Debit	Credit	Debit	Credit	
2000 Jan.	1	Balance				16,000	
Nov.	1	4,000 shares issued for cash		8,000		24,000	

ACCOUNT *Paid-In Capital in Excess of Par—Common Stock*					ACCOUNT NO.		
						Balance	
Date		Item	Debit	Credit	Debit	Credit	
2000 Jan.	1	Balance				80,000	
Nov.	1	4,000 shares issued for cash		40,000		120,000	

This cash inflow is reported in the financing activities section as follows:

Cash flows from financing activities:
    Cash received from sale of common stock $48,000

Bonds Payable

The bonds payable account decreased by $50,000, as shown below. This decrease results from retiring the bonds by a cash payment for their face amount.

ACCOUNT *Bonds Payable*					ACCOUNT NO.		
						Balance	
Date		Item	Debit	Credit	Debit	Credit	
2000 Jan.	1	Balance				150,000	
June	30	Retired by payment of cash at face amount	50,000			100,000	

This cash outflow is reported in the financing activities section as follows:

Cash flows from financing activities:
   Cash paid to retire bonds payable $50,000

Building

The building account increased by $60,000, and the accumulated depreciation—building account increased by $7,000, as shown below.

ACCOUNT Building					ACCOUNT NO.	
					Balance	
Date		**Item**	**Debit**	**Credit**	**Debit**	**Credit**
2000 Jan.	1	Balance			200,000	
Dec.	27	Purchased for cash	60,000		260,000	

ACCOUNT Accumulated Depreciation—Building					ACCOUNT NO.	
					Balance	
Date		**Item**	**Debit**	**Credit**	**Debit**	**Credit**
2000 Jan.	1	Balance				58,300
Dec.	31	Depreciation for the year		7,000		65,300

The purchase of a building for cash of $60,000 is reported as an outflow of cash in the investing activities section, as follows:

Cash flows from investing activities:
   Cash paid for purchase of building $60,000

Q&A *A building with a cost of $145,000 and accumulated depreciation of $35,000 was sold for a $10,000 gain. How much cash was generated from this investing activity?*

$120,000 ($145,000 − $35,000 + $10,000)

The credit in the accumulated depreciation—building account, shown earlier, represents depreciation expense for the year. This depreciation expense of $7,000 on the building has already been considered as an addition to net income in determining cash flows from operating activities, as reported in Exhibit 5.

Land

The $45,000 decline in the land account resulted from two separate transactions, as shown below.

ACCOUNT Land					ACCOUNT NO.	
					Balance	
Date		**Item**	**Debit**	**Credit**	**Debit**	**Credit**
2000 Jan.	1	Balance			125,000	
June	8	Sold for $72,000 cash		60,000	65,000	
Oct.	12	Purchased for $15,000 cash	15,000		80,000	

A negative cash flow from operations would normally be considered a cause for concern. Such a condition could not be sustained indefinitely. However, in the short term, a firm could seek cash through additional financing or liquidating assets. For example, **America Online** (AOL) has had a negative cumulative cash flow from operations from its inception until 1996. However, AOL has been able to grow by obtaining cash from the sale of common stock. Investors are willing to purchase the common stock on the belief that AOL will have a very profitable future as the Internet online market matures.

The first transaction is the sale of land with a cost of $60,000 for $72,000 in cash. The $72,000 proceeds from the sale are reported in the investing activities section, as follows:

Cash flows from investing activities:
 Cash received from sale of land (includes $12,000 gain reported
 in net income) $72,000

The proceeds of $72,000 include the $12,000 gain on the sale of land and the $60,000 cost (book value) of the land. As shown in Exhibit 5, the $12,000 gain is also deducted from net income in the cash flows from operating activities section. This is necessary so that the $12,000 cash inflow related to the gain is not included twice as a cash inflow.

The second transaction is the purchase of land for cash of $15,000. This transaction is reported as an outflow of cash in the investing activities section, as follows:

Cash flows from investing activities:
 Cash paid for purchase of land $15,000

Preparing the Statement of Cash Flows

The statement of cash flows for Rundell Inc. is prepared from the data assembled and analyzed above, using the indirect method. Exhibit 6 shows the statement of cash flows prepared by Rundell Inc. The statement indicates that the cash position

EXHIBIT 6
Statement of Cash Flows—
Indirect Method

Cash management is not only important for businesses, but also for governmental units. The city of Miami faced a cash squeeze, due to an excessive public payroll, graft, and inefficiency. For example, the Miami police were allowed to take their police cruisers home with them, which effectively doubled the number of police cars needed by the city. The cash shortfall was so severe that the city considered merging with Dade County.

Source: Peter Katel, "Miami Goes to the Dogs," *Newsweek,* December 16, 1996.

Rundell Inc. Statement of Cash Flows For the Year Ended December 31, 2000			
Cash flows from operating activities:			
Net income		$108,000	
Add: Depreciation	$ 7,000		
Decrease in inventories	8,000		
Increase in accrued expenses	2,200	17,200	
		$125,200	
Deduct: Increase in accounts receivable	$ 9,000		
Decrease in accounts payable	3,200		
Decrease in income taxes payable	500		
Gain on sale of land	12,000	24,700	
Net cash flow from operating activities			$100,500
Cash flows from investing activities:			
Cash from sale of land		$ 72,000	
Less: Cash paid to purchase land	$15,000		
Cash paid for purchase of building	60,000	75,000	
Net cash flow used for investing activities			(3,000)
Cash flows from financing activities:			
Cash received from sale of common stock		$ 48,000	
Less: Cash paid to retire bonds payable	$50,000		
Cash paid for dividends	24,000	74,000	
Net cash flow used for financing activities			(26,000)
Increase in cash			$ 71,500
Cash at the beginning of the year			26,000
Cash at the end of the year			$ 97,500

increased by $71,500 during the year. The most significant increase in net cash flows, $100,500, was from operating activities. The most significant use of cash, $26,000, was for financing activities.

Statement of Cash Flows— The Direct Method

OBJECTIVE 4

Prepare a statement of cash flows, using the direct method.

As we discussed previously, the manner of reporting cash flows from investing and financing activities is the same under the direct and indirect methods. In addition, the direct method and the indirect method will report the same amount of cash flows from operating activities. However, the methods differ in how the cash flows from operating activities data are obtained, analyzed, and reported.

To illustrate the direct method, we will use the comparative balance sheet and the income statement for Rundell Inc. In this way, we can compare the statement of cash flows under the direct method and the indirect method.

Exhibit 7 shows the changes in the current asset and liability account balances for Rundell Inc. The income statement in Exhibit 7 shows additional data for Rundell Inc.

EXHIBIT 7
Balance Sheet and Income Statement Data for Direct Method

Rundell Inc.
Schedule of Changes in Current Accounts

Accounts	December 31 2000	December 31 1999	Increase Decrease*
Cash	$ 97,500	$ 26,000	$71,500
Accounts receivable (net)	74,000	65,000	9,000
Inventories	172,000	180,000	8,000*
Accounts payable (merchandise creditors)	43,500	46,700	3,200*
Accrued expenses payable (operating expenses)	26,500	24,300	2,200
Income taxes payable	7,900	8,400	500*
Dividends payable	14,000	10,000	4,000

Rundell Inc.
Income Statement
For the Year Ended December 31, 2000

Sales		$1,180,000
Cost of merchandise sold		790,000
Gross profit		$ 390,000
Operating expenses:		
Depreciation expense	$ 7,000	
Other operating expenses	196,000	
Total operating expenses		203,000
Income from operations		$ 187,000
Other income:		
Gain on sale of land	$ 12,000	
Other expense:		
Interest expense	8,000	4,000
Income before income tax		$ 191,000
Income tax expense		83,000
Net income		$ 108,000

The direct method reports cash flows from operating activities by major classes of operating cash receipts and operating cash payments. The difference between the major classes of total operating cash receipts and total operating cash payments is the net cash flow from operating activities.

Cash Received from Customers

The $1,180,000 of sales for Rundell Inc. is reported by using the accrual method. To determine the cash received from sales to customers, the $1,180,000 must be adjusted. The adjustments necessary to convert the sales reported on the income statement to the cash received from customers is summarized below.

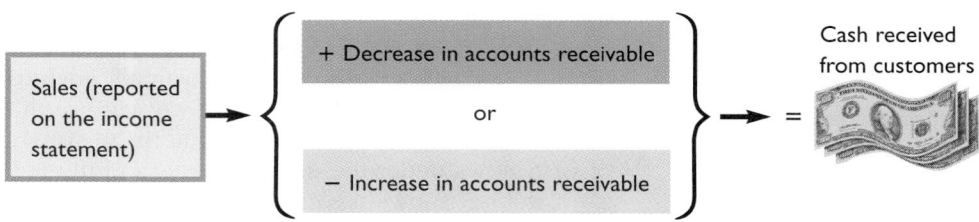

For Rundell Inc., the cash received from customers is $1,171,000, as shown below.

Sales	$1,180,000
Less increase in accounts receivable	9,000
Cash received from customers	$1,171,000

The additions to **accounts receivable** for sales on account during the year were $9,000 more than the amounts collected from customers on account. Sales reported on the income statement therefore included $9,000 that did not result in a cash inflow during the year. In other words, the increase of $9,000 in accounts receivable during 2000 indicates that sales on account exceeded cash received from customers by $9,000. Thus, $9,000 is deducted from sales to determine the cash received from customers. The $1,171,000 of cash received from customers is reported in the cash flows from operating activities section of the cash flow statement.

Cash Payments for Merchandise

The $790,000 of cost of merchandise sold is reported on the income statement for Rundell Inc., using the accrual method. The adjustments necessary to convert the cost of merchandise sold to cash payments for merchandise during 2000 are summarized below.

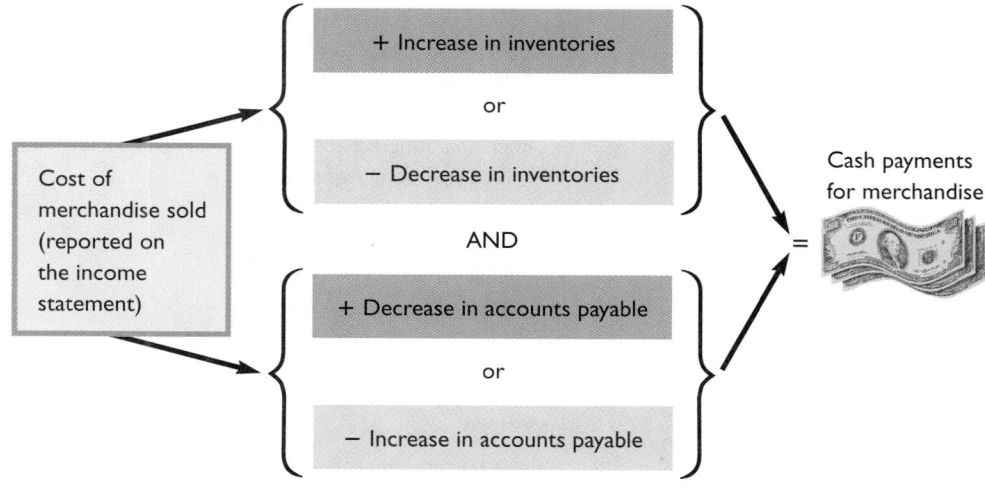

Sales reported on the income statement were $350,000. The accounts receivable balance declined $8,000 over the year. What was the amount of cash received from customers?

$358,000 ($350,000 + $8,000)

For Rundell Inc., the amount of cash payments for merchandise is $785,200, as determined below.

Cost of merchandise sold	$790,000
Deduct decrease in inventories	(8,000)
Add decrease in accounts payable	3,200
Cash payments for merchandise	$785,200

The $8,000 decrease in **inventories** indicates that the merchandise sold exceeded the cost of the merchandise purchased by $8,000. The amount reported on the income statement for cost of merchandise sold therefore includes $8,000 that did not require a cash outflow during the year. Thus, $8,000 is deducted from the cost of merchandise sold in determining the cash payments for merchandise.

The $3,200 decrease in **accounts payable** (merchandise creditors) indicates a cash outflow that is excluded from cost of merchandise sold. In other words, the decrease in accounts payable indicates that cash payments for merchandise were $3,200 more than the purchases on account during 2000. Thus, $3,200 is added to the cost of merchandise sold in determining the cash payments for merchandise.

Cash Payments for Operating Expenses

The $7,000 of depreciation expense reported on the income statement did not require a cash outflow. Thus, under the direct method, it is not reported on the statement of cash flows. The $196,000 reported for other operating expenses is adjusted to reflect the cash payments for operating expenses, as summarized below.

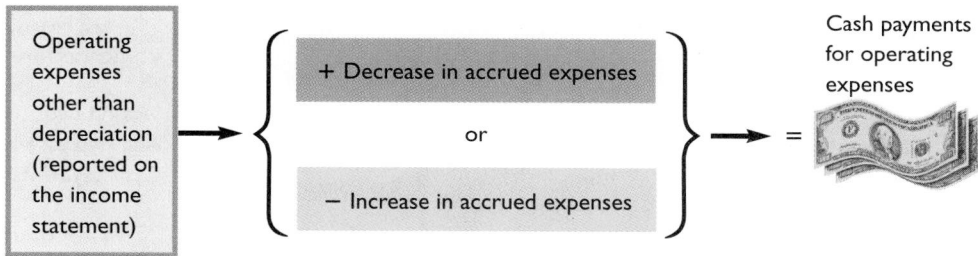

For Rundell Inc., the amount of cash payments for operating expenses is $193,800, determined as follows:

Operating expenses other than depreciation	$196,000
Deduct increase in accrued expenses	2,200
Cash payments for operating expenses	$193,800

The increase in **accrued expenses** (operating expenses) indicates that operating expenses include $2,200 for which there was no cash outflow (payment) during the year. In other words, the increase in accrued expenses indicates that the cash payments for operating expenses were $2,200 less than the amount reported as an expense during the year. Thus, $2,200 is deducted from the operating expenses on the income statement in determining the cash payments for operating expenses.

Gain on Sale of Land

The income statement for Rundell Inc. in Exhibit 7 reports a gain of $12,000 on the sale of land. As we discussed previously, the gain is included in the proceeds from the sale of land, which is reported as part of the cash flows from investing activities.

Interest Expense

The income statement for Rundell Inc. in Exhibit 7 reports interest expense of $8,000. The interest expense is related to the bonds payable that were outstanding during the year. We assume that interest on the bonds is paid on June 30 and December 31. Thus, $8,000 cash outflow for interest expense is reported on the statement of cash flows as an operating activity.

If interest payable had existed at the end of the year, the interest expense would be adjusted for any increase or decrease in interest payable from the beginning to the end of the year. That is, a decrease in interest payable would be added to interest expense and an increase in interest payable would be subtracted from interest expense. This is similar to the adjustment for changes in income taxes payable, which we will illustrate in the following paragraphs.

Cash Payments for Income Taxes

The adjustment to convert the income tax reported on the income statement to the cash basis is summarized below.

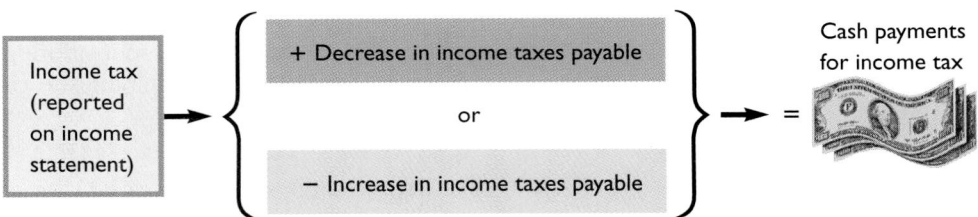

For Rundell Inc., cash payments for income tax are $83,500, determined as follows:

Income tax	$83,000
Add decrease in income taxes payable	500
Cash payments for income tax	$83,500

The cash outflow for income taxes exceeded the income tax deducted as an expense during the period by $500. Thus, $500 is added to the amount of income tax reported on the income statement in determining the cash payments for income tax.

Reporting Cash Flows from Operating Activities—Direct Method

Exhibit 8 is a complete statement of cash flows for Rundell Inc., using the direct method for reporting cash flows from operating activities. The portions of this statement that differ from the indirect method are highlighted in color. Exhibit 8 also includes the separate schedule reconciling net income and net cash flow from operating activities. This schedule must accompany the statement of cash flows when the direct method is used. This schedule is similar to the cash flows from operating activities section of the statement of cash flows prepared using the indirect method.

EXHIBIT 8
Statement of Cash Flows—
Direct Method

Rundell Inc.
Statement of Cash Flows
For the Year Ended December 31, 2000

Cash flows from operating activities:

Cash received from customers		$1,171,000	
Deduct: Cash payments for merchandise	$785,200		
Cash payments for operating expense	193,800		
Cash payments for interest	8,000		
Cash payments for income taxes	83,500	1,070,500	
Net cash flow from operating activities			$100,500

Cash flows from investing activities:

Cash from sale of land		$ 72,000	
Less: Cash paid to purchase land	$ 15,000		
Cash paid for purchase of building	60,000	75,000	
Net cash flow used for investing activities			(3,000)

Cash flows from financing activities:

Cash received from sale of common stock		$ 48,000	
Less: Cash paid to retire bonds payable	$ 50,000		
Cash paid for dividends	24,000	74,000	
Net cash flow used for financing activities			(26,000)
Increase in cash			$ 71,500
Cash at the beginning of the year			26,000
Cash at the end of the year			$ 97,500

Schedule Reconciling Net Income with Cash Flows from Operating Activities:

Net income, per income statement		$108,000
Add: Depreciation	$ 7,000	
Decrease in inventories	8,000	
Increase in accrued expenses	2,200	17,200
		$125,200
Deduct: Increase in accounts receivable	$ 9,000	
Decrease in accounts payable	3,200	
Decrease in income taxes payable	500	
Gain on sale of land	12,000	24,700
Net cash flow from operating activities		$100,500

FINANCIAL ANALYSIS AND INTERPRETATION

OBJECTIVE 5

Calculate and interpret the free cash flow.

A valuable tool for evaluating the cash position of a business is free cash flow. **Free cash flow** is a measure of operating cash flow available for corporate purposes after providing sufficient fixed asset additions to maintain current productive capacity and dividends. Thus, free cash flow can be calculated as follows:

	Cash flow from operations
Less:	Cash used to purchase fixed assets to maintain productive capacity used up in producing income during the period
Less:	Cash used for dividends
	Free cash flow

Many high technology firms must aggressively reinvest in new technology to remain competitive. This can reduce free cash flow. For example, **Motorola's** free cash flow is less than 10% of the cash flow from operating activities. In contrast, **Coca-Cola's** free cash flow is approximately 75% of the cash flow from operating activities.

To illustrate, assume that O'Brien Company had cash flow from operations of $1,400,000. O'Brien Company invested $450,000 in fixed assets to maintain productive capacity, and another $300,000 to expand capacity. Dividends were $100,000. Thus, free cash flow is as follows:

Cash flow from operations		$1,400,000
Less: Cash invested in fixed assets to		
maintain productive capacity . . .	$450,000	
Cash for dividends	100,000	550,000
Free cash flow		$ 850,000

A company that has free cash flow is able to fund internal growth, retire debt, and enjoy financial flexibility. A company with no free cash flow is unable to maintain current productive capacity or dividend payouts to stockholders. Lack of free cash flow can be an early indicator of liquidity problems. Indeed, all three of the major credit rating agencies use a form of free cash flow in evaluating the creditworthiness of businesses.[5]

ENCORE

"The Pack's" Cash Flow

The **Green Bay Packers** NFL football franchise recorded record earnings of $5.4 million for fiscal year 1995. The increased earnings were caused by a strong 13% increase in revenues, combined with a more modest increase in operating costs, thanks to the NFL salary cap. Even so, the Packers ranked only 22nd in total revenues out of 30 NFL clubs. In addition, the record earnings weren't enough to prevent cash from declining by $3.6 million. Why did cash decline in the face of such strong earnings? The answer is simple. The Packers have spent $43.2 million on facilities over the last dozen years, which has caused a negative cash flow for the last three seasons. John Underwood, treasurer, stated to stockholders, "In spite of the record year, we really need to focus our attention on generating higher levels of cash. The reasons are pretty obvious. In the business we're in, cash is king. And every dollar we make in this franchise goes to only one of two purposes: the football team or the facilities. With the reality of the competition, particularly regarding signing bonuses, it's really critical that our strategy now is to build and replenish cash so that we do have the funds to compete." How could the Green Bay Packers increase cash flow? Some ideas might include:

1.   Increase ticket prices. (The Packers presently rank 29th in average ticket prices.)
2.   Expand private box revenue and corporate sponsorships.
3.   Expand the team's pro shop.
4.   Rent Lambeau Field for concerts or festivals during the off-season.
5.   Distribute pay-for-view games over direct TV. ■

Source: Tom Mulhern, "Packer Finances Bittersweet," *Post-Crescent* (Appleton, Wisconsin), May 30, 1996.

[5] Jeff Ryser, "Cash Flow and the Single A," *CFO: The Magazine for Senior Financial Executives* (October 1995), pp. 87–89. The three major credit-rating agencies that rate the bonds (debt) sold to outside investors are **Fitch Investor Services**, **Standard and Poor's**, and **Moody's**. The ratings are used by investors in evaluating the risk of bond default.

APPENDIX: WORK SHEET FOR STATEMENT OF CASH FLOWS

A work sheet may be useful in assembling data for the statement of cash flows. Whether or not a work sheet is used, the concepts of cash flow and the statements of cash flows presented in this chapter are not affected. In this appendix, we will describe and illustrate the use of work sheets for the indirect method and the direct method.

Work Sheet—Indirect Method

We will use the data for Rundell Inc., presented in Exhibit 3, as a basis for illustrating the work sheet for the indirect method. The procedures used in preparing this work sheet, shown in Exhibit 9, are outlined at the top of the next page.

EXHIBIT 9   Work Sheet for Statement of Cash Flows—Indirect Method

Rundell Inc.
Work Sheet for Statement of Cash Flows
For the Year Ended December 31, 2000

	Accounts	Balance Dec. 31, 1999	Transactions Debit	Transactions Credit	Balance Dec. 31, 2000	
1	Cash	26,000	(o) 71,500		97,500	1
2	Accounts receivable (net)	65,000	(n) 9,000		74,000	2
3	Inventories	180,000		(m) 8,000	172,000	3
4	Land	125,000	(k) 15,000	(l) 60,000	80,000	4
5	Building	200,000	(j) 60,000		260,000	5
6	Accumulated depreciation—building	(58,300)		(i) 7,000	(65,300)	6
7	Accounts payable (merchandise creditors)	(46,700)	(h) 3,200		(43,500)	7
8	Accrued expenses payable (operating expenses)	(24,300)		(g) 2,200	(26,500)	8
9	Income taxes payable	(8,400)	(f) 500		(7,900)	9
10	Dividends payable	(10,000)		(e) 4,000	(14,000)	10
11	Bonds payable	(150,000)	(d) 50,000		(100,000)	11
12	Common stock	(16,000)		(c) 8,000	(24,000)	12
13	Paid-in capital in excess of par	(80,000)		(c) 40,000	(120,000)	13
14	Retained earnings	(202,300)	(b) 28,000	(a) 108,000	(282,300)	14
15	Totals	0	237,200	237,200	0	15
16	Operating activities:					16
17	Net income		(a) 108,000			17
18	Depreciation of building		(i) 7,000			18
19	Decrease in inventories		(m) 8,000			19
20	Increase in accrued expenses		(g) 2,200			20
21	Increase in accounts receivable			(n) 9,000		21
22	Decrease in accounts payable			(h) 3,200		22
23	Decrease in income taxes payable			(f) 500		23
24	Gain on sale of land			(l) 12,000		24
25	Investing activities:					25
26	Sale of land		(l) 72,000			26
27	Purchase of land			(k) 15,000		27
28	Purchase of building			(j) 60,000		28
29	Financing activities:					29
30	Issued common stock		(c) 48,000			30
31	Retired bonds payable			(d) 50,000		31
32	Declared cash dividends			(b) 28,000		32
33	Increase in dividends payable		(e) 4,000			33
34	Net increase in cash			(o) 71,500		34
35	Totals		249,200	249,200		35

1. List the title of each balance sheet account in the Accounts column. For each account, enter its balance as of December 31, 1999, in the first column and its balance as of December 31, 2000, in the last column. Place the credit balances in parentheses. The column totals should equal zero, since the total of the debits in a column should equal the total of the credits in a column.
2. Analyze the change during the year in each account to determine the net increase (decrease) in cash and the cash flows from operating activities, investing activities, financing activities, and the noncash investing and financing activities. Show the effect of the change on cash flows by making entries in the Transactions columns.

Analyzing Accounts

An efficient method of analyzing cash flows is to determine the type of cash flow activity that led to changes in balance sheet accounts during the period. As we analyze each noncash account, we will make entries on the work sheet for specific types of cash flow activities related to the noncash accounts. After we have analyzed all the noncash accounts, we will make an entry for the increase (decrease) in cash during the period. These entries, however, are not posted to the ledger. They only aid in assembling the data on the work sheet.

The order in which the accounts are analyzed is unimportant. However, it is more efficient to begin with the retained earnings account and proceed upward in the account listing.

Retained Earnings. The work sheet shows a Retained Earnings balance of $202,300 at December 31, 1999, and $282,300 at December 31, 2000. Thus, Retained Earnings increased $80,000 during the year. This increase resulted from two factors: (1) net income of $108,000 and (2) declaring cash dividends of $28,000. To identify the cash flows by activity, we will make two entries on the work sheet. These entries also serve to account for or explain, in terms of cash flows, the increase of $80,000.

In closing the accounts at the end of the year, the retained earnings account was credited for the net income of $108,000. The $108,000 is reported on the statement of cash flows as "cash flows from operating activities." The following entry is made in the Transactions columns on the work sheet. This entry (1) accounts for the credit portion of the closing entry (to Retained Earnings) and (2) identifies the cash flow in the bottom portion of the work sheet.

| (a) | Operating Activities—Net Income | 108,000 | |
| | Retained Earnings | | 108,000 |

In closing the accounts at the end of the year, the retained earnings account was debited for dividends declared of $28,000. The $28,000 is reported as a financing activity on the statement of cash flows. The following entry on the work sheet (1) accounts for the debit portion of the closing entry (to Retained Earnings) and (2) identifies the cash flow in the bottom portion of the work sheet.

| (b) | Retained Earnings | 28,000 | |
| | Financing Activities—Declared Cash Dividends | | 28,000 |

The $28,000 of declared dividends will be adjusted later for the actual amount of cash dividends paid during the year.

Other Accounts. The entries for the other accounts are made in the work sheet in a manner similar to entries (a) and (b). A summary of these entries is as follows:

(c)	Financing Activities—Issued Common Stock	48,000	
	Common Stock		8,000
	Paid-In Capital in Excess of Par—Common Stock		40,000

(d)	Bonds Payable	50,000	
	Financing Activities—Retired Bonds Payable		50,000
(e)	Financing Activities—Increase in Dividends Payable	4,000	
	Dividends Payable		4,000
(f)	Income Taxes Payable	500	
	Operating Activities—Decrease in Income Taxes Payable		500
(g)	Operating Activities—Increase in Accrued Expenses	2,200	
	Accrued Expenses		2,200
(h)	Accounts Payable	3,200	
	Operating Activities—Decrease in Accounts Payable		3,200
(i)	Operating Activities—Depreciation of Building	7,000	
	Accumulated Depreciation—Building		7,000
(j)	Building	60,000	
	Investing Activities—Purchase of Building		60,000
(k)	Land	15,000	
	Investing Activities—Purchase of Land		15,000
(l)	Investing Activities—Sale of Land	72,000	
	Operating Activities—Gain on Sale of Land		12,000
	Land		60,000
(m)	Operating Activities—Decrease in Inventories	8,000	
	Inventories		8,000
(n)	Accounts Receivable	9,000	
	Operating Activities—Increase in Accounts Receivable		9,000
(o)	Cash	71,500	
	Net Increase in Cash		71,500

Completing the Work Sheet

After we have analyzed all the balance sheet accounts and made the entries on the work sheet, all the operating, investing, and financing activities are identified in the bottom portion of the work sheet. The accuracy of the work sheet entries is verified by the equality of each pair of the totals of the debit and credit Transactions columns.

Preparing the Statement of Cash Flows

The statement of cash flows prepared from the work sheet is identical to the statement in Exhibit 6. The data for the three sections of the statement are obtained from the bottom portion of the work sheet.

In the cash flows from operating activities section, the effect of depreciation is normally presented first. The effects of increases and decreases in current assets and current liabilities are then presented. The effects of any gains and losses on operating activities are normally reported last. The cash paid for dividends is reported as $24,000 instead of the amount of dividends declared ($28,000) less the increase in dividends payable ($4,000). Any noncash investing and financing activities are usually reported in a separate schedule at the bottom of the statement.

Work Sheet—Direct Method

As a basis for illustrating the direct method work sheet, we will use the balance sheet data for Rundell Inc. in Exhibit 3 and the income statement data in Exhibit 7. The procedures used in preparing the work sheet are outlined following Exhibit 10.

EXHIBIT 10   Work Sheet for Statement of Cash Flows—Direct Method

Rundell Inc.
Work Sheet for Statement of Cash Flows
For the Year Ended December 31, 2000

	Accounts	Balance Dec. 31, 1999	Transactions Debit	Transactions Credit	Balance Dec. 31, 2000	
1	**Balance Sheet**					1
2	Cash	26,000	(t) 71,500		97,500	2
3	Accounts receivable (net)	65,000	(s) 9,000		74,000	3
4	Inventories	180,000		(r) 8,000	172,000	4
5	Land	125,000	(q) 15,000	(e) 60,000	80,000	5
6	Building	200,000	(p) 60,000		260,000	6
7	Accumulated depreciation—building	(58,300)		(c) 7,000	(65,300)	7
8	Accounts payable (merchandise creditors)	(46,700)	(o) 3,200		(43,500)	8
9	Accrued expenses payable (operating expenses) . .	(24,300)		(n) 2,200	(26,500)	9
10	Income taxes payable	(8,400)	(m) 500		(7,900)	10
11	Dividends payable	(10,000)		(l) 4,000	(14,000)	11
12	Bonds payable	(150,000)	(k) 50,000		(100,000)	12
13	Common stock	(16,000)		(j) 8,000	(24,000)	13
14	Paid-in capital in excess of par	(80,000)		(j) 40,000	(120,000)	14
15	Retained earnings	(202,300)	(i) 28,000	(h) 108,000	(282,300)	15
16	Totals	0	237,200	237,200	0	16
17	**Income Statement**					17
18	Sales			(a) 1,180,000		18
19	Cost of merchandise sold		(b) 790,000			19
20	Depreciation expense		(c) 7,000			20
21	Other operating expenses		(d) 196,000			21
22	Gain on sale of land			(e) 12,000		22
23	Interest expense		(f) 8,000			23
24	Income taxes		(g) 83,000			24
25	Net income		(h) 108,000			25
26	**Cash Flows**					26
27	Operating activities:					27
28	Cash received from customers		(a) 1,180,000	(s) 9,000		28
29	Cash payments:					29
30	Merchandise		(r) 8,000	(b) 790,000		30
31				(o) 3,200		31
32	Operating expense		(n) 2,200	(d) 196,000		32
33	Interest			(f) 8,000		33
34	Income taxes			(g) 83,000		34
35				(m) 500		35
36	Investing activities:					36
37	Sale of land		(e) 72,000			37
38	Purchase of land			(q) 15,000		38
39	Purchase of building			(p) 60,000		39
40	Financing activities:					40
41	Issued common stock		(j) 48,000			41
42	Retired bonds payable			(k) 50,000		42
43	Declared cash dividends			(i) 28,000		43
44	Increase in dividends payable		(l) 4,000			44
45	Net increase in cash			(t) 71,500		45
46	Totals		2,506,200	2,506,200		46

1. List the title of each balance sheet account in the Accounts column. For each account, enter its balance as of December 31, 1999, in the first column and its balance as of December 31, 2000, in the last column. Place the credit balances in parentheses. The column totals should equal zero, since the total of the debits in a column should equal the total of the credits in a column.
2. List the title of each income statement account and "Net Income" on the work sheet.
3. Analyze the effect of each income statement item on cash flows from operating activities. Beginning with sales, enter the balance of each item in the proper Transactions column. Complete the entry in the Transactions columns to show the effect on cash flows.
4. Analyze the change during the year in each balance sheet account to determine the net increase (decrease) in cash and the cash flows from operating activities, investing activities, financing activities, and the noncash investing and financing activities. Show the effect of the change on cash flows by making entries in the Transactions columns.

Analyzing Accounts

Under the direct method of reporting cash flows from operating activities, analyzing accounts begins with the income statement. As we analyze each income statement account, we will make entries on the work sheet that show the effect on cash flows from operating activities. After we have analyzed the income statement accounts, we will analyze changes in the balance sheet accounts.

The order in which the balance sheet accounts are analyzed is unimportant. However, it is more efficient to begin with the retained earnings account and proceed upward in the account listing. As each noncash balance sheet account is analyzed, we will make entries on the work sheet for the related cash flow activities. After we have analyzed all the noncash accounts, we will make an entry for the increase (decrease) in cash during the period.

Sales. The income statement for Rundell Inc. shows sales of $1,180,000 for the year. Sales for cash provide cash when the sale is made. Sales on account provide cash when customers pay their bills. The entry on the work sheet is as follows:

| (a) | Operating Activities—Receipts from Customers | 1,180,000 | |
| | Sales | | 1,180,000 |

Cost of Merchandise Sold. The income statement for Rundell Inc. shows cost of merchandise sold of $790,000 for the year. The cost of merchandise sold requires cash payments for cash purchases of merchandise. For purchases on account, cash payments are made when the invoices are due. The entry on the work sheet is as follows:

| (b) | Cost of Merchandise Sold | 790,000 | |
| | Operating Activities—Payments for Merchandise | | 790,000 |

Depreciation Expense. The income statement for Rundell Inc. shows depreciation expense of $7,000. Depreciation expense does not require a cash outflow and thus is not reported on the statement of cash flows. The entry on the work sheet to fully account for the depreciation expense is as follows:

| (c) | Depreciation Expense | 7,000 | |
| | Accumulated Depreciation—Building | | 7,000 |

Other Accounts. The entries for the other accounts are made on the work sheet in a manner similar to entries (a), (b), and (c). A summary of these entries is as follows:

(d)	Other Operating Expenses	196,000	
	Operating Activities—Paid Operating Expenses		196,000
(e)	Investing Activities—Sale of Land	72,000	
	Land		60,000
	Gain on Sale of Land		12,000
(f)	Interest Expense	8,000	
	Operating Activities—Paid Interest		8,000
(g)	Income Taxes	83,000	
	Operating Activities—Paid Income Taxes		83,000
(h)	Net Income	108,000	
	Retained Earnings		108,000
(i)	Retained Earnings	28,000	
	Financing Activities—Declared Cash Dividends		28,000
(j)	Financing Activities—Issued Common Stock	48,000	
	Common Stock		8,000
	Paid-In Capital in Excess of Par—Common Stock		40,000
(k)	Bonds Payable	50,000	
	Financing Activities—Retired Bonds Payable		50,000
(l)	Financing Activities—Increase in Dividends Payable	4,000	
	Dividends Payable		4,000
(m)	Income Taxes Payable	500	
	Operating Activities—Cash Paid for Income Taxes		500
(n)	Operating Activities—Cash Paid for Operating Expenses	2,200	
	Accrued Expenses		2,200
(o)	Accounts Payable	3,200	
	Operating Activities—Cash Paid for Merchandise		3,200
(p)	Building	60,000	
	Investing Activities—Purchase of Building		60,000
(q)	Land	15,000	
	Investing Activities—Purchase of Land		15,000
(r)	Operating Activities—Cash Paid for Merchandise	8,000	
	Inventories		8,000
(s)	Accounts Receivable	9,000	
	Operating Activities—Cash Received from Customers		9,000
(t)	Cash	71,500	
	Net Increase in Cash		71,500

Completing the Work Sheet

After we have analyzed all the income statement and balance sheet accounts and have made the entries on the work sheet, all the operating, investing, and financing activities are identified in the bottom portion of the work sheet. The mathematical accuracy of the work sheet entries is verified by the equality of each pair of the totals of the debit and credit Transactions columns.

Preparing the Statement of Cash Flows

The statement of cash flows prepared from the work sheet is identical to the statement in Exhibit 8. The data for the three sections of the statement are obtained from the bottom portion of the work sheet. Some of these data may not be reported exactly as they appear on the work sheet. The cash paid for dividends is reported as

$24,000 instead of the amount of dividends declared ($28,000) less the increase in the dividends payable ($4,000).

KEY POINTS

1 Explain why the statement of cash flows is one of the basic financial statements.

The statement of cash flows reports useful information about a firm's ability to generate cash from operations, maintain and expand its operating capacity, meet its financial obligations, and pay dividends. This information assists investors, creditors, and others in assessing the firm's profit potential and its ability to pay its maturing debt. The statement of cash flows is also useful to managers in evaluating past operations and in planning future operating, investing, and financing activities.

2 Summarize the types of cash flow activities reported in the statement of cash flows.

The statement of cash flows reports cash receipts and cash payments by three types of activities: operating activities, investing activities, and financing activities.

Cash flows from operating activities are cash flows from transactions that affect net income. There are two methods of reporting cash flows from operating activities: (1) the direct method and (2) the indirect method.

Cash inflows from investing activities are cash flows from the sale of investments, fixed assets, and intangible assets. Cash outflows generally include payments to acquire investments, fixed assets, and intangible assets.

Cash inflows from financing activities include proceeds from issuing equity securities, such as preferred and common stock. Cash inflows also arise from issuing bonds, mortgage notes payable, and other long-term debt. Cash outflows from financing activities arise from paying cash dividends, purchasing treasury stock, and repaying amounts borrowed.

Investing and financing for a business may be affected by transactions that do not involve cash. The effect of such transactions should be reported in a separate schedule accompanying the statement of cash flows.

Because it may be misleading, cash flow per share is not reported in the statement of cash flows.

3 Prepare a statement of cash flows, using the indirect method.

To prepare the statement of cash flows, changes in the noncash balance sheet accounts are analyzed. This logic relies on the fact that a change in any balance sheet account can be analyzed in terms of changes in the other balance sheet accounts. Thus, by analyzing the noncash balance sheet accounts, those activities that resulted in cash flows can be identified. Although the noncash balance sheet accounts may be analyzed in any order, it is usually more efficient to begin with retained earnings. Additional data are obtained by analyzing the income statement accounts and supporting records.

4 Prepare a statement of cash flows, using the direct method.

The direct method and the indirect method will report the same amount of cash flows from operating activities. Also, the manner of reporting cash flows from investing and financing activities is the same under both methods. The methods differ in how the cash flows from operating activities data are obtained, analyzed, and reported. The direct method reports cash flows from operating activities by major classes of operating cash receipts and cash payments. The difference between the major classes of total operating cash receipts and total operating cash payments is the net cash flow from operating activities.

The data for reporting cash flows from operating activities by the direct method can be obtained by analyzing the cash flows related to the revenues and expenses reported on the income statement. The revenues and expenses are adjusted from the accrual basis of accounting to the cash basis for purposes of preparing the statement of cash flows.

When the direct method is used, a reconciliation of net income and net cash flow from operating activities is reported in a separate schedule. This schedule is similar to the cash flows from the operating activities section of the statement of cash flows prepared using the indirect method.

5 Calculate and interpret the free cash flow.

Free cash flow is the amount of operating cash flow remaining after replacing current productive capacity and maintaining current dividends. Free cash flow is the amount of cash available to reduce debt, grow the business, or return to shareholders through increased dividends or treasury stock purchases.

ILLUSTRATIVE PROBLEM

The comparative balance sheet of Dowling Company for December 31, 2001 and 2000, is as follows:

Dowling Company
Comparative Balance Sheet
December 31, 2001 and 2000

	2001	2000
Assets		
Cash	$ 140,350	$ 95,900
Accounts receivable (net)	95,300	102,300
Inventories	165,200	157,900
Prepaid expenses	6,240	5,860
Investments (long-term)	35,700	84,700
Land	75,000	90,000
Buildings	375,000	260,000
Accumulated depreciation—buildings	(71,300)	(58,300)
Machinery and equipment	428,300	428,300
Accumulated depreciation—machinery and equipment	(148,500)	(138,000)
Patents	58,000	65,000
Total assets	$1,159,290	$1,093,660
Liabilities and Stockholders' Equity		
Accounts payable (merchandise creditors)	$ 43,500	$ 46,700
Accrued expenses (operating expenses)	14,000	12,500
Income taxes payable	7,900	8,400
Dividends payable	14,000	10,000
Mortgage note payable, due 2001	40,000	0
Bonds payable	150,000	250,000
Common stock, $30 par	450,000	375,000
Excess of issue price over par—common stock	66,250	41,250
Retained earnings	373,640	349,810
Total liabilities and stockholders' equity	$1,159,290	$1,093,660

The income statement for Dowling Company is shown below.

Dowling Company
Income Statement
For the Year Ended December 31, 2001

Sales		$1,100,000
Cost of merchandise sold		710,000
Gross profit		$ 390,000
Operating expenses:		
Depreciation expense	$ 23,500	
Patent amortization	7,000	
Other operating expenses	196,000	
Total operating expenses		226,500
Income from operations		$ 163,500
Other income:		
Gain on sale of investments	$ 11,000	
Other expense:		
Interest expense	26,000	(15,000)
Income before income tax		$ 148,500
Income tax expense		50,000
Net income		$ 98,500

An examination of the accounting records revealed the following additional information applicable to 2001:

a.   Land costing $15,000 was sold for $15,000.
b.   A mortgage note was issued for $40,000.
c.   A building costing $115,000 was constructed.
d.   2,500 shares of common stock were issued at 40 in exchange for the bonds payable.
e.   Cash dividends declared were $74,670.

Instructions

1.   Prepare a statement of cash flows, using the indirect method of reporting cash flows from operating activities.
2.   Prepare a statement of cash flows, using the direct method of reporting cash flows from operating activities.

Solution

1.

Dowling Company
Statement of Cash Flows—Indirect Method
For the Year Ended December 31, 2001

Cash flows from operating activities:			
Net income, per income statement			$ 98,500
Add: Depreciation	$ 23,500		
Amortization of patents	7,000		
Decrease in accounts receivable	7,000		
Increase in accrued expenses	1,500	39,000	
		$137,500	
Deduct: Increase in inventories	$ 7,300		
Increase in prepaid expenses	380		
Decrease in accounts payable	3,200		
Decrease in income taxes payable	500		
Gain on sale of investments	11,000	22,380	
Net cash flow from operating activities			$115,120
Cash flows from investing activities:			
Cash received from sale of:			
Investments	$ 60,000		
Land	15,000	$ 75,000	
Less: Cash paid for construction of building		115,000	
Net cash flow used for investing activities			(40,000)
Cash flows from financing activities:			
Cash received from issuing mortgage note payable		$ 40,000	
Less: Cash paid for dividends		70,670	
Net cash flow used for financing activities			(30,670)
Increase in cash			$ 44,450
Cash at the beginning of the year			95,900
Cash at the end of the year			$140,350

Schedule of Noncash Investing and
Financing Activities:

Issued common stock to retire bonds payable	$100,000

2.

Dowling Company
Statement of Cash Flows—Direct Method
For the Year Ended December 31, 2001

Cash flows from operating activities:			
Cash received from customers[1]		$1,107,000	
Deduct: Cash paid for merchandise[2]	$720,500		
Cash paid for operating expenses[3]	194,880		
Cash paid for interest expense	26,000		
Cash paid for income tax[4]	50,500	991,880	
Net cash flow from operating activities			$115,120
Cash flows from investing activities:			
Cash received from sale of:			
Investments	$ 60,000		
Land	15,000	$ 75,000	
Less: Cash paid for construction of building		115,000	
Net cash flow used for investing activities			(40,000)
Cash flows from financing activities:			
Cash received from issuing mortgage note payable ..		$ 40,000	
Less: Cash paid for dividends[5]		70,670	
Net cash flow used for financing activities			(30,670)
Increase in cash			$ 44,450
Cash at the beginning of the year			95,900
Cash at the end of the year			$140,350
Schedule of Noncash Investing and Financing Activities:			
Issued common stock to retire bonds payable			$100,000

Computations:

[1]$1,100,000 + $7,000 = $1,107,000
[2]$710,000 + $3,200 + $7,300 = $720,500
[3]$196,000 + $380 − $1,500 = $194,880
[4]$50,000 + $500 = $50,500
[5]$74,670 + $10,000 − $14,000 = $70,670

SELF-EXAMINATION QUESTIONS   Answers at End of Chapter

Matching
Match each of the following statements with its proper term. Some terms may not be used.

A. cash flows from financing activities

B. cash flows from investing activities

C. cash flows from operating activities

D. decrease in accounts payable

E. decrease in accounts receivable

F. direct method

____ 1. An addition to sales under the direct method for determining cash flows from operating activities.

____ 2. A statement of cash flows disclosure item.

____ 3. The section of the statement of cash flows that reports cash flows from transactions affecting the equity and debt of the business.

____ 4. A financing activity that increases cash.

____ 5. An addition to net income under the indirect method for determining cash flows from operating activities.

____ 6. The section of the statement of cash flows that reports cash flows from transactions affecting investments in noncurrent assets.

____ 7. A summary of the major cash receipts and cash payments for a period.

G. dividends declared

H. free cash flow

I. loss on sale of land

J. indirect method

K. issuance of common stock

L. purchase of land with common stock

M. sale of land

N. statement of cash flows

___ 8. A deduction from net income under the indirect method for determining cash flows from operating activities.

___ 9. A method of reporting the cash flows from operating activities as the difference between the operating cash receipts and the operating cash payments.

___ 10. The section of the statement of cash flows that reports the cash transactions affecting the determination of net income.

___ 11. A method of reporting the cash flows from operating activities as the net income from operations adjusted for all deferrals of past cash receipts and payments and all accruals of expected future cash receipts and payments.

___ 12. An investing activity.

___ 13. The amount of operating cash flow remaining after replacing current productive capacity and maintaining current dividends.

Multiple Choice

1. An example of a cash flow from an operating activity is:
   A. receipt of cash from the sale of stock
   B. receipt of cash from the sale of bonds
   C. payment of cash for dividends
   D. receipt of cash from customers on account

2. An example of a cash flow from an investing activity is:
   A. receipt of cash from the sale of equipment
   B. receipt of cash from the sale of stock
   C. payment of cash for dividends
   D. payment of cash to acquire treasury stock

3. An example of a cash flow from a financing activity is:
   A. receipt of cash from customers on account
   B. receipt of cash from the sale of equipment
   C. payment of cash for dividends
   D. payment of cash to acquire marketable securities

4. Which of the following methods of reporting cash flows from operating activities adjusts net income for revenues and expenses not involving the receipt or payment of cash?

   A. Direct method   C. Reciprocal method
   B. Purchase method   D. Indirect method

5. The net income reported on the income statement for the year was $55,000, and depreciation of fixed assets for the year was $22,000. The balances of the current asset and current liability accounts at the beginning and end of the year are as follows:

	End	Beginning
Cash	$ 65,000	$ 70,000
Accounts receivable	100,000	90,000
Inventories	145,000	150,000
Prepaid expenses	7,500	8,000
Accounts payable (merchandise creditors)	51,000	58,000

The total amount reported for cash flows from operating activities in the statement of cash flows, using the indirect method, is:
   A. $33,000   C. $65,500
   B. $55,000   D. $77,000

CLASS DISCUSSION QUESTIONS

1. What is the principal disadvantage of the direct method of reporting cash flows from operating activities?
2. What are the major advantages of the indirect method of reporting cash flows from operating activities?
3. A corporation issued $200,000 of common stock in exchange for $200,000 of fixed assets. Where would this transaction be reported on the statement of cash flows?
4. a. What is the effect on cash flows of declaring and issuing a stock dividend?
   b. Is the stock dividend reported on the statement of cash flows?
5. A retail business, using the accrual method of accounting, owed merchandise creditors (accounts payable) $290,000 at the beginning of the year and $315,000 at the end of the year. How would the $25,000 increase be used to adjust net income in determining the amount of cash flows from operating activities by the indirect method? Explain.

6. If salaries payable was $75,000 at the beginning of the year and $65,000 at the end of the year, should $10,000 be added to or deducted from income to determine the amount of cash flows from operating activities by the indirect method? Explain.

7. A long-term investment in bonds with a cost of $75,000 was sold for $80,000 cash. (a) What was the gain or loss on the sale? (b) What was the effect of the transaction on cash flows? (c) How should the transaction be reported in the statement of cash flows if cash flows from operating activities are reported by the indirect method?

8. A corporation issued $5,000,000 of 20-year bonds for cash at 105. How would the transaction be reported on the statement of cash flows?

9. Fully depreciated equipment costing $55,000 was discarded. What was the effect of the transaction on cash flows if (a) $5,000 cash is received, (b) there is no salvage value?

10. For the current year, Accord Company decided to switch from the indirect method to the direct method for reporting cash flows from operating activities on the statement of cash flows. Will the change cause the amount of net cash flow from operating activities to be (a) larger, (b) smaller, or (c) the same as if the indirect method had been used? Explain.

11. Name five common major classes of operating cash receipts or operating cash payments presented on the statement of cash flows when the cash flows from operating activities are reported by the direct method.

12. In a recent annual report, **PepsiCo, Inc.**, reported that during the year it issued treasury stock and debt of $162.7 million for acquisitions. How would this be reported on the statement of cash flows?

Resources for Your Success On-Line at **warren.swcollege.com**

Remember! If you need additional help, visit South-Western's Web site. See page 26 for a description of the online and printed materials that are available.

EXERCISES

Exercise 15–1
Cash flows from operating activities—net loss

Objective 2

On its income statement for the current year, Marconi Company reported a net loss of $65,000 from operations. On its statement of cash flows, it reported $20,000 of cash flows from operating activities.

✏️ Explain this apparent contradiction between the loss and the positive cash flows.

Exercise 15–2
Effect of transactions on cash flows

Objective 2

✓ c. Cash payment, $501,000

State the effect (cash receipt or payment and amount) of each of the following transactions, considered individually, on cash flows:

a. Paid dividends of $1.50 per share. There were 30,000 shares issued and 5,000 shares of treasury stock.

b. Purchased a building by paying $30,000 cash and issuing a $90,000 mortgage note payable.

c. Retired $500,000 of bonds, on which there was $2,500 of unamortized discount, for $501,000.

d. Purchased land for $120,000 cash.

e. Sold a new issue of $100,000 of bonds at 101.

f. Purchased 5,000 shares of $30 par common stock as treasury stock at $50 per share.

g. Sold 5,000 shares of $30 par common stock for $45 per share.

h. Sold equipment with a book value of $42,500 for $41,000.

Exercise 15–3
Classifying cash flows

Objective 2

Identify the type of cash flow activity for each of the following events (operating, investing, or financing):

a. Paid cash dividends.
b. Sold long-term investments.
c. Issued bonds.
d. Issued common stock.
e. Sold equipment.
f. Net income.
g. Issued preferred stock.
h. Redeemed bonds.
i. Purchased patents.
j. Purchased treasury stock.
k. Purchased buildings.

Exercise 15–4
Cash flows from operating activities—indirect method

Objective 3

Indicate whether each of the following would be added to or deducted from net income in determining net cash flow from operating activities by the indirect method:

a. Decrease in accounts receivable
b. Amortization of patent
c. Depreciation of fixed assets
d. Decrease in salaries payable
e. Decrease in accounts payable
f. Loss on disposal of fixed assets
g. Increase in notes payable due in 90 days
h. Amortization of goodwill
i. Increase in notes receivable due in 90 days
j. Decrease in prepaid expenses
k. Increase in merchandise inventory
l. Gain on retirement of long-term debt

Exercise 15–5
Cash flows from operating activities—indirect method

Objectives 2, 3

✓ a. Cash flows from operating activities, $153,850

The net income reported on the income statement for the current year was $134,800. Depreciation recorded on equipment and a building amounted to $27,400 for the year. Balances of the current asset and current liability accounts at the beginning and end of the year are as follows:

	End of Year	Beginning of Year
Cash	$ 23,500	$37,400
Accounts receivable (net)	84,500	80,350
Inventories	100,200	94,300
Prepaid expenses	4,970	5,300
Accounts payable (merchandise creditors)	71,400	68,900
Salaries payable	5,320	6,450

a. Prepare the cash flows from operating activities section of the statement of cash flows, using the indirect method.
b. ▬▬► If the direct method had been used, would the net cash flow from operating activities have been the same? Explain.

Exercise 15–6
Cash flows from operating activities—indirect method

Objective 3

SPREADSHEET

✓ Cash flows from operating activities, $537,800

The net income reported on the income statement for the current year was $465,000. Depreciation recorded on store equipment for the year amounted to $96,800. Balances of the current asset and current liability accounts at the beginning and end of the year are as follows:

	End of Year	Beginning of Year
Cash	$345,000	$386,000
Accounts receivable (net)	554,300	567,800
Merchandise inventory	693,000	672,400
Prepaid expenses	27,000	24,000
Accounts payable (merchandise creditors)	510,000	527,400
Wages payable	39,500	36,000

Prepare the cash flows from operating activities section of a statement of cash flows, using the indirect method.

Exercise 15–7
Determining cash payments to stockholders
Objective 3

The board of directors declared cash dividends totaling $240,000 during the current year. The comparative balance sheet indicates dividends payable of $50,000 at the beginning of the year and $60,000 at the end of the year. What was the amount of cash payments to stockholders during the year?

Exercise 15–8
Reporting changes in equipment on statement of cash flows
Objective 3

An analysis of the general ledger accounts indicates that office equipment, which had cost $245,000 and on which accumulated depreciation totaled $95,000 on the date of sale, was sold for $130,000 during the year. Using this information, indicate the items to be reported on the statement of cash flows.

Exercise 15–9
Reporting changes in equipment on statement of cash flows
Objective 3

An analysis of the general ledger accounts indicates that delivery equipment, which had cost $39,000 and on which accumulated depreciation totaled $23,000 on the date of sale, was sold for $20,000 during the year. Using this information, indicate the items to be reported on the statement of cash flows.

Exercise 15–10
Reporting land transactions on statement of cash flows
Objective 3

On the basis of the details of the following fixed asset account, indicate the items to be reported on the statement of cash flows:

ACCOUNT *Land*   **ACCOUNT NO.**

Date		Item	Debit	Credit	Balance Debit	Balance Credit
2000						
Jan.	1	Balance			400,000	
Feb.	5	Purchased for cash	250,000		650,000	
Oct.	30	Sold for $95,000		80,000	570,000	

Exercise 15–11
Reporting stockholders' equity items on statement of cash flows
Objective 3

On the basis of the following stockholders' equity accounts, indicate the items, exclusive of net income, to be reported on the statement of cash flows. There were no unpaid dividends at either the beginning or the end of the year.

ACCOUNT *Common Stock, $10 Par*   **ACCOUNT NO.**

Date		Item	Debit	Credit	Balance Debit	Balance Credit
2000						
Jan.	1	Balance, 50,000 shares				500,000
Feb.	11	5,000 shares issued for cash		50,000		550,000
June	30	2,750-share stock dividend		27,500		577,500

ACCOUNT *Paid-In Capital in Excess of Par—Common Stock*   **ACCOUNT NO.**

2000						
Jan.	1	Balance				90,000
Feb.	11	5,000 shares issued for cash		200,000		290,000
June	30	Stock dividend		137,500		427,500

ACCOUNT *Retained Earnings*   **ACCOUNT NO.**

2000						
Jan.	1	Balance				475,000
June	30	Stock dividend	165,000			310,000
Dec.	30	Cash dividend	200,000			110,000
	31	Net income		500,000		610,000

Exercise 15–12

Reporting land acquisition for cash and mortgage note on statement of cash flows

Objective 3

On the basis of the details of the following fixed asset account, indicate the items to be reported on the statement of cash flows:

ACCOUNT *Land* **ACCOUNT NO.**

Date		Item	Debit	Credit	Balance Debit	Balance Credit
2000						
Jan.	1	Balance			450,000	
Feb.	10	Purchased for cash	125,000		575,000	
Nov.	20	Purchased with long-term mortgage note	200,000		775,000	

Exercise 15–13

Determining net income from net cash flow from operating activities

Objective 3

✓ Net income, $89,150

Tiger Golf Inc. reported a net cash flow from operating activities of $102,500 on its statement of cash flows for the year ended December 31, 2000. The following information was reported in the cash flows from operating activities section of the statement of cash flows, using the indirect method:

Decrease in income taxes payable	$ 1,400
Decrease in inventories	6,200
Depreciation	15,400
Gain on sale of investments	9,450
Increase in accounts payable	9,100
Increase in prepaid expenses	1,000
Increase in accounts receivable	5,500

Determine the net income reported by Tiger Golf Inc. for the year ended December 31, 2000.

Exercise 15–14

Cash flows from operating activities

Objective 3

✓ Cash flows from operating activities, $743,400

Selected data from the income statement and statement of cash flows of **Toys "R" Us, Inc.,** for the year ending February 1, 1997, are as follows:

Income Statement Data (dollars in thousands)

Net earnings	$427,400
Depreciation and amortization	206,400
Deferred portion of current period tax expense (noncash expense)	23,400

Statement of Cash Flows Data (dollars in thousands)

Increase in accounts receivable	$ 14,300
Increase in merchandise inventories	194,600
Increase in prepaid expenses and other operating assets	10,100
Increase in accounts payable, accrued expenses, and taxes	261,400
Increase in income tax payable	43,800

Prepare the cash flows from operating activities section of the statement of cash flows (using the indirect method) for Toys "R" Us, Inc., for the year ending February 1, 1997.

Exercise 15–15

Cash flows from operating activities—direct method

Objective 4

✓ a. $865,000

The cash flows from operating activities are reported by the direct method on the statement of cash flows. Determine the following:

a. If sales for the current year were $820,000 and accounts receivable decreased by $45,000 during the year, what was the amount of cash received from customers?

b. If income tax expense for the current year was $64,000 and income tax payable decreased by $6,000 during the year, what was the amount of cash payments for income tax?

Exercise 15–16
Determining selected amounts for cash flows from operating activities—direct method

Objective 4

✓ b. $311,700

Selected data taken from the accounting records of Hi Gain Electronics Company for the current year ended December 31 are as follows:

	Balance January 1	Balance December 31
Accrued expenses (operating expenses)	$ 14,300	$11,100
Accounts payable (merchandise creditors)	112,000	90,000
Inventories	83,400	76,500
Prepaid expenses	21,000	19,500

During the current year, the cost of merchandise sold was $870,000 and the operating expenses other than depreciation were $310,000. The direct method is used for presenting the cash flows from operating activities on the statement of cash flows.

Determine the amount reported on the statement of cash flows for (a) cash payments for merchandise and (b) cash payments for operating expenses.

Exercise 15–17
Cash flows from operating activities—direct method

Objective 4

✓ Cash flows from operating activities, $101,800

The income statement of Tru-Blu Greeting Card Company for the current year ended June 30 is as follows:

Sales		$865,000
Cost of merchandise sold		525,000
Gross profit		$340,000
Operating expenses:		
Depreciation expense	$ 45,000	
Other operating expenses	210,400	
Total operating expenses		255,400
Income before income tax		$ 84,600
Income tax expense		35,000
Net income		$ 49,600

Changes in the balances of selected accounts from the beginning to the end of the current year are as follows:

	Increase Decrease*
Accounts receivable (net)	$27,000*
Inventories	11,200
Prepaid expenses	2,400*
Accounts payable (merchandise creditors)	18,300*
Accrued expenses (operating expenses)	10,700
Income tax payable	3,400*

Prepare the cash flows from operating activities section of the statement of cash flows, using the direct method.

Exercise 15–18
Cash flows from operating activities—direct method

Objective 4

✓ Cash flows from operating activities, $75,450

The income statement for Wholly Donut Company for the current year ended June 30 and balances of selected accounts at the beginning and the end of the year are as follows:

Sales		$683,000
Cost of merchandise sold		395,700
Gross profit		$287,300
Operating expenses:		
Depreciation expense	$ 49,500	
Other operating expenses	172,600	
Total operating expenses		222,100
Income before income tax		$ 65,200
Income tax expense		28,600
Net income		$ 36,600

	End of Year	Beginning of Year
Accounts receivable (net)	$85,000	$82,000
Inventories	98,600	85,000
Prepaid expenses	6,100	8,150
Accounts payable (merchandise creditors)	76,600	71,100
Accrued expenses (operating expenses)	4,250	5,850
Income tax payable	1,600	1,600

Prepare the cash flows from operating activities section of the statement of cash flows, using the direct method.

Exercise 15–19
Statement of cash flows

Objective 3

What's Wrong WITH THIS?

List the errors you find in the following statement of cash flows. The cash balance at the beginning of the year was $70,700. All other figures are correct.

Monarch Games Inc.
Statement of Cash Flows
For the Year Ended December 31, 2000

Cash flows from operating activities:			
Net income, per income statement		$100,500	
Add: Depreciation	$ 49,000		
Increase in accounts receivable	9,500		
Gain on sale of investments	5,000	63,500	
		$164,000	
Deduct: Increase in accounts payable	$ 4,400		
Increase in inventories	18,300		
Decrease in accrued expenses	1,600	24,300	
Net cash flow from operating activities			$139,700
Cash flows from investing activities:			
Cash received from sale of investments		$ 85,000	
Less: Cash paid for purchase of land	$ 90,000		
Cash paid for purchase of equipment	150,100	240,100	
Net cash flow used for investing activities			(155,100)
Cash flows from financing activities:			
Cash received from sale of common stock		$107,000	
Cash paid for dividends		36,800	
Net cash flow provided by financing activities			143,800
Increase in cash			$128,400
Cash at the end of the year			105,300
Cash at the beginning of the year			$233,700

Exercise 15–20
Free cash flow

Objective 5

The financial statements for **Hershey Foods Corporation** are presented in Appendix G at the end of the text.

a. Determine the free cash flow for 1995 and 1996 from the statements of cash flows. Assume that 80% of the capital additions for each year are used to maintain productive capacity and that the remaining 20% adds to productive capacity.

b. ✏ What conclusions can you draw from your analysis?

PROBLEMS SERIES A

Problem 15–1A
Statement of cash flows—indirect method

Objective 3

The comparative balance sheet of Idaho Al's Golf Shops Co. for December 31, 2000 and 1999, is as follows:

HAT

✓ Net cash flow from operating activities, $72,800

	Dec. 31, 2000	Dec. 31, 1999
Assets		
Cash	$ 86,400	$ 51,600
Accounts receivable (net)	132,400	112,600
Inventories	153,400	141,300
Investments	0	115,000
Land	85,000	0
Equipment	785,000	635,000
Accumulated depreciation—equipment	(265,000)	(211,500)
	$977,200	$844,000
Liabilities and Stockholders' Equity		
Accounts payable (merchandise creditors)	$ 85,000	$ 70,600
Accrued expenses (operating expenses)	4,700	6,700
Dividends payable	20,000	15,000
Common stock, $10 par	60,000	40,000
Paid-in capital in excess of par—common stock	220,000	100,000
Retained earnings	587,500	611,700
	$977,200	$844,000

The following additional information was taken from the records:

a. The investments were sold for $132,000 cash.
b. Equipment and land were acquired for cash.
c. There were no disposals of equipment during the year.
d. The common stock was issued for cash.
e. There was a $55,800 credit to Retained Earnings for net income.
f. There was an $80,000 debit to Retained Earnings for cash dividends declared.

Instructions

Prepare a statement of cash flows, using the indirect method of presenting cash flows from operating activities.

Problem 15–2A
Statement of cash flows—indirect method

Objective 3

SPREADSHEET

✓ Net cash flow from operating activities, $315,400

The comparative balance sheet of Endless Summer Apparel Inc. at December 31, 2000 and 1999, is as follows:

	Dec. 31, 2000	Dec. 31, 1999
Assets		
Cash	$ 209,500	$ 290,500
Accounts receivable (net)	687,200	765,300
Merchandise inventory	604,100	587,900
Prepaid expenses	14,500	12,000
Equipment	990,000	900,000
Accumulated depreciation—equipment	(315,400)	(365,800)
	$2,189,900	$2,189,900
Liabilities and Stockholders' Equity		
Accounts payable (merchandise creditors)	$ 514,500	$ 465,800
Mortgage note payable	0	220,000
Common stock, $10 par	100,000	70,000
Paid-in capital in excess of par—common stock	810,000	720,000
Retained earnings	765,400	714,100
	$2,189,900	$2,189,900

Additional data obtained from the income statement and from an examination of the accounts in the ledger are as follows:

a. Net income, $111,300.
b. Depreciation reported on the income statement, $96,000.

c. Equipment was purchased at a cost of $236,400, and fully depreciated equipment costing $146,400 was discarded, with no salvage realized.

d. The mortgage note payable was not due until 2003, but the terms permitted earlier payment without penalty.

e. 3,000 shares of common stock were issued at $40 for cash.

f. Cash dividends declared and paid, $60,000.

Instructions

Prepare a statement of cash flows, using the indirect method of presenting cash flows from operating activities.

Problem 15–3A
Statement of cash flows—indirect method

Objective 3

HAT

✓ Net cash flow from operating activities, ($166,000)

The comparative balance sheet of Gates Lumber Company at December 31, 2000 and 1999, is as follows:

	Dec. 31, 2000	Dec. 31, 1999
Assets		
Cash	$ 194,700	$ 211,600
Accounts receivable (net)	347,800	325,700
Inventories	402,100	387,500
Prepaid expenses	6,200	8,000
Land	70,000	100,000
Buildings	525,000	400,000
Accumulated depreciation—buildings	(172,500)	(150,000)
Equipment	167,900	157,000
Accumulated depreciation—equipment	(39,000)	(42,000)
	$1,502,200	$1,397,800
Liabilities and Stockholders' Equity		
Accounts payable (merchandise creditors)	$ 347,900	$ 356,800
Income tax payable	12,400	6,800
Bonds payable	90,000	0
Common stock, $1 par	60,000	50,000
Paid-in capital in excess of par—common stock	400,000	200,000
Retained earnings	591,900	784,200
	$1,502,200	$1,397,800

The noncurrent asset, the noncurrent liability, and the stockholders' equity accounts for 2000 are as follows:

ACCOUNT Land ACCOUNT NO.

Date		Item	Debit	Credit	Balance Debit	Balance Credit
2000						
Jan.	1	Balance			100,000	
April	20	Realized $45,000 cash from sale		30,000	70,000	

ACCOUNT Buildings ACCOUNT NO.

Date		Item	Debit	Credit	Balance Debit	Balance Credit
2000						
Jan.	1	Balance			400,000	
April	20	Acquired for cash	125,000		525,000	

ACCOUNT Accumulated Depreciation—Buildings ACCOUNT NO.

Date		Item	Debit	Credit	Balance Debit	Balance Credit
2000						
Jan.	1	Balance				150,000
Dec.	31	Depreciation for year		22,500		172,500

ACCOUNT *Equipment*   **ACCOUNT NO.**

Date		Item	Debit	Credit	Balance Debit	Balance Credit
2000						
Jan.	1	Balance			157,000	
	26	Discarded, no salvage		40,000	117,000	
Aug.	11	Purchased for cash	50,900		167,900	

ACCOUNT *Accumulated Depreciation—Equipment*   **ACCOUNT NO.**

Date		Item	Debit	Credit	Balance Debit	Balance Credit
2000						
Jan.	1	Balance				42,000
	26	Equipment discarded	40,000			2,000
Dec.	31	Depreciation for year		37,000		39,000

ACCOUNT *Bonds Payable*   **ACCOUNT NO.**

Date		Item	Debit	Credit	Balance Debit	Balance Credit
2000						
May	1	Issued 20-year bonds		90,000		90,000

ACCOUNT *Common Stock, $1 Par*   **ACCOUNT NO.**

Date		Item	Debit	Credit	Balance Debit	Balance Credit
2000						
Jan.	1	Balance				50,000
Dec.	7	Issued 10,000 shares of common stock for $21 per share		10,000		60,000

ACCOUNT *Paid-In Capital in Excess of Par—Common Stock*   **ACCOUNT NO.**

Date		Item	Debit	Credit	Balance Debit	Balance Credit
2000						
Jan.	1	Balance				200,000
Dec.	7	Issued 10,000 shares of common stock for $21 per share		200,000		400,000

ACCOUNT *Retained Earnings*   **ACCOUNT NO.**

Date		Item	Debit	Credit	Balance Debit	Balance Credit
2000						
Jan.	1	Balance				784,200
Dec.	31	Net loss	172,300			611,900
	31	Cash dividends	20,000			591,900

Instructions

Prepare a statement of cash flows, using the indirect method of presenting cash flows from operating activities.

Problem 15–4A

Statement of cash flows— direct method

Objective 4

SPREADSHEET
GENERAL LEDGER

✓ Net cash flow from operating activities, $67,800

The comparative balance sheet of Corning Plumbing Supply Company for December 31, 2001 and 2000, is as follows:

	Dec. 31, 2001	Dec. 31, 2000
Assets		
Cash	$ 69,200	$ 76,500
Accounts receivable (net)	135,700	132,400
Inventories	223,800	201,400
Investments	—	45,000
Land	74,000	—
Equipment	340,000	250,000
Accumulated depreciation	(79,300)	(66,800)
	$763,400	$638,500

Liabilities and Stockholders' Equity

Accounts payable (merchandise creditors)	$194,300	$187,400
Accrued expenses (operating expenses)	5,000	6,400
Dividends payable	3,800	3,000
Common stock, $1 par	14,000	10,000
Paid-in capital in excess of par—common stock	138,000	90,000
Retained earnings	408,300	341,700
	$763,400	$638,500

The income statement for the year ended December 31, 2001, is as follows:

Sales		$867,000
Cost of merchandise sold		553,000
Gross profit		$314,000
Operating expenses:		
Depreciation expense	$ 12,500	
Other operating expenses	198,000	
Total operating expenses		210,500
Operating income		$103,500
Other income:		
Gain on sale of investments . .		9,000
Income before income tax		$112,500
Income tax expense		28,000
Net income		$ 84,500

The following additional information was taken from the records:

a. Equipment and land were acquired for cash.
b. There were no disposals of equipment during the year.
c. The investments were sold for $54,000 cash.
d. The common stock was issued for cash.
e. There was a $17,900 debit to Retained Earnings for cash dividends declared.

Instructions

Prepare a statement of cash flows, using the direct method of presenting cash flows from operating activities.

Problem 15–5A

Statement of cash flows—direct method applied to Problem 15–1A

Objective 4

HAT

✓ Net cash flow from operating activities, $72,800

The comparative balance sheet of Idaho Al's Golf Shops Co. for December 31, 2000 and 1999, is as follows:

	Dec. 31, 2000	Dec. 31, 1999
Assets		
Cash	$ 86,400	$ 51,600
Accounts receivable (net)	132,400	112,600
Inventories	153,400	141,300
Investments	0	115,000
Land	85,000	0
Equipment	785,000	635,000
Accumulated depreciation—equipment	(265,000)	(211,500)
	$977,200	$844,000
Liabilities and Stockholders' Equity		
Accounts payable (merchandise creditors)	$ 85,000	$ 70,600
Accrued expenses (operating expenses)	4,700	6,700
Dividends payable	20,000	15,000
Common stock, $10 par	60,000	40,000
Paid-in capital in excess of par—common stock	220,000	100,000
Retained earnings	587,500	611,700
	$977,200	$844,000

The income statement for the year ended December 31, 2000, is as follows:

Sales		$693,200
Cost of merchandise sold		394,500
Gross profit		$298,700
Operating expenses:		
Depreciation expense	$ 53,500	
Other operating expenses	172,900	
Total operating expenses		226,400
Operating income		$ 72,300
Other income:		
Gain on sale of investments . .		17,000
Income before income tax		$ 89,300
Income tax expense		33,500
Net income		$ 55,800

The following additional information was taken from the records:

a.   The investments were sold for $132,000 cash.
b.   Equipment and land were acquired for cash.
c.   There were no disposals of equipment during the year.
d.   The common stock was issued for cash.
e.   There was an $80,000 debit to Retained Earnings for cash dividends declared.

Instructions
Prepare a statement of cash flows, using the direct method of presenting cash flows from operating activities.

PROBLEMS SERIES B

Problem 15–1B
Statement of cash flows—indirect method

Objective 3

✓ Net cash flow from operating activities, $95,500

The comparative balance sheet of Mother Nature Health Foods Inc. for June 30, 2000 and 1999, is as follows:

	June 30, 2000	June 30, 1999
Assets		
Cash	$ 93,400	$ 57,800
Accounts receivable (net)	125,000	123,500
Inventories	146,500	108,900
Investments	0	65,000
Land	145,000	0
Equipment	367,600	278,600
Accumulated depreciation	(110,900)	(87,400)
	$766,600	$546,400
Liabilities and Stockholders' Equity		
Accounts payable (merchandise creditors)	$ 82,400	$ 74,000
Accrued expenses (operating expenses)	6,700	6,000
Dividends payable	18,400	15,700
Common stock, $10 par	100,000	70,000
Paid-in capital in excess of par—common stock	320,000	200,000
Retained earnings	239,100	180,700
	$766,600	$546,400

The following additional information was taken from the records of Mother Nature Health Foods Inc.:

a. Equipment and land were acquired for cash.
b. There were no disposals of equipment during the year.
c. The investments were sold for $95,000 cash.
d. The common stock was issued for cash.
e. There was a $132,000 credit to Retained Earnings for net income.
f. There was a $73,600 debit to Retained Earnings for cash dividends declared.

Instructions

Prepare a statement of cash flows, using the indirect method of presenting cash flows from operating activities.

Problem 15–2B

*Statement of cash flows—
indirect method*

Objective 3

SPREADSHEET

✓ Net cash flow from operating
activities, $129,600

The comparative balance sheet of Bon Voyage Luggage Company at December 31, 2000 and 1999, is as follows:

	Dec. 31, 2000	Dec. 31, 1999
Assets		
Cash	$ 184,200	$ 124,600
Accounts receivable (net)	202,800	148,700
Inventories	250,500	275,000
Prepaid expenses	5,400	4,500
Land	85,000	85,000
Buildings	575,000	465,000
Accumulated depreciation—buildings	(192,000)	(168,000)
Machinery and equipment	345,800	345,800
Accumulated depreciation—machinery & equipment	(134,000)	(99,000)
Patents	39,500	45,000
	$1,362,200	$1,226,600
Liabilities and Stockholders' Equity		
Accounts payable (merchandise creditors)	$ 114,500	$ 132,400
Dividends payable	14,500	12,000
Salaries payable	8,900	10,900
Mortgage note payable, due 2001	65,000	—
Bonds payable	—	105,000
Common stock, $1 par	25,000	20,000
Paid-in capital in excess of par—common stock	150,000	50,000
Retained earnings	984,300	896,300
	$1,362,200	$1,226,600

An examination of the income statement and the accounting records revealed the following additional information applicable to 2000:

a. Net income, $115,500.
b. Depreciation expense reported on the income statement: buildings, $24,000; machinery and equipment, $35,000.
c. Patent amortization reported on the income statement, $5,500.
d. A building was constructed for $110,000.
e. A mortgage note for $65,000 was issued for cash.
f. 5,000 shares of common stock were issued at $21 in exchange for the bonds payable.
g. Cash dividends declared, $27,500.

Instructions

Prepare a statement of cash flows, using the indirect method of presenting cash flows from operating activities.

Problem 15–3B

*Statement of cash flows—
indirect method*

Objective 3

The comparative balance sheet of Apple Supply Inc. at December 31, 2000 and 1999, is as follows:

	Dec. 31, 2000	Dec. 31, 1999
Assets		
Cash	$ 74,800	$ 99,400
Accounts receivable (net)	136,700	125,300
Inventories	301,200	267,800
Prepaid expenses	5,000	5,500
Land	50,000	75,000
Buildings	285,000	175,000
Accumulated depreciation—buildings	(74,700)	(65,200)
Equipment	259,500	239,500
Accumulated depreciation—equipment	(100,100)	(105,700)
	$937,400	$816,600
Liabilities and Stockholders' Equity		
Accounts payable (merchandise creditors)	$174,800	$185,400
Income tax payable	5,800	4,500
Bonds payable	40,000	—
Common stock, $1 par	35,000	30,000
Paid-in capital in excess of par—common stock	400,000	300,000
Retained earnings	281,800	296,700
	$937,400	$816,600

The noncurrent asset, the noncurrent liability, and the stockholders' equity accounts for 2000 are as follows:

ACCOUNT *Land*   **ACCOUNT NO.**

Date		Item	Debit	Credit	Balance Debit	Balance Credit
2000						
Jan.	1	Balance			75,000	
April	20	Realized $32,000 cash from sale		25,000	50,000	

ACCOUNT *Buildings*   **ACCOUNT NO.**

Date		Item	Debit	Credit	Balance Debit	Balance Credit
2000						
Jan.	1	Balance			175,000	
April	20	Acquired for cash	110,000		285,000	

ACCOUNT *Accumulated Depreciation—Buildings*   **ACCOUNT NO.**

Date		Item	Debit	Credit	Balance Debit	Balance Credit
2000						
Jan.	1	Balance				65,200
Dec.	31	Depreciation for year		9,500		74,700

ACCOUNT *Equipment*   **ACCOUNT NO.**

Date		Item	Debit	Credit	Balance Debit	Balance Credit
2000						
Jan.	1	Balance			239,500	
	26	Discarded, no salvage		25,000	214,500	
Aug.	11	Purchased for cash	45,000		259,500	

ACCOUNT *Accumulated Depreciation—Equipment*   **ACCOUNT NO.**

Date		Item	Debit	Credit	Balance Debit	Balance Credit
2000						
Jan.	1	Balance				105,700
	26	Equipment discarded	25,000			80,700
Dec.	31	Depreciation for year		19,400		100,100

ACCOUNT *Bonds Payable*   **ACCOUNT NO.**

Date		Item	Debit	Credit	Balance Debit	Balance Credit
2000						
May	1	Issued 20-year bonds		40,000		40,000

ACCOUNT *Common Stock, $1 Par* — **ACCOUNT NO.**

Date		Item	Debit	Credit	Balance Debit	Balance Credit
2000						
Jan.	1	Balance				30,000
Dec.	7	Issued 5000 shares of common stock for $21 per share		5,000		35,000

ACCOUNT *Paid-In Capital in Excess of Par—Common Stock* — **ACCOUNT NO.**

Date		Item	Debit	Credit	Balance Debit	Balance Credit
2000						
Jan.	1	Balance				300,000
Dec.	7	Issued 5000 shares of common stock for $21 per share		100,000		400,000

ACCOUNT *Retained Earnings* — **ACCOUNT NO.**

Date		Item	Debit	Credit	Balance Debit	Balance Credit
2000						
Jan.	1	Balance				296,700
Dec.	31	Net loss	9,900			286,800
	31	Cash dividends	5,000			281,800

Instructions

Prepare a statement of cash flows, using the indirect method of presenting cash flows from operating activities.

Problem 15–4B
Statement of cash flows—direct method

Objective 4

GENERAL LEDGER SPREADSHEET

✓ Net cash flow from operating activities, $127,500

The comparative balance sheet of Green Thumb Nursery Inc. for December 31, 2000 and 2001, is as follows:

	Dec. 31, 2001	Dec. 31, 2000
Assets		
Cash	$ 136,700	$147,300
Accounts receivable (net)	220,000	210,500
Inventories	276,200	254,700
Investments	—	60,000
Land	95,000	—
Equipment	575,000	450,000
Accumulated depreciation	(176,500)	(134,000)
	$1,126,400	$988,500
Liabilities and Stockholders' Equity		
Accounts payable (merchandise creditors)	$ 58,400	$ 55,000
Accrued expenses (operating expenses)	7,100	8,000
Dividends payable	16,000	14,500
Common stock, $1 par	30,000	25,000
Paid-in capital in excess of par—common stock	510,000	400,000
Retained earnings	504,900	486,000
	$1,126,400	$988,500

The income statement for the year ended December 31, 2001, is as follows:

Sales		$1,430,000
Cost of merchandise sold		845,000
Gross profit		$ 585,000
Operating expenses:		
Depreciation expense	$ 42,500	
Other operating expenses	345,000	
Total operating expenses		387,500
Operating income		$ 197,500
Other income:		
Gain on sale of investments		15,000
Income before income tax		$ 212,500
Income tax expense		84,000
Net income		$ 128,500

The following additional information was taken from the records:

a. Equipment and land were acquired for cash.
b. There were no disposals of equipment during the year.
c. The investments were sold for $75,000 cash.
d. The common stock was issued for cash.
e. There was a $109,600 debit to Retained Earnings for cash dividends declared.

Instructions

Prepare a statement of cash flows, using the direct method of presenting cash flows from operating activities.

Problem 15–5B

Statement of cash flows—direct method applied to Problem 15–1B

Objective 4

✓ Net cash flow from operating activities, $95,500

The comparative balance sheet of Mother Nature Health Foods Inc. for June 30, 2000 and 1999, is as follows:

	June 30, 2000	June 30, 1999
Assets		
Cash	$ 93,400	$ 57,800
Accounts receivable (net)	125,000	123,500
Inventories	146,500	108,900
Investments	0	65,000
Land	145,000	0
Equipment	367,600	278,600
Accumulated depreciation	(110,900)	(87,400)
	$766,600	$546,400
Liabilities and Stockholders' Equity		
Accounts payable (merchandise creditors)	$ 82,400	$ 74,000
Accrued expenses (operating expenses)	6,700	6,000
Dividends payable	18,400	15,700
Common stock, $10 par	100,000	70,000
Paid-in capital in excess of par—common stock	320,000	200,000
Retained earnings	239,100	180,700
	$766,600	$546,400

The income statement for the year ended June 30, 2000, is as follows:

Sales		$724,700
Cost of merchandise sold		423,100
Gross profit		$301,600
Operating expenses:		
Depreciation expense	$ 23,500	
Other operating expenses	102,900	
Total operating expenses		126,400
Operating income		$175,200
Other income:		
Gain on sale of investments		30,000
Income before income tax		$205,200
Income tax expense		73,200
Net income		$132,000

The following additional information was taken from the records:

a. Equipment and land were acquired for cash.
b. There were no disposals of equipment during the year.
c. The investments were sold for $95,000 cash.
d. The common stock was issued for cash.
e. There was a $73,600 debit to Retained Earnings for cash dividends declared.

Instructions

Prepare a statement of cash flows, using the direct method of presenting cash flows from operating activities.

SPECIAL ACTIVITIES

**Activity 15–1
Elite Fashions Inc.**

*Ethics and professional
conduct in business*

Carl Allsop, president of Elite Fashions Inc., believes that reporting operating cash flow per share on the income statement would be a useful addition to the company's just completed financial statements. The following discussion took place between Carl Allsop and Elite Fashion's controller, Kim Lee, in January, after the close of the fiscal year.

Carl: I have been reviewing our financial statements for the last year. I am disappointed that our net income per share has dropped by 10% from last year. This is not going to look good to our shareholders. Isn't there anything we can do about this?

Kim: What do you mean? The past is the past, and the numbers are in. There isn't much that can be done about it. Our financial statements were prepared according to generally accepted accounting principles, and I don't see much leeway for significant change at this point.

Carl: No, no. I'm not suggesting that we "cook the books." But look at the cash flow from operations on the statement of cash flows. The cash flow from operations has increased by 20%. This is very good news—and, I might add, useful information. The higher cash flow from operations will give our creditors comfort.

Kim: Well, the cash flow from operations is on the statement of cash flows, so I guess users will be able to see the improved cash flow figures there.

Carl: This is true, but somehow I feel that this information should be given a much higher profile. I don't like this information being "buried" in the statement of cash flows. You know as well as I do that many users will focus on the income statement. Therefore, I think we ought to include an operating cash flow per share number on the face of the income statement—someplace under the earnings per share number. In this way users will get the complete picture of our operating performance. Yes, our earnings per share dropped this year, but our cash flow from operations improved! And all the information is in one place where users can see and compare the figures. What do you think?

Kim: I've never really thought about it like that before. I guess we could put the operating cash flow per share on the income statement, under the earnings per share. Users would really benefit from this disclosure. Thanks for the idea—I'll start working on it.

Carl: Glad to be of service.

How would you interpret this situation? Is Kim behaving in an ethical and professional manner?

**Activity 15–2
DiscArcade Inc.**

*Using the statement of cash
flows*

You are considering an investment in a new start-up software company, DiscArcade Inc. A review of the company's financial statements reveals a negative retained earnings. In addition, it appears as though the company has been running a negative cash flow from operations since the company's inception.

How is the company staying in business under these circumstances? Could this be a good investment?

**Activity 15–3
Books and More
Company**

*Analysis of cash flow from
operations*

The Retailing Division of Books and More Company provided the following information on its cash flow from operations:

Net income	$ 450,000
Increase in accounts receivable	(340,000)
Increase in inventory	(300,000)
Decrease in accounts payable	(90,000)
Depreciation	100,000
Cash flow from operations	$(180,000)

The manager of the Retailing Division provided the accompanying memo with this report:

From: Senior Vice President, Retailing Division

I am pleased to report that we had earnings of $450,000 over the last period. This resulted in a return on invested capital of 10%, which is near our targets for this division. I have been aggressive in building the revenue volume in the division. As a result, I am happy to report that we have increased the number of new credit card customers as a result of an aggressive marketing campaign. In addition, we have found some excellent merchandise opportunities. Some of our suppliers have made some of their apparel merchandise available at a deep discount. We have purchased as much of these goods as possible in order to improve profitability. I'm also happy to report that our vendor payment problems have improved. We are nearly caught up on our overdue payables balances.

▸ Comment on the senior vice president's memo in light of the cash flow information.

Activity 15–4
Into the Real World
Statement of cash flows

The activity will require two teams to retrieve statement of cash flow information from the Internet. One team is to obtain the the most recent year's statement of cash flows for **Intel Corporation**, and the other team the most recent year's statement of cash flows for **America Online (AOL).**

The statement of cash flows is part of the annual report information that is a required disclosure to the Securities Exchange Commission (SEC). The SEC, in turn, provides this information on the Internet through its EDGAR (Electronic Data Gathering, Analysis, and Retrieval) service. The Edgar address is **www.sec.gov/edgarhp.htm.**

To obtain annual report information, type in a company name on the "Search EDGAR archives" form. EDGAR will list the reports available for the selected company. A company's annual report (along with much more information) is provided in its annual 10-K report to the SEC. Click on the 10-K (or 10-K405) report for the year you wish to download. If you wish, you can save the whole 10-K report to a file, then open it with your word processor.

As a group, compare the two statements of cash flows. How are Intel and America Online similar or different regarding cash flows?

Activity 15–5
Chrysler Corporation
Analysis of statement of cash flows

The following is the statement of cash flows for **Chrysler Corporation** for the years ended December 31, 1996, 1995, and 1994.

Chrysler Corporation
Statement of Cash Flows (000s)
For the Years Ended December 31, 1996, 1995, and 1994

	1996	1995	1994
Operations:			
Net income	3,529	2,025	3,713
Depreciation	2,312	2,220	1,955
Other adjustments	1,460	2,709	1,125
Cash flows from operations	7,301	6,954	6,793
Investing activities:			
Purchases of marketable securities	(4,346)	(5,160)	(5,425)
Sales and maturities of marketable securities	5,294	6,122	3,519
Finance receivables acquired	(19,906)	(24,437)	(20,149)
Finance receivables collected	3,062	3,795	5,772
Proceeds from sales of finance receivables	16,809	17,602	13,138
Expenditures for property, equipment, and tools	(4,635)	(3,646)	(3,843)
Other	155	(187)	30
Total	(3,567)	(5,911)	(6,958)
Financing activities:			
Change in short-term debt	410	(1,971)	1,348
Proceeds under long-term borrowings and revolving lines of credit	1,390	4,731	1,305
Payments on long-term borrowings and revolving lines of credit	(2,167)	(1,687)	(1,011)
Payment for early extinguishment of debt	(853)	—	—
Repurchases of common stock	(2,041)	(1,047)	—
Dividends paid	(963)	(710)	(399)
Other	105	39	27
Total financing activities	(4,119)	(645)	1,270
Net change in cash	(385)	398	1,105

a. ➤ In 1995 cash increased by $398 million, then decreased by $385 million in 1996. Was 1996 a "bad year" for Chrysler because the cash declined?

b. ➤ Provide an analysis of Chrysler's cash flow performance for the three years.

c. ➤ Within the investing section there are three lines associated with finance receivables. Interpret these lines.

Activity 15–6
Stainless Kitchens, Inc.

Analysis of statement of cash flows

Alan Hoyt is the president and majority shareholder of Stainless Kitchens, Inc., a small retail store chain. Recently, Hoyt submitted a loan application for Stainless Kitchens, Inc. to Montvale National Bank. It called for a $200,000, 11%, ten-year loan to help finance the construction of a building and the purchase of store equipment, costing a total of $250,000, to enable Stainless Kitchens, Inc. to open a store in Montvale. Land for this purpose was acquired last year. The bank's loan officer requested a statement of cash flows in addition to the most recent income statement, balance sheet, and retained earnings statement that Hoyt had submitted with the loan application.

As a close family friend, Hoyt asked you to prepare a statement of cash flows. From the records provided, you prepared the following statement.

Stainless Kitchens, Inc.
Statement of Cash Flows
For the Year Ended December 31, 2000

Cash flows from operating activities:			
Net income, per income statement		$ 86,400	
Add: Depreciation	$31,000		
Decrease in accounts receivable	11,500	42,500	
		$128,900	
Deduct: Increase in inventory	$12,000		
Increase in prepaid expenses	1,500		
Decrease in accounts payable	3,000		
Gain on sale of investments	7,500	24,000	
Net cash flow from operating activities			$104,900
Cash flows from investing activities:			
Cash received from investments sold		$ 42,500	
Less: Cash paid for purchase of store equipment		31,000	
Net cash flow from investing activities			11,500
Cash flows from financing activities:			
Cash paid for dividends		$ 40,000	
Net cash flow used for financing activities			(40,000)
Increase in cash			$ 76,400
Cash at the beginning of the year			27,500
Cash at the end of the year			$103,900

Schedule of Noncash Financing and Investing Activities:

Issued common stock at par for land	$ 40,000

After reviewing the statement, Hoyt telephoned you and commented, "Are you sure this statement is right?" Hoyt then raised the following questions:

1. "How can depreciation be a cash flow?"
2. "Issuing common stock for the land is listed in a separate schedule. This transaction has nothing to do with cash! Shouldn't this transaction be eliminated from the statement?"
3. "How can the gain on sale of investments be a deduction from net income in determining the cash flow from operating activities?"
4. "Why does the bank need this statement anyway? They can compute the increase in cash from the balance sheets for the last two years."

After jotting down Hoyt's questions, you assured him that this statement was "right." However, to alleviate Hoyt's concern, you arranged a meeting for the following day.

a. ▬▬▶ How would you respond to each of Hoyt's questions?
b. ▬▬▶ Do you think that the statement of cash flows enhances the chances of Stainless Kitchens, Inc. receiving the loan? Discuss.

ANSWERS TO SELF-EXAMINATION QUESTIONS

Matching

1. E	3. A	5. I	7. N	9. F	11. J	12. M	13. H
2. L	4. K	6. B	8. D	10. C			

Multiple Choice

1. **D** Cash flows from operating activities affect transactions that enter into the determination of net income, such as the receipt of cash from customers on account (answer D). Receipts of cash from the sale of stock (answer A) and the sale of bonds (answer B) and payments of cash for dividends (answer C) are cash flows from financing activities.

2. **A** Cash flows from investing activities include receipts from the sale of noncurrent assets, such as equipment (answer A), and payments to acquire noncurrent assets. Receipts of cash from the sale of stock (answer B) and payments of cash for dividends (answer C) and to acquire treasury stock (answer D) are cash flows from financing activities.

3. **C** Payment of cash dividends (answer C) is an example of a financing activity. The receipt of cash from customers on account (answer A) is an operating activity. The receipt of cash from the sale of equipment (answer B) is an investing activity. The payment of cash to acquire marketable securities (answer D) is an example of an investing activity.

4. **D** The indirect method (answer D) reports cash flows from operating activities by beginning with net income and adjusting it for revenues and expenses not involving the receipt or payment of cash.

5. **C** The cash flows from operating activities section of the statement of cash flows would report net cash flow from operating activities of $65,500, determined as follows:

Net income		$55,000
Add: Depreciation	$22,000	
Decrease in inventories	5,000	
Decrease in prepaid expenses	500	27,500
		$82,500
Deduct: Increase in accounts receivable	$10,000	
Decrease in accounts payable	7,000	17,000
Net cash flow from operating activities		$65,500

16

Financial Statement Analysis

Setting *the* STAGE

The *Wall Street Journal* (July 17, 1997) reported that the common stock of Microsoft Corporation was selling for $148 per share. If you had funds to invest, would you invest in Microsoft common stock?

Microsoft is a well-known, international company. However, Eastern Airlines, Pan Am, Montgomery Ward, Woolworth's, and Orion Pictures were also well-known companies. These latter companies share the common characteristic of having declared bankruptcy!

Obviously, being well-known is not necessarily a good basis for investing. Knowledge that a company has a good product, by itself, may also be an inadequate basis for investing in the company. Even with a good product, a company may go bankrupt for a variety of reasons, such as inadequate financing. For example, Orion Pictures went bankrupt, even though it produced the award-winning motion pictures *Dances With Wolves* and *Silence of the Lambs*.

How, then, does one decide on the companies in which to invest? This chapter describes and illustrates common financial data that can be analyzed to assist you in making investment decisions. In addition, the contents of corporate annual reports are also discussed.

After studying this chapter, you should be able to:

1 List basic financial statement analytical procedures.

2 Apply financial statement analysis to assess the solvency of a business.

3 Apply financial statement analysis to assess the profitability of a business.

4 Summarize the uses and limitations of analytical measures.

5 Describe the contents of corporate annual reports.

Basic Analytical Procedures

The basic financial statements provide much of the information users need to make economic decisions about businesses. In this chapter, we illustrate how to perform a complete analysis of these statements by integrating individual analytical measures.

Analytical procedures may be used to compare items on a current statement with related items on earlier statements. For example, cash of $150,000 on the current balance sheet may be compared with cash of $100,000 on the balance sheet of a year earlier. The current year's cash may be expressed as 1.5 or 150% of the earlier amount or as an increase of 50% or $50,000.

Analytical procedures are also widely used to examine relationships within a financial statement. To illustrate, assume that cash of $50,000 and inventories of $250,000 are included in the total assets of $1,000,000 on a balance sheet. In relative terms, the cash balance is 5% of the total assets, and the inventories are 25% of the total assets.

In the following discussion, we emphasize the importance of each of the various analytical measures illustrated. The measures are not ends in themselves. They are only guides in evaluating financial and operating data. Many other factors, such as trends in the industry and general economic conditions, should also be considered.

Horizontal Analysis

The percentage analysis of increases and decreases in related items in comparative financial statements is called **horizontal analysis**. The amount of each item on the most recent statement is compared with the related item on one or more earlier statements. The amount of increase or decrease in the item is listed, along with the percent of increase or decrease.

Horizontal analysis may include a comparison between two statements. In this case, the earlier statement is used as the base. Horizontal analysis may also include three or more comparative statements. In this case, the earliest date or period may be used as the base for comparing all later dates or periods. Alternatively, each statement may be compared to the immediately preceding statement. Exhibit 1 is a condensed comparative balance sheet for two years for Lincoln Company, with horizontal analysis.

We cannot fully evaluate the significance of the various increases and decreases in the items shown in Exhibit 1 without additional information. Although total assets at the end of 2000 were $91,000 (7.4%) less than at the beginning of the year, liabilities were reduced by $133,000 (30%), and stockholders' equity increased $42,000

Q&A

Accounts Payable was $600,000 in the current year and $500,000 in the preceding year. What is the amount and the percentage of increase or decrease that would be shown in a balance sheet with horizontal analysis?

$100,000 or 20%
($100,000/$500,000)
increase

EXHIBIT 1
Comparative Balance
Sheet—Horizontal Analysis

Lincoln Company
Comparative Balance Sheet
December 31, 2000 and 1999

	2000	1999	Increase (Decrease) Amount	Percent
Assets				
Current assets	$ 550,000	$ 533,000	$ 17,000	3.2%
Long-term investments	95,000	177,500	(82,500)	(46.5%)
Property, plant, and equipment (net)	444,500	470,000	(25,500)	(5.4%)
Intangible assets	50,000	50,000	—	
Total assets	$1,139,500	$1,230,500	$ (91,000)	(7.4%)
................Liabilities				
Current liabilities	$ 210,000	$ 243,000	$ (33,000)	(13.6%)
Long-term liabilities	100,000	200,000	(100,000)	(50.0%)
Total liabilities	$ 310,000	$ 443,000	$(133,000)	(30.0%)
Stockholders' Equity				
Preferred 6% stock, $100 par	$ 150,000	$ 150,000	—	—
Common stock, $10 par	500,000	500,000	—	—
Retained earnings	179,500	137,500	$ 42,000	30.5%
Total stockholders' equity	$ 829,500	$ 787,500	$ 42,000	5.3%
Total liabilities and stockholders' equity	$1,139,500	$1,230,500	$ (91,000)	(7.4%)

(5.3%). It appears that the reduction of $100,000 in long-term liabilities was achieved mostly through the sale of long-term investments.

The balance sheet in Exhibit 1 may be expanded to include the details of the various categories of assets and liabilities. An alternative is to present the details in separate schedules. Exhibit 2 is a supporting schedule with horizontal analysis.

EXHIBIT 2
Comparative Schedule of
Current Assets—Horizontal
Analysis

Lincoln Company
Comparative Schedule of Current Assets
December 31, 2000 and 1999

	2000	1999	Increase (Decrease) Amount	Percent
Cash	$ 90,500	$ 64,700	$ 25,800	39.9%
Marketable securities	75,000	60,000	15,000	25.0%
Accounts receivable (net)	115,000	120,000	(5,000)	(4.2%)
Inventories	264,000	283,000	(19,000)	(6.7%)
Prepaid expenses	5,500	5,300	200	3.8%
Total current assets	$550,000	$533,000	$ 17,000	3.2%

The decrease in accounts receivable may be due to changes in credit terms or improved collection policies. Likewise, a decrease in inventories during a period of increased sales may indicate an improvement in the management of inventories.

The changes in the current assets in Exhibit 2 appear favorable. This assessment is supported by the 24.8% increase in net sales shown in Exhibit 3.

EXHIBIT 3
Comparative Income Statement—Horizontal Analysis

Lincoln Company
Comparative Income Statement
For the Years Ended December 31, 2000 and 1999

	2000	1999	Increase (Decrease) Amount	Increase (Decrease) Percent
Sales	$1,530,500	$1,234,000	$296,500	24.0%
Sales returns and allowances	32,500	34,000	(1,500)	(4.4%)
Net sales	$1,498,000	$1,200,000	$298,000	24.8%
Cost of goods sold	1,043,000	820,000	223,000	27.2%
Gross profit	$ 455,000	$ 380,000	$ 75,000	19.7%
Selling expenses	$ 191,000	$ 147,000	$ 44,000	29.9%
Administrative expenses	104,000	97,400	6,600	6.8%
Total operating expenses	$ 295,000	$ 244,400	$ 50,600	20.7%
Income from operations	$ 160,000	$ 135,600	$ 24,400	18.0%
Other income	8,500	11,000	(2,500)	(22.7%)
	$ 168,500	$ 146,600	$ 21,900	14.9%
Other expense	6,000	12,000	(6,000)	(50.0%)
Income before income tax	$ 162,500	$ 134,600	$ 27,900	20.7%
Income tax expense	71,500	58,100	13,400	23.1%
Net income	$ 91,000	$ 76,500	$ 14,500	19.0%

An increase in net sales may not have a favorable effect on operating performance. The percentage increase in Lincoln Company's net sales is accompanied by a greater percentage increase in the cost of goods (merchandise) sold.[1] This has the effect of reducing gross profit. Selling expenses increased significantly, and administrative expenses increased slightly. Overall, operating expenses increased by 20.7%, whereas gross profit increased by only 19.7%.

The increase in income from operations and in net income is favorable. However, a study of the expenses and additional analyses and comparisons should be made before reaching a conclusion.

Exhibit 4 illustrates a comparative retained earnings statement with horizontal analysis. It reveals an increase of 30.5% in retained earnings for the year. The increase is due to net income of $91,000 for the year, less dividends of $49,000.

EXHIBIT 4
Comparative Retained Earnings Statement—Horizontal Analysis

Lincoln Company
Comparative Retained Earnings Statement
December 31, 2000 and 1999

	2000	1999	Increase (Decrease) Amount	Increase (Decrease) Percent
Retained earnings, January 1	$137,500	$100,000	$37,500	37.5%
Net income for the year	91,000	76,500	14,500	19.0%
Total	$228,500	$176,500	$52,000	29.5%
Dividends:				
On preferred stock	$ 9,000	$ 9,000	—	—
On common stock	40,000	30,000	$10,000	33.3%
Total	$ 49,000	$ 39,000	$10,000	25.6%
Retained earnings, December 31	$179,500	$137,500	$42,000	30.5%

---

[1] The term *cost of goods sold* is often used in practice in place of *cost of merchandise sold*. Such usage is followed in this chapter.

Vertical Analysis

A percentage analysis may also be used to show the relationship of each component to the total within a single statement. This type of analysis is called **vertical analysis**. Like horizontal analysis, the statements may be prepared in either detailed or condensed form. In the latter case, additional details of the changes in individual items may be presented in supporting schedules. In such schedules, the percentage analysis may be based on either the total of the schedule or the statement total. Although vertical analysis is limited to an individual statement, its significance may be improved by preparing comparative statements.

In vertical analysis of the balance sheet, each asset item is stated as a percent of the total assets. Each liability and stockholders' equity item is stated as a percent of the total liabilities and stockholders' equity. Exhibit 5 is a condensed comparative balance sheet with vertical analysis for Lincoln Company.

EXHIBIT 5
Comparative Balance
Sheet—Vertical Analysis

Lincoln Company Comparative Balance Sheet December 31, 2000 and 1999				
	2000		**1999**	
	Amount	**Percent**	**Amount**	**Percent**
Assets				
Current assets	$ 550,000	48.3%	$ 533,000	43.3%
Long-term investments	95,000	8.3	177,500	14.4
Property, plant, and equipment (net)	444,500	39.0	470,000	38.2
Intangible assets	50,000	4.4	50,000	4.1
Total assets	$1,139,500	100.0%	$1,230,500	100.0%
Liabilities				
Current liabilities	$ 210,000	18.4%	$ 243,000	19.7%
Long-term liabilities	100,000	8.8	200,000	16.3
Total liabilities	$ 310,000	27.2%	$ 443,000	36.0%
Stockholders' Equity				
Preferred 6% stock, $100 par	$ 150,000	13.2%	$ 150,000	12.2%
Common stock, $10 par	500,000	43.9	500,000	40.6
Retained earnings	179,500	15.7	137,500	11.2
Total stockholders' equity	$ 829,500	72.8%	$ 787,500	64.0%
Total liabilities and stockholders' equity	$1,139,500	100.0%	$1,230,500	100.0%

The major percentage changes in Lincoln Company's assets are in the current asset and long-term investment categories. In the Liabilities and Stockholders' Equity sections of the balance sheet, the greatest percentage changes are in long-term liabilities and retained earnings. Stockholders' equity increased from 64% to 72.8% of total liabilities and stockholders' equity in 2000. There is a comparable decrease in liabilities.

In a vertical analysis of the income statement, each item is stated as a percent of net sales. Exhibit 6 is a condensed comparative income statement with vertical analysis for Lincoln Company.

 *At the end of the current year, Accounts Payable was $600,000 and total liabilities and stockholders' equity was $1,200,000. What percent would be shown for Accounts Payable in a balance sheet with vertical analysis?*

50% ($600,000/$1,200,000)

EXHIBIT 6
Comparative Income State-
ment—Vertical Analysis

Lincoln Company Comparative Income Statement For the Years Ended December 31, 2000 and 1999				
	2000		**1999**	
	Amount	**Percent**	**Amount**	**Percent**
Sales	$1,530,500	102.2%	$1,234,000	102.8%
Sales returns and allowances	32,500	2.2	34,000	2.8
Net sales	$1,498,000	100.0%	$1,200,000	100.0%
Cost of goods sold	1,043,000	69.6	820,000	68.3
Gross profit	$ 455,000	30.4%	$ 380,000	31.7%
Selling expenses	$ 191,000	12.8%	$ 147,000	12.3%
Administrative expenses	104,000	6.9	97,400	8.1
Total operating expenses	$ 295,000	19.7%	$ 244,400	20.4%
Income from operations	$ 160,000	10.7%	$ 135,600	11.3%
Other income	8,500	0.6	11,000	0.9
	$ 168,500	11.3%	$ 146,600	12.2%
Other expense	6,000	0.4	12,000	1.0
Income before income tax	$ 162,500	10.9%	$ 134,600	11.2%
Income tax expense	71,500	4.8	58,100	4.8
Net income	$ 91,000	6.1%	$ 76,500	6.4%

We must be careful when judging the significance of differences between percentages for the two years. For example, the decline of the gross profit rate from
31.7% in 1999 to 30.4% in 2000 is only 1.3 percentage points. In terms of dollars of
potential gross profit, however, it represents a decline of approximately $19,500
(1.3% × $1,498,000).

Common-Size Statements

Horizontal and vertical analyses with both dollar and percentage amounts are useful in assessing relationships and trends in financial conditions and operations of a
business. Vertical analysis with both dollar and percentage amounts is also useful
in comparing one company with another or with industry averages. Such comparisons are easier to make with the use of common-size statements. In a **common-
size statement**, all items are expressed in percentages.

The percentages of gross profit and
net income to sales for fiscal year-
end 1996 for **Kmart Corp.** and
Wal-Mart Stores Inc. are shown
below.

	Kmart Corp.	Wal-Mart Stores Inc.
Gross profit to sales	22.4%	20.2%
Net income to sales	0.7%	2.9%

Wal-Mart has a lower gross profit margin than
Kmart, which is likely due to lower prices. However, Wal-Mart has a much leaner operating expense structure, so is able to earn an overall
higher percentage of net income to sales.

Common-size statements are useful in comparing the current
period with prior periods, individual businesses, or one business
with industry percentages. Industry data are often available from
trade associations and financial information services. Exhibit 7 is
a comparative common-size income statement for two businesses.

Exhibit 7 indicates that Lincoln Company has a slightly higher
rate of gross profit than Madison Corporation. However, this advantage is more than offset by Lincoln Company's higher percentage of selling and administrative expenses. As a result, the
operating income of Lincoln Company is 10.7% of net sales, compared with 14.4% for Madison Corporation—an unfavorable difference of 3.7 percentage points.

Other Analytical Measures

In addition to the preceding analyses, other relationships may be
expressed in ratios and percentages. Often, these items are taken

EXHIBIT 7
Common-Size Income Statement

Lincoln Company and Madison Corporation Condensed Common-Size Income Statement For the Year Ended December 31, 2000	Lincoln Company	Madison Corporation
Sales	102.2%	102.3%
Sales returns and allowances	2.2	2.3
Net sales	100.0%	100.0%
Cost of goods sold	69.6	70.0
Gross profit	30.4%	30.0%
Selling expenses	12.8%	11.5%
Administrative expenses	6.9	4.1
Total operating expenses	19.7%	15.6%
Income from operations	10.7%	14.4%
Other income	0.6	0.6
	11.3%	15.0%
Other expense	0.4	0.5
Income before income tax	10.9%	14.5%
Income tax expense	4.8	5.5
Net income	6.1%	9.0%

from the financial statements and thus are a type of vertical analysis. Comparison of these items with items from earlier periods is a type of horizontal analysis.

Solvency Analysis

OBJECTIVE 2

Apply financial statement analysis to assess the solvency of a business.

Some aspects of a business's financial condition and operations are of greater importance to some users than others. However, all users are interested in the ability of a business to pay its debts as they are due and to earn income. The ability of a business to meet its financial obligations (debts) is called **solvency**. The ability of a business to earn income is called **profitability**.

The factors of solvency and profitability are interrelated. A business that cannot pay its debts on a timely basis may experience difficulty in obtaining credit. A lack of available credit may, in turn, lead to a decline in the business's profitability. Eventually, the business may be forced into bankruptcy. Likewise, a business that is less profitable than its competitors is likely to be at a disadvantage in obtaining credit or new capital from stockholders.

In the following paragraphs, we discuss various types of financial analyses that are useful in evaluating the solvency of a business. In the next section, we discuss various types of profitability analyses. The examples in both sections are based on Lincoln Company's financial statements presented earlier. In some cases, data from Lincoln Company's financial statements of the preceding year and from other sources are also used. These historical data are useful in assessing the past performance of a business and in forecasting its future performance. The results of financial analyses may be

 Two popular printed sources for industry ratios are available in *Annual Statement Studies* from **Robert Morris Associates** and *Industry Norms & Key Business Ratios* from **Dun's Analytical Services**. Additional sources are available on the Internet at **www.sunsite.unc.edu/reference/rita/ratios.html**

even more useful when they are compared with those of competing businesses and with industry averages.

Solvency analysis focuses on the ability of a business to pay or otherwise satisfy its current and noncurrent liabilities. It is normally assessed by examining balance sheet relationships, using the following major analyses:

> **Solvency analysis focuses on the ability of a business to pay or otherwise satisfy its current and noncurrent liabilities.**

1. Current position analysis
2. Accounts receivable analysis
3. Inventory analysis
4. The ratio of fixed assets to long-term liabilities
5. The ratio of liabilities to stockholders' equity
6. The number of times interest charges are earned

Current Position Analysis

To be useful in assessing solvency, a ratio or other financial measure must relate to a business's ability to pay or otherwise satisfy its liabilities. The use of such measures to assess the ability of a business to pay its current liabilities is called **current position analysis**. Such analysis is of special interest to short-term creditors.

An analysis of a firm's current position normally includes determining the working capital, the current ratio, and the acid-test ratio. The current and acid-test ratios are most useful when analyzed together and compared to previous periods and other firms in the industry.

Working Capital

The excess of the current assets of a business over its current liabilities is called **working capital**. The working capital is often used in evaluating a company's ability to meet currently maturing debts. It is especially useful in making monthly or other period-to-period comparisons for a company. However, amounts of working capital are difficult to assess when comparing companies of different sizes or in comparing such amounts with industry figures. For example, working capital of $250,000 may be adequate for a small residential contractor, but it may be inadequate for a large commercial contractor.

Current Ratio

Another means of expressing the relationship between current assets and current liabilities is the **current ratio**. This ratio is sometimes called the **working capital ratio** or **bankers' ratio**. The ratio is computed by dividing the total current assets by the total current liabilities. For Lincoln Company, working capital and the current ratio for 2000 and 1999 are as follows:

	2000	1999
Current assets	$550,000	$533,000
Current liabilities	210,000	243,000
Working capital	$340,000	$290,000
Current ratio	2.6	2.2

The current ratio is a more reliable indicator of solvency than is working capital. To illustrate, assume that as of December 31, 2000, the working capital of a competitor is much greater than $340,000, but its current ratio is only 1.3. Considering these facts alone, Lincoln Company, with its current ratio of 2.6, is in a more favorable position to obtain short-term credit than the competitor, which has the greater amount of working capital.

The current ratio for a **Microsoft Corporation** balance sheet (dated June 30, 1996) was 4.17. The explanation for this high current ratio was Microsoft's cash hoard of $4.75 billion. Microsoft essentially generated cash faster than it could profitably invest it.

Acid-Test Ratio

The working capital and the current ratio do not consider the makeup of the current assets. To illustrate the importance of this consideration, the current position data for Lincoln Company and Jefferson Corporation as of December 31, 2000, are as follows:

	Lincoln Company	Jefferson Corporation
Current assets:		
Cash	$ 90,500	$ 45,500
Marketable securities	75,000	25,000
Accounts receivable (net)	115,000	90,000
Inventories	264,000	380,000
Prepaid expenses	5,500	9,500
Total current assets	$550,000	$550,000
Current liabilities	210,000	210,000
Working capital	$340,000	$340,000
Current ratio	2.6	2.6

Both companies have a working capital of $340,000 and a current ratio of 2.6. But the ability of each company to pay its current debts is significantly different. Jefferson Corporation has more of its current assets in inventories. Some of these inventories must be sold and the receivables collected before the current liabilities can be paid in full. Thus, a large amount of time may be necessary to convert these inventories into cash. Declines in market prices and a reduction in demand could also impair its ability to pay current liabilities. In contrast, Lincoln Company has cash and current assets (marketable securities and accounts receivable) that can generally be converted to cash rather quickly to meet its current liabilities.

A ratio that measures the "instant" debt-paying ability of a company is called the **acid-test ratio** or **quick ratio**. It is the ratio of the total quick assets to the total current liabilities. Quick assets are cash and other current assets that can be quickly converted to cash. Quick assets normally include cash, marketable securities, and receivables. The acid-test ratio data for Lincoln Company are as follows:

A balance sheet shows $300,000 of cash, marketable securities, and receivables, and $250,000 of inventories. Current liabilities are $200,000. What are (a) the current ratio and (b) the acid-test ratio?

- - - - - - - - - - - - - - - - - - - -

(a) 2.75 ($550,000/$200,000);
(b) 1.5 ($300,000/$200,000)

	2000	1999
Quick assets:		
Cash	$ 90,500	$ 64,700
Marketable equity securities	75,000	60,000
Accounts receivable (net)	115,000	120,000
Total quick assets	$280,500	$244,700
Current liabilities	$210,000	$243,000
Acid-test ratio	1.3	1.0

Accounts Receivable Analysis

The size and makeup of accounts receivable change constantly during business operations. Sales on account increase accounts receivable, whereas collections from customers decrease accounts receivable. Firms that grant long credit terms usually have larger accounts receivable balances than those granting short credit terms. Increases or decreases in the volume of sales also affect the balance of accounts receivable.

It is desirable to collect receivables as promptly as possible. The cash collected from receivables improves solvency. In addition, the cash generated by prompt collections from customers may be used in operations for such purposes as purchasing merchandise in large quantities at lower prices. The cash may also be used for payment of dividends to stockholders or for other investing or financing purposes. Prompt collection also lessens the risk of loss from uncollectible accounts.

Accounts Receivable Turnover

The relationship between credit sales and accounts receivable may be stated as the **accounts receivable turnover**. This ratio is computed by dividing net sales on account by the average net accounts receivable. It is desirable to base the average on monthly balances, which allows for seasonal changes in sales. When such data are not available, it may be necessary to use the average of the accounts receivable balance at the beginning and the end of the year. If there are trade notes receivable as well as accounts, the two may be combined. The accounts receivable turnover data for Lincoln Company are as follows. All sales were made on account.

	2000	1999
Net sales on account	$1,498,000	$1,200,000
Accounts receivable (net):		
Beginning of year	$ 120,000	$ 140,000
End of year	115,000	120,000
Total	$ 235,000	$ 260,000
Average (Total ÷ 2)	$ 117,500	$ 130,000
Accounts receivable turnover	12.7	9.2

The increase in the accounts receivable turnover for 2000 indicates that there has been an improvement in the collection of receivables. This may be due to a change in the granting of credit or in collection practices or both.

Number of Days' Sales in Receivables

Another measure of the relationship between credit sales and accounts receivable is the **number of days' sales in receivables**. This ratio is computed by dividing the net accounts receivable at the end of the year by the average daily sales on account. Average daily sales on account is determined by dividing net sales on account by 365 days. The number of days' sales in receivables is computed for Lincoln Company as follows:

	2000	1999
Accounts receivable (net), end of year	$ 115,000	$ 120,000
Net sales on account	$1,498,000	$1,200,000
Average daily sales on account (sales ÷ 365)	$ 4,104	$ 3,288
Number of days' sales in receivables	28.0*	36.5*

*Accounts receivable ÷ Average daily sales on account

Q&A

Sales were $1,200,000, of which 80% were on account. The accounts receivable balance at the beginning of the year was $56,000, and at the end of the year it was $40,000. What are (a) the accounts receivable turnover and (b) the number of days' sales in receivables?

(a) 20 [(0.80 × $1,200,000)/($56,000 + $40,000)/2];
(b) 15.2 days [$40,000/($960,000/365)]

The number of days' sales in receivables is an estimate of the length of time the accounts receivable have been outstanding. Comparing this measure with the credit terms provides information on the efficiency in collecting receivables. For example, assume that the number of days' sales in receivables for Grant Inc. is 40. If Grant Inc.'s credit terms are n/45, then its collection process appears to be efficient. On the other hand, if Grant Inc.'s credit terms are n/30, its collection process does not appear to be efficient. A comparison with other firms in the same industry and with prior years also provides useful information. Such comparisons may indicate efficiency of collection procedures and trends in credit management.

Inventory Analysis

A business should keep enough inventory on hand to meet the needs of its customers and its operations. At the same time, however, an excessive amount of inventory reduces solvency by tying up funds. Excess inventories also increase insurance expense, property taxes, storage costs, and other related expenses. These expenses further reduce funds that could be used elsewhere to improve operations. Finally, excess inventory also increases the risk of losses because of price declines or obsolescence of the inventory. Two measures that are useful for evaluating the management of inventory are the inventory turnover and the number of days' sales in inventory.

Inventory Turnover

The relationship between the volume of goods (merchandise) sold and inventory may be stated as the **inventory turnover**. It is computed by dividing the cost of goods sold by the average inventory. If monthly data are not available, the average of the inventories at the beginning and the end of the year may be used. The inventory turnover for Lincoln Company is computed as follows:

	2000	1999
Cost of goods sold	$1,043,000	$820,000
Inventories:		
Beginning of year	$ 283,000	$311,000
End of year	264,000	283,000
Total	$ 547,000	$594,000
Average (Total ÷ 2)	$ 273,500	$297,000
Inventory turnover	3.8	2.8

 The inventory turnover of Mc-Donald's Corporation for a recent year was 40, while for Toys "R" Us Inc., it was 3.27. McDonald's inventory turnover is higher because it sells perishable food products, while toys can sit on the shelf longer without "spoiling."

The inventory turnover improved for Lincoln Company because of an increase in the cost of goods sold and a decrease in the average inventories. Differences across inventories, companies, and industries are too great to allow a general statement on what is a good inventory turnover. For example, a firm selling food should have a higher turnover than a firm selling furniture or jewelry. Likewise, the perishable foods department of a supermarket should have a higher turnover than the soaps and cleansers department. However, for each business or each department within a business, there is a reasonable turnover rate. A turnover lower than this rate could mean that inventory is not being managed properly.

Number of Days' Sales in Inventory

Another measure of the relationship between the cost of goods sold and inventory is the **number of days' sales in inventory**. This measure is computed by dividing the inventory at the end of the year by the average daily cost of goods sold (cost of goods sold divided by 365). The number of days' sales in inventory for Lincoln Company is computed as follows:

	2000	1999
Inventories, end of year	$ 264,000	$283,000
Cost of goods sold	$1,043,000	$820,000
Average daily cost of goods sold (COGS ÷ 365 days)	$ 2,858	$ 2,247
Number of days' sales in inventory	92.4	125.9

The number of days' sales in inventory is a rough measure of the length of time it takes to acquire, sell, and replace the inventory. For Lincoln Company, there is a major improvement in the number of days' sales in inventory during 2000. However, a comparison with earlier years and similar firms would be useful in assessing Lincoln Company's overall inventory management.

Ratio of Fixed Assets to Long-Term Liabilities

Long-term notes and bonds are often secured by mortgages on fixed assets. The **ratio of fixed assets to long-term liabilities** is a solvency measure that indicates the margin of safety of the noteholders or bondholders. It also indicates the ability of the business to borrow additional funds on a long-term basis. The ratio of fixed assets to long-term liabilities for Lincoln Company is as follows:

	2000	1999
Fixed assets (net)	$444,500	$470,000
Long-term liabilities	$100,000	$200,000
Ratio of fixed assets to long-term liabilities	4.4	2.4

The major increase in this ratio at the end of 2000 is mainly due to liquidating one-half of Lincoln Company's long-term liabilities. If the company needs to borrow additional funds on a long-term basis in the future, it is in a strong position to do so.

Ratio of Liabilities to Stockholders' Equity

Claims against the total assets of a business are divided into two groups: (1) claims of creditors and (2) claims of owners. The relationship between the total claims of the creditors and owners—the **ratio of liabilities to stockholders' equity**—is a solvency measure that indicates the margin of safety for creditors. It also indicates the ability of the business to withstand adverse business conditions. When the claims of creditors are large in relation to the equity of the stockholders, there are usually significant interest payments. If earnings decline to the point where the company is unable to meet its interest payments, the business may be taken over by the creditors.

 The ratio of liabilities to stockholders' equity varies across industries. For example, recent annual reports of some selected companies showed the following ratio of liabilities to stockholders' equity:

Delta Air Lines	3.81
Procter & Gamble	1.36
Bell South	0.36

The airline industry generally uses more debt financing than the consumer product or utility industries. Thus, the airline industry is generally considered more risky.

The relationship between creditor and stockholder equity is shown in the vertical analysis of the balance sheet. For example, the balance sheet of Lincoln Company in Exhibit 5 indicates that on December 31, 2000, liabilities represented 27.2% and stockholders' equity represented 72.8% of the total liabilities and stockholders' equity (100.0%). Instead of expressing each item as a percent of the total, this relationship may be expressed as a ratio of one to the other, as follows:

	2000	1999
Total liabilities	$310,000	$443,000
Total stockholders' equity	$829,500	$787,500
Ratio of liabilities to stockholders' equity	0.37	0.56

The balance sheet of Lincoln Company shows that the major factor affecting the change in the ratio was the $100,000 decrease in long-term liabilities during 2000. The ratio at the end of both years shows a large margin of safety for the creditors.

Number of Times Interest Charges Earned

Corporations in some industries, such as airlines, normally have high ratios of debt to stockholders' equity. For such corporations, the relative risk of the debtholders is normally measured as the **number of times interest charges are earned** during the year. The higher the ratio, the lower the risk that interest payments will not be made if earnings decrease. In other words, the higher the ratio, the greater the assurance that interest payments will be made on a continuing basis. This measure also indicates the general financial strength of the business, which is of interest to stockholders and employees as well as creditors.

The amount available to meet interest charges is not affected by taxes on income. This is because interest is deductible in determining taxable income. Thus, the number of times interest charges are earned is computed as shown below.

	2000	1999
Income before income tax	$ 900,000	$ 800,000
Add interest expense	300,000	250,000
Amount available to meet interest charges	$1,200,000	$1,050,000
Number of times interest charges earned	4	4.2

Q&A *What would be the number of times interest charges are earned for a company with $1,500,000, 10% debt; net income of $120,000; and a corporate tax rate of 40%?*

$$\frac{[\$120,000/(1.0 - 0.4)] + \$150,000}{\$150,000} = 2.33$$

Analysis such as this can also be applied to dividends on preferred stock. In such a case, net income is divided by the amount of preferred dividends to yield the **number of times preferred dividends are earned.** This measure indicates the risk that dividends to preferred stockholders may not be paid.

Profitability Analysis

OBJECTIVE 3

Apply financial statement analysis to assess the profitability of a business.

The ability of a business to earn profits depends on the effectiveness and efficiency of its operations as well as the resources available to it. Profitability analysis, therefore, focuses primarily on the relationship between operating results as reported in the income statement and resources available to the business as reported in the balance sheet. Major analyses used in assessing profitability include the following:

1. Ratio of net sales to assets
2. Rate earned on total assets
3. Rate earned on stockholders' equity
4. Rate earned on common stockholders' equity
5. Earnings per share on common stock
6. Price-earnings ratio
7. Dividends per share
8. Dividend yield

Profitability analysis focuses on the relationship between operating results and the resources available to a business.

Ratio of Net Sales to Assets

The **ratio of net sales to assets** is a profitability measure that shows how effectively a firm utilizes its assets. For example, two competing businesses have equal amounts of assets. If the sales of one are twice the sales of the other, the business with the higher sales is making better use of its assets.

In computing the ratio of net sales to assets, any long-term investments are excluded from total assets. This is because such investments are unrelated to normal operations involving the sale of goods or services. Assets may be measured as the total at the end of the year, the average at the beginning and end of the year, or the average of monthly totals. The basic data and the computation of this ratio for Lincoln Company are as follows:

	2000	1999
Net sales	$1,498,000	$1,200,000
Total assets (excluding long-term investments):		
Beginning of year	$1,053,000	$1,010,000
End of year	1,044,500	1,053,000
Total	$2,097,500	$2,063,000
Average (Total ÷ 2)	$1,048,750	$1,031,500
Ratio of net sales to assets	1.4	1.2

There was an improvement in this ratio during 2000. This was primarily due to an increase in sales volume. A comparison with similar companies or industry averages would be helpful in assessing the effectiveness of Lincoln Company's use of its assets.

Rate Earned on Total Assets

The **rate earned on total assets** measures the profitability of total assets, without considering how the assets are financed. This rate is therefore not affected by whether the assets are financed primarily by creditors or stockholders.

The rate earned on total assets is computed by adding interest expense to net income and dividing this sum by the average total assets. The addition of interest expense to net income eliminates the effect of whether the assets are financed by debt or equity. The rate earned by Lincoln Company on total assets is computed as follows:

	2000	1999
Net income	$ 91,000	$ 76,500
Plus interest expense	6,000	12,000
Total	$ 97,000	$ 88,500
Total assets:		
Beginning of year	$1,230,500	$1,187,500
End of year	1,139,500	1,230,500
Total	$2,370,000	$2,418,000
Average (Total ÷ 2)	$1,185,000	$1,209,000
Rate earned on total assets	8.2%	7.3%

The rate earned on total assets of Lincoln Company during 2000 improved over that of 1999. A comparison with similar companies and industry averages would be useful in evaluating Lincoln Company's profitability on total assets.

Sometimes it may be desirable to compute the **rate of income from operations to total assets**. This is especially true if significant amounts of nonoperating income and expense are reported on the income statement. In this case, any assets related to the nonoperating income and expense items should be excluded from total assets in computing the rate. In addition, using income from operations (which is before tax) has the advantage of eliminating the effects of any changes in the tax structure on the rate of earnings. When evaluating published data on rates earned on assets, you should be careful to determine the exact nature of the measure that is reported.

Rate Earned on Stockholders' Equity

Another measure of profitability is the **rate earned on stockholders' equity**. It is computed by dividing net income by average total stockholders' equity. In contrast to the rate earned on total assets, this measure emphasizes the rate of income earned on the amount invested by the stockholders.

The total stockholders' equity may vary throughout a period. For example, a business may issue or retire stock, pay dividends, and earn net income. If monthly amounts are not available, the average of the stockholders' equity at the beginning and the end of the year is normally used to compute this rate. For Lincoln Company, the rate earned on stockholders' equity is computed as follows:

	2000	1999
Net income	$ 91,000	$ 76,500
Stockholders' equity:		
Beginning of year	$ 787,500	$ 750,000
End of year	829,500	787,500
Total	$1,617,000	$1,537,500
Average (Total ÷ 2)	$ 808,500	$ 768,750
Rate earned on stockholders' equity	11.3%	10.0%

The rate earned by a business on the equity of its stockholders is usually higher than the rate earned on total assets. This occurs when the amount earned on assets acquired with creditors' funds is more than the interest paid to creditors. This difference in the rate on stockholders' equity and the rate on total assets is called **leverage**.

Lincoln Company's rate earned on stockholders' equity for 2000, 11.3%, is greater than the rate of 8.2% earned on total assets. The leverage of 3.1% (11.3% − 8.2%) for 2000 compares favorably with the 2.7% (10.0% − 7.3%) leverage for 1999. Exhibit 8 shows the 2000 and 1999 leverages for Lincoln Company.

EXHIBIT 8
Leverage

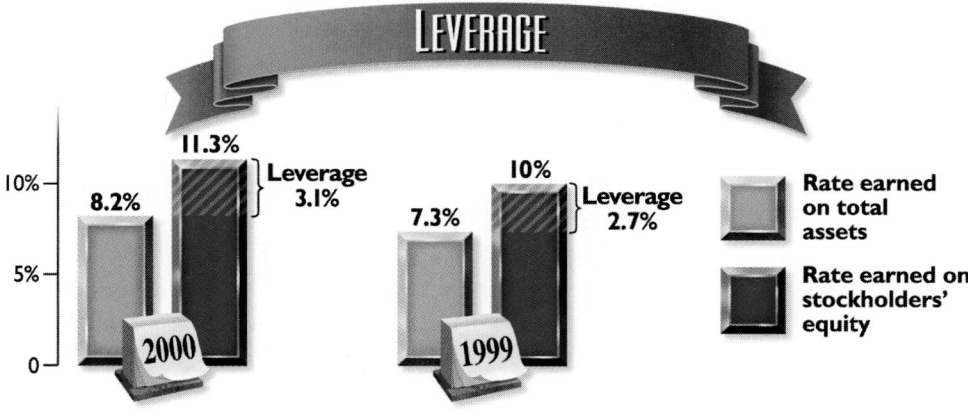

The approximate rates earned on assets and stockholders' equity for **Adolph Coors Company** and **Anheuser-Busch Companies** for a recent fiscal year are shown below.

	Adolph Coors	Anheuser-Busch
Rate earned on assets	3%	11%
Rate earned on stockholders' equity	6%	28%

Anheuser-Busch has been more profitable and has benefited from a greater use of leverage than has Adolph Coors.

Rate Earned on Common Stockholders' Equity

A corporation may have both preferred and common stock outstanding. In this case, the common stockholders have the residual claim on earnings. The **rate earned on common stockholders' equity** focuses only on the rate of profits earned on the amount invested by the common stockholders. It is computed by subtracting preferred dividend requirements from the net income and dividing by the average common stockholders' equity.

Lincoln Company has $150,000 of 6% nonparticipating preferred stock outstanding on December 31, 2000 and 1999. Thus, the annual preferred dividend requirement is $9,000 ($150,000 × 6%). The common stockholders' equity equals the total stockholders' equity, including retained earnings, less the par of the preferred stock ($150,000). The basic data and the rate earned on common stockholders' equity for Lincoln Company are as follows:

	2000	1999
Net income	$ 91,000	$ 76,500
Preferred dividends	9,000	9,000
Remainder—identified with common stock	$ 82,000	$ 67,500
Common stockholders' equity:		
Beginning of year	$ 637,500	$ 600,000
End of year	679,500	637,500
Total	$1,317,000	$1,237,500
Average (Total ÷ 2)	$ 658,500	$ 618,750
Rate earned on common stockholders' equity	12.5%	10.9%

Analysis and Red Flags

An additional source of information about a corporation is the independent auditor's report, which must accompany the financial statements of a public corporation. The purpose of this report is to provide assurance to investors that the financial statements are fairly presented in conformity with generally accepted accounting principles.

The auditor's report may raise "red flags" indicating that profitability and solvency measures should be analyzed further. In such cases, an investor should read the auditor's report carefully to see if the "reliability" of these measures has been affected by one or more of the following factors:

1. There may be substantial doubt as to the ability of the company to continue as a going concern beyond one year.
2. An unusual accounting practice is being followed.
3. The company changed accounting principles from prior years.
4. The auditor wants to call your attention to a specific matter of importance.
5. The financial statements do not conform to generally accepted accounting principles.

The date of the auditor's report is also significant. It represents the last date that the auditor searched for events occurring subsequent to the date of the financial statements—events that might be significant to the interpretation of those statements. For example, the company may have sold a subsidiary after year-end or suffered a substantial loss as a result of some disaster. Such events should be disclosed in notes to the financial statements. ■

The rate earned on common stockholders' equity differs from the rates earned by Lincoln Company on total assets and total stockholders' equity. This occurs if there are borrowed funds and also preferred stock outstanding, which rank ahead of the common shares in their claim on earnings. Thus, the concept of leverage, as we discussed in the preceding section, can also be applied to the use of funds from the sale of preferred stock as well as borrowing. Funds from both sources can be used in an attempt to increase the return on common stockholders' equity.

Earnings per Share on Common Stock

One of the profitability measures often quoted by the financial press is **earnings per share (EPS) on common stock**. It is also normally reported in the income statement in corporate annual reports. If a company has issued only one class of stock, the earnings per share is computed by dividing net income by the number of shares of stock outstanding. If preferred and common stock are outstanding, the net income is first reduced by the amount of preferred dividend requirements.[2]

The data on the earnings per share of common stock for Lincoln Company are as follows:

	2000	1999
Net income	$91,000	$76,500
Preferred dividends	9,000	9,000
Remainder—identified with common stock	$82,000	$67,500
Shares of common stock outstanding	50,000	50,000
Earnings per share on common stock	$1.64	$1.35

Price-Earnings Ratio

Another profitability measure quoted by the financial press is the **price-earnings (P/E) ratio** on common stock. The price-earnings ratio is an indicator of a firm's future earnings prospects. It is computed by dividing the market price per share of common stock at a specific date by the annual earnings per share. To illustrate, assume that the market prices per common share are 20½ at the end of 2000 and 13½ at the end of 1999. The price-earnings ratio on common stock of Lincoln Company is computed as follows:

	2000	1999
Market price per share of common stock	$20.50	$13.50
Earnings per share on common stock	÷ 1.64	÷ 1.35
Price-earnings ratio on common stock	12.5	10.0

---

[2] Additional details related to earnings per share were discussed in a previous chapter.

The price-earnings ratio indicates that a share of common stock of Lincoln Company was selling for 10 times the amount of earnings per share at the end of 1999. At the end of 2000, the common stock was selling for 12.5 times the amount of earnings per share.

Dividends per Share and Dividend Yield

Since the primary basis for dividends is earnings, dividends per share and earnings per share on common stock are commonly used by investors in assessing alternative stock investments. The dividends per share for Lincoln Company were $0.80 ($40,000 ÷ 50,000 shares) for 2000 and $0.60 ($30,000 ÷ 50,000 shares) for 1999.

Dividends per share can be reported with earnings per share to indicate the relationship between dividends and earnings. A comparison of these two per share amounts indicates the extent to which the corporation is retaining its earnings for use in operations. Exhibit 9 shows these relationships for Lincoln Company:

P/E ratios that are much higher than the market averages are generally associated with companies with fast-growing profits. P/E ratios that are much lower than the market averages are generally associated with "out of favor" or declining profit companies.

EXHIBIT 9
Dividends and Earnings per Share of Common Stock

The dividend yield on common stock is a profitability measure that shows the rate of return to common stockholders in terms of cash dividends. It is of special interest to investors whose main investment objective is to receive current returns (dividends) on an investment rather than an increase in the market price of the investment. The dividend yield is computed by dividing the annual dividends paid per share of common stock by the market price per share on a specific date. To illustrate, assume that the market price was 20½ at the end of 2000 and 13½ at the end of 1999. The dividend yield on common stock of Lincoln Company is as follows:

	2000	1999
Dividends per share of common stock	$ 0.80	$ 0.60
Market price per share of common stock	÷ 20.50	÷ 13.50
Dividend yield on common stock	3.9%	4.4%

The earnings per share and dividend yield of a common stock are normally quoted on the daily listing of stock prices in the *Wall Street Journal* and other financial publications.

Summary of Analytical Measures

Exhibit 10 presents a summary of the analytical measures that we have discussed. These measures can be computed for most medium-size businesses. Depending on the specific business being analyzed, some measures might be omitted or additional measures could be developed. The type of industry, the capital structure, and the diversity of the business's operations usually affect the measures used. For example, analysis for an airline might include revenue per passenger mile and cost per available seat as measures. Likewise, analysis for a hotel might focus on occupancy rates.

Percentage analyses, ratios, turnovers, and other measures of financial position and operating results are useful analytical measures. They are helpful in assessing a business's past performance and predicting its future. They are not, however, a substitute for sound judgment. In selecting and interpreting analytical measures, conditions peculiar to a business or its industry should be considered. In addition, the influence of the general economic and business environment should be considered.

In determining trends, the interrelationship of the measures used in assessing a business should be carefully studied. Comparable indexes of earlier periods should also be studied. Data from competing businesses may be useful in assessing the efficiency of operations for the firm under analysis. In making such comparisons, however, the effects of differences in the accounting methods used by the businesses should be considered.

EXHIBIT 10
Summary of Analytical Measures

	Method of Computation	Use
Solvency measures:		
Working capital	Current assets − Current liabilities	To indicate the ability to meet currently maturing obligations
Current ratio	$\dfrac{\text{Current assets}}{\text{Current liabilities}}$	
Acid-test ratio	$\dfrac{\text{Quick assets}}{\text{Current liabilities}}$	To indicate instant debt-paying ability
Accounts receivable turnover	$\dfrac{\text{Net sales on account}}{\text{Average accounts receivable}}$	To assess the efficiency in collecting receivables and in the management of credit
Numbers of days' sales in receivables	$\dfrac{\text{Accounts receivable, end of year}}{\text{Average daily sales on account}}$	
Inventory turnover	$\dfrac{\text{Cost of goods sold}}{\text{Average inventory}}$	To assess the efficiency in the management of inventory
Number of days' sales in inventory	$\dfrac{\text{Inventory, end of year}}{\text{Average daily cost of goods sold}}$	
Ratio of fixed assets to long-term liabilities	$\dfrac{\text{Fixed assets (net)}}{\text{Long-term liabilities}}$	To indicate the margin of safety to long-term creditors
Ratio of liabilities to stockholders' equity	$\dfrac{\text{Total liabilities}}{\text{Total stockholders' equity}}$	To indicate the margin of safety to creditors
Number of times interest charges earned	$\dfrac{\text{Income before income tax + Interest expense}}{\text{Interest expense}}$	To assess the risk to debtholders in terms of number of times interest charges were earned

EXHIBIT 10
(concluded)

Profitability measures:	Method of Computation	Use
Ratio of net sales to assets	$$\dfrac{\text{Net sales}}{\text{Average total assets (excluding long-term investments)}}$$	To assess the effectiveness in the use of assets
Rate earned on total assets	$$\dfrac{\text{Net income + Interest expense}}{\text{Average total assets}}$$	To assess the profitability of the assets
Rate earned on stockholders' equity	$$\dfrac{\text{Net income}}{\text{Average total stockholders' equity}}$$	To assess the profitability of the investment by stockholders
Rate earned on common stockholders' equity	$$\dfrac{\text{Net income} - \text{Preferred dividends}}{\text{Average common stockholders' equity}}$$	To assess the profitability of the investment by common stockholders
Earnings per share on common stock	$$\dfrac{\text{Net income} - \text{Preferred dividends}}{\text{Shares of common stock outstanding}}$$	
Price-earnings ratio	$$\dfrac{\text{Market price per share of common stock}}{\text{Earnings per share of common stock}}$$	To indicate future earnings prospects, based on the relationship between market value of common stock and earnings
Dividends per share of common stock	$$\dfrac{\text{Dividends}}{\text{Shares of common stock outstanding}}$$	To indicate the extent to which earnings are being distributed to common stockholders
Dividend yield	$$\dfrac{\text{Dividends per share of common stock}}{\text{Market price per share of common stock}}$$	To indicate the rate of return to common stockholders in terms of dividends

Corporate Annual Reports

OBJECTIVE 5

Describe the contents of corporate annual reports.

Corporations normally issue annual reports to their stockholders and other interested parties. Such reports summarize the corporation's operating activities for the past year and plans for the future. There are many variations in the order and form for presenting the major sections of annual reports. However, one section of the annual report is devoted to the financial statements, including the accompanying notes. In addition, annual reports usually include the following sections:

1. Financial Highlights
2. President's Letter to the Stockholders
3. Management Report
4. Independent Auditors' Report
5. Historical Summary

In the following paragraphs, we describe these sections. Each section, as well as the financial statements, is illustrated in the 1996 annual report for **Hershey Foods Corporation** in Appendix G.

Financial Highlights

The Financial Highlights section summarizes the operating results for the last year or two. It is sometimes called *Results in Brief*. It is usually presented on the first one or two pages of the annual report.

There are many variations in the format and content of the Financial Highlights section. Such items as sales, net income, net income per common share, cash dividends paid, cash dividends per common share, and the amount of capital expenditures are typically presented. In addition to these data, information about the financial position at the end of the year may be presented. The Financial Highlights section for Hershey Foods Corporation includes the year-end amounts of stockholders' equity, common shares outstanding, book value per share, and the price per share.

President's Letter to the Stockholders

A letter from the company president to the stockholders is also presented in most annual reports. These letters usually discuss such items as reasons for an increase or decrease in net income, changes in existing plants, purchase or construction of new plants, significant new financing commitments, social responsibility issues, and future plans.

Management Report

The management of the corporation is responsible for the corporation's accounting system and financial statements. In the Management Report section, the chief financial officer or other corporate officer normally includes the following:

1. A statement that the financial statements are management's responsibility and that they have been prepared according to generally accepted accounting principles.
2. Management's assessment of the company's internal accounting control system.
3. Comments on any other relevant matters related to the accounting system, the financial statements, and the examination by the independent auditor.

Independent Auditors' Report

Before issuing annual statements, all publicly held corporations are required to have an independent audit (examination) of their financial statements. For the financial statements of most companies, the CPAs who conduct the audit render an opinion on the fairness of the statements, as shown in the Independent Auditors' Report for Hershey Foods Corporation.

Historical Summary

The Historical Summary section reports selected financial and operating data of past periods, usually for five or ten years. It is usually presented near the financial statements for the current year. There are wide variations in the types of data reported and the title of this section. In the annual report for Hershey Foods Corporation, this section is called the "Eleven-Year Consolidated Financial Summary."

Other Information

Some annual reports may include other financial information. For example, some reports may include forecasts that indicate financial plans and expectations for the year ahead and other supplemental data.

 During the mid-1990s, the largest companies in the U.S. and in most parts of the world were audited by six large international accounting firms: **Arthur Andersen, Coopers & Lybrand, Deloitte & Touche, Ernst & Young, KPMG Peat Marwick,** and **Price Waterhouse.** In 1997, Coopers & Lybrand and Price Waterhouse announced their intention to merge, as did Ernst & Young and KPMG Peat Marwick. These mergers were motivated by the firms' desires to grow their consulting practices. However, the business community has expressed the concern that these mergers may jeopardize the competition among auditors, resulting in higher audit fees. In addition, regulators (such as the SEC) are concerned that it will be more difficult for auditors to maintain their independence from clients for whom they also perform consulting services.

ENCORE

A Tale of Two Retailers

Two of the oldest and most venerable names in U.S. retailing are Sears and Montgomery Ward. These two companies virtually defined the "mall-based" retail concept. However, beginning in the mid-1980s, their stories could not be more different. The charts below show the ratio of net income to sales, ratio of liabilities to stockholders' equity, and the rate earned on stockholders' equity for 1992–1996 for the two retailers. As can be seen, their fortunes have diverged significantly over the time period. What happened?

Both companies faced daunting challenges during the mid-80s. First, consumers were becoming very value-conscious. Second, "category killers", such as Home Depot and Circuit City, began their move on U.S. retailing. Third, Wal-Mart began to dominate the price-conscious end of the market. This left both Sears and Montgomery Ward caught in a retailing squeeze. How did these two companies respond to these common threats?

Montgomery Ward failed to find its niche. It reduced prices below other mall-based retailers, but not enough to compete with Wal-Mart. However, at the same time, it failed to modernize its stores or freshen up its brands. Also, it moved away from apparel toward favoring electronics and thus went head to head against Circuit City. Price-conscious retailers shopped at Wal-Mart or Circuit City, while the mall-based shopper chose J.C. Penney or Sears for a more pleasant shopping experience.

Sears, on the other hand, identified its key customer group as the 30- to 50-year-old woman shopping for herself or her family. Then, it launched a $4 billion renovation project to create an appealing atmosphere for women. In addition, it expanded space and launched new brand items for women's apparel. All of this was combined with a new advertising campaign stressing "the softer side of Sears." Lastly, Sears focused on its core merchandising business by eliminating the catalog business and distributing Allstate Insurance back to the shareholders via a special dividend (which is why

the ratio of liabilities to stockholders' equity doubled between 1994 and 1995).

How does the story end? It's not over yet, but Montgomery Ward entered Chapter 11 bankruptcy in the summer of 1997, shed 3,900 workers, and put its Lechmere and Electric Avenue & More units up for sale. Some analysts believe Montgomery Ward may eventually be liquidated. What can be said for Sears? It still faces significant competition, but it's fair to say that Montgomery Ward's pain becomes Sears' gain. ■

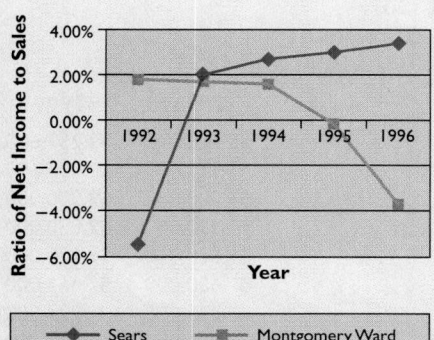

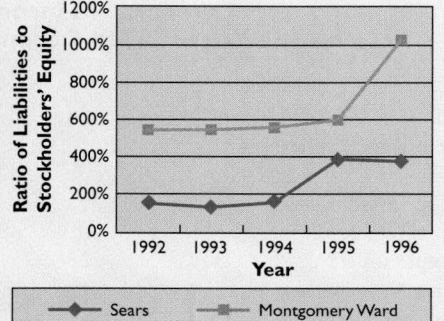

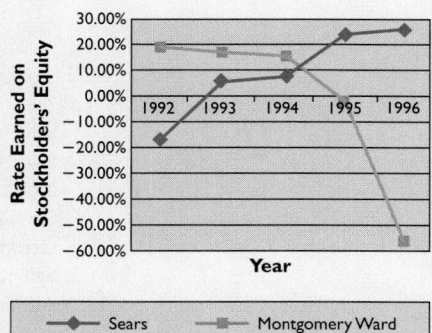

1 **List basic financial statement analytical procedures.**

The analysis of percentage increases and decreases in related items in comparative financial statements is called horizontal analysis. The analysis of percentages of component parts to the total in a single statement is called vertical analysis. Financial statements in which all amounts are expressed in percentages for purposes of analysis are called common-size statements.

2 **Apply financial statement analysis to assess the solvency of a business.**

The primay focus of financial statement analysis is the assessment of solvency and profitability. All users are interested in the ability of a business to pay its debts as they come due (solvency) and to earn income (profitability). Solvency analysis is normally assessed by examining the following balance sheet rela-

tionships: (1) current position analysis, (2) accounts receivable analysis, (3) inventory analysis, (4) the ratio of fixed assets to long-term liabilities, (5) the ratio of liabilities to stockholders' equity, and (6) the number of times interest charges are earned.

3 **Apply financial statement analysis to assess the profitability of a business.**

Profitability analysis focuses mainly on the relationship between operating results (income statement) and resources available (balance sheet). Major analyses used in assessing profitability include (1) the ratio of net sales to assets, (2) the rate earned on total assets, (3) the rate earned on stockholders' equity, (4) the rate earned on common stockholders' equity, (5) earnings per share on common stock, (6) the price-earnings ratio, (7) dividends per share, and (8) dividend yield.

4 **Summarize the uses and limitations of analytical measures.**

In selecting and interpreting analytical measures, conditions peculiar to a business or its industry should be considered. For example, the type of industry, capital structure, and diversity of the business's operations affect the measures used. In addition, the influence of the general economic and business environment should be considered.

5 **Describe the contents of corporate annual reports.**

Corporate annual reports normally include financial statements and the following sections: Financial Highlights, President's Letter to the Stockholders, Management Report, Independent Auditors' Report, and Historical Summary.

Rainbow Paint Co.'s comparative financial statements for the years ending December 31, 2000 and 1999, are as follows. The market price of Rainbow Paint Co.'s common stock was $30 on December 31, 1999, and $25 on December 31, 2000.

Rainbow Paint Co.
Comparative Income Statement
For the Years Ended December 31, 2000 and 1999

	2000	1999
Sales (all on account)	$5,125,000	$3,257,600
Sales returns and allowances	125,000	57,600
Net sales	$5,000,000	$3,200,000
Cost of goods sold	3,400,000	2,080,000
Gross profit	$1,600,000	$1,120,000
Selling expenses	$ 650,000	$ 464,000
Administrative expenses	325,000	224,000
Total operating expenses	$ 975,000	$ 688,000
Income from operations	$ 625,000	$ 432,000
Other income	25,000	19,200
	$ 650,000	$ 451,200
Other expense (interest)	105,000	64,000
Income before income tax	$ 545,000	$ 387,200
Income tax expense	300,000	176,000
Net income	$ 245,000	$ 211,200

Rainbow Paint Co.
Comparative Retained Earnings Statement
For the Years Ended December 31, 2000 and 1999

	2000	1999
Retained earnings, January 1	$723,000	$581,800
Add net income for year	245,000	211,200
Total	$968,000	$793,000
Deduct dividends:		
On preferred stock	$ 40,000	$ 40,000
On common stock	45,000	30,000
Total	$ 85,000	$ 70,000
Retained earnings, December 31	$883,000	$723,000

Rainbow Paint Co.
Comparative Balance Sheet
December 31, 2000 and 1999

	2000	1999
Assets		
Current assets:		
Cash	$ 175,000	$ 125,000
Marketable securities	150,000	50,000
Accounts receivable (net)	425,000	325,000
Inventories	720,000	480,000
Prepaid expenses	30,000	20,000
Total current assets	$1,500,000	$1,000,000
Long-term investments	250,000	225,000
Property, plant, and equipment (net)	2,093,000	1,948,000
Total assets	$3,843,000	$3,173,000
Liabilities		
Current liabilities	$ 750,000	$ 650,000
Long-term liabilities:		
Mortgage note payable, 10%, due 2003	$ 410,000	—
Bonds payable, 8%, due 2006	800,000	$ 800,000
Total long-term liabilities	$1,210,000	$ 800,000
Total liabilities	$1,960,000	$1,450,000
Stockholders' Equity		
Preferred 8% stock, $100 par	$ 500,000	$ 500,000
Common stock, $10 par	500,000	500,000
Retained earnings	883,000	723,000
Total stockholders' equity	$1,883,000	$1,723,000
Total liabilities and stockholders' equity	$3,843,000	$3,173,000

Instructions

Determine the following measures for 2000:

1. Working capital
2. Current ratio
3. Acid-test ratio
4. Accounts receivable turnover
5. Number of days' sales in receivables
6. Inventory turnover
7. Number of days' sales in inventory
8. Ratio of fixed assets to long-term liabilities
9. Ratio of liabilities to stockholders' equity
10. Number of times interest charges earned
11. Number of times preferred dividends earned
12. Ratio of net sales to assets
13. Rate earned on total assets
14. Rate earned on stockholders' equity
15. Rate earned on common stockholders' equity
16. Earnings per share on common stock

17. Price-earnings ratio
18. Dividends per share of common stock
19. Dividend yield

Solution
(Ratios are rounded to the nearest single digit after the decimal point.)

1. Working capital: $750,000
   $1,500,000 − $750,000
2. Current ratio: 2.0
   $1,500,000 ÷ $750,000
3. Acid-test ratio: 1.0
   $750,000 ÷ $750,000
4. Accounts receivable turnover: 13.3
   $5,000,000 ÷ [($425,000 + $325,000) ÷ 2]
5. Number of days' sales in receivables: 31 days
   $5,000,000 ÷ 365 = $13,699
   $425,000 ÷ $13,699
6. Inventory turnover: 5.7
   $3,400,000 ÷ [($720,000 + $480,000) ÷ 2]
7. Number of days' sales in inventory: 77.3 days
   $3,400,000 ÷ 365 = $9,315
   $720,000 ÷ $9,315
8. Ratio of fixed assets to long-term liabilities: 1.7
   $2,093,000 ÷ $1,210,000
9. Ratio of liabilities to stockholders' equity: 1.0
   $1,960,000 ÷ $1,883,000
10. Number of times interest charges earned: 6.2
    ($545,000 + $105,000) ÷ $105,000
11. Number of times preferred dividends earned: 6.1
    $245,000 ÷ $40,000
12. Ratio of net sales to assets: 1.5
    $5,000,000 ÷ [($3,593,000 + $2,948,000) ÷ 2]
13. Rate earned on total assets: 10.0%
    ($245,000 + $105,000) ÷ [($3,843,000 + $3,173,000) ÷ 2]
14. Rate earned on stockholders' equity: 13.6%
    $245,000 ÷ [($1,883,000 + $1,723,000) ÷ 2]
15. Rate earned on common stockholders' equity: 15.7%
    ($245,000 − $40,000) ÷ [($1,383,000 + $1,223,000) ÷ 2]
16. Earnings per share on common stock: $4.10
    ($245,000 − $40,000) ÷ 50,000
17. Price-earnings ratio: 6.1
    $25 ÷ $4.10
18. Dividends per share of common stock: $0.90
    $45,000 ÷ 50,000 shares
19. Dividend yield: 3.6%
    $0.90 ÷ $25

SELF-EXAMINATION QUESTIONS   Answers at End of Chapter

Matching
Match each of the following statements with its proper term. Some terms may not be used.

A. **accounts receivable turnover**	___ 1. The percentage of increases and decreases in corresponding items in comparative financial statements.
B. **acid-test ratio**	___ 2. The sum of cash, receivables, and marketable securities.

C. **common-size statement**
D. **current ratio**
E. **dividends per share**
F. **dividend yield**
G. **earnings per share (EPS) on common stock**
H. **horizontal analysis**
I. **inventory turnover**
J. **leverage**
K. **number of days' sales in inventory**
L. **number of days' sales in receivables**
M. **number of times interest charges earned**
N. **price-earnings (P/E) ratio**
O. **profitability**
P. **quick assets**
Q. **rate earned on common stockholders' equity**
R. **rate earned on stockholders' equity**
S. **rate earned on total assets**
T. **ratio of fixed assets to long-term liabilities**
U. **ratio of liabilities to stockholders' equity**
V. **ratio of net sales to assets**
W. **solvency**
X. **vertical analysis**
Y. **working capital**

____ 3. The relationship between the volume of sales and inventory, computed by dividing the inventory at the end of the year by the average daily cost of goods sold.

____ 4. The ability of a firm to pay its debts as they come due.

____ 5. The relationship between credit sales and accounts receivable, computed by dividing the net accounts receivable at the end of the year by the average daily sales on account.

____ 6. The relationship between credit sales and accounts receivable, computed by dividing net sales on account by the average net accounts receivable.

____ 7. The tendency of the rate earned on stockholders' equity to vary from the rate earned on total assets because the amount earned on assets acquired through the use of funds provided by creditors varies from the interest paid to these creditors.

____ 8. A financial statement in which all items are expressed only in relative terms.

____ 9. A measure of profitability computed by dividing net income by total stockholders' equity.

____ 10. The excess of total current assets over total current liabilities at some point in time.

____ 11. The ratio of the market price per share of common stock, at a specific date, to the annual earnings per share.

____ 12. A measure of the profitability of assets, without regard to the equity of creditors and stockholders in the assets.

____ 13. The profitability ratio of net income available to common shareholders to the number of common shares outstanding.

____ 14. The ratio of the sum of cash, receivables, and marketable securities to current liabilities.

____ 15. The percentage analysis of component parts in relation to the total of the parts in a single financial statement.

____ 16. A measure of profitability computed by dividing net income, reduced by preferred dividend requirements, by common stockholders' equity.

____ 17. The ratio of current assets to current liabilities.

____ 18. The relationship between the volume of goods sold and inventory, computed by dividing the cost of goods sold by the average inventory.

____ 19. The ability of a firm to earn income.

Multiple Choice

1. What type of analysis is indicated by the following?

	Amount	Percent
Current assets	$100,000	20%
Property, plant, and equipment	400,000	80
Total assets	$500,000	100%

   A. Vertical analysis
   B. Horizontal analysis
   C. Profitability analysis
   D. Contribution margin analysis

2. Which of the following measures is useful as an indication of the ability of a firm to pay its current liabilities?
   A. Working capital
   B. Current ratio
   C. Acid-test ratio
   D. All of the above

3. The ratio determined by dividing total current assets by total current liabilities is:
   A. current ratio
   B. working capital ratio
   C. bankers' ratio
   D. all of the above

4. The ratio of the quick assets to current liabilities, which indicates the "instant" debt-paying ability of a firm, is:
   A. current ratio
   B. working capital ratio
   C. acid-test ratio
   D. bankers' ratio

5. A measure useful in evaluating the efficiency in the management of inventories is:
   A. working capital ratio
   B. acid-test ratio
   C. number of days' sales in inventory
   D. ratio of fixed assets to long-term liabilities

CLASS DISCUSSION QUESTIONS

1. What is the difference between horizontal and vertical analysis of financial statements?
2. What is the advantage of using comparative statements for financial analysis rather than statements for a single date or period?
3. The current year's amount of net income (after income tax) is 15% larger than that of the preceding year. Does this indicate an improved operating performance? Discuss.
4. How would you respond to a horizontal analysis that showed an expense increasing by over 100%?
5. a. Name the major ratios useful in assessing solvency and profitability.
   b. Why is it important not to rely on only one ratio or measure in assessing the solvency or profitability of a business?
6. How would the current and acid-test ratios of a service business compare?
7. For Lindsay Corporation, the working capital at the end of the current year is $50,000 greater than the working capital at the end of the preceding year, reported as follows:

	Current Year	Preceding Year
Current assets:		
Cash, marketable securities, and receivables	$340,000	$300,000
Inventories	510,000	325,000
Total current assets	$850,000	$625,000
Current liabilities	425,000	250,000
Working capital	$425,000	$375,000

   Has the current position improved? Explain.
8. A company that grants terms of n/30 on all sales has a yearly accounts receivable turnover, based on monthly averages, of 6. Is this a satisfactory turnover? Discuss.
9. What does an increase in the number of days' sales in receivables ordinarily indicate about the credit and collection policy of the firm?
10. a. Why is it advantageous to have a high inventory turnover?
    b. Is it possible for the inventory turnover to be too high? Discuss.
    c. Is it possible to have a high inventory turnover and a high number of days' sales in inventory? Discuss.
11. What do the following data taken from a comparative balance sheet indicate about the company's ability to borrow additional funds on a long-term basis in the current year as compared to the preceding year?

	Current Year	Preceding Year
Fixed assets (net)	$1,750,000	$1,700,000
Total long-term liabilities	700,000	850,000

12. What does a decrease in the ratio of liabilities to stockholders' equity indicate about the margin of safety for a firm's creditors and the ability of the firm to withstand adverse business conditions?
13. In computing the ratio of net sales to assets, why are long-term investments excluded in determining the amount of the total assets?
14. In determining the number of times interest charges are earned, why are interest charges added to income before income tax?
15. In determining the rate earned on total assets, why is interest expense added to net income before dividing by total assets?
16. a. Why is the rate earned on stockholders' equity by a thriving business ordinarily higher than the rate earned on total assets?
    b. Should the rate earned on common stockholders' equity normally be higher or lower than the rate earned on total stockholders' equity? Explain.

17. The net income (after income tax) of A. L. Gibson Inc. was $25 per common share in the latest year and $40 per common share for the preceding year. At the beginning of the latest year, the number of shares outstanding was doubled by a stock split. There were no other changes in the amount of stock outstanding. What were the earnings per share in the preceding year, adjusted for comparison with the latest year?

18. The price-earnings ratio for the common stock of Essian Company was 10 at December 31, the end of the current fiscal year. What does the ratio indicate about the selling price of the common stock in relation to current earnings?

19. Why would the dividend yield differ significantly from the rate earned on common stockholders' equity?

20. Favorable business conditions may bring about certain seemingly unfavorable ratios, and unfavorable business operations may result in apparently favorable ratios. For example, Sanchez Company increased its sales and net income substantially for the current year, yet the current ratio at the end of the year is lower than at the beginning of the year. Discuss some possible causes of the apparent weakening of the current position, while sales and net income have increased substantially.

21. a. What are the major components of an annual report?
    b. Indicate the purpose of the Financial Highlights section and the President's Letter.

Resources for Your Success On-Line at **warren.swcollege.com**

Remember! If you need additional help, visit South-Western's Web site. See page 26 for a description of the online and printed materials that are available.

EXERCISES

Exercise 16–1
Vertical analysis of income statement

Objective 1

✓ 2000 net income: $52,800; 8% of sales

Revenue and expense data for Cabot Cabinet Co. are as follows:

	2000	1999
Sales	$660,000	$600,000
Cost of goods sold	389,400	384,000
Selling expenses	105,600	84,000
Administrative expenses	66,000	54,000
Income tax expense	46,200	42,000

a. Prepare an income statement in comparative form, stating each item for both 2000 and 1999 as a percent of sales.
b. Comment on the significant changes disclosed by the comparative income statement.

Exercise 16–2
Vertical analysis of income statement

Objective 1

✓ a. 1997 operating income, 9.2% of revenues

The following comparative income statement (in thousands of dollars) for the years ending February 2, 1997, and January 31, 1996, was adapted from the 1997 annual report of **Dell Computer Corporation**:

	1997	1996
Revenues	$7,759,000	$5,296,000
Costs and expenses:		
Cost of sales	6,093,000	4,229,000
Gross profit	$1,666,000	$1,067,000
Selling, distribution, and administrative expenses	952,000	690,000
Operating income	$ 714,000	$ 377,000

a. Prepare a comparative income statement for 1997 and 1996 in vertical form, stating each item as a percent of revenues. Round to one digit after the decimal place.
b. Based upon the 1996 income statement, comment on the significant changes.

Exercise 16–3
Common-size income statement

Objective 1

✓ a. Keystone net income: $642,000; 9.2% of sales

Revenue and expense data for the current calendar year for Keystone Publishing Company and for the publishing industry are as follows. The Keystone Publishing Company data are expressed in dollars. The publishing industry averages are expressed in percentages.

	Keystone Publishing Company	Publishing Industry Average
Sales	$7,070,000	100.5%
Sales returns and allowances	70,000	0.5
Cost of goods sold	4,900,000	69.0
Selling expenses	560,000	9.0
Administrative expenses	490,000	8.2
Other income	42,000	0.6
Other expense	100,000	1.4
Income tax expense	350,000	5.0

a. Prepare a common-size income statement comparing the results of operations for Keystone Publishing Company with the industry average. Round to one digit after the decimal place.
b. As far as the data permit, comment on significant relationships revealed by the comparisons.

Exercise 16–4
Vertical analysis of balance sheet

Objective 1

✓ Retained earnings, Dec. 31, 2000, 33.75%

Balance sheet data for Fisher Fabrics Company on December 31, the end of the fiscal year, are as follows:

	2000	1999
Current assets	$280,000	$260,000
Property, plant, and equipment	480,000	400,000
Intangible assets	40,000	41,000
Current liabilities	100,000	71,000
Long-term liabilities	180,000	220,000
Common stock	250,000	200,000
Retained earnings	270,000	210,000

Prepare a comparative balance sheet for 2000 and 1999, stating each asset as a percent of total assets and each liability and stockholders' equity item as a percent of the total liabilities and stockholders' equity. Round to two digits after the decimal place.

Exercise 16–5
Horizontal analysis of the income statement

Objective 1

✓ a. Net income increase, 73.9%

Income statement data for Neon Flashlight Company for the year ended December 31, 2000 and 1999, are as follows:

	2000	1999
Sales	$940,000	$850,000
Cost of goods sold	610,000	580,000
Gross profit	$330,000	$270,000
Selling expenses	$126,000	$137,000
Administrative expenses	44,000	53,500
Total operating expenses	$170,000	$190,500
Income before income tax	$160,000	$ 79,500
Income tax expense	60,000	22,000
Net income	$100,000	$ 57,500

a. Prepare a comparative income statement with horizontal analysis, indicating the increase (decrease) for 2000 when compared with 1999. Round to one digit after the decimal place.

b. What conclusions can be drawn from the horizontal analysis?

Exercise 16–6
Current position analysis

Objective 2

✓ Current year working capital, $360,000

The following data were taken from the balance sheet of Precision Engine Company:

	Current Year	Preceding Year
Cash	$ 89,500	$139,000
Marketable securities	110,000	98,000
Accounts and notes receivable (net)	190,500	153,000
Inventories	250,500	222,000
Prepaid expenses	19,500	38,000
Accounts and notes payable (short-term)	245,000	203,500
Accrued liabilities	55,000	56,500

a. Determine for each year (1) the working capital, (2) the current ratio, and (3) the acid-test ratio.

b. What conclusions can be drawn from these data as to the company's ability to meet its currently maturing debts?

Exercise 16–7
Current position analysis

Objective 2

What's Wrong WITH THIS?

The bond indenture for the 10-year, 9½% debenture bonds dated January 2, 1999, required working capital of $350,000, a current ratio of 1.5, and an acid-test ratio of 1 at the end of each calendar year until the bonds mature. At December 31, 2000, the three measures were computed as follows:

1. Current assets:
Cash	$295,000	
Marketable securities	148,000	
Accounts and notes receivable (net)	172,000	
Inventories	300,000	
Prepaid expenses	135,000	
Goodwill	150,000	
Total current assets		$1,200,000
Current liabilities:		
Accounts and short-term notes payable	$500,000	
Accrued liabilities	250,000	
Total current liabilities		750,000
Working capital		$ 450,000

2. Current ratio = 1.6 ($1,200,000 ÷ $750,000)
3. Acid-test ratio = 1.2 ($615,000 ÷ $500,000)

a. Can you find any errors in the determination of the three measures of current position analysis?

b. Is the company satisfying the terms of the bond indenture?

Exercise 16–8
Accounts receivable analysis

Objective 2

HAT

✓ a. Accounts receivable turnover, current year, 6.0

The following data are taken from the financial statements of North Company. Terms of all sales are 1/10, n/60.

	Current Year	Preceding Year
Accounts receivable, end of year	$ 572,000	$ 408,333
Monthly average accounts receivable (net)	476,667	350,000
Net sales on account	2,860,000	2,450,000

a. Determine for each year (1) the accounts receivable turnover and (2) the number of days' sales in receivables. Round to one digit after the decimal place.

b. What conclusions can be drawn from these data concerning accounts receivable and credit policies?

Exercise 16–9
Inventory analysis

Objective 2

HAT

✓ a. Inventory turnover, current year, 8.0

The following data were extracted from the income statement of Cascade Instruments Inc.:

	Current Year	Preceding Year
Sales	$7,400,000	$5,200,000
Beginning inventories	642,500	607,500
Cost of goods sold	5,280,000	3,750,000
Ending inventories	677,500	642,500

a.   Determine for each year (1) the inventory turnover and (2) the number of days' sales in inventory. Round to one digit after the decimal place.
b.   What conclusions can be drawn from these data concerning the inventories?

Exercise 16–10
Ratio of liabilities to stockholders' equity and number of times interest charges earned

Objective 2

✓ a. Ratio of liabilities to stockholders' equity, Dec. 31, 2000, 0.56

The following data were taken from the financial statements of Mountain Spring Water Co. for December 31, 2000 and 1999:

	December 31, 2000	December 31, 1999
Accounts payable	$ 200,000	$ 400,000
Current maturities of serial bonds payable	400,000	400,000
Serial bonds payable, 12%, issued 1995, due 2004	1,600,000	2,000,000
Common stock, $1 par value	100,000	100,000
Paid-in capital in excess of par	1,000,000	1,000,000
Retained earnings	2,860,000	2,400,000

The income before income tax was $780,000 and $216,000 for the years 2000 and 1999, respectively.

a.   Determine the ratio of liabilities to stockholders' equity at the end of each year. Round to two digits after the decimal place.
b.   Determine the number of times the bond interest charges are earned during the year for both years.
c.   What conclusions can be drawn from these data as to the company's ability to meet its currently maturing debts?

Exercise 16–11
Profitability ratios

Objective 3

HAT

✓ a. Rate earned on total assets, 2001, 14%

The following selected data were taken from the financial statements of Ohio Cement Co. for December 31, 2001, 2000, and 1999:

	December 31, 2001	December 31, 2000	December 31, 1999
Total assets	$3,200,000	$2,800,000	$2,000,000
Notes payable (8% interest)	500,000	500,000	500,000
Common stock	900,000	900,000	900,000
Preferred $10 stock, $100 par, cumulative, nonparticipating (no change during year)	300,000	300,000	300,000
Retained earnings	1,430,000	1,050,000	250,000

The 2001 net income was $380,000, and the 2000 net income was $800,000. No dividends on common stock were declared between 1999 and 2001.

a.   Determine the rate earned on total assets, the rate earned on stockholders' equity, and the rate earned on common stockholders' equity for the years 2000 and 2001. Round to one digit after the decimal place.
b.   What conclusions can be drawn from these data as to the company's profitability?

Exercise 16–12

Six measures of solvency or profitability

Objectives 2, 3

HAT

✓ c. Ratio of net sales to assets, 1.44

The following data were taken from the financial statements of Premium Printers Inc. for the current fiscal year:

Property, plant, and equipment (net)			$1,000,000
Liabilities:			
Current liabilities		$400,000	
Mortgage note payable, 10%, issued 1990, due 2005 ...		800,000	
Total liabilities			$1,200,000
Stockholders' equity:			
Preferred $4 stock, $80 par, cumulative,			
nonparticipating (no change during year)			$ 400,000
Common stock, $10 par (no change during year)			1,200,000
Retained earnings:			
Balance, beginning of year	$600,000		
Net income	300,000	$900,000	
Preferred dividends	$ 20,000		
Common dividends	80,000	100,000	
Balance, end of year			800,000
Total stockholders' equity			$2,400,000
Net sales			$4,500,000
Interest expense			$ 80,000

Assuming that long-term investments totaled $175,000 throughout the year and that total assets were $3,000,000 at the beginning of the year, determine the following: (a) ratio of fixed assets to long-term liabilities, (b) ratio of liabilities to stockholders' equity, (c) ratio of net sales to assets, (d) rate earned on total assets, (e) rate earned on stockholders' equity, and (f) rate earned on common stockholders' equity. Round to two digits after the decimal place.

Exercise 16–13

Five measures of solvency or profitability

Objectives 2, 3

HAT

✓ d. Price-earnings ratio, 24

The balance sheet for Aspen Avionics Corporation at the end of the current fiscal year indicated the following:

Bonds payable, 10% (issued in 1990, due in 2010)	$4,000,000
Preferred $10 stock, $100 par	1,000,000
Common stock, $20 par	8,000,000

Income before income tax was $1,000,000, and income taxes were $300,000 for the current year. Cash dividends paid on common stock during the current year totaled $288,000. The common stock was selling for $36 per share at the end of the year. Determine each of the following: (a) number of times bond interest charges were earned, (b) number of times preferred dividends were earned, (c) earnings per share on common stock, (d) price-earnings ratio, (e) dividends per share of common stock, and (f) dividend yield.

Exercise 16–14

Earnings per share, price-earnings ratio, dividend yield

Objective 3

✓ b. Price-earnings ratio, 15

The following information was taken from the financial statements of Cool Breeze Air Conditioners Inc. for December 31 of the current fiscal year:

Common stock, $15 par value (no change during the year)	$4,500,000
Preferred $8 stock, $100 par, cumulative, nonparticipating (no change during year) ..	800,000

The net income was $574,000 and the declared dividends on the common stock were $225,000 for the current year. The market price of the common stock is $25.50 per share.

For the common stock, determine the (a) earnings per share, (b) price-earnings ratio, (c) dividends per share, and (d) dividend yield.

Exercise 16–15

Earnings per share

Objective 3

✓ b. Earnings per share on common stock, $6.50

The net income reported on the income statement of United Fruit Co. was $4,200,000. There were 400,000 shares of $20 par common stock and 200,000 shares of $8 cumulative preferred stock outstanding throughout the current year. The income statement included two extraordinary items: a $1,250,000 gain from condemnation of land and a $250,000 loss arising from flood damage, both after applicable income tax. Determine the per share figures for common stock for (a) income before extraordinary items and (b) net income.

Problem 16–1A
Horizontal analysis for income statement

Objective 1

GENERAL LEDGER

✓ 1. Sales, 10% increase

For 2000, Wang Company reported its most significant decline in net income in years. At the end of the year, Hai Wang, the president, is presented with the following condensed comparative income statement:

Wang Company
Comparative Income Statement
For the Years Ended December 31, 2000 and 1999

	2000	1999
Sales	$495,000	$450,000
Sales returns and allowances	5,000	2,000
Net sales	$490,000	$448,000
Cost of goods sold	312,000	260,000
Gross profit	$178,000	$188,000
Selling expenses	$ 84,000	$ 70,000
Administrative expenses	38,500	35,000
Total operating expenses	$122,500	$105,000
Income from operations	$ 55,500	$ 83,000
Other income	2,500	2,000
Income before income tax	$ 58,000	$ 85,000
Income tax expense	20,000	28,000
Net income	$ 38,000	$ 57,000

Instructions

1. Prepare a comparative income statement with horizontal analysis for the two-year period, using 1999 as the base year. Round to one digit after the decimal place.
2. To the extent the data permit, comment on the significant relationships revealed by the horizontal analysis prepared in (1).

Problem 16–2A
Vertical analysis for income statement

Objective 1

GENERAL LEDGER
SPREADSHEET

✓ 1. Net income, 2000, 8.6%

For 2000, Kasouski Company initiated a sales promotion campaign that included the expenditure of an additional $10,000 for advertising. At the end of the year, Leszek Kasouski, the president, is presented with the following condensed comparative income statement:

Kasouski Company
Comparative Income Statement
For the Years Ended December 31, 2000 and 1999

	2000	1999
Sales	$720,000	$650,000
Sales returns and allowances	20,000	15,000
Net sales	$700,000	$635,000
Cost of goods sold	290,000	270,000
Gross profit	$410,000	$365,000
Selling expenses	200,000	190,000
Administrative expenses	125,000	115,000
Total operating expenses	$325,000	$305,000
Income from operations	$ 85,000	$ 60,000
Other income	10,000	9,000
Income before income tax	$ 95,000	$ 69,000
Income tax expense	35,000	26,000
Net income	$ 60,000	$ 43,000

Instructions

1. Prepare a comparative income statement for the two-year period, presenting an analysis of each item in relationship to net sales for each of the years. Round to one digit after the decimal place.

2. To the extent the data permit, comment on the significant relationships revealed by the vertical analysis prepared in (1).

Problem 16–3A
Effect of transactions on current position analysis

Objective 2

✓ 1. Current ratio, 2.5

Data pertaining to the current position of Clarity Glass Company are as follows:

Cash	$256,000
Marketable securities	84,000
Accounts and notes receivable (net)	360,000
Inventories	532,000
Prepaid expenses	18,000
Accounts payable	380,000
Notes payable (short-term)	80,000
Accrued expenses	40,000

Instructions

1. Compute (a) the working capital, (b) the current ratio, and (c) the acid-test ratio.
2. List the following captions on a sheet of paper:

Transaction	Working Capital	Current Ratio	Acid-Test Ratio

Compute the working capital, the current ratio, and the acid-test ratio after each of the following transactions, and record the results in the appropriate columns. Consider each transaction separately and assume that only that transaction affects the data given above. Round to two digits after the decimal point.

a. Sold marketable securities at no gain or loss, $56,000.
b. Paid accounts payable, $40,000.
c. Purchased goods on account, $80,000.
d. Paid notes payable, $30,000.
e. Declared a cash dividend, $25,000.
f. Declared a common stock dividend on common stock, $28,500.
g. Borrowed cash from bank on a long-term note, $140,000.
h. Received cash on account, $164,000.
i. Issued additional shares of stock for cash, $200,000.
j. Paid cash for prepaid expenses, $10,000.

Problem 16–4A
Eighteen measures of solvency and profitability

Objectives 2, 3

HAT
SPREADSHEET

✓ 5. Number of days' sales in receivables, 39.7

The comparative financial statements of Boston Bagel Company are as follows. The market price of Boston Bagel Company common stock was $36 on December 31, 2000.

Boston Bagel Company
Comparative Income Statement
For the Years Ended December 31, 2000 and 1999

	2000	1999
Sales (all on account)	$2,450,000	$2,100,000
Sales returns and allowances	50,000	40,000
Net sales	$2,400,000	$2,060,000
Cost of goods sold	1,100,000	960,000
Gross profit	$1,300,000	$1,100,000
Selling expenses	$ 426,000	$ 395,000
Administrative expenses	354,000	345,000
Total operating expenses	$ 780,000	$ 740,000
Income from operations	$ 520,000	$ 360,000
Other income	80,000	30,000
	$ 600,000	$ 390,000
Other expense (interest)	130,000	90,000
Income before income tax	$ 470,000	$ 300,000
Income tax expense	140,000	100,000
Net income	$ 330,000	$ 200,000

Boston Bagel Company
Comparative Retained Earnings Statement
For the Years Ended December 31, 2000 and 1999

	Dec. 31, 2000	Dec. 31, 1999
Retained earnings, January 1	$275,000	$113,000
Add net income for year	330,000	200,000
Total	$605,000	$313,000
Deduct dividends:		
On preferred stock	$ 30,000	$ 18,000
On common stock	20,000	20,000
Total	$ 50,000	$ 38,000
Retained earnings, December 31	$555,000	$275,000

Boston Bagel Company
Comparative Balance Sheet
December 31, 2000 and 1999

	Dec. 31, 2000	Dec. 31, 1999
Assets		
Current assets:		
Cash	$ 67,000	$ 84,000
Marketable securities	152,000	161,000
Accounts receivable (net)	261,000	295,000
Inventories	325,000	348,000
Prepaid expenses	25,000	22,000
Total current assets	$ 830,000	$ 910,000
Long-term investments	1,000,000	300,000
Property, plant, and equipment (net)	1,675,000	1,290,000
Total assets	$3,505,000	$2,500,000
Liabilities		
Current liabilities	$ 450,000	$ 325,000
Long-term liabilities:		
Mortgage note payable, 10%, due 2005	$ 400,000	—
Bonds payable, 15%, due 2009	600,000	$ 600,000
Total long-term liabilities	$1,000,000	$ 600,000
Total liabilities	$1,450,000	$ 925,000
Stockholders' Equity		
Preferred $6 stock, $100 par	$ 500,000	$ 300,000
Common stock, $10 par	1,000,000	1,000,000
Retained earnings	555,000	275,000
Total stockholders' equity	$2,055,000	$1,575,000
Total liabilities and stockholders' equity	$3,505,000	$2,500,000

Instructions

Determine the following measures for 2000, rounding to the nearest single digit after the decimal point:

1. Working capital
2. Current ratio
3. Acid-test ratio
4. Accounts receivable turnover
5. Number of days' sales in receivables
6. Inventory turnover
7. Number of days' sales in inventory
8. Ratio of fixed assets to long-term liabilities
9. Ratio of liabilities to stockholders' equity
10. Number of times interest charges earned
11. Number of times preferred dividends earned
12. Ratio of net sales to assets
13. Rate earned on total assets
14. Rate earned on stockholders' equity
15. Rate earned on common stockholders' equity
16. Earnings per share on common stock

17. Price-earnings ratio
18. Dividends per share of common stock
19. Dividend yield

Problem 16–5A
Solvency and profitability trend analysis

Objectives 2, 3

Song Shoe Company has provided the following comparative information:

	2000	1999	1998	1997	1996
Net income	$ 600,000	$ 300,000	$ 200,000	$ 100,000	$ 50,000
Income tax expense	150,000	75,000	50,000	25,000	12,500
Interest	140,000	100,000	30,000	20,000	20,000
Average total assets	3,800,000	2,800,000	1,800,000	1,500,000	1,400,000
Average total stockholders' equity	2,400,000	1,800,000	1,500,000	1,300,000	1,200,000

You have been asked to evaluate the historical performance of the company over the last five years. Selected industry ratios have remained relatively steady for the last five years at the following levels:

	1996–2000
Rate earned on total assets	14%
Rate earned on stockholders' equity	18%
Number of times interest charges earned	6.0
Ratio of liabilities to stockholders' equity	0.6

Instructions

1. Prepare four line graphs, with ratio on the vertical axis and years on the horizontal axis for the following four ratios (rounded to two digits after the decimal place):
   a. Rate earned on total assets
   b. Rate earned on stockholders' equity
   c. Number of times interest charges earned
   d. Ratio of liabilities to stockholders' equity (using average balances)
   Display both the company ratio and the industry benchmark on each graph (each graph should have two lines).
2. Prepare an analysis of the graphs in (1).

PROBLEMS SERIES B

Problem 16–1B
Horizontal analysis for income statement

Objective 1

GENERAL LEDGER

✓ 1. Sales, 20% increase

For 1999, Better Biscuit Company reported its most significant increase in net income in years. At the end of the year, John Newton, the president, is presented with the following condensed comparative income statement:

Better Biscuit Company
Comparative Income Statement
For the Years Ended December 31, 2000 and 1999

	2000	1999
Sales	$840,000	$700,000
Sales returns and allowances	5,000	5,000
Net sales	$835,000	$695,000
Cost of goods sold	450,000	400,000
Gross profit	$385,000	$295,000
Selling expenses	$115,000	$100,000
Administrative expenses	49,500	45,000
Total operating expenses	$164,500	$145,000
Income from operations	$220,500	$150,000
Other income	4,500	6,000
Income before income tax	$225,000	$156,000
Income tax expense	70,000	50,000
Net income	$155,000	$106,000

Instructions

1. Prepare a comparative income statement with horizontal analysis for the two-year period, using 1999 as the base year. Round to one digit after the decimal place.
2. To the extent the data permit, comment on the significant relationships revealed by the horizontal analysis prepared in (1).

Problem 16–2B
Vertical analysis for income statement

Objective 1

GENERAL LEDGER
SPREADSHEET

✓ 1. Net income, 2000, 5.4%

For 2000, Stainless Exhaust Systems Inc. initiated a sales promotion campaign that included the expenditure of an additional $50,000 for advertising. At the end of the year, Edmundo Gonzalez, the president, is presented with the following condensed comparative income statement:

Stainless Exhaust Systems Inc.
Comparative Income Statement
For the Years Ended December 31, 2000 and 1999

	2000	1999
Sales	$490,000	$460,000
Sales returns and allowances	10,000	10,000
Net sales	$480,000	$450,000
Cost of goods sold	215,000	200,000
Gross profit	$265,000	$250,000
Selling expenses	$150,000	$100,000
Administrative expenses	85,000	80,000
Total operating expenses	$235,000	$180,000
Income from operations	$ 30,000	$ 70,000
Other income	10,000	9,000
Income before income tax	$ 40,000	$ 79,000
Income tax expense	14,000	30,000
Net income	$ 26,000	$ 49,000

Instructions

1. Prepare a comparative income statement for the two-year period, presenting an analysis of each item in relationship to net sales for each of the years. Round to one digit after the decimal place.
2. To the extent the data permit, comment on the significant relationships revealed by the vertical analysis prepared in (1).

Problem 16–3B
Effect of transactions on current position analysis

Objective 2

✓ 1. Acid-test ratio, 1.8

Data pertaining to the current position of Granular Aggregates Inc. are as follows:

Cash	$143,000
Marketable securities	57,000
Accounts and notes receivable (net)	250,000
Inventories	266,000
Prepaid expenses	9,000
Accounts payable	190,000
Notes payable (short-term)	40,000
Accrued expenses	20,000

Instructions

1. Compute (a) the working capital, (b) the current ratio, and (c) the acid-test ratio.
2. List the following captions on a sheet of paper:

Transaction	Working Capital	Current Ratio	Acid-Test Ratio

Compute the working capital, the current ratio, and the acid-test ratio after each of the following transactions, and record the results in the appropriate columns. Consider each transaction separately and assume that only that transaction affects the data given above. Round to two digits after the decimal point.

a. Sold marketable securities at no gain or loss, $34,000.
b. Paid accounts payable, $60,000.
c. Purchased goods on account, $50,000.
d. Paid notes payable, $20,000.
e. Declared a cash dividend, $15,000.
f. Declared a common stock dividend on common stock, $16,500.
g. Borrowed cash from bank on a long-term note, $120,000.
h. Received cash on account, $86,000.
i. Issued additional shares of stock for cash, $160,000.
j. Paid cash for prepaid expenses, $12,000.

Problem 16–4B
Eighteen measures of solvency and profitability

Objectives 2, 3

HAT
SPREADSHEET

✓ 9. Ratio of liabilities to stock-holders' equity, 0.7

The comparative financial statements of General Grains Company are as follows. The market price of General Grains Company common stock was $18 on December 31, 2000.

General Grains Company
Comparative Income Statement
For the Years Ended December 31, 2000 and 1999

	2000	1999
Sales (all on account)	$5,000,000	$4,200,000
Sales returns and allowances	50,000	50,000
Net sales	$4,950,000	$4,150,000
Cost of goods sold	2,350,000	1,950,000
Gross profit	$2,600,000	$2,200,000
Selling expenses	$1,000,000	$ 950,000
Administrative expenses	700,000	650,000
Total operating expenses	$1,700,000	$1,600,000
Income from operations	$ 900,000	$ 600,000
Other income	80,000	40,000
	$ 980,000	$ 640,000
Other expense (interest)	200,000	120,000
Income before income tax	$ 780,000	$ 520,000
Income tax expense	300,000	200,000
Net income	$ 480,000	$ 320,000

General Grains Company
Comparative Retained Earnings Statement
For the Years Ended December 31, 2000 and 1999

	Dec. 31, 2000	Dec. 31, 1999
Retained earnings, January 1	$350,000	$102,000
Add net income for year	480,000	320,000
Total	$830,000	$422,000
Deduct dividends:		
On preferred stock	$ 48,000	$ 32,000
On common stock	40,000	40,000
Total	$ 88,000	$ 72,000
Retained earnings, December 31	$742,000	$350,000

General Grains Company
Comparative Balance Sheet
December 31, 2000 and 1999

Assets	Dec. 31, 2000	Dec. 31, 1999
Current assets:		
Cash	$ 264,000	$ 124,000
Marketable securities	202,000	182,000
Accounts receivable (net)	364,000	344,000
Inventories	469,000	422,000
Prepaid expenses	31,000	28,000
Total current assets	$1,330,000	$1,100,000
Long-term investments	1,200,000	400,000
Property, plant, and equipment (net)	3,212,000	2,700,000
Total assets	$5,742,000	$4,200,000
Liabilities		
Current liabilities	$ 600,000	$ 450,000
Long-term liabilities:		
Mortgage note payable, 10%, due 2005	$ 800,000	—
Bonds payable, 12%, due 2009	1,000,000	$1,000,000
Total long-term liabilities	$1,800,000	$1,000,000
Total liabilities	$2,400,000	$1,450,000
Stockholders' Equity		
Preferred $8 stock, $100 par	$ 600,000	$ 400,000
Common stock, $10 par	2,000,000	2,000,000
Retained earnings	742,000	350,000
Total stockholders' equity	$3,342,000	$2,750,000
Total liabilities and stockholders' equity	$5,742,000	$4,200,000

Instructions

Determine the following measures for 2000, rounding to nearest single digit after the decimal point:

1. Working capital
2. Current ratio
3. Acid-test ratio
4. Accounts receivable turnover
5. Number of days' sales in receivables
6. Inventory turnover
7. Number of days' sales in inventory
8. Ratio of fixed assets to long-term liabilities
9. Ratio of liabilities to stockholders' equity
10. Number of times interest charges earned
11. Number of times preferred dividends earned
12. Ratio of net sales to assets
13. Rate earned on total assets
14. Rate earned on stockholders' equity
15. Rate earned on common stockholders' equity
16. Earnings per share on common stock
17. Price-earnings ratio
18. Dividends per share of common stock
19. Dividend yield

Problem 16–5B
Solvency and profitability trend analysis

Objectives 2, 3

Asian Arts Company has provided the following comparative information:

	2000	1999	1998	1997	1996
Net income	$ 300,000	$ 500,000	$1,000,000	$ 800,000	$ 500,000
Income tax expense	90,000	150,000	300,000	240,000	150,000
Interest	300,000	200,000	170,000	100,000	50,000
Average total assets	8,600,000	7,300,000	6,500,000	4,800,000	3,500,000
Average total stockholders' equity	5,600,000	5,300,000	4,800,000	3,800,000	3,000,000

You have been asked to evaluate the historical performance of the company over the last five years.

Selected industry ratios have remained relatively steady for the last five years at the following levels:

	1996–2000
Rate earned on total assets	12%
Rate earned on stockholders' equity	15%
Number of times interest charges earned	9.0
Ratio of liabilities to stockholders' equity	0.40

Instructions

1. Prepare four line graphs, with the ratio on the vertical axis and the years on the horizontal axis for the following four ratios (round to two digits after the decimal place):
   a. Rate earned on total assets
   b. Rate earned on stockholders' equity
   c. Number of times interest charges earned
   d. Ratio of liabilities to stockholders' equity (using average balances)
   Display both the company ratio and the industry benchmark on each graph (each graph should have two lines).
2. Prepare an analysis of the graphs in (1).

HERSHEY FOODS CORPORATION PROBLEM

Financial Statement Analysis

HAT

The financial statements for **Hershey Foods Corporation** are presented in Appendix G at the end of the text. The following additional information is available:

Accounts receivable at December 31, 1994	$ 331,670,000
Inventories at December 31, 1994	445,702,000
Total assets at December 31, 1994	2,890,981,000
Stockholders' equity at December 31, 1994	1,441,100,000

Assume that all sales are credit sales.

The makeup of "interest expense, net" is described in Note 6 to the statements. Use only the interest on long-term debt and lease obligations and short-term debt in your computations.

Instructions

1. Determine the following measures for 1996 and 1995:
   a. Working capital
   b. Current ratio
   c. Acid-test ratio
   d. Accounts receivable turnover
   e. Number of days' sales in receivables
   f. Inventory turnover
   g. Number of days' sales in inventory
   h. Ratio of fixed assets (property, plant, and equipment) to long-term liabilities (debt)
   i. Ratio of liabilities to stockholders' equity
   j. Number of times interest charges earned
   k. Ratio of net sales to average total assets
   l. Rate earned on average total assets
   m. Rate earned on average common stockholders' equity
   n. Price-earnings ratio
   o. Dividend yield (on common stock only)
   p. Percentage relationship of net income and net sales

q. Amount of change and percent of change in (1) net sales (revenue for 1996) and (2) selling, marketing, and administrative expense (for 1996)

r. Amount of change and percent of change in net income (for 1996)

2. What conclusions can be drawn from these analyses?

QUICHBOOHS PROBLEM

Vertical Analysis

Use QuickBooks to open the *sample.qbw* file (Larry's Landscaping) for this problem.

1. Use the report feature to print a standard profit and loss report for December 1 to December 15 to your screen. Use the "customize" button to provide a vertical analysis, as a percent of sales, of the standard report.

2. ✏️ Interpret the vertical analysis.

SPECIAL ACTIVITIES

**Activity 16–1
Taylor Equipment
Co.**

*Ethics and professional
conduct in business*

Lee Taylor, president of Taylor Equipment Co., prepared a draft of the President's Letter to be included with Taylor Equipment Co.'s 2000 annual report. The letter mentions a 10% increase in sales and a recent expansion of plant facilities, but fails to mention the net loss of $175,000 for the year. You have been asked to review the letter for inclusion in the annual report.

✏️ How would you respond to the omission of the net loss of $175,000? Specifically, is such an action ethical?

**Activity 16–2
Cascade Brewery**

*Analysis of financing
corporate growth*

Assume that the president of Cascade Brewery made the following statement in the President's Letter to Shareholders:

"The founding family, and majority shareholders, of the company do not believe in using debt to finance future growth. The founding family learned from hard experience during Prohibition and the Great Depression that debt can cause loss of flexibility and eventual loss of corporate control. The company will not place itself at such risk. As such, all future growth will be financed either by stock sales to the public or by internally generated resources."

✏️ As a public shareholder of this company, how would you respond to this policy?

**Activity 16–3
Pinnacle Computer
Company**

*Receivables and inventory
turnover*

Pinnacle Computer Company has completed its fiscal year on December 31, 2000. The auditor, Carol Blake, has approached the CFO, Chase Williams, regarding the year-end receivables and inventory levels of Pinnacle. The following conversation takes place:

Carol: We are beginning our audit of Pinnacle and have prepared ratio analyses to determine if there have been significant changes in operations or financial position. This helps us guide the audit process. This analysis indicates that the inventory turnover has decreased from 5 to 2.8, while the accounts receivable turnover has decreased from 12 to 8. I was wondering if you could explain this change in operations.

Chase: There is little need for concern. The inventory represents computers that we were unable to sell during the holiday buying season. We are confident, however, that we will be able to sell these computers as we move into the next fiscal year.

Carol: What gives you this confidence?

Chase: We will increase our advertising and provide some very attractive price concessions to move these machines. We have no choice. Newer technology is already out there, and we have to unload this inventory.

Carol: . . . and the receivables?

Chase: As you may be aware, the company is under tremendous pressure to expand sales and profits. As a result, we lowered our credit standards to our commercial customers so that we would be able to sell products to a broader customer base. As a result of this policy change, we have been able to expand sales by 35%.

Carol: Your responses have not been reassuring to me.

Chase: I'm a little confused. Assets are good, right? Why don't you look at our current ratio? It has improved, hasn't it? I would think that you would view that very favorably.

> Why is Carol concerned about the inventory and accounts receivable turnover ratios and Chase's responses to them? What action may Carol need to take? How would you respond to Chase's last comment?

**Activity 16–4
Apple Computer
and Dell Computer**
Vertical analysis

The condensed income statements for **Apple Computer Co.** and **Dell Computer Co.** are reproduced below for recent fiscal years:

	Dell Computer Co. For the Year Ended February 2, 1997	Apple Computer Co. For the Year Ended September 27, 1996
Sales (net)	$7,759	$ 9,833
Cost of sales	6,093	8,865
Gross profit	$1,666	$ 968
Selling, general, and administrative expense	826	1,568
Research and development	126	604
Operating income	$ 714	$ (1,204)
Other income and expenses	33	(91)
Income before taxes	$ 747	$ (1,295)
Income tax expense (benefit)	216	(479)
Income before extraordinary items	$ 531	$ (816)

Prepare comparative vertical analyses, rounding to two digits after the decimal point. Interpret the analyses.

**Activity 16–5
Into the Real World**
*Horizontal analysis and
profitability analysis*

Go to the **Microsoft** Web site at **www.microsoft.com** and download Microsoft's comparative income statements for the last three fiscal years as an Excel® file. Next, go to the *Wall Street Journal* and look up Microsoft in the NASDAQ National Market pages. Under this listing, report the price-earnings ratio and dividend yield for Microsoft.

Use the comparative income statement Excel® file to prepare a horizontal analysis for the last two fiscal years (delete the oldest year from the analysis). Use Microsoft's balance sheet and income statement information to determine the rate earned on stockholders' equity for the latest fiscal year. How do these analyses reconcile with Microsoft's price-earnings ratio and dividend yield?

**Activity 16–6
Into the Real World**
*Solvency and profitability
analysis*

One team should obtain the latest annual report for **Wal-Mart Stores Inc.**, and the other team should obtain the latest **Kmart Corp.** annual report. These annual reports can be obtained from a library or the company's 10-K filing with the Securities and Exchange Commission at **www.sec.gov/edgarhp.htm.**

To obtain annual report information, type in the company name on the "Search EDGAR Archives" form. EDGAR will list the reports available for the company. Click on the 10-K (or 10-K405) report for the year you wish to download. If you wish, you can save the whole 10-K report to a file and then open it with your word processor.

Each team should compute the following for their company:

a. Current ratio
b. Inventory turnover
c. Rate earned on stockholders' equity
d. Rate earned on total assets
e. Net income as a percentage of sales
f. Ratio of liabilities to stockholders' equity

As a class, prepare a report comparing the two companies for the latest fiscal period.

ANSWERS TO SELF-EXAMINATION QUESTIONS

Matching

1. H	4. W	7. J	10. Y	13. G	16. Q	18. I
2. P	5. L	8. C	11. N	14. B	17. D	19. O
3. K	6. A	9. R	12. S	15. X		

Multiple Choice

1. **A** Percentage analysis indicating the relationship of the component parts to the total in a financial statement, such as the relationship of current assets to total assets (20% to 100%) in the question, is called vertical analysis (answer A). Percentage analysis of increases and decreases in corresponding items in comparative financial statements is called horizontal analysis (answer B). An example of horizontal analysis would be the presentation of the amount of current assets in the preceding balance sheet, along with the amount of current assets at the end of the current year, with the increase or decrease in current assets between the periods expressed as a percentage. Profitability analysis (answer C) is the analysis of a firm's ability to earn income. Contribution margin analysis (answer D) is discussed in a later managerial accounting chapter.

2. **D** Various solvency measures, categorized as current position analysis, indicate a firm's ability to meet currently maturing obligations. Each measure contributes in the analysis of a firm's current position and is most useful when viewed with other measures and when compared with similar measures for other periods and for other firms. Working capital (answer A) is the excess of current assets over current liabilities; the current ratio (answer B) is the ratio of current assets to current liabilities; and the acid-test ratio (answer C) is the ratio of the sum of cash, receivables, and marketable securities to current liabilities.

3. **D** The ratio of current assets to current liabilities is usually called the current ratio (answer A). It is sometimes called the working capital ratio (answer B) or bankers' ratio (answer C).

4. **C** The ratio of the sum of cash, receivables, and marketable securities (sometimes called quick assets) to current liabilities is called the acid-test ratio (answer C) or quick ratio. The current ratio (answer A), working capital ratio (answer B), and bankers' ratio (answer D) are terms that describe the ratio of current assets to current liabilities.

5. **C** The number of days' sales in inventory (answer C), which is determined by dividing the inventories at the end of the year by the average daily cost of goods sold, expresses the relationship between the cost of goods sold and inventory. It indicates the efficiency in the management of inventory. The working capital ratio (answer A) indicates the ability of the business to meet currently maturing obligations (debt). The acid-test ratio (answer B) indicates the "instant" debt-paying ability of the business. The ratio of fixed assets to long-term liabilities (answer D) indicates the margin of safety for long-term creditors.

Appendices

A. Interest Tables

B. Codes of Professional Ethics

C. Alternative Methods of Recording Deferrals

D. Periodic Inventory Systems for Merchandising Businesses

E. Foreign Currency Transactions

F. Partnerships

G. Hershey Foods Corporation Annual Report

Appendix A: Interest Tables

Present Value of \$1 at Compound Interest Due in n Periods: $p_{\overline{n}|i} = \dfrac{1}{(1 + i)^n}$

$n \backslash i$	5%	5.5%	6%	6.5%	7%	8%
1	0.95238	0.94787	0.94334	0.93897	0.93458	0.92593
2	0.90703	0.89845	0.89000	0.88166	0.87344	0.85734
3	0.86384	0.85161	0.83962	0.82785	0.81630	0.79383
4	0.82270	0.80722	0.79209	0.77732	0.76290	0.73503
5	0.78353	0.76513	0.74726	0.72988	0.71290	0.68058
6	0.74622	0.72525	0.70496	0.68533	0.66634	0.63017
7	0.71068	0.68744	0.66506	0.64351	0.62275	0.58349
8	0.67684	0.65160	0.62741	0.60423	0.58201	0.54027
9	0.64461	0.61763	0.59190	0.56735	0.54393	0.50025
10	0.61391	0.58543	0.55840	0.53273	0.50835	0.46319
11	0.58468	0.55491	0.52679	0.50021	0.47509	0.42888
12	0.55684	0.52598	0.49697	0.46968	0.44401	0.39711
13	0.53032	0.49856	0.46884	0.44102	0.41496	0.36770
14	0.50507	0.47257	0.44230	0.41410	0.38782	0.34046
15	0.48102	0.44793	0.41726	0.38883	0.36245	0.31524
16	0.45811	0.42458	0.39365	0.36510	0.33874	0.29189
17	0.43630	0.40245	0.37136	0.34281	0.31657	0.27027
18	0.41552	0.38147	0.35034	0.32189	0.29586	0.25025
19	0.39573	0.36158	0.33051	0.30224	0.27651	0.23171
20	0.37689	0.34273	0.31180	0.28380	0.25842	0.21455
21	0.35894	0.32486	0.29416	0.26648	0.24151	0.19866
22	0.34185	0.30793	0.27750	0.25021	0.22571	0.18394
23	0.32557	0.29187	0.26180	0.23494	0.21095	0.17032
24	0.31007	0.27666	0.24698	0.22060	0.19715	0.15770
25	0.29530	0.26223	0.23300	0.20714	0.18425	0.14602
26	0.28124	0.24856	0.21981	0.19450	0.17211	0.13520
27	0.26785	0.23560	0.20737	0.18263	0.16093	0.12519
28	0.25509	0.22332	0.19563	0.17148	0.15040	0.11591
29	0.24295	0.21168	0.18456	0.16101	0.14056	0.10733
30	0.23138	0.20064	0.17411	0.15119	0.13137	0.09938
31	0.22036	0.19018	0.16426	0.14196	0.12277	0.09202
32	0.20987	0.18027	0.15496	0.13329	0.11474	0.08520
33	0.19987	0.17087	0.14619	0.12516	0.10724	0.07889
34	0.19036	0.16196	0.13791	0.11752	0.10022	0.07304
35	0.18129	0.15352	0.13010	0.11035	0.09366	0.06764
40	0.14205	0.11746	0.09722	0.08054	0.06678	0.04603
45	0.11130	0.08988	0.07265	0.05879	0.04761	0.03133
50	0.08720	0.06877	0.05429	0.04291	0.03395	0.02132

Present Value of $1 at Compound Interest Due in n Periods: $p_{\overline{n}|i} = \dfrac{1}{(1 + i)^n}$

$n \diagdown i$	9%	10%	11%	12%	13%	14%
1	0.91743	0.90909	0.90090	0.89286	0.88496	0.87719
2	0.84168	0.82645	0.81162	0.79719	0.78315	0.76947
3	0.77218	0.75132	0.73119	0.71178	0.69305	0.67497
4	0.70842	0.68301	0.65873	0.63552	0.61332	0.59208
5	0.64993	0.62092	0.59345	0.56743	0.54276	0.51937
6	0.59627	0.56447	0.53464	0.50663	0.48032	0.45559
7	0.54703	0.51316	0.48166	0.45235	0.42506	0.39964
8	0.50187	0.46651	0.43393	0.40388	0.37616	0.35056
9	0.46043	0.42410	0.39092	0.36061	0.33288	0.30751
10	0.42241	0.38554	0.35218	0.32197	0.29459	0.26974
11	0.38753	0.35049	0.31728	0.28748	0.26070	0.23662
12	0.35554	0.31863	0.28584	0.25668	0.23071	0.20756
13	0.32618	0.28966	0.25751	0.22917	0.20416	0.18207
14	0.29925	0.26333	0.23199	0.20462	0.18068	0.15971
15	0.27454	0.23939	0.20900	0.18270	0.15989	0.14010
16	0.25187	0.21763	0.18829	0.16312	0.14150	0.12289
17	0.23107	0.19784	0.16963	0.14564	0.12522	0.10780
18	0.21199	0.17986	0.15282	0.13004	0.11081	0.09456
19	0.19449	0.16351	0.13768	0.11611	0.09806	0.08295
20	0.17843	0.14864	0.12403	0.10367	0.08678	0.07276
21	0.16370	0.13513	0.11174	0.09256	0.07680	0.06383
22	0.15018	0.12285	0.10067	0.08264	0.06796	0.05599
23	0.13778	0.11168	0.09069	0.07379	0.06014	0.04911
24	0.12640	0.10153	0.08170	0.06588	0.05323	0.04308
25	0.11597	0.09230	0.07361	0.05882	0.04710	0.03779
26	0.10639	0.08390	0.06631	0.05252	0.04168	0.03315
27	0.09761	0.07628	0.05974	0.04689	0.03689	0.02908
28	0.08955	0.06934	0.05382	0.04187	0.03264	0.02551
29	0.08216	0.06304	0.04849	0.03738	0.02889	0.02237
30	0.07537	0.05731	0.04368	0.03338	0.02557	0.01963
31	0.06915	0.05210	0.03935	0.02980	0.02262	0.01722
32	0.06344	0.04736	0.03545	0.02661	0.02002	0.01510
33	0.05820	0.04306	0.03194	0.02376	0.01772	0.01325
34	0.05331	0.03914	0.02878	0.02121	0.01568	0.01162
35	0.04899	0.03558	0.02592	0.01894	0.01388	0.01019
40	0.03184	0.02210	0.01538	0.01075	0.00753	0.00529
45	0.02069	0.01372	0.00913	0.00610	0.00409	0.00275
50	0.01345	0.00852	0.00542	0.00346	0.00222	0.00143

Present Value of Ordinary Annuity of $1 per Period: $p_{\overline{n}|i} = \dfrac{1 - \dfrac{1}{(1 + i)^n}}{i}$

n \ i	5%	5.5%	6%	6.5%	7%	8%
1	0.95238	0.94787	0.94340	0.93897	0.93458	0.92593
2	1.85941	1.84632	1.83339	1.82063	1.80802	1.78326
3	2.72325	2.69793	2.67301	2.64848	2.62432	2.57710
4	3.54595	3.50515	3.46511	3.42580	3.38721	3.31213
5	4.32948	4.27028	4.21236	4.15568	4.10020	3.99271
6	5.07569	4.99553	4.91732	4.84101	4.76654	4.62288
7	5.78637	5.68297	5.58238	5.48452	5.38923	5.20637
8	6.46321	6.33457	6.20979	6.08875	5.97130	5.74664
9	7.10782	6.95220	6.80169	6.65610	6.51523	6.24689
10	7.72174	7.53763	7.36009	7.18883	7.02358	6.71008
11	8.30641	8.09254	7.88688	7.68904	7.49867	7.13896
12	8.86325	8.61852	8.38384	8.15873	7.94269	7.53608
13	9.39357	9.11708	8.85268	8.59974	8.35765	7.90378
14	9.89864	9.58965	9.29498	9.01384	8.74547	8.22424
15	10.37966	10.03758	9.71225	9.40267	9.10791	8.55948
16	10.83777	10.46216	10.10590	9.76776	9.44665	8.85137
17	11.27407	10.86461	10.47726	10.11058	9.76322	9.12164
18	11.68959	11.24607	10.82760	10.43247	10.05909	9.37189
19	12.08532	11.60765	11.15812	10.73471	10.33560	9.60360
20	12.46221	11.95038	11.46992	11.01851	10.59401	9.81815
21	12.82115	12.27524	11.76408	11.28498	10.83553	10.01680
22	13.16300	12.58317	12.04158	11.53520	11.06124	10.20074
23	13.48857	12.87504	12.30338	11.77014	11.27219	10.37106
24	13.79864	13.15170	12.55036	11.99074	11.46933	10.52876
25	14.09394	13.41393	12.78336	12.19788	11.65358	10.67478
26	14.37518	13.66250	13.00317	12.39237	11.82578	10.80998
27	14.64303	13.89810	13.21053	12.57500	11.98671	10.93516
28	14.89813	14.12142	13.40616	12.74648	12.13711	11.05108
29	15.14107	14.33310	13.59072	12.90749	12.27767	11.15841
30	15.37245	14.53375	13.76483	13.05868	12.40904	11.25778
31	15.59281	14.72393	13.92909	13.20063	12.53181	11.34980
32	15.80268	14.90420	14.08404	13.33393	12.64656	11.43500
33	16.00255	15.07507	14.23023	13.45909	12.75379	11.51389
34	16.19290	15.23703	14.36814	13.57661	12.85401	11.58693
35	16.37420	15.39055	14.49825	13.68696	12.94767	11.65457
40	17.15909	16.04612	15.04630	14.14553	13.33171	11.92461
45	17.77407	16.54773	15.45583	14.48023	13.60552	12.10840
50	18.25592	16.93152	15.76186	14.72452	13.80075	12.23348

Present Value of Ordinary Annuity of $1 per Period: $p_{\overline{n}|i} = \dfrac{1 - \dfrac{1}{(1 + i)^n}}{i}$

n \ i	9%	10%	11%	12%	13%	14%
1	0.91743	0.90909	0.90090	0.89286	0.88496	0.87719
2	1.75911	1.73554	1.71252	1.69005	1.66810	1.64666
3	2.53130	2.48685	2.44371	2.40183	2.36115	2.32163
4	3.23972	3.16986	3.10245	3.03735	2.97447	2.91371
5	3.88965	3.79079	3.69590	3.60478	3.51723	3.43308
6	4.48592	4.35526	4.23054	4.11141	3.99755	3.88867
7	5.03295	4.86842	4.71220	4.56376	4.42261	4.28830
8	5.53482	5.33493	5.14612	4.96764	4.79677	4.63886
9	5.99525	5.75902	5.53705	5.32825	5.13166	4.94637
10	6.41766	6.14457	5.88923	5.65022	5.42624	5.21612
11	6.80519	6.49506	6.20652	5.93770	5.68694	5.45273
12	7.16072	6.81369	6.49236	6.19437	5.91765	5.66029
13	7.48690	7.10336	6.74987	6.42355	6.12181	5.84236
14	7.78615	7.36669	6.96187	6.62817	6.30249	6.00207
15	8.06069	7.60608	7.19087	6.81086	6.46238	6.14217
16	8.31256	7.82371	7.37916	6.97399	6.60388	6.26506
17	8.54363	8.02155	7.54879	7.11963	6.72909	6.37286
18	8.75562	8.20141	7.70162	7.24967	6.83991	6.46742
19	8.95012	8.36492	7.83929	7.36578	6.93797	6.55037
20	9.12855	8.51356	7.96333	7.46944	7.02475	6.62313
21	9.29224	8.64869	8.07507	7.56200	7.10155	6.68696
22	9.44242	8.77154	8.17574	7.64465	7.16951	6.74294
23	9.58021	8.88322	8.26643	7.71843	7.22966	6.79206
24	9.70661	8.98474	8.34814	7.78432	7.28288	6.83514
25	9.82258	9.07704	8.42174	7.84314	7.32998	6.87293
26	9.92897	9.16094	8.48806	7.89566	7.37167	6.90608
27	10.02658	9.23722	8.54780	7.94255	7.40856	6.93515
28	10.11613	9.30657	8.60162	7.98442	7.44120	6.96066
29	10.19828	9.36961	8.65011	8.02181	7.47009	6.98304
30	10.27365	9.42691	8.69379	8.05518	7.49565	7.00266
31	10.34280	9.47901	8.73315	8.08499	7.51828	7.01988
32	10.40624	9.52638	8.76860	8.11159	7.53830	7.03498
33	10.46444	9.56943	8.80054	8.13535	7.55602	7.04823
34	10.51784	9.60858	8.82932	8.15656	7.57170	7.05985
35	10.56682	9.64416	8.85524	8.17550	7.58557	7.07005
40	10.75736	9.77905	8.95105	8.24378	7.63438	7.10504
45	10.88118	9.86281	9.00791	8.28252	7.66086	7.12322
50	10.96168	9.91481	9.04165	8.30450	7.67524	7.13266

Future Amount of $1 at Compound Interest Due in n Periods: $A_{\overline{n}|i} = (1 + i)^n$

$n \backslash i$	5%	5.5%	6%	6.5%	7%	8%
1	1.05000	1.05500	1.06000	1.06500	1.07000	1.08000
2	1.10250	1.11303	1.12360	1.13423	1.14490	1.16640
3	1.15762	1.17424	1.19102	1.20795	1.22504	1.25971
4	1.21551	1.23882	1.26248	1.28647	1.31080	1.36049
5	1.27628	1.30696	1.33823	1.37009	1.40255	1.46933
6	1.34100	1.37884	1.41852	1.45914	1.50073	1.58687
7	1.40710	1.45468	1.50363	1.55399	1.60578	1.71382
8	1.54347	1.53469	1.59385	1.65500	1.71819	1.85093
9	1.55133	1.61909	1.68948	1.76257	1.83846	1.99900
10	1.62890	1.70814	1.79085	1.87714	1.96715	2.15892
11	1.71034	1.80209	1.89830	1.99915	2.10485	2.33164
12	1.79586	1.90121	2.01220	2.12910	2.25219	2.51817
13	1.88565	2.00577	2.13293	2.26749	2.40984	2.71962
14	1.97993	2.11609	2.26091	2.41487	2.57853	2.93719
15	2.07893	2.23248	2.39656	2.57184	2.75903	3.17217
16	2.18288	2.35526	2.54035	2.73901	2.95216	3.42594
17	2.29202	2.48480	2.69277	2.91705	3.15882	3.70002
18	2.40662	2.62147	2.85434	3.10665	3.37993	3.99602
19	2.52695	2.76565	3.02560	3.30859	3.61653	4.31570
20	2.65330	2.91776	3.20714	3.52365	3.86968	4.66096
21	2.78596	3.07823	3.39956	3.75268	4.14056	5.03383
22	2.92526	3.24754	3.60354	3.99661	4.43040	5.43654
23	3.07152	3.42615	3.81975	4.25639	4.74053	5.87146
24	3.22510	3.61459	4.04894	4.53305	5.07237	6.34118
25	3.38636	3.81339	4.29187	4.82770	5.42743	6.84848
26	3.55567	4.02313	4.54938	5.14150	5.80735	7.39635
27	3.73346	4.24440	4.82235	5.47570	6.21387	7.98806
28	3.92013	4.47784	5.11169	5.83162	6.64884	8.62711
29	4.11614	4.72412	5.41839	6.21067	7.11426	9.31728
30	4.32194	4.98395	5.74349	6.61437	7.61226	10.06266
31	4.53804	5.25807	6.08810	7.04430	8.14511	10.86767
32	4.76494	5.54726	6.45339	7.50218	8.71527	11.73708
33	5.00319	5.85236	6.84059	7.98982	9.32534	12.67605
34	5.25335	6.17424	7.25102	8.50916	9.97811	13.69013
35	5.51602	6.51383	7.68609	9.06225	10.67658	14.78534
40	7.03999	8.51331	10.28572	12.41607	14.97446	21.72452
45	8.98501	11.12655	13.76461	17.01110	21.00245	31.92045
50	11.46740	14.54196	18.42015	23.30668	29.45702	46.90161

Future Amount of $1 at Compound Interest Due in n Periods: $A_{\overline{n}\backslash i} = (1 + i)^n$

n \ i	9%	10%	11%	12%	13%	14%
1	1.09000	1.10000	1.11000	1.12000	1.13000	1.14000
2	1.18810	1.21000	1.23210	1.25440	1.27690	1.29960
3	1.29503	1.33100	1.36763	1.40493	1.44290	1.48154
4	1.41158	1.46410	1.51807	1.57352	1.63047	1.68896
5	1.53862	1.61051	1.68506	1.76234	1.84244	1.92541
6	1.67710	1.77156	1.87041	1.97382	2.08195	2.19497
7	1.82804	1.94872	2.07616	2.21068	2.35261	2.50227
8	1.99256	2.14359	2.30454	2.47596	2.65844	2.85259
9	2.17189	2.35795	2.55804	2.77308	3.00404	3.25195
10	2.36736	2.59374	2.83942	3.10585	3.39457	3.70722
11	2.58043	2.85312	3.15176	3.47855	3.83586	4.22623
12	2.81266	3.13843	3.49845	3.89598	4.33452	4.81790
13	3.06580	3.45227	3.88328	4.36349	4.89801	5.49241
14	3.34173	3.79750	4.31044	4.88711	5.53475	6.26135
15	3.64248	4.17725	4.78459	5.47357	6.25427	7.13794
16	3.97031	4.59497	5.31089	6.13039	7.06733	8.13725
17	4.32763	5.05447	5.89509	6.86604	7.98608	9.27646
18	4.71712	5.55992	6.54355	7.68997	9.02427	10.57517
19	5.14166	6.11591	7.26334	8.61276	10.19742	12.05569
20	5.60441	6.72750	8.06231	9.64629	11.52309	13.74349
21	6.10881	7.40025	8.94917	10.80385	13.02109	15.66758
22	6.65860	8.14028	9.93357	12.10031	14.71383	17.86104
23	7.25787	8.95430	11.02627	13.55235	16.62663	20.36158
24	7.91108	9.84973	12.23916	15.17863	18.78809	23.21221
25	8.62308	10.83471	13.58546	17.00006	21.23054	26.46192
26	9.39916	11.91818	15.07986	19.04007	23.99051	30.16658
27	10.24508	13.10999	16.73865	21.32488	27.10928	34.38991
28	11.16714	14.42099	18.57990	23.88387	30.63349	39.20449
29	12.17218	15.86309	20.62369	26.74993	34.61584	44.69312
30	13.26768	17.44940	22.89230	29.95992	39.11590	50.95016
31	14.46177	19.19434	25.41045	33.55511	44.20096	58.08318
32	15.76333	21.11378	28.20560	37.58173	49.94709	66.21483
33	17.18203	23.22515	31.30821	42.09153	56.44021	75.48490
34	18.72841	25.54767	34.75212	47.14252	63.77744	86.05279
35	20.41397	28.10244	38.57485	52.79962	72.06851	98.10018
40	31.40942	45.25926	65.00087	93.05097	132.78155	188.88351
45	48.32729	72.89048	109.53024	163.98760	244.64140	363.67907
50	74.35752	117.39085	184.56483	289.00219	450.73593	700.23299

Future Amount of Ordinary Annuity of $1 per Period: $A_{\overline{n}|i} = (1 + i)^n - 1/i$

n \ i	5%	5.5%	6%	6.5%	7%	8%
1	1.00000	1.00000	1.00000	1.00000	1.00000	1.00000
2	2.05000	2.05500	2.06000	2.06500	2.07000	2.08000
3	3.15250	3.16802	3.18360	3.19922	3.21490	3.24640
4	4.31012	4.34227	4.37462	4.40717	4.43994	4.50611
5	5.52563	5.58109	5.63709	5.69364	5.75074	5.86660
6	6.80191	6.88805	6.97532	7.06373	7.15329	7.33593
7	8.14201	8.26689	8.39384	8.52287	8.65402	8.92280
8	9.54911	9.72157	9.89747	10.07688	10.25980	10.63663
9	11.02656	11.25626	11.49132	11.73185	11.97799	12.48756
10	12.57789	12.87535	13.18080	13.49442	13.81645	14.48656
11	14.20679	14.58350	14.97184	15.37156	15.78360	16.64549
12	15.91713	16.38559	16.86994	17.37071	17.88845	18.97713
13	17.71298	18.28680	18.88214	19.49981	20.14064	21.49530
14	19.59863	20.29257	21.01505	21.76730	22.55049	24.21492
15	21.57856	22.40866	23.27597	24.18217	25.12902	27.15211
16	23.65749	24.64114	25.67253	26.75401	27.88805	30.32428
17	25.84037	28.99640	28.21288	29.49302	30.84022	33.75023
18	28.13238	29.48120	30.90565	32.41007	33.99903	37.45024
19	30.53900	32.10267	33.75999	35.51672	37.37896	41.44626
20	33.06595	34.86832	36.78559	38.82531	40.99549	45.76196
21	35.71925	37.78608	39.99273	42.34895	44.86518	50.42292
22	38.50521	40.86431	43.39229	46.10164	49.00574	55.45676
23	41.43048	44.11185	46.99583	50.09824	53.43614	60.89330
24	44.50200	47.53800	50.81558	54.35463	58.17667	66.76476
25	47.72710	51.15259	54.86451	58.88768	63.24904	73.10594
26	51.11345	54.96598	59.15638	63.71538	68.67647	79.95442
27	54.66913	58.98911	63.70577	68.85688	74.48382	87.35077
28	58.40258	63.23351	68.52811	74.33257	80.69769	95.33883
29	62.32271	67.71135	73.62980	80.16419	87.34653	103.96594
30	66.43885	72.43548	79.05819	86.37486	94.46079	113.28321
31	70.76079	77.41943	84.80168	92.98923	102.07304	123.34587
32	75.29883	82.67750	90.88978	100.03353	110.21815	134.21354
33	80.06377	88.22476	97.34316	107.53571	118.93342	145.95062
34	85.06696	94.07712	104.18376	115.52553	128.25876	158.62667
35	90.32031	100.25136	111.43478	124.03469	138.23688	172.31680
40	120.79977	136.60561	154.76197	175.63192	199.63511	259.05652
45	159.70016	184.11917	212.74351	246.32459	285.74931	386.50562
50	209.34800	246.21748	290.33591	343.17967	406.52893	573.77016

Future Amount of Ordinary Annuity of $1 per Period: $A_{\overline{n}|i} = \dfrac{(1 + i)^n - 1}{i}$

n \ i	9%	10%	11%	12%	13%	14%
1	1.00000	1.00000	1.00000	1.00000	1.00000	1.00000
2	2.09000	2.10000	2.11000	2.12000	2.13000	2.14000
3	3.27810	3.31000	3.34210	3.37440	3.40690	3.43960
4	4.57313	4.64100	4.70973	4.77933	4.84980	4.92114
5	5.98471	6.10510	6.22780	6.35285	6.48027	6.61010
6	7.52334	7.71561	7.91286	8.11519	8.32271	8.53552
7	9.20044	9.48717	9.78327	10.08901	10.40466	10.73049
8	11.02847	11.43589	11.85943	12.29969	12.75726	13.23276
9	13.02104	13.57948	14.16397	14.77566	15.41571	16.08535
10	15.19293	15.93742	16.72201	17.54874	18.41975	19.33730
11	17.56029	18.53117	19.56143	20.65458	21.81432	23.04452
12	20.14072	21.38428	22.71319	24.13313	25.65018	27.27075
13	22.95338	24.52271	26.21164	28.02911	29.98470	32.08865
14	26.01919	27.97498	30.09492	32.39260	34.88271	37.58107
15	29.36092	31.77248	34.40536	37.27972	40.41746	43.84241
16	33.00340	35.94973	39.18995	42.75328	46.67173	50.98035
17	36.97370	40.54470	44.50084	48.88367	53.73906	59.11760
18	41.30134	45.59917	50.39594	55.74972	61.72514	68.39407
19	46.01846	51.15909	56.93949	63.43968	70.74941	78.96923
20	51.16012	57.27500	64.20283	72.05244	80.94683	91.02493
21	56.76453	64.00250	72.26514	81.69874	92.46992	104.76842
22	62.87334	71.40275	81.21431	92.50258	105.49101	120.43600
23	69.53194	79.54302	91.14788	104.60289	120.20484	138.29704
24	76.78981	88.49733	102.17415	118.15524	136.83147	158.65862
25	84.70090	98.34706	114.41331	133.33387	155.61956	181.87083
26	93.32398	109.18176	127.99877	150.33393	176.85010	208.33274
27	102.72314	121.09994	143.07864	169.37401	200.84061	238.49933
28	112.96822	134.20994	159.81729	190.69889	227.94989	272.88923
29	124.13536	148.63093	178.39719	214.58275	258.58338	312.09373
30	136.30754	164.49402	199.02088	241.33268	293.19922	356.78685
31	149.57522	181.94342	221.91317	271.29261	332.31511	407.73701
32	164.03699	201.13777	247.32362	304.84772	376.51608	465.82019
33	179.80032	222.25154	275.52922	342.42945	426.46317	532.03501
34	196.98234	245.47670	306.83744	384.52098	482.90338	607.51991
35	215.71076	271.02437	341.58955	431.66350	546.68082	693.57270
40	337.88244	442.59256	581.82607	767.09142	1013.70424	1342.02510
45	525.85873	718.90484	986.63856	1358.23003	1874.16463	2590.56480
50	815.08356	1163.90853	1668.77115	2400.01825	3459.50712	4994.52135

Appendix B: Codes of Professional Ethics for Accountants

In recent years, governments, businesses, and the public have given increased attention to ethical conduct. They have insisted upon a level of human behavior that goes beyond that required by laws and regulations. Thus many businesses, as well as professional groups (such as accountants) and governmental organizations, have established standards of ethical conduct. This text emphasizes the ethical conduct of accountants, who serve various business interests as well as the public.

This appendix sets forth the standards of professional conduct expected of accountants in public accounting and private accounting. For accountants employed in public accounting, the American Institute of Certified Public Accountants' *Code of Professional Conduct* is presented.[1] For accountants employed in private accounting, the Institute of Management Accountants' *Standards of Ethical Conduct for Management Accountants* is presented as a guide to professional conduct.[2]

Supplementing the codes of professional ethics are ethics discussion cases that appear at the end of each chapter. These cases represent "real world" examples of ethical issues facing accountants. It should be noted that codes of professional ethics are general guides to good behavior and their application to specific situations often requires the exercise of professional judgment. In some cases, the line between right and wrong may be quite fine, and reasonable people may disagree. In addition, business is dynamic and everchanging, and what society considers to be acceptable behavior changes from time to time.

Code of Professional Conduct

Composition, Applicability, and Compliance

The Code of Professional Conduct of the American Institute of Certified Public Accountants consists of two sections—(1) the Principles and (2) the Rules. The Principles provide the framework for the Rules, which govern the performance of professional services by members. The Council of the American Institute of Certified Public Accountants is authorized to designate bodies to promulgate technical standards under the Rules, and the bylaws require adherence to those Rules and standards.

The Code of Professional Conduct was adopted by the membership to provide guidance and rules to all members—those in public practice, in industry, in government, and in education—in the performance of their professional responsibilities.

Compliance with the Code of Professional Conduct, as with all standards in an open society, depends primarily on members' understanding and voluntary actions, secondarily on reinforcement by peers and public opinion, and ultimately on disciplinary proceedings, when necessary, against members who fail to comply with the Rules.

Other Guidance

The Principles and Rules as set forth herein are further amplified by interpretations and rulings contained in *AICPA Professional Standards* (Volume 2).

Interpretations of Rules of Conduct consists of interpretations which have been adopted, after exposure to state societies, state boards, practice units, and other interested parties, by the professional ethics division's executive committee to provide guidelines as to the scope and application of the Rules but are not intended to limit

---

[1] *Code of Professional Conduct* (New York: American Institute of Certified Public Accountants, 1994), pp. 3–8.

[2] *Standards of Ethical Conduct for Management Accountants*, Institute of Management Accountants, Montvale, New Jersey, 1994, pp. 1–2.

such scope or application. A member who departs from such guidelines shall have the burden of justifying such departure in any disciplinary hearing.

Ethics Rulings consist of formal rulings made by the professional ethics division's executive committee after exposure to state societies, state boards, practice units, and other interested parties. These rulings summarize the application of Rules of Conduct and interpretations to a particular set of factual circumstances. Members who depart from such rulings in similar circumstances will be requested to justify such departures.

Publication of an interpretation or ethics ruling in the *Journal of Accountancy* constitutes notice to members. Hence, the effective date of the pronouncement is the last day of the month in which the pronouncement is published in the *Journal of Accountancy*. The professional ethics division will take into consideration the time that would have been reasonable for the member to comply with the pronouncement.

Members should also consult, if applicable, the ethical standards of their state CPA society, state board of accountancy, the Securities and Exchange Commission, and any other governmental agency which may regulate their client's business or use their reports to evaluate the client's compliance with applicable laws and related regulations.

Section I—Principles

Preamble

Membership in the American Institute of Certified Public Accountants is voluntary. By accepting membership, a certified public accountant assumes an obligation of self-discipline above and beyond the requirements of laws and regulations.

These Principles of the Code of Professional Conduct of the American Institute of Certified Public Accountants express the profession's recognition of its responsibilities to the public, to clients, and to colleagues. They guide members in the performance of their professional responsibilities and express the basic tenets of ethical and professional conduct. The Principles call for an unswerving commitment to honorable behavior, even at the sacrifice of personal advantage.

Article I—Responsibilities

In carrying out their responsibilities as professionals, members should exercise sensitive professional and moral judgments in all their activities.

As professionals, certified public accountants perform an essential role in society. Consistent with that role, members of the American Institute of Certified Public Accountants have responsibilities to all those who use their professional services. Members also have a continuing responsibility to cooperate with each other to improve the art of accounting, maintain the public's confidence, and carry out the profession's special responsibilities for self-governance. The collective efforts of all members are required to maintain and enhance the traditions of the profession.

Article II—The Public Interest

Members should accept the obligation to act in a way that will serve the public interest, honor the public trust, and demonstrate commitment to professionalism.

A distinguishing mark of a profession is acceptance of its responsibility to the public. The accounting profession's public consists of clients, credit grantors, governments, employers, investors, the business and financial community, and others who rely on the objectivity and integrity of certified public accountants to maintain the orderly functioning of commerce. This reliance imposes a public interest responsibility on certified public accountants. The public interest is defined as the collective well-being of the community of people and institutions the profession serves.

In discharging their professional responsibilities, members may encounter conflicting pressures from among each of those groups. In resolving those conflicts, members should act with integrity, guided by the precept that when members fulfill their responsibility to the public, clients' and employers' interests are best served.

Those who rely on certified public accountants expect them to discharge their responsibilities with integrity, objectivity, due professional care, and a genuine interest in serving the public. They are expected to provide quality services, enter into fee arrangements, and offer a range of services—all in a manner that demonstrates a level of professionalism consistent with these Principles of the Code of Professional Conduct.

All who accept membership in the American Institute of Certified Public Accountants commit themselves to honor the public trust. In return for the faith that the public reposes in them, members should seek continually to demonstrate their dedication to professional excellence.

Article III—Integrity

To maintain and broaden public confidence, members should perform all professional responsibilities with the highest sense of integrity.

Integrity is an element of character fundamental to professional recognition. It is the quality from which the public trust derives and the benchmark against which a member must ultimately test all decisions.

Integrity requires a member to be, among other things, honest and candid within the constraints of client confidentiality. Service and the public trust should not be subordinated to personal gain and advantage. Integrity can accommodate the inadvertent error and the honest difference of opinion; it cannot accommodate deceit or subordination of principle.

Integrity is measured in terms of what is right and just. In the absence of specific rules, standards, or guidance, or in the face of conflicting opinions, a member should test decisions and deeds by asking: "Am I doing what a person of integrity would do? Have I retained my integrity?" Integrity requires a member to observe both the form and the spirit of technical and ethical standards; circumvention of those standards constitutes subordination of judgment.

Integrity also requires a member to observe the principles of objectivity and independence and of due care.

Article IV—Objectivity and Independence

A member should maintain objectivity and be free of conflicts of interest in discharging professional responsibilities. A member in public practice should be independent in fact and appearance when providing auditing and other attestation services.

Objectivity is a state of mind, a quality that lends value to a member's services. It is a distinguishing feature of the profession. The principle of objectivity imposes the obligation to be impartial, intellectually honest, and free of conflicts of interest. Independence precludes relationships that may appear to impair a member's objectivity in rendering attestation services.

Members often serve multiple interests in many different capacities and must demonstrate their objectivity in varying circumstances. Members in public practice render attest, tax, and management advisory services. Other members prepare financial statements in the employment of others, perform internal auditing services, and serve in financial and management capacities in industry, education, and government. They also educate and train those who aspire to admission into the profession. Regardless of service or capacity, members should protect the integrity of their work, maintain objectivity, and avoid any subordination of their judgment.

For a member in public practice, the maintenance of objectivity and independence requires a continuing assessment of client relationships and public responsibility. Such a member who provides auditing and other attestation services should be independent in fact and appearance. In providing all other services, a member should maintain objectivity and avoid conflicts of interest.

Although members not in public practice cannot maintain the appearance of independence, they nevertheless have the responsibility to maintain objectivity in rendering professional services. Members employed by others to prepare financial statements or to perform auditing, tax, or consulting services are charged with the same responsibility for objectivity as members in public practice and must be scrupulous in their application of generally accepted accounting principles and candid in all their dealings with members in public practice.

Activity V—Due Care

A member should observe the profession's technical and ethical standards, strive continually to improve competence and the quality of services, and discharge professional responsibility to the best of the member's ability.

The quest for excellence is the essence of due care. Due care requires a member to discharge professional responsibilities with competence and diligence. It imposes the obligation to perform professional services to the best of a member's ability with concern for the best interest of those for whom the services are performed and consistent with the profession's responsibility to the public.

Competence is derived from a synthesis of education and experience. It begins with a mastery of the common body of knowledge required for designation as a certified public accountant. The maintenance of competence requires a commitment to learning and professional improvement that must continue throughout a member's professional life. It is a member's individual responsibility. In all engagements and in all responsibilities, each member should undertake to achieve a level of competence that will assure that the quality of the member's services meets the high level of professionalism required by these Principles.

Competence represents the attainment and maintenance of a level of understanding and knowledge that enables a member to render services with facility and acumen. It also establishes the limitations of a member's capabilities by dictating that consultation or referral may be required when a professional engagement exceeds the personal competence of a member or a member's firm. Each member is responsible for assessing his or her own competence—of evaluating whether education, experience, and judgment are adequate for the responsibility to be assumed.

Members should be diligent in discharging responsibilities to clients, employers, and the public. Diligence imposes the responsibility to render services promptly and carefully, to be thorough, and to observe applicable technical and ethical standards.

Due care requires a member to plan and supervise adequately any professional activity for which he or she is responsible.

Article VI—Scope and Nature of Services

A member in public practice should observe the Principles of the Code of Professional Conduct in determining the scope and nature of services to be provided.

The public interest aspect of certified public accountants' services requires that such services be consistent with acceptable professional behavior for certified public accountants. Integrity requires that service and the public trust not be subordinated to personal gain and advantage. Objectivity and independence require that members be free from conflicts of interest in discharging professional responsibilities. Due care requires that services be provided with competence and diligence.

Each of these Principles should be considered by members in determining whether or not to provide specific services in individual circumstances. In some instances, they may represent an overall constraint on the nonaudit services that might be offered to a specific client. No hard-and-fast rules can be developed to help members reach these judgments, but they must be satisfied that they are meeting the spirit of the Principles in this regard.

In order to accomplish this, members should:

- Practice in firms that have in place internal quality-control procedures to ensure that services are competently delivered and adequately supervised.

- Determine, in their individual judgments, whether the scope and nature of other services provided to an audit client would create a conflict of interest in the performance of the audit function for that client.
- Assess, in their individual judgments, whether an activity is consistent with their role as professionals (for example, Is such activity a reasonable extension or variation of existing services offered by the member or others in the profession?).

Standards of Ethical Conduct for Management Accountants

Management accountants have an obligation to the organizations they serve, their profession, the public, and themselves to maintain the highest standards of ethical conduct. In recognition of this obligation, the Institute of Management Accountants has promulgated the following standards of ethical conduct for management accountants. Adherence to these standards is integral to achieving the *Objectives of Management Accounting.*[3] Management accountants shall not commit acts contrary to these standards nor shall they condone the commission of such acts by others within their organizations.

Competence

Management accountants have a responsibility to:

- Maintain an appropriate level of professional competence by ongoing development of their knowledge and skills.
- Perform their professional duties in accordance with relevant laws, regulations, and technical standards.
- Prepare complete and clear reports and recommendations after appropriate analyses of relevant and reliable information.

Confidentiality

Management accountants have a responsibility to:

- Refrain from disclosing confidential information acquired in the course of their work except when authorized, unless legally obligated to do so.
- Inform subordinates as appropriate regarding the confidentiality of information acquired in the course of their work and monitor their activities to assure the maintenance of that confidentiality.
- Refrain from using or appearing to use confidential information acquired in the course of their work for unethical or illegal advantage either personally or through third parties.

Integrity

Management accountants have a responsibility to:

- Avoid actual or apparent conflicts of interest and advise all appropriate parties of any potential conflict.
- Refrain from engaging in any activity that would prejudice their ability to carry out their duties ethically.
- Refuse any gift, favor, or hospitality that would influence or would appear to influence their actions.
- Refrain from either actively or passively subverting the attainment of the organization's legitimate and ethical objectives.
- Recognize and communicate professional limitations or other constraints that would preclude responsible judgment or successful performance of an activity.

---

[3] National Association of Accountants, *Statements on Management Accounting: Objectives of Management Accounting,* Statement No. 1B, New York, N.Y., June 17, 1982.

- Communicate unfavorable as well as favorable information and professional judgments or opinions.
- Refrain from engaging in or supporting any activity that would discredit the profession.

Objectivity

Management accountants have a responsibility to:

- Communicate information fairly and objectively.
- Disclose fully all relevant information that could reasonably be expected to influence an intended user's understanding of the reports, comments, and recommendations presented.

Appendix C: Alternative Methods of Recording Deferrals

As discussed in Chapter 3, deferrals are created by recording a transaction in a way that delays or defers the recognition of an expense or a revenue. Deferrals may be either deferred expenses (prepaid expenses) or deferred revenues (unearned revenues).

In Chapter 2, deferred expenses (prepaid expenses) were debited to an *asset* account at the time of payment. As an alternative, deferred expenses may be debited to an *expense* account at the time of payment. In Chapter 2, deferred revenues (unearned revenues) were credited to a *liability* account at the time of receipt. As an alternative, deferred revenues may be credited to a *revenue* account at the time of receipt. This appendix describes and illustrates these alternative methods of recording deferred expenses and deferred revenues.

Deferred Expenses (Prepaid Expenses)

As a basis for illustrating the alternative methods of recording deferred expenses, the insurance premium paid by Computer King in Chapter 2 is used. The amounts related to this insurance are as follows:

Prepayment of insurance for 24 months, starting December 1	$2,400
Insurance premium expired during December	100
Unexpired insurance premium at the end of December	$2,300

Based on the above data, the entries to account for the deferred expense (prepaid insurance) recorded initially as an *asset* are shown in the journal and T accounts in Exhibit 1. The adjusting entry in Exhibit 1 was shown in Chapter 3. The entries to account for the prepaid insurance recorded initially as an *expense* are shown in the journal and T accounts in Exhibit 2.

EXHIBIT 1

Prepaid Expense Recorded Initially as Asset

Initial entry (to record initial payment):

Dec. 1	Prepaid Insurance	2,400	
	Cash		2,400

Adjusting entry (to transfer amount *used* to proper *expense* account):

Dec. 31	Insurance Expense	100	
	Prepaid Insurance		100

Closing entry (to close income statement accounts with debit balances):

Income Summary	XXXX	
Supplies Expense		XXXX
～～～～		
Insurance Expense		100

Prepaid Insurance

Dec. 1		2,400	Dec. 31	Adjusting	100

Insurance Expense

Dec. 31	Adjusting	100	Dec. 31	Closing	100

EXHIBIT 2

Prepaid Expense Recorded Initially as Expense

Initial entry (to record initial payment):

Dec. 1	Insurance Expense	2,400	
	Cash		2,400

Adjusting entry (to transfer amount *unused* to the proper *asset* account):

Dec. 31	Prepaid Insurance	2,300	
	Insurance Expense		2,300

Closing entry (to close income statement accounts with debit balances):

Income Summary	XXXX	
Supplies Expense		XXXX
～～～～		
Insurance Expense		100

Prepaid Insurance

Dec. 31	Adjusting	2,300		

Insurance Expense

Dec. 1		2,400	Dec. 31	Adjusting	2,300
			31	Closing	100

Either of the two methods of recording deferred expenses (prepaid expenses) may be used. As illustrated in Exhibits 1 and 2, both methods result in the same account balances after the adjusting entries have been recorded. Therefore, the amounts reported as expenses in the income statement and as assets on the balance sheet will not be affected by the method used. To avoid confusion, the method used by a business for each kind of prepaid expense should be followed consistently from year to year.

Some businesses record all deferred expenses using one method. Other businesses use one method to record the prepayment of some expenses and the other method for other expenses. Initial debits to the asset account are logical for prepayments of insurance, which are usually for periods of one to three years. On the other hand, rent on a building may be prepaid on the first of each month. The prepaid rent will expire by the end of the month. In this case, it is logical to record the payment of rent by initially debiting an expense account rather than an asset account.

Deferred Revenues (Unearned Revenues)

As a basis for illustrating the alternative methods of recording deferred revenues, the rent received by Computer King in Chapter 2 is used. Computer King rented land on December 1 to a local retailer for use as a parking lot for three months and received $360 for the entire three months. On December 31, $120 (1/3 × $360) of the rent has been earned, and $240 (2/3 × $360) of the rent is still unearned.

Based on the above data, the entries to account for the deferred revenue (unearned rent) recorded initially as a liability are shown in the journal and ledger in Exhibit 3. The adjusting entry in Exhibit 3 was shown in Chapter 3. The entries to account for the unearned rent recorded initially as revenue are shown in the journal and ledger in Exhibit 4.

EXHIBIT 3			**EXHIBIT 4**		
Unearned Revenue Recorded Initially as Liability			Unearned Revenue Recorded Initially as Revenue		
Initial entry (to record initial receipt):			Initial entry (to record initial receipt):		
Dec. 1 Cash	360		Dec. 1 Cash	360	
Unearned Rent		360	Rent Revenue		360
Adjusting entry (to transfer amount *earned* to proper revenue account):			Adjusting entry (to transfer amount *unearned* to proper liability account):		
Dec. 31 Unearned Rent	120		Dec. 31 Rent Revenue	240	
Rent Revenue		120	Unearned Rent		240
Closing entry (to close income statement accounts with credit balances):			Closing entry (to close income statement accounts with credit balances):		
Dec. 31 Fees Earned	XXXX		Dec. 31 Fees Earned	XXXX	
Rent Revenue	120		Rent Revenue	120	
Income Summary		XXXX	Income Summary		XXXX

	Unearned Rent					Unearned Rent			
Dec. 31 Adjusting	120	Dec. 1	360				Dec. 31 Adjusting	240	

	Rent Revenue					Rent Revenue			
Dec. 31 Closing	120	Dec. 31 Adjusting	120		Dec. 31 Adjusting	240	Dec. 1	360
					31 Closing	120		

As illustrated in Exhibits 3 and 4, both methods result in the same account balances after the adjusting entries have been recorded. Therefore, the amounts reported as revenues in the income statement and as liabilities on the balance sheet will not be affected by the method used. Either of the methods may be used for all revenues received in advance. Alternatively, the first method may be used for advance receipts of some kinds of revenue and the second method for other kinds. To avoid confusion, the method used by a business for each kind of unearned revenue should be followed consistently from year to year.

Reversing Entries for Deferrals

As discussed in the appendix at the end of Chapter 4, the use of reversing entries is optional. However, the use of reversing entries generally simplifies the analysis of transactions and reduces the likelihood of errors in the subsequent recording of transactions. Normally, reversing entries are prepared for deferrals in the following two cases:

1. When a deferred expense (prepaid expense) is initially recorded as an expense.
2. When a deferred revenue (unearned revenue) is initially recorded as a revenue.

The entry to reverse the adjustment to record the prepaid insurance in Exhibit 2 is as follows:

Jan.	1	Insurance Expense	2,300	
		Prepaid Insurance		2,300

The entry to reverse the adjustment to record the unearned rent in Exhibit 4 is as follows:

Jan.	1	Unearned Rent	240	
		Rent Revenue		240

EXERCISES

Exercise C–1
Adjusting entries for office supplies

The office supplies purchased during the year total $1,980, and the amount of office supplies on hand at the end of the year is $235.

a. Record the following transactions directly in T accounts for Office Supplies and Office Supplies Expense, using the system of initially recording supplies as an asset: (1) purchases for the period; (2) adjusting entry at the end of the period. Identify each entry by number.

b. Record the following transactions directly in T accounts for Office Supplies and Office Supplies Expense, using the system of initially recording supplies as an expense: (1) purchases for the period; (2) adjusting entry at the end of the period. Identify each entry by number.

Exercise C–2
Adjusting entries for prepaid insurance

During the first year of operations, insurance premiums of $6,750 were paid. At the end of the year, unexpired premiums totaled $4,050. Journalize the adjusting entry at the end of the year, assuming that (a) prepaid expenses were initially recorded as assets and (b) prepaid expenses were initially recorded as expenses.

Exercise C–3
Adjusting entries for advertising revenue

The advertising revenues received during the year total $210,000, and the unearned advertising revenue at the end of the year is $35,900.

a. Record the following transactions directly in T accounts for Unearned Advertising Revenue and Advertising Revenue, using the system of initially recording advertising fees as a liability: (1) revenues received during the period; (2) adjusting entry at the end of the period. Identify each entry by number.

b. Record the following transactions directly in T accounts for Unearned Advertising Revenue and Advertising Revenue, using the system of initially recording advertising fees as revenue: (1) revenues received during the period; (2) adjusting entry at the end of the period. Identify each entry by number.

Exercise C–4
*Year-end entries for
deferred revenues*

In their first year of operation, Snyder Publishing Co. received $1,275,000 from advertising contracts and $3,195,000 from magazine subscriptions, crediting the two amounts to Unearned Advertising Revenue and Circulation Revenue, respectively. At the end of the year, the unearned advertising revenue amounts to $300,000, and the unearned circulation revenue amounts to $542,000. Journalize the adjusting entries that should be made at the end of the year.

Appendix D: Periodic Inventory Systems for Merchandising Businesses

In this text, we emphasize the perpetual inventory system of accounting for purchases and sales of merchandise. Not all merchandise businesses, however, use perpetual inventory systems. For example, some managers/owners of small merchandise businesses, such as locally owned hardware stores, may feel more comfortable using manually kept records. Because a manual perpetual inventory system is time-consuming and costly to maintain, the periodic inventory system is often used in these cases.

Merchandise Transactions in a Periodic Inventory System

In a periodic inventory system, the revenues from sales are recorded when sales are made in the same manner as in a perpetual inventory system. However, no attempt is made on the date of sale to record the cost of the merchandise sold. Instead, the merchandise inventory on hand at the end of the period is counted. This physical inventory is then used to determine (1) the cost of merchandise sold during the period and (2) the cost of merchandise on hand at the end of the period.

In a periodic inventory system, purchases of inventory are recorded in a purchases account rather than in a merchandise inventory account. No attempt is made to keep a detailed record of the amount of inventory on hand at any given time.

The purchases account is normally debited for the amount of the invoice before considering any purchases discounts. Purchases discounts are normally recorded in a separate purchases discounts account.[1] The balance of this account is reported as a deduction from the amount initially recorded in Purchases for the period. Thus, the purchases discounts account is viewed as a contra (or offsetting) account to Purchases.

Purchases returns and allowances are recorded in a similar manner as purchases discounts. A separate account is used to keep a record of the amount of purchases returns and allowances during a period. Purchases returns and allowances are reported as a deduction from the amount initially recorded as Purchases. Like Purchases Discounts, the purchases returns and allowances account is a contra (or offsetting) account to Purchases.

When merchandise is purchased FOB shipping point, the buyer is responsible for paying the freight charges. In a periodic inventory system, freight charges paid when purchasing merchandise FOB shipping point are debited to Transportation In, Freight In, or a similarly titled account.

To illustrate the recording of merchandise transactions in a periodic system, we will use the following selected transactions for Taylor Co. We will also explain how the transaction would have been recorded under a perpetual system.

June 5. Purchased $30,000 of merchandise on account from Owen Clothing, terms 2/10, n/30.

Purchases	30,000	
Accounts Payable—Owen Clothing		30,000

Under the perpetual inventory system, such purchases would be recorded in the merchandise inventory account at their cost, $30,000.

June 8. Returned merchandise purchased on account from Owen Clothing on June 5, $500.

Accounts Payable—Owen Clothing	500	
Purchases Returns and Allowances		500

[1] Some businesses prefer to credit the purchases account. If this alternative is used, the balance of the purchases account will be a net amount—the total purchases less the total purchases discounts for the period.

Under the perpetual inventory system, returns would be recorded as a credit to the merchandise inventory account at their cost of $500.

June 15.   Paid Owen Clothing for purchase of June 5, less return of $500 and discount of $590 [($30,000 − $500) × 2%].

Accounts Payable—Owen Clothing	29,500	
Cash		28,910
Purchases Discounts		590

Under a perpetual inventory system, a purchases discount account is not used. Instead the merchandise inventory account is credited for the amount of the discount, $590.

June 18.   Sold merchandise on account to Jones Co., $12,500, 1/10, n/30. The cost of the merchandise sold was $9,000.

Accounts Receivable—Jones Co.	12,500	
Sales		12,500

The entry to record the sale is the same under both systems. Under the perpetual inventory system, the cost of merchandise sold and the reduction in merchandise inventory would also be recorded on the date of sale.

June 21.   Received merchandise returned on account from Jones Co., $4,000. The cost of the merchandise returned was $2,800.

Sales Returns and Allowances	4,000	
Accounts Receivable—Jones Co.		4,000

The entry to record the sales return is the same under both systems. In addition, the cost of the merchandise returned would be debited to the merchandise inventory account and credited to the cost of merchandise sold account under the perpetual inventory system.

June 22.   Purchased merchandise from Norcross Clothiers, $15,000, terms FOB shipping point, 2/15, n/30, with prepaid transportation charges of $750 added to the invoice.

Purchases	15,000	
Transportation In	750	
Accounts Payable—Norcross Clothiers		15,750

This entry is similar to the June 5 entry for the purchase of merchandise. Since the transportation terms were FOB shipping point, the prepaid freight charges of $750 must be added to the invoice cost of $15,000. Under the perpetual inventory system, the purchase is recorded in the merchandise inventory account at the cost of $15,750 (invoice price plus transportation).

June 28.   Received $8,415 as payment on account from Jones Co., less return of June 21 and less discount of $85 [($12,500 − $4,000) × 1%].

Cash	8,415	
Sales Discounts	85	
Accounts Receivable—Jones Co.		8,500

This entry is the same under the perpetual inventory system.

June 29.   Received $19,600 from cash sales. The cost of the merchandise sold was $13,800.

Cash	19,600	
Sales		19,600

The entry to record the sale is the same under both systems. Under the perpetual inventory system, the cost of merchandise sold and the reduction in merchandise inventory would also be recorded on the date of sale.

Cost of Merchandise Sold

Under the periodic inventory system, the cost of merchandise sold during a period is reported in a separate section in the income statement. To illustrate, assume that on January 3, 2000, Computer King opened a merchandising outlet selling microcomputers and software. During 2000, Computer King purchased $340,000 of merchandise. The inventory on December 31, 2000, is $59,700. The cost of merchandise sold during 2000 is reported as follows:

Cost of merchandise sold:	
Purchases	$340,000
Less merchandise inventory, December 31, 2000	59,700
Cost of merchandise sold	$280,300

To continue the example, assume that during 2001 Computer King purchased additional merchandise of $521,980. Computer King also received credit for purchases returns and allowances of $9,100, took purchases discounts of $2,525, and paid transportation costs of $17,400. The purchases returns and allowances and the purchases discounts are deducted from the total purchases to yield the net purchases. The transportation costs are then added to the net purchases to yield the cost of merchandise purchased. These amounts are reported in the cost of merchandise sold section of the Computer King income statement for 2001 as follows:

Purchases		$521,980	
Less: Purchases returns and allowances	$9,100		
Purchases discounts	2,525	11,625	
Net purchases		$510,355	
Add transportation in		17,400	
Cost of merchandise purchased			$527,755

The ending inventory of Computer King on December 31, 2000, $59,700, becomes the beginning inventory for 2001. In the cost of merchandise sold section of the income statement for 2001, this beginning inventory is added to the cost of merchandise purchased to yield the merchandise available for sale. The ending inventory on December 31, 2001, $62,150, is then subtracted from the merchandise available for sale to yield the cost of merchandise sold. Exhibit 1 shows the cost of merchandise sold during 2001.

EXHIBIT 1
Cost of Merchandise Sold—
Periodic Inventory System

Cost of merchandise sold:			
Merchandise inventory, January 1, 2001 ..			$ 59,700
Purchases		$521,980	
Less: Purchases returns and allowances ..	$9,100		
Purchases discounts	2,525	11,625	
Net purchases		$510,355	
Add transportation in		17,400	
Cost of merchandise purchased			527,755
Merchandise available for sale			$587,455
Less merchandise inventory,			
December 31, 2001			62,150
Cost of merchandise sold			$525,305

The multiple-step income statement under the periodic inventory system is illustrated in Exhibit 2. The multiple-step income statement under a perpetual inventory system is similar, except that the cost of merchandise sold is reported as a single amount.

EXHIBIT 2
Multiple-Step Income
Statement—Periodic
Inventory System

Computer King
Income Statement
For the Year Ended December 31, 2001

Revenue from sales:			
Sales		$720,185	
Less: Sales returns and allowances	$ 6,140		
Sales discounts	5,790	11,930	
Net sales			$708,255
Cost of merchandise sold:			
Merchandise inventory, January 1, 2001		$ 59,700	
Purchases	$521,980		
Less: Purchases returns and allowances	$9,100		
Purchases discounts	2,525	11,625	
Net purchases		$510,355	
Add transportation in		17,400	
Cost of merchandise purchased		527,755	
Merchandise available for sale		$587,455	
Less merchandise inventory,			
December 31, 2001		62,150	
Cost of merchandise sold			525,305
Gross profit			$182,950
Operating expenses:			
Selling expenses:			
Sales salaries expense	$ 60,030		
Advertising expense	10,860		
Depreciation expense—store equipment	3,100		
Miscellaneous selling expense	630		
Total selling expenses		$ 74,620	
Administrative expenses:			
Office salaries expense	$ 21,020		
Rent expense	8,100		
Depreciation expense—office equipment	2,490		
Insurance expense	1,910		
Office supplies expense	610		
Miscellaneous administrative expense	760		
Total administrative expenses		34,890	
Total operating expenses			109,510
Income from operations			$ 73,440
Other income:			
Interest revenue	$ 3,800		
Rent revenue	600		
Total other income		$ 4,400	
Other expense:			
Interest expense		2,440	1,960
Net income			$ 75,400

Chart of Accounts for a Periodic Inventory System

Exhibit 3 is the chart of accounts for Computer King when a periodic inventory system is used. The periodic inventory accounts related to merchandising transactions are shown in color.

EXHIBIT 3
Chart of Accounts—Periodic Inventory System

Balance Sheet Accounts		Income Statement Accounts	
	100 Assets		400 Revenues
110	Cash	410	Sales
111	Notes Receivable	411	Sales Returns and Allowances
112	Accounts Receivable	412	Sales Discounts
113	Interest Receivable		500 Costs and Expenses
115	Merchandise Inventory	510	Purchases
116	Office Supplies	511	Purchases Returns and
117	Prepaid Insurance		Allowances
120	Land	512	Purchases Discounts
123	Store Equipment	513	Transportation In
124	Accumulated Depreciation—	520	Sales Salaries Expenses
	Store Equipment	521	Advertising Expense
125	Office Equipment	522	Depreciation Expense—Store
126	Accumulated Depreciation—		Equipment
	Office Equipment	523	Transportation Out
	200 Liabilities	529	Miscellaneous Selling Expense
210	Accounts Payable	530	Office Salaries Expense
211	Salaries Payable	531	Rent Expense
212	Unearned Rent	532	Depreciation Expense—Office
215	Notes Payable		Equipment
	300 Owner's Equity	533	Insurance Expense
310	Pat King, Capital	534	Office Supplies Expense
311	Pat King, Drawing	539	Misc. Administrative Expense
312	Income Summary		600 Other Income
		610	Rent Revenue
		611	Interest Revenue
			700 Other Expense
		710	Interest Expense

End-of-Period Procedures in a Periodic Inventory System

The end-of-period procedures are generally the same for the periodic and perpetual inventory systems. In the remainder of this appendix, we will discuss the differences in procedures for the two systems which affect the work sheet, the adjusting entries, and the closing entries. As the basis for illustrations, we will use the data for Computer King, presented in Chapter 6.

Work Sheet

The differences in the work sheet for a merchandising business that uses the periodic inventory system are highlighted in the work sheet for Computer King in Exhibit 4. As we illustrated earlier, accounts for purchases, purchases returns and allowances, purchases discounts, and transportation in are used in a periodic inventory system.

Under the periodic inventory system, the merchandise inventory account, throughout the accounting period, shows the inventory at the beginning of the period. As shown in Exhibit 1, the merchandise inventory on January 1, 2001, $59,700, is a part of the merchandise available for sale. At the end of the period, the beginning inventory amount in the ledger is replaced with the ending inventory amount. To update the inventory account, two adjusting entries are used.[2] The first adjust-

---

[2] Another method of updating the merchandise inventory account at the end of the period is called the *closing method*. This method adjusts the merchandise inventory through the use of closing entries. This method may not be appropriate for use in computerized accounting systems. Since the financial statements are the same under both methods and since computerized accounting systems are used by most businesses, the closing method is not illustrated.

ing entry transfers the beginning inventory balance to Income Summary. This entry, shown below, has the effect of increasing the cost of merchandise sold and decreasing net income.

Dec. 31   Income Summary   59,700
               Merchandise Inventory   59,700

After the first adjusting entry has been recorded and posted, the balance of the merchandise inventory account is zero. The second adjusting entry records the cost of the merchandise on hand at the end of the period by debiting Merchandise Inventory. Since the merchandise inventory at December 31, 2001, $62,150, is subtracted from the cost of merchandise available for sale in determining the cost of merchandise sold, Income Summary is credited. This credit has the effect of decreasing the cost of merchandise available for sale during the period, $587,455, by the cost of the unsold merchandise. The second adjusting entry is shown below.

Dec. 31   Merchandise Inventory   62,150
               Income Summary   62,150

After the second adjusting entry has been recorded and posted, the balance of the merchandise inventory account is the amount of the ending inventory. The accounts for Merchandise Inventory and Income Summary after both entries have been posted would appear in T account form as follows:

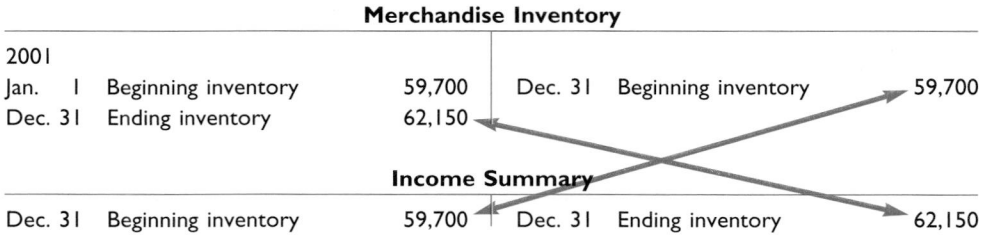

No separate adjusting entry can be made for merchandise inventory shrinkage in a periodic inventory system. This is because no perpetual inventory records are available to show what inventory should be on hand at the end of the period. One disadvantage of the periodic inventory system is that inventory shrinkage cannot be measured.[3]

Completing the Work Sheet

After all of the necessary adjustments have been entered on the work sheet, the work sheet is completed in the normal manner. An exception to the usual practice of extending only account balances is Income Summary. Both the debit and credit amounts for Income Summary are extended to the Adjusted Trial Balance columns. Extending both amounts aids in the preparation of the income statement because the debit adjustment (the beginning inventory of $59,700) and the credit adjustment (the ending inventory of $62,150) are reported as part of the cost of merchandise sold.

The purchases, purchases discounts, purchases returns and allowances, and transportation in accounts are extended to the Income Statement Columns of the work sheet, since they are used in computing the cost of merchandise sold. You should note that the two merchandise inventory amounts in Income Summary are extended to the Income Statement columns. After all of the items have been extended to the statement columns, the four columns are totaled and the net income or net loss is determined.

---

[3] Any inventory shrinkage that does exist is part of the cost of merchandise sold and is reported on the income statement, since a smaller ending inventory is deducted from other merchandise available for sale.

EXHIBIT 4
Work Sheet—Periodic
Inventory System

Computer King
Work Sheet
For the Year Ended December 31, 2001

Account Title	Trial Balance Dr.	Trial Balance Cr.	Adjustments Dr.	Adjustments Cr.	Adjusted Trial Balance Dr.	Adjusted Trial Balance Cr.	Income Statement Dr.	Income Statement Cr.	Balance Sheet Dr.	Balance Sheet Cr.
Cash	52,950				52,950				52,950	
Notes Receivable	40,000				40,000				40,000	
Accounts Receivable	60,880				60,880				60,880	
Interest Receivable			(a) 200		200				200	
Merchandise Inventory	59,700		(c)62,150	(b)59,700	62,150				62,150	
Office Supplies	1,090			(d) 610	480				480	
Prepaid Insurance	4,560			(e) 1,910	2,650				2,650	
Land	10,000				10,000				10,000	
Store Equipment	27,100				27,100				27,100	
Accum. Depr.—Store Equipment		2,600		(f) 3,100		5,700				5,700
Office Equipment	15,570				15,570				15,570	
Accum. Depr.—Office Equipment		2,230		(g) 2,490		4,720				4,720
Accounts Payable		22,420				22,420				22,420
Salaries Payable				(h) 1,140		1,140				1,140
Unearned Rent		2,400	(i) 600			1,800				1,800
Notes Payable (final payment, 2008)		25,000				25,000				25,000
Pat King, Capital		153,800				153,800				153,800
Pat King, Drawing	18,000				18,000				18,000	
Income Summary			(b)59,700	(c)62,150	59,700	62,150	59,700	62,150		
Sales		720,185				720,185		720,185		
Sales Returns and Allowances	6,140				6,140		6,140			
Sales Discounts	5,790				5,790		5,790			
Purchases	521,980				521,980		521,980			
Purchases Returns & Allowances		9,100				9,100		9,100		
Purchases Discounts		2,525				2,525		2,525		
Transportation In	17,400				17,400		17,400			
Sales Salaries Expense	59,250		(h) 780		60,030		60,030			
Advertising Expense	10,860				10,860		10,860			
Depr. Expense—Store Equipment			(f) 3,100		3,100		3,100			
Miscellaneous Selling Expense	630				630		630			
Office Salaries Expense	20,660		(h) 360		21,020		21,020			
Rent Expense	8,100				8,100		8,100			
Depr. Expense—Office Equipment			(g) 2,490		2,490		2,490			
Insurance Expense			(e) 1,910		1,910		1,910			
Office Supplies Expense			(d) 610		610		610			
Misc. Administrative Expense	760				760		760			
Rent Revenue				(i) 600		600		600		
Interest Revenue		3,600		(a) 200		3,800		3,800		
Interest Expense	2,440				2,440		2,440			
	943,860	943,860	131,900	131,900	1,012,940	1,012,940	722,960	798,360	289,980	214,580
Net income							75,400			75,400
							798,360	798,360	289,980	289,980

(a) Interest earned but not received on notes receivable, $200.

(b) Beginning merchandise inventory, $59,700.

(c) Ending merchandise inventory, $62,150.

(d) Office supplies used, $610 ($1,090 − $480).

(e) Insurance expired, $1,910.

(f) Depreciation of store equipment, $3,100.

(g) Depreciation of office equipment, $2,490.

(h) Salaries accrued but not paid (sales salaries, $780; office salaries, $360), $1,140.

(i) Rent earned from amount received in advance, $600.

Financial Statements

The financial statements for Computer King are essentially the same under both the perpetual and periodic inventory systems. The main difference is that the cost of goods is reported as a single amount under the perpetual system. Exhibit 2 illustrates the manner in which cost of merchandise sold is reported in a multiple-step income statement when the periodic inventory system is used.[4]

Adjusting and Closing Entries

The adjusting entries are the same under both inventory systems, except for merchandise inventory. As indicated previously, two adjusting entries for beginning and ending merchandise inventory are necessary in a periodic inventory system.

The closing entries differ in the periodic inventory system in that there is no cost of merchandise sold account to be closed to Income Summary. Instead, the purchases, purchases discounts, purchases returns and allowances, and transportation in accounts are closed to Income Summary.[5] To illustrate, the adjusting and closing entries under a periodic inventory system for Computer King are shown below.

	Date		Description	Post. Ref.	Debit	Credit	
			JOURNAL			**PAGE 16**	
1			Adjusting Entries				1
2	2001 Dec.	31	Interest Receivable	113	2 0 0 00		2
3			Interest Revenue	611		2 0 0 00	3
4							4
5		31	Income Summary	312	59 7 0 0 00		5
6			Merchandise Inventory	115		59 7 0 0 00	6
7							7
8		31	Merchandise Inventory	115	62 1 5 0 00		8
9			Income Summary	312		62 1 5 0 00	9
10							10
11		31	Office Supplies Expense	534	6 1 0 00		11
12			Office Supplies	116		6 1 0 00	12
13							13
14		31	Insurance Expense	533	1 9 1 0 00		14
15			Prepaid Insurance	117		1 9 1 0 00	15
16							16
17		31	Depreciation Expense—Store Equip.	522	3 1 0 0 00		17
18			Accumulated Depr.—Store Equip.	124		3 1 0 0 00	18
19							19
20		31	Depreciation Expense—Office Equip.	532	2 4 9 0 00		20
21			Accumulated Depr.—Office Equip.	126		2 4 9 0 00	21
22							22
23		31	Sales Salaries Expense	520	7 8 0 00		23
24			Office Salaries Expense	530	3 6 0 00		24
25			Salaries Payable	211		1 1 4 0 00	25
26							26
27		31	Unearned Rent	212	6 0 0 00		27
28			Rent Revenue	610		6 0 0 00	28

[4] The single-step income statement would be the same for both the perpetual and the periodic inventory systems.

[5] The balance of Income Summary, after the merchandise inventory adjustments and the first two closing entries have been posted, is the net income or net loss for the period.

	Date		Description	Post. Ref.	Debit	Credit	
			JOURNAL			**PAGE 17**	
1			Closing Entries				1
2	2001 Dec.	31	Sales	410	720 1 8 5 00		2
3			Purchases Returns and Allowances	511	9 1 0 0 00		3
4			Purchases Discounts	512	2 5 2 5 00		4
5			Rent Revenue	610	6 0 0 00		5
6			Interest Revenue	611	3 8 0 0 00		6
7			Income Summary	312		736 2 1 0 00	7
8							8
9		31	Income Summary	312	663 2 6 0 00		9
10			Sales Returns and Allowances	411		6 1 4 0 00	10
11			Sales Discounts	412		5 7 9 0 00	11
12			Purchases	510		521 9 8 0 00	12
13			Transportation In	513		17 4 0 0 00	13
14			Sales Salaries Expense	520		60 0 3 0 00	14
15			Advertising Expense	521		10 8 6 0 00	15
16			Depreciation Exp.—Store Equip.	522		3 1 0 0 00	16
17			Miscellaneous Selling Expense	529		6 3 0 00	17
18			Office Salaries Expense	530		21 0 2 0 00	18
19			Rent Expense	531		8 1 0 0 00	19
20			Depreciation Exp.—Office Equip.	532		2 4 9 0 00	20
21			Insurance Expense	533		1 9 1 0 00	21
22			Office Supplies Expense	534		6 1 0 00	22
23			Miscellaneous Administrative Exp.	539		7 6 0 00	23
24			Interest Expense	710		2 4 4 0 00	24
25							25
26		31	Income Summary	312	75 4 0 0 00		26
27			Pat King, Capital	310		75 4 0 0 00	27
28							28
29		31	Pat King, Capital	310	18 0 0 0 00		29
30			Pat King, Drawing	311		18 0 0 0 00	30

EXERCISES

Exercise D–1

Purchases-related transactions—periodic inventory system

Journalize entries for the following related transactions, assuming that Golf "R" Us Co. uses the periodic inventory system.

a. Purchased $8,000 of merchandise from Cobra Co. on account, terms 2/10, n/30.
b. Discovered that some of the merchandise was defective and returned items with an invoice price of $1,000, receiving credit.
c. Paid the amount owed on the invoice within the discount period.
d. Purchased $5,000 of merchandise from Callaway Co. on account, terms 1/10, n/30.
e. Paid the amount owed on the invoice within the discount period.

Exercise D–2

Sales-related transactions—periodic inventory system

Journalize entries for the following related transactions, assuming that Tedder Company uses the periodic inventory system.

Mar. 8 Sold merchandise to a customer for $7,500, terms FOB shipping point, 2/10, n/30.
     8 Paid the transportation charges of $230, debiting the amounts to Accounts Receivable.

Mar. 12 Issued a credit memorandum for $1,800 to a customer for merchandise returned.
     18 Received a check for the amount due from the sale.

Exercise D–3
Adjusting entries for merchandise inventory—periodic inventory system

Data assembled for preparing the work sheet for Givens Co. for the fiscal year ended December 31, 1999, included the following:

Merchandise inventory as of January 1, 1999 $205,000
Merchandise inventory as of December 31, 1999 $237,200

    Journalize the two adjusting entries for merchandise inventory that would appear on the work sheet, assuming that the periodic inventory system is used.

Exercise D–4
Identification of missing items from income statement—periodic inventory system

For (a) through (i), identify the items designated by "X".

a. Sales − (X + X) = Net sales
b. Purchases − (X + X) = Net purchases
c. Net purchases + X = Cost of merchandise purchased
d. Merchandise inventory (beginning) + cost of merchandise purchased = X
e. Merchandise available for sale − X = Cost of merchandise sold
f. Net sales − cost of merchandise sold = X
g. X + X = Operating expenses
h. Gross profit − operating expenses = X
i. Income from operations + X − X = Net income

Exercise D–5
Multiple-step income statement—periodic inventory system

✓ Gross profit: $145,000

Selected data for Plantstar Company for the current year ended December 31 are as follows:

Merchandise inventory, January 1	$ 51,300
Merchandise inventory, December 31	67,500
Purchases	662,000
Purchases discounts	8,000
Purchases returns and allowances	15,500
Sales	805,000
Sales discounts	6,500
Sales returns and allowances	8,700
Transportation in	22,500

    Prepare a multiple-step income statement through gross profit for Plantstar Company for the current year ended December 31.

Exercise D–6
Adjusting and closing entries—periodic inventory system

Selected account titles and related amounts appearing in the Income Statement and Balance Sheet columns of the work sheet of Delia Company for the year ended December 31 are listed in alphabetical order as follows:

Administrative Expenses	$ 69,500
Building	312,500
Cash	58,500
Delia Williams, Capital	472,580
Delia Williams, Drawing	45,000
Interest Expense	2,500
Merchandise Inventory (1/1)	300,000
Merchandise Inventory (12/31)	315,000
Notes Payable	25,000
Office Supplies	10,600
Purchases	750,000
Purchases Discounts	6,000
Purchases Returns and Allowances	7,000
Salaries Payable	4,220
Sales	1,375,000
Sales Discounts	10,200
Sales Returns and Allowances	44,300
Selling Expenses	232,700
Store Supplies	7,700
Transportation In	21,300

All selling expenses have been recorded in the account entitled Selling Expenses, and all administrative expenses have been recorded in the account entitled Administrative Expenses. Assuming that Delia Company uses the periodic inventory system, journalize (a) the adjusting entries for merchandise inventory and (b) the closing entries.

PROBLEMS

Problem D–1

Sales-related and purchase-related transactions—periodic inventory system

The following were selected from among the transactions completed by The Document Company during April of the current year:

Apr. 4. Purchased merchandise on account from Vela Co., list price $20,000, trade discount 40%, terms FOB destination, 2/10, n/30.
5. Sold merchandise for cash, $4,100.
7. Purchased merchandise on account from Summit Co., $7,500, terms FOB shipping point, 2/10, n/30, with prepaid transportation costs of $200 added to the invoice.
7. Returned $2,500 of merchandise purchased on April 4 from Vela Co.
11. Sold merchandise on account to Bowles Co., list price $2,250, trade discount 20%, terms 1/10, n/30.
14. Paid Vela Co. on account for purchase of April 4, less return of April 7 and discount.
15. Sold merchandise on nonbank credit cards and reported accounts to the card company, American Express, $5,850.
17. Paid Summit Co. on account for purchase of April 7, less discount.
21. Received cash on account from sale of April 11 to Bowles Co., less discount.
25. Sold merchandise on account to Clemons Co., $3,200, terms 1/10, n/30.
28. Received cash from American Express for nonbank credit card sales of April 15, less $280 service fee.
30. Received merchandise returned by Clemons Co. from sale on April 25, $1,700.

Instructions

Journalize the transactions for The Document Co. in a two-column general journal.

Problem D–2

Sales-related and purchase-related transactions—periodic inventory system

The following were selected from among the transactions completed by Taxel Company during March of the current year:

Mar. 2. Purchased merchandise on account from Queen Co., list price $25,000, trade discount 30%, terms FOB shipping point, 2/10, n/30, with prepaid transportation costs of $720 added to the invoice.
4. Purchased merchandise on account from Rossi Co., $6,000, terms FOB destination, 1/10, n/30.
6. Sold merchandise on account to C. F. Howell Co., list price $7,500, trade discount 40%, terms 2/10, n/30.
9. Returned merchandise purchased on March 4 from Rossi Co., $1,300.
12. Paid Queen Co. on account for purchase of March 2, less discount.
14. Paid Rossi Co. on account for purchase of March 4, less return of March 9 and discount.
16. Received cash on account from sale of March 6 to C. F. Howell Co., less discount.
19. Sold merchandise on nonbank credit cards and reported accounts to the card company, American Express, $4,450.
22. Sold merchandise on account to Vantage Co., $3,480, terms 2/10, n/30.
24. Sold merchandise for cash, $4,350.
25. Received merchandise returned by Vantage Co. from sale on March 22, $1,480.
31. Received cash from American Express for nonbank credit card sales of March 19, less $290 service fee.

Instructions

Journalize the transactions for Taxel Co. in a two-column general journal.

Problem D–3

Sales-related and purchase-related transactions for seller and buyer—periodic inventory system

The following selected transactions were completed during July between Servco Company and Barkey Co.:

July 3. Servco Company sold merchandise on account to Barkey Co., $10,500, terms FOB destination, 2/15, n/eom.

3. Servco Company paid transportation costs of $450 for delivery of merchandise sold to Barkey Co. on July 3.

10. Servco Company sold merchandise on account to Barkey Co., $12,000, terms FOB shipping point, n/eom.

11. Barkey Co. returned merchandise purchased on account on July 3 from Servco Company, $2,000.

14. Barkey Co. paid transportation charges of $200 on July 10 purchase from Servco Company.

17. Servco Company sold merchandise on account to Barkey Co., $20,000, terms FOB shipping point, 1/10, n/30. Servco prepaid transportation costs of $1,750, which were added to the invoice.

18. Barkey Co. paid Servco Company for purchase of July 3, less discount and less return of July 11.

27. Barkey Co. paid Servco Company on account for purchase of July 17, less discount.

31. Barkey Co. paid Servco Company on account for purchase of July 10.

Instructions

Journalize the July transactions for (1) Servco Company and for (2) Barkey Co.

Problem D–4

Preparation of work sheet, financial statements, and adjusting and closing entries—periodic inventory system

✓ 1. Net income: $169,250

The accounts and their balances in the ledger of The Shoe Co. on December 31 of the current year are as follows:

Cash	$ 38,000
Accounts Receivable	112,500
Merchandise Inventory	180,000
Prepaid Insurance	9,700
Store Supplies	4,250
Office Supplies	2,100
Store Equipment	132,000
Accumulated Depreciation—Store Equipment	40,300
Office Equipment	50,000
Accumulated Depreciation—Office Equipment	17,200
Accounts Payable	66,700
Salaries Payable	—
Unearned Rent	1,200
Note Payable (final payment, 2010)	105,000
J. Oxford, Capital	174,600
J. Oxford, Drawing	40,000
Income Summary	—
Sales	895,000
Sales Returns and Allowances	11,900
Sales Discounts	7,100
Purchases	535,000
Purchases Returns and Allowances	10,100
Purchases Discounts	4,900
Transportation In	6,200
Sales Salaries Expense	76,400
Advertising Expense	25,000
Depreciation Expense—Store Equipment	—
Store Supplies Expense	—
Miscellaneous Selling Expense	1,600
Office Salaries Expense	44,000
Rent Expense	26,000

Insurance Expense	—
Depreciation Expense—Office Equipment	—
Office Supplies Expense	—
Miscellaneous Administrative Expense	$ 1,650
Rent Revenue	—
Interest Expense	11,600

The data needed for year-end adjustments on December 31 are as follows:

Merchandise inventory on December 31		$212,000
Insurance expired during the year		6,500
Supplies on hand on December 31:		
Store supplies		1,300
Office supplies		750
Depreciation for the year:		
Store equipment		7,500
Office equipment		3,800
Salaries payable on December 31:		
Sales salaries	$3,850	
Office salaries	1,150	5,000
Unearned rent on December 31		400

Instructions

1. Prepare a work sheet for the fiscal year ended December 31, listing all accounts in the order given.
2. Prepare a multiple-step income statement.
3. Prepare a statement of owner's equity.
4. Prepare a report form of balance sheet, assuming that the current portion of the note payable is $15,000.
5. Journalize the adjusting entries.
6. Journalize the closing entries.

Appendix E: Foreign Currency Transactions

In this appendix, we describe and illustrate the accounting for transactions in which a U.S. company sells products or services to foreign companies or buys foreign products or services. If transactions with foreign companies require payment or receipt in U.S. dollars, no special accounting problems arise.[1] Such transactions are recorded as we described and illustrated earlier in this text. For example, the sale of merchandise to a Japanese company that is billed in and paid for in dollars would be recorded by the U.S. company in the normal manner. However, if the transaction is billed and payment is to be received in Japanese yen, the U.S. company may incur an exchange gain or loss. Some foreign manufacturers have begun building manufacturing plants in the United States, which avoids such gains and losses. For example, **BMW** has constructed its first U.S. plant.

Realized Currency Exchange Gains and Losses

When a U.S. company receives foreign currency, the amount must be converted to its equivalent in U.S. dollars for recording in the accounts. When payment is to be made in a foreign currency, U.S. dollars must be exchanged for the foreign currency for payment. To illustrate, assume that a U.S. company purchases merchandise from a British company that requires payment in British pounds. In this case, U.S. dollars ($) must be exchanged for British pounds (£) to pay for the merchandise. This exchange of one currency for another involves using an exchange rate. The **exchange rate** is the rate at which one unit of currency (the dollar, for example) can be converted into another currency (the British pound, for example).

To continue the example, assume that the U.S. company had purchased merchandise for £1,000 from a British company on June 1, when the exchange rate was $1.40 per British pound. Thus, $1,400 must be exchanged for £1,000 to make the purchase.[2] The U.S. company records the transaction in dollars, as follows:

June	1	Merchandise Inventory		1 4 0 0 00	
		Cash			1 4 0 0 00
		Payment of Invoice No. 1725 from			
		W. A. Sterling Co., £1,000; exchange			
		rate, $1.40 per British pound.			

Instead of a cash purchase, the purchase may be made on account. In this case, the exchange rate may change between the date of purchase and the date of payment of the account payable in the foreign currency. In practice, exchange rates vary daily.

To illustrate, assume that the preceding purchase was made on account. The entry to record it is as follows:

June	1	Merchandise Inventory		1 4 0 0 00	
		Accounts Payable—W. A. Sterling Co.			1 4 0 0 00
		Purchase on account; Invoice			
		No. 1725 from W. A. Sterling Co.,			
		£1,000; exchange rate, $1.40 per			
		British pound.			

[1] This discussion is from the point of view of a U.S. company. Unless otherwise indicated, the reference to the dollar refers to the U.S. dollar rather than a dollar of another country, such as Canada.
[2] Foreign exchange rates are quoted in major financial reporting services. Because the exchange rates are quite volatile, those used in this chapter are assumed rates.

Assume that on the date of payment, June 15, the exchange rate was $1.45 per pound. The £1,000 account payable must be settled by exchanging $1,450 (£1,000 × $1.45) for £1,000. In this case, the U.S. company incurs an exchange loss of $50 because $1,450 was needed to settle a $1,400 account payable. The cash payment is recorded as follows:

June	15	Accounts Payable—W. A. Sterling Co.	1 4 0 0 00		
		Exchange Loss	5 0 00		
		Cash		1 4 5 0 00	
		Cash paid on Invoice No. 1725, for			
		£1,000, or $1,400, when exchange			
		rate was $1.45 per pound.			

We can analyze all transactions with foreign companies in the manner described. For example, assume that a sale on account for $1,000 to a Swiss company on May 1 was billed in Swiss francs. The cost of the merchandise sold was $600, and the selling company uses a perpetual inventory system. If the exchange rate was $0.25 per Swiss franc (F) on May 1, the transaction is recorded as follows:

May	1	Accounts Receivable—D. W. Robinson Co.	1 0 0 0 00		
		Sales		1 0 0 0 00	
		Invoice No. 9772, F4,000; exchange			
		rate, $0.25 per Swiss franc.			
	1	Cost of Merchandise Sold	6 0 0 00		
		Merchandise Inventory		6 0 0 00	

Assume that the exchange rate increases to $0.30 per Swiss franc on May 31 when cash is received. In this case, the U.S. company realizes an exchange gain of $200. This gain is realized because the F4,000, which had a value of $1,000 on the date of sale, has increased in value to $1,200 (F4,000 × $0.30) on May 31 when the payment is received. The receipt of the cash is recorded as follows:

May	31	Cash	1 2 0 0 00		
		Accounts Receivable—D. W. Robinson Co.		1 0 0 0 00	
		Exchange Gain		2 0 0 00	
		Cash received on Invoice No. 9772,			
		for F4,000, $1,000, when exchange			
		rate was $0.30 per Swiss franc.			

Unrealized Currency Exchange Gains and Losses

In the previous examples, the transactions were completed by either the receipt or the payment of cash. On the date the cash was received or paid, any related exchange gain or loss was realized and was recorded in the accounts. However, financial statements may be prepared between the date of the sale or purchase on account and the date the cash is received or paid. In this case, any exchange gain or loss created by a change in exchange rates between the date of the original transaction and the balance sheet date must be recorded. Such an exchange gain or loss is reported in the financial statements as an unrealized exchange gain or loss.

To illustrate, assume that a sale on account for $1,000 had been made to a German company on December 20 and had been billed in deutsche marks (DM). The cost of merchandise sold was $700. On this date, the exchange rate was $0.50 per deutsche mark. The transaction is recorded as follows:

Dec.	20	Accounts Receivable—T. A. Mueller Inc.		1 0 0 0 00	
		Sales			1 0 0 0 00
		Invoice No. 1793, DM2,000; exchange			
		rate, $0.50 per deutsche mark.			
	20	Cost of Merchandise Sold		7 0 0 00	
		Merchandise Inventory			7 0 0 00

Assume that the exchange rate decreases to $0.45 per deutsche mark on December 31, the date of the balance sheet. Thus, the $1,000 account receivable on December 31 has a value of only $900 (DM2,000 × $0.45). This unrealized loss of $100 ($1,000 − $900) is recorded as follows:

Dec.	31	Exchange Loss		1 0 0 00	
		Accounts Receivable—T. A. Mueller Inc.			1 0 0 00
		Invoice No. 1793, DM2,000 × $0.05			
		decrease in exchange rate.			

Any additional change in the exchange rate during the following period is recorded when the cash is received. To continue the illustration, assume that the exchange rate declines from $0.45 to $0.42 per deutsche mark by January 19, when the DM2,000 is received. The receipt of the cash on January 19 is recorded as follows:

Jan.	19	Cash (DM2,000 × $0.42)		8 4 0 00	
		Exchange Loss (DM2,000 × $0.03)		6 0 00	
		Accounts Receivable—T. A. Mueller Inc.			9 0 0 00
		Cash received on Invoice No. 1793,			
		for DM2,000, or $900, when exchange			
		rate was $0.42 per deutsche mark.			

In contrast, assume that in the preceding example the exchange rate increases between December 31 and January 19. In this case, an exchange gain would be recorded on January 19. For example, if the exchange rate increases from $0.45 to $0.47 per deutsche mark during this period, Exchange Gain would be credited for $40 (DM2,000 × $0.02).

A balance in the exchange loss account at the end of the fiscal period is reported in the Other Expense section of the income statement. A balance in the exchange gain account is reported in the Other Income section.

EXERCISES

Exercise E–1

Entries for sales made in foreign currency

The Electric Toy Company makes sales on account to several Swedish companies that it bills in kronas. Journalize the entries for the following selected transactions completed during the current year, assuming that Electric uses the perpetual inventory system:

June 2. Sold merchandise on account, 12,000 kronas; exchange rate, $0.13 per krona. The cost of merchandise sold was $1,100.

July 3. Received cash from sale of June 2, 12,000 kronas; exchange rate, $0.14 per krona.

Aug. 30. Sold merchandise on account, 20,000 kronas; exchange rate, $0.14 per krona. The cost of merchandise sold was $1,550.

Sept. 30. Received cash from sale of August 30, 20,000 kronas; exchange rate, $0.12 per krona.

Exercise E–2
Entries for purchases made in foreign currency

Custom Care Inc. sells artificial arms and legs to hospitals and physicians. It purchases merchandise from a German company that requires payment in deutsche marks. Journalize the entries for the following selected transactions completed during the current year, assuming that Custom Care Inc. uses the perpetual inventory system:

Feb. 10. Purchased merchandise on account, net 30, 7,500 deutsche marks; exchange rate, $0.58 per deutsche mark.

Mar. 9. Paid invoice of Feb. 10; exchange rate, $0.59 per deutsche mark.

Apr. 1. Purchased merchandise on account, net 30, 4,000 deutsche marks; exchange rate, $0.59 per deutsche mark.

May 1. Paid invoice of April 1; exchange rate, $0.57 per deutsche mark.

PROBLEMS

Problem E–1
Foreign currency transactions

GENERAL LEDGER

HAT

Global Inc. is a wholesaler of sports equipment, including golf clubs and gym sets. It sells to and purchases from companies in Canada and the Philippines. These transactions are settled in the foreign currency. The following selected transactions were completed during the current fiscal year:

June 10. Sold merchandise on account to Marco Company, net 30, 250,000 pesos; exchange rate, $0.030 per Philippines peso. The cost of merchandise sold was $5,500.

July 10. Received cash from Marco Company; exchange rate, $0.029 per Philippines peso.

15. Purchased merchandise on account from LeRa Inc., net 30, $5,000 Canadian; exchange rate, $0.76 per Canadian dollar.

Aug. 14. Issued check for amount owed to LeRa Inc.; exchange rate, $0.75 per Canadian dollar.

31. Sold merchandise on account to Ramon Company, net 30, 100,000 pesos; exchange rate, $0.031 per Philippines peso. The cost of merchandise sold was $1,200.

Sept. 30. Received cash from Ramon Company; exchange rate, $0.032 per Phillipines peso.

Oct. 8. Purchased merchandise on account from Chevalier Company, net 30, $50,000 Canadian; exchange rate, $0.73 per Canadian dollar.

Nov. 7. Issued check for amount owed to Chevalier Company; exchange rate, $0.74 per Canadian dollar.

Dec. 15. Sold merchandise on account to Jason Company, net 30, $80,000 Canadian; exchange rate, $0.75 per Canadian dollar. The cost of merchandise sold was $32,500.

16. Purchased merchandise on account from Juan Company, net 30, 500,000 pesos; exchange rate, $0.033 per Philippines peso.

31. Recorded unrealized currency exchange gain and/or loss on transactions of December 15 and 16. Exchange rates on December 31: $0.76 per Canadian dollar; $0.034 per Philippines peso.

Instructions

1. Journalize the entries to record the transactions and adjusting entries for the year, assuming that Global uses the perpetual inventory system.

2. Journalize the entries to record the payment of the December 16 purchase, on January 15, when the exchange rate was $0.031 per Philippines peso, and the receipt of cash from the December 15 sale, on January 17, when the exchange rate was $0.77 per Canadian dollar.

Appendix F: Partnerships

The partnership form of business organization allows two or more persons to combine capital, managerial talent, and experience with a minimum of effort. This form is widely used by small businesses. In many cases, the only alternative form of organization for multiple owners is the corporate form. Some states, however, do not permit the corporate form for certain types of businesses. For example, physicians, attorneys, and certified public accountants often organize as partnerships.

Characteristics of Partnerships

A **partnership** is "an association of two or more persons to carry on as co-owners a business for profit."[1] Partnerships have several characteristics with accounting implications.

A partnership has a **limited life**. A partnership dissolves whenever a partner ceases to be a member of the firm. For example, a partnership is dissolved if a partner withdraws due to bankruptcy, incapacity, or death. Likewise, admitting a new partner dissolves the old partnership. When a partnership is dissolved, a new partnership must be formed if operations of the business are to continue.

In most partnerships, the partners have **unlimited liability**. Each partner is individually liable to creditors for debts incurred by the partnership. Thus, if a partnership becomes insolvent, the partners must contribute sufficient personal assets to settle the debts of the partnership.

Partners have **co-ownership of partnership property**. The property invested in a partnership by a partner becomes the property of all the partners jointly. When a partnership is dissolved, the partners' claims against the assets are measured by the amount of the balances in their capital accounts.

Another characteristic of a partnership is **mutual agency**. This means that each partner is an agent of the partnership. Thus, each partner has the authority to enter into contracts for the partnership. The acts of each partner bind the entire partnership and become the obligations of all partners.

An important right of partners is **participation in income** of the partnership. Net income and net loss are distributed among the partners according to their agreement.

A partnership, like a sole proprietorship, is a **nontaxable entity** and thus does not pay federal income taxes. However, revenue and expense and other results of partnership operations must be reported annually to the Internal Revenue Service. The partners must, in turn, report their share of partnership income on their personal tax returns.

A partnership is created by a contract, known as the **partnership agreement** or **articles of partnership**. It should include statements regarding such matters as amounts to be invested, limits on withdrawals, distributions of income and losses, and admission and withdrawal of partners.

Advantages and Disadvantages of Partnerships

The partnership form of business organization is less widely used than are the proprietorship and corporate forms. For many business purposes, however, the advantages of the partnership form are greater than its disadvantages.

A partnership is relatively easy and inexpensive to organize, requiring only an agreement between two or more persons. A partnership has the advantage of bringing together more capital, managerial skills, and experience than does a proprietorship. Since a partnership is a nontaxable entity, the combined income taxes paid by the individual partners may be lower than the income taxes that would be paid by a corporation, which is a taxable entity.

---

[1] This definition of a partnership is included in the Uniform Partnership Act, which has been adopted by over ninety percent of the states.

A major disadvantage of the partnership form of business organization is the unlimited liability feature for partners. Other disadvantages of a partnership are that its life is limited, and one partner can bind the partnership to contracts. Also, raising large amounts of capital is more difficult for a partnership than for a corporation.

Accounting for Partnerships

Most of the day-to-day accounting for a partnership is the same as the accounting for any other form of business organization. The accounting system described in this text may, with little change, be used by a partnership. However, the formation, income distribution, dissolution, and liquidation of partnerships give rise to unique transactions. In the remainder of this appendix, we discuss accounting principles related to these areas.

Forming a Partnership

A separate entry is made for the investment of each partner in a partnership. The assets contributed by a partner are debited to the partnership asset accounts. If liabilities are assumed by the partnership, the partnership liability accounts are credited. The partner's capital account is credited for the net amount.

To illustrate, assume that Joseph A. Stevens and Earl S. Foster, sole owners of competing hardware stores, agree to combine their businesses in a partnership. Each is to contribute certain amounts of cash and other assets. It is also agreed that the partnership is to assume the liabilities of the separate businesses. The entry to record the assets contributed and the liabilities transferred by Stevens is as follows:

Date		Description	Debit	Credit
Apr.	1	Cash	7 2 0 0 00	
		Accounts Receivable	16 3 0 0 00	
		Merchandise Inventory	28 7 0 0 00	
		Store Equipment	5 4 0 0 00	
		Office Equipment	1 5 0 0 00	
		Allowance for Doubtful Accounts		1 5 0 0 00
		Accounts Payable		2 6 0 0 00
		Joseph A. Stevens, Capital		55 0 0 0 00

A similar entry would record the assets contributed and the liabilities transferred by Foster. In each entry, the noncash assets are recorded at values agreed upon by the partners. These values normally represent current market values and therefore usually differ from the book values of the assets in the records of the separate businesses. For example, the store equipment recorded at $5,400 in the preceding entry may have had a book value of $3,500 in Stevens's ledger (cost of $10,000 less accumulated depreciation of $6,500).

Dividing Net Income or Net Loss

Many partnerships have been dissolved because partners could not agree on an equitable distribution of income. Therefore, the method of dividing partnership income should be stated in the partnership agreement. In the absence of an agreement or if the agreement is silent on dividing net income or net losses, all partners share equally. However, if one partner contributes a larger portion of capital than the others, then net income should be divided to reflect the unequal capital contributions. Likewise, if the services rendered by one partner are more important than those of the others, net income should be divided to reflect the unequal service contributions. In the following paragraphs, we illustrate partnership agreements that recognize these differences.

Income Division—Services of Partners

One method of recognizing differences in partners' abilities and in amount of time devoted to the business provides for salary allowances to partners. Since partners are legally not employees of the partnership, such allowances are treated as divisions of the net income and are credited to the partners' capital accounts.

To illustrate, assume that the partnership agreement of Jennifer L. Stone and Crystal R. Mills provides for monthly salary allowances. Jennifer Stone is to receive a monthly allowance of $2,500 ($30,000 annually), and Crystal Mills is to receive $2,000 a month ($24,000 annually). Any net income remaining after the salary allowances is to be divided equally. Assume also that the net income for the year is $75,000.

A report of the division of net income may be presented as a separate statement to accompany the balance sheet and the income statement. Another format is to add the division to the bottom of the income statement. If the latter format is used, the lower part of the income statement would appear as follows:

Net income $75,000

Division of net income:

	J. L. Stone	C. R. Mills	Total
Annual salary allowance	$30,000	$24,000	$54,000
Remaining income	10,500	10,500	21,000
Net income	$40,500	$34,500	$75,000

Net income division is recorded as a closing entry, even if the partners do not actually withdraw the amounts of their salary allowances. The entry for dividing net income is as follows:

Dec.	31	Income Summary	75 0 0 0 00	
		Jennifer L. Stone, Capital		40 5 0 0 00
		Crystal R. Mills, Capital		34 5 0 0 00

If Stone and Mills had withdrawn their salary allowances monthly, the withdrawals would have been debited to their drawing accounts during the year. At the end of the year, the debit balances of $30,000 and $24,000 in their drawing accounts would be transferred as reductions to their capital accounts.

Accountants should be careful to distinguish between salary allowances and partner withdrawals. The amount of net income distributed to each partner's capital account at the end of the year may differ from the amount the partner withdraws during the year. In some cases, the partnership agreement may limit the amount of withdrawals a partner may make during a period.

Income Division—Services of Partners and Investment

Partners may agree that the most equitable plan of dividing income is to provide for (1) salary allowances and (2) interest on capital investments. Any remaining net income is then divided as agreed. For example, assume that the partnership agreement for Stone and Mills divides income as follows:

1. Monthly salary allowances of $2,500 for Stone and $2,000 for Mills.
2. Interest of 12% on each partner's capital balance on January 1.
3. Any remaining net income divided equally between the partners.

Stone had a credit balance of $80,000 in her capital account on January 1 of the current fiscal year, and Mills had a credit balance of $60,000 in her capital account. The $75,000 net income for the year is divided in the following schedule:

Net income $75,000

Division of net income:

	J. L. Stone	C. R. Mills	Total
Annual salary allowance	$30,000	$24,000	$54,000
Interest allowance	9,600[1]	7,200[2]	16,800
Remaining income	2,100	2,100	4,200
Net income	$41,700	$33,300	$75,000

[1]0.12 × $80,000   [2]0.12 × $60,000

For the above example, the entry to close the income summary account is shown below.

Dec.	31	Income Summary	75 0 0 0 00	
		Jennifer L. Stone, Capital		41 7 0 0 00
		Crystal R. Mills, Capital		33 3 0 0 00

Income Division—Allowances Exceed Net Income

In the examples so far, the net income has exceeded the total of the salary and interest allowances. If the net income is less than the total of the allowances, the **remaining balance** will be a negative amount. This amount must be divided among the partners as though it were a net loss.

To illustrate, assume the same salary and interest allowances as in the above example, but assume that the net income is $50,000. The salary and interest allowances total $39,600 for Stone and $31,200 for Mills. The sum of these amounts, $70,800, exceeds the net income of $50,000 by $20,800. It is necessary to divide the $20,800 excess between Stone and Mills. Under the partnership agreement, any net income or net loss remaining after deducting the allowances is divided equally between Stone and Mills. Thus, each partner is allocated one-half of the $20,800, and $10,400 is deducted from each partner's share of the allowances. The final division of net income between Stone and Mills is shown below.

Net income $50,000

Division of net income:

	J. L. Stone	C. R. Mills	Total
Annual salary allowance	$30,000	$24,000	$54,000
Interest allowance	9,600	7,200	16,800
Total	$39,600	$31,200	$70,800
Excess of allowances over income	10,400	10,400	20,800
Net income	$29,200	$20,800	$50,000

In closing Income Summary at the end of the year, $29,200 would be credited to Jennifer L. Stone, Capital, and $20,800 would be credited to Crystal R. Mills, Capital.

Partnership Dissolution

When a partnership dissolves, its affairs are not necessarily wound up. For example, a partnership of two partners may admit a third partner. Or if one of the partners in a business withdraws, the remaining partners may continue to operate the business. In such cases a new partnership is formed and a new partnership agreement should be prepared. Many partnerships provide for the admission of new partners and partner withdrawals in the partnership agreement so that the partnership may continue operations without executing a new agreement.

Admission of a Partner

A person may be admitted to a partnership only with the consent of all the current partners, through either of two methods:[2]

1. Purchasing an interest from one or more of the current partners.
2. Contributing assets to the partnership.

When the first method is used, the capital interest of the incoming partner is obtained from current partners, and *neither the total assets nor the total owner's equity of the business is affected.* When the second method is used, *both the total assets and the total owner's equity of the business are increased.* In the following paragraphs, we discuss each of these methods.

Purchasing an Interest in a Partnership. A person may be admitted to a partnership by buying an interest from one or more of the existing partners. The purchase and sale of the partnership interest occurs between the new partner and the existing partners acting as individuals. The only entry needed is to transfer owner's equity amounts from the capital accounts of the selling partners to the capital account established for the incoming partner.

As an example, assume that partners Tom Andrews and Nathan Bell have capital balances of $50,000 each. On June 1, each sells one-fifth of his equity to Joe Canter for $10,000 in cash. The exchange of cash is not a partnership transaction and thus is not recorded by the partnership. The only entry required in the partnership accounts is as follows:

June	1	Tom Andrews, Capital	10 0 0 0 00	
		Nathan Bell, Capital	10 0 0 0 00	
		Joe Canter, Capital		20 0 0 0 00

The effect of the transaction on the partnership accounts is presented in the following diagram:

Partnership Accounts

The preceding entry is not affected by the amount paid by Canter for the one-fifth interest. Any gain or loss on the sale of the partnership interest accrues to the selling partners as individuals, and not to the partnership. Thus, in either case, the entry to transfer the capital interests is the same as shown above.

After Canter is admitted to the partnership, the total owner's equity of the firm is still $100,000. Canter now has a one-fifth interest, or a $20,000 capital balance. However, Canter may not be entitled to a one-fifth share of the partnership net in-

---

[2] Although an individual cannot become a partner without the consent of the other partners, the rights of a partner, such as the right to share in the income of a partnership, may be assigned to others without the consent of the other partners. Such issues are discussed in business law textbooks.

come. Division of net income or net loss will be made according to the new partnership agreement.

Contributing Assets to a Partnership. Instead of buying an interest from the current partners, the incoming partner may contribute assets to the partnership. In this case, both the assets and the owner's equity of the firm increase. For example, assume that Donald Lewis and Gerald Morton are partners with capital accounts of $35,000 and $25,000. On June 1, Sharon Nelson invests $20,000 cash in the business for an ownership equity of $20,000. The entry to record this transaction is as follows:

June	1	Cash		20 0 0 0 00	
		Sharon Nelson, Capital			20 0 0 0 00

The major difference between the admission of Nelson and the admission of Canter in the preceding examples may be observed by comparing the following diagram with the preceding diagram.

Partnership Accounts

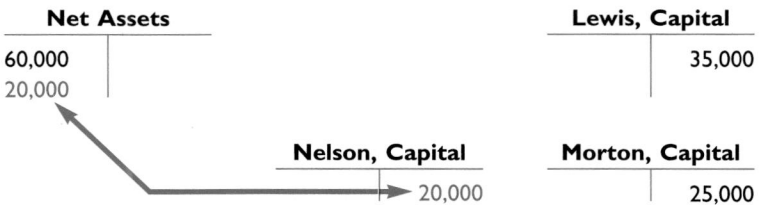

By admitting Nelson, the total owners' equity of the new partnership becomes $80,000, of which Nelson has a one-fourth interest, or $20,000. The extent of Nelson's share in partnership net income will be determined by the partnership agreement.

Revaluation of Assets. A partnership's asset account balances should be stated at current values when a new partner is admitted. If the accounts do not approximate current market values, the accounts should be adjusted. The net adjustment (increase or decrease) in asset values is divided among the capital accounts of the existing partners according to their income-sharing ratio. Failure to adjust the accounts for current values may result in the new partner sharing in asset gains or losses that arose in prior periods.

To illustrate, assume that in the preceding example for the Lewis and Morton partnership, the balance of the merchandise inventory account is $14,000 and the current replacement value is $17,000. Assuming that Lewis and Morton share net income equally, the revaluation is recorded as follows:

June	1	Merchandise Inventory		3 0 0 0 00	
		Donald Lewis, Capital			1 5 0 0 00
		Gerald Morton, Capital			1 5 0 0 00

Partner Bonuses. When a new partner is admitted to a partnership, the incoming partner may pay a bonus to the existing partners for the privilege of joining the partnership. Such a bonus is usually paid in expectation of high partnership profits in the future due to the contributions of the existing partners. Alternatively, the existing partners may pay the incoming partner a bonus to join the partnership. In this case, the bonus is usually paid in recognition of special qualities or skills that the incoming partner is bringing to the partnership. For example, celebrities such as actors, musicians, or sports figures often provide name recognition that is expected to increase partnership profits in the future. The amount of any bonus paid to the partnership is distributed among the partner capital accounts.[3]

To illustrate, assume that on March 1 the partnership of Marsha Jenkins and Helen Kramer is considering admitting a new partner, William Larson. After the assets of the partnership have been adjusted to current market values, the capital balance of Jenkins is $20,000 and the capital balance of Kramer is $24,000. Jenkins and Kramer agree to admit Larson to the partnership for $31,000. In return, Larson will receive a one-third equity in the partnership and will share equally with Jenkins and Kramer in partnership income or losses.

In this case Larson is paying Jenkins and Kramer a $6,000 bonus to join the partnership. This bonus is computed as follows:

Equity of Jenkins	$20,000
Equity of Kramer	24,000
Contribution of Larson	31,000
Total equity after admission of Larson	$75,000
Larson's equity interest after admission	× 1/3
Larson's equity after admission	$25,000
Contribution of Larson	$31,000
Larson's equity after admission	25,000
Bonus paid to Jenkins and Kramer	$ 6,000

The bonus is distributed to Jenkins and Kramer according to their income-sharing ratio. Assuming that Jenkins and Kramer share profits and losses equally, the entry to record the admission of Larson to the partnership is as follows:

Mar.	1	Cash	31 0 0 0 00		
		William Larson, Capital		25 0 0 0 00	
		Marsha Jenkins, Capital		3 0 0 0 00	
		Helen Kramer, Capital		3 0 0 0 00	

If a new partner possesses unique qualities or skills, the existing partners may agree to pay the new partner a bonus to join the partnership. To illustrate, assume that after adjusting assets to market values the capital balance of Janice Cowen is $80,000 and the capital balance of Steve Dodd is $40,000. Cowen and Dodd agree to admit Sandra Ellis to the partnership on June 1 for an investment of $30,000. In return, Ellis will receive a one-fourth equity interest in the partnership and will share in one-fourth of the profits and losses.

In this case Cowen and Dodd are paying Ellis a $7,500 bonus to join the partnership. This bonus is computed as follows:

Equity of Cowen	$ 80,000
Equity of Dodd	40,000
Contribution of Ellis	30,000
Total equity after admission of Ellis	$150,000
Ellis's equity interest after admission	× 25%
Ellis's equity after admission	$ 37,500
Contribution of Ellis	30,000
Bonus paid to Ellis	$ 7,500

[3] Another method is sometimes used to record the admission of partners in situations such as that described in this paragraph. This method attributes goodwill rather than a bonus to the partners. This method is discussed in advanced accounting textbooks.

Assuming that the income-sharing ratio of Cowen and Dodd was 2:1 before the admission of Ellis, the entry to record the bonus and admission of Ellis to the partnership is as follows:

June	1	Cash	30 0 0 0 00		
		Janice Cowen, Capital	5 0 0 0 00		
		Steve Dodd, Capital	2 5 0 0 00		
		Sandra Ellis, Capital		37 5 0 0 00	

Withdrawal of a Partner

When a partner retires or withdraws from a partnership, one or more of the remaining partners may buy the withdrawing partner's interest. The firm may then continue its operations uninterrupted. In such cases the purchase and sale of the partnership interest is between the partners as individuals. The only entry on the partnership's records is to debit the capital account of the partner withdrawing and to credit the capital account of the partner or partners buying the additional interest.

If the withdrawing partner sells the interest directly to the partnership, both the assets and the owner's equity of the partnership are reduced. Before the sale, the asset accounts should be adjusted to current values, so that the withdrawing partner's equity may be accurately determined. The net amount of the adjustment should be divided among the capital accounts of the partners according to their income-sharing ratio. If not enough partnership cash or other assets are available to pay the withdrawing partner, a liability may be created (credited) for the amount owed the withdrawing partner.

Death of a Partner

When a partner dies, the accounts should be closed as of the date of death. The net income for the current year should be determined and divided among the partners' capital accounts. The balance in the capital account of the deceased partner is then transferred to a liability account with the deceased's estate. The remaining partner or partners may continue the business, or the affairs may be terminated. If the partnership continues in business, the procedures for settling with the estate are the same as those discussed for the withdrawal of a partner.

Liquidating Partnerships

When a partnership goes out of business, it usually sells the assets, pays the creditors, and distributes the remaining cash or other assets to the partners. This winding-up process is called the **liquidation** of the partnership. Although liquidating refers to the payment of liabilities, it is often used to include the entire winding-up process.

When the partnership goes out of business and the normal operations are discontinued, the accounts should be adjusted and closed. The only accounts remaining open will be the asset, contra asset, liability, and owner's equity accounts.

The sale of the assets is called **realization**. As cash is realized, it is used to pay the claims of creditors. After all liabilities have been paid, the remaining cash is distributed to the partners based on the balances in their capital accounts.

The liquidating process may extend over a long period of time as individual assets are sold. This delays the distribution of cash to partners, but does not affect the amount each partner will receive.

To illustrate, assume that Farley, Greene, and Hall share income and losses in a ratio of 5:3:2 (5/10, 3/10, 2/10). On April 9, after discontinuing business operations of the partnership and closing the accounts, the following trial balance in summary form was prepared:

Cash	11,000	
Noncash Assets	64,000	
Liabilities		9,000
Jean Farley, Capital		22,000
Brad Greene, Capital		22,000
Alice Hall, Capital		22,000
Total	75,000	75,000

Based on these facts, we will show the accounting for liquidating the partnership by using three different selling prices for the noncash assets. To simplify, we assume that all noncash assets are sold in a single transaction and that all liabilities are paid at one time. In addition, Noncash Assets and Liabilities will be used as account titles in place of the various asset, contra asset, and liability accounts.

Gain on Realization

Between April 10 and April 30 of the current year, Farley, Greene, and Hall sell all noncash assets for $72,000. Thus, a gain of $8,000 ($72,000 − $64,000) is realized. The gain is divided among the capital accounts in the income-sharing ratio of 5:3:2. The liabilities are paid, and the remaining cash is distributed to the partners. *The cash is distributed to the partners based on the balances in their capital accounts.* A statement of partnership liquidation, which summarizes the liquidation process, is shown in Exhibit 1.

EXHIBIT I   Gain on Realization

Farley, Greene, and Hall
Statement of Partnership Liquidation
For Period April 10–30, 20—

	Cash	+	Noncash Assets	=	Liabilities	+	Farley (50%)	+	Greene (30%)	+	Hall (20%)
Balances before realization	$11,000		$64,000		$9,000		$22,000		$22,000		$22,000
Sale of assets and division of gain	+72,000		−64,000		—		+ 4,000		+ 2,400		+ 1,600
Balances after realization	$83,000		$ 0		$9,000		$26,000		$24,400		$23,600
Payment of liabilities	− 9,000		—		−9,000		—		—		—
Balances after payment of liabilities	$74,000		$ 0		$ 0		$26,000		$24,400		$23,600
Cash distributed to partners	−74,000		—		—		−26,000		−24,400		−23,600
Final balances	$ 0		$ 0		$ 0		$ 0		$ 0		$ 0

The entries to record the steps in the liquidating process are as follows:

	Cash		72 0 0 0 00	
	Noncash Assets			64 0 0 0 00
	Gain on Realization			8 0 0 0 00
	Sold assets.			
	Gain on Realization		8 0 0 0 00	
	Jean Farley, Capital			4 0 0 0 00
	Brad Greene, Capital			2 4 0 0 00
	Alice Hall, Capital			1 6 0 0 00
	Divided gain from sale of assets.			

		Liabilities		9 0 0 0 00	
		Cash			9 0 0 0 00
		Paid liabilities.			
		Jean Farley, Capital		26 0 0 0 00	
		Brad Greene, Capital		24 4 0 0 00	
		Alice Hall, Capital		23 6 0 0 00	
		Cash			74 0 0 0 00
		Distributed cash to partners.			

As shown in Exhibit 1, the cash is distributed to the partners based on the balances of their capital accounts. These balances are determined after the gain on realization has been divided among the partners. *The income-sharing ratio should not be used as a basis for distributing the cash to partners.*

Loss on Realization

Assume that in the preceding example, Farley, Greene, and Hall dispose of all noncash assets for $44,000. A loss of $20,000 ($64,000 − $44,000) is realized. The steps in liquidating the partnership are summarized in Exhibit 2.

EXHIBIT 2 Loss on Realization

Farley, Greene, and Hall
Statement of Partnership Liquidation
For Period April 10–30, 20—

	Cash	+	Noncash Assets	=	Liabilities	+	Capital Farley (50%)	+	Greene (30%)	+	Hall (20%)
Balances before realization	$11,000		$64,000		$9,000		$22,000		$22,000		$22,000
Sale of assets and division of loss	+44,000		−64,000		—		−10,000		− 6,000		− 4,000
Balances after realization	$55,000		$ 0		$9,000		$12,000		$16,000		$18,000
Payment of liabilities	− 9,000		—		−9,000		—		—		—
Balances after payment of liabilities	$46,000		$ 0		$ 0		$12,000		$16,000		$18,000
Cash distributed to partners	−46,000		—		—		−12,000		−16,000		−18,000
Final balances	$ 0		$ 0		$ 0		$ 0		$ 0		$ 0

The entries to liquidate the partnership are as follows:

		Cash		44 0 0 0 00	
		Loss on Realization		20 0 0 0 00	
		Noncash Assets			64 0 0 0 00
		Sold assets.			
		Jean Farley, Capital		10 0 0 0 00	
		Brad Greene, Capital		6 0 0 0 00	
		Alice Hall, Capital		4 0 0 0 00	
		Loss on Realization			20 0 0 0 00
		Divided loss from sale of assets.			

	Liabilities			9 0 0 0 00	
	Cash				9 0 0 0 00
	Paid liabilities.				
	Jean Farley, Capital			12 0 0 0 00	
	Brad Greene, Capital			16 0 0 0 00	
	Alice Hall, Capital			18 0 0 0 00	
	Cash				46 0 0 0 00
	Distributed cash to partners.				

Loss on Realization—Capital Deficiency

In the preceding example, the capital account of each partner was large enough to absorb the partner's share of the loss from realization. The partners received cash to the extent of the remaining balances in their capital accounts. The share of loss on realization may exceed, however, the balance in the partner's capital account. The resulting debit balance in the capital account is called a **deficiency**. It represents a claim of the partnership against the partner.

To illustrate, assume that Farley, Greene, and Hall sell all of the noncash assets for $10,000. A loss of $54,000 ($64,000 − $10,000) is realized. The share of the loss allocated to Farley, $27,000 (50% of $54,000), exceeds the $22,000 balance in her capital account. This $5,000 deficiency represents an amount that Farley owes the partnership. Assuming that Farley pays the entire deficiency to the partnership, sufficient cash is available to distribute to the remaining partners according to their capital balances. The steps in liquidating the partnership in this case are summarized in Exhibit 3.

EXHIBIT 3   Loss on Realization—Capital Deficiency

Farley, Greene, and Hall
Statement of Partnership Liquidation
For Period April 10–30, 20—

						Capital		
	Cash	+ Noncash Assets	= Liabilities	+	Farley (50%)	+ Greene (30%)	+	Hall (20%)
Balances before realization	$11,000	$64,000	$9,000		$22,000	$22,000		$22,000
Sale of assets and division of loss	+10,000	−64,000	—		−27,000	−16,200		−10,800
Balances after realization	$21,000	$ 0	$9,000		$ 5,000(Dr.)	$ 5,800		$11,200
Payment of liabilities	− 9,000	—	−9,000		—	—		—
Balances after payment of liabilities	$12,000	$ 0	$ 0		$ 5,000(Dr.)	$ 5,800		$11,200
Receipt of deficiency	+ 5,000	—	—		+ 5,000	—		—
Balances	$17,000	$ 0	$ 0		$ 0	$ 5,800		$11,200
Cash distributed to partners	−17,000	—	—		—	− 5,800		−11,200
Final balances	$ 0	$ 0	$ 0		$ 0	$ 0		$ 0

The entries to record the liquidation are as follows:

	Cash			10 0 0 0 00	
	Loss on Realization			54 0 0 0 00	
	Noncash Assets				64 0 0 0 00
	Sold assets.				

Jean Farley, Capital		27 0 0 0 00		
Brad Greene, Capital		16 2 0 0 00		
Alice Hall, Capital		10 8 0 0 00		
Loss on Realization			54 0 0 0 00	
Divided loss from sale of assets.				
Liabilities		9 0 0 0 00		
Cash			9 0 0 0 00	
Paid liabilities.				
Cash		5 0 0 0 00		
Jean Farley, Capital			5 0 0 0 00	
Received cash from deficient partner.				
Brad Greene, Capital		5 8 0 0 00		
Alice Hall, Capital		11 2 0 0 00		
Cash			17 0 0 0 00	
Distributed cash to partners.				

If cash is not collected from a deficient partner, the partnership cash will not be large enough to pay the other partners in full. Any uncollected deficiency becomes a loss to the partnership and is divided among the remaining partners' capital balances, based on their income-sharing ratio. The cash balance will then equal the sum of the capital account balances. Cash is then distributed to the remaining partners, based on the balances of their capital accounts.[4]

EXERCISES

Exercise F-1

Entry for partner's original investment

Todd Jost and D. Caldwell decide to form a partnership by combining the assets of their separate businesses. Jost contributes the following assets to the partnership: cash, $11,000; accounts receivable with a face amount of $96,000 and an allowance for doubtful accounts of $6,600; merchandise inventory with a cost of $85,000; and equipment with a cost of $140,000 and accumulated depreciation of $90,000.

The partners agree that $7,000 of the accounts receivable are completely worthless and are not to be accepted by the partnership, that $9,000 is a reasonable allowance for the uncollectibility of the remaining accounts, that the merchandise inventory is to be recorded at the current market price of $79,400, and that the equipment is to be valued at $67,600.

Journalize the partnership's entry to record Jost's investment.

Exercise F-2

Dividing partnership income

SPREADSHEET

✓ e. Moore net income, $91,500

Dan Moore and T. J. Knell formed a partnership, investing $300,000 and $150,000 respectively. Determine their participation in the year's net income of $180,000 under each of the following independent assumptions: (a) no agreement concerning division of net income; (b) divided in the ratio of original capital investment; (c) interest at the rate of 12% allowed on original investments and the remainder divided in the ratio of 2:3; (d) salary allowances of $60,000 and $75,000 respectively, and the balance divided equally; (e) allowance of interest at the rate of 12% on original investments, salary allowances of $60,000 and $75,000 respectively, and the remainder divided equally.

---

[4] The accounting for uncollectible deficiencies of partners is discussed and illustrated in advanced accounting texts.

Exercise F–3
Dividing partnership income

✓ d. Knell net income, $127,500

Determine the participation of Moore and Knell in the year's net income of $240,000, according to each of the five assumptions as to income division listed in Exercise F–2.

Exercise F–4
Admitting new partners

Jenny Kirk and Harold Spock are partners who share in the income equally and have capital balances of $120,000 and $62,500, respectively. Kirk, with the consent of Spock, sells one-third of her interest to Benjamin McCoy. What entry is required by the partnership if the sale price is (a) $30,000? (b) $50,000?

Exercise F–5
Admitting new partners who buy an interest and contribute assets

✓ b. Wood, Capital, $100,000

The capital accounts of Susan Laurel and Ben Hardy have balances of $120,000 and $100,000, respectively. Ken Mahl and Jeff Wood are to be admitted to the partnership. Mahl buys one-fourth of Laurel's interest for $32,000 and one-fifth of Hardy's interest for $24,000. Wood contributes $110,000 cash to the partnership, for which he is to receive an ownership equity of $100,000. All partners share equally in income.

a. Journalize the entries to record the admission of (1) Mahl and (2) Wood. Mahl is not credited with any of Wood's bonus.
b. What are the capital balances of each partner after the admission of the new partners?

Exercise F–6
Withdrawal of partner

Glenn Holmes is to retire from the partnership of Holmes and Associates as of March 31, the end of the current fiscal year. After closing the accounts, the capital balances of the partners are as follows: Glenn Holmes, $200,000; Jenny Watson, $125,000; and Pierre Periot, $140,000. They have shared net income and net losses in the ratio of 4:3:3. The partners agree that the merchandise inventory should be increased by $20,000, and the allowance for doubtful accounts should be increased by $2,000. Holmes agrees to accept a note for $130,000 in partial settlement of his ownership equity. The remainder of his claim is to be paid in cash. Watson and Periot are to share equally in the net income or net loss of the new partnership.

Journalize the entries to record (a) the adjustment of the assets to bring them into agreement with current market prices and (b) the withdrawal of Holmes from the partnership.

Exercise F–7
Distribution of cash upon liquidation

✓ a. $8,000 loss

Seinfeld and Kramer are partners, sharing gains and losses equally. At the time they decide to terminate their partnership, their capital balances are $12,000 and $50,000, respectively. After all noncash assets are sold and all liabilities are paid, there is a cash balance of $54,000.

a. What is the amount of a gain or loss on realization?
b. How should the gain or loss be divided between Seinfeld and Kramer?
c. How should the cash be divided between Seinfeld and Kramer?

Exercise F–8
Liquidating partnerships— capital deficiency

✓ b. $51,000

Douglas, Diaz, and Pitt share equally in net income and net losses. After the partnership sells all assets for cash, divides the losses on realization, and pays the liabilities, the balances in the capital accounts are as follows: Douglas, $20,000 Cr.; Diaz, $45,500 Cr.; and Pitt, $14,500 Dr.

a. What term is applied to the debit balance in Pitt's capital account?
b. What is the amount of cash on hand?
c. Journalize the transaction that must take place for Douglas and Diaz to receive cash in the liquidation process equal to their capital account balances.

Exercise F–9
Distribution of cash upon liquidation

✓ a. Grant net income, $100

Allyn Ashton, Jim Card, and Laura Grant arranged to import and sell orchid corsages for a university dance. They agreed to share equally the net income or net loss of the venture. Ashton and Card advanced $260 and $140 of their own respective funds to pay for advertising and other expenses. After collecting for all sales and paying creditors, the partnership has $700 in cash.

a. How should the money be distributed?
b. Assuming that the partnership has only $280 cash instead of $700, do any of the three partners have a capital deficiency? If so, how much?

Exercise F–10
Statement of partnership liquidation

✓ Cash distributed to Chow, $13,500

After closing the accounts on July 1, prior to liquidating the partnership, the capital account balances of Gibbs, Hill, and Chow are $40,000, $29,000, and $18,000, respectively. Cash, noncash assets, and liabilities total $22,000, $105,000, and $40,000, respectively. Between July 1 and July 29, the noncash assets are sold for $78,000, the liabilities are paid, and the remaining cash is distributed to the partners. The partners share net income and loss in the ratio of 3:2:1. Prepare a statement of partnership liquidation for the period July 1–29.

PROBLEMS

Problem F–1
Dividing partnership income

✓ 1. f. Dunn, $140,500

Phil Dunn and Russ Randall have decided to form a partnership. They have agreed that Dunn is to invest $140,000 and that Randall is to invest $210,000. Dunn is to devote full time to the business, and Randall is to devote one-half time. The following plans for the division of income are being considered:

a. Equal division.
b. In the ratio of original investments.
c. In the ratio of time devoted to the business.
d. Interest of 10% on original investments and the remainder in the ratio of 5:3.
e. Interest of 10% on original investments, salary allowances of $90,000 to Dunn and $45,000 to Randall, and the remainder equally.
f. Plan (e), except that Dunn is also to be allowed a bonus equal to 20% of the amount by which net income exceeds the salary allowances.

Instructions
For each plan, determine the division of the net income under each of the following assumptions: (1) net income of $225,000 and (2) net income of $150,000. Present the data in tabular form, using the following columnar headings:

	$225,000		$150,000	
Plan	Dunn	Randall	Dunn	Randall

Problem F–2
Statement of partnership liquidation

SPREADSHEET

✓ 1. d. Langley, $20,000

After the accounts are closed on May 10, prior to liquidating the partnership, the capital accounts of Mark Hernandez, Donna Collins, and Janice Langley are $56,800, $12,400, and $35,600, respectively. Cash and noncash assets total $18,900 and $142,400, respectively. Amounts owed to creditors total $56,500. The partners share income and losses in the ratio of 2:1:1. Between May 10 and May 30, the noncash assets are sold for $80,000, the partner with the capital deficiency pays his or her deficiency to the partnership, and the liabilities are paid.

Instructions

1. Prepare a statement of partnership liquidation, indicating (a) the sale of assets and division of loss, (b) the receipt of the deficiency (from the appropriate partner), and (c) the payment of liabilities.
2. ◀■■■■▶ If the partner with the capital deficiency declares bankruptcy and is unable to pay the deficiency, explain how the deficiency would be divided between the partners.

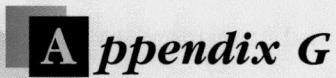

❇ Hershey Foods Corporation

1996 Consolidated Financial Statements

and

Management's Discussion and Analysis

Consolidated Financial Statements and Management's Discussion and Analysis

	Page
Management's Discussion and Analysis	G-3
Consolidated Financial Statements	G-11
Notes to Consolidated Financial Statements	G-15
Responsibility for Financial Statements	G-30
Report of Independent Public Accountants	G-31
Eleven-Year Consolidated Financial Summary	G-32

HERSHEY FOODS CORPORATION

MANAGEMENT'S DISCUSSION AND ANALYSIS

OPERATING RESULTS

The Corporation achieved record sales levels in 1996 and 1995. Net sales during this two-year period increased at a compound annual rate of 5%, primarily reflecting volume growth from the introduction of new confectionery and grocery products and significant volume increases from seasonal packaged candy items. Sales increases also resulted from selected confectionery selling price increases in the United States partially offset by related sales volume declines, increased confectionery sales volume in various international markets and incremental sales from the acquisition of Henry Heide, Incorporated (Henry Heide). These increases were partially offset by lower sales resulting from the divestitures of Hershey Canada, Inc.'s *Planters* nut (Planters) and *Life Savers* and *Breath Savers* hard candy, and *Beech-Nut* cough drops (Life Savers) businesses in January 1996 and Overspecht B.V. (OZF Jamin) in the second quarter of 1995. The discontinuance of the Corporation's refrigerated pudding line in late 1994 also reduced sales during the two-year period.

Hershey Chocolate U.S.A. increased the wholesale price of its standard bar line and king size bars by approximately eleven percent in December 1995. These products represented approximately 25% of the Corporation's 1995 sales. Price increases were intended to offset higher costs for raw materials and packaging, together with the cumulative impact of inflation on other costs since the last standard bar price increase in early 1991. Hershey Pasta Group implemented selected price increases in late 1993, early 1994 and late 1995 in an effort to recover substantial increases in semolina costs. The price increases have not been sufficient to recover the full impact of the higher semolina costs, partly due to competition from subsidized pasta imports shipped into the United States.

The following acquisitions and divestitures occurred during the period:

- December 1996—The acquisition from an affiliate of Huhtamäki Oy (Huhtamaki), the international foods company based in Finland, of Huhtamaki's Leaf North America (Leaf) confectionery operations for $437.2 million, plus the assumption of $17.0 million in debt. In addition, the parties entered into a trademark and technology license agreement under which the Corporation will manufacture and/or market and distribute in North, Central and South America Huhtamaki's confectionery brands including *Good & Plenty, Heath, Jolly Rancher, Milk Duds, PayDay* and *Whoppers*.

- December 1996—The sale to Huhtamaki of the outstanding shares of Gubor Holding GmbH (Gubor) and Sperlari, S.r.l. (Sperlari). Gubor manufactures and markets high-quality assorted pralines and seasonal chocolate products in Germany and Sperlari manufactures and markets various confectionery and grocery products in Italy. The sale resulted in an after-tax loss of $35.4 million, since no tax benefit associated with the transaction was recorded. Combined net sales for Gubor and Sperlari were $216.6 million, $222.0 million and $186.6 million in 1996, 1995 and 1994, respectively.

- January 1996—The sale of the assets of Hershey Canada, Inc.'s Planters and Life Savers businesses to Johnvince Foods Group and Beta Brands Inc., respectively. Both transactions were part of a restructuring program announced by the Corporation in late 1994.

- December 1995—The acquisition of Henry Heide, a confectionery company which manufactures a variety of non-chocolate confectionery products including *Jujyfruits* candy and *Wunderbeans* jellybeans.

- June 1995—The sale of the outstanding shares of OZF Jamin to a management buyout group at OZF Jamin also as part of the restructuring program.

Income, excluding the loss on disposal of businesses in 1996 and the net after-tax effect of restructuring activities recorded in 1994, increased at a compound annual rate of 8% during the two-year period. This increase was a result of the growth in sales, partially offset by a slightly lower gross profit margin and higher selling, marketing and administrative expenses.

The Corporation's net sales, net income and cash flows are affected by the timing of business acquisitions and divestitures, new product introductions, promotional activities, price increases, and a seasonal sales bias toward the second half of the year. These factors, from time to time, cause fluctuations in net sales and net income versus the comparable quarterly periods of prior years.

Net Sales

Net sales rose $298.6 million or 8% in 1996 and $84.4 million or 2% in 1995. The increase in 1996 was primarily due to incremental sales from new confectionery and grocery products, increased confectionery sales volume in the North American seasonal packaged candy line and in various international markets, selected confectionery selling price increases in the United States partially offset by related sales volume declines, and incremental sales from the acquisition of Henry Heide. The increase in 1995 was due to incremental sales from new confectionery and grocery products, volume growth from existing domestic and foreign confectionery brands and pasta products, and selected selling price increases, principally in the Corporation's foreign businesses. These increases were partially offset by lower sales resulting from the divestiture of OZF Jamin in the second quarter of 1995 and the discontinuance of the Corporation's refrigerated pudding line in late 1994.

Costs and Expenses

Cost of sales as a percent of net sales declined from 58.2% in 1994 to 57.6% in 1995, but increased slightly to 57.7% in 1996. The decrease in gross margin in 1996 was principally the result of higher costs for certain major raw materials, primarily cocoa beans, milk, almonds and durum semolina and increased manufacturing labor and overhead rates, substantially offset by selected confectionery price increases, manufacturing efficiency improvements and the favorable impact of the OZF Jamin divestiture. The increase in gross margin in 1995 was primarily the result of manufacturing efficiency improvements, selling price increases in the Corporation's foreign businesses, and the favorable impact of the OZF Jamin divestiture. These increases were partially offset by higher costs for certain major raw materials and packaging, along with inflation in labor and overhead costs.

Selling, marketing and administrative costs increased by 7% in 1996 primarily due to a net increase in advertising and promotion expenses associated with the introduction of new products and higher selling expenses primarily related to international sales volume increases and new product introductions. Selling, marketing and administrative costs increased by 2% in 1995 primarily due to increased advertising for existing confectionery brands and the introduction of new products, partially offset by reduced promotion and administrative expenses.

Restructuring Activities

In the fourth quarter of 1994, the Corporation recorded a pre-tax restructuring charge of $106.1 million ($80.2 million after tax or $.46 per share) following a comprehensive review of domestic and foreign operations designed to enhance performance of operating assets by lowering operating and administrative costs, eliminating underperforming assets and streamlining the overall decision-making process. As of December 31, 1995, $81.8 million of restructuring reserves had been utilized and $16.7 million had been reversed to reflect revisions and changes in estimates to the original restructuring program.

During the third quarter of 1995, a pre-tax restructuring charge of $16.6 million was recorded in connection with a voluntary retirement program announced by the Corporation in August 1995. The charge was primarily related to the funding of retirement benefits for eligible employees who elected early retirement. The impact of this charge was more than offset by the partial reversal of 1994 accrued restructuring reserves, resulting in an increase to income before income taxes of $.2 million and an increase to net income of $2.0 million as the tax benefit associated with the 1995 charge more than offset the tax provision associated with the reversal of 1994 restructuring reserves.

The remaining $7.6 million of accrued restructuring reserves were utilized during 1996 as the restructuring program was completed. A portion of the restructuring reserves were used for severance and relocation benefits related to the consolidation of the pasta and grocery field sales organizations.

Interest Expense, Net

Net interest expense increased $3.2 million in 1996 as higher fixed interest expense was only partially offset by reduced short-term interest expense. Increased fixed interest expense resulted from the issuance of $200 million of 6.7% Notes due 2005 (Notes) in the fourth quarter of 1995. Lower short-term interest expense resulted from lower average borrowing balances and reduced interest rates as compared to 1995.

Net interest expense increased $9.5 million in 1995 primarily as a result of higher short-term interest expense. Short-term interest expense increased due to higher borrowing rates and increased borrowings associated with the purchase of approximately 9.0 million shares, on a pre-split basis, of the Corporation's Common Stock from the Hershey Trust Company, as Trustee for the benefit of Milton Hershey School (Milton Hershey School Trust).

Provision for Income Taxes

The Corporation's effective income tax rate was 43.1%, 39.5%, and 44.7% in 1996, 1995 and 1994, respectively. The higher 1996 rate compared to 1995 was due primarily to the lack of any tax benefit associated with the loss on disposal of businesses. The lower rate in 1995 compared to 1994 was principally due to the impact of restructuring activities.

Net Income

Net income decreased by 3% in 1996. Excluding the loss on the disposal of the Gubor and Sperlari businesses in 1996 and the net after-tax effects of the 1995 restructuring activities, income increased $28.6 million or 10%. Net income increased $15.5 million or 6% in 1995, excluding the net after-tax effects of the 1995 and 1994 restructuring activities. Income as a percent of net sales, after excluding the loss on the sale of the Gubor and Sperlari businesses in 1996 and the net after-tax effects of restructuring activities in 1995 and 1994 was 7.7% in 1996, 7.6% in 1995 and 7.3% in 1994.

FINANCIAL POSITION

The Corporation's financial position remained strong during 1996. The capitalization ratio (total short-term and long-term debt as a percent of stockholders' equity, short-term and long-term debt) was 46% as of December 31, 1996, and 42% as of December 31, 1995. The higher capitalization ratio in 1996 primarily reflected increased borrowings for business acquisitions and share repurchases. The ratio of current assets to current liabilities was 1.2:1 as of December 31, 1996, and 1.1:1 as of December 31, 1995.

Assets

Total assets increased $354.2 million or 13% as of December 31, 1996, primarily as a result of increases in inventories, property, plant and equipment and intangibles resulting from the Leaf acquisition, offset somewhat by decreases associated with the divestitures of Gubor and Sperlari.

Current assets increased by $63.9 million or 7% reflecting increased cash and cash equivalents and higher inventories in existing businesses, partly to support the introduction of new products, and current assets resulting from the Leaf acquisition, substantially offset by decreases associated with the business divestitures.

The $165.9 million net increase in property, plant and equipment principally reflected the Leaf acquisition and capital additions of $159.4 million, partly offset by the divestiture of the Gubor and Sperlari businesses, and depreciation expense of $119.4 million.

The increase in intangibles resulting from business acquisitions primarily reflected preliminary goodwill associated with the acquisition of the Leaf confectionery operations, partially offset by a decrease related to the divestiture of the Gubor and Sperlari businesses and the amortization of intangibles. The decrease in other assets was primarily associated with employee retirement plans.

Liabilities

Total liabilities increased by $276.1 million or 16% as of December 31, 1996, primarily due to an increase in long-term debt. The increase in long-term debt of $298.3 million reflected an increase in commercial paper borrowings associated with the acquisition of Leaf, net of proceeds received from the sale of the Gubor, Sperlari, Planters and Life Savers businesses. As of December 31, 1996, $300.0 million of commercial paper borrowings were reclassified as long-term debt in accordance with the Corporation's intent and ability to refinance such obligations on a long-term basis.

Stockholders' Equity

Total stockholders' equity rose by 7% in 1996, as net income exceeded dividends paid and the repurchase of Common Stock. Total stockholders' equity has increased at a compound annual rate of 5% over the past ten years.

Capital Structure

The Corporation has two classes of stock outstanding, Common Stock and Class B Common Stock (Class B Stock). Holders of the Common Stock and the Class B Stock generally vote together without regard to class on matters submitted to stockholders, including the election of directors, with the Common Stock having one vote per share and the Class B Stock having ten votes per share. However, the Common Stock, voting separately as a class, is entitled to elect one-sixth of the Board of Directors. With respect to dividend rights, the Common Stock is entitled to cash dividends 10% higher than those declared and paid on the Class B Stock.

LIQUIDITY

Historically, the Corporation's major source of financing has been cash generated from operations. The Corporation's income and, consequently, cash provided from operations during the year are affected by seasonal sales patterns, the timing of new product introductions, business acquisitions and divestitures, and price increases. Chocolate, confectionery and grocery seasonal and holiday-related sales have typically been highest during the third and fourth quarters of the year, representing the principal seasonal effect. Generally, seasonal working capital needs peak during the summer months and have been met by issuing commercial paper.

Over the past three years, cash requirements for share repurchases, business acquisitions, capital additions, and dividend payments exceeded cash provided from operating activities and proceeds from business divestitures by $404.6 million. Total debt, including debt assumed, increased during the period by $453.9 million. Cash and cash equivalents increased by $45.5 million during the period.

The Corporation anticipates that capital expenditures will be in the range of $175 million to $225 million per annum during the next several years as a result of continued modernization of existing facilities and capacity expansion to support new products and line extensions. As of December 31, 1996, the Corporation's principal capital commitments included manufacturing capacity expansion and modernization.

In August 1996, the Corporation's Board of Directors declared a two-for-one split of the Common Stock and Class B Common Stock effective September 13, 1996, to stockholders of record as of August 23, 1996. The split was effected as a stock dividend by distributing one additional share for each share held. Unless otherwise indicated, all shares and per share information have been restated to reflect the stock split.

A total of 9,437,770 shares of Common Stock have been repurchased for approximately $263.7 million under share repurchase programs which began in 1993. Of the shares repurchased, 528,000 shares were retired and the remaining 8,909,770 shares were held as Treasury Stock as of December 31, 1996.

In August 1995, the Corporation purchased an additional 18,099,546 shares (9,049,773 shares on a pre-split basis) of its Common Stock to be held as Treasury Stock from the Milton Hershey School Trust for $500.0 million. In connection with the share repurchase program begun in 1993, a total of 4,000,000 shares (2,000,000 shares on a pre-split basis) were also acquired from the Milton Hershey School Trust in 1993 for approximately $103.1 million. As of December 31, 1996, a total of 27,009,316 shares were held as Treasury Stock and $136.3 million remained available for repurchases of Common Stock under a program approved by the Corporation's Board of Directors in February 1996.

In October 1995, the Corporation issued $200 million of Notes under Form S-3 Registration Statements which were declared effective in June 1990 and November 1993. As of December 31, 1996, $300 million of debt securities remained available for issuance under the November 1993 Registration Statement. Proceeds from any offering of the $300 million of debt securities available under the shelf registration may be used for general corporate requirements including, reducing existing commercial paper borrowings, financing capital additions and funding future business acquisitions and working capital requirements.

In March 1997, the Corporation issued $150 million of 6.95% Notes due 2007 under the November 1993 Registration Statement. Proceeds from the debt issuance were used to repay a portion of the commercial paper borrowings associated with the Leaf acquisition.

In order to minimize its financing costs and to manage interest rate exposure, the Corporation, from time to time, enters into interest rate swap agreements to effectively convert a portion of its floating rate debt to fixed rate debt. As of December 31, 1996, the Corporation had agreements outstanding with an aggregate notional amount of $125.0 million, with maturities through October 1997. Any interest rate differential on interest rate swaps is recognized as an adjustment to interest expense over the term of each agreement. The Corporation's risk related to swap agreements is limited to the cost of replacing such agreements at current market rates.

In December 1995, the Corporation entered into committed credit facility agreements with a syndicate of banks under which it could borrow up to $600 million with options to increase borrowings by $1.0 billion with the concurrence of the banks. Lines of credit previously maintained by the Corporation were significantly reduced when the credit facility agreements became effective. Of the total committed credit facility, $200 million is for a renewable 364-day term and $400 million is effective for a five-year term. Both the short-term and long-term committed credit facility agreements were amended and renewed effective December 13, 1996. The credit facilities may be used to fund general corporate requirements, to support commercial paper borrowings and, in certain instances, to finance future business acquisitions.

Cash Flow Activities

Cash provided from operating activities totaled $1.3 billion during the past three years. Over this period, cash used by or provided from accounts receivable and inventories has tended to fluctuate as a result of sales during December and inventory management practices. The change in cash required for or provided from other assets and liabilities between the years was primarily related to variations in the funding status of pension plans, commodities transactions and the timing of payments for accrued liabilities, including income taxes, and in 1995 and 1994, restructuring expenses.

Investing activities included capital additions and business acquisitions and divestitures. Capital additions during the past three years included the purchase of manufacturing equipment, and expansion and modernization of existing facilities. Businesses acquired during the past three years included Leaf in 1996 and Henry Heide in 1995. The Gubor, Sperlari, Planters and Life Savers businesses were sold in 1996 and OZF Jamin was sold in 1995. Cash used for business acquisitions represented the purchase price paid and consisted of the current assets, property, plant and equipment, intangibles and other assets acquired, net of liabilities assumed.

Financing activities included debt borrowings and repayments, payment of dividends, the exercise of stock options, incentive plan transactions and the repurchase of Common Stock. During the past three years, short-term borrowings in the form of commercial paper or bank borrowings were used to fund seasonal working capital requirements, business acquisitions, a share repurchase program and the purchase of Common Stock from the Milton Hershey School Trust. The proceeds from the issuance of $200 million of Notes in October 1995 were used to reduce short-term borrowings. During the past three years, a total of 22,391,116 shares of Common Stock has been repurchased for approximately $631.9 million. Cash requirements for incentive plan transactions were $75.3 million during the past three years, partially offset by cash received from the exercise of stock options of $40.6 million.

Commodity Price Risk Management

The Corporation's most significant raw materials include cocoa, sugar, milk, peanuts, flour and almonds. The Corporation attempts to minimize the effect of price fluctuations related to the purchase of these raw materials primarily through forward purchasing to cover future manufacturing requirements, generally for periods from 3 to 24 months. With regard to cocoa, sugar and corn sweeteners, price risks are also managed by entering into futures and options contracts. At the present time, similar futures and options contracts are not available for use in pricing the Corporation's other major raw materials. Futures contracts are used in combination with forward purchasing of cocoa, sugar and corn sweetener requirements, principally to take advantage of market fluctuations which provide more favorable pricing opportunities and to increase diversity or flexibility in sourcing these raw materials. The Corporation's commodity procurement practices are intended to reduce the risk of future price increases, but also may potentially limit the ability to benefit from possible price decreases.

The cost of cocoa beans and the prices for the related commodity futures contracts historically have been subject to wide fluctuations attributable to a variety of factors, including the effect of weather on crop yield, other imbalances between supply and demand, currency exchange rates and speculative influences. Cocoa prices have been rising since 1992 due to cocoa demand exceeding production. During 1996, prices for cocoa futures were relatively stable as a result of record high cocoa production in West Africa. During 1997, any problems with the development of the West African crop to be harvested beginning in the fall, could result in demand exceeding production, leading to possible cocoa futures price increases. The Corporation's costs during 1997 will not necessarily reflect market price fluctuations because of its forward purchasing practices, premiums and discounts reflective of relative values, varying delivery times, and supply and demand for specific varieties and grades of cocoa beans.

The major raw material used in the manufacture of pasta products is semolina milled from durum wheat. The Corporation purchases semolina from commercial mills and is also engaged in custom milling agreements to obtain sufficient quantities of semolina. In the first half of 1996, the market price for durum semolina remained near historic highs. Durum wheat production during 1996 increased in almost every area of the world, resulting in some price declines in the last quarter of the year. However, prices remained well above long-term historical price levels.

Generally, the Corporation has been able to offset the effects of increases in the cost of its major raw materials, particularly cocoa beans, through selling price increases or reductions in product weights. Conversely, declines in the cost of major raw materials have served as a source of funds to enhance consumer value through increases in product weights, respond to competitive activity, develop new products and markets, and offset rising costs of other raw materials and expenses.

Market Prices and Dividends

Cash dividends paid on the Corporation's Common Stock and Class B Stock were $114.8 million in 1996 and $110.1 million in 1995. After adjustment for the two-for-one stock split, the annual dividend rate on the Common Stock was $.80 per share, an increase of 11% over the 1995 rate of $.72 per share. The 1996 dividend represented the 22nd consecutive year of Common Stock dividend increases.

On February 4, 1997, the Corporation's Board of Directors declared a quarterly dividend of $.20 per share of Common Stock payable on March 14, 1997, to stockholders of record as of February 24, 1997. It is the Corporation's 269th consecutive Common Stock dividend. A quarterly dividend of $.18 per share of Class B Stock also was declared.

Hershey Foods Corporation's Common Stock is listed and traded principally on the New York Stock Exchange (NYSE) under the ticker symbol "HSY." Approximately 47.0 million shares of the Corporation's Common Stock were traded during 1996. The Class B Stock is not publicly traded.

The closing price of the Common Stock on December 31, 1996, was $43¾. There were 42,483 stockholders of record of the Common Stock and the Class B Stock as of December 31, 1996.

The following table shows the dividends paid per share of Common Stock and Class B Stock and the price range of the Common Stock for each quarter of the past two years:

| | Dividends Paid Per Share | | Common Stock Price Range* | |
	Common Stock	Class B Stock	High	Low
1996				
1st Quarter	$ .180	$.1625	40\frac{5}{8}$	31\frac{15}{16}$
2nd Quarter	.180	.1625	38$\frac{15}{16}$	34$\frac{7}{8}$
3rd Quarter	.200	.1800	51$\frac{3}{4}$	35
4th Quarter	.200	.1800	51$\frac{3}{4}$	43$\frac{1}{2}$
Total	$ .760	$.6850		
1995				
1st Quarter	$.1625	$ .1475	26\frac{3}{16}$	$24
2nd Quarter	.1625	.1475	27$\frac{15}{16}$	25$\frac{1}{16}$
3rd Quarter	.1800	.1625	32$\frac{7}{16}$	26$\frac{13}{16}$
4th Quarter	.1800	.1625	33$\frac{15}{16}$	29$\frac{1}{2}$
Total	$.6850	$ .6200		

* NYSE-Composite Quotations for Common Stock by calendar quarter.

RETURN MEASURES

Operating Return on Average Stockholders' Equity

The Corporation's operating return on average stockholders' equity was 27.5% in 1996. Over the most recent five-year period, the return has ranged from 17.3% in 1992 to 27.5% in 1996. For the purpose of calculating operating return on average stockholders' equity, earnings is defined as net income, excluding the catch-up adjustments for accounting changes and the after-tax gain on the sale of the investment in Freia Marabou a.s (Freia) in 1993, the after-tax restructuring activities in 1994 and 1995 and the after-tax loss on the disposal of businesses in 1996.

Operating Return on Average Invested Capital

The Corporation's operating return on average invested capital was 17.8% in 1996. Over the most recent five-year period, the return has ranged from 14.4% in 1992 to 17.8% in 1996. Average invested capital consists of the annual average of beginning and ending balances of long-term debt, deferred income taxes and stockholders' equity. For the purpose of calculating operating return on average invested capital, earnings is defined as net income, excluding the sale of the investment in Freia, the catch-up adjustments for accounting changes, the after-tax restructuring activities in 1994 and 1995, the after-tax loss on disposal of businesses in 1996, and the after-tax effect of interest on long-term debt.

HERSHEY FOODS CORPORATION
CONSOLIDATED STATEMENTS OF INCOME

For the years ended December 31,	1996	1995	1994
In thousands of dollars except per share amounts			
Net Sales	**$3,989,308**	$3,690,667	$3,606,271
Costs and Expenses:			
Cost of sales	**2,302,089**	2,126,274	2,097,556
Selling, marketing and administrative	**1,124,087**	1,053,758	1,034,115
Total costs and expenses	**3,426,176**	3,180,032	3,131,671
Restructuring Credit (Charge)	**—**	151	(106,105)
Loss on Disposal of Businesses	**(35,352)**	—	—
Income before Interest and Income Taxes	**527,780**	510,786	368,495
Interest expense, net	**48,043**	44,833	35,357
Income before Income Taxes	**479,737**	465,953	333,138
Provision for income taxes	**206,551**	184,034	148,919
Net Income	**$ 273,186**	$ 281,919	$ 184,219
Net Income Per Share	**$ 1.77**	$ 1.70	$ 1.06
Cash Dividends Paid Per Share:			
Common Stock	**$ .7600**	$ .6850	$ .6250
Class B Common Stock	**.6850**	.6200	.5675

The notes to consolidated financial statements are an integral part of these statements.

HERSHEY FOODS CORPORATION
CONSOLIDATED BALANCE SHEETS

December 31,	1996	1995
In thousands of dollars		
ASSETS		
Current Assets:		
Cash and cash equivalents	$ 61,422	$ 32,346
Accounts receivable—trade	294,606	326,024
Inventories	474,978	397,570
Deferred income taxes	94,464	84,785
Prepaid expenses and other	60,759	81,598
Total current assets	986,229	922,323
Property, Plant and Equipment, Net	1,601,895	1,436,009
Intangibles Resulting from Business Acquisitions	565,962	428,714
Other Assets	30,710	43,577
Total assets	$3,184,796	$2,830,623
LIABILITIES AND STOCKHOLDERS' EQUITY		
Current Liabilities:		
Accounts payable	$ 134,213	$ 127,067
Accrued liabilities	357,828	308,123
Accrued income taxes	10,254	15,514
Short-term debt	299,469	413,268
Current portion of long-term debt	15,510	383
Total current liabilities	817,274	864,355
Long-term Debt	655,289	357,034
Other Long-term Liabilities	327,209	333,814
Deferred Income Taxes	224,003	192,461
Total liabilities	2,023,775	1,747,664
Stockholders' Equity:		
Preferred Stock, shares issued: none in 1996 and 1995	—	—
Common Stock, shares issued: 149,471,964 in 1996 and 74,733,982 on a pre-split basis in 1995	149,472	74,734
Class B Common Stock, shares issued: 30,478,908 in 1996 and 15,241,454 on a pre-split basis in 1995	30,478	15,241
Additional paid-in capital	42,432	47,732
Cumulative foreign currency translation adjustments	(32,875)	(29,240)
Unearned ESOP compensation	(31,935)	(35,128)
Retained earnings	1,763,144	1,694,696
Treasury—Common Stock shares, at cost: 27,009,316 in 1996 and 12,709,553 on a pre-split basis in 1995	(759,695)	(685,076)
Total stockholders' equity	1,161,021	1,082,959
Total liabilities and stockholders' equity	$3,184,796	$2,830,623

The notes to consolidated financial statements are an integral part of these balance sheets.

HERSHEY FOODS CORPORATION

CONSOLIDATED STATEMENTS OF CASH FLOWS

For the years ended December 31,	1996	1995	1994
In thousands of dollars			
Cash Flows Provided from (Used by) Operating Activities			
Net income	**$ 273,186**	$ 281,919	$ 184,219
Adjustments to reconcile net income to net cash provided from operations:			
Depreciation and amortization	**133,476**	133,884	129,041
Deferred income taxes	**22,863**	26,380	(2,328)
Restructuring (credit) charge	**—**	(151)	106,105
Loss on disposal of businesses	**35,352**	—	—
Changes in assets and liabilities, net of effects from business acquisitions and divestitures:			
Accounts receivable—trade	**5,159**	1,666	(36,696)
Inventories	**(41,038)**	28,147	7,740
Accounts payable	**14,032**	14,767	(10,230)
Other assets and liabilities	**15,120**	(11,297)	(58,146)
Other, net	**5,593**	19,614	20,032
Net Cash Provided from Operating Activities	**463,743**	494,929	339,737
Cash Flows Provided from (Used by) Investing Activities			
Capital additions	**(159,433)**	(140,626)	(138,711)
Business acquisitions	**(437,195)**	(12,500)	—
Proceeds from divestitures	**149,222**	—	—
Other, net	**9,333**	8,720	(4,492)
Net Cash (Used by) Investing Activities	**(438,073)**	(144,406)	(143,203)
Cash Flows Provided from (Used by) Financing Activities			
Net change in short-term borrowings partially classified as long-term debt	**210,929**	103,530	(20,503)
Long-term borrowings	**—**	202,448	102
Repayment of long-term debt	**(3,103)**	(7,887)	(14,413)
Cash dividends paid	**(114,763)**	(110,090)	(106,961)
Exercise of stock options	**22,049**	15,106	3,494
Incentive plan transactions	**(45,634)**	(21,903)	(7,726)
Repurchase of Common Stock	**(66,072)**	(526,119)	(39,748)
Net Cash Provided from (Used by) Financing Activities	**3,406**	(344,915)	(185,755)
Increase in Cash and Cash Equivalents	**29,076**	5,608	10,779
Cash and Cash Equivalents as of January 1	**32,346**	26,738	15,959
Cash and Cash Equivalents as of December 31	**$ 61,422**	$ 32,346	$ 26,738
Interest Paid	**$ 52,143**	$ 43,731	$ 36,803
Income Taxes Paid	**180,347**	148,629	177,876

The notes to consolidated financial statements are an integral part of these statements.

HERSHEY FOODS CORPORATION

CONSOLIDATED STATEMENTS OF STOCKHOLDERS' EQUITY

In thousands of dollars

	Preferred Stock	Common Stock	Class B Common Stock	Additional Paid-in Capital	Cumulative Foreign Currency Translation Adjustments	Unearned ESOP Compensation	Retained Earnings	Treasury Common Stock	Total Stockholders' Equity
Balance as of January 1, 1994	$ —	$ 74,669	$ 15,253	$ 51,196	$ (13,905)	$ (41,515)	$ 1,445,609	$ (118,963)	$ 1,412,344
Net income							184,219		184,219
Dividends:									
Common Stock, $.625 per share							(89,660)		(89,660)
Class B Common Stock, $.5675 per share							(17,301)		(17,301)
Foreign currency translation adjustments					(10,632)				(10,632)
Conversion of Class B Common Stock into Common Stock		10	(10)						—
Incentive plan transactions				(1,264)					(1,264)
Exercise of stock options				(548)					(548)
Employee stock ownership trust transactions				496		3,194			3,690
Repurchase of Common Stock								(39,748)	(39,748)
Balance as of December 31, 1994	—	74,679	15,243	49,880	(24,537)	(38,321)	1,522,867	(158,711)	1,441,100
Net income							281,919		281,919
Dividends:									
Common Stock, $.685 per share							(91,190)		(91,190)
Class B Common Stock, $.62 per share							(18,900)		(18,900)
Foreign currency translation adjustments					(4,703)				(4,703)
Conversion of Class B Common Stock into Common Stock		2	(2)						—
Incentive plan transactions				(180)					(180)
Exercise of stock options		53		(2,456)				(246)	(2,649)
Employee stock ownership trust transactions				488		3,193			3,681
Repurchase of Common Stock								(526,119)	(526,119)
Balance as of December 31, 1995	—	74,734	15,241	47,732	(29,240)	(35,128)	1,694,696	(685,076)	1,082,959
Net income							273,186		273,186
Dividends:									
Common Stock, $.76 per share							(93,884)		(93,884)
Class B Common Stock, $.685 per share							(20,879)		(20,879)
Foreign currency translation adjustments					(3,635)				(3,635)
Two-for-one stock split		74,736	15,239				(89,975)		—
Conversion of Class B Common Stock into Common Stock		2	(2)						
Incentive plan transactions				(426)					(426)
Exercise of stock options				(5,391)				(8,547)	(13,938)
Employee stock ownership trust transactions				517		3,193			3,710
Repurchase of Common Stock								(66,072)	(66,072)
Balance as of December 31, 1996	$ —	$149,472	$30,478	$42,432	$(32,875)	$(31,935)	$1,763,144	$(759,695)	$1,161,021

The notes to consolidated financial statements are an integral part of these statements.

HERSHEY FOODS CORPORATION
NOTES TO CONSOLIDATED FINANCIAL STATEMENTS

1. SUMMARY OF SIGNIFICANT ACCOUNTING POLICIES

Significant accounting policies employed by the Corporation are discussed below and in other notes to the consolidated financial statements. Certain reclassifications have been made to prior year amounts to conform to the 1996 presentation. Unless otherwise indicated, all shares and per share information have been restated for the two-for-one stock split effective September 13, 1996.

Principles of Consolidation

The consolidated financial statements include the accounts of the Corporation and its subsidiaries after elimination of intercompany accounts and transactions.

Use of Estimates

The preparation of financial statements in conformity with generally accepted accounting principles requires management to make estimates and assumptions that affect the reported amounts of assets and liabilities, the disclosure of contingent assets and liabilities at the date of the financial statements and the reported amounts of revenues and expenses during the reporting period. Actual results could differ from those estimates, particularly for accounts receivable and certain current and long-term liabilities.

Cash Equivalents

All highly liquid debt instruments purchased with a maturity of three months or less are classified as cash equivalents.

Commodities Futures and Options Contracts

In connection with the purchasing of cocoa, sugar and corn sweeteners for anticipated manufacturing requirements, the Corporation enters into commodities futures and options contracts as deemed appropriate to reduce the effect of price fluctuations. In accordance with Statement of Financial Accounting Standards No. 80 "Accounting for Futures Contracts," these futures and options contracts meet the hedge criteria and are accounted for as hedges. Accordingly, gains and losses are deferred and recognized in cost of sales as part of the product cost.

Property, Plant and Equipment

Property, plant and equipment are stated at cost. Depreciation of buildings, machinery and equipment is computed using the straight-line method over the estimated useful lives.

Intangibles Resulting from Business Acquisitions

Intangible assets resulting from business acquisitions principally consist of the excess of the acquisition cost over the fair value of the net assets of businesses acquired (goodwill). Goodwill is amortized on a straight-line basis over 40 years. Other intangible assets are amortized on a straight-line basis over the estimated useful lives. The Corporation periodically evaluates whether events or circumstances have occurred indicating that the carrying amount of goodwill may not be recoverable. When factors indicate that goodwill should be evaluated for possible impairment, the Corporation uses an estimate of the acquired business' undiscounted future cash flows compared to the related carrying amount of net assets, including goodwill, to determine if an impairment loss should be recognized.

Accumulated amortization of intangible assets resulting from business acquisitions was $110.1 million and $101.5 million as of December 31, 1996 and 1995, respectively.

Foreign Currency Translation

Results of operations for foreign entities are translated using the average exchange rates during the period. For foreign entities, assets and liabilities are translated to U.S. dollars using the exchange rates in effect at the balance sheet date. Resulting translation adjustments are recorded in a separate component of stockholders' equity, "Cumulative Foreign Currency Translation Adjustments."

Foreign Exchange Contracts

The Corporation enters into foreign exchange forward and options contracts to hedge transactions primarily related to firm commitments to purchase equipment, certain raw materials and finished goods denominated in foreign currencies, and to hedge payment of intercompany transactions with its non-domestic subsidiaries. These contracts reduce currency risk from exchange rate movements.

Foreign exchange forward contracts are intended and effective as hedges of firm, identifiable, foreign currency commitments and foreign exchange options contracts meet required hedge criteria for anticipated transactions. Accordingly, gains and losses are deferred and accounted for as part of the underlying transactions. Gains and losses on terminated derivatives designated as hedges are accounted for as part of the originally hedged transaction. Gains and losses on derivatives designated as hedges of items which mature, are sold or terminated, or of anticipated transactions which are no longer likely to occur, are recorded currently in income. In entering into these contracts the Corporation has assumed the risk which might arise from the possible inability of counterparties to meet the terms of their contracts. The Corporation does not expect any losses as a result of counterparty defaults.

License Agreements

The Corporation has entered into license agreements under which it has access to certain trademarks and proprietary technology, and manufactures and/or markets and distributes certain products. The rights under these agreements are extendable on a long-term basis at the Corporation's option subject to certain conditions, including minimum sales levels, which the Corporation has met. License fees and royalties, payable under the terms of the agreements, are expensed as incurred.

Research and Development

The Corporation expenses research and development costs as incurred. Research and development expense was $26.1 million, $26.2 million and $26.3 million in 1996, 1995 and 1994, respectively.

Advertising

The Corporation expenses advertising costs as incurred. Advertising expense was $174.2 million, $159.2 million and $120.6 million in 1996, 1995 and 1994, respectively. Prepaid advertising as of December 31, 1996 and 1995, was $2.2 million and $3.0 million, respectively.

2. ACQUISITIONS AND DIVESTITURES

In December 1996, the Corporation acquired from an affiliate of Huhtamäki Oy (Huhtamaki), the international foods company based in Finland, Huhtamaki's Leaf North America (Leaf) confectionery operations for $437.2 million, plus the assumption of $17.0 million in debt. In addition, the parties entered into a trademark and technology license agreement under which the Corporation will manufacture and/or market and distribute in North, Central and South America Huhtamaki's confectionery brands including *Good & Plenty, Heath, Jolly Rancher, Milk Duds, PayDay* and *Whoppers*. Leaf's principal manufacturing facilities are located in Denver, Colorado; Memphis, Tennessee; and Robinson, Illinois.

In December 1995, the Corporation completed the acquisition of the outstanding shares of the confectionery company Henry Heide, Incorporated (Henry Heide), for approximately $12.5 million. Henry Heide's headquarters and manufacturing facility are located in New Brunswick, N.J., where it manufactures a variety of non-chocolate confectionery products including *Jujyfruits* candy and *Wunderbeans* jellybeans.

In accordance with the purchase method of accounting, the purchase prices of the acquisitions summarized above were allocated on a preliminary basis to the underlying assets and liabilities at the date of acquisition based on their estimated respective fair values, which may be revised at a later date. Total liabilities assumed, including debt, were $138.0 million in 1996 and $10.6 million in 1995. Results subsequent to the dates of acquisition are included in the consolidated financial statements. Had the results of the Henry Heide acquisition been included in consolidated results for the entire length of each period presented, the effect would not have been material.

Had the acquisition of Leaf occurred at the beginning of 1996, pro forma consolidated results would have been as follows:

For the year ended December 31,	1996
In thousands of dollars except per share amount	(unaudited)
Net sales	$4,473,950
Net income	256,300
Net income per share	1.66

The pro forma results are based on historical financial information provided by Huhtamaki, excluding a business restructuring charge recorded by Huhtamaki in 1996 and adjusted to give effect to certain costs and expenses, including fees under the trademark and technology license agreement, goodwill amortization, interest expense and income taxes which would have been incurred by the Corporation if it had owned and operated the Leaf confectionery business throughout 1996. These results are not necessarily reflective of the actual results which would have occurred if the acquisition had been completed at the beginning of the year, nor are they necessarily indicative of future combined financial results.

In December 1996, the Corporation completed the sale to Huhtamaki of the outstanding shares of Gubor Holding GmbH (Gubor) and Sperlari, S.r.l. (Sperlari). Gubor manufactures and markets high-quality assorted pralines and seasonal chocolate products in Germany and Sperlari manufactures and markets various confectionery and grocery products in Italy. The total proceeds from the sale of the Gubor and Sperlari businesses were $121.7 million. The transaction resulted in an after-tax loss of $35.4 million since no tax benefit associated with the transaction was recorded. Combined net sales for Gubor and Sperlari were $216.6 million, $222.0 million and $186.6 million in 1996, 1995 and 1994, respectively.

In January 1996, the Corporation completed the sale of the assets of Hershey Canada, Inc.'s *Planters* nut (Planters) and *Life Savers* and *Breath Savers* hard candy, and *Beech-Nut* cough drops (Life Savers) businesses to Johnvince Foods Group and Beta Brands Inc., respectively. Both transactions were part of a restructuring program announced by the Corporation in late 1994.

In June 1995, the Corporation completed the sale of the outstanding shares of Overspecht B.V. (OZF Jamin) to a management buyout group at OZF Jamin, as part of the Corporation's restructuring program. OZF Jamin manufactures chocolate and non-chocolate confectionery products, cookies, biscuits and ice cream for distribution primarily to customers in the Netherlands and Belgium.

3. RESTRUCTURING ACTIVITIES

In the fourth quarter of 1994, the Corporation recorded a pre-tax restructuring charge of $106.1 million, following a comprehensive review of domestic and foreign operations designed to enhance performance of operating assets by lowering operating and administrative costs, eliminating underperforming assets and streamlining the overall decision-making process. The charge of $106.1 million resulted in an after-tax charge of $80.2 million or $.46 per share in 1994.

The charge included $34.3 million of severance and termination benefits for the elimination of approximately 500 positions in the manufacturing, technical and administrative areas at both domestic and foreign operations. The charge also included anticipated losses on disposals of certain businesses of $39.1 million, product line discontinuations of $17.5 million and the consolidation of operations and disposal of machinery and equipment of $15.2 million.

As of December 31, 1995, $81.8 million of restructuring reserves had been utilized and $16.7 million had been reversed to reflect revisions and changes in estimates to the original restructuring program. Operating cash flows were used to fund cash requirements which represented approximately 25% of the total reserves utilized. The non-cash portion of restructuring reserve utilization was associated primarily with the divestiture of foreign businesses and the discontinuation of certain product lines.

During the third quarter of 1995, a pre-tax restructuring charge of $16.6 million was recorded in connection with a voluntary retirement program announced by the Corporation in August 1995. The charge was primarily related to the funding of retirement benefits for eligible employees who elected early retirement. This cash charge was funded from operating cash flows. The impact of this charge was more than offset by the partial reversal of 1994 accrued restructuring reserves in the fourth quarter of 1995 resulting in an increase to income before income taxes of $.2 million and an increase to net income of $2.0 million, as the tax benefit associated with the 1995 charge more than offset the tax provision associated with the reversal of 1994 restructuring reserves.

The remaining $7.6 million of accrued restructuring reserves as of December 31, 1995, were utilized during 1996 as the restructuring program was completed. A portion of the restructuring reserves were used for severance and relocation benefits related to the consolidation of the pasta and grocery field sales organizations.

4. RENTAL AND LEASE COMMITMENTS

Rent expense was $25.3 million, $24.9 million and $25.7 million for 1996, 1995 and 1994, respectively. Rent expense pertains to all operating leases, which were principally related to certain administrative buildings, distribution facilities and transportation equipment. Future minimum rental payments under non-cancelable operating leases with a remaining term in excess of one year as of December 31, 1996, were: 1997, $16.4 million; 1998, $15.1 million; 1999, $15.5 million; 2000, $15.1 million; 2001, $15.1 million; 2002 and beyond, $90.8 million.

5. FINANCIAL INSTRUMENTS

The carrying amounts of financial instruments including cash and cash equivalents, accounts receivable, accounts payable and short-term debt approximated fair value as of December 31, 1996 and 1995, because of the relatively short maturity of these instruments. The carrying value of long-term debt, including the current portion, approximated fair value as of December 31, 1996 and 1995, based upon quoted market prices for the same or similar debt issues.

As of December 31, 1996, the Corporation had foreign exchange forward contracts maturing in 1997 and 1998 to purchase $25.0 million in foreign currency, primarily British sterling and German marks, and to sell $24.6 million in foreign currency, primarily Canadian dollars and Japanese yen, at contracted forward rates.

As of December 31, 1995, the Corporation had foreign exchange forward contracts maturing in 1996 and 1997 to purchase $54.7 million in foreign currency, primarily Canadian dollars, British sterling and Swiss francs, and to sell $26.4 million in foreign currency, primarily Italian lira, Canadian dollars and Japanese yen, at contracted forward rates.

To hedge foreign currency exposure related to anticipated transactions associated with the purchase of certain raw materials and finished goods generally covering 3 to 24 months, the Corporation also purchases, from time to time, foreign exchange options which permit, but do not require, the Corporation to exchange foreign currencies at a future date with another party at a contracted exchange rate. To finance premiums paid on such options, the Corporation may also write offsetting options at exercise prices which limit but do not eliminate the effect of purchased options and forward contracts as a hedge. As of December 31, 1995, the Corporation had purchased foreign exchange options of $11.5 million and written foreign exchange options of $8.9 million, principally related to British sterling. Such options expired or were settled in the first quarter of 1996.

The fair value of foreign exchange forward contracts is estimated by obtaining quotes for future contracts with similar terms, adjusted where necessary for maturity differences, and the fair value of foreign exchange options is estimated using active market quotations. As of December 31, 1996 and 1995, the fair value of foreign exchange forward and options contracts approximated carrying value. The Corporation does not hold or issue financial instruments for trading purposes.

In order to minimize its financing costs and to manage interest rate exposure, the Corporation, from time to time, enters into interest rate swap agreements to effectively convert a portion of its floating rate debt to fixed rate debt. Agreements outstanding with an aggregate notional amount of $75.0 million matured during 1996. As of December 31, 1996, the Corporation had agreements outstanding with an aggregate notional amount of $125.0 million with maturities through October 1997. As of December 31, 1996 and 1995, interest rates payable were at weighted average fixed rates of 5.8% and 5.6%, respectively, and interest rates receivable were floating based on 30-day commercial paper composite rates. Any interest rate differential on interest rate swaps is recognized as an adjustment to interest expense over the term of each agreement. The Corporation's risk related to swap agreements is limited to the cost of replacing such agreements at current market rates.

6. INTEREST EXPENSE

Interest expense, net consisted of the following:

For the years ended December 31,	1996	1995	1994
In thousands of dollars			
Long-term debt and lease obligations	$30,818	$20,949	$19,103
Short-term debt	22,752	28,576	21,155
Capitalized interest	(1,534)	(1,957)	(3,009)
Interest expense, gross	52,036	47,568	37,249
Interest income	(3,993)	(2,735)	(1,892)
Interest expense, net	$48,043	$44,833	$35,357

7. SHORT-TERM DEBT

Generally, the Corporation's short-term borrowings are in the form of commercial paper or bank loans with an original maturity of three months or less. In December 1995, the Corporation entered into committed credit facility agreements with a syndicate of banks under which it could borrow up to $600 million as of December 31, 1996, with options to increase borrowings by $1.0 billion with the concurrence of the banks. Of the total committed credit facility, $200 million is for a renewable 364-day term and $400 million is effective for a five-year term. Both the short-term and long-term committed credit facility agreements were amended and renewed effective December 13, 1996. The credit facilities may be used to fund general corporate requirements, to support commercial paper borrowings and, in certain instances, to finance future business acquisitions. As of December 31, 1996, $300.0 million of commercial paper borrowings were reclassified as long-term debt in accordance with the Corporation's intent and ability to refinance such obligations on a long-term basis.

The Corporation also maintains lines of credit arrangements with domestic and international commercial banks, under which it could borrow in various currencies up to approximately $96.1 million and $97.7 million as of December 31, 1996 and 1995, respectively, at the lending banks' prime commercial interest rates or lower. The Corporation had combined domestic commercial paper borrowings, including the portion classified as long-term debt, and short-term foreign bank loans against its credit facilities and lines of credit of $599.5 million as of December 31, 1996, and $413.3 million as of December 31, 1995. The weighted average interest rates on short-term borrowings outstanding as of December 31, 1996 and 1995, were 5.5% and 5.7%, respectively.

The credit facilities and lines of credit were supported by commitment fee arrangements. The average fee during 1996 was approximately .05% per annum of the commitment. The Corporation is in compliance with all covenants included in the credit facility agreements. There were no significant compensating balance agreements which legally restricted these funds.

As a result of maintaining a consolidated cash management system, the Corporation maintains overdraft positions at certain banks. Such overdrafts, which were included in accounts payable, were $25.2 million and $24.8 million as of December 31, 1996 and 1995, respectively.

8. LONG-TERM DEBT

Long-term debt consisted of the following:

December 31,	1996	1995
In thousands of dollars		
Commercial Paper at interest rates ranging from 5.54% to 5.59%	$300,000	$ —
Medium-term Notes, 8.85% to 9.92%, due 1997-1998	40,400	40,400
6.7% Notes due 2005	200,000	200,000
8.8% Debentures due 2021	100,000	100,000
Other obligations, net of unamortized debt discount	30,399	17,017
Total long-term debt	670,799	357,417
Less—current portion	15,510	383
Long-term portion	$655,289	$357,034

As of December 31, 1996, $300.0 million of commercial paper borrowings were reclassified as long-term debt in accordance with the Corporation's intent and ability to refinance such obligations on a long-term basis.

Aggregate annual maturities during the next five years, excluding short-term borrowings reclassified, are: 1997, $15.5 million; 1998, $25.2 million; 1999, $.2 million; 2000, $2.2 million; and 2001, $.2 million. The Corporation's debt is principally unsecured and of equal priority. None of the debt is convertible into stock of the Corporation. The Corporation is in compliance with all covenants included in the related debt agreements.

9. INCOME TAXES

Income before income taxes was as follows:

For the years ended December 31,	1996	1995	1994
In thousands of dollars			
Domestic	$499,607	$452,084	$411,089
Foreign	(19,870)	13,869	(77,951)
Income before income taxes	$479,737	$465,953	$333,138

The provision for income taxes was as follows:

For the years ended December 31,	1996	1995	1994
In thousands of dollars			
Current:			
Federal	$158,040	$135,034	$126,234
State	23,288	22,620	24,712
Foreign	2,360	—	301
Current provision for income taxes	183,688	157,654	151,247
Deferred:			
Federal	12,952	12,455	6,221
State	8,134	8,198	2,652
Foreign	1,777	5,727	(11,201)
Deferred provision for income taxes	22,863	26,380	(2,328)
Total provision for income taxes	$206,551	$184,034	$148,919

The 1994 Foreign deferred income tax benefit was associated primarily with the restructuring charge recorded in the fourth quarter of that year.

The tax effects of the significant temporary differences which comprised the deferred tax assets and liabilities were as follows:

December 31,	1996	1995
In thousands of dollars		
Deferred tax assets:		
Post-retirement benefit obligations	**$ 88,885**	$ 85,907
Accrued expenses and other reserves	**91,675**	78,506
Net operating loss carryforwards, net of valuation allowances		
of $2,663 in 1996 and $25,544 in 1995	**2,663**	7,298
Accrued trade promotion reserves	**22,910**	16,389
Other	**18,013**	27,869
Total deferred tax assets	**224,146**	215,969
Deferred tax liabilities:		
Depreciation	**256,424**	239,389
Other	**97,261**	84,256
Total deferred tax liabilities	**353,685**	323,645
Net deferred tax liabilities	**$129,539**	$107,676
Included in:		
Current deferred tax assets, net	**$ 94,464**	$ 84,785
Non-current deferred tax liabilities, net	**224,003**	192,461
Net deferred tax liabilities	**$129,539**	$107,676

As of December 31, 1996, the Corporation had $15.7 million of operating loss carryforwards available to reduce the future taxable income of a foreign subsidiary. The loss carryforwards must be utilized within the next ten years.

The following table reconciles the Federal statutory income tax rate with the Corporation's effective income tax rate:

For the years ended December 31,	1996	1995	1994
Federal statutory income tax rate	**35.0%**	35.0%	35.0%
Increase (reduction) resulting from:			
State income taxes, net of Federal income tax benefits	**4.7**	4.6	6.0
Restructuring (credit) charge for which no tax benefit was provided	**—**	(.3)	4.5
Non-deductible acquisition costs	**.6**	.6	.8
Loss on disposal of businesses for which no tax benefit was provided	**2.6**	—	—
Other, net	**.2**	(.4)	(1.6)
Effective income tax rate	**43.1%**	39.5%	44.7%

10. RETIREMENT PLANS

The Corporation and its subsidiaries sponsor several defined benefit retirement plans covering substantially all employees. Plans covering most domestic salaried and hourly employees provide retirement benefits based on individual account balances which are increased annually by pay-related and interest credits. Plans covering certain non-domestic employees provide retirement benefits based on career average pay, final pay, or final average pay as defined within the provisions of the individual plans. The Corporation also participates in several multi-employer retirement plans which provide defined benefits to employees covered under certain collective bargaining agreements.

The Corporation's policy is to fund domestic pension liabilities in accordance with the minimum and maximum limits imposed by the Employee Retirement Income Security Act of 1974 and Federal income tax laws, respectively. Non-domestic pension liabilities are funded in accordance with applicable local laws and regulations. Plan assets are invested in a broadly diversified portfolio consisting primarily of domestic and international common stocks and fixed income securities.

Pension expense included the following components:

For the years ended December 31,	1996	1995	1994
In thousands of dollars			
Service cost	$ 29,311	$ 25,311	$ 30,077
Interest cost on projected benefit obligations	35,374	32,531	28,351
Investment (return) loss on plan assets	(51,205)	(71,578)	8,288
Net amortization and deferral	14,844	40,823	(40,550)
Corporate sponsored plans	28,324	27,087	26,166
Multi-employer plans	571	361	374
Other	1,340	615	622
Total pension expense	$ 30,235	$ 28,063	$ 27,162

The funded status and amounts recognized in the consolidated balance sheets for the retirement plans were as follows:

	December 31, 1996		December 31, 1995	
	Assets Exceeded Accumulated Benefits	Accumulated Benefits Exceeded Assets	Assets Exceeded Accumulated Benefits	Accumulated Benefits Exceeded Assets
In thousands of dollars				
Actuarial present value of:				
Vested benefit obligations	$427,839	$27,316	$17,241	$417,027
Accumulated benefit obligations	$452,907	$32,422	$17,833	$447,792
Actuarial present value of projected benefit obligations	$502,371	$34,135	$27,005	$476,439
Plan assets at fair value	488,222	—	19,765	389,064
Plan assets less than projected benefit obligations	14,149	34,135	7,240	87,375
Net gain (loss) unrecognized at date of transition	906	(1,233)	525	(818)
Prior service cost and amendments not yet recognized in earnings	(26,885)	(2,305)	(1,159)	(28,701)
Unrecognized net gain (loss) from past experience different than that assumed	12,386	(2,502)	(3,615)	(3,660)
Minimum liability adjustment	—	4,494	—	21,678
Pension liability	$ 556	$32,589	$ 2,991	$ 75,874

The projected benefit obligations for the plans were determined principally using discount rates of 7.50% as of December 31, 1996, and 7.25% as of December 31, 1995. For both 1996 and 1995 the assumed long-term rate of return on plan assets was 9.5%. The assumed long-term compensation increase rate for 1996 and 1995 was primarily 4.8%.

In the third quarter of 1995, the Corporation offered a voluntary retirement program to domestic eligible employees age 55 and over. The voluntary retirement program gave eligible salaried employees an opportunity to retire with enhanced retirement benefits. The pre-tax impact on pension expense of the 1995 charge was $13.0 million or $7.7 million after tax. This amount has not been included in the disclosure of pension expense by component.

11. POST-RETIREMENT BENEFITS

The Corporation and its subsidiaries provide certain health care and life insurance benefits for retired employees subject to pre-defined limits. Substantially all of the Corporation's domestic employees become eligible for these benefits at retirement with a pre-defined benefit being available at an early retirement date. The post-retirement medical benefit is contributory for pre-Medicare retirees and for most post-Medicare retirees retiring on or after February 1, 1993. Retiree contributions are based upon a combination of years of service and age at retirement. The post-retirement life insurance benefit is non-contributory.

Net post-retirement benefit costs consisted of the following components:

For the years ended December 31,	1996	1995	1994
In thousands of dollars			
Service cost	$ 3,947	$ 3,262	$ 3,642
Interest cost on projected benefit obligations	10,853	12,918	13,334
Amortization	(2,986)	(2,322)	(1,028)
Total	$11,814	$13,858	$15,948

Obligations are unfunded and the actuarial present values of accumulated post-retirement benefit obligations recognized in the consolidated balance sheets were as follows:

December 31,	1996	1995
In thousands of dollars		
Retirees	$ 96,870	$ 78,090
Fully eligible active plan participants	22,096	24,686
Other active plan participants	58,578	57,448
Total	177,544	160,224
Plan amendments	28,903	31,377
Unrecognized net gain from past experience different than that assumed	12,127	20,892
Accrued post-retirement benefits	$218,574	$212,493

The accumulated post-retirement benefit obligations were determined principally using discount rates of 7.50% and 7.25% as of December 31, 1996 and 1995, respectively. The assumed average health care cost trend rate used in measuring the accumulated post-retirement benefit obligation as of December 31, 1996 and 1995, was 6% which was also the ultimate trend rate. A one percentage point increase in the average health care cost trend rate for each year would increase the accumulated post-retirement benefit obligations as of December 31, 1996 and 1995, by $24.4 million and $22.2 million, respectively, and would increase the sum of the net service and interest cost components of net post-retirement benefit costs for 1996 and 1995 by $2.9 million and $2.4 million, respectively.

The pre-tax impact on post-retirement benefits expense and liabilities of the 1995 charge for the voluntary retirement program was $.4 million or $.2 million after tax. This amount has not been included in the disclosure of net post-retirement benefit costs by component.

As part of its long-range financing plans, the Corporation, in 1989, implemented a corporate-owned life insurance program covering most of its domestic employees. After paying employee death benefits, proceeds from this program were available for general corporate purposes and also could be used to offset future employee benefits costs, including retiree medical benefits. During 1996, Federal tax legislation sharply curtailed the financial viability of most corporate-owned life insurance programs. As a result, the Corporation began the phase-out of its corporate-owned life insurance program during 1996. The Corporation's investment in corporate-owned life insurance policies was recorded net of policy loans in other assets, and interest accrued on the policy loans was included in accrued liabilities as of December 31, 1996 and 1995. Net life insurance expense, including interest expense, was included in selling, marketing and administrative expenses.

12. EMPLOYEE STOCK OWNERSHIP TRUST

The Corporation's employee stock ownership trust (ESOP) serves as the primary vehicle for contributions to its existing employee savings and stock investment plan for participating domestic salaried and hourly employees. The ESOP was funded by a 15-year 7.75% loan of $47.9 million from the Corporation. During 1996 and 1995, the ESOP received a combination of dividends on unallocated shares and contributions from the Corporation equal to the amount required to meet its principal and interest payments under the loan. Simultaneously, the ESOP allocated to participants 159,176 shares of Common Stock each year. As of December 31, 1996, the ESOP held 687,610 allocated shares and 1,591,752 unallocated shares. All ESOP shares are considered outstanding for income per share computations.

The Corporation recognized net compensation expense equal to the shares allocated multiplied by the original cost of 20\frac{1}{16}$ per share less dividends received by the ESOP on unallocated shares. Compensation expense related to the ESOP for 1996, 1995 and 1994 was $1.8 million, $1.9 million and $1.7 million, respectively. Dividends paid on unallocated ESOP shares were $1.3 million in 1996 and $1.2 million in 1995 and 1994. The unearned ESOP compensation balance in stockholders' equity represented deferred compensation expense to be recognized by the Corporation in future years as additional shares are allocated to participants.

13. CAPITAL STOCK AND NET INCOME PER SHARE

As of December 31, 1996, the Corporation had 530,000,000 authorized shares of capital stock. Of this total, 450,000,000 shares were designated as Common Stock, 75,000,000 shares as Class B Common Stock (Class B Stock), and 5,000,000 shares as Preferred Stock, each class having a par value of one dollar per share. As of December 31, 1996, a combined total of 179,950,872 shares of both classes of common stock had been issued of which 152,941,556 shares were outstanding. No shares of the Preferred Stock were issued or outstanding during the three-year period ended December 31, 1996.

In August 1996, the Corporation's Board of Directors declared a two-for-one split of the Common Stock and Class B Common Stock effective September 13, 1996, to stockholders of record as of August 23, 1996. The split was effected as a stock dividend by distributing one additional share for each share held.

Holders of the Common Stock and the Class B Stock generally vote together without regard to class on matters submitted to stockholders, including the election of directors, with the Common Stock having one vote per share and the Class B Stock having ten votes per share. However, the Common Stock, voting separately as a class, is entitled to elect one-sixth of the Board of Directors. With respect to dividend rights, the Common Stock is entitled to cash dividends 10% higher than those declared and paid on the Class B Stock.

Class B Stock can be converted into Common Stock on a share-for-share basis at any time. On a pre-split basis during 1996, 1995 and 1994, a total of 2,000 shares, 1,525 shares and 10,300 shares, respectively, of Class B Stock were converted into Common Stock.

Hershey Trust Company, as Trustee for the benefit of Milton Hershey School (Milton Hershey School Trust), as institutional fiduciary for estates and trusts unrelated to Milton Hershey School, and as direct owner of investment shares, held a total of 24,587,025 shares of the Common Stock, and as Trustee for the benefit of Milton Hershey School, held 30,306,006 shares of the Class B Stock as of December 31, 1996, and was entitled to cast approximately 77% of the total votes of both classes of the Corporation's common stock. The Milton Hershey School Trust must approve the issuance of shares of Common Stock or any other action which would result in the Milton Hershey School Trust not continuing to have voting control of the Corporation.

A total of 9,437,770 shares of Common Stock have been repurchased for approximately $263.7 million under share repurchase programs which were approved by the Corporation's Board of Director's in 1993 and 1996. Of the shares repurchased, 528,000 shares were retired and the remaining 8,909,770 shares were held as Treasury Stock as of December 31, 1996. In August 1995, the Corporation purchased an additional 18,099,546 shares (9,049,773 shares on a pre-split basis) of its Common Stock to be held as Treasury Stock from the Milton Hershey School Trust for $500.0 million. A total of 27,009,316 shares were held as Treasury Stock as of December 31, 1996.

Net income per share has been computed based on the weighted average number of shares of the Common Stock and the Class B Stock outstanding during the year. Average shares outstanding were 153,995,307 for 1996, 165,687,082 for 1995 and 174,037,252 for 1994.

14. STOCK COMPENSATION PLAN

The long-term portion of the 1987 Key Employee Incentive Plan (Plan), provides for grants of stock-based compensation awards to senior executives and key employees of one or more of the following: non-qualified stock options (fixed stock options), performance stock units, stock appreciation rights and restricted stock units. The Plan also provides for the deferral of performance stock unit awards by participants. Under the long-term portion of the Plan, the Corporation may grant to its employees up to 6.5 million shares of Common Stock on a pre-split basis. The Corporation applies Accounting Principles Board Opinion No. 25 "Accounting for Stock Issued to Employees," and related Interpretations in accounting for its Plan.

Accordingly, no compensation cost has been recognized for its fixed stock option plan. Had compensation cost for the Corporation's stock-based compensation plan been determined based on the fair value at the grant dates for awards under the Plan consistent with the method of Statement of Financial Accounting Standards No. 123 "Accounting for Stock-Based Compensation," the Corporation's net income and net income per share would have been reduced to the pro forma amounts indicated below:

For the years ended December 31,		1996	1995
In thousands of dollars except per share amounts			
Net income	As reported	**$273,186**	$281,919
	Pro forma	**266,517**	281,015
Net income per share	As reported	**$1.77**	$1.70
	Pro forma	**1.73**	1.70

The fair value of each option grant is estimated on the date of grant using a Black-Scholes option-pricing model with the following weighted-average assumptions used for grants in 1996 and 1995, respectively: dividend yields of 2.4% and 2.7%, expected volatility of 20% and 21%, risk-free interest rates of 5.6% and 7.8%, and expected lives of 7½ and 7 years.

Fixed Stock Options

The exercise price of each option equals the market price of the Corporation's common stock on the date of grant and an option's maximum term is ten years. Options are granted in January and generally vest at the end of the second year.

A summary of the status of the Corporation's fixed stock options as of December 31, 1996, 1995, and 1994, and changes during the years ending on those dates is presented below:

	1996		1995		1994	
Fixed Options	Shares	Weighted-Average Exercise Price	Shares	Weighted-Average Exercise Price	Shares	Weighted-Average Exercise Price
Outstanding at beginning of year	4,435,800	$22.54	5,067,900	$21.62	3,460,850	$19.91
Granted	2,619,200	$33.08	237,400	$24.19	1,927,600	$24.50
Exercised	(1,062,980)	$20.74	(843,100)	$17.43	(209,950)	$18.58
Forfeited	(89,800)	$31.92	(26,400)	$24.24	(110,600)	$24.01
Outstanding at end of year	5,902,220	$27.40	4,435,800	$22.54	5,067,900	$21.62
Options exercisable at year-end	3,670,020		2,901,800		3,469,500	
Weighted-average fair value of options granted during the year (per share)	$8.70		$7.38			

The following table summarizes information about fixed stock options outstanding as of December 31, 1996:

	Options Outstanding			Options Exercisable	
Range of Exercise Prices	Number Outstanding as of 12/31/96	Weighted-Average Remaining Contractual Life in Years	Weighted-Average Exercise Price	Number Exercisable as of 12/31/96	Weighted-Average Exercise Price
$12¹¹⁄₁₆-22⅜	1,370,820	4.5	$21.22	1,370,820	$21.22
$23½ -26½	1,990,000	7.0	$24.40	1,990,000	$24.40
$33¹⁄₁₆ -37⅝	2,541,400	9.0	$33.08	309,200	$33.08
$12¹¹⁄₁₆-37⅝	5,902,220	7.3	$27.40	3,670,020	$23.94

Performance Stock Units

Under the long-term portion of the Plan, each January the Corporation grants selected executives and other key employees performance stock units whose vesting is contingent upon the achievement of certain performance objectives. If at the end of three-year performance cycles, targets for financial measures of earnings per share, return on net assets and free cash flow are met, the full number of shares are awarded to the participants. The performance scores can range from 0% to 150%. The compensation cost charged against income for the performance-based plan was $5.8 million, $3.6 million, and $1.8 million for 1996, 1995, and 1994, respectively.

As of December 31, 1996, a total of 259,730 contingent performance stock units and restricted stock units had been granted for potential future distribution, primarily related to three-year cycles ending December 31, 1996, 1997, and 1998. Deferred performance stock units and accumulated dividend amounts totaled 391,750 shares as of December 31, 1996.

No stock appreciation rights were outstanding as of December 31, 1996.

15. SUPPLEMENTAL BALANCE SHEET INFORMATION

Accounts Receivable—Trade

In the normal course of business, the Corporation extends credit to customers which satisfy pre-defined credit criteria. The Corporation believes that it has little concentration of credit risk due to the diversity of its customer base. Receivables, as shown on the consolidated balance sheets, were net of allowances and anticipated discounts of $14.1 million and $14.8 million as of December 31, 1996 and 1995, respectively.

Inventories

The Corporation values the majority of its inventories under the last-in, first-out (LIFO) method and the remaining inventories at the lower of first-in, first-out (FIFO) cost or market. LIFO cost of inventories valued using the LIFO method was $299.2 million and $282.0 million as of December 31, 1996 and 1995, respectively, and all inventories were stated at amounts that did not exceed realizable values. Total inventories were as follows:

December 31,	1996	1995
In thousands of dollars		
Raw materials	$204,419	$189,371
Goods in process	31,444	28,201
Finished goods	316,726	249,106
Inventories at FIFO	552,589	466,678
Adjustment to LIFO	(77,611)	(69,108)
Total inventories	$474,978	$397,570

Property, Plant and Equipment

Property, plant and equipment balances included construction in progress of $91.9 million and $119.5 million as of December 31, 1996 and 1995, respectively. Major classes of property, plant and equipment were as follows:

December 31,	1996	1995
In thousands of dollars		
Land	$ 34,056	$ 35,385
Buildings	533,559	471,663
Machinery and equipment	1,855,087	1,683,338
Property, plant and equipment, gross	2,422,702	2,190,386
Accumulated depreciation	(820,807)	(754,377)
Property, plant and equipment, net	$1,601,895	$1,436,009

Accrued Liabilities

Accrued liabilities were as follows:

December 31,	1996	1995
In thousands of dollars		
Payroll and other compensation	$ 81,264	$ 97,710
Advertising and promotion	77,351	87,368
Other	199,213	123,045
Total accrued liabilities	$357,828	$308,123

Other Long-term Liabilities

Other long-term liabilities were as follows:

December 31,	1996	1995
In thousands of dollars		
Accrued post-retirement benefits	$207,881	$204,044
Other	119,328	129,770
Total other long-term liabilities	$327,209	$333,814

16. SEGMENT INFORMATION

The Corporation operates in a single consumer foods line of business, encompassing the manufacture, distribution and sale of chocolate, confectionery, grocery and pasta products. The Corporation's principal operations and markets are located in North America. In December 1996, the Corporation sold its Gubor and Sperlari European businesses.

Net sales, income before interest and income taxes and identifiable assets of businesses outside of North America were not significant. Historically, transfers of product between geographic areas have not been significant. In 1996 and 1995, sales to Wal-Mart Stores, Inc. and Subsidiaries amounted to approximately 12% and 11% of total net sales, respectively.

17. QUARTERLY DATA (Unaudited)

Summary quarterly results were as follows:

Year 1996	First	Second	Third	Fourth
In thousands of dollars except per share amounts				
Net sales	$931,514	$796,343	$1,072,336	$1,189,115
Gross profit	381,766	326,545	458,362	520,546
Net income	59,415	40,847	94,270	78,654[a]
Net income per share[b]	.38	.26	.61	.51

Year 1995	First	Second	Third	Fourth
In thousands of dollars except per share amounts				
Net sales	$ 867,446	$ 722,269	$ 981,101	$ 1,119,851
Gross profit	364,085	298,506	408,658	493,144
Net income	60,633	33,323	82,127	105,836[c]
Net income per share[b]	.35	.19	.51	.68

(a) Net income for the fourth quarter and year 1996 included an after-tax loss on the sale of Gubor and Sperlari of $35.4 million. Net income per share was similarly impacted.

(b) Quarterly income per share amounts for 1996 and 1995 do not total to the annual amount due to the changes in weighted average shares outstanding during the year.

(c) Net income for the fourth quarter and year 1995 included a net after-tax credit of $2.0 million associated with adjustments to accrued restructuring reserves. Net income per share was similarly impacted.

RESPONSIBILITY FOR FINANCIAL STATEMENTS

Hershey Foods Corporation is responsible for the financial statements and other financial information contained in this report. The Corporation believes that the financial statements have been prepared in conformity with generally accepted accounting principles appropriate under the circumstances to reflect in all material respects the substance of applicable events and transactions. In preparing the financial statements, it is necessary that management make informed estimates and judgments. The other financial information in this annual report is consistent with the financial statements.

The Corporation maintains a system of internal accounting controls designed to provide reasonable assurance that financial records are reliable for purposes of preparing financial statements and that assets are properly accounted for and safeguarded. The concept of reasonable assurance is based on the recognition that the cost of the system must be related to the benefits to be derived. The Corporation believes its system provides an appropriate balance in this regard. The Corporation maintains an Internal Audit Department which reviews the adequacy and tests the application of internal accounting controls.

The financial statements have been audited by Arthur Andersen LLP, independent public accountants, whose appointment was ratified by stockholder vote at the stockholders' meeting held on April 30, 1996. Their report expresses an opinion that the Corporation's financial statements are fairly stated in conformity with generally accepted accounting principles, and they have indicated to us that their examination was performed in accordance with generally accepted auditing standards which are designed to obtain reasonable assurance about whether the financial statements are free of material misstatement.

The Audit Committee of the Board of Directors of the Corporation, consisting solely of non-management directors, meets regularly with the independent public accountants, internal auditors and management to discuss, among other things, the audit scopes and results. Arthur Andersen LLP and the internal auditors both have full and free access to the Audit Committee, with and without the presence of management.

REPORT OF INDEPENDENT PUBLIC ACCOUNTANTS

To the Stockholders and Board of Directors
of Hershey Foods Corporation:

We have audited the accompanying consolidated balance sheets of Hershey Foods Corporation (a Delaware Corporation) and subsidiaries as of December 31, 1996 and 1995, and the related consolidated statements of income, stockholders' equity and cash flows for each of the three years in the period ended December 31, 1996, appearing on pages B-9 through B-27. These financial statements are the responsibility of the Corporation's management. Our responsibility is to express an opinion on these financial statements based on our audits.

We conducted our audits in accordance with generally accepted auditing standards. Those standards require that we plan and perform the audit to obtain reasonable assurance about whether the financial statements are free of material misstatement. An audit includes examining, on a test basis, evidence supporting the amounts and disclosures in the financial statements. An audit also includes assessing the accounting principles used and significant estimates made by management, as well as evaluating the overall financial statement presentation. We believe that our audits provide a reasonable basis for our opinion.

In our opinion, the financial statements referred to above present fairly, in all material respects, the financial position of Hershey Foods Corporation and subsidiaries as of December 31, 1996 and 1995, and the results of their operations and their cash flows for each of the three years in the period ended December 31, 1996, in conformity with generally accepted accounting principles.

Arthur Andersen LLP

New York, New York
January 27, 1997

HERSHEY FOODS CORPORATION

ELEVEN-YEAR CONSOLIDATED FINANCIAL SUMMARY

All dollar and share amounts in thousands except
market price and per share statistics

	10-Year Compound Growth Rate		1996	1995	1994
Summary of Operations(a)					
Net Sales	9.33%	$	**3,989,308**	3,690,667	3,606,271
Cost of Sales	8.35%	$	**2,302,089**	2,126,274	2,097,556
Selling, Marketing and Administrative	11.25%	$	**1,124,087**	1,053,758	1,034,115
Restructuring Credit, (Charge) and Gain, Net		$	**—**	151	(106,105)
(Loss)/Gain on Sale of Businesses and Investment Interest		$	**(35,352)**	—	—
Interest Expense, Net	19.54%	$	**48,043**	44,833	35,357
Income Taxes	7.42%	$	**206,551**	184,034	148,919
Income from Continuing Operations Before Accounting Changes	9.81%	$	**273,186**	281,919	184,219
Net Cumulative Effect of Accounting Changes		$	**—**	—	—
Discontinued Operations		$	**—**	—	—
Net Income	7.48%	$	**273,186**	281,919	184,219
Income Per Share:(b)					
From Continuing Operations Before Accounting Changes	12.00%	$	**1.77(h)**	1.70(i)	1.06(j)
Net Cumulative Effect of Accounting Changes		$	**—**	—	—
Net Income	9.56%	$	**1.77(h)**	1.70(i)	1.06(j)
Weighted Average Shares Outstanding(b)			**153,995**	165,687	174,037
Dividends Paid on Common Stock	8.66%	$	**93,884**	91,190	89,660
Per Share(b)	11.32%	$	**.760**	.685	.625
Dividends Paid on Class B Common Stock	11.21%	$	**20,879**	18,900	17,301
Per Share(b)	11.24%	$	**.685**	.620	.5675
Income from Continuing Operations Before Accounting Changes as a Percent of Net Sales			**7.7%(c)**	7.6%	7.3%(d)
Depreciation	14.35%	$	**119,443**	119,438	114,821
Advertising	7.62%	$	**174,199**	159,200	120,629
Promotion	13.36%	$	**429,208**	402,454	419,164
Payroll	7.49%	$	**491,677**	461,928	472,997
Year-end Position and Statistics(a)					
Capital Additions	7.91%	$	**159,433**	140,626	138,711
Total Assets	9.70%	$	**3,184,796**	2,830,623	2,890,981
Long-term Portion of Debt	13.44%	$	**655,289**	357,034	157,227
Stockholders' Equity	4.78%	$	**1,161,021**	1,082,959	1,441,100
Net Book Value Per Share(b)	6.51%	$	**7.59**	7.01	8.31
Operating Return on Average Stockholders' Equity			**27.5%**	22.2%	18.5%
Operating Return on Average Invested Capital			**17.8%**	17.1%	15.6%
Full-time Employees			**14,000**	13,300	14,000
Stockholders' Data(b)					
Outstanding Shares of Common Stock and Class B Common Stock at Year-end			**152,942**	154,532	173,470
Market Price of Common Stock at Year-end	13.52%	$	**43¾**	32½	24³⁄₁₆
Range During Year			**$51¾-31¹⁵⁄₁₆**	33¹⁵⁄₁₆-24	26¾-20⁹⁄₁₆

See Notes to the Eleven-Year Consolidated Financial Summary on page B-32.

1993	1992	1991	1990	1989	1988	1987	1986
3,488,249	3,219,805	2,899,165	2,715,609	2,420,988	2,168,048	1,863,816	1,635,486
1,995,502	1,833,388	1,694,404	1,588,360	1,455,612	1,326,458	1,149,663	1,032,061
1,035,519	958,189	814,459	776,668	655,040	575,515	468,062	387,227
—	—	—	35,540	—	—	—	—
80,642	—	—	—	—	—	—	—
26,995	27,240	26,845	24,603	20,414	29,954	22,413	8,061
213,642	158,390	143,929	145,636	118,868	91,615	99,604	100,931
297,233	242,598	219,528	215,882	171,054	144,506	124,074	107,206
(103,908)	—	—	—	—	—	—	—
—	—	—	—	—	69,443	24,097	25,558
193,325	242,598	219,528	215,882	171,054	213,949	148,171	132,764
1.66(k)	1.34	1.22	1.20(l)	.95	.80	.69	.57
(.58)	—	—	—	—	—	—	—
1.08(k)	1.34	1.22	1.20(l)	.95	1.19	.82	.71
179,514	180,373	180,373	180,373	180,373	180,373	180,373	187,017
84,711	77,174	70,426	74,161(f)	55,431	49,433	43,436	40,930
.570	.515	.470	.495(f)	.370	.330	.290	.260
15,788	14,270	12,975	13,596(f)	10,161	9,097	8,031	7,216
.5175	.4675	.425	.445(f)	.3325	.2975	.2625	.236
7.4%(e)	7.5%	7.6%	7.2%(g)	7.1%	6.7%	6.7%	6.6%
100,124	84,434	72,735	61,725	54,543	43,721	35,397	31,254
130,009	137,631	117,049	146,297	121,182	99,082	97,033	83,600
444,546	398,577	325,465	315,242	256,237	230,187	171,162	122,508
469,564	433,162	398,661	372,780	340,129	298,483	263,529	238,742
211,621	249,795	226,071	179,408	162,032	101,682	68,504	74,452
2,855,091	2,672,909	2,341,822	2,078,828	1,814,101	1,764,665	1,544,354	1,262,332
165,757	174,273	282,933	273,442	216,108	233,025	280,900	185,676
1,412,344	1,465,279	1,335,251	1,243,537	1,117,050	1,005,866	832,410	727,941
8.06	8.12	7.40	6.89	6.19	5.58	4.61	4.04
17.8%	17.3%	17.0%	16.6%	16.1%	17.5%	19.0%	18.2%
15.0%	14.4%	13.8%	13.4%	13.2%	13.3%	13.5%	13.5%
14,300	13,700	14,000	12,700	11,800	12,100	10,540	10,210
175,226	180,373	180,373	180,373	180,373	180,373	180,373	180,373
24½	23½	22³⁄₁₆	18¾	17¹⁵⁄₁₆	13	12¼	12⁵⁄₁₆
27¹⁵⁄₁₆-21¾	24³⁄₁₆-19⅛	22¼-17⁹⁄₁₆	19¹³⁄₁₆-14⅛	18⁷⁄₁₆-12⅜	14⁵⁄₁₆-10¹⁵⁄₁₆	18⅞-10⅜	15-7¾

Notes to the Eleven-Year Consolidated Financial Summary

(a) All amounts for years prior to 1988 have been restated for discontinued operations, where applicable. Operating Return on Average Stockholders' Equity and Operating Return on Average Invested Capital have been computed using Net Income, excluding the 1988 gain on disposal included in Discontinued Operations, the 1993 Net Cumulative Effect of Accounting Changes, and the after-tax impacts of the 1990 Restructuring Gain, Net, the 1993 Gain on Sale of the Investment Interest in Freia Marabou a.s (Freia), the 1994 Restructuring Charge, the net 1995 Restructuring Credit and the 1996 Loss on Sale of Businesses.

(b) All shares and per share amounts have been adjusted for the two-for-one stock split effective September 13, 1996.

(c) Calculated percent excludes the 1996 Loss on Sale of Businesses. Including the loss, Income from Continuing Operations Before Accounting Changes as a Percent of Net Sales was 6.8%.

(d) Calculated percent excludes the 1994 Restructuring Charge. Including the charge, Income from Continuing Operations Before Accounting Changes as a Percent of Net Sales was 5.1%.

(e) Calculated percent excludes the 1993 Gain on Sale of Investment Interest in Freia. Including the gain, Income from Continuing Operations Before Accounting Changes as a Percent of Net Sales was 8.5%.

(f) Amounts included a special dividend for 1990 of $11.2 million or $.075 per share of Common Stock and $2.1 million or $.0675 per share of Class B Common Stock.

(g) Calculated percent excludes the 1990 Restructuring Gain, Net. Including the gain, Income from Continuing Operations Before Accounting Changes as a Percent of Net Sales was 7.9%.

(h) Income Per Share from Continuing Operations Before Accounting Changes and Net Income Per Share for 1996 included a $.23 per share loss on the sale of the Gubor and Sperlari businesses. Excluding the impact of this loss, Income Per Share from Continuing Operations Before Accounting Changes and Net Income Per Share would have been $2.00.

(i) Income Per Share from Continuing Operations Before Accounting Changes and Net Income Per Share for 1995 included a net $.01 per share credit associated with adjustments to accrued restructuring reserves. Excluding the impact of this net credit, Income Per Share from Continuing Operations Before Accounting Changes and Net Income Per Share would have been $1.69.

(j) Income Per Share from Continuing Operations Before Accounting Changes and Net Income Per Share for 1994 included a $.46 per share restructuring charge. Excluding the impact of this charge, Income Per Share from Continuing Operations Before Accounting Changes and Net Income Per Share would have been $1.52.

(k) Income Per Share from Continuing Operations Before Accounting Changes and Net Income Per Share for 1993 included a $.23 per share gain on the sale of the investment interest in Freia. Excluding the impact of this gain, Income Per Share from Continuing Operations Before Accounting Changes would have been $1.43.

(l) Income Per Share from Continuing Operations Before Accounting Changes and Net Income Per Share for 1990 included an $.11 per share Restructuring Gain, Net. Excluding the impact of this gain, Income Per Share from Continuing Operations Before Accounting Changes and Net Income Per Share would have been $1.08.

Glossary

A

Accelerated depreciation method. A depreciation method that provides for a high depreciation expense in the first year of use of an asset and a gradually declining expense thereafter. (388)

Account. The form used to record additions and deductions for each individual asset, liability, owner's equity, revenue, and expense. (44)

Account form. The form of balance sheet with the assets section presented on the left-hand side and the liabilities and owner's equity sections presented on the right-hand side. (18, 243)

Account payable. A liability created by a purchase made on credit. (13)

Account receivable. A claim against a customer for services rendered or goods sold on credit. (13, 311)

Accounting. The process of identifying, measuring, and communicating economic information to permit informed judgments and decisions by users of the information. (5)

Accounting cycle. The sequence of basic accounting procedures during a fiscal period. (147)

Accounting equation. The expression of the relationship between assets, liabilities, and owner's equity; it is most commonly stated as Assets = Liabilities + Owner's Equity. (11)

Accounting period concept. An accounting principle that requires accounting reports be prepared at periodic intervals. (98)

Accounting system. The methods and procedures used by a business to record and report financial data for use by management and external users. (178)

Accounts payable subsidiary ledger. The subsidiary ledger containing the individual accounts with suppliers (creditors). (185)

Accounts receivable subsidiary ledger. The subsidiary ledger containing the individual accounts with customers (debtors). (185)

Accounts receivable turnover. The relationship between credit sales and accounts receivable. This ratio is computed by dividing net sales on account by the average net accounts receivable. (323, 634)

Accrual basis. A basis of accounting in which revenues are recognized in the period earned, and expenses are recognized in the period incurred in the process of generating revenues. (98)

Accrued expenses. Expenses that have been incurred but not paid. Sometimes called accrued liabilities. (100)

Accrued revenues. Revenues that have been earned but not collected. Sometimes called accrued assets. (100)

Accumulated depreciation account. The contra asset account used to accumulate the depreciation recognized to date on plant assets. (107)

Acid-test ratio. A ratio that measures the "instant" debt-paying ability of a company. Also known as quick ratio. (633)

Adjusted trial balance. The trial balance which is prepared after all the adjusting entries have been posted. Used to verify the equality of the total debit balances and total credit balances before preparing the financial statements. (111)

Adjusting entries. Entries required at the end of an accounting period to bring the ledger up to date. (99)

Adjusting process. The process of updating the accounts at the end of a period. (99)

Administrative expenses (general expenses). Expenses incurred in the administration or general operations of a business. (240)

Aging the receivables. The process of analyzing the accounts receivable and classifying them according to various age groupings, with the due date being the base point for determining age. (316)

Allowance method. A method of accounting for uncollectible receivables, whereby advance provision for the uncollectibles is made. (314)

Amortization. The periodic expense attributed to the decline in usefulness of an intangible asset. (398)

Annuity. A series of equal cash flows at fixed intervals. (542)

Application software. Computer software that performs a particular task. (197)

Appropriation. The amount of a corporation's retained earnings that has been restricted and therefore is not available for distribution to shareholders as dividends. (506)

Assets. Physical items (tangible) or rights (intangible) that have value and that are owned by the business entity. (11, 44)

Available-for-sale security. A debt or equity security that is not classified as either a held-to-maturity or a trading security. (508)

Average cost method. The method of inventory costing that is based on the assumption that costs should be charged against revenue in accordance with the weighted average unit costs of the items sold. (348)

B

Balance of the account. The amount of difference between the debits and the credits that have been entered into an account. (46)

Balance sheet. A financial statement listing the assets, liabilities, and owner's equity of a business entity as of a specific date. (16)

Bank reconciliation. The analysis that details the items responsible for the difference between the cash balance reported in the bank statement and the balance of the cash account in the ledger. (286)

Betterment. An expenditure that increases operating efficiency or capacity for the remaining useful life of a plant asset. (391)

Bond. A form of interest-bearing note employed by corporations to borrow on a long-term basis. (537)

Bond indenture. The contract between a corporation issuing bonds and the bondholders. (539)

Book value. The amount at which an asset or liability is reported on the balance sheet. Also called basis or carrying value. (387)

Book value of a fixed asset. The difference between the balance of a fixed asset account and its related accumulated depreciation account. (108)

Boot. The cash balance owed the seller when an old asset is traded for a new asset. (393)

Business. An organization in which basic resources (inputs), such as materials and labor, are assembled and processed to provide goods or services (outputs) to customers. (2)

Business entity concept. The concept that accounting applies to individual economic units and that each unit is separate from the persons who supply its assets. (10)

Business stakeholder. A person or entity that has an interest in the economic performance of the business. (4)

Business transaction. The occurrence of an economic event or a condition that must be recorded in the accounting records. (11)

C

Capital expenditures. Costs that add to the usefulness of assets for more than one accounting period. (390)

Capital leases. Leases that treat the leased assets as purchased assets in the accounts. (396)

Carrying amount. The amount at which a long-term investment or a long-term liability is reported on the balance sheet. (548)

Cash. Coins, currency (paper money), checks, money orders, and money on deposit that is available for unrestricted withdrawal from banks or other financial institutions. (278)

Cash basis. A basis of accounting in which revenue is recognized in the period cash is received, and expenses are recognized in the period cash is paid. (98)

Cash dividend. A cash distribution of earnings by a corporation to its shareholders. (476)

Cash equivalents. Highly liquid investments that are usually reported on the balance sheet with cash. (291)

Cash flows from financing activities. The section of the statement of cash flows that reports cash flows from transactions affecting the equity and debt of the entity. (577)

Cash flows from investing activities. The section of the statement of cash flows that reports cash flows from transactions affecting investments in noncurrent assets. (577)

Cash flows from operating activities. The section of the statement of cash flows that reports the cash transactions affecting the determination of net income. (577)

Cash payments journal. The special journal in which all cash payments are recorded. (192)

Cash receipts journal. The special journal in which all cash receipts are recorded. (190)

Cash short and over account. An account which has recorded errors in cash sales or errors in making change causing the amount of actual cash on hand to differ from the beginning amount of cash plus the cash sales for the day. (279)

Chart of accounts. The system of accounts that make up the ledger for a business. (44)

Closing entries. Entries necessary to eliminate the balances of temporary accounts in preparation for the following accounting period. (139)

Common-size statement. A financial statement in which all items are expressed only in relative terms. (630)

Common stock. The basic ownership class of corporate stock. (469)

Comprehensive income. All changes in stockholders' equity during a period, except those resulting from dividends and stockholders' investments. (507)

Consolidated financial statements. Financial statements resulting from combining parent and subsidiary company statements. (514)

Consolidation. The creation of a new corporation by the transfer of assets and liabilities from two or more existing corporations. (513)

Contra accounts. Accounts that are offset against other accounts. (107)

Contra asset. An account that affects an asset account, such as the allowance for uncollectible accounts receivable or accumulated depreciation. (314)

Contract rate. The interest rate specified on a bond; sometimes called the coupon rate of interest. (540)

Controlling account. The account in the general ledger that summarizes the balances of the accounts in a subsidiary ledger. (185)

Copyright. The exclusive right to publish and sell a literary, artistic, or musical composition. (398)

Corporation. A separate legal entity that is organized in accordance with state or federal statutes and in which ownership is divided into shares of stock. (3)

Cost concept. The basis for entering the exchange price, or cost, into the accounting records. (10)

Cost method. A method of accounting for an investment in common stock, by which the investor recognizes as income its share of cash dividends of the investee. (511)

Cost of merchandise sold. The cost of merchandise purchased by a merchandise business and sold. (225)

Credit. (1) The right side of an account; (2) the amount entered on the right side of an account; (3) to enter an amount on the right side of an account. (46)

Credit memorandum. The form issued by a seller to inform a buyer that a credit has been posted to the buyer's account receivable. (232)

Cumulative preferred stock. Preferred stock that is entitled to current and past dividends before dividends may be paid on common stock. (470)

Current assets. Cash or other assets that are expected to be converted to cash or sold or used up, usually within a year or less, through the normal operations of a business. (137)

Current liabilities. Liabilities that will be due within a short time (usually one year or less) and that are to be paid out of current assets. (138)

Current ratio. A financial ratio that is computed by dividing current assets by current liabilities. (149, 632)

D

Debit. (1) The left side of an account; (2) the amount entered on the left side of an account; (3) to enter an amount on the left side of an account. (46)

Debit memorandum. The form issued by a buyer to inform a seller that a debit has been posted to the seller's account payable. (229)

Declining-balance depreciation method. A method of depreciation that provides declining periodic depreciation expense over the estimated life of an asset. (387)

Deferred expenses. Items that are initially recorded as assets but are expected to become expenses over time or through the normal operations of the business. Sometimes called prepaid expenses. (99)

Deferred revenues. Items that are initially recorded as liabilities but are expected to become revenues over time or through the normal operations of the business. Sometimes called unearned revenues. (100)

Deficit. A debit balance in the retained earnings account. (468)

Defined benefit plan. A pension plan that promises employees a fixed annual pension benefit at retirement, based on years of service and compensation levels. (439)

Defined contribution plan. A pension plan that requires a fixed amount of money to be invested for the employee's behalf during the employee's working years. (439)

Depletion. The cost of metal ores and other minerals removed from the earth. (397)

Depreciation. In a general sense, the decrease in usefulness of fixed assets other than land. In accounting, refers to the systematic allocation of a fixed asset's cost to expense. (107, 384)

Depreciation expense. The portion of the cost of a fixed asset that is recorded as an expense each year of its useful life. (107)

Direct method. A method of reporting the cash flows from operating activities as the net income from operations adjusted for all deferrals of past cash receipts and payments and all accruals of expected future cash receipts and payments. (578)

Direct write-off method. A method of accounting for uncollectible receivables, whereby an expense is recognized only when specific accounts are judged to be uncollectible. (314)

Discontinued operations. The operations of a business segment that has been disposed of. (502)

Discount. The interest deducted from the maturity value of a note. (423); The excess of the face amount of bonds over their issue price. (540); The excess of par value of stock over its sales price. (472)

Discount rate. The rate used in computing the interest to be deducted from the maturity value of a note. (423)

Dishonored note receivable. A note that the maker fails to pay on its due date. (321)

Dividends per share. The cash dividends per common shares commonly used by investors in assessing alternative stock investments, computed by dividing dividends by the number of shares of stock outstanding. (641)

Dividend yield. The rate of return to stockholders in terms of cash dividend distributions. (479, 641)

Doomsday ratio. The ratio of cash and cash equivalents to current liabilities. (291)

Double-entry accounting. A system for recording transactions, based on recording increases and decreases in accounts so that debits always equal credits. (50)

Drawing. The account used to record amounts withdrawn by an owner of a proprietorship. (45)

E

Earnings per share (EPS) on common stock. The profitability ratio of net income available to common shareholders to the number of common shares outstanding. (503, 640)

Effective interest rate method. One method of amortizing a bond discount. Also known as the interest method. (545)

Effective rate. The market rate of interest when bonds are issued. (540)

Electronic funds transfer (EFT). A payment system that uses computerized information rather than paper (money, checks, etc.) to effect a cash transaction. (282)

Elements of internal control. The control environment, risk assessment, control activities, information and communication, and monitoring. (180)

Employee fraud. The intentional act of deceiving an employer for personal gain. (179)

Employee's earnings record. A detailed record of each employee's earnings. (433)

Equity method. A method of accounting for investments in common stock, by which the investment account is adjusted for the investor's share of periodic net income and dividends of the investee. (511)

Equity security. A security that represents ownership in a business, such as stock in a corporation. (508)

Ethics. The moral principles that guide the conduct of individuals. (7)

Expenses. Assets used up or services consumed in the process of generating revenues. (13, 45)

Extraordinary items. Events or transactions that are unusual and infrequent. (502)

Extraordinary repair. An expenditure that increases the useful life of an asset beyond the original estimate. (391)

F

FICA tax. Federal Insurance Contributions Act tax used to finance federal programs for old-age and disability benefits (social security) and health insurance for the aged (Medicare). (426)

Financial accounting. The branch of accounting that is concerned with the recording of transactions using generally accepted accounting principles (GAAP) for a business or other economic unit and with a periodic preparation of various statements from such records. (9)

Financial Accounting Standards Board (FASB). An authoritative body for the development of accounting principles. (9)

First-in, first-out (FIFO) method. A method of inventory costing based on the assumption that the costs of merchandise sold should be charged against revenue in the order in which the costs were incurred. (348)

Fiscal year. The annual accounting period adopted by a business. (147)

Fixed assets. Physical resources that are owned and used by a business and are permanent or have a long life. (107, 382)

FOB (free on board) destination. Terms of agreement between buyer and seller whereby ownership passes when merchandise is received by the buyer, and the seller pays the transportation costs. (234)

FOB (free on board) shipping point. Terms of agreement between buyer and seller whereby ownership passes when merchandise is delivered to the freight carrier, and the buyer pays the transportation costs. (234)

Free cash flow. The amount of operating cash flow remaining after replacing current productive capacity and maintaining current dividends. (593)

Fringe benefits. A variety of employee benefits that may take many forms, including vacations, pension plans, and health, life, and disability insurance. (438)

Future value. The estimated worth in the future of an amount of cash on hand today invested at a fixed rate of interest. (541)

G

General journal. The two-column form used for entries that are otherwise not recorded in special journals. (187)

General ledger. The primary ledger, when used in conjunction with subsidiary ledgers, that contains all of the balance sheet and income statement accounts. (185)

Generally accepted accounting principles (GAAP). Generally accepted guidelines for the preparation of financial statements. (9)

Goodwill. An intangible asset of a business due to such favorable factors as location, product superiority, reputation, and managerial skill. (399)

Gross pay. The total earnings of an employee for a payroll period. (426)

Gross profit. The excess of net sales over the cost of merchandise sold. (225)

Gross profit method. A means of estimating inventory based on the relationship of gross profit to sales. (360)

H

Hardware. Computer equipment used for data input/output and internal data management and processing. (196)

Held-to-maturity securities. Investments in bonds or other debt securities that management intends to hold to their maturity. (554)

Horizontal analysis. Financial analysis that compares an item in a current statement with the same item in prior statements. (67, 626)

I

Income from operations (operating income). The excess of gross profit over total operating expenses. (240)

Income statement. A summary of the revenues and expenses of a business entity for a specific period of time. (16)

Income Summary. The account used in the closing process for transferring the revenue and expense account balances to the retained earnings account at the end of the period. (139)

Indirect method. A method of reporting the cash flows from operating activities as the net income from operations adjusted for all deferrals of past cash receipts and payments and all accruals of expected future cash receipts and payments. (579)

Intangible assets. Long-lived assets that are useful in the operations of a business, are not held for sale, and are without physical qualities. (398)

Internal controls. The detailed policies and procedures used to direct operations, ensure accurate reports, and ensure compliance with laws and regulations. (179)

Inventory shrinkage. Loss of inventory due to shoplifting, employee theft, or errors in recording or counting inventory. (242)

Inventory turnover. A ratio that measures the relationship between the volume of goods (merchandise) sold and the amount of inventory carried during the period. (361, 635)

Investments. The balance sheet caption used to report long-term investments in stocks or bonds not intended as a source of cash in the normal operations of the business. (510)

Invoice. The bill provided by the seller (who refers to it as a sales invoice) to a buyer (who refers to it as a purchase invoice) for items purchased. (227)

J

Journal. The initial record in which the effects of a transaction on accounts are recorded. (47)

Journal entry. The form of recording a transaction in a journal. (47)

Journalizing. The process of recording a transaction in a journal. (47)

L

Last-in, first-out (LIFO) method. A method of inventory costing based on the assumption that the most recent merchandise costs incurred should be charged against revenue. (348)

Ledger. The group of accounts used by a business. (44)

Leverage. The tendency of the rate earned on stockholders' equity to vary from the rate earned on total assets because the amount earned on assets acquired through the use of funds provided by creditors varies from the interest paid to these creditors (639)

Liabilities. Debts owed to outsiders (creditors). (11, 44)

Long-term liabilities. Liabilities that are not due for a long time (usually more than one year). (138)

Loss from operations. The excess of operating expenses over gross profit. (240)

Lower-of-cost-or-market (LCM) method. A method of valuing inventory that reports the inventory at the lower of its cost or current market value (replacement cost). (358)

M

Managerial accounting. The branch of accounting that uses both historical and estimated data in providing information that management uses in conducting daily operations, in planning future operations, and in developing overall business strategies. (9)

Managers. Individuals who the owners have authorized to operate the business. (4)

Manufacturing businesses. A type of business that changes basic inputs into products that are sold to individual customers. (2)

Matching concept. The concept that expenses incurred in generating revenue should be matched against the revenue in determining the net income or net loss for the period. (16, 98)

Materiality concept. A concept of accounting that accounts for items that are deemed significant for a given size of operations. (65)

Maturity value. The amount due (face value plus interest) at the maturity or due date of a note. (321)

Merchandise inventory. Merchandise on hand and available for sale to customers. (225)

Merchandising businesses. A type of business that purchases products from other businesses and sells them to customers. (3)

Merger. The combining of two corporations by the acquisition of the properties of one corporation by another, with the dissolution of one of the corporations. (513)

Minority interest. The portion of a subsidiary corporation's stock that is not owned by the parent corporation. (514)

Multiple-step income statement. An income statement with several sections, subsections, and subtotals. (239)

N

Natural business year. A year that ends when a business's activities have reached the lowest point in its annual operating cycle. (147)

Net income. The amount by which revenues exceed expenses. (16)

Net loss. The amount by which expenses exceed revenues. (16)

Net pay. Gross pay less payroll deductions; the amount the employer is obligated to pay the employee. (426)

Net realizable value. The valuation of an asset at an amount equal to the estimated selling price less any direct cost of disposal. (358)

Nonparticipating preferred stock. Preferred stock with a limited dividend preference. (469)

Notes receivable. A written promise to pay by the maker, representing an amount to be received by the payee. (137, 311)

Number of days' sales in inventory. A measure of the length of time it takes to acquire, sell, and replace the inventory. (362)

Number of days' sales in receivables. An estimate of the length of time the accounts receivable have been outstanding. (324, 634)

Number of times the interest charges are earned. A ratio that measures the risk that interest payments to debtholders will continue to be made if earnings decrease. (554, 636)

O

Objectivity concept. Requires that the accounting records and reports be based upon objective evidence. (11)

Operating leases. Leases that do not meet the criteria for capital leases and thus are accounted for as operating expenses. (396)

Operating system. Computer software that provides the basic instructions to the computer and serves as the interface between the user and the computer. (197)

Other expense. An expense that cannot be traced directly to operations. (241)

Other income. Revenue from sources other than the primary operating activity of a business. (241)

Outstanding stock. The stock that is in the hands of stockholders. (468)

Owner's equity. The owner's right to the assets of the business after the total liabilities are deducted. (11, 45)

P

Paid-in capital. The capital acquired from stockholders. (467)

Par. The monetary amount printed on a stock certificate. (468)

Parent company. The company owning a majority of the voting stock of another corporation. (513)

Partnership. An unincorporated business owned by two or more individuals. (3)

Patents. Exclusive rights to produce and sell goods with one or more unique features. (398)

Payroll. The total amount earned by employees for a certain period. (425)

Payroll register. A multicolumn form used to assemble and summarize payroll data at the end of each payroll period. (431)

Periodic inventory system. A system of inventory accounting in which only the revenue from sales is recorded each time a sale is made. The cost of merchandise on hand at the end of a period is determined by a detailed listing (physical inventory) of the merchandise on hand. (226)

Perpetual inventory system. A system of inventory accounting in which both the revenue from sales and the cost of merchandise sold are recorded each time a sale is made, so that the records continually disclose the amount of the inventory on hand. (226)

Petty cash fund. A special cash fund used to pay relatively small amounts. (289)

Physical inventory. The detailed listing of merchandise on hand. (226, 345)

Pooling-of-interests method. A method of accounting for an affiliation of two corporations resulting from an exchange of voting stock of one corporation for substantially all the voting stock of the other corporation. (513)

Post-closing trial balance. A trial balance prepared after all of the temporary accounts have been closed. (146)

Posting. The process of transferring debits and credits from a journal to the accounts. (52)

Postretirement benefits. Rights to benefits that employees earn during their term of employment for themselves and their dependents after they retire. (440)

Preferred stock. A class of stock with preferential rights over common stock. (469)

Premium. The excess of the issue price of bonds over the face amount. (405); The excess of the sales price of stock over its par amount. (472, 540)

Prepaid expenses. Purchased commodities or services that have not been used up at the end of an accounting period. (13)

Present value. The estimated worth today of an amount of cash to be received (or paid) in the future. (540)

Present value of an annuity. The sum of the present values of a series of equal cash flows to be received at fixed intervals. (542)

Price-earnings ratio. The ratio, often called the P/E ratio, computed by dividing the market price per share of common stock at a specific date by the company's earnings per share on common stock. (640)

Prior-period adjustments. Corrections of material errors related to a prior period or periods, excluded from the determination of net income. (507)

Proceeds. The net amount available from discounting a note. (423)

Profitability. The ability of a firm to earn income. (631)

Promissory note. A written promise to pay a sum in money on demand or at a definite time. (319)

Proprietorship. A business owned by one individual. (3)

Purchase method. The accounting method employed when a parent company acquires a controlling share of the voting stock of a subsidiary other than by the exchange of voting common stock. (513)

Purchases discounts. An available discount taken by a buyer for early payment of an invoice. (228)

Purchases journal. The special journal in which all items purchased on account are recorded. (192)

Purchases returns and allowances. Reductions in purchases, resulting from merchandise being returned to the seller or from the seller's reduction in the original purchase price. (229)

Q

Quick ratio. A financial ratio that measures the ability to pay current liabilities within a short period of time. (440)

Quick assets. The sum of cash, receivables, and marketable securities. (633)

R

Rate earned on common stockholders' equity. A measure of profitability computed by dividing net income, reduced by preferred dividend requirements, by common stockholders' equity. (639)

Rate earned on stockholders' equity. A measure of profitability computed by dividing net income by total stockholders' equity. (638)

Rate earned on total assets. A measure of the profitability of assets, computed as net income plus interest expense divided by total average assets. (638)

Ratio of fixed assets to long-term liabilities. A financial ratio that provides a measure indicating the margin of safety to creditors. (400, 635)

Ratio of liabilities to stockholders' equity. The relationship between the total claims of the creditors and owners. (636)

Ratio of net sales to assets. A profitability measure that shows how effectively a firm utilizes its assets. (637)

Real accounts. Balance sheet accounts. (139)

Receivables. All money claims against other entities, including people, business firms, and other organizations. (311)

Report form. The form of balance sheet with the liabilities and owner's equity sections presented below the assets section. (18, 243)

Residual value. The estimated recoverable cost of a depreciable asset as of the time of its removal from service. (385)

Retail inventory method. A means of estimating inventory based on the relationship of the cost and the retail price of merchandise. (359)

Retained earnings. Net income retained in a corporation. (467)

Revenue. The gross increase in owner's equity as a result of business and professional activities that earn income. (13, 45)

Revenue expenditures. Expenditures that benefit only the current period. (390)

Revenue journal. The special journal in which all sales of services on account are recorded. (187)

Revenue recognition concept. The principle by which revenues are recognized in the period in which they are earned. (98)

S

Sales discounts. An available discount granted by a seller for early payment of an invoice; a contra account to Sales. (232)

Sales returns and allowances. Reductions in sales, resulting from merchandise being returned by customers or from the seller's reduction in the original sales price; a contra account to Sales. (232)

Selling expenses. Expenses incurred directly in the sale of merchandise. (240)

Services businesses. A business providing services rather than products to customers. (3)

Single-step income statement. An income statement in which the total of all expenses is deducted in one step from the total of all revenues. (241)

Sinking fund. Assets set aside in a special fund to be used for a specific purpose. (547)

Slide. The erroneous movement of all digits in a number, one or more spaces to the right or the left, such as writing $542 as $5,420. (66)

Software. The programs that provide the computer with instructions. (197)

Solvency. The ability of a business to pay its debts. (148, 631)

Special journals. Journals designed to be used for recording a single type of transaction. (186)

Stated value. A value approved by the board of directors of a corporation for no-par stock. Similar to par value. (469)

Statement of cash flows. A summary of the major cash receipts and cash payments for a period. (16, 577)

Statement of owner's equity. A summary of the changes in the owner's equity of a business that have occurred during a specific period of time. (16)

Statement of stockholders' equity. A summary of the changes in the stockholders' equity of a corporation that have occurred during a specific period of time. (507)

Stock. Shares of ownership of a corporation. (465)

Stock dividend. Distribution of a company's own stock to its shareholders. (478)

Stock split. A reduction in the par or stated value of a share of common stock and the issuance of a proportionate number of additional shares. (475)

Stockholders. The owners of a corporation. (465)

Stockholders' equity. The equity of the stockholders of a corporation. (467)

Straight-line depreciation method. A method of depreciation that provides for equal periodic depreciation expense over the estimated life of an asset. (386)

Subsidiary company. The corporation that is controlled by a parent company. (513)

Subsidiary ledger. A ledger containing individual accounts with a common characteristic. (185)

Sum-of-the-years-digits depreciation method. A method of depreciation that provides for declining periodic depreciation expense over the estimated life of an asset. (401)

T

T account. A form of account resembling the letter T, showing debits on the left and credits on the right. (46)

Taxable income. The base on which the amount of income tax is determined. (499)

Temporary accounts. Revenue, expense, or income summary accounts that are periodically closed; nominal accounts. (139)

Temporary differences. Differences between income before income tax and taxable income created by items that are recognized in one period for income statement purposes and in another period for tax purposes. Such differences reverse, or turn around, in later years. (499)

Temporary investments. Investments in securities that can be readily sold when cash is needed. (508)

Trade discounts. Special discounts from published list prices offered by sellers to certain classes of buyers. (234)

Trade-in allowance. The amount a seller grants a buyer for a fixed asset that is traded in for a similar asset. (393)

Trademark. A name, term, or symbol used to identify a business and its products. (399)

Trading security. A debt or equity security that management intends to actively trade for profit. (508)

Transposition. The erroneous arrangement of digits in a number, such as writing $542 as $524. (66)

Treasury stock. A corporation's issued stock that has been reacquired. (474)

Trial balance. A summary listing of the titles and balances of the accounts in the ledger. (64)

Two-column journal. An all-purpose general journal. (52)

U

Uncollectible accounts expense. The operating expense incurred because of the failure to collect receivables. (314)

Unearned revenue. The liability created by receiving cash in advance of providing goods or services. (54)

Unit of measure concept. A concept of accounting that requires that economic data be recorded in dollars. (11)

Units-of-production depreciation method. A method of depreciation that provides for depreciation expense based on the expected productive capacity of an asset. (387)

Unrealized holding gain or loss. The difference between the fair market values of the securities and their cost. (509)

V

Vertical analysis. An analysis that compares each item in a current statement with a total amount within the same statement. (112, 629)

Voucher. A document that serves as evidence of authority to pay cash. (281)

Voucher system. Records, methods, and procedures used in verifying and recording liabilities and paying and recording cash payments. (281)

W

Working capital. The excess of the current assets of a business over its current liabilities. (148, 632)

Work sheet. A working paper used to summarize adjusting entries and assist in the preparation of financial statements. (136)

Subject Index

A

Absence, compensated, 438
Accelerated depreciation
  method, *def.*, 388
Account,
  allowance, write-offs to, 315
  balance of, *def.*, 46
  business bank, 283
  cash short and over, *def.*, 279
  characteristics of, 46
  clearing, 140
  contra asset, 107
  controlling, *def.*, 185
  def., 44
  fees earned on, 187
  nominal, 139
  perpetual inventory
    Fifo entries, *illus.*, 351
    Lifo entries, *illus.*, 351
  purchases on, 192
  real, *def.*, 139
  sales on, 231
  statement of, 284
  T, *def.*, 46
  temporary, *def.*, 139
  usefulness of, 44–45
Account form, *def.*, 18, 243
Accountancy, state board of, 9
Accountant,
  Certified Management (CMA),
    8
  Certified Public (CPA), 8
Accounting,
  def., 5
  double-entry, *def.*, 50
  financial, *def.*, 9
  for bond investments–
    purchase, interest, and
    amortization, 549
  for bond investments–sale, 551
  for bonds payable, 543–547
  for depreciation, 385–390
  for dividends, 476–479
  for exchanges of similar fixed
    assets, review of, 395
  for exchanges of similar fixed
    assets, summary illustration,
    illus., 395
  for investments in stocks,
    508–512
  for merchandise transactions,
    illustration of, 236–237
  for merchandising businesses,
    224
  for notes receivable, 321–322
  for purchases, 226–230

  for sales, 230–234
  for uncollectibles, allowance
    method of, 314–318
  for uncollectibles, direct write-
    off method of, 318–319
  management, *def.*, 9
  managerial, *def.*, 9
  private, 7, 8
  profession, 7
  public, 7, 8
Accounting cycle,
  completion of, 135
  def., 147
  for a merchandising business,
    241–244
  illus., 148
Accounting equation,
  business transactions and,
    11–15
  def., 11
Accounting fields, specialized, 9
Accounting in business, role of,
  def., 5–6
Accounting information
  and the stakeholders of a
    business, *illus.*, 6
  system, *illus.*, 6
Accounting period concept, *def.*,
  98
Accounting principles,
  changes in, 503
  generally accepted (GAAP),
    def., 9
  need for, *illus.*, 10
Accounting system,
  analysis of, 178
  basic, 178–179
  computerized, 196–200
  computerized, 247
  def., 178
  design of, 178
  feedback for, 178
  for merchandisers, 245–249
  for payroll and payroll taxes,
    430–438
  implementation of, 178
  manual, 184–195, 245
    adapting, 195–196
    purchase and payment cycle,
      191
    revenue and collection cycle,
      187
Accounting treatment of
  contingent liabilities, *illus.*,
  424
Accounts,
  analysis of, 596, 599

analyzing and summarizing
  transactions in, 47–51
balance sheet, transactions
  and, 47
bank, nature and use as a
  control over cash, 282–286
chart of,
  def., 44
  expanded, *illus.*, 101
  for a merchandising
    business, *illus.*, 237–238
  illus., 45
contra, *def.*, 107
doubtful, expense, 314
income statement, 49
normal balances of, 51
other, 596, 599
uncollectible,
  estimate of, *illus.*, 317
  expense, *def.*, 314
Accounts payable, 421, 591
  control and subsidiary ledger,
    195
  decrease in, 584
  def., 13
  subsidiary ledger, *def.*, 185
Accounts receivable, 56, 590
  aging of, *illus.*, 317
  analysis, 633
  control and subsidiary ledger,
    190
  def., 13, 311
  increase in, 584
  subsidiary ledger, *def.*, 185
  turnover,
    def., 323, 633
    equation, 324
Accrual basis, *def.*, 98
Accruals, 100
  and deferrals, *illus.*, 100
Accrued assets, 100, 106
Accrued expenses, 104, 591
  def., 100
  payable, 585
Accrued liabilities, 100, 104
Accrued revenues, 106
  def., 100
Accrued wages, *illus.*, 105,
  150
Accumulated depreciation, *def.*,
  107
Acid-test ratio, 440
  def., 633
Additions to fixed assets, 390
Adjusted trial balance,
  column (work sheet), 136A
  def., 111

entered on work sheet, *illus.*,
  136B
Adjusting entries,
  and closing entries, 139–146
  and closing entries for a
    merchandising business,
    249–252
  def., 99
  illus., 109. 139
  ledger with, *illus.*, 110–111
  recording of, 101–108
Adjusting process,
  def., 99
  nature of, 99–100
Adjustment columns, 136
Adjustment process, summary of,
  108–112
Adjustments,
  basic, summary of, *illus.*, 109
  entered on work sheet, *illus.*,
    136B
  prior period, *def.*, 507
  to net income, indirect
    method, *illus.*, 583
Administrative expenses, *def.*,
  240
Affiliated company, 513
Aging accounts receivable,
  def., 316
  illus., 317
Allowance account, write-offs to,
  315
Allowance method,
  def., 314
  of accounting for
    uncollectibles, 314–318
Allowances,
  purchase,
    def., 229
    returns and, 229
  sales,
    def., 232
    returns and, 232
  trade-in, *def.*, 393
Alternative financing plans,
  effect of, *illus.*, 538
Amortization,
  accounting for bond
    investments, 549
  def., 398
  effective interest rate method
    of, 555
  of a bond discount, 545
  of a bond premium, 546
  of discount,
    by the interest method, 556
    on bonds payable, *illus.*, 556

of premium,
  by the interest method, 557
  on bonds payable, *illus.,* 557
Analysis,
  accounts receivable, 633
  current position, 632
  horizontal,
    comparative balance sheet,
      illus., 627
    comparative income
      statement, *illus.,* 628
    comparative retained
      earnings statement, *illus.,*
      628
    comparative schedule of
      current assets, *illus.,* 627
    def., 67, 626
  inventory, 634
  profitability, 637–641
  solvency, 631–637
  vertical,
    comparative balance sheet,
      illus., 629
    comparative income
      statement, *illus.,* 630
    def., 112, 629
    of income statements, *illus.,*
      113
Analytical measures,
  other, 630
  summary of, *illus.,* 642–643
Analytical procedures, basic,
  626–631
Analyzing and summarizing
  transactions, *illus.,* 51–64
  transactions in accounts, 47–51
Analyzing transactions, 43
Annual reports, corporate,
  643–644
Annuity, *def.,* 542
Application, *def.,* 197
Application of incorporation, 466
Appropriation, *def.,* 506
Articles of incorporation, 466
Assessment, 181
Asset, book value of, *def.,* 108
Assets, 137
  accrued, 100, 106
  contra, *def.,* 314
  current,
    and current liabilities, 584
    comparative schedule of,
      horizontal analysis, *illus.,*
      627
    def., 137
  def., 11, 44
  equation, 581
  fixed, 138
    additions to, 390
    and intangible assets, 381,
      399–400
    costs of acquiring, 382, 383
    def., 107, 382
    discarding, 392
    disposal of, 392–396
    exchanging similar, 393
    internal control of, 396
    leasing, 396

nature of, 382–384
selling, 393
similar, review of, *illus.,* 395
to long-term liabilities, ratio
  of, 635
intangible, 398–399
  fixed assets and, 381,
    399–400
liabilities, and owner's equity,
  11
net, related, excess of cost of
  business acquired over, 514
plant, 107, 138, 382
quick, *def.,* 633
ratio of net sales to, 637
tangible, 382
total,
  rate earned on, *def.,* 638
  rate of income from
    operations to, 638
Assumption,
  cost flow, 348
  inventory cost flow, 347–350
Auditor, Certified Internal (CIA),
  8
Auditors' report, independent,
  644
Available-for-sale securities, *def.,*
  508
Average cost method, 352, 355
  def., 348
  use of, 357

B

Bad debts expense, 314
Balance,
  adjusted trial,
    column (work sheet), 136A
    def., 111
    entered on work sheet,
      illus., 136B
  compensating, 291
  debit, 46
  trial, 64–65
    def., 64
    illus., 64, 112
    post-closing, 146
  unadjusted trial,
    column (work sheet), 136
    entered on work sheet,
      illus., 136B
Balance of accounts,
  def., 46
  normal, 51
Balance sheet, 18, 137, 243
  comparative,
    horizontal analysis, *illus.,*
      627
    illus., 582
    vertical analysis, *illus.,* 629
  corporation, 552–554
  def., 16
  fixed assets and intangible
    assets in, *illus.,* 400
  income statement and, column
    (work sheet), 136A

merchandise inventory on,
  illus., 359
presentation of
  cash, 291
  merchandise inventory on,
    359
receivables on, *illus.,* 322–323
report form of, *illus.,* 243
temporary investments on,
  illus., 510
Balance sheet accounts, 47
Balance sheet and income
  statement data for direct
  method, *illus.,* 589
Balance sheet column, amounts
  extended to, work sheet,
  illus., 136B
Balance sheet of a corporation,
  illus., 553
Balance sheet presentation of
  bond investments, 554
Balance sheet presentation of
  bonds payable, 552
Bank accounts,
  as a control over cash, 285
  business, 283
Bank reconciliation,
  def., 286
  illus., 288
Bank statement, 284
  illus., 285, 286
Bankers' ratio, 632
Basic accounting systems,
  178–179
Basic analytical procedures,
  626–631
Basic earnings per share, 503
Benefit dollars as a percent of
  total, *illus.,* 438
Benefit plan, *def.,* 439
Benefits,
  fringe, 438–440
  def., 438
  postretirement,
    def., 440
    other than pensions, 440
Betterment, *def.,* 391
Board of accountancy, state, 9
Board of directors, 466
Bond,
  debenture, 539
  def., 537
  periodic, interest payments,
    present value of the, 542
Bond discount, amortizing a,
  545
Bond indenture, *def.,* 539
Bond investments,
  accounting for, purchase,
    interest, and amortization,
    549
  accounting for, sale, 551
  balance sheet presentation of,
    554
Bond premium, amortizing a,
  546
Bond redemption, 548–549
Bond sinking funds, 547

Bonds,
  callable, 539, 548
  convertible, 539
  face amount of, present value
    of, 541
  investments in, 549–552
    bonds payable and, 536
  junk, 547
  present value of the face
    amount of, 541
  serial, 539
  term, 539
  zero-coupon, 547
Bonds issued at a discount, 545
Bonds issued at a premium, 546
Bonds issued at face amount,
  543
Bonds payable, 586
  accounting for, 543–547
  amortization of premium on,
    illus., 557
  balance sheet presentation of,
    552
  characteristics of, 539
  discount on, amortization of,
    illus., 556
  present-value concept and,
    539–543
Book value,
  def., 387
  of the asset, *def.,* 108
Boot, *def.,* 393
Business,
  def., 2
  financial history of, *illus.,*
    147
  merchandising, 3
    accounting cycle for,
      241–244
    accounting for, 224
    adjusting and closing entries
      for, 249–252
    cash payments journal for,
      illus., 247
    cash receipts journal for,
      illus., 247
    chart of accounts for,
      237–238
    income statement for,
      238–241
    nature of, 225–226
    purchases journal for, *illus.,*
      246
    sales journal for, *illus.,* 246
    statement of owner's equity
      for, *illus.,* 243
    work sheet for, 249–252
  nature of, *def.,* 2–5
  role of accounting in, *def.,* 5–6
  service, 3
  stakeholders
    def., 4
    of, accounting information
      and, *illus.,* 6
  transactions,
    and the accounting equation,
      11–15
    def., 11

flow of, *illus.,* 52
types of, 2
Business bank accounts, 283
Business combinations, 513–515
Business entity concept, *def.,* 10
Business ethics, 6–7
Business organizations, types of, 3
Business segment, 502
Business year, natural, *def.,* 147
Bylaws, 467

C

Callable bonds, 539, 548
Capital, 467
  contributed, 467
  paid-in,
    def., 467
    other sources of, 471
    reporting, 505
    section of stockholders' equity, *illus.,* 505
    sources of, 468–471
  working, *def.,* 632
Capital and revenue
  expenditures, 390–391
  illus., 391
  summary of, 391
Capital expenditures
  def., 390
  types of, 390
Capital lease, *def.,* 396
Carrying amount, *def.,* 548
Cash, 277
  def., 278
  importance of controls over, 278
  petty, 289
  retailers' sources of, *illus.,* 279
Cash basis, *def.,* 98
Cash dividend, *def.,* 476
Cash equation, 581
Cash equivalents, *def.,* 291
Cash flow,
  free, *def.,* 593
  from operations, direct and indirect methods, *illus.,* 579
  net,
    provided by financing activities, 580
    provided by investing activities, 579
    used for financing activities, 580
    used for investing activities, 579
  per share, 581
Cash flows, *illus.,* 578
  from financing activities, 18, 580
  def., 577
  from investing activities, 18, 579
  def., 577
  from operating activities, 18, 578, 583
  def., 577

indirect method, *illus.,* 585
reporting, direct method, 592
reporting, 577–581
  from operating activities, 585
  statement of, 18,
    def., 16, 577
    direct method, 589, 593
    indirect method, 581, 588
    preparation of, 588, 597, 600
    work sheet for, 595
    work sheet for the indirect method, *illus.,* 595
  used for payment of dividends, 585
Cash on the balance sheet,
  presentation of, 291
Cash payments,
  for income taxes, 592
  for merchandise, 590
  for operating expenses, 591
  internal control of, 280
  journal
    and postings, *illus.,* 194
    def., 192
    for merchandising business, *illus.,* 247
Cash receipts,
  control of, 278
  journal
    and postings, *illus.,* 191
    def., 190
    for merchandising business, *illus.,* 247
Cash received,
  from cash sales, control of, 279
  from customers, 590
  in the mail, control of, 280
Cash sales, 230
  control of cash received from, 279
Cash short and over account, *def.,* 279
Certificates, stock, 468
Certification, CPA, 9
Certified Internal Auditor (CIA), 8
Certified Management Accountant (CMA), 8
Certified Public Accountant (CPA), 8
Change fund, 279
Chart of accounts,
  def., 44
  illus., 45
  expanded, *illus.,* 101
  for a merchandising business, 237–238
Charter, 466
Check and remittance advice, *illus.,* 284
Check, 283
  payroll, 435
  illus., 436
CIA (Certified Internal Auditor), 8
Classification of receivables, 311–312

Clearing account, 140
Closing and adjusting entries, 139–146
Closing entries, 244
  def., 139
  flowchart of, *illus.,* 141
  journalizing and posting, 140
Closing process, 139
  illus., 140
CMA (Certified Management Accountant), 8
Code of professional ethics, B–1
Collection cycle,
  revenue and, 187
  computerized system and, 197
  in QuickBooks®, *illus.,* 199
Combinations, business, 513–515
Common share,
  earnings per (EPS),
    def., 503
    equation, 504
Common stock, 586
  def., 469
  earnings per share (EPS), *def.,* 640
Common stockholders' equity,
  rate earned on, *def.,* 639
Common-size income statement, *illus.,* 631
Common-size statements, *def.,* 630
Company,
  affiliated, 513
  parent, *def.,* 513
  subsidiary, *def.,* 513
Comparative balance sheet,
  horizontal analysis, *illus.,* 627
  illus., 582
  vertical analysis, *illus.,* 629
Comparative income statement,
  horizontal analysis, *illus.,* 628
  vertical analysis, *illus.,* 630
Comparative retained earnings statement, horizontal analysis, *illus.,* 628
Comparative schedule of current assets, horizontal analysis, *illus.,* 627
Compensated absences, 438
Compensating balance, 291
Completed work sheet with net income shown, *illus.,* 136B
Completing the accounting cycle, 135
Composite-rate method, 390
Compound interest, present value of $1 at, *illus.,* 542
Comprehensive income, 507–508
  def., 507
  statement of income and, *illus.,* 510
Computer,
  external hardware, *illus.,* 197
  hardware basics, 196
  software basics, 196, 197
Computer-aided design (CAD) *illus.,* 198

Computer-aided manufacturing (CAM) *illus.,* 198
Computerized accounting systems, 196–200, 247
Computerized perpetual inventory systems, 352
Computerized system, illustration of revenue and collection cycle, 197
Computing employee net pay, 429
Concept,
  accounting period, *def.,* 98
  business entity, *def.,* 10
  cost, *def.,* 10
  financial accounting, statements of, 10
  matching, 98–99
  def., 16, 98
  materiality, *def.,* 65
  objectivity, *def.,* 11
  present-value,
    and bonds payable, 539–543
  revenue recognition, *def.,* 98
  unit of measure, *def.,* 11
Consolidated financial statements, *def.,* 514
Consolidated income statement, *illus.,* 515
Consolidation,
  def., 513
  mergers and, 513
Contingent liability, 325, 423–424
  accounting treatment of, *illus.,* 424
Contra accounts, *def.,* 107
Contra asset, *def.,* 314
Contra asset accounts, 107
Contract rate, *def.,* 540
Contributed capital, 467
Contribution plan, *def.,* 439
Control,
  accounts payable, and subsidiary ledger, 195
  accounts receivable, and subsidiary ledger, 190
  detective, 278
  internal, 179–184
    accounting systems and, 177
    def., 179
    elements of, *def., illus.,* 180
    for payroll systems, 437
    objectives of, 179
    of cash payments, 280
    of fixed assets, 396
  preventive, 278
Control environment, 180
Control of cash
  receipts, 278
  received from cash sales, 279
  received in the mail, 280
Control of receivables, internal, 312
Control over cash,
  bank accounts as a, 282–286
  importance of, 278
Control problems, internal, indicators of, *illus.,* 184

Control procedures, 181
    competent personnel, 181
    internal, *illus.*, 182
    mandatory vacations, 181
    proofs and security measures,
        183
    rotating duties, 181
    separation of
        accounting responsibilities,
            182
        custody of assets, 182
        operations, 182
        responsibilities for related
            operations, 181
Controller, 8
Controlling account, *def.*, 185
Convertible bonds, 539
Copyright and trademarks, *def.*,
    398
Corporate annual reports,
    643–644
Corporate executives, career
    paths of, *illus.*, 8
Corporate income taxes, 498–501
Corporation, 465
    balance sheet, 552–554
    illus., 553
    characteristics of a, 465
    def., 3
    financing, 537–538
    forming a, 466
    income and taxes,
        stockholders' equity, and
        investments in stocks, 497
    nature of, 465–467
    nonpublic, 465
    organization, capital stock
        transactions, and dividends,
        464
    organizational structure of,
        illus., 466
    parent and subsidiary, 513
    private, 465
    public, 465
    states of incorporation, *illus.*,
        467
Correction of errors, 66
    discovery and, 65–67
    procedure for, *illus.*, 66
Corrective maintenance, 390
Cost concept, *def.*, 10
Cost flow assumption, 348
    inventory, 347–350
Cost method, 474, 511
Cost of business, excess of,
    acquired over related net
    assets, 514
Cost of goods sold, 240
Cost of merchandise sold, 240,
    599
    def., 225
Cost of new asset equation,
    394
Cost of sales, 240
Costs,
    flow of,
        first-in, first-out, *illus.*, 354
        last-in, first-out, *illus.*, 355

research and development,
    398
transportation, 234–236
Costs of acquiring fixed assets,
    382
    illus., 383
Coupon rate, 540
CPA (Certified Public
    Accountant), 8
CPA certification, 9
Create invoices form, *illus.*,
    248
Credit,
    and debit, diagram of the
        recording and posting of,
        illus., 53
    def., 46
    memorandum,
        def., 232
        illus., 232
    period, 227
Credit terms, *illus.*, 227
Creditors, 5
    ledger, 185
Cumulative preferred stock,
    def., 470
    dividends to, *illus.*, 471
Current assets
    and current liabilities, 584
    comparative schedule of,
        horizontal analysis, *illus.*,
        627
    def., 137
Current liabilities, 420
    def., 138
Current position analysis, 632
Current ratio, *def.*, 149, 632
Current ratio equation, 149
Customers, 5
Customers, cash received from,
    590
Customers ledger, 185

D

Data,
    flow of, in a payroll system,
        illus., 437
    input, 196
    output, 197
Days' sales, number of,
    in inventory, *def.*, 635
    in receivables, *def.*, 634
Debenture bonds, 539
Debit
    and credit, diagram of the
        recording and posting of,
        illus., 53
    balance, 46
    def., 46
    memorandum,
        def., 229
        illus., 229
Declining-balance method, 387
Deductions, 426
    from employee earnings,
        426
    other, 428

Deferrals, 99
    and accruals, *illus.*, 100
    alternate method, C–1
Deferred expenses, 102
    def., 99
Deferred revenue, 103
    def., 100
Deficit, *def.*, 468
Defined benefit plan, *def.*, 439
Defined contribution plan, *def.*,
    439
Depletion, *def.*, 397
Deposit ticket, 283
Depreciable cost, 385
Depreciation, 584
    accounting for, 385–390
    accumulated, *def.*, 107
    def., 107, 384
    estimates, revision of, 389
    expense, 599
        def., 107
    factors that determine, *illus.*,
        385
    for federal income tax, 388
    functional, 384
    methods,
        accelerated, *def.*, 388
        compared, *illus.*, 388
        use of, *illus.*, 386
    physical, 384
    sum-of-the-years-digits, 401
Detective controls, 278
Development costs, research
    and, 398
Direct and indirect methods,
    cash flow from operations,
    illus., 579
Direct method,
    balance sheet and income
        statement data for, *illus.*,
        589
    def., 578
    statement of cash flows, 589
    work sheet for, 597
    statement of cash flows,
        illus., 598
    of reporting cash flows from
        operating activities, 592
    of statement of cash flows,
        illus., 593
Direct write-off method, 314
Direct write-off method of
    accounting for uncollectibles,
    318–319
Discarding fixed assets, 392
Discontinued operations, *def.*,
    502
Discount, 325
    bond, amortizing a, 545
    bonds issued at a, 545
    by the interest method,
        amortization of, 556
    def., 423, 472, 540
    on bonds payable,
        amortization of, *illus.*, 556
    rate, *def.*, 423
Discounting notes receivable,
    325

Discounts,
    purchase, 227
        def., 228
    sales, *def.*, 232
    trade, *def.*, 234
Dishonored note receivable,
    def., 321
Distribution, payroll, 431
Dividend yield, 641
    def., 479
    equation, 479
Dividends, 466
    accounting for, 476–479
    cash, *def.*, 476
    cash flows used for payment
        of, 585
    cumulative preferred stock,
        illus., 471
    nonparticipating preferred
        stock, *illus.*, 470
    per share, 641
    stock, *def.*, 478
Doomsday ratio,
    def., 291
    equation, 291
Double-entry accounting, *def.*,
    50
Doubtful accounts expense,
    314
Drawee, 283
Drawer, 283
Drawing, *def.*, 45

E

Earned,
    fees, on account, 187
    interest charges, number of
        times, 636
        def., 554
    preferred dividends, number
        of times, 637
Earnings,
    basic, per share, 503
    employee,
        deductions from, 426
        liability for, 425
        recording employees', 431
    retained, 582, 596
        def., 467
    reporting, 506
    statement, *illus.*, 506
Earnings per common share
    (EPS),
    def., 503
    equation, 504
    on common stock, *def.*, 640
Earnings per share, income
    statement with, *illus.*, 504
Earnings record, employee's,
    def., 433
    illus., 434
Edit item form, *illus.*, 247
Effective interest rate method,
    545
    of amortization, 555
Effective rate of interest, *def.*,
    540

Effects of transactions on
    owner's equity, *illus.,* 15
EFT (electronic funds transfer),
    def., 282
Electronic forms, 200
Electronic funds transfer (EFT),
    def., 282
Elements of internal control,
    def., 180
    illus., 180
Employee, 4
Employee earnings,
    deductions from, 426
    liability for, 425
    record,
        def., 433
        illus., 434
    recording, 431
    withholding allowance
        certificate (W–4 Form) *illus.,*
        427
Employee fraud, *def.,* 179
Employee fringe benefits,
    438–440
Employee net pay, computing,
    429
Employer's payroll taxes, liability
    for, 429
Enter bills form, *illus.,* 248
Entrepreneurs, successful,
    illus., 4
Entry,
    adjusting,
        def., 99
        illus., 109, 139
    and perpetual inventory
        account (Fifo), *illus.,* 351
    and perpetual inventory
        account (Lifo), *illus.,* 351
    closing, 244
        def., 139
        illus., 141
        flowchart of, *illus.,* 141
    journalizing and posting,
        140
    reversing, *def.,* 150
Environment, control, 180
EPS (Earnings per common
    share), 640
    def., 503
Equation,
    accounting, business
        transactions and, 11–15
    accounting, *def.,* 11
    accounts receivable turnover,
        324
    assets, 581
    cash, 581
    cost of new asset, 394
    current ratio, 149
    dividend yield, 479
    doomsday ratio, 291
    earnings per common share,
        504
    gross profit, 225
    interest, 321
    inventory turnover, 361
    net income, 225

number of days' sales in
    inventory, 362
number of days' sales in
    receivables, 324
number of times interest
    charges earned, 554
price-earnings ratio, 516
quick ratio, 440
ratio of fixed assets to long-
    term liabilities (debt), 400
ratio of liabilities to owner's
    equity, 19
ratio of net sales to assets,
    244
working capital, 148
Equity,
    common stockholders', rate
        earned on, *def.,* 639
    owner's, 138
        def., 11, 45
        effects of transactions on,
            illus., 15
        statement of, 16, 137, 242
    stockholders', 467–468
        def., 467
        paid-in capital section of,
            illus., 505
        rate earned on, *def.,* 638
        ratio of liabilities to, 636
        reporting, 505
        section with treasury stock,
            illus., 475
        statement of, *def.,* 507
Equity method, *def.,* 511
Equity securities, *def.,* 508
Errors,
    causing unequal trial balance,
        illus., 65
    correction of, 66
    discovery and correction of,
        65–67
    inventory, effect on financial
        statements, 346–347
    procedure for correcting, *illus.,*
        66
Estimate of uncollectible
    accounts, *illus.,* 317
Estimating inventory cost,
    359–361
Estimating uncollectibles, 316
Ethics,
    business, 6–7
    code of professional, B–1
    def., 7
Exchanges,
    gains on, 394
    losses on, 395
Exchanges of similar fixed
    assets, accounting for,
    review of, 395
    illus., 395
Exchanging similar fixed assets,
    393
Executives, corporate, career
    paths of, *illus.,* 8
Expanded chart of accounts,
    illus., 101
Expected useful life, 385

Expenditures,
    capital, *def.,* 390
    capital, types of, 390
    capital and revenue, 390–391
        illus., 391
        summary of, 391
    revenue, *def.,* 390
Expense,
    administrative, *def.,* 240
    bad debts, 314
    deferred (prepaid expense),
        102
        def., 45
    depreciation, 599
        def., 107
        factors that determine, *illus.,*
            385
    doubtful accounts, 314
    interest, 591
    operating, 240
        cash payment for, 591
    other, *def.,* 241
    prepaid, 99, 102
        def., 13
    selling, *def.,* 240
    uncollectible accounts, *def.,*
        314
    wages, 105
Expenses,
    accrued, 104, 591
        def., 100
    deferred, *def.,* 99
        def., 13
    payable, accrued, 585
Extraordinary items, *def.,* 502
Extraordinary repairs, *def.,*
    391

F

Face amount,
    bonds issued at, 543
    of bonds, present value of,
        541
Factor, 313
Factoring, 313
Factors of production, *illus.,* 3
FASB (Financial Accounting
    Standards Board), *def.,* 10
Federal income tax, depreciation
    for, 388
Federal Reserve System, *illus.,*
    287
Federal Unemployment
    Compensation Tax (FUTA),
    430
Fees,
    accrued, column (work sheet),
        136A
    earned, 13, 106
        on account, 187
    protest, 325
FICA tax, 429
    def., 426
Fifo cost method, 350, 354
    def., 348
    flow of costs, *illus.,* 354

use of, 356
Financial accounting,
    concepts, statements of, 10
    def., 9
Financial Accounting Standards
    Board (FASB), *def.,* 10
Financial highlights, 643
Financial reporting for fixed
    assets and intangible assets,
    399–400
Financial statements, 16–18,
    136D–138
    analysis, 625
    consolidated, *def.,* 514
    def., 16
    effect of inventory costing
        methods on, *illus.,* 349
    effect of inventory errors on,
        346–347
        illus., 17
    prepared from work sheet,
        illus., 136C
Financing activities,
    cash flows from, 18, 580
        def., 577
    net cash flow provided by,
        580
    net cash flow used for, 580
    noncash investing and, 580
Financing corporations,
    537–538
Financing plans, alternative,
    effect of, *illus.,* 538
First-in, first-out (Fifo),
    cost method, *def.,* 348
    flow of costs, *illus.,* 354
    method, 350, 354
    use of, 356
Fiscal year, 146
    def., 147
Fixed assets, 138
    additions to, 390
    costs of acquiring, 382
        illus., 383
    def., 107, 382
    discarding, 392
    disposal of, 392–396
    internal control of, 396
    leasing, 396
    selling, 393
    similar, accounting for
        exchanges of,
        review of, 395
        summary illustration, *illus.,*
            395
    similar, exchanging, 393
Fixed assets to long-term
    liabilities, ratio of, 635
    def., 400
Flow of business transactions,
    illus., 52
Flow of costs,
    first-in, first-out, *illus.,* 354
    last-in, first-out, *illus.,* 355
Flow of data in a payroll system,
    illus., 437
Flowchart of closing entries,
    illus., 141

FOB destination, 346
  def., 235
  illus., 235
FOB shipping point, 346
  def., 234
  illus., 235
Form W–2, 433
Forms,
  account, *def.,* 18, 243
  create invoice, *illus.,* 248
  edit item, *illus.,* 247
  electronic, 200
  enter bills, *illus.,* 248
  multi-step, 239
  report,
    def., 18, 243
    of balance sheet, *illus.,* 243
  single-step, 241
Forming a corporation, 466
Fraud, employee, *def.,* 179
Free cash flow, *def.,* 593
Fringe benefits, employees',
  438–440
  def., 438
Functional depreciation, 384
Functions, receivable, separation
  of, *illus.,* 312
Fund,
  change, 279
  petty cash, *def.,* 289
  sinking, *def.,* 547
Funds transfer, electronic (EFT),
  def., 282
FUTA, 430
Future value, *def.,* 541

G

Gain,
  on sale of land, 585, 591
  on exchanges, 394
  unrealized holding, *def.,*
    509
General journal, *def.,* 187
General ledger
  and subsidiary ledger, *illus.,*
    186
  def., 185
Generally accepted accounting
  principles (GAAP), 9–11
  def., 9
Goods sold, cost of, 240
Goodwill, 514
  def., 399
Governments, 5
Gross margin, 240
Gross pay, *def.,* 426
Gross profit,
  def., 225, 240
  equation, 225
  method,
    def., 360
    inventory by, estimating,
      illus., 361
  method of estimating
    inventories, 360
  on sales, 240

H

Hardware,
  computer, basics, 196
  def., 196
  elements, external, of a
    computer, *illus.,* 197
Held-to-maturity securities, *def.,*
  554
Holding gain/loss, unrealized,
  def., 509
Horizontal analysis,
  comparative balance sheet,
    illus., 627
  comparative income statement,
    illus., 628
  comparative retained earnings
    statement, *illus.,* 628
  comparative schedule of
    current assets, *illus.,* 627
  def., 67, 626
  of income statement, *illus.,* 67

I

Identification, specific, method,
  348
In arrears, 470
Income,
  comprehensive, 507–508
    def., 507
    statement of income and,
      illus., 510
  net, 241
    def., 16
    equation, 225
    shown on completed work
      sheet, *illus.,* 136B
  other, and other expense, 241
    def., 241
  statement of, and
    comprehensive income,
    illus., 510
  taxable, *def.,* 499
Income from operations,
  accounts, 49
  and balance sheet columns
    (work sheet), 136A
  common-size, *illus.,* 631
  comparative,
    horizontal analysis, *illus.,*
      628
    vertical analysis, *illus.,* 630
  consolidated, *illus.,* 515
  def., 16, 240
  for a merchandising business,
    238–241
  horizontal analysis of, *illus.,* 67
  illus., 515
  multi-step,
    def., 239
    illus., 239
  single-step,
    def., 241
    illus., 241
  to total assets, rate of, 638
  unusual items in, *illus.,* 501

unusual items that affect the,
  501
vertical analysis of, *illus.,* 113
with earnings per share, *illus.,*
  504
Income statement data, balance
  sheet and, for direct method,
  illus., 589
Income summary, *def.,* 139
Income taxes, 427
  allocation of, 499
  cash payments for, 592
  corporate, 498–501
  federal, depreciation for, 388
  payable, 585
  payment of, 498
Incorporation,
  application of, 466
  articles of, 466
  states of, examples of
    corporations and their, *illus.,*
    467
Independent auditors' report,
  644
Indirect method,
  adjustments to net income,
    illus., 583
  cash flows from operating
    activities, *illus.,* 585
  def., 579
  direct and, cash flow from
    operations, *illus.,* 579
  statement of cash flows, 581
    illus., 588
  work sheet for, 595
  work sheet for statement of
    cash flows, *illus.,* 595
Information and communication,
  183
Information to users, providing,
  illus., 6
Input, data, 196
Input, user, 196
Insurance, prepaid, 102
  column (work sheet), 136A
Intangible assets, 398–399
  def., 398
  financial reporting for, 399–400
  in the balance sheet, *illus.,*
    400
Interest, 320
  accounting for bond
    investments, 549
  charges, number of times
    earned, 554, 636
  compound, present value of
    $1 at, *illus.,* 542
  effective rate of, *def.,* 540
  equation, 321
  expense, 591
  market rate of, 540
  method, 545
    amortization of discount by
      the, 556
    amortization of premium by
      the, 557
  minority, *def.,* 514

payments, periodic bond,
  present value of the, 542
rate, effective, method, 545
  of amortization, 555
  revenue, 13
Interest tables, A–2
Internal control, 179–184
  cash payments, 280
  def., 179
  elements of,
    def., 180
    illus., 180
  for payroll systems, 437
  objectives of, 179
  of fixed assets, 396
  of inventories, 344–346
  receivables, 312
  problems, indicators of, *illus.,*
    184
  procedures, *illus.,* 182
Inventories, 343, 591
  decrease in, 584
  internal control of, 344–346
Inventory,
  account
    Fifo, perpetual, entries and,
      illus., 351
    Lifo, perpetual, entries and,
      illus., 351
  analysis, 634
  at lower of cost or market,
    determining, *illus.,* 358
  at other than cost, valuation
    of, 357–358
  by gross profit method,
    estimating, *illus.,* 361
  by retail method,
    determination of, *illus.,* 360
  cost
    estimating, 359–361
    flow assumptions, 347–350
  costing, retail method of, 359
  def., 344
  errors on financial statements,
    effect of, 346–347
  estimating, gross profit method
    of, 360
  ledger, 345
  merchandise,
    def., 225
    on balance sheet, *illus.,*
      359
  shrinkage, 242
  method, retail, *def.,* 359
  number of days' sales in, *def.,*
    362, 635
  physical, *def.,* 226, 345
  shortage, 242
  shrinkage, *def.,* 242
  turnover,
    def., 361, 635
    equation, 361
Inventory costing method, 348
  comparison of, 356–357
  illus., 349
  on financial statements, effect
    of, *illus.,* 349

under a periodic inventory
system, 353–356
under a perpetual inventory
system, 350–352
Inventory system,
periodic,
def., 226
inventory costing methods
used, 353–356
perpetual,
computerized, 352
def., 226
inventory costing methods
used, 350–352
Investing, noncash, and
financing activities, 580
Investing activities,
cash flows from, 18, 579
def., 577
Investment,
in bonds, bonds payable and,
536
in stocks,
long-term, 508
sale of, 512
Investments,
bond,
accounting for, purchase,
interest, and amortization,
549
accounting for, sale, 551
balance sheet presentation
of, 554
long-term, in stocks, 510
shareholders', 467
temporary,
def., 508
on the balance sheet, illus.,
510
Investments in bonds, 549–552
Investments in stocks,
accounting for, 508–512
Invoice,
def., 227
illus., 227
Invoice form, illus., 248
Issuing stock, 471
Item form, illus., 247

J

Journal, 187
and ledger, illus., 58
cash payments,
and postings, illus., 194
def., 192
for merchandising business,
illus., 247
cash receipts,
and postings, illus., 191
def., 190
for merchandising business,
illus., 247
def., 47
entry, def., 47
general, def., 187

purchases,
and postings, illus., 193
def., 192
for a merchandising
business, illus., 246
revenue,
def., 187
illus., 188
postings to ledgers 9, 189
sales, 188
for a merchandising
business, illus., 246
special, 185
def., 186
modified, 196
two-column, def., 52
Journalizing,
and posting closing entries,
140
def., 47
Junk bonds, 547

L

Land, 587
gain on sale of, 585, 591
Lapses, ethical, avoiding small, 7
Last-in, first-out (lifo)
flow of costs, illus., 355
method, 351, 355
def., 348
use of, 357
LCM method, def., 358
Lease,
capital, def., 396
operating, def., 396
Leasing fixed assets, 396
Ledger,
and journal, illus., 58
creditors, 185
customers, 185
def., 44
general, and subsidiary ledger,
illus., 186
illus., 142–145
inventory, 345
posting to, revenue journal,
illus., 189
subsidiary,
accounts payable control
and, 195
accounts payable, def., 185
accounts receivable control
and, 190
accounts receivable, def.,
185
additional, 195
def., 185
general ledger and, illus.,
186
with adjusting entries, illus.,
110–111
Letter to the stockholders,
president's, 644
Leverage,
def., 639
illus., 639

Liabilities, 138
accrued, 100, 104
and owner's equity, assets
and, 11
contingent, 423–424
accounting treatment of,
illus., 424
current, 420
current assets and, 584
def., 138
def., 11
long-term,
def., 138
ratio of fixed assets to, 400,
635
to stockholders' equity, ratio
of, 636
Liability,
contingent, 325
def., 44
for employee earnings, 425
for employer's payroll taxes,
429
limited, 465
unlimited, 466
Life, expected useful, 385
Lifo (last-in, first-out)
flow of costs, illus., 355
method, 351, 355
def., 348
use of, 357
Limited liability, 465
Long-term investments in stocks,
510
Long-term liabilities,
def., 138
ratio of fixed assets to, 635
def., 400
Loss,
from operations, def., 240
net, 241
def., 16
on exchange, 395
unrealized holding, def., 509
Lower of cost or market (LCM),
inventory at, determining,
illus., 358
method, def., 358
valuation at, 358

M

Maintenance,
corrective, 390
predictive, 390
preventive, 390
Management accounting, def., 9
Management report, 644
Manager, def., 4
Manual accounting system,
184–195, 245
adapting, 195–196
purchase and payment cycle,
191
revenue and collection cycle,
187

Manufacturing
business, 2
computer-aided, illus., 198
Margin, gross, 240
Market rate of interest, 540
Marketable securities, 509
Matching concept, 98–99
and the adjusting process, 97
def., 16, 98
Matching principle, 98
Materiality concept, def., 65
Maturity date, 320
Maturity value, def., 321
Measures,
analytical,
other, 630
summary of, illus., 642–643
Medicare, 426
Memorandum,
credit, def., illus., 232
debit, def., illus., 229
Merchandise, cash payments for,
590
Merchandise inventory,
def., 225
on the balance sheet, 359
shrinkage, 242
Merchandise sold, cost of, 225,
240, 599
Merchandise transactions,
accounting for, illustration
of, 236–237
Merchandisers, accounting
systems for, 245–249
Merchandising business, 3
accounting cycle for, 241–244
accounting for, 224
adjusting and closing entries
for, 249–252
cash payments journal for,
illus., 247
cash receipts journal for, illus.,
247
chart of accounts for, illus.,
237–238
income statement for, 238–241
purchase journal for, illus.,
246
sales journal for, illus., 246
statement of owner's equity
for, illus., 243
work sheet for, 249–252
illus., 250
Merger(s),
and consolidations, 513
def., 513
Method(s),
accelerated depreciation, def.,
388
allowance,
def., 314
of accounting for
uncollectibles, 314–318
average cost, 352, 355
def., 348
use of, 357
composite-rate, 390

cost, 474
  def., 511
declining-balance, *def.,* 387
depreciation, compared, 388
  illus., 388
  use of, *illus.,* 386
direct,
  balance sheet and income
    statement data for, *illus.,*
    589
  def., 578
  of reporting cash flows from
    operating activities, 592
  statement of cash flows, 589,
    593
  work sheet for, 597
  work sheet for statement of
    cash flows, *illus.,* 598
direct write-off,
  accounting for uncollectibles,
    318–319
  def., 314
effective interest rate, 545
equity, *def.,* 511
fifo, 350, 354
  def., 348
  use of, 356
gross profit,
  def., 240
  estimating inventory by,
    illus., 360, 361
  of estimating inventories,
    360
indirect,
  adjustments to net income,
    illus., 583
  cash flows from operating
    activities, *illus.,* 585
  def., 579
  statement of cash flows, 581,
    588
  work sheet for, 595
  work sheet for statement of
    cash flows, *illus.,* 595
interest, 545
  amortization of premium by
    the, 557
inventory costing, 348
  illus., 349
  under a periodic inventory
    system, 353–356
  under a perpetual inventory
    system, 350–352
LCM, *def.,* 358
lifo, 351, 355
  def., 348
  use of, 357
lower-of-cost-or-market, *def.,*
  358
pooling-of-interests, *def.,*
  513
purchase, *def.,* 513
retail inventory method,
  359–360
specific identification, 348
straight-line, 545
  def., 386
sum-of-the-years-digits, 401

units-of-production, 386
  def., 387
weighted average, 355
Minority interest, *def.,* 514
Modified special journals, 196
Monitoring, 183
Multi-step income statement,
  def., 239
  illus., 239
Multiple-step form, 239
Mutual agent, 466

N

Natural business year, *def.,* 147
Natural resources, 397
Net assets, related, excess of
  cost of business acquired
  over, 514
Net cash flow,
  provided by financing
    activities, 580
  provided by investing
    activities, 579
  used for financing activities,
    580
  used for investing activities,
    579
Net income, 241
  adjustments to, indirect
    method, *illus.,* 583
  def., 16
  equation, 225
  shown on completed work
    sheet, *illus.,* 136B
Net loss, 241
  def., 16
Net pay,
  def., 426
  employee, computing, 429
Net profit, *def.,* 16
Net realizable value,
  def., 358
  valuation at, 358
Net sales to assets, ratio of,
  637
Network, 197
No-par stock, 469, 473
Nominal accounts, 139
Noncash investing and financing
  activities, 580
Nonparticipating preferred stock,
  def., 469
  dividends to, *illus.,* 470
Nonpublic corporation, 465
Normal balances of accounts, 51
Note, promissory,
  def., 319
  illus., 319
Notes payable, short-term,
  421–423
Notes receivable,
  accounting for, 321–322
  characteristics of, 319–321
  def., 137, 311
  discounting, 325
  dishonored, *def.,* 321

Number of days' sales in
  inventory,
  def., 362, 635
  equation, 362
Number of days' sales in
  receivables,
  def., 324, 634
  equation, 324
Number of times interest charges
  earned, 636
  def., 554
  equation, 554
Number of times preferred
  dividends are earned, 637

O

Objectives of internal control,
  179
Objectivity concept, *def.,* 11
Operating activities,
  cash flows from 18, 578, 583
  def., 577
  indirect method, *illus.,* 585
  reporting cash flows from, 585
  direct method, 592
Operating cycle, *illus.,* 138
Operating expenses, 240
  cash payments for, 591
Operating lease, *def.,* 396
Operating system, *def.,* 197
Operations,
  cash flow from, direct and
    indirect methods, *illus.,* 579
  discontinued, *def.,* 502
  income from, *def.,* 240
  loss from, *def.,* 240
Organizational structure of a
  corporation, *illus.,* 466
Organizations, business, types
  of, 3
Other deductions, 428
Other expense, *def.,* 241
Other income, *def.,* 241
Other receivables, 312
Other sources of paid-in capital,
  471
Output, data, 197
Outstanding stock, *def.,* 468
Owner's equity, 138
  assets, liabilities, and, 11
  def., 11, 45
  effects of transactions on,
    illus., 15
  statement of, 16, 137, 242
  def., 16
  for merchandising business,
    illus., 243
Owner withdrawals, 50
Owners, 4

P

P/E ratio, 515
  def., 640
Pacioli, Luca, *illus.,* 50
Paid-in capital,
  def., 467

other sources of, 471
reporting, 505
section of stockholders' equity,
  illus., 505
sources of, 468–471
Par, *def.,* 468
Parent and subsidiary
  corporations, 513
Parent company, *def.,* 513
Partnership, 465, F–1
  def., 3
Patents, *def.,* 398
Payee, 283, 319
Payments,
  cash,
    for merchandise, 590
    for operating expenses, 591
    internal control of, 280
    journal, *def.,* 192
  periodic bond interest, present
    value of, 542
  tax, responsibility for, *illus.,*
    429
Payment cycle, purchase and,
  191
Payment of dividends, cash
  flows used for, 585
Payment of income taxes, 498
Payroll,
  and payroll taxes, 425–430
  accounting systems for,
    430–438
  checks, 435
  illus., 436
  def., 425
  distribution, 431
  register,
    def., 431
    illus., 432
  system,
    diagram, 436
    flow of data in a, 437
    internal controls for, 437
  taxes,
    employer's, liability for, 429
    payroll and, 425–430
    recording and paying, 432
Pensions, 439
Periodic bond interest payments,
  present value of the, 542
Periodic inventory system,
  def., 226
  for merchandising business,
    D–1
  inventory costing methods
    used, 353–356
Perpetual inventory account,
  Fifo, entries and, *illus.,* 351
  Lifo, entries and, *illus.,* 351
Perpetual inventory system,
  computerized, 352
  def., 226
  inventory costing methods
    used, 350–352
Petty cash, 289
  fund, *def.,* 289
  receipt, *illus.,* 290
Physical depreciation, 384

Physical inventory, *def.*, 226, 345
Plan, defined benefit, *def.*, 439
Plan, defined contribution, *def.*, 439
Plans, alternative financing, effect of, *illus.*, 538
Plant assets, 107, 138, 382
Plant, property, and equipment, 138
Pooling-of-interests method, *def.*, 513
Post-closing trial balance, *def.*, 146
illus., 146
Posting, 52
and journalizing closing entries, 140
and recording a debit and a credit, diagram of, *illus.*, 53
cash payments journal and, *illus.*, 194
cash receipts journal and, *illus.*, 191
purchases journal and, *illus.*, 193
to ledgers, revenue journal, *illus.*, 189
Postretirement benefits, *def.*, 440
other than pensions, 440
Predictive maintenance, 390
Preferential rights, other, 470
Preferred dividends, number of times earned, 637
Preferred stock,
cumulative,
def., 470
dividends to, *illus.*, 471
def., 469
nonparticipating,
def., 469
dividends to, *illus.*, 470
Premium,
amortization of, by the interest method, 557
bond, amortizing a, 546
bonds issued at a, 546
def., 472, 540
on bonds payable, amortization of, *illus.*, 557
on stock, 473
Prepaid expense, 99, 102
def., 13
Prepaid insurance, 102
column (work sheet), 136A
Present value,
concept and bonds payable, 539–543
def., 540
of $1 at compound interest, *illus.*, 542
of an annuity, *def.*, 542
of the face amount of bonds, 541
of the periodic bond interest payments, 542
Presentation of cash on the balance sheet, 291

President's letter to the stockholders, 644
Preventive controls, 278
Preventive maintenance, 390
Price-earnings (P/E) ratio, *def.*, 515, 640
Principles, 539
accounting,
changes in, 503
generally accepted (GAAP), *def.*, 9
why we need them, *illus.*, 10
Prior period adjustment, *def.*, 507
Private accounting, 7, 8
Private corporation, 465
Problems, internal control, indicators of, *illus.*, 184
Procedures,
basic analytical, 626–631
control, 181
competent personnel, 181
mandatory vacations, 181
proofs and security measures, 183
rotating duties, 181
separating accounting responsibilities, 182
separating custody of assets, 182
separating operations, 182
separating responsibilities for related operations, 181
for correcting errors, *illus.*, 66
internal control, *illus.*, 182
Proceeds, 325
def., 423
Process,
adjusting,
def., 99
adjustment, summary of, 108–112
closing, 139
illus., 140
Processing methods, 179
Professional ethics, codes of, B–1
Profit,
def., 2
gross,
def., 225, 240
equation, 225
on sales, 240
net, *def.*, 16
Profitability,
analysis, 637–641
def., 631
Promissory note,
def., 319
illus., 319
Property, plant, and equipment, 138, 382, 399
Proprietorship, *def.*, 3
Protest fee, 325
Providing information to users, *illus.*, 6
Public accounting, 7, 8

Public corporation, 465
Purchase,
accounting for bond investments, 549
allowance, *def.*, 229
and payment cycle, 191
discounts, 227
def., 228
journal
and postings, *illus.*, 193
def., 192
for a merchandising business, *illus.*, 246
method, *def.*, 513
on account, 192
return, *def.*, 229
returns and allowances, 229
Purchases,
accounting for, 226–230

Q

Quick assets, *def.*, 633
Quick ratio, 633
def., 440
equation, 440
QuickBooks®, revenue and collection cycle in, *illus.*, 199

R

Rate,
contract, *def.*, 540
coupon, 540
discount, *def.*, 423
effective interest, method of amortization, 555
of income from operations to total assets, 638
of interest,
effective, *def.*, 540
market, 540
Rate earned,
on common stockholders' equity, *def.*, 639
on stockholders' equity, *def.*, 638
on total assets, *def.*, 638
Ratio,
acid-test, 440
def., 633
bankers', 632
current, *def.*, 149, 632
doomsday, *def.*, 291
fixed assets to long-term liabilities, 400, 635
liabilities to owner's equity, 19
liabilities to stockholders' equity, 636
net sales to assets, 244, 637
price-earnings (P/E), 516
def., 515, 640
quick, 633
def., 440
working capital, 632
Real accounts, *def.*, 139
Receipts, cash,
control of, 278

journal, and postings, *illus.*, 191
journal, *def.*, 190
petty, *illus.*, 290
Receivable,
accounts, 56, 590
aging of, *illus.*, 317
analysis, 633
def., 13, 311
increase in, 584
subsidiary ledger, *def.*, 185
turnover, *def.*, 323, 633
functions, separation of, *illus.*, 312
note, dishonored, *def.*, 321
notes,
accounting for, 321–322
characteristics of, 319–321
def., 137, 311
discounting, 325
Receivables, 310
aging the, *def.*, 316
classification of, 311–312
def., 311
in balance sheet, *illus.*, 323
internal control of, 312
number of days' sales in, *def.*, 324, 634
on the balance sheet, 322–323
other, 312
trade, 311
uncollectible, 313–314
Reconciliation, bank,
def., 286
illus., 288
Record, employee's earnings, *illus.*, 434
Recording,
adjusting entries, 101–108
and posting a debit and a credit, diagram of, *illus.*, 53
employees' earnings, 431
Redemption, bond, 548–549
Register,
payroll,
def., 431
illus., 432
transactions, 283
Remittance advice, 280, 283
check and, *illus.*, 284
Rent,
revenue, 13
unearned, 103, 421
column, (work sheet), 136A
Repairs, extraordinary, *def.*, 391
Report,
corporate annual, 643–644
form,
def., 18, 243
of balance sheet, *illus.*, 243
independent auditors', 644
management, 644
Reporting,
cash flows from operating activities, 585
financial, for fixed assets and intangible assets, 399–400
paid-in capital, 505

retained earnings, 506
stockholders' equity, 505
Research and development costs, 398
Residual value, *def.*, 385
Resources, natural, 397
Responsibility for tax payments, *illus.*, 429
Retail inventory method, *def.*, 359
inventory by, determination of, *illus.*, 360
of inventory costing, 359
Retailers' sources of cash, *illus.*, 279
Retained earnings, 582, 596
comparative, horizontal analysis, *illus.*, 628
def., 467
illus., 506
reporting, 506
Returns, purchases, and allowances, 229
Returns, sales, and allowances, 232
Revenue,
capital and, expenditures, *illus.*, 391
summary of, 391
deferred (unearned revenue), 103
def., 100
def., 13, 45
expenditures, 390–391
from sales, 240
interest, 13
journal,
def., 187
illus., 188
postings to ledgers, *illus.*, 189
rent, 13
unearned, 103
def., 54
Revenue and collection cycle, 187
computerized system and, 197
in QuickBooks®, *illus.*, 199
Revenue recognition concept, *def.*, 98
Revenues, accrued, 106
def., 100
Reversing entry, *def.*, 150
Revising depreciation estimates, 389
Rights, preferential, other, 470
Risk assessment, 181
Role of accounting in business, *def.*, 5–6

S

Salary, 425
Sale, accounting for bond investments, 551
Sale of investments in stocks, 512

Sale of land, gain on, 585, 591
Sales, 13, 599
accounting for, 230–234
allowance, *def.*, 232
cash, 230
control of cash received from, 279
cost of, 240
discounts, *def.*, 232
gross profit on, 240
journal, 188
for a merchandising business, *illus.*, 246
on account, 231
return, *def.*, 232
returns and allowances, 232
revenue from, 240
taxes, 233
Salvage value, 385
Securities,
available-for-sale, *def.*, 508
equity, *def.*, 508
held-to-maturity, *def.*, 554
marketable, 509
Selling fixed assets, 393
Serial bonds, 539
Service business, 3
Share,
basic earnings per, 503
common, earnings per (EPS), *def.*, 503
dividends per, 641
earnings per common, equation, 504
earnings per,
income statement with, *illus.*, 504
on common stock, *def.*, 640
no cash flow per, 581
Shareholders, 465
Shareholders' investment, 467
Shipping point, FOB, *def.*, 234
Short-term investments in stocks, 508
Short-term notes payable, 421–423
Shortage, inventory, 242
Shrinkage,
inventory, *def.*, 242
merchandise inventory, 242
Signature card, 283
Similar fixed assets, exchanges of, 393, 395
Single-step income statement, def. and *illus.*, 241
Sinking fund, *def.*, 547
Slide, *def.*, 66
Social security, 426
Software,
computer, basics, 196, 197
def., 197
Solvency, *def.*, 148, 631
Solvency analysis, 631–637
Sources of cash, retailers', *illus.*, 279
Sources of paid-in capital, other, 471

Special journals, 185
def., 186
modified, 196
Specialized accounting fields, 9
Specific identification method, 348
Split, stock, *def.*, 475
Stakeholders,
business, *def.*, 4
of a business, accounting information and, *illus.*, 6
State board of accountancy, 9
State of incorporation, examples of corporations, *illus.*, 467
State Unemployment Compensation Tax (SUTA), 430
Stated value, *def.*, 469
Statement,
bank, 284
illus., 285, 286
common-size, *def.*, 630
consolidated financial, *def.*, 514
financial, 16–18, 136D–138
analysis, 625
consolidated, *def.*, 514
def., 16
effect of inventory costing methods on, *illus.*, 349
effect of inventory errors on, 346–347
illus., 17
prepared from work sheet, *illus.*, 136C
income, 16, 136D
accounts, 40
common-size, *illus.*, 631
comparative, horizontal analysis, *illus.*, 628
comparative, vertical analysis, *illus.*, 630
consolidated, *illus.*, 515
def., 16
for a merchandising business, 238–241
horizontal analysis of, *illus.*, 67
illus., 515
multi-step, *def.*, 239
multi-step, *illus.*, 239
unusual items in, *illus.*, 501
unusual items that affect the, 501
with earnings per share, *illus.*, 504
retained earnings, comparative, horizontal analysis, *illus.*, 628
illus., 506
single-step income, *def.*, 241
illus., 241
Statement of account, 284
Statement of cash flows, 18
def., 16, 577

direct method, 589
illus., 593
indirect method, 581
illus., 588
preparation of, 588, 597, 600
purpose of the, 577
work sheet for, 595
direct method, *illus.*, 598
indirect method, *illus.*, 595
Statement of income and comprehensive income, *illus.*, 510
Statement of owner's equity, 16, 137, 242
def., 16
for merchandising business, *illus.*, 243
Statement of stockholders' equity,
def., 507
illus., 507
Statements of financial accounting concepts, 10
Stock, 468
certificates, 468
common, 586
def., 469
earnings per share (EPS) on, *def.*, 640
def., 465
dividend, *def.*, 478
investment in,
accounting for, 508–512
sale of, 512
issuing, 471
long-term investment in, 508, 510
no-par, 469, 473
outstanding, *def.*, 468
preferred,
cumulative, *def.*, 470
cumulative, dividends to, *illus.*, 471
def., 469
nonparticipating, *def.*, 469
nonparticipating, dividends to, *illus.*, 470
premium on, 473
treasury,
def., 474
stockholders' equity section with, *illus.*, 475
transactions, 474–475
Stock split, *def.*, 475
Stockholder, 469
def., 465
Stockholders, president's letter to the, 644
Stockholders' equity, 467–468
common, rate earned on, *def.*, 639
def., 467
paid-in capital section of, *illus.*, 505
rate earned on, *def.*, 638
ratio of liabilities to, 636

reporting, 505
section with treasury stock, *illus.*, 475
statement of,
def and *illus.*, 507
Straight-line method, 545
def., 386
Structure, organizational, of a corporation, *illus.*, 466
Subsidiary company, *def.*, 513
Subsidiary corporations, parent and, 513
Subsidiary ledger,
additional, 195
accounts payable
control and, 195
def., 185
accounts receivable
control and, 190
def., 185
def., 185
general ledger and, *illus.*, 186
Successful entrepreneurs, *illus.*, 4
Sum-of-the-years-digits,
depreciation, 401
method, 401
Summarizing and analyzing transactions,
illustration of, 51–64
in accounts, 47–51
Summary,
income, *def.*, 139
of basic adjustments, *illus.*, 109
Supplies, 102
Supplies column, (work sheet), 136A
System,
accounting,
and internal controls, 177
analysis of, 178
computerized, 196–200, 247
def., 178
design of, 178
feedback for, 178
for merchandisers, 245–249
for payroll and payroll taxes, 430–438
implementation of, 178
information, *illus.*, 6
basic accounting, 178–179
computerized, illustration of
revenue and collection cycle, 197
manual accounting, 184–195, 245
adapting, 195–196
purchase and payment cycle, 191
revenue and collection cycle, 187
operating, *def.*, 197
payroll,
diagram, 436
flow of data in a, 437
internal controls for, 437

periodic inventory,
def., 226
inventory costing methods used, 353–356
perpetual inventory,
computerized, 352
def., 226
inventory costing methods used, 350–352
voucher,
basic features of, 281
def., 281

T

T account, *def.*, 46
Table, wage bracket
withholding, *illus.*, 428
Tangible assets, 382
Tax,
corporate income, 498–501
employer's payroll, liability for, 429
federal, depreciation for, 388
Federal Unemployment Compensation (FUTA), 430
FICA, 429
def., 426
cash payments for, 592
payable, 585
payment of, 498
payments, responsibility for, *illus.*, 429
payroll, 425–430
accounting systems for, 430–438
recording and paying, 432
sales, 233
State Unemployment Compensation (SUTA), 430
Taxable income, *def.*, 499
Temporary
accounts, *def.*, 139
differences,
def., 499
illus., 500
investments,
def., 508
on the balance sheet, *illus.*, 510
Term bonds, 539
Terms,
credit, 227
illus., 227
Total assets,
rate earned on, *def.*, 638
rate of income from
operations to, 638
Trade discounts, *def.*, 234
Trade receivables, 311
Trade-in allowance, *def.*, 393
Trade-in value, 385
Trademark, *def.*, 399
Trademarks, copyrights and, 398
Trading securities, *def.*, 508

Transaction(s),
analysis of, 43
analyzing and summarizing, *illus.*, 51–64
and balance sheet accounts, 47
business, and the accounting equation, 11–15
def., 11
flow of, *illus.*, 52
in accounts, analyzing and summarizing, 47–51
merchandise, accounting for, *illus.*, 236–237
on owner's equity, effects of, *illus.*, 15
register, 283
treasury stock, 474–475
Transfer, electronic funds (EFT), *def.*, 282
Transportation costs, 234–236
Transportation terms, *illus.*, 235
Transposition, *def.*, 66
Treasury stock,
def., 474
stockholders' equity section with, *illus.*, 475
transactions, 474–475
Trial balance, 64–65
adjusted,
column (work sheet), 136A
def., 111
entered on work sheet, *illus.*, 136B
def., 64
illus., 64, 112
post-closing,
def. and *illus.*, 146
unadjusted,
illus., 101
column (work sheet), 136
entered on work sheet, *illus.*, 136B
unequal, errors causing, *illus.*, 65
Trust indenture, 539
Turnover,
accounts receivable, 633
def., 323
equation, 324
inventory, *def.*, 361, 635
Two-column journal, *def.*, 52

U

Unadjusted trial balance,
column (work sheet), 136
entered on work sheet, *illus.*, 136B
illus., 101
Uncollectible accounts,
estimate of, *illus.*, 317
expense, *def.*, 314
receivables, 313–314
Uncollectibles,
accounting for,
allowance method of, 314

direct write-off method of, 318–319
estimate based on analysis of receivables, 316
estimate based on sales, 316
estimating, 316
Unearned rent, 103, 421
Unearned revenue, 100, 103
def., 54
Unemployment compensation taxes, federal and state, 430
Units-of-production method, 386
def., 387
Unlimited liability, 466
Unrealized holding gain or loss, *def.*, 509
Useful life, expected, 385
Usefulness of an account, 44–45
User input, 196
Users, providing information to, *illus.*, 6

V

Vacation pay, 438
Valuation
at lower of cost or market, 358
at net realizable value, 358
of inventory at other than cost, 357–358
Value,
book, *def.*, 387
future, *def.*, 541
net realizable, *def.*, 358
present,
def., 540
of $1 at compound interest, *illus.*, 542
of an annuity, *def.*, 542
of the face amount of bonds, 541
of the periodic bond interest payments, 542
residual, *def.*, 385
salvage, 385
stated, *def.*, 469
trade-in, 385
Vertical analysis,
comparative balance sheet, *illus.*, 629
comparative income statement, *illus.*, 630
def., 112, 629
of income statements, *illus.*, 113
Voucher, def. and *illus.*, 281
Voucher system, *def.*, 281

W

W–4 Form, *illus.*, 427
Wage bracket withholding table, *illus.*, 428
Wages, 425
accrued, *illus.*, 105, 150
expense, 105

Weighted average method, 355
Withdrawals by the owner, 50
Withholding,
    allowance certificate,
        employee's (W–4 Form)
        illus., 427
    table, wage bracket, *illus.*, 428
Work sheet, 136–136D, 242
    completed, with net income
        shown, *illus.*, 136B
    completion of, 597, 600
    def., 136
    direct method, 597

financial statements prepared
    from, *illus.*, 136C
for a merchandising business,
    249–252
    illus., 250
for indirect method, 595
for statement of cash flows,
    595
    direct method, *illus.*, 598
    indirect method, *illus.*,
        595
with amounts extended to
    income statement and

balance sheet columns,
    illus., 136B
with unadjusted trial balance,
    adjustments, and adjusted
    trial balance entered, *illus.*,
    136B
Working capital,
    def., 148, 632
    ratio, 632
Working papers, 136
Write-off,
    direct, method, *def.*, 314
    to the allowance account, 315

Y

Year,
    fiscal, 146
    def., 147
    natural business, *def.*, 147
Yield, dividend, 479, 641

Z

Zero-coupon bonds, 547
Subject Index Financial
    Accounting split@I2:1

Company Index

A

A. G. Edwards & Sons, 537
Adolph Coors Company, 639
Allegis Corp., 539
Allstate Insurance, 181, 645
Amdahl, 477
America Online (AOL), 588, 622
American Airlines, 8, 98
American Express, 231
American Fare, 240
American Greetings Corporation, 102
American Honda, 7
American Telephone & Telegraph (AT&T), 2, 536, 539
Ameritech, 592
Amway, 240
Anheuser-Busch Companies, 639
Antique and Classic Rental Service, 363
Apple Computer Co., 4, 5, 477, 584, 665
Association of Fraud Examiners, 179
Avon, 240

B

Barings Bank, 183
Barnes and Noble, 3
Bass, 240
Bayerische Motoren Werke Aktiengesellschaft (BMW), 149
Bell South, 636
Ben & Jerry's Homemade Inc., 504
Ben Franklin, 240
Berkshire Hathaway Inc., 508
Best, 240
Bethlehem Steel, 440
Bloomingdale's, 240
Boeing Co., 3, 513, 579
Borden, Inc., 467
Boston Celtics, 670
Briggs & Stratton Corporation, 554
Burger King, 279
Business Week, 8

C

Callaway Golf Company, 104
Campbell Soup Company, 477, 522
Canteen, 240
Caterpillar Inc., 467
Chevron U.S.A., 282
Chrysler Corporation, 234, 357, 359, 579, 622
Circle K, 240
Circuit City, 3, 147, 240, 344, 645
Coca-Cola Company, 3, 4, 5, 6, 465, 472, 479, 508, 514, 594
Coldwell Banker Residential Service, 521
Columbia Healthcare Corporation, 316
Compaq Computer Corporation, 223, 445
Conrail, 477
Coopers & Lybrand, 644
Costco, 240
Crazy Eddie Inc., 347

D

Deere & Company, 316, 323
Dell Computer Company, 223, 358, 651, 665
Deloitte & Touche, 7, 644
Delta Air Lines, 3, 467, 503, 636
Disney, 3
Dollar General, 240
Dow Chemical Company, 467
Dun and Bradstreet, 313
Dun's Analytical Services, 631

E

E!, 760
Eastern Airlines, 5, 625
Economic Research Institute, 425
El Paso Electric, 477
Electric Avenue & More, 645
Equity Funding, 205
Ernst & Young, 644
E*TRADE, 514
Exxon Corporation, 30

F

Federal Express Corporation, 4, 425
Federal Reserve System, 287
Federated Department Stores Inc., 158, 341
First Chicago Trust Company of New York, 472
Florida Panthers, 480
Ford Motor Company, 4, 423

G

Gateway 2000, 223
General Electric Company, 4, 467, 579
General Mills, 3
General Motors Corporation, 2, 3, 4, 440, 466, 474, 477, 515, 579
Gillette Company, 4, 508
Goodyear Tire and Rubber Co., 522
Green Bay Packers, 594

H

Hershey Foods Corporation, 31, 82, 123, 222, 262, 334, 372, 412, 450, 488, 528, 565, 643, 663
Hewlett-Packard (HP), 425
Hi-Tech Innovation Institute, 401
Hilton Hotels Corporations, 331
Home Depot, The, 467, 645
Honeywell Corporation, 585
Howard Schultz & Associates (HS&A), 280
Hypermart USA, 240

I

IBM Corporation, 4, 401, 539, 540, 549, 563, 579
Incredible Universe, 106
Indo Rayon, 548
Intel Corporation, 113, 197, 477, 579, 580, 622
Internal Revenue Service (IRS), 178, 385

J

J. Crew, 240
J.C. Penney Company, 4, 158, 181, 225, 240, 244, 313, 316, 384, 645

K

Kellogg Company, 467
Kmart Corporation, 158, 225, 226, 240, 291, 352, 513, 630, 665
Kodak, 4
KPMG Peat Marwick, 179, 644
Kroger, 226, 240

L

L.L. Bean, 240, 279
LA Lakers, 764, 965
La-Z-Boy Chair Company, 292, 311, 361, 362, 399, 406
Lands' End, 3, 240, 279
Lechmere, 645
Lenox, 240
Levi Strauss, 240
Lowe's Companies, Inc. and Subsidiaries, 107, 225
LTV Corporation, 440
Lurias, 240

M

Macy's, 313
Marriott Corporation, 3
Mars Candy Company, 465
MasterCard, 231
Mattel Inc., 20, 516
May Department Stores, 467
McDonald's Corporation, 2, 8, 279, 508, 635
McDonnell Douglas Corporation, 513
Mercantile Stores Co. Inc., 341
Mercedes, 5
Merck, 962
Merrill Lynch, 3, 514, 537
Miami Heat, 480
Micron, 223
Microsoft Corporation, 4, 65, 122, 136, 352, 466, 477, 480, 579, 625, 632, 665
Montgomery Ward, 625, 645
Moody's Investors Service, 504, 548, 555, 574
Motorola, 594

N

National Audubon Society, 466
Nature's Sunshine Products, 475
Navistar, 440
New York University, 183
Nike, Inc., 3

O

Office Depot, 536, 547
OLDE Discount Brokers, 514
Orion Pictures, 625
Orvis, 279
Owens-Corning Fiberglas Corp., 539

P

Pan Am, 625
PepsiCo, Inc., 8, 466, 606
Perini Corporation, 292
Phar-Mor, 180
Philip Morris Companies, Inc., 424
Polo, 240
Price Waterhouse, 644
Procter & Gamble Company, 45, 425, 499, 636
Prudential Insurance Co., 555
Publix, 240

Q

Quaker Oats Company, 65, 121

R

Radio Shack, 106, 240
Rich's, 240

RJR Nabisco, 467
Robert Morris Associates, 631
Ross, 240

S

Safeway, 240
Sam's Club, 240, 345
Saturn Corporation, 423
Scientific-Atlanta Inc., 504
Sears, Roebuck & Co., 4, 6, 104, 181, 240, 244, 313, 352, 357, 384, 440, 477, 521, 539, 645
Service Merchandise, 240
7 Eleven, 240
Sierra Club, 466
Southwest Airlines, 5
Sprint Corporation, 3,
Standard & Poor's, 504, 548
SUPERVALU INC., 361, 362

T

T.J. Maxx, 240
Tandy Corporation, 106, 292, 467
Target, 240
The Limited, Inc., 158
The Studio Theatre, 362
3M, 467
Toyota Motor Company, 235
Toys "R" Us Inc., 3, 4, 158, 240, 635

U

United Airlines, 178

V

VISA, 231

W

Wal-Mart Stores Inc., 3, 4, 225, 226, 240, 245, 345, 352, 473, 630, 645, 665,
Waldenbooks, 513
Wall Street Journal, 10, 625
Warner Bros., 673
Washington Post Company, The, 467
Wendy's, 279
Whirlpool Corporation, 467, 539
Whiskey Dust, 363
Winn-Dixie, 226
Woolworth's, 625

Z

Zales Jewelers, 240
Zayre Corp., 158

Index of Web Site Addresses

Note: These Web site addresses may also be accessed at **warren.swcollege.com**.

A

Accounting
  opportunities, **www.jobweb.com**, 94
  salary information, **www.cfstaffing.com/salary.html**, 462

C

Career guidance, career profiles, and salary information,
  www.tripod.com/work, 462
CIA requirements, **www.rutgers.edu/Accounting/raw/iia**, 40
CMA requirements,
  www.rutgers.edu/Accounting/raw/ima/icma.htm, 40
Compaq, **www.compaq.com**, 223
Computer (engineering, finance, and accounting salary
  information), **www.espan.com/salary**, 462
Copyright applications (Internet site), **www.idresearch.com**, 419

D

Dell Computer Company, **www.dell.com**, 223

E

E*TRADE, **www.etrade.com**, 514
Economic Research Institute, **www.erieri.com**, 425
EDGAR (Electronic Data Gathering, Analysis, and
  Retrieval)(Securities and Exchange Commission),
  www.sec.gov/edgarhp.htm, 176, 379, 495, 534, 622, 665

F

Federated Department Stores Inc., **www.federated-fds.com**, 341

G

Gateway 2000, **www.gateway.com**, 223

I

Industry ratio source,
  www.sunsite.unc.edu/reference/rita/ratios.html, 631

Internal Revenue Service (to download forms), **www.irs.treas.gov**,
  462

M

Mercantile Stores Co. Inc., **www.rootsstore.com**, 341
Micron, **www.micron.com**, 223
Microsoft, **www.microsoft.com**, 665
Moody's Investors Service, **www.Moodys.com**, 574

N

NASDAQ, **www.Nasdaq.com**, 509
New York Stock Exchange, **www.nyse.com**, 495, 509

O

Online Career Center, **www.occ.com**, 462
Opportunities for accountants, **www.jobweb.com**, 94

P

Patent applications (Internet site), **www.idresearch.com**, 419

S

Securities and Exchange Commission (SEC), EDGAR
  (Electronic Data Gathering, Analysis, and Retrieval),
  www.sec.gov/edgarhp.htm, 176, 379, 495, 534, 622, 665
South-Western College Publishing, **warren.swcollege.com**, 118
State Board of Accountancy (for each state), **www.ais-cpa.com**, 40
Stern Stewart & Co., **www.eva.com**, 909

T

T. Rowe Price, **www.troweprice.com**, 442
Trademark applications (Internet site), **www.idresearch.com**, 419

Abbreviations and Acronyms Commonly Used in Business and Accounting

AAA	American Accounting Association
ABC	Activity-based costing
AICPA	American Institute of Certified Public Accountants
CIA	Certified Internal Auditor
CIM	Computer-integrated manufacturing
CMA	Certified Management Accountant
CPA	Certified Public Accountant
Cr.	Credit
Dr.	Debit
EFT	Electronic funds transfer
EPS	Earnings per share
FAF	Financial Accounting Foundation
FASB	Financial Accounting Standards Board
FEI	Financial Executives Institute
FICA tax	Federal Insurance Contributions Act tax
FIFO	First-in, first-out
FOB	Free on board
GAAP	Generally accepted accounting principles
GASB	Governmental Accounting Standards Board
GNP	Gross National Product
IMA	Institute of Management Accountants
IRC	Internal Revenue Code
IRS	Internal Revenue Service
JIT	Just-in-time
LIFO	Last-in, first-out
Lower of C or M	Lower of cost or market
MACRS	Modified Accelerated Cost Recovery System
n/30	Net 30
n/eom	Net, end-of-month
P/E Ratio	Price-earnings ratio
POS	Point of sale
ROI	Return on investment
SEC	Securities and Exchange Commission
TQC	Total quality control

Classification of Accounts

Account Title	Account Classification	Normal Balance	Financial Statement
Accounts Payable	Current liability	Credit	Balance sheet
Accounts Receivable	Current asset	Debit	Balance sheet
Accumulated Depreciation	Fixed asset	Credit	Balance sheet
Accumulated Depletion	Fixed asset	Credit	Balance sheet
Advertising Expense	Operating expense	Debit	Income statement
Allowance for Doubtful Accounts	Current asset	Credit	Balance sheet
Amortization Expense	Operating expense	Debit	Income statement
Bonds Payable	Long-term liability	Credit	Balance sheet
Building	Fixed asset	Debit	Balance sheet
_____ Capital	Owners' equity	Credit	Statement of owner's equity/ Balance sheet
Capital Stock	Stockholders' equity	Credit	Balance sheet
Cash	Current asset	Debit	Balance sheet
Cash Dividends	Stockholders' equity	Debit	Retained earnings statement
Cash Dividends Payable	Current liability	Credit	Balance sheet
Common Stock	Stockholders' equity	Credit	Balance sheet
Cost of Merchandise (Goods) Sold	Cost of merchandise (goods sold)	Debit	Income statement
Deferred Income Tax Payable	Current liability/Long-term liability	Credit	Balance sheet
Depletion Expense	Operating expense	Debit	Income statement
Discount on Bonds Payable	Long-term liability	Debit	Balance sheet
Dividend Revenue	Other income	Credit	Income statement
Dividends	Stockholders' equity	Debit	Retained earnings statement
Donated Capital	Stockholders' equity	Credit	Balance sheet
Employees Federal Income Tax Payable	Current liability	Credit	Balance sheet
Equipment	Fixed asset	Debit	Balance sheet
Exchange Gain	Other income	Credit	Income statement
Exchange Loss	Other expense	Debit	Income statement
Factory Overhead (Overapplied)	Deferred credit	Credit	Balance sheet (interim)
Factory Overhead (Underapplied)	Deferred debit	Debit	Balance sheet (interim)
Federal Income Tax Payable	Current liability	Credit	Balance sheet
Federal Unemployment Tax Payable	Current liability	Credit	Balance sheet
Finished Goods	Current asset	Debit	Balance sheet
Gain on Disposal of Fixed Assets	Other income	Credit	Income statement
Gain on Redemption of Bonds	Extraordinary item	Credit	Income statement
Gain on Sale of Investments	Other income	Credit	Income statement
Goodwill	Intangible asset	Debit	Balance sheet
Income Tax Expense	Income tax	Debit	Income statement
Income Tax Payable	Current liability	Credit	Balance sheet
Insurance Expense	Operating expense	Debit	Income statement
Interest Expense	Other expense	Debit	Income statement
Interest Receivable	Current asset	Debit	Balance sheet
Interest Revenue	Other income	Credit	Income statement
Investment in Bonds	Investment	Debit	Balance sheet
Investment in Stocks	Investment	Debit	Balance sheet
Investment in Subsidiary	Investment	Debit	Balance sheet
Land	Fixed asset	Debit	Balance sheet
Loss on Disposal of Fixed Assets	Other expense	Debit	Income statement
Loss on Redemption of Bonds	Extraordinary item	Debit	Income statement
Loss on Sale of Investments	Other expense	Debit	Income statement